A CONCORDANCE TO *Finnegans Wake*

Clive Hart

licuit semperque licebit
signatum praesente nota producere nomen
Horace, *Ars poetica*

UNIVERSITY OF MINNESOTA PRESS, Minneapolis

Printed in the United States of America at
the William C. Brown Company, Dubuque, Iowa

Library of Congress Catalog Card Number: 63-8226

PUBLISHED IN GREAT BRITAIN, INDIA, AND PAKISTAN BY THE OXFORD UNIVERSITY PRESS,
LONDON, BOMBAY, AND KARACHI, AND IN CANADA BY THOMAS ALLEN, LTD., TORONTO

ACKNOWLEDGMENTS

The work of compiling a concordance is by its nature such that people not actually on the spot cannot contribute greatly to it. Of those who willingly gave of their time when in my vicinity, I owe the greatest debt to the members of my family, all of whom helped to alleviate the tedium of the dullest aspects of the task. My parents helped with the sorting, my wife did much of the typing, and my brother-in-law, an entomologist, wittily dissected "The Ondt and the Gracehoper" for me. Among the many friends who gave me advice and encouragement I must mention especially Adaline Glasheen, James Atherton, Frank Budgen, Matthew Hodgart, J. Mitchell Morse, and Fritz Senn. I am particularly grateful to Miss Anna Russell, of the Poetry Collection at the Lockwood Memorial Library, who, with unfailing courtesy, made it possible for me to examine a photographic copy of the typescript of the "Corrections of Misprints" and gave me willing and valuable assistance with some of the collations.

Parts of this work were carried out with the aid of a bursary from the French Government and a Hackett Studentship from the University of Western Australia.

I am grateful to the editors of *The Journal of English and Germanic Philology* for permission to reprint some of my notes on the text, which first appeared in that periodical, and to the Lockwood Memorial Library and the Administrators of the Joyce Estate for permission to quote the textual emendations. Finally, I must thank Mr. Peter du Sautoy, of Faber & Faber, and Mr. Marshall A. Best, of Viking Press, for very kindly supplying me with bibliographical information.

Clive Hart
University of Lund

TABLE OF CONTENTS

A Concordance to *Finnegans Wake*

INTRODUCTION

The student of Finnegans Wake needs to be a humble person. In few fields of criticism can he so quickly reveal the limitations of his reading and general knowledge and the restricted scope of his vocabulary. In over six years spent, on and off, at the more or less harmless drudgery of compiling this concordance I have learned a great deal and shamed myself many times, but there must still be a very large number of yawning gaps in it to betray my ignorance. I take refuge in the thought that the content of Finnegans Wake is still a very long way from being exhausted by any scholar. Joyce intended that it should never grow out of date and, as is true of all great works of art, each generation will inevitably find a wealth of new relations to explore and record. The list of pun-contents will always be growing; any concordance of Finnegans Wake is doomed to be a Work eternally in Progress.

Finnegans Wake is a highly denotative book. Its references, though overwhelmingly multitudinous, are on the whole precise. Thirty years ago it was common to talk of Work in Progress in the same breath as the vertigralist, sonorist, and other more connotative productions. This error of critical perspective is slowly being corrected but it dies hard outside the inbred society of Joyce scholars, with the result that Joyce's aims in Finnegans Wake are still constantly misrepresented. Joyce told us to listen to the music of his prose, but he also told us to pay some attention to what it means. Consider, for example, his letter to Miss Weaver, dated November 15, 1926.[1] The book is no simple linguistic puzzle to be untangled once and for all by a devoted panel of experts, but it will never be properly understood until its denotative richness is fully appreciated. The methods of word-formation are usually simple; no special mental or psychological equipment is needed in order to appreciate Finnegans Wake. "Now, patience; and remember patience is the great thing"; the rewards speak for themselves.

Something like fifty per cent of the semantic units are built up out of English materials; it is these that the concordance attempts to sort out. It does not aim at supplying any kind of glossary of individual words in Finnegans Wake but is, rather, a finding-list—a time-saver and relatively compact substitute for the reader's own card-index. For some time there have been suggestions about the possible appearance one day of a much more ambitious work—a complete "Dictionary of Finnegans Wake." If prepared with discretion it would clearly save every student of Joyce a great deal of effort and frustration, though the enormous bulk and intricacy of such a volume is terrifying in its absurdity. The reader who has just begun to dip into Finnegans Wake tends to think that if only somebody would compile that Dictionary all our troubles would be at an end. But a little later, after he has been hacking his own way through the forest for a time, he discovers that such is far from being the case. Only a part of the difficulty of understanding Finnegans Wake—and perhaps not the major part—stems from the obscurity of its vocabulary. As one learns from assiduous toil with dictionaries and reference books, a knowledge of what went into the individual words rarely clarifies anything beyond local cruces. The really difficult work of intelligent critical interpretation still remains to be done.

PARTS OF THE CONCORDANCE

This concordance should help the reader to trace the symbolic and thematic development of the intertwining verbal motifs out of which the book is constructed. It is divided into three main parts which provide page/line references for (1) all the words Joyce uses in the book: the "Primary Index"; (2) most of the words and important syllables contained in compounds: the "Syllabifications"; (3) the English words suggested by Joyce's puns, distortions, etc.: the "Overtones."

Primary Index. However vast the semantic field in Finnegans Wake, we may be thankful that the morphological field is finite; part at any rate of the work of charting the book has been done once for all when the vocabulary has been listed. This Primary Index is a fully referenced list of the occurrences of all but 141 of the 63,924 different words forming the vocabulary. Since the appearance of the words on the page is often so important, each is listed just as it occurs—that is, with all italics and capitalization retained—except that no distinctions of type-size are made. As many of the words as possible have been included in the main body of the Index, which is arranged throughout in strictly alphabetical order. It would clearly be absurd to attempt to draw up any separate list of "Foreign Words and Phrases." After "Z" will be found (1) a list of "Numbers," arranged in decimal order so as to keep together such thematic figures as 1132 and 11.32; (2) a list of "Symbols," arranged in order of their occurrence in the text. Abbreviations have been included in the main body of the Index; when I have understood what they mean I have provided a note in parentheses following the page/line number.

Syllabifications. I have used this term to designate an alphabetically arranged list of the inner parts of compounds and portmanteau-words. Thus from "paltipsypote" (listed under "P" in the Primary Index), "tipsypote" and "pote" are listed under "T" and "P"

[1] Letters of James Joyce, ed. S. Gilbert, London, 1957, p. 247

respectively in the Syllabifications. Usually the whole latter part of a word is printed, in order to include as much as possible of the context of the relevant syllable or word-part. Thus "tipsypote" is listed, rather than "tipsy." With some very long words, however, the inclusive method grows rather unwieldy; in these cases the existence of further syllables after the one listed is indicated by a hyphen: e.g., "skawn-" (from the 100-letter word on page 3). The page/line number given is always that on which the whole word starts.

My principal object in syllabifying has been to put on show the English words hidden away in the portmanteaux, together with some of the most obvious of the other meaningful syllables. The points of syllabification are necessarily limited to what seem to me to be the most useful ones. The alternative, brute-force method of including everything by syllabifying at each letter would produce a hopelessly cumbersome list containing about half a million items—just twenty times as many as the present index.

Overtones. Under this heading are listed English words suggested by, but not orthographically present in, Joyce's distorted and compound words. (I use the word "suggest" here for want of a better. There is nothing vague about Joyce's method which, at the level of individual words, usually amounts to quite clear-cut statement by indirect means.) Thus "paltipsypote," already quoted, is intended to suggest by sound and context, "participate," which is accordingly listed under "P" in the Overtones. With a very few exceptions only English words have been listed. Of course many foreign words are similarly suggested but to make a really adequate list of them would call for more linguistic attainments than I can boast and, in any case, they present special problems of their own, such as conventions of transliteration. They are therefore ignored here, although I hope that it may one day be possible to prepare a foreign supplement to this concordance.

I have not attempted to include all the semantic correspondences made possible by common homophones. As a matter of principle, "son" and "sun" are always equivalent; similarly "maid" and "made" (from Adam's rib), and there are hosts of other possibilities. The reader himself will readily know where to look for the most important of these in the concordance. For the others, I have included those specific examples which seem to me to be functional in context; to attempt a blanket coverage would over-load the list with what, for practical purposes, is a lot of dead wood. Almost all proper names have been omitted, except for a small handful of highly important place-names such as Dublin and Howth.[2] The number of different words suggested is something over ten thousand. Where a Joycean distortion is still sufficiently close to the normal form to be easily recognized, that normal form is usually omitted from the Overtones to avoid unnecessary duplication. At the end of this part of the concordance will be found a list of suggested abbreviations and sets of initials, ignoring the obvious "HCE" and "ALP."

My approach to the language of Finnegans Wake is on the whole conservative. Rich, complex, and tortuous though it is, the book has, I believe, been over-read in recent years—in a few cases grotesquely so. The limits of relevancy are difficult to establish but when in doubt I have usually preferred to omit rather than include, though in my ignorance I must have thrown out much that is useful or perhaps essential. Even more dangerous than ignorance is interpretative blindness and lack of imaginative insight. It is remarkable how long and how often one can read certain passages in Finnegans Wake and still miss the most obvious meanings. There is something about the density of Joyce's writing which makes it difficult to maintain a sufficiently broad point of view. He is so constantly rubbing our noses in the "litterage" that it is by no means easy to see the text in the best perspective. I doubt whether any one person can ever see enough of Joyce's linguistic panorama. Finnegans Wake needs, in fact, to be read communally; certainly the greatest weakness of this concordance is that, despite my profound debt to all previously published exegeses and critical commentaries, it remains essentially the product of one man's view of the book. Nevertheless I think that, with all its limitations, it forms a reasonably solid foundation on which the individual user can build.

COMMON WORDS NOT REFERENCED

The following 123 common words are quoted in their correct places in the Primary Index, but without page/line references:

about	I'm	these
again	in	they
all	into	this
an	isn't	those
and	it	thou
any	its	though
are	it's	through
as	I've	thy
at	let	till
been	like	'tis
being	must	to
but	none	too
by	nor	under
cannot	not	up
can't	now	upon
could	of	us
did	off	used
does	often	very
doing	on	was
done	once	we
don't	one	we'll
down	only	were
for	ought	what
from	our	when
had	out	where
has	over	which
have	said	while
having	shall	who
he	she	whom
he'd	she's	why
he'll	should	with
her	so	would
here	some	ye
here's	that	yes
he's	that's	yet
him	thee	you
his	their	you'd
how	them	you'll
I'd	then	your
if	there	you're
I'll	there's	you've

[2] I understand that an "Atlas of Finnegans Wake" is at the moment under preparation, compiled on similar principles to those of Mrs. Adaline Glasheen's indispensable A Census of Finnegans Wake, Evanston, 1956.

In addition the following 18 common words have been only partially referenced:

a	is	O
am	man	or
be	me	than
can	men	the
do	my	whose
I	no	will

STATISTICS

Since this work is primarily designed as a finding-list rather than a linguistic survey, only a few basic statistics have been compiled which should, however, suffice to summarize the over-all picture of the language of Finnegans Wake. The tables below offer a qualitative comparison with Ulysses and Stephen Hero. The gross totals ("FW as listed") take account of every typographical unit in the book, including "Numbers" and "Symbols." The figures shown for "FW with corrections" are corrected to conform, as far as possible, with the editorial procedure adopted in the Ulysses Index. These corrections include the ignoring of italicized and capitalized forms as separate items. It is, however, extremely difficult to know if the capitalization of words in Finnegans Wake is significant, and the corrected figures given below are therefore by no means absolutely accurate.[3]

	W	V	Words Occurring Once Only
FW as listed	218,077	63,924	51,922
FW with corrections	217,937	60,810	49,200
Ulysses	260,430	29,899	16,432
Stephen Hero	74,459	8,740	No figure available

	Total Number of Different Numbers, Symbols, and Money Expressions	Common Words	
		Total No.	% of W
FW	84	100,497	46%
Ul	305	120,769	46%

W = running words; V = vocabulary

It is remarkable that, despite the highly unusual character of the vocabulary of Finnegans Wake, the proportion of the 141 common words, taken together, should be identical with that in Ulysses, to within one per cent. I have made no individual counts of these words, which were ignored not on considerations of frequency alone, but on a combined estimate of usefulness and frequency (using conventional sampling methods). Their omission from the referencing saves many hundreds of pages of space and makes only a negligible difference to the value of the concordance. According to Dewey's Relativ Frequency of English Speech Sounds[4] these 141 words (which include all of Dewey's first 50, and 83 of which fall within Dewey's first 100) would be expected to make up something over sixty per cent of normal English. In Appendix II of Word Index to James Joyce's Ulysses Martin Joos has shown in detail that the basic vocabulary of Ulysses is not radically divergent from normal English. It is apparent that in his last book also Joyce held together the bricks of his curious edifice with the usual mortar.

The average numbers of letters per word for running-words and for the vocabulary-list are about 5 and 7.5 respectively—or about the same as in normal literary English—suggesting that Joyce's portmanteaux, though well stuffed, do not bulge.

CONVENTIONS ADOPTED

Page/line numbers are designated as in the following example: 175.12 (page 175, line 12).

Left- and right-hand marginal notes on pp. 260–308 are designated L and R respectively, after the point: e.g., 260.L2 (page 260, second left-hand note).

Footnotes on pp. 260–308 are designated F, after the point. A single number follows the F and is the number of the footnote, with one exception: for the single 37-line note on page 279 the F is followed by two numbers, giving the line of that note on which the word occurs: e.g., 279.F31.

THE TEXT

The text used is that of the First Editions, emended according to the "Corrections of Misprints in Finnegans Wake," after the latter had itself been emended by collation with a photo-copy of the typescript in the Lockwood Memorial Library, University of Buffalo, and by partial collation with the copy of Finnegans Wake on which Joyce made the original MS corrections, also in that Library. The typescript is very rough indeed, with many overstrikes and inconsistencies, and it is often difficult to draw firm conclusions where discrepancies with the manuscript and/or printed versions occur. For the present purpose I have ignored a number of rather doubtful conjectural changes which might be made, but there are six clear cases of misprint or mistyping which affect the text:

267.02 correction should read: "for 'multimim-' read 'Multimim-'"
285.25 last word of correction should read: "bully-"
301.F2 correction should read: "replace stop by exclamation at end of note"
309.18 correction should read: "for 'distance, getting' read 'distancegetting'"
365.12 correction should read: "for 'dollymaukins.' read 'dollymaukins!'"
458.32 correction should read: "for 'Flee a girl' read 'Flea a girl,'"

These changes should therefore be made in all published texts of Finnegans Wake.

Later American printings through the seventh (March, 1957) are identical with the first. All other editions, English and American, contain further errors which the following notes seek to emend.

[3] For a scholarly comparison of the vocabularies of Ulysses and of certain other English texts, see A. Ellegård, "Estimating Vocabulary Size," Word, vol. XVI, no. 2, August 1960, pp. 219–44. The figures quoted for Ulysses and Stephen Hero are derived from M. L. Hanley, Word Index to James Joyce's Ulysses, 4th printing, Madison, 1953, and C. G. Anderson, Word Index to James Joyce's Stephen Hero, Ridgefield, Conn., 1958.

[4] Rev. edn., Cambridge, Mass., 1950.

American 8th Printing (1958) and Compass Paperback. The "Corrections of Misprints," as published, have been incorporated in these texts, but the following errors remain, or have been newly introduced:

42.07 for "firestuffostered" read "firestufffostered"
98.25 delete "of"
127.26 for first "or" read "of" and for second "or" read "on"
136.36 for "mountaen" read "moontaen"
183.25 for "schoolgirls'" read "schoolgirl's"
272.F1 for "ma'am? says" read "ma'am?, says"
305.F3 for "M" read "Mac"
342.04 for "howbeit;" read "howbeit," (perhaps not a printing error but only a blemish on the plate)
390.17 for "Deaddleconch" read "Deaddleconche"
406.01 for "or" read "of"
438.28-29 for "therein-/under" read "therin-/under"
566.28 for "Then," read "Then."

The "error" at 183.25 probably represents what Joyce intended, but as there is no authority for the reading I have preferred not to adopt it. These printings also incorporate the correction at 267.02 which I have noted above.

English Printings of 1946, 1948, 1949. Referring to these printings in their A Bibliography of James Joyce 1882-1941,[5] Messrs. Slocum and Cahoon state that "Some of the misprints have been corrected in the text and omitted from the 'Corrections of Misprints.'" A collation reveals that this is not so. The major change in these texts is the resetting in smaller type of the marginal notes on pages 260-308, which results in a number of mislineations, some of them serious:

Right-hand Notes: In every case align the first word of the note with the first line of the paragraph to which it refers.
Left-hand Notes: Re-align as follows:
262.L2 opposite line 15 of text
267.L3 opposite line 27 of text
269.L2 opposite line 24 of text
277.L2 opposite space between lines 6 and 7 of text
277.L3 opposite space between lines 9 and 10 of text
277.L4 opposite line 13 of text
277.L5 opposite line 15 of text
278.L5 opposite line 22 of text
306-308 the 52 sets of names (306-8) and the other 11 items (308) should be opposite the relevant phrase or word in the text (52 essay topics, and 11 items on p. 308)

There are three other errors in these texts whose origin is not altogether clear:

305.R1 above "CUNCTITI-" add "COME SI/COMPITA" and align "COME SI" with line 3 of the text; also delete the second "IOIOMISS" (opposite line 20 of the text; this error does not occur in the 1946 text)
305.F3 for "M" read "Mac"
406.01 for "or" read "of"

English "New Edition" of 1950, and all Later Printings. Most of the "Corrections of Misprints" were incorporated into this text, but the following errors remain (in addition to the shortened "Corrections of Misprints" list in the Appendix):

8.27 for "'MacDyke'" read "MacDyke"
8.27 for "'O'Hurry" read "O'Hurry"
14.07 indent paragraph beginning "566 A.D."
22.07 for "'a forethought'" read "a forethought"
32.32 for "of problem" read "of the problem"
114.03 "than" badly printed
132.36 before "hecklebury" insert comma
158.05 before "I see" place dash and indent
219.17 "cellelleneteutoslavzend-latinsoundscript"—delete hyphen and close
229.29 "his" badly printed
261.F4 note in "Corrections of Misprints" in the Appendix should read "for 'the burglar's' read 'her burglar's'" (last word of note already deleted)
271.L4 after "sake" insert comma, and for "chawley." read "chawley!"
274.L3 for "olive hunkered" read "olivehunkered"
290.26 for "for'twas" read "for 'twas"
299.L2 italicize colon
305.R1 above "CUNCTITI-" add "COME SI/COMPITA" and align "COME SI" with line 3 of the text; also delete the second "IOIOMISS" (opposite line 20 of the text)
305.F3 for "M" read "Mac"
310.09 for "(that)" read ", (that)"
322.01 indent
399.12 delete the relevant note in "Corrections of Misprints" in the Appendix (already incorporated)
406.01 for "or" read "of"
425.08 "trouble" badly printed
566.26 for "porkego." read "porkego!"
626.34 for "isht" read "wisht"

The marginal notes on pages 260-308 are misplaced in the same way as those in the 1946-49 printings.

Pagination and lineation are identical in all texts except the latest American printings which have a number of very minor differences. These will not affect users of the concordance. Finnegans Wake is published in the United States by the Viking Press, Inc., and in England by Faber & Faber, Ltd.

METHOD OF PRODUCTION

The following outline of the general mechanics of production is provided for readers who may be interested in such things.

As the concordance was to be produced by one person, with only occasional mechanical help, a simple series of successive operations had to be planned after the editorial procedure had been decided on and the text established.

1. The complete text was typed on small cards (3" x 2 1/2")—one word (with page/line number) to a card. These cards were filed in order of the words' occurrence in the text. After the first few pages considerable mechanical speed can be achieved in this process, so that the typing was completed in about two months.[6]

2. The cards were then checked for accuracy against the text, using a clean copy of the book. As each word was checked it was marked out on the book with heavy

[5] London, 1953, p. 60.

[6] Mr. Richard Fisher, of the University of Lund, is preparing a similar concordance to the works of Faulkner. He has considerably streamlined the first process by typing the text on long rolls of heavy paper, such as are used in cash-registers. After checking, the rolls are guillotined before sorting. This method considerably speeds up the whole task.

pencil. Errors and omissions (about thirty in number at this stage) were then rectified.

3. The cards were hand-sorted into alphabetical order—a process requiring some weeks of work. It is at this stage that the lack of electronic equipment is most seriously felt.

4. The MS of the Primary Index was then typed out and checked against the cards.

5. The first four processes were repeated for the Syllabifications and Overtones, these two lists being produced simultaneously in a single run through the text. My working copy of Finnegans Wake is interleaved throughout with annotations which were consulted for the preparation of these lists.

6. Several further readings of the text produced a new crop of Syllabifications and Overtones which were added in.

7. The word-counts were made with a small hand-tally and twice checked for accuracy.

8. After completion of the first typescripts, a small flow of new material was constantly added to the Syllabifications and Overtones during a long period of study of the text.

PRIMARY INDEX

a a A A
a 140.10 140.15 287.14 369.25
A 226.31 (A is Arancia)
293.18 (A is for Anna)
336.12 (Mr A)
359.21 (Group A)
A. 263.07 (Major A. Shaw)
514.26 (A. Briggs Carlisle)
541.03 (A. Costofino)
'a 415.16 (he)
a' 024.01 038.16
à 007.07 124.09 124.11 184.27
184.27 184.28 184.29 184.30
184.31 184.32
à 081.29 150.03 165.29 292.18
aa 254.16
A.A. 240.30 (Anaks Andrum)
Aarlund 069.08
aab 263.F1
aabs 283.26
aaherra 326.26
aal 403.16
aandt 331.15
aardappel 078.20
aars 214.09
aas 127.19
Aasas 343.10
aasbukividdy 327.34
Aasdocktor 241.15
aase 326.10
aasgaars 221.15
aaskart 377.33
aastalled 088.19
a.a.t.s.o.t. 180.16 (and all
that sort of thing)
ab 154.35 254.16 421.10 479.33
Ab 518.31
A.B, 421.10
ababs 314.30
aback 204.25 309.02 586.17
abad 268.19
abaft 137.23 508.02
abaft 123.21
abaht 093.20
abandon 198.27
abandoned 181.27 625.25
Abarm's 531.10
abarrel 351.03
Abase 154.12
abaseth 249.14
abasourdly 430.14
abast 016.09
abate 547.26
abated 607.25
abbels 584.02
abbely 028.19
abbess's 183.26
abbey 483.09
Abbey 290.F1
Abbeygate 105.26
Abbeytotte 609.17
abbles 005.30 201.33
abblokooken 170.16
abbosed 345.34
Abbot 539.27
Abbotabishop 392.14
Abbrace 106.32
Abbreciades 534.02
abbroaching 324.36
Abby 167.18
A. B. C. 065.28
abcd 141.04
abcedminded 018.17
abdominal 437.10
Abdul 355.10
Abdullah 034.02
abe 005.29 167.08
Abe 106.28
a-be 105.03
abeam 091.18
abeat 328.05
abeat 255.15
abecedeed 140.14
abed 565.36
abedder 252.12
Abedicate 379.19
a'beggars 510.19
abel 455.21
Abel 237.34
Abelbody 063.16
abelboobied 416.03
Abelite 446.29
abery 364.31
abeyance 358.08
abfalltree 088.02
abgod 091.28
Abgott 188.31
Abha 496.27
abhears 023.26
abhor 539.15
abhord 243.34
abhors 581.15
abhout 033.36
abiad 254.16
abide 078.07
Abide 040.03
abiding 484.01
Abies 100.14
abijance 389.03
ability 306.05 324.34
abject 161.02
abjects 340.05
abjourned 585.27
abjure 350.20
ablations 606.24
ablaze 021.17
able 033.20 034.13 041.03
047.29 055.01 063.09 102.03
287.12 303.21 336.13 357.25
364.27 410.30 410.33 427.19
495.21 567.32 616.19
Able 306.F6
abler 154.36
ablished 290.27
ablong 415.32
ablution 235.04
abnegand 573.31
Abnegation 306.L1
abnihilisation 353.22
abnormal 034.28
aboard 469.18
aboarder 358.20
abob 005.02
abock 037.06
abode 040.17
abog 376.03
aboil 604.24
aboleshqvick 302.18
abomasum 097.15
aboo 373.25 464.07
aboon 029.11 181.25
abooned 323.33
abooth 394.27
aboove 110.17
aboriginally 169.02
ABORTISEMENT 181.33
abought 415.17
abound 055.27 323.32 439.15
aboundin 110.03
about about About
aboutobloss 237.12
abouts 603.05
abouve 333.20
above 032.26 035.29 036.14
065.14 077.24 082.20 108.09
135.31 148.07 152.04 164.04
263.21 331.24 377.36 415.22
432.19 472.32 476.18 484.29
492.14 494.02 494.09 494.18
495.30 512.22 516.07 552.06
557.21 559.05 607.29 616.19
above 349.26 418.18
abovebeugled 284.19
abovemansioned 265.04
abover 351.18

abower 450.16
aboy 277.23
abracadabra 184.26
Abraham 078.15 167.25 294.24 421.05
Abraham 307.L1
Abrahamsk 481.24
abram 546.17
abramanation 026.19
Abride 501.03
a'bride 013.27
abridge 097.22
abridged 547.25
abroad 024.17 024.22 058.11 198.30 244.11 362.13 372.20 477.11 567.14 568.01 620.10
Abroad 289.29
abromette 022.20
abrood 129.10
abrowtobayse 602.15
absantee 198.16
abscissan 298.26
absconded 545.02 589.33
absedes 552.07
absence 108.30 189.31 506.17
Absence 536.05
absences 355.04
absendee 228.22 458.10
absent 039.29 173.30 389.19 413.18
absent 342.01
absenter 453.21
absents 348.13
absexed 525.08
absintheminded 464.17
absolation 228.07
absolent 609.02
absolete 575.05
absolute 164.10 390.33 391.16
absolute 276.L5
Absolutely 458.35 502.23 509.16
absolutionally 341.31
absorbable 604.09
absorbere 611.19
absorbing 035.01
absquelitteris 512.17
abstainer 489.17
abstrew 395.01
Absurd 538.19
absurdly 120.06
abu 254.16 500.06
a'buckets 005.03
Abulbul 355.10
abuliousness 255.28
abunda 577.15
abundant 062.13
abunk 267.F6
abuse 183.03
abused 149.34 429.08 547.01
Abuses 306.30
abushed 034.33
abusing 173.20 520.07
abusive 071.05
abutt 415.18
abuy 247.18
abuzz 534.04
abwaited 364.20
abyss 056.04
ac 113.30 185.21
academy 494.21
Academy 221.02
acape 317.36
acarras 320.18
accacians 160.12
accampaigning 356.31
Accanite 158.03
acce'l 182.20
accelerated 099.18
accent 093.10 253.04 376.04 461.03 520.30
accents 140.23 270.03
accentuated 124.07 333.07
accentually 421.26
accept 457.36
Accept 032.22
accepted 049.04 120.17
accepting 447.05
accessit 153.21
Accesstopartnuzz 571.28
accidence 078.16 288.12 472.31
accidens 487.02
accident 038.28 038.29 269.14 539.10 566.30
Accident 418.28
accidental 134.20
Accidental 222.01
accidents 150.32 452.03
acclammitation 153.25
acclapadad 347.27
acclivisciously 437.04
accolated 031.34
accomodate 498.08
accomodation 615.30
accomodationnooks 235.23
accomondation 382.19
accompanied 037.12 108.03 189.24 575.22 605.22
accompaniment 128.26
accompanying 484.04
accomplasses 295.27
accompliced 587.32
accomplished 051.30 174.08 189.14 274.04
accomplishment 368.23
accord 446.16 509.02
accorded 143.09 608.02
according 031.20 046.28 063.31 239.16 253.22 290.05 313.11 387.24 388.30 391.12 393.20 519.08 529.26 573.26
ACCORDING 303.R1
accordingly 088.04
Accordingly 569.29
accornish 151.19
accorsaired 600.11
accostant 567.21
accosted 035.15
accoster 230.11
accouched 542.28
account 061.36 146.16 150.16 181.10 229.35 243.32 391.06 392.36 435.32 445.21 525.12 536.25 574.03 575.13
Account 107.02
accountibus 253.36
accountrements 507.11
accounts 036.11 471.25 519.29 589.31
accounts 338.13
accourdant 236.36
Accourting 094.28
accoustomology 598.23
accowding 061.07
accretions 114.28
accrue 547.02
accuracy 143.07
accurate 525.11
accurect 242.03
accusant 223.19
accusation 036.04
accusative 122.03
Accusative 019.30
accusatives 269.09
accuse 241.23
accused 522.08
Accusing 107.07
accwmwladed 590.16
ace 122.10 134.07 463.07
ace 342.03
Ace 283.04
Ace 071.24
ace's 108.23
aceticist 417.16
Acetius 161.25
aceupper 352.12
ach 090.28 250.34
achamed 143.34
achance 363.29
achaura 345.02
Achburn 059.17
Achdung 100.05
ache 120.30
acheporeoozers 156.13
achershous 536.13
aches 229.01
acheseyeld 148.33
Aches-les-Pains 213.18
Acheve 466.30
Achevre 276.13
achewing 587.31
achieve 596.34
achievement 304.25
achilles 154.18
Achill's 248.11
Achin 257.21
Aching 395.25
Achinhead 262.F6
Achmed 492.22
Achoch 392.15
acid 185.33 210.09 231.14 393.01
acids 036.01 240.19
acidulateds 220.04
acity 094.18
ack 065.34 065.34
Ack 065.34
acknowledging 129.25
acknowledgment 124.30
acknowledgments 358.31
acknuckledownedgment 344.08
ackshan 344.22
aclacking 256.06
a'clog 127.07
aclucking 256.06
acnomina 098.27
acolyte 605.24
Acomedy 425.24
acoming 022.31 194.22
a-coming 264.10
acommon 276.24
acoo 245.18
acoolsha 626.35
acope-acurly 140.19
acordant 180.05
acordial 313.07
acorns 043.11 505.04
acorpolous 541.25
acorss 056.03
A'Cothraige 054.14

acoughawhooping 128.10
acounts 368.05
acountstrick 180.05
acoustic 165.08 393.11
Acoustic 071.18
acoustrolobe 419.21
Acquae 147.07
acquaintance 020.12 095.25 109.18 389.11 398.14 440.16
acquainted 506.27
acquainters 532.26
acquarate 601.33
acqueduced 128.09
acqueducked 471.18
acquiester 145.10
acquinntence 514.17
acquire 435.32
acquired 114.28 413.09 610.23 610.25 610.26
ACQUIRED 268.R1
acquitted 057.36
acquointance 145.10
acrash 382.19
acrawl 074.14
acre 553.08
Acre 073.23 618.08
Acre 105.35
acres 135.05 135.21 189.13 231.21
acropoll 167.13
across 015.10 035.07 053.04 055.09 097.02 122.02 173.33 178.24 185.06 202.32 231.10 367.34 428.21 449.30 529.22 574.29 605.16
acrumbling 415.21
acrux 173.02
act 055.14 061.08 061.10 061.10 061.15 078.34 109.16 162.04 182.19 198.23 332.10 424.18 436.02 443.08 456.33 495.29 510.22 528.24 529.08 532.07 558.16 575.27 576.04 585.25 597.24
act 341.03 345.04
Act 184.16 447.36 501.07 559.18 616.25 617.35
acta 085.13
actaman 598.34
acted 470.03 532.21
action 009.25 167.28 356.31 559.22 574.06 583.02
actionable 519.28
acting 164.03 341.15 486.32
actionneers 028.32
actiums 272.11
active 114.34 134.26 137.33 269.28 386.28 392.35 523.11 543.34 570.22
Active 301.L2
activescent 597.32
actors 569.29
actress 227.07
acts 127.12 137.33 222.06 325.33 384.01 435.36
Acts 222.30
actual 253.17
actually 169.10 184.05 380.17 417.35 611.23
actuary 294.14
acup 138.29
acuredent 184.23
acurraghed 322.19
acushla 480.23
acushla 399.18
acute 624.09
acutebacked 608.24
acùtely 124.10
ad 124.09 254.16 283.15 302.22 441.09 467.34 541.28
ad 068.06 165.34 185.14 355.06 497.23 497.23 551.13
Ad 610.21
Ad 418.04 481.16 497.05
A.D. 013.33 (1132 A.D.)
013.36 (566 A.D.)
014.07 (566 A.D.)
014.11 (1132 A.D.)
272.14
420.20 (1132 A.D.)
Ada 147.11
Adam 021.06 083.22 197.12 246.28 251.28 420.35 514.23 549.33 558.10 619.03
Adam 124.34 176.04 306.L2
adamale 031.12
adamant 626.03
Adamantaya 498.15
adamelegy 077.26
Adam-he-used-to 291.03
Adamman 267.18
adamologists 113.04
adams 551.22
Adams 028.32 039.24 070.05 313.12
Adams 381.19
Adam's 003.01 559.02
adapt 375.34
Adaptation 306.L1
adapted 028.27 284.F4 599.28
adaptive 325.14
Adar 013.24
adazillahs 102.03
adceterus 379.31
adcraft 241.23
add 033.21 033.33 055.01 076.15 115.02 184.03 222.05 270.F3 273.13 283.F1 336.02 396.04 469.30 526.34 575.07 586.24 598.08 599.33 615.12 619.09
add 346.10
Add 074.07 113.18 561.22
adda 200.31
added 043.31 059.14 109.15 156.33 448.34 552.26
addedto 153.30
Adder 535.31
adder's 303.29
addict 179.21
addicted 161.20
adding 035.34 189.02 189.09 369.13 586.12
addition 114.21 165.20
additional 077.21
addle 004.28
addled 205.24 315.03
addlefoes 487.10
addling 082.26
Addmundson 325.22
addn't 297.18
address 077.25 085.24 087.18 187.30 407.28 563.18
Address 375.35
addresse 464.17
addressed 109.08
addresses 173.06
addressing 407.33
Addressing 485.04
adds 117.13
addurge 570.04
adeal 280.26
adear 013.27
Adear 013.27
Adelaide's 040.36 450.17
Adelphi 219.14
Adelphus 234.35
Aden 324.36
Adenoiks 242.02
adepted 320.04
adestance 602.14
Adew 244.29
Adgigasta 081.05
adhere 432.26
adheres 018.27
adhesively 575.18
adi 029.27
adiaptotously 157.21
adie 472.21
Adie 409.30 613.03
adieu 286.13 563.37
Adieu 563.36
adim 395.01
adimadim 552.25
adimdim 552.25
adin 236.10
adipose 499.16
adjacencies 597.13
adjacent 043.02
adjugers 057.18
adjutant 348.12
administers 597.34
administrants 492.16
admirable 041.31 326.26 553.13 607.28
admirable 341.18
admiracion 144.11 451.31
admiralty 123.25
admiration 092.26 374.09 526.29 564.09
admire 570.30
admired 229.35 405.27 495.28 506.33 551.06 617.33
admirer 165.13
admirers 051.35
admiring 025.15 046.28
admittance 322.28
admitted 173.15
admittedly 034.26
Admittedly 109.08
admonish 444.06
Admortal 105.17
admoyers 539.07
adn't 345.02
ado 560.16 560.17
adolescent 188.28
adolls 249.01
Adolphos 093.33
adolphted 234.35
adomic 615.06
adondering 623.24
adoom 552.25
adoptation 446.29
adopted 219.19 575.25
adorable 125.13 527.15
adorables 237.18
adore 145.36 562.32
adored 146.03 302.20
adores 028.17 249.19 527.29
adorest 146.19

adoring 563.33
adornment 077.34 382.18
adown 404.01
adpropinquans 185.16
adraft 598.05
adranse 199.10
a'Dream's 061.04
Adrian 153.20
adrift 598.05
adrone 074.14
Adry 469.27
ads 130.16 235.14 312.35
adsaturas 379.31
adullescence 054.35
Adultereux 250.12
adumbrace 220.15
a'duna 094.31
advance 083.01 114.13 163.14 249.21
advanced 034.15 545.10
advancing 475.12
advantage 544.13 547.02 599.33
Advantages 307.01
advauncement 608.03
advenements 564.33
Advent 130.07
adventuring 279.F20
adverb 115.29
Adversarian 535.14
Adversary 081.19
Adversed 378.13
Adversus 167.34
Advert 599.24
advertisement 004.14
advertisers 163.14
advertising 053.19
advice 299.31 432.06 439.27 506.30
advices 141.20 356.07
advicies 534.15
advise 164.35 188.01 447.35 469.08
advised 193.05 448.26 481.22 618.11
advisers 160.03 185.02
advocate 572.34
advocatesses 093.12
advokaat 256.08
advokaatoes 116.28
advowtried 534.35
Adya 598.14
adyatants 598.25
Adyoe 073.22
adze 169.11 486.28
aebel 303.F1
Aecquotincts 599.20
aegis 276.L3
Aegypt 104.22
aeone 552.08
aeones 552.08
aequal 141.04 300.04
Aequalllllllll 141.07
aerger 281.21
aerial 077.07
Aerial 449.30
Aerials 099.10
aerian 316.04
Aerian's 379.11
aerily 057.22
Aerin 338.36
aerios 540.35
aeropagods 005.33
aers 231.30
Aerwenger's 445.36
Aeships 625.04
Aestmand 325.22
aestumation 204.02
aether 462.34
Aetius 266.25
af 252.35 265.14 479.32
af 491.20
Afamado 492.22
afar 176.32 407.14 589.10
afarfrom 565.32
afarred 278.26
Afartodays 622.15
afeald 602.15
afear 279.01
Afeared 475.03
afeartonights 622.15
afeerd 497.16
Aferican 387.02
aff 491.19
affact 474.05
affair 082.16 118.07 166.06 535.20
affair 201.07
affaird 497.17
affairs 149.36 438.18 442.01
affect 116.01
affectable 618.27
affected 120.23
Affected 602.25
affection 431.24 513.17
affectionate 111.19 461.16 616.15
affectioned 043.22
affections 432.02 445.36
affection's 533.19
affects 483.01
Afferik 320.28
Afferyank 191.04
affianced 433.05
affianxed 235.22
affinitatively 613.35
affirm 033.19 241.33 519.26 520.28 573.21
affirmative 524.10
affirmed 520.29
affirmly 520.32
affixed 545.16
afflictedly 427.30
Affluence 207.12
affluvial 404.01
afford 532.18 586.04
affranchisant 101.24
Affrian 497.12
affrication 573.25
affront 204.25 339.07 415.28
affsang 346.22
affubling 346.01
affusion 606.11
afinger 246.08
afire 003.09
aflash 246.08
afloat 065.29
aflod 209.30
aflower 237.31
aflowering 406.24
aflutter 121.05
aflutter-afraida 272.03
afore 014.31 091.07 130.02 332.20 372.13 378.17 587.16 587.35 594.29
aforefelt 163.09
aforegoing 599.33
aforetime 108.22 478.04
afoul 515.26
afraid 411.30 481.26 495.35
Afram 317.09
Afrantic 297.32
afreet 011.06
Africa 129.32
African 520.17
africot 489.27
afrightened 521.24
Afrothdizzying 203.27
afstef 366.31
aft 254.21 384.27
aftabournes 365.34
aftanon 183.07
aften 338.14
Aftening 099.34
after 013.36 014.28 021.23 024.19 025.11 027.01 028.19 029.31 032.13 035.06 036.19 037.28 037.30 039.08 039.33 040.33 041.03 041.14 041.29 042.05 043.15 049.02 049.09 049.24 055.07 061.15 062.27 063.18 064.15 066.24 066.25 067.16 067.34 070.13 070.16 070.18 070.29 072.29 073.03 073.12 076.24 079.15 082.10 083.20 086.25 091.12 091.32 095.09 102.01 102.05 108.16 109.22 110.16 113.25 113.31 114.36 118.12 118.35 119.01 119.18 119.23 123.19 124.27 124.35 125.06 125.09 129.29 130.08 132.26 136.31 138.15 140.32 144.04 145.03 147.31 150.25 151.18 151.30 152.21 155.35 157.36 159.21 163.33 165.36 170.19 170.36 171.35 174.31 175.01 176.33 178.25 178.34 179.23 180.03 181.07 186.09 186.11 186.34 190.22 192.36 197.21 198.15 199.07 200.08 202.17 203.35 205.09 205.16 205.18 207.01 219.15 220.16 220.21 221.05 222.34 224.02 224.11 226.18 230.13 230.22 231.23 235.11 236.05 237.16 238.26 239.14 240.32 241.15 241.25 244.36 245.33 254.27 256.35 257.21 262.F5 263.08 270.14 275.F5 277.13 280.13 280.33 282.18 286.04 290.11 291.19 300.26 303.18 305.15 311.05 311.06 311.36 313.08 313.11 313.20 315.09 315.13 316.16 316.20 316.26 320.03 323.07 323.09 325.33 327.17 328.10 329.34 331.24 333.31 336.01 343.25 343.26 347.05 347.23 352.12 355.34 358.14 359.05 359.09 359.36 360.35 363.28 368.36 369.36 370.11 372.18 374.26 376.08 376.25 377.22 379.22 380.04 380.08 380.10 380.14 380.20 380.35 382.14 382.15 384.16 385.01 385.20 385.22 386.16 386.27 387.20 387.22 388.10 388.12 388.15 388.22 389.23 391.29 392.05 393.21 394.12 394.20 396.32 396.35 397.09 397.25 398.07 398.07 398.12 405.22 406.08 406.17 408.15

411.02 411.31 412.08 416.12
417.08 417.33 422.35 423.23
428.02 430.17 430.34 431.04
431.14 432.04 432.33 436.20
438.05 439.09 441.10 443.03
453.05 453.31 454.25 454.31
455.06 455.34 460.07 461.17
461.21 462.29 462.34 463.23
465.13 465.28 467.24 468.07
471.14 471.21 472.16 472.36
475.28 477.21 480.31 483.13
488.31 490.34 496.14 497.06
498.17 498.35 499.02 501.10
505.06 507.05 508.01 510.07
510.22 516.33 517.02 517.05
517.13 517.29 519.04 519.22
519.23 519.31 519.34 526.07
526.31 527.14 528.07 530.06
530.07 537.07 539.01 544.30
544.33 550.08 557.36 560.01
560.06 560.22 563.24 566.14
571.22 573.15 574.32 575.03
577.24 579.19 580.06 580.12
581.26 583.36 585.33 588.10
590.06 593.21 594.20 596.27
599.14 603.22 603.26 604.18
605.02 606.29 609.06 609.07
609.07 609.09 612.05 616.30
619.01 620.15 620.24 621.07
621.13 621.27 622.17 622.36
624.34 625.34 626.20
after 340.04 340.14 343.01
345.06 345.06 350.08 353.07
354.17 525.24
After 009.20 059.35 178.08
201.26 266.18 275.F4 294.13
325.09 355.19 409.28 435.26
469.26 469.29 509.24 521.29
528.23 590.17 590.26 623.36
afterdoon 461.13
afterduepoise 407.06
afterdusk 419.21
afterenactment 222.16
afterfall 078.07
afterhis 343.33
Afterhour 221.01
aftermeal 017.16
aftermoon 280.07
aftermorn 346.12
afternoon 030.14 070.33
187.05 309.15
460.29
afternunch 127.31
Afterpiece 455.26
afters 271.17
aftertale 038.10
afterthought 258.32 475.32
afterthoughtfully 342.34
afterwards 032.09 034.05 077.14
110.27 120.21
Afterwheres 477.33
afterwite 066.17
afterworse 416.10
aftoms 598.21
Aftreck 240.17
aftscents 527.29
afume 542.22
afurz 294.23
ag 389.32
A. G. 539.06 (Aktiengesellschaft)
again again Again
agains 241.33
again's 093.35
against 007.33 024.24 061.32
062.15 062.33 063.28 063.34
067.15 067.19 070.32 086.36
097.20 107.32 108.01 112.31
113.21 119.04 123.34 127.11
133.11 146.34 155.19 188.05
190.30 192.32 197.19 205.21
227.28 247.22 254.02 301.F3
316.03 331.20 364.02 365.08
366.02 366.20 374.32 429.18
430.04 451.02 467.25 507.06
523.09 532.19 534.17 541.14
541.18 544.04 544.13 553.23
578.31 587.31 615.33 616.01
626.14
against 354.21
againstm 036.04
againus 361.03
agam 346.17
agamb 346.17
agame 569.17 614.18
Agapemonides 007.16
agapo 202.07
agate 625.35
Agatha's 430.35
age 019.10 020.28 061.30
075.06 078.06 089.28 112.19
136.15 162.02 170.08 173.07
211.13 213.14 227.34 242.26
251.10 289.25 324.10 357.17
362.16 365.18 371.19 380.01
380.14 389.13 392.03 423.26
426.23 433.32 438.22 483.09
489.19 489.36 494.30 513.23
535.30 559.26 559.29 562.18
562.19 595.35 598.33
aged 043.04 136.26 333.06
341.13 463.27
Aged 414.36
ageing 487.16
agelong 102.28
agen 326.18 378.19 551.29
agen 346.17
agence 524.06
agenst 326.21
agent 069.01
agentlike 005.13
Ager 142.13
ages 005.16 007.16 035.05
035.05 051.11 066.05 093.08
101.12 112.09 117.01 144.15
144.15 193.26 198.30 202.36
207.36 255.06 262.18 272.09
291.08 316.16 427.32 453.29
485.18 497.09 582.02 622.14
âges 281.11
aggala 475.02
Aggala 475.13
aggere 287.26
agglaggagglomeratively 186.10
agglutinative 465.12
agglutinatively 120.30
aggravated 063.07
aggregate 497.09
aggrily 120.22
Aghatharept 250.27
aghist 343.34
aghom 338.22
Agiapommenites 498.10
agin 139.27 209.21
agin 176.14
agincourting 009.07
aging 617.17
agins 292.08
aginsst 056.07
aginst 089.01
agirlies 094.01
agitatating 242.14
agitated 114.34
agitator 313.04
Agitator 056.06
Agithetta 569.14
agleement 348.13
aglo 528.23
aglove 374.12
agnates 115.33
agnelows 470.30
Agnes 212.14
Agnes' 548.22
Agni 080.24
Agni 497.05
agnitest 594.02
agnols 223.03
agnomen 030.03
agnomes 283.27
agnoscere 287.27
AGNOSIS 262.R2
ago 020.22 174.23 188.03
252.13 263.13 323.13 357.24
387.17 452.08
agoad 624.17
agob 232.32
Agog 006.19
a-going 264.10
agon 593.10
agone 021.05 336.06
agonising 190.15
Agonising 302.L1
agony 075.18 122.04 333.20
agooding 379.22
agora 062.16
agore 553.07
Agrah 358.32
agrammatical 307.F7
agree 102.23 164.10 174.10
312.34 419.29 616.18
agree 399.15
agreeable 347.18 619.10
agreed 362.03 410.20 537.18
Agreed 590.13
agreem 017.17
agreement 112.11 318.27 612.26
agreenable 609.01
Agreest 514.28
agres 625.20
agricolous 173.16
agricultural 405.11
agrin 139.01
agripment 084.16
Agrippa 094.13
agrog 006.19
aguaducks 553.22
Ague 112.20 150.08
aguepe 417.22
agues 505.17 555.08
Aguilar 184.35
agulp 190.18
agum 422.28
agun 336.06 350.32
agus 378.19
Agus 265.06
agush 178.12
ah 005.11 069.02 069.02 080.09
089.27 121.26 140.09 161.25
180.15 225.32 249.18 278.10
279.07 279.F36 287.15 300.12

301.16 365.35 379.19 391.27 392.02 392.09 395.30 461.32 461.32 461.32 461.32 499.10 521.17 556.21 565.12 608.36
Ah 013.26 090.28 094.14 094.33 096.21 117.10 143.22 158.20 158.20 184.33 184.36 215.12 224.09 224.20 244.11 257.23 279.07 340.16 352.25 372.22 385.17 386.12 389.20 389.31 390.30 391.12 392.12 392.35 393.05 404.12 404.34 410.30 427.08 433.30 434.16 455.23 456.07 464.15 481.08 515.30 515.32 561.06 562.02 562.03 563.10 571.13 581.20 581.24 601.19 606.23 608.36 609.09
Aha 293.19 298.22 352.25
Ahahn 110.21
ahahs 183.14
ahake 240.18
Aham 422.18
A'Hara 049.03
ahat 059.06
ahaza 176.27
Ahdahm 205.31
Ahday's 506.10
Ahdostay 058.11
ahead 004.30 119.29 178.34 274.04 450.06 589.06 589.15
ahear 486.30
ahem 484.36
Ahem 147.11 374.04
ahems 183.14
ahike 603.16
Ahim 458.10
Ahlen 594.18
Ahmohn 377.31
ahnsire 019.30
ahold 281.24 438.20
ahome 215.32 473.05
ahone 176.27
a-hooded 588.16
ahorace 325.13
ahore 481.26
Ahorror 311.25
ahoy 054.26 077.06 460.27
ahoykling 384.05
ahquickyessed 365.11
ahriman 426.03
ahrtides 502.23
ahs 184.01 453.09
ahs 352.29
ahull 370.34
ahumming 198.01 549.20
ahunt 332.04
AI 130.13
A.I. 329.05 (Sir A.I. Magnus) 456.07 (Ah Ireland!)
Aiaiaiai 293.22
aich 537.34
aiches 121.16
aid 029.27 114.12 264.01 337.05 348.02 363.24
aid 346.10
aidant 241.23
aiden 327.34
aiding 571.07
aidress 568.31
Aiduolcis 568.10
aiger 132.07
aight 405.18
aigrydoucks 456.15
Ailbey 484.23
Aileen 320.24
Ailesbury 235.13 615.20
Ailing 148.33
ailment 098.18
ailmint 241.06
ails 015.18
ail's 418.34
aim 126.07 210.18 510.02 548.16
aimai 202.06
aime 372.04
aimed 272.05 545.08
Aimee 335.30
aimees 351.33
aimer's 463.07
Aimihi 213.07
aims 366.26 622.18
aim's 122.10
Aimstirdames 509.24
Aimswell 040.01
ain 138.01 209.23 594.21
Ainée 289.25
ainsell 581.06
Ainsoph 261.23
aint 299.07
Aint 171.29
ain't 248.18 430.25
ainway 021.08
aiopen 165.05
air 067.08 115.06 117.01 132.07 250.32 255.25 256.36 280.21 281.26 304.25 316.14 318.02 351.13 381.23 385.26 397.13 413.21 437.19 437.19 471.24 475.36 488.13 521.05 528.29 534.32 541.31 561.26 602.06 604.24 623.19 624.28 627.09
Air 258.20
Aira 353.32
airabouts 010.26
aird 204.35
aire 201.19
aireating 061.15
aired 004.08
Aireen 421.14
airest 514.36
airforce 461.06
airish 055.24 223.03 327.31 344.18
Airish 192.26
airly 129.14 155.12 224.16 360.14 435.23
Airman 144.33
Airmienious 296.08
airs 222.36 330.14 437.07 450.19 452.13 500.14 511.20 595.13
air's 469.04
airse 489.09
airsighs 502.19
airth 615.24
airwaked 560.15
airweek's 393.13
airwhackers 042.31
Airwinger's 028.15
airy 009.30 119.15 207.08 254.15 414.28 467.22
Airy 106.31
Airyanna 275.14
airywhugger 360.32
aisch 209.27
aisle 122.20
aisles 254.33
aisling 179.31
aisne 204.02
aisy 024.16 152.01
Aisy 027.22
aisy-oisy 198.12
ait 294.04
aitch 382.13
aither 029.09
Aithne 394.26
ajaciulations 089.10
Ajaculate 338.27
Ajax 306.L2
ajaxious 053.16
ajew 250.07 250.07
ajog 414.22
ajustilloosing 180.03
akes 184.13
akimbo 249.23
a'kind 117.17
akiss 203.35
akkant 414.22
akkount 178.32
akkurat 056.19
aks 123.02
akstiom 296.02
akter 241.01
akwart 291.22
al 052.14 160.30
AL 294.03
Ala 335.17
Alabye 225.34
alack 166.30 285.01 428.22
aladdin 407.27
alaguerre 233.30
Alam 347.21
alamam 331.17
alancey 360.34
Aland 601.35
alanglast 006.26
alanna 270.04
alannah 477.05
Alannah 377.19
alarming 549.11
alarms 468.23
alarums 566.13
alas 119.15 270.20 294.16 322.06 453.01 528.18 533.08
alas 231.05
Alas 496.01
alasalah 084.11
alass 293.22 407.27
alast 354.03
alaterelly 337.04
alaughing 361.18
alawd 490.04
alb 605.10 611.08
Alba 463.24
albas 593.13
Albatrus 558.27
albedinous 414.36
albeit 084.09 558.02
Albern 202.20
albert 126.15
Alberths 598.06
albies 456.16
Albiogenselman 173.13
Albionias 343.09
Albiony 137.07
Albo 152.26
albowcrural 557.17
albs 520.15
album 382.18
albut 293.05

albutisle 017.18
Alby 488.29 620.05
alce 618.23
Alcibiades 306.L4
alcoh 040.05
alcoherently 040.05
alcoho 040.05
alcohol 070.27 134.33 444.02
Alcohol 255.24
alcoholic 545.10
alcohoran 020.09
alcovan 597.15
alcove 185.01 491.14 604.08
ald 004.15
aldanabal 186.10
aldays 133.18 282.27
Aldborougham 104.20
Alddaublin 373.19
alderbirk 553.03
alderman 013.25 253.10
Alderman 160.15
aldest 540.19
aldritch 548.35
ale 199.19 264.03 310.31 381.28 382.06
aleal 339.31
aleashing 623.02
aleaves 389.20
alebrill 015.36
aleconner 319.04
aleconnerman 141.25
aled 136.15
alefru's 245.33
alegobrew 283.24
aleguere 233.30
aleland 088.30
Alemaney 423.04
alemon 331.17
ales 192.08 379.25 501.19
Ales 587.09
Alesse 203.08
alest 354.03
Aletheometry 370.13
aleveens 201.27
aleven 388.12
alevilla 388.22
alevoila 388.22
Alexis 073.25
alextronite 349.14
alfa 296.24
Alfaiate 180.12
alfi 568.32
alfred 392.32 600.28
alfrids 019.09
algebrars 270.24
algebrist 443.19
Algy 434.35
alhome 531.13
Ali 319.18
alias 518.15
alias 443.26
Alibany 489.32
Alibey 346.05
alibi 190.30 488.16
alice 321.31
Alice 214.24
alicence 032.03
'alices 115.22
Alicious 528.17
alick 166.30 416.15
alicubi 034.08
alien 197.03
alienation 558.08
Alieni 600.11
Alif 318.24
alift 361.18
aliftle 504.14
alight 208.28 378.17 417.07 427.16
align 296.27
alike 021.18 022.05 022.29 178.15 263.16 317.22 358.13 372.04 503.35 532.14
ALIKE 165.15
aliment 163.02
alimentation 557.26
aliments 130.16
aliments 286.L4
alimoney 344.21
alimony 192.32
Alina 608.18
alio 488.10
alionola 488.09
alios 240.33
alip 397.19
aliquitudinis 100.34
Alis 270.20
alisten 237.09
Alitten's 528.04
alittle 144.13
aliudpiam 287.27
alive 041.27 083.05 139.19 311.22 533.27 538.21 551.22
aliven 341.20
aljambras 550.35
alkalike 167.19
alkolic 393.02
all all All All ALL
alla 184.31 213.33 261.F1 406.03 531.16
Alla 569.12
allabalmy 578.21
allaboardshoops 077.28
allabout 101.02
allabouter 101.03
allaboy 488.21
Allaboy 152.13 159.21
allabroad 417.20
allabroad's 115.28
allabuff 022.35
allacook 214.23
allad 496.11
Allad 231.29
alladim 560.19
all-a-dreams 597.20
Allaf 352.34
allafranka 343.28
allahallahallah 597.14
Allahballah 317.12
Allahblah 340.12
allahlah 235.07
allahthallacamellated 285.21
Allaliefest 562.07
allalilty 373.34
Allalivial 213.32
allallahbath 417.27
allalluvial 213.32
allalong 312.27
allaloserem 304.31
allamarsch 332.18
Allamin 311.02
Allan 588.28
allanights 283.26
allaniuvia 627.27
Allapalla 316.21
allaph 242.31 297.32
allaphbed 018.18
Allapolloosa 494.25
Allare 534.31
allaready 602.33
allarmes 426.14
allaround 355.09
allaroundside 612.14
allasif 331.06
allasundery 339.25
allassundrian 439.34
allasvitally 354.05
allatheses 309.08
allathome 457.35
allathome's 111.11
allatwanst 346.33
allauding 234.21
allaughed 492.04
allaughing 283.18
allavalonche 028.09
allaverred 343.30
allay 311.33 569.23 598.25
Allay 598.25
Allbart 105.14
allbe 537.03
allbegeneses 350.31
allbeit 362.31 524.01
allbeleaved 625.30
allbethey 412.25
allbigenesis 240.13
allbleakest 365.18
allblind 119.31
allbrant 198.31
Allbrecht 539.30
Allbrewham 097.16
Allbroggt 600.12
allbum's 535.10
allburt 598.07
allbust 156.10
allcalling 543.09
allcasually 005.25
Allclose 207.32
allcotten 434.05
allcunct 497.10
Alldaybrandy's 155.36
alldconfusalem 355.11
alle 213.30
Alle 118.21
alleance 242.34
allearth's 068.34
alleged 035.06 244.29 493.01 495.29 574.11
alleghant 129.17
allegiance 344.27
allegibelling 031.32
alleging 070.28 375.01
alleman 485.07
allemanden 467.27
Allen 057.13 618.23
allenalaw 083.34
Allenglisches 532.10
aller 578.34
allergrossest 425.15
allerthings 368.20
alleven 283.F1
allexpected 324.27
alley 119.31 178.06 228.23 372.20 373.33
Alley 043.03 147.32 260.11
alleyeoneyesed 323.29
alleyou 339.26
Alleypulley 492.23
allfalling 535.33
allfaulters 355.35

allfinesof 289.05
allfirst 539.03
allflesh 186.05
Allfor 026.36
Allfor 106.30
allforabit 019.02
allfore 160.33
Allfou 197.25
allgas 496.13
Allgearls 626.03
allgood 021.30
allhallowed 587.14.
allhealths 280.13
Allhighest 080.20
Allhim 295.20
allhorrors 019.25
alliance 007.33 144.12 351.31
Allibuster 535.09
allied 288.F4 333.10 574.33
allieged 617.31
allies 272.10 359.35 491.24
Allies 307.13
Alligator 440.06
Alliman 594.34
allimmanence 394.33
allin 502.07
allinall 154.05 242.31
allinoilia 456.03 456.04
allirish 309.24
alliving 283.17
alljawbreakical 293.16
Allkey 317.05
Allma 268.L3
allmade 581.36
allmanox 512.04
allmarken 126.23
Allmarshy 017.08
Allmaun 479.35
Allmaziful 104.01
allmeals 283.23
Allmen 419.10
Allmeneck's 334.25
allmichael 279.F34
Allmichael 459.02
allmicheal 011.23
Allmookse 153.21
allmurk 404.10
allmysty 155.24
allness 568.26
allnight 153.34
allnight 399.23
allnights 489.35
allno 484.02
allo 430.10
alloaf 134.27
allocution 155.08
allocutioning 381.18
Alloe 321.14
allof 013.18
allohn 324.16
alloilable 153.27
Allolosha 106.23
Allothesis 298.L3
allours 251.27
allover 066.06 206.35 224.14 301.F3 353.16 455.08
allow 034.33 036.33 295.23 297.13 360.11
Allow 293.16 294.05 294.10 295.23
allowance 425.14
allowances 437.10
allowed 033.21 161.07 173.32 312.27 537.26
allower 064.10
allowing 573.16
allows 603.25
Alloy 311.33
alloyed 577.04
alloyiss 453.26
allphannd 129.17
allpointed 550.30
allporterous 560.31
Allprohome 074.06 074.07
allpurgers' 556.28
allriddle 274.02
allround 084.24 618.15
Allrouts 153.22
allruddy 274.03
alls 077.20 237.02 279.05 469.24
Alls 304.F5 304.F5
all's 003.11 125.18 187.25 263.22 382.14 427.17 563.32
All's 107.20 225.31 246.03 295.21
allsall 154.05
Allsap's 264.03
allsea 143.21
allsecure 022.17
allsee 239.05
Allself 395.02
allselse 503.22
allsfare 518.02
allside 611.22
allso 414.32 571.16 609.01
Allso 617.21
allsods 289.04
allsole 365.07
allsoonome 158.10
allsop 377.34
allsort 540.01
Allso's 488.24
allsosiftly 018.08
allsouls 243.06
Allspace 455.29
allstar 176.20
Allsup 377.33
allsweetheartening 189.26
Allswill 150.30
alltheways 602.31
Allthing 133.35
allthose 356.35
alltides 365.14
alltitude 004.33
allto 586.24
alltogether 523.13
alltogotter 349.32
alltolonely 152.19
alltomatetam 336.09
alltoocommon 435.33
all-too-ghoulish 615.04
alltoolyrical 452.03
alluded 051.08
alluding 090.21 507.26
alluring 528.17
allus 295.27 422.30
allvoyous 116.28
allways 020.06
Allwhichhole 278.03
Allwhichwhile 274.27
Allwhile 228.03
allwhite 187.02
ally 133.11 391.15 415.21
Ally 426.17
Allysloper 248.10
alma 348.11
Alma 619.16
Almagnian 352.11
Almayne 363.08
almaynoother 371.26
almeanium 113.03
almeans 465.11
Almeidagad 009.26
almightily 263.25
Almighty' 383.04
almistips 351.16
almonders 497.31
almonder's 234.12
almonds 064.36 183.12 235.34
almonence 337.04
almonthst 015.34
almost 016.23 052.30 111.26 120.24 171.20 276.F6 574.19 575.10 626.29
Almost 007.16 360.01 410.06
alms 098.14 454.03
almsdish 243.15
almshouse 043.19
alo 054.15
Alo 407.27
aloafen 378.23
Alocutionist 072.16
aloer 151.31
aloft 017.28 031.01 191.16 204.19 361.18 506.02 569.19
alohned 049.06
alok 051.16
alomdree 600.20
alone 048.21 118.10 157.13 180.34 190.24 194.05 194.14 199.04 223.33 289.30 305.31 380.35 439.24 450.20 450.22 465.31 561.35 579.23 623.29
Alone 394.33 561.33 561.34
Alone 303.L3
alonely 092.25
alones 113.06 378.23 603.26
alonety 598.18
along 006.02 012.33 019.15 030.18 037.19 039.26 042.01 056.23 081.06 084.08 084.25 084.30 107.28 107.32 114.08 158.08 158.31 205.13 207.21 214.36 236.22 257.06 268.F2 274.26 289.18 310.05 333.08 343.07 344.13 347.02 364.10 385.13 386.28 389.01 404.03 405.08 406.01 413.28 426.25 432.28 447.13 447.35 459.20 471.26 474.19 475.26 479.09 586.10 602.28 611.07 615.21 628.08
Along 047.23
alongement 132.03
alonging 495.23
alongside 114.06 311.03 314.32 405.05
alongsidethat 612.07
alongsoons 606.29
alongst 085.09
aloof 274.26 476.07
Aloof 623.19
aloofer's 395.34
alooflest 265.29
alook 021.18 022.05 022.29
aloon 327.33
aloose 029.03

Alopysius 155.31
aloquent 283.08
alore 539.24
alors 290.18
aloss 018.22
a'lot 063.22
alottylike 101.03
aloud 180.34 305.26 440.08 441.25 522.26
Alouset 323.04
alout 010.04 314.29
alove 021.09 328.07
aloven 220.21
alover 294.27
alow 316.03
Alow 296.27
alowing 175.04
alown 333.14
Aloyse 038.32
alp 017.34 119.20 287.09
Alp 420.18
Alp 209.09
A.L.P. 102.23 297.11
alpenstuck 085.11
alphabeater 553.02
alphabetters 107.09
alphabites 263.F1
alpheubett 208.20
Alphos 064.23
alphybettyformed 183.13
alpilla 194.22
alpin 148.22
alpine 553.25
Alpine 624.25
alplapping 057.11
alpman 478.10
Alpoleary 243.29
alps 008.28 008.30 256.34
Alps 340.06
alpsulumply 595.19
alptrack 577.23
alpy 332.03
alpybecca's 483.19
Alpyssinia 318.32
alraschil 358.28
already 018.19 028.36 051.09 052.30 078.34 189.10 274.04 473.19 593.07
Already 175.06
alright 090.33
Alris 396.03
als 077.20
alse 241.32
alshemist 185.35
also 005.15 029.29 030.19 061.24 065.36 076.34 077.33 104.17 109.32 116.05 116.19 163.04 165.23 174.13 290.08 291.14 315.29 390.26 412.30 413.13 510.31 564.31 571.17 573.09 574.02 574.09 578.08 596.28 606.20
Also 181.32 462.01 514.29 604.17 619.35
Also 281.L3
alsoliuto 043.33
alsos 255.33
also's 368.14
Alta 549.28
altar 088.04 210.24 273.F4 279.F27 409.19 605.14 605.21 605.32
altare 605.08
altared 331.03
altars 276.04
altar's 463.07
altarstane 552.30
alter 156.01 263.20 581.32 603.14
altered 051.02 089.12 429.13
altereffects 483.01
alteregoases 576.33
altermobile 483.24
alternate 357.18
alternately 033.25
alternating 189.04
alternatively 059.20 362.27
alternatives 063.03
alternativomentally 149.32
alters 229.01
altfrumpishly 242.19
althe 138.33
although 061.18 071.01 537.25 595.24
althrough 225.19
altipaltar 344.27
altitude 540.18
altitudinous 416.04
altknoll 499.23
Altmuehler 213.02
alto 407.33
altogether 109.20 155.31 181.20 425.34 438.18 451.23 470.23 484.24 509.14 533.18 574.34
altolà 332.18
altoogooder 358.16
altosonority 062.04
altrettanth 266.23
Altrues 191.14
altruis 247.10
altruism 604.33
altus 185.14
aluck 417.07
Aludin's 108.27
alull 246.03
alum 160.15 393.24 423.23
Alum 086.04
Alum 377.16
alup 397.19
alustre 528.19
alustrelike 032.26
alusty 508.29
alve 600.07
Alvemmarea 244.14
alveum 287.26
alwagers 312.26
always 023.08 025.12 032.15 032.19 037.22 049.22 056.05 064.10 066.19 067.01 069.30 108.35 112.09 115.01 115.27 118.16 120.35 121.18 144.27 144.27 144.27 145.30 146.19 148.31 151.21 153.28 154.15 155.07 159.02 159.02 159.02 166.26 171.20 173.06 173.24 173.28 174.08 177.23 186.27 219.02 226.02 264.F3 268.23 279.F16 279.F33 282.18 286.08 287.F2 300.02 302.20 351.10 351.24 362.36 368.15 369.31 373.30 379.14 393.14 393.18 397.09 410.35 411.20 414.22 414.24 414.35 421.34 423.15 435.14 443.30 457.20 458.34 459.19 461.08 466.21 472.14 479.01 484.08 507.11 507.36 513.34 526.26 527.13 528.28 533.09 539.05 544.31 561.36 570.12 570.15 570.19 570.28 578.09 581.34 606.35 618.28 619.23 620.10 621.23 623.07 624.22 624.33 625.11 626.10 627.10 627.14 627.21
always 349.29 399.22
Always 066.23 148.31 282.23 461.11 465.19 571.25
Alwayswelly 365.30
alwise 352.20
alws 302.26
Alys 057.28 359.32
Alysaloe 359.33
Alzette 578.36
am am Am
Am 324.23 (Am. Dg.) 404.30 (M)
a'm 057.08
A.M. 150.28 (Anno Mundi)
amack 358.21
amad 038.14
amadst 086.18
amaid 014.33 257.01
amain 024.06
amain 352.21
Amain 081.08 473.25
amak 498.16
amalgam 035.01
Amallagamated 308.L2
amaltheouse 338.20
Amam 528.10
aman 406.22
Aman 213.21
amanseprated 239.21
Amanti 237.26
amanygoround 525.17
A'Mara 460.17
amaranth 561.21
amare 279.F09
amarellous 180.10
Amarilla 184.20
amarm 291.22
Amaryllis 609.12
amat 262.F4
Amaxodias 498.04
Amazia 627.28
amazing 550.22
amazingly 336.03 557.19
Ambages 298.L1
amber 387.04 474.20 546.35 619.19
Amberhann 446.01
ambersandalled 241.15
amberulla 024.33
ambiamphions 222.07
ambidextrous 107.11
ambidual 528.24
AMBIDUAL 282.R1
ambiembellishing 119.16
ambijacent 036.15
ambilaterally 323.29
ambit 311.02
ambitions 533.25
ambitious 032.34
ambitrickster 423.06
ambivalent 164.03
ambiviolent 518.02
amble 568.25
ambling 468.26 580.25
ambly 409.31
amblyopia 545.10

ambo 159.29
amboadipates 163.31
amborium 287.24
ambos 247.03
ambo's 291.21
ambothed 230.02
ambows 304.28
Ambras 467.05
ambries 127.36
ambrosian 605.30
ambrosiaurealised 085.32
ambullished 356.30
ambush 087.35
ambushed 085.03
ambusheers 163.12
ambushure 201.20
amd 479.15 542.08
Ameal 457.04
Amean 448.33 538.18
ameet 339.24
ameising 417.28
Amelakins 355.22
ameltingmoult 241.24
Amem 518.33
Amems 235.05
Amen 070.35 384.15 393.03 395.24 411.11 558.20 570.13 578.29
Amen 105.02
amenable 581.36
Amene 439.14
amenessy 513.31
ameng 414.28
amengst 476.20
amengst 123.21
Amengst 505.16
amenities 502.25 502.25 502.25 502.26
Amenius 155.34
Amensch 397.23
Amenta 613.18
Amenti 062.26
America 130.28 497.11
american 117.25
American 307.11
American 176.05
americle 326.31
Amerigas 171.35
amess 613.25
Amessican 105.36
Ametallikos 252.15
amethyst 245.07
Amharican 489.20
amiable 406.26
amiably 564.15
Amicably 287.12
Amick 358.21
amid 031.01 032.22 048.09 051.34 062.29 121.03 127.15 179.25 190.33 191.09 221.19 388.24 392.27 429.23 594.08
Amid 624.10
Amid 349.17
amiddle 605.12
amidships 605.14
amidwhiches 353.25
amiens 549.31
amilikan 318.15
Amin 139.28
amind 379.26
aminglement 092.28
Amingst 462.04
Aminxt 222.32
Amir 355.11 365.16
Amiracles 427.23
amirican 132.02
amiss 145.06
amission 545.12
Amm 495.33
ammatures 239.11
ammi 258.11
ammonia 077.08
ammongled 345.01
Amn 495.33
amnaes 493.18
amnem 287.27
amnesia 122.06
amnessly 562.16
amnest 333.27
Amni 018.11
amnibushes 542.35
Amnios 264.07
Amnis 513.05
Amnis 153.02
Amnist 256.24
Amnisty 207.28
amnium 264.07
Amnium 287.08
Amn't 214.22
amobus 407.27
amock 358.21
Amodicum 362.31
amoist 044.01
amok 102.25 125.19 247.06 498.15
amokst 518.33
a'mona 498.18
among 020.24 031.30 038.13 041.01 043.34 048.02 053.10 059.23 066.04 076.22 076.23 079.04 092.23 096.06 115.12 122.11 128.20 132.27 133.05 164.36 169.05 171.07 172.12 173.28 174.03 174.08 188.13 189.01 193.01 226.13 229.23 235.13 235.30 237.30 248.06 259.01 267.24 282.F1 287.30 357.01 357.10 359.31 364.32 366.06 367.31 403.20 405.08 409.02 414.04 428.09 449.18 451.31 453.32 470.25 477.13 489.05 539.23 539.23 557.23 574.28 575.04 585.28 587.33 595.23 602.30 602.32 603.33 605.19 608.26 613.20 627.16 627.27
among 105.19 342.12
Among 526.05
Amongded 418.06
amongst 059.02 239.25 253.31 328.13 475.09 558.21 581.26 586.02
amonkst 609.30
amont 264.16
Amook 231.07
Amoor 211.26
amoosed 158.03
amor 148.31
Amor 487.23
amore 336.16
amoret 350.05
Amorica 562.31
Amoricas 395.35
amorist 463.18
amorous 189.17 391.05
amorrow 244.34
Amory 148.31
Amos 372.09 550.34
amossive 031.32
amot 396.06
amother 125.12
amotion 365.27
amount 050.16 066.02 514.30 558.03 588.22
amounting 382.08
amounts 521.05
amourlight 147.25
amourmeant 231.08
Amoury 104.10
Amousin 107.23
amove 404.10
amown 557.19
amp 533.33 533.33
ampersands 122.01
amphitheatre 033.10
Amphitheayter 214.14
amphybed 619.07
ampire 549.16
ample 203.25 345.32 574.21
amplecti 287.28
amplification 312.33 551.19
amplify 533.33
amply 429.13 545.19
amplyheaving 190.31
amproperly 337.22
Ampsterdampster 319.16
ampullar 177.03
amputation 558.14
amreeta 091.22
Amrikaans 387.02
Amrique 133.02
ams 376.16
Amsad 496.13
amsered 156.21
Amslu 595.21
amsolookly 404.32
amstel 205.15
Amsteldam 117.24
amstell 548.07
Amsterdam 565.09
amstophere 452.01
Amsulummmm 595.19
Amties 517.33
Amtsadam 532.06
amuckst 449.35
amudst 332.26
amulet 207.05
amullium 613.25
Amum 279.F34 279.F34 279.F34
Amune 244.26
amung 057.14 258.16
amusance 616.18
amuse 120.18 452.33
amusedly 082.31
amusedment 341.26
amusements 524.05
amusers 032.10
amusical 365.08
amusin 539.16
Amusing 261.F2
amustering 364.09
amuzement 125.13
Amy 227.14
Amy 106.32
amygdaleine 094.16
amygdaloid 183.12
an an An An
A.N. 280.09
an' 017.32

ana 094.16 553.02
Ana 311.12
anabaptist 388.14
Anabasis 304.L2
anaccanponied 607.32
anacheronistic 202.35
anachronism 393.20
anaclete 013.30
Anacletus 155.34
anaglyptics 419.19
anagrim 093.29
anakars 113.07
Anaks 240.27
Analbe 364.22
analectralyse 067.08
analectual 268.28
analist 395.04
analists 095.27
analyse 291.21
analytical 299.26
Anam 024.15
Anama 267.F4
anamaba 267.F4
anamabapa 267.F4
anan 284.15
anander 581.33
Ananias' 170.31
Ananymus 423.02
anarch 188.16
anarchistically 072.16
anartful 378.33
anarthur 375.08
anarxaquy 388.29
Anastashie 403.11
anastomosically 615.05
Anathem 348.28
anathomy 154.11
Anatolia 494.13
anatolies 504.30
anayance 233.29
ancelles' 227.18
ancestor 024.08
Ancestor 481.05
ancestors 030.06 134.03 173.20 382.14 442.06
ancestral 124.16
ancestralolosis 054.32
anchor 193.26
Anchor 479.11
anchore 294.05
anchorite 605.27
ancient 007.16 076.25 078.02 111.22 270.17 277.F4 289.08 318.06 357.08 386.21 390.17 396.07 503.05 575.01 614.09 614.36 624.01
ancientest 036.16
anciently 564.29
ancientry 019.33
ancients 254.08 498.34
Ancient's 281.21
ancillars 005.07
ancomartins 467.33
and and And And AND
andallthatsortofthing 178.05
andanding 484.07
andat 483.13
andbut 601.13
Andcommincio 432.04
andeanupper 501.32
Andecoy 226.28
anded 320.01
andens 578.34
Anders 414.02
Andersdaughter 389.10
Andersen 413.15
Andersoon 318.28
andesiters 387.13
andevil 194.15
andies 129.17
anding 141.10 484.06
andmore 148.31
Andoo 144.12
andor 601.14
Andoring 368.34
andouterthus 414.12
andrainit 414.13
Andraws 328.05
Andrée's 147.26
Andrew 393.05 468.32
Andrew 471.34
andrewmartins 392.03
andrewpaulmurphyc 031.35
Andrum 240.27
ands 463.28
andt 087.23 418.09 418.09
andthisishis 177.33
And'tis 046.07
andt's 268.11
Andure 234.29
andwell 036.28
andy 279.F31 409.31
Andy 142.27 210.21 504.20
Andy 072.01
Andycox 124.36
anear 026.07 095.30
aneath 503.13
aneber 209.07
anegreon 279.F32
aneither 101.06
Anem 015.29
Anemone 597.32
anemone's 563.17
Anems 226.35
anending 276.11
anent 060.02 115.11 269.06 365.16 431.02 558.05 617.30
Anent 089.10
anequal 017.35
anerous 318.04
anew 143.03 215.23 226.14 534.02
angalach 596.14
Angar 599.20
angardsmanlake 599.19
angars 538.05
Ange 252.31
Angealousmei 068.18
angel 147.02 170.12 303.F1 367.32 395.30 472.29 474.15 562.25
Angel 056.26
angeleens 443.35
angelers 526.11
Angeles 154.24
Angèles 238.10
Angèle's 238.11
angelets 191.19
angelhood 251.10
angelic 430.28 516.35
Angelinas 233.05
angeline 239.29
angell 141.11
Angell 578.29
angelland 257.01
angelous 296.16
angels 405.07 505.16 605.06
angel's 226.22
Angel's 090.13
Angels' 026.06
angelsexonism 363.35
angelskin 166.08
angelus 053.17
Angelus 211.16
anger 126.23 227.20 354.35
angered 188.36
anger's 373.09 457.07
angerus 517.05
angeu 158.35
anggreget 343.15
angin 207.29
angiol 143.33
angle 036.17 254.30 315.09 508.22
anglease 016.06
angled 224.30 337.10
angler 386.28 472.09
anglers 296.23 526.11
angles 021.25 150.35 284.02 390.14
Angles 183.07
angleseaboard 582.07
Anglesen 600.25
Anglesey 387.10
Angleshman 284.L1
Angleslachsen 532.11
Anglian 306.26
Anglia's 447.06
Anglican 185.10
Anglicey 484.36
angly 485.29
Angly 520.22
anglyother 300.05
Anglys 512.23
Angoisse 265.20
Angricultural 086.20
angry 444.01 465.16
Angry 028.22
angryman 412.19
angskt 224.31
angst 027.28
Angst 145.06
anguille 207.01
anguish 603.21
Anguish 189.19
anguished 256.24
angurr 351.30
Angus 248.04 377.01 377.01 377.01
angush 346.34
Angustissimost 104.06
Ani 243.04 493.32
anilancinant 597.24
Anileen 102.26
Anima 307.04
Animadiabolum 074.08
animal 154.11 221.19 263.F1 301.15 480.33 544.36 611.15
Animal 196.19
animale 185.18
animals 506.01
animal's 086.28
Animandovites 048.24
Animas 214.06
animated 403.23
animos 553.21
animule 417.35
Animus 307.03
aniseed 475.29

Anisette 105.17
anisine 222.26
anit 332.16
Anita 572.26 572.31 572.31 573.03 573.05 573.10 573.18 573.23 573.29
anjerichol 470.18
anker 329.09 375.03
Anker 599.20
ankered 098.06 225.10
ankerrides 548.12
Ankers 030.07
ankle 404.33
Anklegazer 193.12
ankles 140.26
anklets 207.04
Anlone 520.18
An-Lyph 355.32
Anm 495.33
anmal 294.F5
ann 009.14 020.35 063.13 286.19 293.15
Ann 054.04 139.19 207.28 293.19 302.01 422.26 454.06 495.33 575.06 575.07
Ann 106.31
ANN 220.19
anna 182.27
Anna 007.26 028.31 128.14 195.04 196.03 196.04 196.04 196.05 198.10 198.10 199.11 200.16 200.36 207.19 209.35 215.12 215.24 277.12 293.18 325.04 506.34 562.14
Anna 104.08
Annabella 512.10
annacrwatter 135.06
annadominant 014.17
Annadromus 451.11
annagolorum 498.19
Annah 104.01
annal 340.22
annalive 293.20
annals 013.22 013.31 202.23 452.18
annalykeses 280.03
annam 347.19
annamation 568.04
Annamite 179.14
Annamores 626.01
annams 243.02
Annan 205.09
Anna-na-Poghue's 203.36
Annanmeses 452.34
annaone 010.26
annapal 337.08
Annapolis 222.07 318.24
Annar 503.31
annaryllies 268.L1
annas 170.01 170.01 328.19
annastomoses 585.22
annaversary 493.05
Annchen 209.34
anne 584.32
Anne 210.24 308.02 392.32 406.27
Anneliuia 236.17
anner 199.36
annesleyg 130.21
annettes 504.33
annew 594.15
annews 277.18
Annexandreian 318.11
annexation 551.19
annexes 242.08
Annexing 484.10
anngreen 101.36
anni 333.04
annias 575.24
annie 038.21 548.10
Annie 004.28 378.02 492.08
anniece 532.24
Annie's 514.06
Annie's 072.01
annis 463.03
anniums 553.16
anniversary 035.03 380.09 583.23
anniverse 607.11
anno 190.17
Anno 398.31 481.06
Annona 199.34
Annona's 044.06
Annone 614.02
Annos 100.18
announce 422.35
announced 030.17
announcer 534.07
announcing 593.17
annoy 085.16 332.04
annoyance 181.20
annoyimgmost 495.02
Annoyin 546.30
annoying 033.26
annoynted 548.03
annoys 138.26
Ann's 139.22 501.09
Annshee 571.26
anntisquattor 019.26
annual 384.35
annuals 520.34
annuary 221.02
annuhulation 058.08
annuitants' 043.10
Annupciacion 528.19
Annushka 207.08
annusual 516.32
annuysed 342.28
anny 301.07 327.06 361.15 463.10
Anny 007.25 052.01 287.07 327.12 585.30
Anny 105.09
Annybettyelsas 444.31
annyblack 451.15
Annybody's 521.24
annyma 426.03
annyone 464.01
annywom 475.21
anodes 549.17
anointed 203.23 605.22
anointeds 570.33
anointer 252.18
Anol 490.27
anomorous 112.29
Anomyn 326.19
anon 086.32 203.31 282.27 403.24 556.20
Anon 302.30
anondation 372.23
anone 224.16
anonest 411.29
anononously 367.35
Anonymay's 374.07
anonymos 034.02
Anonymoses 047.19
anoof 623.20
anoopanadoon 543.30
anore 273.12
anothel 485.31
another 015.19 021.33 022.21 029.21 069.16 087.17 096.18 109.01 109.06 109.17 110.35 119.06 122.17 133.23 148.18 159.21 162.07 170.13 170.14 170.18 170.19 170.19 171.23 173.25 190.10 197.17 238.34 275.06 288.04 289.16 303.25 312.34 335.27 343.26 347.01 357.13 367.26 368.28 375.22 379.12 385.13 386.28 390.26 396.05 397.07 398.24 411.11 412.15 431.06 452.05 455.35 476.36 479.07 508.16 518.20 571.10 581.32 589.20 619.12
another 345.22
Another 114.21 294.12
another's 181.21
anotherum 609.09
Anow 311.12
anoyato 339.03
anquished 490.01
anruly 332.07
ans 458.29
ansars 005.25
anscessers 600.24
anschluss 095.28
Anser 202.20
Ansighosa 246.10
answer 011.02 033.19 057.07 068.28 074.07 089.27 116.15 144.26 167.27 172.25 179.17 255.34 258.12 286.26 286.27 314.03 360.19 373.22 477.33 487.06 487.28 487.35 515.19 619.11 622.32
Answer 139.14 139.16 140.06 140.15 141.27 141.30 142.29 142.31 143.28 143.31 149.11 168.13
answered 031.09 063.07 154.19 154.28 157.07
ANSWERER 302.R1
answerers 410.35
answering 487.24 487.26 519.06
answers 101.05 512.32
Answers 284.16 542.26
answerth 262.F1
answring 470.14
ant 018.21 395.05
ant 346.10
Ant 307.16
an't 093.05
antar 596.34
antargumends 245.10
antboat 418.05
ante 181.34
ante 423.21
Ante 293.19
Anteach 228.35
antechristian 114.11
antecistral 109.19
antediluvial 047.04
antediluvious 014.16
antelithual 512.16
antemeridian 430.04
antenaughties 537.08
antennas 309.18
antepost 090.06
antepostdating 256.22

antepropreviousday's 407.29
anteproresurrectionism 483.10
Antepummelites 498.10
anterestedness 055.25
anterevolitionary 234.11
anterim 529.15
anterior 589.26
antes 508.27
antesedents 284.22
Anthea 354.22
antheap 057.13
anthem 498.06
anthems 041.10
Anthemy 271.06
anthill 360.34
Anthony 086.13 409.07
anthrapologise 151.07
anti 347.28
antiabecedarian 198.20
Antiann 293.22
antiants 343.23
anticheirst 308.F1
antichill 099.12
anticidingly 606.26
anticipated 078.06
anticipating 043.33
anticipation 036.08 142.16 232.08 405.31 557.18
ANTICIPATION 282.R1
anticollaborators 118.25
antics 229.02
antidulibnium 310.07
antient 243.11 536.32
antifouling 206.33
antigreenst 346.04
antilibellous 048.18
antilopes 622.09
antimonian 184.36
antinomian 172.17
antinos 190.33
antipathies 092.11 163.15 489.10
antipodal 060.28
antipodes 183.31 472.17
antipop 013.30
antipopees 422.02
antiquissimam 287.23
antis 450.07
anti-sexuous 175.31
antisipiences 261.19
ANTITHESIS 282.R1
antitopically 415.29
antlets 224.12
antomine 167.03
Anton 081.07
Antonius 167.01
Antonius-Burrus-Caseous 167.04
Antony 152.21
antries 235.28
Antrim 266.F2
ants 013.33 253.07
ant's 340.33
antsgrain 197.28
Antwarp 140.02
Anty 147.17
anular 131.36
anulas 511.31
Anumque 389.28
anun 431.30
anuncing 409.27
anune 569.07
Anunska 585.22
anvil 197.11 375.28
Anville 235.18
anxious 075.16 113.34 451.35 570.35
anxioust 611.32
any any Any
Anya 537.07
anybloody 070.25
anybody 160.07 309.16 482.25
anybroddy 234.06
anygo 163.09 570.29
anyhow 108.01 215.12 380.07 380.32 521.14 602.08
Anyhow 118.11 380.06 581.01
anyhows 282.18
anymeade 286.07
anyold 075.20
anyon 113.06 113.07
anyone 033.28 085.21 095.19 107.26 111.26 122.27 177.13 254.05 298.F1 313.19 478.36 570.09
anyone 399.20
Anyone 379.09
anyons 113.06
anyour 366.07
anyposs 495.06
anyseed 271.13
anysides 041.03 463.33
anysin 368.21
anysing 251.10
anysing 345.12
anythesious 266.L1
anything 061.10 064.08 064.15 108.09 115.06 165.35 174.05 174.20 244.16 298.19 357.26 374.11 380.13 386.07 409.05 410.18 419.25 425.33 452.30 486.16 503.22 515.02 517.12 603.26 615.13
Anything 247.16 438.31
anythongue 117.15
anytom 088.36
anywas 586.20
anyway 118.22 119.30 174.05 262.01 263.F4 303.28 412.18 414.09
Anyway 146.30 627.12
anywhat 357.09
anywhen 427.34
anywhere 082.34 083.24 099.07 140.22 173.03 226.08 427.36 489.10 491.15 597.22
anywheres 084.07 283.25
anywing 505.17
anyworn 596.36
Anzi 172.22
A.1. 287.08
aoriest 269.05
aosch 286.02
ap 151.32 398.01 398.01 398.01 484.19 484.19 484.19 484.19
Ap 010.17
A.P, 498.10 (Agiapommenites A.P,)
apabhramsa 481.18
apad 595.22
Apagemonite 403.17
apairently 081.36
Apaleogos 349.22
apan 151.14
Apang 231.17
aparrently 081.22
apart 109.35 122.26 123.20 163.24 226.30 253.23 270.03 358.33 458.17 459.17 487.04 557.24 561.24
Apart 567.31
apartita 412.29
apasafello 174.14
apatstrophied 612.19
apauper's 422.15
ape 125.19 192.04 293.20 546.18
apeace 301.F1
apeal 004.07 335.11
aped 314.10 378.36
Apeegeequanee 072.08
apeel 508.29
Apep 494.15
Aper 179.14
aperrytiff 493.03
apersonal 135.26
apert 487.11
aperybally 460.12
apes 245.04
apeupresiosity 132.03
apexojesus 296.10
aphasia 122.04
apholster's 276.F5
Aphrodite 299.L1
apically 116.31
apiece 161.11 209.27 619.02
aping 530.02
apip 314.26
Apis 262.F4
apl 298.01
aplantad 564.22
Aples 106.24
aplompervious 348.06
Apnorval 570.01
apoclogypst 364.18
apocryphul 242.30
apodictic 524.33
apointlex 083.09
apolkaloops 557.02
apologetic 426.15
apologetically 166.09
apologia 189.08
apological 469.25
apologuise 414.16
Apology 104.15
apolojigs 302.04
apoo 561.32
Apophanypes 626.05
apophotorejected 251.07
apopo 319.21
aportion 397.18
aposcals 446.36
apossels 411.16
apostate 171.33
aposterioprismically 612.19
aposteriorious 083.11
aposteriorly 343.16
apostles 607.10
apostolic 062.13
Apostolopolos 134.22
apostrophes 126.06
apostrophised 289.13
apotamus 210.35
APOTHEOSIS 286.R2
apotria 243.29
apout 288.09
apoxyomenously 353.06

appal 320.12
appall 528.21
appalled 334.14
appalling 004.07 339.22 549.12
apparatus 520.08
apparentations 600.09
apparently 033.22 171.09
apparient 336.31
apparition 431.15 528.25
apparoxemete 132.03
apparting 454.26
appatently 085.32
appauling 131.12
appeal 133.35 194.27 240.20 366.02 575.32
appealance 338.11
appealed 090.09
appealing 167.12 268.02
appealingness 056.17
appealling 527.26
appeals 026.25 115.10 466.15
Appeals 105.31
appear 011.08 167.01 522.17 611.15
appearance 127.12 158.26 253.30 309.15 441.31 575.03
appearances 431.02
appearant 490.07
appeared 038.17 077.12 084.24 085.32 136.14 164.26
appearing 585.01
appears 163.20 164.08 487.35 596.26
appease 417.07 573.12
appeased 319.24
appeasement 610.27
appeers 570.22
appellavit 185.19
appelled 606.32
Appelredt's 406.09
append 425.29 484.13
appendix 270.06
appentices 315.18
appetising 164.16
appetite 083.21 153.35 406.35
Appetites 305.L1
appi 417.17
appia 297.25
Appia 548.06
appierce 512.24
applaud 110.18
applause 159.19
apple 113.16 124.18 247.35 330.31 452.07
Apple 051.34
applecheeks 041.11
applegate 069.21
applehooley 340.20
applejack 171.17
applepine 287.16
apples 433.35 436.07 466.05
Apples 532.21
Apples 175.19
Appletree 176.08
appletweed 210.30
applied 336.03
applies 048.19
appling 237.05
appliques 271.F5
applissiate 271.F5
apply 042.02 115.24 550.33 576.04
Apply 440.01
applying 530.05
appoint 355.14 367.30
appointed 443.19
appointment 084.06 449.10 460.07
appondage 271.02
appop 067.22
apposed 276.07
apposite 436.17
Apposite 420.21
apposition 527.12
appraisiate 337.23
appraisiation 041.28
appreciable 232.31
appreciably 151.16
appreciate 238.02
appreciated 114.35 616.24
appreciates 181.32 532.15
apprehended 342.12
apprencisses 365.28
apprentice 590.18
apprising 532.26
approach 032.33 053.19 363.26
Approach 262.02 561.27
approached 220.08 524.07
approaches 248.31
Approaches 604.26
approaching 174.06 505.02
appropriately 185.34
approval 470.05
Approval 071.34
approve 364.08
Approve 306.29
approved 524.12
approxemetely 295.31
appullcelery 586.27
appunkment 536.03
appurtenance 035.05
appurtenant 363.30
appy 041.23
aprican 350.21
april 556.14
April 207.33
aprils 415.11
apriori 343.18
aprioric 083.11
aproham 570.19
apron 147.01 158.30 200.32 213.26 491.35
aproper's 422.20
apropos 433.17
aprowl 139.31
apsaras 060.20
apsence 432.25
apt 044.12 293.20 412.32 436.36 612.35
apter 025.24 354.24
aptist 328.29
aptly 052.34 162.28
apuckalips 455.01
Apud 007.23
apullajibed 317.30
Apun 224.36
apurr 597.16
apuss 597.16
Aput 016.20
apuzzler's 326.11
aqua 296.30
aquaface 003.14
aquaint 139.07
aqualavant 285.16
aquart 139.07
Aquasancta 380.03
aquascutum 133.09
aquiassent 037.22
Aquila 158.29
Aquileone 418.26
Aquileyria 255.10
aquilittoral 286.19
aquinatance 417.08
A'Quite 088.14
ar 034.10 520.27
ara 492.12
arab 098.13 286.06
arabesque 115.03
Arabia 135.15 275.F2
arabinstreeds 553.35
arafatas 005.15
araflammed 080.24
aragan 395.36
aram 262.F4
Aram 228.15
aramny 335.36
Aran 121.14 392.17 475.12
Arancia 226.31
Arancita 572.36
aranging 596.08
Aranman 121.12
arans 087.25
Arans 595.22
Aratar 059.24
araun 042.12
Araxes 296.04
arbatos 512.22
Arber 504.16
arbitrary 524.03
arbor 160.14
Arbor 579.05
arboriginally 314.16
arborised 310.18
arboro 053.14
arbour 227.20 508.17 588.32
Arbour 079.25 136.32
Arbourhill 012.27
arbuties 131.20
arbutus 121.10
arc 129.32 321.27 507.33
Arc 202.18
arcane 552.16
arcanisation 135.27
Arcdesedo 351.05
arcglow's 245.08
arch 186.28 264.F2 403.06 459.16 494.02 590.10
Arch 140.02 490.23 508.01
ARCHAIC 264.R1
archangelical 605.11
archbishopric 134.29
archdeacon 055.17
archdeaconess 209.06
archdeaconry 254.06
archdiochesse 171.25
archdruid 611.05
Archdukon 071.35
arche 102.03
arched 446.05
archer 080.09
Archer 063.13
archers 005.08 254.11 283.19
Archer's 440.04
arches 127.36
archetypt 263.30
Archfieldchaplain 564.32
archgoose 026.05
Archicadenus 055.30
archicitadel 073.24
archimade 230.34

Archimandrite 496.08
Archimimus 219.09
archipelago 605.05
archipelago's 029.23
architecht 076.36
archives 390.12
archsee 531.33
archunsitslike 152.19
archway 043.28
Archway 302.14
Arck 223.02
arclight 003.13
Arcobaleine 175.16
Arcoforty 068.19
Arcoiris 186.28
arcs 284.03
Arcs 104.13
Arcthuris 594.02
arctic 353.13
Arctic 385.34
Arctur 621.08
Arctura 494.13
Ardagh 110.35
Ardechious 578.20
Ardeevin 264.28
ardent 269.17
ardently 436.20
Arderleys 373.23
ardilaun 407.04
Ardite 044.22
arditi 044.22
ardking 025.29
Ardonis 494.11
Ardor 614.09
ardour 606.10
Ardour 106.05
ardouries 577.03
ardree 133.36
ardree's 049.04
Ardreetsar 612.06
Ardrey 261.L3
ards 101.06
Ards 612.35
arduus 487.33
are are Are Are
area 042.22 051.09 331.23 578.22
Area 289.28 485.21
areading 270.29
aream 440.07
areas 205.24
Areas 069.15
arecreating 282.28
Areed 566.36
areekeransy 453.09
Areesh 467.05 467.05 467.11
Areinette 471.01
Arena 320.28
arenary 605.25
arenotts 580.01
areopage 206.01
arered 107.21
ares 088.17 421.23
Ares 269.17
arestocrank 424.10
areyou 102.06
argan 234.33
argaumunt 008.25
arge 344.34
argent 005.07 546.07 586.23
Argentine 559.04
Argloe-Noremen 309.11
argon 165.11
Argos 481.22
arguing 523.26
argument 078.26 174.07 222.21
arguments 172.34
Arhone 210.32
aria 513.22 597.26
aria 164.34
arianautic 530.18
arias 011.34
Arias 435.02
aright 297.13
arimaining 239.34
Arin 112.33
arinam 163.01
aring 391.01
aringarouma 209.18
aringarung 210.03
Arioun 075.02
ariring 496.23
arise 055.05 463.09 571.02
Arise 248.08 532.04 568.25
arises 202.19 235.06
Arishe 104.09
arising 573.36 623.26
aristmystic 293.18
Aristocrat 071.31
aristotaller 417.16
Aristotle 306.L2
arisus 440.07
arith 282.09
arithmosophy 134.14
Ariuz 075.02
ark 230.07 529.21
ark 383.09
Ark 244.26
Ark 104.19
Arkangels 628.10
Arkaway 493.25
arkbashap 491.19
arked 552.06
arkens 364.29
arklast 186.11
Arklow 203.18 290.24
Arklow's 549.18
arklyst 186.11
arks 275.F5 281.F1
arkway 022.28 022.33
arkwright 560.09
arky 606.26
arkypelicans 601.34
arley 257.10
arm 146.30 169.12 305.22 331.24 398.09 438.11 474.03 597.01
Arm 089.33
arma 389.19
armada 234.05 388.11
Armagh 057.08 482.27
armaurs 595.16
armbour 135.02
armed 051.24 134.06
armeemonds 343.05
armelians 038.11
Armen 069.11
armenable 181.23
armenial 190.25
Armenian 559.25
Armenian 072.11
armenities 530.36
Armentières 230.15
armer 353.20 486.14
Armerica 228.19
armful 450.15
Armigerend 584.28
arming 018.33 018.34
arminus-varminus 008.28
Armitage 379.34
armitides 011.13
armjaws 300.13
armlet 148.22
armlets 207.05
armor 361.14
Armor 446.06 623.15
Armorica 003.05
Armoricus 211.26
armour 023.08
Armourican's 447.06
Armoury 096.07
armpacts 470.36
arms 005.05 090.06 157.33 193.24 209.24 249.23 268.01 372.09 389.26 446.17 459.17 485.02 486.24 527.20 546.05 546.09 628.04
Arms 004.07 420.33 444.09 587.09
arms' 518.12
armsaxters 393.32
armsbrace 328.30
armschair 251.22
armslength 166.18
armsore 320.12
Armsworks 618.02
armsworths 363.06
army 091.32 599.20
Army 156.28
Arnolff's 443.22
arnoment 208.08
aroger 554.03 554.03
aroint 492.34
Aromal 346.04
aromatose 427.11
arome 444.09
arongwith 407.04
aroof 101.17
aroon 311.17
arooned 355.19
aroont 012.22
aroostokrat 199.34
arose 094.18 174.35 250.01 541.16 574.10 605.10
aroun 011.18
around 006.03 025.12 044.07 066.13 080.31 082.02 087.36 092.14 094.24 094.26 108.05 124.34 131.35 139.08 141.11 144.32 164.06 176.33 177.20 178.15 189.12 192.34 198.11 199.12 206.01 207.35 212.05 232.14 234.20 243.08 274.27 277.21 300.29 310.18 311.25 361.32 363.25 365.32 368.09 370.09 374.17 375.22 386.05 391.01 394.11 394.14 415.09 426.16 439.01 444.15 452.01 453.09 479.22 484.11 501.31 506.34 510.24 511.09 513.14 515.21 515.30 532.30 548.33 576.14 596.04 596.35 602.16 615.34 619.07 622.12
around 107.05 383.06
Around 172.11 560.19 564.15
aroundabout 448.04
aroundabrupth 242.19
aroundisements 536.10
arount 406.13

Arountown 142.13
Arouse 165.06
arpists 508.33
arr 269.21
Arra 497.04
arrah 068.12 096.05 346.29 376.19 381.25 404.04 425.18 600.33
Arrah 007.25 028.01 044.15 045.19 297.04 460.02 588.29
arrahbeejee 234.31
arrahbejibbers 187.11
Arrahland 378.06
Arrahnacuddle 391.03
Arrah-na-poghue 384.34 385.22
Arrah-na-Poghue 388.25
Arrah-na-pogue 385.03
arrahquinonthiance 296.20
arraigned 127.27
arraignment 219.05
arraky 368.10 368.14
Arram 344.31
arrams 445.24
Arran 204.31
arranged 221.25 222.01 412.03
arrangement 123.11 161.35 260.F2
arranges 386.23
arranging 127.21 127.22
Arranked 246.25
arrant 229.11
arras 568.36
Arras 053.02
array 068.08 246.25 569.25
Array 593.02
arrears 086.30 457.02 586.18
arrears 278.L3
arred 599.05
arrest 348.15 367.30 505.31
Arrest 223.19
arride 265.15
arripple 076.30
arrivaliste 161.20
arrive 088.16 160.33 462.18 564.10
Arrive 613.27
arrivées 281.12
arriving 497.04
arrivisme 189.15
arrogate 149.32
arrohs 626.06
arronged 203.27
arroroots 138.14
Arrorsure 378.06
arrosas 561.19
arrow 093.28 353.21
arrows 094.19 285.05 520.22
Arrusted 420.31
ars 122.06 122.07 299.24 487.33 514.34
Ars 357.15
Arsa 098.07
arsched 547.29
Arschmann 071.34
Arsdiken's 440.01
arse 122.11
arsenal 438.33
arsenic 577.04
arsenicful 242.13
Arser 359.15
arson 328.10 421.05
arsoncheep 357.03
arsoned 127.05
Arssia 026.04
art 066.28 094.10 146.10 167.03 188.31 224.35 237.21 386.01 427.18 440.26 467.36 496.07 534.25 579.08 601.11
Art 199.35 306.13 325.04 468.09 488.03
Art 184.24
artained 512.30
Artahut 043.23
Artalone 418.01
Artaxerxes 337.36
arter 076.08
artesaned 209.33
Artesia 135.15
artful 126.09 137.11
Arth 044.12 380.22 608.07
Arth 175.11
Artha 093.22
Arthar 059.07
arthataxis 235.18
artheynes 353.34
Arthiz 009.26
Artho 254.36
Arthor 052.17
arthou 088.28 621.20
arthouducks 358.29
arthre 246.07
Arthre 093.07
arthroposophia 394.19
arthruseat 577.28
Arths 112.29
Arthur 361.03 420.36 514.06
Arthur 071.23
Arthurduke 335.30
Arthurgink's 285.L2
Arthurhonoured 073.36
arthurious 498.23
arthurs 229.07
artickles 437.31
article 466.23 559.16 614.04
articles 109.23 130.11 283.11 534.12 574.06 596.08
artifacts 110.01
artificial 169.15
artillery 519.06
artis 495.34
artist 374.27 560.13
Artist 071.21
artist's 435.05
artless 114.32 458.36
arts 134.07 152.01 188.31 259.07 345.03 440.20 490.05
Artsa 029.13
artsaccord 415.18
artsed 315.01
Artsichekes 390.09
artstouchups 171.27
artthoudux 252.20
Artur 272.27
Arty 065.16 230.26
aruah 428.15
arubyat 247.03
Aruc-Ituc 237.29
arue 558.29
Arumbian 346.06
arums 566.13
Aruna 210.31 613.34
arundgirond 209.18
arundo 158.07
Arupee 442.25
aruse 619.29
Arvanda 037.22
arver 205.23
arx 583.02
aryan 567.22
Aryania 129.34
a'rye 137.31
arzurian 387.32
as as As As AS
A's 245.35
Asa 279.F20
asama 130.05
asame 356.14
asamed 489.18
asamples 280.23
asarch 203.04
Asa's 246.07
asaspenking 186.11
asawfulas 156.11
asbestas 352.35
Asbestos 517.21
Asbestopoulos 424.07
Ascalon 550.16
Ascare 374.29
ascend 032.06 483.28 536.24
Ascend 601.31
ascendances 037.26
ascendant 108.20
ascending 165.24
Ascending 298.L2
ascertain 447.31
ascertained 237.20
asches 055.30
aschu 187.10
ascowl 223.18
Ascription 301.L2
Asea 447.25
aseesaw 375.31
asfar 234.28
ash 028.30 084.28 130.25 160.05 361.07
ashaker 254.32
ashamed 457.33 463.01 506.33 609.26
ashaped 373.13
Ashburner 369.08
ashe 097.26
Ashe 311.24 321.34 328.04
ashed 356.25
asheen 284.30
ashen 341.15
ashens 436.32
ashes 164.12 189.36 206.27 301.26 584.10
Ashe's 503.32
ashhopperminded 041.12
Ashias 608.31
Ashiffle 371.28
ashipwracked 275.18
ashleep 435.26
ashley 213.14
ashore 026.14 232.20 623.30
ashored 370.36
ashpit 211.22
ashpits 544.14
ashpots 616.12
Ashreborn 059.18
Ashtoumers 497.18
Ashtown 129.24 142.14
ashtray 503.07
ashtun 006.33
ashu 058.20
ashuffle 041.17 371.28
ashunned 489.18
ashure 058.20

ashwald 264.27
Asia 068.29 098.10 182.31 285.F5 497.12
Asias 548.02
aside 032.06 055.31 082.23 336.14 356.23 431.06 444.09 455.23 487.24 604.34
Aside 321.29
asidled 315.05
asikin 113.08
Asitas 060.16
ask 011.35 020.26 035.18 074.06 091.24 112.09 141.32 148.04 165.32 185.08 220.07 255.09 323.12 412.21 420.01 424.15 424.17 433.26 445.06 449.12 453.02 460.24 486.35 519.20 519.30 521.11 522.03 529.19 547.02 561.18 625.10
Ask 093.22 154.18 197.06 205.04 301.05 492.02 507.24 515.19 604.02
Ask 105.13
askan 606.15
askance 204.20
askapot 494.34
askarigal 201.25
aske 320.08
asked 051.11 059.18 063.05 082.11 101.12 110.03 191.20 315.27 322.26 330.15 487.29 575.20
askes 004.15
askew 583.31
asking 022.29 031.06 101.11 111.27 115.19 164.21 170.05 174.18 430.33 431.04 432.06 435.03 465.13 465.22 485.09 490.12 490.34 517.27
asking 342.02 345.12
Asking 225.11 444.30
Askins 281.L2
Askinses 125.11
Askinwhose 276.F4
askit 223.29
askmes 504.28
Askold 310.16
askormiles' 350.21
askors 241.31
asks 133.05 185.23 233.18 286.25 286.27 357.04
askt 535.31
Askt 089.08
askull 384.01
asky 233.27 233.27
Asky 233.27
aslant 608.24
aslegs 225.09
asleep 204.16 307.F5 403.18 424.30 429.15 469.17 476.22 519.18 561.31
a'sleep 064.01
asleeping 157.14
asleeps 116.20
aslick 225.09
aslight 383.20
aslike 100.11
Aslim-all-Muslim 068.12
aslimed 506.07
aslip 377.26 597.12
aslooped 423.06
aslumbered 007.20
aslung 331.25
aslyke 413.07
asmuch 349.33
asnake 100.11 139.31
Asnoch 476.06
asnuh 620.16
a. s. o. 080.11 (and so on)
asong 450.21
asousiated 151.29
aspace 015.18
aspear 340.10
Aspect 604.18
aspectable 362.34
asped 417.04
aspen 361.07
aspenstalk 131.13
aspersed 203.19
asphalt 332.34 481.12
aspillouts 156.13
aspinne 417.24
aspirations 049.16
aspire 166.17 254.31
aspiring 423.06
aspolootly 372.34
aspoor 340.11
asprawl 476.19
asprewl 437.11
ass 020.26 050.25 086.18 127.18 214.33 243.32 252.13 405.06 441.25 475.31 475.35 476.27 480.06 567.27 602.14 609.09
Ass 408.26
assailant 062.33
assalt 331.30
Assass 488.26
assasserted 357.31
assassiations 146.14
Assassor 242.01
assatiated 314.33
assauciations 413.18
assaucyetiams 384.27
assault 130.26 132.20 366.19
assaulted 063.08
assay 601.08
assaye 008.26
Assaye 008.26
assays 137.25
assback 084.03
assbawlveldts 032.27
assemblage 032.25 264.32 432.04
assembled 136.06
assemblements 614.25
Assembly 097.28
assent 144.10 252.29
assented 355.23
assertant 481.20
assertitoff 524.29
asserts 558.08
asservaged 267.18
asservent 364.19
asses 164.13 334.25
assessors 608.06
assets 167.21
asseveralation 523.22
assideration 451.36
Assiegates 004.06
assignation 524.16
assignations 575.15
assigned 136.12
assimilated 615.05
assist 181.31 423.13 579.26
assistance 381.31 433.08
assisted 098.15 181.19
assistents 529.12
assisters 608.06
assistershood 351.29
assisting 393.15
assoars 266.09
associate 419.28
associated 085.23 123.23 441.13 495.01
Associations 270.13
assoiling 146.08
Assoluta 527.13
assombred 570.07
assonance 477.13
Assorceration 608.02
assotted 028.20
assortail 444.17
assphalt 285.F5
assuan 332.30
assuary 341.28
assumbling 514.06
assumed 049.08 263.02
assumptinome 153.20
assumption 035.04 238.27
assune 234.28
assure 571.23
Assure 027.33
assuredly 112.23
ast 240.34 313.20 316.04
Astale 624.27
astamite 594.05
astand 489.02
astarted 232.12
astea 062.16
asteer 598.05
astench 450.07
astensably 151.14
aster 609.30
asterisks 426.32
astern 560.25
asteroid 475.16
Asterr 069.14
asters 248.07
astewte 236.28
Asther's 184.22
asthma 578.05
asthone 460.17
asthore 197.21 397.05
Asthoreths 601.08
astir 246.13
astirrup 245.36
Astley's 214.14
aston 205.13
astone 123.14
astoneaged 018.15
astonish 564.06
astonishment 098.15
astonishments 187.09
astonissment 067.19
Aston's 447.35
astore 327.05 556.33
astoreen 528.32
astoun 624.27
astounded 499.02
astoutsalliesemoutioun 354.20
Astralia 552.07
astray 472.13 506.21
astraylians 321.09
Astrelea 064.23
astrid 279.F27
astride 208.23
astrode 356.04
astroglodynamonologos 194.16
astrollajerries 064.23

astrolobe 551.25
astronomically 596.29
astumbling 514.05
astundished 187.03
astunshed 448.06
astuteness 075.23
asunder 213.16 328.08
asundered 136.07
asundurst 347.09
aswarmer 365.14
aswas 369.21
aswhen 327.05
aswim 170.36
asylum 124.07 172.23
at at At At AT
Atabey 541.17
atac 089.35
Atac 270.14
atack 315.19
atake 097.25
atalaclamoured 100.02
atalantic's 336.27
atam 333.25
atantivy 359.29
ate 019.34 086.26 086.28 091.06 145.07 225.21 227.26 240.01 258.06 258.06 300.16 301.16 303.21 330.01 368.20 378.03 397.20 412.28 432.15 456.03 479.32 490.33 538.20
ate 346.09
Ate 471.34
atem 459.27
Atem 224.07
Atems 353.29
aten 318.15
aterman 572.01
ates 161.31 354.29
atever 461.11
ath 138.10 594.22
Ath 346.22
àth 124.09
Athacleeath 539.17
athall 117.16
athands 194.05
athanor 184.18
athar 599.07
Athclee 498.12
athclete 279.07
athel 459.14
athemisthued 167.10
athems 326.16
athemystsprinkled 153.27
Athens 120.20
Athiacaro 409.14
athletes 222.31
athlone 450.28
Athlone 498.12
Athma 033.18
athome 434.03 446.35
athome's 363.22
athors 578.34
athos 494.06
athug 344.04
athwart 564.24
athwartships 311.08
atillarery 070.31
atime 368.34
ating 376.36 385.16 480.22
atkings 436.11
Atkins 588.18
atkinscum's 534.33
Atkinson 043.10
Atlangthis 232.32
atlanst 601.05
Atlanta 140.35
atlantic 085.20
Atlantic 482.09
atlas 049.26 324.03 368.30 626.13
atlast's 132.03
atman 596.24
atole 603.30
atolk 130.21
atoms 455.17
atoned 246.29 488.03
atop 031.02 475.20
a'top 063.29
atosst 108.05
atous 286.13
atout 286.13
atque 185.15
atramental 452.03
atrance 397.28
Atreeatic 062.02
Atreox 055.03
Atriathroughwards 594.19
Atrocity 072.11
atrot 469.03
Atroxity 179.15
atsweeeep 041.29
att 088.19
atta 079.08
attabom 103.02 103.04
Attabom 103.02 103.04
attabombomboom 103.02 103.04
Attaboy 442.05 466.29
attach 266.29
Attach 255.03
attachatouchy 552.04
attached 050.25 124.13 542.20
attaching 484.03
attachment 018.27 574.35
attack 165.01 202.13 254.29 410.05
attackler 081.18
Attahilloupa 339.32
attaim 367.30
attainted 127.27
attashees 348.17
Attattilad 251.01
attawonder 388.02
attax 097.22
atte 083.21
attempt 149.17 392.05
attempted 086.07 391.25 392.01 392.04 607.28
attempting 091.34 344.14
Attemption 364.12
attempts 469.36
attend 382.16
attendance 579.06
attendantess 220.07
attended 086.22 174.22 415.12
attender 188.07
attending 026.34 060.16 491.01
attends 543.23
Attenshune 100.05
Attent 543.11
attention 070.19 120.15 174.17
Attention 359.30 586.15
attentions 164.32 616.25 618.06
attenuating 034.27
atter 022.09 553.03
attestation 557.32
atthems 272.L4
Attilad 251.01
Attil's 266.25
attitudes 061.08
attomed 367.30
Attonsure 364.14
attouch 171.02
attract 068.32 070.19
attractable 477.20
attracted 064.02 430.05
attraction 449.03 461.14 530.08
attractionable 042.15
Attraente 105.25
attraverse 609.14
attraxity 391.07
Attributive 036.12
attrite 194.03
attrition 231.26
atvoiced 225.02
atwaimen 279.F23
atween 355.30 600.06
atwixt 108.04
au 077.33
au 201.18
Au 335.04 335.04 335.23 335.23
Aubain 499.31
aube 538.23 593.09
aubens 244.33
auberginiste 163.19
aubette 209.14
Aubeyron 357.02
Auborne-to-Auborne 174.31
aubrey 604.19
Aubumn 617.36
auburn 013.26 265.07 552.22
Auburn 280.27
Auburnia 275.05
auburnt 139.23
a.u.c. 077.23 (ab urbe condita or anno urbis conditae)
auchnomes 098.27
aucthor 148.17
auction 362.10 365.10 390.18
auctionable 419.33
auctioneer 386.19 386.24
Auctioneer 268.L3
Auctioneer's 391.03
auctions 386.23
Auction's 538.10
auctual 143.07
auctumned 065.02
Aud 484.21
Audacior 267.06
Auden 279.F26
Audeon's 484.03
Audi 152.14
audialterand 569.09
audible 425.23
audible-visible-gnosible-edible 088.06
audibly 031.26 478.07
audience 092.01 147.02
Audiens 528.06
auditers 229.31
auditor 374.06
auditors' 584.29
auditressee 369.30
audiurient 023.21
audorable 562.33
Aue 335.04 335.23
aues 207.36
aufroofs 006.06
aught 107.22 151.36

aught 341.34
Aught 276.19
aughter 411.34
augmentation 551.18
augmentatively 152.05
augmented 151.16
Augs 090.28
augstritch 162.32
augumentationed 611.31
augur 249.17 356.27 379.29 479.19
Augurer 155.34
AUGURIA 282.R3
auguries 189.34
augurs 330.22
Augusburgh 384.17
august 521.33
Augusta 104.06
augustan 053.15 468.04
Augustanus 532.11
Aujourd'hui 281.04
aulburntress 137.23
auld 088.02 112.08 197.24 257.14 305.29 336.10 384.17 389.11 393.16 398.14 398.26 406.28
Auld 415.03 421.14
auldancients 498.34
auldstane 021.05
Aulidic 299.L1
Auliffe 290.06 582.09
Auliffe's 427.04
aulne 154.04
Aulus 255.19
Aun 308.05
aunt 026.27 063.04 134.27 388.04 465.01
Aunt 376.16 519.33
Aunt 105.28
auntey 314.24
Auntie 306.F1
auntieparthenopes 542.21
aunties 347.28
aunts 224.04 620.18
aunts' 183.27
auntskippers 257.05
aunty 293.20
Aunty 292.F3 496.02 585.32
auntybride 561.16
auracles 467.29
auradrama 517.02
aural 492.21 623.18
aurals 344.26
Auravoles 627.32
Aure 500.19
aureal 568.20
aureas 482.03
Aurelius 132.19
Aurelius 306.L3
Aurell 496.15
aurellian 478.14
aurellum 038.35
aureoles 306.01
aureolies 341.01
aures 113.30
Aures 482.03
auricles 412.15
auricular 157.22 310.10 585.11
auriculars 055.31
auriforasti 512.27
aurignacian 153.21
aurilucens 234.08
aurinos 253.27
auriscenting 294.23
auroholes 241.12
aurorbean 357.06
Aurore 244.33
aurowoch 318.22
Ausone 209.35
Ausonius 267.06
auspicable 325.06
Auspicably 362.23
auspice 024.04 112.18
Auspice 514.25
auspicer 537.09
auspices 189.33 384.03 392.27 397.29 555.18
auspiciis 287.23
auspicious 380.33
AUSPICIUM 282.R2
aussies 567.17
Austelle 048.12
Auster 464.27
austereways 153.22
austers 479.21
austral 050.10
austrasia 489.10
austrologer 601.34
aut 110.09
autamnesically 251.04
authenticated 030.10
authenticitatem 100.34
author 034.14 108.35 517.11
Author 357.28
authordux 425.20
authorised 179.28
authoritativeness 118.04
authorities 387.01
authority 263.24 440.23
authorsagastions 369.27
authorship 118.03
authorways 219.20
Autist 434.35
autobiography 413.31
autocart 434.31
Autocrat 612.12
autocratic 303.19
autodidact 050.36
autointaxication 447.29
autokinaton 235.27
autokinatonetically 614.30
autokinotons 005.32
automoboil 448.29
automutativeness 112.12
Auton 077.07
autonaut 242.07
autonement 568.09
Autore 182.21
autosotorisation 352.19
autotone 158.35
Autum 271.12
aux 281.04 281.13
auxiliaire 471.30
auxiliar 530.18
auxiliary 117.13
auxiliis 188.09
Auxilium 496.13
Auxonian 463.07
auxter 085.11
auxy 587.04
auza 088.26
available 185.36
avalunch 240.32 406.09
avant 074.01
avarice 268.12
avatar 042.16 089.02
avaunt 593.09
ave 059.30
Ave 305.27 420.25
avec 406.22
Avegnue 448.17
Aveh 445.13
aveiled 375.29
Avelaval 628.06
Aveling 613.30
Avenance 374.32
avenge 178.22
Avenlith 242.28
avensung 350.08
Avenue 060.02 (Death Avenue) 191.10 (Novara Avenue) 261.F2 (Amusing Avenue) 497.11 (America Avenue)
avenyue 549.20
aver 347.07 488.15 547.04
average 051.01 051.27 491.27 532.17
averging 055.04
averlaunched 162.31
averred 036.19
averthisment 434.29
averyburies 113.34
aves 069.11
Aves 147.06
avgs 184.27
Avia 230.30
aviar 505.17
aviary 206.20
avic 406.14
avicendas 488.06
avick 188.05
avicuum's 473.06
avider 455.07
avidously 166.11
avikkeen 565.19
avilky 621.21
avis 504.16
Avis 250.01
avocation 178.18
avoice 003.09
avoid 108.09
avoirdupoider 169.18
avond 244.31
Avondale's 209.06
avoopf 177.31
avourneen 140.28
avowals 249.13
avowal's 412.30
avowdeed 424.05
avowels 023.36
avragetopeace 364.17
avtokinatown 484.16
avunculusts 367.14
Avus 230.29
aw 031.10 533.22
Aw 533.21
Awabeg 248.34
awage 247.05
awagering 098.33
awail 344.25
awailable 228.24
awailing 474.11
Awaindhoo's 371.33
awaiting 122.25
awake 174.33 311.16 393.25 473.23
awake 350.01
Awake 510.16
Awake 106.31

awakening 597.26
awallow 398.17
awalt'zaround 010.30
awan 498.13
award 471.13
awards 532.34
aware 177.31 429.01
awary 342.33
awash 133.08 319.25
awater 534.04
away 007.18 009.28 012.03 028.29 049.23 064.25 073.21 078.03 080.34 094.04 095.13 095.29 095.30 098.06 111.21 122.22 136.07 146.12 151.31 158.28 158.36 160.16 161.36 171.04 185.06 186.06 197.36 200.15 202.26 207.17 224.13 233.29 243.02 244.11 258.07 265.09 268.F6 279.F11 289.F2 302.18 305.04 360.29 373.10 375.21 379.35 382.27 389.02 394.11 395.04 410.12 411.24 426.14 430.08 433.14 439.18 445.29 450.12 458.32 459.34 467.36 469.06 470.10 471.20 479.35 480.08 497.17 510.04 528.20 544.17 585.31 586.06 615.22 622.14 625.30 626.01 627.35
Away 188.25 371.09 619.25
Awaywrong 606.31
awe 016.22 117.03 207.36 224.21 294.06 357.06 426.01 520.23 560.34
awebrume 336.15
awed 167.36 531.10
Awed 613.02
Aweek 106.31
Aweghost 353.03
aweigh 312.05
awen 372.28
awer 326.19
awes 055.23 143.13 458.36
awethorrorty 516.19
awflorated 088.17
awfly 458.17
awful 039.20 136.21 148.12 192.10 196.11 296.16 411.13 432.12 451.35 503.07 529.18 541.06 626.16
Awful 009.01
awfully 167.10 386.15 398.20 456.02 577.15
awhile 179.07 327.18 460.35 469.19 478.35 561.05
Awhile 415.15
awhits 088.28
awhore 154.21
awhoyle 323.02
awike 596.06
Awind 534.04
awinking 333.29
awknees 554.06
awkward 012.13
awkwardlike 120.19
Awl 072.02
Awlining 275.01
awlphul 348.05
awlrite 303.22
awlus 581.22
Awmawm 193.30
awn 154.05 160.15 456.12 480.04
awning 249.08
Awnt 071.35
Awny 200.20
awoh 115.17
awondering 336.16
aworn 614.14
awound 226.05
awristed 532.27
awriting 464.22
awry 119.35
awstooloo 343.16
axe 432.35 433.28 451.14 579.09 623.34
Axe 019.20
axecutes 346.06
axehand 534.20
axenwise 019.20
axes 256.25 468.11
aximones 285.29
axin 083.29
axiom 253.23
axiomatic 055.36
axplanation 063.31
axpoxtelating 581.13
ay 013.25 046.22 068.16 079.10 124.09 125.17 168.06 194.15 240.04 267.24 279.F10 326.05 351.04 388.09 390.29 390.30 390.33 395.25 397.06 405.01 406.23 409.03 450.03 468.21 472.01 520.31 558.30 608.15
Ay 013.25 087.32 198.10 208.04 212.26 213.21 296.17 326.05 353.17 388.08 390.29 390.30 390.33 393.06 393.06 395.25 397.06 404.15 473.19 508.16 513.28 518.14 520.32 608.15
aya 595.34 595.35
ayand 601.14
aye 056.14 114.01 114.02 117.20 227.34 239.06 247.31 251.36 271.19 320.27 356.16 360.31 379.11 434.13 440.26 455.22 482.35 499.12 505.18 512.11 520.32 606.33 608.15 620.15
Aye 484.29 512.11 608.15
ayear 113.35
ayearn 364.10
ayelips 533.02
Ayerland 347.11
ayes 143.14 202.02 493.26
Ayessha 105.20
ayewitnessed 254.10
ayi 009.13 009.13
Ayi 009.13
aying 189.20
ayle 007.12
Aylesburg 387.09
ayr 483.29
Aysha 284.24
aysore 107.23
Ayternitay 406.28
ayther 201.34
az 171.25 346.21
Azava 073.36
azores 468.34
Azrael 258.07
azulblu 180.12
azurespotted 477.19
azylium 152.36

b 140.11 140.21 369.29
B 165.23 (Burrus)
226.31 (B is Boyblue)
458.33 (Bienie)
B. 184.28
184.28 (Mistress B. de B. Meinfelde)
251.33 (B. Rohan)
518.10 (B. Dunn)
ba 224.28
Ba 284.L3
B.A. 087.13 (Hyacinth O'Donnell, B.A.)
088.16
B.A.A. 467.27 (swift B.A.A.)
baabaa 133.25
Baaboo 191.35
baaded 178.15
baalamb's 178.13
Baalastartey 091.14
Baalfire's 013.36
baallad 593.15
baar 313.15
baas 127.18 283.26 608.15
Baas 442.08
baases 131.08
baass 141.15
Baass 311.17
bababadalgharaghtakamminarronnkonnbronntonnerronntuonnthunntrovarrhounawnskawntoohoohoordenenthurnuk 003.15
Bababadkessy 471.02
babad 534.10
babalong 103.11
Babau 466.01
babazounded 552.28
Babbau 481.20
babbeing 344.28
babbel 254.17
Babbel 199.31
babbelers 015.12
babbers 262.27
babbishkis 568.19
babble 064.11 354.27
babbling 164.11 195.01 306.F1
babbly 173.27
babblyebubblye 526.09
Babby 230.04
Babbyl 532.25
babbyrags 583.01
babe 026.16 080.17 291.28 483.20 562.22
babel 064.10 499.34
babel 278.L4
Babel 258.11
babeling 006.31 314.02
babes 220.19 308.25 336.16 561.03 619.23
babeteasing 276.F1
babetise 537.08
babies 273.F5 413.10 504.22
babilonias 460.23
Baboon 176.12
babooshkees 417.12
Babs 561.32
bab's 194.24
babskissed 156.17
babu 133.28
Babwith 241.36

baby 099.07 194.24 501.14
babybag 444.20
babybell 346.33
babyboy 242.08
babycurls 024.30
Babylon 139.12 185.12
babylone 017.33
babyma's 166.16
baby's 213.29 253.15
baccbuccus 118.16
bacchante 247.35
Bacchulus 365.06
Bacchus 262.26
baccle 011.02
baccon 363.17
baccy 056.27
baccypipes 243.21
bach 176.34 213.17 287.06 328.10 508.34
Bach 073.21
Bachelor's 214.03
bachelure's 061.04
baches 083.03
bachspilled 526.30
back 003.02 005.27 010.21 012.04 021.23 021.31 022.10 022.19 030.03 030.06 033.07 040.04 051.28 055.23 055.23 061.05 067.05 080.22 080.32 082.27 102.24 110.18 110.31 112.01 116.04 118.06 120.20 126.03 135.03 136.07 137.20 139.05 144.24 145.15 151.15 160.17 165.25 166.34 169.07 169.24 174.32 178.34 187.34 207.15 207.18 211.05 212.25 213.17 213.17 215.03 222.36 223.10 223.32 227.12 227.15 240.29 243.06 244.28 247.05 270.09 271.F1 275.04 275.10 279.F10 287.06 289.07 290.17 292.25 295.11 312.16 315.12 315.19 316.27 320.21 320.24 320.34 322.01 333.08 336.03 348.09 355.22 362.26 367.02 368.18 377.10 382.07 385.19 389.21 411.08 427.35 428.19 428.22 431.07 433.15 434.05 435.14 435.17 435.30 436.34 441.03 442.13 446.17 446.21 449.09 458.21 459.01 464.19 466.08 477.18 481.30 484.08 485.15 492.15 496.25 496.30 498.20 498.25 502.29 508.04 513.27 516.16 517.16 519.23 523.25 529.22 533.21 541.19 544.27 544.27 546.31 566.14 575.01 576.11 580.13 585.32 586.23 588.10 589.16 597.27 610.26 614.02 618.07 619.35 621.24 628.01
back 340.19 344.03 349.35
Back 361.35 421.03 421.07 559.02 615.25
Back 105.31 106.28 106.35
backballed 232.15
backblocks 072.36
backboard 451.03
backbone 036.32 603.23
backclack 423.05
backed 134.01 249.20 615.25
backers' 064.18
backfrish 264.06
backfrisking 572.04
backfronted 280.23
backgammoner 560.11
backing 524.22
Backlane 287.30
backleg 361.25
Backlegs 341.28
backly 444.18
backonham 318.21
backoning 603.01
backroom 557.08
backs 176.23 563.13
backscrat 397.26
backscratching 391.10
Backscuttling 470.22
backsight 249.02
backsights 352.32
backslapping 276.02
backslibris 477.23
backslop 363.29
backsteps 157.15
backthought 359.02
Back-to-Bunk 258.36
backtowards 084.30
backtrap 047.09
backturns 369.03
backward 161.33
backwards 135.30 190.29 248.18 368.02 419.24 426.34
backway 543.30
backwoods 374.28
Backwoods 244.01
backwords 073.19 100.28 487.32 624.18
bacon 141.21 406.03 615.31
bacon 345.30
Bacon 071.24
bad 023.25 026.26 037.02 046.12 087.20 096.21 117.02 117.05 172.03 176.26 178.02 186.29 189.16 192.12 219.24 220.13 221.07 246.32 252.23 263.29 365.18 371.07 379.26 391.13 391.13 392.05 392.07 392.11 392.35 397.25 410.05 419.27 433.11 435.32 437.21 443.03 471.08 489.08 513.10 520.04 526.29 549.23 564.28 565.20 598.22 616.27 617.19 627.25
Bad 499.12
Bad 072.12
Badannas 071.12
Badanuweir 448.31
badazmy 492.32
badbad 179.16
Badbols 376.27
badbrat 555.20
badchthumpered 360.09
badday 378.20
Baddelaries 004.03
badder 242.23 298.22 303.29 314.18
Baddersdown 132.04
baddlefall 348.04
baddy 485.15
bade 547.23
Baden 422.29
badend 138.18
Badeniveagh 408.28
badfather 094.33
badge 470.30
badgeler's 516.04
badher 198.09
badily 425.18
badley 354.35
badly 172.13 176.31
badly 201.05
Badly's 421.06
Badman 113.20
badness 152.29 152.29
badoldkarakter 098.09
Badsheetbaths 188.26
badst 597.05
baedeker 123.27
Baernfather's 099.12
baffle 246.27
baffled 354.09
bafflelost 118.07
baffling 119.17 320.35 373.06 585.35
bafforyou 148.01
bag 008.26 026.10 027.06 054.22 211.14 227.03 237.14 288.11 300.F3 304.17 312.01 320.08 320.22 416.18 433.21 452.05 458.19 494.18 603.08 607.18 625.03
Bag 300.F3
bagabroth 398.02
bagateller 415.25
bagawards 018.32
bagdad 286.04 590.21
bagful 212.20
baggage 444.16 589.15
bagged 058.17 334.23
bagger 186.20
baggermalster 062.03
baggermen 494.36
Baggot 490.20
Baggotty's 071.12
Baggut's 491.06
baggutstract 346.33
baggy 051.07 443.27
baggyrhatty 209.10
Baghus 351.24
Bagnabun 294.F4
bagoderts 394.18
bagot 345.15
bagpipes 499.29
bagpuddingpodded 498.32
bags 220.14
bags 471.33
Bags 264.L1
bagses 420.03
bagsides 007.34
bagslops 583.36
bagsmall 490.04
bahad 532.24
bail 032.03 045.20 073.08 455.06 508.32
bailby 624.19
Baile-Atha-Cliath 420.20
baile's 013.22
bailey 317.30
Bailey 085.26 448.19 480.18
Bailey 071.21 342.23
baileycliaver 159.30
bailiff's 046.09 153.16
bailiwick 031.27
baillybeacons 358.25
bails 584.04
Bailywick 006.33
baint 285.17
bairdboard 349.08
bairn 198.07 477.03 576.16

bairns 244.09
baised 203.34
bait 031.08 089.32 180.31 448.18 451.02
baited 043.01 336.25 492.04
baith 281.01
baiting 144.08
bake 450.15 498.20
Baked 421.14
baken 007.10 320.29
bakenbeggfuss 041.13
Baker 603.06
bakereen's 212.20
Bakerloo 348.31
baker's 257.19
bakes 542.30
bakin 257.22
baking 172.07
bakk 323.23
bakset 277.F7
bakvandets 198.11
balaaming 566.09
Balaclava 170.33
balacleivka 341.09
balance 293.06 426.28 471.06 589.13
balance 399.16
Balance 308.L2
balay 531.20
balaying 451.18
Balbaccio 045.28
balbearians 285.L3
balbettised 192.36
balbly 037.16
balbose 287.19
Balbriggan 399.14
balbriggans 530.12
balbuccio 045.28
balbulous 004.30
Balbus 467.16 518.34
bald 164.27 380.28 390.08 501.22 555.21 606.14
Baldawl 342.06
balder 331.14
baldness 051.09
Baldowl 074.16
Baldoygle 142.15
Baldoyle 039.02
baldyqueens 154.12
baledale 342.07
balefires 052.19
Balenoarch 612.27 612.27 612.28
bales 198.31
balfy 199.29
balifuson 019.19
baling 480.13
balk 309.03
balkan 501.33
balked 296.07
Balkelly 611.05
Balkis 543.14
balkonladies 569.02
ball 009.11 066.37 098.31 209.13 314.13 321.17 377.06 454.11 512.10 518.01 622.24
Ball 130.10 464.28
Ballaclay 314.21
ballad 042.13 043.22 211.19 381.23 580.36
Ballad 044.24
Ballade 177.27
balladproof 616.32
Ballantine 106.09
ballast 313.21 518.01 551.01
ballasted 304.13
Ballat 175.27
ballay 510.14
ballbearing 426.29
Balldole 144.10
balled 037.34
balledder 042.13
Ballera 088.19
ballest 390.03
ballet 253.21 346.20 366.03 565.36
balletbattle 221.18
balletlines 235.23
ballets 495.03
balloon 212.05
ballooned 339.28
balloons 378.01 438.20
ballot 531.29
ballotboxes 122.26
Ballotin 060.28
ballround 096.14
balls 009.19 042.33 118.29 130.21 366.10 498.18 529.11 589.08
balls 339.20
Balls 264.L1
ballsbluffed 084.09
Ballsbridge 306.25
Ballscodden 326.34
Ballses 447.17
ballshee 316.21
Ballshossers 146.13
balltossic 187.02
ballwearied 543.01
bally 136.33 279.08 436.27 523.11 560.30
Ballyaughacleeaghbally 014.09
Ballybock 095.02
Ballybough 236.21
ballybricken 086.24
Ballyclee 210.19
ballyfermont 183.05
Ballygarry 346.24
ballyheart 536.10
Ballyhooly 100.07 608.08
ballyhooric 555.10
ballyhouraised 262.25
Ballyhuntus 622.27
Ballymacarett 501.04
Ballymooney 219.19
Ballymun 014.36
Ballymunites 497.20
balm 204.04 241.16 366.22 442.24 580.10
balmbearer 115.18
balmheartzyheat 102.19
balmoil 440.25
balmybeam 237.14
balneo 605.08
Balrothery 405.27
balsam 100.13
balsamboards 262.25
balsinbal 420.12
Balt 423.03
Baltersby 387.24
Baltic 491.35 544.03
Baltiskeeamore 338.19
baltitude 040.32
baltxebec 323.04
Bam 536.11
Bambam's 389.12
bambolina 561.23
bamboozelem 515.28
bamer 035.13
bames 348.26
bamp 176.34
ban 020.01
Ban 072.03
bana 199.20
Banagher 087.31
bananas 447.12
Banba 132.26 325.24 596.08
Banbasday 294.F4
Banbashore 469.06
banbax 330.21
banck 127.28
banck 338.36
bancorot 266.23
band 008.34 009.09 032.34 047.20 055.13 189.25 198.26 205.06 208.08 333.12 407.33 448.22 533.10 573.06 589.19 601.13
band 349.24
bandanna 030.22
banders 250.03 565.03
bandished 224.34
bandol 073.17
bandolair 022.36
bands 556.29
bandstand 070.11 230.27
Bandusian 280.32
bandy 012.18 187.26
bane 102.22 180.24 363.13 437.34 580.27 614.08
banes 595.01
banes 353.07
bang 008.13 098.02
Bang 341.01 378.18 378.18
Bangbong 245.26
bangd 320.10
banged 014.20 334.23
Bangen-op-Zoom 073.26
bangkok's 008.20
bangled 620.08
bangles 207.07
bangs 544.03
Bangs 100.07
bangslanging 445.10
bang-the-change 577.12
banished 121.21 288.F6
banishee's 581.09
banishment 228.19
banister 544.20
banjo 262.L1
banjopeddlars 347.27
bank 076.08 084.31 087.31 090.24 153.09 158.25 158.32 213.22 235.11 510.21 547.30 574.18 589.12
bank 273.L2 398.33
Bank 083.17 420.32
B A N K 379.30
bankaloan 624.07
bankers 578.10
bankrompers 510.20
bankrump 590.03
bankrupt 024.22
banks 004.28 158.08 246.09 272.12 372.16
bankside 201.05
bann 137.13 210.07 363.12
Bannalanna 100.07
bannan 145.35
bannars 563.14

banned 588.16
bannistars 157.09 159.08
bannock 318.16
bannocks 053.29
banns 197.12
bannucks 136.28
ban's 228.16
Bansh 528.04
banshee 347.15
Banshee 306.17
'Bansheeba 468.36
bantams 262.L1
bantlings 110.24
bantur 204.03
Banza 609.35
Banzaine 351.14
Bap 481.19 481.19
bapka 481.25
Bappy 277.18
Bappy-go-gully 499.04
Bapsbaps 506.18
bapt 044.13
baptism 606.11
Baptiste 204.36
Baptister 255.27
baquets 059.07
bar 016.35 021.34 046.17 057.33 081.31 092.12 177.23 197.35 245.25 291.01 321.07 336.07 440.03 457.06 487.02 512.26 544.35 587.17
Bar 219.02 323.12 529.34 594.35 607.30
barangaparang 345.05
Barass 342.10
Baraton 180.08
Baraza 237.31
Barbados 525.06
barbar 108.19
Barbar 261.L1
barbaras 335.27
Barbaras 105.15
Barbarassa 280.L1
barbarihams 518.28
barbarism 114.13
Barbaropolis 181.06
barbarous 394.03
barbarousse 154.23
barbe 081.29
Barbe 410.26
barbecue 380.10
barbed 569.27
barbels 169.14
barcelonas 273.19 288.18
Barclay 569.07
bard 277.F3 465.28
barde 251.35
barded 373.33
bardic 172.28
bards 037.17 048.07 363.05
bard's 504.16
bare 005.05 055.25 055.25 079.20 079.36 085.14 176.27 177.11 229.17 247.22 302.26 351.20 364.01 391.32 409.19 416.16 416.26 428.04 434.26 454.12 480.14 530.12 538.18 546.36 548.26 561.12 600.27 615.33
bare 348.04
Bare 360.07
Barebarean 071.30
Barec 420.14
bared 251.35 352.32 536.28
barefaced 050.21
barefacedness 091.18
Barefoot 204.06
barefooted 160.19
baregams 075.02
baregazed 069.12
barekely 287.19
barelean 550.08
barely 067.28 126.14 363.35 430.10 436.12 481.31 535.18 541.01 556.04 564.24
baremaids 526.23
Bareniece 038.09
barents 331.12
bares 241.36 377.28
baresark 547.26
baresides 507.10
Baretherootsch 222.12
baretholobruised 021.35
bargain 115.09 242.04 406.14 538.19 589.14
bargainboutbarrows 595.23
Bargainweg 046.04
barge 204.09 328.02
Bargearse 046.20
bargeness 549.35
Bargomuster 393.08
barheated 415.19
Barindens 600.28
baring 049.29
barishnyas 193.14
bark 077.15 168.05 182.36 312.04 358.17 360.10 449.27 467.01 504.01 580.28 626.22
bark 383.02
Barke 303.06
barkers 127.11
barkes 256.12
barketree 588.30
barkeys 552.09
barking 494.35 505.04
barkiss 062.31
barks 272.31
barkst 089.09
Barktholed 535.02
barlady 528.24
Bar-le-Duc 073.26
barley 318.16 362.20 494.16
Barley 257.10
barleybag 514.34
barleyfields 203.06
Barleyhome 382.26
barley's 026.33
barleystraw 589.36
barleywind 428.13
barlow 553.20
Barmabrac's 274.12
barmaid's 059.36
barmaisigheds 387.21
barmhearts 563.29
barmicidal 079.06
barmon 051.33
barn 385.01
barn 339.34
Barna 057.10
barnabarnabarn 481.27
Barnabas 337.36 572.34
barnaboy 237.15
barnacle 399.10
barnacled 423.22
Barnado's 253.31
Barncar 434.27
Barnehulme 130.24
barnet 480.02
barnets 020.28 141.14
barney 453.06
barney 354.15
Barneycorrall 285.F2
barneydansked 330.34
Barnstaple 253.34
Barnum 029.05
Barny-the-Bark 211.02
baroccidents 288.11
Baroke 024.34
baron 365.04 577.18
baronet 266.23
baronets 568.21
baronies 525.18
baronoath 006.33
barons 137.29 566.12
barony 543.18
barony 399.28
baroque 230.36
baroun 107.36
barque 373.10
barqued 197.28
barquentine 479.29
barra 063.36
barrabelowther 266.10
barrack 507.24
barracker 495.01
barracks 530.04
barracksers 348.20
barrackybuller 584.08
barrage 048.05
barragio 048.01
barrakraval 366.20
barral 088.31
barran 365.19
barrancos 386.30
Barratt's 155.26
barraw 491.19
barrel 080.32 179.03 255.11 304.14 419.18 426.31 529.18 565.31 596.17
Barrel 041.17 376.31 510.18
Barrel 072.15 105.16
barrelhours 429.08
barrels 311.11 414.13 506.04
barren 145.05
Barren 575.02
Barrentone 536.32
barreny 265.20
barricade 349.10
barriers 114.07
barring 080.02 309.05
Barringoy 310.15
barrow 198.33 210.07 477.36 479.24 568.24
Barrow 024.20 057.13
barrowload 006.27
Barry 093.28 134.11
Barry's 184.21
bars 118.29 492.10 519.36 558.09
barsalooner 625.11
barstool 443.29
Bart 393.08
barter 311.34
barters 575.01
Barth 044.13
Barthalamou 314.22
barthelemew 541.15
Bartholoman's 100.04
Bartholomew 560.24

Barth-the-Grete-by-the-Exchange 135.10
Bartley 323.13
Barto 247.10
bartrossers 246.27
barttler 372.07
Barty 142.27
Baruch 284.F4
barytinette 562.03
Ba's 415.31
basal 577.15
Basast 364.29
baschfellors 221.12
basco 230.06
base 156.12 187.18 298.19 343.29 543.02 547.34 580.23
Base 105.09
based 314.11
basel 088.05
baselgia 243.29
basemeant 535.18
basement 242.04
basemiddelism 344.22
baseness 367.02
baser 033.14
bash 034.11 063.05 240.01
bashed 292.18 466.28 518.28
bashfully 465.11
Bashfulness 238.20
bashman's 353.07
basia 122.21
basically 116.26
basidens 133.36
Basil 374.31
Basilica 569.16
Basilico's 025.09
basilikerks 005.33
basilisk 577.02
Basilius 463.22
basium 122.32
bask 263.F2
baskatchairch 358.27
baskerboy 417.17
basketfild 273.L3
basketful 492.33
baskib 549.34
basking 143.03 437.36
baskly 233.35
Baskside 106.03
basky 374.19
Baslesbridge 136.30
basque 121.05 507.15
Basqueesh 287.F4
basquibezigues 350.20
basquing 556.33
bass 049.32 222.08
bass 286.L3
bassabosuned 313.04
bassed 312.13
bassein 207.19
basses 311.03
basset 097.05
bassoons 565.04
Bass's 492.03
bassvoco 032.24
Bast 159.19
Bastabasco 329.01
Bastard 072.15
bastardtitle 440.08
baste 311.32 487.17
Bastienne 254.14
bastille 275.10
Basucker 010.19
bat 151.23 584.23
batailles 281.13
batblack 405.36
batch 292.03
Batch 603.06
bate 199.30 231.23 283.27
bateau 065.36
batell 073.12
Bates 209.08
batflea 417.03
batforlake 348.04
bath 255.24 355.13 363.08 394.11 605.15 605.21 605.32
bathandbaddend 541.27
bathar 599.05
bathboites 235.24
bathershins 428.14
bathfeet 279.08
bathing 209.26
bathouse 597.14
bathtub 542.05
batin 029.29
Batiste 054.15
batman's 337.03
batom 296.06
baton 098.29
bats 180.27 215.32 215.33 272.08 446.11
Bats 276.20
batsleeve 289.27
batt 625.18
Batt 374.19
Batt 349.08
battam 594.12
batter 025.35 374.29 583.34
battercops 428.27
battered 287.31 493.04 553.29
Batteries 372.31
battering 064.09 208.04 328.02
Battersby 386.24
batter-the-bolster 577.12
battery 025.17 077.11 310.02
Batterysby 497.18
battle 114.36 129.11 196.17 209.13 329.21 355.20 580.12
Battle 176.10
battleaxes 344.24
Battlecock 051.22
battles 348.01
Battleshore 390.16
Battlewatschers 105.33
battonstaff 366.19
Batty 098.29
Batty 177.29
baubble 536.08
bauble 273.07
baubleclass 359.12
baublelight 224.12
baubletop 005.02
bauchees 370.31
bauchspeech 100.28
bauck 365.13
Baudwin 184.35
baugh 447.23
Baughkley 447.24
Baulacleeva 134.01
Bauliaughacleeagh 310.12
baulk 085.13
Baum's 364.08
Baus 187.27
bausnabeatha 384.09
Bauv 420.10
baver 052.24
bawbees 398.34
bawd 227.03 296.07
bawds 481.06
bawdy 547.27
bawk 215.32 215.33
bawl 056.01 101.17 154.01 475.34 617.25
Bawlawayo 353.29
Bawle 099.32
bawley 239.32
bawlful 464.21
bawling 072.32 309.22 422.36 468.32 517.09
bawll 337.35
Bawlonabraggat 060.12
bawls 046.18 058.12 273.02
bawn 009.22 130.13 252.21 384.21 397.05
bawnee 586.14
bawneen 394.11
bawns 438.34
bawny 472.04
Baws 262.25
Bawse 499.06
Bawshaw 366.34
bax 542.29
baxingmotch 415.13
baxters 136.04 603.06
Baxters 050.01
bay 003.02 046.14 251.01 327.34 360.10 409.02 466.28 567.16 571.08
bay 201.19
Bay 141.34 523.17 543.04 601.17
Bayamouth 071.19
bayers 097.07
Bayleaffs 421.12
bayleaves 121.05
baylight's 626.34
bayondes 327.21
bayrings 287.10
Bayroyt 500.24
bays 095.06 263.10 339.08 366.34
Baywindaws 141.18
baywinds' 006.36
bazaar 597.14
bazar 497.25
bazeness's 378.16
Bb 121.34
B. B. 266.F2 (B. B. Brophy)
Bbyrdwood 169.05
B.C. 272.13
bcome 344.12
bdly 448.28
Bdur 165.07
be be Be
be 284.L3
beach 146.25 323.11
beach 399.03
beachalured 548.11
beachbusker 040.21
beached 292.18 316.04 358.17 605.21
Beacher 365.36
beachwalker 110.36
beacon 257.15 267.12
Beacon 179.14
Beacon 342.23
beaconegg 382.11
beaconings 222.36
beaconphires 553.10
beacons 199.17

beaconsfarafield 100.19
beacsate 590.13
beadells 549.32
Beadle 071.32
beadroll 276.01
beads 210.29 214.01 376.06
Beads 530.33
beagles 245.03 567.23
beagling 096.36
beak 066.24 496.31 548.36
beaker 091.22
beakerings 118.05
beaks 080.21
beall 533.36
beallpersuasions 537.03
bealting 346.15
beam 056.19 093.28 113.25 289.09 315.12 356.17 408.16 472.16 512.09 602.29
beamed 324.33 359.22
beamer 380.16 469.05
beaming 349.08
beamish 405.16
beamstark 615.25
beamy 223.13
bean 279.F24
beandbe 297.14
beanfeast 380.10
beans 133.24 406.16 411.17 425.19
beanstale 126.11
bear 032.14 118.16 177.04 178.03 272.29 339.27 410.22 430.07 450.09 458.08 479.26 495.05 512.05 628.07
Bear 032.04 284.F4 447.11
Bear 267.L2
bearagain 272.30
Bearara 255.15
bearb 209.14
beard 033.32 077.12 229.20 260.F1 352.04 391.01 443.26
Beardall 587.32
bearded 192.25 291.23 435.03
Bearded 222.12
beards 501.27 581.04
beardsboosoloom 012.13
beardslie 357.08
beardwig 625.02
bearer 408.13 575.17 590.04
Bearer 463.05
bearers 043.01
bearers' 200.01
bearfellsed 373.14
bearing 031.01 065.36 097.04 340.17 510.23 536.27 602.30 628.09
bearings 283.25 576.35
Bearn 539.31
Bearring 320.28
bears 136.12 239.30 583.04
bear's 516.14
bears' 358.30
bearserk 582.29
bearskin 253.31
Bearskin 051.15
bearspaw 110.03 621.21
Bearstone 176.08
beast 089.16 099.14 292.28 317.08 466.06 476.16 480.24 541.31 594.27
beast' 150.12
Beastalk 307.F1
beastful 566.33
beasties 227.28
beastly 559.23
beastman 511.02
beasts 347.06
beastskin 262.24
beat 145.34 165.04 167.27 175.05 180.30 190.28 279.F01 328.02 344.30 445.02 445.18 460.12 530.17 586.21
beat 419.08
Beat 071.14
Beata 569.16
Beate 228.25
beaten 080.04 590.06
beatend 600.36
beatenest 299.07
beaters 097.06
beatified 210.29
beating 410.03
Beatrice 227.14
beats 347.23 347.25
Beats 027.20
Beatsoon 286.24
beatties 019.09
beau 143.24 233.05 584.29 585.23
beau 399.11 576.16
beaubirds 180.28
beauchamp 077.19
Beaufort 567.25
beaufu 396.36
beauhind 564.08
beauman's 226.07
beaunes 058.15
Beaus' 405.13
beaushelled 292.18
beausome 449.22
beautfour 393.22
beautibus 445.23
beauties 200.01 541.30
Beauties 622.32
beautifell 558.28
beautific 452.19
beautified 262.F6
beautiful 111.13 116.21 143.24 166.13 194.15 337.17 366.07 393.17 403.14 435.14 460.32 556.04 556.06 556.06 619.04
beautonhole 350.11
beautsy 092.29
beauty 121.30 157.34 192.28 271.09 289.30 331.25 366.35 385.22 389.12 435.21 458.06 476.23 477.23 528.11 533.03 534.24
Beauty 454.19
Beauty 071.11
beautycapes 562.05
Beauty's 355.13
beauw 322.36
beaux 568.22 618.23
beauyne 372.07
beauys 245.20
beaver 260.F1 392.23 396.17
beavers 100.12 537.32
beavery 450.03
bebattersbid 515.30
bebattled 272.28
Bebebekka 471.02
Bebel 118.18
beblive 481.25
bebold 053.14
Bebold 451.17
becakes 370.01
became 016.17 021.30 022.17 050.24 057.31 082.21 083.07 137.23 171.04 235.11 251.28 506.15 618.04
becamedump 332.17
becauld 152.26
because 012.06 014.08 017.03 038.17 055.34 066.36 072.21 086.27 087.21 087.22 087.23 088.08 146.05 146.06 146.17 146.18 151.15 160.19 167.20 191.30 191.31 194.20 194.20 194.21 220.01 230.06 235.20 241.07 317.05 317.28 351.28 368.02 372.13 375.01 391.08 391.17 391.19 391.24 391.26 391.34 405.27 423.11 459.10 473.06 489.28 505.34 510.05 556.12 563.09 564.03 566.34 567.07 608.03 622.36 624.33
because 349.27 349.28 349.31 349.33 350.03
Because 067.32 078.24 118.18 253.21 288.F3 372.35 425.34 442.21 597.09
Because 342.12
becaused 176.30
becauses 596.25
Becchus 276.13
becco 403.13
Becco 412.29
beck 194.30 415.10
beckburn 134.29
beckerbrose 608.20
becket 543.11
beckline 223.32
beckon 267.12
beckside 090.07
become 070.09 099.36 112.19 132.16 132.17 162.01 188.14 238.20 259.01 325.15 362.11 446.13 451.35 457.06 459.32 472.03 487.19 523.07 563.29 570.34
Become 016.24 359.27 485.14
becomes 247.23 267.16 293.04 378.11
becomes 354.05
becoming 108.09 143.20 193.36 235.11 269.08 298.31 333.03 410.02 410.07 427.35 431.10 438.25 438.29 487.20 523.12 526.36 562.35 608.27 627.17
Becoming 331.03
becomingly 487.19
becomings 491.23
becon 405.33 406.15
becorpse 509.32
Becracking 376.09
becrimed 078.32
Bective's 451.10
becups 144.09
Becups 568.14
becursekissed 078.33
bed 003.17 006.26 040.36 064.04 076.32 101.34 148.14 168.10 210.25 276.F5 279.F36 291.06 314.32 327.14 334.05 379.17 394.04 409.18 415.23 422.35 431.36 444.26 475.08 486.24 495.18 533.28 546.36

558.26 559.12 559.20 561.07 576.17 577.36 601.32 622.20
bed 201.17 383.12 399.23
Bed 559.06 559.12
Bed 072.15 105.34
bedamnbut 381.25
bedamp 201.06
bedang 185.31
bedattle 353.11
bedaweens 241.26
bedboards 098.06
bedded 579.27
beddest 311.25
bedding 024.13 362.24 511.08 559.13 586.06
beddingnights 446.05
bedeafdom 236.30
bedeave 476.21
bedeed 185.31
bedelias 266.01
bedemmed 239.33
bedes 548.30
bedevere 266.10
bedewing 463.09
bedfellow 422.11
bedgo 441.29
bediabbled 239.33
bediamondise 428.11
bedizzled 234.02
bedknob 559.09
bedood 185.31
bedoueen 005.23
Bedouix 200.22
bedower'd 371.18
bedowern 427.18
bedpain 328.36
bedpan 581.09
bedreamt 075.05
bedroom 041.16 137.29 396.11 559.01 627.09
bedrooms 362.33
beds 020.25 041.25 265.08
Beds 105.04
bedscrappers 049.28
bedshead 241.20
bedsores 397.26
bedspread 559.06
bedst 356.26 531.05 560.20
bedstead 069.22
bedstead 430.15
bedtick 176.35
bedumbtoit 078.33
bedung 185.32
bee 120.07 133.01 238.34 256.18 263.F3 313.06 360.29 461.08 494.25
Bee 248.19
beeble 313.05
beebread 416.18
beech 112.05
beeches 160.01
beedles 373.23
BEEEFTAY'S 308.R1
beef 423.18
beehiviour 430.19
beeline 555.14
beelyingplace 262.F1
beem 285.10
been been Been
beer 068.27 136.15 171.14 328.02 559.25
Beer 464.28
beerbarrel 439.12
beerbest 536.21
beerchen 503.33
beerchurls 381.33
beerd 373.29
beerings 321.13
beerlitz 182.07
Beerman's 422.31
beers 498.18
beersgrace 468.32
Beery 064.33
bees 422.29
beesabouties 496.33
beesknees 026.35 330.34
beesnest 070.03
beest 411.18
beeswax 141.31 184.20
beeswaxing 261.L3
beeswixed 333.22
Beet 521.19
beeter 138.12
beethoken 360.08
beetle 171.31 358.36 417.04
beetles 248.18
beetly 100.01
Beetom 333.34
Beeton 154.24
beets 019.08
beetyrossy 094.30
beeves 398.03 538.35
beeyed 341.07
befaddle 323.08
befair 515.27
befallhim 251.11
befear 403.10
befell 238.14
befells 380.04
befier 128.19
befinding 261.07
befit 501.26
befitting 052.31
beflore 364.14
befodt 339.34
befogged 536.19
befond 212.18
befor 366.06
Befor 215.18
before 004.20 005.20 007.06 019.21 020.03 022.04 036.27 040.10 043.36 049.01 052.04 052.05 052.13 054.29 055.01 055.32 057.24 067.14 067.23 067.35 069.31 072.26 076.16 083.04 083.34 087.20 091.12 091.24 091.32 094.36 095.19 096.08 107.27 112.18 114.35 115.33 116.17 118.11 121.08 121.25 127.08 128.27 128.28 132.01 132.25 134.13 144.04 144.22 146.36 148.24 149.14 155.26 160.36 164.18 171.36 173.16 175.36 179.07 179.32 191.15 193.06 194.05 194.26 198.24 202.09 203.01 204.06 204.07 204.17 207.24 212.16 226.35 228.29 232.16 232.32 236.04 238.07 241.27 241.34 243.27 247.18 248.11 250.26 252.30 253.19 256.34 261.12 291.F8 292.07 297.10 311.07 311.08 317.33 318.26 328.24 332.23 335.02 335.30 352.02 352.14 355.23 356.03 356.36 357.29 359.08 359.25 360.36 361.21 364.21 366.08 369.32 375.11 380.21 380.25 384.16 385.27 385.29 386.27 389.25 390.19 391.21 391.22 391.23 394.20 395.21 395.22 397.28 404.16 405.11 411.14 417.14 421.25 421.30 422.04 424.27 424.31 427.05 429.01 429.05 432.24 433.34 434.34 435.06 437.05 437.08 439.06 439.25 442.13 442.26 443.11 443.19 451.18 455.34 456.36 461.22 461.29 463.23 463.25 463.32 465.23 467.02 467.06 468.07 473.16 484.03 484.16 485.22 488.31 489.25 490.11 493.04 494.19 497.21 506.02 511.03 516.16 516.23 517.35 519.24 522.15 523.34 525.30 530.13 534.12 535.05 542.04 544.09 549.03 553.04 553.29 565.16 566.34 568.03 579.18 579.22 586.03 586.03 600.15 607.06 607.09 609.27 612.21 613.13 616.27 616.33 617.27 621.34 623.06 626.20 627.35
before 071.17 071.27 345.07 349.33 399.20
Before 057.10 219.15 376.24 452.28 477.32 624.18
Before 105.16
BEFORE 286.R2
beforeaboots 288.25
beforehand 253.14 576.23
beforetime 323.30
befoul 212.19 520.25
befour 250.12 517.30
befriends 460.18
Befurcht 481.09
beg 008.24 082.05 099.33 146.26 168.05 221.35 257.19 264.F2 279.F17 332.26 377.11 410.28 422.10 492.14 517.08 562.36
beg 399.19
Beg 210.13 227.30
begad 024.07 612.32
begad 346.33
begadag 186.21
begalla 520.03
begame 373.26
began 020.26 021.19 048.22 061.11 077.15 078.21 080.16 147.18 158.08 158.21 414.16 431.23 477.01 539.34 547.19 584.21
begatem 506.10
begath 286.06
begay 020.26
begayment 236.30
begeds 241.27
Begetting 373.26
begeylywayled 331.32
begfirst 413.16
begg 007.07
beggar 007.24 145.22 163.13 269.23
Beggards 579.12
beggars 130.06 388.15
beggar's 588.02
beggars' 079.31
Begge 058.16 262.F7 262.F7 262.F7 262.F7 262.F7

beggelaut 484.09
beggered 542.35
beggin 205.19 311.31
begging 093.26 149.15 239.06 584.35
beggybaggy 011.11
begidding 346.09
begiddy 132.20
begin 119.05 121.15 155.13 170.21 173.14 181.34 347.23 409.09 420.15 423.17 428.05 434.03 452.22 455.28 501.17 560.35 565.06 618.17 625.32
Begin 614.20
beginall 090.23
beginners 407.10
beginning 030.12 222.03 255.35 277.12 287.06 425.10 452.35 456.21 468.05 540.19
beginnings 597.10
begins 122.03 295.11 308.15 337.12 472.34 490.09 594.12 600.20 603.35 621.25
begirlified 329.17
begob 463.01 467.18
Begob 047.03 466.34
begod 046.24
Begog 025.23
begolla 485.33
begor 439.15 450.36 454.29 516.17 522.33
Begor 436.08 578.11
begottom 582.01
begrained 026.34
begraved 560.18
begripe 141.21
begrudged 534.22
begs 302.06 309.06
begum 526.26
Begum 590.24
begun 422.31
begyndelse 282.05
Behailed 417.10
behaitch 443.01
behalf 067.17 173.30 290.26 574.22
beham 040.11
behame 319.30
Behan 027.31 063.35 212.03
behangd 391.08
behanged 049.26
behanshrub 588.31
behaste 317.20
behaunt 368.07
behave 327.01
behaved 034.18
behaveyous 068.20
behaving 275.F5
behaviour 534.31
behaviourising 110.25
behaviouristically 149.25
behaviourite 012.18
behazyheld 625.26
beheasts 367.32
beheaving 353.16
beheeding 397.22
beheighten 336.08
beheild 326.05
beheiss 347.34
beheld 055.24 322.23 417.10
behemoth 007.14
behemuth 244.36
behent 388.05
behest 313.14
behicked 049.27
behidden 284.25
behide 340.11
behidin 486.30
behigh 319.30
behind 009.33 012.04 019.22 020.24 052.24 058.21 061.26 068.36 071.02 080.35 081.05 084.09 094.35 098.34 101.12 116.33 127.09 134.36 135.13 136.31 143.06 154.13 175.35 175.36 184.25 189.15 202.36 208.26 227.12 234.08 236.16 260.F3 261.12 267.22 271.F1 284.04 290.F7 319.23 357.04 363.09 377.33 381.35 384.22 386.22 388.27 393.36 419.21 427.04 428.13 429.23 433.09 438.01 445.02 451.18 455.15 458.19 462.16 463.25 464.15 467.06 476.27 488.23 489.25 513.01 522.20 554.05 558.09 560.06 568.03 568.03 576.25 583.05 583.35 586.03 588.01
behind 071.26 349.34 419.04
Behind 049.25 248.33 250.25
behindaside 082.14
behinding 285.F5
behinds 146.08
behindscenes 358.04
behing 607.08
behoiled 324.17
behold 007.14 139.17 185.11 215.02 367.24 412.01 414.29 561.25 596.03
Behold 322.24
beholden 340.26
beholders 355.13 530.26
beholding 489.20
beholdings 616.14
behome 382.20
behomeans 333.15
behond 462.21
behooved 049.27
Behose 239.10
behoughted 018.02
behound 343.15
behounding 352.20
Behove 012.36
behoves 278.11
behowl 567.36
behulked 049.27
behund 339.07
behung 058.04
behunt 320.11
behush 628.12
bei 263.18
beillybursts 295.F1
being being Being
beingstalk 504.19
beingtime 612.21
beiug 297.07
Bejacob's 089.15
bejetties 358.24
bejimboed 238.18
bejupers 279.F22
bekant 432.32
bekase 282.09
Bekel 347.04
bekersse 322.09
bekicks 370.02
bel 412.07
Bel 405.13
belabour 436.20
belaboured 489.31
belaburt 339.06
belame 438.23
belated 395.03 410.22
belave 439.32
belaw 333.19
belch 095.26 492.36
belcher 037.29
belches 381.22 507.05
Belches 447.20
belching 199.10
Belchum 009.01 009.04 009.10 009.13 009.15
Belchum's 009.30
belchybubhub 239.33
belease 534.22
beleave 610.05
Beleave 610.05
beleaved 243.13
Beleaves 106.25
beleeme 351.20
belessk 361.13
belested 299.16
belevin 299.12
belfry 173.16 180.27 403.21
belge 239.32
Belgradia 534.22
belgroved 265.01
Belial 175.05
belied 289.04
belief 369.27 421.30 470.30 616.28
Belief 306.16 533.24
beliefd 077.21
beliek 409.24
believe 007.07 062.01 082.35 113.28 113.29 148.25 150.36 158.26 177.13 179.26 193.25 199.26 252.27 263.27 266.F1 411.12 411.13 411.21 431.24 470.12 470.12 503.19 509.18 512.20 519.20 536.05 557.33 563.22 567.31 622.16
Believe 500.33
Believe 105.13
believed 033.35 114.14 600.15
believer 352.22
believes 020.26 098.29 129.31 221.14
believing 101.28
Belinda 111.05
belined 156.20
Belisha 267.12
belittled 358.07
belittlers 083.35
belive 092.21
belived 534.26
bell 088.10 112.12 141.04 141.04 276.15 297.19 327.24 339.08 393.26 433.03 455.15 512.09 552.23 560.14 568.15 588.23
Bell 328.26
be'll 141.05
bella 518.33
bella 178.17
Bella 346.05
Belladama 450.32
bellance 506.08
bellas 224.28
Bellavistura's 601.25

bellax 486.32
Bellax 486.32
bellbearing 186.15
bellbox 393.28
bellcantos 381.18
Bellchimbers 369.08
belle 144.12 246.20 290.02 351.30 384.22 398.29 515.02 584.29
Belle 137.36 213.18 556.10
Belle 106.16
belleeks 449.33
belles 093.19 147.18 176.28 194.26 372.01
belles' 007.33
BELLETRISTICKS 281.R1
Bellevenue 625.06
Bellezza 211.14
bellhopping 194.34
Bellial 301.10
bellical 122.07
bellicose 018.34
bellied 324.02 387.09
bellies 618.07
belligerent 574.33
Bellina 576.06
belling 053.18
Belling 006.22
Bellini-Tosti 309.19
bellmaster 035.30
bellock 368.15
belloky 368.10
bellomport 549.22
Bellona 494.06
Bellona's 078.31
bellow 438.23
bellows 211.34 234.32 273.01 323.17 365.06
Bellows 292.F1
bellowsed 003.09
bells 011.25 128.01 205.12 244.07 244.22 329.21 483.06 568.05 598.13 621.34
bellseyes 310.29
Bellua 153.29
belluas 541.32
BELLUM-PAX-BELLUM 281.R1
belly 054.22 075.21 107.15 225.10 225.10 323.07 390.07 426.16 463.32 542.35 567.05
Belly 026.28 177.24 464.28
bellybone 085.08
bellyguds 275.10
bellyhooting 263.04
bellyswain's 248.21
Bellyup 072.11
bellyvoid 475.13
bellywash 529.18
belong 052.24 052.25 240.27 426.16 440.36
belongahim 374.35 611.08 612.03
belongame 485.33
belongashe 485.33
belongers 178.21
belonging 024.04 199.09 392.29 489.14
belongings 389.34
belongs 155.17 305.31 472.35 489.05 507.02
belove 022.24 289.04 325.30
beloved 296.23 410.26 413.25 488.04 524.06 533.28 619.03
below 022.01 029.05 041.20 108.01 160.26 164.09 200.14 211.34 213.05 262.F1 263.21 299.18 308.18 310.25 392.21 431.06 457.17 463.04 467.08 492.36 494.12 494.18 526.06 582.09
Below 312.03
belowes 343.17
belowing 154.35
belt 035.09 159.36 208.21 237.14 331.25 368.32 450.04 457.17 475.17 524.17 587.16 620.02
belt 349.24
belted 404.13
beltilla 194.22
belting 227.33
Belting 077.05
beltings 564.25
belts 507.10
beltspanners 534.31
belttry 053.12
beltts 390.08
belubdead 488.20
Belvaros 541.36
Belvedarean 205.05
belves 244.15
belzey 064.11
bemark 222.03
Bemark 567.12
Bembracken 319.04
Beme 144.04
bemember 493.27
beminded 427.33
beminding 528.08
Bemine 105.12
bemolly 450.25
benared 551.35
Benathere 081.16
bench 024.24 090.35 091.19 575.23
Bench 423.13
benches 137.13 161.34 166.11
bend 003.01 196.09 206.23 298.29 476.10
Bend 193.16 553.06
Bend 071.12
bended 035.34
benders 200.24
bending 447.34
bends 194.35 580.27
bene 453.18
Bene 287.16 294.26 295.17
beneadher 560.18
beneath 024.04 031.13 036.06 077.18 147.33 171.13 442.15 468.31 540.32
Beneathere 081.16
benedicat 569.21
benedict 431.18
benedicted 596.17
benedictine 452.17
benediction 204.32 219.08
benedictively 613.15
Benedictus 569.21
benedixed 248.30
benefactresses 544.34
Benefice 371.22
beneficiaries 058.02
benefiction 185.03
benefit 058.01 527.14
benefits 539.11
Benefits 306.22
beneighbour 193.27
Benent 430.02
benevolence 132.31
benevolence's 075.23
Bengalese 179.14
benighted 241.22 489.31
benighth 450.17
benison 410.26
benjamin 038.02 372.07 457.29
Benjamin's 140.01
Benjermine 289.10
B E N K 379.27 379.30
Benkletter 060.10
benn 244.23 623.25
Benn 007.28 128.01
bennbranch 029.03
Benns 606.14
Bennu 473.17
bennyache 302.28
Bennydick 469.23
bens 299.F1
bent 053.17 088.27 233.06 275.23
Bentamai 471.01
Bentley 088.23
bents 316.12
benuvolent 450.11
beogrefright 423.17
beorbtracktors 221.20
beotitubes 158.36
bepestered 098.13
bepiastered 098.12
Beppy's 415.36
bequeathed 579.32
beques 350.01
bequest 130.09
bequiet 137.06
bequined 607.33
bequother 336.24
ber 345.18
beraddy 335.15
Béranger 372.12
berayed 493.28
berbecked 064.31
Berber 106.31
berberutters 241.26
Berched's 430.02
berd 364.31
bereaved 324.19
berebelling 518.19
bereft 453.28 489.05
Berenice 243.26
bereppelling 518.20
beret 507.15
bergagambols 012.27
bergamoors 012.27
bergened 206.09
bergincellies 012.28
bergins 012.26
bergones 012.29
bergoo 276.15
bergs 139.20
berial 415.31
Berkeley 260.11 423.32
Berkeleyites 391.31
Berkness 375.28
Berlin 036.15
Bernadetta's 430.35
Bernesson 340.17
beromst 339.14
berow 541.17
berrathon 254.33

Berrboel 437.08
berriberries 542.01
berried 421.06
berries 464.20
berry 329.03 613.30
Berry 406.25
berrying 622.17
Bert 065.16
berth 330.28
Berthe 221.24
berthed 373.05 525.36
berths 199.02
berting 035.12
Berueme 541.17
beruffled 243.18
beryl 494.04
bes 624.32
besant 234.05 432.32
besated 452.09
besaying 246.11
besch 020.35
beschotten 138.13
beseach 576.30
beseal 454.27
beseated 108.01 430.05
beseech 259.03
Beseek 479.34
beseeked 418.28
beseem 567.35
beset 434.06
besets 583.19
besetting 076.02
beside 026.08 026.31 073.28 101.27 119.21 191.09 193.23 213.06 257.07 313.36 386.21 437.18 455.25 457.18 460.08 549.28 586.33 621.30
beside 383.03
Beside 216.04 503.31
besides 085.33 368.32 384.07 412.17 524.12 618.18
Besides 316.07 419.32 522.12 526.09
besidus 615.23
besieged 075.05 127.13 352.25
besighed 261.24
Besights 100.05
besitteth 546.22
beskilk 133.33
Besoakers 604.08
besogar 497.12
besom 079.36 471.32
besoms 621.01
besoops 491.06
besought 409.08
besouns 230.03
bespaking 066.15
bespeaking 355.35
bespectable 386.16
bespilled 563.05
bespokes 085.36
bespoking 322.01
bess 286.L3
Bess 604.17
bessermettle 359.04
Bess's 187.26
Bessy 434.08
best 008.20 028.11 030.10 038.33 064.36 076.21 082.15 083.29 084.12 086.10 088.05 100.26 114.35 124.18 139.11 143.36 144.28 152.03 162.23 165.01 166.12 183.19 189.20 211.13 230.10 235.36 238.09 240.07 254.33 256.16 260.F3 280.21 291.14 302.04 305.02 308.17 381.01 385.24 388.08 390.23 404.33 406.02 406.22 411.05 411.16 430.19 440.13 450.08 456.05 456.12 457.13 468.18 479.19 480.29 484.07 488.33 498.01 533.02 534.22 538.09 539.08 548.23 557.32 568.18 570.16 582.04 602.10 616.28 616.34 617.03 623.27 625.12 627.13
best 354.20
Best 076.33
Best 105.07
bestank 548.08
bestback 160.21
bestbehaved 464.33
bester 053.28 361.25 517.20
Bester 072.02
besterfar 096.05
Besterfarther 414.35
besters 540.29
besterwhole 247.07
bestia 305.15
Bestir 368.25
bestly 096.34
bestman 356.09
bestness 321.20 618.36
bestpreserved 533.04
bestride 023.18
bestteller 123.23
besure 550.03
bet 061.26 143.36 145.02 155.20 176.24 301.07 325.07 369.04 376.09 425.14 443.07 446.20 469.06 500.27 508.07 508.07 526.04 586.11 624.18
bet 345.07
Bet 266.L1
betaught 153.31
beth 250.34 278.F2
bethehailey 329.36
bethel 542.28
Bethel 607.08
bethels 186.30
Bethgelert 177.22
Bethicket 112.05
bethink 162.21
bethinkful 543.13
betholder 517.09
bethroat 279.F33
bethrust 574.24
betied 563.18
betimes 463.12
betoken 350.18
betold 396.23
Betoun 023.12
betray 459.22
betrayal 466.29
betrayed 120.24
Betreffender 069.32
betreu 459.21
betrue 459.20 459.21
bets 039.01
bett 297.32
Bett 147.11
Bett 342.30 342.31
better 005.21 011.17 024.08 024.28 025.35 042.30 101.30 109.29 115.09 116.03 124.13 172.06 174.30 176.26 180.08 181.18 184.33 237.32 255.26 269.10 282.10 286.07 299.29 328.09 359.07 359.08 369.25 380.26 382.09 406.29 406.29 425.16 429.20 432.28 440.32 444.14 445.33 452.03 455.03 457.14 464.35 478.04 478.36 482.30 488.21 490.25 522.10 557.34 626.34
better 200.11
Better 490.26 501.13 501.14 501.18 501.23
betteraved 164.28
betterlies 293.F1
betterman 161.19
betterment 150.34
bettern 467.18
betters 435.32
Betters 498.09
better's 116.04
betters' 572.03
betterwomen 087.27
bettest 329.11
bettle 354.33
Bettlermensch 161.03
bettlers 497.20
Bettlimbraves 246.33
bettlle 337.34
Betty 211.13 420.10
bettydoaty 094.30
bettygallaghers 090.10
bettyship 583.21
betune 222.06 426.25 581.07
betving 325.20
betwain 287.13
between 010.06 012.32 014.16 020.02 031.36 037.17 038.20 038.32 053.10 065.20 078.04 079.07 081.19 083.02 083.33 084.07 087.19 088.25 090.14 098.27 116.20 116.25 119.08 128.30 130.03 152.32 157.19 164.06 169.03 170.29 176.21 186.30 207.36 210.11 213.04 213.25 214.04 219.22 229.09 238.30 246.17 247.04 259.02 293.03 303.12 321.10 332.31 333.10 335.12 368.14 375.22 376.09 380.13 407.01 410.34 423.07 434.29 436.01 446.32 454.05 458.04 461.26 462.23 467.23 471.07 473.08 483.07 490.13 491.31 506.20 512.02 517.14 522.30 527.36 528.31 538.36 544.20 563.30 566.16 573.17 574.24 575.21 578.09 582.06 584.35 587.18 588.27 599.29 612.22 615.20
between 340.26 525.24
Between 246.04 264.11 348.05 375.12 375.32 445.25 485.10 511.26
Between 209.08
BETWEEN 286.R3
betweenly 247.30
betwides 360.05
betwink 426.32
betwinks 341.15
betwinst 518.21
betwixt 126.18 581.17
Betwixt 306.06
betwixtween 184.07
beunder 140.24

beuraly 017.13
Beurla 132.27
beurlads 467.25
beutel 565.11
Beve 295.29
bevel 606.13
Bevradge 289.23
bevyhum 618.14
bewailing 194.01
beware 085.13 433.36 436.30
Beware 167.31 270.15 567.28 570.35
bewept 498.33
Bewey 277.F4
bewheedling 415.02
bewilderblissed 107.16
Bewise 278.07
bewitching 220.07
bewitthered 134.22
Bewley 487.16
bewonderment 300.19
bewonders 564.16
bewray 068.31
bey 113.25
Bey 433.16
Bey 029.22
beyant 215.01 308.19 327.21
beyashmakt 547.14
beyawnd 511.17
beyeind 160.28
beyessed 061.34
beygoad 346.34
beyind 007.33
beyond 019.14 025.10 062.02 063.05 072.18 100.29 102.19 135.17 161.36 174.27 211.22 213.35 263.09 344.19 364.32 419.33 427.20 460.27 471.16 476.08 488.13 489.05 510.32 512.35 575.34 586.34 599.32 627.25
beyond 340.05
Beyond 049.25 379.35
bezouts 301.28
Bhagafat 035.10
Bhagavat 302.01
Bheri-Bheri 200.14
bheura 091.04
Bhi 050.17
Bhing 261.F4
Bhoy 377.27
bhuoys 491.36
bi 124.07 543.10
bi 284.L3
Bianca 238.23
bianconi 321.09
bianconies 240.18
biangle 165.13
biasement 365.10
bib 568.18
bibbelboy 344.29
bibbering 343.35
bibbers 262.28
bibbing 542.11
bibby 052.20 329.22 520.26 529.33
bibel 523.32
Bibelous 280.L1
biber 577.10
bible 192.28 212.33 256.18 330.01 579.10
Bible 036.27
Bible 071.16
biblous 549.32
bibrondas 243.16
bibs 103.10 161.31 551.09
Bichop 241.36
bicirculars 295.31
bickbuck 469.11
bicker 208.01
bickerrstaffs 178.23
bickhive 561.07
bickybacky 011.11
bicon 339.04
bicycles 208.09
bid 206.23 368.25
biddenland 078.13
biddies 079.30 457.05
bidding 530.14
Bidding 620.25
Biddles 561.36 562.02 562.03
biddy 039.34 321.27 453.04 519.08
Biddy 112.27 210.29
Biddyhouse 427.36
Biddy's 213.36 305.19 305.19
bide 244.22 354.35
bide 399.09
Bide 305.24 305.25
bided 605.23
bides 339.08
bidetree 503.13
bidimetoloves 004.09
bidivil 050.02
bids 224.15
bie 430.20
biekerers 252.16
bien 420.12 420.13
bien 184.20
Bieni 417.18
Bienie 414.25 417.30
Bienie 418.14
bier 006.24 130.12 297.32 496.29
Bier 256.07
Bier 175.22
bierchepes 077.29
bierd 070.16
bierhiven 315.22
biestings 406.34 406.34
biff 023.34 337.03
Bifur 215.19
bifurking 302.15
big 008.17 008.21 008.34 010.02 010.11 010.21 019.22 028.36 033.29 053.12 064.30 079.11 080.30 095.17 095.26 097.19 123.01 126.19 128.35 141.35 144.18 186.20 191.22 194.23 208.03 210.26 211.04 211.33 228.06 229.20 251.22 271.23 274.F4 286.14 287.06 291.F7 295.F1 317.30 320.08 320.08 332.02 338.26 358.15 368.03 383.18 384.06 392.17 393.13 395.09 406.23 410.28 426.06 434.10 445.35 450.06 454.09 464.25 468.34 475.35 485.23 511.18 534.07 565.23 567.06 568.34 569.34 576.15 577.12 596.15 596.27 617.19 620.02 622.08
big 106.25 344.11
Big 047.17 098.01 219.20 241.01 281.F4 284.25 316.25 331.26 361.06 421.13 507.36 514.06 533.36 534.07 568.18 576.28 581.07 612.12
Big 104.16 106.20 267.L2
biga 469.34
Bigamy 048.03
bigbagbone 567.06
Bigbawl 147.04
bigboss 052.24
bigbug 326.22
Bigdud 294.17
bigfeller 247.23
bigger 141.22 269.23 404.24 406.23 464.32
bigger'll 444.14
biggermaster 337.18
Biggerstiff 413.29
biggest 412.26
biggod 111.03
bigguard 260.06
bight 336.28
Bight 594.24
Big-man-up-in-the-Sky 543.29
bigmaster 624.11
Bigmesser's 530.32
bigmost 187.09
bigmouthed 429.18
bigness 565.22
bigotes 352.27
bigrented 372.08
Bigrob 583.09
Bigseer 612.16
bigslaps 370.27
Bigtempered 167.27
bigtider 626.02
bigtimers 398.24
bigtimer's 037.15
bigtree 146.34
bigugly 384.25
biguidd 366.12
biguinnengs 129.10
bigyttens 239.23
bihan 412.18
bij 245.36
bike 085.10 270.23 520.24
bikestool 229.29
bikeygels 567.33
bil 520.24
Bil 331.26
bilabials 465.26
bilaws 310.25
bilder 062.08
bile 447.05
bilge 310.36
bilgenses 488.35
bilgetalking 438.08
bilingual 424.02
bilk 183.30
bilked 511.34
bilker's 435.09
Bilkilly-Belkelly 611.27
Bilkilly-Belkelly-Balkally 612.32
bilking 416.11
bilks 305.02
bill 006.35 023.03 128.22 215.18 242.21 317.30 344.27 568.14 584.28
Bill 230.04 289.14 360.07 480.18 494.20
billbailey 127.06
billed 162.09 219.04 509.33
billet 190.28 507.24
billeted 023.17 137.13
Billey 593.15

billfaust 160.27
Billi 082.29
billiardhalls 125.13
billing 436.27
Billing 047.05
billion 179.35
billions 231.19
billiousness 117.21 117.21
billowfighting 453.03
billowing 035.07
billows 056.06 626.22
billpasses 407.35
bills 579.14
Bill-the-Bustonly 135.13
Billups 537.20
billy 014.18 210.07 236.14 320.34 337.16 438.05 491.10
Billy 177.23 211.34 568.18
billybobbis 334.04
billyboots 466.34 467.01
Billyclub 197.07
billycoose 018.33
billyfell 350.21
Billyhealy 608.08
billy's 559.36
Biloxity 179.14
Bimbam 046.10
bimbamb 251.18
Bimbambombumb 341.06
bimbies 420.12
bimbim 314.13
Bimbim 310.03 314.13
bimblebeaks 416.10
bimboowood 239.01
Bimbushi 561.32
bimedallised 551.32
bimiselves 487.18
Bimutualism 308.L2
bin 173.13 257.01
bîn 124.09
Bina 212.12 279.F24
bind 062.10 148.30 333.12 355.13 414.31 435.22 461.23
bind 341.18
binding 366.34
Bindmerollingeyes 011.06
bing 191.21 328.25
Bing 245.25 379.07
bingbang 304.F1
bingbanging 140.16
binge 148.33 375.15 481.29
bingkan 206.02
B I N K 379.28
binn 130.21
binnoculises 394.30
binocular 068.01 235.25
Binomeans 285.27
binomial 156.02
bint 491.12
biografiend 055.06
Biorwik's 550.18
Bios 445.01
birch 204.09
birchenrods 456.16
birchentop 376.25
birchleaves 275.11
bird 011.09 024.11 037.13 089.33 111.05 112.09 135.15 187.26 225.20 282.10 291.05 369.25 473.17 504.23 584.23 593.04
birde 251.35
Birdflights 324.36
birdies 562.18
birding 117.03
birds 095.09 134.18 139.31 244.30 276.19 383.17 384.03 432.08 447.15 490.35 621.35
birds' 449.17
birdseye 564.07
Birdslay 357.03
birdsmaids 514.26
birdsnests 450.33
Birdsnests 450.33
birdsong 204.13
birdsplace 231.24
birdyhands 330.33
biribarbebeway 348.36
biribiri 345.19
biribiyas 114.28
Birkett 077.02
birman 040.24
birnies 215.20
bironthiarn 296.23
birstol 353.34
birtch 543.10
birth 011.33 018.27 134.20 138.34 188.35 309.12 408.17 509.30
Birth 184.15
Birth 038.34
Birtha 514.24
birthday 145.01 209.28
birthdays 127.25
Birthplate 104.11
birthright 333.24
birthspot 135.17
birthwrong 190.12
Biryina 561.19
bis 047.29 174.26 363.17 389.13
bisaacles 058.04
bisbuiting 433.20
bisco 230.06
biscuits 376.29
biscums 542.30
biscuts 284.02
bisectualism 524.12 524.36
bisexes 564.11
bisextine 364.11
bisexycle 115.16
bishop 110.13 228.05 387.25 432.20 445.08
Bishop 036.28
Bishop 340.27
bishopregionary 533.08
bishops 440.12
bishop's 201.33 377.14
Bishop's 291.19
bisifings 238.17
biskbask 102.17
biskop 302.01
Biskop 374.16
Bismillafoulties 357.04
bisnisgels 601.01
bisons 016.29
Bisons 016.29
biss 093.16 242.16 407.04 465.10
Bissavolo 068.19
Bissbasses 351.14
Bisse 279.F24
bissed 550.01
bissemate 577.04
bisses 124.27
Bisships 606.13
bissing 467.06
bissmark 009.32
bissyclitties 284.23
bistrispissing 302.06
bit 020.23 038.09 049.07 052.33 068.08 072.34 073.16 074.13 088.18 089.36 093.35 115.22 119.06 129.07 132.34 141.30 143.22 160.24 164.24 168.10 173.08 190.20 190.23 194.34 199.29 208.21 208.29 209.36 212.29 227.27 229.25 234.26 254.24 306.13 311.35 316.35 408.16 429.05 443.36 469.36 507.30 547.20 580.10 608.08 618.17 625.16
bit 267.L2
Bit 514.22
bitch 005.35 537.30
Bitch 379.04
bitches 018.27 060.15
bitchfanciers 438.35
Bitchorbotchum 610.11
Bitchson 149.20
bite 005.35 168.05 179.35 182.36 243.21 253.13 316.35 339.08 422.25 465.11 581.09
Bite 145.18
Bite 104.11
bitem 618.25
biter's 434.14
biting 231.36 417.18
bitly 338.16
Bitrial 466.28
bits 040.31 394.09 450.23 539.12
bitskin 016.24
bitte 506.04
bitten 424.09
bitten 175.19
bitter 148.29 155.21 182.36 237.33 291.06 422.25 467.33 506.03 548.36 627.35
bitteraccents 344.25
bitterhalves 540.32
bittering 167.21
bittermint 440.23
bittern 569.22
bitterness 561.15
bitternly 138.35
bitters 036.02 211.03 434.14
bitter's 143.29
bitterstiff 366.19
bittersweet 170.07
bitther 093.24
bittock 431.07
bitts 214.22
bitts 349.11
bittstoff 359.11
bitty 075.11
bitvalike 348.03
bivitellines 252.15
bivouac 581.23
bixed 166.14
bizaas 209.12
bizar 499.21
bjoerne 471.30
B.L. 420.22 (B.L. Guineys)
blaablaablack 301.06
blabber 224.19 484.08
blabs 586.07
Blabus 552.19
blabushing 431.17

black 034.34 034.34 043.28 046.15 055.14 062.27 063.26 066.19 066.20 069.02 085.02 164.27 169.08 176.24 182.33 188.05 193.34 196.12 204.18 242.06 247.32 276.F4 277.16 321.11 361.19 381.17 425.23 439.32 441.04 442.01 447.27 454.22 459.08 495.10 508.33 511.10 517.09 540.21 545.35 549.16 556.10 559.25 564.23 626.24
black 286.L2
Black 059.04 059.04 078.31 158.26 269.F4 403.17 438.15 517.15 546.33 588.18
Blackamoor's 059.02
Blackarss 251.11
blackartful 121.27
blackberd's 381.23
blackboard 180.36
blackbudds 450.18
blackburry 214.32
blackcullen 141.35
blackcurrant 460.33
Blackdillain 219.20
blackeye 183.17
blackfaced 076.01
Blackfordrock 541.02
Blackfriars 048.03
blackfrinch 486.17
blackguarded 464.12
blackguardise 005.17
blackguardism 180.32
blackhaired 147.35
blackham's 584.02
blackhand 495.02
Blackheathen 549.07
blackholes 549.05
blacking 171.31 230.10
blackinwhitepaddynger 612.18
blackleaded 144.06
blackmail 240.12 457.02 563.16
blackman 236.16
blackout 617.14
Blackout 560.02
blackpool 085.15
Blackpool 088.34
Blackrock 083.20
blackseer 340.13
blackshape 608.29
blacksheep 133.25
blackstripe 208.16
blackth 594.33
blackthorn 114.11
blackthorns 057.23
blackwalls 448.08
blackwatchwomen 379.33
bladder 169.20 212.05 355.32 467.20
bladdhers 408.27
bladdy 303.27 345.25
blade 566.22
bladey 553.08
Bladyughfoulmoecklenburgwhura-whorascortastrumpaporna-nennykocksapastippatappatup-perstrippuckputtanach 090.31
blaetther 077.15
blaff 508.17
blagpikes 286.15
blaguardargoos 347.14
blague 112.35 153.29
blah 435.16
blains 043.10
Blaire 607.29
Blaize 372.10
blake 563.15
Blake 563.13
Blake-Roche 294.22
blame 060.10 061.23 061.24 119.33 119.34 212.28 212.29 396.13 411.05 423.11 468.19 509.17 584.26
blameall 289.20
blamed 122.35 627.26
Blamefool 175.17
blanca 184.19 184.19
Blanchardstown 607.34
blanche 083.26
blanche 370.06
Blanche 248.33 485.12
blanched 237.22
Blanchemain 527.21
blanchemanged 164.28
blanches 145.01 614.04
Blanche's 248.33
blanchessance 066.14
Blanchette 537.24
blanching 279.F30 571.15
Blanchisse's 210.24
blanck 350.11
blancking 333.21
blancmange 494.21
Blanco 049.08
blancovide 043.24
bland 003.11 057.26 484.21
blanding 321.24
blank 022.27 063.05 128.04 149.11 176.24 232.02 247.31 356.35 379.09 387.20 413.33 473.06 566.01 575.15
blank 340.15
Blank 515.33
blankards 188.13
Blankdeblank 253.34
blanket 502.19 520.21
blanketed 172.14
blanketer 603.31
blankets 040.18 210.11 395.15 397.16
blanking 242.07
blankit 313.08
blankmerges 428.17
blanko 064.31
blankpoint 468.17
blanks 349.27
blare 562.29
Blare 256.11
blarmey 472.06
blarney 453.06
Blarney 211.11
blarneyest 419.16
blarneying 371.16 483.16
blarneys 061.26
Blashwhite 380.03
Blasil 316.28
blasphematory 183.24
blaspheming 177.23
blasphemously 572.28
blasphorus 167.14
Blass 325.32
blasses 077.29
blast 122.14 303.22
Blast 154.10
blasted 010.30 077.04 167.14 375.06
blaster 184.21
blastfumed 320.25
blasting 250.25
blasts 316.15
blastun 606.15
blatant 167.14
Blath 277.21
blather 197.05 419.16
blatherumskite 453.21
blathrehoot 354.18
Blau 071.17
Blaubarb 169.04
Blaublaze 540.29
blaufunx 035.09
blause 176.23
blautoothdmand 403.12
blawcauld 213.04
Blawland 320.28
Blawlawnd-via-Brigstow 537.24
blay 014.02
Blayncy's 099.34
blaze 037.12 052.19
blazer 144.34
blazerskate 200.04
blazes 189.36 540.35
Blazes 063.23
blazier 558.30
blaziness 012.12
blazing 065.13 411.31 411.32 411.32 454.22 589.06
blazings 382.15
blazoned 546.08
blazy 322.19
bldns 130.34
bldy 448.27
bleachin 353.07
bleaching 214.26 359.10
bleak 054.09 112.26 219.24 220.13 410.09 563.13 563.15
bleakablue 142.10
bleakbardfields 010.34
bleakeyed 327.29
bleakfrost 338.31
bleakhusen 337.11
bleakmealers 545.27
Bleakrooky 040.30
bleary 627.26
bleated 070.19
bleather 479.18
bleating 167.14
Bleating 305.05 499.30
bleaueyedeal 384.24
Blech 563.31
bled 373.36
bleday 070.26
bledded 553.07
bledprusshers 608.10
blee 562.12
bleeding 084.21
bleenk 617.01
bleethered 022.09
bleime 348.08
bleives 155.06
blem 098.03 098.04 098.04
Blemish 157.17
blench 066.29
blend 312.28 571.03 572.36
blending 288.02
blends 221.32
Blennercassel 376.32

blepharospasmockical 515.16
Bleseyblasey 485.13
Blesht 441.07
Blesius 528.08
blesphorous 167.14
bless 134.17 148.20 238.12 275.26 325.32 404.13 405.32 432.34 462.30 469.24 526.16
blesse 539.27
blessed 009.21 056.10 091.33 154.02 206.26 250.24 256.05 289.21 299.15 306.01 412.26 424.18 490.23 605.36 606.02
Blessed 146.12 264.08 404.14 624.21
blessersef 557.05
blesses 590.28
blessing 078.22 328.36 457.10 471.11 552.35 562.25 563.30
blessings 021.27 404.34 617.04
Blessington 194.36
blessons 156.04
blessted 303.24
blessure 070.03
blest 273.F2 279.07 426.26
bletchendmacht 240.13
blethering 192.04
bleu 458.24
bleucotts 543.21
blew 043.27 070.18 129.15 231.31 470.28 471.13
blewblack 457.18
blewy 267.15
bleyes 344.12
blezzard 318.30
B.L.G. 131.03 (Benjamin Lee Guinness; also, P.L.G.: Poor Law Guardian)
bliakings 316.27
blick 139.03 155.23
blickblackblobs 339.21
blickfeast 528.06
blid 553.07
bliddy 014.20
blievend 155.06
blight 055.04 519.36
blightblack 006.01
blighted 453.27
blighter 149.02 488.29
blighting 504.30
blighty 173.27 263.09 347.25 553.08
blimp 129.07
blind 064.08 068.34 116.34 132.14 136.29 149.02 169.17 182.33 189.31 211.25 417.03 530.02 583.15
Blind 559.05
Blinders 501.07
blindfold 462.35
blindly 092.27
blindness 122.36
blindquarters 410.04
blink 017.17 093.04 274.25 468.17
blink 419.01
Blinkensope's 290.12
blinketey 603.31
blinkhard's 109.21
blinking 179.03 449.07
blinkins 568.02
blinkpoint 149.18
blinks 232.02
blinkth 251.08
bliss 235.04 321.02 325.08 335.27 446.24 590.28
blissed 398.20 562.25
blissfilled 417.27
blissforhers 547.29
blissim 156.27
blissup 451.28
blistered 262.F6
blisters 189.32 475.26
blithe 281.03 360.35
blithehaired 265.19
blither 488.18
Blitzenkopfs 272.16
blitzh 314.28
blixom 606.15
blizky 563.23
blizz 442.32
blizzard's 063.06
bll 600.27
bloadonages 241.03
bloasted 340.08
bloaten 167.14
Bloater 524.21
bloater's 305.16
bloats 029.29
Blob 624.02
Bloccus's 105.01
block 025.18 127.30 229.34 549.16
Block 040.03
Blockbeddum 200.23
blockcheap 300.F3
blocked 119.13 543.33
blocks 170.02
blocks 349.28
blocksmitt 197.11
blodestained 341.05
blodidens 347.06
bloedaxe 323.04
Bloem 203.10
blog 510.19
blogas 511.21
Blogg 169.05
blohablasting 416.35
bloke 039.26 177.04 278.F1 596.16
blomsterbohm 055.28
blond 015.16 186.17 559.25
blondblubber 329.11
blonde 220.08
Blonderboss 442.27
blondes 257.11
Blondman's 508.17
blonds 290.F4
blondy 034.09
blong 240.25 247.24 247.24 247.25 257.08 285.07 285.08 303.32
Blong's 406.02
bloo 241.04
blooches 009.22
blood 036.03 039.18 084.20 087.20 130.32 149.05 175.32 185.32 240.28 359.09 376.19 405.33 424.08 425.10 456.32 467.06 508.02 513.18 534.34
Blood 175.09
bloodanoobs 550.35
bloodathirst 052.06
bloodeagle 024.29
blooded 231.16
blooders' 325.26
bloodfadder 496.26
bloodiblabstard 241.29
bloodied 077.20 131.20
blooding 101.20 255.18
bloodlekar 301.01
bloodooth 323.04
bloodorange 208.15
Bloodriddon 219.20
bloods 178.11
bloodshot 288.20
bloodstaned 011.22
bloodvein 212.16
bloody 080.29 099.12 099.31 129.19 178.08 231.21 276.04 303.32 549.10
Bloody 014.09 421.13 530.28 582.16
bloodysibby 465.31
blooff 346.25
blookers 609.04
bloomancowls 456.16
bloombiered 560.20
bloomers 249.36
blooming 134.24
Blooming 620.02
bloomingrund 223.31
bloomkins 600.23
blooms 199.15 385.25 587.27
bloot 288.26
blooty 016.09
blosh 279.F01
bloss 479.17 528.05
blossful 235.04
blossom 051.34 180.13 227.18
blossoming 556.11
blossomly 357.31
blossoms 146.01 279.F02
blossomtime's 064.36
blossomy 475.08
blossy 454.09
blost 276.05
blotch 229.27
blotchwall 013.07
blotchy 263.09
blothoms 069.03
Blotogaff 522.22
blots 118.29
Blotsbloshblothe 280.33
Blott 302.10
blotto 039.33
blottom 281.F2
blottout 134.26
Blotty 014.14
blottyeyed 361.36
bloughs 265.F5
Blount's 039.08
blouse 063.16
blousebosom 180.12
blousejagged 339.12
blouseman 088.12
blousom 338.34
blousyfrock 467.11
blow 010.19 040.31 158.34 176.29 211.34 267.15 271.18 293.F1 344.07 352.11 392.30 502.06 562.11 585.30 600.14 604.24
blowaway 208.22
blowbags 252.02
blowbierd 332.22
Blowcher 133.22
blowdelling 562.26
blowed 251.31 290.F7

bloweyed 534.18
blowfish 312.02
blowharding 273.23
Blowhole 351.18
blowick 243.19
blowicks 135.14
blowie 345.07
blowing 011.04 028.28 056.29 166.14 294.F3 367.35 417.19 556.20 620.26 621.06
blown 016.05 108.05 313.12 321.10 583.01
blown 262.L1
Blown 421.01
blowne 037.23
Blownose 540.35
Blownowse 453.17
blowreaper 555.10
blowrious 498.36
blows 020.35 028.10 117.18 139.08 274.24 366.29 369.35 376.25 448.20 478.12 626.19
blowsheet 180.12
Blowyhart 275.14
Blubby 013.34
blubbywail 081.30
blubles 626.19
blucher 587.16
bluchface 095.04
bluckbells 282.F1
blucky 350.06
bludded 553.07
bludderings 388.25
bluddle 010.08
Bluddymuddymuzzle 352.29
bludgeon's 044.02 372.25
bludgeony 176.19
bludger 351.34
bludgey 063.34
bludyn 593.03
blue 027.11 028.15 039.34 096.29 120.30 143.25 149.05 167.11 215.06 238.29 260.F1 267.14 305.15 327.29 351.08 384.31 396.12 398.19 449.06 458.13 461.06 469.05 479.22 501.27 504.28 511.10 562.10 564.23 567.25 627.09
blue 418.31
Blue 179.27 435.15
Blue 516.08
bluebells 028.28
blueberry 566.04
blueblack 398.32
blueblacksliding 405.09
bluebleeding 370.23
Blueblitzbolted 078.07
blueblooded 170.33
bluebutterbust 165.28
Bluechin 219.20
bluecoat 043.06
Bluecoat 193.19
blued 351.13 515.34 614.11
blued 341.33
bluedomer 319.06
bluedye 305.F1
bluefunkfires 581.14
bluegum 126.12
blueild 155.24
bluemin 078.27
bluemoondag 453.13
bluepaw 100.21
bluerybells 007.02
blues 067.15 176.34 211.14 475.01
Blues 285.F6
blue's 148.09
bluesackin 368.31
bluest 013.21
bluetoothed 387.08
blueybells 361.22
blueygreen 443.36
blueygreyned 603.35
bluff 127.30 422.31
bluffet 535.17
bluffs 051.31
Bluffs 524.15
bluffy 329.11
bluggy 031.11
Blugpuddels 621.13
bluid 122.14
bluidstreams 074.14
bluishing 299.17
bluming 245.07
blump 129.07 577.35
Blunder 221.21
blundered 179.31
blunderguns 173.22
blundering 422.15 596.03
blunders 188.12 589.18
Blunk 355.07
blunkets 503.03
blunt 031.08 510.21
bluntblank 474.14
blunterbusted 600.19
bluntly 088.04 101.14
blup 137.02
blurbeous 477.28
blurney 381.22
blurred 337.13
blurried 013.11
blurring 013.07
blurry 425.13
Blurry 014.05
blurs 118.29
blurtingly 033.15
blurtubruskblunt 116.02
blurty 338.09
blush 015.22 015.23 047.01 093.29 130.23 227.16 268.F4 433.29 445.16 494.31
blusher 194.18
blushfed 185.10
blushing 204.20 241.19 463.01 556.02
blushmantle 024.09
Blushred 380.03
blussing 392.20
Blusterboss 273.23
blusterbuss 327.18
Blut 106.31
blutcherudd 338.09
blutchy 491.28
Bluvv 593.06
bluzzid 352.35
Blyant 069.06
Blymey 366.27
blyth 202.25
blzb 194.17
bmm 600.27
bn 302.25
Bnibrthirhd 310.15
bo 623.12
bo 284.L3
Bo' 032.35
boa 102.11 435.20
boaboa 019.22
boaconstrictor 085.18
boags 396.21
Boald 028.05
Boanerges 022.32
boar 132.05
board 060.10 322.20 363.31 395.09 408.01 409.19 524.04 529.15 569.21
boardcloth 456.14
boarded 141.16
boardelhouse 186.31
boarder 081.32
boards 166.22 173.18 316.04
boardschool 051.11
boardsoldereds 356.04
boare 297.31
boarhorse 370.23
Boaro 136.14
boast 180.34 298.F3
boasterdes 315.21
boasting 421.34
boaston 011.22
boastonmess 364.35
boasts 129.33
Boast's 469.29
boastsung 352.17
boasum 371.02
boat 026.19 146.24 197.28 367.21 370.17 395.22 479.25 479.31
boater 054.31
Boaterstown 507.35
boath 320.24 332.12
Boathes 325.25
boatloads 525.23
boatshaped 502.19
Boawwll's 072.16
bob 170.02 459.34 607.13 624.02 624.02
Bob 048.03
bobbedhair 166.15
bobbing 214.01 316.12
bobby 214.14 329.21 520.26 584.02
bobbycop 338.32
bobbyguard's 093.06
Boblesse 277.11
Bobow 576.27
bobs 611.04
boccat 393.13
Boccuccia's 561.24
boche 458.34 478.20
bock 536.16
bockalips 006.26
bockknickers 208.15
Bockleyshuts 388.33
bockstump 070.17
boddily 337.33
bode 009.10 364.09 562.24
bodemen 258.34
bodey 007.14
bodgbox 276.25
bodice 438.05
bodies 076.14 367.29 394.35 627.20
bodikin 268.15 578.16
bodily 062.17 169.11
bodiment 475.20
Bodingtown 622.35
bodkins 500.02
bodley 354.35
bodom 564.34

body 004.13 051.06 076.20 096.29 098.09 132.07 165.27 185.29 185.36 271.09 285.F5 289.F2 298.F2 356.10 381.15 412.16 417.25 485.04 516.16 549.35 613.13
Boehernapark 321.08
boelgein 316.19
boer 180.35 430.07
Boergemester 607.30
boerne 263.19
boer's 087.21
Boese 499.07
boesen 345.33
bog 008.24 014.01 026.33 058.17 186.20 194.34 203.26 220.14 281.F2 287.06 346.27 516.25 539.25 567.06 582.25 604.03
Bog 076.31 339.06 416.19
Bogaleen 343.12
bogans 198.26
bogchaps 370.27
bogcotton 612.31
bogdoxy 225.21
bogey 340.03 499.01 549.23
Bogey 421.06
bogeyer 042.15
boggers 208.16
Boggey 560.14
boggled 208.09
boggylooking 153.03
Boghas 075.02
bogholders 488.04
bogoakgravy 171.01
bogorror 423.16
bogre's 373.10
bogs 309.06
Bog's 485.06
Bogside 071.11
boguaqueesthers 476.36
bogue 626.06
boguey 589.14
bogus 129.16 425.22
bogusbagwindburster 359.13
Bogy 576.27
boheem 404.26
Bohemeand 170.10
Bohemey 246.18
boher 081.09
bohereen 390.09
Bohermore 399.28
bohernabreen 087.31
Bohnaparts 238.26
boil 210.07 434.10 528.37 600.03
Boildawl 322.02
Boildoyle 017.13
Boileau's 527.13
boiled 456.03 502.23 611.36
boiler 214.26
boilers 190.19
boiling 265.F2 466.09
boiling 354.12
boils 137.29 349.01 444.01
boing 054.16
boinyn 137.01
Bois 414.06
boissboissy 485.06
boîte 165.29
Bok 347.20
boke 013.30
bokes 597.06
Bokes' 156.06
bokk 323.34
bokks 537.31
boko 282.12
bokswoods 337.19
bola 247.10
Boland's 406.13
Bolche 330.23
bold 015.20 046.31 116.16 148.12 204.04 219.24 220.13 257.17 353.13 491.36 549.28 565.20 565.23 627.25
Bold 039.07 624.18
bolder 436.34
bolderdash 233.17
boldfaced 120.36
boldly 187.32
Boldmans 361.22
boldylugged 343.27
boldywell 040.32
bole 265.23 559.25
bolero 102.11 206.04
boleros 066.37
boles 160.01
bolgaboyo 329.17
bolgylines 299.19
bolivars 189.22
boll 024.06
bollas 389.04
bollets 238.32
bollhead 373.33
bollion 575.11
Bollivar's 453.13
bolls 415.05
bollworm 492.25
Bolly 177.25
bolo 151.23
bolshy 425.22
bolsillos 302.16
bolssloose 498.23
bolster 558.26
bolt 014.19 080.28 153.10 279.F26 299.12 483.15
Bolt 579.08
boltaballs 406.34
bolted 119.13
boltoned 548.05
bolts 060.21
bom 007.34 046.09
Bom 072.03
bomb 167.15 599.31
bombambum 273.L4
Bombard 072.02
bombardment 349.08
bombashaw 527.08
Bombay 037.32
bombed 255.11
bombing 371.25
bombingpost 077.05
bombinubble 181.11
bombolts 135.25
bomboosting 320.06
bombossities 493.22
bombs 510.01
bombshoob 010.09
bombtomb 366.32
bomler 341.27
bommptaterre 504.24
bompriss's 525.34
Bompromifazzio 345.23
bompyre 439.34
Bomslinger 506.18
Bomthomanew 623.16
bon 448.30
Bon 207.26
Bon 112.32
Bonaboche 388.21
bonafacies 337.06
bonafay 321.05
bonafide 178.18 485.20
bonafides 087.03
Bonafieries 501.26
Bonaparte 334.09
bond 346.28 362.22
bond 344.03
bonded 467.20
bonders 543.19
bondery 296.29
bondholders 574.19
bonding 614.01
bondman 435.22
bonds 585.26
bondstrict 156.29
bondwoman 101.32
bone 020.05 036.03 184.08 256.03 368.14 373.36 406.16 455.15 516.08 522.22
boneash 359.11
bonedstiff 264.F1
boneless 387.09
Boneless 100.26
bones 056.10 084.26 091.05 149.05 453.29 464.19 485.27 543.31 605.01
bones 341.08
Bones 515.32 515.36
Bones 293.L1
boneshaker 285.F4 447.31
bonetry 494.25
bonewash 192.16
boney 083.26 337.16 340.03 368.10
boney's 084.33
bonfire 046.06
bonfires 501.25
bong 379.08
Bong 245.26
Bonhamme 351.16
bonhams 455.07
bonhom 459.24
boniface 577.11
Boniface 046.20
bonings 607.13
B O N K 379.30
bonnamours 593.08
Bonnbtail 105.16
bonnefacies 380.03
bonnet 009.10 063.28 209.06 392.23 417.19
bonnets 283.F1 552.29
bonnick 363.19
bonnies 494.11
bonniest 389.12
bonny 009.21 039.10
Bonnybrook 514.25
bonnyfeatures 577.11
bonofide 480.09
bonum 023.16
bonum 063.33 163.04 341.28
bonums 540.34
Bonum's 513.24
bonzar 411.17
bonze 483.09 536.09
bonzer 351.20
bonzeye 329.10
Bonzeye 408.26

bonzos 609.33
bonzour 199.14
boo 232.22 333.16 423.22
Boo 247.12
boob 167.08 314.06
Boob 106.06
booble 273.07
booboob 366.25
boob's 531.02
booby 333.16
Booby 104.07
boobybabies 584.14
boobytrap 033.32
booche 341.02
boodle 348.07
boof 333.15
Boohoohoo 379.13
boohoomeo 485.34
Boohooru 016.26
Booil 049.15
booing 589.10
book 008.32 013.21 020.15 050.12 057.31 086.14 123.35 211.09 228.16 251.24 258.31 277.F1 286.09 305.01 305.31 313.13 356.20 397.30 410.01 422.13 448.09 453.18 482.33 524.11 550.03 553.01 562.34 563.04 570.08 580.16 621.03
Book 122.23 178.17 179.27 374.31 415.23 425.20
Book 106.13
bookflood 118.12
bookley 290.F7 611.02
bookmaker 060.27
books 026.36 439.34 529.13 537.27 544.16
Books 409.35
booksafe 082.02
Bookshrine 559.07
bookstaff 571.05
booksyful 268.14
booky 368.31
boola 073.13
Boolies 097.10
boolyhooly 520.33
boom 247.28 326.04 329.20 388.25 498.16 535.34 578.25
Boomaport 133.21
boomarattling 356.32
boomaringing 348.10
boomarpoorter 327.33
boomeringstroms 004.06
booming 263.F2
boomomouths 367.34
boomooster 576.18
Booms 510.01
boomslanging 209.01
Boomster 053.01
boon 136.04 137.13 546.19
Boon 282.05
boonamorse 313.11
boontoday 513.12
boony 597.15
boor 072.36 130.02 167.03 282.04
booraascal 323.32
boord 007.09 557.15
Boore 062.30
boorgomaister 568.17
Boorman's 257.09
boors 430.07
boors' 314.23
boortholomas 352.05
Booru 016.26
boos 127.18
boose 064.11 509.30 581.08
Boose 072.15
boosed 477.05
boosegas 176.31
booseleers 193.17
boosers' 147.04
booseworthies 127.18
booseys 448.36
boosh 189.18
boosiness 497.24
Booslaeugh 005.05
boosome 231.08
boost 116.25 140.10 485.23
Boost 533.36
boosted 167.13
boosting 626.10
boosy 555.13 588.01
boot 019.33 067.12 088.05 181.32 212.21 374.20 425.14 444.05 489.23 497.29 522.29 579.08
Boot 464.28 618.08
Boot 071.33
bootblacked 429.21
Bootenfly 291.F4
Bootersbay 386.24
Boote's 262.21
booth 032.36 072.20 188.07 257.19 262.24 314.21 316.33 351.28 368.24
Booth 552.15
Bootherbrowth 121.33
booths 332.35 332.35 332.35 332.35
Booth's 480.30
Bootiestown 235.36
bootifull 011.29
bootmaker 618.30
bootmarks 080.10
boots 010.22 030.24 063.34 074.12 145.23 151.22 284.F2 351.19 372.21 443.28 461.15 472.21 544.18 548.30 586.32
Boots 032.24 176.17
booty 122.09 300.22 560.20 600.16
bootybutton 391.34
bootyfilly 395.20
booty's 291.F7
Boox 308.L2
booz 257.21
Boozer's 342.05
boozum 449.16
bopeep 227.12
bopeeped 508.27
borab 237.16
Boraborayellers 416.34
borderation 528.31
bordereau 107.24
bordered 080.02
bordering 173.34
bordles 029.01
bore 005.36 081.23 084.10 088.20 094.06 193.33 223.30 367.20 508.30 583.10 585.36
bore 201.11
Boreas 269.18
bored 093.35 136.08 468.32 619.32
boredom 292.28
borers 183.12
borgeously 152.27
borgiess 130.12
boric 182.28
Boriorum 013.21
Boris 385.15
born 004.34 014.11 026.14 079.09 091.12 111.13 112.13 116.25 138.20 142.35 157.36 172.21 175.03 197.09 198.01 211.21 224.11 240.12 274.19 275.F6 290.26 301.11 305.22 334.14 385.20 460.34 471.36 513.07 521.10 546.20 562.19 563.25 576.02 615.19
born 150.26
Born 072.13
bornabarbar 120.34
borne 471.30 546.14
borne 349.12
Borneholm 331.36
borning 437.01
bornstable 010.17
bornybarnies 584.14
boro 133.28
Borrel 071.26
borrid 578.26
Borrisalooner 337.33
borrlefull 348.04
borrough 538.08
borrow 469.08 512.24 610.30
borrowed 149.22 150.09 183.17 183.32 607.09
borrowing 422.32 463.23 495.16
Borrowing 093.25
borrows 279.F36
borrowsaloaner 520.09
Borry 569.30
Borsaiolini's 483.11
borsaline 471.12
borst 197.35
borstel 391.09
bort 493.15
borthday 497.27
borting 452.02
Bortolo 527.25
Borumborad 492.22
Borumoter 331.27
borus 283.03
bosbully 490.35
Boscoor 414.06
bosh 125.22
boshiman 594.23
boshop's 158.30
boskage 564.16
boskiest 235.15
boskop 190.19
bosky 465.03
bosom 134.24 139.17 189.29 191.30 215.28 336.31 355.20 527.04 586.08
bosomfoes 571.35
bosom's 056.02
Bosquet 523.25
boss 268.15 338.27 363.07 417.07 546.07
Boss 129.11 623.36
Boss 342.25
bossaloner 032.36
Bossbrute 255.13
bosse 325.16 584.16
Bosse 221.30 602.20
bosser 344.35

bosses 146.12 325.29
Bossford 583.12
bosso 148.21
bossom 204.08
bossoms 535.33
boss's 286.L3
bosthoon 301.05
bosthoon 273.L1
Bostion 347.13
Boston 111.09 421.10 617.23
bostoons 490.01
bosun 579.01
B.O.T. 060.09 (Board of Trade)
Botany 543.04 601.17
botch 322.05
botchalover 356.09
botchbons 542.22
botchy 180.17
boterham 397.18
both 031.12 031.34 034.22 038.06 039.19 039.20 054.33 078.25 082.08 085.28 087.18 089.04 096.13 108.14 109.34 112.27 114.35 117.33 128.19 129.21 158.15 163.34 165.15 190.28 191.35 203.23 220.16 243.13 274.F2 284.03 316.12 319.16 325.17 392.01 396.01 413.07 417.07 429.04 444.05 457.01 479.31 481.23 491.05 495.24 497.21 536.29 539.01 543.36 565.15 577.25 584.12 617.13
Both 508.33 563.29
Bothallchoractorschumminaround-gansumuminarumdrumstrum-truminahumptadumpwaultopoo-fooloderamaunsturnup 314.08
Botham 369.12
Bothar 200.14
botheared 156.23
bothem 340.09
bothem 350.14
bother 045.13 225.12 225.13 225.13 276.F2 459.22 469.26
botherbumbose 623.17
bothered 256.20 381.28 496.34 619.08
Botherhim 406.10
Bothersby 372.36
bothersome 485.15
Bothnians 025.11
bothom 278.F2
both's 413.23
bothsforus 465.09
bothsides 370.26
bothstiesed 363.12
bothways 576.34
bothwise 281.22
Botlettle 198.22
bott 155.01
bottery 358.12
bottes 141.15 288.20 568.19
botthends 343.25
Bottisilly 435.07
bottle 038.04 040.33 063.17 064.11 065.35 222.10 272.28 304.13 407.03 413.11 419.32 429.24 445.23 488.32 492.18 510.22 556.26 618.10
Bottle 205.24 579.18
bottlebreaker 054.30
bottled 067.10 544.17 549.22
bottledby 624.02
bottlefilled 310.26
bottleholders 366.05
bottlenim 539.19
bottler 118.05
bottles 023.22 052.05 082.07 348.01 380.16 518.21 588.11
Bottles 176.05
bottloggers 019.19
bottlop 063.32
bottol 085.01
bottom 065.18 098.07 163.21 173.28 304.16 391.06
Bottom 078.32 342.31 375.03 503.21
bottombay 313.26
Bottome 093.18
bottomlie 534.10
bottoms 312.07 381.33
bottom's 248.12
bottomsside 565.23
Bott's 268.26
botulism 170.30
Boubou 415.08
bouc 094.29
bouchal 091.06 314.32 471.22
boucher 111.32
bouchers 183.12
bouchers' 064.18
bouchesave 234.27
bouchicaulture 569.35
Boucicault 385.03
bouckaleens 042.11
bouckuet 531.12
boucled 208.11
boudeloire 207.11
boudeville 294.18
bouf 445.22
Bouf 421.09
boufeither 566.10
bough 465.14 503.33
boughpee 248.18
boughs 058.07 275.15
bought 069.16 081.14 144.25 434.18 459.36 580.36
boughtem 061.26
boughtenland 078.13
bouillis 038.02
Boukeleff 081.35
Boulanger 190.29
bould 139.11 188.33 336.04 362.19 469.14
Bould 303.05
boulder 209.19 600.27
Boule 082.29
boules 341.13
boulevard 491.10
boulevards 447.10
boullowards 553.31
boultter 136.35
Boumce 370.30
Bouncer 455.14
bounce-the-baller's 262.L1
bouncing 055.21 473.14
bound 020.14 148.30 165.20 192.18 227.12 243.11 248.29 253.11 355.13 362.10 376.17 435.23 452.31 468.31 471.13 479.29 525.34 556.13 585.18 598.03 613.29
bound 175.17
Bound 211.03 316.06
boundaried 208.20
boundary 264.30 448.33 543.04
bounden 267.18
bounder 495.20
bounder's 583.36
boundin 110.03
bounding 513.18
boundles 349.32
boundless 132.31
boundlessly 417.27
bounds 055.05 136.06 139.27 339.08 367.29 458.12 553.06 586.22
bounquet 038.06
bountiful 227.07
bountifully 614.04
bounty 088.30 300.23 565.31
Bouououmce 370.35
bourd 539.20
bourgeoismeister 191.35
bourighevisien 423.05
Bourn 031.33
bourne 190.21 365.05 366.14
Bourne 321.08 513.09
bournes 379.35
Bourneum 415.08
bourse 448.30 540.26 589.09
bourseday 027.11
bourst 224.18
bout 043.05 075.17 118.35 129.29 176.20 227.33 310.27 541.19
bouteilles 162.11
bouts 014.35
'bove 075.14
boviality 058.14
bow 052.25 055.17 137.06 198.27 206.23 228.09 235.03 321.25 364.12 445.19 476.10 623.12
Bow 458.34
Bowal 106.30
Bowandcoat 391.14
bowbays 550.24
bowdler 179.28
bowe 584.28
Bowe 027.01
bowed 025.18 060.34 091.16 154.14 264.20 385.33 430.18
Bowed 199.27
bowel 164.27 437.13 613.25
bowels 185.33 563.14
bowels 398.33
bowen 371.23
bower 228.09 265.17 389.20
Bower 024.21
bowers 354.27 379.35
bowery 363.34 553.20
Bowery's-without-his-Walls 153.01
bowing 316.12 618.21
bowknots 225.36
bowl 082.05 161.32 239.07 245.11 317.19 397.17 613.24 619.27
bowl 164.20
Bowl 231.33
Bowlbeggar 135.13
bowlderblow 517.08
bowldstrong 626.02
bowle 542.35
bowled 337.02
bowlers 607.36
bowler's 363.08
bowling 584.07

bowls 025.13 107.32
bowls 355.02
bowman 198.30
bowman's 023.03
bowmpriss 197.35
bows 283.F1 372.01
bowstrung 087.28
box 013.09 060.12 179.36 209.27 210.31 362.26 375.11 433.21 472.19
box 261.L3
Box 517.17
boxed 176.33 465.04
Boxed 559.01
Boxer 105.05
Boxerising 347.29
boxes 165.30
boxes 341.33
boxing 201.33 412.34
boxomeneness 266.01
boxst 382.20
boy 008.25 010.06 065.21 083.03 083.18 086.08 112.03 148.10 187.27 211.15 219.24 220.13 224.24 240.22 247.24 249.19 249.30 249.30 257.07 285.06 287.19 303.12 333.09 351.18 370.30 409.09 412.14 460.05 461.04 470.07 472.05 473.12 485.17 499.22 506.27 507.01 514.34 528.32 562.29 589.32 603.16 621.30
boy 338.05 341.09
Boy 039.07 197.07 374.16 508.30
Boyana 198.05
Boyards 497.19
Boyarka 198.05
boyars 348.10
boyazhness 565.13
Boyblue 226.32
boyblue's 556.10
boybold 474.15
boyce 536.22
boycotted 185.04 496.03
boycottoncrezy 009.08
boyd 180.07
boydskinned 609.04
boyg 313.13
boyish 459.34
boyjones 275.F5
Boyle 343.03
boyles 034.11
Boyles 044.08 617.14
boyne 008.22 126.22 341.06 361.25 538.21
Boyne 114.36
boyo 053.25
boyplay 569.34
boyproof 527.19
boyrun 465.17
Boyrut 229.34
boys 027.24 041.16 054.01 059.03 078.22 085.08 099.17 128.10 130.36 133.28 134.26 147.15 208.32 209.34 240.05 304.28 304.F1 336.19 338.03 343.06 359.14 361.36 366.03 374.30 380.06 381.29 385.10 385.10 396.01 434.04 438.33 440.06 504.26 527.09 595.01 620.12
boys 346.07 353.34
boy's 487.11 549.23
boys' 044.04 124.18
boyscript 374.03
boysforus 460.27
boytom 561.04
boyuk 234.32
Bozun 389.31
B.P, 498.09 (Brehons B.P,)
b —— r 081.27 (bugger)
brabanson 138.12
brabble 315.10 315.10 315.10
brac 077.33
brace 021.32 042.34 134.09 172.35 208.19 267.17 408.30 446.33
Brace 245.20
braced 098.21
braceleans 291.21
braceleting 140.25
bracelets 060.17 207.04 235.34
bracelonettes 273.18
braceoelanders 398.05
braces 059.01 065.19 085.34 435.34 559.09
braceth 389.31
brach 422.07
Brache 260.11
braches 265.F5
bracing 524.22
brack 017.24 531.10
bracken 130.25
brackfest 563.30
bracksullied 525.03
Bracqueytuitte 609.17
brad 616.31
bradaun 573.33
Braddon 059.35
Bradley 294.24
Bradogue 212.09
bradsted 593.12
bradys 035.20
Brady's 381.12
Brae 246.26
brag 069.30 183.04 600.27
bragadore-gunneral 352.23
brage 386.19
braggart 453.06
bragged 333.20 624.32
bragger 303.27
bragget 451.08
braggs 211.11 340.03
Braglodyte 252.34
Bragshaw 132.10
Bragspear 152.33
bragues 329.21
Brahaam's 441.25
Braham 284.F4 284.F4 422.26
Brahm 081.07
Brahm 106.29
brahming 200.04
Braid 541.02
braim 288.26
brain 015.33 061.17 127.29 327.34 381.04
brainbox 299.18
braincap 541.12
brainpan 486.18
brains 223.26 392.30
brain's 409.13
brainskin 565.13
braintree 180.22
braintrust 529.05
brainy 425.05 436.35
braise 187.27 338.33
braising 531.08
brake 247.06 263.06 377.25
Brakeforth's 575.11
bramblers 366.22
brambles 507.13
brambling 624.14
bramborry 333.33
bran 232.28 376.29 486.31
branch 364.08
Branch 069.33
Brancherds 609.16
branches 059.13 213.13 244.04 264.12 267.25 397.15 416.26 505.10 626.23
branchings 280.05 571.05
brancomongepadenopie 179.34
brand 185.11 374.32 566.24 583.29 594.01 617.16
brand 354.13
Brandan's 488.25
branded 194.13
Brandenborgenthor 246.06
brandihands 080.14
brandishing 186.14
brandisong 462.03
brandnew 182.25 471.10 529.05 620.02
brandnew 201.05
brandnewburgher 265.13
brandold 553.26
Brandonius 327.02
brandylogged 344.14
brandywine 510.19
Brani 373.16
branlish 009.34
Brannan's 276.21
brannewail 021.25
brao 431.20
braod 483.24
brarkfarsts 613.23
brash 442.35 627.20
brass 183.05 246.04 315.07 439.18 617.08
Brass 408.29
brassard 570.10
brasse 245.20 579.11
Brassenaarse 301.02
Brassey's 357.07
brasshat 351.18
brassiere 446.33
Brasslattin 519.16
brassmade 084.28
Brassolis 228.12
Brassup 443.02
Brast 316.28
brat 239.36 270.04
Brat 424.01
Braten's 406.09
brather 468.03
Brathwacker 594.19
Bratislavoff 219.14
bratton 313.31
brauchbarred 481.18
Braudribnob's 491.21
braught 224.31 269.30 333.19
Brautchers 106.09
brave 047.21 117.02 303.08 303.10 303.12 625.31
Brave 473.20
braved 541.17
bravevow 065.23
Bravo 211.07 463.32

bravor 038.33
Bravose 569.36
Bravossimost 570.02
Bravure 181.02
braw 404.18
Braw 398.34
brawdawn 006.26
brawl 354.15
brawlmiddle 253.31
brawly 607.18
brawn 084.28 288.26
Brawn 187.24
Brawne 050.23
braxy 043.06
bray 325.33 522.30 537.34 550.27
Bray 624.32
Braye 203.11
brayed 154.01
Brayers 342.11
Brayhowth 448.18
braying 441.25
Brayned 104.13
braynes 074.13
brayvoh 313.31
braz 425.18
Brazel 464.07
brazen 210.12 320.29
brazenaze 398.30
brazenlockt 014.07
brazenness 437.08
Brazil 488.25
breach 058.10 096.19 136.24 239.35 374.20 442.13 491.34 589.34
Breach 447.17
breached 274.32
breaches 440.30
breachesmaker 317.23
breachsuit 613.31
bread 007.11 168.08 210.18 230.13 256.18 301.11 430.27 543.24 603.07
breadchestviousness 156.14
breadcost 510.26
breadcrumbs 430.29
breadfruit 428.01
bread's 623.19
breadth 324.03 344.19 439.16 452.25 475.04
breadwinning 055.07
bready 550.14
breaf 165.10
break 059.32 070.21 070.23 148.02 165.30 212.23 374.18 394.09 566.04 584.08
Break 469.26
Brèak 124.09
breakages 184.03
breakfarts 453.12
breakfast 026.27 255.24 405.32 458.23 510.25
Breakfast 575.29
Breakfates 131.04
breakfedes 597.16
breaking 009.10 321.07 335.17 404.32 442.23 517.22
breakmiddles 077.31
breakneck 039.10
breakparts 252.30
breaks 137.28 290.15
breaksin 459.15
breans 463.35
Breasil 549.26
breast 040.20 067.11 083.33 292.02 434.26 486.29 535.13 627.29
Breast 023.17
breastbare 312.06
breastbrother 168.07
breasthigh 097.01
breasths 148.30
breastlaw 464.34
breastpaps 480.14
breastplate 486.29
breastplates 231.24
breasts 325.24 532.35
breastsack 240.21
breastswells 336.27
breath 035.35 061.19 095.13 133.01 156.34 180.21 225.12 225.13 248.09 250.18 328.19 336.25 393.06 404.05 429.02 461.05 474.09 510.04 550.09 561.25 608.04 625.28
Breath 167.30 225.12 261.13
breathe 023.18
Breathe 206.25
breather 488.18
breathes 606.23
breathing 088.08 100.27 315.10 445.30
breathings 249.06 249.10
Breathings 415.23
breathless 244.22
breaths 318.03
breathtaking 389.12
breaving 228.12
brebe 079.09
brebreeches 539.02
bred 062.22 075.19 127.01 188.09 198.06 268.06 287.31 523.16
bredder 620.16
bredscrums 563.24
breechbowls 080.11
breeches 183.18 204.06 434.08 529.32
breechettes 210.25
breed 023.34 237.32 268.06 328.29 420.04 445.36 531.01 573.33
Breedabrooda 078.17
breeder 309.12
Breeders' 077.23
breeding 593.12
breedings 410.02
breeds 096.36
breeks 011.22 022.36
Breeks 228.02
breeze 544.27
Breeze 482.03
breezed 315.14 452.25
breezes 095.19 264.18 449.25
breezing 197.34
breezy 029.04 039.02
bref 143.30
Bref 338.28
Breffnian 099.26
Bregia's 604.04
brehemons 059.28
brehons 133.24
Brehons 498.09 608.02
breiches 234.09
breide 367.28
breit 187.25
Brek 121.34
Brékkek 004.02
brekkers 012.14
brella 007.26
Brendan 491.11
Brendan's 213.35 442.14
Brennan 211.27
Brennan's 081.14
brennt 578.28
breretonbiking 437.06
brerfox's 245.09
Brerfuchs 574.04
Bretagne 157.33
breth 578.31
brethern 483.21
brethren 389.01 488.04
Bretish 228.19
Brettaine 292.F2
Brettland 025.28
brevet 411.01
brevetnamed 100.20
brew 117.23 272.28 371.31 608.21
brewbarrett 171.14
brewbeer 617.21
brewed 003.13 553.25
brewer's 095.26 508.04
brewery 382.04
Brewery 307.01
Brewinbaroon 316.09
brewing 140.11 589.06
brews 258.08
Brewster 071.08 537.24
Brewster's 029.04 039.36
Breyfawkes 574.36
Bri 053.30
briam 524.33
brian 337.15
Brian 017.12 060.11 211.06 388.27
Brian's 485.18 498.25
brianslog 073.07
briar 474.04
briar 341.24
briars 319.04 518.17
bribe 622.03
bribes 366.02 465.05
bribing 375.25
bric 077.33
Brices 390.01
brichashert 352.05
brick 005.26 041.25 059.24 067.12 130.23 463.36 507.32
Brick 238.10
Brick 106.14
Brickbaths 284.04
brickdust 018.04 108.25
bricket 024.32
Brickfaced 359.28
brickfields 174.27
bricking 584.06
bricklayers 043.03
bricks 077.17 139.11 235.14 245.34
bricksnumber 325.14
brid 597.16
bridable 261.27
bridawl 237.06
bride 024.13 028.15 066.36 147.18 158.01 194.25 213.24 328.28 362.09 469.19 510.35 547.26 563.11 595.05
Bride 388.27 465.02

Bride 071.29
Bride-and-Audeons-behind-Wardborg 569.11
brideen 377.19
bridelittle 526.34
bridely 207.16
bridemuredemeanour 189.26
brideness 223.06
brider 324.34
brides 066.36
bride's 309.04
Bride's 220.03
bridest 563.17
brideth 034.28
bridewell 172.03
brideworship 433.11
bridge 006.07 084.03 119.28 125.17 203.02 262.03 265.25 332.27 361.22 443.28 471.16 512.34 567.03 626.07
Bridge 063.13 170.29 286.11 447.20 538.10
Bridge 103.01
bridgecloths 569.01
bridges 085.15 194.34 560.05 583.01
bridges 277.L1
bridge's 322.11
Bridge's 521.05
bridgesmaker 126.10
bridle's 462.09
bridling 589.11
Bridomay 471.01
Brie 163.28
brieck 266.04
brief 049.31 348.16 432.25 433.24 473.01 474.03 493.01 509.04 585.08
briefdragger 126.04
briefed 529.05
briefest 267.10
brieffrocked 166.15
briefly 515.22 540.13
Briefly 090.23
briefs 093.12 407.35
Brien 110.02 541.17
Brie-on-Arrosa 207.15
briers 074.02
briery 301.F3
Briery 212.07
brieve 276.10
brieved 396.29
brievingbust 075.04
brieze 407.17
brigade 137.18 159.32 359.15 474.16 555.17 618.09
brigadier-general 567.22
Briganteen 329.05
Briggs 514.26
bright 066.21 100.09 108.28 134.23 186.18 239.28 267.12 271.09 276.18 300.02 311.12 336.28 354.26 362.22 385.28 469.33 473.17 520.36 529.05 562.22 610.28
Bright 147.22
brightened 157.10 237.29
Brightening 626.36
Brighten-pon-the-Baltic 320.21
brighter 429.13 598.12
brightly 053.20
brightning 290.04
brighton 448.18
brights 245.05 621.23
Brights 245.04 368.30
brigid 256.06
Brigid 039.36
brigidschool 562.13
brigstoll 133.29
brile 288.26
brillant 059.30
brillers 556.29
brilliance 490.07
brilliant 569.01
brilliants 449.23
brilling 571.01
brim 042.24
brime 366.15
brimfall 225.36
Brimgem 542.27
brimless 056.09
brimmers 055.21
brimming 331.09
Brimstoker 145.32
Brimstone 182.31
brimsts 505.33
brinabath 312.06
Brinabride 500.21 500.22 500.22 500.27 500.27 500.30
Brinabride 399.03
Brinbrou's 148.19
brindishing 382.02
brindising 462.02
brindled 164.28
brine 198.07
brine 399.07
Brine 331.26
brinegroom 362.09
brine's 469.19
bring 013.32 024.13 025.08 055.21 067.04 096.27 164.30 200.25 220.19 233.06 235.10 279.07 294.05 295.17 329.34 445.16 473.08 533.32 576.24 576.31 615.16 616.19 621.07 621.13
Bring 226.10 244.04 378.17 601.04 603.07
bringback 324.19
bringem 542.27 542.27
bringer 187.12
Bringer 104.02
bringfast 434.31
bringing 024.36 092.17 141.31 240.36 283.17 319.04 443.11 490.21 492.19 608.20 622.17
brings 003.02 116.19 285.15 299.02 414.10 474.16 606.36
bringthee 442.24
bringtheecease 118.04
brink 085.13 197.14 322.32
brinks 615.26
brinkspondy 430.05
brisees 241.20
brisées 281.10
brisha 073.12
brisk 041.29 149.25 467.16 627.04
brisken 242.27
briskly 235.36
Briss 587.31
bristelings 442.10
bristling 352.28
Bristol 405.27 421.13 606.17
Bristolhut 392.31
bristolry 021.34
Britain 062.36 434.15
brite 542.19
britgits 093.05
britting 156.29
British 036.32 054.26 085.08
Britoness 104.14
britsh 362.10
Brittas 375.08
Brittas 201.17
brittle 565.29
brittled 015.05
Britus 568.08
brividies 222.27
brixtol 539.21
Brixton 538.09
bro 489.16
Bro 423.36
broached 088.04
broaching 042.24
broad 029.05 187.24 274.31 406.16 415.35 430.26 439.16 494.18 582.05 602.01 602.03
broad 260.L1
broadawake 041.15 476.11
broadcaster 108.22
broadchurch 533.27
broadcloth 536.30
broadcussed 526.27
broader 153.31
broaders-in-laugh 312.13
broadest 004.19
broadginger 022.34
broads 264.19
broadside 134.01
broadsteyne 075.14
broadstone 568.23
broadstretched 033.05
broadtail 397.32
broadth 318.11
broadtone 404.04
broadway 565.36
broadwhite 136.05
broady 152.20
broather 425.30
brocade 348.25
broched 239.35
Brock 272.25
brockendootsch 070.04
brodar 022.02 481.33
brodhe 356.18
brodo 307.F7
broeks 199.07
Brofèsor 124.09
brofkost 320.09
brogue 051.25 056.24 376.32 378.31
broguen 070.04
brogues 014.04 102.10 183.17 404.20 429.05 451.12 619.35
broguish 421.21
broil 052.18
broin 625.18
Broin 024.34
broke 038.12 043.07 081.32 094.05 168.12 258.05 258.07 270.21 274.02 426.08
broke 278.L5
brokecurst 311.36
brokeforths 343.33
broken 092.01 183.34 261.28 274.32 312.03 406.13 442.34 449.21 503.05 567.10 618.32
Broken 182.24

Broken 175.19 176.05
brokenarched 156.29
brokerheartened 535.19
brokerly 439.27
broking 149.08 596.21
Brolano 569.32
brollies 511.11
bron 054.14
bron 352.16
bronchial 396.16
bronchos 554.01
brone 601.33
bronnanoleum 391.21
Bronto 007.22
brontoichthyan 007.20
Brontolone 007.28
bronxitic 536.13
bronze 054.10 164.27 207.01 241.08 288.02 329.27 531.04
bronzily 274.31
brooch 211.10 213.33
broochbronze 242.34
brooche 531.16
brooched 127.14
brooches 011.21
brood 004.06 237.32 240.12 271.20 288.08 318.22 378.04 621.14
broodcast 567.20
brooder-on-low 153.18
brooder's 561.16
broods 121.03
broody 073.06
brooher 425.31
brook 159.17 306.F1 526.31
Brook 264.06
Brookbear 481.24
brookcells 017.06
Brooke 210.23
brooked 134.30
brookfisht 621.12
brooking 247.01
brooklined 140.29
brookpebbles 072.33
brooks 236.25 247.01 440.29
brooled 184.17
broom 231.32 361.08 550.21
broon 344.12
broons 522.34
broothes 590.25
Brophy 266.F2
bror 099.11
Broree 373.25
Bros 141.19 (Brothers)
Bros. 461.07 (Brothers)
Brosna 212.07
Brosna's 474.20
Brostal 624.33
Brotfressor 124.15
broth 211.15 265.F2 406.13 411.19
brothel 489.30
brother 031.25 039.18 086.22 090.20 121.01 172.24 193.22 224.33 232.22 343.20 394.24 420.17 421.19 425.23 457.29 467.21 488.21 488.22 488.31 523.14
brother 526.15
Brother 307.05 464.16 495.11
brotherbesides 431.18
brotherkeeper 443.04
brothermilk 624.32
brothers 083.33 108.14 191.22 307.F9 311.03 325.25 447.18 465.16 490.07 520.23 551.15 617.11
Brothers 219.14 325.25
brothers' 052.18
brothron 170.04
broths 368.19
brottels 328.22
Brotus 278.L3
brought 005.13 097.32 128.08 131.12 134.21 161.24 174.34 185.32 220.17 237.26 248.11 255.29 288.F2 326.30 337.30 385.18 390.21 484.24 520.20 532.07 571.09 579.28 586.32 601.04 618.09 624.13
broughton 569.33
broughts 181.01
Brounemouth 578.25
brow 056.09 135.13 185.12 187.25 291.27 374.33 405.17 452.15 470.30 563.12 583.30
brow 399.07
Brow 366.36
browbenders 130.02
browbrand 582.31
browd 286.L3
browen 334.14
brown 028.33 043.26 050.05 053.25 056.33 076.29 095.17 114.31 130.24 153.05 164.27 271.F5 392.33 394.09 397.17 406.25 443.20 550.20 583.09 588.13
brown 341.04
Brown 187.26 520.17 546.34
Brownaboy 372.29
browne 300.29
browne 341.27
Browne 038.26 050.18 144.31 159.22 211.32 268.08 334.07 537.06 567.23 599.23
Browne-Browne 303.F3
browned 113.28
Browne-Nowlan 176.20
Brownes 303.F3 380.32
Browne's 042.08 503.34
brownesberrow 391.14
Brownhazelwood 372.15
brownie 368.31 586.14
brownie's 449.13
browning 516.18
brownings 351.01
Browno 412.36
browrings 467.09
brows 470.34 551.25 622.08
browse 073.30
browsers 433.31
browses 264.17
browsing 183.07
browthered 248.32
brozaozaozing 407.18
Brozzo 560.32
brr 502.09 600.27
Brr 502.09
b —— r's 081.26 (bugger's)
brubblemm'as 182.21
bruce 228.10
Bruce 108.14
brucer 596.15
bruck 090.24
Bruda 424.01
bruddy 234.04
bruder 427.19
brueburnt 384.28
brugh 136.23
brugk 347.21
bruin 097.06
Bruin 328.02 461.12 488.14
Bruinoboroff 340.20
Bruisanose 125.20
bruise 187.27 238.11
Bruise 457.17
bruised 065.01 084.11 429.04
bruiselivid 432.31
bruisy 247.24 247.25
bruited 033.16
bruk 141.34 372.25
brukasloop 562.16
Bruko 416.15
brulobrulo 117.12
Brum 009.26 009.27
bruma 502.19
Brumans 093.01
brume 271.21
brumming 044.19
brune 015.16 158.11 187.26 271.21
Brune 246.32
brunette 546.32
Bruneyes 418.31
brung 230.23 310.08
Bruni 373.16
Bruno 050.19 152.11 336.35 488.04 488.07 488.10 569.09
brunoipso 488.09
Bruno's 369.08
brunt 417.12
Brunt 594.11
Brunto 007.22
brunzewig 578.04
brupper 191.20
brush 096.34 127.24 149.24 302.11 507.30 594.23
brusk 575.10
bruskly 072.36
brusque 269.17
brustall 512.05
brut 060.26 060.26 292.F2 451.24
brutals 366.25
brute 481.13
brutest 254.05
brutherscutch 163.08
Bruto 281.15
Bruton 595.18
brutstrenth 359.17
Bruyant 338.28
bruzeup 266.26
brwn 130.34
Bryan 275.01
Bryant's 080.02
Bryllars 151.33
bryllupswibe 547.28
Bryne 595.05
bryns 051.29
Bryony 450.32
Brystal 378.19
brythe 389.31
Brythonic 091.03
Brythyc 310.14
Bu 087.32
buaboababbaun 126.12
buaboabaybohm 029.02
buah 198.05

Buahbuah 622.12
Bubabipibambuli 306.F5
bubbering 344.29
bubbily 367.34
bubble 273.07
bubbleblown 461.34
bubbles 088.33 162.07 246.11 427.02
bubblets 462.12
bubblin 583.25
bubbling 195.02
bubblingplace 134.32
bubblye 526.09
bubby 443.04
bubel 624.09
Bubo 243.24
buboes 198.30
bubub 532.07
Bubye 215.07
buccaneer-admiral 567.22
Buccas 378.03
buccat 296.30
Buccinate 412.08
Buccleuch 346.19
Bucclis 518.25
buch 210.06
buchan 081.13
buchel 562.25
buchstubs 157.28
buck 054.22 055.24 059.24 205.07 320.34 326.18 375.16 436.33
buck 350.01 350.12
Buck 210.17
buckarestive 554.01
buckbeshottered 352.30
bucked 117.21 275.10 398.21 580.33
buckeley 138.14
buckely 536.15
bucker 055.24
buckers 134.04
bucker's 119.30
bucket 070.27 170.12 211.09 312.12 359.15 617.13
bucketing 471.14
bucketroom 079.25
buckets 272.08 443.07
bucketshop 046.03
buckgoat 215.27
buckily 341.05
Buckily 341.05
bucking 146.08 524.23
Buckle 346.23
bucklecatch 328.16
buckled 579.27
buckler 127.10 242.03
bucklesome 325.29
Buckley 101.15 101.21 221.36
buckleybackers 530.02
Buckley's 375.23
Buckleyself 101.19
bucklied 011.26
buckling 310.19 432.16
Buckling 105.21
bucklings 349.24
Bucklovitch 049.08
buckly 620.04
bucknesst 363.07
buckons 508.04
buckoo 351.19
buckos 476.08
buckram 568.19
buckrom 059.20
bucks 272.31 339.07
buckseaseilers 319.21
buckshee 052.21
buckshotbackshattered 137.13
buckside 010.11
buckskin 253.16 295.F1
buckstiff 374.19
buckthurnstock 346.14
bucktooth 242.08
buckup 517.33
BUCKUP 304.R3
buckwoulds 339.16
bucky 583.09
bud 224.23 329.03 355.08
Bud 337.32 337.32 337.32
budd 346.30 445.07
Budd 620.03
Buddapest 131.13
Buddaree 100.08
Budderly 337.32 337.32
budders 277.L5
buddhas 544.24
buddhoch 025.25
buddhy 234.14 602.27
buddies 340.11
buddy 199.08 485.16
budge 511.30
budged 194.09
budgerigars 180.27
budget 099.11
budinholder 320.05
budkley 361.25
Budlim 337.26
budly 354.34
buds 095.36 465.10
budsome 364.13
bueh 198.05
buel 441.28
Buellas 435.01
Buen 536.21
Buf 226.09
bufeteer 511.10
buff 397.33 567.25
Buffalo 275.L3
buffeteers 023.26
buffkid 441.09
Buffler 398.01
bug 008.26 145.34 246.08 270.F2 345.25 596.27
Bug 044.12
Bug 134.36
bugaboo 304.12
bugbear 275.F3
Buggaloffs 026.04
bugganeering 323.01
Bugge 058.17
buggelawrs 141.14
bugger 047.09
Buggered 522.18
buggey 262.F7
buggy 085.10
bugigle 562.27
buginning 378.29
bugle 475.36
Bugle 379.04
buglehorners 589.32
bugler 587.20
bugler's 335.06
bugles 097.01
Bugley 622.25
bugling 236.04
buglooking 128.06
bugs 029.08
bugsby 516.09
bugsmess 535.17
bugtwug 349.11
Buickly 292.F1
buikdanseuses 098.12
build 027.33 073.09 246.12 559.25 578.05 605.23
builded 262.18
builder 560.30 576.18
building 155.06 286.F1 541.06
buildn 624.07
buildung 004.27 004.27
built 135.33 137.09 181.32 274.22 375.04 543.10 551.24
Buinness's 443.32
bujibuji 533.28
buk 114.26
Bukarahast 114.04
Buke 255.21
Bulafests 541.16
bulb 125.16
bulbenboss 013.24
bulbsbyg 339.11
bulbubly 384.29
bulbul 476.02
Bulbul 360.23
bulbulone 360.23
bulby 406.07
bulching 224.13
bulchrichudes 340.26
bulg 347.01
bulgar 563.14
Bulgarad 114.05
bulge 097.19 457.17 620.05
bulgeglarying 339.19
bulgen 376.04
bulgic 204.09
bulgiest 138.18
bulgy 498.36
bulk 006.31 313.30 324.05 415.11 578.05
Bulk 102.20
bulked 057.33
Bulkeley 327.26 435.11
bulkhead 511.24
bulkier 445.20
bulkihood 029.29
bulkily 192.02 310.26
Bulkily 610.01
bulkis 102.20
bulkside 153.16
bull 017.09 039.34 045.21 077.19 087.21 118.07 188.07 344.28 353.13 490.35 491.01 522.15 562.22 568.14
Bull 008.13 098.31 272.29 448.19
Bullavogue 100.08
bullbeadle 511.09
Bullbeck 609.16
bullbeef 190.05
bullbraggin 022.35
bulldog 030.24 179.04
bulledicted 458.03
bullet 008.12 035.26 190.28 522.01
bulletaction 310.36
bulletist 130.10
bullets 079.31
Bulley 378.15
bullfight 464.27
bullfist 534.19
bullfolly 157.07

Bullfoost 070.15
bullgine 529.22
Bullhead 525.28
bulligan 272.30
bullin 445.24
bulling 206.04
Bullingdong 333.18
Bulljon 255.13
bullock 522.02
bullocker 154.34
bullocks 135.14 337.30
bullock's 429.16
bullocky 072.26 611.04
bulloge 583.04
bullowed 154.07
bullpen 359.01
bulls 198.04
bull's 084.02 464.18
bulls' 358.31
bullseaboob 580.14
Bullsear 009.24
Bullseye 010.21
Bullsfoot 008.15
bullsfooted 120.07
Bullsrag 010.15
bullsrusshius 494.19
bullugs 180.24
bully 079.04 082.05 083.28 319.06 375.17 426.17 456.03 550.04 566.04
Bully 073.23 177.27 210.16 511.24
bullycassidy 087.15
bullyclaver 352.23
bullyclavers 285.25
Bullyclubber 335.13
Bullydamestough 485.16
Bullyfamous 229.15
Bullyhowley 608.09
bullyon 313.29
bullyoungs 595.11
Bully's 618.08
Bullysacre 320.33
bullyum 393.12
bulopent 612.06
bulper 468.27
bulrush 207.03
bulsheywigger's 070.21
Bulsklivism 116.06
bulweh 513.07
bum 046.11 168.11 251.18 316.24 338.27
bum 284.L3
Bum 102.35
bumaround 039.21
bumbac 054.16
bumbashaws 098.13
bumbellye 568.23
Bumble 176.04
bumbler 370.02
bumblin 555.14
bumboards 375.06
bumbosolom 180.27
Bumbty 496.06
Bumchub 342.19
bumfit 339.26
bumgalowre 496.13
Bumm 421.14
bummel 491.21
bummell 323.01
bump 055.32 176.34 312.29 315.12 442.32 494.03 547.19
Bump 314.07
bumped 203.13
Bumped 071.13
bumper 462.12 607.13
bumpersprinkler 180.34
bumpily 107.33
bumping 045.21
Bumping 437.03
bumpinstrass 556.25
bumpkin 627.23
Bumps 273.01
bumpsed 393.29 493.20
bumpsetty 562.07
bumpslump 332.17
bumrush 029.21
bun 320.09 433.20
Bun 546.25
bunbaked 139.11
Bunbath 198.05
bunch 097.20 220.04 253.18 323.30 351.19 443.12
Bunch 106.23
buncskleydoodle 258.05
bundle 192.36 221.03 414.02
bundukiboi 201.25
bung 025.29 049.32 205.23 352.10
Bung 378.17 421.13 421.13
bungaloid 471.12
bungalow 265.12
bungbarrel 138.18
bunged 498.36
bungelars 197.19
bunghole 428.13
bungle 320.19
bungless 157.25
bungley 368.08
bung's 187.26
bunificence 302.07
bunk 040.19 055.07 374.18 525.35 559.34
Bunk 420.34
B U N K 379.29
bunkers' 542.26
Bunkers' 228.20
bunkersheels 009.29
bunket 397.06
bunkledoodle 376.24
bunkum 422.30 608.04
Bunnicombe 254.35
bunny 321.27
bunnyboy 177.36
bunnyhugging 384.21
buns 121.32 455.07 498.20
buntad 366.09
bunting 198.15
Bunting 607.28
buntingcap 567.07
buntingpall 549.05
buntings 529.33
buntz 215.13
buon 412.29
buona 264.24
buoy 204.10 318.11 328.29 380.28 606.13
buoyant 098.22
buoyantly 426.34
buoyed 097.15
Burb 479.05 479.05 479.05
burberry 444.28
burble 504.17
burden 040.06 112.20 190.21 607.19
burdened 273.21
burdens 536.27
Bure 163.27
Burgaans 072.03
burgage 539.21
burgages 358.08
Burgearse 371.22
burgeon 239.02
burger 023.15
burgess 277.10 516.32
Burgess 062.30
burgesses 567.08
burgh 541.36
burgherbooh 372.30
burgherly 335.13
Burghley 338.02
burghmote 484.21
burglar 390.02
burglar's 261.F4
burglary 133.12
burgley's 070.14
burgomaster 587.33
burial 311.19 479.19 486.15 596.08
Burial 325.01
burialbattell 479.25
burialplot 135.17
Burials 262.25
buried 038.23 078.09 078.18 131.15 171.35 397.03 429.21 434.14 499.25 624.04
Buried 595.28
burk 060.14 542.19
Burke 343.03 420.29 580.31
burked 132.33
Burke-Lees 330.17
burkeley 610.12
Burkeley's 346.11
burkes 443.16
Burke's 235.13
Burke's 071.30
Burklley 312.29
Burkos 064.23
burl 266.26
burlap 404.25
burled 182.26
Burleigh 257.17
burley 511.24
burleyhearthed 602.16
burleys 362.03
burlingtons 055.15
burly 270.26 492.03
burm 348.26
burman 523.31
burn 439.34 549.29
Burn 204.06 447.04
burn'd 122.12
burned 516.22 527.14
burner 093.11
burners 526.17
Burnham 071.21
Burnias 345.05
Burniface 315.09
burning 005.02 132.07 143.30 145.36 182.11 244.12 250.16 322.15 427.15 450.14 474.17 602.18
burning 341.24 354.13
burnous 197.34
burns 189.32 232.16 520.26
burnt 021.10 464.09 621.26
burnzburn 102.07
burqued 503.36
burr 034.36

burral 085.02
burre 130.12
burro 163.15
burrocks 005.35
Burroman 163.35
burroow 625.19
burrow 512.24 565.36 602.17
burrowed 011.17 375.28
burrowing 078.09 275.06
burrs 453.16
Burrus 161.12 161.15 162.22 162.33 165.12 166.30 166.35
Burrus's 164.24
burryberries 376.28
Burrymecarott 390.25
burryripe 291.11
burst 052.20 073.07 135.25 139.26 183.11 202.13 277.03 356.32 429.12 442.29 584.13 589.26
Burst 072.13
burstall 504.26
burstday 059.11
bursters 621.11
bursthright 300.32
bursting 516.14
burstteself 187.04
Burtt 293.F2
Burud 406.21
bury 047.22 410.13 414.31
buryings 117.28
Burymeleg 011.06
bus 540.16
busby 009.10 205.33
bush 005.02 089.31 095.36 112.03 165.18 301.F3 408.08 433.29 445.03 588.02 628.12
Bush 438.15
Bush 176.10
bushboys 129.13
bushbrows 371.03
Bushe 331.10
bushel 529.17
bushellors 010.03
bushes 522.12
bushies 256.12
bushle 504.03
bushman 207.34
bushman's 110.28
bushment's 248.28
Bushmillah 521.15
Bushmills 577.21
business 005.14 012.11 031.23 037.09 063.06 088.12 108.10 127.20 127.23 156.35 248.29 268.06 410.16 452.35 522.02 536.30 543.34
Business 062.21 321.20 559.24
buskbutts 434.25
busker 041.13 580.32
busket 614.15
buskin 429.17
busnis 174.30 174.30
Bussave 017.17
busses 092.17
bussing 417.18
Bussing 467.06
Bussmullah 292.F3
bussness 618.19
Bussoftlhee 628.14
busspleaches 553.11
Bussup 435.11
bussybozzy 040.07
bussycat 445.19
bust 452.21 527.32 531.16
busted 498.24
bustle 455.04
bustle 348.31
bustles 243.05
bustling 041.09
busy 020.23 042.34 398.09 477.14 588.24
busybody 438.16
busynext 580.28
but but But But
butagain 354.34
butch 190.05 351.19
butcheler 315.01
butcher 067.15 265.F5
butcherblue 063.16
butcher's 172.05 213.26
butcherswood 080.08
butchery 070.11
Butchery 406.02
butchup's 600.29
buthbach 346.22
buthock 311.33
butlegger 166.17
butler 519.06
butlered 266.10
butler's 189.08
butly 372.06
Butly 338.16
butnot 124.01
butrose 433.11
buts 436.34
But's 251.08
butstillone 581.34
butt 006.07 008.07 023.32 045.04 088.36 196.09 221.11 254.13 321.03 525.35
butt 044.27
Butt 302.13 421.04 529.17
BUTT 338.11 338.34 339.24 340.04 340.19 341.03 341.10 343.13 344.08 345.10 345.26 346.31 348.03 350.10 352.27 353.06 354.03 354.07
buttall 035.34
Buttbutterbust 106.33
butte 013.14
butted 580.32
butteler's 012.04
buttend 315.12 498.35
buttended 003.11
butter 027.31 045.22 045.23 140.34 162.17 230.23 256.35 406.30 406.30 464.20 543.24 603.07 615.31
Butter 045.24 533.36 603.07
Butter 071.13
butterblond 429.19
Butterbrot 163.06 163.06
buttercup 321.16
Buttercup 561.12
buttercups 145.14
buttered 320.29 356.22
butterfly 232.11
butteries 192.09
Butterman's 210.33
buttermilt 277.F5
buttermore 586.36
butternat 160.04
butterscatch 206.33
buttertower 100.17
Buttery 498.08
buttes 536.04
butthering 444.17
butting 186.29 315.12 603.13
Butting 524.22
buttinghole 464.13
buttins 011.19
buttle 016.20 130.13
buttler 385.15
buttles 245.32 283.F1 419.26
buttocks 169.18
buttom 048.18 163.19
button 316.18 508.16
buttoncups 433.25
buttonhaled 311.08
buttonholes 015.09
buttonlegs 188.29
buttons 208.20 392.10 393.20 404.23 458.24 559.10
buttons 339.20
buttress 135.34 471.17
butts 214.22 271.19
Butt's 085.15
butty 039.26
buttyr 483.24
buttywalch 338.09
Butyrum 163.03
Butys 220.07
buum 550.04
Buvard 302.09
buxers 090.02
buxon 266.26
buy 009.18 025.03 065.15 083.03 161.14 161.14 253.18 273.F5 279.07 290.22 291.12 363.14 391.02 422.16 431.20 432.08 444.05 456.11 466.29 474.11 530.12 583.21 610.12 621.18
buy 342.23
Buy 376.29 420.36 507.24 521.36 569.35 579.20
Buy 104.11
buybibles 539.02
Buybuy 146.33
Buycout 060.30
buying 354.31
buyings 597.18
Buylan 435.10
buylawyer 374.20
buys 279.F36 354.31
buyshop 130.33
Buythebanks 006.34
buytings 250.08
buzz 180.22 393.13
Buzz 227.11
buzzard 361.16
buzzard 383.05
buzzed 099.10
buzzer 417.06 474.16
buzzerd 277.F1
buzzers 604.13
Buzzersbee 387.24
buzzim 348.07
buzzle 102.10
buzzling 223.25
buzztle 578.22
buzzy 238.34 430.20
BVD 238.01 238.01
B.V.H. 131.03
by by By By BY
b —— y 081.26 081.27 (bloody)
byandby 203.04
byaway 432.17

bybyscuttlings 095.33
bycause 536.24
byck 423.14
bycorn 348.11
bye 545.33 584.12
byeboys 369.07
byebye 304.F1
Byebye 228.12
byelegs 594.28
byelo 064.06
byes 011.08 011.08
Byfall 257.29
byg 262.19
bygger 324.27
Byggning 017.22
Byggotstrade 602.21
Bygmester 004.18
Bygning 056.20
bygone 310.18 385.03 386.07
bygones 263.17
bygotter 612.31
Bygrad 491.35
byhangs 224.08
byhold 143.17
bylaws 524.04 589.34
byleave 289.01
bymby 290.17
bymeby 611.26
Bymeby 611.04
bynames 029.31
bynear 416.04
byng 008.12
Bynight 089.16
byorn 392.12
byre 340.12
Byrightofoaptz 571.28
byrn-and-bushe 586.11
Byrne's 289.13
byrni 568.32
byrnie 525.36
Byrns 455.02
Byron 041.16
byscent 165.10
bysistance 469.31
bysone 275.L3
byspills 356.14
bytheway 063.01
byusucapiture 537.23
bywan 201.29 201.30
byward 077.19
byway 043.27
byway 338.07
bywaymen 546.36
byways 012.01
byword 129.08 390.20
Byzantium 294.27

c 140.12 140.27 370.01
C̄ 165.23 (Caseous)
C. 230.04 (Bill C. Babby)
C. 342.20 (Hermyn C. Entwhistle)
ca 496.34 577.30
caabman's 542.14
cab 391.35
cabaleer 234.03
cabalstone 132.01
cabbage 095.17 144.26 271.F2 406.18 520.36
cabbageblad 056.25
cabbageous 409.13
cabbages 132.28
cabbaging 030.12
Cabbanger 071.35
cabbangers 390.12
cabbis 419.32
cabbuchin 568.28
cabful 034.11
Cabin 205.35
Cabinhogan 388.17
cabins 244.05 395.09
cabinteeny 533.19
cable 025.35 289.09 434.31
cabled 172.22
Cablen 315.32
Cabler 488.21 488.28
cables 542.06
cabman 529.23
Cabo 312.08
caboosh 586.26
cabootle 315.22
cabotinesque 512.18
Cabra 142.14
Cabraists 497.19
Cabranke 420.36
cabrattlefield 609.34
cabronne 352.21
cabs 613.06
cac 250.34
caca 534.26
Cacao 073.10
cacchinated 261.12
cacchinic 511.14
cache 586.34
cacheton 224.27
cachucha 027.20
cackle 415.04
Cackler 237.34
cackling 200.27 364.30 452.05
cacumen 415.04
cacuminal 055.29
cad 035.11 088.13 127.07 178.02 270.07 332.25 511.32 534.26 588.10 618.03
Cad 520.10
cadbully's 587.07
Cadbury 193.15
cadder 303.29
Cadderpollard 350.10
caddishly 101.21
caddy 167.08 624.01
Caddy 014.12 014.13
cadenus 413.27
cadenzando 226.30
cadet 069.18 101.35
cadge 450.24
cadging 358.02
Cadman 113.20
Cadmillersfolly 625.06
Cadmus 307.L1
cads 520.21
cad's 038.09 358.09
Caducus 211.16
Cadwallon 152.06
Cadwalloner 152.06
Cadwan 152.06
caecodedition 512.17
caecos 100.18
Caer 171.34
Caerholme 341.19
Caesar 161.36
Caesar 306.L2
Caesar-in-Chief 219.13
caeseine 349.16
Café 372.12
Cafeteria 433.16
Caffirs 614.10
cafflers 615.29
caftan 343.10
caftan's 187.08
cagacity 108.28
cage 197.22
Cage 563.19
cagehaused 533.18
cagnan 206.02
Caherlehome-upon-Eskur 220.35
Cahills 044.08
Cahlls 423.36
Cailcainnin 391.33
cain 287.11
Cain 047.29 193.32
Cain 307.L1
Cainandabler 071.13
cainapple 121.11
Caines 106.33
Cainfully 374.33
Cainmaker's 583.28
cainozoic 101.15
cairns 073.29 594.24
Cairns 604.06
Cairo 509.19
Caius 128.15 467.13
caiuscounting 282.29
cajoleries 139.24
cake 147.24 170.22 287.29 333.33 620.36
Cake 261.F2
cakeeater 192.33
cakes 111.14 116.09 131.15 279.F33 392.32 619.02
Cal 534.01
Calabashes 336.33
calaboose 052.24
calaboosh 240.24
calam 363.18
Calaman 059.24
calamitance 119.11
calamite's 119.11
calamities 128.29 438.23
calamitous 119.11
calamity 207.28
calamolumen 255.19
calamum 302.16
calamus 185.22
calanders 040.34
Calavera 255.14
Calculating 108.15
cald 219.18 414.34
caldin 117.31
calding 327.20
caldor 188.27
caldron 528.37
caledosian 187.07
calef 426.13
Calembaurnus 240.21
calendar 033.24 087.13 456.34
calendarias 553.16
calends 085.27
calends 274.L3
calf 294.11 332.13
calfloving 438.02
calico 240.25
calicohydrants 182.36
calicolum 298.31
calicub 516.16
calid 502.18
calif 367.33
Calif 576.03
Caligula 060.26

caligulate 004.32
calipers 332.32
calisenic 499.05
call 035.32 037.16 041.32 054.23 059.36 064.26 073.34 074.06 088.35 121.11 132.14 150.23 163.01 164.10 166.05 185.28 190.30 194.36 198.19 207.14 212.21 222.36 223.13 232.11 232.11 243.02 244.17 249.29 262.26 276.F4 299.F2 301.01 310.22 313.15 314.28 318.05 318.36 323.25 326.01 328.21 337.35 347.26 352.24 362.08 362.31 364.31 407.18 420.01 457.35 459.10 464.31 466.03 474.17 479.25 480.03 487.30 489.28 501.13 514.17 521.04 538.20 547.30 612.17 612.17 622.22 623.04 624.22
Call 207.28 361.15 480.04 488.14 530.32 569.28
Call 048.14
callback 294.28
Callboy 559.30
callby 248.34
calle 549.30
called 014.12 018.35 027.15 034.14 041.16 044.14 052.13 066.11 071.06 079.15 080.06 108.34 110.34 119.18 119.20 123.15 137.29 141.33 174.07 192.28 197.08 287.14 310.02 313.15 335.10 421.26 431.11 486.35 491.10 506.05 512.34 536.01 539.28 540.07 564.04 565.02 575.24 581.02 598.17 602.18 616.03 617.11 619.29
Called 106.36
callen 324.21
caller 136.26
Caller 394.34
callers 235.30
callhim 126.03
calligraphy 114.12
calling 025.11 040.08 056.09 119.11 120.15 198.10 335.25 335.35 364.36 373.21 389.10 442.32 501.21 580.17
Calling 200.22 593.02 593.02 593.11 593.11
callit 058.34
callours 146.16
callous 037.28
callouses 419.28
calls 026.03 049.34 065.06 127.30 129.35 131.28 133.35 245.36 246.06 246.21 428.07 587.21 628.13
Calls 108.23
Calls 105.19
Call'st 442.19
calm 079.17 083.07 132.30 262.01
Calm 534.07 534.07
calmleaved 600.36
calmly 006.35
calms 427.20
calmy 223.13 237.31
Calomella's 354.26
Calomnequiller's 050.09
calories 544.34
caloripeia 611.32
calorrubordolor 445.18
Calottica 349.21
calour 051.26 223.06
calpered 297.10
Calton 541.03
calubra 184.26
Calumdonia 241.30
Calumnia 199.28
Calumnious 179.13
calvary 024.19
calvers 019.23
calves 210.17 339.27
calvescatcher 461.15
Calvinic 519.26
calvitousness 318.34
calyptrous 613.17
calyzettes 237.02
calzium 035.02
cam 202.07
Camac 212.08
camber 340.30
Cambriannus 151.32
Cambridge 587.08
Cambronses 573.21
camcam 531.24
came 019.13 022.32 029.20 030.12 032.09 042.07 049.12 058.06 063.36 064.16 073.23 110.02 123.31 130.32 132.05 153.01 154.22 158.25 158.32 168.03 171.23 173.02 207.20 223.19 250.30 256.06 282.12 288.20 315.11 334.28 334.32 361.27 362.02 382.19 387.12 404.09 406.01 410.17 430.27 442.12 474.17 483.29 496.30 510.32 512.08 541.34 556.34 580.28 588.10 589.32 605.10 605.18 623.02 627.08
came 349.35
Came 421.14
Camebreech 182.24
camel 046.23 086.18 245.04 313.36 494.03 532.07
camelback 067.29
cameleer's 197.34
camelia 113.17
camell 549.35
Camellus 090.18 090.19
camelot 143.07
camelottery 359.16
camelry 009.24
camel's 201.09
camels' 551.34
camelsensing 352.16
cameltemper 553.02
camelump 323.23
camera 137.12 171.33
camera 115.25 575.23
Camerad 602.23
Camerade 551.15
cameras 375.14
Camhelsson 124.29
camibalistics 004.05
camiflag 339.13 463.22
Camilla 211.08
camises 551.06
Camlenstrete 132.06
camlin 202.07
cammelskins 320.26
Cammmels 104.21
cammocking 205.28
Cammomile 553.05
camnabel 362.05
camouflaged 494.21
camp 009.17 258.28 343.04 343.04 343.05
campaign 515.27
campaniles 541.07
campanulae 601.16
camparative 598.23
Campbell 073.10 343.03
campbells 022.31
campdens 517.22
campos 142.12
camps 078.25
Camps 058.28
campus 246.21
can can Can Can
can 225.16 227.04 233.13 330.26 373.09 392.31 568.14 571.07 579.08
Canaan 264.09
canaille 173.02
canailles 548.04
canal 100.30 179.18 228.30 551.23
canalised 436.18
canalles 494.32
canaries 260.F1
canary 050.28
canat 604.19
canavan 602.28
Canavan 031.21
Canbe 048.09
canbung 098.10
cancan 331.11 436.35
cancanzanies 236.29
canceal 366.01
cancelled 159.08
Candia 408.11
candid 241.03
candidacy 336.30
Candidately 396.05
candidates 122.24
Candidatus 234.08
candiedights 498.32
candle 214.02 257.16 271.10 295.09 376.06 459.30
candled 382.17
candleliked 434.12
candlelittle 010.27
Candlemas 460.35
candles 028.31 185.05 246.05 626.14
candlestock 050.05
candy 092.20
Candy 176.14
candykissing 300.15
candylock 409.13
candywhistle 556.15
cane 029.28 201.33 424.28 568.20 587.29
canease 595.32
canem 060.15
caneseated 559.07
Canicula 573.30
canicular 512.36
canine 132.02
Canine 299.L1
canins 334.26 334.26
canis 157.01
canister 009.32
cankle 463.34 557.04
Canmakenoise 031.21
canna 159.18

cannasure 162.14
cannibal 193.32 600.01
cannier 114.15
Canniley 518.29
Cannmatha 329.14
cannoball 339.10
Cannon 104.09
cannonise 081.26
cannons' 330.08
cannos 154.31
cannot
Cannought 389.05
Cannut 520.23
canny 097.08 496.34 577.30
canoedler 204.09
canon 222.05 465.24 596.09 625.09
Canon 009.19
canonicity 100.34
canonisator's 428.22
canonise 467.21
canons 121.28
canon's 206.27
canoodle 065.24 065.26 065.32
canooter 325.23
canopies 173.12
canopy 249.08
Canorian 287.F3
cans 170.31 183.30 483.17 581.05
Cans 501.09
canseels 373.29
cansill 538.14
cant 109.01 339.07 381.12
cant 282.L2 349.35
Cant 572.16
can't can't Can't
cantab 467.31
Cantaberra 569.17
Cantalamesse 236.07
cantalang 148.23
cantanberous 463.13
cantatrickee 165.06
canteen 214.21
canteenhus 267.05
Canter 440.17
canterberry 310.29
Canterel 137.07
canticle 263.22
Cantilene 441.11
canting 167.17 311.25
cantins 496.09
cantitans 185.23
canto 044.05
cantonnatal 091.23
cantons 472.24
cantoridettes 415.09
cantraps 184.26
cantreds 189.11
canty 232.06
canule 568.36
Canwyll 464.06
canyouseehim 129.09
canzoned 548.04
Caoch 043.20
caoutchouc 035.08
cap 039.12 093.10 126.15 166.08 232.14 253.27 283.02 365.04 515.35
Cap 008.12 330.18
capable 033.23 039.03 049.20 109.27 309.20
capacity 154.25 187.07
capahand 042.09
Capalisoot 487.32
capalleens 039.30
capallo 565.20
capapee 583.29
cap-a-pipe 220.26
capapole 622.30
cape 389.35 619.27
Cape 312.19 491.11 573.33
capecast 060.31
capecloaked 339.29
Capeinhope 010.02
Capel 325.14 515.21
Capeler 488.33
capelist's 051.27
Capellisato 255.01
Capels 161.29 448.09
capercallzie 383.17
caperchasing 475.28
capered 286.09
capers 233.03 563.08
Capilla 492.13
capital 181.07 227.11 255.22 296.05 302.09 368.03 528.29 589.08 625.21
capitaletter 397.29
capItallsed 120.04
capitally 461.34
Capite 101.13
capitol 131.02 140.08 548.17
Caplan 060.30
capman 292.19 322.25
Capn 082.29
capo 044.28 466.19
capocapo 506.19
Capolic 370.36
caponchin 447.19
capons 569.27
cappa 606.05
cappapee 058.25
capped 467.24 607.32
cappon 316.34 319.18
Cappon's 155.35
cappunchers 386.30
capri 412.33
capricious 121.20
capriole 331.28
capritious 276.F5
caps 119.35 205.06 220.14 226.25 260.04 374.10
capsflap 452.04
capsized 123.26
capsizer 418.05
capstan 311.09 311.27 312.02
capsules 403.06
capsy 470.32
capt 360.19 540.18
Capt. 169.04
captain 137.18 197.13 325.27 495.14
Captain 039.08 067.22 622.25 624.28
Captain 106.15
Capteen 323.13
captious 109.24
captivating 092.15
captive 246.19 318.11
Captive 607.28
captivities 364.16
captn 587.05
captol 023.11
capture 082.01 100.33 325.19
captured 039.06 200.30
capturing 309.20
Caput 197.08
car 042.27 053.11 055.24 110.10 623.22
Car 308.08
cara 358.31 625.24
Cara 327.02
caractacurs 518.22
caracul 397.32
Caraculacticors 048.07
Carambas 512.07
caramel 235.35
Caramis 064.23
caratimaney 207.25
caravan 079.25 285.21
Caray's 370.06
carberry 228.18
Carbo 232.03
carbolic 067.34
carbon 336.23 579.05
carbonoxside 128.10
carbons 183.33
carbunckley 224.36
carcass 479.19
carcasses 067.16 344.20
Carchingarri 180.14
card 039.03 221.13 281.F3 405.14
cardigans 339.12
cardinal 114.07 131.01 474.19 504.15 555.20 605.25
Cardinal 180.13 180.14 180.14 180.15
cardinal's 243.30
cardinals' 200.03
cardinhands 286.13
cardonals 484.19
cardriver 059.25
cards 127.25 201.36 304.28
care 012.15 031.03 054.20 062.24 098.33 115.25 144.02 145.16 145.20 149.10 151.36 165.11 198.16 228.19 320.33 351.26 355.12 381.07 387.22 414.12 421.27 438.05 441.15 442.03 457.11 560.31 589.03
cared 100.31 332.30
careened 426.30
career 091.30
Career 306.19
careero 209.21
careers 032.28 078.35
careful 037.24 148.07 460.32
Careful 572.13
carefully 077.17 163.36 176.34 297.07 449.36
carelessest 317.12
Careous 167.24
cares 326.01 473.07 624.14 627.14
caressed 041.23
caressimus 238.33
Carfax 260.12
cargon 019.15
carhacks 005.31
cariad 158.36
caries 523.29
Carilloners 569.04
carina 007.03 007.03
caring 314.21
carishy 207.25
cark 050.29
carl 015.29

carlen 550.08
Carlisle 514.26
Carlow 214.30 379.10
Carlowman's 334.36
Carlow's 538.29
Carlton 622.29
carlysle 517.22
carm 354.32
Carme 418.03
carmelite 050.21
Carmen 360.13 448.12
Carminia 239.24
carmp 392.05
carnage 582.15
carnal 427.21 573.21
carnation 040.09 557.21
carnier 349.12
carnium 287.22
Carnival 440.09
Carnsore 580.34
Caro 238.33
carol 501.34
Carolan 369.09
Carolinas 226.02
caroline 460.10
caroll 601.17
carollaries 294.07
Carolus 360.27
Caron 496.32
carp 164.17 335.06
Carpam 525.20
Carpenger 294.F1
carpers 450.07
Carpery 390.35
carpet 553.09
Carprimustimus 108.12
Carpulenta 099.09
carpus 616.06
carr 264.16
Carr 279.F22
Carrageehouse 108.19
Carrageen 184.21
carrawain 276.26
carriage 079.25 627.22
carriageable 584.32
carried 061.32 082.31 146.24 158.02 158.28 220.16 379.35 404.31 420.17 542.07 545.07 546.14 558.17
Carried 624.01
carrier 385.05 407.30
carriero 230.27
carrier's 066.11
carries 584.23
Carrigacurra 214.21
carrion 131.17 189.28
Carrison 532.01
carrot 404.24
Carrot 501.09
Carrothagenuine 087.28
carrots 190.03 476.17
carrotty 300.08
carry 020.14 079.16 115.36 171.23 239.31 283.05 294.06 442.16 444.31 445.25 456.05 460.25 463.02 511.03 548.06 577.09
carry 268.L2
Carry 562.13 628.08
carrycam 550.20
carryfour 581.22
carryin 035.13
carrying 082.06 165.25 278.16 479.08 486.17 529.21 593.21 605.31
Carryone 588.02
cars 542.08
carsed 319.29
carsse 339.06
carsst 343.02
cart 116.35
cartage 538.12
cartager 064.03
cartel 362.02
Cartesian 301.25
cartomance 310.22
cartridge 210.07
cartridges 347.31
cartwheel 059.06
Carty 142.28
Carubdish 229.14
carucates 128.05
carusal 406.15
carvers 078.35
Casabianca 342.09
Casaconcordia 054.10
Casanuova 230.15
cascadas 152.27
cascades 567.06
caschal 397.26
case 031.22 033.25 033.34 039.24 061.03 067.10 111.05 115.14 122.34 123.22 124.26 150.07 151.14 159.26 161.20 162.19 166.33 179.16 251.32 253.13 269.07 428.25 443.17 458.21 458.25 468.07 484.18 544.06 557.25 573.24 577.24 617.25
casehardened 087.34
Casemate 387.23
casematter 478.17
casement 559.04
Caseous 161.12 161.18 162.21 163.08 164.24 165.12 166.36 167.24
cases 048.02 181.09 381.31 573.36 575.18
Casey's 206.12 286.09
cash 024.01 024.01 065.15 133.13 134.19 150.24 161.06 161.07 404.30 451.05 492.20 574.30 577.09
cash 201.14
Cash 538.16
cash-and-cash-can-again 451.19
cashcash 149.21
cashdime 161.04
cashdraper's 040.15
cashel 228.26
cashellum 283.L1
Cashelmagh 381.22
cashels 004.08
cashla 483.26
cashy 562.31
cask 452.24
casket 098.33 312.23 545.09
caskles 128.17
Caspi 256.35
caspian 578.05
cassack 311.29
cassay 018.31
Cassels 552.11
cassey 538.14
Cassidy 098.31
Cassidys 045.21
Cassio 281.16
Cassiodorus 255.21
Cassius 391.23
cassock 212.31 611.09
cast 030.18 033.11 099.15 183.21 230.13 313.22 399.33 514.07 515.20 547.29 567.11 571.04 601.33 612.30 623.30
castastrophear 222.12
castaway 062.19
caste 484.28 519.29
casted 538.32
castellated 594.09
castelles 037.22
Castillian-Emeratic-Hebridian 263.13
Castello 135.29
caster 007.29
Castilian 092.01
casting 127.15
Casting 202.08 583.14
castle 021.13 183.05 230.35 246.05 262.05 301.27 387.29 440.03 537.02 560.09
Castle 003.03 045.07 242.33 266.03 530.33
Castlebar 055.32
Castlecostello 072.05
Castlecowards 276.F1
Castlehacknolan 303.F3
Castleknock 447.15
castleknocker's 091.34
castlemallards 080.09
castles 022.34 101.23 380.36 623.19
Castlevillainous 077.03
Castlewoos 420.31
castoff 273.F6
castomercies 349.25
castor 489.16
Castor 307.L1
Castor's 432.01
castrament 080.13
Castrucci 533.16
casts 138.14
castwhores 418.22
casual 042.02 161.20
casualised 150.03
casualitas 175.29
casuality 178.03
casuallty 357.22
casuaway 227.05
Casudas 043.23
casus 414.18
casus 508.12
cat 048.02 082.18 116.02 118.35 145.09 278.17 285.16 420.06 461.19 509.19 544.32
cat 275.L1
Cat 436.23 563.19
Cat 071.24
catacalamitumbling 514.11
catachumens 484.12
catachysm 282.25
catalaunic 266.24
cataleptic 481.04
Catalick 158.04
catalogue 047.03 548.21
catalogued 129.12
catapelting 004.04
catara 395.11
cataraction 332.30

cataracts 192.23
catasthmatic 366.23
catastripes 504.31
Catastrophe 304.L2
catastrophes 614.36
catatheristic 357.13
catch 143.17 174.18 199.11 223.05 228.22 257.13 321.22 324.12 331.11 372.32 411.08 439.03 458.11 582.18 611.25
catchaleens 189.11
catchalot 410.11
catchcup 237.01
Catchecatche 502.28
catched 197.22 285.09
Catchering 498.13
catcher's 210.27
catches 127.28
catching 081.31 449.23 450.14
catchment 205.01
Catchmire 226.24
catclub 528.07
categoric 524.16
categorically 119.08 176.25
cater 317.08
caterpillar 033.23
cates 011.24 280.16
cathalogue 440.04
cathargic 344.15
catharic 310.36
Cathay 119.23
cathedral 486.18
cathedris 573.21
catheis 522.30
cathering 382.17
Catheringnettes 538.22
Cathlin 329.15
Cathmon-Carbery 194.02
cathodes 549.17
catholeens 239.21
catholic 032.25 128.27
Catholic 050.24 215.20 389.26
catholick 126.21 292.10
Catilina 307.L1
catkins 397.28
catlick 409.12
Catlick's 485.01
Cato 306.L2
catoninelives 462.31
cats 069.25
cat's 028.05 115.05 116.02 116.03 116.03 116.04 223.23 459.09
cats' 227.06 567.27
catseye 423.07
catspew 520.05
catsup 265.F2
cattagut 548.15
cattegut 022.36 507.10
Cattelaxes 516.05
Cattermole 129.04
Cattie 239.24
cattiness 458.18
cattle 276.F4 316.20 548.26
cattlemen's 172.06
cattlepillar 063.29
cattleraiders 387.02
catz 350.01
Caubeen 622.07
Caubeenhaubeen 568.28
cauchman 133.24
Caucuses 392.23
cauda 239.10 477.22
caudal 333.35 485.03
caudant 350.01
caudle 271.11
Caudledayed 415.14
caught 047.10 078.34 095.01 135.08 147.16 156.12 272.F4 283.23 291.F5 302.15 333.18 344.25 372.19 423.35 438.12 519.05 535.29 564.27 584.12 607.19
Caught 421.05
caughtalock 230.10
Caughterect 600.14
caughtnapping 336.25
caul 254.19
Caulis 553.14
caulking 375.34
Caulofat's 533.28
caun 496.34
cauntry 253.29
causas 342.10
causcaus 378.15
cause 016.18 025.33 056.31 076.13 191.13 198.21 220.27 316.07 380.30 392.22 439.14 474.05 482.36 527.15 545.16 573.17 585.28 589.05 612.26 615.11
caused 029.35 031.05 072.32 092.34 092.34 255.27 310.02 310.08 314.01 483.28 503.01 557.23
caused 354.12
causeries 543.08
Causeries 437.23
causes 067.30 233.25 422.27
causeway 031.06 198.32 448.05
Causeway 080.02
causeways 576.19
Causin 071.30
causing 067.30 111.35 482.36
caustick 336.24
caution 255.14 306.F6 503.24
Caution 013.05
cautioned 086.36
cautiouses 366.26
cauwl 578.10
cavalcaders 567.18
cavaliery 370.07
cavalries 564.26
cavalry 519.06
Cavantry 150.21
cavarnan 333.10
cave 586.34
Cave 016.03 261.15 579.08
caveat 534.16
cavedin 262.11
cavehill 529.24
caveman 060.14
cavemouth 131.18
cavern 037.01 332.16 601.32 615.34
caves 365.02
cavileer 465.16
caviller 162.22
cavin 132.02
caving 368.16
cavity 605.33
caw 371.07
Cawcaught 329.13
cawcaw 357.20
cawcaws 327.36
cawer 049.09
cawing 622.01
cawld 367.28
cawls 495.18
cawraidd's 344.07
cawthrick 486.02
Caxons 397.13
Caxton 229.31
cayennepeppercast 120.14
C.C.D.D. 432.08
Cead 016.34
Ceadurbar-atta-Cleath 057.31
cearc 011.27
cease 050.02 146.01 256.12 368.22 449.24 568.01
Cease 165.06 193.12 361.32
ceased 086.16 158.14 158.14 256.24 360.11
ceaselessly 108.25
ceasing 031.12 279.03
cecelticocommediant 033.03
cecialism 230.09
Cecilia's 424.07
cecilies 279.F03
Cecily 041.33
cedarous 470.15
Ceder 244.05
cederbalm 558.35
Cedric 016.34 348.18
Cee 048.01
ceen 549.20
ceilidhe 312.30
ceiling 362.24 559.26
Ceiling 104.13
ceilinged 032.36
ceive 237.19
Celana 351.30
cele 360.30
celeberrimates 535.33
celebesty 191.17
celebrand 484.13
celebrate 042.06 250.02
CelebrAted 421.21
celebrating 037.36
celebration 006.20
celebridging 305.08
celescalating 005.01
celestial 242.14 612.20
Celestial 298.L2
celestials 071.09 552.16
celestian 154.20
celestine 191.15 288.21
celestious 178.35
Celia 147.11
Celibacy 092.24
celibate 605.09
celibated 422.04
celibrate 600.35
celicolar 516.35
celiculation 135.28
cell 012.02 182.35 323.25
Cell 295.L1
cellar 209.30 544.23
cellaring 373.18
cellarmalt 021.35
Cellbridge 129.09
cellelleneteutoslavzendlatinsound-script 219.17
celluloid 534.25
celt 018.30
celtech 237.20
Celtiberian 078.25
celtslinger 520.22
celves 049.33

cement 004.26
cemented 059.24 221.27 587.18
CENOGENETIC 275.R1
Cenograph 488.24
cense 130.01
censered 440.11
censor 179.28 422.03 476.30
census 129.16 230.32
cent 529.02 538.09 538.09
centelinnates 345.28
centiblade 063.02
Centimachus' 100.16
centiments 239.03
Centinel 585.02
central 321.13 491.24
centre 564.10 594.22 605.19 606.03
Centres 303.L1
centries 497.09
centripetally 605.15
centripunts 541.01
centrum 294.09
cents 375.10
centuple 049.33
centuries 015.10 129.19 337.02 385.07 386.27 473.16
century 055.12 188.14 388.27 507.35 606.17
centy 240.28
Ceolleges 594.36
Ceolmore 041.33
cerberating 343.04
cerebralised 292.13
cerebrated 421.19
cerebrum 172.18
ceremonially 237.21
Ceremonialness 623.13
ceremonies 568.15
ceremony 109.19
Cerisia 128.14
Cernilius 228.34
Cerosia 128.14
cerpaintime 365.07
cert 407.14 587.03
certain 033.16 033.19 068.06 099.35 100.32 118.08 119.20 120.23 150.20 173.05 190.13 190.14 190.15 250.02 254.01 444.01 455.22 460.03 490.10 522.08 574.06 587.22 618.09
certainly 032.17 312.27 363.12 502.17 502.32 519.27 560.10 582.16 625.04
certainty 051.05 363.15
certayn 481.20
certes 057.30
certified 492.32
Certified 088.13 619.09
certify 083.13
certiorari 530.05
certitude 057.17
CERTITUDE 282.R4
certney 234.31
certo 263.28
Cerularius 573.04
cesarella 468.04
Cesarevitch 498.02
cess 029.28 263.29
cessed 229.22
cesses 155.30
cesspull 338.15
C'est 478.19
Ceteroom 105.04
cettehis 578.35
cf. 123.20 (confer)
cgar 341.17
Cha 054.12
chabelshoveller 013.08
Chacer 245.35
chach 333.35
chades 167.02
chafes 278.F2
chaff 037.35 266.24 517.13
chafferings 597.18
chaffing 095.04
chaffit 351.27
chaffs 371.12
chafingdish 607.09
chagreenold 186.08
Chaichairs 357.06
chain 066.14 254.09 278.F5 494.36 498.29 568.21 623.17
chained 548.07 618.24
chainganger's 126.15
chains 283.14
chair 028.20 061.05 198.24 287.29 338.01 394.01 455.23 469.35 492.20 559.08 618.25
Chair 559.08
chairful 515.36
chairmanlooking 416.05
chairs 043.01 045.29 200.03 362.26 453.13 562.20
Chaka 424.10
chal 332.14
chalce 613.27
chalice 044.03 110.35
chalished 461.35
chalix 552.36
chalk 200.16 220.11 529.02
chalked 030.04
chalkem 372.19
chalkfull 152.26
chalkin 428.03
chalking 027.05
challenge 081.25
challenge 346.34
challenged 067.20
Challenger's 501.11
Chalwador 189.14
chamba 198.11
chambadory 395.22
chamber 272.20 408.21 455.06 585.27
Chamber 559.01
chambercushy 556.32
chambered 073.29
chamberlain 129.25
chambermade 184.04
chambermate 461.24
chambers 045.30 094.25 395.10 451.32 456.19
Chambers 246.02
Chambers 105.04
chamber's 334.02
chambrett 548.08
chambrette 561.35
chambro 160.30
chameleon 590.07
chamermissies 075.08
champ 142.14 305.30
champ 162.11
Champ 119.32
champagne 462.09
champaign 162.08
Champaign 539.32
champain 540.05
champdamors 551.10
champed 115.05
Champelysied 607.14
champgnon 377.04
champion 214.27 254.06 384.23 398.05 473.13 578.12 582.26
Champius 395.35
champouree 236.15 236.15 236.16 236.17
champs 478.21
chance 004.08 082.33 085.08 149.27 184.05 212.05 269.07 318.36 357.24 438.07 438.11 443.05 480.20 501.34 518.20
Chance 065.16
chanced 039.22 363.22 487.13 589.26
chancedrifting 100.33
chancellory 308.03
chancerisk 582.04
chancers 238.26
chancery 091.31 423.14
chances 052.22 062.23 127.07 254.24
chancetrying 442.25
chancey 451.02
chanching 288.01
chandeleure 064.19
chandner's 542.33
chang 322.06 608.20
Chang 130.35
change 045.25 072.32 073.13 082.23 082.25 119.20 160.16 167.31 186.16 211.25 232.17 242.03 247.29 318.36 324.14 374.12 419.17 422.13 459.31 496.23 582.33 589.20 618.33
Change 625.07
changé 281.08
changeable 200.02 332.21 405.10
changeably 118.27
change-a-pennies 313.16
Changechild 481.02
changecors 344.10
changed 051.16 110.27 136.28 518.16 603.23 617.13
changelings 087.18
changeover 607.10
changers 022.18
changes 135.14 165.17 165.27 620.14
changeth 032.05 486.10
changez 203.11
changful 355.28
changing 029.28 062.02 090.05 118.23 177.07 189.03 253.06 394.03 551.32 626.35 626.35 627.01
Chang-li-meng 338.26
channel 595.05
channels 422.28 436.14 501.12
channon 451.14
chant 234.36 412.07
chanted 407.15
chantermale 594.31
chantied 044.05 350.32
chanting 178.16 184.24
chantreying 533.16
chants 279.F03
chanza 206.19
chaos 186.05 518.31
chaosfoedted 137.14

chaosmos 118.21
chap 004.25 020.06 028.03 028.03 028.25 049.14 092.30 125.07 135.28 227.09 425.34 434.02 477.17 608.20 609.36 620.22
chaparound 269.05
chapboucqs 206.12
Chapchopchap 304.F2
chape 297.F1
chapel 127.29 444.33 544.05
chapelgoer 587.36
chapelgoers 086.33
Chapelldiseut 236.20
Chapelle 290.02
chapellledeosy 396.31
chapelofeases 571.11
chapelry 528.06
chaperon 128.21
Chaperon 147.22
chapes 600.25
chapjappy 054.23
chaplain 533.08
Chaplain 039.08
chaplain's 166.14
chaplan 467.26
chaplet 265.14
chaplets 410.34 459.01
chapot 059.06
Chappielassies 607.15
chapplie 430.31
chappy 065.29 237.20
chaps 099.28 137.11 172.27 275.F4 333.24 523.25 529.05
chap's 040.28 093.10
chap's 383.14
chapstuck 035.36
chaptel 395.23
chapter 062.27 452.02 461.01
chapters 134.34
Chapters 156.06 156.06
Chapwellswendows 382.11
charabang 469.35
Charachthercuss 054.04
characktericksticks 149.22
character 084.21 306.F3 428.09 444.02 487.03
charactering 533.13
characteristically 298.20
Characteristics 072.12
characters 033.14 578.33
characticuls 617.14
chare 148.10 245.03
chareman 500.15
charge 113.22 138.33 159.32 255.11 406.22
charge 349.10
charged 014.18 615.07
chargehand 371.25
chargehard 034.08
chargeleyden 585.16
charger 535.09
charges 254.23 522.09
charging 153.14 524.22
charictures 302.31
charily 268.10
Charis 561.22
Charissima 561.22
charitable 178.25 192.09
charities 362.25 543.02
chariton 208.33
charity 075.19 115.10 193.27 251.08 417.29 434.03 448.22 503.20 519.28
Charity 461.07
Charlatan 037.19
charlattinas 059.12
Charles 291.F8
charley 494.15
Charley 065.16 252.28 419.35 443.18
Charley's 426.25
Charleys' 183.27
charlock 587.28
charlotte 504.28
Charlotte 051.35
charm 022.21 082.20 179.01 224.29 371.19 396.12
Charmadouiro 327.04
charmaunt 384.30
charme 348.25
charmed 382.02 549.30
charmeen 527.18
charmer 132.16 376.18 493.09
charmermaid 148.24
charmers 267.24 267.25
charmeuse 271.F5
Charmeuses 236.01
charmful 008.02
charmhim 288.10
charmian 020.03
charmig 458.17
charming 096.35 430.11 472.07 562.13 606.21
charmingly 013.06
charms 138.15 144.28 386.01
charnelcysts 613.20
charred 208.31
chars 544.10
chart 215.06 593.19
Chart 603.22
chartarums 566.15
charter 020.07 117.35 266.03
Charterhouse's 137.21
charties 551.32
chartula 287.21
chartularies 545.14
chary 434.03
chase 060.14 185.06 494.15
Chase 097.03
chased 394.07
chasing 417.29
chassetitties 093.19
chasta 147.24
chaste 115.20 227.33 227.33 350.17 414.28 606.01
chastemate 548.07
chastener 553.01
chastenot 246.36 247.26
chastisement 572.29
chastisements 573.29
chastity 440.32 572.31
chat 057.35 133.14 485.36 611.02
Chat 618.03
chatbags 064.35
chatchatchat 043.19
chateaubottled 382.03
chato 327.04
chats 274.08
chattahoochee 209.22
Chattaway 369.09
chattels 068.36 598.36
chattering 195.02 504.29 583.03
chatters 271.25
Chattertone 573.34
chattiry 324.26
chatty 076.27 523.27 528.31
Chatty 307.15
Chau 551.15
chauffed 551.03
chauk 542.34
chaunting 055.24
chavi 172.02
Chavvyout 245.35
chaw 045.29 045.29
chawchaw 036.02
chawclates 049.14
chawing 455.35
Chawleses 303.11
chawley 271.L4
chayney 213.05 371.12
chayr 530.11
chchch 394.30
che 284.01
cheadmilias 081.06
cheakinlevers 370.35
cheap 215.19 253.15 330.22 330.22 330.22 339.22 343.31 374.27 444.21 529.10 623.16
cheapened 163.27
cheapest 140.35
cheaply 495.04 589.17
Cheapner 029.18
cheapshein 387.05
cheat 278.02
Cheat 046.01
cheateary 343.32
cheats 394.18
cheayat 365.35
cheb 196.06
check 097.11 127.28 198.36 266.25 315.11
Check 332.36 559.22
checkenbrooth 243.13
checker 114.10
checking 485.36
checkinlossegg 129.14
checks 575.09
checkself 036.35
chee 038.16 053.36 166.31 221.08
Chee 053.36
Chee 106.19 106.19
cheeckchubby 461.24
cheeckin 205.18
cheef 198.12
cheek 027.05 057.28 122.34 153.28 161.11 185.13 268.F5 290.20 411.14 528.37 617.01
Cheek 066.17
cheekacheek 439.29
cheekadeekchimple 282.14
cheekars 332.08
cheekas 442.35
Cheekee's 155.35
cheekmee 205.31
cheekmole 242.31
cheeks 025.12 068.10 092.18 125.15 177.06 199.13 210.10 214.20 365.36 373.32 544.01 564.14 619.06 626.07
cheeks 340.04
Cheek's 140.30
cheekside 230.03
Cheekspeer 257.20
Cheels 106.19

Cheepalizzy's 111.06
cheeped 153.35
cheeping 200.08
cheeps 161.10
cheer 406.27 469.33 536.03
cheer 399.03
cheered 564.16
cheerfully 575.08
cheerfulness 551.21
cheeringly 324.08
cheerio 052.34 131.31
cheeriot 279.F32
cheeriubicundenances 382.02
cheers 053.36 494.26 512.23 542.06
Cheerup 469.10
cheerus 406.26
cheery 114.24 162.35
cheeryboyum 258.34
cheerycherrily 031.30
Cheeryman 516.03
chees 167.02
cheese 162.17 180.09 456.08
cheesechalk 233.35
cheesse 292.09
Cheesugh 163.10
cheesus 511.18
Cheeverstown 097.09
Cheevio 321.35
chef 236.27
chef's 463.34
cheic 205.30
chelet 117.11
Chelli 199.28
Chelly 484.33
Cheloven 339.04
Chelsies 587.26
chemical 616.08
chemicalled 621.27
chemicots 111.26
chemins 376.06
chemise 333.20
chemise 290.19
chemist 492.21
chemistry 306.14
chemney 364.27
chempel 026.17
chems 177.10 464.03
chenchen 329.10
chenlemagne 280.28
cheoilboys 543.09
Cheops 062.21
chepachap 237.15
chepelure 560.27
chepped 025.17
chepps 467.17
cheque 181.16 574.14 574.25
chequered 560.09
cherchant 568.27
Cherchons 064.28
chère 239.09
Chérie 239.25
cherierapest 508.23
cheriffs 006.17
cheriotiers 595.23
cherished 038.06 614.23
Cherna 537.24
cheroot 053.23
Cheroot 321.35
cherries 446.21
cherripickers 538.21
Cherry 009.13
cherrybum 065.28
cherryderry 058.36
cherrywhisks 436.22
cherrywickerkishabrack 495.23
cher's 213.14
cherub 027.05
cherubcake 175.29
cherubical 606.06
cherubs 469.34
cherubum 177.14
chesnut 453.16
chessganglions 571.36
chest 069.27 144.06 164.17 616.14
Chest 048.01
Chesterfield 553.19
chestfront 055.10
chesth 377.04
chesthouse 179.18
chestnote 363.09
chestnut's 341.31
chest-o-wars 133.17
chesty 333.35
Cheveluir 458.34
chew 278.03 512.31
chewable 406.33
chew-chin-grin 082.12
chewchow 474.10
chewed 025.17 115.05 416.22
chewer 231.17
chewing 045.29 205.18 494.36
chewly 162.05
chewn 456.21
chews 279.F07
cheyned 542.10
chez 244.12
chi 332.14
chiaroscuro 107.29
chic 538.33
Chic 527.17
Chichester 390.18
chichiu 209.23
chickchilds 244.10
Chickchilds 244.09
chicken 569.22
chickenestegg 081.23
chickenpox 045.29
chickens 148.13
chicken's 192.13
chickerow 425.19
chicking 313.22
chickle 028.25
chickled 212.33
chicks 020.25 446.10
Chickspeer's 145.24
chid 145.17
chidden 061.20
chief 042.27 088.02 099.24 237.20 326.09 380.12 463.32 494.27 495.29 545.09 555.17 564.15 566.12 574.19
Chief 546.33 546.33 546.34 546.34
chiefest 373.12
chiefly 052.34 547.04
Chiefly 440.21
Chiefoverseer 409.35
chiefs 475.12
chiefsmith 342.08
chieftain 310.32 362.05
chieftains 131.07
chieftaness 384.23
Chiel 490.06
chiffchaff 444.29
Chiggenchugger's 379.03
chigs 441.34
Chilblaimend 074.15
child 027.11 043.20 080.19 085.22 094.09 101.34 110.31 115.20 194.17 199.12 205.10 327.07 375.20 429.11 487.34 487.35 520.17 531.33 533.25 556.19 575.25 595.34 595.34 616.13 621.30 621.31 626.12
Child 059.03
Childaman 304.F2
Childared 480.20
childbearer 511.21
childe 166.14
Childe 423.08
childer 209.28 213.30 598.35
childergarten 253.31
Childeric 004.32
childerness 355.34
childers 598.36
Childers 481.22 535.34
childerun 386.30
childfather 234.11
childher 011.16 620.11
childhide 483.31
childhood 163.05 188.10
childhood's 227.34 483.05
childish 589.03
childishly 157.10 178.20
childlight 266.13
childlinen 198.36
childream's 219.05
children 047.13 076.01 132.08 258.27 258.29 258.31 285.F2 545.18 572.31
children 341.35
children's 545.17 545.17
Childs 246.21
child's 088.04 480.25 529.32
childsfather 015.08
Childsize 106.14
childspies 088.25
childsplay 501.11
childy 159.09
chilia 078.04
chiliad 015.05
chilidrin 498.33
chilikin 369.28
chilired 068.10
chill 213.23 259.05 355.34 462.06 580.23
chilldays 473.09
chilled 041.18 338.31 365.35 527.35
chills 158.26 608.16
chilly 040.13 415.28
chillybombom 552.29
chilterlings 243.32
chiltern 359.04
Chiltern 105.02
chiltren's 589.02
chim 598.30
chimant 569.11
Chimbers 032.16
chimbes 538.31
chimbley 345.26
chimbleys 250.06
chimbneys 380.17
chime 605.10
chimebells 371.12
chimed 058.14
Chimepiece 590.11

chimerahunter 107.14
chimers' 596.05
chimes 140.22 268.02 275.24 403.21
chimiche 417.31
chimista 233.30
Chimmuck 072.08
chimney's 190.27
Chimney's 141.20
Chimpden 046.02
Chimpden's 030.02
chimpney 029.05
chin 034.17 034.17 058.13 058.13 117.07 169.14
Chin 058.13 058.13
china 045.30 433.07
China 028.24
China 106.19
chinarpot 305.27
china's 583.18
chinatins 533.06
chinchin 034.17 131.34 485.36 585.08
Chinchin 304.F2
chinchinatibus 367.04
chinchinjoss 611.05
chine 435.27
chined 569.27
chineknees 461.24
ching 322.06 338.32 608.19
Ching 057.05
chingchong 299.F3
chink 311.26 465.28 484.16 486.11
Chink 465.28
chinkaminx 261.01
chinook's 212.33
Chinx 104.13
chiny 224.31
chip 020.05 083.10 110.26 146.35 240.23 416.26 566.03
chipper 300.19 467.31
chipperchapper 439.30
chipping 351.04
Chipping 209.36
chipps 371.11
chippy 621.15
chips 025.17
chir 209.36
chirography 482.17
chirp 146.35
chirped 532.20
Chirpings 098.17
chirps 175.27
chirpsies 359.18
Chirpy 477.15
Chirripa-Chirruta 204.12
chirrub 226.19
chirrup 146.35
chirrupeth 098.36
chirryboth 258.34
chirrywill 446.23
chirsines 207.12
chiseller 482.06
chisellers 043.05
Chistayas 539.01
chit 199.12
chithouse 057.34
chito 327.04
chiton 131.30
chitschats 494.25
chittering 215.31
chittinous 416.25
chiuff 239.29
chivalries 254.07
chivee 065.27
chivily 546.35
Chivitats 481.21
chivoo 065.27
chivvychace 335.10
Chivychas 030.14
chlamydophagian 227.36
chloereydes 035.02
chloes 236.01
Chlora 102.26
chloras 616.12
chlorid 613.26
cho 224.30
chocolat 013.09
chocolate 144.15 236.03 528.06
choculars 587.07
chogfulled 590.13
choice 126.18 161.16 184.11 246.17 384.24 427.32 432.36 522.09 522.15 563.02
choicest 039.34 140.35 596.07
choicey 200.08
choir 048.13
choirage 287.30
choirboys' 555.17
chokanchuckers 310.32
choke 079.11 193.27 319.31 397.23
Choke 500.17
choked 470.27
chokee 396.28
chokefull 494.36
choker 064.02 404.26
chokered 292.03
chokers 614.06
choker's 278.02
chokes 131.18
chokewill 266.25
cholaroguled 341.11
cholera 463.30
cholers 322.36
Cholk 319.10
chollar 022.34
Chollyman 539.32
cholonder 347.02
chomicalest 334.20
Chomp 102.16
chonchambre 182.09
chonks 603.20
choo 198.11 270.F2
choochoo 538.19
chooldrengs 343.11
choorch 067.13
choose 012.26 027.12 161.19 270.05 620.28
choosed 015.01
chooses 120.29
choosing 394.29
chop 190.04 208.03 467.14
chopes 553.10
Choplain 351.13
chopp 034.08
choppy 556.24 612.07
chops 045.29 406.04
Chops 106.32
chopstuck 036.16
chopwife 020.29
choquées 281.10
chor 234.36
choractoristic 334.07
chorale 222.05
chorams 343.30
chorecho 584.34
choree 584.34 585.03 585.04
choreographer 472.09
choreopiscopally 513.11
chores 068.01 586.08
chorias 349.05
chorico 585.04
chorines 468.35
Chorles 181.02
chorley 016.05
chorming 162.34
Chorney 351.13
choroh 585.04
chorous 417.36
chors 391.08
Chorsles 603.22
chort 541.04
chorus 048.14 178.16 266.15 430.18
Chorus 045.05 045.11 045.17 045.23 046.03 046.10 046.16 046.23 046.32 047.05 047.11 047.17 047.24 322.14
chorush 360.15
chorussed 044.05
choruysh 005.16
chory 265.F5
chosen 156.24 222.28 375.07
chosen's 252.23
choucolout 286.F5
choughs 449.19
Chours 236.12
chouse 432.36
chousen 551.36
chow 228.32 354.35
chowchow 612.14
chowdar 357.02
chp 227.09
chrest 596.06
Chrest 173.12
chrestend 312.32
Chrestien 245.28
Chriesty 111.14
chris 245.29
Chris 481.06
chrisan 326.15
chrism 289.03
Chrisman 480.15
chrisman's 455.27
chrismon 119.17
chrismy 578.04
Chris-na-Murty 472.15
Chrissman's 059.08
chrissormiss 006.15
christ 481.09
Christ 384.15 393.02 500.14 500.14 500.15 500.15
christchurch 082.19
Christcross 412.36
christen 419.22 433.35
christened 044.05 188.34
christener 605.06
christening 307.F7 387.24
Christi 398.31
christian 003.18 127.29 605.36
christianbrothers 301.F2
Christianier 053.08
christianismus 325.11 325.12
Christian's 419.19
christie 515.29
Christienmas 130.07
christies 086.23

Christie's 130.31
Christina 537.06
Christinette 280.22
christlikeness 033.29
christmas 186.35
Christmas 113.35 209.27 490.22 513.21 542.16 556.08
christmass 289.03
christmastyde 590.22
christmians 518.36
christous 552.28
Christpatrick's 026.22
Christ's 301.09 535.25
Christy 062.30 482.01 496.30
christymansboxer 142.11
Chromaticus 304.18
chrome 494.02
Chromean 339.09
chromes 477.26
chromitis 232.02
chromo 334.24
Chromophilomos 123.14
chromous 477.12
chroncher 254.07
chronic 150.07 241.07
chronicler 042.28
chronicles 240.36
chronic's 417.35
Chronides 231.23
chronology 358.06
chronometer 391.15
chronometrum 036.14
chronos 517.36
chry 535.03
Chrysalmas 416.26
chrysmed 138.25
chrysming 562.09
chrysolite 494.04
chrystal 319.16
chrystalisations 086.04
Chrystanthemlander 609.32
chthonic 261.18 450.18
chuam 482.09
chub 141.03
chubbs 371.11
chubby 474.15
Chubby 235.27
Chubgoodchob 357.03
chuch 533.23
chuchuffuous 131.34
chuck 085.08 364.34 579.20
chuckal 594.28
chucked 543.36
chucking 141.03 504.32
chuckinpucks 371.12
chuckle 028.26
chuckler 110.07
chuckles 212.34
chucklesome 538.19
chucklings 370.06
chucks 212.31 405.25
Chudley 088.24
Chuff 205.22 225.30
CHUFF 220.11
Chuffchuff's 225.30
chuffeur 235.28
Chuffs 235.27
Chuffy 222.22
Chuffy's 226.19
chugged 122.26
chum 085.08 191.18
chumbers 354.01
chumming 280.22 280.25 435.34
chummy 466.28
Chummy 210.08
chump 142.05 231.17 261.14
Chump 560.16
chumps 129.01
Chung 374.34
chunk 311.26 484.15
church 035.32 147.16 198.32 264.31 403.21 463.05 495.10 574.07 603.30 606.08 621.34
Church 036.29 044.06 301.09
churchal 587.16
churchclose 102.14
churchdome 147.26
churchees 312.32
churchen 593.16
churcher 619.04
churches 488.23 525.17 569.12
Churches 307.18
churchman 234.11
churchmode 409.11
churchprince 416.13
church's 137.10
churchwarden 544.08
churchyard 068.08 221.15 467.24
churl 168.11
churls 398.03
churneroil 390.02
churning 140.34 213.23
Churopodvas 343.34
churpelizod 096.08
churring 474.17
Churstry's 601.25
chuse 522.01
chute 368.08
chuthor 300.19
chuthoring 181.12
chuting 220.15
chutney 456.20
Chutney 405.26
chymerical 067.08
chyst 596.28
ci 456.08
Ciaho 172.02
Cian 078.18
ciappacioppachew 233.33
Ciardeclan 484.23
cicada 416.25
ciccalick 456.08
Cicely 224.21
Cicilian 354.14
cicles 134.16
ciders 058.15
cieclest 245.21
ciel 184.28
ciello 043.32
cielung 155.24
Ciesa 472.08
cif 327.04
Cigalette 563.28
cigals 417.13
cigar 127.21 127.23
Cigar 501.08
cigare 536.17
cigarette 443.31
cigolo 146.35
Ciliegia 207.12
ciltilla 194.22
cimadoro 263.F3
Cimmerian 504.07
Cincinnati 285.L1
Cincinnatis 456.08
Cincinnatus 030.13 139.05
Cincinnatus 307.L1
cinder 280.21
Cinderella 440.27
cinderenda 331.26
cinders 566.17
cindery 551.09
Cinderynelly 224.30
cinemen 006.18
cinerary 077.29
cineres 128.35
cinnabar 030.24
cinnamon 097.17 184.20 419.21 456.20
cinnamondhued 288.F5
cinsero 182.09
cintrum 183.29
Ciondolone's 161.03
cipher 248.35
Circas 600.29
circiter 077.06
circle 033.11 098.19 362.01 453.07 484.31 594.22
Circle 545.35
circles 191.15 280.15 320.35
circling 080.08 186.12 292.02 383.20
Circos 132.01
circuiting 476.13
circuitise 552.08
circuits 442.07
circular 219.23 321.13 427.07
circulated 079.04
circulating 085.07 410.07 440.15 574.27
circulatio 427.08
circulation 151.16 159.20 356.28 585.03
circuls 480.24
circulums 553.30
circuly 505.13
circumassembled 498.27
circumcentric 310.07
circumcised 483.33
circumcivicise 446.35
circumconversioning 512.16
circumdeditioned 484.24
circumference 541.02
circumflexuous 124.06
circumflicksrent 298.15
circumfluent 605.19
circumformation 599.17
circuminiuminluminatedhave 278.04
circuminsistence 354.14
circumpictified 230.32
circumscript 294.10
Circumspection 307.13
circumspicious 433.34
circumstance 055.20
circumstances 034.27 113.24
circumstancias 350.16
Circumstantial 307.24
circumstantiating 109.14
circumvallator 139.18
circumveiloped 244.15
circus 529.34
Circus 307.08 469.16 560.03
circusalley 532.32
circusdances 342.12
circuses 005.33
circusfix 102.13
circuts 460.09
cirque 079.01
cirrchus 375.28

Cis 267.L1
Cisamis 240.06
cissies 234.14
cissiest 561.16
cisternbrothelly 436.14
cit 012.02 205.24 332.33
citadear 062.01
citch 461.01
citchin 009.31
citchincarry 494.34
cited 031.21
cites 574.04
citherers 006.17
citherior 158.11
citie 017.21 075.14
cities 448.12
citing 524.12
Citizen 338.04 447.22
citizens 076.09 288.F5
citrawn 303.21
citron 474.03
Citronelle 223.06
citronnades 058.15
citta 098.29
città 228.23
cittas 532.06
citters 012.02
citting 603.23
city 061.36 079.15 116.13 127.20 140.08 155.07 181.07 181.29 264.19 277.21 318.25 318.26 364.22 412.35 437.06 481.16 488.21 530.07 530.31 539.25 540.04 545.21 545.21 559.01 575.20 606.19 619.20
City 015.08 306.16 420.33 482.09 553.09
citye 372.08 601.05
city's 535.07
ciudad 435.01
civic 022.34
civicised 550.23
civicity 277.08
civics 221.04
civil 014.24 109.10 193.12 426.24 444.23 574.08
Civil 306.20
civiles 353.04
civilian 140.06 618.26
civilisation 081.15 438.25
Civilisation 420.32
civilisations 281.10
civilised 138.06
civille 320.07
civil-to-civil 283.16
Civis 215.27
civvy 208.20
Ciwareke 602.21
cla 044.19
C. L. A. 061.10 (Criminal Law Amendment)
clackdish 210.22
clad 055.25 437.36 503.36 532.26
cladagain 055.26
claddagh 497.33
Claddagh 464.24
claddaghs 606.32
cladstone 031.32
Claffey's 625.09
claim 358.09 577.16
claimed 098.19
claimhis 353.17
claiming 538.26 581.13
claims 573.10 614.12
clairaudience 533.31
claire 479.06
claire's 290.21
clam 362.02 540.13
Clam 515.03
clamast 243.29
clamatising 371.24
clambake 453.06
clamour 110.36
clan 070.14 391.04
Clan 500.02
clanagirls 601.13
Clancarbry 144.05
Clancartys 027.25
Clancy'll 046.07
clandestinely 436.11 572.33
Clandibblon 362.02
clandoilskins 370.35
Clandorf 071.33
Clane 212.25 381.06 625.17
Clane's 274.29
clanetourf 086.10
clang 339.22 518.35
clangalied 601.20
clankatachankata 024.23
clanked 152.33
Clanruckard 376.32
clansakiltic 326.09
clansdestinies 497.04
clap 065.34 090.28 093.10 117.05
Clap 248.08 453.36 622.31
Clap 104.23
clapped 376.17
clapperclaws 491.07
clappercoupling 614.30
clapping 507.07
clapplaud 032.27
claps 538.14
claptrap 084.34
Clara 572.36
claractinism 611.31
clare 488.25
Clare 226.10 381.22
Clarence's 209.07
clarenx 489.17
claret 443.24 544.23
clarety 162.30
claribel 232.16
clarience 266.12
clarify 594.12
Clarinda's 601.22
clark 130.11
Clarke 558.20
Clarksome 625.03
clash 627.31
clashcloshant 552.24
clashes 004.01
clashing 084.28
clasp 174.09 272.09 464.24 468.21 482.23 580.17
clasped 249.21
claspers 292.10
class 049.29 090.17 099.32 111.23 237.32 279.F05 431.34 475.03 489.19 494.20 575.05 587.17
classbirds 147.07
classes 076.06 388.35 427.26 526.36
classic 039.05 481.28
classically 241.12
classics 165.34
classicum 185.18
classies 357.16
classified 160.02
classroom 159.22
classy 404.17 477.29
Clatchka 623.22
claub 141.31
claud 126.14 509.30
claudesdales 553.35
Claudian 121.01
claudication 444.03
Claus 209.23 307.16
clause 558.16
clauses 269.29
Clausetter's 141.19
Clauthes 434.23
clav 038.12
clavicures 011.20
claw 038.12 311.10 505.03
clawhammers 033.09
claxonise 255.07
clay 007.30 024.31 127.26 136.33 184.12 186.23 255.04 372.26 514.07
Clay 071.17
clayblade 222.29
claybook 018.17
Clayed 546.01
claylayers 165.26
claymen 475.18
claypot 117.18
clayroses 498.23
Clays 468.33
Clay's 278.F7
cleah 138.10
clean 024.26 065.20 071.10 160.01 177.14 188.06 196.17 240.21 274.29 408.03 433.25 447.02 460.02 464.09 484.02 516.12 533.13
clean 342.26
Clean 376.22 377.21 614.12
cleaned 079.36 580.35
Cleaned 509.36
cleaner 142.09 150.06 252.17
Cleaner 211.19
cleaners 309.21
cleanliving 532.14 532.16
cleanlooking 442.02
cleanly 162.34
cleanminded 033.29
cleans 544.21
cleansers 362.26
cleansing 252.01
cleantarriffs 539.28
cleanup 144.04
cleany 250.11
clear 069.23 099.23 115.06 119.05 124.22 190.27 457.33 469.10 501.25 546.28 571.02 571.04 595.14
Clear 016.07 501.13 580.34
clearance 431.22
cleared 128.31 289.F1
Clearer 258.20
clearly 034.35 034.35 035.20 522.05 602.09
Clearly 533.21
clearness 132.31
clearobscure 247.34
Cleaver 254.02

cleavunto 548.09
clect 059.34
clee 478.21
Cleethabala 600.10
Cleftfoot 175.17
cleftoft 394.18
clement 154.20
clenching 441.26
clene 548.15
Cleopater's 104.20
cleopatrician 166.34
cleped 537.22
clere 014.28
clergical 338.11
clergimanths 421.34
clergy 058.01 492.32
clergyman 520.11
clergymen 544.15
cleric 485.36
clerical 190.15 419.34 617.30
clericalease 057.25
cleric's 146.10
clericy 424.03
clerk 027.17 270.06 599.03 618.14
clerking 425.17
clerks 015.15
clerricals 302.06
Clery 520.03 520.15
cleryng's 459.08
Clesiastes 139.26
cleur 092.18
clever 012.30 039.08 225.03 294.15 517.03
cleverly 035.20 123.26
cley 475.35
click 296.12 457.22 468.14 517.25
clickclack 469.10
clicking 207.05 464.18
clickings 309.21
client 534.16 574.23
Clifden 407.20
cliff 241.06
cliffed 505.18
cliffs 601.10
cliffscaur 577.17
Clifftop 315.32
climactogram 165.23
climate 173.23 404.21
Climate 141.36
climatitis 059.13
climax 032.34 471.10
climb 059.34 152.02
climbacks 222.11
climbed 159.08
climber 506.02
climbing 059.02 086.08 318.03 470.05 504.27
climbs 377.11
climes 076.03 474.22
cling 119.03 152.02 519.01
clingarounds 261.F1
clingleclangle 456.22
clings 043.19 043.19 043.19 628.07
clink 118.05
clinkars 360.12
clinked 102.14
clinkers 029.08
clinking 152.33
Cliopatria 271.L2
Cliopatrick 091.06
Clio's 254.07
clip 044.19 395.28
clipperbuilt 394.17
clipperclappers 614.13
clipperclipperclipper-clipper 088.10
clippings 135.34 183.29 254.07
cliptbuss 291.14
clister 406.19
clittering 005.03
Clive 219.11
cllng 502.11 (calling)
Clo 453.15
cloack 243.26
Cloack 211.01
cloak 099.12 130.06 135.21 200.15 329.27
cloaked 185.09
cloaks 033.11
cloakses 322.12
cloasts 510.29
Cloaxity 179.14
clobber 039.23
clock 027.34 033.11 035.18 035.19 037.07 257.09 457.22 567.17
clocka 502.04
clockback 579.05
clocks 077.11
clocks 353.30
clocksure 551.01
Clod 070.34 457.11
clodded 069.29
clods 151.17
Clodshoppers 105.28
cloes 053.12
cloever 508.33
Clogan 593.14
clogh 213.16
clogs 208.06 329.24 410.13
cloister 026.13 155.25 467.24 571.13
cloitered 231.08
cloke 276.12
clomb 475.18 506.02
clompturf 017.09
Clonakilty 057.09
Clondalkin 201.26
clonk 328.11 599.04
Clonliffe 210.18
clonmellian 443.10
Clontalk 420.30
Clontarf 307.05 324.20 376.08 497.20
Clontarf 201.19
clontarfminded 099.32
clookey 557.10
Cloon's 616.21
cloose 366.33
clooshed 582.07
cloover 478.25
clop 044.19
Clopatrick's 508.23
clopped 023.03 333.07 333.07 333.07
clops 476.16
Cloran 040.16 212.03
clorks 510.21
close 068.08 073.24 085.04 097.14 109.21 111.17 181.24 404.02 407.34 413.33 432.22 451.08 468.24 531.27 558.01 571.16 580.16 604.07 616.34 621.29
Close 147.29 201.28 439.33 442.36 614.13
closechop 311.24
closed 098.19 107.28 129.20 133.19 258.29
Closed 621.03
closehended 438.01
closely 163.32 166.20 174.24 440.34
closer 144.13 429.10
Closer 107.23
closes 552.17 552.18
closest 464.03
closet 184.33 445.05 543.25 544.01 545.02
Closet 421.03
closeth 020.17
closets 068.05
Closeup 559.19 559.29
closing 255.07 474.08 507.06
Closure 585.27
cloth 021.13 038.24 362.32 377.29 503.01 605.10
Cloth 141.30 317.11
Clothea 528.03
clothed 194.15 586.04 601.02
clothes 070.20 086.34 132.11 166.25 213.20 226.11 263.F4 279.F37 333.24 483.34 508.04 620.21
clotheshorse 522.16
clothespeg 208.22
clothiering 109.31
clothildies 325.28
clothing 109.10 109.23 448.13 493.19 539.16 544.32
clothnails 283.18
cloths 560.05
clothse 148.23 311.28
clothyheaded 152.09
clots 186.23 397.18 489.19
clottering 005.03 621.16
clou 528.14
cloud 048.05 127.26 178.31 189.33 220.09 256.33 281.15 541.07 546.14 588.22 593.19 599.30 599.30 615.22 627.09
Cloud 082.20 546.34 597.31
cloudberry 430.25
clouded 568.19
cloudhued 043.20
Cloudia 568.10
cloudious 581.23
cloudletlitter 073.29
clouds 007.36 029.11 324.30 344.23 358.14 407.15 425.36 453.30 615.17
cloudscrums 449.36
cloudsing 390.06
cloudweed 013.23
cloudy 159.09 236.22
cloudy 201.05
Cloudy 070.17 500.19
cloudyphiz 051.01
Clouonaskieym's 601.25
clout 607.32
clouth 320.17
clouthses 375.29
clouts 138.32 279.F29
clove 115.05

clover 080.03 139.31 145.13 210.26 372.26 451.21
cloverfields 043.02
clovery 110.04
cloves 175.30 456.20 526.27
clown 315.31
clowns 345.05
clownsillies 537.35
Clowntalkin 414.04
clownturkish 051.27
club 063.34 376.27 514.09 529.33 572.06
Club 092.25 219.03
clubmoss 550.21
clubpubber 594.18
clubs 134.07 222.29 405.25 497.32 510.21
Clubs 307.01
clubsessel 559.06
cluck 237.34 296.12
cluckclock 531.24
clucken 371.04
cluckers 273.F3
clue 124.06 311.10 528.12
cluekey 100.29
clues 062.03
cluft 229.23
Clummensy 344.30
clump 404.10
Clump 409.24
clumpstump 544.09
Clumpthump 385.15
Clunkthurf 388.17
clup 023.05
cluse 165.04
Cluse 528.22 602.24
cluster 249.09
clustered 498.31
clutch 192.24 225.29 228.35
clutcharm 186.35
clutches 477.26
clutchless 609.01
cluttering 621.15
clyding 202.12
Cnut 139.05
Co 497.26 518.16 518.29 557.01 (Company)
Co. 261.F2 318.28 (Company)
coaccoackey 516.20
coach 143.01 228.17 468.02 589.15
Coach 079.25 461.30
Coach 359.24
coached 287.29
coachers 284.F3
coacher's 011.17
coaches 045.14
coaching 476.24 565.33
Coachmaher 221.23
Coachyard 213.01
coaculates 349.17
co-affianced 061.19
coagulation 557.35
coal 068.08 127.08 232.01 244.17 289.17 316.14
Coalcutter 492.15
coald 187.19 365.13
coalding 596.32
coalesce 107.29
COALESCING 279.R1
coalhole 194.18 434.09
Coalmansbell 278.11
Coalprince 139.35
coals 447.05 604.35
Coal's 026.32
coant 408.35
Coarbs 219.11
coarse 116.35 161.35 172.15 586.02
coarsehair 323.03
coarser 089.11
coast 068.11 138.21 245.07 316.06 317.35 388.13 601.11
coastal 099.10
coastguard 232.30
coasting 215.02
coastmap 287.14
coasts 116.14
coat 005.34 097.12 149.26 180.10 192.11 208.20 220.27 428.09 456.12 485.02 507.06
coataways 548.16
coate 322.14
coathemmed 320.14
Coathes 325.26
coatings 349.16
coatmawther 146.05
coats 051.12 447.27 579.34
coat's 411.31
coatschemes 364.05
coatsleeves 343.13
coax 392.10
Coax 271.24 472.06
coaxes 509.20
coaxfonder 328.04
coaxing 512.09 582.03
coaxyorum 241.02
cobbeler 265.12
cobbler 357.19
Cobbler 060.29
cobbler's 214.02
cobbles 207.05 315.33 565.35
cobbleway 178.10
cobbold 606.18
Cobra 271.24 370.07
cobs 613.06
cobsmoking 586.01
cobwebbed 544.23
cobwebcrusted 038.07
cobwebs 214.16
Coccola 382.05
Coccolanius 118.13
coccyx 084.11
cochineal 235.35
cock 026.05 207.15 363.03 379.23 464.27 473.22 482.27 504.34 516.06 519.08 584.25
cock 383.10
Cock 039.36 053.28
Cock 104.22 440.20
cockaded 050.26
cockaleak 058.25
cockaleekie 210.08
Cockalooralooraloomenos 615.08
Cockardes 348.35
cockchafers 435.35
cockcock 192.21
cocke 362.16
cocked 012.17 180.08 184.17 205.36 437.26
cockeedoodle 244.33
cocker 030.19 232.27
COCKER 303.R1
Cocker's 537.36
cockful 450.27
cocking 471.18
cockle 199.31 249.01
cocklehat 041.02
cockles 012.10
cocklesent 321.15
cocklesong 390.24
cocklyhearted 608.18
cockney 042.27
cockneze 102.13
cockofthewalking 086.25
Cockotte 239.23
Cockpit 427.34
Cockran 137.08
cocks 088.06 276.18 509.20
cock's 035.19 113.12
Cock's 071.27
cockshock 353.21
cockshot 524.34
Cockshott 524.14 524.16
cockshy 234.04
cockshyshooter's 056.04
Cocksnark 353.11
Cockspur 124.17
cockspurt 050.03
cocksure 459.25
Cocksure 146.10
cocktails 436.30
Cockywocky 612.12
cocoa 073.05 128.24 538.04
Cocoa 467.13
cocoahouse 042.24
cococancancacacanotioun 354.21
Cococream 236.04
cocoincidences 597.01
co-comeraid 036.20
cocommend 356.27
cocomoss 409.12
Cocoree 584.30
Cocorico 584.27
cocottch 439.04
cocquette 548.22
coctable 083.15
cocto 185.24
cod 046.22 046.23 577.09 587.02
Cod 054.20 121.34 313.08
C. O. D. 102.34 (Cash on Delivery)
coda 466.20
codant 349.35
Codde 536.33
coddeau 015.18
codding 467.26
coddlam 577.29
coddle 271.14
coddled 192.07
coddlelecherskithers' 323.18
coddlepot 593.23
coddlin 499.20
coddling 091.22
code 014.21 213.28 324.21
coded 482.35
codes 614.32
code's 364.01
codestruces 108.12
codex 397.30
Codex 185.03
codfisck 198.09
codgers 214.33
codhead's 233.16
Codinhand 467.13
Codling 145.10
codliverside 563.01
codnops 356.07

codroy 208.20
cods 579.21
cods' 427.20
coeds 561.04
Co-Education 307.03
Coeli 159.01
coelicola 237.12
coelo 150.18
Coemghem 603.34
Coemghen 602.09
coerce 410.02
coerogenal 616.20
coersion 378.27
coexes 041.15
coexistent 526.12
coextensive 356.28
Coffee 043.08
coffin 056.19 066.28 076.11 089.23 231.14
coffinnail 115.05
coffins 077.28 595.15
cog 304.31 464.04
Cog 440.28
Cogan 516.20
cogged 049.32
cogitabundantly 088.07
coglionial 488.31
cognac 083.36
cognance 599.01
cognates 115.33
cognisances 575.30
cognitively 088.07
cogodparents 189.01
cohabit 624.08
cohabitation 550.30
Cohabited 421.08
cohalething 029.16
cohlorine 359.10
Cohortyard 455.01
coif 250.13 556.04
coif 342.11
coiffs 548.22
coiffure 304.20
coifs 204.29 397.28
coign 566.23
coignings 118.36
coil 331.23 393.08 433.28 566.19
Coil 360.14
coiled 057.12 506.06
coils 206.30 365.32
coin 127.14 450.35 574.30
coincidance 049.36
coincident 060.23
coincidental 109.28
coined 102.27 358.10
coining 338.23
coits 572.24
coke 089.18 319.31
cokeblack 447.05
coked 359.09
Cokenhape 008.17
Cokerycokes 232.01
col 042.18 281.19 348.01
colander 432.36 513.12
cold 021.11 042.36 061.17 081.13 110.25 110.33 131.05 145.09 149.04 158.33 169.19 176.24 213.14 214.26 219.18 347.24 369.14 374.32 397.15 405.35 406.18 415.29 441.18 451.04 458.12 478.32 502.18 503.24 525.03 571.15 579.06 595.13 628.01 628.01 628.02
cold 399.12
Cold 188.26
coldblood 171.32
coldcream 527.13
colder 040.20
coldfashion 227.08
coldness 506.20
Coldours 250.17
coldpalled 506.09
coldporters 221.03
colds 151.24
Cold's 597.24
coldspell's 343.08
Coldstream 058.25
coldstreams 526.29
coldtbrundt 318.31
Cole 328.24 619.28
Coleman 048.12
coleopter 546.07
Coleraine 210.33
Coll 044.13 433.16
collage 279.F14
collapsed 176.34
collar 137.20 292.29 377.08 404.19 428.06 443.26 527.30 559.09 619.35
collarbow 381.13
collared 256.02
collarette 040.08
collars 183.33 567.26
Collars 214.29
collarwork 189.22
collaspsed 426.33
collateral 031.35
collation 059.19 405.32
collaughsed 580.07
colleagues 189.35
Colleagues 106.35
collect 394.09 456.29 470.24
collected 529.20 605.30
collecting 375.30
collecting 341.33
Collecting 307.25
collection 155.35
collection 350.07
collectium 153.30
collective 585.28
COLLECTIVE 268.R1
collector 192.05
collector's 099.11
collects 544.24
colleen 101.17 384.21 433.29 438.34
colleenbawl 039.23
Colleenkiller's 409.28
college 146.20 438.32 450.15
College 386.23 390.18
colleges 385.13 386.23 387.07 389.04 389.06
Colleges 388.26
collegians 385.08 388.35
collegions 228.32
collegtium 550.06
collemullas 319.08
collera 211.01
colles 468.11
Collesons 129.35
Colley 065.04
colliberated 342.34
collidabanter 082.15
Collide 433.32
collideorscape 143.28
collie 468.33
colliens 153.04
collier 343.02
Colliguchuna 346.15
Collin 203.12
colline 224.11
collines 012.21
Collinses 508.32
collion 438.33
Collis 256.25
collision 071.08
collispendent 602.20
Collopys 457.02
Collosul 241.08
colluction 162.13
collude 433.33
colluded 332.25
collupsus 005.27
colmans 443.27
Colo 204.33
colombinas 527.26
colombinations 361.01
Colombo 129.31
colombophile 358.12
colonel 466.36 535.36
Colonel 099.32
colonial 212.20 544.33
colonies 393.14
colophon 123.05
coloratura 226.30
coloraturas 466.24
Colores 063.13
colori 178.24
coloribus 611.23
colories 365.36
coloroform 158.10
colossets 553.10
Colossus 132.27
coloumba 549.14
colour 038.17 089.33 109.26 177.07 230.01 248.36 256.10 318.03 329.28 458.33 561.23 596.27 611.34
Colour 610.34
coloured 120.06 147.33 604.14
colours 081.19 182.07 187.33 205.06 224.26 360.20 481.30 557.20 587.21 590.08
Colours 176.10 626.17
colp 238.21 238.21 238.21
Colpa 412.29
colpo 165.02 455.27
Colporal 346.35
colt 039.07 190.24 194.29 289.F5 323.22 352.09 410.14
Colt 084.24
Colt's 534.08
coluber 157.01
Columb 496.30
Columbarium 049.10
Columbia 548.02
Columbian 433.18
columbillas 430.36
Columbkisses 105.32
Columbsisle 463.31
columbuses 409.15
Columcellas 615.02
Columelle 281.05
columitas 119.11
Columkiller 122.26
column 068.35
Column 179.13

columna 131.30
columnkill 347.21
Colunnfiller 324.26
Coma 395.08
comaleon 136.27
comb 025.06 458.35
Comb 409.14
combarative 140.33
combat 036.21 202.14 388.24
610.25 610.26
combatants 099.29
combed 190.29 199.06
combies 200.35
combinaisies 284.12
combination 067.08
combinations 034.23 616.08
combined 408.05 435.23
combinedly 235.02
combing 065.10
combing 341.22
combitsch 141.23
combled 117.29
combly 550.20
Combria 327.21
combrune 352.22
combs 238.33
combuccinate 156.12
comburenda 232.03
combustion 604.18
comdoom 613.03
come 004.17 011.26 012.14
021.14 021.23 021.34 022.10
026.27 038.22 039.15 039.20
049.33 051.19 061.31 067.01
068.13 069.12 070.34 073.05
078.16 091.15 124.36 132.08
134.13 136.07 138.03 138.30
138.30 158.16 159.11 160.25
164.13 166.34 172.06 187.32
192.20 194.20 202.16 204.35
205.04 213.31 215.03 227.15
228.08 233.30 234.36 236.12
236.26 236.29 239.11 240.14
242.30 243.01 244.32 250.16
253.17 254.21 256.14 258.03
262.05 263.F2 272.07 272.08
274.F1 290.25 290.25 293.09
312.01 322.01 324.10 329.01
331.36 346.30 347.16 347.26
348.09 351.36 358.31 371.36
377.10 379.22 382.28 388.22
389.21 392.33 393.27 393.27
393.28 393.32 415.08 415.30
416.31 424.24 442.11 446.13
446.18 446.21 446.21 446.27
448.31 451.08 454.34 455.16
459.01 461.25 466.27 468.22
473.16 477.15 478.06 478.22
480.09 496.11 516.03 527.10
529.17 536.35 539.08 545.13
550.12 560.33 561.14 562.19
566.25 567.15 567.21 568.01
570.10 577.19 583.20 585.15
585.15 587.35 594.17 597.25
598.10 605.05 606.29 613.09
615.09 615.16 618.12 619.35
621.32 623.10 625.14 625.19
627.05 627.13 628.10
come 040.06 350.01 350.05
399.01 399.03 399.27 418.31
Come 011.16 016.04 064.30
144.18 193.12 252.04 257.13
279.F01 284.F3 320.24 339.26
403.17 442.33 446.34 465.06
469.12 472.06 485.15 510.14
510.16 515.36 521.10 527.04
585.14 595.18 608.35 620.10
621.03 621.20
Come 071.29 176.05
COME 305.R1
Comeallyedimseldamsels 432.21
comeallyoum 295.12
comeallyous 334.17
comeback 060.13 510.27
Comeday 005.10
comedet 163.03
comedy 283.07
comeether 325.30
comefeast 147.16
comeho 244.09
Comehome 244.10
comeing 594.02
Come-Inn 512.34
comeliewithhers 143.16
comely 015.14 158.33 446.10
comeplay 484.18
comepression 115.24
comepull 552.10
comepulsing 434.28
comequeers 357.08
comer 311.11 311.13
comes 011.03 011.09 023.16
088.28 100.11 113.35
128.24 148.02 162.04
185.28 190.02 201.25
231.26 237.34 244.03
246.01 260.04 269.02
298.21 328.13 328.28
337.12 356.10 360.26
361.03 364.09 369.33
409.29 473.05 537.34
602.31 606.28
Comes 031.33 032.18 289.29
comeseekwenchers 284.23
comesend 326.28
comesilencers 143.16
comest 026.20
comestabulish 429.19
Comestipple 015.35
Comestowntonobble 074.11
comet 054.08
cometh 143.01 224.25 265.07
287.07 328.33
comethers 135.05
comets 100.33
comet's 065.10
cometshair 475.15
comeundermends 326.02
comf 136.32
comfany 230.20
comfirts 521.01
comfoderacies 349.34
comfort 142.20 230.07
comfortable 540.04 543.26
comfortably 166.33
comforter 619.36
comfortism 268.29
Comforts 437.22
comfortumble 417.14
comfreshenall 619.15
comfy 523.27
comfytousness 620.06
comic 127.24 286.08 440.06
537.33
comicalbottomed 110.26
comicsongbook 380.24
cominations 351.26
coming 024.36 026.20 027.12
058.33 122.20 132.35
137.20 238.07 242.09
246.11 248.25 249.19
253.14 256.18 257.03
277.20 308.21 323.11
323.35 333.13 392.03
409.36 445.10 446.13
448.15 457.16 462.32
493.34 508.09 543.35
578.32 588.21 598.10
614.02 615.35 618.35
623.30 624.06 627.03
Coming 628.13
Cominghome 388.13
comings 595.16 599.29
comings 346.04
Comither 325.13
comm 132.36
command 032.30 032.36 174.11
545.15
commandant 609.28
commanded 545.15
commandeering 555.16
commander 612.05
commanding 248.31 564.06
commandment 062.12
commandments 181.31 432.26
commando 350.19
commands 127.30
commas 108.34
comme 281.04 281.12
Comme 420.12 420.13
commen 617.21
commence 266.24 414.26 566.30
commencement 266.24
commendable 085.12
commended 304.10
commender 034.05
commendmant 615.32
comment 521.23
Comments 261.F2
Commerces 420.20
commercial 433.17 572.30 589.10
commercially 054.26
commercio's 264.01
commet 177.26
commeylad 343.08
comminates 573.23
commind 552.24
comming 481.12
comminxed 130.11
commission 147.06 426.02
commissioners 448.20
commit 357.22 435.36 507.16
587.22
commit 176.14
Commit 579.13
commited 181.30
committal 479.20
Committalman 529.08
committe 395.12
committed 004.21 504.11 520.18
572.22 573.03
committee 034.04 616.18
committees 076.15 122.27
committled 428.07
commix 433.23
commodity 354.21
commodius 003.02
Commodore 093.06
Commodus 157.26

common 039.31 051.21 062.19 160.13 178.13 186.05 256.28 292.28 315.34 432.36 503.04 523.36 558.13 562.12 574.09
common 341.25
Common 124.17 214.13 372.17 385.05
Common 106.29
commoner 120.08 224.24 224.32
Commoner 072.12
commonest 050.36 573.35
COMMONEST 286.R2
commonface 159.15
Commong 478.23
commoniser 132.19
commonknounest 269.26
commononguardiant 151.20
commonorrong 098.10
commonplace 052.10
commonpleas 422.29
commons 091.08
Commons 161.27
commontoryism 162.06
commonturn 354.19
commoted 172.31
commotion 436.36
Commudicate 536.04
commulion 380.10
commune 029.30 539.23
communial 600.34
communic 385.12
communicake 239.01
communicanting 498.21
COMMUNICATED 172.10
Communicator 535.36
communion 345.27
communionism 035.28
communionistically 453.32
community 222.04 397.10
commutative 036.32
commuted 434.34
Como 154.27
Comong 396.06
comp 348.02
companies 376.30
companion 082.23
companion 201.08
companionate 192.28
companions 044.03 157.14 255.32 498.16
companionship 545.07
company 023.17 026.21 046.08 122.30 369.23 436.16 437.28 450.08 454.01 510.17 584.32 616.15
Company 141.20 495.11 529.13 576.03
companykeeper 438.30
comparative 114.09 362.30
Compare 307.19 447.19
compared 164.29 455.25
comparison 163.26
comparisoning 059.10
compartments 451.32
compass 025.33 057.02
compasses 287.11
Compasses 275.16
Compassionate 052.13
compatriate 602.34
compeer 337.36
compellably 529.06
compelled 071.06
compels 033.33
compensation 369.06 442.29
competence 551.21
competition 166.13
competitioning 356.07
compiled 071.04
COMPITA 305.R1
complacent 057.22
complain 163.10
complaining 407.34 530.04
complaint 448.09 618.31
complaisance 532.26
comple 553.16
compleasely 232.20
compleat 296.23
compleet 617.01
complement 333.09 516.33
complementary 227.21 248.03 487.03
complet 495.29
completamentarily 612.21
complete 165.19 302.19 413.28 443.17 557.34 616.14
completed 161.34
completely 033.07 057.21 387.27 387.29
completing 446.29
completion 368.23 407.07
complex 128.36 581.29
complexe 291.F8
complexion 090.34 241.19 398.11 423.29
complexious 421.34
complexus 114.33
complicates 166.35
complications 109.05
compliment 516.33
complimentary 533.12
complimenting 092.15
compliments 290.11
Compliments 106.30
compline 194.04 606.06
complinement 271.F4
complore 557.34
complussed 410.10
compolitely 540.01
compompounded 036.02
component 142.08
Components 221.01
compors 313.19
Comport 192.31
composed 165.22 175.32
compositor 162.02
composs 382.20
Compost 447.23
compote 155.21
compound 178.13 412.32 415.02
Compree 065.14
comprehendurient 611.30
comprehension 604.32
comprendered 285.28
compresent 526.12
comprised 165.23
comprises 435.07
Compromise 303.L2
comprong 370.01
compunction 433.24
compuss 516.29
compyhandy 612.01
comrades 587.13
comrhade 329.04
Comsy 021.02
Comtesse 441.11
Comty 186.25
Comyn 130.21 367.10
Comyng 295.08
con 019.25 156.19 532.19 552.03
con 466.19 518.05
Con 457.01
Conal 625.12
Conall 553.14
conals 525.18
Conan 322.03 617.14
conansdream 228.13
conatively 088.07
conavent 527.22
Concaving 508.21
conceal 166.24 188.02 190.34
concealed 484.14
concealer 484.14
conceive 033.22 535.18
conceived 617.28
concelebrated 470.06
concensus 523.30
concentrate 109.12
concentric 606.03
Concepcion 527.36
Concepta 213.19
Conception 303.L2
concern 099.02 126.04 309.01 574.28 618.29
concerned 187.10 315.08 363.32 371.14 516.26
concerning 026.22 030.02 060.23 410.18 524.11
Concerning 506.27
concerns 364.23
concertina 028.18
concertiums 310.14
concertone 354.15
concerts 438.20
Concessas 327.24
conch 310.12
conchitas 268.03
conciliabulite 054.34
conciliabulum 496.10
CONCILIANCE 275.R1
conciliation 126.14 178.34
concionator 154.07
conclaiming 093.19
conclamazzione 173.15
conclave 504.17
conclaved 157.26
concloose 617.04
concloud 590.17
concludded 155.09
conclude 108.29 222.04
concluded 523.32
concluding 489.01
conclusion 049.05 108.32
conclusium 084.15
conclusively 149.14
Concoct 286.21
concocted 137.25
CONCOMITANCE 270.R1
concomitantly 523.36
concomitated 280.29
conconey's 449.08
conconundrums 506.03
concoon 519.03
Concorant 328.25
concord 582.30
Concord 197.10
concordant 405.04
Concordant 409.36
concreated 605.35

concreation 581.28
concreke 285.F5
concrete 481.12 582.17
concrude 358.06
concupiscent 572.21
concurred 058.28
condam 142.22
condamn 252.34
Condamned 421.02
condeal 585.17
condemn 062.20
condemned 188.15 409.34 544.11 559.03
condensed 183.30
condenser 310.01
condign 172.29
condiments 456.06
condition 092.09 489.14
conditions 078.29 386.34 599.09
conditiously 232.23
Conditor 211.28
condolences 280.11
condomnation 362.03
condonable 058.19
condone 142.21 510.06
condor 332.13
Condra's 532.12
condrition 229.29
conducible 605.14
conduct 099.10 449.12 524.03 573.17 585.13
conducted 386.01
conduict 537.14
coner 533.24
cones 261.09 405.12
coney 068.09 577.09
Coney 436.23 553.06
coneyfarm 257.05
coneywink 198.15
confabulation 558.01
confarreating 432.11
confarreation 390.11
confects 595.10
confederate 084.09
confederates 397.13
conference 445.01
confermentated 537.18
confesh 459.07
confess 271.14 411.28 484.01 494.31
confessed 058.31 322.30 572.28
confessed 350.03
confessedly 365.04
confesses 344.32
confesses 349.28 349.29 349.31 349.33
confession 150.24 188.01 391.30
confessioners 339.15
confessions 467.04
confessor 237.11 432.07
confidante 059.05
confidence 432.09
confident 619.14
confidentials 038.31
Confindention 593.16
confine 412.15
confined 201.29 492.17
confinement 150.25
confiners 433.23
confirm 324.36
confirmed 290.08 533.28 605.35
confisieur 531.02
confiteor 188.04 322.09
conflict 132.06 314.04
conflingent 142.18
confoederated 537.18
conformant 185.27
conformed 417.16
conformity 312.26
conforted 340.23
confounded 125.11 564.14
confoundyous 412.13
confraternitisers 608.06
confronted 529.29
confronts 564.12
confucion 417.15
Confucium 485.35
confused 120.05 536.08
confusianist 131.33
confusion 119.33 131.24
confusional 520.12
confusionaries 387.01
confusionary 333.06
confusioning 035.05
confusium 015.12
confussed 193.21
confussion 353.25
confute 149.15
cong 167.16 306.07 325.32
Cong 399.25
Congan's 538.32
congealed 229.22 453.02
congeners 267.17
Conger 525.26
congested 189.12 580.03
congesters 379.08
conglomerate 614.25
congorool 165.21
Congoswood 211.05
congrandyoulikethems 535.12
congratulate 150.21
congregant 177.24
Congregational 466.18
congress 115.33 128.28
congressulations 234.21
congsmen 087.25
conical 131.33
Coninghams 058.30
conjoint 108.14
conjugal 573.10
conjugate 279.F08
conjugation 121.31 465.24 557.20
conjunct 573.20
conjunction 078.35 251.12 595.25
Conjunctive 305.L1
conjure 617.10
conjured 595.36
conk 170.14 388.01
Conk 031.14 595.30
CONKERY 305.R1
Conn 051.12 203.12 289.24 528.33 549.33
Conna 160.12
Connacht 047.28 451.14 528.29
Connachy 392.04
connected 037.26 118.22 309.18 557.35
Connecticut 271.L1
connecting 483.32
connection 063.12 069.31 150.18 240.26 362.28 438.27 524.02 544.20 573.36
connections 060.07 169.06
conned 261.09 278.F5 334.32
connellic 326.13
connemaras 076.01
connexion 374.08
Connibell 311.18
Connie 239.24
Connies 071.29
conning 077.10 374.02
Conning 156.07 479.36
conningnesses 590.14
Conno 348.19
Connolly 303.09 303.12
Connolly's 457.01
Connor's 507.29
connow 154.31
Conn's 475.06
connubial 386.04
connundurumchuff 352.34
conny 140.20 365.12
conprovocative 162.20
conquered 058.06 512.08
conquering 584.24
conquerods 355.19
conquest 318.11
conquists 167.36
Conry 398.01
cons 078.29
con's 117.15
consanguineous 572.26
conscia 581.18
conscience 070.02 180.22 240.07 486.11
Consciencia 542.20
conscientious 067.12
conscious 075.15
consciousness 186.04
consciquenchers 178.03
conscraptions 364.19
Conscribe 338.17
consecants 298.24
consecrandable 596.09
consecrated 503.33
consecutive 513.34
consent 193.11 396.13 544.22
consentconsorted 239.28
consequence 060.18 438.28 618.31
consequentially 149.16
conservancy 358.18
conservancy's 198.21
conservative 076.14
conservatory 071.02 110.08
Conshy 424.09
consider 414.18 506.32 572.18
Consider 506.29
considerable 081.36 240.31 317.23 326.21
considerably 072.26 382.08
considerate 145.09
consideration 373.30 538.02 574.23 599.15
considered 109.35 543.13 572.22
considering 438.21 452.04 459.15 524.27 606.09
considewed 061.08
consients 368.21
consigned 472.18
consinent 337.08
consinnantes 485.11
consinuously 294.31
consisted 052.34 082.07
consistent 406.15
consistently 085.06 313.12 320.24 326.27
consistorous 155.07
consociately 224.23
consolation 280.20 532.32 558.02

console 291.08 441.25
Console 457.15
consolering 462.17
consollation 581.13
consomation 339.28
consommation 432.14
consonant 115.02
consonantia 249.13
consort 119.22 243.11 255.29 584.02
conspectrum 329.36
conspicuously 033.13
Conspirators 107.04
conspued 496.06
conspuent 187.11
consstated 070.06
constable 186.19
constably 618.32
constabulary 530.16
constancy 616.08
CONSTANCY 271.R1
constant 120.26 132.02 238.11 297.29 542.31 577.11
constantineal 442.05
constantinently 155.09
constantly 032.20
constantonoble's 548.16
constellations 405.10 476.24
constellatria 157.19
consternation 006.16 142.24 450.13
consternations 340.30
constituting 405.31
CONSTITUTION 261.R1
CONSTITUTIONABLE 261.R1
CONSTITUTIONAL 261.R1
constitutionally 108.35
Constitutionhill 012.29
constoutuent 537.22
constrains 355.28
construct 286.19
constructor 180.35
Consuelas 528.25
consult 149.16 221.02
consultation 509.34
consulted 206.12
consumed 034.17 189.17
consumers 497.01
consummate 573.22
consummated 368.23
consummation 194.07
Consummation 308.L2
consummatory 052.01
consummed 336.35
consumption 256.07 422.07
consurgent 287.23
contact 265.24 374.20 511.16 538.24
contacted 077.07
contacts 018.26
contaimns 355.28
contained 052.04 161.08
contains 289.06
contango 534.11
contanto 419.13
Conte 418.03
contemp 175.01
contempibles 175.01
contemplate 497.20
contemplated 109.34
contemplating 357.33
contemplation 209.02
contemporaries 100.09
contempt 145.16 322.29 422.08 424.08 513.30
contemption 155.13
contending 166.36
content 109.13 606.23 624.06
contenters 058.32
contention 256.03
contents 318.20
contentsed 348.12
contest 597.18
contested 473.15
contestimony 057.36
contexts 115.26
contey 538.28
conticinium 244.31
continence 198.35 252.14 462.33
continencies 585.28
continent 191.32 411.12
continental 173.01 398.13 539.06
continental's 289.12
continents 177.09
continually 032.21 051.10 118.24 543.32
continuant 598.29
Continuarration 205.14
continuatingly 609.13
continuation 006.20 523.21
continue 083.32 166.05 405.10
continued 066.08 155.15 294.03 302.30 452.11 454.07 557.26
continues 018.30 066.33 164.32 261.17
continuing 067.11 484.12
CONTINUITY 275.R1
continuous 186.01
continuously 520.33 606.10
continuum 472.30
contonuation 284.20
contours 538.04
Contrabally 440.25
contraceptives 045.14
contract 146.21
contractations 584.33
contracted 362.07
contractors 077.01 414.30
contractual 358.14 576.02
contradicting 390.02 393.18
contradrinking 096.03
contrairy 620.12
contraman 490.28
CONTRAPULSIVENESS 286.R4
contraries 049.36
contrarieties 107.29
contrarium 287.27
contrary 151.36 241.35 431.02 529.28
contrasta 242.25
Contrastations 071.08
contrasting 483.27
contravention 524.04 558.12 616.07
contrawatchwise 119.18
Contrescene 321.21
contribe 341.25
contributting 142.18
contrite 231.26
contrited 416.19
contritely 081.27
contrivance 516.07 596.19
contrive 443.18
control 123.13 247.08 310.06
controlled 123.09
controversies 142.18
contumacy 115.27
contumellas 255.19
contusiones 612.11
contusiums 084.11
contwawy 061.10
convaynience 024.02
convened 086.20
convenience 433.24
conveniences 219.02
convenient 113.24 165.11 550.16
convent 213.28 528.01 577.30
Convent 027.15
convention 128.27
conventional 054.26
CONVERGENCE 286.R4
conversa 238.24
conversant 425.23
conversation 148.12 443.33 618.35
conversazione 172.31
converse 144.31
conversion 132.26 378.14
conversions 530.32
convert 082.15 251.19 435.19 537.07
converted 288.16 332.23 439.08 573.15
Converted 420.31
convertedness 037.24
converters 263.11
convertible 183.33
converting 388.15
convexly 508.21
convey 018.26
conveyed 542.05
convibrational 394.03
convict 034.13 465.36
convict 231.07
convicted 050.28 425.13
convince 062.20
convocacaon 179.12
convolvuli 292.16
convolvulis 292.19
convorted 021.29
convoy 055.26
convulsion 261.L3
convulsionary 193.35
convultures 138.34
Conway 479.07
Conway's 083.20 214.20
Conyngham 434.12
coo 204.18 236.14
Coo 047.05 482.01
Coocaged 329.13
cooch 568.04
cooched 476.31
cooclaim 129.22
coocome 238.32
coocoo 327.35 358.01 417.36
Coocoohandler 072.13
coocoomb 516.13
cooed 371.06
cooefficient 284.12
Coogan 093.28
cooin 008.33 579.16
cooing 577.17
cooinsight 551.34
cook 079.07 199.15 284.F4 333.17 395.28
Cookcook 269.22
cooked 192.06 233.03 339.03 424.12 436.08
cookerynook 184.17
cooking 364.18 455.31 589.31

cookingclass 294.08
cookinghagar 530.34
Cookingha'pence 046.18
cookmaids 181.10
cooks 374.26
Cooks 409.35
cool 009.32 017.26 057.12 203.20 226.07 303.09 354.27 360.13 434.02 440.31 465.33 495.19 578.06
coolcellar 410.13
coolcold 290.15
coold 086.06 367.28 452.01
Coole 068.11 531.33 622.01
cooledas 279.F27
cooler 572.35
Cooley-Couley 242.36
Coolie 330.18
coolies 413.22
coolinder 408.34
cooling 033.06 151.15 211.10 526.31
cooll 346.25
Coollimbeina 221.25
coolly 362.07 626.23
Coolock 073.31 616.02
coolocked 552.22
Cooloosus 625.22
Coolp 344.31
coolpigeons 029.10
coolpose 618.01
coolpressus 470.16
cools 315.20
cool's 581.11
coolskittle 160.27
coolsome 318.02
coolt 074.13
coolun 394.22 493.35
cooly 520.32
coomb 442.35
coombe 073.30 423.25 506.12 529.19
Coombe 255.22
Coombing 104.21
coon 175.30 187.12 187.16 483.35
Cooney 194.29
Cooney 176.14
coop 319.20
Cooper 439.12
cooperation 568.20
coops 606.17
coordinal 157.27
coordination 551.17
coort 557.12
Coort 373.01
coos 471.34
cooshes 622.01
coosine 238.25
cootcoops 537.23
coowner 529.34
Coox 308.L2
cop 112.30 186.17 491.09 580.28
COP 306.R1
coparcenors 096.35
cope 248.25 328.35
Cope 098.30
Copeman 321.20
copener's 329.03
Copenhagen 010.21
Copenhague-Marengo 223.16
copers 555.11
cophetuise 537.32
copied 055.17
copies 099.34
Copies 181.33
coping 132.02
copiosity 472.03
copious 545.08
copoll 053.10
Coppal 446.24
coppall 432.13
coppeecuffs 542.13
coppeehouses 416.36
coppels 313.24
copper 170.08 489.24 617.34
copperads 299.30
copperas 086.03
Coppercheap 574.13 574.22
coppers 399.19
copper's 140.31
coppersmith 228.05
copperstick 035.35
copperwise 563.30
coppin 095.08
Coppinger 055.18 211.20 524.08 524.18 525.01
coppingers 524.27
coppingers 280.L2
Coppingers 341.34
Coppinger's 575.06 575.24
coppy 464.05
coppyl 607.34
Copricapron 026.12
copriright 185.30
coprulation 525.06
copsjute 110.26
Copt 241.26
copy 181.01 181.15 424.32 447.35 574.16
copycus's 056.01
copyhold 133.18
copying 374.02
copyist 014.17 121.30
copyngink 294.02
copyright 537.27
coq 136.17
Coquette 239.23
cor 061.21
corage 395.28
Coraggio 435.08
Coraio 466.24
coral 225.26
coram 089.05
coram 586.05
coranto 597.26
corapusse 416.15
coras 363.03
corass 006.21
corbicule 416.19
Corcor 504.20
cord 278.24 433.28 566.19
cordial 140.20
Cordial 205.16
cordiality 431.21
cordiallest 585.08
cordially 054.35
cordon 459.26
corduroy 559.09
cordwainers 313.01
core 056.03 203.23 377.30 447.06 590.27
corespondent 314.03
coricome 623.01
coriolano 228.11
cork 027.25 052.03 095.11 161.32
Cork 009.23 221.35 236.07 451.13
Corkcuttas 541.17
corked 155.01 624.01
corkedagains 333.11
Corkhill 012.27
corkhorse 121.23
corkiness 588.11
corknered 116.11
corks 038.08 427.02 465.16
corkscrew 085.35
corkscrewed 491.10
corkscrewn 576.20
Corkshire 406.03
corksown 197.05
corkyshows 443.35
Cormac 329.18
cormacks 019.09
cormorant 479.21
Cormwell's 260.F1
corn 034.18 059.03 137.30 380.11
cornaille 173.20
corncrake 493.32
corne 021.03
Cornelius 098.09 389.28
corner 036.31 071.01 111.18 122.20 173.06 278.06 301.F5 367.12 382.17 413.14 426.35 442.04 445.35 455.20 465.04 475.29 516.27 527.09 560.12 623.03
Corner 006.03 062.31 170.32 447.17 461.08 531.35 578.30
cornerboys 205.28
cornered 174.02
corners 095.11
cornerwall 135.01 581.09
cornets 212.30
Corneywall 419.16
cornflowers 014.36
corngold 075.10
cornish 586.27
Cornish 126.24
Cornix 049.13
cornquake 144.33
corns 081.02 223.32 419.27
Cornwallis-West 157.34
cornwer 291.01
Cornyngwham 387.28
corocured 541.27
coroll 601.16
corollanes' 354.33
corollas 321.05 414.36
coronaichon 230.24
coroner 067.13
coroners 219.10
coronetcrimsoned 180.02
Corpo 048.01
corporal 558.14
corporators 586.10
corporeity 471.06
corporelezzo 336.24
corpse 254.32 343.08 576.05
Corpse 105.20
corpses 037.10
Corpses 423.31
Corpsica 175.11
corpsus 362.17
corpular 310.19
corpulums 288.19

corpus 047.27 376.15
Corrack-on-Sharon 526.28
corralsome 254.12
correct 037.27 151.08 164.22 170.22 404.17 484.17
Correct 350.19
corrected 180.36
correctingly 576.29
correctional 375.11 575.34
correctly 124.04 617.15
correlations 557.17
correspondance 452.09
correspondant 041.19
correspondence 543.36
correspondent 617.35
Correspondents 164.21
corribly 202.35
corricators 602.23
corridor 333.08
Corridor 560.03
Corrie 220.19
Corriendo 220.19
Corrig 513.05
Corrigan's 214.23
corrigidly 162.28
corrispondee 457.28
corrobberating 082.24
corrosive 185.36
corrubberation 575.13
corructive 300.24
corrugitate 057.27
corrupted 373.24 466.07 572.35
corruptible 062.18
corry 372.28
Corry's 140.02
Corsages 096.05
corsair 577.10
corsar 343.03
corse 037.10 336.02
corsehairs 444.27
corselage 437.08
Corsergoth 626.28
corset 575.09
corsets 222.30
Corsicos 561.06
corso 084.27 089.11
corsorily 447.07
corss 542.14
corsslands 097.03
cortege 479.34
Corth 519.24
corthage 468.31
Corthy 310.13
cortoppled 549.34
Corumbas 513.16
corveeture 409.17
corves 178.36
corvinophobe 358.12
cos 240.33
Cos 433.21
coseries 145.28
cosh 620.05
cosied 368.36
cosin 298.23
cosm 151.01
cospolite 309.10
Cospol's 155.19
coss 459.24
Coss 293.01
cossa 089.10
cossakes 350.20
Cossist 293.01
cost 148.10 153.32 188.31 189.22 451.01 521.07
Cost 440.15
costard 464.30
costarred 563.25
Costello 133.01
costellous 132.13
coster 279.F23
costing 492.27
costive 184.36
costly 544.12
Costofino 541.04
Costollo 254.25
costs 313.29
costumance 560.33
costume 322.07 611.35
costumes 181.27 453.08
Coswarn 397.13
cosy 114.31 417.19 627.18
cosyn 354.33
cot 330.28 556.14
cotangincies 298.24
cotched 019.16 531.20
cotchin 031.10
Cotchme 106.24
cothurminous 429.02
coton 234.09
cots 039.33
cottage 079.29 179.32 265.12 414.34 620.36 624.07
cottages 545.03
Cottages 575.07
cotted 429.11
cottemptable 352.01
Cotter 071.22
Cottericks' 024.22
cotton 108.24 130.26
cottonwood 277.L2
couard 480.27
couch 355.32
Couch 479.34 543.11
couchamed 502.28
couchman 420.06
couchmare 576.28
Coucous 378.14
Coucousien 162.14
couddled 376.23
cough 147.12 210.09 385.23 444.03 458.11 555.13
coughan 482.10
coughed 253.03
coughin 444.14
coughing 022.02
Coughings 026.26
coughs 322.36 488.34 571.25
Couhounin's 035.32
could could Could
couldn't 025.30 038.18 045.19 061.11 192.11 208.34 322.13 344.20 390.12 427.15 427.16 458.21 509.32
Couldn't 456.11
coulinclouted 049.26
coulpure 311.26
coulter 246.36
coume 230.11
coumfry 035.14
coumplegs 607.20
Councillors-om-Trent 531.03
councils 077.21
coundedtouts 272.27
counsel 605.28
COUNSEL 271.R1
counsels 374.23
count 099.24 188.35 313.29 392.10 396.28 548.35
count 418.16
Count 374.09
Countenance 427.29
countenants 056.02
counter 029.34 174.28 328.12 498.02 574.30
counterbezzled 589.32
counterclaimed 574.13
countered 015.17
counterfeit 183.19 483.05
counterfeuille 191.18
counterhand 240.10
counterination 352.26
counterpoint 482.34
counterscarp 539.26
countess 578.36
counties 039.30 049.19 500.36
counting 237.33 286.16 393.18 396.35 436.05 516.17
countinghands 304.01
countless 189.01 189.11 523.15
Countlessness 017.26
countmortial 349.02
countrary 148.35
Countries 620.10
country 008.03 052.32 056.35 066.07 098.05 110.02 116.33 124.30 277.20 277.21 322.07 427.27 442.02 446.25 446.35 472.29 574.27 575.07 583.07 587.12
country 345.05
Country 181.05
countrybossed 012.28
countrymouse 553.02
countryports 187.07
countryside 102.09 205.26
counts 062.02 085.28 128.06 270.02
county 202.36 465.21 481.17 545.21 583.25
County 025.28 284.05 284.08 361.20 479.07 526.28
County's 003.08
coup 406.36
coupe 165.29 462.06 542.10
couple 053.11 090.16 134.30 151.24 154.26 242.28 433.10 499.17 503.09 587.06
coupled 107.16 577.10
couples 435.34 589.02 623.22
couplet 073.14 081.28 284.10
coupling 309.19 314.20
coupoll 242.04
courage 313.29 351.11
COURAGE 270.R1
courants 075.12
Courcy 370.22 370.22
courier 092.21
course 006.09 030.04 049.35 058.14 066.33 077.35 078.29 082.04 088.35 110.27 114.11 128.29 143.12 143.31 144.04 144.20 145.08 146.19 148.25 149.18 161.17 163.04 164.32 172.27 174.01 184.11 196.04 230.24 245.13 283.05 289.20 296.16 322.36 406.08 406.15 410.18 419.17 426.33 431.08 443.08 443.26 448.03 457.32

458.08 458.15 458.17 458.18 459.30 516.11 527.05 527.24 574.15 588.26 588.26 594.07 603.21 608.07 625.08
course 342.09
Courser 481.02
courser's 469.10
courses 172.33 543.36 546.31
Courses 221.01
coursets 236.36
courseway 391.19
coursing 479.04
coursse 372.03
court 031.28 087.30 094.31 220.02 264.29 369.18 375.20 391.03 448.36 476.12 498.28 536.31 566.07 566.25 589.28
Court 040.04 049.10 087.34 434.15 515.21 563.27
Court 350.12
courteous 032.30 480.30
courtesy 383.21
Courther 452.09
courtin 319.22
courting 145.16 321.18 395.15 466.04 514.06 586.02
courting 399.01
courtinghousie 575.26
courtlike 093.06
Courtmilits' 567.11
courts 422.05 442.07 460.12 561.33 574.01 575.33
courtships 147.04
coushcouch 597.17
cousin 020.03 235.29 479.10 526.30 625.02
cousines 532.21
cousins 021.11 130.28 466.04
cousins 265.L2
cousis 414.18
cousterclother 549.33
couverfowl 586.21
couvrefeu 436.02
cove 382.21 501.24 528.31 620.34
Cove 108.27
covenant 507.33
Covenant 510.26
covenanter 061.32 590.07
covenience 551.27
covennanters 552.06
coventry 353.26
cover 101.25 129.22 180.18 255.13 351.25 438.19 446.10 574.14
Cover 072.01
coverchaf 274.01
coverdisk 086.35
covered 014.22 084.19 188.25 374.36 408.07 444.28
Coverfew 244.08
coverlets 558.27
coverpoint 583.34
covers 397.33
coverswised 298.23
covert 097.14
covertly 014.26 554.04 554.04
coverture 243.11
coves 324.11
Covetfilles 434.28
covethand 321.27
covetous 172.30
covets 331.28
Covey 528.03
covin 538.24
cow 233.35 337.05 394.25 427.03 455.24
Cow 083.19 412.25
Cow 176.03
coward 449.21
cowardice 558.27
cowardly 171.33 521.34
cowbeamer 508.03
cowbelly 485.32
cowcarlows 129.01
cowchooks 009.16
Cowdung 273.L3
cowe 534.05
cowery 382.16
cowhaendel 054.27
cowhandler 444.21
cowheel 319.03 410.32
Cowhowling 547.21
cowknucks 467.30
cowld 139.26 593.20
cowled 502.24 581.13
Cowlie 378.16
cowly 275.26
cowmate 243.32
Cowpoyride 105.35
cowrie 281.F3
cowrieosity 014.02
cowruads 344.18
cowrymaid 164.08
cows 277.14 292.11 380.29
cow's 063.28
cowse 615.27
cowshots 037.23
cowslips 577.26
cowsway 284.F5
cowtaw 090.01
Cowtends 448.10
Cox 517.18
Coxenhagen 328.22
Coxer 105.05
coxerusing 347.29
Coxon 039.09
Cox's 066.23
coxswain 289.25
coxyt 198.22
coy 139.24 157.21 354.33 431.04 433.29
Coyle 210.21 370.21
Coyle-Finns 330.17
coyly 057.12
coynds 538.16
coyne 016.31 313.17
coyner 186.29
coynth 579.16
coyquailing 552.22
cozenkerries 577.25
cozes 608.07
cozydozy 061.03
crab 170.07 392.11
crabbed 138.03
crabeyes 257.23
crabround 417.28
Crabtree 062.34
craching 017.25
crack 059.32 070.24 086.16 090.24 221.35 323.26 476.13 497.06
cracka 212.30
Crackajolking 094.04
Crackasider 418.02
cracked 136.02 441.19 544.21
crackerhack 190.06
crackers 193.15
crackery 353.35
cracket 056.24
cracking 463.08
crackler 082.34
crackles 512.23
crackling 455.35 528.27
Cracklings 099.04
cracks 139.07
cracksmith 304.F4
Craddock 098.31
cradle 080.17 081.36 098.33 282.10 427.20
cradlenames 201.32
cradler 315.02
cradles 211.20 227.07
craft 290.28 309.20
crafty 263.02 333.06
craftygild 549.32
crag 566.29
craggy 244.24
Craig 096.24 210.14 541.03
craigs 095.34
crake 251.06
cram 323.34 424.12 515.03
crambs 304.29
crame 292.22
cramkrieged 539.11
crammer 155.09
cramp 312.18 397.25
crampton 204.36
Crampton's 291.05
cramwell 512.17
cramwells 053.36
cran 504.01 504.01
cranberries 504.33
crane 331.28 569.22 596.22
cranic 007.29
crank 317.19
cranking 377.15
crankly 275.27
crannock 507.36
crans 504.02
Crany's 105.32
craogs 051.28
crap 185.17
crapes 009.31
crappidamn 326.32
crash 044.20 289.08 324.36 569.30
crashed 136.33
Crashedafar 513.16
crashing 581.04
Crasnian 492.10
crass 455.13
Crass 546.10
crate 049.32
crater 410.10
Craterium 150.04
crates 604.11
cravat 101.14
crave 240.04
craved 426.27
craven 563.04
craven 354.11
craving 055.31
crawl 134.02
crawler 506.06
Crawleys 288.F6
crawling 027.36 448.12
crawls 135.36
craws 615.30

crawsake 007.08
crawsbomb 424.18
crawsick 193.02
crawsopper 063.01
craythur 004.29 487.20
crazed 417.22
crazedledaze 562.16
Crazier 104.14
crazing 065.13
crazy 192.34 231.17
crazyheaded 513.07
crazyquilt 556.16
creactive 300.20
creaking 144.32
creakish 019.10
creakorheuman 214.22
cream 039.07 064.27 207.09 461.03 531.13 555.18
cream 164.19
creamclotted 097.16
creamery 036.22
creamings 144.02
Creampuffs 065.11
creams 462.06 621.16
creamsourer 457.14
Creamtartery 346.01
creamtocustard 475.15
creamy 215.20
crease 136.04 404.32 584.19
creased 179.07
Creases 204.35
create 453.02
created 029.14 058.03 238.13
creater 129.34
creaters 386.25
creation 029.15 032.33 035.06 273.F1 431.12 457.24 505.09 512.02 546.19
Creation 132.15
creations 109.23
Creations 221.24
Creator 029.14 604.27
creature 036.06 060.06 101.31 155.06 214.32 230.07 279.F36 585.19
Creature 437.22
creatured 029.14
creatures 505.02
credibel 536.32
credidisti 074.08
credit 036.23 133.13 367.13 538.06
Credit 579.19
creditable 051.14
creditor 574.14
creditors 172.15
credits 054.27
cree 209.23
creed 525.02
creedle 276.F5
Creedless 252.33
creek 288.F4 547.17
creeked 332.07
creeks 016.09
creeped 170.25
creepered 264.30
creepers 290.F1 404.05
creepfoxed 087.22
creeping 039.34 178.19 589.16
Creeping 288.F6 494.18
creeps 019.16 617.21
creepsake 145.33
crekking 449.32
Creman 342.20
cremation 350.14
Creme 461.03
crème-de-citron 575.16
cremoaning 041.22
creppt 427.11
crept 037.20
crerdulous 568.03
Crescent 260.11 369.09
cress 130.25
cressets 549.02
cressloggedlike 297.28
crest 005.06 220.27 546.05
cresta 485.02
crested 026.12 074.02 079.09 318.34
crestfallen 049.03
cresties 519.22
Crestofer 512.07
crests 198.31
crevices 151.18
crew 024.04 133.05 167.17 313.32
crewn 610.11
crews 619.24
crewsers 085.01
crewth 041.22
criados 325.34
crib 190.23 302.22 464.04 476.32
cribbed 205.35
cribcracking 076.05
cribful 329.03
cribibber 423.05
cribies 103.05
cribro 155.04
crick 557.03
crickcrackcruck 426.05
cricked 099.04
cricket 138.26
Cricketbutt 160.02
crickler 082.26
Crick's 416.18
cricquette 249.35
cricri 146.33
crid 256.29
cried 086.16 100.14 256.10 292.F3 454.24
Cried 566.02
cries 034.05 087.30 152.21 182.08 359.19 427.04 469.01 558.23 620.17 622.19 627.32
crig 532.19
crihumph 328.34
crim 532.19
crime 085.22 094.08 107.26 242.11 275.20 410.06 419.33 603.16
Crimealian 347.10
crimealine 008.30
Crimean 049.05
Crimeans 522.08
crimemummers 356.06
crimes 107.26 138.16
crimeslaved 478.15
criminal 049.16 076.05 165.33
crimm 334.25
crimms 334.25
crimosing 569.02
crimp 312.18
crimsend 350.28
crimson 087.28 387.04
crimstone 570.34
Criniculture 164.25
criniman 422.12
crinklydoodle 404.28
crinoline 212.22 548.29
Crippled-with-Children 102.29
cripples 579.32
crisis 395.32
crismion 326.33
crisp 206.24 455.35
crispianity 618.34
crispin 491.06
crispness 236.14
Criss 011.27 011.27
crisscouple 613.10
crisscrossed 120.19
crither 549.29
critic 109.24
critically 241.13
criticism 163.36
croak 296.12 532.03
croak 344.03
croaked 177.07
croaker 391.16
croakers 197.30
croakpartridge 301.30
croaks 377.22
crocelips 511.31
crock 142.01
crockard 537.29
crockery 353.35
crocodile 183.24 273.22
crocs 199.04
crocus 546.36
Crocus 254.20
Croesus 231.18 564.05
crofting 507.02
croixes 376.07
crom 595.18
cromagnom 020.07
cromcruwell 022.14
cromlech 061.14
Cromlechheight 132.22
cromlecks 343.31
cromlin 353.33
Crommalhill 132.22
Cromwell 039.08 500.06
Cromwell's 068.15
Cromwelly 009.02
cronauning 041.22
crone 013.36
cronies 032.16
croniony 390.07
Cronwall 261.L3
crony 620.18
crook 014.32 142.09 549.19
Crookback 134.11
crookcrook 546.35
crooked 183.34 190.36 594.31
Crookedribs 038.31
Crooker 221.28
crookodeyled 570.34
crookolevante 228.10
croon 366.28 491.05
Croona 602.14
Croonacreena 376.34
crooner 381.22 471.36
croonless 252.33
croons 388.01
crop 317.09
cropatkin 081.18
cropherb 005.23
cropped 506.25
croppied 580.30

croppis's 099.14
Croppy 229.12
crops 076.35 084.34 373.36
cropse 055.08
cropulence 294.22
crores 256.31
cross 009.04 016.30 041.17 042.23 192.18 193.25 211.05 250.24 448.08 471.12 577.26 605.09
cross 349.22 399.25
Cross 011.27 011.27 228.05 262.04 574.16
crossbelt 559.09
crossbones 504.25
crossbugled 589.32
crossbuns 308.F2
Crosscann 089.10
crosscomplimentary 613.11
crossed 060.34 098.18 546.09 574.14 589.05
crossexanimation 087.34
crossgrained 088.16
Crossgunn 008.14
crosshurdles 570.05
crossing 114.11 393.35 492.33
crosskisses 111.17
crossknoll 552.23
crossmess 619.05
crossqueets 487.27
crossroads 119.28 475.03
Crostiguns 177.09
croststyx 206.04
crosty 144.33
crotch 504.27
crotts 548.15
crotty 141.14
Crouch 480.03
crouched 483.36
croucher 485.17
crould 206.08
croust 042.33
croven 262.F3
crow 053.36 360.28 473.22
Crow 496.32
Crowalley 105.27
Crowbar 086.08
crowcock 468.30
crowd 012.29 048.07 107.15 464.15 467.13 580.32 596.17
Crowd 186.13
crowdblast 219.17
crowder 567.30
crowders 206.02
crowds 049.06
Crowds 310.16
crowed 199.30
Crowhore 229.12
crown 086.07 128.21 152.25 167.30 192.11 200.27 206.32 211.04 252.15 331.36 371.31 385.16 392.17 430.15 430.18 463.26 549.20 561.21 587.09 610.12
Crown 399.07
Crownd 420.36
crowndest 503.33
crowned 208.33
crowner 474.19
crowning 038.01 397.14 589.36
crowns 521.07
crowplucking 084.06
crows 011.01 131.31 192.21
crowy 232.28
crozier 180.13
Crozier 464.03
crozzier 353.20
cru 053.36
Cruachan 526.20
cruaching 173.25
cruces 375.05
crucethouse 427.04
crucian 122.25
crucifer's 477.22
crucifix 465.26
crucifixioners 377.24
cruciform 122.20
Crucis 243.31
crucket 375.19
crucycrooks 155.17
crude 070.15
crudelty 538.10
crudities 505.36
cruelfiction 192.19
cruelly 448.05
cruetstand 165.17
Cruise 123.26
cruised 388.01
cruisery 205.06
cruisk 326.06
cruize 339.32
Crum 500.06
crumb 147.24 172.30
crumbed 304.30
crumbends 102.06
crumbling 018.07
crumbs 193.03
Crumglen's 142.13
crumlin 555.13 555.15 586.29
Crumlin 073.06
crumm 241.01
Crummwiliam 347.32
Crump 176.07
crumple 577.19
Crumple 045.03
Crum-ple 044.27
Crumwall 088.21
crunch 142.20
crunchbracken 005.23
crupper 382.19 445.15
crupping 323.05
crusade 480.07
crusader 055.11
crusaders 434.36
cruschinly 344.16
Cruses 530.13
crush 059.23 102.17 193.25 200.03 461.09 622.09
crush 271.L4
crushmess 534.01
crushts 624.36
Crusoe's 211.16
Crusos 538.13
crusswords 178.04
crust 166.01 462.19 473.05
crusted 031.30 385.33
crusts 142.20
crutch 215.16 600.03
crutches 215.16
crux 047.03 326.04 409.18 525.02 623.34
cruxader 464.14
cruxway 478.15
cry 009.26 009.27 010.16 041.26 117.03 118.19 159.09 190.05 215.17 315.04 412.21 462.24 470.09 478.15 493.32 500.12 525.30 548.35 558.32 608.16 609.21 622.33
cry 344.04
Cry 020.19 559.30
Cry 106.02
crydle 444.13
crying 043.28 160.33 178.11 482.25 501.17 517.19 530.05 563.01
Crying 621.16
crylove 159.14
crypt 190.23
cryptmahs 346.05
cryptoconchoidsiphonostomata 135.16
cryptogam 261.27
cry's 248.16
crystal 127.03 229.12 579.05
Crystal 528.09
crystalline 186.07
cryzy 528.07
cstorrap 310.20
cub 060.11
cuba 208.12
cubane 117.15
cubarola 618.22
cubat 007.22
cubblin 328.03
cubbyhole 386.03
cube 151.02
cubehouse 005.14
cubical 476.32
cubid 284.14 321.28
cubilibum 194.18
cubin 384.23
cubital 369.36
cubits 449.17
cublic 604.05
cubs 480.31
cucconut 376.09
cuckhold 278.F7
cuckling 260.18
cuckoo 446.20
cuckoospit 033.01
Cucullus 248.16
Cucumber 536.33
cud 064.18 164.02 278.03 371.07 381.01
cudd 233.35
cuddle 203.32 271.13 593.22
Cuddle 147.02
Cuddle 105.03
cuddlebath 290.13
cuddled 096.17
cuddlepuller 241.09
cuddleys 004.08
cuddling 384.21 384.29 385.01 389.22
cuddy 020.27 555.12
cuddycoalman's 326.10
cudgel 043.06 119.34 268.07
cudgelplayers' 056.35
cudgin 320.15
cuds 205.18
cue 035.27 044.23 054.11 227.24 319.24
cue 344.03
cued 019.02
cuffed 580.10
cuffes 300.25
cuffs 410.32 527.18 556.07 614.06

Cuffs 214.29
cuirscrween 587.13
cuistha 422.18
Cujas 041.32
cul 178.12
cul 153.17
Culapert 536.09
culculpuration 368.12
culcumbre 279.F27
culdee 210.01
Culex 418.23
culious 278.F2 508.11
culkilt 414.07
cull 174.05 337.17 571.08
Cull 015.21
Culla 154.29
cullchaw 303.21
cullebuone 368.13
culled 267.L1
Cullege 315.01
Cullen 033.02 200.03 440.09
Cullen's 385.01
culler 624.20
cullies 348.12
Cullin 203.12
cullions 174.34
culls 614.10
culmination 551.20
culminwillth 593.12
culms 378.05
culonelle 351.32
culorum 184.26
Culossal 181.03
culosses 261.12
culoteer 275.02
culothone 353.18
culottes 181.29
culotticism 374.13
culp 322.35
culpability 263.29
culpable 305.11 310.12
culpads 483.35
culpas 246.31
Culpenhelp 010.13
culping 515.01
Culpo 357.15
culponed 569.26
culpows 363.20
Culpreints 105.18
culprik's 538.15
culprines 504.26
culprit 023.16
Culsen 310.32
cult 279.02
Culthur's 523.14
cultic 344.12
cultous 288.24
culubosh 051.36
culunder 102.10 578.22
cum 406.20
cum 185.24 189.19 189.19
496.22 605.08
Cum 485.16
cumannity 042.14
cumb 350.25
cumbeck 232.16
Cumberer 071.34
Cumbilum 088.28
cumbottes 023.01
cumbrum 134.08 134.08
Cumbrum 009.27
Cumbulent 352.32
cumfused 156.31
cumfusium 035.36
cumhulments 624.28
cumjustled 092.06
Cumm 421.13
cummal 289.11 334.15
cumman 228.12
cummanisht 320.05
cumming 044.19
cummulium 498.30
cumpohlstery 271.F3
cumps 612.15
cumsceptres 032.03
Cumsensation 616.25
cumule 073.35 525.31
cumulikick 344.09
cumuliously 449.35
Cumulonubulocirrhonimbant
599.25
cunctant 288.04
cuncties 189.19
cunctipotentem 185.14
CUNCTITITITILATIO 305.R1
cundoctor 553.33
cunduncing 310.13
cungunitals 525.05
Cunha 159.32
cunifarm 524.20
Cunina 561.09
CUNK 305.R1
cunldron 151.13
Cunn 203.12
cunneth 581.16
cunniform 198.25
Cunnig's 549.01
cunning 094.08 099.22 372.32
cunning 346.08
Cunning 156.06
Cunningham 095.09 393.05
cunningly 120.05
cunnyngnest 576.28
cunstabless 443.05
Cunstuntonopolies 357.30
cunundrum 085.22
cunvesser 534.20
cunvy 430.28
cunziehowffse 538.16
Cuoholson 332.08
cup 025.07 056.24 098.31
115.04 117.30 221.05 245.36
318.02 373.10 386.09 397.19
443.14 455.36 456.01 462.09
515.35 613.26 615.09
Cup 040.01 122.13 334.36
Cup 342.16
cupahurling 455.01
cupandnaggin 548.32
cupenhave 199.17
cuperation 251.13
cupgirls 367.01
cupid 268.10 445.22
cupiosity 434.30
cupital 369.32
cupla 606.23
cupolar 151.17
cupoled 541.07
cupped 321.22 407.23
cuppinjars 621.15
cuppled 038.21 433.30
cupplerts 331.03
cuppy 138.14 584.12
cupric 241.14
cups 304.F4
cupslips 171.18
cupstoomerries 312.28
cupteam 511.02
cuptin 362.09
cuptosser 520.13
cupturing 371.15
cur 132.33 594.29
Cur 038.05 594.27
Cur 073.19 188.08
curach 131.25
curara 209.21
curate 116.18 188.34 573.04
Curate 210.36
curate-author 533.29
curate's 115.16
curb 085.10 198.02
Curchies 051.14
curchycurchy 476.35
curdinal 282.20 282.21 282.22
282.23
curdinals 282.20
curdnal 600.34
curds 374.05
cure 027.25 102.28 334.01
432.19 448.31 460.33 492.11
618.07
Cure 104.23
cured 463.04 482.30 498.36
555.21
curefully 289.11
Curer 440.10
cures 137.28
cure's 622.13
curfe 145.34
curia 044.04
curial 093.06
curiasity 157.26
Curier 125.14
curillass 159.30
curing 429.23
curiolater 043.20
curios 018.17
curiose 458.22
curiosing 107.12
curiositease 576.24
curiosity 285.F2
curious 096.34 121.08 426.36
577.31 577.32 577.32
curiously 041.19 210.09 574.31
curks 160.27
curkscraw 341.18
curl 044.01 169.16 318.10
469.32 588.10
curled 045.03 054.35
curled 044.26
curlew 383.16
Curlew 466.02
curlews 167.30 595.13
Curley 239.24
curlicabbis 612.02
curlicornies 102.11
curliest 365.32
curling 112.35 392.29 602.03
curlingthongues 511.31
curlpins 559.20
curls 057.12 092.17 283.F1
430.23 448.24 469.32 491.31
curly 280.18 360.14 457.10
465.28
Curly 105.32
curlyflower 409.14
Curlymane 310.20
curman 142.10
curname 441.29

curner 190.25
curolent 052.11
curpse 224.05
curragh 399.05
Curragh 387.01
Curragh 273.L1
Curraghchasa 160.06
curraghcoombs 542.03
Curraghman 202.29
Curran 093.32
currant 623.19
Currens 550.32
current 183.22 187.05 212.27 498.02 575.13
currgans 348.17
curried 183.19 542.08
currier 570.10
curries 595.13
currish 534.34
curry 138.12 295.18 351.02 456.20
currycombs 152.28
curse 046.14 062.17 073.07 130.02 134.18 143.11 287.F4 305.17 374.33 414.29 453.11 469.33 470.27 485.25 507.05 516.33 557.35 577.15 582.09
curse 342.06
Curse 252.11
cursed 029.09 083.21
Cursed 090.25
curser 060.12
curserbog 556.25
cursery 162.11
curses 022.14 176.28 289.12
curseway 343.07
cursigan 010.18
cursing 247.20
Cursits 106.23
cursives 099.18
cursowarries 263.F2
curst 076.32 222.24 482.13
cursu 089.11
curt 120.02 534.32
curtailment 353.04 543.03
curtain 257.31 290.F7 467.07
Curtain 501.07
curtains 049.01 461.19 559.05
curtain's 049.02
curter 063.33 317.25
curtrages 011.19
curtsey 038.13 249.22 301.F3 476.11
Curtsey 249.22
curtsies 571.16
curve 527.18
curve 340.29
curveachord 284.03
curves 203.22 524.31
curvy 470.32
Cusack 049.34
Cusanus 163.17
Cush 308.09
cushats 085.30
cushingloo 200.36
cushion 236.05 568.24
cushionettes 474.14
cushlas 203.24
cushlin 136.03
cushlows 346.31
Cussacke 550.30
cusses 459.24
custard 247.35 406.26
custodian 410.05
custody 443.04
Custody 072.16
custom 055.13 069.24 122.30
customary 463.26 470.05
customed 312.29
customers 580.10
CUSTOMERS 221.01
customhouse 220.35
customs 136.23 189.36 545.20
Customs 106.19
custos 532.01
cut 020.06 026.02 065.15 123.02 137.04 145.02 171.34 180.11 191.31 197.02 199.30 248.17 320.19 425.27 433.26 440.22 445.05 453.34 477.06 484.28 495.07 548.10
Cut 156.28 377.34
cutattrapped 372.01
cute 011.18 208.01 254.30 297.13 403.21
cutely 181.15 189.31
cutey 314.03
Cutey 364.31
cuthone 190.30
cuthulic 603.30
cuticatura 291.F6
Cuticura 164.30
cuticure 550.18
cutlass 136.25
cutless 063.02
cutletsized 255.29
Cutprice 072.04
Cutpurse 042.30
cuts 137.04 286.08 320.03 392.32 493.24 553.06
cutter 317.24 375.30 385.06
cuttered 322.10
cutthroat 183.19
cutting 182.25 233.02 250.08 423.15
Cutting 444.32
cuttinrunner 076.19
cuttlefishing 173.36
Cuxhaven 060.22
C. W. 099.15 (Code Wave)
cweamy 337.16
cwold 110.16
cworn 110.17
cwympty 314.16
cycl 339.32
cycled 461.09
cyclefinishing 543.29
cycles 013.31 452.23 462.34
cyclewheeling 186.02
cyclic 285.01
cycling 099.05 394.14
cycloannalism 254.26
cyclological 220.30
cyclone 294.10
cyclopes 300.26
Cycloptically 055.22
cyclorums 336.01
cyclums 336.01
cygncygn 511.13
cygnet's 204.11
cylindrical 347.18
cymbaloosing 607.10
Cymry 464.06
cymtrymanx 085.36
Cymylaya 329.32
cynarettes 236.02
cyphalos 422.07
cyprissis 460.23
cyrcles 119.23
Cyrus 263.07
Czardanser 513.16
Czeschs 423.36
czitr 171.11
czitround 171.08
czurnying 362.33

d 370.11
420.25 (1014 d.)
d 140.12 140.36
D 574.26
574.26 (D you D)
D. 099.34 (D. Blayncy's)
d' 017.12 (d' of Linn)
da 051.16 101.21 101.21 159.32 271.03 271.03 338.13 496.20 609.35
da 560.32
Da 518.30
Da 044.28 342.11
daadooped 326.24
daarlingt 242.08
dab 186.10 282.07 311.32
dabal 186.09 186.10
dabardin 245.14
dabbed 037.31
dabble 250.36
dabbles 342.25
dabblin 016.35 139.24
dabbling 196.08
dabblingtime 550.34
Dablena 057.32
dabnal 186.09
dace 141.03 450.04
dace 201.14
dacent 006.23
Dacent 405.28
d'action 274.L2
dactyl 282.L2
dactylise 468.16
dactylogram 430.11
dad 136.21 178.02
Dad 258.03
dada 065.17 338.14
dadaddy 496.28
dadad's 561.15
daddam 346.16
dadden 254.04
dadder 294.17
daddies 564.18
daddle 315.02
Daddy 094.35 257.14 398.02 439.20
Daddy 072.13
daddyho 431.32
daddyoak 446.13
Dadeney 284.F1
Dadgerson's 374.02
dadging 394.07
d'adieu 580.17
dads 528.15
dads 341.33
dadtid 498.32
Daemper 332.18
Daery 200.20
dafe 136.29
daff 491.30
daff 268.L4
daffs 350.17
dafft 225.17

daffy 366.24
daffydowndillies 475.09
daft 087.24 200.11 232.18
571.03 578.13
daft 175.23
Daft 274.05
dag 279.F26 349.04 607.18
dagabout 035.12
Daganasanavitch 278.23
Dagdasson 248.04
dagger 526.24
daggers 176.23 191.05
daggily 411.19
Dagobert 274.29
dagos 144.08 603.18
dagrene 228.08
dags 240.09
Dagsdogs 385.34
daguerre 339.23
Dah 594.02
dahet 531.36
dahlias 596.28
daildialler 309.14
daily 118.02 219.08 221.08
282.06 457.03 543.23 604.34
619.15
Daily 177.05
Daimon 261.L1
daimond 365.04 365.04
daimons 142.23 476.15
daindy 276.16
dainly 060.36
daintical 295.27
daintied 340.29
daintiness 548.32
daintree 492.09
dainty 034.19 200.25 238.03
248.28 337.26 533.06 604.34
Dainty 360.08
daintylines 587.26
Daintytrees 244.02
d'airain 338.26
dairmaidens 601.08
Dair's 069.08
dairy 161.14 409.18 604.35
Dairy 295.13
dairyman 045.20
daisies 428.27
daisy 053.09 272.09
Daisy 212.14
Daisy 105.15
daisy's 158.02
daiyrudder 379.20
daktar 277.L4
dakyo 160.16
dal 186.10 281.19
Dalaveras 009.36
Dalbania 114.25
Dalchi 570.03
dale 074.04 203.17 327.18
Dalem 350.03
Dalems 351.30
dales 331.22
Daleth 020.17
dalgo 281.F3
Dalicious 421.04
dalickey 422.07
dalkeys 087.25
Dalkin 532.13
Dalkymont 390.29
dall 427.17
dallkey 317.05
Dally 562.07
dallydandle 328.31
dallytaunties 435.01
Dalough 039.09
dalppling 007.02
Dalton 248.22
D'Alton 572.36
daltons 019.09
Dalway 140.36
Daly 526.20
Dalymount's 375.23
Daly's 042.35
dam 139.18 215.16 277.F6
339.06 625.20
Dam 409.21
Dama 471.02
Damadam 019.30
Damadomina 471.03
damages 070.09
damas 341.33
damasker's 404.27
damazon 199.13
Damb 006.10
damdam 353.36
dame 034.21 226.15 226.16
548.13 566.18 566.21
577.10
Dame 124.23 206.06 386.21
387.07 388.20 428.17
Dame 102.18 112.32
damedeaconesses 366.24
damename 244.08
dames 022.32 092.22 102.26
135.11 568.06
Dames 106.34
damesman 504.02
Damester 283.F2
damid 357.07
damimonds 134.07
damm 332.30
Dammad 291.24
damman 243.12
dammat 137.04
dammias 347.19
dammymonde 438.30
damn 042.05 118.31 120.30
145.14 323.26 455.36
damn 399.01
Damn 009.14
D'amn 514.23
damned 077.04 148.19 185.13
359.05 489.11
damning 288.13
damns 183.24
damnty 344.06
damnymite 349.13
d'amores 003.04
damp 051.21 214.23
311.18 331.05 453.14
534.06 534.06 534.06
619.09
dampers 410.25
dampfbulls 547.35
dampkookin 550.15
dampned 300.06
damprauch 157.28
Dampsterdamp 138.24
dams 215.15
damse 595.06
damsel 014.07
damsells 554.03
damson 568.03
Damyouwell 093.34
dan 317.14 523.17
Dan 044.12 060.31 094.02
133.03 147.30 199.14 317.31
367.12 466.20 494.26
Dana 386.22
Danaan 381.06
Danabrog 549.01
Danadune 079.15
danage 541.19
Danaides 094.14
Danamaraca 255.15
dance 065.17 070.16 128.25
147.31 250.16 337.20 415.10
417.31 579.25 602.33
dance 399.07
danceadeils 236.29
danced 175.32
Dancekerl 462.17
dancer 439.03
dances 570.05 627.27
Dances 221.25
dancetongues 404.06
dancing 159.12 208.08 226.34
354.29
dancings 235.35
Dancings 113.15
Dancingtree 371.30
Dandeliond 361.23
dander 199.05 303.F2
dandleass 141.34
dandruff 037.11
dandy 092.20 172.14 345.24
464.24
dandydainty 238.03
dandyforth 473.10
dandymount 247.34
dandypanies 234.16
dane 086.22 139.22 323.36
385.16
Dane 077.14 288.19 330.06
452.02 503.21 594.27
Dane 201.08
danegeld 084.04
Danegreven 622.20
Danelagh 334.13
Daneland 480.10
Danelly 379.36
Danelope 359.14
Danemork 479.32
danery 261.16
Danes 015.06 047.23 047.24
129.12 420.29
dane's 562.30
Dane's 496.08
Danesbury 372.17
Daneygaul 237.18
dang 478.21
Dang 377.35 528.26
dangelous 296.17
danger 112.15 246.35 364.01
370.04 439.03 579.29
DANGER 271.R1
dangered 363.33
dangerfield 080.08
dangerous 544.14
Dangerous 308.01 420.22
dangers 113.23
dangieling 322.03
d'anglas 485.12
Dangle 534.36
dangling 347.12
daniel 354.03
Daniel 160.18 541.16
Daniel's 468.33

Danis 336.03 617.06
Danish 433.06
dank 129.06 151.35 252.09
danked 469.20
dankyshin 585.08
Danl 060.26
Danmark 192.21
dann 347.29
Dann 352.27
Dannamen 014.20
danned 326.13
dannies 378.01
Danno 330.06 348.19
d'Anno 246.32
dannoy 162.16
Dann's 139.22
Danny 303.08 303.10 303.12 604.13
dannyboy 051.33
dannymans 621.07
Danos 518.23
dans 054.16 478.20 478.23 525.18
dans 281.05 281.09
Dansh 105.18
dantellising 251.23
Dantsigirls 105.10
Danu 007.12
Danubierhome 181.06
Danuboyes 435.15
danworld 102.08
danzing 333.08
danzzling 089.28
Dapes 497.05
daphdaph 203.30
daphnedews 556.18
dapifer 136.17
dapper 464.24
dapperent 614.05
dapping 450.13
dapple 113.18 609.09
dapplebellied 245.30
dappled 294.01
dapplegray 585.20
dapplehued 336.12
dapplepied 276.F5
dappy 023.05
Dar 433.16 575.24
Daradora 434.07
darblun 385.35
darby 180.15
darby's 473.09
Darby's 374.25
d'Arcy 587.04
dard 357.09
dare 022.23 034.16 093.14 142.34 149.16 212.23 252.04 289.30 323.36 365.20 366.07 382.23 394.22 436.30 440.30 463.34 472.26 527.07 561.30 562.08 571.08 576.08
dare 341.22
Dare 022.23
darearing 466.11
dared 181.23 353.10
daredevil 281.F3
darely 600.24
daremood's 369.31
darent 199.11
dares 253.02 535.13
d'Arezzo's 260.13
dargle 206.18
Dargle 460.15
dargman 340.32
Dargul 327.18
Dariaumaurius 113.04
darik 096.01
daring 098.22 142.34 274.08 347.12 451.17
Dariou 257.07
Darius 138.27
Darius 307.L1
dark 020.20 063.18 092.32 093.27 108.16 130.13 135.14 136.31 148.04 228.09 246.30 251.24 297.15 328.28 383.19 511.22 526.07 527.07 533.14 544.31 549.09 571.14 598.07 598.07 603.09 606.22
dark 383.05
Dark 087.33 215.36 272.09 620.09
darka 114.24
darkened 020.16 131.27
darkener 418.05
darkenings 037.19
darkens 439.24
darker 387.18
darkest 487.32 545.29
darkfall 570.06
darkies 293.13 603.27
Darkies 175.30
darkist 290.12
darklane 568.22
darkled 434.31
darkles 244.13
darkling 023.23 404.01
darkly 122.31 355.09 626.24
darkness 014.29 079.01 107.21 136.21 139.30 258.32 321.19 493.35
Darkpark's 245.17
darks 226.13 276.20 603.26
darktongues 223.28
darkumen 350.28
darkumound 386.20
darky 515.34
darling 045.20 095.10 147.25 208.35 443.18 459.14 462.16 462.30 463.34 470.10 478.03 478.05 478.29 502.13 505.09 531.01 556.14
Darling 159.28 159.28
darlings 504.28
Darly 137.03
darm 513.27
darnall 108.18
darnels 198.34
darning 201.15
DARNING 300.R1
darr 584.07
darras 388.01
darsey 333.08
darsy 543.20
dart 209.26 285.04 457.27 547.20 599.25
dartars 135.24
darters 558.22
Darthoola 329.17
darting 317.34 496.24 524.23
dartry 305.07
darty 521.19
darwing 252.28
das 130.16 481.33 482.04
Da's 496.20
Da's 105.15
dash 065.16 182.25 232.27 360.01 444.02 446.04 470.31
Dash 210.26 450.31
Dashe 532.21
dashes 120.03 252.24
dasht 199.36
dass 273.06 603.10
dastard 188.14 586.15
dastychappy 357.05
dat 375.32 379.07 477.04 528.27
date 020.03 032.13 039.02 054.02 112.26 120.20 121.29 136.02 167.26 190.16 309.17 329.25 347.07 355.22 395.32 473.08 536.04 575.12 581.35
Date 513.03
dates 087.06 127.36 444.33 580.16
dates 275.L4
datetree 274.15
datey 502.15
dath 517.36
dathe 377.35
dather 396.26
dathering 245.22
Dathy 274.05
dating 575.01
datish 318.16
dative 268.22
datter 583.10
Dattery 550.32
daub 332.11 623.15
Dauber 466.20
dauberg 333.35
daubing 153.04
dauby 492.13
Dauby 492.13
dauctors 413.07
daughter 028.07 117.05 133.26 157.35 212.15 226.10 265.19 284.F4 289.29 294.29 306.15 329.18 366.14 408.31 436.23 500.17
daughter 399.05
daughterpearl 561.15
daughters 036.23 125.09 189.18 210.05 215.29 216.02 430.01 470.04 498.27 505.30 572.16 589.11 601.10
Daughters 060.10 469.02
Daughters 175.23
daughters-in-trade 532.25
daughtersons 215.35
daughterwife 627.02
daughts 327.06
daulimbs 337.26
daulphin 566.20
daulphins 211.21
daum 455.24
daun 350.28
Dauncy 499.06
daunt 229.04 373.32
Daunty 539.06
Dauran's 060.33
Daurdour 238.35
d'autel 462.01
dauvening 365.23
Dav 300.F2
Dave 134.11 462.17 462.30 463.36 494.23
Daveran 146.08
David 172.26 464.03

Davies 391.28
davit 464.36
davors 315.01
davy 008.23 412.05
Davy 070.14 177.20 210.29
davy's 557.10
Daw 496.02
dawdled 250.13
dawdling 306.08 404.04
Dawdy 282.F2
Dawe 554.04
dawk 207.08
dawn 087.36 143.17 169.21 214.23 328.28 523.07 585.20 593.11
Dawn 222.18 293.20 590.25
Dawncing 513.11
dawnfire 594.21
dawnflakes 570.06
dawning 118.32
dawns 194.11
dawnsong 276.19
dawnybreak 353.31
day 011.16 020.05 034.17 036.25 037.06 046.14 051.21 067.33 068.01 068.27 073.36 083.35 095.03 111.03 118.09 125.06 136.30 138.22 144.03 146.24 170.06 175.33 178.08 181.16 182.36 183.02 186.14 192.33 193.07 195.01 202.04 228.08 238.12 238.14 239.11 243.20 248.13 250.13 261.26 270.28 279.F17 281.F1 281.F4 286.F1 290.12 292.25 295.03 306.12 306.F2 321.35 330.11 334.33 340.16 347.15 347.16 347.16 347.17 347.18 360.35 365.05 371.19 374.18 377.21 380.09 382.15 387.19 409.26 413.11 415.20 420.16 425.11 428.22 432.13 456.11 458.29 461.11 472.34 472.34 479.01 491.34 501.17 508.06 517.31 517.33 517.35 520.28 536.25 544.06 548.27 556.02 569.13 578.34 598.12 598.12 606.25 613.29 615.18 617.28 618.13 619.34 623.07 626.08
day 342.07
Day 026.06 027.14 035.24 122.13 226.12 236.08 292.05 444.13 618.26
Day 530.23
Dayagreening 607.24
daybowbreak 546.23
daybroken 191.27
daydreamsed 615.24
daye 338.13
dayeleyves 608.28
dayety 143.04
daying 392.08
daylast 304.21
dayle 366.30
dayleash 613.08
daylight 030.13 321.18 425.21
daylighted 135.30
daylit 083.27
daylives 617.15
dayman 577.32
dayne 079.35 593.02
daynes 593.11 593.11
daynoight 412.06
daynurse 147.21
days 004.34 018.23 056.20 058.22 062.13 064.14 078.01 079.07 097.29 118.11 127.25 136.20 161.14 194.04 203.08 211.06 236.19 237.31 241.07 300.07 312.09 318.08 351.05 351.17 355.25 385.03 390.20 393.07 397.05 422.35 425.26 448.26 468.04 472.32 474.23 506.20 514.11 549.06 549.06 555.06 555.06 568.29 589.20 603.08 615.02 624.01 624.20
days 275.L3 280.L2 399.16
Days 229.13
day's 194.11 347.24 579.35
days' 009.20 101.26
daysends 610.28
daysent 578.14
dayses 398.21
daze 051.01 316.26
dazecrazemazed 389.27
dazed 240.03 550.36
dazes 231.07
dazzle 364.24
dazzlers 444.27
dazzling 145.18
dazzly 234.14
D.B.C. 149.25 (Dublin Bakery Co.)
Dbln 013.14 (Dublin)
de 011.01 012.36 027.16 042.18 049.34 054.16 054.16 081.34 088.26 092.20 119.32 150.04 165.29 169.05 177.30 184.27 184.28 184.28 211.15 212.15 213.35 230.06 230.06 230.06 234.16 234.16 246.01 248.33 272.29 274.23 279.F09 279.F24 291.F8 300.14 303.F3 329.30 329.30 332.19 335.08 357.07 370.22 372.10 377.32 381.06 398.02 420.14 440.17 445.01 465.21 478.23 481.15 494.20 497.15 520.19 543.18 544.36 553.14
de 036.18 043.23 102.18 104.14 153.17 157.32 162.11 165.34 179.27 192.14 204.33 229.02 274.L2 280.L4 281.04 281.04 281.07 281.08 281.08 285.L3 287.20 290.19 291.17 339.33 357.15 376.07 548.28
De 084.36 245.36 285.F6 325.03 334.05 533.16
De 152.26 159.01
d.e. 066.12 (det er)
dea 140.08 140.08
Deacon 257.14
dead 007.18 014.01 062.07 068.25 073.33 079.16 100.01 116.11 165.04 176.35 187.10 194.20 251.26 269.F1 272.23 297.20 303.31 315.04 321.08 323.19 347.23 352.32 378.02 392.06 452.20 455.21 467.22 483.36 489.01 500.01 543.24 560.08 612.04
dead 430.15
Dead 105.29
deadbeat 151.18
deadbest 173.11
Deaddleconche 390.17
deader 170.18
deadheads 407.36
deadhorse 521.12
deading 024.14
deadleaf 271.F5
deadliness 052.01
deadlop 029.03
deadlost 239.03
deadly 358.05 549.09
deadman's 121.36
Deadman's 087.33
deadported 536.02
deadsea 029.24
deadwar 370.32
deady 499.06
deaf 047.24 068.34 097.13 132.14 169.17 200.15 309.03 323.19 331.05 379.20 395.29 582.07
Deaf 307.21 376.33
Deaf 134.36
deafadumped 590.01
deafeeled 335.06
deaferended 284.19
Deafir 352.27
deafman's 467.17
deafspot 498.32
deafths 407.12
deah 407.02
deal 070.03 232.07 253.26 286.14 311.15 462.23 517.05 570.16 599.33
Deal 437.16
Deal 180.05
dealer 451.34
dealered 319.25
dealing 579.19
dealinsh 243.25
dealt 623.35
dealter 568.32
dean 287.18 460.31 485.03 562.32
Deane 211.02 552.11
Deanns 248.26
deans 368.21
dean's 180.13
Deansgrange 057.09
deap 095.30 277.13
dear 049.15 065.12 067.35 076.25 095.10 096.07 102.01 111.14 112.30 116.09 117.09 123.01 131.07 143.31 146.27 148.25 154.03 163.27 171.15 188.22 199.14 204.26 228.30 237.11 269.12 280.34 294.11 294.12 295.25 299.03 302.10 360.14 366.05 384.35 384.35 385.18 386.14 389.20 389.31 390.20 390.20 391.12 392.13 394.22 395.03 395.33 396.22 404.29 409.08 410.29 411.23 414.18 425.26 439.29 442.31 457.32 459.13 459.30 462.18 471.29 474.06 489.36 493.36 500.23 507.19 527.20 533.25 535.31 565.18 565.20 565.30 571.13 581.20 608.03 621.01 625.17 627.07
dear 231.05
Dear 111.10 135.29 215.13 270.F3 280.09 286.15 301.10 301.F5 306.F1 364.11 439.26 535.27 615.12
Dear 107.04 278.L3

dearagadye 313.18
dearast 493.35
dearbraithers 052.11
dearbrathairs 052.12
dearby 180.15
deared 353.10
dearer 101.31 237.11
dearest 207.34 237.12 431.21 448.34 452.08 461.06 472.20 505.09 561.17 577.33
dearest 200.10
dearies 411.08
dearling 146.19 478.05
dearly 413.24 548.06
Dearly 488.04
dearmate 125.08 232.19
dearmud 068.14
dearo 389.20 389.31 389.31 392.12 392.12 581.20
Dearo 581.20
dearome 095.06
dears 093.17 148.11 365.28 433.34 564.27
dearsee 558.34
dearstreaming 148.27
dearth 128.24 130.23 410.16 571.15
Dearthy 370.09
deary 200.16 393.22
deas 466.23
Deataceas 213.30
death 018.27 047.10 078.06 097.33 117.20 132.29 134.21 170.12 172.21 189.34 243.13 274.06 291.F8 293.03 311.15 347.08 369.29 398.10 422.09 466.24 472.29 571.14 573.16 580.03 585.17 605.03
death 201.08
Death 028.22 060.02 595.01
Death 440.02
deathbone 193.29
deathcap 198.32
deathcup 450.31
deathdealing 333.10
deathfête 186.12
deathhow 304.03
Deaubaleau 383.21
debauched 573.01 573.18
debauchly 319.35
Debbling 603.27
debelledem 545.29
debit 172.17
debituary 189.21
deblancer 049.22
deblinite 160.27 160.29
Deblinity 373.20
deborah 415.04
debouch 169.21
deboutcheries 350.16
debt 011.32 173.24 496.04 574.10
debths 199.01
debtor 464.02
debts 123.17 416.09
debuzzled 234.03
Debwickweck 552.02
decade 292.26 444.04
decadendecads 601.14
decades 472.36
decans 261.31
decan's 423.06
decartilaged 437.08
decasualisation 076.07
decay 247.28
decayed 211.24
deceased 173.20 573.30 573.34
deceit 405.14
Deceit 241.29
deceitfold 375.35
Deceitful 436.07
deceive 573.09
deceivers 547.02
Decemberer 201.10
decembs 087.07
decemt 262.01
decemvers 282.26
Decencies 104.07
decency 033.15
decency 340.15
decennia 473.01
decent 014.13 027.22 042.02 042.05 049.21 173.13 419.17 537.13
decentest 050.07
decentius 287.20
decentsoort 043.35
deceptered 290.01
Decer 139.36
decide 005.24 513.31
decided 415.30
decidedly 404.28
deciduously 468.21
decimating 289.F1
deciphered 118.01
decisions 163.33
decisive 063.17 375.23
deck 214.27
deck 342.03
Deck 453.34
Deckel 530.20
deckhuman 619.19
decks 135.22 245.24
Declaim 497.03
declaination 603.23
Declaney 083.24
declaratory 523.06
declare 125.18 153.09 205.03 423.16 452.35 587.24
Declare 584.09
declared 091.03
declareer 075.09
declaret 411.14
declaring 120.07
decline 079.17 214.25
declined 574.20
declosed 063.27
Decoded 232.26
decomposition 614.34
decontaminated 292.15
decorated 545.08
decorded 482.35
decorousness 151.05
decoy 339.22
decoying 028.09
decree 279.F13 390.33 391.16
decrepitude 078.02
decretal 290.11
decretals 155.14
dectroscophonious 123.12
decumans 369.24
D.E.D. 420.30
dedal 179.17
deday 613.08
deductio 165.34
Deductive 363.08
dee 198.26 299.21 299.21 327.10 382.24
Dee 054.11 133.36 226.15 525.33
deed 006.13 011.07 089.28 214.08 214.08 246.30 251.16 258.18 283.F2 310.24 328.28 346.27 347.05 378.18 416.30 440.26 461.30 473.13
Deed 503.12
D.e.e.d 054.05
deedpoll 524.17
deeds 013.31 055.05 137.11 427.24 531.32
deedsetton 239.05
deef 021.23 200.16 512.14 619.10
Deel 206.24
deeleet 272.08
deelight 450.12
deelish 266.F3 457.15
deelishas 351.23
deem 388.05
deemed 545.29
deempeys 532.28
Deemsday 602.20
deemsterhood 362.21
deep 062.08 064.12 095.30 100.04 127.16 135.26 137.07 137.15 206.25 255.27 257.32 301.24 305.07 317.06 328.34 339.23 374.18 410.14 425.25 431.24 454.12 475.24 503.26 530.35 539.17 582.06 588.25 595.28 595.28 605.26
Deep 100.04 321.18 501.11 570.03
deepbrow 006.25
deepdark 203.25
deepdeep 092.32
deepen 385.35
deepend 199.02
deeper 110.28 118.15 404.08 407.13
Deepereras 595.28
deepest 445.28
deepings 428.05
deepknee 067.23
deeplinns 076.25
deeply 035.34 357.15 358.10 406.27 412.22 460.20 488.20 489.29 492.27 511.26 556.21 585.17
Deeply 124.12
deepraised 536.25
deeps 158.15 226.13 387.32 595.28 626.01
Deeps 546.34
deepsea 495.04
deepseeing 075.13
deepseep 366.14
deepseepeepers 389.26
Deepsleep 037.18
deepunded 310.05
deer 079.24
deer 277.L4
Deer 344.32
deerdrive 449.08
deergarth 580.11
deerhaven 244.29
deers 053.18 603.26
Deers 105.34
deeseesee 386.35
deesperation 257.25

deevlin 566.20
defaulter 334.12
defdum 089.33
defeater 334.12
defecalties 366.20
defecate 193.22
defect 081.24
defective 177.16
defeme 092.24
defence 574.11
defenceless 189.09
defences 016.02 588.05
defend 194.01 305.30 411.09
Defend 254.29
defender 334.12
defendy 222.23
Defense 350.16
defensive 162.23
Deferred 488.25
deff 244.17 517.02 535.31
deff 175.25
deffodates 088.25
deffwedoff 123.24
deffydowndummies 530.03
defiance 090.03 184.15
defience 084.22
defile 237.24 365.08 469.13
defileth 034.11
define 256.28
definite 109.23
deflowret 360.30
Defmut 593.21
deformation 509.28
deformer 334.12
deft 109.29 578.12
defunct 413.05
degabug 186.21
deglutables 151.28
degrace 057.23
degree 408.11 438.29 522.27 572.26 611.20
degrees 036.07 036.18 495.34 597.31
Dehlia 415.02
dehlivered 542.31
dei 178.24
deiectiones 185.19
deiffel 314.01
deification 498.21
deified 530.31
deign 252.19
Deimetuus 514.23
dein 163.06
deinderivative 084.16
deispiration 257.25
Deity 036.28 444.01
DEITY 282.R4
dejected 182.35 185.23
dejectedly 121.04
dejester 338.12
dejeunerate 422.08
del 206.06 247.10
Delacey 043.33
Delamode 221.24
Delandy 064.03
delaney 084.08
Delaney 043.33
Delap 378.02
delated 484.08
delayed 040.06
Delays 308.01
Delba 200.09
deleberate 300.21
delectation 558.07
delectations 189.05
delected 223.21
deleteful 118.32
deleteriousness 151.05
deletious 247.20
Delfas 140.15
delfian 378.36
Delgany 334.08
Delhi 501.20
delhightful 497.24
delia 208.29
Delia 147.11
Delian 008.28
deliberate 142.26
deliberatively 115.15
delicacy 515.36
delicate 037.04 172.32 243.25 598.12 602.04
delicately 516.08
delicatissima 562.06
deliciated 486.34
delicious 143.32
delicted 504.21
delictuous 128.29
delight 315.02 329.10 362.21
delightafellay 395.19
delighted 148.06 261.11
delightedly 179.30
delighter 248.20
delightered 296.F1
delightful 495.21
delightfully 220.08 398.18
delights 043.10 350.22 547.14
Delights 071.25
delightsome 224.22
Delightsome 144.13
delimitator 334.15
delimited 132.24
deliquescent 107.10
deliric 513.32
Delisle 578.25
delited 540.06
delitious 616.10
Delittle 492.08
deliver 041.02 576.35
delivered 024.06 027.03 038.23 382.14 431.21 575.09 623.35
Delivered 614.10
deliverer 237.13
deliveried 358.23
delivering 067.16
delivery 431.22 439.19
Delivver 097.30
dell 244.24 555.13 588.24
Dell 203.16
della 009.36
della 162.16 201.18
Dellabelliney 432.21
delldale 007.02
d'elles 281.07
delltangle 465.03
deloothering 195.02
deloused 175.03
delph 304.26
Delphin 376.11
Delphin's 513.09 601.22
delt 229.23
delta 119.21 297.24
d'Elta 221.13
deltas 318.13
Deltas 600.06
delth 626.31
deltic 140.09 492.09
deltilla 194.23
deltoïd 210.09
delts 197.22
delty 614.25
delubberate 300.23
Delude 331.18 331.19
deluded 136.07
deluge 013.36 086.24 214.07 315.13
delugion 367.24
delugium 502.30*
deluscious 148.01
delusional 164.03
deluxiously 038.04
delvan 197.20
delville 503.17
Delville 043.26
delvin 021.06
Delvin 622.35
Delvin 106.26
delving 108.16
delysiums 379.17
dem 172.36 234.16 249.20
Demaasch 491.15
deman 577.32
demand 052.18 076.22 220.04
Demand 105.32
demanded 070.27 573.10
demands 521.21 575.10
Demani 237.30
demasiada 054.17
demask 131.12
demb 073.20 619.06
demented 463.36 507.31
Demetrius 319.05
demi 230.18
demidetached 079.06
Demidoff's 329.23
demifrish 098.24
demilitery 166.04
demise 582.17
demisfairs 129.21
demission 049.35
demivoyelles 116.28
demmed 607.02
demmet 417.21
demnye 376.16
demobbed 501.12
democriticos 551.31
demolition 110.28
demonal 281.17
Demoncracy 167.25
demonetised 574.29
demonican 424.03
demons 274.21
Demon's 056.21
demoralizing 434.01
demosthrenated 542.18
dempty 319.36 386.08
demselle 226.16 226.16
demum 185.24
demun 287.27
demure 569.14
demysell 585.07
den 038.15 179.26 242.02 262.28 278.20 333.35
Den 176.05
denary 261.16
denayed 061.34
denays 043.30
d'engien 146.20
denier 256.29

denighted 615.15
Denis 200.34
Denmark 421.29 529.35
Dennis 316.36
dennises 378.01
denounce 139.27 235.29
dense 062.29 231.15 292.26
densed 365.18
dent 162.24
dentelles 116.29
Denti 440.06
denudation 557.22
deny 034.16 271.15 460.16 537.16 569.26
denying 557.29
Deo 353.18
deodarty 160.08
deossiphysing 277.L5
deoxodised 183.33
deparkment 364.07
depart 167.31 472.33
departamenty 607.26
departed 295.10 381.36 489.07
department 398.26
departure 174.22 543.28
depend 411.10
depended 270.19
depends 487.06 522.18
Dephilim 258.09
dephlegmatised 394.21
depleted 574.36
deplorable 544.23
deplore 536.11
deplored 412.22
deplurabel 224.10
deponent 187.30 523.07
depontify 097.23
Deposed 072.16
deposend 070.17
deposing 085.36 568.30
deposit 574.03
deposited 091.10
depraved 421.36
depravities 573.30
depredation 142.20
depredations 510.27
depressed 136.06 189.09
depression 324.27 565.01
depressors 414.30
deprofound 058.09
deprofundity 394.31
depth 132.30 186.17 255.11 605.26 621.03
depths 029.25 194.03 467.24 516.25
deputiliser 514.26
deputised 092.24
deputising 476.04
der 365.29 530.20 607.08
Der 070.05 213.23 222.10
Der 163.05
derail 097.23
deranged 379.29
derby 446.20 577.28
Derby 454.32
dere 372.22
derelict 292.17
deretane 228.28 557.22
derevatov 505.26
derg 198.25
Derg 582.28
derivative 076.07
derivatur 478.16
derive 527.14
Dermod 137.03
dermot 021.14
derringdo 431.32
Derry 484.33
derryjellybies 006.02
derry's 197.04
Dervilish 513.16
dervish 184.06
Derzherr 289.09
des 256.20 289.26
des 131.09 281.13
desarted 013.27
descanting 140.24
descend 255.28
descendance 289.17
descendant 230.30
descendants 582.10
descended 290.F6 440.33
Descending 298.L2
descends 249.09
descent 150.31 552.06
desception 270.F4
describe 109.24 421.25 422.10
Describe 207.21 306.25
described 048.19 087.13
describes 191.03
describing 430.11 573.29
description 056.01 066.34 080.12
descriptions 585.35
descry 475.08
desdaign 153.15
dese 528.27
desert 321.32 505.03
Desert 421.07
Deserta 309.09
deserted 162.11 174.25
desertions 129.03
deserve 304.14 409.05
deserving 159.26
desh 007.09 172.01
design 066.01 336.01 472.11 559.13 606.21 621.29
Design 297.L1
designate 027.17
designed 190.11 221.24
designing 484.10
desippated 026.31
Desirable 307.04
desire 018.26 125.08 366.35 585.25 599.26
Desire 502.32
desired 121.13 145.06 280.09
desires 226.16 280.23 573.07
desk 235.11
Desmond 514.02
desolate 549.10
Desombres 312.09
despair 263.11 366.35 417.35 448.19 544.34
despatch 343.12
Despenseme 054.13
desperanto 582.08
desperate 064.16 520.04 549.10
desperate 343.15
despertieu 289.22
despite 440.03
desployed 009.12
despondful 110.32
Despond's 018.02
desponent 269.31
despot 386.18
desprit 267.F3
desprot 354.07
despyneedis 433.36
dessed 555.19
destady 598.11
desterrado 289.22
d'Esterre 052.29
destined 455.17
Destinied 421.10
destiny 040.20 413.01
Destiny 297.L1
DESTINY 271.R1
destraction 140.18
destroy 339.23
destroyed 137.10
destroyer 480.13
desultory 118.06
det 054.11
detachably 585.10
detail 188.26
detailed 186.21
details 039.04 606.21 611.03
detarmined 170.11
detch 008.22
detect 165.34
detected 124.20 533.13
detective 061.01
detectors 355.36
deteened 174.29
determination 120.32
DETERMINATION 262.R2
determined 386.18
Determined 536.33
determining 355.02
determinised 150.07
DETERMINISM 262.R2
deterred 189.16
detestificated 438.30
detonation 129.15
detour 228.23
detractors 033.21
detrained 567.33
Detter 490.26
deturbaned 353.06
Deublan 569.20
Deucalion 179.09
deuce 043.11 134.07 253.19 283.04 586.25
Deuce 071.25
Deucollion 538.29 538.30 538.33
deur 092.17
Deus 162.36 162.36
Deus 524.15
Deusdedit 153.28
Deuterogamy 537.26
deuteronomy 004.21
deuterous 478.07
deux 222.09
dev 626.31
Dev 051.13
Deva 287.04 614.25
devaleurised 543.02
develop 172.13
developed 389.16
developing 443.36
development 265.24
devere 492.16
Devereux 563.20
devide 212.17
devil 027.08 046.25 047.23 089.02 196.15 246.28 251.12 252.34 268.F6 314.28 473.08 549.24 579.17
Devil 457.10

devilances 346.06
devilbobs 540.29
devilish 113.29
devilry 417.32
devils 273.F6 439.05 449.26
devil's 051.34 172.21 518.06 582.06
Devil's 204.15
deviltries 365.02
devine 062.07
Devine 290.10
devined 373.20
Devine's 325.01
devious 123.31 197.22
devise 550.25
devisers 585.16
devising 040.26 288.03
devitalised 448.16
Devitt 489.30
Devlin 024.25
devlins 243.22
devlinsfirst 003.24
devoiled 546.06
devorers 023.32
devoted 090.15 159.27 182.18 586.03
devotees 249.23
devotes 616.15
Devotion 306.23
devotionally 424.18
devotions 461.21
devouces 243.35
devoucha 466.20
devour 079.09 538.11
devourced 370.05
devoured 099.15 128.24 392.35 416.21
Devours 388.07
devoused 340.22
devouted 413.20
devouts 348.15 365.29
devowtion 072.24
Devoyd 072.11
dew 095.25 158.20 158.20 213.20 277.07 331.34 375.32 588.17
Dew 372.28
dewed 057.27 568.10
dewfolded 359.32
dewood 293.13
dewry 603.17
dews 409.28 428.11
dew's 024.21
dewscent 330.07
dewstuckacqmirage 470.20
Dewvale 457.11
dewydress 331.09
dewyfully 237.08
dexter 099.30
dexterity 384.26
dextremity 464.23
dextro 198.15
deyes 074.06
Deyus 074.06
dez 187.20
Dg. 324.23 (Am. Dg.)
dgiaour 068.18
dhamnk 365.21
dhaoul 499.18
dharma 093.22
dhee 123.02
dhink 608.22
d'Hiver 548.29
dho 037.25
Dhorough's 341.27
dhouche 462.07
dhoul 024.15
Dhoult 105.12
dhove's 403.16
dhow 029.22
dhrone 417.11
dhruimadhreamdhrue 320.21
Dhu 282.32
dhumnk 365.21
dhymful 536.16
di 048.01 289.02
di 165.02 305.15 412.29
di' 588.17
dia 178.26
diablen 072.34
diabolically 518.04
diabolo 205.10
diaconal 605.15
diademmed 353.08
diadumenos 174.19
Diaeblen-Balkley 326.25
diagelegenaitoikon 416.12
diagnosing 036.35
diagonally 084.19
diagonising 260.10
DIAGONISTIC 275.R1
diagonoser's 290.21
dial 193.16 306.08
dialytically 614.33
diamants 453.34 528.06
diamindwaiting 377.20
diamond 137.03 150.24 406.16 433.15 464.08 578.32
diamondcuts 572.04
diamondinah's 250.31
diamonds 342.02
diamondskulled 498.14
diamoned 359.09
Diana 276.19
dianablowing 476.01
dianaphous 261.11
dianas 043.11
Diander 613.36
diaper 145.11
diapered 121.04
diaphragm 164.36
diar 608.36 608.36
diarmuee 291.28
Diarmuid 306.28
diarrhio 467.19
diary 489.35
Dias 492.08
diasporation 257.25 463.21
diavolo 466.19
Diavoloh 466.27
dib 311.32
dibble 149.07 505.32
Dibble 028.04
dibbler 495.04
dibble's 578.13
dice 283.09
Dicebox 122.13
dice's 433.30
DICHOTOMY 275.R1
Dichter 213.01
dicint 413.05
dick 494.23 604.29
Dick 210.28
dickens 157.27
dickette's 434.27
dickey 568.08
dickhuns 610.03
Dick's 069.34
dicksturping 457.12
dicky 055.15
dictaphone 059.15
dictas 183.14
dictators 185.02
diction 431.22
dictited 170.03
did did Did
didando 232.31
didaredonit 353.11
diddely 466.26
diddest 235.10
Diddiddy 257.21
diddies 179.17
diddled 172.21
Diddled 315.02
Diddlem 219.03
diddydid 554.08
Dideney 284.F1
Didget 519.18
didhithim 358.36
Didicism 294.L2
didits 258.09
did'nt 381.29
didn't 027.35 040.03 073.10 143.34 148.15 148.22 198.16 199.25 200.17 214.07 273.24 320.13 320.30 381.29 409.06 496.29 522.25 587.19
Didn't 198.23 304.19
dido 291.F3
Dido 357.15
dids 539.12
didst 190.01
didulceydovely 327.35
Didymus 258.30
die 111.02 196.05 215.04 223.12 283.F2 293.04 358.36 453.34 456.09 466.26 480.34 536.13 628.11
die 200.07 353.08
Die 215.04 441.13
Die 212.36
died 291.F8
died 399.18
Diehards 443.05
dielate 083.27
dielectrick 322.31
Dieman's 225.26
Diener 131.04
dieobscure 431.32
dieoguinnsis 421.26
dies 302.27
Dies 226.36 609.28
Dies 481.05
diesmal 301.26
diesparation 257.26
diet 544.36
Diet 026.29 307.26
dietcess 433.05
Dietician 437.22
dieting 097.20
dieudonnay 478.26
Dieudonney 369.10
Dieuf 149.03
dieva 147.24
dieybos 019.31
differ 096.17
difference 130.29 269.15 528.30 581.35
differenciabus 481.18

differended 357.29
different 082.11 092.11 156.01 172.05 173.35 335.25 381.33 381.34 382.07 576.22
Different 179.28
differentiation 142.19
differently 118.26 481.11
differents 417.10
differing 077.11 215.17
differs 150.18
difficoltous 348.03
difficult 251.25
difficultads 302.17
difficulties 151.30 510.05
diffle 149.06
diffpair 059.34
diffused 056.17
diffusing 359.31
difinely 389.16
dig 186.20 282.F3 320.33 320.33 607.17
Dig 261.L2
digaditchies 241.01
digamma 120.34
digarced 338.13
digesting 163.36
digests 183.21
digged 373.01
digger 180.11
Diggerydiggerydock 378.16
Digges 313.26
diggin 326.17
Diggin 069.09
digging 069.33 428.23
diggings 027.07 239.25
Diggins 596.12
diggy 430.15
digit 321.26
dignagging 583.09
dignified 055.17
dignisties 567.15
Digteter 423.18
diie 006.13
Dijke 100.31
dik 104.11
Dik 578.06
dilalah 067.33
dilalahs 523.16
dilapidating 544.13
dilatation 558.06
dilate 027.21
dilates 345.31
diligence 228.17
Diligence 457.23
diligences 167.26
dilisk 392.33
diliskious 370.18
diliskydrear 209.20
Dilke 090.04
dillisks 550.11
dillon 288.01
Dillon 586.15
dilltoyds 531.05
Dilluvia 585.32
Dilmun 136.01
dilsydulsily 031.24
dilute 232.01
diluv's 315.13
dim 088.03 096.28 330.10 565.29 565.30 593.14 614.25 625.21
dimb 053.02 237.08
Dimb 006.09
dimbelowstard 607.26
dimdom 594.06
dime 065.11 109.02 138.15 138.15 150.23 161.06 364.15 454.03
dime-cash 149.17
dime-dime 149.21
dimension 420.02 467.23
dimensional 154.26
dimensions 442.26 498.28
dimentioned 299.06
dimeshow 163.13
diminishing 611.31
diminitive 278.F2
diminuendoing 354.04
Diminussed 609.30
dimissage 298.07
dimities 067.28
Dimitrius 027.25
dimkims 373.34
dimm 143.27
dimmed 424.32
dimmen 606.15
dimmering 014.30
dimmers 501.18
dimming 462.09
dimned 484.16
dimpled 273.14
dimpler 282.19
dimples 220.08
dimpling 028.19
dimply 398.20
dims 226.12
dimsdzey 347.08
dimsweet 357.24
dimtop 449.23
dimtwinklers 131.28
din 006.25 058.14 112.15 586.13 627.27
din 346.16
Dina 175.35
Dinah 141.29
Dinahs 226.02
Dinamarqueza 328.14
dinar 170.03
dinars 243.25
dindians 483.08
dindin 110.03
dindy 092.20
dine 457.21
dined 117.25
dinful 140.18
ding 249.21 293.13 586.13
Ding 028.24 377.35 528.18 611.21
dingbushed 285.17
dingbut 349.04
dinggyings 256.31
dingle 327.17
Dingle 499.29
Dingle 399.03
dingnant 014.28
dingo 168.11
Dingoldell 360.33
Dingy 093.16
Dining 420.29
dinkel 203.17
dinkety 395.05
dinkum 108.28 384.22
dinkun's 258.09
dinky 115.15
Dinky 469.17
dinmurk 143.07
dinn 023.22 262.F5
Dinn 121.34
dinna 116.19 391.05
dinnasdoolins 372.16
dinned 312.12 378.22
dinner 035.16 127.30 406.01 434.10
dinnerchime 026.28
dinners 205.18 544.14
Dinnin 377.36
dinny 558.31
Dinny 232.06 327.17 332.33
dinsiduously 580.19
dint 547.30
dinties 583.03
dio 466.19
Diobell 434.25
diocesan 062.35
diodying 171.17
Diogenes 307.L1
diogneses 411.29
Dion 385.03 391.23
Dionysius 070.36
Dionysius 307.L1
dioram 156.02
diorems 292.05
dip 397.26 427.06 433.30 587.21
dip 201.14
Dip 333.18 334.08 334.11 334.16
dipandump 223.04
dipdip 483.08
dipdippingdownes 549.04
diplussedly 156.09
dipped 138.25 493.09
dipper 577.06 581.14
dipperend 342.35
dippies 524.34
dipping 447.07
dippy 065.20 065.29 065.32
dips 226.15
diputy 277.09
dirckle-me-ondenees 139.21
dire 136.20 224.10 224.10 362.29 366.24 427.17
direct 069.01 167.28 187.32 268.21 438.27 490.11
directing 529.26
direction 051.09 084.01 249.28 427.04 491.11
direction 342.35
directions 073.19 114.04 298.29 432.05 618.21
directly 076.07 232.30 252.16
director 038.19 050.20
directory 118.13
Directory 534.21
Directus 261.21
Diremood 125.06
direst 617.07
dirging 276.04
dirgle 206.17
dirigible 112.19
Dirk 550.31
dirkandurk 055.21
Dirke 485.11
dirls 601.18
dirly 601.17
Dirouchy 344.32

dirt 043.31 175.02 187.10
196.12 374.27 407.03 437.16
444.22 503.07 506.36 507.21
543.33
Dirt 072.13
dirtby 062.06
Dirtdump 615.12
dirted 141.11
dirth 130.23
dirthdags 484.14
dirther 392.34
dirtiment 353.04
dirts 242.22
dirty 060.35 080.30 131.06
139.22 171.30 173.28 286.10
339.02 362.24 433.25 444.14
490.23 524.28 535.29 584.24
620.21
Dirty 008.27 069.34 094.34
209.26 215.13
dirtynine 534.12
Dis 528.27
disabled 409.26
disagreed 574.32
disagreeing 574.33
disagreement 574.33
disagrees 214.22 323.18
disappainted 090.16
disappaled 427.07
disappear 615.17
disappeared 050.08
disappointed 286.28
disappointing 437.22
disappointments 107.33
disarranging 438.03
disasperaguss 448.17
disassembling 358.33
disaster 143.22 189.34
disbarred 411.02
discalced 448.30
discarding 030.05
discarnate 292.15
discharge 313.20
discharged 040.16 529.14 586.05
dischurch 431.25
discinct 297.21
discinctis 185.15
disciple 166.22
discipline 306.15 520.28
Discipline 411.14
discipular 112.22
disclothe 543.14
discoastedself 321.06
discobely 294.12
Disconnection 228.17
disconnections 348.06
discontent 407.34
discontinue 537.16
disconvulsing 231.16
discord 564.04
discordance 564.02
discounted 575.11
discountenanced 537.03
discouraged 070.30
discourse 485.14
discover 220.01
discovered 188.15 482.32 573.11
Discovered 559.21
discredit 033.24
discrimination 358.34
discurverself 540.33
discussing 187.22
discusst 275.19
disdag 531.01
disdain 079.14
disdoon 472.06
disdotted 121.16
disease 033.18
diseased 242.02
Diseased 069.15
diseasinesses 223.01
disembers 024.11
disemvowelled 515.12
disengaged 306.F3
diserecordant 450.28
disgeneration 331.31
disgenically 436.09
disghosted 136.07
disgrace 220.02 227.23 391.02
434.21 530.28
disgrace 260.L1
Disgrace 413.03
disguides 363.09
disguise 457.10
disguised 038.26 099.07 527.25
disguising 086.10
disgust 544.32
disgusted 060.25 408.05
disgustedly 174.32
disgustered 212.33
disgusting 521.08
dish 037.31 172.36 276.16
455.31
dishcover 577.18
dished 068.10 408.09 426.14
457.15
disheen 114.24
dishes 123.17 544.03
dishevelled 395.03
dishonest 572.21
dishorned 112.22
disigraible 301.F4
disimally 440.15
disincarnated 535.36
disinfected 436.15
disinterestingly 179.12
disjointed 104.05
disjunctively 524.19
disk 317.12 408.29
disliked 174.05
Disliken 050.06
dislocated 189.30
dismal 549.09
dismantled 125.02
dismay 483.14
dismissed 252.30
dismissem 364.02
dismissing 364.33
disoluded 081.12
disorded 286.F3
disorder 126.09
disossed 415.11
disparition 427.30
disparito 289.22
dispatch 009.03
Dispatch 009.03
dispensation 037.24 310.33
337.04
dispensations 495.10
dispenses 573.18
Dispersal 101.01
dispillsation 095.01
Dispitch 009.12
dispitchback 009.12
displace 612.08
displaced 090.03
displaid 227.22
display 495.25 569.22
Display 206.13
displayed 431.03 557.27
displeaced 292.04
disposal 491.33
disposale 149.17
disposed 538.02
disposition 546.12
disqualifications 529.07
disrespects 460.09
Disrobe 586.04
disrobing 238.16
diss 603.09
dissassents 575.35
disseized 574.05
disselving 608.05
disseminating 425.11
dissent 504.29
dissentant 313.33
dissenting 073.02
disserve 366.11
dissimulant 298.10
dissimulating 384.34
dissipated 453.30
dissolution 362.30
distance 008.02 228.25 309.05
429.09
distancegetting 309.18
distances 539.25
distant 123.13 169.06 458.34
distend 358.03
distented 317.31
distilleries 589.36
distillery 082.06 373.25 543.33
Distillery 122.12
distilling 196.21
distinct 114.13 150.16 306.F7
distinction 122.28
distinction 295.L2
distinctly 086.24 131.06 272.21
Distinctly 092.11
distinguish 463.25 522.29
distinguished 075.24 219.09
463.24
distorted 111.29
Distorted 265.28
distortions 184.04
distracted 092.33
distrain 153.16
distress 164.18 470.09
Distressed 270.12
distressful 533.14
distressfully 474.06
Distributary 089.26
distribute 302.28
DISTRIBUTION 271.R1
distributory 472.18
district 085.26 265.F2 507.02
599.27 624.32
districts 580.03
disturb 620.36
Disturbance 071.18
disturbed 070.07 573.23
disturbing 544.04
disumbunking 388.20
disunited 188.16 394.34 395.33
ditch 079.25 209.15 517.14
ditcher 318.13
ditchers 053.17
ditcher's 586.15
ditches 108.16
ditches 341.22

dite 504.19
dither 396.25
ditherer 438.08
dithering 245.22
dito 442.27
dito 212.35 212.35
ditties 255.33
ditto 489.09 559.11
Ditto 213.02
dittoes 449.20
dittoh 019.21
diu 159.20
Diu 598.09
diublin's 331.19
diupetriark 153.27
diurn 598.32
div 626.33
diva 415.04 466.20 492.09
Diva 560.02
divane 536.18
divans 177.10
divarts 203.11
divases 598.12
dive 040.29 210.01 282.07 314.10
diveline 202.08
divelsion 285.F3
Diveltaking 627.04
divergent 034.24
divers 039.33 066.14 099.13
diverse 517.04
diversed 381.20
diversified 061.31
diversion 395.26
diversity 610.24 610.25
diverted 179.24
diverting 164.31
dives 078.29 321.04 579.20
divested 132.09
divi 185.24
Divi 418.04
divided 522.10
dividends 585.16
dividual 186.04
divil 147.02 473.21 580.14
Divilcult 303.F1
divileen 511.12
diviliouker 183.33
divine 078.11 337.05 435.15 440.06 451.17 527.11 527.19 560.35 563.33 598.12
Divine 082.04
Divine 106.28
divinely 148.01
divine's 190.22
divining 233.36 279.F26 599.13
DIVINITY 282.R4
division 536.30
divisional 268.09 523.35
divisions 333.11
divlin's 329.03
divlun 227.22
divorce 260.F3 422.05 441.29 586.06
Divorce 032.33 071.28
divorced 172.07 220.01 390.19 391.11 392.07
divorcee 095.10
divorces 423.03 442.07
divorsion 009.35
Divulge 340.31 441.24
divulse 255.24
divver's 300.04
divvy 306.F1
divy 451.19
Divy 316.19
Dix 370.09
dixtinguish 063.26
di'yegut 455.10
di'yesmellygut 455.10
di'yesmellyspatterygut 455.11
dizzed 550.36
Dizzier 471.07
Dizzier's 408.23
dizzledazzle 113.01
dizzy 073.07 373.27
Djadja 348.23
Djamja 537.24
Djanaral 492.29
Djinpalast 597.13
Djowl 222.31
Djoytsch 485.13
Djublian 340.06
d'lin 448.11
Dmn 515.06
Dmuggies 342.02
dmzn 113.05
dneepers 196.18
do do Do Do
Do 308.06
d'o 478.20
doaked 601.02
doalittle 010.32
doat 027.05
doatereen's 376.10
doaters 526.35
doatty 330.07
doaty 398.19
dob 480.30 480.30
Dobbelin 007.12
dobblenotch 353.19
dobbling 480.30
dobblins 316.36
dobelon 208.33
doblinganger 490.17
D'Oblong's 266.06
dobrey 333.08
doc 256.27
Doc 287.F3 485.29
docence 155.27
Docetism 294.L2
dochter 199.35
docile 473.14
dock 023.36 085.32 569.17
Dock 569.17
dockandoilish 466.23
Dockrell 294.23
doctator 170.22
doctor 269.25 394.12 432.07
doctor 606.07
Doctor 025.04 140.30 193.06
doctored 438.36
doctors 031.07 290.06
doctor's 215.18
doctrina 031.23
doctrine 108.12 440.16 476.25 482.36
document 107.25 109.13 123.32
documents 107.25
Dod 389.32
Dodd 191.23
Doddercan 523.26
dodderer 201.08
Dodderick 498.23
doddhunters 283.25
Doddpebble 620.19
dode 100.30
dodear 492.16
dodecanesian 123.27
dodewodedook 340.20
dodge 277.26
dodged 285.09
dodgemyeyes 025.03
dodgers 321.29
dodges 374.02
Dodgesome 228.16
Dodgfather 482.01
dodginess 184.17
dodging 068.01 194.34 363.30 625.22
dodgsomely 057.26
Dodgson 482.01
dodo 199.09 397.28 531.07
Dodo 533.20
dodos 367.34
dodwell 212.33
doe 139.03 338.25 372.04
doed 392.11
Doeit 105.34
Doelsy 398.18
doer 246.30 333.01 333.03
doerehmoose 053.18
does Does
doesend 335.27
doeslike 226.35 226.36 227.01 227.01
doesn't 134.13 458.17
doevre 164.18
doez 562.17
doff 457.22 457.22
Doff 532.05
doffed 430.17
doffensive 078.30
doffer 415.13
doffered 620.16
doffers 183.34
doffing 136.23
dog 039.34 043.04 068.18 177.08 186.20 186.32 233.13 279.F26 376.29 411.19 479.03 506.36 508.02 517.36 589.16
Dog 436.23 567.19 567.19
Dog-an-Doras 073.26
dogdhis 596.02
doge 074.16
doges 578.13
dogess 391.36
dogfox 030.18
Doggies 039.35
Dogging 620.33
doggo 454.10
Doggymens' 528.33
doglegs 351.20
dogmad 158.03
dogmarks 161.08
dogmestic 411.23
dognosed 254.01
dogpoet 177.21
dogril 498.16
dogs 018.27 285.16 380.29 623.02
dog's 054.07 171.30 355.32
Dogs' 276.11
dogshunds' 548.15
dogstar 194.14
dogumen 482.20
doherlynt 232.13
doil 256.28
doin 231.34

doing doing
doings 139.27
Dola 621.21
Dolando 570.03
doldorboys 266.18
Dole 060.01
doleful 549.09
Dolekey 533.08
doles 130.16 541.10
dolightful 291.25
dolings 597.18
doll 197.20 210.23 266.18 268.F7 328.31 444.35 575.24
Doll 298.09 298.11 469.17
dollar 288.01
Dollarmighty 562.33
Dolldy 339.03
dolled 397.16
Dolled 492.08
dollies 019.09
dollimonde 327.25
dollmanovers 570.05
dolls' 294.F1
dolly 166.12 226.16 226.17 451.01
Dolly 246.26 294.21 562.06
dollybegs 430.34
dollymaukins 365.12
dollymount 580.22
dolmeny 499.12
dolomite 241.19
dolores 609.05
Dolores 601.22
doloriferous 274.15
dolour 588.14
dolours 278.F2
Dolph 286.25 287.18
dolphin 160.19
dolphins 275.F6
Dolphin's 434.27
dolthood 492.08
dom 022.18
Dom 197.18 352.33 568.23 625.20
Domas 258.31
domb 022.10 599.31
Domb 149.03
Dombdomb 197.18
dombell 604.11
dombkey 020.25
Dombly 415.15
dombs 595.02
dombstom 346.16
domday's 588.34
domdom 354.01
dome 240.11 541.05
domecreepers 006.05
domefool 299.16
domesday 485.06
domestic 114.15 181.32 280.15 438.23 545.05 616.36
domestication 539.34
domestics 166.16
dometry 230.05
domfine 547.25
Domhnall 129.26 129.26
Dominae 513.05
dominate 194.12
dominators 498.34
Domine 193.31
domineered 551.05
Domini 398.31
Dominic 261.20
dominical 187.11
Dominical 342.11
dominican 072.23 432.07
Dominic's 580.05
domino 554.08
Domino 485.19 496.13
Dominoc's 422.29
dominos 433.07
domisole 267.15
Domitian 306.L2
domm 261.17
dommed 353.01
Domnall 420.28
domnas 492.08
domnatory 593.21
Domne 239.15
Domnial 322.34
Domnkirk 326.25
domov 411.18
Domoyno 609.24
domp 325.23
Dompkey 568.26
dompling 333.33
domstered 545.30
domstoole 352.03
domum 230.06
domunum 165.34
don 121.22
Don 050.19 084.36 094.02 197.17 365.16 375.23 428.18 496.02
Dona 388.15
Doña 297.F1
Donachie's 624.16
donahbella 585.24
donal 499.11
Donald 071.24
donalds 087.25
donated 309.12
donation 551.17
donatrices 093.16
Donatus 563.18
Donauwatter 578.19
Donawhu 076.32
donconfounder 323.06
Dondderwedder 283.L2
dondhering 525.20
done done
dones 341.01
dong 249.21 366.32 528.18
Dong 377.35
dongdong 238.31
donggie 373.04
dongu 206.08
donk 555.13
donker 383.23
donkers 566.31
donkey 024.22 234.04
Donkeybrook 537.35
donkeyman 477.22
donkeys 069.22 459.34
donkey's 014.35
donkeyschott 482.14
donkness 427.11
Donn 211.32 337.30
Donnaurwatteur 078.05
donnelly 281.F3
Donnelly 039.17
Donnelly's 585.28
Donnerbruch 323.09
Donnerbruck 499.33
donnery 261.16
Donnez-moi 046.18
Donnicoombe 334.35
donning 191.27
Donnuley 518.30
Donnybrook 142.12 563.26
donochs 328.10
Donogh 106.02
donor 425.10
donours 318.22
Dons 281.L2
donsk 016.06
dont 044.18 263.F2 332.03
Dont 260.L3
don't don't Don't
Donyahzade 032.08
doo 046.32 244.10 382.24 595.30
doob 287.08
dood 264.F1 479.13 499.06 499.06
Dood 479.13 499.06
doodah 524.36
doodle 299.F4
doodledoo 584.22
doodler 421.33 464.22
Doodles 299.F4
doodling 306.08
doodlum 337.29
doodly 040.12
dooforhim 010.19
doofpoosts 221.32
doog 354.03
dooing 394.14
dook 595.30
dook 354.19 354.19
Dook 032.15 127.17 330.26 371.36
Dook 071.19
dooley 010.05 010.06
Doolin 210.19 332.10
dooly 240.12
doom 049.02 091.22 127.28 255.12 309.03 351.35 483.18 496.04 517.31 552.25 593.14
Doom 598.11
doombody 289.15
doomed 017.16 056.05 194.11 294.16 323.26
doomering 316.17
doominoom 613.03
dooms 128.07
doom's 049.02 583.23
doomsdag 199.04
doomster 049.17
doon 200.17 370.14
Doon 369.12
Doone 614.03
doonloop 394.14
doon's 340.09
door 043.09 046.09 046.10 064.10 073.28 075.12 078.25 116.17 137.19 209.29 316.20 333.02 385.08 388.27 394.01 405.28 442.31 486.30 544.10 559.36 572.09 606.08 615.34 622.26 623.06
Door 427.05
doorak 354.03
doorbell 059.35
doorboy 142.09
doorbrasses 041.11
doorknobs 378.01
doornail 024.15
doornoggers 572.03

doorplate 182.33
doorpost 178.09
doors 129.20 135.22 186.30 377.02 438.01
doorstep 455.19 456.36
Doorsteps 141.18
doorway 040.18 535.10
doorweg 086.26
doos 438.05
doot 357.20
dootch 021.20
dooty 568.25
dooves 579.15
dope 068.21 241.24 320.01 511.32 537.05
Dope 287.F3 336.08
doped 209.09 339.26
dopedope 104.11
doper 320.02
doppeldoorknockers 445.31
dopter 314.30
dopy 603.20
dor 349.01
Dor 020.18
Dora 211.10 228.16 519.05
Doran 112.27
Dorans 111.05 372.31 518.26
doran's 584.21
doraphobian 478.32
Dora's 443.05
dorass 067.19
dorckaness 470.07
d'oreiller 572.23
Doremon's 433.04
dores 249.19
dorfy 374.18
Dorhqk 140.21
Dorian 450.18
doriangrayer 186.08
Doris 462.07
dorkeys 285.14
dorkland 313.19
dorksey 322.17
dormant 066.26 474.02
dormas 565.26
dormer 192.30 551.05
dormerwindow 118.18
Dormidy 598.10
dormimust 158.20
dorming 091.24
Dorminus 609.28
dormis 565.25
dormition 561.28
dormont 012.35 386.20
dororrhea 283.28
doroughbread 317.01
Dorsan 417.31
dorsay 405.05
dorse 448.35
dorst 565.06
dorter 333.29
dorters 572.16
dorty 333.33
dos 339.08 376.13
dose 170.20 178.26 528.27 601.17
Dose 535.13
dosed 438.36
dosiriously 470.13
doss 267.F6 329.23 435.27 580.31 603.09
dosshouse 481.29
dossier 374.25
dossies 524.24
Dost 518.13
dot 232.27 238.01 532.23 626.09
Dot 210.25
Dotch 140.03
dote 052.15 395.31 459.27
doth 032.06 139.17 454.03 512.22 534.22 561.28 565.13
Doth 224.28 254.21 562.06
dothe 143.30
dother 396.26
doting 148.25
dots 127.36 446.04
dot's 444.35
Dotsh 290.F6
dotted 589.02
dotter 068.14 372.03 595.05
Dotter 430.15
dotthergills 215.14
dotties 296.25
dottrin 326.33
dotty 360.01
Dotty 527.17
Doubbllinnbbayyates 303.07
double 134.04 185.32 319.24 328.32 365.18 441.25 450.21 471.20 490.06 523.31 534.29 560.12 573.03 579.09 595.24 619.35
double 349.13
Double 528.19
doublecressing 288.03
doubled 168.07 180.15 578.08
doubledasguesched 232.33
doubleface 363.21
Doublefirst 450.34
doublejoynted 027.02
doublemonth's 329.19
Doublends 020.16
doubleparalleled 286.F4
doubles 039.04 138.03
doublesixing 048.13
doublet 578.08
doubleviewed 296.01
doubleyous 120.28
doublin 003.08 578.14
doubling 097.09 197.05 290.16 295.31 413.25 462.19 543.01
doubloons 086.30
Doubly 489.21
doubt 089.12 100.31 153.11 160.09 365.20 394.23 421.30 456.13 466.11 471.29 531.29 567.23 575.34
doubt 345.22
Doubt 202.19
doubtful 114.09 183.11 188.17
doubtlings 374.18
Doubtlynn 248.07
doubts 109.30 117.35 416.10 458.19
douce 462.09 577.06
douche 211.10 290.16 326.11 605.02 605.02
douches 171.26
douching 411.04
Douchka 106.17
douchy 371.06
Doug 397.02
Dougal 479.10
Dougall's 405.06
Dougals 391.04
Douge 290.11
dough 407.30 441.35 498.20 531.07
dough 530.24
doughboys 529.24
doughboys 349.26
doughdoughty 363.21
doughdy 531.07
Doughertys' 374.15
doughtier 132.28
douh 396.06
douls 588.28
doulse 588.28
doun 069.11
douncestears 219.03
dour 021.16 021.17 021.19 049.21 333.33 556.34 577.06
Dour 371.06
dourest 577.33
dournailed 329.24
douro 200.18
doused 624.14
douters 616.04
douth-the-candle 188.34
douze 175.25
dove 067.36 203.08 227.29 232.12 247.35 266.F3 276.05 457.27 515.34
Dove 521.17
dovecotes 129.22
dovedoves 459.03
Dovegall 500.04
Doveland 061.02
doveling 550.23
dovely 357.17
doves 136.29
dovesandraves 363.07
dovesgall 021.23
dovessoild 336.30
dovetimid 093.17
dovey 147.01
Doveyed 434.28
Dovlen 377.22
Dovolnoisers 350.15
dowager 566.18
Dowager 390.36
dowager's 566.21
dowan 009.29 566.11
dowandshe 556.35
dowanouet 408.04
dowanstairs 556.34
dowce 208.29
dowdycameramen 435.09
dower 327.28
dowerstrip 233.06
dowling 624.23
Dowling 492.21
down down Down Down
Downaboo 054.01
Downadown 010.28 010.28
downadowns 509.34
downalupping 395.06
downand 557.04
downandoutermost 194.19
Downbellow 383.22
Downes 139.36 603.09
downfall 273.10
downfumbed 482.21
downg 072.32
downin 060.36
Downlairy 040.30
downlook 570.32
downpour 043.34 174.23

downright 065.25 118.16 153.11 527.24
downs 101.06 427.06 593.02 593.02
Downs 221.08
downsaduck 135.26
downsaw 542.16
downslyder 505.07
down-to-the-ground 161.34
downtrodden 056.24
downtrodding 151.10
downupon 289.01
downwards 210.23
downy 562.01
dowon 334.14
dowser 577.05
doxarchology 388.29
doxologers 454.30
doying 392.11
doyle 322.16
Doyle 574.09 575.06 575.07
Doyler 575.32
doyles 142.26 574.32
Doyle's 575.07
doylish 575.09
d'Oyly 279.F21
D'Oyly 574.01
doyne 052.17
Doyne 485.20
doze 329.11 367.24 415.06 597.22
doze 201.11 345.08
Doze 566.04 614.13
dozed 310.18
dozedeams 293.12
dozen 006.01 109.02 155.20 155.21 161.28 179.08 211.20 221.03 327.35 335.06 385.24 435.09 446.20 451.06 472.28 498.26 511.06 524.19 574.31 589.26
dozen 265.L2
dozendest 050.07
dozens 135.22
Dozi 262.F2
dozing 404.04
D.P, 498.09 (Druids D.P,)
dr 456.30 (debtor)
Dr 026.30 (Dr Tipple's)
150.11 (Dr Gedankje)
150.17 (Dr Hydes)
163.35 (Dr Burroman)
301.02 (Dr Brassenaarse)
405.05 (Dr Tarpey's)
475.27 (Dr Shunadure Tarpey)
505.24 (Dr Melamanessy)
525.04 (Dr Rutty)
603.22 (Dr Chart)
Dr. 179.28 (Dr. Poindejenk)
drab 436.26
drabs 060.36
Draco 343.02
Dracula's 145.32
Drade's 601.27
draeper 608.05
draff 535.21
draft 574.20
drag 616.25
draggedasunder 546.12
dragging 102.08 121.07 321.11 516.10
draggletail 436.26
dragoman 479.09 486.08
dragon 015.34 024.05 480.26 540.01 559.12 583.18
dragonfly 244.27
dragon-the-market 316.30
dragooned 134.05
drags 585.20
drahereen 096.13
draiming 406.27
draims 623.31
drain 134.17 142.20 214.02 320.31 332.10 363.29
Drain 074.19
drainer 311.03
draining 031.11
Drainophilias 110.11
drains 541.10
drake 142.02 197.13 466.05
drakeling 406.17
draken 358.29
Draken 479.32
drakes 123.17 364.34 390.08
dram 314.23 521.08
drama 474.05
dramas 577.32
dramatic 342.20
dramdrinker 107.32
drame 110.11 302.32
drames 049.32 277.17
dramhead 349.02
drammen 198.34
dramn 464.21 615.26
dramped 488.19
dranchmas 182.24
drang 262.28
Drang 300.L2
drank 023.07 067.34 240.22
drankasup 009.17
draped 225.35 462.32 550.24
Draper 211.02 421.25
drapery 120.06
draphole 521.08
drapier-cut-dean 550.27
drapped 491.18
drapyery 422.01
draraks 491.18
drars 065.19
drary 491.30
drat 239.36
draught 311.19 412.08 419.26 579.17
draught 340.16
draughtness 549.21
draughts 385.26 578.24
draughty 150.29
drauma 115.32
Draumcondra's 293.F1
drave 276.F2
draves 214.35
draw 035.26 238.17 292.31 377.08 445.14 456.25 521.01
Draw 145.33 621.24
drawadust 447.13
drawars 205.12
drawbreeches 389.35
drawen 224.23
drawens 224.23 224.27
drawers 014.26
drawes 143.30
Drawg 377.16
drawhead 254.12
drawher 457.26
drawhure 457.15
drawing 447.16 622.18
Drawing 113.30
drawings 308.F2
drawl 197.05 381.21
drawling 338.34
drawls 622.25
drawly 333.14
drawn 078.31 114.10 212.34 306.28 559.05 566.22 566.24 574.16
drawoffs 465.06
drawpairs 238.01
drawpers 608.06
drawringroam 126.20
draws 068.33 162.08 172.08 246.23 457.09 561.31 610.36
draym 527.06
dread 020.05 024.05 161.01 480.26 528.04
dreaded 577.10
dreadful 177.30 238.14 549.10
dreads 531.04
dreadths 349.26
dream 028.07 189.15 280.35 297.F3 304.21 397.01 404.03 460.21 470.11 470.11 472.13 474.04 480.22 502.29
dream 153.07
Dream 307.12 481.07 602.24
dreamadoory 377.02
dreambookpage 428.16
Dreamcolohour 176.10
Dreamcountry 293.F1
dreamed 064.04 577.09
dreamend 565.18
dreamerish 608.19
dreamers 577.31
dreamily 449.29
dreaming 230.27 295.10 444.31 468.34
dreamings 427.13 556.32
dreamland 615.28
dreamlifeboat 065.30
dreamoneire 280.01
dreams 081.16 130.32 139.25 143.06 146.06 192.27 277.17 338.30 393.36 398.22 532.33
Dreams 176.11
dreamskhwindel 426.27
dreamt 203.01 209.28 264.F2 404.13 449.18 481.07
dreamwings 576.14
dreamydeary 005.26
dreamyums 089.03
Dreans 381.19
drear 329.17 476.21
dreardrizzle 552.35
dreariodreama 079.28
drears 145.12
dreary 136.21
dredgerous 197.22
dreeing 199.05
dreemplace 527.06
dreeper's 529.12
dreeping 571.13
Dreeping 441.13
dreevy 333.14
dregs 321.29
drema 069.14
drench 139.25 533.03
drenched 051.12 461.16
drengs 025.14

dress 024.29 148.07 165.15 167.09 182.26 219.23 235.34 261.F1 420.24 498.28 505.08 624.22
Dress 435.24
dressed 166.12 404.16
dresser 578.35 622.07
dresser's 153.15
dresses 226.16
dressing 279.F22 311.07
dressparading 327.16
dressy 055.14 166.06
drest 250.31
dreven 098.03
drew 190.22 238.24 311.07 314.04 329.23 476.32 582.34
drewbryf 418.27
Drewitt's 279.F27
drey 133.29
dreyfussed 078.21
Dreyschluss 139.33
dribble 370.20
dribbled 153.06
dribblederry 210.04
dribbling 209.19
dried 118.33 153.11
drier 209.20 540.36
dries 136.05
drift 128.20 424.31
driftbombs 304.16
drifted 628.06
drifter 477.12
drifting 159.07
drifts 212.30
drikking 416.10
drill 253.27 544.24
drilled 014.13
drills 315.05
Drily 406.21
drim 223.10
Drimicumtra's 601.24
dring 094.28 348.11
dringing 376.11
drink 023.33 024.15 063.23 070.26 145.19 180.20 247.28 311.03 376.26 380.29 423.11 451.15 461.35 561.14 566.03 579.19 580.09 611.11
Drink 009.17 051.20 453.35
Drink 105.12
drinkards 312.31
Drinkbattle's 093.16
drinking 020.04 174.12 177.18 311.15 381.34 385.26 507.05 513.33 624.34
drinklords 141.24
drinks 098.25 130.04 511.26
drinkthedregs 129.01
drip 192.15 204.22 362.24
dripdropdrap 073.17
drippeling 337.24
drippindhrue 378.28
dripping 086.05 136.10 277.F5 315.14 330.16 441.08 461.16 578.28
Dripping 260.F2
drisheens 164.22
driv 136.29
drive 129.32 193.14 377.07 510.08 531.31 533.15 547.18
Drive 369.08
drivel 173.33
driven 142.23 149.20 525.13
driver 089.01
drives 018.26
driving 225.17 436.31
drizzle 428.03 428.04
drizzles 324.33
drob 370.20
drobs 344.09
droemer 327.22
Drogheda 031.18 518.06
droghedars 566.11
drogist 102.20
drogueries 358.35
drohneth 099.16
drohnings 321.28
droit 017.21
droit 572.23
droll 362.21
drolleries 139.24 587.08
drollo 230.05
dromed 295.13
Dromedaries 241.29
Dromilla 211.08
droming 199.06
dromium 089.03
drommen 198.35
Drommhiem 277.15
dromo 598.02
droners 585.21
drones 485.27 498.34
droning 389.01
dronk 408.36
dronnings 333.22
drooght 413.25
drool 619.31
droomodose 351.17
droop 204.24 278.F3
droopadwindle 122.35
drooped 225.35
droopers 608.06
drooping 291.F3
Droopink 441.13
droopleaflong 470.25
drooplin 370.19
drop 026.32 113.26 115.04 151.25 171.23 180.19 192.10 210.28 220.12 248.08 255.25 289.15 315.02 323.19 412.19 413.25 431.01 470.27 501.07 509.06 623.11
Drop 026.16 204.21
drope 319.18
dropeen 056.16
dropes 371.15
dropped 119.14 125.20 205.23 492.03 590.02
dropping 149.01 362.24 403.18 467.19 470.06 604.35
droppings 037.11 079.30 542.31
Dropping-with-Sweat 102.30
drops 194.31 210.09 257.32 289.15 439.18 558.31 596.35
Drops 074.18
dropt 049.32
dross 014.23
drought 094.13 316.26 513.03
Droughty 361.35
Drouth 336.20
drouthdropping 208.36
drove 028.12 136.29 204.19
drown 056.18 319.31 335.02 351.15 589.06
drownd 313.36
drowned 021.35 145.11 153.13 210.23 387.27 387.29 388.11 391.23 526.29
Drowned 420.34
drowner 191.05 539.17
drowning 119.03 387.26
Drownings 132.09
drows 262.F2
drowse 585.21
drowsers 396.18
drowsing 140.36
Drr 244.17
Dr's 150.09 (Dr's Het Ubeleeft) 151.33 (Professor Llewellys ap Bryllars, F.D., Ph. Dr's)
druck 364.34
druckhouse 256.34
Drudge 454.10 579.19
drug 179.20 280.34
drugged 602.26
drugger 492.21
druggeted 571.06
Drughad 197.01
Drugmallt 240.29
drugs 355.36 550.15
drugtails 545.29
druid 362.01
druider 288.05
druidesses 271.04
druidful 347.16 609.35
Druidia 037.18
druids 025.02 362.28
Druids 498.09
druiven 078.24
drukn 017.35
druly 094.28
drum 134.08 211.33 372.25 398.30 500.01
Drumadunderry 323.21
drumbume 340.23
Drumcollakill 060.08
Drumcollogher 540.09 540.11 540.12
Drumcollogher-la-Belle 540.10
Drumcondriac 181.35
drumdrum 036.14
Drumes 614.03
Drumgondola 447.32
Drumleek 623.26
drummatoysed 133.26
drummed 590.26
Drummer 039.09
drummers 061.27 545.26
drumming 223.10
drummling 449.29
drums 107.17 325.07 485.27
Drumsally 449.26
drunk 194.07 453.20 453.20 510.18 515.26 618.29
Drunk 089.08
drunkard 114.22
drunken 436.26
drunkery 179.20
drunkishly 072.26
druping 415.02
druriodrama 050.06
drury 543.20 600.02
druv 583.35
druve 395.36
dry 038.16 045.15 074.10 085.32 094.28 123.12 128.12 155.30 194.27 273.F4 313.35 321.29

323.25 382.09 416.16 434.16 460.15 492.29 502.19 506.20 590.01 605.35
Dry 462.04
dryankle 286.20
dryfilthyheat 492.29
dryflooring 577.34
drying 111.28
Drysalter 512.02
drysick 155.30
dspl 124.08
Dthat 089.18
dthclangavore 393.29
dtheir 089.17
dtin 350.09 350.09 350.09
Dtin 350.09
du 433.06
du 112.32 124.34
duad 253.24
dual 111.02 269.03
Dual 105.20
duan 594.29
Duanna 551.06
duary 603.17
duasdestinies 092.11
dub 044.11 129.20 254.17 596.12
Dub 329.14 484.21
dubbed 177.28
Dubbeldorp 383.23
dubbeltye 138.23
dubber 199.14
dubbing 219.08
dubble 250.36 311.16
dubblebrasterd 320.07
dubbledecoys 603.29
Dubblenn 066.18
dubeurry 461.02
dubhlet 367.22
dubildin 546.17
dubiosity 118.03
dubious 544.11
dubiously 034.23
duble 297.22
dubliboused 158.04
Dublin 014.15 039.04 049.18 084.31 091.22 101.18 266.F1 306.24 321.07 372.02 382.06 410.11 436.26 446.35 451.13 512.26 515.29 523.17 553.27 585.21
Dublin 071.19
Dublinn 482.07
dublinos 042.30
Dublin's 236.10 255.21 447.20
Dublire 488.26
dublnotch 037.03
Dubloonik 432.20
dubrin 346.15
dubs 060.35
Dubs 610.35
Dub's 098.28
dubuny 232.05
Dubville 153.18
duc 036.18
duchtars 358.21
duchy 309.16
duck 171.26 197.13 224.07 466.04 478.35 506.01 531.06 584.08 622.30
Duck 039.35
duckasaloppics 386.06
duckboard 374.15
duckhouse 395.29
duckindonche 255.23
ducking 141.03 194.33
Ducking 176.12
duckings 177.35
duckish 350.22
duck-on-the-rock 579.02
ducks 123.17 277.F5 315.05 449.06 519.32
ducksruns 594.30
duckwhite 137.21
ducky 398.19
ducky 200.07
duckydowndivvy 331.24
duckyheim 533.18
ducomans 358.30
ducose 156.15
Ducrow 133.22
Ductor 044.02
dud 006.10 129.07 221.07 258.09 323.36
duddandgunne 025.23
dudder 540.24
duddurty 196.15
Duddy 161.23
Duddy 104.08
Dudeney 284.F1
Dudge 105.23
dudheen 200.18
dudhud 186.08
duds 342.03
dudst 190.01
dudud 534.12
due 005.27 142.20 220.29 243.09 309.21 392.25 398.09 439.18 482.28 492.18 501.12 508.08 574.09 589.29
Due 314.29
duedesmally 566.12
duel 089.04 111.02 238.31 269.04 290.23
duels 251.33 453.04
dueluct 374.12
dues 549.25 586.12
duetted 556.16
duetting 377.19
Dufblin 447.23
duff 073.20 250.34 313.19 354.33 467.17
duffed 549.33 583.34
Dufferin 093.30
duffgerent 566.21 566.24
duffmatt 415.13
Duff-Muggli 123.11
duffs 438.35
duffyeyed 609.05
Duffy's 589.18
duft 334.29
dug 024.03 024.03 068.18 197.20
duggedy 277.07
Duggelduggel 368.33
dugger 186.21
duggies 079.30
dugong 029.24
dugouts 358.04
dugters 019.29
duhans 343.25
Duhkha 595.22
dui 570.36
Duignan 390.11
duindleeng 549.13
duinnafear 318.05
duiparate 157.29
duist 550.21
duiv 136.13
duk 395.06
duke 100.12 128.16 197.03
Duke 405.18 541.21
duke's 620.09
dulay 492.14
Dulby 362.36
dulcarnons 276.L1
Dulce 562.06
dulcets 460.21
dulcid 427.13
dulcifair 360.05
dulcitude 474.13
dulcydamble 226.17
duldrum 051.34
Dulkey 616.11
dull 109.02
dullakeykongsbyogblagroggers-wagginline 582.32
dullaphone 485.22
dullard 305.07
dullcisamica 254.16
dulled 337.11
dullemitter 317.34
dullfuoco 387.03
Dullkey 040.29
dullmarks 283.23
dullokbloon 389.27
dully 500.15
Dully 228.13
dulpeners 193.02
dulse 130.25 406.21
dulsy 234.23
dulwich 352.12
duly 143.04 150.06 457.19 519.26 529.13
Dulyn 064.03
dumagirls 054.09
dumb 047.24 053.02 088.25 100.36 132.14 195.05 288.23 350.25 355.08 372.05 391.28 442.22 521.09 617.31
Dumb 006.10
Dumbaling 034.01
dumbbawls 284.19
dumbed 262.09
dumbelles 237.08
dumbestic 038.11
dumbfounder 121.27
dumbillsilly 015.18
Dumbil's 116.13
Dumble 350.08
dumbly 628.11
dumblynass 625.27
dumbnation 068.34
dumbs 604.11
dumbshow 559.18
Dumlat 030.10
dumm 223.21 241.01 351.01 517.04
dumm 175.25
dummed 545.36
dummpshow 120.07
dummy 021.12 022.01 022.24 334.22 411.17
Dummy 373.24
dummydeaf 329.27
dummyship 023.13
dumnation 058.08
dumnb 225.18

Dumnlimn 443.16
dump 018.36 110.26 129.18 242.22 296.21 316.17 351.21 352.15 479.20
Dump 289.F4
dumped 371.19
dumpertree 184.14
dumpest 426.18
Dumping's 447.17
dumplan 079.29
dumple 441.09
Dumpling 215.14
dumplings 544.35
dumps 523.30 624.13
dumpsea 317.24
dumpsey 466.26 466.26
dumpsydiddle 493.20
dumpteen 219.15
dumptied 017.04
Dumpty 045.01
Dump-ty 044.25
dumptydum 567.12
dumpy 606.34
dumque 287.20
Dumstdumbdrummers 497.17
dun 017.17 067.19 074.03 093.19 206.35 278.20 317.34 367.23 590.26
Dun 083.17
Duna 392.30
dunas 203.08
Dunboyne 211.34
dunce 517.08
duncingk 550.35
Dunckle 248.22
duncledames 015.17
Dundalgan 091.08
dunderfunder 596.03
Dunderhead 274.08
Dunders 213.34
dundrearies 042.35
dundrum 553.03
Dundrums 135.31
Dune 330.06
Dunelli 084.36
dunes 014.30
dune's 594.12
dung 031.36 447.14 509.09
Dung 377.36
Dungbin 370.09
dungcairn 479.34
dungcart 079.26
dungflies 118.32
dungfork 087.14
dungheap 124.24
DUNGMOUND 276.R1
Dungtarf 016.22
dunhill 050.30
dunk 269.03
Dunker's 497.29
dunkey 405.06
dunlearies 370.19
dunleary 566.36
Dunlin 479.18
Dunlip 539.24
Dunlob 437.06
dunloop 295.32
Dunlop 058.04 420.27 497.36
dunlops 584.13
Dunmow's 579.01
Dunn 518.10
dunnage 329.23
Dunne 210.35 337.36
dunner 624.05
Dunnes 213.35
dunneth 334.29
Dunnohoo's 439.20
Dunn's 516.20
Dunphy's 549.02
Dun's 040.35
Dunshanagan 417.31
Dunsink 518.01
dunsker's 378.31
dunsky 185.11
dunstung 135.09
duntalking 566.11
duo 271.04
Duodecimoroon 207.25
duodisimally 006.16
duohs 626.14
duol 360.10 565.03
duoly 372.18
duominous 552.24
duotrigesumy 234.12
Dupe 337.03
duped 142.23
dupes 367.35
dupest 367.35 506.06
duplex 123.30 292.24
duplicitly 156.09
Dupling 586.15
duppy 023.05
dupsydurby 448.14
duran 014.20
durance 199.10
durant 243.11
Duras 334.30
duration 362.04
Durbalanars 594.05
Durban 602.19
durbar 497.29
durblinly 347.35
durck 351.09
durc's 138.27
durdicky 178.28
durdin 548.06
dure 371.16 395.13
durian 257.06
during 004.26 015.04 039.01 040.14 046.27 051.36 059.19 075.17 078.27 090.07 117.22 144.03 172.31 173.04 187.09 190.14 221.14 347.11 482.24 495.29 517.04 518.12 518.17 573.25 588.05 617.14 625.20
during 345.35
During 432.25
durk 580.15
durknass 607.25
durkness 407.12
durlbin 019.12
durmed 199.09
durn 107.36 448.07
duro 054.18
durrydunglecks 416.11
durst 234.28 331.10 567.32
dursted 333.32
dursus 159.20
dusess 461.09
dusind 212.20
dusk 056.08 087.36 095.22 158.15 213.13
duskcended 222.35
duskfoil 359.35
duskguise 532.27
duskish 052.33
duskness 276.20
duskrose 015.01
dusks 226.13
duskt 004.12
dusky 206.17 593.14
Dusort 219.12
duspurudo 289.22
duss 603.10
dussard 323.02
dust 130.24 140.09 140.10 176.30 180.28 227.11 280.35 424.04 440.26 518.06 544.20 580.11
dustamount 359.12
dustbins 409.02 625.23
Dustbin's 181.17
dustcovered 291.16
duster 432.24
Dustheap 307.23
Dustify 488.17
dustiny 162.03
dustman 059.16
dusts 255.06 370.26
dustungwashed 342.13
dustwhisk 050.12
dusty 006.25 416.25
dustydust 314.16
dustyfeets 545.30
dustyrust 357.06
dutc 553.33 622.20 (Dublin United Tramway Co.)
D.U.T.C. 256.30 (Dublin United Tramway Co.)
dutch 098.07 244.02 459.05
Dutch 602.24
Dutchener's 430.14
Dutches 420.13
Dutchlord 135.08 135.09
dutchuncler 314.22
dutchy 076.25 117.31
duteoused 617.29
duther 396.26
Duthless 481.22
duthsthrows 240.16
duties 141.22 497.21 621.01
Dutiful 603.15
Dutiful 106.18
duty 012.04 019.01 037.07 162.35 245.28 313.19 374.19 396.15 429.23 431.26 457.17 493.04 573.10 576.36 622.30
Duty 306.15
DUTY 271.R1
dutyful 452.24
Duum 013.25
duusk 158.08 158.09 158.19 158.20
duv 136.30 626.33
duvetyne 148.07
duvlin 197.20 222.25 364.25
Duvvelsache 178.35
dux 008.19
Duyvil 535.15
Duzinascu 064.32
D.V. 287.01 527.26 (Deo Volente)
DVbLIn 293.12
Dvershen 332.36
dvine 212.31
Dvoinabrathran 252.04
dwarfees 494.28
dwarfs 128.18
dwealth 449.18

dweam 601.17
dwell 266.14
Dwell 466.14
dweller 194.19
dwelling 158.28 483.29 558.36
dwellinghouses 116.34
dwellings 543.26
Dwellings 093.16
dwells 551.06
dwellst 239.25
dwelt 203.18
Dweyr 600.18
dwibble 555.19
dwilights 492.09
dwyergray 214.33
dwympty 314.16
Dyas 055.34
Dyb 480.28 480.28
Dybblin 326.34
Dybbling 029.22
dye 185.32 327.34 375.13 407.36 506.06
dyed 130.24 143.26 335.02 464.23
Dyed 106.24
dyedyedaintee 102.32
dyeing 276.F2
Dyer 226.12
Dyfflinarsky 013.22
Dyfflinsborg 582.21
dyfflun's 314.05
dyin 420.13
dyinboosycough 095.08
dying 146.03 200.35 235.18 376.29 408.32 465.02 555.12
Dyk 607.31
dyke 558.31 597.06
Dyke 517.15
dykes 202.31
dym 625.21
dynamight 210.36
dynamitisation 189.35
Dynamon 077.07
dynasdescendanced 109.06
dynast 202.24 393.07
DYNASTIC 275.R1
dynasties 532.07
dynasty 075.24 084.32 380.21
dyode 319.24
Dyoublong 013.04
dyply 320.01
dyrby 325.06
dyrchace 553.23
dyrt 600.25
Dysart 088.23
Dyspeptist 453.15
dystomy 597.21
d'yu 521.01
D'yu 499.19 519.18
dzoupgan 199.18

e 054.16
e 178.17 370.12 540.12
E 051.19
E 212.35
E. 489.13 (E. Obiit Nolan)
é 301.16
è 199.28 292.12
each 012.30 049.11 060.35 068.02 078.29 085.28 102.03 109.35 117.13 135.26 147.24 155.12 157.01 162.27 172.29 186.06 191.05 193.23 208.21 210.06 210.16 215.17 219.04 221.04 234.27 236.34 252.14 252.16 255.35 259.03 261.27 265.05 268.05 268.06 274.25 287.F2 299.F3 330.03 335.24 356.02 436.24 436.27 451.29 488.06 503.09 505.10 540.22 557.13 567.26 585.36 595.01 609.21 609.21 614.05 614.21
Each 538.29
eachone 215.25
Eachovos 133.35
each's 160.26 256.10 275.27
eachway 178.31 281.22
eachwise 235.02
eacla 568.32
eacy 023.04
eadem 287.25
eaden 597.35
Eads 106.32
eagelly 231.13
eager 364.29
Eager 620.28
eagerly 356.22
eaght 617.27
eagle 505.17
Eagle 053.28 059.03 622.08
eagles 080.21 302.14
eagle's 493.04
eagle's 342.22
Ealdermann 503.10
Ealing 446.21
ealsth 313.36
ealth 076.09
eaps 456.22
ear 005.35 009.11 023.23 038.10 039.23 043.28 048.21 059.22 062.08 070.36 074.11 086.32 098.28 108.21 113.27 129.27 138.27 180.06 193.13 254.18 280.03 300.12 302.02 311.11 326.25 333.28 370.01 384.36 394.22 433.09 449.29 457.29 464.18 467.32 468.25 477.18 482.35 486.21 492.03 509.29 512.24 572.16 576.29 582.07 622.32
Ear 097.08 409.03 409.03 568.26 568.26
Ear 175.24
Earalend 546.33
earbig 091.11
earer 180.25
earin 021.24
earing 390.04
earish 130.19
earl 128.05 404.17 620.08
Earl 394.28 447.13 514.23
earlier 083.14 274.16
earliest 570.27 616.28
earling 291.21
early 003.17 033.10 034.33 037.14 101.32 120.29 134.12 172.13 210.18 230.28 243.04 271.24 356.36 393.19 408.16 524.12 524.36 533.26 551.36 575.01 581.35 589.21
early 342.25
Early 127.33 294.15 300.F2
EARLY 268.R1
Earlytouler 197.08
earmarks 066.01
earn 190.20 590.13
Earn 579.18
earnasyoulearning 389.04
earned 134.20 467.26
earnest 426.18
earnestly 490.12 617.28
earning 408.01
earnst 141.23 452.07
earny 125.22
earong 267.13
earopean 598.15
earopen 419.14
earpicker 312.16
earpiercing 474.12
earps 191.20
earring 022.10 465.27
ears 014.29 041.24 083.06 147.34 149.13 152.23 158.13 164.33 169.15 173.24 180.28 244.22 290.F4 291.27 337.25 382.25 384.19 386.10 452.12 467.28 475.36 496.15 565.16 580.30 620.08
Ears 364.14
earse 375.19
earsend 024.09 024.10
earsequack 221.09
earshare 018.31
earshells 435.19
earshot 426.35
earsighted 143.09
earstoear 539.01
earswathed 547.14
earth 018.24 050.10 096.31 119.01 138.26 239.17 255.05 258.22 303.28 311.18 331.32 404.05 425.36 435.22 454.25 455.24 472.33 550.17 588.20
earth 201.05 481.03
earthapples 271.24
earthball 079.16
earthborn 137.14
earthcall 494.06
earthcrust 018.31
earthenhouse 021.13
earthernborn 084.29
earthing 434.09
earthlight 449.07
earthlost 596.10
earthly 621.34
earthnight 427.10
earthpresence 499.28
earthquake 133.12
earths 309.24
earth's 329.36 469.03
earthsbest 414.33
earthside 031.03
Earthsigh 601.08
earthsleep 074.02
earthspake 014.20
earthveins 571.36
earthwight 262.11
earthwork 358.04
earthworm 509.29
earwakers 351.25
earwaker's 173.09
earwanker 520.06
earwax 025.06
Earwicker 033.30 034.14 035.21 036.12 047.15 070.35 073.03 073.04 108.22 119.16
Earwicker 107.02 107.06
Earwickers 030.07
earwig 017.34 164.29

earwigger 031.28
earwigger's 579.25
earwigs 047.16 047.17 079.16
earwitness 005.14
earwuggers 031.11
earwugs 485.21
easancies 545.26
ease 136.03 143.14 228.29 262.17 271.23 337.26 454.34 579.26 597.33
Ease 359.30
eased 018.35
Easehouse 523.26
easger 340.18
easier 138.22
easiest 286.29
easily 039.03 042.22 070.30 115.09 115.23 121.16 123.09 138.06 150.36 304.24 419.14
easiness 571.19
easing 128.07
east 076.12 140.32 251.14 321.13 329.08 473.22 541.34 583.18 593.05
East 035.30 160.12
eastanglian 042.28
eastasian 166.32
Eastchept 347.12
eastend 586.27
easter 043.12 188.10 376.36 483.10 513.11
Easter 236.08 556.08
easteredman 590.22
Easterheld 480.20
eastering 315.26
Easterling 130.09
Easterlings 378.13
easterly 085.15
eastern 453.22
Easther's 413.08
easthmost 326.34
easting 471.11
Eastman 067.18
eastmidlands 474.18
eastmoreland 553.30
Eastrailian 060.27
eastuards 017.25
eastward 605.29
eastway 202.12
easty 228.23
easy 020.36 025.21 061.05 072.19 126.24 205.01 364.28 377.21 425.19 427.03 431.17 449.06 471.15 622.13
Easy 262.01 439.28
Easyathic 072.14
easyfree 152.12
eat 111.19 239.17 262.19 279.F07 376.36 485.04 485.04 624.36
Eat 163.02 247.10 271.24 456.18
eatables 150.27
eatalittle 010.33
eaten 416.21 455.33
eatenly 616.24
eater 180.25
Eates 306.F1
eath 149.03 295.33
eather 016.08
eating 127.21 127.22 157.17 321.03 455.34 544.14 579.18
Eating 292.29
eatlust 077.31
eatmost 058.14
eats 129.19 130.05 136.05 318.20 437.19 535.32
Eats 373.03
eatsother 527.29
Eatsoup 246.31
Eatster 623.08
Eatsup 563.24
eatupus 128.36
eatwords 569.28
eau 295.18
eau 204.33
Eaudelusk 576.03
eaulande 158.11
Eavens 173.24
eaveswater 173.30
eavy 421.07
Eavybrolly 315.20
Ebahi-Ahuri 165.28
ebb 017.26 118.12
Ebba 103.03
ebbing 235.06 290.28
ebblanes 135.28
Ebbiannah 138.23
Ebblawn 139.36
Ebblinn's 041.18
Ebblybally 612.15
ebblynuncies 373.12
Ebbraios 497.24
ebbrous 049.24
Ebell 491.16
Eblana 046.14
Eblanamagna 625.26
Eblanensis 215.27
Eblania's 614.25
eblanite 553.29
Eblinn 264.15
EBONISER 304.R1
ebony 341.09
Eboracum 442.08
ebribadies 228.36
ebro 198.19
Eburnea's 396.01
ecad 518.12
Ecce 480.14
eccentric 544.07
eccentricities 614.36
eccentricity 284.L1
Ecclasiastical 298.L2
ecclastics 447.34
Ecclectiastes 038.29
Eccles 179.27
ecclesency 535.12
Ecclesia 604.19
Ecclesiast 374.23
Ecclesiastes 514.14
ecclesiastic 426.24
Eccles's 514.15
Eccls 567.27
Eccolo 462.27
ech 264.03 284.01 623.09
Eche 302.28
echo 093.12 126.03 158.20 379.01 409.12 485.04
Echo 468.20 584.33
echoating 404.07
echobank 547.30
echoed 060.36
Echoland 013.05
Echolo 585.03
eckcot 242.33
Ecko 477.33
eclectrically 309.24
eclipses 264.05 564.03
eclosed 450.21
ecnumina 098.27
ecolites 490.04
ecolube 599.18
economantarchy 167.06
economical 114.15 163.31
economy 306.14 545.05
Economy 432.35
ecotaph 420.11
ecou 054.15
ecrazyaztecs 242.11
ecrooksman 556.27
Ecstasies 066.09
ecstasy 231.09
ectoplasm 133.24
ecunemical 131.31 496.10
ecus 538.16
eczema 260.F1 380.25
ed 466.19
Edam 183.08
Edar 326.18
Edar's 594.28
edcedras 235.17
Eddaminiva's 601.23
eddams 069.10
eddas 597.06
eddaying 389.21
Eddems 278.F7
eddiketsflaskers 556.30
eddistoon 127.15
Eddy 210.33
eddying 055.23
Eddy's 482.01
Ede 324.07
edelweissed 378.24
Edem 396.21
Eden 172.15 282.18
Edenberry 066.17
Edenborough 029.35
edereider 209.22
edge 202.15 238.16 294.21
edges 456.15
edgewiped 120.10
edgings 374.26
edicted 167.23
ediculous 553.15
edifice 100.25
edifices 004.26
edify 568.35
edifying 356.29
Ediles 421.03
edilis 007.23
Edipus 306.L2
edith 034.10
edition 063.01 164.01 291.27 292.07 397.33
édition 179.27
editor 596.19
Edned 054.05
Edomite 072.11
Educande 246.24
educanded 189.14
educandees 182.08
educated 178.23
education 138.25 166.22 166.27
educe 355.12
Edulia 561.09
edventyres 051.14
Edwin 513.21
Edzo 039.24 039.24

ee 021.02 029.34 198.09 254.30
Eebrydime 610.11
eegs 019.09
eel 141.02
Eel 525.26
eelfare 209.04
eelpie 296.26
eelsblood 169.19
Eelwhipper 496.12
Eelwick 134.16
eely 234.14
eelyotripes 303.F1
een 249.36
e'en 235.03 262.26 366.20 458.08
E'en 105.03
eer 073.17 292.13
e'er 098.32 165.07 407.14 408.08 454.01 496.29 496.35 510.27 528.22
E'erawan 046.01
E'erawhere 006.24
Eeric 359.26
eeridreme 342.30
eerie 020.23 053.05 266.04
eeriebleak 316.22
eeriesh 070.04
eeriesk 320.13
eeriewhigg 360.32
Eer's 238.31
ees 120.19 262.F2
ef 222.09
Ef 522.01
Efas-Taem 311.12
eff 120.33
effaces 352.19
effect 031.05 092.33 092.34 148.08 162.04 238.35 277.F5 295.04 305.12 322.26 385.29 569.11 597.35 607.04 615.11
effect 342.21 345.07
effected 574.17
effecting 076.13
effective 056.19 523.06 574.12 615.08
effects 186.23 483.01 503.01
Effendi 131.08
effered 342.30
efferfreshpainted 452.19
efficiencies 550.22
efficient 581.29
effigies 340.14
effigy 567.10
effingee 018.34
effluvia 107.17
effluvious 182.11
effluvium 095.16
effort 164.24
effort 352.18
efforts 093.32
effrays 090.07
effused 605.34
effusion 432.14
efteased 266.30
efter 079.20 141.13 209.13 226.36 315.09 394.28 509.27
Efter 156.19
Eftsoon 473.18
egad 180.04
egal 297.F2
Egan 447.23
Egari's 408.26
Egbert 088.21
Egen 604.06
egg 120.11 144.09 210.35 220.29 269.28 294.11 376.07 394.27 434.13 483.23 489.19 527.14
Egg 205.36
Egg 440.20
eggblend 614.32
eggbrooms 403.11
eggburial 614.32
eggburst 614.32
eggcup 616.20
eggday 069.28
eggdrazzles 504.35
Eggeberth 004.32
egged 087.27
Egged 106.18
eggfactor 380.11
egglips 603.02
Egglyfella 374.34
eggoarchicism 525.10
eggons 613.11
eggotisters 137.08
eggs 054.24 112.14 151.13 161.31 163.27 167.07 329.01 373.24 437.21 447.12 524.33 615.10
Eggs 071.27 175.19 176.10 484.36
eggschicker 423.19
eggscumuddher-in-chaff 240.15
eggseggs 537.28
eggshaped 529.21
eggshells 183.12 420.15
eggshill 415.09
eggsized 457.16
Eggsmather 296.21
eggspilled 230.05
eggtentical 016.36
eggways 288.05
eggynaggy 026.03
Eglandine's 039.34
ego 051.02 184.07 463.07
egoarch 188.16
egobruno 488.08
Egon 102.14
Egoname 485.05
egondoom 343.26
Egory 397.06
egotum 394.30
egourge 049.34
egregious 090.20
egregiunt 143.11
Egypsians 355.23
egypt 551.30
Egyptus 263.06
eh 068.17 068.17 068.17 090.33 161.25 192.04 278.10 485.18 485.19 485.19 485.20 485.20 485.21 487.23 506.11 510.29 513.35
eh 058.26 058.28
Eh 307.F8 319.16 340.16 470.13 559.22
eher 256.01
Eher 057.30
Eheu 058.18
ehim 060.07 060.08
Ehim 060.03
ehren 510.24
Ehren 338.03
Ehren 537.10
ehrltogether 155.36
Ei 481.21
Ei 049.02
eiderdown 399.23
eiers 184.28
Eiffel 088.24
eight 142.02 169.12 170.02 430.09 443.23 543.26 544.29 559.35 559.35 622.23
eighteen 040.34 169.13 178.27 556.09
eighteenthly 123.03
eighth 119.24 253.23
Eighth 071.14
eightpence 069.18
eighty 129.33 265.26
Eilder 603.09
Eileen 210.31
eilerdich 132.36
eiligh 553.14
eilish 410.33
Eilish 144.10
ein 246.15
ein 163.06
Eins 152.18
eira 331.23
Eirae 227.01
Eirae 481.05
eire 565.17
Eire 256.23 275.05 496.15
Eireann 312.01 503.23
Eireen 620.06
eirenarch's 532.01
Eirenesians 025.17
eirenical 014.30
Eire's 013.23
eirest 514.36
Eireweeker 593.03
Eirewhiggs 175.25
Eirinishmhan 616.03
Eironesia 411.12
Eirzerum 344.31
eisen 536.15
Eiskaffier 059.29
Eisold 607.31
eitch 376.19
either 004.16 031.22 031.34 058.27 063.03 066.30 067.30 081.02 085.16 091.12 091.25 091.32 100.24 109.30 134.01 159.03 166.03 171.08 171.14 177.32 223.34 281.27 292.09 298.12 316.08 325.19 427.36 439.29 441.31 462.33 475.32 481.30 482.14 491.15 510.34 521.13 533.18 563.34 564.31
eitheranny 586.31
eithers 605.13
eitherways 289.16
eithou 452.07
eius 515.09
Eivin 493.27
ejaculating 520.05
ejaculations 183.23 253.27
ejector 551.26
ejist 258.04
ejoculated 129.10
ejus 610.06
ek 039.06
eke 332.29 505.19 579.08 588.16
ekeascent 538.33
ekenames 098.27

ekewilled 297.07
ekksprezzion 064.31
ekonome 230.34
ekspedient 317.10
Ekspedient 317.15
ekstras 324.29
ekumene 440.35
el 034.32
El 060.30 084.36 198.13 246.06
El 339.33
ἔλαβον 269.L2
elaborative 109.19
elacock 447.12
Elanio 221.22
elapse 418.33
elation 528.08 528.09 528.09
Elation 528.09
elazilee 232.35
elb 208.01
Elba 283.L1
elbaroom 052.25
Elberfeld's 108.15
elbiduubled 583.27
elbow 166.13 190.08 214.20 274.10 321.02 444.06 459.18
elbowdints 080.11
elbownunsense 245.21
elbows 195.03
Elcock 031.18
Elcock's 329.26
eld 021.05 197.03 412.01
Eld 481.03
elder 024.12 076.01 385.03 412.23 546.11 568.27
Elder 137.21 255.19 295.20 579.04
elderens 604.16
eldering 562.19
elderman 325.13
elders 179.19 428.03 484.22
Elders 064.36
Elderships 219.10
eldest 408.31 543.29
eldfar 058.31 581.31
elding 328.17
elding 346.08
Elding 328.16
eldorado 134.01
Eldorado 276.16
Eldsfells 316.31
eleathury 536.11 536.11
eleaxir 133.19
elect 160.18 453.33 594.04
elected 613.35
electing 599.25
election 253.30
elections 111.12
Elector 365.19
electress 156.24 207.29
electric 451.30
Electricity 307.10
electrickery 579.06
electrifies 207.28
electrolatiginous 475.17
electrons 615.07
elects 239.28
elecutioner 058.34
eleft 510.35
Elegance 050.27
elegant 065.06 321.13 534.24
elegies 192.34
Elelijiacks 156.26
element 175.34 282.20 526.32
elementator 302.12
elements 188.06 614.34
Elements 485.35
elenchate 189.02
elenders 551.02
Elenfant 244.35
elephant 300.F4 564.05
elephants 513.35
elephant's 461.05 537.01
Eleutheriodendron 042.20
Elevating 155.23
elevation 389.24
Elevato 387.06
eleven 038.13 070.33 073.20 077.06 098.11 120.25 147.04 201.29 256.22 325.05 425.32 447.18 448.03 516.17 517.30 544.02 544.31 617.03
eleven 338.05
eleventh 084.32
Eleventh 274.13
elf 403.02 577.14
Elf 073.15
elfinbone 249.07
elfkin's 578.33
elfshot 274.17
elfun 203.31
Elga 596.22
Elgin's 549.15
eliceam 453.32
eliciter 087.02
elicitous 622.03
elicted 622.03
Elien 408.26
eligere 163.04
eligible 442.01
elimbinated 131.32
eliminated 107.30
eliminating 076.06
eliminium 309.23
Elin 364.21
Elin's 130.34
Eliphas 244.35
elipsities 298.16
Elisabbess 289.26
elisaboth 542.23
Elissabed 156.34
élite 453.33
elixir 237.09
elizabeetons 437.24
Elizabeliza 328.36
elk 014.18
elkox 567.24
ell 578.33 586.25
Ell 176.04
ellboge 036.16
elle 281.L1
Elleb 237.26
ellegedly 086.14
eller 281.26 552.36
Ellers 324.21
Elletrouvetout 211.35
Elliot 043.09
Ellis 205.07 294.08 586.14
Ellishly 289.14
Ellme 572.17
ellpow 535.31
ells 011.25 347.19 475.05 475.05
Elly 212.13
elm 094.04 215.35 216.03 235.19 265.04 503.32 542.07 563.21
Elm 507.36 571.07
elmer 074.02
elmer's 243.15
elmme 572.17
elmoes 460.17
elms 004.15 267.26 553.19
elmstree 025.30
Elmstree 247.04
elmtree 159.04
Elochlannensis 600.29
elois 086.07
elope 143.01
elopement 559.03
elopes 418.33
eloping 330.24
elp 076.09
Elpis 267.04
elrington 055.36
else 020.09 021.09 044.14 061.26 067.02 073.11 083.26 108.09 146.13 178.14 220.16 332.16 424.19 463.33 468.26
Else 213.25 246.35
Elsebett 495.25
elsecare 330.07
Elsekiss 015.16
elserground 546.11
else's 070.26 565.16
Elsewere 099.02
elsewhere 012.20 066.06 149.17 505.02
elſewhere 238.08
Elsie 211.12
Elsies 587.26
elskede 551.24
Elsker 388.06
elskerelks' 243.01
elskmestoon 572.17
elsor 623.15
elster 197.07
elter 350.15
eltered 483.30
eltering 552.20
Elters 017.19
elucidation 109.05
eluded 083.14
eluding 090.22 507.28
elued 448.27
elusive 167.01
elv 261.03
elvanstone 079.29
elve 347.04
Elvenland 215.22
elventurns 606.18
elvery 565.31
elves 357.32 566.05
elvishness 238.14
elwys 202.15
elytrical 415.01
em 011.22 018.36 035.33 043.13 052.03 079.22 254.26 262.15 282.28 288.02 288.21 324.17 334.26 334.26 355.35 466.15 524.27 545.34 545.34 549.22 579.08
em 526.14
Em 419.19
'em 418.22
emaciated 078.35
émail 575.16

Emailia 410.23
emanating 064.07
emanation 425.11
emanations 157.19 600.09
emancipated 386.25
Emancipator 342.19
emanence 494.27
Emania 480.21 521.32
emballem 277.F1
embalmed 078.06
embalsemate 499.01
embankment 547.18
embaraced 354.17
Embark 446.30
embarras 207.35
embarrassment 491.33
embattled 403.06
embazzlement 375.26
embelliching 407.32
embellished 386.01
emberose 324.04
embers 473.09
emblem 274.01
emblence 220.33
emblushing 357.32
embossed 574.25
embottled 140.33
embouscher 156.35
embowed 270.16
embrace 083.32 348.35 398.10
Embrace 465.11
embraced 213.25
embracer 122.33
embracing 483.33
embracings 429.24
Embrassador-at-Large 472.10
embrassured 235.25
embrasures 550.24
embre 527.29
embrocation 184.22
embrothred 404.29
Embulence 352.33
embushed 470.04
embusked 546.10
Emen 222.24
emended 163.35
Emenia 412.08
emerald 068.12 263.22 440.33 603.09
Emeraldilluim 062.11
emeralds 492.11
emergency 574.07
emergency 338.07
emergent 033.13
emerges 032.12 593.19
Emeritus 392.14
emery 128.25
emetic 192.15
Emfang 494.20
Emhe 267.19
emigrant 190.36 463.04
emillian 129.16
eminence 408.12
eminent 033.01 149.18 282.23 380.19 432.20
eminently 181.10 356.21 544.21 599.27
emir 582.27
emirate 133.27
emittences 309.20
emitting 545.08
emma 517.25
Emma 306.F1 306.F1
emmas 328.21
Emme 198.18
emmerhim 581.34
Emmet 136.14 417.21
emmets 013.33
emollient 409.25
emolument 165.12
emotion 437.21
emotional 492.33
emotion's 036.20
Emp 175.11
empalmover 601.01
empanelled 529.06
empathies 487.23
empathy 522.30
Emperor 549.36 612.09
Emperour 157.35
empirative 187.31
empire 099.26 362.07 393.14 587.23
Empire 278.23 543.05
emplacement 599.10
employ 059.17
employed 028.14
employment 133.10
empoisoned 339.33
empores 367.25
emporialist 589.10
emprisoms 127.03
empsyseas 584.09
empthood 298.12
emptied 363.29
empties 052.03 445.30
emptors 059.03
emptout 141.08
empty 319.36 433.22 559.02
emptybloddy 324.11
Emptybolly 321.15
empyreal 353.29
empyrean 014.19
ems 123.01 207.35
emt 339.36
emugee 588.02
emulous 572.30
emulously 371.14
emulsipotion 310.36
emurgency 241.06
en 054.13 160.30 234.36
en 058.26 058.28 281.06
En 261.03
En 100.18
E. N. 354.16 (E. N. Sheilmartin)
Ena 094.14 147.11 212.08
enabling 077.36
Enactment 423.31
enamel 612.08
enamelled 203.28
Enameron 561.24
Enastella 278.F3
enaunter 069.27
encampassed 543.12
encampness 470.19
encaust 424.08
encaustum 185.25
ences 623.34
encestor 096.34
Enchainted 237.11
enchantement 028.08
enchanting 594.09
enchelonce 352.02
encho 146.21
encient 324.08 538.12
encircle 505.13
encircling 209.24
encirculingly 055.27
encloded 356.07
enclosed 411.18
Enclosed 072.06
enclosing 484.11
enclosure 605.24
encloud 296.27
enclouded 277.15
encompass 480.26
encore 466.17 581.34
Encore 351.16
encored 192.26
encostive 027.10
encounter 596.17
encountered 050.31
encourage 198.36 462.24
Encourage 039.05
encouraged 061.18 573.27
encouraging 077.20
Encroachement 479.18
encuoniams 278.04
encyclical 605.04
encyclicling 153.26
end 003.14 018.21 019.26 048.24 112.18 114.16 114.16 114.17 114.17 115.03 117.25 120.24 127.08 132.05 140.09 144.25 167.23 185.07 192.12 215.09 232.21 233.14 239.32 252.33 270.31 279.06 279.F04 296.10 303.21 316.24 331.06 335.27 337.13 347.05 361.29 368.35 369.35 373.35 380.01 392.33 393.04 393.22 397.09 410.21 414.02 433.16 435.36 436.03 461.01 468.05 491.15 493.08 501.14 505.13 515.36 540.18 582.05 582.21 582.21 598.15 606.15
end 072.06 419.05
End 028.29 534.01 628.13
'end 011.28
endadjustables 236.28
endall 481.03
endearment 571.04
endeavour 426.03
ended 010.22 026.16 054.05 061.12 069.10 080.16 093.22
Endee 598.09
enderer 320.01
Enders 412.23
Endersen 138.16
endeth 257.31 346.23 367.04
ending 253.26 368.23 468.20 469.30 484.15 627.35
endings 089.26 200.06
endknown 091.28
Endles 226.36
endless 213.15 604.15
endlessly 182.18
endlike 020.12
endmost 547.04
endnessnessessity 613.27
endnew 315.29
endnot 604.05
endnow 370.34
endocrine 136.28
endocrine-pineal 115.31
endonational 128.28
endorse 091.16 575.17
endorsed 447.33
endorsement 163.16

endow 134.27
endowment 532.35
endphthisis 305.21
endright 098.19
ends 122.04 128.19 149.22 278.F2 291.25 306.07 449.04 455.18 496.18 614.19
ends 418.28
Endsland's 304.21
endso 283.01
endspeaking 267.08
endswell 150.31
endth 298.21 312.17
Endth 579.12
Endues 338.20
endupped 022.30
endupper 489.04
endurable 598.07
enduring 519.20
endurses 127.28
endurtaking 625.09
Eneas 185.27
Enel-Rah 237.28
enemay 352.10
enement 282.21
enemies 075.15
enemy 155.19 328.35 442.02 469.23 509.05 539.23
energuman 512.17
energument 305.13
energy 177.01 264.01
enerretur 478.17
eneugh 308.02
enevy 620.06
enfamillias 395.15
Enfilmung 375.01
enfins 483.27
enfranchisable 024.27
enfranchised 548.19
enfysis 329.34
eng 537.12
engage 305.13 618.06
engaged 080.09 081.19 109.18 177.03 220.34 459.32
engagement 332.28
engagements 014.24 272.11
Engagements 454.27
engaging 081.34 140.23
engauzements 159.08
engels 519.01
Engels 533.29
engelsk 233.33
engenerand 372.06
engiles 416.32
engindear 146.19
engine 063.26 457.32 604.10
engined 355.23
engineer 459.35
Engineers 518.16
engineral 292.F1
engines 230.25
enginium 310.01
engl 124.07 607.22
England 036.29 524.14
England's 420.34
Englandwales 242.33
Englend 170.32
engles 075.19
Englesemen 181.01
Engleterre 175.11
Englisch 539.36
english 178.06 579.21
English 013.01 052.09 093.02 116.26 124.19 127.33 271.F3 327.23 357.02
engraved 120.10
engraving 495.28
engravure 013.07
engrish 351.08
engrossing 423.08
Engrvakon 394.26
enhance 458.07
enigma 135.27
enjoined 584.30
enjoineth 533.24
enjoining 060.08
enjoins 185.28
Enjombyourselves 465.10
enjoy 172.06 298.F1
Enjoy 312.10
enjoyable 008.01
enjoyed 229.34 361.29 557.18 615.13
enjoyed 273.L3
enjoyimsolff 308.F2
enjoying 147.35 148.03 187.36 488.17 536.13
enjoyment 133.09
enjoys 129.30 544.08
enjurious 234.29
enkel 480.17
Enkelchums 051.15
enlarged 069.16 622.33
enlargement 310.06
enlisted 049.07
enlivened 357.28 564.17
enlivening 468.21
enliventh 032.31
enlocked 268.02
enmity 597.19
enmivallupped 339.09
enmy 542.18
enn 293.15
ennemberable 608.31
ennempties 549.22
Enniskerry 073.31
ennoviacion 230.16
ennoy 148.05
ennoyed 460.36
Enobarbarus 157.27
enoch 442.06
Enoch 283.01
enormally 538.28
enormanous 360.33
enormity 033.23
enormous 419.05
enormously 463.14
enormousness 102.06
enos 030.04
Enos 577.21
Enouch 535.21
enough 027.26 040.18 085.21 107.27 111.28 116.22 122.27 130.17 171.21 187.17 199.27 226.07 265.F2 282.09 292.15 304.17 311.35 355.21 381.30 384.09 387.16 393.23 397.04 397.04 422.02 427.03 449.05 450.32 468.34 479.15 495.05 503.31 510.36 519.16 530.25 531.28 555.21 557.33 571.26 616.08 621.05
enough 399.18
Enough 164.22 356.26 623.03
enoupes 158.18
enow 246.11
enquick 537.31
enquiries 280.13
enrate 097.23
enrich 095.25
enriched 076.25
enrouted 371.33
ens 483.21
ens 157.23
ensallycopodium 334.03
enscayed 156.20
enscure 326.17
ensectuous 029.30
ensemble 384.30 426.33 493.05
ensembled 225.03 451.14
ensemple 254.01
ensevelised 334.01
ensign 182.07
ensigned 261.06
Ensigning 498.12
ensorcelled 476.29
Ensouling 302.L1
ensuance 018.28
ensue 547.05
ensuer 266.30
entail 564.03
entailed 003.19
entailing 492.30
entails 018.27
entducked 294.14
Enten 281.26
enter 534.15
ENTER 306.R1
entered 258.27 419.34 534.07 574.36 575.02
Entered 106.11
enterellbo 336.02
Enterest 388.02
entering 321.07 483.36
enternatural 240.14
enterrooms 278.F4
Enterruption 332.36
entertaining 220.34
entertainment 173.23
Entertainment 307.08
entertainments 433.18
entertermentdags 413.10
entertrained 348.29
Entertrainer 106.09
enthewsyass 260.18
enthreateningly 246.06
enthroned 606.03
enthroproise 318.05
enthusiasm 341.21
enthusiastic 180.01
enthusiastically 050.25
entibus 287.20
enticers 561.33
enticing 459.14
entilely 299.25
entire 173.20 179.35 502.36 599.27 605.29
entirely 027.04 027.35 050.11 131.21 139.09 156.33 326.02 391.13 392.35 423.11 574.19
entirely 399.23
entirety 033.05
entiringly 261.17
entis 376.15
Entis-Onton 611.20
entitled 033.08 414.05
entity 599.16
entomate 417.20

entomophilust 107.13
entoutcas 129.06
entowerly 004.36
entrails 231.35 475.17
entrammed 567.33
entrance 057.20 063.15 115.16 134.29
entrancing 226.34 566.29
Entrancings 219.03
entre 274.08
entreats 021.03
entrée 128.29
entrees 220.21
entrées 281.09
entrenched 357.33
entrenous 603.18
entrust 483.10
entry 164.16
Entry 248.31
entumuled 133.30
entwine 259.07
entwined 488.03
Entwhistle 342.20
entychologist 059.15
entymology 417.04
entyrely 537.16
enumerated 128.05
enumerating 439.31
envelope 066.14 109.08 212.22 437.26
enveloped 176.35 414.11
enveloping 109.14
envenomoloped 099.19
enver 582.12
envery 367.35
envil 514.11
enville 310.20
Enville 420.21
enviolated 285.02
Environs 003.03
envolving 080.12
envy 058.06
Envyeyes 235.24
Enwreak 545.23
enysled 605.20
eocene 165.26
eodem 185.20
eolders 372.34
eolithostroton 073.30
eon 159.11 228.15
eonion 078.04
Eonochs 357.30
Eons 226.36
eon's 585.01
eorl 130.33
epaulettes 208.18
epening 067.16
epexegesis 511.16
ephemeral 417.33 583.23
ephemerides 087.07
ephemerids 416.23
epheud 498.14
epheus 097.36
Ephialtes 493.23
ephort 560.16
Ephthah 240.06
ephumeral 369.33
Epi 054.15
epic 515.21
epical 181.16
epicentric 605.16
epickthalamorous 040.14
epics 438.18
epicures 475.11
epiepistle 108.24
Epiphanes 341.26
epiphany 508.11
epipsychidically 041.05
episcopalian 559.26
episcoping 484.23
Epistlemadethemology 374.17
epistol 228.33
epistola 117.27
epistolear 038.23
epithet 191.02
epiwo 611.24
epizzles 411.15
epochs 101.14
epolettes 623.17
epoostles 617.05
epples 504.24
epscene 523.34
epsilene 019.11
epsut 333.34
epte 208.04
epulence 126.16
epulent 282.22
Equadocta 134.18
equal 017.35 032.20 036.21 306.F7 488.09
Equal 286.02
equality 283.11
equally 032.17 081.36 097.33 292.22 488.10 564.14
equalobe 599.18
equals 092.08 116.08 253.01
equate 167.04
equator 131.32 435.13
Equerry 102.14 135.29
equestrian 388.16
equilab 599.18
equilebriated 429.23
equilibbrium 599.18
equilines 380.17
equinarx 347.02
equinous 093.09
equinoxious 085.28
equip 188.21
equipped 309.17
equitable 362.28
equivalent 167.05
equo 572.36
equoangular 286.21
equonomic 599.17
er 070.06 262.F2 263.18
era 014.24 068.25 121.29 473.08
Era 228.15
eranthus 092.13
eraphon 131.30
eras 138.31 582.18
era's 244.25
Erasmus 504.26
Erat 140.04
erbas 230.07
erbole 451.07
Erchdeakin 369.11
Erchenwyne 088.21
ercked 410.08
erdcloset 551.25
erde 017.30 017.30
Erdnacrusha 262.15
erdor 285.02
erdours 360.30
ere 004.22 015.21 037.17 078.02 116.13 152.18 187.34 194.04 204.10 232.17 238.05 244.31 256.24 266.24 275.03 276.14 280.19 289.09 293.03 315.04 318.19 324.07 324.12 360.28 361.28 366.31 427.06 427.19 432.18 472.34 473.07 479.24 481.06 482.35 488.06 535.17 582.17
Ere 004.14 053.04 069.08 307.F9 358.21 371.16 420.32 433.33 547.10 599.08
Ere 418.32
Erebia 473.16
erebusqued 038.03
erect 036.14 619.14
Erect 108.01
erecta 242.13
erecta 131.30
erected 606.16
erectheion 539.03
erection 006.09 310.23 506.07
Erectus 101.13
Eregobragh 303.14
erehim 017.23
ere-in-garden 062.19
Ereland 264.31
erely 390.06 507.31
eren 053.13
Eren 398.05
erenoon 079.20
ereperse 117.15
eres 365.13 371.25
ereshiningem 586.30
erestationed 515.01
Erething 415.22
erewaken 255.05
Ereweak 126.07
Ereweaker 421.12
Erewhig 301.08
erewhile 426.26
erewold 588.34
erewone 213.15
Ergastulus 532.12
erge 594.24
Ergen 381.19
ergo 263.28
ergons 167.07
Erho 328.25
eric 316.08 537.14
Eric 030.10 277.23
erica's 498.30
Ericoricori 623.01
erics 456.22
ericulous 487.15
Ericus 220.25 373.24
Erie 601.06
Erievikkingr 326.07
erigenal 431.35
erigenating 004.36
Erigureen 279.03
Erill 493.03
Erin 203.01 347.21 384.06 387.29 408.08 452.28 462.04 547.32
Eringrowback 389.04
Erinly 316.18
Erinmonker 610.32
Erinnes 025.27
Erin's 275.01 428.20 467.32
Erio 021.26 022.13
Eristocras 534.34
erit 279.F08
Erit 140.05

erithmatic 537.36
Eriweddyng 327.32
erixtion 343.18
Erminia 391.01
Erminia's 339.29
ern 433.31
Erne 459.18
erned 198.05
ernest 233.20
Ernin 042.26
erning 324.03
ernst 127.32 238.19 264.03 534.08
Erobinson 434.12
eroes 146.24
erogenously 115.14
Eroico 271.L3
eroscope 431.14
erosion 479.18
Erosmas 301.F5
erpressgangs 068.31
err 258.32 273.06 300.12 332.01 405.19 578.34
errand 452.17 484.06
Errands 601.23
errears 140.32
erred 531.01
Erred 491.16
Errian 525.06
errible 381.23
Errick 530.21
erriff 205.23
Errin 394.34
errind 232.16
errindwards 371.36
erring 058.19 198.12 288.F6
erringnesses 279.F05
errings 272.20 524.26
errol 312.19
erronymously 617.30
error 067.23 089.03 433.30
erroriboose 140.33
Errorland 062.25
errorooth 231.11
erroroots 285.12
errors 120.15 434.04
errthors 036.35
Erryn 389.06
Ers 494.12
ersatz 518.18
erse 003.20 178.07 620.09
erse 268.L4
Erse 488.25
ersebest 253.01
ersed 285.11 484.09
ersed 540.11
ersekind 596.05
erseroyal 353.18
Erserum 240.28
Erse's 575.24
ersewild 319.04
Erssia's 354.10
erst 076.32 263.02
erstborn 178.10
ersther 500.21
erstwhile 034.36 412.23
erstwort 490.18
erthe 069.03
eruberuption 612.23
erubescent 055.29
Eruct 097.30
eructation 558.05
eructions 545.33
erudite 179.22
erumping 386.35
erupting 494.08
eruptious 079.18
erver 344.20
ervics 610.08
ervigheds 547.34
Ervigsen 616.03
eryan 215.27
Eryan's 580.34
Eryen 508.02
Erynnana 469.21
es 054.17 222.09 246.06 407.15 470.01 562.03
es 291.24 342.10
Es 245.16 301.02
é's 124.09
Esa 088.22
Esahur 359.17
esaltarshoming 470.15 470.17
Esau 093.17
Esaup 414.17
Esaus 433.20
esausted 542.30
Esc 029.19
escapa 464.11
escape 038.01 150.25 163.12 489.06 582.15
escaped 580.02
escapemaster-in-chief 127.10
escapes 291.16
escaping 232.12
escapology 428.22
Esch 588.28
eschatological 134.34
eschatology 482.33
eschess 588.28
escipe 158.17
escribibis 300.17
esculapuloids 540.33
escumo 198.02
escupement 151.19
escusado 485.21
Escuterre 541.35
Esellus 478.08
esercizism 231.27
Eset 029.13
eshtree 503.30
esimple 561.09
esiop's 422.22
esk 199.27 202.15
esker 126.15 475.22 555.13 555.15
eskermillas 350.21
eskimo 247.35
eskipping 579.05
eskmeno 572.16
eslaap 398.14
eslats 206.35
eslucylamp 327.05
Esme 088.22
Esmeralde 223.07
Esnekerry 038.22
esobhrakonton 508.12
Esop 307.L1
esophagous 558.03
esoupcans 289.05
esox 525.12
Espanol-Cymric-Helleniky 263.14
espart 626.32
especially 150.21 224.33 275.F3 492.31 557.30
Especially 433.36
especious 296.28
espellor 179.30
espera 497.15
Esperations 105.30
espicially 440.19
espied 375.31
Espionia 348.30
esplanadas 553.12
espos 144.05
espousals 129.03
espousing 605.08
espy 139.26
Esquara 557.01
esqueer 420.22
Esquilocus 254.20
esquimeena 585.24
esquire 485.21
esquirial 550.24
Esquoro 102.16
Esra 116.02
ess 111.18 479.36 609.09
Ess 479.36 479.36
Essastessa 278.F3
Essav 607.08
essavans 007.04
essayes 447.07
essaying 486.27
essenes 546.13
essenesse 608.04
essentience 600.22
Essex 125.17
Essexelcy 521.04
Essia 605.12
Essie 027.14 027.15 257.02
essied 484.06
essies 234.30
essixcoloured 611.35
Essonne 201.04
esster 528.12
est 273.06 611.21
est 081.29 281.L1 488.09 496.36
Est 116.16 140.04 481.04
establish 151.05 511.15
establisher 055.09
establishing 114.33
establishment 041.30 580.25
Establishment 220.03
establishments 036.22
estably 523.27
Estarr 069.14
estas 052.15 160.30
estate 182.24
Estates 105.36
Estchapel 374.31
esteem 225.07
esteemed 145.07
Estella 101.08
estelles 365.28
estellos 471.08
ester 327.13
Esterelles 462.07
esthate 343.17
estheryear's 212.31
esthetic 435.06
estimate 154.25
estimation 558.10
esto 168.13
Estoesto 540.17
estomach 192.22
Estote 540.17
Estout 099.04
estreated 575.30

estreme 432.31
estuarine 549.20
esually 089.13
Esuan 185.34
Eswuards' 026.31
et 178.17 201.30 261.03 384.27
414.14 514.14 610.21
et 028.27 041.05 077.23 092.07
104.11 113.30 157.01 163.03
163.04 185.14 185.17 185.21
251.29 281.04 281.07 281.08
281.10 281.11 281.12 287.24
419.34 443.13
Et 223.21 246.16
Et 073.19
ET 260.R1
etc 586.02
etc. 411.19 411.20
411.20 (et cetera)
etcaetera 514.20
etcaeterorum 514.20
etcera 568.32
etcetera 071.07 127.22 127.22
etceterogenious 595.23
etchy 418.23
etcicero 152.10
ete 397.25
Etem 224.03
eten 392.05
eternal 107.14 251.12 296.31
298.33 454.32
eternally 488.09 488.10
eternals 078.30
Eternest 532.06
eternity 035.25 273.F1
eternuel 499.11
ethel 166.07 614.01
etheling 031.17
ethelred 439.36
Ethelwulf 088.22
ether 059.09 098.03 197.13
476.07
Etheria 309.09
ethernal 527.23
etherways 458.23
Ethiaop 223.28
ethical 523.33
ethics 037.02 525.02
ethiquethical 109.21
Ethna 318.12
ethnarch 030.20
ethnic 089.33
ethnicist 578.12
ethur 349.05
etnat 494.06
etoiled 546.06
Etoudies 508.34
Etrurian 215.20
Etruscan 120.23
etsched 205.27
etsitaraw 152.10
etym 353.22
Eu 307.26 307.F8
eucharistic 605.31
eucherised 462.01
EUCHRE 304.R3
euchring 110.34
euchs 299.02
Euclid 206.13
eugenious 154.20
Eugenius 572.24 572.25 573.05
573.11 573.17
Euh 601.30
Eulalina's 430.36
Eulogia 527.12
Eulumu 499.09
eunique 562.33
eupeptic 050.21
euphemiasly 528.24
Euphonia 446.30
euphonise 515.11
euphonium 533.17
euphorious 353.08
Eurasian 610.12
eure 215.26
eurekason 326.30
eurhythmytic 147.08
eurn 291.06
Euro 228.26
Europa 497.12
Europasianised 191.04
europe 466.13
Europe 003.06 138.07 171.06
Europeic 088.01
europicolas 423.35
eurus 283.03
Eusapia 528.14
Eusebian 409.36
Eustace 535.26
eustacetube 036.36
Eustache 310.12 361.11
Euston 192.29 578.30
Eva 210.30 251.28
Eva 288.15
evabusies 568.04
evacuan 362.25
evacuated 127.12
evacuavit 185.17
Evan 482.18
evangel 551.15
evangelical 040.07
evangelion 223.19
Evangelist 391.33
Evans's 533.05
evar 595.06 626.03
evars 596.24
Evas 379.15
Eva's 494.15
evasive 254.19
eve 005.11 015.11 019.25
104.02 117.19 215.04 215.04
314.25 321.16 389.20 397.30
410.35 455.03
Eve 003.01 030.14 293.21
366.16 488.24
Eve 106.29 306.L2 377.16
evec 578.35
evectuals 405.36
eveling 186.24
evelings 222.32
evelo 039.07
evelopment 394.10
evelyns 094.28
evelytime 130.35
even 007.21 012.12 029.33
034.05 036.26 058.36 062.35
068.13 070.33 073.31 076.23
079.02 079.21 079.22 084.32
087.26 093.09 096.26 098.08
099.33 109.13 113.29 117.26
118.09 118.33 118.36 120.07
124.15 134.11 143.16 144.29
145.22 148.24 156.31 157.24
159.25 160.36 166.01 171.04
172.17 172.21 179.27 181.22
181.34 182.15 183.03 187.08
189.08 192.11 205.20 223.07
225.31 232.17 241.01 247.27
252.08 253.14 254.25 254.31
258.30 268.22 269.04 318.07
325.05 336.31 338.14 348.12
393.34 395.32 414.28 425.17
427.25 442.04 442.34 443.08
453.28 454.10 456.27 476.16
478.12 489.05 490.31 496.04
527.07 527.31 533.13 536.29
537.14 563.23 573.25 578.28
594.27 597.04 599.06 599.13
604.10 607.07 611.26 617.01
even 105.29
Even 086.04 130.03 235.04
241.26 255.22 264.09 278.08
329.22 360.32 527.27 547.07
568.06 594.08 612.32 624.26
evenbread 550.25
evenbreads 310.22
evencalm 556.22
evenchime 051.32
evenements 398.13
evenif 595.24
evenin 138.16 182.26
Evenine's 285.27
evening 109.02 149.10 152.21
156.36 174.32 219.01 268.14
589.33
Evening 028.20
evenlode 215.08
evens 090.02
evens 342.27
even's 405.12
evenso 474.09
evensong 056.05
evenstarde 312.08
event 253.14 443.13 583.15
Event 341.19
eventide 034.22
events 013.31 039.04 110.19
274.19 581.26
eventualising 051.22
eventually 118.09
eventuals 559.15
Eventyr 100.06
ever 005.17 011.36 019.36
021.08 025.06 025.16 026.20
028.33 029.14 029.26 030.01
039.13 042.16 047.18 055.21
060.03 061.15 061.33 066.10
066.23 068.32 078.21 087.19
091.30 092.04 101.19 108.31
109.07 110.21 110.33 120.12
121.23 138.19 144.34 148.27
148.29 153.03 157.02 159.27
162.35 170.28 170.30 171.10
172.31 173.01 177.15 179.24
179.33 180.31 182.14 185.11
187.34 193.34 194.30 200.29
203.01 204.03 207.34 208.03
208.32 210.06 234.18 234.23
240.08 240.22 242.09 243.12
246.01 248.12 249.36 250.31
251.27 253.23 259.02 260.04
264.10 264.F2 267.29 270.20
276.F1 277.22 279.03 279.F11
279.F20 283.F1 287.F2
291.F4 294.08 296.21 299.07
299.12 300.11 302.17 307.12
317.13 319.03 331.10 332.30
337.12 338.09 344.30 356.10
357.04 359.01 363.22 366.18

373.34 375.33 376.32 382.23 390.08 395.18 396.21 404.31 405.09 405.14 407.17 408.08 409.05 409.08 412.24 413.09 419.35 425.05 425.14 426.03 426.32 427.25 430.13 431.11 435.22 439.03 453.19 455.03 456.03 458.26 462.21 463.08 463.25 467.31 472.27 475.19 476.07 486.36 494.28 500.11 501.29 505.36 507.01 507.36 508.27 515.34 516.11 517.20 517.21 523.02 528.02 530.08 534.14 547.05 552.17 553.01 562.11 563.22 563.33 564.04 569.30 570.21 570.33 574.29 575.36 580.16 582.04 582.11 586.20 597.04 597.22 609.31 615.14 615.36 616.02 616.14 621.08 621.09 621.32 623.27 623.34 624.36 625.34 626.11
ever 338.13 340.07 346.31 383.09 383.13
Ever 146.26 191.34 192.01 192.03 264.10 299.30 406.27 461.36
everabody 597.21
everadayde 538.20
Everallin 228.04
everdevoting 408.18
everdue 604.17
evereachbird 098.36
everest 548.09
everfasting 584.28
everflowing 117.03
everglaning 221.19
everglass 252.07
evergrey 014.34
evergrim 455.13
Everguin's 285.L2
everie 360.03
everintermutuomergent 055.11
everlapsing 333.06
everlasting 220.29
everliking 483.19
everlistings 414.29
Everliving 104.01
evermixed 194.04
evermore 049.11 084.05 315.35 585.22
evernasty 503.07
evernew 460.36
everplanned 489.34
everpresent 151.21
Everready 523.14
evers 622.29
Everscepistic 536.04
everseen 029.09
eversides 568.26
everso 328.19 555.09
eversore 304.05
Eversought 512.30
eversower 593.20
eversure 054.08
evertheless 581.36
everthelest 619.36
everthemore 180.01
everthrown 570.36
Evertomind 329.35
evertwo 298.15
everurge 524.32
evervirens 088.02
everwere 011.16
everwhalmed 356.35
everwhy 415.23
everwore 234.09
every 010.30 012.29 012.30 019.27 019.29 020.14 020.23 025.13 025.20 027.18 032.21 033.08 033.23 036.30 036.30 052.22 066.04 066.15 066.34 078.31 080.22 091.33 098.29 101.16 101.17 101.17 112.17 115.02 115.07 118.01 118.21 118.23 120.34 125.05 136.23 138.17 142.21 144.02 146.27 152.34 153.14 162.20 162.24 169.06 172.30 173.36 174.10 177.07 177.25 178.09 178.10 179.30 180.02 183.02 185.35 187.25 189.34 191.17 200.18 201.21 201.22 205.23 210.01 210.28 210.28 213.12 215.16 215.16 221.05 228.26 239.18 239.19 247.27 256.05 264.F3 265.05 268.05 270.F4 274.16 277.05 283.30 283.31 283.F2 311.35 317.08 325.34 327.17 328.21 330.02 330.02 336.26 340.02 350.16 350.33 364.15 366.18 374.24 393.19 393.30 397.27 405.22 407.33 414.05 421.30 426.06 436.27 438.06 438.34 444.08 450.36 463.07 463.24 473.24 481.23 486.11 488.24 491.11 496.35 501.22 506.01 523.11 525.02 531.34 535.10 544.05 544.27 544.38 557.13 575.25 576.21 581.29 583.23 585.19 600.03 601.15 607.10 607.13 609.20 609.21 613.10 614.04 614.20 614.28 625.06
every 525.24
Every 065.11 165.13 219.01 228.26 269.17 378.26 424.32 486.11 510.16 586.15 597.19 598.01 623.33
everybiddy 021.09
everybilly 021.09
everybody 032.19 093.23 182.14 241.17 264.02 279.F19 391.16 396.06 463.24 502.21 527.11 557.35 618.21
Everybody 032.19
everybothy's 354.15
everybuddy 021.08
everybug 475.20
everybully 021.07
everydaily 136.26
Everyday 460.19
everydaylooking 109.07
everyelsesbody 329.18
everyhe 079.22
everyhow 378.27
everyknight 126.18
everyman 129.31
everynight 017.33 452.26
everyone 147.19 178.14 222.04 234.27 386.30 440.29 452.30 626.26
Everyone 208.29
everyone's 183.02 190.33
everysee 360.31
everyside 019.12
everysing 299.02
every-tale-a-treat-in-itself 123.27
everything 040.24 069.20 112.17 154.04 166.32 255.34 285.17 384.25 404.33 410.26 451.34 452.31 502.20 527.19 560.31 623.09
Everything 306.17 306.18
everythingling 395.19
everythings 599.01
Everything's 026.25
everythinks 242.04
everytime 455.31
everywans 557.09
everyway 153.30
Everywhair 108.23
everywhencewithersoever 613.20
everywhere 394.08 581.05 585.19
Everywhere 205.23 514.30 535.34
everywheres 349.29
everywince 624.26
eves 266.27 424.29
Eve's 083.22 197.12 226.13
evesdrip 023.22
evesdripping 089.01
evew 061.06
evicted 414.06
evidence 086.32 314.04 534.10 544.16
Evidence 307.24
evidenced 164.18
evidencegivers 057.17
evident 016.01 398.24
Evidentament 253.19
evidential 096.27
evidently 043.16
evil 052.29 142.21 169.19 172.33 189.29 210.06 250.25 281.02 390.30 465.13 523.02
evildoer 532.04
Evil-it-is 418.06
Evilling 538.31
evillyboldy's 361.12
evils 616.29
evilsmeller 182.17
evince 137.16
evings 235.03
evinxed 090.06
eviparated 004.24
evitated 035.20
Evlyn 062.34
evmans 327.12
evocation 056.05
evoe 508.09
Evohodie 546.11
evoke 165.18
evoker 472.01
Evol 262.F2
evoluation 073.32
evolution 462.34
evolutionary 109.23
evolved 092.08
Evora 623.27
evorage 539.22
Evovae 505.13
evremberried 264.26
Evropeahahn 205.29
evrywehr 131.07
evums 261.14
evurdyburdy 378.05
Ewacka 079.05
ewe 145.05
Ewe 396.14
eweheart 336.34

ewer 180.06
ewes 279.F02
ewesed 580.05
ewigs 552.21
ewon 601.03
ex 183.26 284.17 529.16 609.24
ex 075.18 162.29 185.24 287.25 355.06 407.33 572.36 573.21 586.05
Ex 023.16 172.08 294.F1 424.13 424.13 424.13 424.13
Ex 513.08
exact 408.13
exactly 089.21 108.26 122.24 564.14
Exactly 089.14
exactlyso 598.31
exaggerated 003.07
exagmination 497.02
exaltated 505.14
exaltation 558.11
exalted 068.23 136.06 605.09
exalts 249.14
Examen 240.06
examhoops 450.35
examinations 468.02
examiner 519.24
example 150.06 524.13 561.08 616.27
EXAMPLES 282.R4
examplum 198.21
exanimation 143.08
Exarchas 062.21
exarx 285.09
exaspirated 251.31
Exat 106.26
Exaudi 152.14
Exbelled 420.25
Exby 369.11
excavated 605.26 605.27 605.33
excavators 573.08
excavement 596.28
exceed 425.22
exceeded 493.23
exceeding 183.02 396.19 431.29 548.36
exceedingly 048.21 252.22 252.22 258.15 570.16
excelcism 083.31
excellency 031.20 033.30 258.16
excellent 070.15 163.34 263.23 347.17 560.26
Excellent 582.30
Excellent 106.36
excelling 037.33
Excelsior 411.05
excelsis 165.22
excelsissimost 014.19
excelsius 597.31
excelssiorising 505.14
except 067.26 234.23 560.31
excerpt 359.23
excess 558.11 581.30
excesses 067.29
excessively 043.24 537.28 561.13
exchange 464.20 538.08 574.24 575.11
Exchange 252.10
Exchange 106.18
exchanged 083.32
exchanging 042.36 394.18
excheck 016.08
exchequer 375.20
exchequered 091.30
exchullard 392.15
excise 159.25
excisively 138.09
excitation 557.22
excited 234.21 242.10 527.31
excitement 091.36
exciting 453.11
excits 368.19
excivily 055.13
exclaimed 177.12
EXCLAMATION 281.R4
excluded 537.27
exclusive 584.36
exclusively 544.34
Exclusivism 299.L2
ex-Colonel 600.17
excommunicated 181.35
excomologosis 341.30
excramation 342.19
excremuncted 227.32
excrescence 138.06
excruciated 137.13 192.18
exculpatory 056.15
excursions 566.13
excuse 096.18 357.27 411.36 421.19
Excuse 148.21 301.F2 518.18
excusethems 474.24
Excutes 607.22
exe 205.09
execrated 544.11
Execration 035.20
Executed 070.35
executing 052.01
execution 366.17
executive 040.15
exegious 057.22
exemple 521.32
exemptied 313.21
exemption 362.17
exeomnosunt 258.02
exercise 085.12
exercised 166.31
exercitise 347.30
exers 529.25
exerxeses 286.08
exes 281.F3 625.02
exess 524.01
exestuance 387.12
exetur 073.23
Exeunc 388.01
exeunt 171.36
Exex 172.09
Exexex 172.10
ex-ex-executive 042.08
exexive 363.09
ex-gardener 133.06
exgust 616.16
exhabiting 602.22
exhaling 449.22
exhaust 408.04
exhausted 292.06
exhaustive 132.06
exhib 607.32
exhibisces 349.20
exhibit 403.10
Exhibit 087.32
exhibited 084.18
exhibiting 550.34
exhibitioners 205.05
exhibitionism 121.19
exhibitiveness 304.11
exhibits 109.09 559.24 559.27
Exhibits 106.09
exhorting 073.03
exhumed 032.13
exile 098.05 233.13
exiled 184.06
exiles 163.12
exilicy's 084.14
eximious 505.14
exist 033.35 069.08 576.05
existed 013.12 087.20 088.07
existence 033.30 076.18 098.15 100.35 173.20
existencies 133.07
existentiality 018.28
existents 578.14
existers 222.28
existing 560.29
Existing 306.29
existings 187.22
exists 186.08
exit 127.29 431.25
exite 368.16
exitous 353.18
exits 057.21 280.27
exking 187.11
exlegged 167.10
Exmooth 595.01
exmountain 129.04
exnun 099.07
exodus 004.24 222.05
exonerated 185.23
exoneratus 185.18
exorcise 437.12
exorcised 605.36
exordium 432.05
exotic 100.13 121.20
expancian 488.32
expanded 593.19
expanding 263.26
expanse 035.08 302.29
expansion 440.13
expansive 140.12
expansive 350.10
Expatiate 555.03
expatriate 100.10
expect 326.15 410.20 553.33
expectancy 362.23
expectant 077.07
expectation 404.03
expectations 614.23
expected 398.25 439.19 471.09 545.13
expecting 286.27 489.17 616.35
expectorate 037.28
expectoration 245.31
expectoratiously 470.28
expects 502.30
expectungpelick 020.34
expedience 156.04
expeltsion 518.23
expending 410.17
expenditures 358.14
expense 182.35 298.27 385.36
expensive 140.11 461.05
expercatered 219.06
experdition 455.06
experience 436.21 509.02 573.26
experienced 165.19
experiences 398.13
EXPERIENCES 286.R2
experiencing 107.33
experimenter 582.03

experiments 151.12
Experssly 240.10
expert 109.30 522.31 522.33
expiating 062.06
expiatory 392.22
expired 089.20
expiry 089.20
explain 028.10 042.16 253.21 362.06 523.19
Explain 447.24
Explain 105.14
explained 072.21 159.24 409.31
explaining 173.33 488.06
explaining 343.16
explains 163.04 179.21
explanation 051.24
explanations 152.04 524.09
explaud 172.19
expletion 316.34
expletive 152.07
explex 149.30
explication 523.21
explique 148.17
explode 063.14
exploded 077.05
exploder 326.23 606.23
exploits 196.22 620.23
exploser 512.18
explosion 078.04 133.11
explosition 419.11
explosium 589.36
explots 124.29
explunderer 326.09
explutor 387.13
Expolled 176.07
expolodotonates 353.23
exponents 260.F3
exponse 167.29
export 471.36
Exports 497.26
exposant 549.34
expose 089.06
exposed 159.35 413.21
exposition 589.17
Exposition 111.07
exposito 185.25
expositoed 498.35
exposure 034.26 057.24
expound 167.29
expounding 151.27
expoused 548.11
expousing 344.16
express 135.34 431.21 567.32
expressed 034.35 060.01 144.21 500.16
expression 069.01 173.01 265.F2 559.23 559.27
expressionism 467.07
expressions 293.17
exprivate 040.16
exprogressive 614.31
exprussians 135.16
expulled 488.22
expulsed 501.20
expurgative 356.30
exqueezit 412.08
exquisite 013.06 143.33 458.24
Exquisite 302.19
exquisitely 039.19 624.21
exquisitive 505.09
Exquovis 484.34
exrace 051.25
exsearfaceman 429.20
exservicemajor 572.21
Ex-Skaerer-Sissers 375.25
exsogerraider 619.30
exsponging 440.07
exspoused 503.18
Exsquire 205.22
exsystems 148.18
extand 005.28
extell 258.15 258.15
extempore 606.09
extemporised 137.18
extench 524.30
extend 235.31 461.03
extended 381.02
extending 408.15
extends 254.09
extense 418.33
extension 150.08 582.36
extensions 144.23
extensive 140.10
extensolies 006.35
extensors 414.31
extent 558.04 599.11
exterior 261.18
exteriorises 394.34
exterminate 081.25
extermination 006.21
exterra 601.33
exthro 092.01
extlicker 308.04
Extinct 494.06
extinction 155.31
extincts 387.20
extinguish 606.13
extinsion 371.24
extinuation 558.12
extol 258.07 258.10
extorreor 254.13
Extorreor 105.11
extra 207.11 375.15
extrahand 435.08
extramurals 579.31
extraoldandairy 505.14
extraomnes 497.10
extraordinary 176.21 263.F4 408.13 516.34
Extraordinary 144.16
extraprofessional 456.29
extravagance 193.02
extravent 314.20
extravert 412.05
extremely 074.15 425.17 558.05 605.22
extremes 254.04 440.34
extremeties 074.15 154.16 426.29
extremity 360.32
extremum 575.36
extructed 284.15
extruding 189.08
extrusion 386.19
Exuber 612.03
Exuberant 381.25
exude 100.12 247.21
Exultations' 066.09
exution 086.01
ex-voto 413.36
ey 207.08
eyballds 075.17
eye 006.35 023.36 025.26 027.31 061.24 081.20 086.32 093.28 101.33 107.16 113.28 118.17 120.26 124.18 143.09 145.17 174.18 180.20 182.06 183.36 197.17 202.34 210.26 213.15 215.05 225.32 240.33 248.06 249.16 252.34 271.18 279.F33 280.04 293.11 299.F3 300.12 309.04 330.26 332.21 336.30 348.26 360.31 363.03 366.36 370.15 377.04 437.01 441.17 464.12 466.35 482.35 486.13 512.09 515.23 524.19 533.05 624.19
eye 303.L1 344.03
Eye 162.32 301.07 409.03 409.03
Eye 106.24
eyebags 616.14
eyeball 541.19
eyeballs 523.12
eyebold 091.11
eyebrow 093.25
eyebrowns 020.02
eyebulbs 531.08 557.12
eyebush 012.08
eyed 239.06
eyedulls 351.25
eyeeye 532.14
eyefeast 357.17
eyeforsight 417.23
eyeful 004.36
eyegonblack 016.29
Eyeinstye 305.06
eyelids 234.16 248.16
eyeluscious 482.05
eyenbowls 389.28
eyeness 623.18
eyer 406.15
eyerim 247.22
eyes 014.29 020.34 021.09 051.26 052.18 055.22 055.23 056.23 068.26 094.17 107.28 109.21 121.17 121.25 130.19 152.23 153.04 158.12 162.08 165.04 167.13 176.22 183.36 203.28 208.10 208.32 214.16 230.33 231.30 234.07 240.05 240.16 290.04 302.11 328.05 368.31 372.03 384.20 395.07 396.11 405.29 415.03 423.23 424.04 434.31 443.01 443.36 449.03 457.28 459.01 463.27 490.22 509.27 509.30 512.25 515.21 522.13 542.26 556.17 558.07 559.23 562.27 564.34 612.06 618.01 621.29 626.15
eyes 262.L2 339.19
Eyes 106.27
eye's 189.26
eyesalt 484.05
eyesoult 222.27
eyespy 237.03
eye-to-eye 254.10
eyetrompit 247.32
eyeux 102.12
eyewinker 320.27
eyewitless 515.30
eygs 199.06 199.16
eyis 499.12
eyne 275.18
eynes 534.26
eyoldhyms 183.15
Eyolf 201.34
eyols 182.22
eyot 463.30

Eyot 604.25
eyots 040.10
Eyrawyggla 048.16
Eyrewaker's 581.06
eyriewinging 367.33
Eyrlands 604.24
eys 038.16
eysolt 394.30
ez 245.17
Ezekiel 027.23
Ezekiel 307.L1

f 370.13
F 266.22
468.03 (P? F?)
fa 448.35 466.26
Fa 532.03
F . . . A . . . 059.04 (Mrs F . . . A . . .)
Faagher 536.34
faathern 565.20
Fabius 307.L1
fable 245.09 275.20 319.14 414.17
Fable 307.15
fablebodied 160.34
fables 159.14 385.11
fablings 061.28
fabrication 054.28
fabrications 036.34
fabulafigured 596.29
fabulist's 152.13
face 051.19 063.05 084.19 086.09 086.22 090.02 101.30 109.08 111.13 115.35 118.05 120.30 138.18 160.20 173.09 176.35 178.07 179.07 210.23 223.15 237.28 240.19 263.16 265.F1 271.15 274.31 276.F2 279.01 291.06 303.32 307.F7 310.27 330.17 355.09 355.09 361.35 368.30 392.26 407.08 411.10 434.32 434.32 442.23 444.09 448.11 458.16 459.34 550.19 561.31 570.34 574.27 582.28 602.12 602.12 615.24
face 209.09 260.L1 344.11
Face 018.35 018.35
Face 106.19
Ⅎace 018.36
Ⅎace 018.36
f.a.c.e. 450.10
faceage 296.12
faceback 023.31
facebuts 612.12
faced 062.32 139.04 315.18
facefronts 369.04
facepails 250.09
faces 042.23 148.27 173.25 230.33 427.21 496.14 526.30
face's 588.04
facessà 212.36
facetious 147.31
facetowel 559.07
facets 061.03 298.30
facewall 135.16
Faciasi 212.35 212.35
facing 223.15 367.26 375.11
faciofacey 279.F08
Facktotem 071.31
Facst 607.03
fact 032.12 039.31 050.36 055.06 060.18 066.01 107.28 109.06 109.21 113.05 124.01 129.04 161.18 162.16 163.08 192.33 199.33 242.21 358.07 385.30 407.35 411.20 422.04 515.14 517.11 529.31 537.16 586.20 596.05 615.06
Fact 079.19
factferreters 055.13
factification 497.02
faction 229.20 320.07 336.20
factionables 285.26
factions 289.F1
factitation 467.26
factor 451.09
Factor 420.31
factory 110.26 243.02 409.25
FACTORY 282.R1
facts 031.33 038.27 109.14 109.31 109.32 152.14 179.07 447.31
factual 529.31
factual 308.L2
faculties 206.20
fad 178.02 626.10
faddles 531.29
fade 473.10
fade 349.06
faded 051.02 268.01 543.31
fadeless 395.30 493.27
fader 333.26
fadervor 276.14
fades 427.17
Fadgestfudgist 323.23
fading 005.21 226.11 235.07 486.33 528.11
fadograph 007.15
fads 437.10
faengers 349.30
faery 281.03 319.12
fafafather 045.13
fag 322.30
fagbutt 435.33
fagged 097.32
fagroaster 421.31
fags 130.36
faher 481.32
faher's 467.12
Faherty 025.04
fahr 260.15 471.19
fahrman 577.13
fahrt 248.14
fahrts 553.34
fail 013.22 077.15 083.13 151.26 271.07 462.08 558.34 565.01 566.25
Fail 131.10
failed 025.31 026.32 253.19 539.10
failend 535.30
failing 063.04 189.02 190.18 445.21 490.05
failing 339.33 353.01
fails 116.34 133.35 142.15 627.11
failure 114.30
failures 589.17
faime 163.02
fain 037.36 061.30 069.03 083.22 135.02 149.07 165.06 227.25 254.36 313.27 333.27 366.11 498.13 556.20 621.14
Fain 257.02
Fain 105.03
faineans 546.18
Faineant 254.20
fainéants 131.09
fainfully 124.32
fainmain 346.27
faint 038.14 204.10 278.26 403.22 626.01
faint 354.05
fainted 208.28
faintly 109.04
fair 003.11 028.23 043.17 065.25 069.17 086.11 087.14 089.08 093.32 094.09 116.13 117.02 125.10 137.16 146.11 146.25 158.02 184.05 207.25 212.32 215.22 246.19 251.20 279.07 280.28 295.21 321.35 355.20 363.19 365.36 374.03 385.27 394.18 432.04 451.08 472.13 479.28 481.06 484.22 501.17 521.16 532.17 543.22 569.33 582.23 588.29 607.13 625.28 625.32 628.09
fair 340.26
Fair 018.08 028.13 337.21 387.19 445.09 537.35 563.26
Fair 072.08
Fairbrother's 585.29
faire 532.33
fairer 178.21 472.04
fairescapading 388.03
fairest 011.26 360.26 430.24
faireviews 541.25
fairground 128.31
fairhailed 234.27
Fairhair 572.21
fairhaired 220.12
fairhead 490.15
fairies 069.03
fairies 268.L2
fairiest 204.11
Fairing 334.35
fairioes 326.18
fairish 427.03
fairlove 300.28
fairly 076.24 079.04 083.13 099.08 279.F03 292.21 372.18 431.36 453.20 456.13 503.18 626.22
fairly 399.08
fairlygosmotherthemselves 353.27
Fairlys 176.07
fairmesse 596.02
fairmoneys 595.15
fairness 249.06 249.10 249.11 249.11 249.12 249.12
fairnesse 547.06
Fairplay 521.33
fairs 361.02
Fairshee 486.33
fairsized 602.02 602.05
fairskin 552.36
Fairview 447.20
Fairwail 345.14
fairway 206.26
Fairwell 225.30
fairworded 077.25
fairy 009.14 203.16 328.03 454.28 580.12 583.14
fairyaciodes 450.19
fairygeyed 015.03
fairyhees 029.12
Fairynelly's 151.07

fairypair 606.23
fairytales 220.13
Fais-le 528.14
faist 311.31
faith 129.36 199.33 255.10 263.11 405.01 417.30 425.21 434.02 463.06 468.31 476.25 482.30 519.27 522.27 579.23
Faith 461.07 464.36 516.03
faithful 056.09 069.26 190.26 391.12 546.30
Faithful 295.10
faithfully 489.07
faithly 185.34 503.19
faiths 151.15 331.03
faix 091.36 381.09
Faixgood 369.08
fake 206.07 311.27 375.17 463.21
Fake 013.03
faked 185.25
fakes 300.03
fakesimilar 484.34
faketotem 516.24
fal 206.29
falchioned 135.25
Falconer 185.04
falconplumes 026.10
fald 386.08
Falias 219.11
fall 003.15 003.18 011.36 012.12 019.36 028.09 053.09 064.36 083.21 102.02 129.09 130.15 131.06 156.27 158.21 163.27 166.08 170.17 184.14 190.12 198.01 223.16 293.21 294.25 312.11 323.15 335.33 357.27 382.01 382.01 382.07 407.27 411.05 425.11 434.11 439.07 469.13 469.34 470.27 502.02 504.32 568.10 579.26 583.23 588.22 589.17 589.20 596.02 602.32 627.11
fall 073.16 175.18
Fall 070.05 366.30 379.12 600.13
Fall 105.23 106.20 106.21 107.05
fallacy 032.06 150.24 151.27
falladelfian 073.18
Fallareen 214.13
falled 619.21
fallen 007.08 015.19 055.03 058.10 086.03 122.29 183.16 207.03 313.33 407.24 476.13 611.16
fallener 352.03
fallensickners 530.02
faller 368.29
fallimineers 112.33
falling 021.25 063.27 064.34 096.21 120.34 143.20 178.34 180.16 391.26 392.18 394.05 460.20 483.31 534.04 566.17 619.22
Falling 072.07
fall-of-the-trick 577.08
fallow 053.18 204.18
fallowing 602.19
falls 051.06 080.22 139.09 210.24 214.31 242.20 247.22 285.11 286.04 317.09 327.14 419.14 423.28 427.02 434.33 563.33
falls 348.04 354.13
fallse 534.20
fallth 619.08
fallthere 302.26
false 004.11 041.31 068.20 129.15 131.18 210.26 241.32 465.27 467.34 508.03 566.13
falsehair 183.18
falseheaven 590.08
falsehood 452.06
falseleep 345.11
falsely 107.07
falsemeaning 077.26
falsesighted 079.03
falsetissues 048.18
falsetook 063.29
falskin 621.25
falsoletto 281.19
falted 606.27
falter 270.03
falter 354.18
fam. 299.F4
Fama 098.02
famalgia 314.36
famas 314.36
famblings 582.05
fame 025.09 192.20 375.16
famellicurbs 303.19
famiksed 451.35
familiar 288.21 317.17 389.33 470.26 514.01 515.29 564.33
familiarities 392.05 395.21
familiars 333.15 608.08
familiarum 496.22
familias 386.13
families 033.25 181.04
family 031.22 048.06 052.04 052.33 067.25 078.35 085.23 098.16 119.29 121.34 129.35 132.32 134.03 141.23 183.17 213.34 230.29 242.03 244.19 252.11 284.04 299.F4 330.13 381.36 392.23 440.34 444.04 454.36 492.21 522.17 522.18 543.23 560.28 560.33 578.15 581.06 601.13 607.05
Family 106.22
familyans 382.18
Familyman's 391.03
famine 094.12 130.26 196.15 539.36
faminebuilt 071.02
faminy 340.15
Faminy 441.02
famish 422.18
famished 192.24
Famm 420.10
Fammfamm 064.28 064.29
fammished 251.12
fammy 020.29
Famose 463.33
famous 036.08 060.30 197.03 382.05 502.26 540.07
famous 342.21
fan 058.12 147.33 184.25 199.36 254.36 434.28 438.17 559.03 626.23
Fanagan 503.10
fanagan's 351.02
Fanagan's 276.22 537.34
fancied 031.08 177.34 425.07 616.04
fancies 623.18
fancie's 115.35
Fanciesland 440.21
Fanciulla 278.08
Fanciulla's 278.07
fancy 130.36 132.30 171.03 171.28 239.13 375.30 376.21 395.14 425.04 568.17 570.07 588.36 598.24 606.32
fancydress 529.32
fancyfastened 208.16
fancyflame 301.05
fancyfought 086.26
fancymud 006.05
fand 224.26 315.28
Fanden 516.19
Fanden's 282.25
fands 617.31
fane 056.08 081.11 139.23
Fane 600.15
fane's 122.10
fanespanned 004.13
fanest 506.17
fanfare 130.09
fang 333.22
Fangaluvu 594.23
fanky 302.31
fanmail 471.26
fann 616.01
fannacies 340.29
fanned 130.14 241.19 493.22 535.10
fanny 204.08
Fanny 171.28
fans 159.14 236.02 279.F09
Fans 464.15
fansaties 112.36
fantastic 415.11
Fantastic 294.15
fantasy 493.18
Fantasy 493.18
fantods 283.29
faotre 473.17
far 023.22 032.13 033.08 048.23 052.09 055.33 069.27 099.33 107.27 116.12 118.01 127.32 136.05 138.05 149.15 171.05 174.27 180.06 184.14 189.15 213.08 240.31 242.16 251.01 320.27 357.23 360.10 395.14 404.18 419.28 421.35 425.22 429.06 440.32 440.32 440.33 445.29 453.01 455.03 459.01 463.04 467.35 469.06 475.23 476.22 480.08 506.21 506.21 516.26 525.11 532.24 533.21 540.05 548.18 570.29 583.16 603.24 622.14 627.25 628.13
far 350.12
Far 244.22 628.13
farabove 468.13
farabroads 333.15
faraclacks, 595.33
farahead 234.27
farback 385.06 386.09
Farber 065.32
farbetween 250.35
farbiger 613.11
farbung 235.05

farce 014.14 162.02 285.12 374.11 509.32
farced 120.11 228.33
farceson 423.01
Farcing 518.25
fard 371.05
fare 018.07 083.22 242.21 317.20 327.09 365.22 367.23 454.01
Fare 454.27
farecard 228.23
fared 225.33 320.27 326.18
Farer 203.11
farerne 382.28
farest 112.06 206.17
Farety 312.09
farewell 038.07 472.13
Farewell 468.28 469.19 521.35
farfalling 417.13
farfamed 132.23 173.22
farfar 068.19 139.06 482.27
Farfar 052.16
Farfassa 398.15
farfatch'd 014.28
farfather 095.20
farfetched 473.13
farflung 419.11
fargazer 143.26
fargobawlers 005.31
fargoneahead 426.23
farheard 562.24
farinadays 542.33
fark 581.09
Farley 257.24
farlook 418.35
farm 053.18 129.26 545.23
farmament 494.03
farmer 351.04 413.16 455.04 614.31
Farmer 257.17
farmerette 200.19
farmers 096.16
farmer's 164.12 589.21
farmfrow's 119.10
farnights 357.24
farning 320.20
Farnum's 532.12
faroots 303.20
faroscope 150.32
farout 463.30
farranoch 502.01
Farrel 176.17
Farrell 552.12
Farrell 270.L2
Farrelly 013.13
farrer 241.20
farrest 418.27
farrier's 433.07
farruler 547.23
farsed 138.32
farseeing 157.21
Farseeingetherich 054.03
farseeker 548.14
farshook 601.35
farsoonerite 171.04
farst 340.35 356.12
fartas 160.32
farternoiser 530.36
farth 128.10 597.12
farther 112.01 115.21 147.20 166.34 213.32 229.01 329.07 378.35 396.22 426.35 481.19 483.16 545.17 595.06
farther 339.36
Farther 071.20
farthest 545.17
farthing 397.26 574.29
farthingales 468.14
farting 451.01 567.34
fartoomanyness 122.36
fartykket 604.14
farums 566.14
farused 339.24
farvel 471.34
Farvel 382.28
Farvver 093.20
farwailed 590.16
farwellens 371.28
fas 098.26
fas 031.36 167.34 443.13
Fas 273.06
fascinated 220.10
fascinator 398.17
fascion 333.21
fash 137.11 318.20
fashion 037.29 510.20
Fashion 206.13
fashionaping 505.08
fassed 077.18
fassilwise 013.32
fast 064.34 101.01 124.10 172.03 174.35 189.30 208.13 211.16 318.13 423.06 449.24 497.16 540.07 577.36 611.09 620.11
fast 350.13
Fast 072.15
fastalbarnstone 280.31
fastbroke 541.25
faste 405.31 598.11
fasten 444.11
Fastened 532.36
faster 584.05 584.05
fasting 069.35
Fastintide 453.36
fastion 339.10
Fastland 070.06
fastness 297.20
fastra 061.20
fat 023.08 079.13 099.08 136.09 171.24 275.F5 275.13 378.27 413.09 430.30 491.09 494.23 497.34 603.04 626.13
fat 260.L3 418.15
Fat 485.20
Fat 176.17
fata 031.35
fatal 058.29 110.25 122.34 563.10
fatally 220.10
fate 056.18 066.12 136.12 157.25 345.13 408.01 472.30 482.31 540.18 578.27
fated 223.16
Fatefully 424.12
Fateha 235.02
fates 004.22 344.35 383.21 449.13
fate's 432.32
Fathach 100.07 329.33
fathe 379.21
Fathe 105.30
father 004.12 043.03 137.15 139.06 155.01 194.17 204.36 263.05 285.F4 369.33 420.10 420.18 439.07 440.14 448.24 457.07 481.34 483.28 500.19 512.03 565.21 590.06 628.01 628.02 628.02
father 115.26
Father 050.18 089.25 096.10 111.15 116.07 150.27 184.34 185.04 214.12 223.04 255.28 257.10 330.05 350.27 382.12 420.30 432.07 442.08 443.28 464.29 520.04 520.10 520.16 528.08 562.27 600.02
Father 104.22 341.26
fatherick 478.28
fathering 267.F5
father-in-law 545.05
fatherjohnson 440.08
fatherlow 141.24
fathers 426.30 545.17 558.29
father's 152.31 210.18
fathers' 447.18
fatherthyme's 090.07
fathom 394.10 605.27
fathomglasses 386.16
fathoms 386.17
fatigued 143.04
fatiguing 409.16
Fatiguing 409.16
Fatima 205.31 389.15
Fatimiliafamilias 389.15
fatlike 136.09
Fatmate 072.15
fat's 064.34
fatspitters 616.23
fatt 354.35
fattafottafutt 599.08
fatted 210.17
fatten 437.24
fattened 188.10
Fattens 172.07
fatter 150.11 319.21
fatthoms 312.07
faturity 292.19
fauces 418.11
faugh 324.28
Faugh 382.22
fauh 352.29
faulker 316.32
faullt 558.08
faulscrescendied 492.07
fault 171.27 193.31 193.31 193.32 202.34
Fault 106.25
faulterer 131.27
faultering 081.06
faulter-in-law 323.15
faulters 233.15
faults 392.01 627.34
faulty 016.35
Faultyfindth 153.34
Faun 033.28 354.06
Fauna 212.09
Faunagon 337.28
faunayman 025.32
faunonfleetfoot 128.04
fauns' 250.32
Faurore 587.01
faus 323.16
fauss 127.04
faust 083.29 160.29 288.09 356.01
faustian 292.22
fausties 252.02
faustive 074.09

Faut 106.12
fauve 238.10
Fauxfitzhuorson 529.20
favorite 263.05
Favorite 306.21
favour 110.01 129.02 470.23
favour 352.19
Favour 054.05
favourable 470.11
favoured 076.03 534.16 590.01
favourests 357.11
favourite 385.24 444.04 447.20
539.05
favourites 243.18
favours 068.05 470.11 566.16
567.29 584.30
favour's 396.13
faw 291.02
Fawkes 177.29
fawned 547.07
fawngest 489.11
fawthery 586.27
fawthrig 565.18
faxes 567.25
fay 018.11 018.35 292.08
328.03 528.13
Fay 101.08
fayboys 526.17
faye 020.33
Faynean 481.13
fays 569.35 603.24
fayst 141.06
fazzolotto 281.19
fb 124.07
F.D. 151.11
151.33 (Fidei Defensor)
fe 089.27
Fe 011.07 532.03
feacemaker 301.04
feacht 086.05
feactures 493.02
feale 201.19
fealse 144.13
fealty 030.20 038.33
fear 004.06 013.23 134.07
168.12 182.06 189.07 204.25
222.30 258.05 258.06 260.15
263.F2 279.F31 301.22 324.21
344.35 368.07 379.32 434.25
438.31 460.06 481.32 487.18
487.22 497.14 525.36 533.15
541.35 559.28 562.09 566.31
583.17 584.13 626.29
Fear 009.05 566.31
feared 071.05 086.06 097.29
299.03 312.18
feared 418.11
fearer 604.28
fearfeel 290.15
fearfilled 481.08
fearful 549.11
fearfully 297.12
fearfurther 288.F7
Fearhoure 587.01
fearing 313.32
fearless 031.09
fearly 278.F4
Fearmanagh 284.06
fearra 091.04
fears 197.15 361.02 573.16
576.15 587.36
fearse 018.02
fearsome 316.16 555.11
Fearson's 359.27
fearstung 085.18
fearty 312.10
Fearview 420.26
Fearwealing 345.14
feary 628.02
feasible 544.13
feast 005.24 189.30 244.05
316.23 434.16 450.04 550.12
605.05
Feast 306.23
feaster 317.11
feaster's 277.05
feastking 231.12
feat 473.15
feather 085.24 589.29
feather 383.13
feathered 579.36
feathers 299.11 454.10 463.04
538.07
Feathers 072.05
featherweighed 417.34
featly 292.21
feats 382.24 514.04
feats 419.05
feature 187.25 263.16 314.25
494.11
featured 443.34
featureful 109.09
features 056.15 111.35 602.04
612.35
featuring 107.29 219.21
Febber 372.09
febrewery 015.35
february 544.36
February 470.04
fecit 185.25
fecking 253.27 257.17
Fecks 425.23
fect 248.26
fecundclass 444.04
Fecundus 574.12
fed 168.01 188.09 257.36 333.24
410.07 503.36 550.08
fed 338.36
federal 443.14
Federals' 066.08
fee 054.18 295.33 457.04
586.25
Fee 466.29 528.03 545.23
feeatre 059.09
feeble 414.18 507.08
feebles 113.15
feebly 177.01
feebought 115.25
feed 083.18 242.02 243.14
276.F6 308.15 317.09 320.16
376.28 437.27 441.12 448.21
489.30 579.24 602.35
feed 484.36
Feed 472.05
feedailyones 058.11
feedchute 200.05
feeders 188.30
feeding 078.33 079.13 350.29
550.16
feeds 239.17
feedst 408.23
feefee 204.16
Feefee 475.01
Feefeel 420.13 420.13
feeh 352.29
feehn 593.09
Feejeean 546.18
feekeepers 142.24
feel 058.11 065.27 066.35
098.24 113.05 115.18 122.01
128.16 132.18 142.33 155.13
159.26 160.34 164.06 167.34
185.12 215.34 215.36 224.35
238.36 248.26 250.25 254.20
261.F1 296.16 336.26 365.30
366.18 408.31 421.24 426.23
431.25 437.11 439.04 439.22
441.19 452.23 466.07 466.10
468.18 469.15 473.10 486.07
486.22 486.23 486.35 506.19
506.33 528.05 532.23 565.11
585.19 590.28 625.34 626.01
626.36 627.02 627.11
feel 418.19 418.23
Feel 172.08 172.09 337.24
491.30
feeled 006.08 158.17 274.18
434.12
feeler 115.35 588.01
feelful 613.19
feelhers 414.30
feelimbs 537.29
feelin 035.27
feeling 004.10 079.05 096.12
112.03 115.33 135.02 142.33
160.24 161.33 203.23 224.02
227.24 269.F1 276.24 303.16
315.17 370.02 426.12 430.30
436.09 442.26 487.15 502.30
549.27 566.05 570.27 597.12
597.33
Feeling 252.09 377.17
feelings 351.27 466.12
feelins 072.22
feelmick's 520.01
feelplay 095.21
feels 031.31 112.13 142.15
193.22 211.04 334.10 382.25
410.05 427.30 489.18
feels 348.03
feel-this-feather 577.06
feelyfooling 584.18
feen 092.17
Feeney's 518.27
Feenichts 219.02
feeofeeds 336.13
feepence 141.07
Feeries 048.14
feers 451.17
feery 340.10
feet 006.27 007.30 024.21
026.13 052.09 063.10 132.13
136.33 143.06 158.26 177.01
178.24 200.36 204.02 206.29
222.30 288.13 302.26 423.29
462.33 467.22 486.30 489.22
516.10 518.16 578.08 628.11
Feet 072.13
feeters's 337.20
feetrests 132.23
feets 076.12
Feghin 593.15
feherbour 171.27
Feigenbaumblatt 150.27
feightened 243.06
feign 346.25 366.36
feigned 031.04 579.31
feigns 279.01
feignt 157.24

Feilbogen 464.30
feinder 223.26
feine 593.08
feines 330.18
feint 278.F4 331.29 603.36
feinting 008.31 269.F1
feishts 086.12
feist 600.34
Feist 613.09
felched 594.09
feldgrau 247.35
feldt 366.25
felibrine 043.22
Felicia 572.23 572.25 573.07 573.15
felicias 347.35
felicious 618.01
felicitates 023.15
felicitous 263.29
felicitude 140.06
felicity 277.08
Felim 211.23
Felin 488.14
Felix 027.13 536.08
felixed 246.31 454.34
felixity 540.26
fell 014.07 015.19 025.30 035.04 045.02 049.31 052.03 053.01 057.11 067.27 082.18 090.25 144.14 146.27 159.13 172.16 198.16 204.16 224.06 252.14 253.21 257.12 282.19 323.15 335.31 360.26 361.18 374.36 416.12 426.28 454.10 459.28 462.31 465.14 465.20 502.02 502.22 535.04 551.01 589.35 621.29 624.30
fell 044.26 390.26
Fell 379.18
fella 041.12 485.31 611.05
Fellagulphia 320.20
fellah 028.22 355.30
fellas 611.09
felled 126.17 131.10 246.04 340.08
feller 322.25 322.25 347.25 347.26
fellhellows 569.25
fellhim 439.11
felloes 447.04
fellonem 007.31
fellow 036.19 037.26 042.17 054.23 055.18 109.01 109.16 109.17 125.08 146.06 150.29 220.12 239.14 299.23 313.32 357.07 384.13 385.13 386.28 390.04 397.31 405.13 416.03 421.31 452.31 465.20 466.35 471.36 485.17 486.12 507.13 598.20 611.36 612.10
fellow 390.27
Fellow 044.03 379.10
fellowchap 349.18
fellowcommuter's 056.01
fellowed 343.07
fellower's 364.04
fellows 015.17 059.23 202.08 248.24 257.12 335.31 351.06 363.20 543.03 574.31 596.16
fellow's 085.29
fells 331.21
felon 278.F1 436.19
Felon 106.26
felons 577.34
felony 543.21
felt 035.25 061.17 069.27 088.10 110.01 131.05 295.29 319.33 323.33 330.13 363.20 407.03 455.34 459.28 469.13 487.08 487.15 537.23 542.19 599.32
female 164.07 166.05 181.27 413.18 465.05 508.22 559.22 590.24
Female 582.30
Female 302.L1
females 165.18 524.01 530.07
femaline 251.31
feme 243.10 577.18
femecovert 564.03
Femelles 617.23
Femilies 273.L2
feminiairity 606.22
feminine 109.31 109.32 123.08 490.11 505.25
femininny 166.25
feminisible 073.04
feminite 237.01
femme 081.29
femmiliar 237.35
Femorafamilla 434.11
femorniser 242.13
femtyfem 241.10
femtyfyx 200.05
femurl 437.31
fen 264.16 278.20
fenced 553.19
fences 291.19
fend 110.01
fender 063.07 063.11 065.35 084.09 518.15 522.08
fending 575.35
fends 302.F2
Fenegans 358.23
Fenella 184.32
fenemine 093.14
Fengless 074.15
fenian 035.24 525.15
fenians 025.01 131.09 332.27 504.25
fenian's 580.28
fenicitas 610.08
fenland 589.22
Fenlanns 229.03
Fenn 297.20 376.33 376.33
Fenn 048.14
Fennella 291.F6
Fenns 376.33
Fennsense 614.14
fenny 242.29
Fenny 208.31
Fennyana 055.05
feodal 354.07
feof 323.20 370.28
fer 290.19
feracity 151.06
ferax 525.12 606.23
feraxiously 423.04
Ferchios 231.29
Ferdinand 457.03
fere 519.15
Fere 171.34
ferial 600.34
feriaquintaism 245.12
ferm 571.10
fermament 029.21 274.23
ferment 078.27
fermentarian 555.09
fermented 184.26
Fermers 424.04
fern 095.30 219.18 375.31 625.15
ferns 199.19
Ferns 212.09
fernspreak 536.02
ferrier 404.19
Ferris-Fender 369.12
ferroconcrete 077.17
Ferry 211.24 547.19
Ferr-y-Bree 375.32
Fer's 036.18
fersch 117.29
ferse 203.16
ferst 286.19
fert 258.04 596.15
Fert 369.12
F.E.R.T. 127.10 (Fortitudo Eius Rhodum Tenuit)
fervently 472.32
fervid 266.28
fervour 124.31
fervxamplus 099.33
fesces 358.35 461.02
feshest 543.09
fessed 005.08
fesses 085.30
fest 354.20
fester 453.19
festering 079.31
festfix 551.28
festination 557.33
Festive 041.24
Festives 094.29
Festus 212.01
Festy 085.23 091.01
festyknees 023.20
fetch 027.27 085.29 344.13 429.02
Fetch 027.26 579.19
fetched 256.25
fetching 261.F1
fetid 436.21
fett 239.17
fetted 619.17
fetter 153.31
fetters 585.25
fettle 058.13
feud 134.02 374.13 564.30
feudal 493.22
feuded 326.18
feuer 347.35
Feueragusaria 117.04
feugtig 432.26
fever 597.26 597.26
fevercases 544.26
fevers 597.25
fever's 201.23
few 016.08 042.06 043.06 043.14 057.17 072.27 084.01 086.26 091.02 099.31 100.30 110.01 110.29 115.02 155.24 165.08 169.01 182.01 213.24 250.35 313.22 316.26 343.35 409.20 424.32 431.01 431.14 439.05 441.20 451.24 455.34 456.16 459.12 476.05 482.23 487.13 510.22 521.29 523.24 619.01 620.20
few 032.23

Few 421.03
fewd 141.23 323.13 330.13
fewer 123.05 465.04 598.31
Fewer 374.13
fewnrally 277.04
fews 551.36
fex 516.12
feyrieglenn 553.22
fez 056.09 083.36
Fez 028.22
feza 198.16
fezzy 044.02
ff 037.20
ffff 468.01
ffiffty 208.26
ffogg 607.31
fforvell 626.33
ffrench 296.F1 392.15
ffrenchllatin 495.27
ffrinch 008.11 008.13
fhronehflord 336.13
fhroneroom 498.07
Fi 532.03
Fia 481.09 481.09
fiacckles 468.29
Fiacre 081.11
Fiammelle 560.01
fiancee 061.22
fiancy 226.14 458.07
Fianna's 076.24
fiannaship 354.19
fiannians 277.05
fiansees 015.15
Fiatfuit 017.32
fibbing 319.14
fibble 029.13
fibfib 036.34
Fibsburrow 147.26
fibule 242.34
Fibyouare 473.03
Fication 241.36
ficfect 532.29
fichers 173.33
fickers 298.17
Fickle 186.13
fickles 079.19
Fickleyes 176.13
fickling 439.01
ficsimilar 358.03
fict 523.33 532.15
fiction 109.32 279.F35 440.08
fictionable 345.35
ficts 288.09
Ficturing 104.20
Fidaris 202.18
fidd 099.29
fiddan 198.26
fiddeley 466.26
fiddle 041.22 198.25 312.24
fiddler 546.04 619.28
fiddling 531.28
fideism 162.23
fidelios 006.26
Fidelisat 369.17
fidelity 309.14
Fidge 257.36
fidget 120.33
fidgets 468.29
fidhil 131.28
fidies 080.21
fido 068.17 068.17 068.17
fie 018.36 257.02 332.03
528.03
Fie 257.20
fief 015.35 543.16
fiefeofhome 133.17
fiefie 204.16
fiefighs 588.10
fiehigh 451.22
fiehigher 451.22
fiehighest 451.22
field 015.21 025.04 049.13
052.33 058.30 085.31 112.16
119.30 135.18 135.27 205.09
246.23 250.23 264.24 281.03
340.07 440.03 443.05 454.12
501.15 514.06 516.20 546.08
583.08 585.29
field 350.08
Field 545.11
Field 055.31
Fieldgaze 009.05
fieldgosongingon 274.24
fieldmarshal 099.24
fieldmice 215.32
fieldmouse 120.06
fieldnights 453.32
fieldpost 422.03
fields 024.27 075.10 096.29
131.26 142.14 142.14 142.14
142.15 195.02 244.28 331.35
545.34 567.13 584.11
Fields 057.35 328.25
Fieluhr 213.14
fiend 224.24 408.18
fiend 273.L1
Fiendish 196.11
fiennd 345.33
Fierappel 483.15
fierce 292.F2 608.31
fierceas 196.21
Fierceendgiddyex 066.12
fiercelier 252.17
fiercemarchands 352.26
fiercer 190.07
fiercest 626.11
fiercst 298.11
fierifornax 319.34
fiertey 243.04 493.22
fiery 024.11 149.22 242.25
328.31 412.13 611.33
Fiery 013.13
fierythroats 128.09
fiet 344.30
fiety 125.22
fife 282.11 323.20
fifeing 199.30
fiferer 398.30
fifteen 082.13 086.30 135.21
246.12 384.22 483.21
fifth 119.24 343.36 513.34
558.16
Fifth 153.33
Fifthly 063.20
fifths 169.17
Fiftines 601.13
fifty 010.31 430.09 506.34
fiftyeven 380.14
fiftyfifty 589.02
fiftyodd 380.14
Fiftyseven 620.04
fiftysix 443.22
fiftytwo 513.23
fig 145.16 322.30 583.23
FIG 303.R3
Fig. 294.03 (Figure)
Figas 440.17
figblabbers 042.04
figends 452.34
figger 335.30
figgers 420.09
figgies 354.30
figgy 368.10
fight 040.13 085.34 090.12
246.29 300.22 303.30 313.30
379.31 439.33 521.31
fight 268.L2 354.08
fighting 062.23 082.02 176.25
443.17
fightning 263.F2
fights 060.22
figments 096.26
Figtreeyou 009.13
Figura 463.05
figurants 279.F16
figuratleavely 296.31
figure 038.36 133.03 133.04
181.34 191.31 237.05 271.14
532.34 574.26
figure 349.18
Figure 154.17
figurehead 029.24
figures 201.29
figurines 018.33 018.34
fiho 297.24
Fik 469.27
Fikup 034.32
filch 371.31
file 071.05
filest 390.12
filfths 616.10
filiabus 496.22
filial 260.16 604.28
filiality 428.12
filial's 139.17
filiform 099.19 462.07
filimentation 209.03
filius 327.02
Filius 443.12
fill 124.33 201.29 317.28
335.31 429.12 431.08 445.35
455.33 606.02 607.13
Fill 595.32
Fillagain's 006.14
Filldyke 470.04
filled 057.11 066.25 109.27
130.14 153.25 249.10 541.28
fillerouters 603.19
fillfull 229.30
fillibustered 324.01
fillies 297.10 524.01
filling 006.22 174.14
Fillstup 020.13
fillth 128.24
fillthefluthered 063.27
Fillthepot 093.32
filly 194.30 255.30 415.21
fillyings 246.24
film 221.21 298.16 458.16
filmacoulored 443.34
filmly 610.05
Filons 064.28
filoosh 064.28
Filou 213.14
filt 006.08
filtered 309.24
filth 010.09 087.04 183.04
419.35
filthdump 080.06

filthered 324.30 537.06
Filthered 492.18
filthily 288.11
filtred 561.14
fimament 258.23
Fime 499.18
fimfim 013.15
Fimfim 013.15
fiminin 434.20
fimmel 539.22
fimmieras 009.36
fin 035.16 053.01 317.14
331.24 495.09 525.31
Fin 236.09 297.04 388.06
Fin 103.03
final 028.29 072.27 119.14
121.18 163.16 221.05 246.16
397.33 531.29 590.23
finale 230.27
finalised 381.26
finalley 291.04
finally 020.11 072.32 090.23
115.30 119.17 174.29
310.08 370.10 406.08
454.25 581.29
finaly 569.32 569.32
finas 230.07
fincarnate 596.04
Finckers 617.02
find 008.07 063.09 096.12
113.29 137.04 138.23 163.32
191.32 202.18 215.06 232.35
248.03 260.05 265.F2 267.01
283.09 284.11 287.09 335.09
337.12 356.16 368.28 374.27
386.16 387.06 379.03 416.15
426.24 440.07 444.27 507.31
531.35 556.31 563.20 581.11
618.18
find 072.07 346.18 355.05
419.03
Find 233.09 378.15 480.33
Find 106.05 626.17
findblasts 504.31
finder 320.34 481.34
finders 128.23
findest 357.01
findhorn's 204.21
finding 025.24 067.36 110.35
178.32 465.27
Finding 303.L2
findingos 187.01
findings 476.13 523.33 575.33
Findlater 170.32 558.10
Findlater's 533.23
findlestilts 414.23
Findlings 620.29
Findrias 219.11
findring 511.31
Findrinny 028.12
finds 018.25 128.30 151.12
412.04
fine 014.22 014.26 028.02
045.20 063.22 067.11 068.09
116.10 122.15 126.09 134.24
144.34 173.22 191.29 193.08
205.04 220.12 269.29 288.12
296.19 316.20 319.03 347.17
385.28 425.26 430.25 430.25
452.36 456.02 457.04 463.36
477.20 486.23 529.02 556.31
556.31 560.08 564.07 570.23
578.14 589.28 606.17 615.18
618.30 620.01 621.12 621.18
623.05 624.20 624.35
Fine 008.15 095.21 332.08
fined 005.12 325.15 340.22
finefeelingfit 431.01
finegale 022.10
fineglas 550.24
fineglass 100.23
finehued 234.26
finel 455.14
finely 368.22
finely 398.35
fineounce 541.07
finer 531.20
finery 066.37 166.25
fines 173.25 521.12
fines 418.15
Fine's 256.19
Fine's 106.25
finest 376.30 491.10
Finest 461.10 590.23
Finewell's 080.07
finfin 094.19
Finfoefom 007.09
Finfria's 430.24
fing 621.04
Fing 388.08 610.05 610.05
617.16 617.17
Fingal 046.20 329.14 503.13
596.36
Fingal 072.07
Fingale 469.15
fingall 480.34
fingallian 138.11
Fingallians 106.17
fingalls 215.14
fingall's 496.18
fingathumbs 337.25
finger 147.08 226.26 375.02
423.07 519.11
fingerbuttons 061.22
fingerfondler 612.09
fingerforce 484.02
fingerhals 557.10
fingerhot 406.20
fingering 251.23
fingerpats 436.02
fingers 138.22 180.18 265.F2
408.03 533.11
fingersigns 080.11
fingerthick 199.12
finges 250.08
fingey 144.35
Finging 519.16
Finglas 075.16 142.14 502.35
Finglas 625.13
Finglossies 497.19
fingon 230.21
Fingool 371.22
fingringmaries 435.30
fingures 282.11
Finiche 007.15
finickin 102.09
finicking 314.01 531.28
Finight 505.24
finikin 032.06
finis 230.07 291.13
finish 032.25 039.06 193.09
246.30 285.22 288.04 303.31
347.26 367.04 465.34 611.07
622.31
finished 118.08 205.20 507.12
560.08
finisher 439.11
finishes 128.29
Finishing 220.03
Finishthere 017.23
finisky 006.27
Finist 455.29
finister 516.35 566.32
finixed 311.26
finker 357.11
finklers 419.26
Finks 177.29
Finlandia 098.07
Finlay's 506.09
Finmark's 553.23
finn 362.12
Finn 005.10 028.34 074.01
074.01 089.30 093.35 139.14
203.09 246.19 532.02 564.08
574.02 628.14
Finnados 178.26
Finnagain 005.10
Finnan 393.10
Finncoole 569.23
finnd 332.04
Finndlader's 334.33
finndrinn 052.27
finnecies 377.16
Finneen 232.06
Finnegan 003.19 004.18 221.27
531.28 580.19
Finnegan's 607.16
finnence 313.30
Finner 058.28 589.11
Finnerty 041.24
Finnfannfawners 309.09
Finnfinn 254.20
Finnfinnotus 285.L1
finngures 352.29
Finnians 521.33
finnic 017.14
Finnican 287.F4
Finnimore 024.16
finnisch 325.12
finnish 518.26
Finnish 039.17 374.21
finnishfurst 238.24
Finnius 615.07
Finnk 499.18
Finnlambs 009.28
Finnland 340.24
Finnlatter 619.03
Finnleader 214.11
finnoc 578.10
Finns 105.21
Finn's 330.24 420.25 440.10
Finnsen 481.13
finnsonse 614.14
Finntown 078.18
Finntown's 265.28
Finnuala 559.33
finny 450.04 519.14
Finny 065.33 519.14
Finnykin 576.28
Finnyking 495.20
Finnyland 245.16
fino 588.12
Fino 447.24
Finoglam 506.29
fins 015.25
Fins 390.35
Finsbury 374.28
Finsen 624.28
finshark 500.04

finsky 524.35
finst 380.10
finsterest 050.17
Fintan 025.09 359.05
fintasies 493.18
Fintona 617.06
Finucane-Law 324.22
Finucane-Lee 324.22
Finvara 621.11
finweeds 527.03
fion 042.11
fionghalian 564.30
Fionia 257.36
Fionn 108.21
Fionnachan 398.16
fionnling 367.22
fion's 042.12
fiord 350.25
Fiord 330.24
fiounaregal 332.26
Fiounnisgehaven 100.07
fippence 142.01 425.14
fippence 266.L1
fir 100.14
firbalk 054.30
Firbolgs 381.05
firdstwise 113.06
fire 008.13 009.23 016.02 028.08 036.20 039.33 052.21 058.23 080.27 086.05 091.11 091.29 094.04 128.34 131.14 133.12 137.18 139.20 145.05 168.08 172.18 180.23 190.07 190.26 213.28 228.32 239.31 280.35 319.30 323.09 324.17 327.33 333.11 348.26 362.14 367.23 370.31 426.04 436.09 442.16 453.21 455.27 516.14 524.08 527.24 543.34
Fire 306.16 499.33
Fire 106.27 175.14 303.L1
firearmed 557.23
fireball 316.23
fireboat 215.01
Firebugs 015.06 540.35
fired 289.09 405.15 419.35 616.21
firefill'd 122.13
firefinders 585.16
firefing 018.35
firefly 528.28
fireglims 141.15
fireguard 084.34
firelamp 613.01
fireland 021.16
fireleaved 055.27
fireless 469.29
Fireless 172.25
fireman's 530.14
firement 221.36
firenibblers 572.01
fireplace 362.34
fireplease 461.19
fireplug 428.12
firepool 311.31
fires 134.02 186.04 409.29 474.17 501.22
fire's 083.04
fireshield 223.29
fireside 138.01
firespot 349.14
firestufffostered 042.07
firethere 612.30
firetrench 344.09
firewater 171.13
firewaterloover 093.07
fireworker 080.08
firile 564.22
firing 336.08
firing-on-me 174.15
firkin 381.36
firm 131.25 297.20 385.23 434.02 454.18 483.11 547.13 574.05 574.35 590.16
firma 290.27
Firma 261.F2
firman 185.27
firmforhold 365.03
firmly 437.02 545.15 545.15 545.19
firmness 502.26
firm's 616.23
firn 219.18
firrum 476.12
firs 235.17
firsht 435.25
first 005.05 009.14 021.07 022.01 023.09 029.23 034.07 034.25 035.04 038.14 042.08 042.17 046.02 052.23 055.20 058.29 062.20 063.20 066.28 070.03 070.21 073.14 075.24 077.03 079.02 079.14 080.17 083.05 083.20 084.01 085.06 097.06 098.11 101.31 111.10 114.10 116.20 119.24 120.21 121.31 123.15 124.18 124.31 126.11 126.17 131.09 132.21 141.01 144.03 144.11 147.32 149.20 153.32 155.12 156.24 156.32 158.21 163.32 164.23 164.26 169.21 170.04 170.06 170.26 173.24 175.02 180.16 182.03 185.34 190.22 197.20 202.12 204.14 212.26 222.33 228.08 230.02 231.01 235.28 238.20 242.36 247.30 248.04 249.03 263.F1 269.01 270.14 279.F13 283.30 287.06 289.25 290.11 297.27 311.15 313.01 314.02 315.22 317.23 318.12 320.15 322.36 324.01 326.02 331.10 331.27 331.33 332.29 346.35 347.02 354.22 364.03 364.32 365.09 369.18 388.16 391.36 393.09 405.32 408.11 411.31 421.24 422.18 423.27 429.02 430.06 430.17 432.29 433.26 433.29 438.05 439.08 439.27 440.03 440.33 443.04 447.16 454.23 459.33 460.06 461.27 465.21 468.08 469.20 470.01 472.08 472.16 474.21 483.27 485.05 486.10 488.01 491.34 502.27 503.09 503.09 509.35 516.03 517.12 519.12 519.13 520.30 526.27 527.10 528.16 528.20 528.34 528.34 528.36 530.01 531.33 532.08 532.32 534.11 535.07 536.30 537.07 539.34 540.20 542.15 556.13 557.20 563.02 564.29 566.19 566.24 570.31 573.14 575.11 576.25 577.05 577.24 578.34 579.35 580.21 581.29 585.12 585.34 587.06 600.14 604.13 604.20 606.23 606.25 607.11 615.19 616.03 617.34 619.03 623.15
first 342.33 350.13 353.23
First 026.28 206.29 282.12 286.31 300.F2 339.30 374.22 408.31 433.22 456.33 475.23 477.35 480.17 515.18 533.20 535.15 539.32 559.21 589.20 616.21 625.34 627.11 628.12
First 106.13 107.01
firstaiding 098.23
firstborn 194.12
firstclass 395.13 396.11 451.34
firstcoming 602.19
firstfruit 194.12
firstings 303.26
firstlings 012.19
firstly 368.18
firstmeeting 051.10
Firstnighter 071.10
firstnighting 095.21
firstparted 087.21
firstrate 497.21
first's 130.30
firstserved 171.13
firstshot 058.23 171.14
firth 200.13 608.29
firths 549.21
firtree 439.11
fischial 064.31
fish 127.02 148.19 209.07 240.31 254.12 299.F3 316.20 321.03 377.30 384.15 384.16 391.22 410.15 451.06 463.12 482.26 520.09 535.25 563.34 578.13 597.36
Fish 408.25
fishabed 051.13
fishandblood 049.27
fishball 317.13
fishdrunks 263.04
fished 229.24 563.03
fishery 525.13
fishle 243.17
fishmummer 029.26
fishnetzeveil 208.10
fishngaman 256.25
fishnoo 525.27
fish's 339.25
fishshambles 061.14
Fisht 376.34
fishup 089.08
fishy 076.24 245.09 507.02 559.23
fishygods 004.01
fisk 180.30 199.16 320.16 325.21
fisstball 557.10
fissure 386.32
fist 112.31 123.10 269.16 286.F5 607.05
fisterman's 393.29
fistful 310.31 376.28
Fistic 307.19
fistiknots 202.20
fists 426.28
fit 058.12 067.34 076.17 117.33 153.11 154.34 176.26 231.30 317.28 453.18 495.05 558.13
fit 163.15
Fit 240.17 420.27

fitchid 340.02
fitful 552.24
fithery 559.27
fitlier 471.31
fits 203.09 273.F6 351.04
560.29
fitted 133.06 292.21 447.34
fitten 316.25
fitter 149.15
fittest 614.11
fitther 322.12
fitting 359.13 617.36
fittings 524.08
Fitz 008.26 097.05 211.14
Fitzadam 514.23
Fitzgibbets 420.21
Fitzmary 389.13
fitzpatricks 133.27
fiuming 243.02 548.08
fiumy 208.24
fiunn 095.18
five 036.21 043.29 084.26
088.33 122.18 126.23 128.32
134.02 180.07 211.21 255.31
255.31 285.23 386.32 386.32
394.17 409.25 440.01 443.23
475.07 476.29 495.30 497.26
550.34 589.19
Five 274.05 515.10
fiveaxled 359.23
fived 141.23
fivefinger 067.29
fivefirearms 353.35
fiveful 396.27
fiver 586.24
fives 158.22 285.23 285.24
285.25 285.25
fives' 589.27
fivestoried 544.36
Fivs 024.20
fix 332.21 412.18 434.30
480.23 482.14 486.12
fixation 164.03
fixed 031.02 031.03 040.17
100.32 568.21
fixings 317.14
fixtures 231.16 403.09
fize 333.23
fizz 041.32 231.17 451.24
462.09
FIZZIN 308.R1
fizzle 436.25
fjaell 261.03
fjeld 136.13
fjell 006.36
fjord 006.36
fjorg 343.36
Fjorgn 124.29
Fjorn 622.06
flabbergaze 084.12
flabberghosted 494.03
flabbies 453.12
Flabbius 278.L2
flabel 071.03
flabelled 152.23
flackering 022.03
flag 008.11 008.12 008.14
128.25 210.13 480.01 503.24
503.25 547.35
Flageolettes 440.20
flagfall 090.06
flagged 552.18
flaggin 139.07
Flaggy 063.13
flagons 043.18
Flagpatch 559.13
flagrant 031.01 294.F2
flags 007.23 323.08 448.23
flagstone 503.26
flagway 473.05
flaherty 080.09
flail 436.36
flair 119.10
flairs 128.30
flam 499.13
flambe 473.19
flambs 246.05
flame 027.13 145.23 145.35
232.04 232.04 232.04 232.14
329.20 614.09 621.02
Flame 269.16 537.30
flamefaces 589.23
flamen 242.34
flamend 023.10
flamenfan 080.27
flames 426.02
flamifestouned 256.09
flaming 265.09
flamingans 504.23
flaminulinorum 264.07
flaminum 287.24
Flammagen's 321.17
flammballs 502.20
flamme 464.06
flamme 064.28
Flammeus 185.04
Flamming's 289.13
flank 112.23 202.11 351.23
flanks 008.36
Flannagan 357.35
flannel 147.31
Flannelfeet 422.09
flannelly 584.17
flannels 059.34 214.28
flap 109.12 245.16 313.08
Flap 214.17 534.36
flappant 546.06
flapped 011.01
flappent 468.10
flappered 207.33
flappergangsted 496.15
flappernooser 329.05
flappery 139.04
Flappia 278.L2
flapping 394.13 507.10
flare 028.31 483.25
flares 250.32
flasch 594.16
flash 011.04 066.36 135.26
188.12 188.13 220.28 267.16
289.08 314.26 323.27 597.28
626.16
flash 342.35
Flash 106.26
flashback 057.25
flashed 341.23
flasher 215.01 404.11
flashermind's 339.01
flashing 338.08 450.05
457.27
flashlight 320.26
flashly 185.33
flashmurket 378.08
Flashnose 549.13
flasht 227.05
flashy 281.F3
flask 011.11 024.32 071.02
426.29
flaskneck 056.24
flasks 011.20 263.21
flasky 430.16
flat 027.21 061.04 113.05
275.F5 291.04 325.22 437.03
439.12 450.29 481.31 492.03
544.19
flatch 506.07
flatchested 109.03
flatfish 221.07
flating 320.25
Flatnose 073.08
flats 560.04
flatten 278.L4
flatter 254.36 335.31 425.04
536.28
Flatter 512.31
flattered 092.14
Flatterfun 060.34
flattering 028.30 395.27 506.03
flattery 580.19
flattest 034.12
flatty 098.11
Flattyro 422.09
flatulent 109.04
flatuous 023.10
flaunt 279.F14 374.03
flaunting 166.24
flaus 359.14
flautish 536.22
Flavin 337.36 460.27
flavory 041.25
flavour 456.05
flavoured 052.33 166.33 179.18
460.33
flavourite 294.19
flavours 533.01
flaw 191.26
flawhoolagh 128.33
Flawhoolags 498.10
flaxafloyeds 536.23
flaxed 379.33
flaxen 036.13 583.20
flay 072.34 090.02 436.09
flayed 525.30
flayfell 119.10
flayflutter 117.14
flayful 067.26
flays 172.08
flea 168.10 487.08 516.09
531.21
Flea 458.32
fleabesides 523.24
Fleapow 015.27
fleas 137.09 180.19 320.10
394.19 506.36
flea's 558.05
FLEBBY 304.R3
flech 149.05
fleckflinging 011.11
fled 014.17 062.03 098.04
176.27 244.21 258.06 258.06
258.07 365.36
Fled 225.34
fledge 378.04
flee 019.33 071.09 130.34
434.24 468.29 546.23
Flee 104.13
fleece 112.23 603.22
fleeest 266.28
flees 347.05

fleet 135.06 238.10
fleet-as-spindhrift 418.07
fleetfooted 341.21
fleeting 444.24
fleetly 209.29
fleets 331.34
flegm 072.35
fleischcurers 422.03
fleming 043.04
Flemingtown 622.34
Flemish 388.10
flemsh 376.05
flen 034.32
flenders 204.22
flens 185.17
Flep 213.23
Fleppety 015.26
flesch 138.08
flesh 034.32 036.03 067.05 079.02 129.05 175.31 256.04 275.13 374.01 561.27 563.35
flesh 265.L1
fleshambles 494.32
fleshasplush 474.14
fleshblood 292.09
fleshcoloured 434.08
fleshed 222.22
fleshener 072.35
fleshers 607.12
fleshfettered 411.15
fleshlumpfleeter 377.27
fleshly 547.27
Fleshmans 050.01
fleshmeats 550.14
fleshmonger 144.30
Fleshshambles 538.22
fleshskin 229.30
flesh-without-word 468.06
flesk 325.21
fletch 137.11 621.33
fletcherbowyers 312.36
Fletcher-Flemmings 542.23
fletches 263.F2
fleur 268.01
Fleur 252.31
fleurelly 250.27
fleurettes 226.32
fleurt 449.26
fleurting 145.03
fleurty 561.34
flew 022.03 098.04 407.12
flewmen 202.05
flewn 010.36
flexible 290.F4
flexibly 192.09
flexors 414.30
flic 197.23
flick 011.11 017.27 320.08 584.04
flickars 606.33
flicked 304.29
flickered 179.20
flickerflapper 266.31
flickers 501.18
flicklesome 266.28
flied 393.10
Flieflie 273.L4
flies 060.36 170.21 514.28
flies 418.18
Flies 213.09
Flies 106.26
flight 071.04 222.33
flightening 626.16
flights 416.22
Flimsy 193.23
flimsyfilmsies 279.F14
flinchgreef 565.13
Flinders 562.14
fling 134.16 223.12 331.11 438.12
fling 338.35
flingamejig 479.14
flinging 121.06 180.02
flink 282.07
Flinn 240.23
flinnered 179.20
flint 625.15
Flint 083.10
Flinter 240.23
flintforall 018.35
flints 183.12
fliorten 315.32
flip 207.33 245.16 419.13
Flip 213.22
flippant 133.14
flippers 015.25
Flippety 015.27
flipping 524.27
flirt 204.11 436.32 469.31
flirties 524.28
flirting 096.15
flirtsome 028.16
flirty 139.23
flishguds 073.06
flispering 580.19
flister 546.04
flit 364.14
flitch 456.18
flitcher 579.01
flitmansfluh 037.20
flitsy 440.18
flittaflute 007.03
Flittering 215.31
flitters 007.23
flittsbit 469.01
flitty 441.20
flivvers 404.05
Flo 248.17
float 027.26 095.11 213.09 263.F2 571.05
floatable 268.F7
floating 486.23 511.29
floats 032.26
flocaflake 561.19
flock 362.24
flockfuyant 502.35
flocking 246.25 416.33 497.16
flock's 455.09
floedy 072.35
floflo 360.02
flog 584.07
flogs 267.14
Floh 414.25 417.17 417.29
Floh 418.14
Flonnels 452.09
flonting 050.34
flood 014.18 078.23 081.18 133.12 230.09 359.05 386.28 387.23 388.12 583.19 583.20
Flood 202.17 511.10
Flood 625.13
flooded 580.33
floodens 009.24
Floodlift 318.06
floodlight 498.25
floodlights 134.18 260.F3
floodlit 494.02
floodmud 552.05
floodplain 036.15
floods 028.24 060.04 330.10
Floods 221.28 289.28
Flood's 514.32
floodsupplier 135.28
floody 023.10
flooing 327.10
floon 370.14
floor 046.02 390.22 420.15 504.26 544.14 605.25
floored 227.24 301.23
flooring 183.09
floot 388.18
floote 012.08
flooting 224.20
flop 029.02 162.09 271.F2 288.22 455.18
Flop 214.21
flopped 383.09
floppens 231.15
floprightdown 120.32
flopsome 513.32
Flora 033.28 212.09
florahs 339.25
floral 471.27
floralora 458.14
florals 227.15
floral's 250.33
floran 594.25
floras 015.20
FLORAS 220.03
flore 107.18 107.18
floreal 406.36
floreflorence 360.02
Florence 137.05 200.34
Florenza 026.27
flores 143.04 606.34
Florestan 246.18
Florian's 385.11
florid 276.03
Florida 158.02
florileague 224.23
florilingua 117.14
floriners 541.14
florists 172.02
florizel 621.30
florry 204.25
floruerunts 053.34
floskons 370.33
Floss 532.31
Floss 213.02
flossies 213.03 225.35
flossim 354.31
flossity 524.32
flossy 365.12
flosting 501.31
flotilla 496.05
Flott 547.19
flou 276.20
Flou 020.35
flouer 531.12
flounced 493.22
flouncies 588.08
flounder 006.31
floundering 525.23
flour 320.11 529.03
flourish 360.14 360.15 415.36 415.36 416.02 420.11
flourished 462.21
flourishing 029.02 235.20
flout 082.20

flouter 363.15
flouting 023.35
flouts 058.12 128.30
flow 020.35 132.31 271.18
315.09 332.16 444.07 481.15
586.34 588.23
Flow 206.27
Flow 105.25
flowandflow 404.01
flowed 361.35
floweers 337.25
flower 140.26 141.32 248.13
265.07 280.25 331.34 556.20
598.13
flowerfeeding 209.01
flowerfleckled 602.04
flowerfruityfrond 609.12
flowerheads 236.33
flowerpot 031.03 194.08
flowers 096.11 227.18 237.05
301.F3 318.28 475.09 534.25
Flowers 281.15
flowersports 386.26
flowerwhite 007.14
flowery 562.05
Flowey 197.14
flowflakes 017.28
flowing 246.36 281.03
flowing 159.18
flown 049.05 407.12
flowns 092.21
flowowered 370.19
flowre 313.05
flowrish 171.10
flows 390.30 390.30 621.22
floxy 140.16
flshpst 395.36
flu 197.19 327.32 523.28
Flu 464.15
Flucher's 058.12
fluctuant 189.13
fluctuated 574.29
fluctuation 209.02
fluctuous 496.26
flue 028.09 456.18
fluefoul 183.15
fluencies 494.16
fluere 287.25
fluff 227.27 460.03
fluffballs 112.15
fluffy 276.24
flugged 514.06
fluid 006.28 480.16 599.11
fluke 451.08
Flukie 539.35
fluking 520.27
flument 297.22
flumingworthily 547.15
Fluminian 081.03
Fluminian 277.L1
fluminiculum 264.07
Flummery 420.01
flummoxed 438.29
flundered 334.27
flung 026.11 119.02 297.01
547.28
Flunkey 418.02
Flunkey 071.32
fluorescence 349.17
fluorescent 498.29
fluors 086.01
flup 341.02
Flur 104.14
Flura's 623.21
flure 021.13 136.09 382.24
flureofthe 142.07
flurewaltzer 443.21
flurrish 416.01
flurtation 352.07
flush 145.33 182.12 279.F15
437.12 527.07 576.31
flushcaloured 205.08
flushed 042.07
flushing 457.27
flushpots 192.29
flussed 206.29
flusther 457.28
flut 200.35
flute 043.32
Flute 343.36
fluted 541.33
Fluteful 513.08
fluteous 297.23
fluter 230.21
flutes 520.20
fluther's 444.08
flutter 039.01
flutterby 262.13
fluttered 043.26 092.14 159.09
fluttering 359.14
fluttersome 028.16
fluve 208.25
fluvey 297.22
Fluvia 546.35 547.05
fluvii 287.25
fluwed 319.12
flux 103.03
Flux 464.15
fluxion 297.29
fly 112.10 129.21 146.33
147.23 201.22 246.24 248.18
250.35 352.07 352.07 425.34
448.09 450.26 451.28 560.04
588.08
Fly 378.01 493.31
flyblow 407.05
flyday 005.24
flyend 327.23
flyfire 029.07 542.26
flying 080.35 085.29 148.05
432.16
Flying 358.19
flyleaf 153.15
flyswatter 270.07
F.M. 280.13 (Finn MacCool or
Father Michael)
fnow 302.F2
fo 011.07
Fo 532.03
fò 212.35
foam 331.35
foamed 124.33
foamer 310.33
Foamflakes 502.35
foaming 203.02
foaminine 241.15
foamous 007.12
Foamous 272.28
fob 327.05 602.34
Fochlut 479.13
Fockeyvilla 609.18
focoal 411.32 411.32
focse 382.22
focus 164.07 191.31 452.11
focus 349.13
focuss 174.16
focussed 324.24
fodder 126.23 551.14
foddy 622.09
foder 011.23
foe 156.35 191.30 273.06
278.25 291.18 316.24 411.10
411.33 596.05
foeburghers 543.19
foef 370.28
foegutfulls 350.34
Foehn 394.15
foeman 354.07
foemoe 353.14
foenix 023.16
foerses 345.32
foerst 506.15
foes 151.11 254.21
foes' 579.36
foetal 563.10
foetotype 324.01
fofavour 364.06
foft 302.F2
fog 180.21 415.21 502.22
502.27 522.35 599.30 599.30
Fog 555.01
fogabawlers 497.05
fogbow 403.06
fogeyboren 525.21
fogging 587.28
foggus 515.30
foggy 024.21 263.03 367.24
428.11
Foght 090.13
fogloot 478.34
Fogloot 290.18
foh 149.03 202.20
foi 131.22
foible 422.22
foibleminded 160.33
foibler 419.13
foie 059.30
foify 403.04
foil 230.21 363.15 464.05
foiled 326.04 424.01
Foinn 343.25
foinne 071.07
foison 568.28
foist 291.27
foisted 616.26
Fokes 106.22
fokloire 419.12
fol 208.31 343.21 382.24
621.21
folced 365.36
Folchu 480.04 480.05
fold 076.01 193.04 235.02
Fold 500.33
folded 094.08 213.25 244.28
271.27 566.13
folding 576.14
folds 392.18
foles 143.19
Foley 552.12
folgor 613.28
Foli 243.16
foliated 096.30 124.02
folk 108.11 178.19 221.21
316.33 549.06
folkenfather 382.18
folkers 057.04 308.18
folkfarthers 281.F1
folklore's 480.06
folkmood 590.16

folkrich 101.11
folks 059.28 390.10 472.28
folksfiendship 542.18
folksforefather 033.04
folksstone 068.30
follay 510.15
follest 339.25
Folletta 422.33
Follettes 193.23
folley 526.21
folleys 357.32
folliagenous 361.27
follicity 494.22
follied 623.22
folliedays 553.16
follies 397.12
Follies 374.28
Follies 106.12
folloged 091.09
follopon 443.06
follow 077.35 082.29 121.13
187.28 191.05 239.14 269.F2
276.27 382.30 435.24 440.18
452.31 458.36 472.17 486.13
506.27 522.35 525.11
follow 399.24
Follow 053.13 432.22 479.05
501.14 555.14 579.19
followay 565.21
followed 030.18 038.05 069.04
372.11 449.03 449.34 510.25
590.17 618.25 626.12
follower 323.22
followers 130.09
followeup 267.08
following 030.15 039.16 057.30
062.17 076.17 119.20 124.06
161.35 230.20 313.12 406.18
471.27 483.32 501.16 543.36
546.31
following 349.06
Following 588.15
Following 105.06
followis 598.20
follows 222.21 284.22 367.30
519.36 563.18 599.34
Follows 602.25
follow's 085.29 162.24
follteedee 342.29
folly 334.04 340.33 466.02
563.28
Folly 012.23 291.19 503.15
follyages 008.04
follyo 197.18
folly's 526.15
fols 112.33
folsage 119.05
folsoletto 281.18
folty 020.28 619.21
Folty 619.20
foluminous 155.20
fom 011.07
fombly 357.14
fomefing 226.26
fomentation 084.17
fomiliours 345.02
Fomor's 236.09
Fonar 231.12
foncey 227.16
foncey 346.18
fond 065.25 156.16 166.30
166.31 266.28 315.30 359.01
396.13 408.25 417.19 427.30
431.15 471.27 489.13 575.28
585.01 605.01 619.23 626.17
Fond 028.17 468.18
fondance 249.11
fonder 282.19
fondest 111.17 458.02
fondlepets 436.02
fondlers 107.17
fondling 200.05 227.26 362.18
410.31
fondlinger 346.32
fondly 165.24 171.34 235.22
fondnes 468.12
fondseed 004.31
fondstare 461.22
fong 394.21
fongered 357.14
fongster 186.31
Fonn 345.09
fonngeena 354.15
Fonnumagula 162.12
font 337.19 435.17 507.11
fontanella 303.L1
fontaneously 542.09
fontannoy 009.06
Fonte-in-Monte 202.09
fontly 119.19
fontmouther 224.10
fonx 449.06
foochoor 608.21
food 025.06 028.10 163.35
246.12 300.23 317.19 405.30
455.09 550.05 550.16
foodbrawler 144.05
foods 239.17
foodstuffs 170.26
fooi 075.07
Fooi 075.07
fook 262.L1
fool 016.04 144.25 164.17
167.09 188.15 262.18
fool 201.10
Fool 370.13 568.14
fooled 161.01
fooling 224.03 343.35
foolish 210.34 244.19 433.30
foolproof 165.32
fools 238.24 283.19
Fools 222.23
fool's 460.08
foolscap 185.35
foolth 160.12
foolufool 430.09
foon 617.19
Foon 617.11
fooneral 617.20 617.26
foorchtha 475.02
foorsitter 390.36
foos 215.34 603.24
foostherfather 215.14
foot 006.34 137.09 168.06
169.16 191.14 203.16 227.10
294.F4 300.02 318.28 343.36
429.15 434.19 443.23 462.33
518.04 519.12 519.21 544.20
580.11 590.04
Foot 499.31
Footage 559.31
footback 381.01
footbatter 080.02
footblows 049.26
footer 376.23
footgear 429.08
footh 239.32
footing 009.17
footinmouther 424.19
Footle 418.02
footles 139.09 363.14
footlights 032.26 475.10
footloose 314.26
footplate 284.25
footprinse 137.16
footprints 080.10
foots 233.31 243.14 333.03
Foots 501.07
footsey 131.35
footslips 442.15
footsore 473.20
footsteps 475.25
footsy 255.31
foottreats 141.12
footure 518.28
footwash 550.33
footwear 115.11 448.29
Foozle 496.02
for for For For FOR
Foraignghistan 493.02
forain 500.35 570.05
foran 323.22
forasmuch 484.16
forbear 614.07
forbed 376.35 541.36
Forbeer 614.07
forbidden 423.29 459.19 492.31
615.32
forbids 128.34
force 063.15 223.15 223.15
278.26 413.01 439.24 465.17
608.31
Force 617.12
Force 303.L1
forcecaused 332.27
forced 309.13 366.01 374.11
444.18 546.12 576.27 580.07
forced 175.11
forceglass 167.20
forceps 107.17
forces 085.30 518.13 557.23
ford 289.01 364.16 503.31
570.32
Ford 622.35
fordeed 315.31
forders 614.09
fordofhurdlestown 203.07
fordone 560.21
Fords 447.30
fore 005.36 006.27 016.29
020.01 023.11 025.20 078.14
117.05 134.08 139.09 157.20
186.11 199.03 230.22 240.11
266.31 271.F2 315.05 332.15
355.33 359.05 367.23 377.29
382.20 384.27 408.03 414.30
484.20 498.05 513.30 516.20
559.20 588.10 612.35 613.08
fore 287.26
Fore 209.13 293.14 336.10
346.29 546.28
foreback 426.22
forebanned 247.30
forebare 030.01
forebe 596.12
forebears 572.06
forebeer 084.36
forebidden 011.29
forebitten 303.16

foreboden 466.22
forecasts 128.30
foreclosed 586.17
foreconsciously 174.01
forecoroners 602.16
forecotes 232.13
forecourts 030.23
forecursing 516.19
foredreamed 551.11
forefarther 057.04
forefather 560.26
forefelt 290.14
forefivest 596.16
foregather 548.13
foregathered 587.29
foreget 433.33
foregiftness 498.27
foregiver 345.28
forego 096.20
foregodden 339.24
foregone 265.03
foregot 338.30
foregotthened 345.34
forehead 020.16 031.10 204.01
275.13 452.15 482.23
forehearingly 096.30
forehengist 214.12
foreign 064.13 172.21 173.35
281.F3 419.34 461.25 484.35
544.09 574.05
foreigner 463.15
forelooper 327.01
foreman 076.24
foremasters 385.35
Foremaster's 305.31
foremost 009.16 434.19 450.35
Foremost 072.14
foremouthst 519.21
forenenst 188.15 299.15 382.17
476.19 608.05 618.28
forengistanters 357.05
Forening 267.L3
foreninst 021.16 504.05
forequarters 285.F5 559.32
forere 613.23
foreretyred 395.06
fores 113.08
foresake-me-nought 227.16
foresaw 596.30
forescut 076.19
foreshorten 479.17
foresmellt 436.18
forespoken 175.16
forest 128.03 294.03 331.33
410.09 465.36 503.36
Forest 306.21
Forestallings 123.18
forestand 434.13
forests 524.04
Forests 088.27
foresupposed 424.25
Foresygth 290.10
foretaste 083.17 409.13
foretellers 135.04
forethought 022.07 080.16
foretold 189.31 247.02 596.04
foretolk 390.24
forever 455.22
forewaken 576.12
forewarred 421.05
Foreweal 225.30
forewheel 286.17
forewhen 343.10
forewhere 614.24
forfear 492.27
forfeit 453.28
Forfet 440.24
forfickle 310.10
Forficules 018.11
forfor 326.08
forforget 231.24
forforgetting 231.24
forfummed 370.28
forgate 128.34
forgave 476.27
Forge 305.04
forged 181.16 182.02 589.05
forgein 374.24
forget 062.06 075.02 094.30
111.15 116.20 144.22 144.23
146.11 161.07 164.36 203.33
212.26 231.20 279.F26 315.01
325.06 364.11 384.13 390.01
390.15 391.05 392.02 398.21
431.17 441.31 458.10 460.14
498.18 522.13 614.20 615.36
617.09 617.26
Forget 340.08 614.22 614.26
forgetful 396.35
Forgetful 030.19
forgetmenot 215.08
forgetmenots 389.02
forgetness 291.16
forgetting 043.11 114.35 137.20
184.35 194.21 208.04 272.16
350.18 388.10 393.15 395.21
428.02 462.15 464.29 526.17
forget-uf-knots 302.F2
forging 178.34
forgive 175.02 392.02 507.17
527.11
forgive 418.12
Forgive 409.33
Forgivemequick 215.07
forgiving 315.06
Forglim 434.13
forgodden 625.18
forgot 390.23 391.17 391.19
394.20 397.24
forgotten 055.11 061.29 096.21
488.28
forherself 526.29
forim 224.02
foriver 013.17
foriverever 242.31
forivor 295.02
fork 008.15 022.31 124.09
250.23 450.27 618.26
Fork 105.06
forkbearded 387.08
forkenpootsies 077.32
forker 507.35
forkflank 561.02
forkful 626.12
forkings 221.12
forkpiece 328.16
Forks 273.L3
forksfrogs 121.05
Forky 176.13
forlongs 545.24
form 007.20 036.06 045.18
076.31 123.03 128.06 150.09
187.29 220.05 412.33 431.08
505.25 523.12 523.13 578.14
581.30 603.12
form 342.21
formal 056.31
Formalisa 304.03
formally 606.09
formarly 242.02
formast 590.15
formation 076.03 165.26
formed 120.21 309.21 536.14
Formelly 125.11
forment 132.29
former 119.27 164.11 240.31
372.29 419.09 535.36 580.24
619.03
Former 530.36
Former 440.20
formerly 490.20 551.20 570.18
573.03 573.18
formers 342.22
formicolation 417.27
Formio 563.28
formolon 155.36
formor 331.25
Formoreans 015.05
formose 154.20
formous 502.26
Formula 303.L2
formule 230.04
formwhite 241.14
forn 367.23
fornenst 626.22
fornication 142.25
fornicationists 004.12
fornicolopulation 557.17
fornicular 319.28
forninehalf 533.34
fornix 116.18
forover 013.18
forrarder 113.09
Forrester 257.24
fors 359.11
Fors 299.L2
for's 228.15 228.16 550.06
forsailoshe 095.06
forsake 359.04 561.14
forsake 418.22
forsakenly 368.17
forsehn 245.23
Forshapen 015.30
Forsin 018.21
forsoaken 405.35
forsooks 344.27
forsooth 188.13
forsstand 017.14
forstake 441.06
forstfellfoss 202.32
forstold 411.01
Forstowelsy 444.11
forsunkener 241.24
forswore 193.33
Forswundled 598.03
fort 007.34 083.10 089.33
090.17 127.09 286.18 516.13
596.15
Fort 369.12 500.24 500.24
539.24
forte 327.19 438.04 450.23
517.22
fortepiano 176.33
Fortescue 194.30
fortethurd 156.33
fortey 519.07 519.07
forth 042.18 062.27 102.07
126.03 130.31 187.28 187.32
200.13 207.19 225.34 311.11

311.13 321.32 372.06 378.17 414.15 452.15 461.25 474.01 493.34 589.15
forth 338.34 340.28
forthe 377.14
forthemore 314.15
forther 617.25
Forthink 570.27
forthright 083.07
forthstretched 054.30
forties 039.01 099.09 326.31
fortiffed 548.16
fortifine 188.07
fortines 601.13
Fortissa 572.27 572.32 573.27
fortitude 605.24
fortitudinous 053.16
fortitudo 099.23
Fortitudo 515.09
fortnichts 409.21
fortnight 170.07
fortnightly 142.24
fortody 533.36
fortorest 279.08
Fortress 567.11
fortuitous 279.F35
fortuitously 096.27
fortunate 084.25 360.10
fortunately 050.24
Fortunatus 327.26
fortune 050.33 109.09 327.14 512.29
Fortune 149.23 235.21 405.24
fortunes 025.32 227.10 589.27
fortunous 175.29
forty 021.26 022.13 028.18 129.32 135.05 136.28 183.01 237.14 265.F2 283.F1 310.13 333.25 397.02 416.22 453.31 458.05 458.05 495.22 511.31 519.32 552.29 595.08
Forty 068.14
Forty 072.08
fortycantle 379.23
fortyinch 362.09
fortyish 109.04
fortyshilling 255.30
fortysixths 149.12
fortytooth 177.26
fortytudor 093.08
fortytwo 169.13
Forum 097.34 542.18
forward 131.25 343.11 410.03 458.20 582.19
Forward 206.23
Forward 105.31
forwards 396.01 615.17
Forwards 375.17
Forwhat 225.29
forx 089.12
foss 281.F1
fossed 077.18
fosses 331.21
fossette 559.28
fossickers 321.31
fossil 080.10
Fossilisation 264.11
fossilyears 040.10
fossyending 298.05
fost 473.24
fostard 603.34
foster 076.35 327.07
Foster 280.17 300.14 542.18
fostered 188.10
fosterlings 446.30
fostermother 439.08
fostermothers' 183.28
foster's 277.05 490.23
fostertailor 255.30
fostfath 596.07
fosther 489.13
fother 279.F32
fou 130.15 134.02 230.11 338.25
Foueh 520.21
fought 229.25 272.F4 375.18 579.31 588.11
Foughtarundser 078.16
Foughty 283.01
foul 082.14 119.10 186.23 215.19 251.16 373.17 378.36 418.03 425.11 445.09 465.20 516.19
foul 352.29 354.12
Foul 010.15 212.32
foulardy 434.19
fould 224.05
foule 475.09
fouled 579.36
foulen 234.02
foulend 239.35
foulfamed 085.25
fouling 471.17
Foulke's 545.31
foull 228.33 322.08 603.22
foully 113.13 313.33
foulplace 624.34
foulplay 589.27
foulshoulders 490.15
foulty 243.24
found 014.03 054.02 068.03 086.05 096.32 099.13 126.23 127.08 128.28 129.31 132.12 137.29 138.23 164.12 171.22 179.02 197.09 202.19 204.17 205.27 224.06 240.01 241.17 241.23 257.26 294.F5 306.F4 307.23 380.34 449.06 476.09 482.20 530.25 540.03 557.16 575.02 575.34 625.03 625.23
founded 030.09 095.30 136.11 136.12
founder 310.11 481.33
foundingpen 563.06
foundling 255.30 291.14
Foundlitter 420.35
foundly 445.30
fount 280.32
fountain 267.04
Fountainoy 212.14
founter 328.08
founts 088.30 171.11
fountybuckets 372.18
four 010.31 021.29 022.15 043.07 043.14 048.13 057.08 080.16 083.02 084.04 091.20 092.35 094.24 094.31 096.10 111.17 121.36 124.03 126.09 130.27 131.22 143.01 147.03 157.31 170.02 177.25 182.16 184.33 214.33 214.35 219.10 219.17 223.08 224.01 224.04 250.34 264.20 282.20 335.06 367.08 367.14 377.23 384.04 384.06 384.06 384.07 384.08 384.10 384.11 384.14 384.20 384.35 385.08 385.27 386.04 386.09 386.10 386.14 387.15 387.16 389.04 389.06 389.25 389.33 390.13 390.15 390.19 391.07 393.16 393.17 393.21 393.31 396.26 396.36 397.03 397.12 422.04 424.29 428.04 440.01 472.24 474.21 475.18 475.34 482.14 490.21 496.09 499.16 503.18 513.35 517.36 533.35 543.05 545.06 552.01 552.15 555.08 557.01 558.06 558.16 566.08 573.08 574.19 589.30 604.34 607.07 612.26 617.02 621.05 625.11
four 175.25 530.23
Four 013.20 256.21 377.34 588.36 608.35 622.34
fourale 405.19
fourbottle 095.27
fourd 224.06
fourdimmansions 367.27
fourfettering 475.10
four-flights-the-charmer 290.16
fourfootlers 029.10
fourinhanced 460.30
fourinhand 052.25 572.06
four-in-hand 168.06
fourks 370.12
fourleaved 124.20
fourlegged 123.01
fourlike 560.24
fourlings 368.05
fourmaster 479.29
fourmasters 394.17
fourmillierly 414.34
fourmish 414.32
fourpart 405.06
fourpence 165.31
fourpenny 099.14 208.21
fourposter 325.10 533.16
fourpriest 483.13
fours 018.06 030.24 158.22 178.19 295.21 535.14
fourscore 346.24 580.06
foursome 395.05
foursquare 363.24
fourstar 352.33
fourteen 144.07 255.35 545.02
fourteenth 266.22
fourth 062.12 064.05 119.24 171.31 467.23 479.01 519.12 537.25 567.16 607.06
fourth 342.18
Fourth 303.04 387.24 590.22
fourthermore 288.10
fourtiered 194.27
fourwheedler 119.30
fourwords 279.F21
fouvenirs 302.F2
fouyoufoukou 320.05
fow 061.08
fowl 110.25 112.09 124.25 380.24 544.17
fowlhouse 184.13
Fowls 383.11
fox 124.33 132.17 149.01 323.17 446.18 449.21 515.02 557.14
Fox 035.30 156.07 159.23 289.F5 514.33
Fox 176.05
foxed 177.36

foxes 603.32
foxfetor 119.10
Fox-Goodman 212.09
foxold 590.14
Foxrock 502.35
foxrogues 547.01
foxtrotting 180.18
foxy 192.03 516.14 622.24
foxyjack 528.36
foyer 538.27
foyer's 244.12
Foyle 212.13
Foyn 593.12
foyne 301.07
foyneboyne 041.26
F.P, 498.10 (Flawhoolags F.P,)
Fr 458.03 (Father)
fra 141.09
fra 466.24
Fra 553.13
fracassing 206.01
fraction 462.19
fractions 211.13
fracture 386.32
Fracture 073.08
fractures 285.22
fragment 165.36
fragments 066.25 110.29
fragolance 265.08
fragoromboassity 353.25
fragrance 427.12
fragrant 460.05
fragrend 051.36
fraguant 206.31
fraher 510.10
frai 094.15
fraîches 281.12
fraid 172.21
frail 204.11 572.21 551.12
frails 129.09
frailyshees 029.12
fraimd 315.30
fraiseberry 041.25
fraisey 265.08
fram 312.07 596.07
frame 206.07
framed 085.27 266.20
frameshape 313.27
framing 096.26
framm 094.18
framous 550.29
Fran 423.36
franca 198.18
Frances 212.15
France's 226.09
Franch 495.03
franchisables 062.15
Francie 420.09
Francie's 086.27
Francisco 433.01
Francist 372.10
frangipani 182.28
frangipanned 493.22
frank 121.20 220.12 413.30
452.15 465.12 521.23 557.20
Frank 048.11 521.24 562.23
frankay 234.32
frankeyed 134.26
frankfurters 332.08
Frankfurters 533.15
frankily 282.08
franking 410.21
frankish 315.36
Frankish 388.18
frankling 372.08
franklings 606.20
frankly 615.13
Frankly 478.17
Frankofurto 070.05
franks 127.29 183.19
franksman 070.10
frankson 303.30
frantling 245.03
Franz 312.07
frasques 020.32
fraternibus 489.06
fraternitrees 504.21
Fratomistor 050.23
fratrorum 185.20
frau 094.15
fraud 172.21 573.25
fraudstuff 007.13
Fraufrau 510.35
fraufrau's 127.17
fraught 099.23
fraulino 052.16
fraur 038.33
frausch 505.32
fray 128.31 246.26 330.26
335.15 471.27
frayed 274.17
frayshouters 378.26
fraywhaling 284.F4
freak 057.19 225.04 424.02
516.14
freakandesias 542.31
freakfog 048.02
freakings 603.29
freaksily 172.27
freakwing 121.21
freaky 626.11
Frech 268.F6
freck 282.07
freck 525.24
freckened 521.23
freckled 204.01
frecklefully 615.35
frecklesome 376.19
frecklessness 435.11
Fred 330.04 445.32 587.20
587.20 588.06 588.12
Freda 470.36 588.02
Fredborg 529.21
fredeland's 014.31
fredonnance 184.19
free 008.05 019.22 023.08
025.21 036.13 047.20 051.11
057.21 058.24 060.36 067.08
069.34 094.09 094.15 117.34
126.08 132.23 166.10 178.10
208.16 229.25 270.06 276.03
281.25 308.F1 346.28 346.28
356.07 377.22 378.02 398.20
399.33 406.19 406.22 433.27
437.06 439.28 446.34 451.09
496.28 515.13 528.11 538.36
540.28 542.03 545.20 553.27
559.29 569.24 576.02 577.05
579.07 581.08 588.36 600.25
604.23 621.04 627.32
Free 145.29 228.36 323.12
372.28
freeandies 535.33
freeboots' 469.08
freebutter 388.19
freed 078.23 205.01 299.02
Freeday's 487.34
freedman's 500.15
freedom 137.32 448.16
freeflawforms 596.24
freeholdit 535.06
freely 028.27 069.29 079.04
111.30 227.32 437.14 495.22
551.11 552.05 597.33
freeman's 291.F6 546.20
freemen's 004.18
freequuntly 357.14
freer 432.23 468.31 489.28
588.13
freers 338.05
frees 137.09 250.25 576.36
Freeshots 464.30
freespeech 273.19
Freestouters 329.31
freeswinging 404.19
freethinker 107.32
Freetime's 348.27
freewritten 280.02
freeze 269.16
freezigrade 108.02
freightfullness 224.10
freipforter 548.12
freiung 538.27
frem 229.02 434.03
fremble 462.26
fremdling 442.01
french 464.36
French 050.09 083.31 146.20
192.15 246.32 256.19 412.19
462.34 498.01
French-Egyptian 130.30
Frenchman 479.30
frenchy 138.12
frenge 233.09
frensheets 603.08
frequency 256.30 312.33
frequent 149.36 263.01
frequenting 039.31 435.33
frequently 051.02 152.07 161.03
544.17
frere 487.21
fresch 113.25
fresco 597.34
fresh 015.10 042.35 046.27
183.35 243.02 292.09 327.31
336.17 385.19 394.25 413.13
414.10 428.25 440.31 498.17
510.23 524.27 540.06 581.32
fresh 341.33
freshcheeky 376.20
freshed 606.22
freshener 553.27
freshet 201.27
fresheth 561.29
freshets 264.18
freshfallen 426.13
freshly 543.27
freshprosts 347.11
freshwatties 315.21
fresk 540.23
fresky 059.36
fress 300.15
fret 257.13 452.24
fretful 120.33
Fretta 147.12
freudened 115.23
freudful 411.35
freudzay 337.07
freund 579.20

frew 047.15 578.23
frey 211.04 335.15
freytherem 231.13
friar 338.12
friarbird 595.33
friars 099.15
Friars 447.18 569.09
friar's 439.07
friarylayman 472.03
frickans 054.11
frickled 204.23
Frick's 537.30
frickyfrockies 431.03
frictions 269.F3 385.12
Frida 470.36
friday 433.12
Friday 211.16
Friday 399.21
Frideggs 184.32
fried-at-belief-stakes 170.33
friedhoffer 087.16
friend 035.06 053.32 079.15 082.17 109.17 115.08 124.18 131.21 145.09 159.27 188.02 239.13 279.F36 291.18 311.25 356.27 366.06 384.24 411.09 412.23 437.29 458.05 467.21 476.17 479.23 484.08 485.23 489.26 509.05 519.31 523.23 524.13 532.20 537.20 545.02 558.09 586.08 605.01
friend 418.20
Friend 307.15
friendeen 561.17
friendly 082.21 137.19 362.29 437.29 440.26
friendlylike 523.26
friends 065.35 459.15 463.23 546.29
Friends 477.35 495.11
Friends 105.02
friend's 083.30
friends' 363.19
friendshapes 565.07
friendship 042.07 174.35
frier 117.26
frieren 244.16
frieze 602.35
Frieze 404.17
frifrif 532.20
frifty 025.34
fright 178.08 309.02 395.25 459.04
frightday 301.21
frighted 555.19
frightened 391.05 393.28
frighteousness 343.34
frightfools 613.28
frightful 034.06 549.12
frightfully 409.01 506.33
frigid 549.14
frigorique 185.25
frilldress 360.35
frilled 563.27
frilles-in-pleyurs 224.22
frillick 537.33
frills 205.02
frimosa 549.14
frind 449.16
fringe 199.05 311.33
fringes 548.19
frish 407.17 546.05
frisherman's 153.29
frishfrey 356.17
frisk 209.13
friskiest 170.28
frisking 095.22
friskly 419.15
frisko 564.17
frisky 039.19 470.33
Frisky 039.18 212.02 523.23 523.30
frisque 020.32
Frist 607.28
frithstool 358.36
frittling 078.20
fritz 138.13
Fritzie 420.09
frivolish 166.25
frivolity 270.F3
Frivulteeny 298.27
frizette 112.36
frizzle 380.28
frizzy 430.23
Frizzy 510.35
fro 011.26 121.06 226.21 317.02
fro' 062.36 250.07
frock 053.22
frockenhalted 241.32
frockful 079.19
frocks 226.25 233.09 548.25
frocks 342.07
froggy 116.12
frogmarchers 469.12
froh 553.27
frohim 510.09
frohn 594.25
frokerfoskerfuskar 178.36
frole 430.32
frolic 064.28
frolicky 301.13 451.09
from from From From FROM
frome 199.24
fromm 094.18 272.01
fromming 483.28
fromoud 010.08
fromout 007.16
froms 601.06
fron 214.28
Fronces 527.17
frond 079.15 107.14
frondest 601.02
frondeur 266.29
frondoak 460.24
fronds 100.36 278.09 571.05
frons 153.15 358.35
front 022.28 032.22 214.05 223.09 235.22 271.F1 315.19 362.25 377.10 386.20 404.28 469.13 533.21 541.20 559.12 582.30 620.19
front 340.25
Front 106.28
fronting 524.15
frontispecs 191.32
fronts 069.06
frontyard 191.06
froods 034.07
frore 055.26 055.26
froren 495.10
froriose 016.01
frost 264.13 286.09 464.20 581.14
Frost 424.30
frostivying 199.36
frostwork 502.17
frosty 044.15 045.25
froth 587.12
frothblower 227.32
Frothblowers 270.13
frothearnity 133.31
frother 310.35 464.24
frothwhiskered 558.15
frothy 553.27
froubadour 462.26
froufrous 127.17
froutiknow 366.06
fr'over 003.04
frow 009.05
frown 121.06 392.11
frowned 023.21 252.17
frowner 301.13
frowns 175.21
froze 552.36
frozen 502.18 549.08 626.25
Frozen 421.09
frozenmeat 211.23
frucht 148.29
fruchte 094.14
fructed 604.05
fructification 232.09
fructos 155.22
fruent 310.19
frugal 201.09
Frui 495.34
fruit 011.32 116.34 150.19 181.15 192.07 271.28 303.17 492.32 597.36 609.12
Fruit 071.10 106.21
fruiterers 172.01
fruiteyeing 209.01
fruitflavoured 444.22
fruitflowerleaf 121.10
fruitful 068.03
fruitfully 167.11
fruits 132.28 318.16 336.26 535.32 535.34
fruit's 357.26
frull 451.24
frullatullepleats 530.27
frulling 184.19
Frullini's 531.21
fruminy 276.15
frumped 405.28
frumpier 208.32
frumpty 012.12
frush 588.08
frusker 050.07
frust 569.22
frustate 352.33
Frustrations 123.21
frut 376.13
fruting 012.19
fruur 110.22
Fruzian 346.01
fry 525.16
Fry 043.09 413.35
Fry 342.10
fryggabet 577.17
f.t. 013.22 (four things)
ftofty 114.23
fu 212.35
Fu 426.17
fù 049.02
fuchs 489.02
Fuchs 328.26
fuchser 578.13
fuchser's 097.13

fuchsia 279.F15
fuchsiar 072.23
fuchu 466.04
Fudd 499.18
fudden 339.05
Fudder 415.20
fudding 375.02
fuddle 603.04
fuddled 006.28
fuddlers 569.24
Fuddling 531.26
fuderal 336.22
fudgem 456.22
Fudgesons 257.36
fué 481.35 481.35
fuellest 419.35
fuercilier 335.18
fuere 287.26
Fuerst 157.15
Fuert 154.27
fuesies 551.03
fuffing 199.29
fufuf 533.11
Fugabollags 541.18
Fugger's 097.32
fugle 374.13
fuglers 250.11
fuglewards 504.23
fuguall 073.14
fui 481.11 481.11
Fuinn 427.30
Fuinnninuinn's 372.29
Fuisfinister 228.28
fuissent 185.16
fuit 128.01
fuitefuite 235.10
Fuitfiat 613.14
Fuitfuit 050.32
Fukien 468.03
fuko 416.16
Fulcrum 481.04
fuld 238.35
Fulfest 388.04
fulgar 242.29
Fulgitudes 258.04
Fulgitudo 610.06
full 006.08 020.29 024.29 028.21 036.14 061.09 075.03 095.15 097.12 109.25 115.10 118.14 120.12 129.32 132.21 133.24 139.04 160.27 161.16 170.18 181.09 181.28 183.01 187.13 214.18 228.27 235.31 239.17 240.36 248.24 254.20 275.13 312.07 315.08 328.14 330.18 333.23 344.22 348.07 360.05 361.18 390.07 390.07 390.08 391.06 399.33 404.03 430.30 431.30 434.24 446.17 463.15 467.08 469.17 471.31 473.24 484.18 543.07 566.22 566.25 568.14 568.20 596.02 596.13 604.10 604.36 605.26 611.15 615.33 617.08 618.15 623.19
full 339.19 339.20 339.20 339.20 339.20 339.20 339.21 418.18
Full 452.24 588.21
Fullacan's 531.26
fullback 144.07 564.07
fullbelow 569.03
fullblacks 129.32
fullblown 059.35 422.04
fullbottom 164.29 390.36
fullchantedly 461.33
fullconsciousness 421.22
fulldress 455.05
fulled 323.17 561.15
fullen 377.26
fullends 376.14
fuller's 130.25
fullest 141.16 153.25
fullexampling 356.14
fullface 550.29
fullfeatured 602.02 602.05
fullfour 353.35
fullfrength 341.11
fullfully 490.16
fullgets 467.27
Fullgrapce 489.04
fullin 344.34
fullmaked 551.11
fullmin 283.13
fullness 275.11 336.04
fullnights 365.31
fullpried 101.22
fullscore 170.01
fullsoot 411.22
fullstandingly 141.21
fullstoppers 152.16
fulltroth 162.33
fullup 177.06
Fullup 121.35
fullvide 568.02
fullvixen 603.29
fully 050.30 051.23 166.32 180.07 189.14 324.02 345.31 398.12 478.08 533.27 606.20
fullybigs 099.11
fullyfilling 042.21
fullyfleeced 578.10
Fullyhum 613.04
fulmament 449.02
fulmenbomb 588.20
fulmfilming 398.25
fulminance 599.12
fulminant 185.27
fulmoon 167.34
fulse 378.12
fulsomeness 534.32
Fulvia 546.30 547.05
fulvurite 347.36
fum 596.06
Fum 532.03
Fumadory 395.10
fumant 043.04
fumb 283.20 533.11
fumbelums 323.15
fumbles 269.16
fumbling 180.18 438.04
fume 031.26
fumes 006.03 128.18 190.08 382.25
fumfing 341.11
fumfum 013.15
Fumfum 013.15
fumiform 413.31
fuming 476.30 608.31
fumings 256.12
fummer 302.F2
Fummuccumul 375.29
fumous 502.27
fumusiste 609.24
fun 083.22 128.31 160.32 175.34 184.25 187.10 197.32 236.13 278.20 297.04 301.13 351.02 364.24 431.09 444.07 454.02 460.15 473.09 512.23 531.26 558.24
Fun 176.16
Funagin 503.11
funantics 450.27
funcktas 160.31
functionary 067.14
functionist 270.06
functions 284.07 590.29
fund 108.13 574.08 574.12 574.22
Fundally 200.20
fundament 180.23 258.23
fundamental 035.22
fundamentalist 072.21
fundamentally 115.33
Fundemaintalish 296.L1
fundementially 610.01
fundigs 006.25
fundness 542.07
funds 116.09 192.08
fundus 564.35
funebral 077.24
funeral 025.33 066.34 083.22 190.03 243.14 280.11 477.09 491.03 515.23 602.22
funereels 414.35
funfer 304.12
funferal 120.10
funferall 013.15 111.15
funforall 458.22
funfun 094.19
Fung 109.06
Funglus 198.33
fungoalgaceous 613.18
fungopark 051.20
fungstif 456.24
funickin 102.09
funicking 314.01
fun-in-the-corner 577.08
funk 010.05 150.05 176.26 451.16
funkleblue 171.17
funkling 199.35
Funkling 289.10
funn 321.17 617.11
Funn 005.12 600.10
funnaminal 244.13
funnel 471.26
funner's 096.31
funnet 302.17
funning 392.03
Funniral 137.12
funnish 040.18 288.09
funnity 327.09
funny 038.17 127.02 171.27 227.24 414.35 519.15 596.27
Funny 144.35 211.14
Funnycoon's 499.13
Funnycoon's 105.21
Funnyface 071.12
funnyfeelbelong 569.03
Funnylegs 251.18
funnyman's 590.29
Funnymore 439.12
funpowtherplother 142.11
funst 334.13
funster's 050.17
funtasy 493.18
funts 241.10
fur 166.07 311.33 611.18

furbear 132.32
furbelovs 468.13
furbishing 041.11
furchte 094.14
furframed 022.36 241.18
furibound 243.05
furibouts 163.23
furies 320.26
Furioso 271.L3
furiosos 548.09
furious 174.35 460.11 549.11
furiously 570.14
furlan 327.19
furlong 473.12
furlongs 567.01
Furlong's 071.35
furloughed 418.03
furnaced 412.17
furnished 437.27 451.32
Furniss's 289.13
furnit 611.18
furniture 184.10 412.11 543.23 611.14
furnitures 081.32
Furphy 065.22
furrinarr 254.21
furrinfrowned 555.22
furrow 323.22
furrow 353.01
furrowards 018.32
Furrows 535.02
furry 135.02 340.09 456.12 526.22
furry 338.16
Furr-y-Benn 375.32
furscht 262.12
Fursday 182.26
fursed 282.25
furses 346.01
furst 162.04 326.08 481.34
Furstin 342.24
furt 316.28
furth 608.30
further 038.24 042.01 082.15 149.25 160.24 219.01 357.26 365.01 397.29 494.31 538.04 541.07
furthermore 438.10 585.05
furtive 432.25
furtivefree 173.07
furtivfired 514.27
furtz 116.29
fury 567.14 617.18
furze 330.17
furzeborn 210.04
furzed 338.16
furzy 474.20
fuseboxes 077.11
fused 077.09 593.11
Fusees 451.14
fusefiressence 378.08
fuselage 479.19 529.21
fuselaiding 348.11
fush 359.01
Fush 007.10
fusiliers 033.27 047.10
Fusilovna 049.08
fusky 426.07
Fuss 329.07
fussfor 415.05
fussforus 505.33
fust 049.32 303.03
fustfed 456.24
fustian 035.09 292.22
fut 291.04
futherer 566.24
Futhorc 018.34
futile 389.35
Futilears 176.13
Futs 408.36
futt 196.06
Futt 181.19
futter 129.04
Futter 009.20
Futtfishy 480.16
futuerism 130.01
futule 143.08
futules 348.06
futuous 527.34
futura 287.26
future 004.22 048.09 110.34 246.12 270.01 276.03 364.07 398.07 445.28 460.08 483.30 496.35 525.13 536.04 597.28
future 355.03
Future 303.L3
FUTURE 272.R1
futurepip 314.25
futures 123.13 407.33
future's 234.24
futurist 221.18
fututa 287.26
Fuvver 157.16
fux 177.36 177.36
fuyerescaper 228.29
fuzz 044.02
fuzzolezzo 281.19
fweet 302.F2
F. X. 055.18 (F. X. Preserved Coppinger)
Fy 621.20
Fyat-Fyat 235.26
fyats 520.28
fylkers 264.22
Fyne 622.35
Fynlogue 327.03
Fyn's 510.24
Fyon 558.35
fyre 394.09
Fyre 370.34
fyrsty 328.19

ga 270.31 270.31
ga 212.34 212.35 212.36
Gaa 514.33
gaames 332.26
gaarden 140.36
Gaascooker 323.13
gaasy 175.31
gaauspices 332.14
gab 237.16 436.26
gabbalots 324.14
gabbard 197.28
Gabbarnaur-Jaggarnath 342.13
gabber 213.08
gabbercoat 150.28
Gabbiano's 424.10
gabble 453.04
gabe 209.28
gabgut 490.14
gabhard 276.12
gable 100.16
Gabrielle 184.27
Gach 422.03
gackles 511.11
gad 284.29
Gad 597.09
gadabount 202.04
gadden 354.22
gadder 602.11
gaddered 155.26
gaddeth 034.27
gadding 418.32
gaddy 275.F2
Gadeway 260.13
gadgets 597.09
Gadolmagtog 246.05
gads 219.03
gaeilish 063.06
gael 267.07 321.12 515.07
Gael 500.03 604.24
Gaelers' 510.15
gaelic 549.36
Gaelic 384.23
Gaelicise 514.33
gaels 011.05 043.27
Gaels' 047.20
gaelstorms 339.13
Gaeltact 087.14
gaff 366.29 499.04
gaffed 170.29
gaffer 215.15
gaffneysaffron 560.27
gafr 330.01
gaft 093.20
gag 322.26 515.32 516.03 580.18
Gag 302.F3
gagag 482.20
gagagniagnian 389.22
gagainst 178.01
gagar's 102.08
gage 036.19 070.23 331.27
Gage 105.32
Gage's 600.15
gageure 272.29
gagged 049.30
gaggin 004.01
gaggles 069.14 270.F1
gags 308.F2
Gags 485.10
gagster 219.23
Gaieties 455.25
gaiety 180.04
Gaiety 513.22
Gaij 565.11
gail 321.23
gaily 035.15 054.14 507.05 554.02
gailydhe 312.30
gain 310.06 355.28 358.19 431.23
gaingangers 540.24
gaingridando 093.20
gaining 240.31
gainous 325.04
gains 607.24
gainsay 192.33
Gainsborough 260.12
gainst 366.11
gainsts 321.06
gait 318.01 473.14 521.14 579.32 616.30
gaiters 035.10
gaiter's 531.04
gaits 258.08
gait's 214.22
gala 408.28 453.18
galahat 389.23

galandhar 492.26
galantifloures 256.09
Galasia 105.26
Galata 547.31 547.31
Galathee 032.12
galawater 206.31
galaxy 432.05
galbs 203.28
gale 070.20 134.22 241.06 276.05
Gale 087.17
galehus 294.16
Galen 424.07
gales 062.02 502.06 567.14 589.30
Galilleotto 251.25
gall 063.06 108.25 134.22 267.07 276.05 364.15
Gall 510.16
Galla 622.06
gallant 322.03
gallants 283.17
Gallawghurs 008.25
gallaxion 604.15
galled 515.07
galleon 602.35
galleonman 583.08
galler 321.11
gallery 219.23 438.35
gallews 489.07
galley 546.14
galleyliers 540.23
gallic 185.33 315.36
gallicry 143.17
galligo 208.13
Galliver 620.13
gallockers 524.29
Gallocks 256.36
Gallon 412.25
gallonts 187.13
gallop 583.12 583.12
Galloper 048.15
galloper's 457.14
galloroman 288.24
Gallotaurus 118.13
gallous 014.20
gallowglasses 031.17 387.06
gallows 584.23
gallowsbirds 388.25
gallpitch 566.03
Gall's 046.14
Gallstonebelly 393.18
gallus 377.21
Gallus 594.30
Gallus's 256.02
Gallwegian 089.07
galohery 557.04
Galopping 039.35
galore 397.05 439.16
galore 398.34
Galorius 219.12
Galory 141.30
galorybit 557.03
galumphantes 502.10
Galway 190.29 495.12
galways 458.09
Galway's 141.02
Galwegian 343.10
gam 339.06
Gam 271.18 599.18
Gambanman 344.06
Gambariste 009.35
gambeson 578.31
gambills 414.28
gambit 266.26 559.34
Gambleden 541.13
gambling 341.17
Gambrinus 134.06
game 025.21 039.21 070.11 090.04 112.16 123.29 128.18 209.10 239.09 252.18 269.22 269.22 279.F20 295.09 301.F4 334.28 375.23 408.29 433.13 444.08 460.15 472.14 512.15 520.26 532.17 545.31 560.12 582.24 584.14
game 266.L1 340.07 399.18
Game 010.21 184.16 257.31 302.19
gamebold 615.06
gameboy 451.27
gamecox 234.17
gamefellow 191.19 350.35
Gamellaxarksky 034.03
gamely 271.03
gamen 389.32
games 066.37 175.32 175.34 176.01 368.35 515.23 621.11
Games 602.22
gamest 279.F19
Gamester 283.F2
gamesy 606.33
gamey 334.21 446.26
gamier 026.05
gamings 427.31 461.12
gamman 568.32
gammat 492.04
gammel 275.05
gammeldags 096.09
gammelhole 046.21
gammelhore 046.22
Gammer 215.14
gammon 112.16 152.22
Gamp 449.14
Gamper 268.L4
gamps 057.23
Gamuels 318.22
gamut 450.17
gamy 083.23
gan 129.10 246.21 503.23
gander 123.29 197.14 249.18 410.15 482.16
gander 399.10
Gander 557.07
gandered 389.3[illegible]
ganderpan 423.09
gandfarder 378.25
Gandon 552.11
gang 232.06 247.10 289.18 316.22 323.36 359.36 454.29 532.02
Gangang 487.30
Ganger 263.15 444.32
ganghorn 479.35
gangin 487.29
gangrene 397.35
gangres 196.18
gangrung 576.31
gangs 334.28 586.24
gangstairs 373.09
Gangster 263.15
gangsters 215.15
ganna 330.29
gannets 384.02
gannies 452.27
ganswer 287.02
gansyfett 531.07
gantlets 567.31
ganymede 583.11
Ganymede 269.18
ganz 098.28 407.06
Gaogaogaone 427.09
gaols 139.02
gaon 413.29
Gaoy 425.23
gap 014.16 191.07 204.15 229.24 232.33 305.09 580.06 617.19
Gap 090.14
gape 069.24 192.13 248.30 257.24 446.35 461.22 478.14 508.30 576.29
Gape 369.09
gaped 449.02
Gaper 037.08
gapers 620.24
gaping 299.13
Gaping 036.35
gapman 136.20
gar 098.28 252.24 273.20
Gar 499.33
garb 377.12
garbage 093.20 550.09
garbagecans 019.16
garble 069.09
garce 509.30
garcielasso 423.02
Gard 377.31 445.02
Garda 197.07 258.30 258.30
garde 471.30
gardeenen 564.35
garden 030.16 046.27 052.10 096.14 138.04 145.25 160.21 166.06 169.23 203.01 227.18 235.26 263.20 271.29 309.07 357.34 446.34 450.30 464.30 487.11 503.04 553.25 568.28 577.30
gardener 030.13 266.F2
Gardener 569.07
Gardener's 547.18
Gardener's 175.17
gardenfillers 475.11
Gardenia's 601.21
gardens 152.27 265.14 454.30 553.09 558.22
Gardens 043.03
gardiner 133.23
garding 552.19
Gardoun 252.32
gards 596.22
garerden 350.02
gargantast 319.26
gargle 206.17 206.17
gargling 088.32
garland 140.19 207.01 226.23
garlands 393.25
garleeks 550.10
garlens 622.36
garlic 462.29
garment 166.10 208.15 238.11 532.35
garmentguy 339.21
garments 192.29 200.25 404.02 465.29 508.14 559.08
Garnd 146.35
garner 253.17
garnered 564.31
garnet 137.04

garnish 164.22
garnishee 574.34
garonne 205.15
Garonne 205.15
garotted 467.13
garou 352.31
garret 180.27
garrickson's 055.35
garrison 076.17
garron 471.20
garrotted 078.36
garrulous 139.18
Garry 215.03
garrymore 583.11
gart 089.19
gartener 336.21
Garterd 423.35
gartergazer 471.09
garters 183.28 208.19 226.24 347.12 445.06
garth 090.15
Garth 558.35
garthen 034.27 069.10
garths 331.22
Garvey 176.18
garzelle 362.16
gas 577.07
gasbag 067.09
Gascon 403.08
gaseytotum 426.21
gash 093.11 500.07
Gash 251.20 444.17
gashes 124.02
gasometer 095.08 131.36
gasped 116.25
gaspel 349.16
gaspers 208.19
Gaspey 485.03
gasping 375.13
gaspower 521.24
gaspy 485.09
gassies 058.18
gastricks 437.01
gastronomy 449.11
gastspiels 393.35
Gasty 346.20
gaswind 281.F2
gat 177.07 541.08 569.34 599.19
gat 344.11
gatch 288.F7
gate 063.34 065.35 069.15 089.19 433.32 459.27 466.29 569.30 583.06
Gate 140.32 329.25 535.05
gates 129.20 136.19 145.13 149.33 606.36
gates 341.23
Gates 493.27
gate's 063.19
gatestone 063.28
gateway 063.19
gather 428.11 502.03 509.06
Gather 154.13
gathered 032.25 073.34 158.27 412.11 545.34
gathering 086.20
gatherings 609.31
gatherings 353.33
gatherumed 345.18
gathery 051.17
gatovit 339.04
gats 220.14
Gattabuia 424.10
gattling 246.21 377.06
Gau 233.27
gauche 467.27
Gaud 207.23
Gaudio 134.06
gaudy 450.31
Gaudyanna 294.29
gaudyquiviry 208.07
gauge 029.31 057.02
gauged 130.16
gauger 313.29
gaul 321.23
Gaul 043.36 070.01 509.20
Gaules 281.05
gaulish 291.23
Gaulls 604.22
gaulusch 406.06
gaunt 121.04
Gaunt 594.25
gauntlet 036.16 052.28
gaunts 381.13
gause 531.19
Gautamed 277.L5
Gauze 566.28
gav 056.34 365.31 423.10
gave 019.33 032.17 054.32 060.13 068.23 078.22 085.24 098.26 102.02 126.17 128.13 133.10 159.09 177.22 202.26 202.33 212.15 214.30 227.29 243.34 271.29 290.12 310.35 317.10 352.06 353.19 362.12 380.15 385.23 409.10 438.07 463.03 471.22 477.27 479.03 483.06 535.32 535.32 542.29 546.26 548.20 549.24 550.17 576.02 579.28 580.11 582.04 615.28 625.31
Gave 105.36
gavel 444.21
Gavelkind 268.L4
gaving 175.02
gawan 208.25
gawds 257.34
Gawin 398.06
gawk 225.18
gawking 476.35
gay 083.05 083.05 116.14 133.14 173.05 198.04 227.15 242.16 244.11 257.06 263.F4 273.13 334.32 337.20 358.07 364.35 412.23 438.36 566.17 571.16
gay 201.19
Gay 193.19 419.30 433.05
gayatsee 297.18
gayboys 179.08
gaye 020.33
gayed 239.36
gayet 300.09
gayl 352.31
gaylabouring 006.23
Gaylad 442.24
gayleague 378.28
Gaylegs 256.36
gays 092.30
Gay's 601.23
gaze 043.22 070.11 266.22 362.26 389.22 448.01
Gaze 582.36
gazebocroticon 614.28
gazed 389.26
gazelle 595.04
gazer 193.10
gazet 293.09
gazette 559.14
Gazette 602.19
gazework 224.26
Gazey 369.10
gazing 065.13 461.22
gazious 227.25
g.b.d. 450.10
G. B. W. 369.07 (Mr G. B. W. Ashburner)
gcourts 089.17
gd 302.25 (good)
geallachers 502.14
Geamatron 257.05
Gearge 599.18
geasa 392.24
gebroren 199.34
Gedankje 150.11
gee 042.05 133.10 284.F5 409.14
Gee 112.06 188.27 299.F3 420.19 421.30 436.08
geegaws 548.24
geegees 120.21
geek 275.07
geen 606.36
Geenar 552.02
geepy 454.16
gees 042.05 223.12
Gee's 340.19
geese 026.06 049.06 124.34 384.02 557.14 602.36
Geese 104.24
geeser 065.05
geeses 233.12
geesing 527.08
Geesyhus 464.32
geewhiz 180.06
Geg 308.14
gegging 249.36
gegifting 246.28
gegs 379.19
Geh 378.21
gehamerat 127.31
Gehinnon 078.09
geil 321.23
geing 296.11
geip 597.27
geit 141.09
Geit 071.11
Geity's 411.15
gel 065.23
Gelagala 233.36
gelatine 155.35
gelb 143.25
Gelchasser 228.14
gelded 279.F01
gelding 020.30
geldings 432.13
geldings 342.23
gell 375.12 445.09
Gellius 255.19
Gellover 620.14
gells 283.17 354.31
gels 065.18 361.17
Gels 508.34
gem 159.28 441.18 612.09
gember 182.09
Gemellus 090.18 090.19
gemenal 352.01
gemens 185.17

geminally 220.14
gemination 505.12
Gemini 409.01
geminorum 185.20
Gemiti 290.27
Gemma 092.25
gemman's 202.20
gemmynosed 498.13
Gemral 116.06
Gemuas 358.32
gemurrmal 251.36
gen 004.01 323.36
gendarm 530.17
gender 251.32 275.F3 505.25
genderous 268.25
genderymen 510.31
generable 436.15
general 036.31 040.24 046.33 081.35 098.14 099.24 122.06 141.12 165.19 192.05 229.05 253.28 253.30 335.14 357.31 369.26 391.31 407.28 431.22 444.02 462.02 467.04 471.20 523.21 594.19
general 353.25
General 050.31 221.35 229.05 329.05 388.21
generales 351.22
Generalissimo 610.13
generality 539.07
generally 042.11 120.17 172.11 447.02 603.12
generalman 325.16
generals 101.21 529.09
general's 111.12 567.02
generand 335.20
generation 098.09 546.13 589.19 595.28
generations 107.35 107.35 107.35 484.30 589.26
générations 281.11
generose 362.16
generous 178.10 265.28 380.23
genesic 112.16
genesis 030.02
Genesius 219.09
genewality 523.04
genghis 593.17
gengstermen 350.09
genial 031.14 097.03 132.30 334.05
Genik 228.07
genitalmen 569.31
genitricksling 230.29
genius 048.20 159.26
Genius 167.24
genmen 371.26
Genoaman 113.21
genral 531.28
Genral 501.20
genre 165.17
genrously 423.33
genstries 609.03
gent 089.15 388.05
Gent 278.L5
genteel 093.05 161.04 557.31
genteelician 546.05
gentes 552.14
Gentes 152.16
Gentia 092.25
gentian 023.20
Gentileman 150.26
gentilemen 573.35
gentilhomme 365.04
gentium 089.27
gentle 020.36 292.01 515.34 570.04 580.18 618.27 622.12
Gentlehomme's 106.12
gentlemale 617.25
gentleman 035.14 086.27 111.13 116.25 126.02 128.17 269.21 432.24 460.34
Gentleman 300.F2
gentleman's 112.17 584.17
gentlemeants 318.26
gentlemen 042.34 091.20 224.01 224.04 356.03 368.11 412.03
Gentlemen 221.02
gentlemens 325.16
gentlemen's 165.24 455.33 564.17
gentlemine 301.11
gentlenest 561.31
gentlenuns 177.08
gentlerman 120.09
gentlermen 462.02
gentlest 470.24
gentlewomanly 067.24
gentlewriter 063.10
gentlman 524.07
gently 037.19 164.13 165.30 280.19 431.05 522.04 566.06
Gently 522.04 627.12
gentryman 322.17
gentrymen 236.12
gents 043.07 554.03
genua 269.06
genuane 053.19
Genuas 274.F2
genuflected 120.21
genuflecting 605.29
genuflections 411.18
genuflexions 519.35
genuine 111.22 118.03 161.15 470.09 470.30
genuinely 065.27 099.36
genus 160.03
genus 419.07
geodetic 114.15
Geoff 488.29
Geoglyphy's 595.07
geography 275.F2
geolgian 242.06
geomater 297.01
Georgeous 303.17
George-le-Greek 569.07
Georges 428.19
Georgian 140.30
gerachknell 388.34
gerandiums 269.10
Gereland 337.34
gerils 434.07
German 083.28 497.35 543.25
germane 230.33
Germanon 338.03
germhuns 127.13
germinal 354.35
Germinal 134.13
germinating 130.28
germination 505.12
germogall 176.20
germs 079.32
Gerontes 573.21
gerontophils 115.12
gert 287.19
gertles 618.03
ges 245.17
geselles 352.31
geshing 093.11
geshotten 420.35
gest 468.05
Gestapose 332.07
gestare 361.32
geste 227.27
gested 407.25
gests 414.17
gesture 036.17 377.20
gestures 614.21
gesweest 431.33
get 036.26 040.34 061.11 061.19 079.07 086.25 111.28 131.31 134.12 137.27 141.23 141.23 145.12 206.21 209.13 232.20 233.29 275.F3 279.F13 287.09 317.04 334.22 337.17 348.17 372.13 378.21 386.33 389.22 411.05 411.09 411.10 423.16 434.18 435.17 436.24 437.35 438.07 438.20 441.30 443.06 446.32 448.13 448.29 452.35 456.17 469.06 482.06 490.09 500.30 509.01 525.34 530.20 553.32 604.02 607.01 613.33 616.02 619.13
Get 095.05 233.27 251.01 280.24 387.08 466.08 477.14 507.21 522.31 534.32
getatable 169.02
getaway 039.08
gethobbyhorsical 434.07
Getobodoff 370.17
getrennty 228.24
getrunner 337.01
gets 047.15 074.12 243.07 276.18 341.13 375.14 428.18 441.20 467.27 581.29 586.12 598.25
gets 399.11
getsome 312.18
gettin 500.35
getting 040.27 064.32 069.25 109.16 153.14 176.26 206.19 247.07 347.28 350.34 376.14 393.24 394.02 406.13 426.08 453.27 458.30 496.27 529.10 543.26 543.33 626.36
getting 345.18
Gettle 104.24
gettogether 380.08
getup 169.11
geulant 136.13
geust 369.04
gev 394.27
geyser 497.35
Geyser 305.F3
geyswerks 221.09
gezumpher 278.F1
ghariwallahs 609.33
gharters 008.19
ghast 349.19
ghastcold 265.03
ghastern 598.10
ghastly 467.10
ghates 551.35
ghazi 056.11
Ghazi 521.22
ghazometron 559.24
ghee 411.19
gheist 299.14
ghem 193.09

ghem's 318.05
Ghenter's 381.13
ghentleman 010.18
gheol 228.33
gherman 392.15
ghets 182.13
ghetto 286.06
Ghibeline 071.26
ghiberring 504.30
ghimbelling 567.36
ghimel 120.26
ghinee 182.12
Ghinees 016.31
Ghinis 272.27
ghiornal 228.33
ghirk 182.12
ghoasts 551.03
ghoats 051.15 081.30
ghoatstory 051.13
ghools 377.34
ghoom 318.06
ghoon 593.18
ghosses 397.22
ghost 024.27 056.16 057.06 173.26 295.08 426.20 561.28
Ghost 399.02
ghosters 219.08
ghosting 501.32
ghostly 062.17 594.26
ghostmark 473.09
Ghoststown 329.25
ghostus 532.04
ghostwhite 214.15
ghouly 057.06
ghuest 414.08
Ghugugoothoyou 471.02
ghustorily 323.35
Ghyllygully 518.09
Giacinta 615.03
Giallia 102.25
giamond's 391.18
gianed 006.18
gianerant 368.08
giant 033.29 134.21 277.06 494.27 500.01 504.15 540.17 576.18
Giant 324.36
giantar 243.15
giantle 509.19
Giants 306.17
giant's 198.32 343.06 578.33
giantstand 616.30
Giaourmany 355.22
giaours 107.22
giardarner 108.17
gias 184.02
Gibbering 071.19
gibbet 119.29
Gibbet 079.11
gibbetmeade 568.22
gibbonses 504.29
gibbous 136.23 314.19 377.08 531.01
gibits 334.04
gibos 148.20
Gibsen's 170.26
gickling 511.11
gidday 284.29
giddersh 617.12
giddied 568.07
giddies 375.13 435.11
Gidding 347.27
giddle 508.30
giddles 448.25
giddy 387.33 597.09 603.17 624.12
giddygaddy 195.03
gidflirts 418.32
gidgad 202.05
gie 367.13
giel 321.23
gielgaulgalls 326.08
gients 241.17
gif 231.03
gifs 007.06
gift 005.25 031.12 075.17 093.19 306.04 327.28 351.03 457.34 562.04
giftake 062.10
gifted 548.15
gifting 239.13
giftname 358.07
gifts 209.28
gig 206.14 322.26 515.32 516.04
giganteous 126.12
gigantesquesque 253.29
Gigantic 242.21
gigantig's 055.27
giggag 363.36
gigging 554.02
giggle 275.F2
giggle-for-giggle 377.19
gigglehouse 289.18
gigglesomes 008.04
gigglibly 079.18
Gigglotte's 532.22
gigguels 206.14
gigirl 532.20
Giglamps 305.F3
gigls 341.07
gigot 404.31
gigscrew 523.31
gihon 213.08
Gilbert 573.14
Gilbey's 558.02
gild 076.30
Gilda 147.12
gildthegap 037.08
Giliette 391.21
gill 278.26 382.09
Gill 036.35 244.23 312.29 440.14 440.14 578.06
Gillaroo 450.06
Gillia 572.33 572.35 573.16
gillie 267.07
gillie 354.13
Gillie 227.30
Gilligan 229.11 622.22
Gilligan-Goll 370.22
Gilligan's 421.32
Gillooly 178.16
Gilly 617.19
gillybrighteners 524.28
Gillydehooly's 440.15
gillyflowrets 254.36
gilt 016.30
giltedged 550.25
giming 344.01
gimlets 454.22
gimme 456.08
gimmy 334.21
gin 114.01 171.14 182.10 231.03 319.07
ginabawdy 095.07
ging 444.32
ginger 036.01 065.01 076.35 447.02 526.16 535.14
Ginger 059.26
gingerine 052.26
gingering 512.26
gingerly 115.18
gingin 116.19 116.19
gink 388.02
ginkus 081.22
ginnandgo 014.16
gins 302.11
gints 540.23
gip 597.27
Gipoo 276.17
gipsy 121.31
Gipsy 210.07 563.20
gipsylike 261.01
gipsy's 177.23
gir . . . 571.31 (girl)
Girahash 075.20
girde 437.01
girded 152.32 606.05
girder 138.36
girders 247.19
girdle 059.01 272.03 486.28 621.18
girdlers 313.01
girdles 134.10 245.20
girds 138.36
giregargoh 245.14
Girilis 112.30
girl 043.17 061.01 095.21 146.06 171.32 175.36 186.28 211.15 227.08 240.21 257.07 271.26 291.05 395.29 397.31 449.10 451.25 458.32 459.04 480.03 527.05 556.11 603.14 620.27 626.27
girl 341.09
Girl 082.20 220.03
Girl 032.35 342.24
girlalove 288.10
girlcutted 496.03
girleen 397.05
girleen 398.34
girlery 493.21
Girles 051.15
girlglee 182.08
girlic 260.F1
girlic-on-you 174.15
girling 034.28
girlish 562.05
girls 011.04 023.09 040.08 063.12 134.23 226.22 227.24 246.22 252.18 252.22 290.22 297.26 358.31 363.33 366.03 380.32 430.19 432.05 440.21 446.26 457.30 561.33
girl's 148.23 253.15 296.F5 384.24 463.10
girlsfuss 430.22
girly 068.03 112.06 203.08 222.33 272.15
girlycums 234.34
girlyhead 143.20
girnirilles 346.20
Giroflaa 129.30
Giroflee 129.30
girtel 349.21
girters 144.27
girth 319.21
girther 130.27 130.27 130.27
girton 211.01

gish 080.33
gist 483.03 483.03 599.36
gisture 350.10
git 008.34 009.09 023.14
059.08 097.19 138.08
git 344.01
gitter 320.14
Giubilei 031.20
Giv 056.34
give 035.35 049.14 070.25
096.20 117.26 145.32 152.12
154.27 154.32 155.23 163.23
170.23 187.34 192.16 212.06
224.04 232.02 234.33 246.09
247.28 257.16 266.26 273.F8
280.36 295.07 314.02 314.27
317.05 321.13 347.24 348.13
351.21 377.04 388.28 389.18
406.20 422.12 436.29 439.05
440.04 445.15 445.21 448.36
450.20 450.21 450.22 450.22
455.08 455.27 459.33 465.24
470.02 480.14 483.09 499.11
508.08 534.08 570.04 586.06
607.35 609.20 614.15 620.26
623.08 624.03 626.30 626.32
give 345.10
Give 047.12 080.18 087.33
283.29 377.03 379.12 434.05
436.06 455.35 463.30 464.23
466.02 521.16 535.24 536.29
540.08 621.20
GIVE 282.R1
giveme 345.21
given 004.20 018.22 051.03
056.29 061.34 086.32 097.01
101.33 109.04 133.29 141.13
165.29 184.05 251.12 291.05
326.14 406.35 423.13 425.21
458.28 493.01 493.28 496.05
524.10 524.13 526.25 529.02
531.12 546.03 604.28
given 341.20 352.16 399.21
Given 293.15 628.15
givers 023.34
gives 193.11 276.F1 279.05
293.20 328.26 356.11 375.21
465.35 563.35 563.36 565.03
570.14 595.03 619.10
Gives 321.35 581.26
giveth 133.31
givin 223.11
giving 084.13 117.23 153.16
153.33 163.16 173.29 254.04
282.11 287.03 305.07 329.33
333.12 396.24 432.17 443.04
462.05 477.03 515.20 587.28
589.07
giving 339.25 344.08
Giving 623.22
givnergenral 243.10
gizzard 558.05
Gizzards 370.36
Gizzygay 451.30
Gizzygazelle 238.36
Glacianivia's 601.27
glaciator 232.32
glad 095.17 113.35 272.15
299.05 301.F5 394.12 398.21
438.09 513.17 523.25 536.20
625.33
Gladdays 470.17
gladdened 271.26
gladdens 608.18
gladdest 200.25
gladdied 555.15
glades 014.31
Gladeys 387.35
gladful 524.26
gladhander 276.02
gladrags 267.10
gladrolleries 507.16
Gladshouse 428.08
gladshouses 537.01
gladsighted 600.13
gladsome 061.13 189.26 562.05
Gladstone 334.06
Gladstone's 170.32
Gladstools 373.28
gladyst 365.11
glaives 329.31
glamourie 493.36
Glamours 250.16
glance 334.13 470.33
glance 346.17
glancefull 512.09
glances 626.34
glaned 038.10
glans 526.23
glants 226.28
glaow 404.12
glaring 412.15
glashaboys 209.30
glass 007.12 059.05 070.10
145.03 183.36 249.26 270.21
274.F3 355.09 441.35 521.06
528.18 622.31
Glass 044.19 292.F1
Glassarse 027.01
glasseries 113.02
glasses 160.14
glasshouse 409.22
Glassthure 529.23
glasstone 077.34
Glasstone 041.35
Glasthule 321.08
glatsch 327.13
glatt 072.27
Glattstoneburg 261.16
glaubering 157.11
glaubrous 012.08
glaucous 179.26
glaum 600.36
glav 010.35
glave 621.24
glaze 548.31
glazy 214.20
gleam 099.01 130.22 197.23
226.06 404.01 600.31
Gleam 105.29
gleamens 232.07
gleaming 052.33 226.04 274.F4
566.06
gleamy 477.12
gleaner 364.34
gleanermonth 553.23
Gleannaulinn 264.28
glebe 354.11
glee 223.12
gleechoreal 145.25
gleeful 178.20 443.12 558.23
gleefully 079.32
gleeglom 533.22
gleemen 374.13
gleet 523.29
gleetsteen 169.18
gleison 146.16
glen 204.15 264.27
Glen 221.08
Glen 106.01
glenagearries 529.26
Glenasmole 223.17
Glendalough 062.35 248.30
Glendalough-le-vert 605.11
Glenfinnisk-en-la-Valle 380.09
Glens 266.F2
glete 183.36
gleve 006.29
glib 173.30 269.18 436.25
Glibt 063.24
glidder 158.08
gliddinyss 318.35
glide 618.22
Glideon 325.27
glider 271.26
gliders 404.05
glike 284.10
glim 379.23
Glimglow 585.05
glimmer 558.26
glimpse 267.10 447.16
glimpse 346.17
glimpsed 588.21
glimse 130.03
glimt 049.29
Glinaduna 623.28
glint 264.29
Glintalook 059.18
glints 226.28
Glintylook 130.33
glistening 384.20
glistering 182.28
glistery 403.24
glitter 551.09
glitteraglatteraglutt 349.12
glittergates 249.07
glittering 627.22
gllll 054.29
gloamering 014.31
gloaming 158.09 226.04 318.14
474.21
Gloamy 433.06
gloat 056.18 500.07
Gloatsdane's 438.14
globbtrottel 229.18
globe 006.29 036.31 275.F2
438.09 559.14
globeful 131.35
globelettes 532.30
globes 151.03 532.31
globetopper 435.12
globetrotter 475.31
globing 272.01
globoes 455.26
globule 057.27
globules 183.35
glommen 198.29
glomsk 089.33
gloom 411.27 473.20 600.31
Gloom 342.06
gloomerie 493.36
glooming 158.09 226.04 226.06
gloompourers 112.24
gloomy 549.11
glooves 434.06
Glor 439.16
gloria 213.31 611.23
Gloria 228.20
gloriam 418.04

gloria's 454.29
gloriaspanquost 388.28
glories 313.28
glorietta's 553.15
glorification 438.14
glorifires 304.22
glorioles 119.15
glorious 452.18 527.36 577.02
Glorious 411.20
gloriously 461.36
glorisol 108.27
glory 025.07 068.23 099.01 235.06 243.26 281.22 304.30 309.06 329.16 439.16 444.32 473.01 526.22 543.15 552.26 627.24
Glory 130.10 307.22
gloryaims 282.06
glos 230.33
gloss 146.16 183.36 334.32 390.18
glossary 324.21
glossery 083.11
glosses 304.F3
glossing 050.29
glottal 171.10
glottide 165.02
glouch 252.21
glouglou 345.19
glovars' 540.31
glove 333.04 586.06
gloved 607.05
glover's 567.08
gloves 024.32 253.16 412.34 469.32
gloving 144.28
glow 052.21 130.22 182.05 215.02 329.14 334.05 421.22 427.15 428.13 472.26 594.26
glowing 079.28
glowrings 338.28
glowru 327.17
glowry 372.29
glows 204.25 231.20
glows 344.11
glowstop 144.01
glowworld's 318.14
glowworm 099.01
glozery 339.24
gluckglucky 360.09
gluckspeels 569.04
glue 135.33 234.17 412.05 531.14 596.21
Glue 375.03
gluecose 537.13
glueglue 537.13
gluepot 329.08
glues 097.20
Glues 030.06
Glugg 220.10 220.14 223.05 224.09 224.16 225.29 225.29
GLUGG 219.22
Glugger 222.25 240.03
Glugg's 226.20
glume 613.17
glumsome 301.14
glunn 340.10
glut 399.12
glutany 370.36
glutinously 416.24
gluttened 358.10
Glutton 007.06
gluttony 406.33
Glwlwd 482.13
glycering 236.02
glycorawman 242.13
glypse 122.01
Gmax 342.02
gmere 243.05
gmountains 243.05
G.M.P.'s 603.12 (P.M.G. and Get My Price)
gnaas 344.29
Gnaccus 159.28
gnarld 345.30
gnarlybird 010.32 010.34
gnasty 556.29
gnat 140.02
gnatives 274.F2
gnatsching 222.27
gnaw 143.34
gnawstick 170.11
gnawthing 231.22
gneesgnobs 274.F2
gneiss 556.28
gnewgnawns 605.01
gnid 607.18
Gnig 607.18
gnir 319.07
gnit 416.15
Gnoccovitch 159.28
gnockmeggs 333.33
gnome 533.22
gnomeosulphidosalamermauderman 596.14
gnomes 243.05 552.10
gnosegates 612.24
gnoses 157.25
gnose's 182.04
GNOSIS 262.R2
gnot 060.10 140.02
gnows 274.F2
Gnug 607.18
gnwrng 349.27 (gone wrong)
go 011.19 027.21 038.24 040.31 041.12 045.20 047.02 058.30 063.09 073.08 075.20 080.32 082.09 083.09 083.13 096.15 098.31 099.21 110.18 114.04 117.25 125.18 132.08 136.07 140.18 141.05 145.03 146.36 148.28 152.20 159.19 159.31 160.16 163.33 169.24 193.10 193.15 196.07 198.12 198.20 200.17 203.02 204.27 204.27 204.27 206.26 213.18 219.24 221.16 223.35 225.04 226.09 226.21 233.08 237.02 239.26 240.24 244.02 245.17 247.09 249.01 251.26 252.29 252.30 256.11 260.F1 262.F7 262.F7 276.F3 280.10 281.F4 293.09 296.08 297.04 314.15 322.25 327.07 334.22 337.12 347.18 350.27 354.31 359.29 366.08 368.07 381.24 381.30 384.13 390.29 391.27 394.11 411.07 424.03 425.18 437.15 438.05 442.23 444.08 452.15 455.16 462.04 467.04 473.04 474.13 481.32 482.10 485.14 495.06 496.19 508.27 512.15 515.32 520.09 526.21 527.05 528.07 566.07 566.14 570.26 571.30 576.11 585.12 585.12 585.32 598.21 615.12 618.21 620.10 621.18 622.20 623.12 625.15 626.21 627.14 628.01
go 270.L1 418.26 418.31
Go 200.15 229.07 231.29 232.18 252.04 258.07 258.14 274.F1 313.04 411.06 424.11 435.27 441.08 515.36
Go 071.28
goad 379.19 445.02 450.30
Goad 305.05
goal 396.02 435.18 576.21
Goal 233.04 374.21
Goalball 083.27
goalbind 093.18
goaldkeeper 129.31
goaling 147.15 602.11
Goals 175.05
goan 008.09 010.22
goaneggbetter 298.03
goang 340.33
goat 054.23 069.18 087.26 094.29 136.19 156.22 319.29 330.28 347.15 373.14 413.28 463.15 580.12
Goat 009.27 275.16 330.01 579.12
goatfathers 585.14
goatheye 344.05
goats 048.02 380.32 412.28
goat's 025.08 089.21 132.13 520.12
goatsbeard 464.12
goatservant 097.34
goatsman 370.01
Goatstown's 015.01
goatswhey 558.02
goattanned 441.33
goatweigh 372.13
gob 191.07 312.29
Gob 034.10 095.13 530.25
gobbenses 504.29
gobbet 278.01
gobbit 061.19
Gobblasst 071.18
gobble 310.34 453.04
Gobble 308.01 501.09
gobbless 087.03
gobblydumped 118.22
gobbos 319.20
gobed 441.29
go-be-dee 437.07
gobelimned 357.29
gobelins 552.13
gobleege 277.12
goblin 301.27
goblins 183.22
Goborro 095.18
gobrawl 338.03
gobs 453.07
gobstick 242.09
Gobugga 095.18
goby 436.29 535.27
goche 251.26
god 024.17 083.35 123.01 131.17 188.18 237.28 253.33 285.29 325.28 327.17 355.27 451.11 497.07
God 027.24 057.09 091.07 122.16 122.17 138.28 146.04 246.06 380.23 384.12 385.31 387.31 390.19 393.05 398.07 404.34 486.10 487.26 499.15 499.16 526.16 604.27

<u>God</u> 231.05
<u>Godamedy</u> 503.17
<u>Godardi</u> 185.21
Godavari 213.20
Godd 254.28 578.03
goddam 111.03
Godde 560.15
godden 593.07
goddess 237.29 366.12
goddesses 025.20 508.31
goddestfar 476.04
goddinpotty 059.12
gode 076.10 076.11
Godeown 313.05
godfather 266.F2 313.09 431.18
godforgiven 490.24
Godforsaken 183.18
Godfrey 550.02
Godhelic 091.35
godhsbattaring 326.16
godinats 347.06
godkin 079.20 446.05
godliness 141.17
godmothers' 183.28
Godnotch 534.01
godolphing 300.28
Godolphing 555.20
godolphinglad 563.26
godoms 361.23
godown 456.05 565.21
godrolling 449.35
gods 058.18 162.35 179.10 188.15 221.36 365.01 382.15 427.29 551.08
God's 037.07 316.26 429.03
godsend 269.17
godsends 478.05
<u>Godsoilman</u> 071.14
godsons' 476.04
godsun 117.04
godthaab 312.19
Goeasyosey 584.11
goed 256.16
goeligum 296.F3
Goerz 577.22
goes 011.08 011.18 011.18 039.02 065.18 085.15 118.18 135.04 139.09 162.22 196.13 226.34 232.15 245.17 254.12 268.F2 269.22 269.F2 275.F2 304.31 320.05 332.22 352.10 369.31 379.33 419.14 419.28 433.20 441.01 445.01 452.21 453.15 465.23 469.23 488.14 540.14 583.12 618.18 620.32 627.14
<u>goes</u> 341.05 345.12
<u>Goes</u> 359.26 546.33
<u>Goes</u> 072.09
goesbelly 270.F2
goest 347.03
goff 334.18 375.17
goflooded 126.24
G.O.G. 025.23 (game old Gunne)
gogemble 343.03
gogetter 451.04
goggle 206.14
gogoing 292.29
gogor's 102.08
Gog's 073.06
goh 361.07
goharksome 080.26
goheerd 538.29
gohellt 077.27
goholden 234.36
goin 371.26
going 005.10 005.12 026.25 054.16 055.05 062.27 066.03 087.06 096.09 117.08 125.09 146.32 148.15 207.31 215.07 223.25 224.29 226.09 236.07 245.15 254.34 257.03 276.22 293.F2 301.F5 333.09 333.12 336.23 365.15 367.25 374.30 380.30 386.27 395.22 397.28 410.07 438.06 448.31 452.26 460.31 461.15 468.01 469.05 473.14 487.19 507.09 507.18 517.24 529.36 555.16 566.30 578.29 583.06 598.24 600.25 613.32 625.09
<u>going</u> 340.28 345.06 346.33 383.14 390.25
Going 589.15
<u>Going</u> 177.29
goingaways 028.23
goings 096.08 595.16 599.29
Golazy 360.07
gold 027.13 189.24 206.36 438.31 460.19 477.26 483.09 486.24 527.23 538.13 563.17 564.05 605.10
<u>gold</u> 164.20 398.34
<u>Gold</u> 493.27
Goldarskield 567.19
goldcapped 448.14
golddawn 099.01
golded 148.08
golden 020.30 112.18 193.11 203.06 214.31 263.F3 336.21 360.24 395.34 412.21 428.18 433.32 450.01 461.17 542.24 561.19 562.05 567.23 589.08 612.02
<u>golden</u> 342.27
<u>Golden</u> 521.05
<u>Golden</u> 104.09 105.05
goldenest 234.10
goldeny 211.34
goldfashioned 276.F2
goldies 384.31
goldrush 366.11
Goldselforelump 613.01
goldtin 008.18
goldways 595.14
goldwhite 569.19
<u>Goldy</u> 071.11
goldylocks 615.23
golf 357.31
golfchild's 167.08
Golfe 312.09
Golforgilhisjurylegs 060.11
goliar's 008.20
Goliath 491.01
golliwog 430.23
<u>Gollovar's</u> 294.18
golls 240.13
<u>Goll's</u> 354.13
golly 083.27
gololy 089.35
goloshes 008.20
golten 225.16
Gomagh 054.19
gombolier 317.15
gomeet 259.06
gomenon 116.33
Gomez 545.32
gommas 374.10
Gomorrha 579.23
gon 068.27 141.06 546.32
<u>Gonder</u> 104.23
gone 028.17 050.34 065.12 069.31 075.06 096.16 104.05 119.01 129.11 154.15 159.10 159.11 172.24 187.04 187.26 213.14 213.31 215.32 226.07 236.27 250.28 254.34 280.06 291.15 295.05 306.F2 316.16 347.21 359.25 369.02 376.17 380.36 396.32 398.22 416.32 449.25 467.01 474.23 481.25 508.16 526.26 527.08 528.32 535.27 540.30 549.09 555.06 558.24 595.26 598.09 602.29 613.08 614.19 623.28
<u>gone</u> 104.18 399.22
<u>Gone</u> 095.06 130.10 220.24 420.19 472.14
gonemost 066.32
goney 306.F2
Goney 306.F2
gong 244.25 441.01 446.11
gonging 607.07
<u>gongos</u> 345.20
<u>goning</u> 598.09
gonk 181.22
gonlannludder 370.28
gonn 009.08
Gonn 072.25 257.34
<u>gonna</u> 292.12
<u>Gonna</u> 271.18
Gonne 398.06
gonning 508.28
gonorrhal 349.02
gonz 245.02
goo 230.19
<u>Goo</u> 102.33
gooandfrighthisdualman 442.27
goobes 603.25
goochlipped 609.04
good 016.31 020.35 024.16 028.04 032.15 032.24 034.13 037.02 041.02 043.14 047.06 054.24 065.08 069.13 075.12 075.13 079.35 083.09 086.25 091.21 091.23 097.11 108.10 116.14 117.05 119.01 129.29 140.22 142.22 152.22 154.20 162.01 162.36 163.34 174.11 174.16 189.29 193.22 197.20 208.30 209.15 211.19 221.21 222.06 223.36 226.07 235.14 238.26 241.17 251.22 255.32 274.28 276.17 279.F32 279.F34 281.F2 298.F1 299.20 306.F3 311.35 313.20 313.24 315.26 315.27 316.11 316.11 317.11 324.19 324.24 327.31 328.08 329.06 338.24 347.10 351.24 356.26 358.15 364.02 366.30 368.02 371.36 376.22 377.36 378.34 380.18 380.30 385.02 390.29 393.05 394.15 397.35 404.23 405.17 406.36 409.09 409.12 411.13 417.04 419.11 428.23 429.05 431.20 433.12 436.19 440.04 440.20 441.07 443.12 443.32 445.11 445.21 448.01 448.20 448.27

450.30 453.20 455.32 455.36 456.09 456.13 458.24 460.05 465.26 466.16 469.12 471.25 471.35 476.29 477.16 478.01 479.15 480.06 483.24 490.29 490.32 494.33 495.08 498.18 501.15 508.16 510.08 515.13 516.10 523.04 524.11 528.05 532.10 539.13 539.31 540.27 540.35 551.15 555.05 557.25 566.04 567.03 568.10 574.25 574.26 575.06 598.11 603.32 607.04 612.17 613.31 615.17 617.01 618.05 618.15 619.01 619.33 620.20 622.01 622.11
good 278.L4 345.23 398.34 399.21
Good 059.31 083.19 153.35 193.06 213.29 240.17 278.F1 312.19 315.21 316.11 375.21 409.15 472.10 509.04 595.21 613.01 616.10 617.17
Good 071.18 105.28
Goodbark 382.28
Goodbeg 262.F7
goodbett 595.07
Goodboy 453.16
goodboy's 471.32
goodbroomirish 600.33
goodbuy 077.29 537.23
goodbye 382.29 454.04 500.22
Goodbye 409.11 454.03
goodbyte 073.16
goodcheap 406.36
goodda 224.02
gooden 025.05 113.03 326.17
gooder 326.17 625.35
goodess 242.09
goodfilips 463.36
goodfor 209.17
goodfornobody 292.14
Goodfox 360.11
goodiest 622.10
goodishsized 111.08
goodless 460.06
goodlooker 191.25
goodly 004.30
goodman 014.11 492.01 515.02
Goodman 035.30
Good-man 511.09
goodmantrue 403.22
goodmen 557.13
Goodmens 621.35
Goodmen's 545.10
goodmiss 237.07
goodmorrow 568.24
goodmother 149.23
goodness 118.10 169.06 245.27 256.01 424.16 427.24 537.02 561.18 607.34
goodnight's 041.14
goodrid 262.F3
goodridhirring 007.19
goods 011.19 107.16 171.36 174.13 230.14 455.12 547.04 548.20 573.33 590.01
good's 480.02
goodself 140.34
goodsend 327.02
goodsforetombed 586.30
goodsforseeking 346.31
goodship 428.19
Goodspeed 600.14
goodwalldabout 539.25
goodwill 184.05 430.19
goody 014.04 240.21 256.18 332.01
Goof 234.33
Googlaa 265.F4
googlie 584.09
googling 231.12 620.22
googoo 557.07
googoos 472.02
googs 381.06 405.34
goold 602.11
Goold 390.35
goolden 619.24 619.29 619.30
Goonness's 414.12
goose 123.29 322.35 626.14
goosebellies 142.02
gooseberry 544.17
goosebosom 170.35
goosegaze 548.03
goosegreasing 399.23
goosemother 242.25 449.36
gooses 389.31
goosey's 287.02
goosling 233.12
Goosna 533.19
goosseys 227.25
goosth 557.07
goosybone 425.01
goot 155.19
Gootch 197.01
gooth 394.27
gopeep 624.09
Gophar 325.26
Gopheph 125.17
goragorridgorballyed 323.16
gorban 031.12
Gorbotipacco 069.36
Gordon 392.34
gordons 438.36
gore 128.22 178.10 500.07
gored 599.26
Gores 348.21
Gorey 246.04
gorge 073.21 151.29 180.24 341.02
gorgeous 179.31 181.09 385.36 562.29
gorger 191.08
gorger's 406.07
gorgers' 324.31
gorges 541.34
gorgeups 011.15
gorggony 102.07
gorgios 003.08
gorgiose 458.25
gorgon 137.34
Gorham 277.F4
Gorias 219.11
gorky 132.35
Gormagareen 376.18
Gorman 349.24
gormandising 407.01
Gormleyson 348.18
Gorotsky 294.18
gorse 208.08 330.28 450.30
gorsecone 403.08
gorsecopper's 338.35
gorsedd 361.23
gorsegrowth 128.20
Gort 053.30
gortan 602.18
Gorteen 379.28
Gortigern 565.12
gory 181.08 333.31
Gory 305.F3
Gosem 278.F1
gosh 352.35
Gosh 070.02
goslingnecked 152.09
gospeds 343.32
gospellers 112.06
gospelly 552.27
gospfather 325.18
Gospolis 345.02
gossan 253.23
gossans 271.18
gosse 325.16
gossip 118.19 125.18 316.12 450.33
gossipaceous 195.04
gossiple 038.23
gossipocracy 476.04
gossips 594.26
gosson 377.25
gossoon 300.04
Gosterstown 390.03
got 052.21 055.32 061.12 065.18 069.20 080.32 084.01 096.02 108.18 110.03 132.20 143.22 143.23 144.02 146.15 148.09 156.17 159.01 162.07 166.04 178.08 179.01 181.32 184.12 188.29 193.14 205.05 226.20 231.03 233.01 242.08 248.10 257.10 263.08 273.F6 275.06 275.08 278.02 296.22 317.09 344.21 352.10 362.11 365.02 376.02 377.35 393.13 398.08 422.25 436.35 460.01 494.03 494.16 505.24 516.05 527.31 541.08 541.19 579.27 582.16 590.11 613.31 618.08 626.32
got 383.02
Got 463.15
Got 106.15
Gota 198.13
gotafit 339.04
Gotahelv 262.F1
Gotellus 527.01
Goteshoppard 276.12
goth 332.10
Gothabobus 352.11
gothakrauts 550.11
Gothamm 538.33
gotheny 394.27
Gothewishegoths 148.20
Gothgorod 565.21
Gothius 568.08
goths 415.27
Goth's 251.02
gothsprogue 053.27
gotliness 378.04
Gotopoxy 386.31
gots 487.17
gotsquantity 114.25
gott 326.17
gottalike 551.29
gotten 232.33 281.24
Gottgab 490.08
gotye 501.09
gougerotty 498.17
Gough 211.25 271.29
gougouzoug 438.08
goulache 165.14

gould 140.15 327.28
goulewed 531.14
goumeral's 369.34
goupons 170.35
gourd 373.20
gourds 171.19
gourgling 088.31
gourmand 235.29
gourmeteering 407.02
gouspils 480.33
gout 069.25 412.31 530.11
Gout 229.03
Goute 596.36
gouttelette 194.07
gouty 143.05 211.25 389.23
Gouty 539.06
Gouty 071.26
gouvernament 301.20
Gouverneur 375.23
Gov 258.28
govalise 345.11
government 178.26 210.20
gow 346.21 599.06
Gow 356.03
Gowan 398.05
Gowans 624.08
gowgow 552.11
gown 034.20 146.11 200.02 559.10
Gown 071.36
gowndabout 057.25
goy 273.14
goyls 182.22
goyt 199.22
G.P.O. 256.29 (General Post Office)
graab 018.13
graatched 541.17
Grab 464.31
Grab 072.01
Grabar 113.03
Grabashag 492.11
grabbed 528.29
graben 545.34
grabs 137.10
Grabstone 221.34
Gracchus 614.01
grace 021.20 021.20 083.23 115.20 119.20 141.02 186.35 201.32 213.21 240.32 312.27 318.01 335.31 366.21 377.30 384.09 384.16 391.22 393.15 395.21 395.21 395.24 408.36 424.14 428.16 465.17 550.35 561.17 577.15 584.11 603.01
Grace 007.06 025.36 329.30 387.25
Grace 071.19
gracecup 561.14
graced 365.15 427.29 597.09
graceful 273.F6
Gracefully 146.30
Gracehoper 414.21 414.22 416.08 417.03 417.22 417.33
Gracehoper 418.11 418.12
gracehoppers 257.05
graceless 460.06
gracer 512.28
Graces 440.12
Graces 105.27 419.06
gracc's 568.25
Grace's 289.21 570.06
gracesold 337.01
gracest 387.34
Gracest 607.34
gracewindow'd 291.09
Gracias 364.25
graciast 623.11
gracies 095.04 242.09 273.19 356.07
gracious 069.28 089.11 118.10 144.26 224.34 252.20 424.15 429.11
graciously 236.03 258.26 406.26
Gracius 361.12
grackles 142.01
gradationes 611.17
grade 446.36
graded 161.06
gradual 165.26
gradually 084.30 124.04 441.27 599.10
grafe 353.10
grafficking 300.25
grafted 221.31 546.18
Grafton's 198.32
gragh 317.36
Gragious 353.03
Grahot 140.04
grain 184.05 311.36 550.06
grain 338.36
grained 339.28
grainpopaw 587.32
grains 207.01 415.06 508.04
grainwaster 203.03
graith 113.01
grakeshoots 366.20
grame 457.09
gramercy 534.13
graminivorous 128.07
graminopalmular 613.18
gramma 268.24
Grammaires 256.20
grammar 268.17
grammarians 026.22
gramma's 268.17
Gramm's 378.28
Grampupus 007.08
grampurpoise 362.08
grampus 198.29
gran 197.31
Gran 132.29 257.04
Granby 569.36
grand 008.18 012.13 013.15 013.21 013.32 030.13 055.36 078.06 111.14 121.32 132.27 176.20 230.27 242.18 249.03 281.F1 294.12 347.17 352.11 352.24 367.03 375.23 380.35 390.11 394.25 405.15 442.34 452.26 454.09 468.29 472.30 497.27 504.15 519.19 519.26 551.23 557.27 577.08 590.09 617.26 618.16 618.20
Grand 008.29 037.20 038.05 137.36 140.04 294.F3 506.05 607.35 610.35 624.27
Grand 399.23
Grandbeyond 570.01
granddaucher 498.14
Grande 207.12 232.36
grandegaffe 268.12
Grander 309.09
grandest 329.35 388.28 389.06 389.09
grandeur 197.04
grandfallar 029.07
Grandfarthring 202.02
grandfer 027.03
Grandicellies 250.12
grandiose 412.01
grandma 580.20
Grandmère 256.20
grandmother 167.32 253.02 253.02 253.03 545.09
grandmother's 253.03 479.01
grandmothers' 183.27
grandnational 448.14
grandoper 343.23
grandpassia 527.07
grandsire 510.29
grandson 053.33 252.36
grandson's 252.36 252.36 252.36
grandsourd 464.13
grandsumer 152.21
grandthinked 343.25
grandy 113.03
grandydad's 439.13
graneen 375.29
granfather's 070.28
Grangegorman 236.24
Grania 306.28
granite 061.14
granite 209.09
Granjook 329.29
grannewwail 022.12
grannom 450.04
granny 146.29
Granny 105.03
grannyamother 299.10
grannyma 195.04
Granny-stream-Auborne 495.18
grant 078.28 213.21 361.30 463.13 566.32
Grant 259.04 301.F5 336.21
granted 298.09 515.14
granting 078.25
granvilled 553.26
granyou 292.01
grapbed 457.28
grapce 432.35
grapcias 568.11
grape 117.23 249.09
Grape 497.28
grapefruice 171.18
grapejuice 261.F3
grapeling 456.15
grapes 072.28 212.16
graph 107.08
graphplot 284.07
grappa 268.26
grappes 360.25
grapple 151.31
graps 561.26
grasp 004.31 136.04
grasped 121.30
grasping 128.33
graspis 405.26
Grasps 579.13
grass 019.12 028.03 111.32 134.31 165.29 190.29 223.22 366.22 380.26 491.27 516.01 516.01 557.19 588.09 597.34 604.28 615.29 628.12
grassbelonghead 611.33
grasscircle 132.13
grasses 014.34
grassgross 556.25
grasshoop 197.27

Grasshopper 307.16
grassies 024.10 360.30
grasswinter's 209.05
grassy 142.13
Grassy 252.13
grassyass 174.15
Grasyaplaina 158.19
grate 559.02 586.05
grateful 220.09
gratefully 181.28 459.17 582.07
graters 199.21 332.29
grates 421.23
gratias 174.12 584.35
gratiasagam 093.15
gratification 142.22 409.26
gratifications 593.16
gratifying 398.13
gratiis 415.20
Gratings 288.19
gratitude 116.10
Grattan 202.17
grattaned 580.32
gratuitouses 496.06
graundplotting 624.12
graunt 513.28
graunted 605.07
Graunya 068.10
Graunya's 058.11
Graussssss 417.01 417.02
grauws 506.13
grave 020.29 076.21 078.19 117.03 124.09 133.13 134.21 198.33 240.04 243.30 283.18 463.20 503.27 548.06
Grave 134.07
gravedigger 189.28
gravedigging 121.32
gravel 024.36
graveleek 568.27
graveller 202.24
gravemure 013.10
graven 429.13
graver 034.15
graves 352.31
Gravesend 434.34
gravesobbers 364.23
gravespoil 102.21
gravest 375.26
gravetrench 572.05
gravies 097.20
gravitates 151.28 418.01
gravitational 100.32
gravstone 146.34
gravy 224.06 406.06
gravydock 329.08
Gravys 030.07
Graw 200.20 488.36
grawndest 503.33
gray 031.29 371.07
Gray 228.13
graycloak 567.18
graye 322.14
grayling 197.36
Grays 609.10
graze 339.27
graze 176.17
grazeheifer 614.01
grazing 064.06 089.19
grazious 186.31
greace 161.16
greak 343.17
Greaney 212.10
Greanteavvents 603.28
greas 464.29
grease 190.08 214.18
Grease 071.13
greased 395.35 520.10
greasefulness 136.09 136.10
greaseshaper 339.36
greaseways 140.20
greasilygristly 170.34
Greasouwea 552.02
greasy 204.30
great 003.18 020.08 025.25 032.12 033.23 034.13 035.09 039.10 049.25 053.20 079.09 094.34 097.24 108.08 108.20 122.28 135.21 152.21 160.35 172.09 173.21 182.25 194.23 198.33 203.02 206.01 214.11 229.20 241.10 242.03 252.25 253.26 277.13 278.F7 313.30 347.16 348.24 367.36 377.36 378.14 385.27 389.12 398.25 404.23 405.22 434.11 435.31 437.16 441.26 469.04 472.19 497.07 525.31 540.28 543.02 543.02 545.16 549.01 552.15 568.34 577.07 582.34 587.33 594.22 599.11 599.33 617.05 618.26 619.31 621.20 622.18 625.10 626.24 627.09 627.23
great 340.30 349.24
Great 025.27 036.27 055.01 211.29 237.34 245.27 258.17 293.14 295.04 306.16 415.17 431.26 456.33 514.34 529.35 594.27 607.04 612.27 612.18
Great 106.09 244.35
greataunt 031.16
greatbritish 403.23
Greatchrist 569.15
greater 034.05 036.07 252.25 269.24 298.13 318.08
greater 354.04
Greates 343.21
greatest 035.08 109.05 228.29 417.25 527.14 543.02 587.33 616.07
Greatest 612.28
greatgrand 191.34
greatgrandgosterfosters 368.04
greatgrandhotelled 017.33
greatly 090.04 292.04 348.14 352.04 380.15 470.01
greatmess 237.07
greats 310.34 502.22 507.09 546.02 567.08
greatsire 068.11
Greatwheel 058.03
Grecian 561.18
gred 407.12
greeces 267.04
greed 412.29
greediguss 362.16
greeding 377.01
greedings 308.17
greedly 037.03
Greedo 411.21
greedy 627.19
greedypuss 445.23
greeft 241.31
greek 043.13 604.12
Greek 120.19 235.17 390.18 419.20 509.19
greekenhearted 171.01
Greeks 409.19
greem 143.25
green 003.23 031.04 034.27 043.29 047.16 047.17 055.26 055.26 058.07 064.36 074.09 087.14 131.21 162.32 167.11 180.09 193.10 194.35 234.09 317.36 335.32 364.08 388.35 395.07 403.11 406.19 407.11 434.07 441.04 466.35 480.08 491.27 517.09 534.28 549.26 571.16 575.26 589.02 600.20 620.02
green 344.11
Green 015.08 045.09 057.35 070.17 174.27 292.10 386.26 507.04
Green 106.35
greenafang 563.31
greenawn 068.06
greendgold 289.06
greendy 360.30
greene 094.01
Greene 277.F4 533.19
greeneriN 226.31
Greene's 381.13
greenest 447.27
greeneyed 088.15 249.03
greengageflavoured 556.15
greengeese 446.19
greengoaters 522.16
greengrocer 437.17
greengrown 407.13
greenhouse 362.34 377.05
greenily 532.23
greenish 008.02
Greenislender 378.11
Greenland's 199.18
Greenman's 074.02
greenmould 582.10
greenridinghued 411.24
greensleeves 161.30
greenwished 553.20
greenwood's 450.33
greeping 467.10
greepsing 158.08 158.08
greese 549.02
greesed 206.32
greesiously 379.29
greet 037.08 177.35 245.07 444.20 550.06
Greet 409.15 603.22
greeted 097.35
greeter 324.21
greethims 535.11
greeting 186.31 241.11
greetings 567.08
Greets 254.28 598.10
Greevy 375.03
greeze 278.F1
Greg 397.02 397.02
gregarious 099.21
gregary 156.21
gregational 167.16
gregorian 605.30
Gregorio 533.21
Gregorius 573.08 573.28
gregoromaios 553.16
Gregorovitch 368.33
Gregory 214.34 384.07 384.10 386.13 397.05 398.02 405.04 475.24 476.25
gregos 551.31

grekish 564.09
gren 596.21
Grenadiers 526.11
grenadier's 192.15
grenadines 060.24
grenadite 349.13
grene 267.13
grenoulls 449.33
greppies 450.05
gresk 155.27
Greste 344.27
gretched 538.24
Gretecloke 553.14
gretnass 094.01
Grettna 212.10
grevey 041.23
grew 130.27 133.25 191.09 271.28 367.02 392.17 406.29 541.08 555.17
Grex's 170.34
grey 008.23 170.17 278.10 329.28 387.03 388.21 423.21 424.29 441.04 461.05 479.02 536.32 580.21 594.25
grey 399.09
Grey 376.27
greybeard 086.18
greybounding 190.31
greyed 241.09 578.04
Greyglens 602.15
greyleg 478.35
greyne 503.23
greys 344.11
greysfriaryfamily 611.09
greyt 601.05
greytcloak 016.34
Gri 158.17
grianblachk 503.23
gribes 331.17
gribgrobgrab 332.15
grice 158.17
gricks 620.30
Gricks 011.35
grid 406.05
grida 058.09
griddle 012.35 455.33
Griddle-the-Sink 531.21
grief 056.16 180.21 358.15 366.36 413.22 426.06 452.14 453.27 457.35 472.15 589.07
griefer 269.25
Griefotrofio 169.23
griefs 207.03
griesouper 393.12
grievance 024.28
grievances 220.27
grieve 223.36 439.34
grieved 014.07 482.35
grievingfrue 370.04
griffeen 450.14
Griffith's 041.34
grig 139.19 279.F14
grigs 113.02
grill 436.09 522.01
grilled 060.17 087.01 456.16
grillies 416.29
grilsy 016.35
grim 134.06 176.24 278.F1 292.03 580.20
grimacing 055.35
grimaldism 055.35
Grimbarb 480.24
grime 179.25 243.09
Grimes 370.20
grimm 335.05 335.05 414.17
grimmacticals 388.31
grimmed 330.06
Grimmest 009.02
Grimmfather 206.02
Grimshaw 132.10
Grimstad 602.35
grin 012.06 567.26 580.20
Grin 252.07
grind 203.05
grinden 579.08
grinder 353.23
grinders 408.03
grinding 208.23
Grindings 290.28
grindstone 141.15
gringrin 272.30
Gringrin 272.30
grinner 301.14 443.26
grinner 348.33
grinning 171.28 272.25
grinny 007.09
Grinwicker 517.25
grip 047.15 523.29 584.17
gripe 523.29
griper 301.26
gripes 072.20 231.36 465.35
Gripes 152.15 153.11 153.21 153.36 154.06 154.14 154.32 155.10 155.13 156.19 156.21 156.31 157.21 158.04 158.13 158.35 159.01 159.02
Gripes's 155.32
gripins 193.08
Gripos 156.10
griposly 234.02
grippe 231.36 548.08
gripped 396.29
grippes 581.31
gripping 392.29
Grippiths' 619.04
Grischun 220.19
grisly 115.21 577.17
grisning 353.22
grist 314.19
Gristle 040.34
grit 083.28 327.09
grits 270.F2
grizzild 410.09
grizzlies 516.13
grizzliest 340.21
grl 302.25 (girl)
groan 296.11 345.14 499.28
groaned 019.32
groaner 611.09
groaning 453.13
groanmothers 585.14
groans 239.32
Groans 104.14
groany 137.04
Groany 291.24
groat 170.03 589.13
groatsupper 360.36
grobbling 356.05
grobsmid 357.01
grocer 139.34
grocerest 619.04
groceries 507.09
Groceries 254.28
grocer's 227.03
grocery 411.16
Grocery 387.34
Groenmund's 469.16
grog 428.19
Grog 449.05
Grog 032.23
grognt 177.17
grogory 154.21
grogram 399.09
Grogram 609.10
groin 319.18
groinscrubbers 550.19
grommelants 130.02
gromwelled 116.32
gronde 332.20
grondt 418.12
groogy 492.11
groom 096.16 224.31 377.05 514.27
——groom 189.27 (bridegroom)
groomed 523.16
grooming 391.09
grooms 067.01
groont 365.06
grooser's 268.11
groot 013.33 317.30
groot 102.33
grootvatter 361.21
groove 206.32
Groove 559.01
grooves 371.16
groovy 329.09
grope 107.21 312.31
groped 182.35 414.34
gropes 418.32
gropesarching 167.12
grose 158.07
grosning 353.22
gross 007.07 407.06 431.28 559.25
Gross 417.11
Gross 342.14
grossed 132.25
grossery 367.02
grosses 567.09
grossgrown 478.14
Grossguy 598.33
grosskopp 078.05
grosskropper 331.16
grossly 082.32 111.36 426.13
grossman's 565.22
grossopper's 268.12
grossscruple 541.08
Grot 345.08
grotesquely 111.29
grouching 008.22
groun 500.01
ground 056.10 077.11 084.19 087.20 119.02 202.33 263.05 293.15 300.10 319.36 330.11 334.11 335.11 366.18 392.21 404.07 415.23 452.13 585.23
ground 341.22
Ground 071.34
groundloftfan 262.22
groundould 072.34
grounds 577.29
groundsapper 338.18
groundwet 076.18
grouns 477.35
group 546.13
Group 312.31 359.21
Groupname 261.F3
groupography 476.33
Groups 365.20

groupsuppers 147.16
grouptriad 167.04
Grouscious 415.25
grouse 112.24
Grouseus 449.27
grousuppers 087.23
grove 354.26
groves 364.09 472.07
groves 271.L4
grow 019.01 031.24 069.19 247.27 272.03 293.10 318.14 341.13 406.29 416.01 427.23 428.26 467.21 472.04
Grow 104.23
growed 556.02
growing 029.27 125.12 179.21 213.13 375.17 404.15 429.11 504.22 594.26 604.28 626.35
Growler 071.20
Growley 197.07
growlsy 016.35
grown 051.20 117.08 124.24 265.F5 318.08 541.08 599.27
grownian 369.31
growning 223.32
grownup 261.F1 621.16
Grownup 221.02
grows 026.08 143.25 208.02 251.10 283.F2
growth 214.33 274.17
Grozarktic 339.21
gruarso 054.17
grub 416.14
grubbed 110.16 407.02
grubber 594.26
grubbiness 268.11
grube 056.35
grubs 306.09
grubstake 537.22
gruebleen 023.01
gruel 190.08 441.29
gruen 117.07
gruff 052.27
Gruff 271.17
grum 065.20 065.23
Grum 065.23
grumble 483.07
Grumbledum's 273.01
grumbling 272.26
Grumby 413.21
grumes 006.17
grummelung 057.14
grumpapar 065.12 065.19
grumus 072.33
grunder 353.23
Grundtsagar 423.18
Grunny 301.F5
grunt 296.11 580.20
Grunt 466.22
Grunt 071.31
grunted 078.29 116.32
gruntens 078.24
grunters' 170.35
grunts 581.26
Grusham 376.11
grusomehed's 229.36
Grwpp 482.13
gryffygryffygryffs 358.22
g. s. M. 230.21 (go to sleep Music)
gttrdmmrng 258.02 (Götterdämmerung)
Gu 287.12
guage 366.01
guaranteed 065.09
guard 008.07 055.19 063.18 220.06 246.13 380.23 552.13 576.16
Guard 356.34 441.18
Guardacosta 172.22
guardafew 570.35
guarded 237.05
guardian 042.29 224.24 224.32 514.26
guardiance 258.33
guardiant 187.02
guardient 538.24
guardin 324.07
guarding 066.20
guardroom 492.17
guards 135.03 258.30 258.33 318.26
Guards 058.25 340.24
Guardsman 210.08
Gubbernathor 525.15
Gubbs 558.15
GUBERNANT 306.R1
gubernier-gerenal 338.19
Gudd 551.02
Gudfodren 326.24
gudgeon 102.33
gudhe 356.18
Gudstruce 613.12
gudth 241.28
gué 332.18 332.18
guegerre 272.29
guelfing 504.29
guelflinks 567.36
guenesis 006.27
guenneses 004.24
guerdon 302.06
Guerdon 553.09
guerillaman 340.10
gueroligue 256.36
guess 089.03 200.09 286.28 287.08 313.23 562.33 562.34
Guess 442.19
guesse 137.10
guessed 177.34
guessing 233.11
guessmasque 603.03
guessp 624.17
guest 369.04 611.07
Guest 561.07
Guestermed 536.12
guestfriendly 076.04
guesthouse 054.27
guests 323.30 543.32
Guesturn's 470.13
guett 614.16
guey 570.28
guff 231.31 616.22
guffalawd 341.30
guffalled 149.04
guffaw 470.28
guffawably 079.18
guffer 229.19
gugglet 031.11
Guggy's 363.36
Guglielmus 553.14 573.24
Gugnir 221.09
Gugurtha 403.12 403.13
gui 360.26 360.27
guid 519.16 520.35
Guid 521.31
guidance 151.04 432.28 605.11
guiddus 621.08
guide 146.25 449.11 541.05 576.32
Guide 409.07
guidness 345.22
guidneys 464.36
Guido 260.12
guilbey 406.33
guild 446.34
Guild 077.23 310.14
guildered 208.09
guilders 037.05
guiles 240.31
guillotened 567.28
guillotine 211.26
guilphy 072.29
guilt 305.09 375.16 627.23
Guilteypig's 072.14
guiltfeather 355.12
Guiltless 034.34
guiltshouters 356.06
guilty 211.34 438.25 532.19 557.16
Guilty 363.20
Guimea 105.15
guimpes 204.29
guinea 182.25 452.32 589.13
guineagold 179.34
Guinea-Gooseberry's 342.15
guineagould 479.05
guineas 236.25
Guineas 106.30
guineases 361.05
guineese 071.04
guineeser 565.10
Guiness's 382.03
Guiney 482.19
Guineys 420.22
Guinn 044.12
Guinnass 549.34
guinness 009.18
Guinness 035.15 408.27 510.13
Guinness' 307.01
Guinnesses 099.03 309.01
Guinness's 190.17 299.30
Guinney's 090.13
Guinnghis 024.35
guised 357.08
gulch 254.17
guld 340.01
Guld 593.09
gulden 079.35
guldenselver 028.11
gulfed 171.19
gull 095.17 377.05 628.13
gullaby 462.15
gullaway 197.06
gullery 057.21
gullet 396.02 521.27
gulletburn 171.14
gullible's 173.03
gullies 582.18
gulling 354.31
gulls 462.36
Gulls 628.13
gulp 191.07 426.15 519.33 566.04
Gulp 468.27
gulpa 426.17
gulpable 396.23 406.33
gulped 102.33
gulpstroom 319.27
gulughurutty 493.13

gum 045.29 160.04 253.13
564.19 587.32
gumboil 231.13
gumboots 210.16
gummalicked 470.29
gummer 229.22
gummibacks 066.13
gummy 559.15
gumpower 410.25
gumptyum 208.27
gun 135.04 171.33 317.14
331.01 439.05 500.07
Gun 377.06 481.19
gunbarrel 444.15
Gund 596.15
Gundhur 351.32
Gundogs 096.36
gundy 316.33 368.02
gunerally 220.15
gunfree 387.35
Gunger 443.21
gunman 083.06
gunn 008.11 130.26
Gunnar 596.15
gunnard 177.18
Gunnar's 257.34
gunne 531.05 590.24 625.32
Gunne 025.22 044.12 271.17
Gunne 104.08
gunnell 379.10
gunner 497.17 588.11
Gunner 510.13
Gunne's 263.18
gunnfodder 242.10
Gunning 495.26
gunnings 567.11
Gunnings 596.15
gunnong 343.23
gunorrhal 192.03
gunpocket 035.27
gunpowdered 190.01
gunrun 136.20
guns 064.02 107.17 116.15
622.23
Guns 368.01 368.03 368.04
368.04 368.06
gun's 434.10
gunshop 338.24
Gunting 376.18
guntinued 067.16
gunwale 077.09 133.33
gunwielder 056.11
gup 529.14
guranium 349.09
gurdly 354.14
gurg 341.02
gurgle 039.26 206.17 206.17
378.25 406.12
gurgles 234.31
gurk 378.26
Gurk 365.25
gurragrunch 342.17
Gurragrunch 342.17
gurs 258.01
Gus 125.22 332.32 555.12
gush 093.11 095.02 097.30
180.23
Gush 087.17 251.19
gushed 080.34
gushes 627.19
gushgasps 568.07
gushious 394.35
gushy 234.33
gusset 320.14
gussies 231.03
gust 234.33 321.31 552.18
gustoms 534.02
Gustsofairy 621.06
gustspells 257.34
Gusty 305.F3
gut 339.04 344.28 524.26
Gut 017.16
Gutenmorg 020.07
Gutmann 328.26
gutmurdherers 617.18
guts 378.12 495.05
gutter 166.15 199.03
gutterful 394.21
guttergloomering 565.02
gutterhowls 116.29
gutterish 518.25
gutthroat 091.11
guttural 365.07
guvnor 531.29
guy 016.05 205.28 273.13
388.02 499.24
Guy 177.29
Guygas 494.23
Guy's 545.31
G. V. 210.23 (G. V. Brooke)
Gwds 258.01
gweatness 061.07
gwen 406.11
gwendolenes 609.04
Gwenn 433.06
gwistel 406.11
Gwyfyn 418.27
gyant 018.11
Gyant 069.06
gygantogyres 596.23
Gygas 036.13
Gygasta 099.09
gym 437.02
gymnufleshed 271.F4
gynecollege 389.09
gynecure 014.25
gypseyeyed 444.16
gypsing 586.34
gypsyjuliennes 553.17
gyre 295.24
Gyre 295.23
gyribouts 298.16
gyrographically 292.28
gyrogyrorondo 239.27
gyrotundo 295.24

h 257.34
H 284.F4 (H for Lona the
Konkubine)
492.18 (H and J. C. S.)
H. 386.26 (James H. Tickell)
ha 023.25 044.17 121.26
160.09 378.34 378.36 485.28
608.13
Ha 092.03 092.05 092.05
144.34 212.36 212.36 244.18
259.09 335.04 335.23 378.36
471.04 559.22 607.23 608.13
Haar 536.34
haard 332.20
haardly 051.14
haares 317.34
Haarington's 447.09
hab 200.32
habakuk 116.32
habasund 494.35
habben 075.11
Habberdasherisher 176.11
habby 285.01
habe 538.29
habenny 041.20
Haberdasher 051.14
Habes 113.29 113.30
habiliments 052.16 546.06
habit 039.31 057.25 114.36
435.33 483.32 533.30 614.08
habitacularly 004.31
habitand 483.26
Habitant 604.25
habitat 160.09 506.29
habitationlesness 078.08
habitations 258.27 258.29 557.14
habits 115.09 289.08 625.09
Habituels 033.12
hable 560.36
habt 541.01
haccent 180.35
hace 478.11
hack 549.25
Hack 623.34
hacked 130.19 286.10
Hacker 485.11
Hackett 197.06
hacking 395.03 565.35
hackleberries 130.14
hackney 529.19
Hackney 039.05
hacks 042.28
had had Had Had
hadbeen 042.03
hadde 014.01
hadded 371.04 491.31
Haddem 538.25
haddies 393.10
hadding 597.02
Haddocks 034.09
haddock's 533.11
hade 358.36
Hades 183.35
hadn't 066.36 233.01 319.33
392.19 587.04
Hadn't 215.15 330.01
hads 187.06
hadtobe 229.33
haec 269.06
haemicycles 375.13
Haensli 163.05
Hafid 595.03
hafogate 234.01
haftara 343.33
hafts 329.31
hag 014.12 244.08 406.16
423.25
Hag 030.14
Hagaba 276.09
Hagakhroustioun 396.19
haggards 580.06
haggiography 234.12
haggis 456.09 456.09
Haggis 456.09
haggish 559.26
Haggispatrick 404.35
haggyown 156.13
Hagiasofia 552.07
Hagiographice 604.19
hagiohygiecynicism 353.08
hagion 131.30
Hagios 409.27 480.14
hagious 096.34

Hague 436.30
hah 522.20 522.20
Hah 522.13 522.19
haha 494.24 558.25
Haha 117.30 145.04 244.19
hahah 293.19
Hahah 522.23
Hahahaha 005.11
hahands 038.33
hahititahiti 337.29
Hahn 066.23
hahnreich 138.32
haihaihail 398.27
haikon 322.16
hail 044.11 128.23 133.28 200.34 228.21 276.19 311.36 343.06 344.13
Hail 189.25 189.25 271.25 502.22 607.25
Hail 481.01
hailcannon 174.22
hailed 324.08 590.16 596.05 613.01
hailfellow 039.32
Hailfellow 447.30
hailies 435.30
hailing 062.36 379.32
hails 415.34
hailsohame 326.18
hailstorms 392.28
hailth 091.28
haily 616.32
haine 416.01
haint 191.13
hair 008.34 026.08 044.01 065.06 087.22 087.28 101.36 141.13 146.25 157.32 186.34 194.32 203.24 204.08 205.21 206.29 207.02 305.19 305.19 328.05 332.16 333.17 363.26 368.32 393.26 396.10 416.29 426.10 430.23 457.11 459.10 460.27 468.30 472.04 486.24 495.19 527.16 556.17 563.17 566.17 578.28 619.21 627.30
hair 344.11
Hair 069.08
Hair 106.27
hairafall 140.25
hairbrow 012.08
hairclip 210.22
haircut 240.34
Hairductor 492.22
haires 489.03
Hairfluke 023.25
Hairhorehounds 531.25
hairing 268.F6 313.17 464.22
hairmaierians 345.01
hairmejig 146.02
hairpin 211.12
hairpins 144.17 312.21
hairs 043.30 065.03 084.23 149.28 169.13 483.34 516.14 535.30
hair's 028.33
Hair's 420.10
hairshirt 387.05
hairtrigger 540.30
hairweed 512.25
Hairwigger 491.30
hairwigs 221.28
Hairwire 169.04
hairy 093.07 137.22 454.19 455.13 511.22 616.14 621.24
hairy 260.L1
Hairy 008.27
Hairy 071.15
hairydary 303.26
hairydittary 410.02
hairyfair 134.27
hairyg 396.16
hairyman 425.34
Hairyman 014.36
hairyoddities 275.F5
hairyparts 373.17
hairytop 483.19
Hajizfijjiz 347.19
hakemouth 263.02
Hake's 180.30
hakusay 036.04
hal 358.20
Hal 234.04 440.36 535.05 576.06
halas 077.35
hald 063.36 481.05 598.03
hale 014.01 577.03 583.28
hale 418.35
haled 085.26 604.10
halemerry 488.32
half 005.26 010.08 010.10 010.14 010.20 043.18 053.26 059.04 065.18 087.36 101.31 114.03 116.03 116.04 125.19 129.16 137.35 141.04 161.11 174.11 191.26 200.27 201.32 205.31 207.17 269.11 281.25 285.25 292.27 335.26 372.08 386.17 387.03 388.21 389.34 390.17 394.05 405.33 406.01 436.08 443.18 446.19 451.03 452.03 452.36 470.25 470.32 475.06 475.06 487.15 489.04 503.20 509.31 516.15 517.25 531.04 544.36 566.07 567.03 583.30 586.23 588.04 596.30
Halfa 497.33
halfahead 494.24
halfaloafonwashed 159.27
halfbend 578.20
halfbit 312.14
halfbrother 489.28
Halfcentre 106.36
halfcousin 422.17
halfcrown 329.29
Halfdreamt 307.12
half-halted 121.07
halfkneed 091.34
halfmoon 375.12
Halfmoon 059.01
halfpast 041.29
halfpence 413.36
halfprice 530.01
halfpricers 375.25
halfsinster 051.18
halfsovereign 221.07
halfviewed 329.16
halfwayhoist 268.F4
halfwife 532.15
halibut 382.06
halibutt 023.32
halifskin 367.33
haliodraping 509.22
halk 426.18
hall 028.01 057.34 364.22 405.25 497.25 511.12 602.13
Hall 237.27 379.34 421.12 510.14
Hall 106.12 354.18 377.16
Hallall 499.08
hallaw 553.22
halle 498.07
Halled 613.02
halles 549.15
Halley 090.04
Halley's 054.08
hallhagal 107.36
halliday 264.04
Halliday's 573.02
Halligan 622.22
hallmark 137.25
hallmirks 078.08
hallow 025.14
hallowed 122.08
hallowe'en 049.24
halls 049.09 064.05 074.09 215.36
hallthundered 547.28
halltraps 030.04
hallucinate 310.23
hallucination 133.24
hallucinian 478.13
halluxes 429.17
hallway 544.03
hallways 435.35
halmet 530.14
halo 136.13 612.30
haloday 353.07
haloease 237.35
haloed 104.02
halohedge 475.10
Halome 256.11
Halosobuth 561.08
halp 300.20 463.26
Halp 590.26
halpbrother 066.26
Halpin 266.F2
halt 022.20 081.16 114.08 279.09 335.10 367.05 531.27
Halt 469.20 486.01
Halte 081.11
halted 030.17 035.26 042.27 429.02
haltedly 368.17
halter 062.11 248.14 434.17
halth 222.28
haltid 326.21
haltin 457.31
halton 569.28
Haltstille 482.07
halty 132.14
halunkenend 248.15
halve 121.17 145.35 309.17 526.02
ham 037.04 049.22 079.01 082.11 253.24 275.22 317.16 322.35 359.22 359.22 364.31 406.32 431.05 489.15 586.35 586.36
Ham 143.23 187.22 497.34
hamage 623.12
hamalags 043.02
Hamazum's 494.35
hamble 214.32
hambledown 584.18
hambone 177.21

hamd 320.09 464.25
hame 244.09 316.33
hamefame 619.13
hames 093.15
hamid 357.07
hamilkcars 192.06
Hamiltan 274.09
hamiltons 438.36
Hamilton's 513.21
Hamis 181.36
hamissim 029.33
hamjambo 199.20
Hamlaugh 084.32
Hamlaugh's 079.35
hamlet 041.18 465.32
hamlock 031.24
hamman 205.30
Hammeltones 299.22
hammer 316.25 511.04 544.19
hammered 404.20
hammerfast 046.13
hammering 063.33 064.07
hammerlegs 582.22
hammers 565.34
hammersmith 043.05
hammet 193.11
Hammisandivis 468.10
hammocks 235.23
Hammurabi 139.25
hamo 247.14
Hamovs 499.11
hamps 616.14
hampty 619.08
hams 531.19
Hams 552.08
Ham's 076.05
hamshack 309.22
han 318.14 594.30
Han 050.05
Hanah 273.11
Hanandhunigan's 006.20
Hanar 350.08
hanbathtub 606.02
hance 376.24
hand 008.33 023.03 023.22 043.05 043.28 052.28 066.13 091.31 109.29 114.34 116.11 121.25 127.29 130.18 135.11 138.21 140.32 141.21 146.25 180.16 185.18 191.24 191.25 191.29 192.25 196.15 202.21 203.15 224.34 227.03 240.10 244.06 249.16 255.07 277.F1 283.06 302.20 308.F1 313.07 315.17 317.05 318.24 321.24 333.22 351.09 351.09 357.12 392.09 392.10 394.24 397.19 404.03 404.16 404.16 407.25 433.27 439.24 441.35 461.35 467.32 471.32 472.01 474.14 476.08 483.03 483.04 483.16 484.17 490.22 493.09 508.34 522.04 526.24 528.08 534.27 537.04 540.08 563.09 564.31 565.07 580.14 580.26 582.04 593.19 596.01 617.29 621.25
hand 345.17
Hand 004.18 094.06 419.20 499.31
handacross 470.35
handard 389.25
handaxe 407.24
handbag 232.12
handbathtub 606.07
handcaughtscheaf 612.25
handcomplishies 349.34
handcoup 099.30
handcuffs 149.02
handed 575.23 576.01
handel 295.28
handewers 550.19
handful 076.25 169.16
handgripper 535.13
handgrips 183.32
handharp 066.29
handheart 407.24
handicapped 481.30 532.34
handiest 129.17
handihap 022.33
Handiman 102.16
handle 180.10 618.02
handleaf 407.24
handlebars 437.07
handled 179.04 414.01
handlegs 316.32
handles 482.27
handling 005.09
handly 550.05
handmade 561.26
handmades 239.10
handmade's 008.32
handmake 278.12
Handmarried 176.13
handmud 420.08
handpainted 504.34
handpalm 407.23
handpicked 364.36
hands 021.11 021.36 028.14 038.32 042.31 080.16 097.31 098.23 119.03 129.18 131.20 143.05 143.33 151.13 162.19 188.03 188.03 203.23 213.04 235.03 239.26 239.26 248.23 249.21 251.23 333.12 356.29 384.18 396.08 408.25 409.22 410.18 421.01 453.36 458.01 470.01 486.08 489.23 505.11 507.07 523.06 523.15 527.16 527.16 527.17 529.28 566.18 568.22 574.19 618.05
hands 345.27 354.16
Hands 244.20
handsboon 556.29
handscabby 487.10
handsel 618.02
Handsel 105.15
handself 020.21
handsetl 199.01
handshakey 535.11
handshell 407.23
handshut 395.29
handsign 407.23
handsome 134.26 182.21 188.29 191.16 239.29 391.35 495.22 564.12 564.14 570.19 627.28
handsomst 364.25
handson 384.28
handstoe 286.20
handsup 446.09
handtouch 174.10
Handwalled 518.33
handwarp 066.29
handwedown 380.35
handworded 021.20
handwording 022.06
handwriting 135.15
handy 082.06 089.34 229.02
Handy 408.30
handygrabbed 498.05
Hane 111.07
hang 006.28 143.15 154.11 243.26 248.15 442.03 516.15 588.20 596.13 627.31
Hang 378.27 627.31
hangars 380.16
hanged 103.10 119.07 130.20
hanger 550.01
hanging 024.23 069.23 102.24 122.27 192.29 603.25 617.36
Hanging 534.34
Hangkang 457.08
hangle 050.27
hangname 177.22
hangnomen 206.03
hangovers 567.12
Hangry 539.33
hangs 172.08 249.09 252.33 256.33 327.14 622.22
hangsters 355.28
hanguest 063.22
hanigen 332.04
hank 158.34
hankerwaves 471.23
hanking 010.10
hankinhunkn 553.34
hankowchaff 089.36
hankypanks 600.24
Hanner 478.08
Hannibal 274.09
Hannibal's 081.03
Hanno 123.32
Hanno 182.20
Hanny's 455.11
Hanoukan's 245.05
hanry 316.05
Hans 125.14 603.16
Hans 382.27
Hans' 209.26
Hansard 098.28
Hansbaad's 104.18
hansbailis 540.20
Hansen 529.25 602.31
hansome 161.31
hant 044.18 365.23
hantitat 057.07
Hanway 449.14
Hanzas 497.34
hap 082.26 145.27 328.18
hapagodlap 344.02
Hapapoosiesobjibway 134.14
hapaxle 116.33
hapence 321.25
hapenced 348.18
hapless 143.06
haply 261.05
hapney 284.F3
haporth 578.27
happen 107.28 109.11 165.01 173.04 397.23 457.26 502.11
Happen 534.26
happened 082.25 116.10 256.22 307.F5 386.12 395.26 470.22 561.29 597.07 625.29
Happened 307.04
happening 036.15 609.22
happens 082.32 111.27 165.35 171.02 435.27 458.22
happering 426.31
happier 558.24

happiest 250.34
happily 393.17 397.03 562.24
Happily 515.15
happiness 191.06 255.35
happinest 011.15
happinext 302.19
Happinice 471.04
happnessised 261.F1
happy 032.25 038.01 065.09 065.27 069.19 140.28 156.36 178.21 195.01 197.15 202.34 215.23 266.02 280.11 358.08 429.15 446.16 450.04 451.25 453.32 457.25 489.24 535.33 558.21 627.07
Happy 234.34 411.19 578.22
happyass 581.22
happygogusty 035.03
happynghome 602.33
happytight 441.08
Haps 233.21 233.23 233.25
hapsalap 325.08
hapsnots 358.02
hapspurus 557.06
har 054.11 059.34
Har 579.28
haraflare 610.03
Haraharem 331.19
haralded 324.28
Haraldsby 139.34
haram's 532.32
harangued 263.04
harauspices 100.18
harbitrary 099.09
harbour 046.17 170.15 309.20 550.07
harboured 243.09
Harbourer-cum-Enheritance 264.09
harbourless 197.29
Harbourstown 622.34
hard 024.26 081.12 095.11 113.29 120.08 134.19 146.14 170.11 198.06 201.24 245.22 275.23 278.F2 313.27 327.09 375.14 383.22 391.29 404.30 409.18 432.02 505.23 533.10 538.31 574.30 614.15 623.33
hard 341.35 342.16
hardalone 588.05
harder 190.07
hardest 427.20 623.33
hardey 199.24
hardhearingness 581.31
hardily 035.15 107.12
hardly 020.14 041.26 082.09 100.24 202.23 405.15 427.26 446.26 455.03 455.19 511.24 622.10
Hardmuth's 042.27
Hardress 246.18
hardset 180.29 223.35
hardshape 448.23
hardship 558.26
hardup 396.11
hardware 066.31 548.20
Hardware 420.19
hardworking 441.24 603.10
hardy 325.23
Hardy 372.10
hare 097.08 118.24 210.15 238.22 285.04 313.22 408.04
hare 338.16
Hare 466.30
harefoot 330.33 444.05
Harem 611.01
haremhorde 285.F3
haremscarems 102.25
hares 083.01 136.19 449.20
harestary 280.L1
harff 225.04
haricot 227.03
Harik 096.01 096.01 096.01
Harington's 266.12
Haristobulus 219.14
hark 068.26 246.09 292.25 569.07 624.28
Hark 021.03 057.08 233.11 403.01
Harkabuddy 346.25
harks 258.08
Harleem 577.22
Harlene 164.31
Harlequinade 455.28
harleqwind 360.36
Harley 221.25
harlot 094.08
Harlots' 252.11
Harlotte 434.15
harlottes 113.16
Harlyadrope 089.19
harm 199.31 229.01 337.07 521.21 529.18
harm 344.04
Harman 394.29
harmanize 466.25
harmed 615.31
harmless 544.27
harmonic 310.01
harmonical 012.31 426.28
harmonise 140.14
harmony 559.21
harms 608.17
harm's 246.31
harness 207.27 387.04 441.02
Harnett 176.03
harns 256.07
Harold 030.02 030.21
Haromphrey 032.14
Haromphreyld 031.08
Haroun 004.32
haround 033.36
haroween 537.28
harp 013.12 325.10 475.36 570.04
harped 152.25 486.06
harpened 600.15
harpermaster 358.18
harpoons 332.31
harps 329.16 449.30
harpsdischord 013.18
Harreng 187.19
harricana 233.31
harried 425.25
harrier 132.17 227.07 445.03
harriers 480.34
harrily 176.20
Harring 289.F6
harriot 301.17
Harris 326.32
harrobrew 419.27
Harrod's 536.35
harrogate 149.32
harrow 127.08 355.16
harrowd 527.03
harruad 599.05
harrums 566.16
harry 414.31
Harry 028.03 028.03 028.25 117.17 431.26 484.21
Harryng 578.07
Harrystotalies 110.17
harse 008.17 008.21 010.02 010.11 010.13 010.21
harsh 035.30
Harshoe 447.17
harss 602.23
hart 011.26 037.11 300.16 339.08 622.29
Hart 499.30
Harte's 251.28
harth 348.26
hartiest 616.02
Hartigan 210.16
harts 460.17
hartyly 547.04
Haru 418.05 418.08
harum 485.26
haruspical 345.29
harvey 426.12
Harvey 471.33
haryman 390.31
has has Has Has
Hasaboobrawbees 146.17
hasard 107.21 357.04
Hasatency 016.26
haschish 359.09
ha'scint 563.16
hascupth's 516.19
hash 171.05
hashbill 115.28
hashes 067.06
hashhoush 059.20
hash-say-ugh 407.30
hasitancy 016.30
hasitate 149.16
Hasitatense 296.F4
hasitense 097.26
hasn't 122.18 270.F2 463.29
hasn't 383.02
Hasn't 209.36
hast 095.33 237.20 258.29 258.30 325.25 369.03
Hast 224.35
hastaluego 470.33
Hastan 485.06
haste 173.08 244.09 262.02 461.31
Haste 494.14
hastehater 408.11
hasten 075.09
hastencraft 604.13
haster 523.05
hastes 083.31
hastily 063.35
hasting 030.22
hastings 009.02 562.07
hastroubles 192.16
hasty 372.23
hastywasty 080.26
hasvey 313.19
hat 008.15 010.08 010.10 010.14 010.20 022.34 036.27 043.35 050.26 054.01 056.30 068.03 081.11 083.28 121.14 180.09 208.07 221.29 225.19 229.25 243.28 250.14 275.27 278.F7 290.F7 291.F3 302.12 321.10 335.35 337.07 363.08

372.26 381.12 386.17 387.03 388.22 389.34 390.17 392.16 394.05 396.09 422.26 430.17 452.07 453.25 480.34 509.07 515.31 545.04 587.11 623.09
hat 032.23 121.12
Hat 464.23
Hat 176.02
hatache 127.31
hatboxes 165.21
hatch 018.30 112.11 315.29
Hatch 465.09 578.26
hatch-as-hatch 614.33
hatched 129.09
hatches 604.05
Hatches 071.27
hatchet 171.36
Hatchett 325.01
Hatchettsbury 080.33
hatching 504.35
hatcraft 483.11
hate 111.11 116.23 142.33 146.18 168.07 168.12 269.01 345.14 421.15 433.11 463.17 468.23
hatefilled 101.23
Hateful 264.10
Hatenot 579.16
hates 075.23 162.20 233.15 328.09 506.26
Hatesbury's 578.26
hatfuls 192.07
hath 004.13 015.31 038.10 116.36 170.20 250.16 270.29 270.29 303.13 326.01 338.31 388.06 403.13 411.27 561.29 623.34
hathatansy 026.35
Hathed 539.33
hather 566.36
hatinaring 087.05
hating 142.32
hatless 515.33
hatpinny 437.18
hats 008.09 016.08 077.21 213.36 476.12 548.22 622.28
hatsnatcher 445.03
hatsoff 552.18
hattajocky 383.24
Hattentats 540.29
hattention 099.09
hatter's 083.01
hattracted 099.09
hattrick 288.22 486.07
Hatup 415.34
hauberkhelm 273.28
Hauburnea's 381.04
haud 419.03
Haud 263.28
haudworth 019.11
Haugh 454.04 454.04
haughs 331.21
haught 074.02
Haught's 289.14
haughty 055.29 252.33 438.36 627.30
haughtypitched 121.16
hauhauhauhaudibble 016.18
haul 051.28 137.28 153.31 250.36 273.16 298.06 312.11 492.15
Haul 441.04
hauled 581.12
haulin 180.30
haulm 613.32
haulted 359.23
Haun 471.35 472.14 472.20 473.21
haunder 352.31
Hauneen 472.11
haunt 029.01 295.09 332.04 560.17
haunted 049.22 193.35 272.19 435.12 544.10
Haunted 182.31 340.34
haunter 132.16
haunting 096.02 151.18 233.08 319.06
haunts 031.29 039.29 393.09 551.12
Haurousians 344.33
hauru 335.16
haururu 335.16
Hau's 482.03
Hausman 205.35
hausmann 129.16
haute 536.14
hauwck 133.01
Havana 053.26
havd 541.01
have have Have Have
Haveajube 231.18
Haveandholdpp 571.29
havebeen 531.32
havel 231.01
Havelook 556.23
havemercyonhurs 234.28
Havemmarea 198.08
haven 049.11 139.08 200.32 258.14 496.04 620.34
Haven 321.12 610.17
havenliness 548.11
havenots 579.16 599.14
havenots 295.L2
haven't 144.14 205.05 213.11 294.15 460.01 465.05
Haventyne 608.12
Havers 421.32
haves 599.14
haves 295.L2
Haves 603.15
Haveth 535.34
Haveyou-caught-emerod's 063.18
havind 250.03
having Having
havoc 405.29
havonfalled 258.14
havsousedovers 370.31
Havv 593.06
Havvah-ban-Annah 038.30
havvents 604.12
havvermashed 110.14
haw 057.10 347.32 347.33
Haw 399.30
hawhawhawrd 023.28
hawk 493.32
hawked 120.20 363.27 507.36
hawker's 158.34
hawkins 316.27
Hawkins 034.09
Hawkinsonia 542.01
hawks 091.29 215.36 280.17 420.08
hawkspower 178.27
hawrors 184.07
haws 622.18
Haws 257.11
hawsehole 323.06
hawthorndene 553.22
hawthorns 135.02 204.20
hay 033.27 033.27 059.03 202.29 307.F9 338.25 346.23 514.15 516.22
Hay 033.27 444.35 478.21
hayair 004.10
hayamatt 560.25
hayastdanars 387.11
Haycock 136.14
Hayden 482.17 529.01
haydyng 359.33
hayels 243.18
Hayes 210.16 434.12
hayfork's 028.04
haygue 367.05
hayheaded 047.01
Haying 560.06
hayir 498.31
haymaking 192.36
haymow 068.05
haypence 586.23
haypennies 011.21
hayre 004.29
Hayre 239.24
hayrope 208.19
hayseed 452.32
Hayses's 289.14
haythen 424.11
Haywarden 515.35
hazbane 162.21
Haze 593.05
hazel 250.23 622.18
Hazel 064.34
hazelhatchery 201.25
hazelight 587.03
Hazelridge 469.18
hazels 235.17
Hazelton 515.12
hazelwood 135.13
hazevaipar 208.13
hazeydency 305.04
hazzy 162.20
H. C. 033.30 (H. C. Earwicker) 036.12 (H. C. Earwicker) 138.16 (H. C. Endersen)
hce 284.01 291.F1 291.F1
H.C.E. 032.14 198.08
H' dk' fs' 265.F3 (Handkerchiefs)
he he He He
H. E. 141.20 (H. E. Chimney's)
he' 408.29
hea 068.26
heacups 616.23
head 006.27 007.10 007.29 021.10 026.12 034.06 043.13 049.31 064.30 070.22 070.23 084.24 089.31 090.05 091.16 101.24 102.17 110.15 144.26 152.14 154.15 162.22 164.27 168.02 180.10 188.36 191.14 197.03 213.30 215.36 227.29 231.36 235.03 237.27 248.14 249.17 256.35 261.F4 270.09 275.23 275.26 277.10 291.26 318.30 320.08 325.18 351.36 354.29 370.24 377.09 381.28 407.31 408.18 416.29 424.02 442.25 444.17 450.34 454.12 471.29 517.16 527.32 544.04

545.05 560.08 565.03 578.26 594.36 607.03 615.29 617.10
Head 004.06 053.30 059.02 127.33 377.04 501.14 609.25 620.12
headandheelless 081.22
headawag 274.17
headboddylwatcher 026.17
headd 603.13
headdress 102.12 297.01 529.33
headed 043.24
header 257.12
Headfire 409.23
Head-in-Clouds 018.23
Headiness 236.06
heading 352.17
headless 471.15
headlight 011.17
headlong 518.10
Headmaster 251.28
Headmound 135.09
headnoise 535.23
headquarters 202.16
heads 065.02 178.18 250.09 272.18 333.13 373.35 376.22 476.12
headsake 453.28
headstrength 120.24
headth 317.32
headup 454.36
headway 085.21
headwood 136.33
headygabblers 540.24
heaering 332.20
heahear 337.26
heal 191.07 595.07 620.13
heal 418.35 481.01
healed 498.36
Healer's 551.16
Heali 176.12
healing 246.32 289.01 426.15 472.01
Healiopolis 024.18
heall 092.03
healped 356.26
healps 352.35
heals 407.25
health 084.24 111.11 113.23 363.22 391.26 405.16 452.04 454.17 462.03 570.16 589.21 618.32 622.11
health 276.L4
Health 613.27
healtheous 483.23
health's 322.29
healthy 437.12 452.25
healthytobedder 253.09
Healy 329.34
heap 259.07 277.02
heaps 124.19 270.10 270.10 596.18
hear 005.15 006.25 008.03 012.26 028.24 054.07 057.01 059.35 065.14 068.25 068.26 068.33 076.11 080.20 087.11 101.02 104.05 111.16 112.29 140.15 147.19 154.09 155.03 157.21 158.13 160.23 171.18 181.27 192.03 193.10 194.29 196.03 196.06 198.14 204.26 206.16 206.20 207.23 209.24 214.07 215.31 215.33 215.36 219.22 238.16 242.20 245.15 246.11 254.34 258.13 258.25 258.26 259.03 263.F2 271.25 278.09 324.29 327.20 329.32 331.09 338.32 340.36 351.15 357.20 359.18 361.06 361.11 374.16 376.04 389.22 394.33 394.33 396.30 398.29 398.29 410.22 411.25 435.20 442.32 444.16 445.18 451.25 458.25 467.08 468.25 472.13 475.36 477.08 478.02 478.04 479.35 486.29 488.01 488.03 488.13 494.01 499.29 504.16 505.27 508.31 513.14 521.22 522.12 536.02 543.11 561.11 562.28 571.03 571.22 588.28 617.24 621.02 624.10 624.31
Hear 013.14 057.07 068.25 108.23 146.33 151.22 244.01 299.19 398.29 454.19 528.16 564.34 565.19 571.24 598.30
Hear 105.18
hearable 609.21
Hearasay 263.L4
heard 045.01 048.06 088.10 093.23 099.04 116.10 116.24 119.22 120.34 125.03 137.12 137.35 141.36 149.13 154.28 180.31 197.20 198.28 200.29 206.08 213.33 251.36 263.07 266.F2 296.21 329.36 338.01 343.31 369.16 369.16 369.16 373.23 392.31 403.19 404.04 404.09 407.13 409.01 460.16 485.06 491.14 507.01 511.07 515.18 542.02 547.03 564.04 565.15 567.13 570.08 570.09 574.09 586.10 588.33 596.22 604.30 624.05
heard 044.25
Heard 598.29 603.16
hearer 117.02
Hearhasting 371.11
Hearhere 147.03
hearinat 323.28
hearing 035.29 055.33 063.21 064.07 100.27 172.15 174.13 242.01 269.01 309.15 449.29 468.15 490.09 571.25
hearing 345.10 355.04
Hearing 598.28
hearings 040.15
hearken 134.28
hears 031.30 061.02 068.27 098.30 138.26 364.14 544.20 580.18
hearsake 279.09
hearse 094.04 137.06 377.23
hearsemen 276.26 553.31
hearseyard 621.35
hearsomeness 023.14
heart 026.11 027.21 070.10 085.25 109.30 111.34 112.33 129.36 140.16 146.10 159.17 168.12 169.17 194.03 196.14 210.17 278.07 278.07 312.23 318.24 321.08 326.35 360.35 362.21 381.16 387.21 392.19 405.20 406.23 409.03 426.11 431.19 431.33 433.14 456.19 472.01 488.36 490.31 493.34 493.34 493.35 527.22 534.35 536.34 542.36 556.14 577.16 599.26 605.31 612.26 626.31
heart 303.L1
Heart 083.05 570.35
Heart 199.27
heartaches 270.09
heartbeats 403.05
heartbreakingly 182.21
hearth 303.10 329.07 364.27 531.13 549.30 594.17 594.17
hearths 512.22
Hearths 577.22
hearthsculdus 137.24
hearthside 596.04
hearthstone 037.24
hearthy 235.31
hearties 209.24
heartily 031.13 150.36 416.20
heartpocking 572.03
hearts 103.10 135.33 258.02 286.16 335.01 358.11 366.06 396.11 405.29 446.08 459.33 489.21 529.25 533.10 595.29
Hearts 545.36
heart's 009.30 074.14 122.14 252.24 449.10 450.12 454.27
heartseast 418.29
heartsfoot 199.16
heartshaker 107.31
heartsies 434.24
heartsilly 229.28
heartskewerer 055.21
heartsleeveside 562.23
heartsoul 474.02
heartswise 279.F21
heartvein 020.02
hearty 422.25 454.09
hearz'waves 460.25
heat 012.10 075.10 163.02 181.21 185.32 266.19 538.36 557.25 570.27 597.18 613.25
heat 418.15
Heat 363.10
Heated 111.33
heath 042.36 408.07 468.35
Heath 175.14
heathen 046.30 574.07
heathen 481.01
Heathen 215.20
heather 089.32 126.21 241.06 318.27 329.26 359.34 505.01
Heather 007.28
heathersmoke 013.22
heathery 623.25
Heathtown 622.34
heathvens 426.21
Heaton 552.12
heats 251.07
Heatthen 264.06
heave 228.31 347.14 365.13 382.21 481.26 583.02 607.35
Heave 032.06 296.06 324.11
heaved 053.34 311.02
Heaved 316.08
heaven 004.13 005.18 057.11 076.33 096.28 110.04 144.26 188.11 206.19 223.30 247.31 248.25 279.F32 292.03 331.01 396.22 425.36 431.18 433.03 446.01 483.27 534.13 566.28 571.20 599.25 606.14 609.13
Heaven 026.08 424.34 510.25 514.23 547.28

Heaven 349.21
heavenarches 203.27
Heavencry 494.06
heavened 601.09
heavengendered 137.14
heavenlaid 177.21
heavenlies 251.30
heavenly 157.18 312.23 343.29 454.30 518.08
Heavenly 278.F4 413.32
heavens 029.14 168.04 170.09 469.02 501.27 625.36
heaven's 330.01 467.03
heavenspawn 339.27
heaventalk 261.28
heaviered 247.21
heaviest 362.17 409.17
heavily 172.16 177.18 458.03 518.24
heavilybody's 361.12
heavin 312.03
heaving 095.13 293.16 517.13
heavings 153.17
heavinscent 348.29
heavy 006.08 081.21 134.25 174.23 192.09 202.28 216.01 254.14 325.34 344.36 355.29 439.06 490.22 496.30 503.26 510.01 560.25
heavy 346.01
heavyache 362.20
heavybuilt 063.15
Heavysciusgardaddy 306.03
heavyside 315.10
Heavystost's 514.11
heavysuppers 564.18
heavyweight 046.30
hebdomedaries 443.31
hebdomodary 181.07
hebdromadary 581.27
Hebdromadary 071.16
Hebear 014.35
Hebeneros 346.04
Heber 271.19
hebrew 138.01
Hebrewer 104.12
hec 332.03
Hec 119.18
Hecech 377.03
hecitency 119.18
HeCitEncy 421.23
heckhisway 577.23
hecklar 494.08
Hecklar's 578.12
hecklebury 132.36
heckler 085.05
heckling 522.02
hecky 454.15
hectares 135.21
hectoendecate 273.17
Hector 255.16
he'd
Hedalgoland 388.19
hedcosycasket 578.07
hedd 338.08
Heddadin 601.26
hedge 037.20 215.02 249.16 430.01 445.04 576.33
hedgehung 228.16
hedges 015.01 265.16 449.23
hedgygreen 471.13
hedjes 571.10
hedjeskool 533.26
hedon 268.27
hedrolics 452.01
hee 009.15 009.15 395.12 395.12 395.24 395.24 395.24 512.12
Hee 009.15 057.10 225.20
heed 095.07 157.23 158.33 246.03 258.04 377.09 436.34 540.08 627.32
Heed 005.26 005.26
heeders 160.35 164.36
heeding 041.26
heegills 012.21
heehaw 520.20
Heehaw 202.04
heehills 448.04
heel 174.04 563.08 617.32
Heel 620.13
heeler 604.29
heelers 210.03
heeling 250.30 317.18
heels 020.27 021.35 049.03 144.25 299.25 404.21 415.12 437.07 457.14 476.31 514.36
heeltapper 070.22
heeltapping 381.09
heeltipper 483.19
Heenan 466.29
Heeny 360.07
heer 137.06 485.28
Heer 077.27 098.30 242.01
heerdly 485.27
heering 603.02
heers 342.05 342.05
hee's 092.29
heet 151.23
heft 136.24 316.08
heftiest 211.23
hefty 436.03
hegelstomes 416.33
hegemony 573.32
Hegerite 274.10
Hegesippus 038.16
hegg 059.31
hegheg 347.06
hegoak 005.07
hegoat 240.34
Hegvat 485.10
heh 510.09
Hehr 506.11
hehry 224.12
Heidelberg 037.01
Heidenburgh 018.23
heifer 445.24
heigh 373.15
Heigh 201.36 373.15
Heighland 392.34
heighohs 352.29
height 029.04 044.02 180.23 249.14 264.29 309.03 447.09
Height 284.05
heights 078.15 392.31 501.30
Heights 481.15
heil 247.31 532.06
Heil 273.04
heily 110.35
heimlick 461.14
heimlocked 450.31
heing 238.13
heinousness 126.17
Heinz 581.05
heir 192.04 214.29
heiress 600.17
heiresses 538.26
heirheaps 102.24
heirloom 329.26
heirs 011.31 054.02 096.35 513.23 526.26 545.19 580.02
Heirs 316.09
Heish 335.04 335.23
heissrohgin 228.21
heiterscene 067.10
hejirite 062.03
hek 546.23 584.05
Hek 199.24 411.18 420.17 420.18
Hekkites 484.20
heladies 386.15
held 102.03 113.19 115.27 131.10 166.18 235.18 236.23 257.20 318.24 347.08 356.17 524.02 537.04 545.04 564.22 576.04 620.18
heldin 229.33
Helen 210.32
helf 249.34 292.27
helfalittle 010.34
Heli 073.19
helio 005.08
Heliogobbleus 157.26
heliolatry 237.01
Heliopolitan 530.16
helioscope 341.23
heliose 067.10
heliotrollops 603.28
heliotrope 461.09 533.02 561.20
heliotrope 265.L1
Heliotrope 610.36
heliotropical 349.06
Heliotropolis 594.08
heliots 613.01
Helius 564.05
helixtrolysis 163.31
hell 039.33 047.28 083.26 190.02 270.F3 304.15 323.23 382.06 385.10 393.28 432.15
hell 354.12
Hell 063.23 108.26 273.24
Hell 440.05
he'll He'll
hellabelow 239.33
hellas 419.27
hellbeit 305.11
hellbowl 060.14
Helldsdend 239.34
Hellena 071.29
Hellfeuersteyn 225.24
hellfire 514.09 552.27
Hellicott's 529.31
Hellig 481.20
hellish 015.17 519.01
hellishly 235.14
hellmuirries 081.28
hello 072.20 144.06 388.30
Hello 480.18 500.36 501.02 501.08 536.04
Hello 200.07
hellof 075.18
Hellohello 501.04
hellpelhullpulthebell 245.25
hells 228.06 535.28
hell's 043.10 116.23 117.06 520.20
Hell's 485.35
Hellsbells 208.27
hellscyown 351.05

hellsinky 326.12
hellskirt 200.12
hellstohns 502.20
hellyg 471.31
helm 580.14
helmet 045.06 220.26
hel-met 044.28
Helmingham 088.21
Helmut's 277.L2
helo 377.04
hélos 280.L4
helots 543.19
helotsphilots 062.16
helotwashipper 408.35
heloved 132.24
help 027.33 035.23 040.34
057.09 086.21 094.29 102.05
114.02 155.11 162.36 182.12
191.02 197.18 203.32 214.18
226.18 234.25 245.05 253.12
256.01 286.18 292.04 306.F3
313.13 316.19 328.35 364.24
377.33 410.14 433.23 447.01
449.05 450.08 538.09 569.02
594.16 594.16 610.11 617.28
Help 377.33
helpabit 223.04
helpas 052.14 619.34
helped 061.12 164.01 393.04
445.33
helpen 321.20
helper 191.07
helpers 005.25
helphelped 549.13
helping 096.28 369.35 404.23
helping 338.15
helpings 283.12 429.11 455.32
474.12
helpless 171.07 583.20
Helpless 423.31
Helpmeat 242.25
Helpsome 407.25
Helpunto 619.34
helpyourselftoastrool 622.13
helts 227.05
Helusbelus 594.23
helve 136.24
helve's 285.22
Helviticus 004.21
hem 030.09 079.21 276.09
297.08 319.23 320.09 351.26
371.23 405.19 422.33 431.06
590.24
hemale 581.18
hematite 247.35
hemd 440.25
hemel 435.23
hemhaltshealing 611.28
hemifaces 493.06
hemiparalysed 177.05
hemisemidemicolons 374.09
hemmed 022.35
hemmer 368.15
hemming 166.09
hemoptysia 174.19
hemosphores 081.25
Hemoves 499.11
hemp 495.14 538.16
Hemp 495.13
Hempal 175.17
hempen 211.27
hempshelves 373.13
hempty 386.08
hemptyempty 372.19
hems 315.31
Hemself 557.01
hemselves 547.24
hemsylph 416.14
hemustwhomust 223.27
hemycapnoise 168.11
hen 055.11 064.34 083.31
110.22 111.33 112.02 119.23
199.30 256.02 256.05 273.F3
278.21 336.17 370.02 382.11
584.20 606.17 615.10
hen 350.07
Hen 094.07
henayearn 379.23
hence 017.26 034.36 051.32
067.29 120.02 298.14 427.18
Hence 007.36 036.21 097.17
247.25 374.23 536.25 600.04
619.11
henceforth 441.12
Hencetaking 261.05
henchwench 334.29
henconvention's 516.29
hencoop 405.21
hend 285.10 395.27
hende 318.14
henders 556.25
hendrud 220.21
henesies 240.13
henesy 463.18
Henge 594.36
Hengegst 272.17
Hengler's 307.08
Heng's 143.22
hengster's 529.34
henkerchoff 495.09
henker's 248.14
henna 434.19
hennad 205.36
Hennery 137.07
hennin's 254.31
Hennu 479.33
henpecked 492.09
Henressy 176.06
Henrietta's 447.08
Henry 307.14 447.13
hens 038.18 256.05 321.26
hen's 275.13
Hen's 299.F1
henservants 432.06
hensmoker 200.12
Henson 446.30
hensyne 112.08
henwives 128.32
heoll's 449.27
heoponhurrish 607.20
hep 026.09 436.34
Hep 026.09 478.23 480.18
525.27
heppiness 443.10
Heppy's 416.01
heptachromatic 611.06
heptagon 127.03
HEPTAGRAMMATON 286.R1
heptahundread 347.19
heptarched 273.04
heptarchy 077.18
heptark 590.02
her her Her Her
herafter 533.04
herald 134.27 375.06 567.18
597.34
Herald 498.11
herb 014.34
herba 115.15
herbage 039.35
herbata 102.19
herberge 328.16
herberged 056.26
herbest 277.20
herbgreen 611.34
herblord 254.36
herbrides' 548.03
hercourt 236.22
herculeneous 570.17
Hercules' 081.03
Hercushiccups' 355.12
hercy 326.19
herd 073.35 331.03
Herd 499.31
herdifferent 601.15
herds 227.06 272.31
herdsquatters 344.19
here here Here Here
here' 148.11
hereafters 130.20
herearther 618.30
hereby 334.10 444.06 456.05
468.25
hereby 163.16
hereckons 524.18
hered 044.18
hereditary 031.15 172.13
hereditate 511.22
hereditatis 131.30
herefore 250.17
herehear 237.12 584.36
Herein 566.25
hereinafter 049.35 446.23
Hereinunder 017.32
hereis 349.35
heremite 203.18
Heremon 271.20
Heremonheber 604.04
herenext 598.14
Herenow 579.20
hereon 566.36
herepong 231.10
hereround 552.09
Heres 313.27
here's Here's Here's
hereshealth 622.28
hereticalist 192.01
Hereto 545.22
heretoday 455.24
heretofore 319.19 537.04
hereupon 454.01
herewaker 619.12
Hereweareagain 455.25
Herewhippit 077.27
herewitdnessed 413.23
herewith 584.29 617.31
herewithin 238.28
herfor 550.16
Heri 328.25
Heriness 351.31
hering 453.06
herit 128.02 298.04
herm 066.26 471.17
herman 283.28
hermana 184.19
Hermes 081.07 263.22
hermetic 470.02
hermits 505.03
Hermyn 342.20

hero 127.25 184.11 255.01 275.09 326.09 384.23 398.29 466.14
hero 343.17
Hero 026.09 306.21
herobit 498.22
Herod 260.F1
herodotary 013.20
heroes 074.03 091.29 178.11 234.09
Heroes 106.14
Heroes' 607.12
heroest 398.05
herof 249.07
heroic 073.14 122.04 619.14
heroicised 163.23
heroim 344.24
Heroine 306.21
heroines 067.31 203.13
heronim 131.34
heron's 233.16
herospont 135.17
heroticisms 614.35
herou 107.20
herouns 358.28
herr 548.07
Herr 069.32 164.31 193.13
herreraism 512.18
herrgott 240.35
Herrick 030.09
herrin 587.02
Herrin 525.21
herring 136.26 186.32 213.35 315.12 506.02 524.20
herringabone 330.34
herrings 538.18
herringtons' 101.14
Herrinsilde 391.16
herrors 545.13
Herrschuft 012.09
hers 020.04 080.15 092.29 128.12 233.11 236.07 246.14 251.19 267.F3 352.08 533.03 600.19 612.25 613.36 625.02
Hers 232.16
her's 239.13
Her's 411.21
herself 028.02 089.24 116.17 157.18 157.34 157.36 164.09 166.36 195.02 198.09 201.29 202.23 206.06 206.13 206.30 208.35 236.34 238.06 243.26 269.F1 327.13 363.07 389.15 391.20 447.31 526.31 528.24 528.25 561.35 575.22 575.27 615.10 626.33
herselfs 298.27
hersell 014.03
herselp 333.13
herselves 101.22
hersirrs 355.28
herslF 230.22
hersute 391.20
Hersy 355.15
herth 352.22
herum 295.25
herup 249.14
heruponhim 092.28
herwayferer 365.01
Herwho 084.27
herword 561.27
Hery 546.10
herzian 232.10
Herzog 238.24
hes 119.18 471.11
he's he's He's He's
hesitancy 421.19 483.12
hesitants 097.25
hesitency 082.30 097.25 599.14
Hesitency 035.20
hesitensies 187.30
Hesper 494.13
hespermun 538.23
Hesperons 245.23
Hesperus 306.27
hessians 097.13 459.07
hestened 535.06
hestens 135.11
Hesterdays 104.12
hesterdie 295.01
hesteries 319.06
hesternis 596.07
hesternmost 407.36
het 151.19 407.25 509.22
Het 021.02 150.09 256.16
hetarosexual 120.35
Heteroditheroe's 221.31
heterotropic 252.21
heth 623.34
hetman 137.17
Hetman 243.14
Hetty 027.11
heupanepi 611.18
heuteyleutey 493.21
heva 494.26 494.26
Heva 271.25
hevantonoze 392.06
hevel 557.03
hevens 258.14
heventh 284.10
hevn 416.01
hevnly 234.13
hevre 416.31
hevy 228.31
hew 549.25
Hewitt 135.29
hewn 600.19
hex 208.31
hexengown 297.03
Hexenschuss 221.23
hexenshoes 288.12
hey 162.26 171.29 466.18 590.14
Hey 215.29 226.06 334.33 480.22
heyday 434.17
Heyday 337.28
Heydays 547.28
heyheyheyhey 097.26
heyweywomen 542.36
hezelf 170.17
hi 259.09 485.28 607.17
Hi 163.10 163.10 587.36
hiarwather 600.08
hibat 171.09
Hiberio-Miletians 309.11
hibernating 079.05
Hibernia 388.30 616.05
hiberniad 138.11
hibernian 335.26 605.15
hiberniating 316.15
Hibernicis 104.14
Hibernites 440.12
Hibernonian 212.21
Hibernska 551.32
hibruws 228.34
hic 374.21
hic 179.02
Hic 153.23
Hic 007.22
Hiccupper 276.09
hiccupping 171.08
hiccups 232.35
hice 502.18
hick 067.20
hickerwards 266.08
Hickey's 286.10
hickheckhocks 130.20
hickicked 067.19
hickory 098.36
hickoryhockery 160.13
hicks 423.10
hickstrey's 064.06
hicky 454.15
hicnuncs 407.32
hicstory 280.L1
hid 097.14
hidal 128.05
Hidamo 212.36 212.36
hidded 493.06
hidden 078.12 120.05 188.15 247.23
Hidden 499.15
hide 080.14 171.24 188.32 204.08 211.31 233.05 321.28 330.02 451.26 540.34 576.14 589.16 625.30
Hide 100.26 372.35 372.35 372.36 372.36 373.02 373.02 373.03 373.04 576.13
hidebound 525.01
hideful 186.30
hideinsacks 035.09
hideous 549.11
Hideous 045.18
hidepence 161.22
hider 240.23
hides 020.11 191.12 309.02
hideseeks 462.10
hidest 272.01
hiding 102.06 307.F1 330.36 373.13 445.04 495.19 504.03
hidingplace 504.08
hidings 602.09
hidmost 118.36
hidn't 345.08
hids 284.14
hids 339.24
hie 598.10
hied 097.18
hiehied 449.19
hielt 204.01
Hiemlancollin 533.33
hiena 010.04
Hierarchies 298.L2
hierarchitectitiptitop-loftical 005.01
hierarchy 447.33
hieroglyph 122.07
hieros 551.31
hies 016.31 057.07 255.07 279.09 590.19
hig 390.05 406.16
higgins 517.27
Higgins 604.06
high 004.13 012.01 020.28 021.10 023.18 025.16 025.31 031.02 036.05 053.27 054.26 088.02 131.24 197.03 209.35

214.12 215.06 258.20 277.14 309.14 320.35 331.11 331.18 360.17 388.35 396.08 404.08 404.08 408.23 408.23 408.23 410.01 415.19 415.36 421.30 436.03 439.05 448.35 473.14 498.28 501.28 504.02 516.01 538.09 577.25 580.14 582.15 586.28 595.05 606.05 607.17 609.27 610.29 613.02 621.36 621.36
High 010.28 036.29 062.14 163.10 361.30 373.07 373.07 482.19 484.34 485.02 488.24 611.33 612.04 612.09 612.09
High 105.01 200.12 530.24
highajinks 094.29
highbigpipey 130.36
Highbosomheaving 189.25
highboys 033.09
highbrow 183.30
highbrowed 264.06
higher 169.15 178.22 251.08 404.08 448.21
higherdimissional 395.01
highest 130.13 409.26 464.01 534.23 593.16 616.13
Highest 406.28 612.06
higheye 347.08
Highfee 418.02
highflyer 534.36
Highho 117.16
highhued 602.04
highjacking 581.11
Highjakes 547.22
highlandman's 521.07
highlows 168.02 297.02
highlucky 502.12
highly 083.16 085.12 185.17 230.29 242.03 244.18 357.13 358.10 398.13 426.35 441.27 477.26 499.01 532.16 543.28 570.25 615.07
Highly 247.18
highlyfictional 261.17
highmost 167.25
highness 145.35
Highohigh 373.07
highpitched 179.22
highpowered 557.30
highpriest's 122.07
highroad 030.18 471.26
highs 540.20
highsaydighsayman 323.03
highschoolhorse 413.07
highsteppers 399.18
highstepping 386.31
highstinks 163.09
hight 066.12 275.16
Hight 611.33
Hightime 239.16
hights 158.29
highty 531.23
Highup 612.12
highview 504.16
highway 043.26 321.14 334.34
Highway 607.12
highways 410.08
hijiniks 439.33
hijo 274.23
hike 196.09 247.04 260.05 377.23 621.07
hikely 070.15
hiker 318.29 475.30
hiking 240.18 448.27
hikler's 410.08
hilariohoot 092.06
Hilarion 361.30
hilarious 188.11
hilarity 225.01
Hilary 021.12 021.36
hild 528.22
Hilda 147.12
hill 048.02 057.11 073.30 079.04 094.10 099.26 131.24 132.12 204.13 239.32 323.23 355.16 371.35 406.06 442.04 469.16 496.04 501.22 520.27 541.02
hill 346.17
Hill 023.17 057.13 061.23 082.32 097.11 129.04 182.24 185.08 261.F2 436.29 477.06 532.22 595.03
Hill 105.08
Hillary 314.18 618.23
Hillborough 340.34
Hillcloud 480.26
hillcombs 022.04
Hillel 350.03
hillelulia 083.34
Hillewille 609.18
Hillill 499.08
hillman 376.03
hillmythey 331.09
hillo 430.33
hillock 474.02
Hillock 160.12
hillocks 337.31
hills 194.35 335.28 352.32 469.05 480.08 540.05 569.36 576.25 583.05 627.02
Hills 307.13
Hill's 594.18
hillsaide 542.25
Hillsengals 601.10
hillside 486.33 486.33
hillsir 481.14
hilltapped 318.29
hilly 096.04
Hilly 369.09
hilly-and-even 502.04
hillydroops 626.17
Hillyhollow 319.01
hillymount 623.23
Hilton 048.11
him him Him Him
himals 005.01
Himana 309.14
himashim 029.33
himcell 086.05
himhim 314.14
Himhim 314.14 371.10 371.10
Himkim 598.20
himm 074.07
Himmal 599.05
himmed 371.11
himmels 191.35
himmeltones 138.01
himmertality 580.13
himmulteemiously 285.10
Himmyshimmy 173.27
himother 187.24
himp 619.12
himples 012.20
himpself 313.33
hims 187.06 222.36 249.35 560.13 612.25
himsalves 352.36
himsel 184.10
himself 013.13 021.11 021.36 022.32 024.03 029.25 032.20 034.35 040.31 047.01 047.02 048.07 050.11 055.05 059.32 061.18 076.16 078.17 079.02 083.18 086.10 088.35 093.05 097.31 122.28 131.06 132.26 133.28 134.33 138.18 155.17 161.27 162.21 165.35 169.22 170.22 171.15 172.14 172.19 177.22 177.34 178.32 179.02 179.18 179.30 180.34 182.19 203.33 214.11 214.13 222.04 224.26 225.04 227.36 228.04 228.18 230.02 231.25 232.07 281.F4 293.07 293.07 317.32 320.02 323.28 326.32 343.28 380.20 380.28 380.34 380.35 381.20 388.32 389.36 391.17 391.18 392.24 405.02 406.23 407.33 408.05 411.34 417.05 417.14 417.28 422.09 424.18 426.09 431.21 437.32 449.35 452.28 459.22 461.34 463.08 463.29 467.09 467.22 468.17 470.02 471.11 473.04 477.27 481.31 482.24 501.31 501.31 501.32 505.36 506.08 507.03 516.12 517.06 520.03 520.08 524.19 532.01 543.35 563.06 573.22 574.02 580.25 585.36 589.06 589.35 595.36 596.24 602.32 609.26 611.31 619.13 620.13
himself 175.07 201.11 338.15 346.34 352.19
Himself 197.32
himselfs 234.10
himshelp 157.13
himshemp 317.28
himsilf 497.36
himundher 092.09
himupon 488.07
hin 012.17 236.09 377.29 482.16 590.19
hind 012.17 241.31 267.06 333.17 484.21 500.12 559.20 588.04 617.02
Hind 550.30
hinder 224.24 272.02 445.04
hindergored 339.29
hindies 499.21
hindigan 403.13
hindled 608.29
hindlegs 522.16
hindly 528.22
hindmoist 627.03
hindmost 130.03 246.28 292.04 358.11 445.16
hindquarters 051.32 498.04
hindustand 492.17
hing 391.08
Hing 206.03
hinge 396.20
hinges 252.18
hingeworms 078.08
hinn 151.12
hinndoo 010.06 010.09 010.14
hinnessy 010.04 010.05 010.07

hinnigen 332.05
hinny 039.09 554.05
hinnyhennyhindyou 272.19
hins 483.25
hint 024.02 033.15 173.14 204.08 411.34 436.10 468.14
hinted 109.03 115.13 134.34 374.07
hinterclutch 572.02
hintergrunting 273.20
hinterhand 369.02
hintering 363.34
Hinther 365.22
hints 020.11
hip 022.33 245.33 329.04 329.04
Hip 226.19 236.15 236.16 433.23
hiphigh 582.29
Hiphip 236.15 236.17
hiplength 146.04
hippic 039.02
Hippo 038.30
hippofoxphiz 307.F7
hippohobbilies 005.32
Hippohopparray 341.22
hippopotamians 437.25
hippopopotamuns 047.08
hippychip 329.01
hips 022.22 149.01 225.04 363.23
Hips 257.11
hips' 205.01
hipsalewd 325.08
hir 015.26 063.14
hircohaired 275.01
hircomed 372.01
hirculeads 128.36
Hirculos 016.04
hircum 089.27
Hircups 321.15
Hircus 215.27
hire 012.10 204.02 339.14 502.32
Hireark 409.35
hired 182.26 192.25 362.32
Hired 375.14
Hireling's 270.30
hiremonger 584.05
hires 137.27
hiresiarch 188.16
hireth 282.04
Hirish 126.24
Hirp 175.27 175.27
hirrara 497.04
hirs 246.14
hirsuiter 070.21
hirtly 222.03
his his His His HIS
hisand 432.18
hiscitendency 305.09
hise 299.24
hised 320.19 624.13
hishelp 130.20
hishtakatsch 296.24
hisk 287.18
hisn't 162.26
hisophenguts 319.12
Hispain's 553.36
Hispano-Cathayan-Euxine 263.13
hisphex 415.28
hiss 086.29 125.01 144.06 271.29 460.28
Hiss 587.03
hissarlik 254.30
hissch 506.08
hissed 132.16
hisself 193.31
hissens 228.32
hissent 321.23
hisses 493.10
hissheory 163.25
hisshistenency 146.34
hissindensity 350.12
hissing 456.02
Hissss 297.04
hisstops 422.13
hist 095.33 196.23 270.15 607.27
Hist 571.34
hister 528.11
histereve 214.01
histher 022.02
historic 011.30 032.13 481.13
historical 477.35
historically 452.17
histories 389.09
historiorum 013.21
historique 528.15
history 064.09 087.07 136.28 140.33 173.23 186.02 388.32 389.15 503.34 514.03 573.36
history 271.L2
History 221.19 486.06 602.25
HISTORY 262.R1
historyend 332.01
histrionic 230.29
histry 052.05 161.22
hists 244.08
hisu 092.28
hit 010.12 010.12 051.33 150.13 173.14 224.19 250.05 303.23 307.F9 396.20 405.21 525.20 565.34 566.32 613.34
Hit 010.12
Hit 104.13
hitback 238.05
hitch 023.04 065.19 248.14 315.27 363.02
Hitchcock 044.02
hitched 007.11
hitches 581.19
hitching 291.F4
hith 623.34
hithaways 114.17
hither 158.32
Hither 017.25
hitherandthithering 216.04
hitheris 273.27
Hither-on-Thither 452.27
hitherto 280.30
Hitherzither 360.01
hits 032.28 140.06 174.30 187.06 225.19 353.20
hitter's 084.23
Hittit 346.35
hitz 053.35
hivanhoesed 178.01
hive 025.06
hive 346.17
Hive 139.35
hives 375.20
hiving 590.14
hiz 097.34
hizzars 617.03
Hjalmar 284.F4
hjem 242.33
hleepy 426.18
Hll 349.26
Hlls 258.02
Hm 509.23
hney 010.15 010.15
Hney 010.15
hnmn 623.24
Hnmn 623.24
hnor 243.33
ho 013.26 023.24 059.34 094.33 096.21 117.10 121.14 121.27 180.15 184.33 184.36 201.36 215.29 215.36 224.09 224.21 232.06 259.09 314.18 314.18 379.19 379.19 379.19 385.18 392.35 469.01 581.24 627.31
Ho 018.36 212.35 212.35 215.28 215.32 215.34 305.F2 305.F2 305.F2 314.18 403.13 464.08 471.04 484.33 485.28 532.03 627.31
Ho 415.15
hoa 205.07
Hoa 163.11 163.11
hoagshead 015.31
hoahoahoah 007.01
Hoally 163.11
hoang 322.12
Hoangho 213.06
hoar 060.15 139.06 535.30
hoard 019.08
hoarded 253.07
hoarder 078.11
hoarding 331.03
hoardpayns 533.20
hoariness 158.27
hoaring 205.21 468.36
hoarish 029.27
hoarse 154.10 334.16
hoarsehaar 362.31
hoarsely 037.35
hoarsemen 557.01
Hoarsers 219.15
hoarth 346.31
hoary 310.35
Hoary 071.15
hoath 036.26
Hoath 175.15
hoax 300.06 363.09 511.34
Hoax 071.15
hoaxites 239.12
hobbledehorn 428.15
hobbledyhips 214.21
hobbles 063.30
hobbsy 584.15
hobbyhodge 266.01
hobdoblins' 600.23
hobmop 531.23
hobnobs 274.08
hobo 050.16
Hobos 409.16
hobs 453.07
Hobson's 063.02
hoc 153.24 289.14
hoc 478.18
hoch 053.34 314.18
hochsized 548.09
hochskied 157.11
hock 128.24 454.15
Hock 423.10
Hockeyvilla 609.17

hockinbechers 130.15
hockockles 623.08
Hocksett's 529.17
hocksheat 364.17
hockums 007.35
Hocus 254.20
hod 004.26 098.30 568.18
hod 098.07
Hod 266.04
hodd 621.28
hodden 313.35
hodder 201.08
Hodder's 537.36
hoddit 006.08
Hoddum 296.06
hodge 138.11
hodgepadge 285.06
Hodie 508.12
hodinstag 577.17
hodpiece 131.33
hod's 359.01
hodypoker 558.30
hoe 005.09
Hoe 334.33
Hoebegunne 104.12
hoed 385.33
Hoed 130.33 221.29
Hoel 143.15
Hoeland 169.24
hoep 434.02
hoer 006.27
hoeres 320.22
hoerrisings 449.28
hoerse 273.28
Hoet 254.29
hof 303.20
hofd 588.16
hofdking 359.25
Hofed-ben-Edar 030.11
hog 060.15 199.20 433.12 519.04
Hogam 223.04
Hogan 098.30 552.13
hogarths 435.07
hogcallering 070.20
hogdam 471.34
hogg 069.19
Hoggin 386.26
hogglebully 025.33
hogglepiggle 285.08
hoggs 533.35
hoghill 568.22
hoghly 245.13
hoghly 344.02
hogmanny 455.10
Hogmanny 455.09 455.10
hogo 498.29
hogpew 442.35
hogs 366.26
hogsfat 483.25
hogsford 182.26
hogsheaded 381.35
hogsheads 581.12
hogshole 447.02
hogshome 041.17
Hogsober 186.14
hogwarts 296.19
hoh 510.09
hohallo 485.22
Hohannes 391.05
hohmryk 314.23
Hoho 117.31
Hohohoho 005.09 539.14
Hohohoho 383.08
Hohore 020.36
hohse 373.15 373.15
hoiest 340.22
hoig 264.27
Hoily 138.25
hoist 025.31 031.03 330.21 441.04 549.05
hoisted 044.02 133.03 568.18
hoisted 286.L2
hoisting 338.07
Hoisty 373.09
hoity 466.30
hok 584.05
Hoke 552.31 552.32 552.33 552.34
hokey 256.02
Hokey 089.34
hokidimatzi 234.01
Hokmah 032.04
Hokoway 582.29
hoks 548.01
hold 015.13 023.12 023.32 040.27 101.10 128.05 144.18 146.14 147.27 170.11 188.18 190.26 197.02 207.30 213.27 224.33 224.34 239.19 257.15 288.28 296.15 313.30 357.26 362.20 375.13 389.10 392.09 397.19 425.21 425.35 428.06 438.26 439.24 441.02 451.10 457.11 459.30 463.33 475.18 496.11 500.15 540.17 545.18 570.18 577.05 621.28
Hold 027.23 095.10 245.21 255.03 338.33 414.15 436.09 473.21 509.04 525.28 579.14 621.04
Hold 342.16
hol'd 143.01
holden 102.24
holder 318.24 319.16 330.21 443.32 524.17
holders 574.28
holdfour 022.23
Holdhard 012.36 464.18
holding 077.13 096.19 117.34 123.34 181.21 199.04 200.27 225.05 497.29 534.24 557.09 593.19
holdmenag's 334.25
holds 025.14 096.33 137.32 271.10 337.07 574.02 574.02 582.27
holdup 566.10
hole 085.06 121.13 122.04 163.09 211.19 253.21 266.02 271.F1 323.22 338.20 462.14 467.02 512.28 539.24 556.26 586.28 587.16
hole 037.25 121.12
Hole 041.32 099.13 147.05 531.34 535.20
holedigs 069.32
holemost 407.25
holenpolendom 101.27
holes 198.32 434.22 545.08
holes 339.20
holey 023.35 111.18 312.11
holeydome 155.15
holf 292.27 610.12
holiday 110.28 596.16
Holiday 556.08
holied 552.10
holiest 025.06
holifer 193.04
Holihowlsballs 231.21
holiname 515.25
holiness 520.11
holinight 192.19
holiodrops 235.05
holipoli 111.18
holired 005.30
Holispolis 335.07
Holl 565.02
hollaballoon 322.07
hollegs 059.09
holler 341.30
hollichrost 331.14
hollow 025.14 034.20 067.31 136.34 192.10 436.30 505.03 597.06 607.27
Hollow 156.25 421.06 565.02
hollowy 371.35
holly 147.10 152.03
Holly 027.15
hollyboys 291.11
hollyday 058.05
Hollymerry 588.17
hollywood 265.17
holm 330.24
holmen 200.12
Holmes 276.F2
holmgang 466.29
holmgrewnworsteds 611.35
Holmpatrick 031.31
holmsted 026.26
Holmstock 533.35
holocaust 419.09
holocryptogam 546.13
holoday 129.13
holographs 032.13
Holohan 147.30
Holophullopopulace 342.18
holos 019.01
holp 118.28 300.22
holpenstake 137.32
holst 081.31 374.21
holt 097.02 315.31
holth 619.12
holusbolus 118.04
Holwell 492.18
holy 056.09 062.19 091.33 110.13 111.17 158.29 177.23 188.10 190.14 206.18 228.06 237.20 241.16 256.14 267.F3 272.16 275.05 299.13 405.07 407.25 411.02 426.29 429.16 454.17 464.08 465.13 468.01 470.32 495.16 501.22 504.02 504.26 531.32 600.35 605.05 605.22 605.25 605.36
holy 346.05
Holy 063.24 088.23 141.02 145.34 193.03 214.30 219.09 247.20 282.17 360.25 376.13 439.05 451.22 453.14 490.20 494.15 556.03 562.17 569.15
Holy 071.34 177.06 399.01 419.08
holy-as-ivory 502.02
Holybones 031.25
holyboy's 620.22
holyhagionous 520.33
holymaid 390.31
holymess 091.35

holypolygon 339.35
holypolypools 302.32
Holyryssia 329.20
holystone 481.01
holytroopers 223.11
holyyear's 569.13
hom 324.21 431.05 431.08 482.16
Hom 006.32
homa 201.23
homage 623.12
Homard 351.09
Hombly 415.14
hombres 551.13
Hombreyhambrey 317.10
homd 055.15
homdsmeethes 595.17
home 034.11 049.10 061.12 062.29 097.18 114.01 119.03 133.03 143.01 145.28 161.22 164.13 164.36 174.31 187.12 191.23 197.21 215.10 220.17 228.30 271.F5 275.04 275.20 291.26 294.F1 316.22 323.35 331.16 334.34 362.13 374.15 379.14 390.10 393.14 411.08 427.35 428.11 434.01 436.31 437.32 437.35 442.11 455.09 455.31 462.32 463.04 474.17 479.02 487.29 490.21 494.02 513.20 543.22 576.25 581.12 589.10 617.06
home 231.05 263.L2
Home 228.02 256.11 443.19 627.24
homeborn 114.12
homedromed 032,31
homegoers 381.36
Homelan 536.35
homelessness 040.19
homelet 586.18
homelette 059.31
homelies 525.02
homelike 079.29
homely 188.04 245.34 272.28 343.34 398.12 436.34 467.26 530.28 614.32
Homely 306.26
Homely 071.21
homemade 454.36
homer 129.23
Homer 306.L3
homereek 314.23
homerigh 021.13
homerole 445.32
homer's 515.24
homes 041.25 066.05 277.F4 540.25
Homes 165.33
homeseek 444.35
homespinning 431.31
homespins 499.24
homespund 329.07
homestages 346.32
homesters 539.09
homeswab 245.34
homesweepers 006.05
homesweetened 533.19
homesweetstown 358.08
Homesworth 458.23
hometown 274.30
homety 230.05
homeur 034.12
homey 330.26
homeysweet 398.12
Homfrie 023.20
homiest 266.14
Homilies 409.36
Homin 024.34
homing 317.05
hominous 560.17
hominy 256.18
hommage 543.21
homme-nourrice 081.29
hommers 140.15
homnibus 099.10
homnis 314.34
homo 136.17
Homo 101.12 418.25 422.11 499.05
Homo 342.23
homogallant 168.10
HOMOGENEITY 279.R1
homogenius 034.14
HOMOGENUINE 279.R1
homoheatherous 129.14
homoid 149.26
homolocous 295.01
homoplate 119.03
homoplatts 559.24
Homos 600.29
homosexual 522.30
homosodalism 352.20
homovirtue 318.05
homp 063.36
Homper 491.16
hompety 325.23
homy 380.10
Hon 093.21
Hon. 169.05 (Honourable)
honaryhuest 240.03
Honddu 198.18
honds 004.29
hone 382.21
Hone 536.12
honest 031.08 150.29 169.06 171.14 396.04 410.20 448.32 450.03 590.04
honestly 082.33 431.24 446.12 539.04 539.10 545.19
honey 025.05 133.01 141.33 235.35 267.27 277.F1 318.16 354.32 410.28 512.31 590.14
honey 201.10
Honey 076.04 238.33
honeybeehivehut 605.24
honeycomb 422.25
honeycoombe 243.23
honeyful 474.12
honeyhunting 124.27
honeying 215.03
honeylamb 065.07
honeyman 041.26
honeymeads 558.19
honeymoon 395.09 557.09
honeyoldloom 385.29
honeys 175.34
Honeys 113.17
honeysuckle 504.36
honeysuckler 588.04
Honeysuckler 587.19
honeysugger 141.34
hong 446.11
Hong 206.03
hongkong 119.25
hongue 411.21
honnein 029.32
honnessy 325.08
honnibel 538.10
honnisoid 035.21
honophreum 077.34
Honophrius 572.25 572.27
honorabile 185.20
honorary 137.18 615.32
Honorary 107.02
Honorbright 211.33
honorey 422.27
honorific 179.22
Honorific 484.27
Honoriousness 154.36
honour 064.24 073.06 132.31 181.25 189.16 192.18 212.25 253.11 255.24 311.18 413.19 465.02 488.01 522.03 539.04 585.07
Honour 053.29 237.27 264.01 375.15 413.16
honourable 078.34 381.36 475.28 615.18
Honourable 413.03 622.26
honourably 085.23
honoured 235.03 430.26 590.22
honours 036.23 059.29 091.07 393.14
Honours 304.09 351.28
honour's 027.23 584.36
honourworthy 244.18
hont 365.23
honty 565.23
Honuphrius 572.21 572.28 572.30 572.34 573.02 573.09 573.12 573.19 573.29
hoo 205.06 348.01 426.18
Hoo 247.13 262.11
Hoo 102.34
hood 131.18 152.20 333.25 392.29
hood 342.12
Hood 487.21
hoodendoses 077.30
hoodenwinkle 078.22
hoodie 276.26
Hoodie 004.05
hoodies 468.30
Hoodle 299.F4
hoodlum 337.29 530.18
hoodoodman 339.29
hoodoodoo 149.08
hoods 551.09 589.01
hoody 360.28
hoof 156.17 175.30 222.30 321.32 429.16 599.07 599.08 599.08 599.08
hoofd 077.21
Hoofd 340.06
Hooghly 318.12
hooghoog 069.07
hoogly 207.33
hooh 474.11
Hoojahoo 609.18
hoojahs 282.24
hook 061.24 197.17 233.29 239.05 260.05 305.18 311.22 324.12 431.07 549.19 623.34
Hookbackcrook 127.17
hooked 140.36 453.31
hooker 046.13 377.21
hookercrookers 245.08
hooks 214.05

Hook's 180.30
Hookup 360.16 530.22
hooky 028.35
Hool 568.14
hooley 326.01 584.12
Hooley 424.04
hoolft 506.03
hoolies 138.11
hooligan 622.22
hoolivans 006.15
hoom 624.15
hoompsydoompsy 373.06
hoon 200.11
hooneymoon 329.19
hooneymoonger 340.20
hoonger 586.29
<u>Hoonsbood</u> 104.18
hoop 156.04 328.29 398.19
Hoop 294.10
hooper 255.09
hoopicough 397.24
hooping 008.30 095.08
hoopoe's 449.27
hooprings 428.12
hoops 020.28 118.29 476.34
527.23 552.18
hoopsaloop 325.09
Hooraymost 413.32
hoose 313.05 369.03 369.15
380.07 506.05 530.14
hoosh 112.14 273.F3
hooshed 023.27
<u>Hooshed</u> 071.24
Hooshin 482.16
hooshmoney 489.11
Hoost 147.11
hoot 317.22 415.18
Hootch 005.09
Hootchcopper's 480.17
hooth 126.15
hoothed 223.29
Hoother 021.10 021.22 021.34
022.09 022.22 022.32 023.14
Hoother's 021.32 022.19
hoothoothoo 623.10
hooths 619.25
hoots 117.23 233.31 253.26
351.26 442.04
Hoots 272.01
hoot's 415.18
Hoovedsoon's 394.28
hoovier 376.14 376.14 376.15
hoovthing 359.25
hop 007.11 022.33 199.01
226.19 297.25 328.18 436.34
469.19 470.22 489.30
Hop 015.28 295.24 500.03
hopas 594.06
hope 033.20 040.28 057.06
084.14 091.18 100.02 119.04
123.28 130.01 141.36 146.09
146.12 156.32 160.23 167.19
174.36 178.31 188.23 190.27
193.26 227.17 235.04 252.24
252.24 263.10 385.24 394.04
417.29 431.10 448.22 458.25
489.24 493.08 503.19 508.32
519.28 545.27 567.32 572.17
582.14 604.31 610.32 621.31
625.36
Hope 461.07 463.29
Hopeandwater 211.10
hoped 059.07 172.12 183.03
<u>hoped</u> 419.06
hopeful 164.19
<u>hopeful</u> 267.L1
hopeharrods 159.15
hopeinhaven 143.10
hopeless 410.18
hopelessly 150.22 171.07
hopelessness 544.06
Hopely 280.03
hopen 518.36
hopends 324.35
hopenhaven 478.16
hopening 060.29
hopes 006.04 011.08 111.16
165.34 337.28 369.36 408.22
446.08 602.32 617.28 624.04
hope's 168.02
hopesalot 325.08
hopesend 320.23
hopeseys 320.02
hopesome's 432.35
hopeygoalucrey 358.09
hophazards 615.07
hoping 119.04 128.32 313.02
369.31 616.34
Hoping 471.04
hopitout 506.32
hopjoimt 231.31
Hopkins 026.02 026.02
<u>Hoploits</u> 272.L4
hopolopocattls 386.35
hopon 186.13
Hopopodorme 245.02
hopops 234.36
hopped 334.29 454.11 474.22
489.12 559.34
hopper 486.30
hopping 012.34 083.02 516.01
576.19
Hopping 361.12
hoppinghail 558.19
Hoppity 273.F3
hopptociel 504.24
hoppy 414.22 452.16
hoppy-go-jumpy 332.24
hops 250.34 553.19
Hops 319.30
<u>Hops</u> 176.16
Hopsinbond 510.35
Hopsoloosely 413.27
Hopstout 412.36
hoptohill 288.12
hopy 320.01
hoq 033.27 033.27
Hoq 033.27
hor 426.18
Hora 514.22
<u>Horace</u> 072.06 307.L1
Horace's 319.21
<u>Horam</u> 481.16
<u>Horan</u> 049.15
horasa 325.17
horatia 329.04
horces 322.25
hord 371.05
horde 069.09 362.12 584.28
614.25
hordwanderbaffle 610.30
hore 268.27
hored 485.25
horeilles 102.12
horenpipe 315.24
hores 379.14 435.23
horescens 194.16
horesies 376.05
Horey 502.22
horild 610.03
horing 416.11
horizon 252.24 502.36 590.23
<u>Horizon</u> 340.29
horizons 594.16
horizont 486.21
horizontally 444.18
Hork 403.03
horker 245.14
Horkus 373.12
Horlockstown 097.07
hormonies 456.21
horn 006.36 017.10 020.04
026.27 043.33 074.04 246.05
323.25 326.28 457.01
Horn 039.36 264.05
hornbook 422.15
horne 352.31
horned 005.07 594.24
hornemoonium 377.15
horner 623.03
Horner 465.04
hornerable 050.23
horners 279.F29
hornest 290.22
hornets-two-nest 441.01
horneymen 540.22
horneys 507.25
hornful 120.33
hornhide 403.14
Horniman's 061.23
horning 436.35
hornitosehead 415.03
hornknees 409.16
hornmade 192.27
horns 045.22 045.23 045.24
552.09
hornypipe 231.31
horodities 614.02
horolodgeries 607.07
horologe 128.01
Horoseshoew 159.28
Horrasure 346.34
horrhorrd 378.07
horrible 067.32 188.21 192.10
horrid 005.07 386.02 516.07
Horrid 423.08
horridly 511.06
horrifier 438.10
Horrild 169.04
Horrocks 326.01
horrockses' 491.32
horror 171.23 282.02
Horror 156.33
horrors 005.30 062.24 183.35
419.34
horrorscup 261.25
horrus 455.06
hors 164.18
Horsa's 143.23
horsday 347.01
horse 049.07 111.27 111.30
135.22 201.24 214.12 214.15
487.32 510.30 568.27 600.01
606.35
<u>horse</u> 040.06
horsebags 095.14
<u>horsebrose</u> 201.15
Horsegardens 617.22
<u>horsegift</u> 418.20

horsehappy 111.29
Horsehem 571.25
horseless 446.24
Horsepass 203.02
horsepower 459.33 576.26
horsepowers 387.11
horserie 032.35
horsery 231.14
horses 047.26 116.05 118.06 321.26 377.23 386.36
Horses 108.16
Horsesauce 272.17
horseshow 246.23 386.27
horsey 322.17
Horsibus 498.06
Horssmayres 379.05
hortatrixy 269.31
horthoducts 152.28
horthrug 126.20
hortifex 136.18
Horuscoup 105.28
Horuse 328.34
hory 352.13
horyhistoricold 382.12
hos 528.07
Ho's 422.17
Hosana 417.12
hosch 038.20
hose 128.11 133.08 135.03 143.01 235.35 434.24 577.11 617.02
hosebound 104.16
hosed 059.26 179.07
hosen 429.05
hosenband 062.10
hosenbands 393.16
hoseshoes 595.23
hosetanzies 379.07
Hoseyeh 553.35
hoshoe 063.22
hosiered 016.04 536.15
hosiery 179.33 548.21
hosies 271.L2
hosing 059.25
hospedariaty 345.29
hospes 416.15
hospices 477.16
hospitable 380.11
hospital 618.11
Hospitalism 420.31
hospitality 171.22
hospitals 555.22
Hospitals 176.09
hospodch 620.32
Hossaleen 476.28
hosspittles 040.36
host 133.11 139.04 193.26 234.18 310.26 369.03 394.19 394.19 417.24 609.27 622.29
hostage 166.18
Hostages 518.16
hosteilend 335.12
hostel 135.19 213.24 514.15 535.05
Hostel 053.28
hostem 167.34
hostery 162.12 378.32
hosth 317.32
hosties 566.01
hostilious 468.01
hostillery 371.25
hostily 315.10
hosting 202.18 501.31
hostis 041.05
hostpost 364.06
hosts 580.24
hosty 372.23 523.27
Hosty 040.21 041.08 044.08 044.15 044.15 044.15 045.25 045.25 046.25 211.20 525.19 580.36
Hosty's 497.26
hosy 375.26
hot 055.18 068.09 097.01 139.25 161.23 161.29 203.33 207.22 239.18 272.10 316.14 333.27 363.27 414.09 439.05 456.02 475.28 485.09 553.18 570.08 615.09
hot 399.12
Hot 215.29 420.25 579.06 621.24
Hotchkiss 523.14
Hoteform 623.17
hotel 030.16 036.22 046.05 063.25 578.11
Hotel 050.34 137.05 205.25 289.26 330.24 609.16
hotelmen 539.16
hotels 444.34 542.09
hotface 030.21
hotfoots 469.24
hoth 004.11 167.36
hothehill 607.27
hothel 586.18
Hothelizod 452.11
hother 350.19
hotly 123.07 125.20
hots 233.31
hotted 406.17
hottempered 426.06
hottentot 193.02
hottest 435.13 507.22
hottin 117.30
hottoweyt 583.30
hottyhammyum 613.12
Hotup 415.35
hotwashed 050.29
hou 244.21 322.12 594.30
Hou 011.35 011.35
Houdian 160.31
houdingplaces 127.11
Houdo 042.18
hough 036.16 208.05
houghers 386.31
houhnhymn 015.13
hould 362.19
houlish 518.35
houlm 613.32
Houlth's 624.26
houmonymh 490.13
houn 478.31
hound 037.10 181.22 204.12 471.21 500.13
Hound 244.21
hounded 132.16
hounds 097.17 321.26 334.34
hour 014.11 034.22 036.25 037.17 052.28 053.17 053.26 067.04 069.23 082.16 087.15 091.33 107.22 111.07 118.32 119.06 126.20 148.29 164.10 190.16 194.05 215.06 255.06 276.14 279.09 279.F09 288.08 328.18 334.02 336.15 360.24 365.18 387.18 403.20 409.25 442.18 449.25 461.12 477.27 477.27 519.35 524.22 548.32 563.36 580.15 594.13 598.13 605.23
Hour 307.19
Hour 104.19
houram 609.22
hourglass 455.16
Houri 068.11
hourihaared 468.36
Hourihaleine 156.36
hourihorn 316.15
houris 177.10 417.28
hourly 060.30 421.31 457.03 604.06
hourmony 462.06
houroines 348.29
hours 018.32 028.06 053.20 054.02 087.36 154.26 190.15 219.06 238.12 305.07 368.09 393.30 405.22 427.17 449.27 472.31 507.05 558.01 586.02 598.31 600.16 607.10 608.35 617.27
hour's 259.04
hours' 075.18
hourse 388.17
hourspringlike 535.02
house 013.08 024.09 031.29 032.26 033.05 034.08 041.31 055.03 058.05 062.30 066.32 069.34 096.07 097.13 098.11 101.32 126.21 136.11 136.12 137.30 174.26 176.31 181.02 182.30 183.05 194.09 205.30 220.23 237.26 241.07 244.20 249.06 249.10 257.08 262.18 264.32 285.08 292.14 317.17 327.04 327.28 367.12 369.04 375.04 377.02 380.15 405.26 406.26 431.35 434.03 443.31 452.17 456.27 481.36 483.11 493.30 506.21 510.17 512.34 514.08 537.02 543.18 543.32 552.27 560.17 609.13 622.36 623.11
House 025.15 063.23 070.34 140.03 170.32 261.F2 310.22 397.14 420.21 421.02 558.35 617.22
House 105.05 106.27 176.09 213.01
Houseanna 406.28
Houseboat 139.34
housebonds 617.07
housebound 317.06
housebreaker 107.31
housed 355.15 622.36
Housefather 246.06
houseful 407.35
househalters 054.25
Househelp's 181.18
household 076.02 377.02 544.07
households 025.10 181.12
houseking's 070.19
houseonsample 397.32
housepays 392.07
housepets 279.F18
housery 414.33
houses 155.15 321.10 498.08
House's 600.17
housesleep 411.07 411.07
Housesweep 141.28

housetops 118.19 193.15
housetruewith 598.34
housewalls 589.30
housewarmer 423.15
housingroom 040.02
housings 564.18
houspill 448.15
Houtens 111.12
Houtes 366.27
houthhunters 497.07
houthse 010.27
houx 097.36
hov 346.20
hoved 128.23
Hoved 324.20
Hoved 106.33
hovel 117.31 231.01
hoven 365.13
hovering 475.11 576.14
hoveth 131.07
Hovobovo 234.01
how how How How HOW
howabouts 355.03
howalively 273.20
Howarden's 242.33
howareyous 430.34
howbeit 342.04
Howbeit 125.02
howcameyou-e'enso 065.31
howd 006.08
Howday 517.31
howdeddoh 340.31
howdiedow 455.14
Howdoyoucallem 094.34
how-do-you-do 035.16
howdrocephalous 310.06
howdydos 433.02
howdydowdy 333.26
howdyedo 527.17
howe 261.04 370.08
Howe 018.12 026.23 315.20 553.23
howed 346.26
howelse 260.05
hower 389.20
howe's 081.12
howeth 197.03
however 029.16 116.26 116.31 118.02 161.04 162.03 167.12 356.26 369.06 455.22 468.24 573.27 599.34
However 406.30 422.31 428.01 437.25 439.25
Howforhim 098.36
howhappy 131.15
howitts 015.24
howitzer 011.24
Howke 106.24
howl 426.01 480.28 480.34
howldmoutherhibbert 388.29
howling 443.15
How'll 205.04
Howlong 363.11
Howls 304.F5
howlth 287.09
howly 072.25
howmanyeth 274.20
howme 173.29
howmely 173.29
howmovingth 274.20
Howmuch 261.29
howmulty 215.25
hownow 408.30
Howoft 316.21
howonton 349.31
howorodies 341.11
howover 451.34
howpsadrowsay 597.23
howr 556.34
hows 194.29 312.24
how's 584.23
How's 425.02 451.16 464.27 536.04
howsands 567.02
howses 009.22
howsoclever 426.03
howsoever's 362.18
howsome 330.35
howsomedever 341.35
Howsomendeavour 624.35
Howten 414.04
howth 433.12
Howth 003.03 073.31 514.23
Howth 525.24
Howthe 312.20
howtheners 326.13
howthern 357.32
howthold 242.05
howthorns 160.06
how'tis 140.23
howtosayto 223.27
howyousaw 362.14
hoy 063.30 372.22
Hoy 180.36
hoyden 167.35 260.18 436.03
hoydenname 276.F1
hoydens 504.34
hoyhop 612.35
hoyhra 561.01
hoy's 514.08
Hoy's 563.27
hoyse 005.34
hoyt 536.14
hoyth 004.36 448.02
h'p'y 265.F3 (halfpenny; also perhaps happy)
Hraabhraab 072.13
Hray 372.28
hree 150.02
hriosmas 091.05
Hrom 243.33
hross 342.18
hrossbucked 535.08
hrosspower 008.36
H.R.R. 492.36
hu 257.35 259.09
Huam 499.10
Hubba's 477.10
hubbishobbis 511.28
Hubbleforth 073.18
hubbub 029.35
Huber 394.29
Hubert 031.25 376.06
Hublin 105.18
Hubty 105.18
hubuljoynted 310.31
huc 153.24
huck 068.06
Huck 454.07
huckling 543.05
hucks 066.13 622.18
hucksler 286.11
hucky 584.05
Hucky 410.36
huddle 447.30
huddled 546.15
huddled 341.20
Huddlestown 481.28
huddly 257.18
huddy 622.08
Huddy 257.08
hudson 212.24
hue 034.02 052.26 118.20 215.17 227.25 257.35 588.20 609.20 611.36 622.33
Hue 106.02
huecry 068.20
hued 256.10
huedobrass 373.29
hueful 611.13
hueglut 612.13
huemeramybows 011.12
huemoures 102.27
huepanwor 611.19
huer 257.35
hues 215.17 233.05
hues 103.05
Huesofrichunfoldingmorn 571.32
Huey 063.13
Huff 560.02
Huffsnuff 124.35
Huffy 106.32
hug 145.14 167.01 200.32 315.32 465.22
hug 273.L2
Hugacting 009.05
huge 057.32 066.13 099.08 179.18 553.19
hugely 084.15 417.28
huges 454.15 454.15 454.15
Huges 197.08
hugest 589.09
hugged 511.33
huggerknut 512.16
huggin 327.36
Huggin 292.10 543.17
hugging 065.30 404.33 484.09
Huggins 376.23
Huggisbrigid 404.35
hugglebeddy 616.01
Hugglebelly's 137.12
huggornut 517.07
hugh 006.07 223.13 273.13
Hugh 357.07 388.33
hugheknots 541.14
Hughes 330.05
hughy 454.15 454.16 454.16
hugibum 598.34
hugibus 598.34
hugly 620.26
hugon 371.36 621.25
Hugonot 211.18
hugs 453.17
Huguenot 456.14
Huguenots 133.21
huguenottes 350.29
Huh 378.05 378.05 378.05
Huhneye 273.F3
huhu 558.25
Huhu 117.32
huing 517.20
Huirse 273.28
huis 245.36
hula 297.26
hulk 324.05 471.20 583.01
Hulker's 245.21
hulks 039.20
hulkwight 310.26
hull 029.21 323.23 416.32

Hull 436.30 518.35
hullabaloo 180.28
hulldread 329.09
hullender's 126.16
Hullespond 328.19
hullo 508.09
Hullo 488.23
hullocks 566.29
hullow 596.28
Hullulullu 353.28
hulm 378.04
hulme 594.13
hulp 323.15 348.27
Hulp 348.27
hulstler 521.30
hum 052.23 339.22 369.21 431.07 447.04 465.29 512.22 514.04 611.08
Hum 006.33 114.19 199.32 441.19
human 035.05 051.01 058.19 073.32 079.19 099.04 112.22 115.36 116.30 143.04 164.27 179.13 186.05 254.09 359.02 403.24 430.06 431.09 431.11 481.12 618.36
Human 525.26
humanae 287.23
humand 366.26
humane 429.07
humanity 138.06 306.14 451.20 542.36 599.28
humanity's 577.13
Humans 533.25
humbedumb 619.01
Humber 198.29
humbered 265.26 265.26
Humbermouth 525.25
humbild 588.33
Humblady 018.07
humble 037.07 038.06 472.30 483.36 484.28
Humble 176.04
humbledown 586.11
humbleness 242.22
humbler 427.26
Humbles 296.09
Humblin 018.07
humbly 484.17 615.14 628.11
Humbly 589.17
Humbo 585.30
humbodumbones 387.33
Humborg 072.12
humbs 346.16
humbug 582.10
humbugger 496.03
humburgh 560.07
humdrum 288.22
hume 080.18 080.18 261.05 606.16
Hume 043.01 443.19
humely 450.13
humeplace 481.21
Humfries 097.03
Humhum 173.23
Humid 597.33
Humidia 048.05
humidity 588.25
humile 029.30
humility 427.26
Humilo 499.06
Humme 029.18 338.16
hummed 098.14
Hummels 566.29
hummer 310.19 368.15
hummer 341.10
hummers 404.06
humminbass 295.01
humming 261.04 371.21
hummingsphere 453.22
hummley 356.05
hummock 411.19 622.19
Hummum 416.02
humn 363.05 443.17
humoral 084.04
humoresque 050.16
humour 031.14 511.27
humour 341.10
humours 071.07 154.21 502.07 521.34
hump 129.18 197.03 358.35 549.35 584.18
hump 201.09 352.20
Hump 045.06 242.22 312.13 312.13 352.15 612.15
Hump 044.28
HUMP 220.24
humpbacked 492.29
humpenny 351.21
humpered 577.14
Humperfeldt 585.22
Humpfrey 582.26
Humph 074.16 254.15
humphar 124.33
Humpharey 046.30
Humpheres 062.21
humphing 029.05
Humphrey 030.02 030.20 040.35 196.21 325.28 405.18 430.07 484.09
Humphreys 616.35 616.36
Humphrey's 052.23 070.13 134.34 203.06 275.F4
Humphreystown 270.13
humphriad 053.09
humping 062.28
humple 390.32
humponadimply 097.26
Humpopolamos 327.33
Humprey 441.07 585.32
humps 042.18
Humps 624.13
Hump's 525.19
Humpsea 317.24
humpteen 219.15
humpty 455.24
Humpty 012.12 045.01
Hump-ty 044.25
humptyhillhead 003.20
humpup 355.30
humpy 606.34
Humpy's 200.32
hums 485.27
humself 003.20 168.01 288.08
humuluation 593.15
humuristic 594.28
humus 018.05
hun 275.21 278.21 362.12 616.20
Hun 076.32 251.03 251.03 590.26
Hunanov 038.22
Hunarig 535.02
hunched 312.16
huncher 333.26
hundering 596.02
Hunderthunder 078.05
hundled 608.29
hundreadfilled 019.24
hundreads 243.01
hundred 009.20 038.13 073.20 084.26 084.26 086.15 098.01 101.35 123.06 128.31 156.02 182.23 201.29 201.34 208.08 211.17 283.F1 305.10 347.04 380.16 404.36 405.12 408.06 425.32 478.09 518.04 519.35 544.16 547.12 574.26 584.24 589.03 617.03 627.14
hundred 398.32
Hundred 030.08
hundredaires 564.18
hundredlettered 424.23
hundreds 135.19 264.20 283.16 375.09
hundredth 497.26
hundrick 126.05
hundrund 597.05
hundt 335.10
huneysuckling 329.20
hunfree 017.19
hung 010.03 025.29 127.06 137.23 228.01 245.06 271.28 295.07 306.06 322.12 336.25 485.28 549.12 558.28
Hung 374.34
Hungaria 460.26
hunger 422.24
hungered 188.36
hungerford 576.26
Hungerford-on-Mudway 393.09
Hungerig 623.17
hungerlean 032.15
hunger's 457.07
hungerstriking 199.04
hungery 126.22
hunghoranghoangoly 611.30
Hungkung 457.07
hungray 101.35
Hungreb 068.25
hungred 029.01
hungried 081.04
Hungrig 464.28
hungrily 121.35
hungry 411.11 416.20 465.16
Hungry 539.32
hunguest 325.17
Hungulash 287.F4
hunigen 332.04
hunk 373.17 408.03
Hunkalus 480.20
hunker 321.11
Hunker 065.17
hunkered 541.29
hunkers 225.10
Hunkett 127.19
hunks 094.10
hunky 333.22
hunnerable 325.27
hunnibal 132.06
hunnish 392.05
hunnishmooners 395.13
Hunover 388.17
Hunphydunphyville'll 375.05
huns 135.24
hunsbend 364.36
hunself 171.04
hunselv 199.05
Hunshire 197.10

hunt 043.11 060.15 132.04 134.03 567.25 594.07 603.32
hunt 530.24
Hunt 355.16 530.25
hunt-by-threes 245.19
hunted 134.35
hunter 132.17 435.14 513.05 567.03
hunter 342.20
Hunter 376.06
Hunter 286.L1 440.03
huntered 359.01 618.36
hunterland 276.F7
hunters 139.03
hunter's 310.26
hunthorning 500.13
hunting 031.02 323.07 567.24
hunting 383.06
Hunting 376.18
Huntler 263.F1
huntsem 384.28
huntsfurwards 357.36
huntsome 623.02
hunty 330.36
hup 038.16 302.25
Hup 054.01
Huppy 328.19
hurd 213.16
hurdies 316.29
Hurdlebury 297.20
hurdles 180.16
hurdles 342.18
Hurdlesford 014.05 547.17
hurdley 512.31 570.33
hurdly 354.14
hurgle 378.25
huries 445.04
hurlbat 084.04
hurled 035.25 039.15
Hurleg 337.30
hurley 279.09 511.24
Hurleyquinn 048.15
hurlin 322.16
hurling 144.08
Hurls 574.15
hurlyburlygrowth 558.20
hurlywurly 257.18
hurold 009.11
huroldry 005.06
hurooshoos 084.02
Hurr 602.31
hurrah 026.09 406.25
Hurrah 006.29 045.25
hurrahs 205.02
hurray 377.33 495.14
hurricane 022.22
Hurricane 210.16
hurricanes 455.01
hurriedly 511.03
hurries 233.31
hurrigan 589.30
hurrish 416.01 416.02
hurry 093.04 228.21 238.05 285.06 300.10 356.27 376.26 449.05
Hurry 206.26
hurryaswormarose 302.27
hurry-come-union 227.30
hurrying 555.20
hurry-me-o'er-the-hazy 111.24
hursey 328.15
hurss 323.08
hurt 055.14 062.16 115.19 434.25 445.07 466.12 469.12
hurtful 109.15
hurther 426.19
hurtig 356.15
hurtled 224.06
Hurtleforth 570.21
hurtleturtled 005.17
Hurtreford 353.23
hurts 345.08 476.15 514.35
Huru 054.10
hurusalaming 542.04
husband 049.02 134.27 229.35 272.02 311.21 311.23 311.36 313.09 356.09 358.17 362.27 391.24 536.17 576.25
Husband 071.28 104.16
husband-in-law 436.16
husbandman 005.09
husbandmanvir 465.07
husbandry 038.11
husbands 436.04 504.34
husband's 325.19
husbandship 492.36
husboat 104.16
hush 134.04 134.28 305.25 305.25 333.30 552.09 553.25 553.25 562.35
Hush 013.05 100.36 563.01
hushaby 211.35
husheth 214.10
Hushkah 246.05
hushly 038.34
hushmagandy 276.17
hushtokan 296.24
hushy 250.11
husinclose 545.30
husk 109.08 287.18
huskers 467.28
Huskies 106.04
huskiest 582.03
Huskvy 105.16
husky 077.16 160.24 214.28 253.04 426.07 593.15
huspals 441.12
hussars 214.29
hussies 285.L2
hussif 512.13
hussites 589.33
husstenhasstencaffincoffin-tussemtossemdamandamna-cosaghcusaghhobixhatoux-peswchbechoscashl-carcarcaract 414.19
hussy 166.29
hussyband 226.18
Huster's 184.22
hustings 577.28
Hustings 106.04
Hustle 207.21
hut 254.30 291.09 334.07
hutcaged 600.36
hutch 337.07 543.11
huts 055.13 548.12
huur 077.22
huw 423.02
Huzoor 244.19
huzzars 348.27
hvad 088.29 611.21
hvide 247.31 320.08
Hvidfinns 099.15
hvis 403.14
hvisper 460.07
Hwaad 018.14
hwan 322.06
Hwang 130.35
hwat 538.04
Hwemwednoget 243.03
hwen 073.36 322.06 389.31 586.21
hwere 034.28
Hwere 311.22
hwide 013.34
Hwo 601.08
Hwoah 474.15
Hwoorledes 054.11
hworefore 326.22
hworsoever 364.23
Hwy 601.08
Hy 549.19
Hyacinssies 603.28
hyacinth 086.15
Hyacinth 087.12
Hyacinthinous 281.14
hyacinths 335.06
Hyam 455.23
Hyam's 455.23
hyber 484.15 577.23
hybreds 152.16
hybrid 169.09
hyde 374.21
Hyde 066.17
hydeaspects 208.11
Hyderow 327.10
hydes 603.15
Hydes 150.18
hydraulics 256.28
hydrocomic 580.25
hydromel 451.07
hydromine 077.04
Hydrophilos 606.05
hydrophobe 035.02
hydrostatics 151.30
hye 545.33
Hyededye 340.31
hyelp 141.13 141.13
hyemn 330.07
hyenesmeal 301.28
hygiene 573.21
hygienic 036.25 054.29
hygiennic 596.19
Hyland 073.02
hym 465.29 550.33
Hymanian 261.15
Hymbuktu 288.23
Hymernians 376.12
hymn 093.33 199.27 447.04
Hymn 136.16 609.23
hymned 472.08
hymns 229.28 514.35
Hymnumber 234.34
Hymserf 240.11
Hynes-Joynes 370.21
hyougono 085.05
hyperape 271.L4
hyperchemical 167.06
hypertituitary 037.01
hyphen 248.20
Hyphen 446.04
hypnos 078.03
hypnot 360.24
hypnotised 320.02
hypostasised 055.35
hypothecated 161.03
HYPOTHESES 286.R2
hypothesis 125.19 150.35

hypothetic 524.18
hypsometers 235.17
Hyrcan 219.14
hys 248.20
hyssop 423.10
hysteria 528.14
Hystorical 564.31
hystry 535.18

i 302.25 410.12
i 106.25
I I
I 251.31 (I is a femaline person)
i' 037.20 (in)
275.13 (in)
I' 226.34 (In)
.i..'. 514.18 (Finn's)
Iago 041.02
I'am 278.F3
Iarland 582.25
Iar-Spain 050.20
Ibdullin 309.13
iberborealic 487.01
ibi 167.33
Ibid 034.05
ibipep 540.14
Ibn 488.07
Ibrahim 346.05
Ibscenest 535.19
Icantenue 347.22
ice 451.25 452.36 481.35 621.26
icebox 326.36
iceclad 110.24
Icecold 502.09
icefloe 017.22
iceland 040.19
Iceland 139.20
Iceland's 129.27
icepolled 435.12
iceslant 316.32
ich 113.25
ichabod 116.32
ichnehmon 416.12
ichs 299.02
Ichthyan 485.10
Ichts 343.20
iciclist 145.11
icies 551.05
icing 149.26
icinglass 415.28
Icis 214.31
ick 483.35 555.23 555.23
Ickam 446.03
Ickick 423.10
ickle 483.35
Icknild 042.26
icky 284.17 555.24
Icon 339.03
iconostase 603.35
icoocoon 483.35
iction 603.29
icy 379.23 616.32
Icy 104.10
Icyk 106.28
Icy-la-Belle 246.20
id 611.21
id 488.09
I'd I'd
Ida 060.22 211.35 211.35 227.14 276.F4
Idahore 504.22
Idas 379.15
iday 547.33
iddle 547.05
ide 027.08 031.33
idea 035.19 121.03
ideal 064.22 120.13 120.14 136.33 161.19 560.13
Ideal 303.L3
idealist 490.06
ideally 355.01
IDEAREAL 262.R1
idears 538.19
ideas 037.27 076.02 078.28 160.17 443.22 463.12
Idefyne 510.10
Idem 263.21
idendifine 051.06
identifiable 488.29
identified 575.19
identify 496.25
identifying 482.10
identities 114.33
identity 123.30
Ides 289.27
Ides-of-April 035.03
idies 354.25
idim 019.22
idinhole 581.20
idioglossary 423.09
idiology 352.19
idiom 117.14 253.01
idiot 167.14 438.06
idiotism 299.F3
idle 118.03 455.03
Idle 546.11
Idleness 289.28
idler 527.21
idlers 287.18
idlers' 013.29
idles 128.32
idlish 182.15
idly 588.15
Idneed 201.03
idol 378.24
idolatry 433.23
Idoless 395.02
idolhours 238.17
idoll 527.24
idolon 349.20
idols 594.25
Idos 465.13
idself 611.21
Idyall 325.25
idylly 357.21
Iereny 455.08
iern 207.21 242.34 547.32
if if If If
ifidalicence 040.27
ififif 284.15
ifs 455.17 463.28
ifsuchhewas 079.03
igen 265.06
Igen 538.33
Iggri 193.17
iggs 012.14 339.03
igien 272.29
iglesias 553.21
igloo 207.33
Ignaceous 186.13
ignacio 228.11
ignerants 540.32
ignite 446.36
ignitial's 451.19
ignitious 433.01
ignomen 241.21
ignorance 018.24 115.01 125.04 229.28 446.24
ignorant 238.15 586.09
Ignorant 361.20
ignorants 163.16
ignoratis 442.21
ignore 352.18
Ignorinsers' 321.02
ignorious 498.36
Ignotus 263.03
igone 547.34
Igorladns 353.19
Iguines 088.20
ihis 335.19 335.19
ihm 072.25
ihs 300.18
ii 244.30
I. I. 369.09 (Mr I. I. Chattaway)
ijypt 198.01
Ik 104.10
ikan 312.03
ike 483.25
ikeson 483.20 483.20
ikey 416.06
Ikish 424.03
ikom 205.27
il 230.11 281.18
il 466.19
ilandiskippy 011.10
ilcka 212.15
ild 017.35
Ild 320.25
ildiot 037.14
ile 013.23
ilex 571.08
Ili 566.26
ilk 102.26 588.16
ilkermann 356.02
ilks 599.01
ill 007.34 158.13 223.21 224.06 315.17 328.23 448.20 454.24 527.34 590.19
ill 164.34
Ill 007.33 128.12 165.28
I'll I'll
Illas 626.34
illassorted 503.09
illassumed 086.12
Illbelpaese 129.27
illcertain 340.26
illcome 567.24
illconditioned 521.24
ille 092.07
illed 257.21
illegallooking 518.15
illegible 119.15 421.34 482.21
illegitimate 543.35 572.31
illexpressibles 357.28
illfamed 545.03
illfollowable 325.35
illformation 137.34 374.26
illglands 451.04
illian 581.20
Illicit 029.01
illico 110.31
illicterate 336.31
illigant 014.04
illiterative 023.09
illitterettes 284.15
illness 130.08
illortemporate 082.17

illpogue 303.04
ills 011.24 211.25 279.F02 541.01 579.32
illscents 279.F29
illscribed 496.05
illsell 537.25
illsobordunates 156.11
illspent 563.06
illstarred 040.21
Illstarred 467.29
illth 060.08
illud 153.24
illuding 507.28
illuminatured 568.34
illusiones 611.12
illusionist's 066.28
Illustration 301.L1
illustrationing 570.30
illustred 349.15
illustrious 422.19
illvoodawpeehole 120.31
illwinded 292.13
illwishers' 414.02
illy 609.28
illyrical 615.04
Illyrie 281.06
illysus 196.21
Ilma 621.09
ilond 294.04
ily 411.26
Ilyam 055.03
Ilyum 055.03
im 180.05
I'm I'm
image 157.35 429.14
imageascene 331.30
images 443.02 563.04
imagettes 025.02
IMAGINABLE 260.R3
Imaginaire 177.28
imaginary 449.03
imaginating 487.15
imagination 068.07 487.01 565.29
imagine 056.02 161.15 518.01
Imagine 152.08 284.18 305.06 337.16
imagined 165.24
imago 417.32
imbabe 378.03
Imbandiment 497.05
imbecile 544.27
imberillas 373.21
imbetther 234.29
imbraced 244.29
imbretellated 227.36
Imean 444.05
imeffible 183.14
I'm-free-Down-in-Easia 482.29
imitating 408.24 461.34
imitation 053.21 221.07 487.22
imitationer's 466.18
imitator 423.10
Imlamaya 627.03
Immacolacion 528.20
Immaculacy 247.28
immaculate 045.14
Immaculatus 191.13
immanse 528.09
immarginable 004.19
immartial 149.07
immaterialities 394.32
immature 425.31
Immecula's 601.22
immediata 228.23
immediate 036.30 155.08
immediately 054.27 446.23 544.30
immengine 337.20
immense 096.32 405.21
immense 419.05
immensesness 241.11
Immensipater 342.26
immensity 150.36
immenuensoes 425.18
immer 098.32
immerges 310.24
immergreen 032.29
immermemorial 600.26
immersion 513.03
Immi 258.11
Imminence 504.20
immingled 345.01
immitiate 535.03
immo 287.22
immobile 152.25 163.20
immodst 085.30
immodus 034.18
immor 098.33
immoral 572.34
immoralities 145.26
immortal 152.34
immurables 197.25
immutant 361.20
immutating 460.12
imnage 082.19
imogenation 251.17
imorgans 547.34
impact 133.13
Impalpabunt 023.25
impalsive 386.29
impart 091.19 569.20
imparticular 602.07
imparvious 377.13
Impassable 499.19
impassible 340.05
impeachment 220.29
impedance 322.28
impediments 596.23
impendements 515.33
Impending 279.F18
impenetrablum 178.30
imperative 268.24
imperfect 468.09
imperfectible 122.35
imperfection 109.09 428.07
imperfectly 033.22 582.31
imperial 133.34 382.09 398.16 539.19 560.18
Imperial 498.12
imperious 283.16
impermanent 101.30
impermeable 152.24
impersonating 086.08 490.15
impetiginous 189.32
impetus 268.24
impfang 418.08
impiety 206.20
implicating 033.34 166.36
implicitly 065.36
implied 151.28
implies 018.24
implore 557.33
imploring 100.15 174.18
impluvium 251.02
implying 234.23
impolitely 192.26
imponence 277.02
import 166.32
Import 579.22
importance 035.22 114.32 440.33
important 158.32 166.31 437.19 515.03
importunate 138.05
importunes 151.19
importunity 395.34
impose 378.26
imposed 137.25
imposing 032.19
imposition 533.11
impossible 110.19 417.32
Impossible 617.08
impossive 162.19
Impostolopulos 306.10
imposts 183.10 541.07
impostulance 483.30
impostures 182.02
impotent 573.22
Impovernment 273.06
impracing 365.35
imprecisely 057.16
imprecurious 363.28
Impregnable 411.33
imprescriptible 085.07
Impress 548.02
impressiom 278.F2
impression 018.24 411.34
impressive 069.04
imprincipially 483.20
improbable 110.12 110.12 110.15 499.19 617.09
improctor 366.23
improduce 283.13
impromptued 171.09
improofment 603.03
improper 096.14 131.33 384.29 387.07 391.24 395.15
Improper 269.F3
improperable 538.12
Improperial 484.20
improperies 278.05
Improperty 617.35
impropriety 034.15
impressable 609.06
improvable 530.34
improve 145.28
improved 077.08 386.34
improvement 345.31
improvidence 012.01
improving 292.05 409.24 453.29
impudence 296.F5
impudent 167.35 453.06
impugnable 152.24
impull 418.33
impulsively 059.21
impulsivism 149.11
impulsory 421.27
impure 024.24
impures 234.30
impursuant 594.28
imputant 067.21
imputation 033.26
imputations 557.16
imputed 067.22
in in In In IN
ina 124.08
Inaccessible 159.33
inaddendance 358.35
Inam 237.26

inamagoaded 180.03
inandouting 513.35
inane 250.16
inartistic 182.19
inasdroll 121.17
inaslittle 019.03
inasmuch 350.02
Inasmuch 495.20
inat 017.06 083.20
inatentions 241.05
Inattendance 604.20
inauguration 099.26
inauspiciously 049.13
inbourne 268.16
inbrace 388.05
inbursts 066.19
Inc 534.16 (Incorporated)
Incabus 013.11
incalpable 363.32
incamination 497.02
incapable 108.35 186.33
incapacity 576.02
incarnadined 079.03
incarnations 600.09
Incarnations 308.19
incas 423.01
incautious 034.26
incendiarist 426.02
incendiary 424.31
incense 207.01 235.17
incensed 179.10 336.35 412.14 536.19
incensive 465.12
incenstrobed 263.06
inception 150.30
Incertitude 178.32
incessantlament 614.02
incessantly 462.18
incestuish 115.12
incestuous 573.11
inch 152.34 182.05 185.35 268.05 384.22 590.27
inchamisas 233.30
inchanting 543.08
inchettes 255.32
inchies 155.11
Inchigeela 407.18
inchimings 360.11
inching 438.03
inchly 578.33
inchthick 170.33
incidence 332.24
incident 038.29 081.33
incidentalising 091.13
incidentally 529.35
Incidentally 600.15
incipience 051.09
incipit 185.22
INCIPIT 278.R1
inclinaison 284.06
inclination 266.17
inclined 113.27 228.27 421.24
inclining 478.24
incloted 026.10
incloths 537.15
included 169.11
including 077.31 211.30 222.14 230.22 483.33
incognits 283.27
incoherend 242.15
incomc 448.32
incomeshare 191.18
incommixtion 347.22
incommon 041.04
incompatabililiy 164.02
incompatibly 085.27 533.05
incomplete 560.07
incompletet 119.14
incomputables 367.31
inconoscope 349.18
inconsistency 192.32
incontigruity 607.20
Inconvenient 172.25
incoronate 250.35
incorporate 580.23
incorporated 108.15 332.14
incorruption 062.18
increaminated 366.17
increase 448.29
increasing 173.31 613.19
increate 604.27
incredible 425.21
Incredible 155.03
increscent 276.F3
incubation 112.21 397.34
Incubone 221.23
inculmination 232.08
incunabula 114.06
incur 142.21
incurable 041.01
incurables 197.25
incuriosited 449.01
incursioned 324.31
incut 571.06
ind 071.07 143.25 156.03 313.20
Ind 598.16
indanified 133.28
indead 505.21 560.18
indecency 436.01
indecked 261.02
indecores 432.31
indecorous 608.09
indecorum 092.05
indeed 032.19 034.11 048.05 164.25 189.14 295.06 295.26 360.27 419.30 448.06 503.19 505.21 513.16 537.02 561.10 563.25 570.22 602.03 606.24
Indeed 066.35 099.31
indeedmymy 162.25
indeedust 055.03
indeeth 079.17
indeiterum 247.17
indelibile 185.25
indelible 185.26
Indelond 626.28
indentifide 051.05
indentity 049.36
indenture 524.17
independence 118.02 500.14
independent 129.24 510.24
independant 602.17
indergoading 203.28
Indes 215.03
index 154.18 423.08 440.07 589.13
Indgangd 127.28
India 307.25
Indian 134.13 612.08
Indiana 285.F6
indiapepper 292.07
indiarubber 497.29
indicat 513.01
indicate 487.17 564.24
indicating 121.12 599.32
indices 292.07
indicks 241.09
indictment 085.27
indiejestings 536.07
indienne 215.21
indies 390.25
indigenous 006.04
indigent 542.17
indignant 119.12 171.22
indignation 581.02
indigo 404.18
indigonation 023.02
indiscriminatingly 369.27
indispute 309.10
Inditty 411.29
individual 072.17 160.11 186.03
INDIVIDUAL 268.R1
individuals 066.05
individuone 051.06
indivisibles 472.30
indo 477.30
indoor 257.13
indoubting 468.15
Indra 223.07 573.01
indradiction 060.21
inds 427.22
indtil 310.29
indts 417.23
indulgence 009.20 319.08
Indulgence 306.24
indulgences 432.27 445.09
indulgencies 376.05
indulgent 519.32
indulging 031.14
indulligence 531.02
induments 127.04
induniforms 344.10
induring 368.35
Indus 289.06
industrial 409.25
industries 085.24 574.01
industry 140.11
indwellingness 488.02
inebriates 542.10
inedible 016.23 594.32
Ineen 376.01
ineluctable 184.08
ineluctably 120.32
ineptias 510.06
inessive 162.19
inevitable 110.12 155.03 441.14 599.14
inexactly 515.22
Inexagoras 155.32
inexcellsiored 553.15
Inexcessible 285.28
Inexhaustible 160.04
inexousthausthible 091.27
inexpensive 170.27
inexshellsis 154.35
infairioriboos 154.11
infallible 100.15 201.33
infamatios 059.34
infamous 098.18
infams 621.26
infance 538.30
infancy 022.01 022.26
infanetes 565.28
infant 024.24 420.15 544.18 566.23
Infant 166.18
infanta 166.23
Infanta 211.22

infanted 097.35 184.34
infantina 556.01
Infantulus 166.22
infarover 613.08
infect 510.17
infelicitous 537.14
infernal 505.04
Infernal 320.33
infernals 552.15
Inferos 497.23
inferring 108.33
Inferus 136.08
infested 182.32
infester 600.11
infidel 520.13
infidelities 572.23
infidels 589.34
infinibility 245.12
infinisissimalls 298.30
infinite 037.04 127.04
infinitely 180.07
infinitesimally 597.25
infinities 019.30
infinitive 271.21
infinity 154.14
infirmierity 291.F8
infirmity 375.01
inflammabilis 232.03
inflamtry 348.35
inflected 118.26
Inflexibly 454.06
inflicted 107.25
inflounce 221.11
influence 166.31 438.03
Influence 297.L1
INFLUENCE 268.R1
influences 363.35
influenza 513.18
influx 567.13
inform 229.08
informal 357.27
informally 056.27
information 245.32 356.31 443.06
informations 061.03
informed 572.31 617.15
Informer 071.10
infradig 425.35
INFRALIMINAL 276.R1
infrarational 020.01
infroraids 316.03
infructuosities 348.33
infurioted 138.28
infused 542.11
infuseries 431.13
infusing 242.16
infusion 542.11
infusionism 117.33
infustigation 150.07
infuxes 249.02
ingain 343.09
ingang 560.14
ingate 337.10
Inge 370.03
Ingean 361.11
ingelles 226.22
ingen 496.11
ingenious 425.06
INGENIOUS 286.R3
ingenuinas 209.32
ingenuous 425.17
INGENUOUS 286.R3
ingestion 406.32
ingh 124.11
ingle 233.14
ingles 512.23
ingles 346.18
Inglesante 212.10
ingletears 562.30
inglis 008.23
Inglis 543.18
Inglo-Andean 106.08
ingoyed 456.01
ingperwhis 121.12
Ingram 568.35
ingrate 253.17
ingredient 143.10
ingul 201.22
inhabit 545.18
inhabit 350.04
inhabitands 062.16
inhanger 114.22
inharmonious 109.23 188.26
inhebited 224.11
inher 004.30 546.21
inherdoff 363.26
inherited 031.15 545.04 596.34
inhesitant 542.24
inhibitance 348.16
inhibitating 437.14
inhibited 121.07
inhis 284.10
inhowmuch 414.11
inhumationary 077.33
Iniivdluaritzas 572.15
inimitable 441.14
inimyskilling 008.23
Ininest 241.13
iniquity 421.35
Inisfail 244.06
inish 465.32
Inishfeel 510.33
Inishmacsaint 267.F1
Inishman 091.22
inital 486.15
initial 130.29 486.27
initialled 032.13
Initialled 420.19
initials 100.29 119.16 286.04
initiumwise 483.18
injected 321.06
injective 412.13
injine 224.03
injons 207.30
injoynted 244.29
Injun 008.29
injunction 575.04
ink 066.14 118.33 145.12 183.24 185.07 185.26 186.17 460.19 563.19
Ink 373.19
Ink 342.23
inkbattle 176.31
inkbottle 263.24
Inkbottle 182.31
inked 606.26
inkedup 099.17
inkenstink 183.06
inkeptive 541.02
inkerman 433.09
Inkermann 048.10 071.08
inket 586.30
inkhorn 118.23
inkinghorn 563.06
inkle 295.23
Inklenders 229.03
Inklespill 156.03
inklings 377.28
inkome 182.23
inkpot 152.11
inkstands 173.34
inkum 027.10
Inkupot 424.07
inkware 182.09
inky 182.27
inlaw 169.04
inlay 315.05
inlookers 355.24
inloss 366.03
inmaggin 337.18
inmate 523.23
inmates 049.19
inmid 561.26
inmoodmined 141.25
inmost 056.03
inn 020.35 021.14 113.18 119.27 129.15 221.04 262.26 262.27 315.34 369.18 565.34
Inn 017.22 056.20 064.09 083.20 138.20 205.25 262.26 262.27 626.33
Inn 105.29
Innalavia 600.05
innamorate 092.27
innards 191.33
innasense 391.11
Innate 296.29
innation 414.08
inne 201.04
innebbiated 029.29
innebriated 098.21
inneed 079.16 602.03
innemorous 158.11
inner 373.35 492.02
innereer'd 485.27
innerhalf 100.19
innermals 341.04
innerman 462.16
innermost 194.03 248.32
inners 225.30
innersence 538.30
innersense 229.36
Innholder 313.03
innings 271.23 584.02
Innition 614.17
Innkeeper 376.10
innkeeping 345.20
innkempt 013.08
Innkipper 144.07
innocefree 204.19
innocence 194.01 435.10 621.30
innocency 034.21
innocens 013.29 483.21
innocent 047.13 110.35 115.28 121.19 235.10 425.10 426.12 601.17
Innocent 152.02
innocenth 618.01
innocents 361.20 563.28
Innocident 059.09
innovated 289.02
inns 007.05 534.29
Inns 016.22 201.26
innumantic 615.04
innvalet 320.15
innwhite 510.30
inny 200.30
inoccupation 344.21
Inoperation 604.24
inordinately 437.36

inplayn 609.15
Inprobable 538.05
inquiline 088.17
inquire 031.05 546.12
inquiries 066.10 124.08
inquiring 035.33
inquisition 342.10
inquisitive 458.19
inroad 097.23
ins 291.20
insalt 373.17
insamples 342.08
insane 173.34
inscissors 563.02
inscrewments 043.32
inscribed 099.18
inscythe 415.01
insect 127.03
insectarian 358.08
insects 414.27
Insects 306.30 339.22
insels 604.25
inselt 051.30
insensed 499.25
insensible 291.23
inseparable 032.07
inseuladed 291.05
in'sheaven 469.30
inshore 264.17
inshored 197.18
inside 069.26 145.29 166.25 200.21 292.13 292.29 364.17 377.24 393.26 393.27 404.27 522.26 529.23 564.27 588.21 611.21 611.24
insiders 497.10
insides 141.10 375.24
Insides 359.24
insidesofme 499.26
insiding 483.25
insight 075.13
insighting 437.05
insigni 412.08
insince 499.25
insinuate 225.06
insinuating 033.25
insist 165.03
insister 442.18
insists 557.26 572.36
inso 237.06
insodaintily 254.31
insofarforth 581.28
insolence 121.23
insomnia 120.14
Insomnia 193.29
insoult 010.14
insound 323.27
inspection 107.24 131.33 498.35
inspectors 107.28
inspectorum 596.28
inspiration 032.28 302.19 436.21
inspire 439.11 453.25
inspired 069.05 187.29 519.30
inspiring 122.22
inspissated 179.25
inspiterebbed 374.08
inst 279.F12
installation 551.18
instalmonths 542.32
instance 034.04 077.26 120.27 504.04 574.07
instant 035.21 124.31 394.23 421.17 429.13
instants 517.04
instantt 561.26
instar 287.08
instate 439.36
Instaunton 534.35
instead 101.21 172.36 174.32 225.18 391.10 434.09 442.28 470.35 604.14 618.03
Instead 171.15 181.12
insteadily 053.07
Insteed 598.04
instench 061.13
instents 337.21
instep 166.07
insteppen 077.20
instigated 067.30
instinct 227.05 610.25 610.26
institution 422.01
institutions 073.20
Instopressible 568.16
instructed 572.29
instructor 295.22
instructual 440.23
instrument 124.03 150.33
instrumental 447.01
instrumongs 064.14
instullt 353.18
insue 336.13
insufficient 409.25
insufficiently 125.21
Insul 510.25
insulant 484.15
insularis 606.07
insulation 316.04
insult 042.03 117.02
insultantly 542.29
insuper 041.05
insurance 589.18
insure 159.25 413.05 578.09
insured 442.16
insurrectioned 352.13
Insway 371.21
int 048.17
in't 148.01
intact 585.10
intactas 432.11
intaken 292.02
intartenment 534.08
intectis 364.21
integer 590.15
integerrimost 590.15
integras 131.32
integument 186.01
intellecktuals 161.06
intellect 606.09
intellects 549.30
intellectual 464.02
intellible 016.33
Intelligence 049.18
INTELLIGENCE 276.R1
Intelligentius 464.16
intelligentsia 173.14
intelligow 478.18
intemperance 178.35
intempestuous 143.16
intend 164.30
Intend 268.16
intendant 089.29
intended 076.35 148.15 279.F11 533.27
intendente 542.17
intending 491.02
Intendite 054.06
intensely 188.17 612.13
intensive 052.11
intent 085.16 187.04 557.22
intentended 413.33
intention 114.14
intentional 517.04
intentionally 424.02
intentions 042.02 063.30 072.31 154.01 154.22 183.19 412.30 439.01
inter 287.26
Inter 506.31
interbranching 123.08
intercellular 116.11
intercepted 457.27
Interchangeability 308.L2
intercissous 449.15
intercourse 237.23
interdict 391.11
interdum 033.35
interecting 284.01
interest 019.03 082.09 150.29 167.02 172.32 173.32 268.23 575.31
interesting 398.10 564.33
interfairance 504.18
interferences 522.35
interfering 232.10
interfeud 058.35
interfizzing 060.24
interims 384.16
interior 314.23
Interior 558.36
Interior 106.22
interiors 119.33
interirigate 601.33
interjection 221.36
interjoked 320.23
interlarded 472.31
interlocative 162.19
interlocutor 177.19
interlocutory 575.04
interlooking 289.11
interloopings 551.01
intermediately 178.20
intermidgets 306.13
INTERMISSIO 278.R1
intermisunderstanding 118.25
intermittences 599.12
intermitting 232.10
international 284.13
internatural 128.27
Interpenetrativeness 308.L2
Interplay 293.L1
interpolation 121.32
interpretation 117.36 369.07
interpreter 091.03 478.08
interprovincial 377.23
interquackeringly 542.23
interregnation 224.14
interrimost 050.17
Interrogarius 572.19
interrogation 523.22
INTERROGATION 281.R3
interrupted 108.03
interrupting 121.01
interskips 232.10
interstipital 436.01
intertemporal 303.L1
interval 032.34 070.34
intervener 438.27
intervulve 314.20
interyerear 182.20

intesticle 413.17
intestines 097.19
intestions 301.30
inthro 310.09
inthrusted 356.29
intil 170.21
intimacies 068.06
intimacy 229.35
intimast 248.31
intimate 034.25 417.21
intimelle 563.05
Intimier 105.11
intimologies 101.17
intinuations 412.15
into into Into
intomeet 238.06
intouristing 055.24
intoxication 142.21 171.07 438.26
intra 038.20
intra 326.07
intraduced 607.05
intrance 423.06
Intrance 240.29
intrants 407.05
intrepidation 338.29
intrepider 467.05
intrepifide 157.25
intrieatedly 302.24
intriguant 561.23
intro 109.16
introduce 280.15 527.34
introdùce 124.10
introduced 160.07 370.12 465.01 533.15
introduces 164.09
introducing 435.06 466.23
introit 432.05
introvent 425.28
intruser 082.18
intuitions 394.36
inturned 254.14
intwo 231.15
inuendation 194.32
inunder 209.29 320.03
inundered 127.05
invaded 247.08
invairn 327.12
invalid 519.33 574.13
invalids 008.06
invariable 033.05
invasable 594.33
inveiled 360.35
invened 066.31
invent 033.36 482.31
invented 374.10 423.09 605.09
inventing 165.31 474.24
invention 082.23 133.33 266.12
Inverleffy 332.28
invernal 300.07
inverness 035.10
inversion 076.34 523.17 526.35
inversions 184.04
invert 486.27 604.05
inverted 108.34 115.31
invertedness 522.31
investigations 150.19
investment 341.14
invincible 081.01 121.23
invincibled 132.33
invincibles 361.20
invinsible 367.25
invinsibles 527.12
invisible 081.01 158.28 546.29
invisibly 504.09
invision 626.28
invisors 316.02
invitem 510.34
invocate 479.20
invocation 449.14
invocatione 185.20
invoice 439.19
invoiced 623.08
invoked 026.20 290.28 394.22
invoking 572.23
involted 284.09
involucrum 050.13
involucrumines 613.17
involuptary 358.02
involved 079.01
involving 558.02
invrention 424.20
invulnerable 404.25
invulnerably 077.02
inwader 581.03
inwardness 611.21
inwards 128.18
inwiting 054.35
inwoking 368.13
inwreathed 234.14
inyeborn 585.18
inyon 079.20
in-you 446.04
Inzanzarity 415.26
io 583.10 583.10
Iodina 573.01
iodine 200.36
iodines 253.18
IOIOMISS 305.R1
Iomio 416.18 416.18
Iona-in-the-Fields 569.08
iordenwater 117.04
iorn 614.11
Iosa 562.25
iosals 408.06
iota 120.27 356.01
Ipanzussch 488.07
Ipostila 449.11
Ipse 254.04
Ipsey 230.20
ipsissima 121.09
ipsofacts 156.09
ipsum 287.27
Ir 086.15
Iran 144.18 358.21 491.36
ire 069.08 124.14 320.26 445.26 541.19
Ire 391.28 522.04
ireglint's 006.35
Ireland 078.26 141.36 182.31 214.18 214.18 288.F6 380.13 380.18 380.20 380.20 380.34 429.17 452.29 456.07 456.28 472.35 482.13 501.23 528.31 571.19 608.14
Ireland 260.L1
Irelande 157.36
irelands 455.08
Ireland's 162.32 420.32 466.35
Ireland's 071.14
irelitz 421.27
Irelly 525.16
Iren 127.26 310.20 392.27 620.09
Irene 154.23
Irenean 023.19
Irenews 254.10
irers' 141.21
Ireton 480.08
Irewaker 059.27
Irewick 126.04
iridals 611.17
iridecencies 494.04
iridescent 068.20
iries 354.25
Irine 471.01
Irinwakes 321.17
iris 238.32 528.23
Iris 030.01 285.27
Irise 493.28
irised 318.34
irish 150.02 301.F2 312.30 361.07 465.31 484.15 500.14
Irish 013.01 037.25 038.24 049.07 053.07 063.21 086.01 086.20 086.21 111.23 118.02 119.32 140.08 140.31 176.22 190.09 190.36 207.07 208.26 270.11 283.17 341.20 342.32 381.29 396.08 403.23 404.19 406.11 407.14 431.04 447.04 470.33 498.15 518.22 542.02 559.02
Irish 055.31 072.12
irished 538.01
Irishers 537.07
Irishmen 132.34 488.33
irishsmiled 555.18
irismaimed 489.31
Irismans 612.20
irkdays 553.15
Irl 313.15
irmages 486.34
Irmak 212.13
Irmenial 345.01
Iro-European 037.26
iron 050.02 069.24 185.33 245.25 325.22 351.04 404.21 447.06 518.15 582.22
Iron 138.21 286.11
ironed 008.18 079.14
ironing 531.06
ironing 399.21
irons 422.01
Irons 027.23
ironsides 035.09 362.05
irony 160.22
irony 348.32
Iro's 612.20
irrara 497.04
irrawaddyng 214.09
irredent 484.09
irregular 179.03
irregularshaped 134.25
Irrelevance 249.24
irrelevant 511.04
irremovable 117.35
irreperible 057.18
irrepressible 470.31
irrespectively 119.26
irreverend 511.07
irriconcilible 434.20
irrigate 009.03
irritant 416.36
irritating 109.25
irritation 266.17
Irrlanding 539.18
Irrland's 171.06
irruminate 167.07
Irryland 583.20

irsk 070.30
Irskaholm 132.33
irskusky 070.30
irthing 207.22
I.R.U. 446.18 (why are you? and I am you)
Irush-Irish 322.02
irvingite 491.07
irwell 201.13
is is Is Is IS
Is 269.21 (Is a)
570.30 (Is, is)
601.05 (citye of Is)
620.32 (Is is)
Isa 226.04 556.09
isaac 003.11 253.35
Isaac 408.26
Isaac 307.L1
Isaac's 254.13 293.17 421.04
Isaacsen's 621.19
isabeaubel 146.17
Isabel 210.12
isabella 279.F31
Isabella 566.23
Isabelle 556.07
isabellis 446.07
Isad 580.18
isagrim 448.24
Isas 361.22
isaspell 238.03
isbar 070.29
Iscappellas 527.01
isce 092.07
ischt 113.12
I'se 159.18
Isegrim 244.21
Iseland 323.20
iselands 290.18
Iseult 398.29
Iseut 004.14
isges 017.29 017.30
ish 231.03
Isha 140.27
Ishallassoboundbewilsothoutoosezit 154.33
ishebeau 527.29
Ishekarry 207.24
ishibilley 238.04
ishim 199.13
Isid 026.17
isingglass 247.36
isinglass 084.29 460.21
isisglass 486.24
Isitachapel-Asitalukin 110.08
isits 186.09
isker 213.04
isky 256.33
iskybaush 091.28
islamitic 098.08
island 019.13 046.12 188.11 321.09 325.32 374.19 411.06 411.07 447.27 549.26 626.07
Island 170.29 245.24 355.21 410.13 496.08 553.06
Island 103.01 105.26 175.25
islanders 228.07
islands 351.08 362.07
isle 110.06 159.32 263.F2 287.15 387.12 506.26
Isle 076.23 232.13 496.09
isles 206.35 456.20 501.19 580.34
Isles 387.30
isle's 095.11
Isley 462.15
islish 611.05
Isma 621.08
Ismael 258.13 258.16 258.17
Ismeme 054.16
isnor 236.28
isnoutso 245.01
isn't Isn't
isobaric 133.04
Isobel 556.01 556.05 556.16
isocelating 165.13
isochronism 515.11
isod 444.34
Isod's 087.29
Isolabella 209.24
Isolade 289.28
Isolamisola 384.31
isolate 410.12
Isolde 500.25
isoles 486.20
Isoles 607.31
isonbound 461.23
isoplural 297.21
Isot 223.11
Isout 007.29
iSpace 124.12
Israel 331.19
Israfel 049.23
iss 163.06
Iss 501.04
Issabil 513.25
issavan 007.04
Isset 214.13
issle 394.20 394.20
Isssossianusheen 267.19
isst 128.01
issuance 476.35
issuant 601.05
issue 183.23 255.29 324.07 575.12 585.01 602.20
issue 354.04
Issy 459.06
Issy-la-Chapelle 080.36
ist 245.02 540.19 568.13 597.11
ist 163.05
Ist 349.02
is't 552.09
Is't 621.14
iste 092.09
Isteroprotos 498.04
Isther 069.14
istherdie 295.01
isthmass 197.15
isthmians 594.25
isthmon 017.21
isthmus 003.06
iszoppy 560.27
it it It It IT
Ita 094.12 147.12
ital 089.35
italian 498.30
Italian 031.20 182.27 456.08
italics 550.09
Italicuss 407.17
italiote 504.18
itandthey 481.29
itch 124.08 180.20 231.03 268.04 343.26 548.14
Itch 485.03
itcher 206.33
itchery 439.22
itches 488.34 495.30
itching 423.35
itchother's 546.16
ite 005.30
Item 223.35 306.07 618.24
item's 456.28
iterimpellant 486.35
iteritinerant 594.07
iterum 287.26
ites 542.14
ith 249.35 249.35
Ithalians 569.29
ithel 459.13
ithmuthisthy 623.10
ithpot 262.L2
ITINERARY 260.R3
itiswhatis 223.27
it'll 141.36
its its Its ITS
it's it's It's It's
itself 025.18 025.33 030.17 038.03 068.08 081.33 107.08 109.11 113.29 116.30 122.04 153.04 194.05 294.28 384.16 576.23 585.13 597.33 611.18 614.20
Itself 036.28 394.33 394.33
itsen 488.15
ittle 191.20
Ittle 601.19
itwas 301.02
iucunditate 185.24
iudicat 096.33
Iuld 100.31
Ivan 355.11
ivanmorinthorrorumble 353.24
Ivanne 048.12
ivargraine 019.23
ivary 327.28
Ivaun 138.17
Ive 031.32
I've I've
Ivel 390.30
ively 236.14
iver 139.28
Ivernikan 197.29
iverol 619.36
iveryone 209.27
ives 152.03 291.09
ivfry 446.12
ivies 354.25
ivileagh 557.11
ivoeh 029.04
Ivor 100.25
Ivorbonegorer 255.15
ivoroiled 004.31
Ivor's 012.31
ivory 192.27 396.10 437.32 527.22 545.09
ivory 341.08
Ivory 556.03
ivorymint 235.36
ivvy's 005.30
ivy 027.13 058.06 134.21 265.17 505.03
Ivy 485.21
Ivy 377.16
ivyclad 392.29
ivysad 588.17
ivytod 571.14
ixits 534.30
Iy 446.02
iz 004.14 017.36

Izaak 076.28
Izalond 261.F2
izarres 101.29
izba 335.03
Izd-la-Chapelle 334.36
Izod 203.09 512.03
IZOD 220.07
Izodella 349.21
Izolde 265.13
Izzy 212.17 257.01 431.15
Izzy's 588.24

J. 213.02 (Mill (J.))
ja 325.11
Ja 213.02
Ja 163.07 163.07 163.07
jab 124.21 368.25
jabberjaw 125.19
jabote 297.09
jabule 066.30
jac 466.14 466.14 466.14
jacent 243.15
jacinthe 281.05
jack 168.11 179.08 308.24 320.34 549.23
Jack 211.15 307.20 330.22 459.27 460.27 496.03
jackabox 091.26
jackadandyline 535.01
jackal 211.31
jackalantern's 197.26
jackass 096.01
jackasses 153.36
jackboots 026.10 035.10
jackdaw 360.04
Jacked 511.36
jackeen 210.19 620.24
jackery 535.13
jacket 313.08 368.30 404.22
jackets 183.17
jackhouse 274.22
jackill 589.15
Jackinaboss 485.33
jackinjills 141.09
jackknife 455.31
jackless 462.06
Jacko 414.17
Jackot 465.04
jackstaff 479.27
jackticktating 243.08
Jacob 169.01 420.30
Jacob 307.L1
jacobeaters 542.30
Jacobiters 111.04
jacob's 300.12
Jacob's 026.30 138.14 366.36
Jacobsen 424.27
Jacobus 449.15
Jacoby 303.16
Jacohob 359.17
Jacq 366.36
jacquemin 253.35
Jacqueson's 245.24
jaculation 145.25
jade 200.02 276.F3 436.08 486.15 494.05
jadeses 417.22
jadesses 019.23
Jady 277.L4
jaeger 435.14
jaffas 406.32
jagger 481.36
jaggery-yo 256.19
jaggled 357.21
jags 069.23
jagsthole 201.23
jah 090.18
jail 045.10 045.11
Jail 045.12
jailahim 060.05
jailbird's 496.31
jailbrand 484.34
Jaime 461.31
Jaimesan 470.33
jake 308.24
Jake 026.05 487.10 611.01
Jakeline 447.01
Jakes 142.28
Jakob 607.08
jaladaew 597.31
Jales 387.23
Jalice 105.17
jam 121.18 141.35 406.21 448.08 497.31
jamal 233.32
Jamas 449.14
jamb 027.18
Jambaptistae 287.24
jambe 280.L4
jambebatiste 117.12
jambos 471.23
jambs 068.02 228.27 478.24
Jambs 513.09
jambses 258.08
Jambudvispa 596.29
Jambuwel's 366.20
James 386.26 387.08
jameseslane 373.25
Jameson 382.04
Jamesons 305.17
James's 140.32
Jamessime 588.06
Jamesy 142.28
Jamesy's 521.14
jamey 007.36
jameymock 423.01
jammesons 333.16
jamn 225.17
jampot 496.19
Jampots 219.06
Jams 098.19
Jan 349.22
Jan. 420.20 (January)
Jane 059.26 214.25 254.25 358.32
Jane's 027.11
Janesdanes 389.10
janglage 275.F6
jangled 416.09
jangs 480.33
jangtherapper 361.27
janitor 027.03 224.11
janitrix 008.08
Janiveer 112.26
Jansens 173.12
jantar 316.36
januarious 429.16
january 544.36
January 105.22
Januero 536.01
Janus 133.19 272.16
Janus's 542.16
Janyouare 473.03
jaoneofergs 233.21
jaonickally 430.10
jape 486.12
japers 233.03
japets 583.18
japijap 031.30
japlatin 467.14
jaquejack 422.33
jar 530.12
Jarama 602.13
Jarge 229.03
jargon 108.23
Jargonsen 621.22
Jark 558.17
jarkon 198.18
Jarl 021.10 021.22 021.32 021.34 022.09 022.19 022.22 022.31 313.15
Jarley 061.11
jarred 098.19
jarrety 222.31
jarry 278.F1 463.12 575.26
jars 082.07 183.18
jarvey 407.06
jary 210.01
jas 184.02
Jas 447.22
Jasminia 613.34
jasons 089.34
Jason's 123.26
jasper 249.08 494.05
Jasper 479.10 479.11
jast 599.19
Jaun 429.01 430.17 430.33 431.09 431.13 431.20 431.21 437.35 439.27 441.24 448.34 453.14 454.16 469.29 470.24
Jaunathaun 454.09
jaundice 582.11
Jaunick 457.36
Jaunstown 462.28
jaunted 542.34
jauntingcar 210.19
jauntingly 059.25
jauntings 225.34
jauntlyman 343.14
jaunts 284.F5
jaunty 359.28 407.06
Jaunty 429.01
jauntyjogging 053.07
Java 254.25
javanese 152.12
javel 077.33
javelin 534.35
jaw 162.35 246.09
jawache 423.17
jawballs 463.17
Jawboose 590.19
jawcrockeries 443.25
Jawjon 471.14
jawr 223.08 426.18
jawrode 613.22
jaws 439.18
jay 251.01 284.F5 540.14
jay 478.21
jaypee 386.26 387.06
Jaypees 134.35
jaywalking 121.17
jazz 437.03
Jazzaphoney 388.08
jazzlike 511.11
jazztfancy 292.20
J. B. 497.36 (J. B. Dunlop)
J. C. S, 492.19
je 058.26 058.28
Je 478.20

Jealesies 106.13
Jeallyous 271.03
jealosomines 450.11
jealous 062.33 174.33
jealousjoy 583.17
jealousy 361.12 547.14
jeamses 543.20
Jean 222.08 553.13
jebel 005.23
Jebusite 240.28
Jedburgh 057.36
Jeebies 590.19
Jeejakers 469.11
jeenjakes 463.09
jeer 101.26 127.18
jeeremyhead 229.32
jeerilied 257.06
jeers 117.23 173.26
jeeshee 475.02
Jeeshees 612.33
jeff 016.12 359.18
Jeffet 168.06
jeffmute 016.14
jeffs 273.18
Jeff's 143.23
Jeg 269.20
Jehosophat 255.12
Jehova 035.33
jehovial 405.20
Jehu 053.08 563.07
jehumispheure 346.07
Jehusalem's 469.09
Jeldy 297.16
jelks 321.16
jelly 274.F4
jellybags 430.31
jellybelly 206.36
jellywork 550.12
Jelsey 061.12
Jelupa 550.15
jem 563.07
Jem 169.01
jemassons 229.23
jemcrow 360.04
jemenfichue 268.13
jemes 456.06
Jeminy 564.01
jemmijohns 268.07
Jempson's 245.24
Jenkins' 485.21
jennerously 084.18
jennet 554.05
jennies 271.F2
jenniest 266.27
jennings 271.19
jenny 039.34 097.35 415.11
Jenny 278.12 327.10 490.25
jennyjos 238.33
jennyroll 461.16
jennyrosy 093.07
jenny's 247.33
jennytenny 457.36
Jer 458.15
Jeremias 572.24 572.26 572.35
573.11 573.18
Jeremy 246.36 370.08 372.10
575.32
Jericho 150.20
jerk 138.29 231.31 615.25
jerkin 311.07
jerking 121.06 479.27
Jerkoff 246.30 563.24
jerks 611.01
jerksome 513.32
Jermyn 625.02
Jerne 469.18
Jeroboam 558.15
Jerome 252.11
Jeromesolem 124.35
jerried 288.F5
jerry 274.22 301.17 426.08
565.10
Jerry 027.09 210.21 225.34
555.20 563.07 604.02
jerrybly 283.28
jerrybuilding 015.07
Jerrybuilt 489.14
jerryhatted 265.F2
jerrykin 575.25
jerrywangle 041.03
Jerseys 302.F1
jerumsalemdo 368.09
Jerusalemfaring 026.04
Jervis's 040.35
Jeshuam 452.35
Jess 147.12
jesse 502.03
Jesses 034.29
jessies 236.17
jessim 354.31
jessup 583.33
jest 099.21 233.03 331.36
332.07 359.22 363.10 486.10
509.31 511.35 565.14
jester 171.15
jesterday 570.09
jestnuts 125.20
Jests 221.26 307.F1
Jesu 398.31
jesuistically 120.21
jesuit 182.36
jesuits 382.07
jesuit's 038.24
jesuneral 349.19
Jesuphine's 038.32
jesus 300.29
jet 247.36
jets 548.23
jetsam 292.16
jetty 207.05
Jetty 332.18 420.24
jettyblack 583.22
jeune 430.22
jew 035.16 116.12 180.06
273.14 534.05
Jew 155.34
jewbeggar 070.34
jewel 441.19
jewel 277.L4
jewelled 155.23
jewels 449.23 551.03 587.09
Jewess 133.20
jewr 312.32
jewries 447.09
jew's 086.23
jewses 423.36
Jeyses 480.16
jezabelles 192.25
jezebel 562.03
Jezebel 210.12
J. F. 048.12 (J. F. Jones)
J.F.X.P. 211.20 (J.F.X.P.
Coppinger)
J. H. 529.13 (J. H. North)
Jhamieson 126.05
Jhanaral 375.24
Jhem 003.13
Jhon 126.05
jib 387.04
jibberweek's 565.14
jiboulees 087.05
jibsheets 220.31
jiccup 004.11
jiesis 450.25
Jiff 369.11
jiffey 625.33
jiffies 041.11
jiffy 170.11
jig 122.13 200.24 231.32
236.14 469.04 534.36
jig 399.07
Jig-a-Lanthern 010.27
jiggers 580.33
jiggery 437.03
jiggerypokery 113.26
Jiggety 534.36
jiggilyjugging 351.10
jigging 414.22
jigjagged 180.18
jigotty 531.17
jigs 193.34 221.26
jigsaw 210.11
jigses 375.27
jigsmith 184.15
Jik 376.13
Jilian's 406.24
Jilke 061.11
jill 462.06
Jill 211.15
jilldaw's 276.06
jillies 273.L4
jilling 315.22
jillous 009.07
jilt 318.10
jilt 399.08
Jilt 290.F2
jilted 220.10
jilting 279.F02 465.04
jiltses 417.21
jim 575.26
jiminies 021.11
jiminy 021.21 021.28 021.32
022.07 022.08 022.15 022.24
jimjams 193.35
jimmies 095.10
jimminies 023.13
jimminy 021.36
jimmy 039.21
Jimmy 307.20 587.04 587.05
587.19 587.24 587.30 587.35
588.13
jimpjoyed 068.02
jims 121.18
Jined 020.16
jingaling 430.30
jingelbrett 542.34
jingled 416.08
Jinglejoys 466.18
Jinglesome 229.06
jingling 031.01
jinglish 275.F6
jingo 067.02
jingoobangoist 364.32
jings 246.08 310.25 616.06
jink 062.17
jinking 348.24
Jinko 329.01
jinnies 008.31 008.33 008.33
008.36 009.06 009.07 009.13

009.17 009.21 009.27 009.28 009.33 009.35
jinnies' 009.02
jinnyjones 576.36
jinnyjos 526.17
Jinnyland 359.35
jintyaun 094.30
jirryalimpaloop 302.24
jist 011.07 031.10 038.20
jistr 406.11
jisty 351.09
jitters 377.17
jittinju 352.28
J. J. 083.03 (J. J. and S.)
Jno 447.22
jo 095.10 170.03 171.24 171.24 171.24 171.25 171.25 171.25
Jo 397.03
Jo 199.29
Joahanahanahana 554.10
joakimono 214.11
joan 607.13
Joan 222.07 528.13
joans 323.07
Joan's 223.20
Joax 369.15
job 012.18 090.17 181.30 282.01 301.20 443.32 562.31 563.07
Job 448.22
Job 307.L1
jobbera 088.19
jobduty 235.11
jobs 266.F2
jock 511.36 575.26
Jock 540.27
Jockey 611.01
Jockit 126.07
Jocko 587.36
jocolarinas 361.28
jocosus 433.08
jocubus 251.01
jodelling 455.02
jodhpur 329.02
Joe 141.27 152.14 159.22 175.35 175.36 211.32 215.18 254.24 282.17 328.04 455.11 549.35 590.06
joebiggar 015.30
joepeter's 426.21
joey 460.36
jog 122.13 236.14
jog 341.04
jogahoyaway 285.14
Joge 594.35
jogging 404.03
jogjoy 245.21
Joh 366.35
Johannes 533.21
Johannisburg's 453.33
johl 245.30
john 399.34 399.34
John 061.04 099.32 187.20 215.18 216.01 254.09 255.27 359.23 382.04 395.03 448.32 516.20 526.18
John-a-Donk 614.29
johnajeams 399.34
Johnathan 307.05
Johnheehewheehew 399.29
johnjacobs 188.28
johnny 290.09 347.29 397.25 590.23
Johnny 210.13 214.36 278.13 384.14 386.06 386.12 387.15 389.17 391.04 482.14 521.10
johnnythin 463.27
Johns 172.05 172.07
Johns 281.L2
John's 359.34 408.33
johnsgate 373.25
Johnston-Johnson 377.32
johntily 223.33
join 091.14 206.13 226.08 234.05 296.24 300.01 424.03 488.32 491.36
Join 318.28
joined 042.01 092.05 155.16 255.10 348.01
joint 007.09 059.28 361.11 574.03 574.18
jointly 037.19 574.32
jointoils 564.20
joints 503.01
joint's 455.30
jointspoiler 201.10
jointure 275.12
jointuremen 228.35
jokable 454.16
joke 009.14 010.12 133.16 323.34 511.34 565.14
Joke 290.F2 455.29 458.13
jokepiece 033.03
joker 202.03
jokes 193.09 221.26 502.09 517.08
jokeup 487.22
joking 082.22 569.01
Jokinias 256.21
joki's 208.23
joky 169.01 380.21
Jolio 144.14
Jollification 455.12
jollity 489.30
jolly 043.17 066.21 187.32 380.18 386.03 447.11 454.12 454.15 487.18 533.03 533.06 578.14 587.06
jolly 344.04 350.06
Jolly 395.03
jollybrool 005.34
jollycomes 276.F2
jollygame 569.25
jollyjacques 335.34
jollytan 463.35
jollywell 085,18
jollywelly 250.13
jolt 248.09 318.10
jolting 107.33
jom 241.34
Jom 031.28
jomping 441.03
Jomsborg 310.03
Jon 424.27
jonah 323.07
Jonah 536.32
jonahs 358.24
Jonas 434.27 463.31
jonass 529.23
jonathan 172.24
Jonathan 192.22
Jonathans 540.28
jones 160.18
Jones 048.12 149.10 210.17 487.10
joneses 543.20
Jones's 431.12 521.13
Jong 482.11
jongers 051.16
jonjemsums 325.17
jonnies 095.10
Jonny 476.27
Jonnyjoys 428.20
jonquil 238.10
jontom 252.35
joobileejeu 329.30
Jook 441.07
Jooks 456.31
jool 329.29 394.08
joornee 621.02
jophet 189.31
joq 033.28
jordan 210.30 497.31
Jordan 103.08
Jordani 287.24
jordan's 480.02
Jorden 228.31
Jorgen 621.22
Jorn 142.27 513.07
jornies 428.03
Jorsey 609.16
jorth 496.11
jorums 221.26
Jorum's 316.19
jos 184.02
Josadam 485.32
José 312.07
joseph 208.17
Joseph 274.L3 307.L1
Josephine 071.07 212.13
Josephinus 246.17
Josephs 243.35
Joseph's 366.35
Joshua 053.22 231.18 550.02
joshuan 004.20
Josiah 372.09
joss 089.36 611.04 611.27
Joss 611.14
Joss 177.06
Joss-el-Jovan 472.15
josser 109.03
Jossiph 213.29
jostling 058.21
Josus 091.19
jot 193.19 563.07
jotalpheson 089.34
jotning 344.01
Jotnursfjaell 057.14
jottings 118.30
jotty 112.32
jouay 430.10
jouejous 056.16
joule 315.11
joulting 047.07
Jour 246.32 329.31
jourd'weh 470.13
jourd'woe 470.13
journalwriter 439.10
Journaral 341.07
Journee's 226.11
journeeys 417.34
journey 431.27 456.18
Journey 104.18
journeyall 026.03
journeymanright 546.20
journeyon 594.07

jours 281.13
jousstly 468.05
joussture 535.03
joust 416.12
jousters 531.36
joustle 568.08
jouted 441.24
Jova 351.35
Jove 080.28 231.23 624.10
jove's 206.03
jovesday 050.32
jovial 583.08
joviale 181.08
Jow 302.13
jowel 153.29
jowl 089.25 161.32 248.09
jowld 367.16
jowls 368.27 368.27 368.28
jowly 230.04
joy 045.12 131.23 178.12 331.34 434.27 439.14 472.19 495.21 563.07 588.12 596.20 605.31 626.29
Joy 076.05
joyance 598.25
joyant 310.33 495.20
joybelled 551.12
joybells 566.18
joyboy 443.11
joyboys 094.01
joyclid 302.12
joyday 194.11
joydrinks 277.04
joyfold 527.22
joyful 472.35
joygrantit 004.35
joyicity 414.23
Joynts 015.07
joyntstone 192.35
joyous 134.24 246.13
joyously 470.08
joyoust 414.01
joys 211.25 547.29
joysis 395.32
J.P. 420.31 (Justice of the Peace)
J. P. 524.14 (Mr J. P. Cockshott)
jpysian 005.23
Jr 279.F11 (Junior)
Jr. 087.18 (Roaring O'Crian, Jr.)
Juan 461.31 461.33 470.33
jub 204.30
jubabe 066.30
jubalant 338.17
jubalee 013.12 305.19
jubalharp 466.18
jubilarian 567.22
jubilated 607.30
jubilee 031.18 275.11 447.13
Jubilee 521.19
jubilends 593.13
jublander 141.22
jucal 182.23
Juckey 105.12
jucking 417.30
juckjucking 450.17
Jucundus 574.12
judaces 575.36
Judapest 150.27
judas 193.09
Judascessed 492.05
Judder 175.12
jude 334.21
Jude-at-Gate 569.09
Jude's 205.25
judex 133.23
judge 200.17 303.18 326.04 337.02 535.31 574.33
Judge 574.09 575.32
judgements 058.21 289.21
judgers 582.33
judges 004.20 242.27 263.28
judges' 094.24
judgeship 090.36
Judgity 386.36
judgment 575.33
judicandees 057.19
Judsys 620.26
Judy 358.33
judyqueen 207.36
Judy's 255.26
jug 083.15 122.13 543.34
Jug 246.02
jugful 065.22
juggaleer's 300.31
jugglemonkysh 084.16
jugglywuggly 027.32
jugicants 156.05
jugoslaves 137.33
jugs 406.24 449.32
Juhn 473.10
juice 153.12 180.07 626.15
Juice 501.07
juiced 043.15
juicejelly 170.34
juices 564.20
Juin 569.13
juinnesses 333.17
juju 127.24
jujube 444.22
juju-jaw 256.19
Jukar 209.04
juke 162.04 375.04
Juke 033.24 137.11 367.18
jukely 417.30
jukersmen 337.24
Jukes 295.F1
Jukoleon 367.20
julep 464.29
julepot 559.15
Julepunsch 594.35
Jules 386.30
Juletide's 097.03
Julia 207.24 465.02
juliannes 350.22
julias 242.14
julie 426.04
Julie 502.24
Juliennaw's 430.36
juliettes 148.13
Julius 306.L2
jully 113.35 569.13
jumbjubes 273.17
jumble 416.09
jumbled 430.29
jumbles 459.08
Jumbluffer 590.20
Jumbo 105.17
jumbobricks 042.32
jumboland 528.18
jumeantry 286.L4
jump 145.35 376.22 618.17
Jump 528.35
Jump 176.05
jumped 578.25
jumper 181.28
jumphet 064.01
Jumpiter 342.14
jumpnad 202.26
jumps 145.03 363.10
Jumpst 626.05
Jun. 421.11 (June)
Juncroom 156.06
june 266.27
June 416.32 454.32
junelooking 589.23
juneses 238.29
juness 117.10
jungerl 268.F3
Jungfraud's 460.20
jungle 112.04 416.09
junglegrown 170.30
jungleman 586.11
Junglemen 348.13
jungular 511.35
junior 440.17 575.02
Junior 321.34
juniorees 279.F15
juniper 583.02
junipery 015.35
juniverse 231.02
junk 178.17 511.35
Junkermenn 503.10
junket 127.18
junking 348.24
Juno 087.05 538.01
Junoh 245.12
junojuly 203.20
Junuary 332.25
jup 294.F1
jupan 435.27
jupes 339.26
jupetbackagain 114.19
juppettes 531.19
Jupto 353.18
Jura 356.08
jurats 536.33
jurbulance 084.02
jure 302.13
jure 290.23
jureens 575.25
juremembers 557.15
Jurgensen's 035.28
juridical 557.13
jurily 313.10
jurisdiction 155.08
jurisfiction 574.34
jurna's 215.09
jurors 091.02 519.19 575.04
jurors' 375.05 574.33
jury 242.21 337.02 466.29 574.10 574.30 576.01
juryboxers 575.08
jurymiad 575.09
jurys 257.23
Jury's 091.20
jus 156.04
jused 229.26 229.27
jusfuggading 350.05
jushed 448.06
jusqu'à 281.12
jusse 502.07
just 027.05 030.04 039.16 041.08 042.03 042.06 053.24 059.21 059.27 066.31 067.08 068.07 068.24 069.13 069.23 083.03 089.15 092.33 092.34

108.13 109.15 110.02 112.13
114.32 120.03 122.29 133.23
144.09 144.19 145.20 154.30
162.06 162.20 163.08 165.29
167.06 170.19 181.17 186.29
189.23 190.17 191.02 191.23
198.20 202.27 225.03 229.26
240.35 242.28 244.17 252.19
270.29 270.F2 271.F5 279.F26
284.F5 287.16 289.F2 299.07
303.18 305.11 310.31 331.07
337.07 343.04 356.19 356.33
365.30 370.13 373.33 379.19
381.09 382.26 385.36 386.17
404.17 409.06 411.26 413.05
419.29 421.31 425.28 430.32
431.08 436.34 445.14 449.25
451.32 452.10 454.14 458.14
460.08 460.10 461.20 461.27
462.31 468.16 470.10 470.24
487.07 490.13 491.31 501.10
507.30 523.26 559.34 578.27
581.34 588.10 589.28 597.03
597.03 597.03 598.02 599.34
606.29 608.05 619.22 626.02
Just 017.06 048.11 064.22
193.09 209.10 236.33 291.F7
307.14 352.08 368.25 374.32
375.13 453.21 504.14 511.29
538.07 616.36 618.06 624.10
627.04
Just 241.36
justajiff 501.10
justbeencleaned 091.17
Justesse 134.34
justice 036.32 057.36 134.33
137.30 187.21 458.17 527.22
Justice 390.36
Justice 275.F4
justicers 092.35
justicestjobbers 368.28
Justician 377.31 377.31 377.32
Justiciated 421.05
justickulating 243.19
justifiable 084.14
justification 142.22
justified 112.24
JUSTIFIED 282.R4
Justinian 377.32
JUSTIUS 187.24
justly 357.04 357.35
justness 534.13
justotoryum 153.26
justright 191.22 395.27
justsamelike 612.02
justso 340.29
jute 018.15
Jute 016.07 016.10 016.12
016.14 016.16 016.18 016.21
016.23 016.29 017.03 017.08
017.13 017.31 018.01 018.10
018.12 018.14 018.16
juteyfrieze 327.01
juties 600.25
juts 138.28 491.06
jutstiff 100.15
jutty 202.11
Juva 609.25 609.28 609.32
610.01 610.05 610.07 610.11
610.16 610.18 610.20 610.22
610.28 610.32
juvenile 209.32 617.33
juwelietry 291.12
juwells 236.02
juwels 313.25
juxtajunctor 125.07
juxtaposed 118.30
juxtaposition 419.30
jymes 181.30
Jymes 181.27

K 333.03
K. 066.24 (Owen K.)
kabbakks 034.08
kabisses 475.35
kackle 279.F25
kaddies 350.33
kadem 034.31
Kaemper 332.18
Kaempersally 383.22
Kaer 421.08
Kafa 550.15
Kaffir 095.15
Kaffue 199.18
Kahanan 108.17
kahdeksan 285.19
kai 054.12 054.13
kailkannonkabbis 456.07
kaillykailly 372.14
Kain 455.18
kaind 099.14
Kainly 421.05
Kairokorran 177.09
kak 125.22
KAKAOPOETIC 308.R2
kake 149.06
kakes 448.07
kakography 120.22
kaksi 285.20
kaksitoista 285.17
kal 594.07
Kalastus 325.10
Kalatavala 178.33
kalblionized 483.22
kaldt 198.07
kalebrose 529.01
Kaledon 481.21
Kaledvalch 241.12
Kallikak 137.12
kalospintheochroma-
tokreening 392.28
kama 093.22
Kamen 392.25
kamerad 089.07
kamicha 234.01
kampften 241.18
kamps 491.07
kanddledrum 356.19
Kane 211.30 448.03
Kane 491.16
kanekannan 028.19
Kanel 212.07
kanes 516.23
Kanes 536.27
Kane's 063.07
Kang 052.25
Kangaroose 299.11
kankan 006.21
Kansas 509.24
kants 120.31
kaow 608.20
Kapak 113.12
Kapelavaster 024.19
Kapitayn 295.F1
kapnimancy 117.33
Kappa 221.29
kappines 510.34
kapr 475.35
Kaptan 352.32
kaptor 568.33
kapuk 113.13
karhags 340.08
Karikature 085.33
karkery 577.34
karlikeevna 331.25
karls 613.06
karmalife 338.06
Karmalite 211.29
karman's 237.22
karrig 114.24
Karrs 339.14
Karssens 241.33
kast 199.24
Kat 120.02
katadupe 252.34
Katakasm 533.24
Kate 027.31 079.27 113.21
211.19 245.34
KATE 221.12
Kateclean 448.10
katekattershin 333.07
kater 403.02
kates 116.22 456.22
Kates 423.12
Kate's 421.04
Katey 380.01 380.02
katey's 334.28 334.28
kathareen 330.35
kathartic 185.06
Kathe 008.08
Kathleen 093.31
Kathlins 601.32
katte 394.28
Kattekat 197.10
Katty 147.12 212.07 531.15
Katu 335.19 335.19
katya 040.11
Katya 566.11
Kavanagh 492.28
kavehazs 177.20
Kaven's 382.11
kavos 512.22
Kavya 093.22
kay 093.23 133.09
Kay 095.14 282.23
Kayenne 351.10
kayoed 085.04
K.C. 368.27 368.27 368.28
451.27 (King's Counsel)
kcedron 171.11
ke 052.15
Keane 305.18 305.19
keaoghs 349.03
Keavens 064.24
Keavn 601.18 601.18 601.19
keddle 596.32
Keddle 073.08
keek 296.13 584.20
keel 138.04 206.32 497.15
keelrow 427.03
keeltappers 480.09
Keemun 534.11
keen 097.02 102.02 121.14
145.29 159.14 313.31 336.13
363.05 381.27 562.31
keener 356.23 372.33
keenest 083.21
keenheartened 354.13
keenin 615.34

keening 006.21
keening 340.14
keenly 532.36
keep 021.14 023.13 025.07 034.34 034.34 040.08 069.22 069.26 084.06 131.03 159.36 164.21 166.16 249.17 252.31 252.31 276.26 276.F2 304.26 312.24 333.21 337.07 360.03 372.25 379.23 425.12 437.26 439.27 444.15 444.23 460.04 461.20 469.32 482.22 509.04 552.14 552.14 565.31 566.06 566.11 576.15 576.35 582.34 588.08 615.29
keep 498.06
Keep 368.02 432.22 434.02 435.23 440.31 546.28
Keep 106.03
keeper 320.35 464.25 589.31 606.08
keepers 362.19
keepeth 355.31
keeping 059.33 191.12 410.06 430.08 448.24 474.16 477.28 519.36 580.09
keeping 418.13
keeps 147.24 205.04 313.13 363.10 479.11 578.11
Keepsacre 080.07
keepsakes 498.02
keepsoaking 438.19
keepy 110.32
keesens 316.36
keg 399.32
Kehoe 039.17
Keisserse 534.18
kek 590.19
Kékkek 004.02 004.02 004.02
kekkle 585.30
kelchy 222.28
keld 024.31
keling 010.25
kelkefoje 160.31
Kelkefoje 160.31
Kelleiney 295.F1
Kellikek 033.24
Kells 122.23
Kellsfrieclub 436.29
Kelly 193.24 299.27 361.16 370.20 407.16 484.33
Kelly-Cooks 456.31
Kellyesque 456.30
kellykekkle 372.15
Kelly's 093.29
Kellywick 261.F2
kelp 197.31
kelt 594.03
keltts 390.07
kem 037.19
Kematitis 360.30
kemin 383.24
ken 110.13 110.14 286.26 482.17 560.32
kenalittle 010.33
kend 317.35
kenees 534.19
keng 026.29
Keng 187.20
Kennealey 071.36
Kennedy 007.11
kennedy's 317.01
Kennedy's 498.19
kennel 173.03 324.31
kenneldar 341.29
kennet 213.11
Kenneth 514.02
kenning 313.31
kennot 167.15
Kenny 193.24
Kenny's 332.33
kenspeckled 362.15
kent 584.06
Kentish 553.19
Keogh 193.24
Keogh's 448.03
Keown's 205.09
kep 208.23 403.08
kepi 035.08
Kepin 370.08
Kepp 540.36
kept 071.05 124.34 141.12 172.29 180.01 278.F5 362.36 422.36 516.19 544.04 580.09
ker 408.19
kerchief 024.33 033.06
kerchiefs 213.27
kerilour 234.20
Kerk 533.23
kerkegaard 246.01
kerl 234.07
kerls 331.18
kerosene's 257.16
Kerribrasilian 442.14
kerry 247.14
Kerry 015.16 513.33
kerrybommers 258.34
kerrycoys 469.26
kerryer 515.24
kerryjevin 563.37
kersey 322.17
kersse 137.22 317.22 319.27 320.02 320.12 404.32
Kersse 311.07 312.15 313.07 322.01 322.05 322.18 328.04
Kersse's 085.33
kerssest 180.11
Kerssfesstiydt 510.32
kertssey 623.11
keshaned 534.30
kestrel 383.16
ketch 012.16 311.22
ketchups 405.26
Ket's 151.14
Kettil 549.13
kettle 011.32 137.23 229.25 279.F25 362.10 426.29 600.03
Kettle 219.12 609.25
Kettle-Griffith-Moynihan 307.09
kettlekerry 076.24
Kettlelicker 117.26
kettletom 122.07
ketts 267.F5
ketyl 332.02
Kev 286.27 303.15
Kevanses 015.07
keve 565.15
Keven 482.18
Kevin 110.32 300.15 388.14 483.05 555.16 562.23 604.27 605.07 605.13 605.18 605.22 605.25 605.27 605.34 605.36 606.03 606.04
Kevineen 210.14
kevinly 234.10
kevinour 234.20
Kevin's 027.05 040.36 547.17
Kevvy 303.17
Kew 469.18
kews 119.36
key 236.11 279.F08 302.22 309.20 311.12 385.04 433.32 450.24 516.20 584.21
key 201.09
Key 421.04
Key 302.L2
Keyhoe 379.36
keyhole 070.19 178.29
keying 499.14
keykeeper 377.01
keyman 186.15
keymaster 560.29
keyn 499.13
keys 011.21 031.01 077.11 377.01 568.24 615.28 626.30 628.15
Keysars 061.27
kezom 162.19
khaibits 570.29
khakireinettes 348.22
khalassal 128.32
khan 032.02
Khan 024.35 497.34
khat 415.32
Khorason 347.03
Khuam 499.10
Khubadah 609.32
khul 415.32
Khummer-Phett 355.31
khyber 464.10
Kia 565.27
kiber 321.11
kick 098.34 117.21 149.06 285.06 314.04 348.17 375.03 375.04 415.24 437.03 470.03 498.05 514.32 531.23 583.26
Kick 187.15 379.01 554.09
kickaheeling 021.12
Kickakick 583.26
kickakickkack 531.25
kicked 045.08 298.F2 423.32 514.09
kickee 515.02
kicker 315.36 583.32
Kickhams 208.31
kickin 011.34
kicking 175.35 175.36 433.15 441.24 506.36 511.08 518.06
kickkick 532.36
kicks 138.14 170.12 323.12 515.13
kicksalittle 010.33
kicksheets 116.26
kickshoes 270.24
kicksolock 584.03
kickup 067.21
Kicky 238.23
kickychoses 291.12
kid 392.25 477.14
Kidballacks 315.28
kidd 069.19 587.05
kiddeneys 350.23
kidder 035.33
kiddies 379.28
kidding 413.27
kiddings 370.03
kiddledrum 531.09

kiddling 356.16 384.20 385.01 389.22
kidds 403.15
kiddy 314.05 521.02
kidlings 570.19
kidloves 205.18
kidnapped 595.35
kidney 443.30
kidneys 437.13
kidooleyoon 107.19
Kidoosh 258.05
kidos 172.35
kids 241.23 469.32
kids 276.L3
Kids 261.15
kids' 294.F1
kidscad 003.11
kidsnapped 021.21
Kiel 160.31
kiep 015.34
Kieran 212.08
kik 113.07
Kikikuki 245.02
kikkers 556.29
kikkery 584.21
kikkinmidden 503.08
kiks 210.06
kilalooly 595.17
Kilbarrack 327.24
Kilbride 203.02 576.06
Kildare 202.31 436.31 516.06
kilder 330.33
kilderkins 596.17
kilkenny 142.04
kill 167.20 173.11 223.20 275.21 279.F25 303.31 443.18 516.23 613.33
Killadown 456.26
Killallwho 015.11
killarnies 450.29
Killdoughall 588.29
Killeachother 389.07
killed 126.22 155.11 164.34 424.02
killelulia 083.34
Killesther's 427.01
killim 186.14
Killiney 433.13
killing 202.31 248.24 279.F03 459.09
killingest 430.32
killings 567.27
Killkelly-on-tne-Flure 389.07
killmaimthem 504.31
Killorcure 389.06
Killorglin 087.26
kills 028.22 052.18 055.06 172.08 482.33 509.19
Killthemall 389.07
Killtork 353.11
Killykelly 361.16
killykick 375.04
Killykillkilly 004.07
Killykook 295.F1
Killy's 206.19
kiln 498.20
kilolitre 265.21
kilowatts 490.24
kilt 250.29
Kilt 594.03
kilts 529.32
Kilty 305.F2
kimkim 598.20
Kimmage 072.20 507.02
Kimmage's 142.13
kimmells 019.08
kin 121.15 364.14 463.17
kinagain 594.04
Kinahaun 364.19
kinantics 441.28
kind 027.29 033.34 077.33 086.24 098.25 112.13 123.11 123.15 144.20 269.15 357.19 374.27 409.05 429.07 461.36 462.20 479.28 502.30 564.11 589.35 608.22
Kind 421.15
kindalled 256.12
kinder 283.31 449.12 536.35
kindergardien 483.25
kinderwardens 555.07
kindest 366.05 397.19 617.05
kindhearted 560.28
kindlelight 020.20
kindler 128.33
kindli 276.10
kindlily 430.33
kindling 203.22 290.04 327.31 594.06
kindlings 112.08 453.17
kindly 112.09 327.31 378.23 412.19 433.05 458.09 585.06 585.19
kindness 096.22 386.09 430.33 431.09 445.13 548.18 550.23
kindom 373.15
kinds 066.04 200.05 357.19 506.22
kine 141.22
Kine's 273.L3
king 025.29 025.29 025.29 025.29 031.11 032.07 043.32 044.16 045.27 058.05 087.26 088.12 091.01 098.11 099.24 134.36 135.09 162.35 186.14 240.18 278.17 289.F6 333.21 357.17 380.13 380.18 380.19 380.20 392.23 428.20 430.07 450.12 450.20 452.26 452.27 466.06 499.15 504.01 526.27 531.36 546.03 578.04 587.14 600.01 625.04 626.13
King 041.24 045.07 079.35 085.23 086.07 093.01 139.05 196.21 212.01 220.25 254.29 277.01 294.24 380.11 380.22 381.25 421.06 431.13 447.09 495.12 557.36 558.17 568.23 568.34 583.28 610.05 610.05 612.04 612.06
King 072.03 105.11
kingable 032.02
kingbilly 075.15
kingclud 456.23
kingcomed 369.18
kingcorrier 367.32
kingdom 110.04 130.29 188.16
Kingdom 424.33
kingdome 213.31
Kingen 617.21
kingly 068.22 398.23 499.16 625.13
kingmount 588.15
kings 087.17 087.25 087.26 446.25 474.18 497.29 582.35 613.06
Kings 242.27
king's 032.26 047.26 090.05 091.07 094.28 136.22 252.18 264.32 334.34 450.15 548.35 567.17 567.17 616.29
King's 219.15 374.32 422.05 553.36
kingscouriered 471.15
kingself 032.07
kingship 193.32 390.35
kingsinnturns 539.31
kingsrick 048.05
Kings's 201.26
Kingston 294.22
Kinihoun 108.17
kink 129.01 240.10 296.12 490.05 614.06
kinked 511.32
kinkin 006.21
Kinkincaraborg 316.13
kinkles 603.21
kinkless 458.31
kinks 349.01
Kinkypeard 353.14
kinly 550.23
kinn 376.33
kinne 394.28
kinned 031.28
Kinsella 133.02 549.19 618.04 622.03
Kinsella's 205.11
kiosk 135.18
kiotowing 550.28
kip 243.22
kipper 247.36 305.16
kippers 012.35 053.22 524.26
Kippure 204.13
kipsie 321.07
kiribis 066.25
kirikirikiring 612.11
kirjallisuus 325.11 325.12
kirk 137.10 559.29
kirked 388.02
kirkeyaard 201.31
kirkpeal 141.12
kirles 379.16
Kirschie 207.12
kirssy 023.10
kirtle 320.16
kirtles 250.29 571.16
kirtlies 364.10
kis 026.03
kischabrigies 110.23
kish 007.08 083.13 164.12
Kish 014.01 014.02 308.F1 316.06
kished 512.08
kishes 451.13
Kishtna 215.02
kisker 056.33
Kiskiviikko 325.10
kismet 518.10
kisokushk 203.35
kiss 094.29 119.02 145.14 149.05 203.35 279.F08 288.20 376.22 445.07 459.16 468.19
Kiss 011.27 011.27 011.27 421.04 587.05
Kiss 071.25
kissabelle 571.15
kissabetts 095.22
kissanywhere 072.19
kisschen 531.06

kissed 333.22 507.15 527.32 544.01
kissening 384.19
Kisser 122.19
kisses 183.31 434.05
kisshams 286.29
kisshands 430.21
kissier 234.29
Kissilov's 532.22
kissing 022.25 248.24 384.30 385.02 438.01 465.25 618.05 618.19
kissists 280.27
kisskiss 460.24
Kisslemerched 412.10
kissmans 011.14
kissmiss 624.06
kisstvanes 005.31
kissuahealing 204.03
kissykissy 102.28
Kissykitty 361.16
kitcat 089.24
kitchen 057.34 198.31
kitchenette 184.12
kitchens 409.20
kitchernott 107.20
kitchin 465.28 601.32
kites 476.34
kithagain 594.03
kither 056.34
kithkinish 465.31
kithoguishly 091.34
kitnabudja 056.34
kits 026.10
kitssle 494.29
kitten 269.11
kitteney 059.20
kittering 430.21
kitty 243.17
Kitty 060.09 210.33 328.23 361.15 530.32
kittycasques 431.03
kittycoaxed 192.08
kittyls 340.31
kitz 375.16
Kitzy 330.23 406.09
Kiwasti 056.33
Kjaer 284.F4
kk 037.20
K.K. 365.30 (olderman K.K.)
K. K. 533.24 (K. K. Katakasm)
kknneess 376.10
klakkin 464.19
klanclord 362.09
klanver 422.02
klees 511.30
Kleinsuessmein 330.24
klerds 076.20
klettered 475.23
klikkaklakkaklaskaklopatzklatschabattacreppycrottygraddaghsemmihsammihnouithappluddyappladdypkonpkot 044.20
Klitty 239.18
klokking 111.08
klondykers 181.04
Kloster 265.02
K.M. 122.19 (K.M. O'Mara)
knacked 505.34
knacking 302.F1
knackskey 602.34
knaggs 548.23
knappers 556.29
Knatut 395.23
knave 202.03 229.11 430.07 463.35
knavepaltry 022.26
knaver 520.26
knaves 202.03
knavish 342.01
kne 059.34
knechts 567.18
knechtschaft 505.35
kneck 162.10
kned 498.20
knee 038.09 040.20 232.36 233.07 350.24 468.19 565.08
kneebuckle 214.05
kneecap 247.19 495.30
kneed 580.31
kneedeep 381.10 470.06
kneehigh 408.07
kneehighs 134.31
kneel 139.22
kneeled 227.08 566.19
kneeled 471.33
kneeleths 612.27 612.27 612.28
kneeling 248.25 394.01
kneepants 042.31
kneeprayer 244.36
knees 027.22 397.15 434.33 557.05 607.19
knees'dontelleries 205.02
Kneesknobs 157.12
knew 028.14 033.29 037.27 040.33 070.15 075.06 082.09 093.02 141.32 148.16 154.02 158.31 158.31 158.31 162.10 171.20 172.02 199.31 220.01 226.01 241.18 317.27 317.36 344.21 363.01 385.07 387.21 417.03 419.17 422.27 451.18 457.25 462.29 479.07 487.32 547.26 624.27 626.20
knew 200.11
Knew 106.15
knew't 075.12
Knickerbocker 442.09
knickerbockers 098.21
knickered 192.31
knickers 492.25
knickknaver 505.34
knickknots 162.10
Knickle 104.08
knicks 027.06 527.20
knickt 508.33
kniejinksky 513.11
knife 087.35 162.10 433.12
knife 345.07
knifekanter 561.02
Kniferope 376.30
knifes 087.35
knight 396.31 562.29 623.15
knight 201.13
Knight 245.32
knighters 618.24
knightlamp 559.36
knightmayers' 364.26
knights 335.26
knight's 012.04 497.32
Knight's 225.17
Knightsmore 608.12
knirps 027.09
knit 268.13
Knit 315.03
knits 018.25 227.06
Knittrick 353.14
knive 545.22
knivers 267.06
knives 405.29
Knives 346.06
kniveses 141.16
knobby 550.09
knobkerries 082.22
knobs 448.23
knock 003.22 027.07 330.30 330.31 330.32 456.35 595.03 595.03 625.22
Knock 262.06 330.30 330.31 330.31 528.21
Knock 176.07
knockbrecky 534.19
Knockcastle 379.01
knockdown 174.06
knocked 538.15
knocker 318.30 376.12 376.12
knocking 202.10 212.05 444.19 506.36
knockingshop 322.27
knockling 572.01
Knockmaree 186.25
Knockmaroon 015.04
knockneeghs 393.29
knockonacow 228.32
Knockout 505.34
knocks 443.15
Knocks 622.34
knockside 428.24
knockturn 064.16
knogg 556.34
knogging 557.05
knoll 076.26 267.06 476.06
Knoll 422.32
knollyrock 010.31
knootvindict 370.32
knopfs 052.27
knot 189.21 305.21 441.06 458.27 561.22
knotcracking 143.13
knotknow 224.18
knots 231.35 245.10 288.07
knot's 377.18
knotting 144.23
Knout 353.14
know 005.24 016.33 026.18 026.18 029.11 031.26 036.02 052.23 054.21 059.06 059.30 070.10 073.11 082.22 083.24 090.19 108.29 109.30 116.05 138.24 139.15 143.31 144.01 145.08 145.17 146.34 165.14 186.09 187.35 187.35 188.30 191.12 196.04 196.05 196.06 196.07 196.07 196.14 196.22 198.07 198.10 200.07 201.22 203.17 204.28 204.28 213.03 213.11 214.17 215.19 226.12 227.25 232.15 233.07 234.30 236.06 247.10 248.17 251.25 252.19 252.35 260.17 271.24 275.17 284.F1 286.05 286.05 286.26 289.F6 291.F4 299.04 300.01 300.03 300.06 304.F3 330.35 344.06 351.31 358.18 361.14 363.02 363.12 373.32 374.12 374.30 377.09 377.24 379.02 395.30 395.31 396.10 405.24 408.32 423.19 428.14 435.26 436.26 438.02 438.34

448.25 456.33 457.29 458.04
458.15 458.15 458.23 460.03
460.08 463.12 469.05 470.11
470.12 472.12 476.24 478.36
479.10 481.18 482.22 483.26
487.33 487.35 491.28 493.35
503.08 504.18 507.24 516.22
518.19 518.27 522.03 522.06
522.18 522.21 523.32 527.05
528.02 529.09 533.25 538.24
539.09 547.03 548.30 561.29
563.08 563.21 586.16 590.07
600.21 606.17 615.17 621.23
622.16 623.20 627.36
know 176.08
Know 105.25
knowed 079.24 173.29 279.F21
282.10 290.F7 431.15
knowest 479.28
knowing 078.08 209.21 311.23
485.14 616.20
knowing 345.06
Knowing 485.15
knowledgable 099.22
knowledge 018.25 194.15 245.15
269.01 604.32 605.18
knowledge's 155.21
Knowling 442.05
Knowme 446.26
known 013.13 036.05 036.12
040.17 048.24 052.10 054.24
071.08 072.24 079.06 086.08
111.23 115.08 123.32 126.14
166.07 176.19 177.17 181.18
182.30 191.15 310.10 335.20
363.12 369.25 420.22 435.01
506.28 532.10 544.10 583.16
614.28 614.32 624.36
knowor 460.14
knows 012.04 027.04 037.32
065.16 080.03 101.16 101.19
112.13 118.10 148.11 152.12
169.07 201.28 202.23 213.29
234.16 236.08 239.26 242.35
247.16 247.32 248.21 254.19
269.26 279.F31 286.07 328.27
331.07 347.15 360.20 374.28
387.30 396.22 431.19 439.24
460.13 464.01 467.18 473.07
483.28 508.14 527.11 528.12
539.09 573.02 573.26 600.04
knows 390.28
knowwell 246.24
knox 567.01 596.20
Knox 342.02
Knox-atta-Belle 139.35
knuckle 444.06
knuckles 475.16 613.22
knud 345.30
Knut 221.06
knuts 285.03 613.22
knut's 084.23
Knut's 622.10
knutshedell 276.L2
knutted 377.18
knychts 247.03
knyckle 602.33
Ko 335.16 335.16
K. O. 035.24 (K. O. Sempatrick's
Day)
koa 484.33
Kóax 004.02 004.02 004.02
kobbor 398.27
Kocshis 054.18
Kod 247.16
kodak 171.32
kodseoggs 178.33
Koebi 163.06
Koenigstein's 136.31
kohinor 398.27
kohol 108.25
kokkenhovens 324.29
koldbethizzdryel 241.27
Kollidimus 299.09
kolme 285.20
Kolonsreagh 129.24
kolooney 624.24
kolossa 551.35 551.35
Kommeandine 542.08
kommen 437.30
Kommerzial 069.35
komnate 350.33
konditiens 077.35
kondyl 302.03
kong 446.11
Kong 348.21 498.11 557.06
Kongbullies 322.33
Kongdam 255.22
kongdomain 600.10
kongen 267.05
kongsemma 133.36
Konguerrig 353.31
Konkubine 284.F4
konning 393.07
konservative 535.17
konyglik 578.36
koojahs 282.24
kook 279.F25
kookaburra 393.26
kook-and-dishdrudge 221.14
kookin 420.09
kool 095.22 262.F2
Koombe 390.32
kooper 255.22
koorts 076.17 120.31
kop 243.24
Kopay 221.29
kopfers 416.04
kopfinpot 356.03
kopje 015.29
Korduroy 085.33
Kornalls 351.22
koros 208.36
korps 595.10
korsets 480.12
kosenkissing 436.09
Kosmos 456.07
Kostello 334.03
Kothereen 556.32
koud 244.17
Koughenough 380.22
koursse 322.19
Kovenhow 378.14
Kovnor-Journal 531.36
kow 623.12
kowse 199.07
kowtoros 325.34
Koy 027.27
kozydozy 429.22
kraaking 011.01
kraal 134.02 497.15
kraals 016.02
kracht 262.12
Kraicz 172.23
Kram 388.02
krashning 338.08
krasnapoppsky 404.24
krectly 042.17
Kredas 052.15
kreeksmen 053.26
kreeponskneed 075.21
krenfy 426.07
Kresbyterians 120.02
krias 565.27
krieging 010.05
krigkry 093.13
krikit 055.07
kriowday 233.36
krischnians 080.20
kristansen 053.04
kristianiasation 331.32
Kristlike 267.L3
krk 334.19
krosser 480.12
Kroukaparka 178.33
krow 347.05
krubeems 258.35
Kruis-Kroon-Kraal 186.19
krumlin 536.10
Krumlin 497.19
Krumlin 339.34
Krumwall 299.09
Krzerszonese 347.09
kuang 058.20
kuckkuck 511.08
kuddle 330.25
kudos 057.21
kughs 350.17
kuk 162.15
kukkakould 171.10
Kukkuk 137.12
kuldrum 345.12
kules 178.33
Kullykeg 367.11
kumpavin 316.32
Kund 201.33
kungoloo 131.35
Kung's 108.11
kunject 608.08
kunning 223.28 579.15
kunst 295.28
Kunstful 357.16
kunt 075.16
Kunut 390.31
kuo 058.19
Kuran 242.32
kurds 241.25
kurkle 095.22 296.13
kursses 594.36
Kurt 100.31
kuru 601.03
kuschkars 365.17
kusin 053.03
kuskykorked 176.30
kuss 383.18 475.34 475.35
Kutt 179.11
kuur 110.22
kuusi 285.19
kuvertly 606.27
kvarters 011.02
kveldeve 037.16
kvind 608.23
Kvinne 267.L3
Kvinnes 124.30
kvold 326.17
Kwhat 594.33
kyat 322.22
Kyboshicksal 283.L2
kymmenen 285.18

Kyow 534.02
kyrie 054.12
Kyrielle 528.08 528.09

L 293.19 (L is for liv) 458.33 (Luse)
la 020.33 023.25 052.15 160.30 177.30 184.27 184.27 184.28 184.29 184.30 184.31 184.32 194.12 224.35 246.16 246.20 257.07 293.21 314.18 314.18 327.04 327.04 327.04 398.29 486.25 486.25 560.01
la 064.28 068.09 102.18 150.03 157.32 157.32 158.23 184.19 280.L4 281.05 281.06 281.06 292.12 292.18 376.07 471.30 478.21
La 137.36 198.14 212.12 229.11 235.13 239.24 290.02 293.21 314.18 441.13 495.24 531.22 556.09 579.05 597.01
La 053.14 106.16 199.28 548.28
laa 298.01
Laagen 212.01
laat 242.29
lab 084.13
labaryntos 187.21
Labbeycliath 237.33
label 470.27 579.18
Labia 540.07
labiolingual 122.32
labious 372.16
lable 603.29
labour 120.26 255.17 599.31
labourers 363.21
Labouriter 090.03
labourlasses 025.21
labours 544.33
labour's 014.23 448.21
laboursaving 585.15
LABOURTENACITY 286.R3
labronry 440.05
labrose 520.36
labs 527.31
laburnums 450.31
labyrinth 576.32
lac 162.23 378.04
Lacarthy 137.02
Laccorde 222.02
lace 021.33 022.21 043.13 330.14 434.21
Lace 177.06
laced 282.26
lacers 404.19
lacertinelazily 121.24
lacessive 068.12
laceswinging 417.25
Lacey 238.23
lach 314.18 511.13
lachsembulger 132.29
lacies 071.09
lacings 152.10
lack 088.31 100.03 166.26 173.31 223.24 224.14 245.27 440.31 493.29 540.32 585.28 601.05
Lack 250.17
lacked 596.26
lackin 537.35
lacking 543.30
lacklearning 252.05
lacksleap 547.16
lackslipping 310.05
lacrimal 077.30
lacteal 426.26
lacustrian 388.14
lacustrine 605.20
Lacytynant 388.33
lad 028.36 095.19 311.33 314.17 332.03 332.22 361.07 382.16 395.14 395.28 436.32 440.29 472.11 480.19 519.19 520.36 525.28 526.08 600.04 604.36 620.22
lad 399.27
Lada 272.02
ladbroke 022.36
ladder 089.31 125.14 278.20 314.17 390.05
laddercase 576.30
ladderleap 079.12
ladderproof 548.21
ladders 566.35
laddery 198.15
laddes 568.23
laddios 348.01
laddo 091.36 404.14
laddos 577.35
laddy 315.03 586.28
laddylike 370.10
laddyown 429.21
laddy's 328.24 621.05
lade 232.23
laden 108.07
Lader's 330.10
ladest 285.11
ladgers 489.03
Ladiegent 523.22
ladies 043.01 179.33 186.32 385.18 395.13 453.35 462.02 553.05 570.07 582.34
ladies 200.12
Ladies 033.11 079.14 270.12 307.21
ladies' 068.07 183.25 395.05 395.10 455.32
Ladies' 221.31
ladiest 365.05
Ladigs 228.35
ladins 327.19
ladle 231.32
ladled 253.10
ladlelike 246.14 531.23
ladleliked 437.01
Lad-o'-me-soul 225.01 225.01
ladra 436.06
lads 026.34 046.01 204.05 253.26 371.30 587.11 587.35 589.01
lads 341.32
Lads 105.33
lad's 377.06 459.23
lad's 350.14
ladwigs 243.17
lady 030.19 031.31 059.31 060.34 100.21 102.23 109.18 124.19 127.20 165.22 207.25 227.04 233.12 311.13 311.28 312.20 331.33 334.17 361.09 376.03 389.12 449.11 486.23 495.25 501.30 514.33 535.28 535.31 560.26 587.20 618.17
Lady 145.30 178.22 235.32 236.06 289.26 306.F4 385.36 387.22 389.10 496.02 568.06 622.27
Lady 105.22 288.15
ladybirdies 416.12
Ladycastle 471.16
ladyeater 150.02
ladykants 077.22
ladykiller 430.33
ladylike 092.05 112.16 470.31
ladymaid 428.08
ladymaidesses 011.31
lady's 040.33 042.09 433.13
Ladyseyes 398.18
ladyship 391.10
ladywhite 121.22
laete 185.21
laetich 174.29
laetification 160.21 331.31
laff 175.23
Laffayette 026.16
Laffey 420.34
laffing 011.33
lafft 256.36
lafing 203.30
laftercheeks 463.11
lag 315.09 407.27 603.25
lagan 345.19
Lagener 390.04
lagenloves 530.15
laggards 210.04
lagged 506.12
laggin 292.17
lagging 176.29
lagmen 532.28
lagoon 479.22
lagos 203.08
Lagrima 290.27
lags 415.21
lags-behind-Wall 434.10
lah 235.08
lahlah 235.08
laicness 153.32
laid 003.23 006.26 034.34 080.17 087.36 092.35 097.31 134.02 191.29 209.29 240.04 245.14 289.27 317.11 325.20 328.12 432.01 434.17 537.20 553.28 566.02
Laid 480.13
Laid 440.20
laida 204.10
laiding 344.15
laimen 062.01
lain 097.32
lain 352.21
lair 183.09
laird 242.36 253.32 282.04 457.24
lairdie 550.28
lairdship 312.16
lairking 510.18
lairs 330.15
laities 177.08
laitiest 232.15
laitymen 152.16
laizurely 427.01
Lajambe 422.33
lake 465.36 601.04 605.13 605.16 605.17 605.17
Lake 307.11 433.06
lakelet 605.20
lakemist 131.26
laker 526.36

lakes 395.08
lakeside 605.28
laking 467.03
lala 295.24 335.16 335.17 335.23
Lala 250.21 250.21
lalage 229.10
lalaughed 554.08
laleish 335.17
Lalia 525.14
Lalipat 284.24
lall 310.18
lallance 059.07
lallaryrook 184.16
lally 396.25
Lally 067.11 094.26 387.19 389.34 390.03 394.18 397.34
Lalors 025.10
L'Alouette's 450.16
lamagnage 450.23
lamatory 357.22
lamb 058.07 430.35 527.05 529.32
Lamb 063.24
Lambay 208.03 464.35
lambdad's 486.01
Lambday 294.04
Lambeg 398.29
Lambel 595.06
Lambeyth 533.08
lambkinsback 322.20
lambs 073.33 172.08
lambskip 502.36
lambstoels 350.23
lambtail 294.09
lame 132.14 521.14 576.29
Lame 071.16
lamelookond 520.27
lamely 063.30 414.31
lamentably 539.10
lamentation 100.03
lamented 326.27
lames 355.15
Lamfadar's 597.01
lamm 201.30
lammalelouh 258.03
Lammas 281.01
lamme 524.31
lammswolle 070.07
lamoor 292.01
lamp 010.27 027.06 137.01 198.31 245.05 299.17 404.13 427.15 511.12 514.34 559.14 578.18 580.27 583.31 612.33
lampaddyfair 472.22
lampblack 114.10
lampblick 290.22
lampern 621.05
lamphouse 021.10
Lampi 323.32
lamping 549.15
lampion 206.11
lampless 127.15
lamplight 190.33
lampman 427.01
lampoon's 182.11
Lamppost 193.18
lamps 033.10 088.33 100.19 178.28 252.17 330.02 362.22 560.19
lampsleeve 411.26
lampthorne 321.04
lamusong 595.04
lance 022.31 139.03 559.11
lancer 073.36
lancers 513.34
Lancesters 348.28
Lancey 219.12
lancia 152.31
lanciers 546.09
lancifer 354.32
Lancs 500.11
Lancydancy 282.F4
land 012.07 024.34 028.14 039.29 056.36 062.11 062.11 062.11 064.05 068.25 088.02 100.01 100.22 110.06 134.21 137.10 169.07 181.05 188.35 249.19 288.25 308.20 331.11 355.23 393.16 442.13 453.33 477.34 494.23 501.12 526.01 540.05 545.22 545.26 546.14 605.35
land 278.L3
Land 022.08 056.21 312.08
landadge 485.13
Landaunelegants 353.27
Landauner 568.06
lande 039.15 353.16
landed 019.15 086.17 288.13 589.08
landeguage 478.09
lander 466.14
landescape 053.01
landfall 197.30
landfather 191.34
landhavemiseries 288.25
landing 289.25 316.03 387.22 525.20 544.05
landleague 540.02
landleaper 203.07
landlord 316.06
Landloughed 023.29
landlubber's 173.09
landmark 430.06
lands 197.22 292.16 397.02 510.32 579.24
land's 537.12
Landsend 291.01
landshape 474.02
landshop 332.24
landskip 464.35
landslewder 323.09
landslots 596.12
landsmaul 292.27
landsmoolwashable 577.07
landsown 381.03
landsvague 577.23
landuage 327.20
Land-under-Wave 248.08
landwester 042.29
lane 079.27 107.34 141.04 148.10 242.07 244.08 330.02 491.30 600.04 618.08
Lane 061.27 084.19 093.27 095.21 210.33 248.33 260.09 260.13 371.34 408.33 578.27
lanejoymt 534.18
lanes 116.34 365.24
laneway 544.30
laney 436.09 510.11
lang 021.05 305.29 335.32 384.17 406.28
Lang 244.25 270.F2
langdwage 338.20
Langley 050.06 050.14
langlo 202.22
langscape 595.04
langseling 315.31
langsome 415.12 415.12
langtennas 414.26
langthorn 338.35
langua 198.19
language 037.15 039.24 066.19 083.12 090.27 116.23 185.09 256.14 311.23 333.27 424.17 424.23 488.25 561.18
Language 518.02
languages 029.32 081.24
Languid 434.23
languidoily 083.15
languidous 427.13
languil 298.06
languised 508.34
languish 096.11 232.21 465.02
languished 528.10
languishing 111.23 474.10
Languishing 528.14
languo 621.22
languoaths 116.28
languors 270.08
langurge 141.21
langways 484.25
langwedge 073.01
langwid 367.29
Lanigan 354.17
lank 369.13
lankalivline 178.05
lankaloot 146.17
Lankester 485.12
lanky 442.09
lankyduckling 070.23
Lankyshied 095.18
Lankystare 465.33
Lanner 531.16
Lanner's 027.19
Lannigan's 377.06
Lanno's 373.16
Lansdowne 506.24
Lanteran 152.36
lantern 421.22
lanthorns 549.02
Lanty 381.12
lanv 330.07
lanxiety 087.06
lao 322.04
Laohun 244.32
Laonum 420.20
laotsey 242.25
laow 608.20
lap 068.21 136.03 232.24 242.20 299.17 318.12 362.13 397.19 451.30
Lap 398.01
Lapac 487.31
lapapple 126.17
lapel 404.23
lapes 427.02
lapful 604.35
lapidated 449.15
Lapidous 271.06
lapins 113.02
lapis 293.11
Lapole 390.11
Lapoleon 388.16
lapped 369.15 625.27
lappel 314.33
lapper 393.20 531.14
lappet 043.13

Lappin 212.08
lapping 159.16
lappish 066.18
Lapps 105.21
Lappy 268.F6
laps 025.20
lapsaddlelonglegs 498.03
Lapsang 534.11
lapse 063.24 122.03 155.28 265.25 291.17 291.25
lapses 151.28
lapsing 396.30
lapsis 178.01
lapspan 251.16
Lapsummer 199.13
lapsus 484.25
lapwhelp 441.31
laracor 228.21
Laraseny 618.31
larboard 517.36
larbourd 178.28
larcenlads 075.08
larch 249.31 364.07
L'Archet 222.02
larchly 412.28
lard 260.L3
Lard 409.15
larder 201.09
Lardling 071.23
lards 083.07
large 050.16 051.20 064.30 065.22 086.23 099.07 138.09 177.03 219.04 275.07 290.F4 368.30 417.20 429.06 492.01 498.24 532.15 547.18 580.23
largelimbs 559.36
largelooking 111.19
largely 057.20 250.14 253.32 487.02 487.12 585.28
larger 041.27 132.28
larges 521.13
Larges 276.24
largesse 230.27
largest 047.18 160.11 564.11
largos 519.10
Larix 235.19
lark 115.06 292.25 361.24 450.26
lark 383.04
larking 526.22
larks 047.06 273.21 458.12
larkseye 169.12
larksical 022.15
larksmathes 595.17
larms 004.07
larmsworth 137.35
larn 149.06
larned 288.23 479.23
larnt 255.21
larpnotes 021.03
larries 432.15
larrikins 582.19
larrons 005.03
larruping 594.20
larry 019.28
Larry 086.23 210.19
Larrybird 534.36
Larryhill 022.19
larry's 519.05
Larry's 382.21 517.35
larto 247.10
L'arty 303.13
larved 418.10 418.10
Larynx 419.23
Las 214.06
lashbetasselled 474.08
lashed 077.08 157.02
lasher 450.09
lashes 463.10
lashings 134.02 451.07
Lashlanns 626.06
lashons 029.32
lass 097.35 159.05 177.25 202.06 226.06 227.09 250.21 297.28 333.27 363.19 395.14 440.30 553.18 600.04
Lasse 222.11
lassers 324.09
lasses 589.01
lasses 341.32
lassies 253.25
lassihood 270.08
l'assitude 370.10
lassitudes 441.09
lasslike 562.05
lasso 123.06 257.17
Lasso 279.F14
lassy 328.29 328.29 437.14
last 007.31 010.12 011.25 020.01 025.25 027.10 028.08 028.17 041.36 049.27 049.29 064.14 067.16 070.24 072.22 073.24 076.06 076.31 078.02 080.17 082.28 097.11 098.02 110.29 111.10 116.21 121.31 122.32 123.05 130.33 131.26 138.34 142.02 153.32 156.24 156.32 158.22 159.06 174.09 185.35 186.12 188.01 196.13 197.25 211.22 213.15 214.04 223.32 242.20 247.30 254.34 283.30 286.12 291.16 293.22 302.23 313.01 324.26 331.32 344.07 369.20 371.15 373.04 379.31 380.12 380.15 380.18 380.20 384.01 391.30 406.19 408.32 413.17 421.01 421.33 424.23 424.35 431.27 433.02 433.27 439.30 452.21 453.10 461.11 461.17 468.23 469.29 470.26 472.16 473.22 503.18 517.12 519.11 519.12 519.21 528.34 528.34 528.35 529.14 531.31 540.19 542.16 544.14 545.06 556.31 583.23 587.01 590.08 590.09 596.30 597.20 598.23 601.15 602.23 607.11 615.25 617.20 623.08 628.15
last 201.10
Last 245.28 372.23 610.34
Last 071.36 106.17 107.01 176.12
lasted 178.06 284.27
lasterhalft 247.06
Lastest 106.11
lasting 528.35
lastingness 100.18
lastly 112.15 123.04
lasts 444.24 486.10
lastways 113.06
latakia 450.11
latch 266.15
Latch 493.32
latcher 450.26
latchet 349.22
latchets 183.34
latchkey 146.15
late 021.05 037.14 055.17 060.04 062.29 078.02 213.15 221.27 240.04 244.25 301.05 307.F7 329.26 345.13 389.13 408.17 413.12 454.19 460.10 488.31 544.01 564.36 595.13 624.25
Latearly 502.16 502.16 502.16 502.16
latecomers 142.16
Lateen 205.27
lateenth 567.15
lately 181.30 326.27 490.21
Lately 507.23
latenesses 550.29
latents 461.04
later 003.17 015.22 031.21 055.12 076.12 080.07 086.27 137.29 231.26 280.36 290.08 290.27 312.34 409.20 499.17 518.04
Later 082.10 589.33
Later 123.20
latere 177.19
Laterza 212.12
latest 166.14 242.29 459.23 581.35
latest 349.30
latewiser 253.09
lath 133.34
lather 313.35 380.27 425.01
lathering 200.34 614.04
latification 551.20
LATIFUNDISM 264.R2
Latimer 388.32 388.32
Latin 215.26 234.30
latitat 050.17
latitudinous 052.23
Latouche 067.36
Latouche's 450.36
latten 093.09 183.20
latter 006.10 035.11 100.02 100.02 119.27 337.12 369.32 419.09 423.11
latterday 455.05
latterlig 502.17
latterly 317.31
latterly 390.28
latterman 603.03
latterman's 602.18
latterpress 356.21
latters 114.18 590.15
latter's 109.18
lattice 043.28
lattlebrattons 152.05
lauar 206.31
L'Auberge 124.34
laubes 208.11
laubhing 273.22
lauch 550.10
laud 090.03 136.03 258.13 483.34 485.01 613.15 625.36
laudabiliter 392.36
laudable 306.05
laudibiliter 154.22
lauds 358.24 552.25
laudsnarers 208.12
lauf 314.20
lauffe 299.29
lauffed 319.31
laugh 101.05 103.08 142.31 191.02 226.02 249.33 275.F5

293.21 323.32 335.26 408.28 423.26 454.10 495.17 509.32 544.09 583.26 584.21 617.17
laugh 338.36
Laughable 066.16
laughed 018.21 137.20 154.01 194.21 204.18 426.14
laughin 513.05
laughing 010.04 095.36 142.31 146.02 369.29 390.13 390.16 390.22 440.30 449.28 461.10 462.36 522.28 526.35 626.22
Laughing 162.25 293.F2 330.22
laughings 125.15 361.30 568.05
laughleaking 042.10
laughs 257.02
Laughs 148.32
laughside 301.29
laughsworth 137.34
laughta 031.30
laughtears 015.09
laughter 187.33 190.34 403.20 433.29 575.16 576.07 600.20
laughtered 361.29
laughters 145.19 259.07
Laughty 531.04
laun 325.14
launch 288.15
laundered 033.09
Laundersdale 620.21
laundresses 586.13
laundry 404.02
laundryman 214.27
launer's 292.23
lauphed 254.13
Laura 205.09 212.14 507.29
lauralad 548.10
laurals 203.30
lauralworths 548.25
lauraly 397.15
Laurans 616.34
laurel 612.05
laurency 022.12
laurens 613.15
Laurens 003.08
Laurentie 228.25
laurettas 359.14
laus 027.08 416.06
lausafire 621.03
lauschening 290.08
lauscher 173.10
laut 479.33
laut-lievtonant 338.19
Lautrill 081.14
lautterick's 531.15
lauwering 315.35
lava 494.07
lavabad 240.16
lavabibs 203.19
lavaleer 051.07
lavandaiette 066.15
lavandier 214.28
Lavantaj 325.11
lavariant 431.06
lavas 294.26
lavast 481.15
lavastories 068.07
Lavatery 260.10
Lavatory 530.11
lave 091.30 168.02 203.01 371.17 600.07 621.33
Lave 015.24 080.29
lavender 041.26
laver 552.26
laveries 134.03
lavgiver 545.32
lavguage 466.32
laving 088.34
lavings 027.10
lavinias 040.11
Lavinias 327.12
lavishing 345.18
lavurdy 038.15
lavvander 331.27
lavy 275.12
law 017.21 039.24 055.09 082.01 090.36 094.26 094.28 096.04 097.01 128.08 168.01 206.04 267.F5 268.F3 276.27 290.10 305.25 313.14 318.23 318.23 505.21 576.05 600.22
Law 238.23 301.22
LAW 305.R1
lawanorder 374.16
Lawd 587.15
lawding 605.14
Lawdy 282.F2 554.04
lawful 432.13
Lawless 210.33
lawn 044.07 140.30 204.36 510.10 553.09
lawncastrum 567.36
lawrels 264.26
Lawrence 211.26
lawrie 038.21
laws 028.30 059.29 063.27 142.24 378.28 579.26 623.11
law's 355.14 541.23
lawstift 321.04
Lawyered 421.11
lawyers 173.16 507.14
Lawzenge 405.24
lax 170.28 573.33
lax 525.21
Lax 044.12
laxative 492.31
Laxdalesaga 220.24
Laxembraghs 330.09
laxlaw 536.29
Laxlip 069.34
laxtleap 242.02
lay 004.15 013.34 020.36 022.27 025.35 033.25 042.15 061.22 062.18 080.28 081.26 100.03 112.14 199.16 204.17 213.24 239.35 244.17 282.17 299.07 320.20 328.15 346.28 347.25 374.18 374.25 411.29 434.26 439.18 442.36 450.01 452.32 454.10 457.08 469.32 474.01 474.02 474.11 475.07 476.22 480.01 486.21 498.28 513.09 548.19 551.23 556.18 556.22 573.35 580.36 588.11 596.23 597.32
Lay 436.33 500.01
layaman 254.06
layaman's 359.17
laychief 392.14
laycreated 484.19
laydays 240.29
layen 179.01
layer 091.01 181.32
layers 330.16 454.29 566.02
laying 021.11 082.23 301.27 301.29 316.22 422.35 476.18 476.19 587.09
Laying 377.29
layir 323.30
laylaw 515.13
laylock 279.F02
laylylaw 511.15
layout 271.07
lays 012.35 137.06 277.F4
laysense 373.18
laysure 024.16
layteacher 038.35
Layteacher 184.35
layum 186.14
Lazar 041.02
Lazar's 429.06
Lazarus 398.26
Lazary 484.25
lazatables 580.06
Lazenby's 405.26
Lazer's 209.03
laziest 298.10
lazily 293.11
lazul 494.05
lazy 056.21 126.02 309.05 381.33 393.27 449.28 627.19
lazychair 493.05
L.B. 420.22
L.B.W. 495.13 (Leg Before Wicket and Lynch Brother, Withworkers)
le 626.02
le 281.09 497.22
Le 139.36 140.01 184.34 236.03 372.09 496.32
Le 072.03 280.L4
lea 033.28 057.05 338.27 476.08 491.22 580.05 626.02
Lea 140.01 221.12
leababobed 040.02
leabarrow 244.34
leabhar 080.14
leabhour 484.29
lead 065.04 068.34 122.14 148.18 246.19 262.02 266.27 267.01 317.04 333.30 344.21 358.31 434.17 478.16 523.03 526.08 560.01 595.18 616.12 622.19
Lead 112.09 469.20
leada 204.10
leadder 311.16
leaden 061.30 251.05 313.35
leader 278.21 369.36 477.04 573.06 577.13 593.13 593.13
leaders 074.03
leader's 044.01
leading 119.31 122.05 128.24 331.16 357.27 490.06 560.26 573.27 581.27
LEADING 264.R2
leadlight 100.23
leadown 208.18
leadpencil 056.12
leadpencils 504.27
leads 209.32 436.17 611.01
Leads 559.19
lead's 541.23
leady 465.36
leaf 118.34 227.17 329.03 329.27 467.10 556.19 619.22 619.22

Leafboughnoon 470.15
leafery 270.22
leafeth 274.16
Leafiest 624.22
leaflefts 357.21
leafless 049.14
leaflet 220.07
leafmould 206.34
leafscreen 131.19
leaftime 088.34
leaftimes 361.26
leafy 619.20 619.29
league 025.25 062.09 273.05 283.19 567.03
League 291.F2
leagues 039.12 041.34 100.03
leagues-in-amour 335.07
leak 381.01 433.34 598.22
leak 121.11
leaked 508.17
leaker 137.06
leaking 332.33
Leaking 510.17
leaks 577.15 627.20
leaks 349.16
leaky 034.01
leal 021.07 464.06
lealand 311.05
lealittlesons 019.28
Leally 089.36
leaman's 038.07
lean 007.22 079.35 096.03 497.06 510.21 626.02
lean 344.04 484.36
Lean 014.32 444.29 534.18 579.21
leandros 203.13
leaned 061.05 262.23 527.30
leaning 157.09 195.03 394.01 449.16
leanings 084.35
leanins 351.28
leanly 251.18
leans 491.09
Leanstare 389.05
leap 004.15 020.24 226.26 250.17 250.18 280.08 314.17 327.11 364.11 460.29 469.33 510.15 513.18
leap 175.22
Leap 268.F6 483.14
leaped 108.33
Leaper 009.05
Leapermann 250.21
leapgirl 092.25
leaping 123.06 390.16
Leaping 525.24
leaps 245.06 363.10 367.28 450.06 594.17
leapt 136.08 149.04 375.14
leaptear 159.16
leapy 146.23
leapyourown 127.02
leareyed 590.02
learn 056.25 082.32 193.12 270.17 278.02 307.21 421.32 462.23 468.03 484.23 489.08 553.02 579.21 585.36
Learn 346.07
learned 031.21 099.22 130.18 131.06 147.33 163.16 231.32 252.05 279.F19 327.19 480.28 482.32 579.35 607.03
learning 108.07 120.24 274.31 430.03
learningful 145.08
learns 374.06
leary 582.35 610.09
Leary 367.12 381.12 428.18 442.29 582.35 611.33 612.04
Leas 466.06
lease 040.12 068.07 265.25 329.19 577.05
lease 102.31
leased 264.16 457.32 563.11 600.28
leasekuays 535.07
leash 276.F5 479.04 579.15
leashed 060.15 063.24 323.33
leashes 227.07
leasing 209.03
least 034.35 056.13 073.13 082.33 120.25 121.30 123.04 124.17 146.04 227.09 305.06 379.29 380.17 509.25 558.08 590.07
leastways 310.08
leasward 279.F30 404.02
leather 435.19 510.16
Leatherbags 026.01
leatherbed 005.20
leatherbox 618.12
leathercoats 289.19
leathered 380.22
leathermail 364.05
leathern 387.04
leathersellers 312.35
Leathertogs 071.24
leave 020.06 024.26 044.15 044.15 064.23 067.07 072.32 073.28 076.10 083.30 125.03 133.06 155.18 159.22 172.21 192.20 206.20 229.13 233.13 272.18 281.23 350.27 363.19 368.12 379.36 381.29 382.21 384.13 392.14 405.24 424.11 428.14 431.23 439.26 439.32 457.05 458.19 463.05 504.01 520.17 530.11 563.30 568.07 585.09 607.13 623.20
leave 140.22 354.16
Leave 337.11
leaved 361.26 604.05
leavely 361.26
leaven 506.26
leaver 059.19
Leaver 093.34
Leaverholma's 517.19
leaves 013.30 050.09 068.36 101.07 168.01 194.25 228.36 235.07 255.02 271.27 280.30 293.22 353.10 361.18 435.21 453.18 460.20 505.09 571.06 612.05 619.23 628.06
leaves' 060.20
leavesdroppings 564.31
leavethings 556.28
leavetime 395.34
leaving 012.02 084.28 140.29 165.19 174.01 230.25 233.16 250.20 264.16 449.33 462.16 534.29 580.09 605.01 614.05
Leavybrink 342.25
Lebab 258.12
Lebanon 171.12
lebanus 440.13
lebbensquatsch 270.L1
leber 059.31
leberally 465.25
lebriety 133.31
lech 149.07 209.26 441.22 595.18
lechery 451.31
lecheworked 553.09
lecit 445.10
lecker 407.04
lecking 276.16 551.05
leckle 511.13
l'Ecluse 520.19
lectionary 524.13
lector 374.17 437.15 605.33
Lector 197.06
lecture 504.01
lecturer 150.08
lectures 388.29
led 014.21 034.31 097.06 118.35 132.15 143.16 243.10 281.01 316.02 399.34 432.12 528.34 567.18 594.06 623.21
led 344.09
Led 250.34
Led 105.04
Leda 272.02
ledan 412.10
ledden 620.31
ledder 323.14
ledgings 233.07
ledn 378.23
Ledwidge 538.03
lee 029.03 250.22 315.24 512.12 583.01
Lee 210.07
Leeambye 600.30
leebez 017.36
Leech 302.01
Leecher 537.09
leechers 495.26
Leeds 576.22
leedy 332.22
leek 462.30
leeklickers' 056.36
leekses 595.13
Leelander 487.31
leep 626.02
leer 398.23 567.05 567.06 570.24
Leer 065.04
leering 570.25
leery 093.33 596.12
lees 183.32 405.20 555.23
leeses 379.24
leest 452.06
leetle 417.04
leeward 602.02
Lefanu 213.01
Lefanunian 265.04
leff 142.03
lefftoff's 119.02
left 009.33 018.21 033.12 063.02 069.24 073.02 080.05 084.08 091.21 093.03 099.29 116.35 122.20 126.08 133.04 135.12 136.25 146.25 158.13 159.04 184.25 186.26 188.12 189.16 194.20 212.25 214.03 234.07 250.21 260.08 311.13 315.16 326.03 329.22 329.24 368.12 374.07 381.32 381.34 390.30 391.34 394.23 414.03

425.18 435.06 442.13 458.02 494.35 544.32 546.35 554.07 563.10 575.08 580.08 589.34 616.09 620.28 622.23 624.06
left 164.20 262.L2
Left 071.33
lefthand 271.11
lefting 344.10
leftlead 547.15
lefts 132.04
Leftus 246.28
Lefty 175.29
leg 039.17 081.20 101.10 142.02 205.11 205.12 205.36 338.29 353.20 417.18 417.18 429.02 454.06 495.32 499.20 508.32 525.35 543.04 576.29 584.15
Leg 144.18 536.15
LEG 305.R1
legacy 079.17 614.36
legahorns 008.31
legal 185.02 537.14 574.24
Legalentitled 571.28
LEGALISATION 264.R2
legando 092.19
legate 243.31 337.03
legatine 484.23
Leg-before-Wicked 434.10
legend 314.15 561.18 566.36 603.36
LEGEND 264.R2
legends 156.03 330.12
Legerleger 498.03
leggats 497.08
Legge 127.08
legged 329.24 511.34
legginds 431.04
legging 200.23 343.26
leggions 380.23
legglegels 587.26
leggs 413.08
leggy 289.F5 496.19
legibly 189.09
legintimate 495.25
legion 058.03 167.22 362.01
legionds 277.22
legions 318.22
legislation 558.13
legislator 042.19
legit 262.F4
legitima 085.13
legitimate 047.14
legless 475.32
leglift 495.08
leglifters 130.01
legligible 356.21
l'Eglise 184.27
Lego 131.26
legomena 052.31
legpoll 057.17
legs 088.20 137.22 152.32 170.34 184.25 194.28 331.28 408.11 411.02 471.15 529.11
leg's 064.32
legsplits 237.23
legture 241.16
leguminiferous 135.32
lei 275.21
leib 145.26
leibsters 351.06
leichtly 237.07
leickname 408.18
leidend 508.18
leif 316.27 506.08 580.13
Leimuncononnulstria 229.17
leinconnmuns 521.28
leinster 288.14
Leinster 202.24
Leinsterface 442.30
leinster's 068.13
leinstrel 528.32
leip 451.15
leish 335.16
leisure 160.35 279.06 441.36 622.13
leisureloving 030.18
leisures 083.31
leivnits 416.29
Leix 031.18
leixlep 525.10
Leixlip 170.29 558.22
lekan 053.24
Lel 250.19
Lelia 525.14
lelias 340.22
lellipos 207.09
lelly 396.26
Lelly 096.23
Lelong 371.33
LEMAN 302.R1
lemans 373.23
lemanted 601.05
lemantitions 571.22
lemmas 296.01
Lemmas 421.02
lemoncholic 453.07
lemoncholy 555.23
lemonsized 059.08
lemoronage 596.01
Lena 211.08
Lencs 374.07
lend 206.10 467.02 469.09 564.25
lend 346.09
Lendet 420.19
lends 068.35 285.01
lendtill 302.02
Lenfant 545.36
length 012.07 078.17 079.08 154.25 166.07 207.17 208.14 233.04 281.F4 284.27 303.27 315.07 381.02 417.20 475.04 495.06
length 345.16
Length 261.13 602.25
lengthen 587.15
lengthily 056.23
lengths 028.21 475.34
lenguage 323.05
lenience 078.02
Leninstar 271.L1
lennones 179.02
lenonem 513.08
lens 112.02 293.23
lenses 183.17 241.34 364.18
Lenster 042.21
lent 089.15 173.14 221.26 453.36 512.23
Lent 106.18
lentern 184.17
lentil 612.10
Lentil 440.09
lentils 089.04 171.05
lentling 607.09
lento 546.02
lents 078.02
lenty 130.08
lenz 285.01
leo 300.16
Leo 544.24 573.08 573.28
Leodegarius 498.03
Leon 193.04 272.26
Leonard's 549.02
Leonden 541.16
Leonem 162.29
Leonidas 307.L1
Leonie 246.16
leonine 150.25
leonlike 155.07
Leonocopolos 368.33
leopard 028.22
Leos 466.06
leoves 601.02
lep 136.03 197.11 347.14
lep 201.18
l'Epée 329.30
lepel 397.19
leperd 483.21
leperlean 132.29
lepers 355.33 540.31
lepers 350.04
Leperstower 237.22
Leperstown 462.24
leperties' 577.34
lepes 395.33
leporello 172.23
leporty 338.20
lepossette 484.33
leppers 257.06
leppin 141.04
leppy 041.23
leprous 145.02
leps 499.13
lep's 250.22
lept 334.26
lequou 151.29
Lerck's 203.29
lerking 381.22
lerningstoel 251.22
lerryn 200.36
les 129.35 281.05 281.06 281.08 281.09 281.11 478.21
Les 622.20
Les 028.26
Lesbia 093.27
lesbiels 116.28
L'Escaut 203.21
lese 571.07
lesmended 440.35
less 023.17 033.01 081.20 087.33 108.21 108.21 118.25 125.15 223.16 232.31 281.23 298.13 304.23 311.06 413.35 426.34 443.13 479.16 502.07 529.04 532.01 599.17
Lesscontinuous 501.22
lesser 051.29 115.01
lessions 436.20
lessle 226.29
Lessnatbe 599.19
lesson 430.04 579.35
lessonless 324.18
lessons 539.09
lessontimes 462.24
lest 076.36 364.11 444.10 456.18 566.31
lest 346.34
Lest 576.12

lestage 541.09
leste 232.16
Leste 207.24
Lesten 477.07
let let Let Let
letate 053.20
letdown 025.18
Lethals 450.30
lethargy's 397.08
lethelulled 078.04
lethemuse 272.F3
lether 390.07
lethest 214.10
lethurgies 334.01
letitiae 287.22
letout 152.27
lets 069.30 128.10 278.09 441.06 455.26
Lets 016.02 338.32 359.27 466.04
let's 244.11 244.11 244.11 287.12 297.06 307.F9
Let's 145.31 505.27 515.28 621.02
letter 093.24 112.30 115.07 120.04 129.07 211.22 269.17 288.13 337.12 397.27 410.22 419.23 421.25 424.32 458.27 459.32 489.33 531.35 563.17 615.01 623.29 623.33
Letter 181.02 307.15 420.17
Letter 176.06
letteracettera 339.36
lettercrackers 026.30
lettereens 276.07
letterines 235.22
lettering 617.30
letterish 590.02
lettermaking 124.29
letterman 454.04
Lettermuck 456.27
Letternoosh 456.26
letterpaper 111.09
letterread 425.05
letters 032.18 061.30 082.18 112.24 114.36 140.09 198.25 205.07 237.19 251.31 278.14 278.14 278.16 278.16 278.18 288.01 307.F5 405.01 413.09 425.24 431.29 435.31 478.02 492.35 495.02 543.06 546.10
Letters 066.11
Letters 104.14
lettersday 278.22
Letterspeak 456.26
lettertrumpets 179.22
lettice 020.24
letties 511.22 540.23 603.17
lettin 524.30
letting 086.35 162.03 200.11 233.03 233.19 331.15 450.13 520.02 605.34 627.21
letting 347.34
Letting 198.16
Letting 071.32
Lettland 548.01
letton 155.27
Lettrechaun 419.17
lettruce 424.20
letts 078.28
Lettucia 161.30
Letty 184.25 203.29 415.03
Lettyshape 229.21
leud 580.36
leurs 281.10
leursieuresponsor 542.25
leuther 536.36
levanted 084.02
levantine 480.10
leve 549.01 549.01
levee 209.34 544.01
level 135.32 206.05 508.03
levellaut 609.10
levelled 057.01
levelling 189.36
levels 605.33
Leven 184.25
Lever 594.13
leveret 176.27
levey 041.22
Levey 050.14
Levia 617.01
Levi-Brullo 151.11
levirs 230.34
levity 020.30
levret 458.12
levt 490.25
levy 069.02
Levy 273.11
lew 338.32
lewd 141.16 370.31 435.10 459.28 550.28
lewdbrogue 313.23 343.31
lewdness 573.12
lewdningbluebolteredallucktruck-alltraumconductor 378.09
Lewd's 501.34
lewdy 268.28 624.20
Lewes 087.20
lex 273.05 280.07 460.29 518.31
Lex 044.12
lexical 180.36
lexinction 083.25
lex's 028.05
leymon 488.04
Leytha 212.11
Lezba 212.10
Lff 628.07
lhirondella 359.28
Lhirondella 359.28
lhorde 243.10
Lhugewhite 350.10
l'hummour 331.33
li 565.27
Li 565.25
liability 574.21
liable 492.35 508.31
liaison 270.16 529.27
Liam 025.31 131.10
laimstone 331.04
Liane 212.11
liar 034.10 096.18 331.32 488.01 535.15
liard 054.21 344.20
liarnels 241.32
lib 302.23
libans 460.22
libationally 522.07
libber 097.30 424.11
libbers 531.14
libe 023.33
libel 355.14 419.33 534.17
libelman 250.19
libels 494.32 581.04
Libelulous 415.26
liber 234.30
Liber 250.20
Liber 014.29
Libera 228.25
liberal 035.22 138.25 551.17
liberally 408.09
liberaloider 336.24
liberator 024.07 588.35
liberorumqueue 019.24
liberties 072.17 085.07 371.34 545.20 548.19
Liberties 040.04
libertilands 542.02
libertinam 007.23
libertine 505.21
LIBERTINE 286.R3
libertins 421.36
Liberton 541.03
liberty 041.33 179.33 250.21 611.11 614.23
libertyed 226.24
libidinum 441.09
libido 123.08
Libido 417.17
libidous 524.35
Libidous 106.31
libitate 322.34
libling 250.19
Libnia 540.07
Libnius 250.20
Libnud 600.11
librariums 550.25
library 313.02
librotto 425.20
librum 262.F4
libs 283.15 442.36
Liburnum 509.24
lice 029.08 135.36 149.01 180.19 463.14 589.05
Lice 106.21
liceens 417.05
licence 060.20 068.15 220.06 234.29 255.23 329.19 423.14 523.34 543.13
Licence 421.09
licenced 618.10
license 197.16 589.20
licensed 042.08 132.11 179.10 315.06 440.11 497.24 580.24
licet 440.12
lichee 474.10
lichening 013.17
lick 086.29 241.34 273.F1 286.18 415.05
Lick 311.34
lickam 298.01 298.01
licked 204.11
lickering 583.33
lickfings 455.33
Licking 212.11
lickle 282.F3 461.13 527.11
lickley 577.13
licknames 234.22
Lick-Pa-flai-hai-pa-Pa-li-si-lang-lang 054.15
licks 265.F2 337.29 617.17
Licks 106.32
licksed 096.17
Lickslip 326.35
lickspoon 445.19
lickybudmonth 553.23
licquidance 465.23
lict 437.14

Lictor 197.06 463.06
licture 333.35
lid 437.02 509.27
Lid 509.27
liddel 207.26
Liddell 270.21
liddle 004.28 315.05 448.25
Liddle 208.05
liddled 048.04
Liddlelambe's 440.18
lidging 506.21
lidlylac 461.19
lids 474.08 596.17
lie 004.15 027.22 034.12 057.05 112.22 173.36 192.21 203.07 223.28 241.08 271.07 327.20 344.28 349.02 355.35 371.30 375.01 376.31 409.03 471.08 477.12 488.18 509.07 527.36 528.13 566.20 580.13 599.36 624.06 626.23
lieabed 180.19 544.30
lieabroad 202.29
liealoud 077.29
lieb 250.17
liebeneaus 527.28
liebermann 250.19
lieberretter 365.09
Liebsterpet 133.08
lied 275.21 486.06 598.23
lieder 042.17
lief 107.15 326.30 449.09
Lief 425.20
liefest 117.01 265.14 372.07
lieflang 547.33
lieftime 444.25
liege 191.06 567.15
lien 258.16
lieon's 350.30
lies 010.35 012.07 014.32 055.08 076.31 081.05 135.17 135.21 249.06 249.13 270.16 281.F3 509.27 604.04 615.35
liest 148.25
lieth 367.29 540.06
Lieto 502.10
Lieu 291.17
Lieutuvisky 187.08
lieve 027.08 203.10
lieved 153.30
liever 076.13
lif 328.17
Lif 328.17
Lifay 224.29
life 003.18 017.33 024.24 035.23 036.26 052.07 054.07 059.28 065.21 067.35 068.36 078.01 079.06 081.26 083.25 094.09 113.13 117.20 131.01 132.09 132.28 132.35 138.27 140.21 145.11 145.15 147.36 148.28 149.14 159.06 169.07 170.13 171.16 176.32 179.02 181.29 182.35 186.03 189.08 190.23 191.23 197.28 209.35 212.19 213.10 222.28 231.19 260.F3 264.14 271.09 292.03 293.04 303.05 309.03 310.21 313.21 318.36 328.28 351.34 359.02 382.02 404.29 409.25 411.02 416.10 430.04 431.19 432.12 434.01 444.25 447.08 453.29 455.14 457.33 487.03 490.06 499.02 509.26 512.06 515.26 516.16 516.16 519.10 526.36 551.29 581.07 585.17 586.07 595.02 605.03 618.33 619.30 623.23 627.16
life 201.08 343.14
Life 055.05 063.16 264.06 473.06 499.15
Life 105.05 106.26 175.10 176.14
Lifé 496.27
lifearst 537.10
lifebark 329.06
Lifeboat 321.14
lifeday 079.10
lifelike 593.04
lifeliked 057.20
lifelong 173.19 585.29
lifemayor 138.24
lifeness 621.27
lifepartners 488.05
lifeprivates 351.27
lifer 247.30 548.07
liferight 487.14
life's 012.34 049.24 110.24 111.15 116.22 133.19 458.08 533.25 563.13 582.15 587.13
lifesighs 230.28 571.21
lifesize 529.29
lifesnight 100.22
Lifetenant-Groevener 325.01
lifetime 032.28 083.17 137.36 211.22 427.13
lifetimes 566.02
lifetree 055.27
lifetrees 280.30
lifewand 195.05
lifework 012.01
lifey 203.06
Liff 382.27
Liffalidebankum 445.34
liffe 230.25 447.23
liffey 451.15 512.06
Liffey 026.08 172.19 380.03 576.01
liffeybank 526.01
Liffeyetta's 245.11
liffeyette 126.13
liffeying 215.33
liffeyism 614.24
liffeyside 042.25
liffing 310.05
liffle 018.34 287.07
lifflebed 332.17
liffopotamus 064.17
liffs 175.23
liffsloup 547.16
lifing 495.21
Lifp 302.F2
lifstack 279.F12
lift 012.32 014.29 036.27 046.25 056.22 138.21 171.08 183.29 198.15 297.08 326.28 371.09 394.23 408.29 474.20 498.05 499.14 554.07 583.06 622.28
Lift 046.25 247.30 250.20 371.09 525.19
Lift 105.27
lifted 271.27 407.23 454.11 548.04 562.25
lifted 209.09
lifting 029.03 139.04 214.20 319.01
Lifting 106.04
lifts 195.05 283.F3 355.14 440.30 445.12
lift-ye-landsmen 311.01
ligatureliablous 186.23
liggen 357.29 390.05
ligger 228.27
LIGGERILAG 305.R1
liggy 496.18
lighning 367.28
light 025.08 066.23 082.20 088.03 091.25 096.27 119.04 123.13 123.31 123.36 130.01 133.29 136.20 158.13 180.17 182.04 203.30 206.10 207.14 214.31 222.22 226.27 233.05 233.06 235.07 251.07 258.32 266.18 267.01 290.12 297.15 309.02 313.35 338.27 366.02 384.26 385.28 399.31 404.11 411.27 427.20 438.35 439.34 442.02 466.09 472.08 472.16 472.23 474.16 500.15 535.09 546.21 580.14 586.30 589.09 593.20 594.06 594.06 603.36 606.22 610.28 611.17 611.23 621.04 623.14 626.14
light 349.10
Light 256.34 440.24
light-a-leaves 551.12
lightandgayle 360.02
lightbreakfastbringer 473.23
lightburnes 549.04
lightdress 157.08 159.09
Lighted 559.14
lightened 080.27
lightening 607.26
lighters 551.23
lightest 561.22
lightfoot 457.11
lighthouse 345.19
Lighthouse 390.04
lighting 040.29 219.01 292.18 415.20
lighting 347.34
lightingshaft 241.13
lightly 076.30 336.30 428.27 486.22 532.25
lightness 327.11
lightning 022.31 073.36 117.03 131.14 133.11 246.08 426.30 449.28 501.17 509.34 585.12
Lightnints 351.32
Lightowler 585.02
lights 127.34 137.27 245.04 249.09 324.04 341.16 344.23 379.13 549.19 615.15
Lights 245.04 445.22
light's 493.08
lightseyes 404.14
lightsome 292.23
lightthrowers 192.30
lightweight 390.08
lighty 173.27 242.02
ligious 576.34
ligious 344.02
ligname 414.03
Lignifer 250.34
lignum 084.05
Lignum 499.32
ligooms 456.15

ligtning 335.11
Ligue 310.17
likable 399.27
like like Like
likeas 017.35
liked 079.20 224.36 389.14 425.14 483.19 538.33
likedbylike 171.13
likeless 271.11
likeliest 137.07
likelihood 012.33
likelings 339.17
likelong 296.04
likely 110.21 324.01 441.31 475.04
likemelong 111.33
likenand 332.16
likeness 133.30 276.04 463.06 526.31
likening 222.22
likequid 234.17
liker 562.35 601.12
likers 613.34
likes 138.29 163.12 196.14 309.06 326.29 441.01 457.24 513.23 619.02 620.14 627.12 627.12
likes 418.18
likesome 424.28
likeward 394.35
likewise 519.34 558.06
Likewise 437.25
LIKEWISE 293.R1
liking 022.11 115.34 462.14
liking 352.21
likkypuggers 613.27
likon 279.F12
lil 295.05 331.27 332.01 621.24
Lil 298.23
Lil 180.06
lilady 318.04
Lilegas 160.30
Lili 030.01 052.03 058.30
Lilia 525.14
liliens 422.32
lilienyounger 548.20
lilies 543.14
lililiths 075.05
lilipath 022.08
Lilith 205.11
lilithe 241.04
lill 310.21
Lillabil 513.25
lillabilla 333.30
lillabilling 450.29
lille 198.05
lillias 561.19
lilliths 366.25
lills 068.26
lilly 396.26
lilly 352.22
Lilly 373.03
lillypets 491.22
Lillytrilly 096.04
lilt 091.35 189.23 273.21 450.24
Lilt 206.04
lilting 627.21
lily 066.37 246.18 434.18
Lily 032.11 212.14 306.F4 618.04 618.16
Lily 032.35
lilybit 561.24
lilygem 566.06
lilyhung 200.12
lilying 291.21
lilylike 436.33
lilypond 098.20
lilyth 034.33
Lima 376.01
limb 058.07 068.36 153.10 155.01 158.36 562.24
Limba 518.24
limbaloft 340.30
limber 203.20 236.31
limberlimbed 270.08
limberly 550.26
Limbers 339.07
limbersome 613.36
limbfree 236.31
limbo 256.23
limbopool 224.17
limbs 025.25 204.19 331.28 354.23
limbs 433.18
limbs-to-lave 290.03
lime 415.05 462.36 489.12
limelooking 095.14
Limen 560.14
limenick's 434.21
limerick 183.23
Limerick 444.36
Limericked 067.18
limericks 595.12
limes 146.34
Limes 221.28 559.13
Limestone 100.13
limfy 580.25
Limibig 398.30
Limina 153.02
limit 119.09 448.33
limitated 137.08
limitative 524.10
limited 291.24 356.21
Limited 066.11 123.15 141.18 325.04 425.06 574.05 618.02
limits 436.10
limitsing 298.26
limmat 198.13
limmenings 571.22
limn 129.21
limniphobes 076.23
limolitmious 184.36
limon 110.28 171.12 296.03 604.09
limonladies 361.24
limony 215.20
limousine 376.03
limp 214.28 549.16
limpalove 338.31
limper 057.29
limpet 361.09
limpidy 624.15
limply 156.31
limpopo 214.28
limpshades 445.04
limricked 410.21
lin 310.09
linch 293.15
Linda 527.27
Lindendelly 089.18
Lindley's 269.29
lindsays 438.36
lindub 553.27
Linduff 469.21
Lindundarri 180.13
line 044.10 134.16 162.34 292.31 296.18 302.23 308.F2 324.12 340.33 357.17 389.10 439.17 449.12 465.14 475.25 501.13 538.20 538.20 621.20
Line 060.02
Line 105.01
linea 041.19
lineal 289.16
lineal 277.L6
lined 077.17 208.14 395.11
linefree 276.F2
linen 026.15 196.16 433.13
linenhall 458.02
liners 319.19
lines 009.04 114.03 114.17 169.03 197.16 265.27 333.11 386.32 389.25 396.01 454.05 548.21
lines 349.15
line's 120.24
lineup 224.32
Linfian 600.13
lingas 485.29
linger 553.05
lingering 056.23
lingerous 251.24
lingery 434.23
lingling 560.15
Lingling 560.15
lingo 116.25
lingua 248.08
lingua 167.33 287.21
Lingua 185.22
linguified 228.21
linguish 584.04
linguo 147.34
liniments 442.30
lining 315.06 457.23 520.10
link 030.06 054.02 226.26 254.08 462.22 493.29 623.14
Link 250.21 311.16
Link 106.10
linkboy's 041.12
linked 118.30 369.13
Linked 205.08
linking 499.35
Linking 202.10
linkingclass 459.04
linkless 264.02
linklink 500.13
linkman 427.01
links 135.32 283.13 309.19 596.23
linn 626.33
Linn 017.12
linnet 381.13
linnuts 162.25
linquo 178.02
linsteer 550.08
lintel 508.17
lintels 540.21
linth 208.05
lintil 625.23
lintils 138.14
Linzen 440.12
Lio 153.34
liofant 599.06
liogotenente 228.27
lion 075.01 077.19 099.30
lioness 112.22
liongrass 494.19

lionndub 072.34
lionroar 488.13
lions 236.25
lion's 528.30
lions' 477.34
lionses 178.01
lip 050.33 062.22 087.33 136.03 169.13 486.22
lipalip 023.33
lipe 334.36
lipes 042.10 409.33
liplove 486.22
Lipmasks 221.27
lipoleum 008.22 008.24 008.24 008.25
Lipoleum 008.16
Lipoleumhat 008.16
lipoleums 008.30 009.08 009.08 009.22 010.01 010.08 010.10 010.14 010.20
Lipoleums 010.03
lippeleens 207.09
Lipperfull 342.16
lippes 203.35
lippeyear's 327.07
lippia 297.25
Lippia 548.06
lipping 578.24
lipple 471.10
lippling 068.26
lipponease 339.01
LIPPUDENIES 308.R2
lipreaders 091.17
lips 027.16 028.11 038.21 084.22 147.29 148.07 170.10 345.26 357.23 384.33 444.22 459.28 477.28 501.17 520.33 527.34 528.03 610.10 626.29
Lips 105.32
lipsabuss 147.30
lipsolution 147.17
lipstering 467.29
lipstipple 093.25
lipsus 120.35
lipsyg 010.05
liptails 054.34
lipth 023.23 461.26
Lipton's 288.15
liptum 541.28
liquefied 430.13
liquescing 251.09
liquick 280.32
liquid 313.29 382.09 409.33 574.30
liquidamber 100.12
liquidation 012.07 580.02
liquids 051.28
liquor 004.34 043.16
liquor 530.24
liquorally 321.01
liquorice 184.21
liretta 170.02
lirra 359.29
liryc 528.23
Li's 426.17
Lisa 040.17 041.03
lisbing 553.18
liseias 154.05
Liselle 290.02
lishener 013.13
lisieuse 432.29
Lismore 491.11
lisn't 162.26
lisp 139.19 396.30 404.23 459.28 528.13
Lisp 206.24
lispes 571.26
lispias 348.26
lisping 173.10 384.32
lisplips 276.F6
Lispn 619.22
liss 053.05 101.06 148.26 276.F7
Liss 148.26
lissaned 245.09
lissle 226.29 432.21
Lissnaluhy 340.06
lissom 021.02
Lissom 021.02
lissome 236.07
lissomer 477.18
lissy 525.24
Lissy 538.22
list 054.07 071.05 103.10 271.26 415.31 493.05 548.14 571.34
List 013.16 238.23
listed 101.06 127.27 223.32 289.11 323.28
listen 065.04 143.31 177.27 203.17 207.31 213.08 251.35 457.26 457.30 457.36 458.07 458.09 458.33 460.35 461.10 461.31 528.11 571.24
Listen 144.20 201.03 460.31 527.21 571.24 588.25
Listeneath 318.17
listened 093.23 157.17 184.33 465.19 594.20
listeners 099.10 580.36
listener's 174.18
Listenest 527.03
Listeneth 564.21
listening 013.09 056.04 146.27 157.09 201.03 203.22 359.22 383.22 384.05 384.07 384.19 385.02 385.35 386.10 387.16 395.12 546.27 555.15
Listening 595.33
listeningin 304.20
listeth 138.10
listing 407.22
listleto 588.26
listnin 277.L2
Listowel 513.33
Listun 376.04
liszted 508.34
lit 021.16 022.03 022.27 123.34 135.20 321.16 355.09 543.32
Lit 114.19
litanate 593.08
litany 179.22 234.22
litcherous 181.08
lited 127.27
litel 533.23
literal 033.14 109.12 575.13
literally 187.03 284.11
literary 049.16
literature 112.27 306.14
literatured 183.10
lithargogalenu 184.13
lithe 236.31 457.32 512.12 602.01 602.02
Lithia 493.14
lithial 154.04
lithium 131.36
lithpeth 023.23
lithurgy 432.32
litigants 087.24
litigation • 574.01
litigimate 364.29
litlee 265.14
lits 284.30
litt 545.27
litted 542.22
litten 100.22
litter 093.24 202.02 615.01
litterage 292.16
litterarumque 495.34
littered 534.34
litterery 422.35
litteringture 570.18
litterish 066.25
litters 017.28 114.17 370.06 413.16
litterydistributer 530.10
litting 029.02
little 004.29 007.25 015.22 020.13 021.11 025.02 027.06 033.28 037.06 039.10 039.10 039.11 062.23 068.10 080.35 083.24 085.21 100.09 102.11 102.23 109.33 110.32 113.16 114.31 115.36 125.15 128.36 133.07 135.18 135.22 143.35 146.36 147.36 149.24 153.05 155.13 159.06 163.32 166.21 166.34 170.04 170.08 171.06 171.31 173.26 177.14 178.19 186.23 186.27 188.02 188.04 190.19 192.32 193.09 194.32 194.33 200.29 206.36 207.34 208.29 209.34 211.04 215.04 220.22 225.01 226.29 228.26 234.23 234.34 241.10 250.11 256.33 265.F1 269.03 270.07 277.16 291.26 296.29 307.F1 308.24 313.31 318.03 327.12 329.03 332.19 332.24 360.33 365.27 365.34 368.10 368.10 375.25 376.02 398.19 406.04 410.28 413.22 414.18 435.04 435.04 435.25 444.13 451.11 457.08 458.11 458.19 461.29 463.11 465.29 466.05 479.02 486.12 486.13 486.22 491.31 507.30 524.27 524.28 524.28 524.29 524.32 524.34 527.31 532.35 536.03 536.07 538.36 543.22 547.19 549.29 551.30 553.02 561.03 561.28 561.36 563.24 564.15 565.29 567.34 575.26 581.35 583.03 586.25 600.23 602.11 607.07 613.11 618.17 624.12 627.17
little 339.36 339.36 341.04 345.21
Little 015.08 040.01 062.36 068.29 307.07 415.18 514.22
Little 153.07
littlebilker 037.35
littleeasechapel 571.18
Littlegame 445.34
littlegets 507.09
littlego 567.24
Littlehorn 084.08
littleknown 123.22
littlenist 298.08

Littlepeace 503.13
littleritt 551.08
littlesons 019.28
littlest 360.33 528.02
littlewinter 502.02
littleyest 331.23
Littleylady 598.33
littliest 170.15
littlums 532.30
Littorananima 456.27
Litty 184.25
Litvian 382.13
liubbocks 222.28
Liubokovskva 498.15
liv 011.05 063.14 293.19 595.08
Liv 200.16 583.21
Livania's 549.16
live 029.20 044.09 074.03 078.01 091.02 091.09 110.04 138.24 142.36 144.29 148.26 159.31 231.19 242.04 253.25 289.09 318.04 346.21 351.04 368.12 397.22 455.20 458.30 466.05 499.24 529.29 544.36 545.06 555.04 594.17 602.21 604.35 605.24 608.14
Live 273.05 572.15
lived 004.19 018.21 021.09 129.28 153.17 230.28 293.04 303.23 372.36 389.12 452.29 477.03 480.27 532.04 535.28 546.16 549.09 565.09 619.11 627.16
liveliest 381.04
lively 153.07 330.02 429.07 525.14 554.06
liven 131.19
livepelts 344.15
livepower 274.10
liver 169.17 172.09 301.16 436.19 437.11
liveries 017.01
Liverpoor 074.13
liverpooser 379.13
livers 004.28 540.03
livery 313.17 586.35 586.36 587.01
lives 010.26 011.28 083.14 145.32 148.23 173.07 176.27 191.23 208.02 246.17 257.35 277.13 293.21 311.06 398.26 406.05 438.12 440.22 489.10 525.07 540.27 600.08 614.11 618.27
liveside 564.22
livesliving 597.07
livestories 017.27
livetree 420.11
Livia 023.20 128.14 195.04 196.03 196.04 196.04 196.05 198.10 198.10 199.11 207.19 215.12 215.24
Liviam 208.05
liviana 287.21
Livia's 200.36 215.35
Liviau 042.18
livibel 337.08
livicking 463.28
livid 626.29
livid 339.25
Lividus 014.29
Livienbad 211.23
living 008.22 013.30 024.05 036.30 068.25 073.33 088.08 095.35 131.14 216.02 269.F1 297.19 358.18 376.28 408.31 446.08 455.19 462.04 462.04 463.10 562.20 614.10
living 354.10
Living 514.25
livings 531.32
livings 350.02
livings' 496.01
livingsmeansunium-getherum 186.25
livit 055.07
livite 578.06
Livius 260.09 260.13
livivorous 613.19
livland 081.17
Livland 548.01
livlianess 568.04
Livmouth 245.23
Livpoomark 533.35
livramentoed 545.24
Liv's 289.28
livsadventure 138.31
livves 340.22
livvey 308.20
livving 011.32 327.06
livvly 204.14
livvy 003.24
Livvy 204.05 553.04
livvying 254.11
livvylong 007.01
livy 452.19
liyers 499.19
Liza 388.04
lizards 242.28
lizod 324.04
lizzy 200.31
Lizzy 538.22
Lizzy 399.11
lizzyboy 530.21
'll 399.19
llad 051.08
llane 051.08
Llarge 017.32
Llawnroc 388.02
Llewellys 151.32
Llewelyn 210.12
Llong 269.F4
lloydhaired 609.03
Lloyd's 590.05
lloyrge 533.35
Lludd 331.09
Lludillongi 519.08
Llwyd 091.19
Llyn 044.11
l'm 222.09
lmp 427.16 (lamp and last menstrual period)
lo 007.13 058.18 058.18 194.02 194.11 244.26 282.03 293.21 322.01 404.09 407.11 620.27
lo 053.14
Lo 053.14 293.21 453.29 545.25 613.15
Lo 106.14
L. O. 077.02 (L. O. Tuohalls)
loa 198.23
loab 023.32
Loab 587.02
load 025.19 170.36 214.19 278.12 431.27 565.22 604.10
Load 017.08
loaded 063.02
loadenbrogued 444.05
loading 346.01
loadpoker 493.10
loads 064.13 244.34 426.12 622.21
loaf 007.10 065.35 136.28 210.18 392.33 393.02 393.04 466.25 531.11
loafer 544.22
loafers 319.32 372.20
loaferst 283.07
loafs 393.27
loal 098.03
loam 469.03
loamed 578.26
loamsome 026.15
loan 012.09 099.33 112.01 206.10 587.14
loans 173.07 514.29
loanshark 193.05
loathe 518.02
Loathe 450.31
Loathers' 229.13
loathing 204.26
loathsome 551.16
Loaved 539.33
loavely 182.27
loaves 406.24 418.06
lob 584.08
Lob 297.15
lobbard 422.13
lobby 437.15 557.08
lobbywith 142.07
lobe 055.01 305.31
lobed 354.28
lobestir 311.10
lobscouse 467.17
lobstarts 337.21
lobster 122.15 138.03 249.03
Lobsterpot 071.23
lobsters 569.27 624.36
lobstertrapping 031.08
local 046.01 087.25 108.23 109.26 120.16 127.24 203.18 205.32 435.06 438.16
LOCALISATION 264.R2
locality 599.32
locally 040.17 172.17 365.02
localoption 449.17
locate 574.35
locative 135.26 481.19
loch 196.20
Loch 048.14
lochkneeghed 241.24
Lochlanner 100.06
Lochlaunstown 291.10
Lochlunn 370.28
lock 110.16 135.32 211.33 224.15 242.17 376.21 410.26 423.25 445.05 542.29 560.30 585.30
Lock 460.04
locked 085.01 153.03 371.16 386.02 438.01 493.07 520.06 545.09
Lockhart's 541.03
Locklane 390.04
Locklaun 268.F6
locks 122.16 474.07 617.34

lockt 099.16
locktoes 015.31
lockup 060.05
Loco 420.21
locofoco 231.32
locomotive 221.04
locquor 316.19
locum 537.21
locums 056.03
locus 287.09
locus 418.24
locust 111.18 546.14
locusts 184.20
locutey 484.07
lodascircles 228.13
loddon 201.36
lode 248.07
Lodenbroke 373.29
lodes 201.36 497.16
Lodewijk 361.21
lodge 027.29 136.16 564.13 618.31 622.06
Lodge 130.08 191.10 369.11 421.02 428.09 494.34 614.03
lodged 129.27 264.26
lodgepole 160.07
lodgers 437.27
lodging 173.18 449.17
lodginghouse 545.03
lodginghouses 039.31
Lodgings 261.F2
lodgment 574.17
loe 327.27
Loellisotoelles 601.28
loes 245.07
loevdom 244.34
loeven 136.28
Loewensteil 097.05
Loewy-Brueller 150.15
lofed 375.33
lofetime 230.19
loff 073.18
loffin 420.13
loffs 011.25
lofobsed 408.19
loft 198.15 199.06 249.30 397.11
lofter 162.24
loftet 415.34
lofting 593.07
loftleaved 265.04
loftly 407.20
Loftonant-Cornel 607.29
lofts 567.19
loftust 549.33
lofty 213.13 355.15
log 244.12 430.12
Log 531.04
Log 032.24 105.09
logans 450.31
logansome 450.09
logged 123.13
loggerthuds 156.15
logh 229.04
logoical 296.26
logos 298.19
logs 512.23 580.04
loguy 528.26
lohaned 212.27
loidies 071.07
loin 406.18
loins 333.29 549.08 606.06
loinsprung 600.18
loisy 516.09
loiter 369.35 604.08
loitering 114.29
loiternan's 299.16
loits 199.08
Lok 597.24
Loka 598.28
loke 601.04
loki 237.22
lokil 051.26
lokistroki 221.09
Lokk 013.13
lokker 270.21
Lokman 367.01
lol 034.31
Lola 525.14
Lola's 434.23
lolave 244.04
loll 096.20 568.07
Lollapaloosa 254.23
lolleywide 584.15
Lollgoll 512.01
lollies 326.03
lolling 209.03 244.22
lolllike 100.21
lolls 553.05
lolly 331.27 365.12 396.25
lolly 352.21
Lolly 096.20
lollypops 304.23
Lolo 250.19 250.19
lols 250.19
lomba 207.23
Lombog 398.30
lomdom 568.33
lomondations 340.09
lon 167.27
L.O.N. 131.04 (League of Nations)
Lona 284.F4
Lonan 024.34
Londan 602.28
londmear 372.02
London's 253.10
Londsend 535.15
Londub 625.36
lone 015.30 093.28 271.11 382.21 601.15 605.13 628.15
Lonedom's 239.34
lonee 088.14
lonely 225.18 289.28 291.05 478.28
Lonely 444.34
loneness 627.34
lonesome 453.34
lonesome 399.11
lonestime 319.10
Loney 071.33
long 006.11 025.26 032.15 033.30 049.21 051.01 052.04 060.19 062.13 068.33 068.33 070.16 071.05 079.22 085.23 095.19 096.08 100.22 100.22 100.31 107.34 115.07 130.26 132.36 145.09 146.23 148.32 158.07 159.06 171.36 177.02 182.27 190.24 196.19 224.01 238.13 242.23 244.25 252.05 263.13 270.26 271.09 274.F1 276.18 276.F5 283.32 284.29 286.12 286.28 288.08 300.10 301.29 304.14 311.05 312.32 314.28 321.28 322.22 327.11 328.21 347.17 351.08 356.20 360.15 360.34 366.04 370.11 387.17 387.17 395.06 399.31 409.06 412.36 422.13 422.28 431.27 432.27 436.33 439.17 440.21 442.23 443.25 452.08 452.10 459.20 459.20 462.14 472.13 472.33 478.04 479.03 495.07 499.24 519.20 523.12 532.04 532.07 547.18 553.07 556.10 556.25 567.09 570.20 570.21 574.03 575.09 575.23 576.15 577.28 582.11 584.24 587.13 595.09 595.09 598.06 598.07 617.08 619.21 622.09 622.14 622.14 625.27 628.16
long 176.15 399.20 525.24
Long 067.11 127.07 208.05 248.31 260.09
'long 191.22
longa 028.03 041.13 257.08 292.17 303.31 347.26
Longabed 254.34
longarmed 507.12
longawaited 041.28
Longbow 376.31
longcar 615.21
longdistance 457.24
Longeal 525.29
Longears 148.04
longed 225.33 385.29 626.21
longer 038.18 121.23 153.30 187.28 190.07 285.08 434.23
longerous 251.24
longertubes 542.06
longest 381.03
Longfellow's 261.F2
longfoot 222.31
Longhorns 528.28
longing 204.26 204.26 448.01 609.09
longingly 056.25
longlugs 449.20
longly 109.07 337.20 474.01
Longman 373.29
longos 100.18
longroutes 457.23
longs 237.33
Long's 088.31
longsephyring 418.29
Longshots 221.22
longside 551.23
longsighted 031.04
longsome 206.24
Longsome 601.10
longstanding 184.01
longstone 539.03
longsuffering 070.36 253.32 473.01
longsufferings 184.01
longtailed 236.16
length 023.02 238.24
longtimes 254.22
longtobechronickled 380.08
Longtong's 058.10
longuardness 357.18
longuer 509.05
longuewedge 339.01
longurn 479.35
lonly 194.21
Lonni's 373.16
Lonu 623.28
loo 069.22 071.09 082.33 120.30

Loo 051.24
Lood 469.21
loof 196.24
loofs 140.25
looft 170.21
loogoont 327.29
looiscurrals 234.15
loojing 125.09
look 020.21 033.10 035.14 047.14 053.11 065.03 068.04 086.22 117.03 120.09 125.13 131.25 144.01 144.25 147.29 157.20 160.06 160.17 163.32 166.11 169.10 179.07 208.01 210.23 213.13 223.24 226.27 239.06 240.32 245.07 247.25 253.04 273.F8 275.F3 277.22 285.F4 292.15 299.04 300.09 322.04 327.11 330.26 339.16 347.25 365.34 377.34 394.08 394.08 404.11 410.03 429.10 432.16 433.34 434.34 439.02 441.10 456.11 458.06 461.17 468.23 484.33 507.19 519.15 523.10 527.12 542.13 561.36 576.23 600.36 605.02 611.36 612.02 618.12 625.23
Look 081.02 193.05 193.15 193.16 196.11 196.12 198.06 213.12 248.06 248.32 251.25 267.F6 301.22 301.24 367.01 367.10 419.22 435.20 453.23 457.20 515.36 586.03 621.36 625.20 625.23
Look 105.22
lookbehinder 379.24
looked 005.28 032.19 049.11 101.03 109.07 111.08 112.27 153.05 153.32 203.21 208.29 234.03 234.07 330.06 344.33 386.15 405.13 405.28 415.33 430.12 430.31 472.16 508.13 517.19 545.25 556.05 580.06 626.29
Lookery 231.34
lookin 581.22
looking 040.12 043.35 062.08 066.20 131.24 135.30 150.32 157.09 164.05 175.01 187.09 188.04 204.20 275.F2 275.F4 304.07 370.25 405.15 409.01 426.19 429.04 445.19 457.05 461.20 463.27 468.04 488.23 490.28 496.32 528.04 559.23 578.12 582.18 607.31 615.17 615.21 618.19 620.01
looking 338.05
Looking 058.36
lookingfor 102.06
lookit 014.01
lookmelittle 111.33
lookout 442.17
looks 114.06 115.29 118.31 129.27 129.34 136.35 152.02 186.24 219.13 229.19 231.35 274.13 323.03 408.24 455.24 462.14 527.35 536.26 548.28 559.26 560.07 562.25
Lookt 339.30
lookwhyse 369.34
loom 197.29 286.20 358.05
loomends 548.27
loomening 625.26
Loomis 372.10
loomph 583.33
looms 058.21
loomy 276.25
loon 202.22
Loona 465.21
Loonacied 492.05
loone 507.17
Loonely 627.34
loop 250.22
loop 343.14
looping 578.18
looply 226.26 226.26
loops 458.31
loopy 146.23
Loos 448.22
loose 009.26 030.22 099.06 140.24 169.17 179.21 208.11 222.23 223.10 292.29 294.07 296.25 323.32 357.21 379.09 388.04 454.23 471.22 474.03 520.02
Loose 181.03 378.17 462.05
Loose 071.27
looseaffair 505.32
loosebrick 552.05
loosed 197.30 484.21 525.05 567.19 623.01
loosen 196.08 429.03 499.12
Loosen 106.23
loosened 197.12
looser 057.29 366.03
looses 128.11
loose's 376.17
looset 372.14
Loosh 295.19
Looshe 093.28
loost 547.07
looswallawer 151.23
loot 108.07 443.31
Looted 009.02
Lootherstown 582.33
loothing 627.33
looties 350.08
lootin 205.27
loots 082.25
Loots 032.24
looty 415.21
loovahgloovah 369.19
loovelit 226.27
loovely 226.27 273.19
looves 357.21 385.15
Lop 044.12
Loper 440.17
lopes 395.33
lopping 587.11
lopp's 415.30
loquacity 049.17
Loquor 263.03
loquos 398.08
Lora 131.24
Lorcan 617.12
Lorcans 518.11
Lorcansby 448.19
lord 031.17 060.33 198.04 237.34 248.30 311.11 312.17 318.23 319.33 323.27 355.25 381.16 418.06 452.29 486.14 501.30 527.33 546.03 593.23
lord 201.13 350.14 353.23
Lord 045.03 144.09 214.18 215.28 215.28 226.19 244.31 250.20 292.F3 307.07 332.22 388.33 476.24 549.35 553.05 562.24 566.35 570.20 604.27 611.14 623.04
Lord 044.26
lordbeeron 563.12
Lordedward 088.31
lordherry's 584.01
lordmade 581.17
lordmajor 029.02
lord's 596.09
Lord's 051.21 433.14
Lord's 071.34 105.34
lordship 027.23 129.25
lordsure 373.19
lordy 011.31 200.28
Lordy 200.28 496.02
lore 107.20 142.35 223.28 250.19 314.15
Lore 440.09
Loreas 561.19
loreley 201.35
Lorencao 179.12
Lorencz 537.10
Lorenz-by-the-Toolechest 569.06
Lorenzo 053.29
loretos 528.01
loretta 312.20
Lorette 067.33
Lorimers 312.35
Loriotuli 180.14
Loritz 312.19
lorking 534.31
lorkmakor 342.28
lorn 142.35
Lorne 089.10
lorning 378.25
Lorry 059.26
lors 547.08
Loryon 136.27
Los 154.24
Losdoor 054.11
lose 024.18 117.06 433.14 436.24 577.30 625.28
losed 285.12
losel 066.12
loser 408.29
losers 523.16
loses 138.35
loseth 247.26
losing 624.34
loss 088.31 093.36 133.12 133.13 140.16 188.21 318.35 375.16 423.26 576.34
lossassinated 241.02
lossie 200.31
lost 046.33 054.01 069.10 071.05 074.03 095.29 097.11 112.03 118.36 122.24 139.12 147.02 149.23 154.36 176.32 192.16 213.06 213.33 214.01 225.28 232.06 255.23 257.36 270.20 292.16 293.07 293.23 294.F4 307.F4 356.01 364.32 377.20 389.34 414.03 443.35 449.06 453.12 453.33 457.33 462.17 467.13 471.28 480.20 489.05 515.26 527.04 543.33 551.16 556.27 566.31 589.21 621.03
lost 342.13
Lost 421.09
lostfully 080.15
losthappy 556.19

lostsomewhere 433.10
lost-to-lurning 222.25
lot 062.09 117.06 117.36 144.16 189.36 249.36 285.01 336.33 379.26 399.33 409.18 445.10 453.19 484.27 509.31 535.04 570.17
lot 341.32 381.23
Lot 307.L1
lote 267.01
lotetree 191.18
loth 204.26 263.23 428.14
lothe 627.33
lothed 627.17
lothing 627.17 627.18
lothlied 470.14
lothst 300.11
lotion 084.17
lotions 183.31
lots 188.32 257.35 281.F3 312.05 364.35 377.24 459.24 519.33
Lots 579.24 599.21
Lot's 436.24
Lotsy 208.30
Lotta 062.34 241.33
lottance 388.15
lotteries 238.02
lottheringcan 518.18
lottiest 561.15
lotts 321.17
lottuse 062.11
lotus 492.02
Lotus 598.14
lotust 620.03
lou 257.07 352.31
Lou 058.06 058.06 147.12 360.13
louched 545.27
loud 022.10 064.05 258.13 279.F32 306.05 371.06 404.26 533.12 576.06 624.05
Loud 044.03 258.25 258.26 259.03 259.04 259.07 358.24
Loudbrags 360.17
loudburst 091.03
louden 141.12
louder 177.03
loudest 358.11
loudly 336.07
louds 114.18
Loud's 485.25
loudship 332.23
Loudship 053.31
loudy 154.33
loue 541.14
loue 418.24
louee 016.33
Louee 016.33
Lough 076.21 272.23 526.33 601.07
loughladd 141.08
Loughlin 271.01
Loughlins 541.18
Loughlin's 596.36
Loughlinstown 097.10
Lougk 310.34
Louigi's 059.29
Louisan 223.02
louisequean's 102.10
louistone 276.F3
Loulou 293.23
loulous 358.22
lound 257.26
Loundin 342.33
Loundres 543.18
lounge 579.07
loungelizards 101.25
loungeon 322.02
lounger 142.09
loungey 427.01
loup 097.08 214.04
louping 097.08
loups 484.25
lour 107.20
Lour 343.02
Lourde 299.06 299.06
lous 417.05
lousadoor 107.36
lousaforitch 069.12
louse 024.06 210.21
louseboob 442.36
lousers 381.33
lousiany 368.32
lously 336.07
loust 408.10
lousy 393.28 555.05
Lousyfear 439.07
lout 132.23 336.36 456.10 526.08
lout 390.26
loutgout 180.07
Louth 290.24
louther 460.11
louthly 023.31 336.06
louthmouthing 329.33
louties 510.31
loutll 399.01
louts 393.28 595.12
louvers 546.32
Lovabella 512.10
lovabilities 240.20
lovable 268.F7
lovablest 375.36
lovalit 241.13
lovasteamadorion 398.18
lovat 213.08
lov'd 450.10
love 007.25 033.28 045.16 064.24 090.04 096.11 112.14 116.36 129.36 133.19 142.31 142.35 143.29 145.27 145.34 147.32 147.36 148.07 148.21 148.26 151.36 159.29 168.07 182.22 189.05 197.16 212.18 215.04 234.31 238.09 238.28 247.17 253.25 263.F2 266.14 268.F1 269.02 269.26 269.F1 271.09 276.08 279.F10 281.23 281.F3 289.27 293.21 304.11 324.07 324.20 332.03 334.03 344.32 352.06 355.35 357.10 360.25 365.27 366.10 366.12 395.29 397.08 398.10 411.28 416.09 426.09 431.15 433.23 436.17 436.18 437.01 438.31 444.24 445.28 451.26 454.02 459.07 459.26 460.05 460.13 461.16 463.18 463.19 464.32 466.06 466.11 474.15 489.25 526.33 532.36 547.07 569.32 588.01 589.01 604.32 618.18 621.31
love 153.08 399.11
Love 307.07 361.09 372.09 436.14 499.30 522.04 578.27 579.18
Love 106.25
lovearm 027.04
lovebird 451.16
lovebirds 527.26
loveblast 471.13
lovecalls 337.10
lovecharming 561.13
lovecurling 345.26
loved 003.24 007.22 018.21 033.29 040.26 122.05 179.23 250.20 279.F10 302.F1 351.17 408.07 471.07 489.26 556.12 563.10 588.29 603.32 628.15
loved 200.10
Loved 420.23
lovedroyd 282.20
lovejelly 486.18
lovelade 617.24
lovelast 527.35
loveleavest 624.22
loveletter 080.14
loveletters 183.11 430.24
loveliaks 292.30
loveliest 159.13 446.03 461.06
lovelilletter 459.23
loveliness 145.21 220.09 458.31
lovelinoise 226.05
lovelittle 007.26
lovelives 272.F4
lovelooking 092.25
lovely 096.10 138.05 143.32 146.06 170.14 226.02 273.F6 280.15 299.22 299.25 304.18 361.05 379.27 386.01 387.30 388.12 393.19 395.16 397.04 397.20 405.29 437.33 450.22 459.33 525.14 527.12 562.09
lovely 111.13
lovelyt 615.24
Lovelyt 237.09
lovemaker's 335.11
Loveme 208.05
lovemountjoy 460.09
lovemutch 143.29
lovenaned 041.17
lovenest 065.09
lovenext 290.15
lovensoft 531.08
lover 131.20 432.32 460.11
Lover 093.34
loveribboned 147.23
loverlucky 055.28
lovers 015.21 359.31 385.20
lovers' 556.27
loverslowlap 437.36
loves 179.01 245.18 249.27 251.07 274.F4 303.18 321.19 398.22 459.15 461.08 491.29 584.35 624.18
Loves 304.03
Loves 028.26
love's 438.33 462.08 585.12
lovesaking 021.08
loveseat 384.22 600.21
lovesend 617.07
lovesick 235.22
lovesoftfun 607.16
loves-o'women 436.13
lovespots 021.27
lovest 148.31

lovestalk 236.34
loviest 144.20
lovinardor 374.16
loving 088.08 140.25 142.31 336.30 431.11 458.21 487.34 548.18
lovingest 146.03
lovleg 613.29
lovly 528.04
lovom 187.21
lovsang 328.06
lovver 327.32
Lovvey 231.12
low 051.04 057.05 079.01 170.25 170.26 171.20 172.28 173.20 177.08 178.12 179.13 184.11 186.14 191.29 229.24 240.05 240.05 248.11 259.08 301.26 302.13 312.33 316.22 324.32 339.22 355.15 359.03 363.13 364.12 403.05 404.08 435.03 441.22 474.01 480.03 483.36 547.35 587.11 588.24 615.36 618.17
Low 173.05 528.04
lowbelt 534.19
lowbrown 424.36
lowcasts 318.15
lowcusses 435.35
lowd 232.22
lowdelph 403.11
lowdown 180.32
Lowe 034.09
lowease 365.29
lower 036.07 450.28 453.35 543.03 546.08 575.34 589.19
Lower 046.04 284.07 456.26 459.19 507.26 602.21
lowered 286.L2
lowering 381.26
lowest 572.26 623.13
Lowest 535.18
Lowlaid 499.31
lowliness 014.34
Lowly 474.01
Lowman 485.01
loweness 187.17
lowness 170.25 171.12 171.29 174.36 177.09 249.14
Lowness 192.05
lownest 177.17
lowquacity 424.34
lowquacks 099.02
lowry 154.02
lowsense 422.06
lowsome 347.22
lowtownian 167.10
loy 545.32
loyable 425.13
loyal 122.14 243.35 351.06 423.03 511.14
loyally 451.20
loyd 326.19
Loyd 413.05
Loye 428.07
lozenge 299.28
lozenges 148.12
lpa 298.01
Lpf 619.20
l'pool 448.13 (Liverpool)
Lps 628.15
Lptit 054.16
Ls. 325.03 (Ls. De.)
l.s.d. 418.04
L.S.D. 107.02
Lsp 619.20
Lss 624.06
Lst 621.17
Ltd 421.10 (Limited)
lu 461.30
Lu 397.03 485.30
Luahah 554.10
Luathan 244.30
Lubar 132.24
lubbed 341.07
lubber 305.20 513.32
lubberds 152.17
lubberendth 310.21
lubberintly 485.26
lubberly 300.F4
Lubbernabohore 245.13
Lubbers 540.35
lubberty 233.18
lubbock's 189.07
Lubbock's 292.05
lubded 551.02
lubeen 042.17
lubilashings 211.07
Lublin 565.22
Lubliner 339.31
lubrication 584.04
lubricitous 115.34 121.31
lubs 324.09
Luc 377.32 541.16
lucal 051.26 324.32
Lucalamplight 438.30
Lucalised 565.33
Lucalizod 032.16 062.35 101.11 178.09
Lucalizod 107.05
lucan 474.07
Lucan 048.12 203.15 359.28 452.29 521.06 620.08
Lucanhof 253.32
Lucanias 256.21
lucans 080.36
lucan's 143.17
Lucan's 419.35 564.33
Lucas 184.35 389.10 390.34 476.26 482.07
Luccan 295.20
Luccanicans 497.18
lucciolys 155.25
Luccombe 235.16
lucerne 472.23
lucid 477.26
luciferant 035.11
lucifericiously 182.05
lucifers 183.16
lucifug 354.32
Lucihere. 295.33
lucile 247.36
luciphro 140.05
lucisphere 239.34
lucius 525.12
luck 035.19 046.12 079.22 119.02 134.05 158.17 320.25 321.14 325.09 355.35 428.13 453.11 465.23 471.08 493.29 622.01
Luck 249.05 290.25 299.20 578.17
Luck 071.27
luckat 485.09
luckchange 491.07
luckhump 358.24
luckiest 440.14
Luckily 109.01
lucklock 531.24
Lucklucklucklucklucklluckluck 342.14
lucks 469.02
luck's 262.16 314.17 499.12
lucksloop 597.20
lucksmith 148.32
lucksome 556.10
lucky 028.23 088.06 232.36 355.29 438.11 438.35 496.20 565.22 606.24
Lucky 374.21
luckybock 310.28
Luckypig 176.03
luckystruck 155.24
lucre 207.23 578.18
lucreasious 277.F2
Lucretius 306.L4
luctuous 062.11
lucy 262.16
lucydlac 203.26
ludd 540.34
lude 337.09
Lude 105.27
Ludegude 626.06
luderman 021.30
ludicrous 033.26
ludiments 485.30
ludmers 498.29
Ludmilla 211.08
ludo 261.F1
Ludstown 152.28
ludubility 607.03
lues 347.15
luff 417.18
luffing 311.05
luft 223.30 540.35
luftcat 388.03
lufted 037.02 118.34
luftstream 427.12
luftsucks 452.01
lug 146.36 162.26 165.02 315.24 500.01
Lug 044.11 130.04
LUG 305.R1
lugahoy 285.14
Luggelaw 203.17
lugger 312.01
lugging 344.15 417.18
lugh 507.12
Lugh 594.19
lugly 011.23 416.34
Lugnaquillia's 204.07
lugod 079.21
lugodoo 079.21
lugs 088.12
lugwags 243.17
lui 275.21
Luisome 236.06
luistening 384.19
Luiz-Marios 243.35
Lujah 614.28
Lujius 013.20
Luk 130.04 377.32
LUK 308.R1
lukan 053.24
Lukan 255.21
Lukanpukan 037.32
luke 398.26
Luke 329.26 384.11 386.06 398.22 447.14

lukeareyou 142.06
luked 223.31 245.30
Lukeehew 399.29
lukes 127.19
lukesummer 501.16
Lukey 614.29
Lukie 485.32
luking 428.03
lukked 604.07
Lukkedoerendunandurra-skewdylooshoofermoyporter-tooryzooysphalnabortansport-thaokansakroidverjkapak-kapuk 257.27
Lukky 326.35
Lulia 525.14
Lulie 502.24
lull 369.36
Lull 324.25
lullaby 333.30
lullobaw's 176.36
Lully 096.19
lulul 534.33
Lumbag 390.16 398.30
Lumbage 410.13
lumber 063.11 068.05 276.25
lumbers 339.07
lumbojumbo 359.04
lumbos 027.28
lumbs 346.16
lumbsmall 323.06
Lumdrum 178.01
Lumen 476.24
lumerous 282.29
lumililts 112.33
lumin 136.36
lumineused 548.27
luminous 178.28
lump 005.20 065.04 170.36 180.20 207.18 248.19 318.14 411.28 447.21 455.08 509.31
lump 164.20 418.18
lumpblock 277.02
lumpend 019.31
lumpenpack 324.13
lumpky 094.17
Lumproar 010.35
lumps 068.35 275.07
Lumps 294.25
Lumpsome 270.01
lumpsum 270.02
lumpty 550.36
Lumptytumtumpty 106.20
lumpy 352.20
Lums 249.35
lumtum 462.26
Lumtum 462.25
Lun 121.34
luna 340.32
Luna 262.F4
lunacy 049.17
lunar 264.04
Lunar 092.24
lunarised 092.12
lunary 601.15
lunas 549.13
Luna's 027.15
lunch 026.28 260.08 499.17 579.21
luncheon 042.06 456.02
luncheonette 070.33
Luncher 229.13
lunchlight 441.16
lunds 331.21
lund's 320.22
Lund's 137.09
lundsmin 372.23
lune 215.04
Luney 049.06
lung 439.16
Lung 499.14 578.06
lungachers 579.33
lungarhodes 208.26
lungd 367.16
lunge 302.22
lungeon 248.20
lunger 165.10 331.06
lunger 349.35
Lunger 131.04
lungfortes 595.14
lungfush 525.31
lunghalloon 323.25
lungible 394.21
lungitube 566.35
lungorge 378.23
lungs 488.31
lunguam 095.28
lunguings 396.29
Luntum 012.05
Luperca 067.36 444.36
Lupita 067.33
lupitally 444.28
lupo 192.03
luppas 403.16
lupps 489.27
lupsqueezer 376.20
lupstucks 460.02
Lupton 257.13
lupus 480.35
lur 310.24
lurch 073.21 132.23 316.30 365.27
lurched 186.26
lurchers 283.19
lurching 202.29
lure 245.08 497.14 549.18
lured 239.10 297.29
Luredogged 492.06
luridity 131.36
lurk 007.34 066.26 361.24 450.30
lurked 476.27
lurkin 346.28
lurking 292.28 337.21
lurks 245.25
luscious 170.35
Luse 414.25 417.18 417.29
Luse 418.14
lushier 024.26
lushiness 095.23
Lusk 211.23
lusky 339.31
lusosing 426.28
Lusqu'au 541.19
lusspillerindernees 234.19
lust 051.09 080.15 176.29 211.07 443.17 603.01
lust 263.L4 530.24
Lust 433.23
lusteth 138.10
lustiest 439.13
lustily 337.19
LUSTRAL 286.R2
lustres 055.30 231.20 416.21 607.02
lustsleuth 033.31
lusty 176.16
lustyg 127.32
lute 006.11 224.15
lutean 239.07
luters 492.15
lutestring 533.09
lutetiae 287.22
lutetias 542.29
Lutetiavitch 207.08
Lutharius 263.F4
Luther 071.27
lutification 372.24
luting 448.35
lutran 110.08
Luttrell 081.14
luttrelly 534.09
luusk 325.32
luv 017.36
Luvia 619.16
luvial 086.09
Luvillicit 385.25
Luvium 226.35
luvvomony 172.11
lux 083.09
luxories 548.27
luxure 328.09
luxuriotiating 613.19
luxury 192.05
Luxuumburgher 578.35
luy 340.17
Luz 528.13
lyasher 322.22
Lycanthrope 071.32
lyceum 480.27
lydialight 236.02
lydialike 111.23
lydias 294.20
lyer 013.17
lyethey 017.32
lyewdsky 340.02
lyffing-in-wait 007.35
lying 088.13 095.35 135.28 213.05 244.32 301.26 301.29 357.19 498.28 504.12 534.33 567.14 608.25
Lying 213.06
lyingin 572.04
lyingplace 504.09
lyk 099.15
Lyke 245.33
lykkehud 312.03
Lylian 563.20
lylyputtana 583.09
lymph 309.05 577.11
lymphing 367.13
lymphyamphyre 137.24
lynch 545.32
Lynch 392.32 406.27 495.11
lyncheon 372.30
Lynchya 325.04
Lynd 206.26
Lyndhurst 351.29
lyne 209.18
Lynn 070.07
Lynn-Duff 313.34
Lynne 266.03
Lynsha's 506.34
Lynsky 060.11
lyoking 343.27
Lyon 148.36
Lyones 371.36
lyonesses 229.10
lyonesslooting 359.16

lyonine 155.06
lyonised 465.15
Lyons 214.34 384.08 387.14
388.34 397.21 405.04 449.11
475.25 476.26 519.33 520.13
lyow 181.26
lyrars 364.32
lyre 139.22
lyrical 385.24
lyricism 164.15
lyrics 182.22
lyse 348.25
lyst 364.29

M. 031.19 (Michael M. Manning)
164.08
534.32 (Private M.)
M. 269.L1
ma 094.11 236.32 239.09
496.20 562.03 562.03 571.12
571.12 601.33
ma 499.30
Ma 080.15 206.03 527.30
Maace 165.02
maaks 312.31
maam 485.32
Maam 085.23
ma'am 272.F1
maaned 598.32
Maass 203.31
Maassy 212.08
maaster 384.06
maasters 391.08
maateskippey 076.19
mabbing 329.22
Mabbot's 174.27
Mabbul 136.08
mabby 280.20 335.08
Mabhrodaphne 406.25
mac 274.09 (Hannibal mac
Hamiltan)
404.17 (mac Frieze)
570.23 (fine mac sons)
586.29
Mac 025.36 (Mac Magnus)
046.20 (Mac Oscar)
077.25 (Mac Pelah)
080.32 (Mac Shane's)
087.17 (Mac Gale)
126.04 (Mac Irewick)
133.26 (Mac Milligan's)
142.28 (Mac Carty)
168.05 (Mac Jeffet)
271.01 (Mac Loughlin)
271.02 (Mac Namara)
290.06 (Mac Auliffe)
305.F3 (Mac Gusty)
325.23 (Mac Namara)
340.17 (Mac Mahahon)
365.24 (Mac Gurk)
398.01 (Mac Gregory)
405.05 (Mac Dougall's)
427.04 (Mac Auliffe's)
452.09 (Mac Courther)
Mac 048.14 (Mac Call)
072.01 (Mac Noon)
176.18 (Mac Garvey)
M.A.C.A, 492.22
Macadam 469.20
macadamised 080.01
Macadamson 187.35
MacAdoo 290.09
Macaires 065.04
MacAlister 370.21
MacArty 463.22
MacAuscullpth 532.09
MacBeth 290.06
Macbeths 302.F1
MacBlacks 409.23
MacBlakes 409.23
MacBruiser 376.09
Maccabe 033.02
MacCabe 200.03
MacCarthy's 200.35
MacCawley 025.36
MacCawley's 392.08
MacCawthelock 587.30
Macchevuole 089.06
Macclefield's 381.14
MacClouds 519.07
MacConn 376.01
MacCool 139.14
MacCoort 376.01
MacCormack 137.02
MacCormick 376.01
MacCowell 607.04
MacCrawl 617.11
MacCrawls 618.01
Maccullaghmore 025.31
MacCumhal 243.14
MacDollett 290.09
Macdonagh 490.06
Macdougal 482.09
MacDougal 214.36 475.30
MacDougall 384.14 386.06 389.18
macdublins 087.30
Macdugalius 573.08
MacDyke 008.27
mace 375.28 547.21 558.28
583.29
MacEels 450.06
MacElligut 365.26
macfarlane 180.10
Macfarlane 100.03
MacFarlane 210.10
MacFearsome 227.32
MacFewney 622.05
Macfinnan's 578.06
MacGarath 622.04
MacGarry 526.24
MacGhimley 290.07
MacGhoul 354.06
MacGolly 395.03
MacGregor 520.04 520.10
MacGuiney's 381.19
MacHammud's 156.22
machelar's 064.32
machina 055.34
machine 163.30
machineries 253.33
machinery 320.33
machines 410.21
Machinsky 064.31
Machonochie 228.01
MacHooley 125.04
MacHooligan 593.12
machree 456.35
machree 096.13 273.L1 399.13
machrees 542.21
machreether 093.32
macht 150.11
MacHugh 382.22
MacIsaac 227.33
MacJobber 178.22
mack 133.08 296.05 476.26
570.23
Mack 575.24
mackavicks 101.33
MacKenna's 589.18
Mackenzie 210.21
mackerel 316.31 453.05 560.25
mackerglosia 525.08
Mackeys 106.11
mackin 537.35
mackinamucks 465.33
Mackinerny 264.L2
MacKishgmard 371.22
MackPartland 067.25
mackrel 597.32
macks 543.20
MacKundred 376.02
Macleay 212.15
MacMahon 099.28
MacMannigan's 523.18
MacMichael 382.12
MacMuhun 254.03
Macnoon 228.04
macoghamade 089.30
Macool 006.13 006.13
macotther 275.09
MacPacem 212.04
MacPerson's 123.25
macroborg 012.35
macroliths 594.22
macromass 111.29
macroscope 275.L2
MacShane 437.33
MacShine 437.33
MacShunny 475.29
MacSiccaries 228.02
MacSmashall 516.05
Macsorley 408.25
mad 082.36 129.15 139.09
178.02 193.28 251.17 252.04
269.F3 276.F2 285.F4 364.26
385.16 507.13 509.07 509.11
526.26 628.01 628.02
mad 399.22
Mad 279.F24 502.29
madahoy 285.14
madam 180.16
Madam 040.34 067.23 221.13
Madama 224.29 224.30
madamanvantora 598.33
madamaud 451.03
Madame 032.10 184.27 200.09
221.24 242.36 541.13 556.09
madameen 021.06
Madammangut 214.19
madam's 436.07
Madam's 057.20
madapolam 396.09
madar 358.20
Madas 496.21
maddeling 352.08
madden 232.18
maddened 367.16
Madderhorn 274.07
maddlemass 413.24
made 020.11 020.31 021.16
022.04 022.28 023.11 024.06
033.21 036.04 039.28 044.08
051.30 056.31 062.17 067.04
076.20 077.02 081.08 085.04
085.22 088.10 094.02 094.10
098.26 102.03 107.26 116.15
123.20 124.02 126.24 127.09
128.08 128.15 131.16 132.05
132.11 132.20 137.02 137.03

138.28 146.04 149.04 151.12 159.07 169.09 173.23 185.06 193.02 197.31 200.33 201.22 206.13 207.04 215.24 215.25 222.35 225.09 229.10 229.24 236.26 236.27 261.08 263.20 286.29 287.F3 288.07 300.03 309.22 312.04 312.10 315.23 316.25 317.11 319.10 327.27 330.26 331.29 332.03 336.01 336.17 363.07 369.27 373.28 374.01 384.35 385.07 386.27 391.17 391.30 392.12 395.10 405.29 411.35 416.23 416.29 420.06 423.20 423.22 429.01 429.05 431.14 441.07 448.28 464.34 464.34 470.34 470.36 472.10 476.14 509.35 510.06 529.21 530.34 539.12 541.24 542.09 542.11 542.24 551.10 551.22 551.33 552.10 558.23 558.24 567.20 574.11 575.14 580.36 587.17 589.01 589.04 596.34 614.04 621.10 624.15
made 105.17 105.33 175.12 343.18 530.24
Made 046.31
Made 105.08 106.27 342.23
made-at-all-hours 117.29
Madeleine 586.09
mademark 114.32
Mademoisselle 230.15
maden 240.12
made-of-all-smiles 015.11
maderaheads 288.17
madernacerution 107.19
mades 289.19
Mades 436.32
made's 201.17
madesty 022.07 022.07
Madge 459.04 586.14
madges 420.07
Madges 369.30
madgestoo 334.18
madgetcy 112.28
madh 110.09
madhouse 177.13 353.13
madhowiatrees 259.06
madhugh 325.32
madiens' 235.01
madison 025.04
madjestky 335.02
madlley 335.31
madonine 158.01
Madonna 549.02
madorn 395.10
madornaments 291.12
madrashattaras 010.16
Madre 408.32
madre's 212.15
madridden 553.36
Madsons 175.21
madthing 058.02
Madwakemiherculossed 492.05
Mae 330.27
maenneritsch 247.27
Maeromor 055.03
Maery 200.20
Maester 576.28
maeud 335.36
mag 199.32 228.05 267.20
Mag 232.05 461.28 586.15
magazine 007.31 310.02 497.25 497.25
Magazine 045.04 045.05
Mag-a-zine 044.27 044.28
magd 129.04
magda 139.32
Magda 528.12
Magdalena 211.08
magdalenian 576.36
magdelenes 237.36
magdies 289.20
Magdugalius 573.28
Magellanic 358.14
Magennis 497.27
magentic 008.18
maggalenes 453.19
maggers 031.10 478.07
maggers 120.17
Maggerstick 535.07
maggets 011.24
Maggi 211.22
maggias 199.15
maggies 039.13 048.11 142.30 560.15 586.14
Maggies 219.19
Maggiestraps 106.23
magginbottle 458.18
maggis 145.02
Maggis 054.21
maggot 410.05
maggot 471.33
Maggot 399.26
maggots 562.21
maggoty 228.05
maggy 007.32 280.14
Maggy 111.11 111.16 273.F6 273.F6 458.10
Maggyer 066.19
Maggy's 116.24
magic 013.17 421.22 451.08 470.03 565.29 608.19
magical 220.26
magicianer's 547.22
magicscene 553.24
magill 588.32
Magis 478.09
Magis 478.17
magisquammythical 354.10
Magistra 089.20
magistrades 495.30
magistrafes 443.12
magistrite 607.02
Magistrodontos 244.35
Mag'll 292.F3
magmasine 294.25
magmonimoss 545.32
magna 185.22 606.05
Magnaffica 463.06
Magnall 088.24
Magnam 525.20
magnate's 008.19
magnegnousioum 397.27
Magnes 375.28
magnete 246.23
magnetic 309.18 501.15
magnetically 430.09
magnets 616.25
magnetude 298.09
Magnifica 100.14
magnificent 060.26 377.20 539.25
Magnificent 222.17
magnificently 032.20
magnifying 183.21
magnon 530.21
magnoperous 057.33
magnum 566.15
magnum 063.33
magnumoore 609.03
magnus 136.18
Magnus 025.36 248.34 329.05 480.12 535.07
Magnus 307.L1
Magnusson 574.02
magog 006.19
Magogagog 071.26
Magongty 366.32
magories 397.25
magorios 454.15
Magory 303.13
magot's 254.32
Magpeg 210.25
magpyre's 354.27
Magrath 060.26 145.22 212.03 584.05
magrathmagreeth 243.03
Magrath's 098.09 204.34 495.03
Magravius 572.30 572.33 573.02 573.05 573.15
Magraw 494.26 511.02 511.07
magreedy 373.14
magrees 397.12
magretta 067.31
Magtmorken 378.14
mague 206.09
magyansty 171.25
magyerstrape 623.16
Mah 365.35
Mahahon 340.17
mahamayability 597.28
Mahamewetma 297.30
mahamoth 244.36
mahan 016.01
Mahar 549.28
Maharashers 497.34
Maha's 059.14
mahatmas 243.27
Mahazar 389.32
Mahmato 499.07
Mahmullagh 390.09
Mahnung 378.36
Maho 482.11
mahoganies 159.34
Mahogany 261.F2
mahomahouma 020.17
mahonagyan 334.11
Mahony 133.02
mahun 201.24
Mahun 254.26
Mai 281.L1
maid 025.08 046.31 056.33 129.07 200.26 245.06 251.06 269.23 304.22 388.24 395.19 440.26 495.06 495.06 513.25 526.21 537.32
Maid 586.06
Maidadate 267.02
maidan 547.26
Maidanvale 502.27
maidavale 581.19
maidbrides 566.16
maidcap 257.06
maiden 137.35 204.19 397.01 490.11 528.19 571.10 584.18
maidenloo 046.33
maidenly 562.04
maidenna 384.30

maidens 220.04 250.09 323.07 602.33
maideve 513.25
maidfree 239.22
maidies 092.12 314.13
maidinettes 241.04
maiding 305.28
maids 020.20 202.17 207.11 208.34 509.22
maids' 453.08
maidsapron 297.11
maidservants 034.19
Maidykins 222.13
maikar 352.36
mail 069.02 281.F3 579.09 603.04
Mail 404.30
mailbag 350.11
mailde 394.26
Mailed 221.35
Mailers' 510.15
mailing 372.34
mailman 408.10
mails 237.14 449.30 465.15
mailsack 206.10
mailstanes 462.25
maily 304.17 603.08
Maily 177.06
maim 223.20 515.10 581.34
maimed 325.33
maimeries 348.07
maimoomeining 267.03
main 115.16 118.20 132.25 143.18 186.18 214.02 325.21 331.35 434.04 512.14 589.26
Main 025.27
mainest 396.21
mainges 145.01
mainhirr 492.17
mainingstaying 312.15
mainland 042.25
mains 086.26 541.09 623.31
mainsay 431.35
maintenance 100.19
maintenante 281.L1
Mainylands 600.35
maircanny 408.16
Mairie 135.23
mairmaid 352.08
Mairrion 615.20
mais 478.21
maisonette 524.14
maisonry 004.35
Maisons 197.24
Maistre 177.30
maître 462.01
maîtres 281.08
maize 244.21
Maizenhead 582.26
majar 088.20
majers 568.25
majestate 478.12
majesty 031.03 043.31 116.24 304.22 615.13
majesty 120.17
Majesty 166.19 380.05 381.25 457.23
majesty's 408.14
majik 203.31
major 048.22 062.32 232.09 335.33 355.12 516.04
Major 098.10 159.21 263.07 561.07
Major 342.20
MAJOR 278.R2
majorchy 555.09
majorem 418.04
majuscule 119.16
Majuscules 535.06
Mak 258.10 258.17
Makal 258.10 258.14 258.15
make 011.31 012.17 019.03 019.21 023.36 035.02 036.26 036.36 039.23 041.13 070.10 074.07 078.23 091.35 094.11 099.35 116.22 120.26 121.15 133.07 139.21 141.01 144.01 145.15 145.33 145.35 146.11 147.12 150.29 154.31 157.20 157.21 159.33 161.36 162.09 162.31 166.19 193.10 194.26 196.10 196.16 200.21 205.31 209.16 212.32 219.18 225.06 228.31 229.05 233.08 235.24 240.02 240.21 240.26 242.20 242.22 243.24 243.27 248.03 249.35 252.11 293.01 296.13 296.30 304.27 311.27 313.28 316.20 328.14 329.02 335.34 357.23 358.08 360.15 364.29 376.03 376.16 406.32 411.10 434.23 435.31 439.02 439.28 445.07 451.04 453.22 458.09 459.06 467.03 475.30 488.14 491.02 495.17 510.15 521.31 525.30 527.35 536.03 558.09 560.21 565.22 567.25 571.19 576.22 580.20 594.11 596.36 600.22 606.24 613.31 614.12 616.06 616.09 617.11 617.18 618.23 620.06 621.02 625.04 626.16
make 340.07 383.14
Make 012.25 206.16 222.24 249.20 251.17 374.21 433.15 528.04 571.30
Make 071.28 176.16 264.L2
makeacting 157.12
Makeacakeache 294.F1
Makeall 220.24
Makefearsome's 294.13
Makegiddyculling 092.26
Makehalpence 338.28
makeleash 461.23
maker 041.36 261.08 362.11
Maker 098.17
makes 012.01 029.18 069.23 128.29 133.32 144.10 147.04 162.03 197.15 222.29 238.31 242.12 250.06 256.04 266.01 269.F3 283.F1 295.26 314.29 319.08 354.33 361.02 366.30 417.08 418.03 451.12 460.17 463.16 477.33 484.28 571.03 572.21 594.30 604.08 620.29 624.28 628.03
makes 271.L3 275.L2 339.35 354.16
makeshift 325.21
maketh 369.20 487.21
maketomake 240.16
makeup 625.05
makeussin 116.18
makewater 420.07
makin 345.17
making 008.32 027.10 027.19 039.22 070.04 081.24 085.30 096.11 179.26 181.24 196.24 200.26 201.30 202.29 209.22 214.15 230.14 233.17 251.35 253.08 305.33 327.17 328.32 328.34 341.14 360.35 364.13 386.11 389.33 391.17 397.10 409.24 414.24 415.28 416.05 416.06 417.25 420.05 423.08 424.18 430.21 437.09 438.08 439.22 442.24 447.12 453.09 463.23 464.33 471.10 475.05 476.08 484.01 506.22 509.09 526.30 542.03 563.02 584.14 589.08 593.22 599.13
making 346.08 353.07
Making 208.32 268.F2 422.12 514.02
makings 412.32
makkar 054.13
makkers 535.14
makmerriers 619.28
Makoto 233.35
mal 478.19
mal 192.14
mala 094.16 577.23
Malachus 004.04
Malachy 155.34
maladies 492.34
maladik 057.32
maladventure 231.10
malady 229.09
malafides 141.13
Malagassy 207.26
malahide 583.21
malaise 343.01
malakoiffed 339.11
Malawinga 499.10
Malawunga 499.10
malbellulo 052.14
Malbone 565.26
malbongusta 438.02
Malbruk 073.13
malchick 565.21
Maldelikato 566.26
Maldemaer 317.18
Maldon 094.02
male 069.01 123.10 166.17 222.07 392.07 457.28 523.35 539.22 564.03 575.04 582.31
Male 391.03 421.02 559.22 590.24
maledictions 269.F3 439.06
maledictive 612.09
Maleesh 229.17
malefactors 127.16
malers 034.33
males 128.33 164.04 164.06 333.31 448.16 461.25
malestimated 125.21
malestream 547.31
maleybags 337.11
malfeasance 532.19
malgranda 160.30
malherbal 478.09
malice 189.03
Maligns 364.03
Malin 525.29 580.34
malinchily 565.20
Malincurred 380.05
Malingerer 192.05
Maliziies 114.05

Malket 532.25
Malkos 512.22
mall 373.28
Mall 037.19 147.22 174.27 260.10 510.15 547.18
mallardmissing 042.36
mallaura's 327.15
Mallinger 475.22
Mallon 094.02
Mallon's 034.03
Mallow 199.28
Mallowlane 491.15
mallsight 540.33
malltitude 004.33
mallymedears' 328.20
malmalaid 285.F6
Malmarriedad 020.31
malo 023.16
malodi 229.10
malody 279.F04
Malone 215.33
Malorazzias 338.22
malorum 075.18
Malpasplace 081.15
malpractices 050.28
malrecapturable 058.22
Malster 337.28 338.01
malt 003.13 151.26 498.18 558.19
Malt 106.27
malters 229.23
Malthos 231.28
Malthouse 271.06
Malthus 585.11 604.07
maltknights 381.33
Maltomeetim 336.09
malts 362.03
maltsight 405.23
malttreating 322.29
malum 163.04
Maly 177.06
mam 085.04
Mam 287.07 535.06
Mama 243.04
mamafesta 104.04
mamain 224.34
mamalujo 398.04 476.32
Mamalujo 397.11
Mamalujorum 290.F3
Maman 535.06
Mamaw 146.04
mamertime 085.36
Mamie 491.29
Mamilla 211.08
Mamma 614.28
mammalian 084.20
Mammamanet 272.05
mammamuscles 015.32
Mammon 013.20 205.11
mammy 421.35
Mammy 226.14
Mammy 176.12
Mamnesty 570.07
mamooth 054.25
Mamor 499.11
mamourneen's 428.08
mams 290.25
mamy's 576.04
man man Man Man MAN
Man 026.29 062.23 076.23 138.28 145.30 150.31 156.28 205.29 291.09 339.27 360.11 421.04 507.04 535.06 576.03
Man 418.28 433.20
manage 045.19 112.01
managed 107.28 174.17 579.36
management 165.09
managers 609.18
manajar 305.F2
manalive 500.02
mananas 170.20
manausteriums 387.14
manawife 451.29
Manbutton 607.35
Manchem 617.22
manchind's 252.05
manchokuffs 339.12
mancipelles 545.25
mancipium 576.04
mand 067.15 146.35 162.27 285.11 332.20 387.35 590.20
mandaboutwoman 151.06
Mandame 530.33
mandamus 220.20
mandamus 574.35
mandarimus 432.30
mandate 601.36
mandelays 577.24
mandibles 385.21
Mandig 324.33
mandragon 577.01
mandrake 138.33
Mandrake 486.13
manducabimus 306.12
Manducare 433.06
manducators 408.02
mandy 279.F31
mane 100.20
manege 330.28
Manelagh 235.19
manewanting 112.21
maney 138.29
manfally 053.24
manfolker 038.15
mang 338.32
Mangain's 434.15
manganese 184.36
mangay 273.17
manger 188.18 267.F6
mangle 199.33
mangled 439.09
mango 060.19
mangoat 353.02
mangolds 211.03
mangraphique 339.23
mangrovemazes 221.20
mangy 242.06
Mangy 136.15
Manhead 339.02
manhere 539.03
manhood 098.01 264.21 430.32 459.29 512.24 596.03
Manhood 030.08
manhoods 375.09
manhor 365.05
manias 289.18
manier 298.31 298.31
manifest 343.36 497.21
manifestation 092.10 266.17
manigilt 127.34
maniplumbs 041.20
manipulator 472.20
manjack 177.24
manjester's 073.14
Mankaylands 595.26
mankey 337.29
mankind 096.30 585.34
manlies 096.06 441.26
Manlius 336.22
manly 495.29 527.32
manmade 357.30
manmichal 340.21
manmote 128.19
mann 044.16
Mann 211.01
manna 160.05 242.36
Mannagad 258.03
mannarks 369.20
mannepalpabuat 113.30
Mannequins 058.10 532.33
Mannequins' 267.F2
manner 054.36 185.08 322.11 336.24 348.20 389.35 435.04 470.06 486.26 516.09 516.34 546.21
mannered 386.02
manners 040.26 057.03 099.08 161.10 373.36 443.03 457.14 573.20
mannikin 576.15
manning 447.14
Manning 031.19 311.27 329.24
mannings 182.25
mannish 189.11
mannleich 037.01
mannork 378.06
mannormillor 614.13
manny 291.20 303.25 432.14 463.20
manoark 468.29
Manoel 440.17
Manofisle 529.20
manoirs 128.08
manomano 427.25
manomen 576.15
manonna 433.04
manor 057.34 464.33
manor 201.13
Manor 026.04
Manorlord 106.33
manorwombanborn 055.10
manosymples 338.25
manoverboard 159.32
man-o'-war 046.15 046.16
manowhood 329.09
manowife's 117.06
manowoman 396.05
manplanting 579.33
manram 112.22
manroot 169.18
mans 141.09 361.13
man's 040.20 056.17 059.30 151.34 251.29 380.24 411.29 433.29 456.17 486.09 548.18 559.15
Man's 040.01 397.14 559.08 559.09
mans' 511.23
manse 197.24
Mansianhase 491.18
mansiemagd 540.22
mansion 099.25
Mansion 380.05
mansioner 235.12
mansionhome 022.21
mansions 426.26 494.14
mansion's 140.30
mansk 317.34
manslaughter 062.06

manslayer's 056.11
mansuetude 484.03
mansuetudinous 472.19
mansway 493.11
mantel 559.03
mantelpiece 559.11
Manthly 387.35
mantis 417.34
mantissa 298.20
mantle 131.21 442.14 596.35 611.07
mantle 399.06
mantles 267.29
mantram 553.32
Manu 525.32
manual 282.08
manucupes 349.32
manufraudurers 173.17
manum 185.17
manument 025.16
manunknown 616.30
manure 095.03 447.16
manurevring 344.17
manuscribe 179.23
Manuum 476.08
manuvres 480.17
Manx 391.29
Manxmaid 433.19
many 012.21 020.19 037.15 037.21 041.11 051.18 053.34 057.23 059.14 061.33 068.15 073.28 079.10 082.17 084.31 104.05 108.11 112.36 115.02 116.20 118.11 135.19 135.20 149.34 161.31 170.29 173.18 173.25 181.36 182.01 182.02 189.12 189.32 196.13 201.27 203.19 227.01 229.34 236.22 238.19 238.19 270.05 278.22 291.07 306.11 306.11 306.11 306.12 325.05 367.15 369.23 369.23 389.14 430.01 432.10 432.26 437.21 458.26 475.05 482.34 484.16 496.27 502.22 509.18 510.06 516.17 523.15 540.02 544.15 544.34 551.10 551.36 567.08 569.12 577.24 589.04 598.31 603.33 605.31 609.05 611.12 623.22
Many 018.20 306.11 466.20
manyfathom 362.08
manyfeast 261.21
Manyfestoons 106.34
manyheaded 127.01
manymirth 074.10
manyoumeant 318.31
many's 267.F5 435.12 581.02
manzinahurries 214.03
maomant 353.06
maomette 312.20
Maomi 491.29
maormaoring 335.18
map 211.30 476.33 564.10 623.35
maple 494.21 587.32
Maples 155.25
Maply 098.35
mappamund 253.05
Mapqiq 029.18
maps 011.20
mar 102.22 254.18 406.04 438.24 456.17 582.09
Mar 397.03
Mara 062.05 407.16
Marahah 554.10
Maraia 158.19
Marak 491.17 491.17 491.17
maramara 595.27
marashy 624.24
marathon 009.33
marauder 624.27
marauding 457.12 464.26
marble 049.09 264.F2 549.15
marbled 055.22
marbles 476.34
marbletopped 033.09
Marcantonio 483.17
marcella 112.28
marcellewaved 204.23
march 041.35 070.14 114.08 180.29 187.20 292.27 343.05 438.25 540.15 590.09 603.15
March 420.32 500.24
marchadant 327.18
marchant 061.28
marchantman 197.33
marchants 536.31
marche 280.L4
Marché 112.32
marchers 364.12
marches 479.04
Marchessvan 013.27
marching 020.22 473.05
marchint 340.23
Marchison 058.32
marchpane 235.33
March's 442.15
Marcon 192.01
marconimasts 407.20
marcus 096.06
Marcus 384.08 384.11 385.19 387.14 388.10 388.34 391.14 397.21 398.02 476.26 513.05
Marcus 306.L3
marcy 517.33
mard 374.01
mardal 317.33
mardhyr 326.02
mardred 517.11
mardyk 325.32
mare 381.02 471.21 510.11 559.32 623.23
marecurious 484.36
marelupe 325.30
Marely 245.28
maremen 312.10
marents 388.16
Marera 334.05
mares 502.33
mare's 549.01
Mare's 045.15
mareschalled 132.24
marfellows 148.24
Margan 594.05
Margarasticandeatar 406.07
Margareen 164.14
Margareen 164.19
Margareena 166.30
Margareena 164.19 164.20
Margaret 116.08 615.03
Margaretar 406.07
Margareter 406.07
Margaritomancy 281.14
margarseen 615.31
margary 247.21
marge 600.06 614.17 624.15
Marge 165.14 165.22 166.05
Margees 166.01
margery 496.23
margey 495.30
margin 121.04
marginal 122.25
margins 182.17
Margrate 387.19 460.26
marguerite 281.06
Marguerite 146.12
marhaba 418.17
Maria 214.18 411.20
marian 257.06
Marian 366.35
Marian 274.L3
Marianne 106.17
maricles 425.20
marie 300.12
Marie 212.14 434.16 444.08 618.14
Marienne 625.01
maries 088.34
marigold 127.34 214.02
Marina 162.16
marine 030.16 441.16 548.34
mariner 123.24
marines 264.F3 325.18 502.36
Marinka 102.26
marinned 319.26
Marino 607.01
Marinuzza 573.01
Mario-Louis 246.17
marital 573.16
maritory 599.16
Maritza 469.14
Marius 307.L1
mark 025.16 070.01 076.08 101.09 121.02 135.01 223.31 245.29 292.04 305.32 336.23 348.24 363.15 378.13 425.29 425.29 480.11 525.19 541.15 563.18 565.08 568.09 608.01
mark 383.03 383.14
Mark 021.18 022.05 022.29 391.14 403.06 444.35 455.29 464.03 564.02 569.05
Mark 383.01 383.08
Markandeyn 525.28
Markarthy 091.13
marked 111.21 134.31 431.22 484.34
markedly 036.36
Markeehew 399.29
marken 539.29
market 091.23 212.22 440.14 499.22 529.01
market 530.23
Market 621.18
markets 215.19
Markets 306.16
marking 119.28 428.03
marking 350.13
markiss 096.05
Markland's 213.35
markmakers 585.15
marks 014.22 108.34 446.17 564.23
Marks 377.32
markshaire 423.03
markt 442.18
Markwalther 519.24
Marky 614.29
marl 031.01

Marlborough 057.35 132.22
Marlborough-the-Less 569.14
Marlborry 105.08
marly 365.29
marmade's 464.06
Marmarazalles 075.03
Marmela 235.32 236.06
Marmeniere 075.03
marmorial 009.34
Marmouselles 113.11
marn 374.04
marne 212.26
marooned 588.03
marousers 319.26
marquess 544.01
marracks 015.36
marrage 196.24 514.04 607.21
marrams 315.21 316.11
marred 312.11 544.29
marrer 250.35 361.27
marrer 345.04
marriage 117.05 260.16 279.F18 328.04 438.21 441.01 546.13
marrid 232.15
married 075.22 124.19 131.14 146.22 147.18 213.34 215.19 284.F4 393.17 394.26 438.27 510.07 570.20 626.31
Married 391.03 617.34
Married 071.33
marriedann 012.06
marrier 132.17
marrimoney 423.30
marrimont 375.27
marringaar 370.27
marrit 256.08
marritime 209.05
marrogbones 016.03
marrolebone 550.10
marrons 264.27
Marrowbone 347.12
marrowbones 391.32
marrues 344.29
marry 015.23 079.25 414.31 432.15
Marry 562.02
marryd 537.31
marrye 525.16
Marryetta 495.26
marrying 038.03 441.35
marryingman 570.21
marryings 117.28
marrymay's 227.17
marryng 282.21
Marryonn 538.01
marryvoising 186.01
mars 133.33
Mars 085.27 134.12
Mars 263.L1
marse 366.30
Marsellas 151.31
marses 064.13
Marses 518.02
marsh 212.31 349.03
marshalaisy 176.22
marshall 541.23
marshalled 343.06
marshalsea 094.25 456.32
marshalsing 371.34
marsheyls 089.18
marshmallow 575.17
marshpond 244.14
Marsiful 353.02
mart 451.09 517.34
Mart 105.03
martar 341.12
martas 040.10
martell 073.12
Marterdyed 492.05
marthared 214.23
Marthe 528.12
marthyrs 348.11
martial 227.31 577.04
martiallawsey 064.13
martian's 581.14
martiell 539.27
martimorphysed 434.32
Martin 026.05 266.F2 393.05 520.15 624.21
Martinetta 089.20
martyr 060.16 135.09 431.25 465.34
Martyr 392.08
Martyrology 349.24
martyrs 617.12
Marusias 256.21
Marvel 479.09
marvelling 123.07
marvellosity 177.15
marvels 119.12 193.07
marx 083.10
Marx 365.20
mary 206.36 214.23 492.31
Mary 027.12 052.20 206.06 223.02 229.03 239.26 260.F2 262.F6 294.20 404.34 440.18 440.36 555.16 569.10
Mary 274.L3
maryamyriameliamurphies 293.10
maryangs 276.F2
maryboy 563.26
maryfruit 495.24
marygales 562.12
marygold 561.21
marygoraumd 309.24
Marylebone 192.29
marypose 417.28
Mas 256.08
Mas 184.19
Ma's 496.20
mascarete 206.14
mascarine 268.18
maschine 495.23
mascot 475.34
mascoteers 412.35
mascular 166.24
masculine 092.18 099.08 190.35 505.25
mash 240.01 407.09
Mash 140.22
mashboy 439.30
mashed 065.25
mashter 516.26
masikal 237.30
mask 011.34 210.35 520.16 531.34
Mask 367.08 367.08 367.08 367.08
masked 062.33 512.10
maskers 367.25
masket 517.09
masking 559.22 582.31
masks 042.23
mason 113.34
masoned 552.05
Masons 223.05
mass 008.01 047.20 193.34 300.21 304.07 343.29 432.12 433.10 517.34 519.32 519.35 543.23
Mass 054.21 301.05 421.11 456.17 481.22
Mass. 111.10
massa 178.15 243.24
Massa 079.05 274.22
Massach 284.F4
massacre 111.02
massacreedoed 515.25
massage 510.12
massalltolled 376.13
massangrey 288.28
massas 275.F5
Massas 607.01
Massa's 511.28
massed 330.33 336.05 408.06 540.15
masses 011.22 076.06 111.30 221.21 410.34
massgo 552.23
massgoing 042.36
massicious 249.08
massimust 532.09
massinees 219.05
massive 277.24 395.36 446.15
massmuled 234.25
massness 454.14
massoeurses 432.23
Massores 256.21
massplon 141.05
massproduct 546.15
massquantities 447.03
massstab 493.23
massus 376.28
Masta 515.32
mastabadtomm 006.11
Mastabatoom 006.10
master 108.11 133.23 168.09 230.08 239.04 311.28 329.06 356.36 390.03 483.08 484.30 570.09 589.15 609.28
Master 053.27 123.20 166.20 169.20 209.08 212.03 241.22 288.20 485.19 585.06 615.18 622.25
masterbilker 111.21
Masterers 091.20
masterhands 137.25
masterplasters 152.26
masters 021.29 184.33 435.06 477.02 587.36 618.14
master's 539.08
Master's 531.04
mastersinging 513.34
masterthief 459.33
masthard 322.11
masthigh 547.21
mastic 055.19
mastication 108.03
mastiff 534.34
Maston 623.36
mastress 326.10
mastrodantic 510.03
masttop 320.27
mastufractured 466.12
mat 055.32 131.17 466.28
mat 411.17
Mat 397.03
Mata 609.06
matadear 060.31

Matamaru 609.07
Matamaruluka 609.07
Matamarulukajoni 609.08
matarial 205.20
match 023.08 041.35 048.21 233.18 413.24 440.24 441.21 461.19 483.23
Match 294.17
matcher's 620.29
matches 280.L3
Matches 421.01
matchhead 131.13
matching 248.22
matchless 134.23 148.28
matchness 294.17
mate 036.35 049.28 113.26 245.23 270.F2 298.07 459.35 520.26 583.28 616.03
mate 346.09
mated 407.24 579.27
matelote 531.17
mater 225.32
Mater 260.F2
materfamilias 391.10
material 378.34
materialist 529.04
materially 076.13
maternal 529.06
materny 397.16
mates 261.08 377.34 545.07
Matey 142.27
math 288.08
Mathematics 307.22
Mather 370.06
mathers 089.26
Mathers 268.L3
Mathew 184.34 476.03 520.16
Mathew's 443.28
mathmaster 004.04
mathness 182.07
Mathurin 335.35
Matieto 257.07
matin 596.05 605.09
mating 121.31 129.13 190.34 295.31 332.28
matinmarked 581.21
matres 166.27
matriarch 392.20
matrimony 605.09
matrmatron 086.19
matrons 242.22
Matrosenhosens 133.16
mats 366.08 428.04 553.08
matsch 366.13
matt 209.29 245.29 541.15
Matt 142.28 330.05 384.07 384.08 384.10 385.19 386.13 388.30 392.14 392.16 392.19 393.04 476.25 477.20 559.22
Mattahah 554.10
Mattatias 256.21
matter 026.23 038.12 051.03 060.06 066.24 077.33 085.04 090.35 113.13 114.29 119.22 129.03 150.08 185.08 185.30 200.30 253.13 294.F5 337.06 359.10 360.26 373.18 375.07 382.03 382.05 412.34 419.35 429.08 443.06 456.31 460.03 473.02 508.08 522.28 524.09 532.14 532.29 537.15 575.33 576.01 581.01 581.30
Matter 292.F2
matteroffactness 123.10
matters 019.36 167.19 290.14 358.30 405.23 593.05
Mattheehew 399.29
matther 389.06
Matthew 122.28
Matthews 377.31
matthued 223.30
matting 464.10
mattinmummur 604.11
Mattins 328.24
Mattom 333.34
mattonchepps 067.17
Matty 398.01 482.27 614.29
maturin 549.23
maturing 282.06
Maucepan 562.14
Maud 586.07
maudelenian 153.36
maudlin 586.12
Mäudlin 434.16
maugdleness 057.27
maugher 542.20
maught 315.06
maul 437.31
mauldrin 206.01
mauled 082.30
mauler 269.24
maulers 144.07
mauling 115.20
maulth 172.22
maun 496.35
maundarin 089.24 171.16
maundered 148.36
maundering 056.22
maundy 210.02
maun't 233.07
maurdering 449.21
maure 213.08
maurer 004.18
Maurice 063.35 123.04
Mauritius 572.29 572.32 573.31
mauromormo 253.35
Maurya's 494.20
Mauser 568.01
mausers 372.02
Mauses' 354.12
mausey 127.32
mausoleum 056.14 081.05
mausolime 013.14
Maut 319.09
mauve 253.17
mauveport 407.21 407.21
mauves 215.21 556.18
mauwe 232.02
mave 326.19
Mavis 441.11
mavone 291.03
mavourneens 290.24
Mavro 203.29
mavrone 232.24 247.14
mavrue 291.03
maw 553.28
Mawgraw 377.04
MAWMAW 308.R1
mawn 091.24
maws 064.06
mawshe 037.25
Max 248.34
maxbotch 010.18
maxim 228.16
Maximagnetic 497.16
maximollient 607.02
maximost 126.10
maxims 176.25
maximum 440.18
Maximus 088.22 153.18
Maxwell 130.11
Maxwelton 038.09
maxy 010.03
may 005.26 006.06 007.20 011.35 012.19 012.25 015.16 015.22 018.06 020.16 024.11 025.07 026.06 027.24 029.31 033.11 035.17 043.30 044.09 049.20 050.01 050.14 052.20 052.21 053.11 054.07 055.18 056.18 075.03 075.08 075.11 076.30 078.15 078.36 079.11 081.10 081.35 084.36 096.15 097.16 100.12 103.08 108.11 109.11 109.33 109.34 109.35 110.20 111.18 112.07 112.08 112.10 112.28 113.27 113.32 114.14 117.33 117.35 119.05 120.18 121.13 122.34 123.11 123.13 129.03 138.02 141.23 145.01 148.04 148.27 149.33 149.36 150.02 156.22 159.22 161.05 162.21 164.35 165.05 165.11 165.23 165.30 166.05 167.04 167.10 167.30 169.09 182.04 184.09 185.11 190.17 193.25 193.25 193.27 194.20 197.17 205.10 208.34 212.21 219.18 226.22 232.01 232.05 233.05 237.01 238.19 238.21 238.21 247.34 251.11 252.07 252.11 255.26 258.31 266.F3 267.21 267.22 269.06 269.13 270.22 270.F3 270.F3 271.07 271.18 274.13 275.25 277.26 279.F16 284.09 304.10 305.16 309.01 312.33 323.02 327.25 334.10 335.21 337.23 338.29 339.23 361.07 361.31 363.27 364.25 369.36 382.16 393.10 404.34 404.36 405.09 406.36 410.21 411.34 420.11 422.23 425.27 428.10 428.26 434.25 436.31 437.34 439.06 442.19 444.07 445.36 448.02 450.22 451.03 452.14 455.16 460.03 463.05 471.35 472.23 472.25 472.32 476.21 484.17 489.06 496.25 499.28 501.24 507.16 513.23 515.13 517.01 519.15 523.08 523.09 525.04 525.31 528.25 536.02 536.26 540.21 545.36 549.25 558.18 561.28 562.19 563.21 564.31 569.03 569.04 569.13 569.18 573.17 577.18 577.18 577.19 577.19 581.34 582.07 582.18 585.32 594.27 595.07 597.02 598.21 599.09 602.21 604.33 604.33 606.34 606.34 614.16 615.08 615.36 618.12 618.29 619.09 619.30 623.30 624.03 625.29
may 340.07 352.21
May 065.09 144.36 145.04 191.29 235.03 238.21 264.24 320.24 341.12 360.14 413.25 415.34 415.35 422.19 428.11 428.12 428.13 436.28 453.19 472.04 481.08 527.34 533.06

552.30 610.30 615.12 616.03 627.07
May 378.35 419.06
mayamutras 080.24
Mayaqueenies 234.13
mayarannies 493.06
Mayasdaysed 617.29
Maya-Thaya 294.L2
maybe 024.21 209.16 267.29 309.01 357.35 410.15 429.08 445.33 487.12 597.28
Maybe 125.12 520.35 620.18 621.27
maybole 596.21
mayde 013.26
Mayde 243.26
mayds 135.02
Maye 020.33
mayers 550.28
mayhap 395.27 404.11
Mayhap 514.22
Mayhapnot 110.07
Mayhappy 110.07
mayhem 115.14
Mayhem 514.29
mayhope 236.07
mayit 624.29
mayjaunties 233.23
maymay 053.13 546.29
maymeaminning 267.03
maymoon's 201.10
maynoon 050.32
Maynooth 553.13
maynoother 370.34
Mayo 085.25 141.01 479.03
mayom 589.07
mayor 031.18
Mayor 307.08
Mayour 568.16
maypole 044.04 249.26 358.34 503.33
maypoleriding 589.01
maypoles 421.32
mayridinghim 524.21
mayst 366.01
mayvalleys 015.03
maywhatmay 230.17
maze 120.05 285.03 552.17
mazing 364.13 477.27
Mazourikawitch 437.29
Mazzaccio 435.09
Mbv 568.04
McAdoo 227.33
McCaper 415.10
McCarthy's 381.02
McEndicoth 277.F4
McGluckin 180.08
McGree 488.36
Mch 625.19
m'chester 448.14 (Manchester)
McKraw 284.F4
McQuillad 219.22
M.D. 423.20 493.14 (Lithia, M.D.)
M.D.D. O.D. 413.25 (May doubling drop of droought)
m.ds. 232.25
me me Me Me
Me 471.04 579.22
mea 296.01
mea 185.22 499.30 549.14 549.14
Mea 186.25
Mea 472.08
meac 344.31
meace 087.24
mead 097.16 142.20 316.23 374.01 451.07 474.02 475.23 558.35 563.03
meadabawdy 095.07
meade 314.03
Meade-Reid 313.34
meaders 336.07
Meades 018.22
Meade's 590.06
meadewy 600.06
meadow 443.09
Meadow 076.04
meadowgrass 207.02
meadows 353.13 532.13
Meads 479.09
meager 287.18
Meagher 061.13 061.22 211.11 508.15
Meaghers 214.04
meal 034.12 110.30 407.03 529.04
Meal 273.L3
mealiebag 207.18
meals 127.21 127.22 132.26 161.19 405.30 405.32
meal's 007.18
mealsight 569.21
Mealterum 572.19
mealtime 192.06
mealtub 312.25
Mealwhile 243.14
mealy 016.34
Mealy 329.34
mean 007.26 015.16 024.25 053.27 059.07 065.28 068.20 116.09 124.04 145.15 145.26 148.12 148.22 149.30 150.13 159.14 161.08 204.27 204.28 209.16 249.30 308.25 318.19 406.32 412.09 427.08 437.09 437.19 444.35 447.22 461.22 468.18 480.27 483.36 488.15 488.20 499.19 499.23 505.27 510.14 518.26 519.18 521.33 522.20 531.30 534.14 539.22 546.30 561.34 563.15 586.14 586.27 588.21 597.01 617.10 620.09 627.18
mean 430.15
Mean 104.12
meanacuminamoyas 201.30
meanam 214.34
meander 209.05
meandering 123.10
meandertale 018.22
meanderthalltale 019.25
meaned 225.15 225.16 225.16
meang 108.12
meaning 028.10 031.05 033.14 036.17 038.19 095.23 118.01 118.27 150.01 173.01 225.03 237.04 384.25 482.01 495.28 517.24 523.28
Meaning 370.20 617.02
meanings 173.35
Meanings 234.29
meaningwhile 568.33
meanit 538.17
Meanly 313.23
means 040.26 069.21 077.04 086.10 092.09 112.06 119.01 130.31 141.28 144.11 161.09 232.21 253.05 254.05 309.04 373.36 374.12 407.27 411.36 475.32 538.08 594.34 601.01
means 352.20
meansigns 369.01
meansort 186.32
meanst 134.31
meant 089.14 089.30 090.25 119.17 146.19 163.20 184.12 184.32 193.36 239.03 370.03 586.18
meantime 557.31
meanwhile 173.31 448.07
meanwhilome 345.16
mear 108.18 297.15 316.07 471.19
mearbound 292.26
meared 081.17
mearest 460.04 527.03
mearing 239.30
Mearingstone 293.14
mearly 224.19
Mearmerge 017.24
mear's 156.34
meas 483.35
measenmanonger 108.18
measlers 336.07
measles 459.05
measlest 142.03
Measly 106.21
meassurers 608.17
meassures 356.20
meast 224.07
measure 154.24 255.23 328.24 382.09 493.24 560.18
measured 097.36 303.28
measures 336.05
meat 060.29 172.07 380.29 411.36 443.26 456.17
meat 260.L3 399.12 419.04
Meat 026.32
Meat 273.L3
meataerial 274.32
meataxe 229.23
meath 352.12
meathe 087.24
meathers 336.06
meathewersoftened 077.32
Meathman 051.25
meatierities 518.12
meatjutes 067.17
meatman's 067.25
meatous 310.12
meats 249.12
meattrap 465.21
meaty 435.13
Mebbe 093.31
Mebbuck 344.16
Meblizzered 416.20
mebold 315.03
mecback 412.21
meccamaniac 471.14
Meccan 051.25
Mecckrass 323.21
mech 297.16
mechanics 012.30
mechree 092.20
meckamockame 542.13
Meckl 329.29
mecklenburk 005.35

meckling 541.35
med 007.27 073.28 101.10
187.10 231.17 279.F23 290.12
Med 100.06
medal 111.06
medals 067.12
medals 339.20
medams 351.31
Medardi 185.21
medascene 413.11
meddery 199.16
meddlar 145.16
meddlars 094.17
meddle 086.19 171.06 357.05
410.17
Meddle 088.01 191.29
meddlement 014.26
meddlied 303.20
meddlist 336.21
medears 348.07
Medem 624.08
medeoturanian 289.20
Medeurscodeignus 624.26
medhe 356.18
medial 121.18
median 284.01
medical 146.14 290.09 557.32
Medical 086.34
medicals 333.24
medicine 193.06 618.09
medicis 517.06
medios 398.08
meditabound 338.34
meditarenias 263.F2
meditated 261.09 606.10
meditation 606.08
Meditations 307.06
medium 081.18 273.F4 288.18
315.36 439.22 490.17
medlard 433.35
medley 516.32
Medoleys 106.08
medsdreams 366.14
medway 209.21
mee 456.12 576.15
Mee 147.15 156.33 322.17
meeck 423.13
meed 020.10 041.10 236.21
305.32 448.21 518.31
551.22
meednight 470.07
meeds 316.15
Meehan 466.33
meeingseeing 179.01
meek 145.10 271.F4 277.09
614.06
meekly 222.23
meekname 567.14
meekst 365.14
meelisha's 351.23
meelk 613.11
meemly 527.24
meeow 409.15
meepotsi 276.F4
meer 061.28 317.19 484.15
Meereschal 254.03
meerschaundize 210.02
mees 354.29
Mees 607.19
meesh 457.25
Meesh 457.25
meest 352.12
Meesta 516.03
meet 020.12 060.31 067.03
098.21 113.26 143.19 159.15
164.09 164.13 201.25 212.05
215.05 226.14 230.18 264.31
266.23 269.15 320.10 328.18
330.07 340.36 440.35 452.22
452.26 460.07 464.31 475.21
479.36 513.32 520.03 538.30
540.22 547.09 567.04 568.24
571.09 574.21 583.28 626.08
Meet 242.27 618.26
meeter 116.02 116.04
meeter's 116.03 116.03 116.04
meeth 436.28
meetheeng 395.02
meeting 042.21 047.20 096.14
159.34 254.26 258.28 320.18
409.21 446.14 505.11 513.31
527.25 581.02 587.25 605.12
Meeting 024.22
Meetinghouse 354.17
Meetingless 247.16
meetings 245.22 336.29
meets 251.34 523.05 598.15
meetual 434.28
mefood 437.20
meg 532.01
Meg 106.10
Megacene 137.17
megacycles 310.07
megafundum 229.21
megageg 169.14
megallant 620.07
megalogue 467.08
Megalomagellan 512.05
megalomane 179.21
Megalopolis 128.03
megalopolitan 543.01
Meganesia 604.25
Megan's 243.27 378.19
Megantic 379.31
megaphoggs 005.32
megapod 078.05
megaron 582.20
megee 231.14
Meggeg 054.23
Meggers 379.30
meggs 351.03
Meggy 363.36
megis 478.17
megnominous 331.22
Megrievy 227.06
megs 532.01
Meg's 537.34
meh 331.13
mehaunt 224.03
mehind 350.15
mehokeypoo 256.02
mehrer 506.24
mehrkurios 261.25
Mehs 593.22
mehynte 224.03
mei 466.32
Mei 245.06
meias 054.16
meiblume 267.29
meid 496.11
Meideveide 340.21
meidinogues 601.31
Meignysthy 239.22
Meiklejohn 060.31
mein 059.31 113.25 155.19
538.28
mein 163.06
Meinfelde 184.28
meinkind 297.F4
Meins 594.14
meinungs 151.31
meiosis 115.34
Meirdreach 090.34
meiresses 550.28
meis 483.27
meise 568.12
meisies 056.14 535.16
Meistr 323.13
Meistral 241.18
Meithne 394.26
mejical 514.02
mekanek 258.17
mel 163.03
Melained 247.19
Melamanessy 505.24
melancholia 040.24
melancholic 449.01 611.32
melancholy 097.33
Melancholy 056.30
melanctholy 416.19
melanite 475.15
melanmoon 233.34
melanodactylism 522.07
Melarancitrone 132.28
melbaw 494.29
Melcamomilla 492.13
melding 477.30
Meldon 094.02
Meldundleize 018.02
melegoturny 309.23
Melekmans 366.17
Meleky 086.08
Meliorism 447.02
Melissa 212.09
melissciously 414.30
melittleme 446.02
melk 141.09
melking 135.01
melkkaart 538.08
Mell 131.01
mellay 510.14
Mellay 351.32
mellems 567.16
melliflue 185.21
mellifond 477.30
mellisponds 238.34
mellonge 406.03
Mellos 533.17
mellow 569.24
melma 595.27
melmelode 223.08
Melmoth 587.21
melodeontic 151.34
melodest 468.28
melodi 229.10
melodies 439.09
Melodiotiosities 222.02
melody 418.04
melomap 042.15
melomon 094.14
Melooney 331.12
melos 057.02
Melosedible 422.26
Melosiosus 437.33
melost 334.03
melovelance 350.13
melt 050.05 111.27 139.20
147.34 228.19 277.F5 450.03
melted 092.31

melting 132.07
meltingly 161.20
meltingpoint 134.32
meltoned 070.07
Meltons 328.06
melts 143.19
meltwhile 111.30
melumps 380.07
mem 422.33
Mem 242.28
member 128.03 438.27 585.26
members 026.29 237.26 291.07 385.12 475.16 498.21 550.05
membore 396.36
membrance 220.32
meme 527.03 527.21 527.24 528.10
mememormee 628.14
memento 457.34
Meminerva 061.01
memmas 092.30
memmer 447.14
Memmy 308.18
memoirias 507.30
memoiries 270.30
memoirs 490.14
Memoland 318.32
memorial 567.03
memorialising 104.04
memorialorum 610.04
memories 266.20 407.31
memorise 280.02
memory 025.13 037.16 069.05 080.25 147.31 172.28 240.07 266.19 295.16 318.01 471.29 503.27 515.33 558.27 606.08
Memory 413.03
memory's 083.04
memostinmust 394.30
memphis 516.29
men men Men
MEN 461.33
menags 069.11
men-a'war 436.13
menbrace 316.09
mench 279.F30
mend 230.08
mendaciis 493.24
menday's 117.05
mended 033.25
mendiants 448.12
Mendicants' 205.16
mendicity 541.27
mene 074.08
Menestrels 062.31
meng 396.06 568.21
Mengarments 311.30
mengle 594.16
menhere's 025.11
menial 227.31
menialstrait 083.36
men-in-the 300.F4
menkind 270.F4
menlike 505.16
Menly 260.L2
Menn 015.15
mennage 239.13
menner 158.05
menody 341.04
mens 040.11 269.F3 505.24 537.01
mens 581.17
men's 039.32 063.17 124.07 166.25 339.15 408.06
Men's 412.24
mensas 416.22
Menschavik 185.34
mensuring 331.22
mensy 607.35
mental 165.20 177.16 491.09 545.07 606.19
mentalists 096.32
mentally 543.24
mentibus 287.24
mention 042.25 111.11 177.11 204.09 256.28 280.12 491.14 517.03 585.14
mentioned 118.12 545.05
mentioning 062.36 599.34 608.03
mentioningahem 421.19
mentis 365.19
menuly 406.31
meny 229.34
meoptics 139.16
meother 238.25
Meould 348.17
mepetition 492.28
mephiticism 349.17
mequeues 280.18
Mer 349.02
Mer 292.18
mercaseus 163.15
Merced 212.26
mercenaries 573.07
mercenary 012.06
mercernariness 573.13
mercers 313.01
mercery 184.09
Mercerycordial 260.F2
merchamtur 496.26
merchand 246.23
merchant 173.16
Merchants 077.23
MERCI 304.R3
Mercia 565.12
mercias 385.18
mercies 391.07
merciless 252.06
MERCIUS 193.31
mercury 183.35 454.20
mercy 062.05 062.14 075.22 102.19 137.30 187.21 256.01 458.16 558.19 585.13
Mercy 054.18
mercy's 528.02
mercystroke 303.27
merd 418.10
merder 259.05
mere 033.31 053.05 112.28 127.12 149.29 161.04 213.10 238.34 240.08 248.07 252.26 273.10 318.08 350.18 360.07 408.10 411.25 433.11 518.21 520.25 532.29 608.01 608.26 628.02
Mere 486.09 507.23
Mère 038.32 184.31
merelimb 358.15
merely 063.32 070.11 174.35 226.33 359.06 363.35 541.11
merendally 406.01
Mereshame 241.14
merest 110.24 434.22
mereswin 404.19
merfish 546.18
merge 614.17
merged 116.15
merger 305.12
mergers 364.12
mergey 495.30
merging 364.09
Mergue 499.09
Mergyt 186.28
Mericy 205.16
merit 425.29
meritary 048.22
merited 429.09
merits 356.28 409.04 524.12
merk 551.07
Merkery 494.12
Merkin 387.28
merkins 364.28
merlin 028.20
merlinburrow 005.35
Mermaids' 229.14
merman 171.03 324.09
mermen 399.31
mermeries 551.04
mermers 254.18
mermon 262.F1
Merodach 254.28
Merquus 386.18
Merreytrickx 211.33
merrier 190.08 202.01
merries 006.11
Merries 105.20
merrily 615.21
Merrimake 197.10
merriment 253.26
merrimynn 584.14
Merrionites 497.17
merror 310.24
merry 009.33 094.11 182.27 183.26 291.20 308.19 335.34 361.30 440.36 463.09 501.32 620.30
Merry 027.15 270.12 529.12 562.14
merryaunt 364.23
Merryfalls 503.15
merryfoule 602.32
merrymeg 086.19
merrymen 048.16
merrymills 316.11
merrymoney 302.05
merrytime 325.30
merrytricks 060.06
Merryvirgin 376.35
Mersey 208.36
mersscenary 609.03
merthe 392.34
merumber 339.31
Merus 167.23
Mery 428.07
Merzmard 345.13
mes 183.15 232.22 543.05
Mes 410.12
me's 321.22 494.08
mesa 179.11
mesaw 407.11
mescemed 404.09
Mescerfs 113.11
Meschiameschianah 358.19
Mesdaims 113.11
mesdames 194.28
mesdamines 451.03
Mesdememdes 542.24
meseedo 564.04

meseemim 353.15
meself 095.13 168.05 410.13 469.12 487.18 623.33 627.21 627.27
Mesembria 494.13
mesfull 415.06
mesh 237.05 464.10
Mesh 385.06
meshallehs 550.12
meshes 203.31
meshing 477.24
mesical 492.24
mesleems 619.26
Mesme 212.12 254.26
Mesmer's 476.07
Mesopotomac 559.35
Mespil 497.13
mespilt 535.24
mess 184.22 199.09 300.24 336.02 382.13 391.18 514.27 604.06
Messa 211.14
Messafissi 356.09
message 019.23 147.23 223.31 232.09 333.19 571.08
messaged 531.05
Messagepostumia 607.09
Messamisery 202.03
messanger 609.19
Messar 344.16
messas 114.28
messchef 058.20
messer's 336.05
messes 183.22 290.25 391.36
messger 352.10
Messherrn 272.25
messiager 235.01
Messiagh 041.28
messiah 478.24
messicals 497.07
messieurs 336.05
messing 439.01
messio 478.17
messmate 487.13
messmother 560.28
Messoirs 219.11
Messongebook 460.20
messonger 405.07
Messop 569.30
Messrs 059.17 067.17 073.04 077.01 126.04 178.25 185.03 221.20 405.04
Messrs. 047.05
messuages 004.20 506.35 536.02
messy 605.02 605.02
mest 536.19
mester 395.03
Mester 058.16 222.08 291.F4
Mesthress 406.30
mestreamed 407.11
met 004.11 004.24 026.29 035.11 037.13 053.27 077.34 113.31 148.33 150.25 155.12 166.06 176.23 182.14 223.15 241.20 257.11 315.28 316.06 329.21 345.13 347.01 361.22 372.29 393.10 405.34 408.17 417.09 430.08 464.24 472.27 503.09 503.13 548.13 556.13 562.34 579.27
met 103.01
metagonistic 040.14
metal 616.05
metalmen 014.22
metals 041.12
Metamnisia 158.10
metamorphoseous 190.31
metandmorefussed 513.31
metanoic 341.30
metaphor 466.10
metaphores 070.32
metaphysicians 116.27
metauwero 199.23
Metcalfe 476.26
metch 584.10
metchennacht 339.05
Metellus 252.15
metenergic 349.07
meteor 475.12
meteoromancy 228.20
meter 398.14 531.19
meth 039.32
methaglin 092.04
methanks 316.10
Methanks 239.22
metheg 032.04
methera 457.13
metherjar 026.18
methim 232.17
methinks 556.13
method 141.16 152.07
methodiousness 159.31
methodist 391.11 507.33
methought 316.31 404.04 405.07
Methought 403.18
methylated 085.31 555.23
methylogical 373.21
methyr 132.34
meticulosity 173.34
metinkus 322.30
metins 540.31
metre 043.22
metro 041.20 128.22
metromyriams 265.22
metronome 451.21
metroosers 280.L3
metropoliarchialisation 181.07
metropolitan 524.02
Metropolitan 306.25
metropolonians 616.24
Mettenchough 249.30
metter 037.10
mettle 604.36
mettles 313.27
Mettresson 585.06
mettrollops 582.34
metuor 194.16
metween 570.24
Meum 496.13
meunders 333.23
meurther 206.09
Meusdeus 341.24
meusic 198.24
Mevrouw 413.15
mew 468.31
mewill 620.27
mewithout 238.27
mewmew 036.23
mews 061.04
mews 341.22
mewses 541.32
mewseyfume 333.16
mewspeppers 607.34
mey 075.17
meye 484.05
meyne 214.34
Meynhir 568.16
Mezha 214.07
Mezienius 483.32
Mezosius 483.32
Mezouzalem 258.08
mezzo 243.34
Mezzofanti 260.09
m'gay 054.23
Mghtwg 482.13
Mgr 076.36
mhos 322.30 322.30
mhost 396.24
mhuise 091.04
mhuith 091.04
mhutton 549.04
Mi 052.15 224.35 297.F2 297.F2 471.04 607.19
mia 160.32
mia 147.33
mic 570.22
Mic 126.07 (Jockit Mic Ereweak)
Micaco 233.27
micahlike 153.32
Micawber 131.16
Miccheruni's 407.33
mice 545.08
Micgranes 004.04
Mich 307.F6
Michael 031.17 031.19 094.36 111.15 116.07 203.18 296.14 398.15 447.12 520.03 533.29 533.29 533.32 559.11 573.04 573.15 573.18 573.23
Michaeleen 407.16
Michaelly 115.29
Michal 369.32
Michales 461.21
Michalsmas 567.16
Michan 036.29 443.35 541.05
michelangelines 161.01
Michelangelo 230.03
Michelangiolesque 081.23
Michele's 199.28
Michelides 349.22
michemiche 117.11
micher's 291.23
michi 140.05
michindaddy 016.01
miching 291.22
Miching 072.13
Micholas 049.34
micies 019.32
mick 048.10 296.08 301.08 434.13 538.04 570.23
Mick 025.36 087.31 330.16
Mick 219.19 399.26
Mickil 175.05
micking 251.35
mickle 369.35 576.22
Micklemans 618.03
micklemassed 023.16
mickly 234.14
Mickmichael's 090.10
micknick 240.02
mickos 012.24
mickroocyphyllicks 525.08
micks 133.09
mickwhite 596.32
micky 444.27
Micmacrobius 255.20
micramacrees 343.11
microamp 123.15
microbemost 151.01

microbirg 012.36
microchasm 229.24
Miction 106.19
micture 184.22
micturious 166.28
mid 007.26 057.34 067.03
076.26 092.31 095.22 260.09
344.24 369.27 407.15 437.32
449.18 463.09 474.02 505.03
557.19 597.36 599.07
Mid 231.26
midcap 415.07
midday 059.19 502.13
middayevil 423.28
midday's 540.33
middelhav 324.30
midden 110.25 141.33 297.23
488.25
middenhide 019.08
middenprivet 363.30
middenst 350.02
middinest 342.09
middle 012.34 038.36 070.14
090.15 098.20 164.06 248.11
270.18 337.15 391.12 487.16
middle 399.15
Middle 228.01
mIddle 120.05
middleaged 390.14
middleclassed 089.16
middlepoint 038.03
middlesex 523.28
middlesins 110.05
middlewhite 086.11
middling 084.25
middlishneck 136.26
middy 480.09
midgers 011.24
midges 416.14
midget 112.28
midgetsy 334.17
midgit 029.08
midgreys 603.18
midheight 606.02
midhill 506.02
midhook 228.30
midias 158.07
midinfinite 505.24
midland 235.11
midland's 203.03
Midleinster 381.16
midlimb 447.33
midmost 605.11
midness 032.05
midnight 053.19 381.27 480.09
510.07 520.16
Midnight 071.15
midnights 325.09
midnight's 403.20
midril 347.01
midst 011.32 019.14 135.02
163.02 224.20 616.26
midway 605.16
Midweeks 063.08
Midwinter 110.22
midwives 128.27
mie 361.13
Mieliodories 025.04
mielodorous 412.07
mien 021.01 068.22 511.22
mienerism 608.01
miening 313.23
miens 333.02
mierelin 285.02
mies 031.32
Mieux 140.01
Mifgreawis 552.02
mig 446.09 607.18
Mig 281.F4
mighshe 038.21
might 004.23 013.01 025.19
050.03 050.14 052.29 052.36
055.09 062.20 066.22 067.07
070.08 072.25 072.31 075.22
076.19 083.03 083.08 083.12
090.30 090.30 090.31 091.13
091.14 091.14 096.28 099.07
107.26 109.02 109.24 115.14
122.32 137.04 141.14 145.06
156.36 158.02 164.28 175.02
190.18 193.36 207.14 207.32
229.19 232.03 232.08 234.27
254.05 292.26 304.24 304.25
317.07 318.35 321.11 321.28
323.33 356.25 362.07 365.15
379.24 395.28 404.02 404.10
407.09 409.32 410.06 410.30
413.36 415.18 420.02 424.28
426.24 436.28 443.05 450.28
453.01 466.01 481.23 487.02
487.08 488.13 494.29 511.21
517.20 521.04 523.03 527.33
529.22 547.02 548.19 548.30
557.34 558.28 567.32 575.21
612.26 623.04 623.15
might 274.L4 341.23 345.11
355.04
Might 191.30 570.03
mighthavebeen 052.29
mightier 512.15
Mightier 306.19
mightiest 462.21
mightif 408.16
mightmace 568.30
mightmountain 019.32
mightn't 443.07
mights 603.26
mightwhomight 230.17
mighty 004.26 024.07 074.04
136.04 235.09 325.13 328.33
430.25 430.25 542.06 545.28
582.05
Mighty 490.03
Mighty 378.35
mightyevil 538.12
mightyfine 426.31
migniss 415.06
mignons 157.33
Migo 146.36
migratories 384.02
mihimihi 104.11
miho 297.24
mike 054.22 139.15 422.11
468.22
Mike 044.11 099.20 270.23
277.09 378.17 381.12 432.07
443.02 602.17
mikeadvice 432.18
mikealls 113.27
Mikealy's 441.05
Mikel 176.02
mikely 445.14
mikes 287.29 602.19
mikey 296.19
Mikey 300.F1
Mikkelraved 097.17
miklamanded 326.23
miladies 348.22
milady 229.10 301.11
milady's 537.32
Milchbroke 420.33
milchcamel 020.01
Milchcow 105.26
milchgoat 596.01
Milchku 241.22
milchmand 435.28
Milcho 366.17
mild 057.27 111.12 388.04
602.29 618.07
Mild 372.28
Mildbut 424.28
mildest 161.16
mildew 582.11
Mildew 040.17 598.22
mildewstaned 128.02
mildly 439.22
mild's 157.23
mile 150.06 473.12 491.11
529.04 622.11
Miledd 540.33
Milenesia 601.36
miles 084.31 123.20 135.05
135.20 144.29 208.26 467.18
524.19
Miles 343.11 516.12
Milesia 347.09
milesian 253.35
Milesian 518.07
milestone 036.18
milestones 081.06 375.31 504.32
milg 243.32
Milice 451.13
Miliken's 176.16
Miliodorus 032.12
milisk 370.19
militant 433.09
military 014.24 084.13 109.10
529.28 599.16 616.27
militia 518.08 543.24
militopucos 011.14
milk 025.08 027.07 037.34
039.18 045.15 075.22 243.23
249.11 321.24 323.21 438.09
506.35 604.14 615.27
milk 201.16 390.28
milked 321.04
milkee 608.20
milkfeeding 337.05
milkidmass 215.21
milking 113.08 456.32
Milkinghoneybeaverbrooker 072.10
milkjuggles 557.05
milkless 396.15
milkmaids' 183.25
milkman's 480.35
milkmike 116.23
milkmudder 496.26
milk's 215.07 260.F2
milksoep 240.22
milksoup 428.01
milkstoffs 161.16
milky 053.19 162.25 397.18
480.27 555.18
mill 075.16 183.20 265.02
285.24 285.25
Mill 213.02
milla 073.12
millamills 285.24
milldieuw 221.11

Millecientotrigintadue 054.12
millenary 599.16
millenions 117.22
Millenium 397.14
millennium 386.11
millentury 032.32
millery 314.19
milles 545.24 545.24
millestones 322.33
milletestudinous 609.14
milliards 589.07
millicentime 123.15
Millickmaam's 277.F1
milliems 239.03
Milligan's 133.26
Millikin's 334.35
millikinstool 559.07
millimetre 194.09
millinary 125.10
milliner 495.10
million 317.09 451.33
million 398.32
Million 496.07
millioncandled 025.26
millions 231.19 421.17 479.26
Millions 478.05
millipeeds 416.33
millium 265.25
milliums 117.22
millner 341.05
millrace 089.32
mills 375.10
mills'money 140.28
Millstream 175.21
Milltown 071.07
millwheeling 614.27
milo 094.14
milreys 541.15
Milster 338.01
Miltiades 307.L1
Milton's 096.10
Milucre 200.20
mim 367.01
mimage 053.03
miman 096.15
mimber 277.09
mime 048.10 486.09
Mime 219.18
mimic 313.23
Mimic 106.10
mimine 194.04
miming 048.11
Mimmim 310.02
Mimmy 226.15
mimmykin 329.04
mimograph 467.33
mimosa 247.36
Mimosa 267.02
min 012.03 046.21 068.24 547.27 619.34
Mina 147.13 318.18
minaaehe 206.15
Minace 095.01
mincethrill 515.28
m'incline 478.20
mind 019.35 025.07 032.04 038.19 095.02 095.02 108.03 118.07 118.16 143.32 144.34 146.26 161.11 165.17 192.10 200.25 205.19 208.30 228.04 230.08 232.18 248.27 251.30 258.32 268.25 300.21 314.27 315.31 357.11 358.11 364.02 371.19 377.07 385.23 390.21 410.28 423.28 431.31 439.02 439.04 447.11 450.23 457.16 458.14 459.29 461.10 466.30 468.12 472.05 473.01 477.35 482.25 483.12 486.12 487.05 487.24 487.26 506.32 507.32 508.08 520.35 536.09 539.18 565.30 616.28
Mind 008.09 010.22 087.31 148.07 206.02 349.03 387.35 406.31 426.17 484.27 485.05 501.18 579.12 625.22
MIND 282.R1 304.R3
minded 089.09 317.23 508.14 555.07
Mindelsinn 528.08
minder 394.23
mindered 540.29
mindfag 180.22
minding 266.21 272.13
mindmouldered 143.14
minds 114.34 118.25 137.33 157.25 159.07 203.11 293.06 477.23
mind's 254.18 477.18 515.23
mindself 161.01
mine 016.27 062.10 117.02 191.02 197.13 207.16 213.22 213.22 233.19 238.25 263.19 268.28 302.13 313.07 313.25 317.15 357.08 373.22 408.25 418.08 422.17 426.04 427.19 450.34 451.16 454.03 459.34 462.18 484.04 509.28 515.22 530.14 535.01 535.30 536.35 537.20 538.36 539.20 539.30 539.30 543.15 547.33 565.16 578.35 588.14 604.02 626.32
Mine 151.35 487.30 536.35 570.01
Mined 421.11
minefield 077.08
minely 313.28
Mineninecyhandsy 621.21
miner 082.05 263.08
mineral 493.01 611.15
minerals 127.24
mines 007.24 016.27 340.16
mine's 294.01 412.27 425.25
Mine's 144.15
minest 321.23
minestrary 228.14
ming 259.05
Ming 057.05 623.12
mingen 361.11
mingerals 556.36
mingle 579.36
mingling 203.25 326.06 446.14
minglings 594.16
minhatton 539.02
miniated 568.32
miniature 463.07
minimas 483.35
minion 014.08
minions' 268.10
ministel 609.11
ministerbuilding 274.11
ministers 242.11
ministers' 080.31
ministrance 060.03
ministring 345.22
ministriss 442.01
mink 271.L4
minkerstary 338.35
minkst 339.34
minnas 012.25
minne 519.04 528.07 551.24
minneful 189.12
Minneha 206.15
minnehi 206.15
minneho 206.16
minnelisp 254.13
Minnelisp 105.11
minners 444.26
minnestirring 508.22
minney 284.12
minnies 177.27 238.34 488.34
minnikin 207.14
Minnikin 017.02
Minnimiss 278.L2
minnions 354.11
minnow 079.10
minnowahaw 450.05
Minnowaurs 272.10
minnshogue's 037.34
minny 054.10
minnyhahing 600.07
minor 034.24 561.07
Minor 003.06 152.13 515.36
MINOR 278.R2
minorchy 555.09
minority 042.25
min's 197.24
Minssions 620.21
Minster 095.02
minstrel 521.22
minstrelsers 371.34
minstrelsy 003.18
minstress 370.05
mint 007.24 313.28 541.11
Mint 472.05
mintage 355.29
Mintargisia's 601.24
minted 138.29
minth 146.31
minthe 417.16
mints 418.04
Minucius 486.13
Minuinette 540.34
minus 057.19 298.21
Minuscoline's 226.15
minute 079.11 083.04 091.26 143.36 153.14 210.28 270.18 309.15 432.34 492.02 625.28
minutes 051.33 180.07 246.03 436.05 482.23 490.14 598.31
minutes 353.30
Minutes 421.03
minute's 411.22
minutes' 448.04
minutia 011.15
minx 080.30 376.03 496.08
Minxing 196.24
minxit 185.21
minxmingled 363.26
minxt 008.04
Minxy 095.09
Minxy 433.19
miny 621.21
minymony 250.36
minzies 113.13
mio 527.26
mio 455.27
mios 054.17
Mippa's 280.18

miracle 467.19 536.06
Miracle 384.10
miracles 579.14 605.02
Miracula 440.02
miraculising 352.27
Miraculone 132.15
miraculous 410.16
miraculously 097.14
mirage 265.29 310.24
mircle 066.22
mircles 365.01
mire 520.25
mireiclles 327.30
mirely 119.23
mires 410.34
mirgery 496.23
Miriam 366.35
miriamsweet 561.21
mirification 372.23
Mirillovis 388.08
Mirist 447.18
Mirra 471.04
mirrage 340.28
mirrages 613.29
Mirrdo 353.20
mirror 208.35 220.09 271.10 458.35 561.16 618.19
Mirror 527.22
Mirror 046.28
mirrorable 291.09
mirrorhand 177.31
mirrorminded 576.24
mirrow 548.31
Mirrylamb 223.01
mirrymouth 493.07
Mirsu 107.02
mirth 329.19 361.27 408.16
Mirtha 529.11
mirthday 035.04
mirthpeals 253.28
mirthprovoker 466.22
miry 239.31 453.19
Miry 013.09 594.11
Miryburrow 577.14
mis 396.23 478.34
misalignments 120.16
misappearance 186.12
misappropriating 108.36
misbadgered 097.06
misbelieving 301.04
miscegenations 018.20
Miscegenations 018.20
misches 027.29
mischief 251.29 483.18
mischiefmaker 206.07
mischievmiss 020.31
Mischnary 228.14
miscisprinks 537.05
misconception 444.11
misdemean 494.31
misdemeanour 035.06
Mise 087.20
miseffectual 118.28
misenary 348.09
miser 144.20
miserable 558.25
miserecordation 142.25
miserendissimest 154.06
Miserere 466.32
miseribilibus 466.32
miseries 259.07 527.10
Miserius 128.13
misery 142.21 185.33 466.34 467.01 470.21 574.18
Misery 229.15
Miseryhill 012.28
miseryme 455.24
misface 357.23
misflooded 589.27
misfortune 113.32 357.23 476.02 566.34
misfutthered 322.10
mish 241.16
Mish 131.01
Misha 249.29 249.29 485.08
Misha-La-Valse's 601.25
mishe 003.09 003.09
misheard 121.36
mishmash 466.12
Mishy 277.11
mishymissy 145.07
misi 148.02
Misi 148.02
Miskinguette 032.11
mislaid 239.03 311.12
misled 124.19 495.36 588.25
mislikes 163.12
misliness 148.36
Misma 568.01
mismy 236.22
misnomering 122.06
misocain 303.32
misonesans 076.22
misoxenetic 175.31
mispatriate 490.16
mispeschyites 365.09
misplaced 079.13
misquewhite 235.06
Misrs 534.15
miss 089.11 190.03 207.22 220.22 226.36 236.01 272.14 290.18 389.18 427.36 431.24 433.10 457.18 487.31 565.34 568.27 588.26 627.36
Miss 137.02 149.23 220.07 220.19 221.12 226.35 277.10 290.F6 327.26 330.18 398.17 412.23 414.02 420.26 423.35 444.11 445.11 468.10 501.04 502.29 523.18 532.21 585.05 620.19
Miss 340.28
missa 303.03
Missa 211.14
missado 504.35
missage 324.18
missal 236.15 456.18
missammen 454.13
missas 243.35
Missas 607.01
Missaunderstaid 363.36
missbelovers 520.19
missbrand 068.19
missed 129.30 132.27 135.07 208.27 224.20 286.14 314.05 324.32 424.31 471.17 525.33 566.36 621.28
Missed 175.27
missers 017.01
misses 020.11 127.32 162.27 362.11 364.13
Misses 351.29 375.12 529.11
Misses 106.34
missfired 005.26
misshapes 313.32
Missiers 058.23
missies 247.24 430.34
missiled 299.F1
missiles 097.36 115.03
missilethroes 616.32
Missing 421.05
mission 072.23 242.06 356.30 373.21 452.18 468.03
Missioner 060.22
missioners 529.01
missions 154.22 289.19
missis 285.07
Missisliffi 159.12
missive 111.31 238.05 408.14
missivemaids' 066.13
missledhropes 349.11
Missmisstress 189.25
Missmolly 360.28
missness 578.19
missnomer 562.04
missnot 267.02
missoccurs 391.13
Missrs 073.04
misstery 166.36
missuies 228.03
missus 028.01 047.14 207.13 275.F5 333.19 352.14 446.29 511.11
Missus 208.30 274.22 379.27
missuse 289.F4
missusses 075.22
missy 272.13 543.15
Missy 257.20
missymackenzies 065.12
missymissy 065.31
missyname 561.13
missywives 588.36
mist 007.17 214.36 318.30 337.13 607.27
Mista 485.32 590.11
mistaenk 317.26
mistake 134.21 162.03 229.05 411.36 509.09 513.29 620.14
mistaken 089.21 448.05 488.36
mistakenly 085.03
mistakes 276.02
mistaking 405.16
mistandew 501.34
Mistel 485.30
mistellose 360.25
mister 088.16 181.26 361.25 611.07
Mister 005.09 005.10 005.12 020.12 095.05 133.22 167.18 319.09 587.32 608.14
Mister 072.15
misterbilder 077.03
mistermysterion 301.18
misters 393.17
mistery 270.22
Misthra 578.10
Misthress 112.29
misties 027.28
mistiles 586.26
mistle 147.10
mistlemam 491.29
Mistlemas 556.05
mistlethrush 385.02
mistlethrushes 384.03
mistletoe 147.23 265.17
mistletoes 393.30
mistletots 588.35
mistletouch 465.27

mistletropes 009.19
mistmusk 267.28
misto 430.10
Misto 355.30
mistomist 340.05
mistook 081.21
Mistral 453.17
mistraversers 538.06
mistress 008.08
Mistress 020.13 184.27 241.14
Mistress 105.13
mistributed 371.12
mistributes 220.20
mistridden 110.31
Mistro 437.33
misturbing 585.34
misty 602.28
Misty's 224.20
misunderstood 470.01
misunderstord 163.22
misunderstruck 126.07
misused 173.36 344.30
mit 411.17
mitch 446.09
Mitchel 013.09
Mitchells 147.06 281.F4
mitching 468.26
mite 457.36
Mite 304.19
mites 166.28 625.24
mite's 133.07
mitey 416.26
Mithra 080.24
mithre 004.30
mithyphallic 481.04
mitigation 557.25 616.29
Mitleid 151.19
mitre 233.16
mitrogenerand 604.23
Mitropolitos 316.15
mitryman 578.03
mitsch 366.13
Mitsch 222.11
mitsmillers 084.01
mittens 210.13
mittle 491.12
mitts 290.13
Mitzymitzy 225.20
mivver 157.14
mix 050.34 079.11 194.29 437.32 515.20
Mix 193.06
mixandmass 238.21
mixcuits 166.14
mixed 048.02 117.22 151.30 209.10 251.33 626.36
mixer 087.13 088.04
mixers 065.28
mixes 160.12
miximhost 345.29
mixing 281.26 507.08 609.02
mixness 505.20
mixplace 418.11
mixter 328.04
mixto 185.24
mixture 083.32 275.23
mixum 385.12
Mixymost 567.31
mizpah 306.07
Mizpah 588.24
mizzatint 334.24
mizzle 468.26
mizzles 523.29
Ml 458.03 (Michael)
mlachy 341.17
mladies 054.11
mleckman 337.06
Mm 115.35
mmany 131.08
Mmarriage 210.12
M.M.L.J. 397.30 (Matthew, Mark, Luke, John)
mmmmany 171.19
mmmmuch 171.19
m'm'ry's 460.20 (memory's)
mmummy 547.04
mnakes 019.08
mnames 595.34
Mnepos 389.28 392.18
mness 019.07
mnice 019.07
mo 292.04 485.29 621.24
Mo 491.29
M.O. 421.08 (Money Order)
Moabit 547.01
moan 141.06 281.23 333.31
moananoaning 628.03
moanday 301.20
moaning 023.31 177.01
moanolothe 254.14
moans 094.05 184.01
moarning 512.26
moat 162.32
Moate 094.03
moatst 198.28
mob 261.21
Mob 602.25
mobbed 329.22
Mobbely 210.30
mobbily 009.25
mobbing 379.18
mobbu 178.15
mobcap 583.05
mobhouse 030.16
mobile 309.21
mobile 292.12
mobiling 403.09
mobility 235.13
mobmauling 186.23
mob's 466.33
mock 169.13 296.09 406.11 580.21 581.02
Mock 515.08
mockamill 531.10
mockbelief 484.15
MockComic 222.07
Mocked 380.04
Mockerloo 073.05
mocking 251.35 322.06 498.31
mockingbird 476.01
Mockmacmahonitch 529.16
Mockmorrow 380.22
Mocknitza 228.07
mocks 053.11 072.27
mocks 418.32
mocktitles 567.14
mod 058.31 118.20
Mod 058.01 523.19
modareds 132.05
Modder 294.04
moddereen 558.29
moddle 311.07
mode 057.02 057.02 247.27 426.36 493.21 540.30
model 181.12 191.25
modeln 289.F6
moder 330.36
modern 055.14 151.06 270.18 309.14 396.07
moders 330.36
modes 165.25 165.25
MODES 279.R1
modest 124.28 210.24 296.09 569.02 585.05
modest 116.16
modesties 278.F6 438.04
modestuous 054.34
modesty 146.05 494.01
modified 073.03
modning 593.09
modo 287.25
moe 177.27 202.06 252.33 302.F2 569.28
Moe 426.19
Moedl's 435.15
Moels 390.09
moest 075.09
Moffat 087.10
Mofsovitz 514.30
Moggie's 176.04
moggies' 079.30
Mogoul 277.03
mogul 097.24
moguphonoised 258.21
moher 198.28
Moherboher 373.05
mohns 245.07
Mohomadhawn 443.02
mohomoment 082.34
Mohorat 033.16
moidered 345.07
moidered's 250.17
moidhered 445.31
moiety 232.22
moighty 623.05
moil 199.02
Moirgan's 060.33
moist 157.23 204.35 347.07 475.01 581.11
moisten 028.12
Moisten 501.17
moistened 408.02
moister 550.22
moistly 502.19
moistnostrilled 115.26
moisturologist 608.02
Moitered 569.08
moither 433.30
mokau 199.18
moke 528.33
Moke 372.04
mokes 331.16
moksa 093.22
mokst 432.34
molars 408.02 467.01
mole 206.33 426.16 509.26
mole 271.L4
Mole 310.01
molehill 474.22
molehunter 576.25
mole's 076.33
molested 530.06 573.05
Molesworth 057.35
moletons 353.26
moliamordhar 099.25
moliman 240.27
moll 260.17 521.35
Moll 299.27 569.29
Mollanny 370.21

Mollies 338.28
mollification 092.03
Molloyd 616.01
mollvogels 113.16
molly 093.35
Molly 600.33
Molly's 495.28
molniacs' 289.18
Molochy 473.07
Molodeztious 339.05
Molroe 087.02
moltapuke 040.05
molten 170.34 477.29
Moltens 494.07
Moltern 355.21
molting 378.12
Molyneux 569.10
Molyvdokondylon 056.13
mom 365.26
Mom 365.26
Mom 106.03
moma 207.34
mombition 366.29
momence 404.14
moment 056.29 058.34 063.25 064.22 082.26 111.22 166.28 173.21 173.25 176.32 181.21 188.02 202.21 280.13 289.24 309.10 325.20 360.11 395.27 396.14 396.27 405.22 406.33 421.28 431.25 449.17 453.23 469.08 471.22 479.17 479.23 486.16 501.11 521.15 555.17 565.07 570.27 626.08
moments 107.23 128.07 252.25 446.16 489.29 534.23
moment's 457.34
momentum 155.19 304.08 582.36
momentums 108.11
Momerry 378.33
momie 236.31
Momie 466.01
Momonian 387.18
Momor's 236.09
momou 144.35
momourning 247.18
momouth 364.15 437.20
momstchance 345.22
Momuluius 484.11
mon 006.11 083.01 095.02 167.36
mon 576.16
Mon 493.35 493.36 527.29
Mon 059.30
mona 061.01
Mona 449.10 464.32
Monabella 368.12
monach 525.17
Monachan 284.08
Monacheena 616.12
monad 341.13
Monade 236.03
monads 078.19
monarch 380.34 478.11
monasticism 456.17
Monastir 271.L1
monatan 227.20
monbreamstone 225.22
Mondamoiseau 230.14
Monday 407.08 433.07
mondayne 333.23
mone 315.28
Moneta 538.01
monetary 108.30 599.16
monetone 312.21
money 042.10 070.02 101.13 138.29 227.10 232.27 271.05 279.F35 307.F3 418.04 421.16 433.33 458.29 529.10 541.13 589.04 610.17
money 383.14
mong 138.29 427.11 587.02
Mong 623.13
mongafesh 256.25
Mongan 041.04
mongoloid 550.17
mongrel 214.25
MONGREL 276.R1
Mongrieff 536.12
monies 220.20
moniker 046.21
moning 608.19
monished 080.24
monitorology 251.28
monitress 561.12
monitrix 022.16
monk 016.05 203.33 228.26 487.26 577.31
Monk 485.19
monkafellas 611.10
monkax 192.03
monkblinkers 612.21
monkeys 046.28
monkey's 070.09
monkeywrench 070.24
Monkish 532.13
monkishouse 139.32
monkmarian 177.02
Monkmesserag 239.07
monks 254.11
Monks 294.21 579.13
monkshood 571.14
monkst 339.35
Monn 528.33
monofractured 310.10
Monogynes 613.35
monolith 053.15
monologue 474.04
monologuy 119.32
monolook 182.20
Monolothe 105.12
Monomark 017.01
monomyth 581.24
monophone 462.16
monophysicking 156.11
monopoleums 094.35
monopolises 488.07
monopolized 429.24
monosyllables 190.35
Monosyllables 306.26
monotheme 177.02
monothoid 029.15
monothong 424.34
monowards 338.24
mons 332.19
Mons 008.29 113.19 537.34
Monsaigneur 243.31
Monseigneur 184.30
monsie 228.03
Monsieur 133.22 188.31 307.F8 307.F8 307.F8 307.F8
Monsigneur 569.20
Monsignore 575.29
monster 244.34 276.08 606.25
Monster 178.16
monsterbilker 296.07
monstrous 177.15
Monstrucceleen 132.15
Mont 008.28 008.29
Montague 516.21
Montan 260.17
Monte 274.02
Monte 339.33
montey 328.15
Montez 525.14
Montgomery 058.26
Montgomeryite 525.07
Montgomery's 426.11
month 010.27 034.07 180.29 211.30 264.04 364.13 395.23 517.34
monthage 223.08
monthlies 437.17
monthly 142.25
Monthly 537.34
months 082.14 194.25 238.19 260.F1 405.18 520.07 536.29 544.18 558.14 575.12
Months 071.31
month's 220.04
monticules 037.11
Montmalency 318.02
montrumeny 010.03
Montybunkum 316.14
monument 036.24 042.19 047.07 057.22
monumentally 056.13
monumentalness 543.07
monument's 054.28
mony 451.12
Moo 158.15
moochy 011.06
mood 203.35 414.14 425.26 448.28 467.31
Mood 536.26 536.26
Moodend 153.22
moodmoulded 186.02
moods 187.30 268.19 421.17
mooherhead 426.08
moohooed 230.21
moohootch 485.35
Moohr 106.08
Mookery 231.35
mooks 231.35
Mookse 152.15 152.19 152.20 153.18 153.20 153.35 154.07 154.17 154.19 155.07 156.20 156.22 156.25 157.20 158.03 158.12 158.27 158.30
Mooksey 154.30
Mooksius 156.08
mookst 234.10
moon 065.09 088.03 138.36 144.25 244.04 271.F1 271.F1 285.F5 341.16 360.25 385.28 413.13 436.28 449.35 493.19 504.36 519.21 538.23 623.27
Moonan 157.15
moonbeams 566.05
Moondy 060.19
mooner 190.32
mooner's 478.15
Moonface 071.15
moonflower 212.16
moonful 347.07
Moonis 540.12
moonled 011.21
moonlight 064.06 495.14
moonlight's 091.18

moonlike 428.08
moonlit 053.16
moonmist 477.30
moonmounded 588.19
moonplastered 181.08
moons 101.16 408.34 409.28
moon's 276.F3
moonshane 489.27
moonshee 192.30
moonshine 138.31 439.08
moonshiny 073.21
Moonster 389.05 528.28
moontaen 136.36
moontime 528.05
moony 017.02
moonyhaunts 595.15
Moopetsi 276.F4
moor 020.03 276.21 316.07 449.31 449.32 477.29 516.31
Moor 211.28
moore 468.27
Moore 024.21 101.08 206.12 447.13
mooremoore 160.25
Mooreparque 359.35
Moore's 439.09
moorhens 478.15
Moorning 222.18
moors 078.28 430.08
moor's 492.34
moos 215.34
Mooseyeare 414.12
moostarshes 182.27
moother 426.04
Mooting 610.34
Moove 377.14
mooxed 070.32 299.13
Moppa 207.29
moppamound 464.26
mop's 335.08
mopsa's 550.21
Mopsus 614.01
mor 078.29 087.33 179.30 247.10 577.01
Mor 142.28 397.31 398.23 497.27
mora 287.20
Mora 131.23
moracles 617.25
moraculous 229.32
morahoy 285.14
moral 122.36 177.16 435.05 491.08 522.14 523.28
Moral 434.18 550.03 616.34
morally 342.01
Morals 306.27
moraltack 602.10
moramor 247.27
Moramor 231.28
Moran 133.02
Morandmor 102.18
moratorium 575.01
moravar 172.11 213.09
morbid 182.03
morbidisation 151.05
morbous 211.01
morbus 466.31
Morbus 088.14
Mord 499.07
mordant 412.16
morder 131.07
mordering 008.24
mordern 353.29
Mordvealive 162.18
more 005.36 006.21 010.31 016.24 020.09 028.09 028.34 031.08 035.14 035.35 042.06 042.17 043.35 044.04 046.11 048.08 054.34 056.06 057.20 058.36 059.24 060.13 064.13 070.27 072.25 074.17 076.03 077.13 080.18 081.09 081.20 083.16 084.35 085.18 088.24 088.32 094.32 100.28 101.15 101.16 107.35 107.35 108.17 108.32 109.27 111.05 112.01 114.03 114.34 115.08 116.13 116.22 118.25 119.34 120.17 121.10 121.23 121.24 124.21 129.21 134.11 143.02 145.11 146.31 146.31 146.31 148.17 149.28 150.34 152.06 156.22 159.26 160.14 161.04 161.20 161.29 163.20 163.31 163.32 164.19 165.31 166.24 166.34 174.21 177.04 179.31 180.29 183.02 183.08 186.26 187.08 190.03 190.04 190.04 190.05 190.05 190.06 190.06 190.08 199.32 201.21 202.01 202.05 206.28 208.02 212.22 213.32 213.32 213.32 215.05 220.31 221.05 223.02 225.12 225.13 228.14 228.35 234.25 237.30 237.35 237.36 239.12 239.13 240.09 240.19 241.32 243.01 243.27 249.22 250.17 250.18 251.21 254.35 256.11 257.07 261.21 263.25 263.25 267.F5 274.10 274.16 276.F5 279.F03 283.F2 285.07 296.25 301.25 304.F4 305.08 313.21 315.05 321.01 322.04 325.33 330.09 336.14 350.20 352.30 360.08 367.13 369.26 375.08 378.02 382.06 382.08 384.12 384.14 385.31 387.32 390.21 394.05 395.19 398.24 405.16 406.18 407.16 408.13 411.35 412.18 413.34 417.32 420.16 423.12 424.35 427.02 427.23 428.10 435.21 437.19 443.13 446.15 449.12 454.26 457.18 459.12 459.13 460.32 466.16 467.20 471.29 476.20 476.22 482.32 487.12 489.02 489.08 501.21 506.35 507.03 507.15 515.04 517.13 519.07 520.19 522.05 524.29 527.18 527.32 529.02 542.11 543.10 543.10 543.26 545.03 549.08 549.10 550.22 551.11 557.30 560.29 561.23 562.11 568.08 568.15 570.14 571.24 575.16 581.24 586.13 588.32 599.17 602.11 604.02 615.13 618.35 620.21 620.29 624.12 628.05 628.06
more 140.34 276.L1 340.20 343.14
More 062.34 145.24 299.29 476.29 586.31 590.27
moreafter 612.02
moreblue 253.36
moreboy 410.29
moreen 528.32
morefar 139.06
moregruggy 418.19
Morehampton 354.16
Moreigner 385.32
moreinausland's 116.21
morely 541.12
moremens 628.06
moremon 534.14
moren 404.12
Moreover 443.02
morepork 407.19 407.19
mores 273.05
Mores 494.12
moresome 534.08
moretis 378.20
morey 502.22
Morfydd 529.25
Morganas 570.12
morgans 584.25
Morgans 518.26
Morganspost 036.05
Morgen 221.30
morgenattics 545.27
Morgen's 127.31
Morgh 546.02
morgning 598.10
Morgue 530.13
morgued 367.16
morhor 377.25
Morialtay 376.30
moriartsky 338.09
moriarty 453.04
moribus 251.29
Morion 398.01
Morionmale 577.01
Moriture 167.24
morkernwindup 090.08
morkning 525.03
Morkret 594.11
Morland-West 514.24
morm 005.10 584.03
mormon 064.04
mormon's 199.01
mormor 354.18
mormorial 008.35
morn 100.10 101.32 138.17 139.10 332.25 338.30 382.10 407.36 410.34 458.08 473.23 605.23
Morna 189.25
mornal 597.33
mornin 609.25
morning 027.03 033.17 035.03 050.32 063.25 066.10 073.18 087.02 152.22 188.01 191.29 210.28 249.26 253.18 257.10 294.F3 300.F2 319.02 388.12 391.20 427.20 428.17 428.18 436.27 461.27 475.22 485.02 485.26 490.27 493.07 499.16 561.29 565.32 566.07 566.25 581.36 583.30 589.16 619.20 621.08 622.12 628.08
Morning 481.14 617.22
Morning 176.16
morningrise 543.12
mornings 242.11 446.12 510.07 556.08
Morningtop's 266.11
moromelodious 184.15
morosity 121.24 189.04
Morphios 142.29
morphological 165.27 599.16
morphomelosophopancreates 088.09

morphyl 080.22
Morra 104.12
morrals 583.24
morrder 224.18
morrienbaths 333.36
morries 604.10
Morris 205.28
Morrisons 192.04
Morrissey's 410.14
morrokse 158.16
morrow 125.06 279.F09 570.10 625.14
morroweth 473.24
morrowing 100.10
morrowy 295.17
Mors 119.32
morse 087.03
Morse 099.06
morse-erse 530.19
morsel 550.10
Morses 123.35
mort 460.22 511.33
Mortadarthella 151.20
mortal 067.02 091.31 186.06 488.08 501.29 606.24
mortals' 264.13
mortar 077.18 314.15
Mortar 341.12
mortarboard 551.28
mortem 510.33
mortem 423.21
mortgage 577.05
Morthering 017.24
mortiality 277.24
mortially 063.33
morticians 172.12
morties 499.04
mortification 540.18
mortified 558.28
Mortimer 210.24
Mortimor 316.21
mortinatality 447.08
mortisection 253.34
mortuorum 287.21
mortuum 074.08
Morty 329.24
morvaloos 443.36
morvenlight 131.28
Morya 053.30 316.21
mosaic 495.09
Moscas 084.01
mose 399.27
mosel 207.23
Moselems 319.11
moses 004.23 167.36
Moses 307.L1
Moseses 463.30
mosest 540.19
moseys 313.05
moskats 347.15 366.08
Moskiosk 597.13
moskors 622.24
moslemans 243.28
mosoleum 261.13
mosque 390.10
moss 184.21 556.18 626.23
Moss 347.13
mossacre 390.01
mosse 428.10
mosselman's 422.16
mosses 209.20
Mosses 069.09
Mosse's 043.03
mosshungry 288.28
mossies 225.35
mossroses 127.08
mossyhonours 552.30
most 004.13 004.36 009.01 015.32 024.08 025.34 031.13 040.23 042.15 052.11 062.22 063.17 064.15 076.02 079.34 080.12 084.25 085.15 088.09 091.33 092.31 096.14 111.03 111.36 112.04 115.19 121.17 123.31 123.35 124.31 129.17 131.33 140.10 140.11 140.12 140.13 149.35 150.36 153.03 154.07 155.07 160.22 162.11 169.06 171.25 177.30 179.18 181.09 182.01 188.17 191.17 202.05 229.31 234.02 234.24 240.32 247.11 247.20 251.10 251.23 257.02 263.01 279.F20 279.F23 292.05 294.07 298.20 305.02 310.08 312.27 317.13 320.12 322.10 326.01 356.01 361.26 361.26 362.17 370.18 371.14 381.21 391.24 391.24 396.11 403.14 404.31 416.24 422.21 425.16 425.21 431.11 432.19 440.11 451.31 452.17 464.07 468.01 469.27 488.08 489.20 499.01 504.35 507.04 519.27 524.09 524.33 526.27 529.35 530.26 532.16 532.23 532.24 533.01 534.07 535.08 542.29 544.06 546.22 551.26 560.28 575.18 576.29 590.01 603.30 605.25 605.33 606.02 607.21 607.31 616.23 617.29 625.04
Most 179.28 240.29 353.02 381.24 413.03 474.05 612.06
mostfortunes 492.28
Mosthighest 104.04
mostly 099.32 112.15 232.03 280.16 410.29 410.32 440.06 586.09 598.08
mostmonolith 539.01
mot 396.06
mot 411.17
Mot 206.12
motamourfully 158.27
mote 044.10 118.20
moth 561.27
Moth 526.23
Motham 388.21
Mothelup 177.06
mother 041.07 050.12 133.33 137.16 187.15 191.20 207.29 213.29 223.23 294.29 329.08 393.19 420.03 420.10 420.18 444.34 452.32 493.34 506.32 526.24 527.36 559.35 598.34 627.09
mother 399.01
Mother 026.31 035.30 144.31 229.15 299.03 391.32 492.11 500.33 561.27 600.03
Mother 105.08 106.25
mother-in-lieu 220.22
mother-in-waders 089.22
mothernaked 206.30
motherour's 155.14
motherpeributts 396.35
mothers 316.11 366.13 457.08
mother's 463.09
mothers'-in-laws' 183.28
mothers-in-load 448.15
mothersmothered 191.25
motherwaters 084.30
Mothrapurl 443.34
Moths 360.25
mothst 416.07
motion 151.04 330.23 426.36 455.06 484.12 575.03 575.04 622.12
motions 020.22
motive 110.34
motives 483.34
Motometusolum 378.15
motophosically 319.34
motor 039.23
motru 114.27
mots 333.26
mot's 146.27
mottage 183.22
mottams 485.03
mottes 288.02
motther 608.16
mottled 075.21
mottledged 338.11
motto 404.28 495.27 506.30 508.05 607.04
motto 338.12
Motto 546.10
mottob 445.13
motto-in-lieu 139.29
motts 138.08
mottu 358.09
motylucky 417.10
mou 267.22 562.26
mouche 416.07
moucreas 345.02
moues 354.34
mouf 587.34
mought 005.27
mould 146.13 362.19
mouldaw 196.17
moulday 338.18
mouldem 377.12
moulder 018.08
mouldern 396.36
mouldhering 354.25
moulding 280.18
mouldy 037.09 381.05
mouldystoned 128.02
Moulsaybaysse 464.21
moult 061.13 112.10 455.18
moultain 136.35 317.34
moulting 044.01
moulty 383.08
moultylousy 301.08
mound 017.29 018.03 102.22 420.14 479.23 499.34 564.29
Mound 175.12
mounded 405.30
mounden 331.18 331.20
mounding's 008.01
mounds 012.20
mount 206.19 245.15 262.21 290.18 347.03
Mount 051.20 131.01 137.36 197.14 235.18 359.34 494.16 497.16 562.10
Mount 418.17
Mountagnone 225.15

mountain 032.05 090.17 095.25 132.07 241.17 277.07 288.F3 309.04 564.27 596.11
Mountain 076.04 479.11
Mountain 222.12
mountains 139.19 171.11 446.15 462.32
Mountains 070.16 329.33 455.32 557.07 570.01
mountainy 333.26 474.22
mountback 108.01
mounted 137.09 581.04
Mountgomery 543.28
mounth 331.29 536.22
mounthings 338.17
mounting 018.33
Mounting 018.33
Mountjoy 045.10 045.11
Mountjoys 587.06
Mountone 372.28
mount's 324.26
Mountsackvilles 375.12
Mountstill 175.21
mountunmighty 128.03
mountynotty 021.07
mouph 088.18
mour 238.26
mourn 462.32 489.01 541.22 602.13
Mourne 203.10 549.17
mourned 071.04
mournenslaund 614.08
mournful 549.11
mournhim 012.14
mournin 006.14
mourning 031.29 131.27 139.11 277.07 331.06 387.31 395.16 470.26 623.27
Mourning 106.08
Mournomates 055.04
mous 023.22
mouschical 417.09
mouse 082.19 318.08 456.01 563.34
mousefarm 183.04
mousework 397.10
mousey 048.03
moush 228.03
mousoo 478.20
Mousoumeselles 339.16
mousselimes 553.10
moustache 125.12 443.25
moustaches 031.13 291.23
moustacheteasing 437.36
mouster 154.03
mousterious 015.33
mouth 068.32 130.18 133.36 138.20 143.24 146.31 151.26 173.07 199.32 208.24 235.24 243.02 246.13 258.12 277.F1 292.26 311.18 325.36 348.16 366.36 381.08 385.21 393.01 442.29 469.36 474.09 477.30 480.07 480.25 490.19 493.28 512.26 525.33 559.27 577.12 578.05 626.05
mouth 354.04
Mouth 105.24
mouthart 253.04
mouthbrand 311.30
mouthbuds 459.03
mouther 055.19 423.01
mouther 349.30
mouther-in-louth 049.15
mouthfilled 248.24
mouthful 163.01
mouthfull 231.09
mouthless 101.30 537.23
mouthparts 414.27
mouthpull 441.15
mouths 019.24 041.27 116.27 120.01 124.28 208.28 315.24 386.04 386.11 486.08
mouth's 140.26 159.26
mouthshine 440.31
mouthspeech 484.02
Moutmaro 499.07
moutonlegs 233.02
movables 443.30
move 187.33 213.03 437.13 480.24 494.17 559.30 560.02
Move 099.19 146.30
Move 264.L2
moved 119.18 287.28 383.21 425.28 483.16 541.14 541.31
movely 318.01
movemens 351.23
movement 310.36 343.11 357.12 432.35
movements 115.10
movent 568.13
mover 483.27
moves 134.16 253.06 256.13 385.20 399.31
moveyovering 609.34
movibile 165.35
movibles 020.21
Moviefigure 602.27
movies 166.13
Movies 194.02
movietone 062.09
moving 091.29 118.22 376.02 484.12 499.34 522.22 565.06
Moving 281.25
mow 233.08 330.05 374.33 596.06
mower 409.14
Mower 106.06
moweress 510.11
mowlding 142.03
Mowlted 181.19
mownself 447.10
Mowy 252.07
Mox 308.02
moy 141.07 340.16 416.19
Moy 131.01 203.11 312.01 427.27 455.18 485.06
Moy 478.21
moya 375.36
Moyelta 076.21
moyety 310.33
Moyhammlet 418.17
Moyhard's 412.05
Moykill 255.13
Moykle 384.05
Moylamore 600.11
Moyle 136.09 315.12
Moylean 025.27
Moylendsea 428.21
moyles 548.34 628.03 628.03
moyliffey 054.24
moyne 469.11
moyvalley 215.10
Mozos 455.36
mozzed 440.35
M.P. 290.05 (4.32 M.P.)
M.P, 498.09 (Orange and Betters M.P,)
mpe 120.09
mporn 120.09
Mr 024.16 032.29 037.27 037.28 038.26 039.24 043.33 043.33 048.11 048.12 056.30 060.26 065.04 065.17 097.05 098.25 130.08 144.30 150.17 160.28 169.05 173.22 173.27 174.26 193.11 219.22 220.11 220.24 221.06 221.27 242.01 245.32 255.27 261.19 274.F3 288.19 303.F1 327.26 334.06 334.09 335.34 336.12 357.02 361.11 365.24 365.25 365.26 369.07 369.08 369.09 369.10 369.11 369.11 377.31 377.31 377.32 377.32 383.21 387.07 405.05 413.35 414.04 420.04 421.25 434.11 434.36 435.34 466.18 466.33 479.10 481.14 487.23 490.08 490.08 490.26 490.27 491.30 493.36 496.12 510.35 511.07 519.16 520.03 520.15 524.08 524.13 524.16 524.18 537.20 542.26 546.29 558.14 558.29 560.14 560.24 569.30 569.30 570.15 571.20 575.11 578.11 588.18 602.31 616.36 618.05
Mr 341.24 342.10 342.22 350.10
Mr. 420.27
Mria 495.34
Mrknrk 621.20
mrowkas 516.10
Mrs 036.29 059.04 066.23 087.02 089.20 096.04 132.09 157.15 157.33 193.20 204.34 227.04 228.19 257.13 268.F6 375.25 386.22 390.35 392.08 392.30 397.31 413.05 413.06 413.12 413.21 434.15 440.17 460.17 460.18 494.35 511.29 519.33 520.13 546.29 550.32 550.32 550.32 550.32 560.26 616.34 620.19
Mrs 342.24
Mrs's 523.18
msch 459.03 459.04
MSS. 121.34 (manuscripts)
Mti 204.21
Mtu 204.21
Mu 051.20
much 029.16 034.34 035.18 041.04 048.08 056.29 063.22 076.22 083.16 088.03 092.02 093.15 109.27 112.02 115.08 125.18 125.22 127.02 133.05 150.01 153.22 157.22 161.04 166.04 169.20 190.17 199.25 207.27 232.25 239.22 248.22 252.12 279.F02 281.F1 304.05 309.10 336.35 336.05 367.15 369.33 370.11 370.12 381.32 384.25 385.25 395.18 395.19 405.15 405.16 408.06 408.12 412.27 417.36 421.15 421.30 425.33 437.23 438.08 454.06 458.02 466.12 466.34 475.33 481.29 482.30 489.09 490.17 495.28 498.07 504.18 508.24 509.06 520.36 521.06 522.18

523.09 528.37 555.03 560.35 562.04 562.06 562.11 564.08 568.15 568.15 571.12 595.09 607.30 611.12 617.33 620.20
much 383.02
Much 375.30 599.03 623.07
much-altered 201.09
muchas 174.14 273.18
muchears 011.24
muched 541.12
muchee 608.20
muchmore 504.35
muchrooms 625.19
Muchsias 568.11
muchtried 178.09
muchy 311.26
Mucias 364.25
muck 024.15 086.21 211.19 437.23 499.22 563.03
Muck 379.01
Muckers 312.26
muckinstushes 346.02
Muckinurney 264.L2
muckle 576.21
muckloved 448.11
muckrake 448.10
Muckross 290.F1
muck's 576.23
Mucksrats 615.16
muckstails 393.11
muckswinish 535.20
mucktub 358.22
muckwits 273.25
mucky 144.16 442.03
mucky 277.L1
mucuses 453.11
mud 018.16 020.16 039.12 064.17 087.26 206.31 244.04 277.26 286.31 287.07 381.01 517.03
mudapplication 026.36
mudded 240.11
mudden 595.25
mudder 240.23
Mudder 535.35
muddest 296.20
muddied 159.12
muddies 314.13
muddle 171.05 285.05 378.29 586.13
Muddle 071.27
muddleage 491.08
muddlecrass 152.08
muddles 125.01
muddlingisms 303.20
muddy 011.14 093.18 120.29 297.24 301.09 534.01
muddyass 423.18
muddyhorsebroth 482.05
mude 037.21
mudfacepacket 492.20
Mudford 086.11
mudhead's 190.02
mudheeldy 230.12
mudhen 393.23
mudical 413.07
mudland 295.19
Mudlin 136.02
mudmound 111.34
Mudquirt 376.04
Mudson 133.22
mudstorm 086.20
mudstuskers 459.06
mudwake 349.25
Muerther 499.07
muertification 058.08
muezzatinties 552.24
muezzin 442.32
Muezzin's 056.08
muff 467.21
Muffed 442.20
muffetee 300.25
muffin 166.08
muffinbell 121.36 324.25
muffinstuffinaches 225.11
muffle 603.20
mufflers 397.17
mufti 462.32
muftilife 261.19
muftis 497.30
mufto 523.11
mug 144.32 337.15 368.26
mugfull 286.31
mugger's 054.20
Muggleton 312.26
Muggy 111.15
mugisstosst 624.02
Mugn 520.23
mugnum 536.16
mugpunters 439.33
mugs 245.30 306.09 526.07 619.01
mug's 268.11 355.35
mugurdy 231.15
muinnuit 469.01
muirre 091.04
mujic 518.28
mujikal 013.09
Mujiksy's 340.34
Mukk's 016.11
Mul 398.01
Mulachy 032.01
mulattomilitiaman 354.10
mulbrey 265.01
Mulbreys 553.06
mulct 388.06
mulctman 586.16
mulde 212.26
Muldoons 094.03
mule 411.33 554.05
muleback 498.04
Mulelo 499.05
mules 564.29
Mulhuddart 206.18
mulicules 353.26
mulierage 243.27
muliercula 494.09
mulimuli 427.25
mulk 021.07
mull 286.31 371.31
Mull 193.18
Mullabury 237.05
Mullah 193.18
Mullans 279.F24
Mullarty 390.10
mulled 193.06
Mullen 094.01
mullet's 208.32
mullified 462.05
mulligar 321.33
mulligrubs 245.26
Mullinahob 097.03
Mullingar 138.19
Mullingar 286.L3
Mullingaria 345.34
Mullingcan 064.09
Mullinguard 371.34
mullmud 228.33
Mullocky 151.24
Mulo 499.05
mulsum 245.27
mult 555.01
Multaferry 580.12
Multalusi 290.19
multaphoniaksically 178.06
multaplussed 586.24
Multifarnham 090.24
multilingual 392.24
multimathematical 394.31
Multimimetica 267.02
multimirror 582.20
multimony 451.12
multinotcheralled 348.33
multipede 446.01
multiple 410.12
Multiple 369.11
multiplease 270.23
multiplest 322.10
multiplicables 004.32
multiplicating 281.18
multiplication 119.28
multiplicity 107.24
multiply 405.01
multipopulipater 081.05
multitude 073.05
mults 488.20
multvult 057.32
mum 300.18 360.07 365.26 538.19
Mum 219.16 491.29
Mum 105.35
mumble 462.25
Mumblesome 377.15
mumbo 273.17
Mumfsen 155.33
Mumm 451.23 569.28
mummed 082.30 236.32
mummer 114.30
mummeries 535.27
mummers 569.28
mummery 310.23 535.30
mumming 048.10
mummouth's 510.04
Mummum 144.35 259.10
mummur 373.34
mummurrlubejubes 396.34
mummy 194.22 194.33 194.33 411.17
mummyscrips 156.05
mumorise 180.29
mumper 003.08
mumpos 380.07
Mumpty 099.20
Mum's 053.03 228.15
Mumsell 185.01
Mumtiplay 283.05
mun 251.04
Mun 287.15
Muna 502.12
munch 164.01 318.21
munchables 121.33
munchantman 317.24
munchaowl 240.12
muncipated 322.35
Muncius 092.35
mund 007.31 154.18 300.24 413.22
Munda 172.31
Mundai 532.31

mundamanu 364.33
mundaynism 350.12
mundballs 416.23
Mundelonde 609.17
mundering 320.13
Mundi 481.06
mundibanks 055.04
mundo 034.32
mundo 287.25
mundom 330.29
mundy 149.05
mundyfoot 128.13
Mundzucker 071.20
mungy 228.03
municipal 005.14
munificent 261.21
muniment 094.25 595.22
munin 327.36
munipicence 549.21
munkybown 397.20
Munster's 498.11
munt 245.15
Munting 376.18
muntons 327.22
muore 419.13
murage 541.09
muravyingly 416.07
murble 319.10
murcery 548.31
Murch 377.15
murder 099.27 100.10 187.13 254.32 341.14 411.25 460.06
murder 345.07 399.02
murdered 078.18 093.02
Murderer 071.15
murdering 498.15
murderous 177.31
murders 564.29
murdhering 354.25
Murdoch 274.L1
Murdrus 374.12
mured 261.10
murgessly 160.25
murhersson 319.29
murial 027.33
Murias 219.11
Muriel 212.08
murk 266.09 318.29 506.24 598.22
Murk 023.23
murkblankered 612.22
murkery 251.15
Murkesty 175.23
murketplots 368.09
Murkiss 533.20
murky 180.17 395.01 448.34
murmars 540.15
murmel 541.31
murmoaned 430.13
murmoirs 387.34
murmur 501.32
murmurable 294.07
murmurand 473.04
murmured 060.10 062.14 097.28 471.31
murmurladen 586.36
murmurously 385.22
murmurrandoms 358.03
murmurulentous 611.29
murmury 254.18
Murnane 613.30
Murph 272.24
murphies 190.04 625.08
murphy 293.09 293.09 293.10 293.10
Murphy 446.30
Murphybuds 161.29
murphyplantz 542.01
Murphy's 333.32
murrainer 324.08
Murray 063.27
murrayed 208.35
murrerof 295.05
Murrey 227.29
Murrey's 269.29
murrmurr 101.33
murrough 037.02
Murrough 330.16
murry 135.01
Murry 433.19
mursque 136.01
murtagh 314.30
murther 340.16 397.12
Murther 219.20
murthers 412.31
murty 088.17 289.20
murumd 006.06
mus 190.36 238.22
musaic 037.24
musband 146.20
Musca 140.02
muscafilicial 613.18
muscalone 237.03
muscle 036.03 084.28
musclebound 064.33
musclemum 491.28
muscles 084.26
muscowmoney 416.17
musculink 166.26
mused 096.16
musefed 037.30
museomound 008.05
museum 008.02
museyroom 008.09 010.22
Museyroom 008.10
Musforget 147.01
mush 145.06 208.32 448.08 487.24
Mush 098.24
Musha 427.33
Mushame 481.26 481.26
mushe 505.20
Mushe 505.20
mushn't 090.15
mushroofs 543.13
mushroom 265.F2 315.18 618.27
mushrooms 198.33
Mushure 464.02
Mushy 277.11
mushymushy 096.12
music 075.22 133.26 145.25 164.16 184.04 222.01 230.19 280.32 377.17 472.01 490.22 508.22 548.03 562.32 575.21 601.19
Music 044.23 307.22 321.16 617.15
musical 048.20 124.25 172.01
musicall 450.19
musically 092.31
musichall 408.26 588.09
musicianlessness 121.26
Musicianship 472.09
musickers 373.31
musics 407.32
musies 565.17
musik 437.32
musikants' 064.13
musk 191.24 280.33 359.09
muskat 354.26
muskating 078.24
musked 512.09
musketeering 245.20
musketeers 064.22
muskished 527.31
muskrateers 379.36
musky 541.31
muslim 497.30
musnoo 144.12
musquodoboits 211.28
muss 148.26 265.F1
Muss 329.08
Mussabotomia 318.25
mussed 191.30
musselman 491.28
mussels 531.06
mussing 430.23
mussmass 125.01
mussna 010.26
mussroomsniffer 142.10
mussymussy 240.25
must must
mustaccents 087.03
mustangs 553.36
mustard 381.27 409.16 455.32 554.05
Mustard 270.12
mustardpunge 050.04
musted 446.22
muster 324.28 603.12
Muster 499.15 506.05
Muster 383.01
mustered 230.08
mustied 279.F23
mustn't 236.01
musts 325.19
mut 287.05
Muta 609.24 609.26 609.30 609.35 610.03 610.06 610.09 610.14 610.17 610.19 610.21 610.23 610.30
mutandis 508.23
mutandus 060.33
Mutantini 238.23
mutatis 508.23
mutatus 060.33
mutch 220.01
mutchtatches 288.F7
mute 087.24 120.08 415.16 508.27
Mute 496.07
mutely 092.27 189.20
Mutemalice 488.16
muters 270.26
muthar 411.17
mutherer 566.19
mutismuser 612.01
mutsohito 054.33
Mutt 016.11 016.13 016.15 016.17 016.19 016.20 016.22 016.26 016.33 017.06 017.09 017.17 017.32 018.02 018.11 018.13 018.15
muttan 467.16
mutter 016.16 139.15 415.13 615.04
Mutter 213.30
muttering 063.21
muttermelk 425.09

mutther 469.14
Mutther 223.05
mutthergoosip 623.03
mutthering 354.24
muttheringpot 020.07
Mutti 161.24 161.24
muttiny 323.11
mutton 064.32 170.34 190.06 246.05 265.F2
mutton 343.13
muttonbrooch 413.15
muttonsuet 185.04
mutts 273.18
Mutua 271.10
mutual 036.23 065.35 082.25 574.04
mutualiter 247.02
mutuearly 164.02
MUTUOMORPHOMUTATION 281.R1
mutuurity 230.14
mutyness 053.03
mux 193.05
Mux 287.13
Muximus 278.L2
muxy 489.04
muy 141.07 411.18 565.20
muy 184.20
muzzing 245.03
muzzinmessed 310.25
muzzlenimiissilehims 005.16
muzzling 319.11
mwilshsuni 338.14
my my My My MY
My 491.29
Myama's 253.28
myandthys 354.32
Mycock 538.22
mycoscoups 300.17
mygh 297.19
myhind 295.06
myles 567.01
Myles 099.24 246.19 433.10
Mymiddle 468.26
myn 378.14
myne 538.27
Mynfadher 180.35
mynhosts 314.22
mynus 478.17
myodorers 459.27
myopper 454.01
Myramy 063.12
myraw 553.03
myrds 375.10
myre 417.33
Myre 569.06
Myrha 471.04
myriabellous 539.29
myriads 159.07
myriadth 238.20
myriamilia 427.25
myrioheartzed 331.23
Myriom 285.F4
myriopoods 416.34
myrioscope 127.35
myrmidins 415.13
Myrrdin 151.31
myrrh 267.28 477.29
myrries 241.16
myrrmyrred 092.13
myrtle 147.17 226.10 346.27
Myrtle 291.F4
Myrtles 105.01
mys 248.21
myself 095.20 145.28 150.22 160.18 160.18 163.32 187.31 188.20 189.20 279.F04 347.30 351.25 356.03 357.33 358.07 364.10 365.08 408.09 410.06 419.28 421.24 452.08 452.11 453.23 454.06 460.04 461.04 481.23 483.02 483.31 484.01 487.15 487.17 495.16 499.24 507.32 509.13 519.31 522.26 522.34 532.29 534.13 536.28 539.15 541.12 571.18 579.18
myselfish 238.28
myselfwhose 439.21
myselx 444.18
mystagogue 477.21
myster 466.30
mysterbolder 309.13
mystery 184.09 221.10 294.28 600.35 617.11
mystries 027.29
mysttetry 060.20
myterbilder 377.26
myth 070.04 561.26
mythametical 286.23
mythed 197.23
mythelated 266.09
myther 126.10
mythical 052.16
mythified 393.33
mything 238.27
mytinbeddy 243.06

n 333.03 334.19
N 226.31 (N for greeneriN)
N. 016.06
251.34 (N. Ohlan)
na 248.36 330.16 343.11 476.27 478.23 496.27 502.09 622.06
naaman 103.08
Naama's 204.05
naas 516.11
nab 187.13 235.15
nabir 005.21
Nabis 235.01
nabobs 414.05
naboc 456.22
nabour 091.14
nabs 490.18
nabsack 011.19
Nabuch 103.08
nace 295.26
nacessory 237.36
nach 552.29
nachasach 595.03
nacht 556.23
nachtingale 406.24
nachtistag 066.04
Nacion 297.F1
nacks 011.23
nackt 067.03 502.12
Nackt 229.16
naclenude 359.10
nacre 559.10
nad 178.03 625.33
nada 470.01 521.06
nadianods 112.34
nadir 297.12
naemaer 444.32
naeme 601.30
nag 266.15 554.06
naggin 075.04 382.09
nagging 572.01
nagginneck 581.12
naggins 560.19
nagles 516.12
nahars 241.27
naif 107.09
Naif 526.20
naightily 222.35
nail 022.15 377.34 404.30 558.29 559.10 571.35
nailed 099.17
nails 110.14 143.34
Nailscissor 388.23
nailstudded 208.06
naivebride 022.26
naked 357.33 601.01 624.19
Naked 107.04
Nakedbucker 139.06
nakedness 096.29 109.11
Nakel 438.13
nakeshift 603.14
nakest 461.26
naket 067.03 555.05
naktlives 538.11
Nakulon 258.18
nam 607.11 607.12
Namantanai 595.20
Namar 374.22
Namara 271.02 325.23
namas 512.25 599.05
namby 614.07
name 005.05 015.29 039.16 040.21 044.14 049.08 049.19 056.32 058.04 067.26 073.04 093.29 099.17 102.08 102.23 104.01 118.12 121.29 125.07 134.14 141.07 141.33 147.10 159.12 173.05 179.24 187.24 188.26 203.19 204.21 237.27 240.26 249.29 253.15 254.19 255.01 263.03 268.F1 272.02 280.09 286.22 288.16 290.19 293.02 299.11 330.13 352.24 353.02 355.24 360.06 378.07 393.13 393.23 397.01 398.24 419.09 419.17 422.34 424.23 426.01 439.28 441.17 442.16 444.19 450.32 451.27 453.23 455.08 459.31 461.25 482.18 487.30 488.22 491.14 493.33 494.26 495.36 501.26 507.34 521.22 524.07 524.13 529.15 548.05 558.33 561.12 563.08 569.35 574.15 606.20 618.05 624.17 627.33
name 390.26 399.26
Name 477.35 514.17
namecousin 055.17
named 031.20 257.11 262.14 403.12 409.22 528.33 561.11 574.31 625.11
Named 525.16
nameform 018.25
nameless 182.14 410.08
namely 187.12 187.16 253.23 615.30
Namely 355.10 368.33
nameofsen 142.06
namer 468.18
names 025.11 071.06 086.12 088.12 104.05 108.14 123.23 165.29 179.09 232.11 237.21

286.F4 320.14 331.14 348.20 409.23 441.13 445.30 460.19 472.26 574.03 574.18 576.34
Names 105.25
name's 457.03 570.01
namesake 043.36 130.29
namesakely 313.33
namesame 619.13
nameshielder's 590.25
namesick 489.20
namesuch 442.05
nan 583.22
Nan 019.30 254.15 567.15 567.15
nana 331.25
Nance 203.21
nancies 376.24
nancing 007.27
Nancy 211.09 244.20 422.32 576.08
nancyfree 439.08
Nancy's 568.17
Nancy's 071.36
Nanenities 538.07
Nanetta 567.15
Nanette 117.16
nangel 222.22
nangles 390.14
nankeen 321.34
nanna 463.16
Nanny 328.14
nannygoes 007.27
nanny's 559.34
Nanny's 568.18
Nannywater 205.26
nano 040.25
Nanon 203.21
nansen 477.20
nansence 535.19
Nansense 326.21
Nansy 382.27
Nao 233.22
Naohao 233.24
Naohaohao 233.26
nap 131.30 202.03 313.08 478.21 550.27
Nap 009.06 516.31
Nap 176.11
nape 033.06 137.23 247.19 461.16 590.25
naperied 345.21
naperon 011.34
napex 297.14
napier 300.32
napirs 598.35 598.36
napirs' 598.35
napkins 213.28
Napoleon 033.02
napollyon 273.27
Napoo 389.29
napper 040.31 408.30
nappies 039.11
nappin 329.10
Nappiwenk 105.10
napple 239.04
nappotondus 273.L4
nappy 011.19
Narancy 102.25
narar 339.02
narcissism 522.30
narcissus 212.32
narcolepts 395.08
narcosis 475.10
nare 012.08 202.06
narev 203.14
nargleygargley 234.31
nark 581.08
narked 034.10
narks 368.22
narrated 431.33
narratives 031.35
narrator 314.27
narrowa 209.19
narrowedknee 230.05
narrowing 457.18
narrowly 471.17
narrows 153.05
narse 340.24
Narsty 395.02
Narwhealian 023.11
nary 279.F16
nasal 051.27 281.F1 463.08 559.28
Nasal 156.28
Nascitur 512.36
nascituris 287.20
nase 088.18 154.19
Nash 075.20 290.28
nasoes 403.07
nass-and-pair 522.19
Nassau 135.12
Nassaustrass 178.29
nassy 074.14
Naster 455.14
nastilow 301.F4
nastily 185.34
nasturtium 463.19
nasturtls 624.26
nasty 386.03 510.21
nat 083.12 555.05
natal 281.F1
Natal 587.21
nataves 288.16
nate 181.36
nate 339.24
natecup 334.10
nates 440.18
nateswipe 281.F2
nathandjoe 003.12
nathem's 588.16
nati 185.16
natibus 185.16
natigal's 040.25
nation 006.15 040.27 043.21 052.30 062.19 177.02 190.20 229.08 409.06 419.18 471.27 514.36 557.24 565.30 615.04
national 008.01 013.32 039.04 041.34 099.18 116.10 165.16 171.33 220.22 385.25 428.18 430.02 467.11 570.31 574.18 615.27
nationalist 133.15
nationals 190.12
nationglad 258.28
nationists 190.13
nations 011.20 042.21 243.33 540.02
nation's 172.32
native 051.24 081.19 235.20 288.F6 374.30 408.07 430.14 617.34 624.36
natives 455.35
native's 556.32
natsirt 388.03
natteldster 318.31
Nattenden 608.29
Nattenlaender 382.28
nattes 236.33
nattleshaker 159.19
nattonbuff 336.19
natty 558.21
natural 066.33 109.20 117.28 126.08 149.14 161.16 169.16 178.19 189.20 208.16 251.04 260.16 291.F8 357.29 385.19 411.26 428.17 437.21 462.36 472.11 489.30 498.06 546.20 595.34 618.36
Natural 610.35
naturalborn 159.24
Naturale 450.27
naturalest 120.33
naturalistically 149.18
Naturality 308.L2
naturally 066.29 077.35 124.23 412.14 510.31 574.32
naturally 284.L2
naturals 530.01
nàture 029.31 034.21 034.25 037.05 049.25 092.08 119.20 120.33 124.12 139.01 181.19 185.01 187.25 189.03 235.20 345.32 385.20 389.16 454.08 463.16 472.10 523.11 564.17 597.33
Nature 279.F19 306.20 357.28 437.16
Nature 072.12
naturel 252.28
natures 593.12 615.14
Natures 106.10
nature's 057.31 570.03
naturlikevice 085.16
naturpark 524.06
Nau 093.21
naught 241.13 356.12 536.18 555.05
naughties 147.28
naughtingels 359.32
naughtingerls 450.17
Naughtsycalves 229.15
naughty 204.05 540.03
naughtygay 578.22
Naul 310.13 333.36 622.25
naun 482.03 536.35
nauseous 613.23
nauses 418.10
nausy 233.36
nautaey 512.21
Nautaey 512.21
nautchy 068.03
Nautic 204.05
nautonects 416.11
Nautsen 479.36
naval 061.13 272.11 377.07 544.08 583.03
naval's 297.13
Navan 436.29
nave 127.36 552.07
Nave 420.23
navel 018.29 323.05 447.04 475.14 480.17
navel 303.L1
Navellicky 392.25
naver 241.20
naves 211.25
n'avez 478.20
navico 179.19

navigable 605.13
navigants 398.15
Naville 061.21
navious 414.05
navn 204.05
navvies 179.19
navvygaiterd 320.07
Naw 031.10
nawboggaleesh 192.26
nawful 159.30
Nawlanmore 050.23
nay 023.36 079.02 079.09 136.22 141.07 141.25 172.14 188.15 193.12 279.F17 312.23 337.15 337.15 339.23 440.35 472.28 520.31 586.07 606.34
Nay 020.35 231.26 239.13 281.29
nayer 234.23
Naylar-Traynor 370.22
naym 029.19
Nayman 187.28
nayophight 425.31
Naysayers 108.29
Naytellmeknot 361.10
nayther 008.26 027.27 140.04 201.34
naze 208.28
Naze 524.21
Nazi 375.18
nazil 577.11
nazional 440.05
nck 334.19 (neck)
N.C.R. 256.32 (North Circular Road)
N.D. 520.19 (Notre Dame)
nday 089.18
ndays 089.18
ne 052.14 068.29 223.30 223.31 333.03 417.34 567.36 567.36
ne 565.25
Ne 388.06
Neach 048.14
neagh 196.20
Neagh 076.22
neaghboormistress 023.29
Neagk 310.34
neaheaheahear 466.25
neahere 027.27
Neandser 600.12
néant 281.09
neantas 598.06
neanzas 598.06
neap 196.23
neappearance 483.10
near 013.21 032.33 076.12 080.06 088.01 116.18 152.36 154.36 159.33 186.24 204.26 213.07 223.12 234.14 276.F2 297.15 320.28 340.35 361.23 386.20 424.24 435.01 451.33 460.07 466.36 482.10 506.19 518.05 526.28 529.35 559.12 571.03 580.23 588.31 601.12 602.02 620.04 624.30 626.01 628.02
near 262.L2
Near 214.31
Nearapoblican 172.23
nearby 448.01
neared 077.16
nearer 101.31 111.36 113.31 478.06 601.12
nearest 035.23 084.18 457.26 528.10 544.16 583.19
nearing 267.23 585.20 590.18
nearly 198.09 433.22 454.24 510.03 582.35
nears 565.32
nearstout 038.36
nearvanashed 061.18
Nearwicked 539.04
neat 075.17 151.25 311.19 339.06 436.15 518.32 525.20 558.21 585.05
neath 014.32 556.19 577.28 588.15
neathe 202.33
neatlight 004.33
neatly 092.06 153.13 165.29
neats 361.17 380.32
neatschknee 346.02
Neaves 577.21
neb 210.01
neberls 536.19
Neblas 011.05
Neblonovi's 230.15
Nebnos 250.27
nebo 011.16
Nebob 270.27 590.17
nebohood 235.16
nebuless 050.36
nebulose 475.14
nec 185.15 283.L1
necess 508.14
necessarily 521.16
necessary 033.35 109.24 488.30
necessitades 553.21
necessity 133.32 188.21 266.11 518.20
Necessity 207.29 307.27
neck 017.11 033.06 049.32 091.16 092.19 125.10 133.04 395.17 438.09 454.32 496.26
neckanicholas' 090.11
neckar 202.08
necking 068.04
neckkandcropfs 306.02
necklace 207.05 235.34 387.04
necklassoed 426.27
necklike 454.32
neckloth 542.34
necknamesh 546.04
necknoose 568.20
neckplace 548.33
necks 147.23
nectar 025.07
nectarial 613.36
ned 273.11 288.05
Ned 082.17 330.04 368.36 477.06
Neddos 325.33
nedenfor 395.05
Nedlework 104.20
Nee 054.10
Neeblow's 552.19
neece 092.18
need 020.14 052.31 101.19 109.17 109.27 112.01 115.35 122.23 124.35 151.07 184.11 188.06 193.22 214.09 214.09 222.03 233.08 263.19 294.F2 440.26 482.26 503.22 528.02 535.09 621.19
need 399.11
needatellye 492.07
needed 066.34 066.34 066.35 185.01 328.15 437.12
Needer 508.14
Neederthorpe 541.25
needle 494.04
needles 210.11 369.23
needless 162.29
Needlesswoman 165.16
needn't 622.29
needs 068.28 150.33 159.36 316.24 523.19 551.27
Neeinsee 600.13
Neelson 242.01
neer 385.09 388.26
ne'er 013.22 098.32 405.17 462.13 472.23 488.22 496.28 496.34
ne'er-do-wells 544.29
neese 388.04
nefand 167.19
nefarious 389.24
nefas 031.36 443.13
Nefersenless 415.33
Neffin 376.17
Neg 106.10
Negas 423.33
negasti 423.33
negatise 241.34
negative 111.27 111.35 524.10
negatively 108.29
negativisticists 612.03
negertoby 423.33
negertoe 423.33
negertop 423.33
neglect 109.14
neglecting 222.16
negociated 574.22
Negoist 488.21
negotiations 084.16
Negro 198.13
Negru 540.21
negrunter 423.33
negus 058.15 489.17
nehm 270.28
nei 286.25
Neid 222.18
neigh 584.22 584.22
Neighboulotts 625.25
neighbour 024.27 163.13 275.07 299.27 311.35 477.21
neighbouring 054.28
neighbours 492.12 544.04
neighbour's 014.27 172.30
neighing 530.07
neighs 338.36
nein 488.26
neins 202.02
neiss 200.29
neither 068.30 068.30 101.20 188.19 198.30 230.09 384.25 508.14 521.25 536.06 563.34 616.31
Neither 102.21 177.13 298.F2
Nej 230.25
nek 039.06
Nek 258.10
nekropolitan 080.01
Nekulon 258.10 258.14
nel 281.18

nelja 285.20
nelliza 291.14
Nells 423.12
nelly 034.32
Nelly 227.14 361.14 604.36
Nelson 422.30 466.24
neltts 390.07
Nema 395.23
nember 390.29
nemcon 352.02
nemesisplotsch 343.28
neming 505.22
Nemo 229.13
nemon 318.06
Nemon 175.33
nemone 274.25
Nemorn 347.04
Nemzes 114.04
nen 203.14
neniatwantyng 499.05
nenni 452.27
Nenni 307.F8
nenuphars 075.01
neoclassical 179.23
neoitalian 151.08
neoliffic 576.36
Neomenie 244.05
Neomugglian 123.21
neonovene 291.28
neople 141.06
neow 289.F6
nepertheloss 318.18
nephew 210.09 314.27
Nephew 066.32 484.09
nephews 465.09
Nephilim 590.17
nephos 536.19
nepmen's 558.07
nepogreasymost 156.17
Nepomuk 349.23
nepos 134.28
Nepos 389.28
nepotists 230.31
Neptune 203.12
Neptune's 391.18 585.02
n'er 457.31
nera 198.31
Nerbu 445.01
nere 318.06 403.17
ne're 479.30
Nereids 267.24
Nero 177.14
Nero 306.L2
Nerone 212.04
nerses 242.09
nerthe 207.22
nerve 146.08 188.20 361.13
nerver 344.20
nerves 274.18 456.18 461.11
ness 141.06
nessans 026.34
Nessau 488.05
nesse 295.26
Nessies 365.28 379.16
nest 112.11 120.06 189.28 265.10 276.06 364.26
nestegg 192.32
nesters 028.09
nestle 330.04
nestlings 131.19
Nestor 073.25
Nestor 307.L1
nests 579.36
net 384.31 407.05 444.32
nether 297.12 415.31
netherfallen 017.27
netherheart 539.15
netherlights 095.24
netherlumbs 319.17
nethermore 057.26
nethermost 154.32 576.31
netherworld's 571.35
nets 136.31 148.04 388.08 477.12 477.12 477.20 477.20
Nett 312.16
Netta 527.27
netted 132.25 262.14
Nettie 104.24
nettle 306.F4
Nettle 604.36
nettlerash 439.07
nettles 136.16
nettleses 243.23
nettlesome 412.28
nettly 469.12
nettus 286.07
neuchoristic 234.20
Neuclidius 155.32
neuhumorisation 331.31
Neuilands 348.16
neuphraties 199.14
neuralgiabrown 286.01
neurasthene 115.30
Neuropaths 488.26
neuropeans 519.01
neuter 523.36
Neuter 106.29
neuthing 455.22
neutral 117.14 574.35
Neutrals 529.08
neutric 167.21
neutriment 416.25
neutrolysis 612.22
neuw 076.20
neuziel 335.13
nevar 203.36
nevay 322.04
nevelo 039.07
never 025.27 026.07 026.36 028.14 029.10 034.12 038.21 050.35 051.06 054.35 055.11 064.09 086.16 090.30 090.31 091.24 096.06 110.21 111.19 112.25 114.35 119.05 119.09 120.03 144.36 148.23 153.18 154.36 159.03 162.07 168.01 175.30 178.12 181.13 182.10 185.01 190.01 197.12 198.19 198.27 200.09 203.16 205.36 208.13 229.22 230.08 242.32 246.15 252.17 253.25 255.23 257.15 269.30 270.27 271.23 276.07 276.F1 290.14 298.16 305.16 309.09 318.21 323.19 327.10 327.14 328.28 337.12 351.33 351.35 361.28 368.04 368.16 368.20 368.22 375.19 376.29 376.36 377.18 390.21 391.35 398.21 411.09 411.10 411.10 411.35 414.08 425.33 433.15 434.26 435.21 437.20 448.19 451.28 452.05 452.24 453.34 456.09 457.05 458.08 458.10 459.14 459.24 459.32 461.10 465.18 468.18 472.32 476.27 479.07 485.36 488.19 489.08 493.04 517.01 517.19 517.21 519.27 520.20 525.36 531.20 532.18 535.01 544.31 545.05 552.01 553.07 558.25 561.35 563.21 570.11 579.10 579.35 581.08 585.31 590.05 596.35 615.26 616.17 618.12 618.24 622.04 622.31 622.33 625.18 626.20 627.32 627.35
never 176.14 342.27 346.08 346.09 346.09 346.10 346.10 346.10 433.19
Never 148.27 148.28 205.14 343.19 368.19 368.19 377.07 411.08 417.31 423.28 433.10 433.11 433.12 433.13 433.14 433.24 433.25 433.26 433.27 433.30 433.31 433.34 506.32 586.05 590.10 615.36 618.03
Never 104.19
neverheedthemhorseluggars-andlistletomine 023.28
Nevermore 129.30
neverperfect 489.34
neverreached 523.14
neverrip 039.11
nevers 451.29
neverso 586.31
neversoever 158.14
neverstop 475.14
nevertheleast 237.04
nevertheless 091.10 380.26 475.06 481.23 557.29 599.10
Nevertheless 057.19
Nevertoletta 329.35
nevertoolatetolove 472.19
neverwithstanding 347.30
neverworn 183.18
nevewtheless 523.03
Nevewtheless 061.07
neviewscope 449.34
Neville 552.12
new 013.14 055.33 055.34 061.14 090.34 092.19 123.35 126.17 129.18 136.23 136.24 136.24 137.32 139.07 144.27 188.25 190.09 232.28 308.22 324.03 333.16 344.22 347.13 387.36 406.29 410.08 443.31 450.01 455.04 472.14 505.11 516.30 531.18 543.28 575.29 580.04 585.25 621.18
New 078.26 130.08 130.21 145.29 197.10 260.13 307.10 412.02 509.24 540.20
New 104.22 346.08
newbridge 063.14
newbucklenoosers 319.29
Newbuddies 415.19
newcasters 388.07
newcommers 322.26
newcsle 555.13 555.15
Newer 601.35
newera's 623.07
Neweryork 569.18
newest 148.08
Newestlatter 382.13
newfolly 279.F12
Newgade 551.34
newhame 098.08
Newhigherland 392.31
Newirgland's 595.10
newisland 525.30

newknow 246.24
newlaidills 124.14
newlaids 438.23
newleaved 140.34
newleavos 470.19
newled 405.34
newly 203.23 457.19 560.21
Newly 219.04
newlywet 452.31
newman 596.36
newmanmaun 614.17
newnesboys 363.06
news 028.21 028.21 194.23 333.36 377.25 420.05
news 278.L5
News 028.21
newsbaggers 560.23
Newschool 327.08
newseryreel 489.35
newses 141.11 196.20
Newses 385.34
newsky 442.11
Newslaters 390.01
Newsletter 097.32
newspaper 127.20 127.23
newstage 610.35
newt 021.02
newthing 253:08
newtown 625.25
newwhere 155.12
newyearspray 561.20
nex 273.05
Nex 163.15
nexally 035.22
nexistence 366.02
nexmouth 177.25
next 005.01 038.15 066.10 070.22 112.10 119.06 122.06 128.25 136.31 167.27 170.12 174.17 202.10 205.05 224.32 231.02 231.02 231.02 238.18 248.27 327.15 336.16 374.22 403.10 405.33 413.24 417.08 429.01 431.01 438.12 439.25 446.21 456.28 460.04 460.07 466.06 470.28 471.08 487.03 487.05 496.12 556.05 556.31 577.25 585.01 621.18 625.08
next 399.16
Next 172.05 206.32 238.08 456.14 589.29 622.02
nextdoored 369.14
nextfirst 452.20
nexth 207.33
nexword 487.12
ney 337.16 337.16 567.20
Ney 154.05
Neya 203.14
neys 184.02
neyther 256.05
ni 499.30
Ni 137.02 225.06 308.13 328.14 607.18
N.I. 553.21 (necessitades iglesias)
Niall 096.04 282.32
niallist 346.32
Nibble 106.29
nibbleh 300.18
nibbleth 014.33
nibbling 132.25
Nibs 182.10
nibulissa 256.33
Nic 251.01
nice 010.03 011.32 022.21 028.11 035.16 065.12 092.19 227.26 236.14 242.17 252.22 253.18 270.28 271.F5 323.03 361.09 374.30 386.15 419.31 421.33 430:27 430.28 430.29 431.29 435.04 435.04 439.26 444.13 459.14 459.18 464.05 492.01 492.02 502.29 515.35 522.27 558.21 558.23 560.23 560.32 562.03 563.37 590.11 597.05
Nice 415.14
nicechild 555.16
niced 048.21 528.04
niceliest 413.08
nicelookers 125.09
nicely 115.19 255.36 368.16 386.02 472.24
nicenames 468.13
nicest 235.15 502.04
nicesth 327.03
Nicey 485.29
niche 290.01
Nichiabelli's 182.20
Nichil 175.05
nichilite 349.14
Nicholas 012.25 163.17 541.04 569.06
nicholists 113.27
Nicholls 147.06
nicht 244.33
nichthemerically 185.29
Nichtia 376.16
Nichtian 083.10
nichts 343.20 343.20
Nichtsnichtsundnichts 416.17
nicies 196.21
nick 019.27 048.11 054.21 067.26 330.13 422.12
Nick 307.F6
Nick 219.19 399.26
Nickagain 300.F1
Nickekellous 099.20
Nickel 296.17
Nickel 176.03
nickelly 011.23
nickelname 506.01
nickendbookers 549.04
nickers 301.09
Nickies 422.33
Nickil 412.36
nickleless 281.F4
nickname 032.18 094.34
nicknamed 046.01
nicknumber 318.30
nicks 540.30
nickst 445.14
nicky 116.24
nickylow 023.16
niece 312.24 373.26 558.21
Niece 608.08
nieceless 532.24
niece-of-his-in-law 021.14
nieces 349.28
Niecia 278.L2
niedelig 265.10
Nielsen 553.13
Nieman 202.19
nieows 141.17
niester 210.35
niet 312.19
Niet 565.10
nieu 148.18
Nieuw 117.24
niever 206.08
nievre 273.12
nig 250.36 266.15
Niger 212.01
Nigerian 181.13
nigg 374.05
niggar 281.F4
niggard 297.26
nigger 177.04 208.16
niggerblonker 611.34
niggerd's 444.21
niggeress 537.24
niggerhead 316.24
niggers 040.13
niggs 183.06 183.06
Niggs 183.05
nigh 099.13 153.19 282.13 282.13 282.14 282.14 306.F2 451.21 457.09 496.12 501.30 585.20
nighadays 561.06
nighboor 585.34
nighboors 552.20
nighboor's 487.12 615.33
nighbrood 248.35
nighing 476.33
nighs 590.18
night 005.20 007.02 007.02 007.02 013.36 021.05 021.25 021.33 022.12 028.28 038.15 040.13 040.24 049.24 055.18 064.20 065.10 067.03 083.27 087.12 090.10 090.31 107.17 117.01 120.13 135.34 136.31 138.36 139.11 139.18 139.28 147.32 158.21 159.32 162.27 172.14 174.22 182.36 188.12 192.24 207.32 216.03 226.28 245.16 256.34 277.14 277.F1 295.03 310.23 319.01 320.28 321.16 328.18 328.31 328.32 328.34 329.14 337.14 371.19 379.17 385.28 393.19 393.30 394.13 397.27 405.36 414.03 429.23 432.01 436.27 436.28 442.33 449.22 452.14 458.13 461.17 473.10 473.23 475.01 479.36 481.28 484.10 488.24 501.16 501.23 501.28 501.29 505.10 514.17 517.32 519.04 519.05 519.22 519.22 527.07 530.01 549.06 555.05 555.21 556.01 556.01 556.13 556.28 556.31 556.31 556.31 557.13 564.36 589.16 593.21 593.22 598.09 620.24 625.01 625.20 626.04 626.21
Night 215.36 215.36 216.02 216.03 216.05 546.34 626.20
Night 107.01
nightbirds 438.35
nightcap 321.10 406.14 559.20
nightcap's 306.F2
Nightclothesed 355.19
nightcoover 141.15
nightdress 560.27
nightfallen 191.27
nightgarters 011.22
nighthood's 403.22
nighties 147.28

nightinesses 051.05
nightinveils 541.30
nightjoys 357.18
nightle 066.22
nightleaves 580.19
NIGHTLETTER 308.16
nightlife 150.33 407.20
nightlights 135.20
nightlong 184.07
nightly 126.06 142.24 219.07 261.27
Nightly 359.27
nightmail 565.32
nightmale 485.26
nightmarching 210.15
nightmare 583.09
nightmaze 411.08
nightout 145.33
nightplots 033.17
nightprayers 081.27
nightrives 449.30
nights 015.20 032.36 040.18 080.02 083.27 255.17 312.10 433.18 458.05 495.15 506.21 549.06 619.21 627.16
night's 062.04 074.11 360.12 461.25 597.02 604.18
Night's 122.12
nightschool 430.02
nightsend 614.04
nightshared 603.13
nightshirt 251.13
nightslong 188.03
nightsoil 544.07
nightstride 429.02
nighttalkers 032.08
nighttim 284.09
nighttime 007.21
nightwatch 576.30
nighty 435.24 451.21
nightynovel 054.21
nighumpledan 420.26
nigra 160.32
nigro 185.18
nihil 493.19
Nihil 202.19
nihilant 143.20
nihilnulls 318.32
nik 625.33
Nike 270.24 296.28
Nikkelsaved 097.17
Niklaus 155.31 155.31
nikrokosmikon 468.21
nikte 565.27
nil 361.02 493.05
Nil 598.06
Nilbud 024.01
Nile 075.02 328.22 494.34
Nilfit's 194.17
nill 620.03
nillohs 019.31
nilly 332.29
nilobstant 485.01
Nils 520.22
Nilsens 322.32
Niluna 627.30
nimb 143.20 375.31
nimbum 155.32
nimm 270.28
nimmer 469.23 528.34
nin 257.08 257.08 257.08 257.08 257.09 257.09 257.09 257.10
Nin 600.10
ninan 246.21
Ninan 246.21
nine 051.17 077.13 086.15 100.14 101.26 213.27 213.36 255.36 260.F1 265.26 377.12 429.08 473.12 517.32 558.22 567.04 575.12 580.24 584.24
Nine 096.05 535.29
Nine 398.32
ninehundred 133.17
ninelived 235.31
nineninenineteee 102.31
ninepace 618.07
ninepins 014.22 549.36
ninequires 229.31
ninethest 326.33
ninety 237.23 364.35 413.12
ninetynine 086.16
ninetynine 398.32
ninned 257.09
ninnies 586.07
ninny 173.28 286.27
Ninny 514.15
ninnygoes 007.27
Ninon 153.04
ninsloes 583.22
ninth 119.26 317.26 317.26
ninth 346.32
Ninth 347.18
ninthly 606.03
ninyananya 578.21
Niomon 236.08
nip 009.29 009.29 239.04
Nip 187.13
Nippa 147.13
nipped 022.03
nipper 345.24
nippers 366.28
nippies 114.28
Nipples 260.F2
nippling 462.11
Nippoluono 081.33
Nippon 276.15
nipponnippers 485.36
nippy 009.29 087.23 449.10
Nippy 388.08
Nircississies 526.34
Nirgends 202.19
nirshe 370.05
Niscemus 175.33
nissunitimost 417.04
nistling 209.24
nistlingsloes 571.17
nith 200.01 273.26
nitrience 067.07
Nitscht 222.11
nitshnykopfgoknob 344.14
nittle 029.08
nittlewoman 327.03
Niutirenis 335.16 335.16
niver 011.03 203.36 203.36
nivia 583.22
Nivia 199.34
niviceny 596.19
Nivonovio 230.16
nivulon 148.18
Nivynubies' 066.37
nix 050.35 361.02
Nixie 203.21
Nixies 365.28
Nixnixundnix 415.29
Nixy 011.04
Nizam 013.25
Nmr 502.11 (Number)
Nn 016.06
nngnr 318.35 (anger)
Nnn 016.07 515.05
Nnnn 016.07
nnow 626.33
no no No No
No 574.26 (No 11)
no. 420.25 (number)
No. 389.13 (No. 1132) 389.13 (No. 1169)
Noah 036.11 064.33
Noah 307.L1
Noahnsy 105.14
noahs 178.12
Noah's 047.06
Noah's 383.09
Noahsdobahs 388.18
Noal 393.11
noane 275.F5
Noanswa 023.20 023.20
noarch 020.29
noarchic 080.25
noas 531.11
noa's 420.23
noase 098.03
Noasies 463.30
noavy 396.21
Noball 584.23
Nobbio 230.16
nobble 498.22
nobblynape 371.03
nobbut 355.33
nobelities 536.12
nobilees 356.11
nobiloroman 084.15
nobily 156.25
nobirdy 505.17
nobis 228.26
nobit 247.09
noble 100.14 171.24 211.03 222.08 535.08
Noble 184.34 413.04 488.14
nobleman 173.05
nobler 434.04
noblesse 204.07 495.26
noblest 028.32 627.22
Noblett's 306.04
noblewomen 180.01
noblige 567.26
noblish 187.12
nobly 419.22
Nobnut 376.09
nobody 073.11 077.12 110.16 208.27 239.26 249.27 393.34 463.33 471.09 624.30
Nobody 377.09
nobodyatall 073.09
Nobookisonester 177.14
nobottle 569.25
Nobru 490.26
Nobucketnozzler 024.35
nocadont 338.21
Nocelettres 534.21
nocense 378.33
noces 224.14
Nock 301.09 515.07
nocknamed 059.16
noclass 125.13
Noctuber 481.28
noctules 276.23
nocturnal 449.36

nocturne 238.10 428.17
nocturnefield 360.12
nocturnes 430.11 603.19
nod 005.21 273.26 287.12 337.22 385.09 439.29 476.10 554.02 554.02 585.08
Nod 181.05
Nodderlands 385.09
noddies 554.02
nodding 058.27 207.35 316.06 389.02 440.16
Nodding 529.08
noddle 120.13
noddling 369.24
noddy 024.02
nodebinding 143.14
nodje 345.16
nods 131.30 226.22 288.25 365.26
nodsloddledome 379.15
nodst 621.23
Nodt 608.21
nodunder 370.33
noe 561.05
Noe 125.18 387.21 514.14
noebroed 378.34
Noeh 513.23 549.34
noel 337.15
Noel 588.27
noelan 097.05
Noel's 490.23 594.35
Noeman's 321.14
noen 414.07
noer 286.28
noes 053.13 102.03 114.02 114.02 245.17 493.26
noesmall 581.15
noewhemoe 007.15
Nogen 560.18
nogent 496.10
nogeysokey 315.22
nogg 374.05
Noggens 370.26
nogger 188.13
noght 475.21
nogs 366.09
nogumtreeumption 191.13
noh 611.11
Noh 244.26
Noho 016.15
Nohoholan 341.24
Nohomiah 032.01
Nohow 317.22
noirse-made-earsy 314.27
noisance 479.20
Noisdanger 168.05
noise 028.25 200.27 214.32 242.20 404.09 551.27 571.30
noised 099.06 511.33
noiselisslesoughts 379.15
noisense 147.06
noises 225.05 625.04
noisies 386.02
noisy 136.01 422.36
Noksagt 535.19
Nola 488.04 488.07 488.11
Nolagh 321.08
Nolan 038.28 159.22 211.32 334.10 336.33 489.13 490.07 490.08 567.22
Noland 187.28 599.23
noland's 300.29
nolandsland 391.15
Nolaner 412.36
Nolans 093.01 488.15 558.18
Nolans 418.31
Nolan's 050.05 268.09 380.31 503.35
Nolanus 163.24
nolens 271.20
nolensed 113.28
Noll 044.13
nollcromforemost 362.05
Nollwelshian 618.34
nolly 621.18
nom 040.06
nom 291.17
Nom 229.02 285.L3
nomad 190.32 473.07
Nomad 103.08 374.22
nomads 386.28 410.32
nomanclatter 147.21
Nomario 450.24
nomatter 258.33
nomber 373.02
nombre 222.32
nombres 529.24
nombres 285.L3
nome 279.05
nomen 546.04
nomened 075.20
nominally 490.07
nominating 092.14
nominator 283.07
nominigentilisation 031.33
nomme 146.20
Nomo 370.35
Nomomorphemy 599.18
Nomon 374.23
nomore 073.11 473.07
nompos 365.19
noms 281.08
non 141.07 566.32 626.19
non 301.16 496.36 586.05
Non 140.05 263.L3 283.L1
nonactionable 048.18
Nonanno 182.20
nonation 036.22
nonbar 358.30
nonbehavers 520.18
nonce 131.31 149.22 333.32
noncommunicables 087.19
noncredible 301.04
nonday 481.07 489.35
nondepict 039.09
nondescript 121.09
nondesirable 456.30
Nondum 020.19
none none None None
noneknown 596.10
nonesuch 534.23
non-excretory 175.31
nonfatal 084.20
Nongood 500.19
noninvasive 072.17
nonirishblooder 378.11
nonland 403.18
nonne 514.14
nonneither 230.09
nonni 203.14
nonobli 064.30
nonobstaclant 345.21
nonot 056.06
nonoun 104.16
nonpaps 583.22
nonparile 283.22
nonparticular 613.33
nonparty 413.08
nonpenal 398.07
nonplush 516.27
nonplussing 475.04
nonpresence 108.33
Nonsense 056.28
nonsensical 487.28
nonsery 619.18
nonsolance 562.32
nonstop 375.27
nonthings 598.01
nontrue 063.10
nonviewable 403.23
noo 047.06 198.11 388.21 520.29 568.33
Noo 332.01 497.13
noobibusses 006.01
noodle 143.09 320.17
noodles 369.23
noodlum 334.14
noods 468.13
Noodynaady's 253.16
Nooikke 221.28
nooks 553.20
nook's 330.04
Noolahn 128.26
noon 232.18 517.25 542.10
noon 353.30
Noon 420.24
Noon 072.01
nooncheon 191.28
noondayterrorised 184.08
noondrunkard's 125.02
no-one 181.22 583.20 588.27
nooning 042.35
nooningless 064.15
noonmeal 397.33
noonstroom 613.03
noonstruck 261.26
noor 140.05
Noord 387.02
Noordeece 375.03
Noordwogen's 241.18
noose 241.04 524.34
noose 278.L1
noosebag 377.08
noosed 226.27
nooth 509.19
nope 271.14
Nope 424.30
nopebobbies 113.36
Nopper 105.10
nopussy 028.10
nor nor Nor Nor
noran 037.23
norange 450.09
Norawain 452.36
norcely 552.04
nordest 097.13
nordic 529.32
nordsihkes 202.01
nordsoud 553.30
nordth 324.25
Nore 203.10
noreast 447.20
noreaster 091.17
noreland 446.25
Norening 330.25
Noreway 535.10
norewere 626.04
Norewheezian 067.13
norewhig 021.01

Norganson 530.31
Norgean 312.05
norgels 015.14
Norgeyborgey 327.30
norjankeltian 311.22
Norkmann 578.11
norlandes 564.23
normal 117.26
normalcy 112.13
Norman 264.29
Normand 514.02
Normandy 443.33
normative 032.18
Normend 510.20
norms 345.21
norone 348.26
norphan 060.07
Norreys 311.35 557.02
Norris 376.09 534.15
Norronesen 023.19
nors 620.16
norse 017.08 064.02 329.07 329.08
Norse 420.23
norsebloodheartened 577.07
norsect's 523.34
norsemanship 547.25
norsery 584.16
Norsker 480.01
Norsker 106.04
nort 371.28
nort 418.26
north 127.30 251.14 317.06 482.27 567.35
North 003.05 024.19 095.05 209.03 372.36 529.13 529.35 534.27 546.33 559.04
northcliffs 010.36
northe 105.19
Northeasts 030.07
northern 042.28 049.19 494.12
Northern 522.04
northers 437.05
Northmen's 215.24
northquain 141.22
northroomer 069.32
north-south 114.03
Northumberland 387.09
Northwegian 049.28
Northwhiggern 511.02
nortons 351.04
Norveegickers 046.21 046.22
Norvena's 619.29
Norwall 621.19
Norweeger's 311.09 312.02
Norwegian 046.23
Norwood's 157.16 578.30
nos 203.14 322.34 422.17 612.08 622.21
nose 086.32 095.13 096.02 133.16 143.23 169.12 200.06 204.32 208.23 210.12 322.13 340.17 368.31 369.05 379.01 379.02 403.07 413.28 436.18 447.08 449.06 463.19 495.07 529.10 559.27 579.23 624.26
nosed 079.29
noseheavy 587.10
noseknaving 091.11
Noselong 461.12
nosepaper 457.34
noses 039.06 039.25 522.28 530.16
nosestorsioms 320.04
nosethrills 450.11
nosetice 164.31
nosibos 112.31
nosing 033.31
nosoes 349.28
nosoever 342.12
nossow 021.20
nossowl 361.16
nostalgia 228.25
nostop 144.01
nostorey 452.16
nostri 398.31
nostril 171.08 509.28
nostrils 084.22 152.23
nostrils' 558.06
nostrums 288.23 439.31
Nostrums 149.03
nosty 536.36
not not Not Not NOT
notables 581.04
notary 290.10 574.23
notation 533.18
notcase 356.23
note 112.31 233.12 241.30 311.06 448.36 467.07
Note 065.06 270.11 374.08
noted 043.36 058.34 066.32 410.11 429.07 557.28
notefew 607.02
Notep 237.27
notepaper 419.29
notes 183.19 236.11 319.35 374.09
Notes 101.04
notesnatcher 125.21
notever 048.08
noth 249.35 294.06 346.23
Noth 494.14
nothalf 161.11
nothave 161.09
nother 356.13
notherslogging 151.17
nothing 005.01 012.20 012.26 042.30 050.35 057.10 063.36 082.08 130.21 140.03 140.04 146.32 161.04 179.33 183.10 198.01 227.34 288.06 322.25 336.14 361.03 362.14 391.05 396.09 410.03 423.20 436.04 439.29 441.14 441.20 443.24 451.11 452.36 455.02 458.26 458.30 462.23 465.26 499.03 503.35 512.02 515.08 516.30 521.03 536.36 560.31
nothing 399.16
Nothing 052.20 419.33 448.23 522.22
nothings 599.35
nothums 281.L4
nothung 295.18
notice 003.19 049.21 091.05 149.19 219.02 421.33 464.04 470.03 470.35 562.22 564.02 575.03 616.16 616.19
Notice 104.08
noticeably 031.04
noticed 163.35
noticing 114.03
noting 316.06
notion 124.11 128.16 358.02 436.35 475.21
notional 057.21
notions 112.05
NOTIONS 268.R1
notmuchers 381.07
notmust 147.29
notnoys 349.26
notomise 356.12
notoriety 291.27 398.24
notorious 230.31 540.03
Notorious 421.24
notoriously 176.19
notplease 256.26
Notpossible 175.05
Notre 388.20
Notre 102.18 112.32
nots 267.09
Notshall 455.29
Notshoh 353.05
nott 245.17
notto 523.31
notus 283.03
Notwildebeestsch 571.28
notwithstanding 061.11 100.09 171.21 240.31 429.15
notwithstempting 356.20
notwithstumbling 560.10
Notylytl 105.10
nough 078.36
nought 067.04 223.34 277.F3 312.17 361.02 368.36 403.07 407.05 415.16 495.06 536.27 548.11 607.11 614.07 616.02 616.02
Nought 244.26 613.14
Nought 106.03
Noughtnoughtnought 488.25
noughttime 349.06
noughty 261.24 284.11 597.15
noun 042.04 245.17 523.10
nourritures 406.31
nourse 279.F20
nous 222.23
nous 281.12
Nous 056.29
nouse 154.10
nouveautays 435.12
nouvelles 129.35
nouyou 027.27
nov 034.32 187.20
Nova 267.23 330.25 407.21 494.10 535.08
novanas 601.14
Novara 191.10
Novarome 155.05
novel 145.29 463.12 569.36
noveletta 087.23 561.11
novels 283.09
novelties 548.24
November 087.04
novembrance 226.32
Novena 191.10
novence 268.10
novene 528.01
novened 603.35
Noverca 230.31
Novgolosh 346.02
noviality 351.15
novicer 322.04
novices 266.15
noviny 333.36
novit 496.36
novo 292.20
Novo 024.01
Novus 365.19

Novvergin's 028.27
now now Now
nowadays 101.15
nowan 173.29
nowand 141.30
nowanights 015.20
nowedding 325.27
nowells 351.01
nowet 298.22
nowface 370.25
Nowhare's 335.29
nowhere 010.26 202.36 226.08 372.32 512.21
Nowhere 175.07 175.09
Nowhergs 533.22
Nowlan 152.11
Nowlong 587.36
nown 481.12
Nowno 569.32
nowraging 320.25
now's 153.20 598.29
Now's 377.18 469.22
nowt 238.27
nowter 228.12
nowth 556.23
Nowthen 084.28
nowtime 290.17
now'twas 404.11
Nox 143.17
noxally 035.23
noxe 594.29
noxer 602.35
noxious 174.35
Noxt 614.13
noying 533.36
noyr 176.24
noy's 343.15
noyth 059.13
noze 162.21
nozzy 117.16
N.S.W. 489.13 (New South Wales)
Ntamplin 593.24
Nth 033.02 (Napoleon the Nth)
Nu 240.08
Nuad 344.36
Nuah-Nuah 590.17
Nuahs 593.22
Nuancee 202.21
Nuancee 105.14
nuasilver 138.20
Nuathan 244.31
Nubian 559.28
nubied 157.13
nubila 506.31
nubilee 205.07
nubilettes 073.35
Nubilina 304.19
Nubis 514.22
Nublid 140.27
nubo 011.05
nubtials 324.36
Nuby 230.16
nuck 379.01
nuckling 406.31
nucleuds 283.24
nucleus 472.26
Nuctumbulumbumus 598.05
nude 039.32 208.12 248.03 395.17 546.17
nuder 268.18 493.19
nudes 493.26
nudge 038.15 143.35
nudgemeroughgorude 240.18
nudging 144.19 405.08
nudgment 185.02
nudiboots 126.13
nudies 435.05
nudis 185.16
nudity 109.11
nue 527.18
Nuée 159.09 159.09
nuemaid 138.08
Nuffolk 283.14
Nugent 024.26
nuggently 537.19
nuggets 366.28
Nuggets 107.03
nuhlan 352.16
nuinous 140.09
nuisance 099.06 524.03 587.25
nuisances 520.18
nula 623.28
null 282.20
nullahs 202.36
nullatinenties 336.32
nulled 613.14
nullity 059.22 441.02 573.27
nullius 443.13
Nullnull 086.34
nullum 298.21
nult 110.09
num 040.06
num 113.30 163.15
Numah 374.22
numan 467.33
Numance 281.07
numb 169.12 286.25 288.23 546.25 546.26
number 058.03 065.23 065.25 065.26 069.33 076.14 076.15 076.16 084.10 085.12 118.10 121.28 122.05 126.08 134.14 151.15 151.25 182.31 213.36 235.26 245.35 247.08 275.17 283.06 292.05 307.F7 310.03 320.33 372.35 373.01 385.14 385.34 447.24 447.25 447.26 447.26 448.02 482.20 561.08 562.17 570.29 588.24
Number 157.16 159.33 274.12 482.14 529.09 588.21
Number 072.04
numbered 369.24 557.14
numberous 450.19
numbers 004.20 086.23 290.24 586.25
numborines 533.15
numbulous 367.28
numbum 506.31
numbur 386.21
numen 142.23 162.13 282.21
Nu-Men 493.31
numerable 561.07
numerical 190.35
numerose 407.17
numerous 124.02
Numerous 472.28
numfit 512.36
nummer 171.36 242.05
Nummer 531.04
nummered 010.28
Nummers 313.25
nummifeed 333.06
numpa 311.27 485.30 611.19
numps 523.29
numptywumpty 374.34
nun 366.36 523.17 556.04
nun 484.36
Nun 296.01
nunc 469.23
nuncandtunc 290.23
nunce 004.17 239.10
nunch 405.17
Nunch 222.10
nuncheon 015.33
nuncio 445.26
nuncupassit 167.33
nuncupiscent 432.10
nunguam 095.28
Nunn 231.18
nuns' 183.26 278.10
Nunsbelly 095.36
nunsibellies 233.25
nunsongs 457.29
Nunsturk 346.07
Nuntius' 464.09
Nuotabene 606.13
Nup 377.29
nupersaturals 341.30
Nupiter 390.22
nuptial 080.21 442.26
nuptialism 599.12
nuptiallers 553.32
nuptials 038.05
nuptias 167.30
nuptious 226.27
Nur 310.24
Nuremberg 151.13
nurse 204.15 397.20 457.04 459.04 556.07
nursed 177.15 376.26
nurse'll 257.16
nursely 242.09
nursemagd 436.12
nursepin 561.32
nursery 169.23 227.11 496.12 520.02
Nursery 222.13
nurserymen 160.03
nurses 361.14
nursetender 399.17
nursetendered 392.09
Nursing 046.28
nursis 522.33
Nurskery 385.09
nurssmaid 364.03
nursured 252.22
nursus 019.21
nurtural 313.21
Nurus 230.31
nusance 551.10
nusances 275.F6
Nuseht 593.23
Nush 385.05
nusick 570.02
nut 070.24 136.02 225.19 247.36 349.04
Nut 360.15 370.15
nutalled 550.14
nutbrown 243.25
Nutcracker 304.F1
nutmeg 199.21
nutre 243.15
nutrients 550.13
nutritius 230.29
nuts 082.36 270.F2 273.F3 337.29

Nuts 456.18
Nutsky 360.16
nutslost 238.29
nutsnolleges 623.32
Nutstown 097.10
nutter 080.09
nutties 032.23
Nuttings 113.03
nutty 435.17 587.07
nuver 241.20
Nuvoletta 157.08 157.17 159.05
159.06
Nuvoluccia 157.24
Nuzuland 156.30
nuzzled 120.12
nwan 233.28
n'wc'stle 018.06 (Newcastle)
nwo 483.15
Nwo 483.15
ny 502.09
Nyamnyam 306.F5
Nyanza 558.28
Nyanzer 558.27
nyar 215.02
nyche 563.35
Nye 340.10
nyet 353.10
Nyets 608.21
nymphant 202.33
nympholept 115.30
nymphosis 107.13
nymphs 415.02
nymphs 399.03
nyne 206.04
nyumba 198.11

o 014.14 019.11 140.08 333.01
333.03 528.03
o 096.13 182.20
O O
O 196.01
226.32 (odalisque O)
251.31
270.25 (the O of woman)
287.10 287.10 287.16
o' 024.01 (o' tall)
024.02 (o' toll)
064.12 (out o' slumber)
226.34 (view o' th'avignue)
261.02 (o' voylets)
273.24 (Hell o' your troop)
510.18 (o' tootlers)
O' 424.25 (Shaun O')
oach 016.08
oaf 191.11 251.21 322.08
oafsprung 162.14
oak 016.31 316.16 338.25
361.08 370.24 448.25
Oak 545.36 577.22
oakanknee 211.28
oakboys 385.09
oakey 601.02
oakleaves 336.15
Oakley 052.01 503.32
oakmulberryeke 221.33
oaks 004.14 053.15 235.16
oakses 498.04
oaktree 100.11
oaktrees 202.30
Oalgoak's 339.04
oaproariose 121.27
oar 154.10 320.19 482.26
535.09
oarsclub 205.06
oasis 112.26
Oasis 470.15 470.17 470.19
oasthouse 319.23 319.30
Oates 070.18
oath 067.22 091.04 165.05
426.01 519.19
Oath 175.16
oathes 325.26
oathhead 538.34
oathily 193.32
oathiose 552.15
oathmassed 332.26
oaths 100.17 239.32
oathword 227.23
oats 406.35 587.01 602.36
oatshus 320.11
Oaxmealturn 621.14
ob 481.17
O. B. 212.02 (O. B. Behan)
Obadiah 531.11
obasiant 347.35
O'Bawlar 382.22
obayre 333.34
Obbligado 464.02
obcaecated 076.36
obcecity 236.30
obdurately 038.07
Obealbe 459.27
obedience 076.09 343.36 476.10
obedient 277.08
obeisance 566.23
Obeisance 494.21
obeisant 235.12
O'Bejorumsen 529.16
obeli 120.14
obelise 068.29
obelisk 335.33 567.01
oben 395.12
obening 349.31
Obeold 015.32
Ober 612.04
oberflake 041.20
obertosend 070.09
obesendean 494.19
obesity 140.06
Obesume 371.22
obey 488.01
obeyance 073.15
Obeyance 540.25
obi 064.02
Obiit 489.13
obintentional 151.08
OBIT 271.R1
obitered 059.15
object 268.21 490.11
objected 181.10
objectionable 050.25
objects 019.08 060.02 183.21
403.23 460.14 598.01 611.22
oblate 043.03
oblative 268.22
obliffious 317.32
obligation 574.04
oblige 458.07
Oblige 057.23
obliged 037.03 154.14 357.25
599.03
obliges 341.08
obliging 524.09
oblious 251.04
oblique 270.03
obliquelike 187.29
obliterate 445.20
obliterated 111.34
obliteration 050.12 558.09
oblivion 424.19
obliviscent 158.04
oblong 081.31
obloquohy 290.F6
obluvial 080.25
Obning 609.19
Obnoximost 422.14
oboboes 006.36
oboboomaround 613.23
obolum 154.18
obote 458.16
obras 343.25
O'Breen's 056.32
Obriania's 339.14
O'Brien 070.07 270.31 370.21
385.15
o'briertree 588.31
o'brine 013.26
O'Briny 095.04
O'Bruin's 128.25
O'Bryan 376.08
O'Bryony 450.32
obs 611.24
obscene 185.30 194.18
obscenity 150.31
obscides 008.35
obscidian 403.16
obscindgemeinded 252.16
obscuritads 244.15
obscurity 546.19
obsecration 557.35
obseen 068.33
obselved 156.25
obsen 378.25
obsequient 422.21
obsequies 198.36
Obsequies 408.26
observation 123.19 282.12 411.22
observational 087.09
observed 110.24 433.05
Obsit 318.06
obsolete 268.23
obsoletely 161.17
Obsoletely 502.24
obsoletion 322.32
Obsolutely 090.20
obstacles 437.04
obstain 141.24 546.01
obster 094.17
obstruct 378.32
obstruction 529.29
obtaining 084.33
obtains 481.11 482.36
obtemperate 542.12
obtundity 190.02
obtuse 284.02
obuses 070.12
obverse 067.28 133.32
obversely 161.18
obvious 031.12 151.27
obviously 186.34 374.08 443.27
515.12
Oc 286.30
O'Cannell 392.30
O'Cannochar 348.19
occasion 034.29 038.01 107.27
177.18 248.04 250.02 508.05
575.22
occasional 312.26 443.33
444.03

occasionally 050.26 134.12 362.27 483.01
occasioned 448.08
occasioning 482.36
occasions 062.22 189.02 585.09
occeanyclived 481.13
occident 120.22
Occidentaccia 180.15
occidentally 589.22
occiput 107.12
Occitantitempoli 230.16
occluded 267.22 494.09
occumule 198.34
occupancy 052.08
occupante 575.36
occupanters 609.13
occupants 545.06
occupational 030.03
occupies 544.05
occupying 098.08 166.29
occur 092.34 121.33 160.11 254.05 486.36 536.34 566.30 617.26
occurance 084.12
occurred 111.31 454.08
occurs 190.10
ocean 185.06 227.20 365.32 392.06 467.23
Ocean 294.13 326.06 600.11
oceanfuls 388.35
oceanic 125.03
oceans 157.17 384.19
Oceans 207.23
ocean's 426.21
ocher 295.33
ochiuri 184.29
ochlocracy 484.32
Ochonal 277.02
Ochone 277.01
ochtroyed 538.07
Ockt 308.12
o'clerk 382.13
O'Clery 385.07
O'Clery's 386.20
o'cloak 155.02
oclock 406.09
o'clock 087.15 219.01 427.34 517.25 519.31 558.18 617.21
o'coat 404.17
ocolombs 335.28
O'Colonel 317.30
Ocone 297.11 297.11
Oconee 003.07 140.35
O'Connee 549.28
o'connell 070.29
O'Connell 081.09 386.22 507.26 580.31
o'connell's 310.28
O'Connell's 382.05
O'Conner 317.31
O'Connor 271.01
O'Conor 380.12 380.33 381.25
o'copious 137.30
O'Cormacan 463.22
o'corneltree 588.31
o'cousin 313.09
O'Crian 087.18
O'Cronione 415.21
O'c'stle 018.06 (Oldcastle)
octagonal 174.07
octagonist 174.17
octavium 467.08
octette 279.F15
octettes 601.14
octo 520.24
October 144.32 410.09
octopods 484.02
octopuds 477.11
O'Cullagh 622.04
oculos 113.30
O'Cunnuc 378.13
od 114.23
odable 053.04
O'Daffy 084.14
O'Daley 048.13
odalisks 335.33
odalisque 226.32
Odam 254.25
O'dan 056.14
O'Daniel 625.12
odarkery 231.14
o'darnel 094.31
odd 004.26 051.10 082.27 088.17 145.07 155.20 155.21 199.15 208.26 266.F2 409.14 410.33 476.17 497.32 507.23 607.07 620.19
odda 609.26
oddaugghter 444.26
odder 180.16 598.20
odderkop 417.33
oddes 597.06
oddfellow's 205.33
odding 334.15
oddity 207.27
oddman 061.29
oddments 453.08
oddmitted 222.15
oddmund 256.11
oddrabbit 366.18
odds 035.12 039.10 090.02 155.27 227.28 405.12 453.31 470.23
odd's 455.17
Odd's 505.13
oddsbones 122.08
Oddsbones 569.03
oddstodds 370.23
oddwinters 580.06
ode 250.23
O'Dea 210.14
o'dears 395.34
O'Dea's 059.23
O'Deavis 041.04
O'Delawarr 212.04
o'dendron 588.32
oder 204.34
Odet 200.33 200.33
odia 108.30
Odin 069.10 088.21
odinburgh 487.09
odiose 163.26
odious 125.21 352.07
ODIUM 264.R1
O'Domnally 420.28
O'Donnell 087.12
O'Donner 087.32
O'Donogh 106.02
O'Donoshough 349.19
odor 332.08 477.34
odor 041.05
Odor 538.31
Odorozone 321.23
odour 051.26 603.07
odours 153.14 280.33 450.13
O'Dowd 089.13 439.20
O'Doyles 048.13
odrer 287.17
odrous 059.10
O'Duane 365.25
O'Dungaschiff 350.07
O'Dunnochoo 348.19
odvices 390.32
O'Dwyer 446.31 602.14
O' Dwyer 116.16
O'Dyar 529.25
O'echolowing 510.26
oedor 053.04
oel 596.13
oelkenner 321.01
oels 498.18
Oelsvinger 221.06
o'er 014.24 017.20 056.06 056.18 058.07 074.03 086.09 101.07 114.01 116.14 250.23 387.33 403.05 407.18 424.11 445.26 445.30 453.07 525.31 535.10 570.01 588.20
o'er 344.04
O'er 373.10
oerasound 315.23
o'erem 469.22
o'erflown 405.36
o'ering 244.25
oerkussens 393.32
oertax 099.11
o'erthemore 238.06
Oetzmann 066.32
oewfs 184.27
of of Of Of OF
O'Farrell 212.13 516.31
O'Faynix 139.35
ofe 572.16
ofen 541.35
off off Off
offa 082.13
offal 320.16 419.32
offalia 465.32
offals 134.17 304.28
Offaly 031.18
offarings 241.03
offdealings 077.21
offed 483.26
offence 034.25 238.07 522.09
offended 069.02
offender 029.30 356.13
Offenders 456.33
offensive 078.15 352.05 558.05
offer 396.20
offercings 364.08
offered 243.35 300.21 325.05
offering 164.29 170.07 279.F29 484.05
offerings 025.03
offers 127.07 306.03 435.03 530.06
offertory 432.17
offgott 346.22
offhand 085.04
office 190.13 190.14 190.15 265.28 278.F6 412.22 484.10 539.34
officer 529.27 544.08
officers 042.33
offices 556.28
official 060.09 387.22 387.28
officially 066.11 388.11
officials 603.11
offils 374.24

offing 110.23
offly 619.32
offon 202.26
offpoint 576.19
offrand 432.09 601.02
OFFRANDES 276.R1
offrom 581.15
offs 230.28 363.36
offsides 384.28
offsprout 030.08
offsprung 023.30
offthedocks 491.07
offwall 003.19
O'Flagonan 027.25
O'Flanagan 210.20
O'Fluctuary 080.29
ofmalt 086.06
Ofman 034.30
O'Ford 512.31
ofsins 499.25
oft 040.13 117.17 318.20
366.25 430.13 445.28 552.01
583.28 620.15
Oft 192.23
oftafter 053.07
oftebeen 075.13
often
oftentimes 384.08 557.32
ofter 140.27 235.10 254.22
Ofter 156.21 589.20
Oftwhile 004.30
ofver 595.24
og 162.26 556.28 610.22
Og 046.22
Oga 203.32
ogas 556.29
oges 525.18 543.19
oggles 349.27
oggly 082.12
oggog 366.26
oggs 069.13
Ogh 249.31 249.31
ogham 123.08
Oghrem 340.09
oghres 027.05
ogle 297.F2
ogled 261.10
oglers 283.09
Oglethorpe 081.21
Oglores 286.31
o'gloriously 063.22
o'goblin 039.21
o'gong 026.27
Ogonoch 498.23
ogos 316.35
Ogowe 207.24
o'gratises 409.26
ogre 014.09
Ogrowdnyk's 102.19
ogry 317.16
ogs 267.20
ogso 539.14
ogsowearit 331.15
oh 080.08 121.27 140.09
229.20 278.10 279.F35 363.36
461.13
Oh 067.32 067.32 099.07
158.19 162.18 222.10 249.20
277.F7 340.16 365.35 372.22
379.18 456.07 470.13 480.16
483.34 499.10 506.09 601.20
O'Haggans 299.23
ohahnthenth 608.24
O'Hara 580.32
O'Hefferns 519.06
Ohere 117.02
Ohiboh 078.32
Ohibow 442.27
OHIO 305.R1 305.R1
Ohlan 251.34
Ohldhbhoy 624.23
ohmes 310.01
ohny 064.02
oho 058.16 352.26
Oho 058.16 352.23
ohoh 054.28
ohoho 590.04
ohold 352.24
ohole 163.01
O'Hollerins 291.11
Oholy 352.22
ohosililesvienne 348.36
ohr 311.06
Ohr 302.21
ohrs 090.28
ohs 184.01 453.09
O'Huggins 519.05
O'Hurry 008.27
O'Hyens 291.10
Oi 551.35
Oiboe 359.36
Oikey 306.09
Oikkont 286.26
oil 021.13 108.28 133.08
230.36 276.17 286.30 365.01
382.06 432.01 438.22 520.24
580.07 605.22 615.31
Oil 448.21
Oilbeam 054.01
oilclothed 550.29
oiled 624.24
oils 464.29 550.18
oils 338.36
Oil's 579.24
oilthan 461.29
oily 234.15 291.26 570.22
Oincuish 090.34
oinnos 456.23
ointment 025.09
Oirasesheorebukujibun 484.26
Oirish 347.08
Oirisher 092.18
Oisis 470.16 470.18 470.20
o'it 057.09 063.29
O'Jerusalem 105.06
O.K. 299.08 (Omnius Kollidimus)
456.07 (Oh Kosmos)
Okaroff 049.03
O'Kay 282.23
okaysure 063.04
okeamic 102.05
Okean 197.29
O'Keef-Rosses 310.16
O'Keepers 370.08
O'kehley 090.28
okey 368.10 368.14
O'Khorwan 352.34
o'kindling 117.17
O'Kneels 291.10
okodeboko 051.17
okt 187.20
. o . . l 514.18 (Hotel)
Olaf 100.26 294.08 443.30
O-la-fa 044.26
Olaf's 012.31 294.09
olala 026.13 450.26
Olaph 132.17 201.30
olave 564.21
Olbion 264.F3
olchedolche 302.22
old 003.11 005.36 008.06 010.03
010.07 013.14 013.21 013.25
015.24 018.23 019.07 022.12
022.32 024.22 025.21 026.26
027.31 029.30 030.13 033.28
034.08 035.30 038.18 043.15
044.05 044.06 045.08 046.23
047.01 047.15 048.03 049.02
049.10 049.14 049.15 053.27
053.33 055.36 057.24 062.06
062.31 063.14 064.16 065.05
065.12 065.20 065.23 068.14
069.14 069.19 069.24 073.06
073.25 076.26 079.02 079.28
080.01 080.33 082.17 083.10
085.25 087.17 093.35 094.10
094.17 094.26 094.34 095.01
095.07 096.05 096.07 096.09
097.13 102.08 110.24 112.25
113.03 113.18 114.18 115.21
116.08 119.29 122.17 122.28
124.35 124.35 124.35 124.36
125.04 129.19 132.27 136.10
136.10 136.25 137.19 139.05
139.06 140.22 141.09 143.10
144.32 144.33 146.06 148.19
151.31 152.13 160.26 163.17
163.19 167.26 170.17 175.34
175.35 175.36 177.24 182.19
188.25 189.15 193.05 193.20
194.23 194.27 196.06 196.11
196.24 198.28 200.16 200.18
204.13 204.30 205.03 206.12
207.29 209.15 211.13 213.01
214.33 214.36 215.12 215.13
215.34 220.22 224.09 229.08
230.28 231.33 234.32 234.33
240.23 246.26 248.26 249.03
249.18 253.09 254.24 256.29
257.10 260.F1 261.07 263.03
263.08 265.20 266.F2 267.F5
270.18 270.F2 273.01 273.23
275.F3 277.F1 279.F20 288.17
289.01 289.08 290.05 290.09
291.03 293.17 293.F2 295.09
297.24 301.F5 305.10 305.19
308.18 312.17 316.13 316.18
316.32 317.02 319.07 321.17
322.03 322.11 323.11 323.26
324.02 327.33 327.36 329.04
329.27 332.20 332.35 334.11
336.16 336.19 336.21 338.24
339.03 339.05 344.16 344.22
347.13 348.10 348.23 352.03
354.22 356.13 357.35 359.11
359.12 360.17 362.05 363.05
364.34 365.07 365.32 366.23
367.25 370.08 370.08 374.01
375.05 378.35 380.11 380.21
380.33 380.35 381.11 381.20
382.05 384.07 384.07 384.08
384.10 384.11 384.11 384.13
385.03 386.04 386.05 386.15
386.17 386.18 388.01 388.07
388.36 389.23 389.35 390.04
390.06 390.10 390.16 390.24
391.11 391.15 391.19 391.29
392.03 392.07 392.10 392.19

392.29 393.07 393.09 393.18
393.27 393.31 394.15 395.12
396.07 396.15 396.16 396.17
396.27 397.29 397.30 397.30
398.02 398.16 398.22 403.21
406.10 408.23 408.24 408.32
415.19 422.28 423.19 426.26
427.27 428.19 432.16 434.30
435.06 435.16 438.14 440.16
440.24 441.18 444.14 449.30
452.16 452.33 454.30 455.04
457.01 459.05 460.36 462.13
462.18 462.33 463.19 464.13
464.27 465.03 467.12 468.29
468.33 472.36 472.36 474.23
475.29 476.25 480.18 480.30
481.16 481.27 484.09 485.17
486.10 491.36 494.35 496.03
496.15 497.27 498.22 503.24
506.36 507.01 507.35 509.18
509.27 510.16 510.17 511.08
513.20 514.34 523.27 530.28
532.02 536.13 537.08 538.13
544.15 549.25 552.01 555.05
555.11 555.12 557.06 557.15
559.35 560.07 560.33 568.28
569.24 578.19 578.27 578.27
581.32 583.12 583.26 584.06
584.07 584.14 586.10 586.19
586.20 586.21 586.28 587.10
587.12 588.04 588.13 593.12
596.25 599.34 599.35 602.35
606.18 607.01 607.14 607.18
607.35 608.17 610.30 615.07
616.23 617.06 617.19 619.14
620.18 621.05 621.33 623.03
623.06 627.36 627.36 627.36
old 199.29 201.08 261.L3
340.15 346.16 350.07 383.05
383.09 390.27 399.13 525.21
Old 016.35 040.01 041.32
085.26 147.05 161.26 169.23
171.02 232.27 242.18 260.14
287.F4 290.F3 305.18 330.13
397.14 422.31 442.08 535.26
569.23 595.18 598.20 600.30
606.29 609.25 623.04
Old 071.10 104.06 104.23
105.18 268.L4 273.L3 346.07
354.10
Oldanelang's 353.31
Oldbally 350.12
Oldboof 609.16
oldboy 377.13
oldbrawn 590.25
oldbuoyant 415.01
oldbyrdes 348.34
oldcant 359.19
oldcoat 451.02
olddaisers 035.17
olde 007.12 017.18 027.08
030.16 352.01
oldeborre 248.17
oldeborre's 415.32
olden 387.18
Olden 307.11
Oldens 219.10
older 030.05 051.30 101.36
135.32 135.33 153.14 162.01
167.05 254.25
Older 105.19
olderly's 125.11
olderman 365.30
oldermen 358.26
olders 513.09 562.20
olderwise 056.20 263.19
oldest 067.25 123.36 129.34
189.23 290.26 472.36
oldfashioned 194.33
oldfellow's 410.04
oldhame 616.04
oldher 337.05
oldivirdual 396.20
Oldloafs 498.07
oldowth 116.15
oldparr 003.17
Oldpatrick 394.12
oldpoetryck 393.10
oldpollocks 418.22
old's 014.21
oldself 627.06
oldshouldered 136.25
Oldsire 105.29
oldsteinsong 231.29
oldsteirs 533.17
oldsters 393.31
oldstrums 362.33
oldtime 390.06 610.35
olduman 593.07
olduman's 593.07
oldun 586.19
oldways 318.19
oldwollday 019.11
oldworld 117.27 431.31 463.16
oldy 469.04 469.05 481.31
ole 024.34 076.09 141.27
303.03
ole 350.06
Ole 453.15
oleaginosity 054.32
O'Leary 043.21
oleas 434.36
Olecasandrum 124.36
Olefoh 353.14
Olegsonder 310.16
Oleosus 161.25
oleotorium 503.05
oles 124.11
olesoleself 329.19
olewidgeon 329.11
oleypoe 427.27
olfa 287.15
olfac 524.30
olfact 341.12
olff 225.09
Olff 225.08
o'liefing 361.18
olim 185.19
Olim 006.23
oliphants 427.22
olive 038.02 395.17 612.10
Olive 227.14 279.F21 525.29
olivehunkered 274.L3
Oliver 211.03 334.15 499.28
oliverian 381.18
Olivers 073.33
olives 335.28
Olives 019.08 138.25
olivetion 160.11
Oliviero 456.10
oll 382.24
olla 092.02
ollas 287.22
ollaves 013.19 499.26
olld 089.29
olled 580.04
Olley's 060.32
ollguns 552.28
ollo 126.08
ollollowed 007.33
Ollover 299.09
olly 236.13
olmond 118.05
Olobobo 622.23
Olofa 045.03
ologies 468.02
olold 117.10
Olona 211.07
O'Looniys 464.07
olorium 410.04
oloroso 588.12
olorum 287.01
olosheen 389.27
oloss 410.04 548.35
O'Loughlin 106.07
O'Loughlins 049.33
olover 056.15
olso 017.33 533.11
olt 437.30
olt 231.05
oltrigger 335.13
olty 469.14
O'Luinn 328.02
olum 153.10
olymp 261.11
Olymp 167.22
olympiading 084.31
olympically 613.28
olympics 625.21
O'Lynn 148.36
olyovyover 350.06
om 078.10 282.29 543.06
594.12 607.22
Om 607.22
O'Mailey 220.11
o'malice 021.21
Omama 586.07
Omar 319.34
O'Mara 040.16 122.16 122.19
O'Mara 270.L2
O'Mario 407.16
omber 164.05
ombre 024.36
Ombrellone 361.19
Ombrilla 492.23
ombushes 007.35
Omebound 560.01
O'Meghisthest 269.19
omegrims 348.05
omen 279.05
Omen 007.08
OMEN 271.R1
omens 328.23
omething 295.28
O'Michael's 600.18
omination 299.05
Ominence 504.20
ominies 453.26
omiss 245.34
omission 121.28
omissions 120.16
omit 042.25 437.02 519.29
Ommes 567.26
omnem 287.27
omnia 269.06
omnianimalism 127.14
omniannual 142.25
Omnibil 337.19
omnibobs 189.19

omniboose 488.11
omniboss 020.08
Omniboss 415.17
omnibox 098.12
omnibus 047.09 081.07 444.02
omnibus 251.29 419.34
omnient 551.15
Omnitudes 276.L2
Omnius 299.09
omniwomen 581.18
omo 212.35
Omo 212.35
O'Mollies 106.34
omominous 543.06
o'monkynous 417.15
O'Morum 460.18
O'Moyly 095.03
ompiter 183.13
omportent 464.07
O'Muirk 622.05
O'mulanchonry 482.12
O'Mulcnory 397.36
omulette 230.07
on on On On ON
Ona 481.07
onage 555.19
onaglibtograbakelly 463.02
onagrass 482.09
Onamassofmancynaves 370.15
onamatterpoetic 468.10
onamuttony 241.16
onangonamed 361.21
onanymous 435.31
onappealed 452.22
onasmuck 386.33
onasum 097.15
onawares 371.26
onbelieving 468.16
onboiassed 110.18
Oncaill's 235.16
once once Once
onceaday 066.03
onceagain 614.11
onced 370.04 424.06
oncemaid 433.28
once-upon-a-four 430.03
onconditionally 326.08
oncontinent 388.05
oncounter 321.28
ond 141.05 146.35
ond 418.10
onder 213.09 324.03
ondown 291.17
ondrawer 266.30
Ond's 505.12
Ondslosby 244.07
Ondt 414.20 415.27 416.03 417.08 417.11 417.24
Ondt 418.12
Ondtship 419.06
ondulate 243.28
one one One One
Oneanother 040.03
onebumper 087.01
onebut 604.25
onecertain 022.17
onecrooned 043.32
oneday 457.19
oneeyed 214.25
onefriend 289.23
onegugulp 613.22
onehorse 221.18
O'Neill 495.27
oneir 486.35
onelike 302.16
onely 372.18
onem 370.34
oner 025.19
onerable 328.13
ones 023.17 029.15 036.21 042.06 052.03 143.18 145.18 148.17 158.21 158.22 166.17 200.29 215.28 224.36 232.33 239.21 259.04 284.17 285.23 300.02 315.06 322.27 328.07 336.07 368.24 378.29 383.16 450.04 454.19 519.11 532.23 563.35 564.09 586.25 594.21 627.07
ones 341.34 418.15
Ones 230.35 278.02
one's 051.04 122.06 125.19 245.35 252.27 334.18 374.02 489.33 564.34 597.27
One's 020.23 248.34 597.16
onesame 092.08
onescuppered 155.28
oneself 114.31
oneselves 607.19
oneship 344.13
onesidemissing 119.31
Onesine 046.20
onesomeness 152.19
onestone 100.26
onesure 021.30
oneth 153.02
onething 561.04
onetime 099.35 314.31
Onetwo 628.05
oneven 475.33
onewinker 174.19
oneydge 506.26
Oneyone's 176.09
oneysucker 417.17
onfell 541.15
ongentilmensky 034.18
ongle 076.28
ongly 223.31
ongoad 097.23
onhapje 257.02
Onheard 017.15
O'Niell 550.31
onimpudent 469.24
onion 406.07
onions 190.05 288.F1 506.22
onkel 467.12
onkring 279.05
onleft 054.11
onliest 384.24
onliness 325.35
only only Only Only
onlymergeant 318.34
Onlyromans 582.33
onme 451.15
Onmen 612.30
onmountof 470.16
onni 162.25
Onon 201.21 201.21
O'Nonhanno's 123.32
onrush 353.12
ons 075.09
onsaturncast 449.02
onsens 162.18
onset 078.25
onsk 562.08
Onslought 329.06
onsway 371.21
onswers 257.35
ont 281.08 281.11
ontesantes 611.28
ontheboards 058.33
onthelongsidethat 612.10
onthergarmenteries 181.29
onthy 361.13
ontime 496.29
onto 009.08 100.11 126.15 155.28 236.34 310.07 359.13 360.29 422.12 463.10
ontophanes 013.16
ontorsed 010.36
ontowhom 369.12
onus 457.12
ONUS 271.R1
onvied 541.16
onward 292.27
onwards 347.14
ony 177.27
Onzel 361.21
oo 260.03
Oo 090.28
O.O. 054.17
ooah 553.04
Oodles 226.35
oodlum 337.29
oofbird 039.21
ooft 427.24
oogling 426.16
oogs 088.17 184.30
oogst 406.36
Oogster 584.09
ooh 149.08
ook 302.31 302.31 302.31
ool 328.01
oom 101.09 376.16
Oom 200.14 578.03
ooman 122.15
oonagh 064.08 064.08
oooom 371.01 371.01
OOOOOOOO 096.22
Oop 437.19
ooridiminy 475.02
Ooridiminy 475.16
Oorlog 077.13
oos 127.18
oose 379.13
ooze 236.21
oozed 087.33 171.30
oozies 283.15
Oozle 332.33
oozy 190.32
op 101.10 161.24 346.27 535.06 565.17
Op. 093.33 (Opus and off)
o.p. 289.07 (our people)
opacities 473.20
opal 220.10
opals 276.16
opanoff 116.32
ope 231.03 239.11 248.11 273.10 358.01 441.06 477.28 598.32
Ope 459.27 535.26 572.10
oped 020.17
open 041.27 054.28 063.32 069.24 085.09 098.04 120.28 129.20 133.18 137.19 145.27 147.29 199.03 219.03 235.20 236.35 240.29 258.12 277.F1 316.32 333.01 344.17 410.22

425.30 431.07 437.20 437.26 461.26 529.27 540.02 544.03 551.27 562.11 564.36 586.17 604.06 613.30 623.07
Open 036.27 321.14 442.31
Open 427.05
Openair 045.16
Opendoor 071.13
openear 425.16
opened 070.31 082.05 519.01
Opened 420.26
opening 083.16 144.11 258.31 355.23 488.27
Opening 105.24
openly 077.03 543.10
opennine 618.24
openwide 171.24
operahouse 179.35
operated 510.21 539.21 544.22
operating 247.08
operation 232.09
operatops 532.35
opering 395.23
operoar 442.34
opes 254.22 302.02
opheld 586.26
Ophelia's 105.18
O'Phelim's 072.04
ophis 289.07
Ophiuchus 494.09
Opian 448.18
opifex 185.14
Opima 273.02
opine 050.14
opinion 058.27 177.15 420.02 529.11 538.05 563.25
opinions 421.26
oplooked 542.15
opop 565.20
Opop 565.20
oppedemics 539.36
oppelong 315.32
oppen 342.26
oppersite 581.19
oppidumic 497.15
Opportunity 028.23
opposed 488.11
opposite 034.19 134.09 220.23 488.09 488.10 564.14
oppositely 082.01
opposites 092.08
opposition 079.05
Oppositional 305.L1
Opprimor's 273.02
opprobrious 172.34
opprobro 188.27
Opr 417.01 417.02
O'Prayins 291.10
ops 425.30
opsits 324.14
opslo 553.32
Opsy 147.13
opt 546.22
opten 349.31
opter 354.23
optical 179.01
optimately 150.01
optimominous 613.28
Optimus 153.17
option 139.02
optophone 013.16
O'Puckins 376.01
opulence 078.02 098.12
opulent 581.11
opulose 488.35
O'Purcell 187.18
Opus 073.15
Opvarts 317.16
or or Or Or
or 482.04
Or 404.30 (R)
Or 548.28
orable 545.12
oracular 115.24
orafferteed 345.25
oragel 552.25
oragious 143.25
oral 036.09 302.22
o'ralereality 289.04
orally 420.03
Oralmus 447.29
Oram 211.12
Oran 390.10
O'Rangans 030.01
orange 043.08 059.08 069.35 140.19 405.33 495.09 556.11
Orange 063.23 135.12 374.31 498.08
orangeboat 479.31
oranged 528.05
orangeflavoured 111.34
orangeman 023.01
orangepeel 110.29
orangepeelers 522.16
orangeray 246.26
orangery 110.27 477.36 478.01
oranges 003.23
orangetawneymen 361.24
orangey 488.05
orangogran 396.16
orangotangos 019.05
orangultonia 343.01
Orani 049.19
Orania 504.24
orankastank 344.26
O'Rann 372.32
Orara 214.06
O'Rarelys 354.14
oras 186.31
Orasmus 155.33
orational 432.07
orations 270.03 620.24
orb 140.07 263.28
orbal 601.06
orbe 230.08
Orbe 214.06
orbis 096.33
orbit 311.02
Orbiter 257.35
orbits 481.20 583.02
orbs 598.28
Orca 494.06
orchafts 133.30
orchard 453.29 585.29
Orchards 264.25
orchid 530.25
orchid 530.24
Orchid 421.02
orchidectural 165.09
orchids 059.08
orchistruss 128.26
Orcotron 468.36
ord 378.13
order 009.23 012.25 045.09 048.22 076.18 086.29 089.35 096.27 099.20 121.13 156.01 156.01 165.17 167.33 187.11 255.17 277.19 296.11 337.35 337.35 337.35 338.01 338.01 381.02 385.23 409.32 447.25 447.26 456.13 486.10 511.16 529.13 530.05 548.36 587.29 596.09 613.14 614.09
order 338.06
Order 337.35 338.01 616.33
ordered 026.22 181.09 574.34
orders 113.23 140.31 314.02 367.21 411.02 447.25 448.29 492.19 605.15
orders 349.20
Orders 221.35
order's 277.20
ordilawn 498.14
ordinailed 288.06
ordinal 185.10
ordinarily 190.11
ordinary 034.13 064.30 077.35 192.14 573.24 574.15
Ordinary 559.01
ORDINATION 271.R1
ordnance 073.02
ordnands 288.16
ordo 512.36
Ordovices 051.29
Ordovico 215.23
ordurd 023.04
ordure 344.17
ore 069.08 185.33 197.28 201.04 311.05 445.34 538.16
Ore 018.15
orefice 414.27
orefices 357.01
orege 132.29
oreillental 357.18
oreilles 270.16
O'Reilly 044.14 044.24 616.01
O'Reilly's 071.25
oreils 482.04
orel 310.27
Orel 105.11 105.11
oreland 352.09
Oreland 359.26
Orelli 243.34
orelode 097.31
Oremunds 105.02
oremus 398.12
Oremus 489.06
O'Remus 122.09
orenore 359.03
orerotundity 055.36
ores 239.12 497.16
Orexes 305.L1
orf 463.03
orfishfellows' 056.35
organ 082.19 439.36
Organ 105.16
organic 599.15
organisation 551.18
organs 315.25
orgias 538.11
Orgiasts 254.03
orgibald 065.03
orhowwhen 394.29
oriel 552.27 609.20
orielising 613.15
orience 418.29
orient 450.02
orients 343.01
origen 161.08

origin 056.18 120.29 140.09 504.28
original 051.03 110.22 114.21 123.31 239.02 263.27
originally 150.13 482.32 575.05
originating 111.09
origins 579.35
orileys 467.29
Orimis 418.05
orioled 310.27
Oriolopos 107.14
Orion 254.03
Orionis 185.24
oriorts 069.09
orison 235.06
orisons 191.09 552.07
oriuolate 035.11
orkan 513.08
orland 074.05
Orlbrdsz 105.11
orlog 154.23
orlop 232.34
orm 054.14
Ormepierre 614.03
ormolus 467.35
ormonde 519.05
ormuzd 163.02 425.28
ornamental 098.20
ornaments 183.16
ornates 165.16
ornery 109.03
Ornery 533.34
Ornery's 144.09
O'Roarke 099.33
orofaces 356.06
orologium 410.04
Oronoko 214.10
Oropos 513.21
Orops 343.10
oround 386.35
Orp 494.22
orpentings 492.30
orphalines 595.14
orphan 313.21
orphans 215.28 500.10
orra 006.13
orranged 203.27
Ors 299.L2
orse 373.16
orseriders 581.19
orses 067.05
orso 298.21
ortchert 613.30
orther 397.34 593.11
Orther 510.30
orthodox 390.27 573.06
Orthodox 307.18
orthophonethics 038.36
Orthor 009.05
orthough 426.18
Ortovito 513.17
orts 069.09 599.01
orussheying 347.31
Orwin 397.06
O'Ryan's 185.25
o'ryely 498.19
O'Ryne 372.32
os 053.04 378.26 408.19 547.24
Os 054.17
osa 416.16
Osbornes 429.22
Oscan 419.24
oscar 066.36 384.22
Oscar 046.20 068.11
Oscarshal's 536.21
Oscarvaughther 326.07
oscasleep 476.22
osco 230.06
oscula 122.21
Oscur 602.23
osghirs 241.32
O'Shame 182.30
O'Shaun 211.31
O'Shea 182.30
Oshean 123.25
O'Sheen 223.18
O'Shem 421.25
o'shouker 415.06
osi 416.16
osiery 076.27 198.24
osion 326.18
Osirises 493.28
oska 511.20
osker 326.16
o'skirt 335.09
Osler 317.16
Osman 235.06
Osmund 088.23 514.02
oso 203.20
O' Somebody 088.14
O'Sorgmann 578.11
Ospices 071.13
Osro 340.17
ossas 128.36
Ossean 139.22
Osseania 593.05
osseletion 279.04
Ossian 385.36
ossicles 453.14
osstheology 341.28
ost 595.01
Ostbys 595.01
Ostelinda 445.32
ostenditur 287.21
ostensible 381.08
ostensibly 508.05
ostentatiously 166.09
Ostenton 135.25
Osterich 070.01 136.15
Osthern 604.26
Ostia 371.09 371.09
Ostiak 162.15
ostiary 437.15
Osti-Fosti 048.19
Ostman 131.07
Ostmannstown 243.26
Ostmanorum 543.16
ostmen's 062.05
ostralian 488.20
O'Strap 070.12
ostrogothic 263.10
Ostrogothic 120.22
Ostrov 136.08
ostrovgods 289.16
ostscent 502.06
osturs 317.12
osure 234.13
o.s.v. 221.09 310.17 (og så videre)
ot 365.31
o't 037.36
Ota 493.19
otay 262.L2
Otem 224.01
other 004.34 039.12 040.27 049.11 049.12 060.24 061.24 064.32 066.04 067.35 068.02 070.08 076.15 078.15 081.22 082.01 082.29 084.04 085.19 085.29 090.21 091.09 091.25 095.11 109.34 109.36 113.23 114.06 115.11 119.25 125.05 136.20 144.07 147.28 148.19 150.22 155.12 157.01 160.26 162.24 164.05 167.11 174.01 177.32 177.32 182.06 188.11 189.07 191.13 191.14 191.24 193.23 220.16 247.25 248.24 249.17 252.14 253.15 255.10 268.08 270.11 276.03 277.05 283.06 288.21 290.23 316.08 361.29 362.29 367.23 374.31 374.35 381.36 384.13 395.04 404.34 404.36 408.17 408.25 411.07 412.16 413.19 425.32 427.34 428.22 436.17 436.24 437.29 446.20 447.26 451.29 461.26 476.06 476.18 484.12 486.11 488.06 489.34 490.35 501.26 503.09 511.10 514.04 516.32 517.03 518.05 522.06 522.36 532.05 536.27 543.26 544.02 544.05 558.07 561.06 561.06 562.12 562.22 563.01 563.10 564.13 577.27 586.33 598.11 603.20 606.15 609.20 611.28 612.01 617.04 617.30 620.25 627.29
other 345.34
Other 241.23 300.20
Other 342.24
otherchurch's 546.21
otherdogs 312.32
othered 613.14
Otherman 419.25
otherman's 151.35
others 005.28 038.13 044.11 051.10 078.34 108.17 108.36 110.20 113.28 114.04 178.11 180.03 183.03 191.05 357.10 357.16 371.14 386.14 398.25 430.18 507.34 554.02 597.17 626.19
Others 044.18 044.18 585.35
other's 060.35 061.21 276.01 567.27
othersites 228.31
otherso 301.14
othertimes 593.08
otherwales 040.10
otherwards 280.26
Otherways 005.22
otherwise 084.24 118.27 146.28 253.05 405.19 411.04 439.01 525.11 547.03 596.25
Otherwise 413.30
Otherwised 225.05
otherworld 385.04
otho 132.06
othour 364.24
otion 309.12
otiumic 489.29
otological 310.21
O'Toole 433.05 557.07
o'toolers 005.03
Otooles 138.26
ottawark 544.21

otter 121.10 245.05
Otters 214.12
otther 275.09 450.03
Otto 051.12 067.17 485.03
ottoman 451.30
ottomanic 263.10
ottomantic 284.27
ottorly 229.35
Otulass 179.12
O'Tuli 228.25
ou 081.29
Où 307.F8
oubworn 597.18
ouchyotchy 344.10
oud 207.26 245.36 586.26
oudchd 354.20
Ouer 481.20
Ouerlord's 541.09
ough 276.10
Ough 276.09
ought ought
Ouhr 530.36
oui 286.30
Ouida 221.28
ouija 532.18 532.18
ouis 184.02
ouishguss 326.05
οὐκ 269.L2
oukosouso 345.24
oukraydoubray 340.01
ould 087.06 117.30 381.21 536.09
Ould 329.33
ouldmouldy 382.15
ouldstrow 617.16
ounce 451.02
ounceworth 288.F1
ounckel 101.09
our our Our Our OUR
oura 599.05
ouragan 504.14
Ouraganisations 086.21
ourangoontangues 541.34
Ourang's 096.23
Ourania 185.31
ourdeaned 291.F4
ourder 089.25
oure 215.27
ourest 514.36
Ourguile 071.19
ourherenow 394.34
ourish 498.01
Ourishman 463.25
ourland's 288.13
ourloud's 353.16
ourly 060.31
ourmenial 321.23
ourn 021.12
ournhisn 442.30
ours 017.19 035.28 067.03 077.26 129.03 147.34 161.05 165.09 238.13 239.14 270.22 277.F7 375.09 378.01 398.19 427.12 467.23 472.29 489.05 489.07 566.32 582.15 600.02 608.35 628.08
ourself 261.07
ourselfsake 617.06
ourselves 118.34 118.34 119.08 122.01 235.15 398.08 431.36 432.10 508.26 576.13 582.18 622.21
Ourselves 623.28
oursforownly 235.27
oursouls 623.28
ourtales 224.08
ourth 018.04
ourthe 208.03
ouryour 446.16
ous 114.23
Ous 538.26
ouse 201.04
ouses 007.05
oust 084.29 156.32
Ousterholm 139.33
ousterlists 009.28
Ousterrike 462.29
oustman 310.30
ousts 427.23
out out Out Out
outa 289.10
outandin 050.05
outandouts 509.33
outathat 477.10
outback's 321.08
outblacks 221.22
outbreak 160.35
outbreighten 537.11
outbroke 092.02
outcast 534.34
Outcaste 237.21
Outcasts 307.25
outching 439.22
outcome 280.07
outdoor 110.30 579.12
outdoors 385.27
outed 053.21
outer 091.01 109.08 150.35 173.10 245.06 378.33 509.29
Outer 072.21 297.07
outerly 485.25
outermost 278.23
outerrand 113.08
outers 482.18
outflash 210.32
outgate 337.10
outgift 187.10
outgoing 294.L1
outharrods 127.11
outher 222.28 285.22
outhired 359.03
outhue 182.08
outing 135.30
outings 141.23 221.04 538.09
Outis 493.24
outlander 057.32
Outlawrie 550.31
outlex 169.03
outlier 097.05
outlined 007.20
outlook 162.36 324.33 544.29
outlusts 444.25
outmost 424.08
outnullused 161.36
outofman 019.17
outofwork 191.11
outozone 542.07
Outpassed 489.21
outpriams 131.08
outpuffs 038.30
outraciously 285.02
outrage 048.04
Outrage 602.25
outraged 339.28 369.01
Outragedy 425.24
outrager's 434.04
outrages 061.31
outratted 097.02
outraved 062.02
outreachesly 541.08
outs 031.32 239.16 320.26 354.30
outsends 505.06
outset 505.13
outsewed 507.07
outshriek 141.13
outside 070.20 073.05 079.07 127.03 135.32 456.17 521.28 533.05 557.36 574.34 578.01
Outsider 610.18
outsiders 141.10
outsider's 442.23
outsize 333.20
outsizinned 374.14
outskirts 558.36
Outstamp 302.28
outstanding 100.21 530.08
Outstanding 106.35
outstarching 033.08
outstretcheds 600.18
outstripperous 232.28
outturned 091.16
outumn 178.30
outwalls 262.24
outwardly 544.19
outwashed 013.06
outworn 013.10
ouveralls 085.30
ouverleaved 448.36
ouze 474.09
ouzel 035.16 546.14
ov 199.29 346.21
ova 525.16
oval 152.20 435.18 458.36 470.30
ovalled 584.19
ovally 144.10
ovas 423.04
ovasleep 397.16
ove 154.35
oven 070.30 151.14 239.18
ovenfor 395.05
ovenly 603.07
over over Over Over OVER
overabroad 066.07
overagait 051.13
overall 567.27
overalls 004.31 251.13 392.18 614.11
overawall 051.12
overawes 135.09
overblaseed 237.19
overborder 025.10
overcarefully 122.22
overcast 364.33
overcautelousness 111.20
overclothes 064.02
overclused 157.12
overcrowded 543.22
overdoing 165.03
overdrave 539.29
Overdrawn 419.32
overdress 384.31
overdressed 441.05
overed 057.30
overflauwing 397.01
overflow 042.20 174.20
overgestern 407.30
overgiven 077.27

overgoat 035.13
overgrind 128.08
overground 494.24
overgrown 006.31 036.18 056.12
overhawl 315.16
overheard 038.27
overhinduce 289.06
Overhoved 383.15
overhowe 365.11
overinsured 333.06
overking 452.27
overland 547.16
overlasting 499.02
overlisting 503.30
overlistingness 355.05
overlive 316.14
overload 193.01
overlooking 061.04
overlord 097.24 355.25
Overlord 565.12
overlorded 472.30
overlusting 222.30
Overman 302.L1
overnight 136.27 378.11
overopposides 382.16
overpast 151.22
overpowered 426.09
overraskelled 324.13
overreaching 110.05
o'verse 288.01
oversear 328.33
overseas 130.33
overseen 029.19
overseer 493.30 550.34
oversense 378.06
Overset 447.28
overshirt 404.27
oversire 493.31
overspat 329.12
overspoiled 038.25
overstand 444.30
overstep 016.02
overt 039.15
overthepoise 206.24
overthepoise 277.L6
overthere 479.01
overthirties 494.33
overthrew 356.02
overthrewer 064.14
overthrown 504.32
overtime 137.15 571.36
overtrow 326.22
overtspeaking 486.08
overtupped 547.29
Overture 407.10
overtures 414.24 438.33
overus 316.21
Overwayed 421.07
overwhelmed 381.17
Overwhere 594.25
overwide 228.08
oves 184.29 393.24
ovful 361.13
Ovid 306.L2
ovidently 166.11
oving 178.33
ovipository 415.33
Ovlergroamlius 322.34
Ovoca 203.15
ovocal 466.35
Ovocation 305.28
Ovocnas 537.06
ow 052.34 173.24
Ow 203.14
O.W. 535.29 (Old Whitehowth)
owe 058.22 183.15 299.F3
357.09 363.16 364.27 421.08
oweand 464.01
owed 561.05 600.28
Owel 549.34
owelglass 408.24
owen 202.06 223.13 601.03
Owen 066.24
owenglass 101.29
Owenmore's 475.07
Owens 294.21 574.01 574.04
Ower 206.27
owes 042.14 458.36
owfally 329.28
owing 381.01 456.29 520.07
owl 006.29 037.07 107.22 489.36
owld 230.03 331.19 593.20
621.11 624.27
owldfrow 486.06
owledclock 449.24
owlers 021.29
Owlets' 019.09
owlglassy 208.09
Owllaugh 532.08
owls 120.20
Owl's 071.31
owlseller 467.15
owlwise 078.30
own 007.21 012.31 019.36
033.04 039.18 039.26 041.25
051.21 053.33 059.23 063.31
065.07 068.10 079.08 079.13
100.28 108.21 110.01 112.07
115.08 119.26 122.06 126.09
126.22 128.26 129.31 132.34
140.29 142.22 148.25 150.19
150.36 154.34 159.24 159.29
159.36 164.13 166.24 166.35
168.06 181.14 181.16 185.03
185.07 185.11 185.13 185.36
186.03 188.17 189.31 192.18
197.05 206.22 215.10 224.33
228.26 228.27 243.19 276.01
287.30 289.16 289.23 292.19
300.04 306.F5 313.32 315.13
322.12 329.03 334.18 336.36
337.09 355.14 368.12 376.27
378.27 381.18 408.35 421.28
422.20 422.23 428.19 428.21
442.05 445.11 446.19 450.08
457.35 459.19 464.32 466.23
470.28 472.04 473.18 480.22
481.27 490.17 506.01 515.29
517.35 518.06 526.34 530.30
533.31 537.17 539.13 553.18
568.18 575.20 578.13 579.18
580.01 582.27 583.08 587.34
588.01 605.11 608.08 623.07
627.06
own 150.27 399.17
ownconsciously 300.25
owned 140.29 205.36 252.28
528.07
Owned 613.36
owneirist 397.02
owner 048.20 242.32
owners 092.03
Ownes 421.08
ownest 627.30
ownhouse 151.01
owning 229.29 484.03
owning 354.11
ownkind 465.31
owns 138.18 214.33
335.29 524.14
544.26
own's 569.13
owntown 523.12
owreglias 256.03
owrithy 231.13
owther 053.12
oxagiants 067.07
Oxatown 288.11
oxbelled 618.34
oxe 623.34
oxers 291.20
oxesother 252.16
oxeter 051.07
oxeyed 480.10
oxgangs 032.27
oxhide 127.26
oxhousehumper 107.34
Oxman 015.06 132.17
oxmanstongue 355.24
Oxmanstown 047.22
Oxmanswold 073.28
oxmaster 596.18
oxmaul 317.16
oxmen's 088.28
oxon 467.31
oxsight 392.27
oxtail 133.14
Oxthievious 271.05
oxtrabeeforeness 419.04
oxus 197.17
oxyggent 281.24
oxygon 284.L2
Oy 485.13
oye 426.16
Oye 018.16
oyeglances 405.20
Oyeh 085.31 085.31
oyes 419.26
Oyes 604.22
Oyeses 604.22
Oyesesyeses 604.22
Oyessoyess 488.19
oyir 553.04 553.04
553.04
Oylrubber 069.36
oyne 310.30
oyster 049.26 385.01
Oyster 407.08
oysterette 247.36
oysterface 207.19
oysters 179.35 479.06
oystrygods 004.01
oz 243.12
ozeone 241.19

P 284.F4 (P for shift)
468.03 (P? F?)
492.03 (P flat)
P. 265.F5 (P. Shuter)
300.15 (P. Kevin)
508.23 (P. and Q.)
pa 478.23
Pa 095.17
Paa 298.01
paaralone 236.09 236.10
Paas 550.13
Paatryk 425.28
pac 283.02
Pacata 275.04

pace 030.19 154.16 272.24 329.28 361.04 547.16 583.07 612.03
pace 076.02 513.30
paces 072.34 121.05 622.13
pacifettes 470.36
pacific 085.07
Pacific 502.11
pacis 549.07
pack 025.19 030.19 076.20 194.08 201.31 227.15 269.F2 278.13 323.28 437.20 458.35 476.17 480.31
Pack 350.17
Packen 356.24
Packenham's 039.17
packet 211.09 507.28
packetboat 131.02 136.20
packetshape 471.25
packing 068.16
packnumbers 286.17
packt 007.17
pacnincstricken 599.28
Paco 286.L1
pact 576.06
pacts 325.20 614.07
pacts' 011.12
pad 368.07 423.25
Pad 333.04
padapodopudupedding 599.08
padar 358.20
padbun 531.17
padder 621.21
padderjagmartin 086.02
Paddeus 326.03
paddies 325.07
paddin 311.32
padding 405.34
paddish 031.24
Paddishaw 131.08
paddle 297.F5 486.09
paddled 430.08
paddlewicking 086.17
Paddley 325.23
paddock 396.08
paddocks 341.21
Paddrock 611.02
paddy 231.03
Paddy 008.06 019.15 254.10 351.16
Paddybanners 084.13
Paddybarke's 378.36
paddybird 256.26
paddycoats 407.36
paddyflaherty 520.30
paddygoeasy 123.16
Paddyouare 463.04
paddypalace 552.23
paddypatched 596.31
paddyplanters 025.19
paddystool 130.06
padham 492.23
Padma 598.12
padouasoys 059.01
padre 439.31 612.16
Padre 050.19 184.35
padredges 478.34
padre's 060.30
pads 097.12 584.19
paff 341.16
Paff 012.11
pagan 079.14 451.27
Pagan 447.22
paganelles 512.16
paganinism 050.15
pagans 549.07
pagany 506.28
pagar 464.11
page 108.31 108.35 111.21 115.03 121.03 122.23 180.18 182.05 270.25 286.10 289.25 397.30 513.27 553.01 624.04
pageans 597.05
Pageant 221.18
pageantfiller 338.27
pageantmaster 237.13 568.35
pageantries 549.33
pageboy 245.04
pages 013.29 013.29 057.31 116.05 236.04
Pagets 622.27
pagne 344.22
pagoda 228.10 466.19 466.21
pah 034.08 173.26 296.28
paid 277.24 330.18 586.16
pail 197.11
pailleté 149.26
pain 088.30 270.22 307.F6
Pain 192.23
painapple 167.15 246.29
pained 108.06
paineth 247.25 356.24
painful 183.21 187.03
painfully 511.26
painfully 354.04
painlessly 049.23
pains 065.03 456.34
paint 162.17 230.36 455.05 459.05 613.24
paintbox 207.10
painted 121.26 139.30 248.16 411.24
Painter 085.05
painters 453.10
paintings 095.32
paints 113.17 617.35
pair 010.36 022.18 034.19 079.21 081.33 094.16 137.26 148.29 181.28 182.27 187.16 208.06 211.11 230.30 250.08 275.15 291.21 295.27 320.36 329.02 362.26 370.05 382.23 392.29 395.07 396.11 406.04 408.27 409.21 412.33 414.23 430.26 430.26 433.25 434.30 457.13 502.13 563.31 578.09 588.09
Pair 107.06
pairamere 583.12
pairanymphs 548.02
Pairaskivvymenassed 492.06
pairc 324.07
pairfact 404.32
pairk 373.20
pairless 092.12
pairofhids 342.26
pairs 028.18 052.02 229.18 602.35
pair's 334.15
pairsadrawsing 379.04
pairsecluded 503.29
Paisdinernes 100.06
paisibles 281.11
paisibly 014.30
paisley 497.30
Paisy 471.01
pal 113.20 177.20 264.03 318.13 451.23 462.18 528.18
palace 275.15 403.16
Palace 378.19
paladays 069.10 615.25
paladin 073.35
palam 363.18
palashe 246.14
palast 551.01
palastered 543.10
palate 084.22
palatin 596.25
palatine 444.36
palce 299.14
pale 026.02 092.26 136.36 202.27 209.23 269.08 332.11 451.25 539.26 563.11 563.15
Pale 128.13 618.07
paleale 296.26
paled 067.35
palegrim 483.33
paleographers 121.11
paleologic 073.01
paleoparisien 151.09
palers 323.30
pales 143.24
Pales 289.09
palesmen 042.34
palestrine 407.14
palfrey 566.08
palfrycraft 120.25
Pa-li-di 345.23
palignol 338.21
palimpsests 182.02
paling 472.22
palinode 374.07
palisades 539.26
pall 013.23 588.23
Pall 349.23
pallet 248.08
palling 202.11
palliumed 152.24
palls 143.24 284.10
pallups 339.34
pallyass 380.25 495.15
pallyollogass 555.11
palm 020.04 062.09 180.21 235.17 318.17 619.26
palmassing 457.30
palmer 221.13
Palmer 254.10
palmer's 539.08
Palmerstown 383.06
palming 514.20
palmost 470.17
palms 227.19 384.18 411.15
palms 354.20
palmspread 365.31
palmsweat 025.15
palmtailed 121.10
Palmwine 428.01
palmy 112.26 136.02
palmyways 117.16
paloola 475.02
Paloola 475.14
palpably 111.35 384.29
palpabrows 394.23
palpitating 050.21
palposes 348.24
palpruy 154.15
pals 065.08 523.22
palseyputred 350.17
palships 587.18

parambolator 490.03
paramilintary 338.20
paramount 380.12
parapangle 190.32
parapets 266.05
paraphe 123.05
parapilagian 387.05
parapolylogic 474.05
parapotacarry's 492.19
para's 098.14
parasama 596.24
parasangs 586.27
paraseuls 315.19
parasites 493.13
Paraskivee 192.21
parasol 568.07
Parasol 525.16
parasoliloquisingly 063.20
parasollieras 361.19
paratonnerwetter 585.11
paravis 435.18
parawag 423.03
parcel 062.29 369.34
parcels 444.31
parcequeue 151.10
parched 153.10
parchels' 364.07
parching 078.22
parchment 364.18 395.04
parciful 545.28
parco 201.02
pard 483.14
pardee 452.28
pardon 146.26 422.10 517.08 584.36 615.23
pardon 354.04
Pardon 342.10
pardonable 119.33
pardone 145.23
pardoned 270.F3
Pardonell 553.12
pardonership 575.28
pardoning 113.25
pardonnez 058.27
pardonnez-leur 058.26
pardons 570.25
pardonsky 303.01
pardoosled 331.33
pardun 083.29
parent 265.22 306.03 480.07 496.33
parentage 115.31
parently 014.16
parents 052.35 441.10 562.31 624.33
parents' 589.03
Parfaitly 090.19
parfect 242.23
Parfey 501.10
Pariah 193.32
paridicynical 610.14
parik 096.03
parilegs 284.02
Parimiknie 194.28
Paris 307.F3 453.25 464.17
parises 155.17
parish 041.32 091.23 475.22 525.17 543.27 625.10
Parish 093.14 192.08 199.08
parishclerks 312.36
parishlife 589.22
Parishmoslattary 350.27
Parisienne's 102.13
Parisise 230.13
parisites 131.09 418.01
park 003.22 033.27 035.08 060.25 134.17 136.34 138.05 140.10 196.11 364.16 371.13 433.24 449.31 449.32 506.03 512.28 520.01 540.34 558.15 564.08 564.08 564.11 564.35 571.03
Park 080.06 085.10 096.10 369.10 370.07 421.06 461.10 534.12 610.34 624.15
Park 383.07
parked 091.07 454.34
parker 138.13
Parkes 497.18 576.29
Parkes 354.14
parkies 587.27
parkiest 502.24
Parkland 335.07
parks 110.10 116.17 242.10 606.24
park's 020.20 583.24
parkside 394.27
parlament 189.34
parlements 252.05
parler 346.18
parles 467.29
parley 288.F6 518.12
Parley 276.F4
parleyglutton 240.27
parleysprig 365.32
parliamentary 059.29 151.04
Parliamentary 306.29
parlour 058.36
parlourmade 432.24
Parlourmaids 104.21
parlourmen 392.35
parlous 454.20
Parme 102.26
parn 177.31 177.34 293.01
parnella 173.11
Parnellites 307.14
parochial 186.20
parodies 296.07
parody's 011.09
Parolas 565.28
parole 180.36 246.16
Paronama 502.36
paroply 530.16
paroqial 029.20
parparaparnelligoes 303.11
parr 036.06 170.28 205.02
Parr 081.22
parriage 458.04
parricombating 597.17
parridge 281.L4
parring 584.09
Parrio 484.32
Parrish's 432.01
parritch 074.13
Parrot 063.23
parrotbook 275.L4
parroteyes 493.05
parrots 534.28
parrotsprate's 334.01
parruchially 533.28
parry 252.04 332.07
parrylewis 352.14
parryshoots 237.02
parse 044.14 204.01
parsecs 152.35
parsed 270.04
Parsee 296.F1 495.03
parsenaps 256.20
parses 467.29
parshes 625.20
parsley 430.29 612.07
parsnip 045.08
parson 011.23 063.11 420.24 532.19 617.25
Parson 299.31
parsonal 174.24
parsonfired 589.24
parsonifier 378.24
parson's 479.11
parssed 373.33
Parsuralia 353.24
part 004.29 019.01 024.25 055.34 058.03 065.24 071.05 082.15 083.26 087.14 112.17 118.23 130.32 135.28 201.26 215.05 222.29 253.11 331.05 365.10 382.09 389.34 393.20 421.28 427.27 440.32 445.20 446.15 450.26 454.01 461.14 507.21 537.25 539.16 546.30 547.10 563.25 577.10 590.16 605.26 611.17 611.18 625.21 627.07
part 175.07
Part 390.33 494.13
PART 281.R1
partaking 484.01
parted 147.30 371.07 371.20 371.32 372.26 373.10 390.22 390.28 505.23 563.32 541.33 625.31
Parteen-a-lax 100.13
parter 311.34
parterre 033.12
parth 015.30
Parthalonians 381.05
Parthenopea 494.11
partial 034.26 149.09 360.02
partially 220.28 564.03
partial's 445.08
participle 269.30 467.25
Partick 378.18
particular 038.18 062.29 164.26 381.31 412.24 444.33 501.16 523.21
PARTICULAR 260.R3
particularised 574.18
particularist 043.12
particularly 033.32 066.07 362.34 443.20 533.01 543.32 617.10
particulars 055.32
parties 082.08 197.19 243.13 436.24
partifesswise 546.07
parting 087.01 203.24 369.33 468.27 486.07
Parting's 454.02
Partiprise 419.01
partisans 004.03
partition 475.25
partitional 264.22
partitioned 132.33
Partlet 124.24
partly 061.32 111.34 422.23 543.35 559.22
partner 414.23 574.16 575.02
partners 142.08 607.16
partnership 123.16
partnick 478.26

partridge's 344.07
parts 040.09 048.13 049.21 084.18 101.11 108.32 109.28 173.35 219.07 245.06 283.08 297.22 307.F7 324.32 358.12 380.23 434.08 474.19 489.15 495.29 540.06 566.32
Partsymasters 186.36
parturience 166.27
party 031.02 091.15 116.09 127.20 133.12 144.06 190.15 240.02 243.04 309.06 359.15 413.16 415.30 434.01 435.07 441.30 447.19 523.28 559.05 587.30 589.08
Party 066.17 161.26
partying 068.04
partyng 372.30
partywall 108.01
parva 287.21
parvulam 007.23
Parysis 155.16
parzel 619.05
pas 478.20
pas 192.14 272.L1
Pas 256.08
Pas 106.13 274.L2 479.29
pa's 003.13 236.31
Pa's 136.24
pasch 594.17
paschal 128.34
pascol's 302.03
pascua 262.F4
pashes 269.27
pasht 096.20 516.26
pasphault 581.30
pasqualines 432.30
pass 007.07 013.32 030.12 054.09 077.36 080.18 081.15 094.32 120.26 186.06 191.24 192.35 213.27 224.15 233.19 237.33 266.07 279.F06 296.F2 340.10 377.30 379.32 384.15 393.02 395.23 397.22 421.26 422.03 449.08 458.12 463.29 507.24 527.16 550.16 551.33 556.26 577.23 581.12 603.12 610.24 610.26 615.22 625.06 628.12
Pass 334.35 373.31 531.36 535.25 553.05
passabed 600.08
passable 602.34
passably 161.21
passage 048.23 251.25 262.02 301.07 462.35 473.15
paſs'd 238.08
passdoor 146.36
passe 017.02 207.14
Passe 532.33
passed 040.17 049.23 133.25 223.17 231.26 320.34 454.31 499.14 528.02 580.29 610.24
passencore 003.04
passent 324.19
passer 294.15
passes 486.33
passession 198.17
passibility 189.06
passim 561.11
passim 123.22 548.21
passims 149.34
passing 028.18 125.08 145.22 277.19 313.16 358.35 385.04 427.18 449.17 470.26 524.20 604.34 608.33 608.33 608.34 627.34
passing 348.32
Passing 608.33
passinggeering 372.20
passings 563.36
passioflower 459.35
passiom 356.32
passion 032.32 115.13 148.09 189.17 394.25
passionate 457.06
passionpallid 109.10
passionpanting 394.36
passions 076.03 142.17
passive 072.19 269.28 523.09
Passive 301.L3
passivism 137.33
Passivucant 553.15
passkey 008.08
passkeys 460.02
passmore 197.17
passon 039.23
passport 025.05
passthecupper 330.09
password 262.07 441.36
past 003.01 011.30 048.15 081.08 099.05 110.31 114.29 115.32 120.28 145.13 170.08 179.21 197.24 212.19 263.17 266.11 275.20 276.04 307.F6 348.06 356.33 389.17 389.19 390.01 407.32 412.22 420.32 438.11 446.22 467.25 472.18 473.24 484.01 496.35 533.03 536.28 539.08 577.26 583.30 584.24 587.02 615.01
past 340.14 346.14 355.03
Past 221.19 594.26
Past 071.36
PAST 272.R1
pastcast 314.26
paste 413.34
Paster 329.30
pastime 052.01
Pastimes 263.17
pastipreaching 292.09
pastor 014.32 185.04
Pastor 184.34
pastry 412.20
pastryart's 531.11
pastured 062.12
pastures 141.10
pastureuration 356.24
pasty 197.27
pat 058.23 191.24 249.18 490.10 563.07 596.02
Pat 027.27 051.24 058.32 094.01 326.04 361.07 479.12
Pat 176.17
Patagoreyan 310.32
patapet 461.35
patata 495.10
Patatapadatback 289.F3
Patatapapaveri's 172.01
patates 595.11
Patathicus 602.27
patch 083.26 251.26 253.24 316.23 452.28 488.30 559.25
Patch 174.27 223.17
Patchbox 562.14
patcher 515.35
patches 051.18 085.34 200.04
patching 623.31
patchpurple 111.02
Patch's 063.05
patchy 379.09
pate 462.35
Pate-by-the-Neva 205.34
patenly 253.20
patent 108.23 165.31 310.03 419.19 463.18
pater 386.13 507.31
Pater 496.22
pateramater 560.28
paternoster 031.07
Patersen's 421.01
Paterson 529.30
patfella 611.27
path 080.30 311.14 432.28 469.09 478.13
path 294.L1
pathetic 421.33
pathetically 100.30
Patholic 611.07 611.10 611.24
pathoricks 027.02
pathos 164.23
pathways 244.27
patience 108.08 108.08 108.10 108.13 123.05 567.02
patient 585.08
Patientia 154.28
patimur 100.18
Patkinses 008.06
patly 076.12 410.24
patmost 526.18
Patomkin 290.F7
patpun 301.13
patrarc 269.24
patrecknocksters 081.28
Patria 229.13
Patriack 408.32
patriarch 581.05
patriarchal 075.14
Patrice 442.36
patrician 387.15 485.01
patricianly 179.23
patricius 129.18
Patricius' 221.02
Patrick 040.35 307.23 388.13 411.20
patrick's 582.29
Patrick's 491.11 530.10
patrified 087.11
Patriki 317.02
patrilinear 279.04
patrions 328.08
patriots 488.36
Patripodium-am-Bummel 191.10
Patrisky 347.17
patriss 230.32
patristic 483.34
patrizien 078.23
Patrol 380.04
patrolman 586.28
patrona 495.35
patronage 219.09
patronning 347.31
patrons' 337.05
patroonshaap 539.31
patruum 496.22
patruuts 230.34
Pat's 080.07 463.01
pats' 051.30

Patsch 516.23
Patself 073.21
patsy 475.35
Patsy 070.11 210.27
Patt 593.06
patte 062.09
pattedyr 321.25
pattens 548.29
patter 333.14
Patter 516.31
pattered 209.18
pattering 207.06
patterjackmartins 007.04
pattern 076.22 123.24 179.04 213.05 220.16 253.06 257.04 311.29 362.12 408.15 472.25 508.04 519.03
Pattern 237.13
patternmind 070.35
patties 133.04
Pattorn 537.10
pattrin 068.35
patty 184.23
patwhat 017.14
pau' 246.16
Paud 335.24
paudeen 464.14
Paudheen 332.32 600.32
Paudraic's 550.07
paul 111.18
Paul 043.09 049.15
Pauline 034.33 154.23
Paullabucca 369.26
Paullock 039.05
Paull-the-Aposteln 569.08
paulpoison 101.22
paulse 157.13
Paulus 274.07 438.19
paumee 099.31
paump 340.19
paumpshop 516.28
paunch 066.26 133.23 583.27
paunches 422.05
paunchjab 498.16
paunchon 435.33
paunschaup 209.31
paupe 269.27
pauper 086.19
Pauper 523.25
Paupering 071.25
paupers 316.23
paupulation 140.13
pausably 619.08
pause 036.19 041.29 058.10 082.10 128.22 235.06 320.32 586.32
paused 051.32 057.24
pauses 316.27
pauses 345.30
pausse 256.15
Pautheen 082.09
pavanos 236.19
Pave 531.03
paved 131.05 582.25
paven 205.35
pavilion 084.22
paviour 534.23
Pavl 210.36
paw 115.05 315.35 462.36
Paw 060.13 060.16 546.33
pawdrag 565.18
pawdry's 177.04
Pawerschoof 386.18
pawkytalk 037.21
Pawmbroke 074.15
pawn 042.34 192.11 560.08
pawnbreaking 164.23
pawnbroking 041.29
pawned 322.15 579.30 596.30
pawns 102.15 507.05
Pawpaw 378.33
Pawr 535.19
paws 091.35 438.04
pawsdeen 095.17
pawses 221.14
pawty 182.27
pax 083.32
Pax 406.20 508.06 621.35
paxsealing 015.09
pay 009.32 019.04 061.08 082.27 086.29 141.07 144.17 172.05 177.24 188.20 207.14 375.33 413.36 419.30 436.26 437.17 438.26 448.35 451.04 458.30 497.21 537.12 542.14 545.01 553.34 568.14 574.20 583.25 589.35
pay 418.16
Pay 590.04
Paybads 541.14
paycook's 551.04
payee-drawee 575.14
payees 480.01
payers-drawers 575.18
paying 070.01 385.14 437.27 493.04 588.09
payings 339.16
paykelt 413.01
payment 230.19 574.08 574.11 574.13
paynattention 434.28
Payne 370.03
paynims 564.21
payono 362.32
paypaypay 249.17
payrents 576.27
payrodicule 070.06
pays 270.02 457.04 543.31 622.33
Pays 145.31
paysecurers 366.28
paythronosed 032.12
Paza 471.01
P.C. 086.07 (P.C. Robort)
P.C. 277.L2 (P.C. Helmut's)
P.C.Q. 618.13
P.D. 421.11
pea 171.06 296.24 391.27 496.19 625.23
Peabody's 101.13
peacable 158.10
peace 014.14 023.09 025.25 030.15 040.32 094.07 096.19 124.34 133.16 149.02 189.06 207.31 225.06 244.05 273.05 276.27 295.15 360.01 364.20 364.20 374.15 378.21 397.18 408.10 429.19 443.15 463.27 465.14 493.30 500.13 518.31 549.12 549.12 552.14 571.20 583.10 583.10 586.32 620.17 627.10
Peace 202.14 222.19 332.09 471.05 502.11 616.12
Peace 346.04
peaceablest 063.29
peacebetothem 053.15
peaced 372.05
peacefed 449.32
peacefugle 011.09
peaceful 290.20
Peacefully 098.14
peacegreen 086.35
Peacepeace 175.16
Peacer 503.27
peaces 391.27
peacesmokes 350.26
peacewave 023.13
peach 238.18 360.28 508.24 556.06
Peach 037.31
peached 337.27
peaches 057.04 065.26 113.17 251.24
peachest 145.15
peaching 365.07
peachskin 240.30
peachumpidgeonlover 485.20
peacience 568.05
peacies 496.32
peacifold 043.31
Peacisely 089.04
peacocks 245.03 303.F2
Peacockstown 097.04
peadar 326.26
Peadhar 464.31
Peadhar 346.14
peahen 578.20
peahenning 234.19
peajagd 055.16
peak 070.13 130.04 208.07 273.15 317.35 547.34 548.26
peakload 199.23
peaky 559.27
Peaky 368.31
peal 330.08 403.20
Peal 568.14
pealabells 569.12
pealer 347.15 603.31
Peamengro 171.29
peanas 360.09
peanats 314.35
Peannlueamoore 069.06
peanut 587.10
peanzanzangan 389.01
pear 292.08 360.29
pearced 090.30
Pearcey 493.03
pearcin 363.06
Pearidge 084.07
pearl 225.26 556.12
pearl 399.05
pearlagraph 226.01 226.01
Pearlfar 102.07
pearlies 462.11
pearlmothers 083.17
pearlogs 461.20
pearls 276.15 363.03 446.26
pearly 139.10
pears 571.17
pearse 262.08 620.24
peartree 291.06
peas 019.02 037.33 138.04 267.11 363.27 404.29 406.19 432.09 456.04 472.06
peasant 062.12
peascod 578.08
pease 022.30 191.21 257.22 412.31 549.31

Pease 440.10
peasemeal 582.16
peat 004.15 012.10 521.19
peat 338.05
peater 076.29
peaters 622.02
peaties 117.18
peatrefired 405.35
peatrick's 361.03
peatrol 340.19
peats 202.30
peatsmoor 086.09
Peax 424.26 424.26
pebble 020.05 031.30 245.12 255.31
pebbled 463.27
pebbledropper 494.24
pebbles 207.06 442.15 562.08
pebblets 134.04
pebils 424.27
peccadilly 577.05
peccaminous 288.19
peccat 240.11
peck 003.13 112.08 278.12 396.16 420.14 489.36
peckadillies 336.29
Peck-at-my-Heart 143.02
pecked 623.32
pecker 111.36
pecking 011.12 199.03 452.12
pecklapitschens 038.22
pectoral 015.32
pectoralium 524.32
pectorals 137.26
peculiar 120.28 423.19 544.06
Peculiar 071.30
Pecundus 574.12
pecuniar 019.03
pecuniarity 241.05
pedal 360.06
pedalettes 430.09
pedarrests 349.33
Peddlars 310.15
peddle 582.24
peddled 551.10
peddles 137.33
pede 619.27
pedeiculosus 466.31
Peder 344.27
pederast 089.15
pederect 153.28 155.23
pederestians 565.01
Pedersen 221.29
Pedersill 161.28
pedestarolies 368.11
pedestrians 387.26
pedestriasts 410.35
Pedher 142.27
pediculously 088.13
pedigree 086.14
peduncle 211.29
Pedwar 403.04
pee 111.18 204.12
Pee 296.05
peeas 602.36
peebles 537.13
peebles 260.L2
Peebles 390.26
peeby 370.15
peechy 604.01
Peechy 603.36
peecieve 609.30
peegee 006.32
peekaboo 580.15
peeking 452.11
peekweeny 519.11
peel 167.35 171.08 190.04 255.16 274.F3 302.11 327.02 332.11 441.34
Peeld 206.36
peeled 552.04
peeler 005.34 067.27 374.26
Peeler 086.12 535.19
Peeler 176.02
peeling 418.02 430.28 468.36 621.30
peels 447.12 583.24
Peena 377.18
peep 006.32 096.13 131.02 292.13 296.13 330.05 335.09 385.10 420.07
Peep 248.19 540.14
peepair 462.10
peepat 327.29
peepee 533.26
peepeestrilling 276.20
peeper 279.F23
peepers 237.04 541.29
peepestrella 178.27
peepet 449.31 449.31
peepette 096.14
Peepette 248.19
peeping 351.34 438.15
peepingpartner 580.26
peeplers 567.33
peeps 248.17 255.17
Peeps 614.15
peeptomine 361.01
Peequeen 508.26
peequuliar 606.30
peer 007.29 039.05 075.17 199.08 311.29 365.06 389.23 445.24 490.22 626.34
Peer 330.05 369.10
peered 322.22
peerer 124.20
peeress 124.20 529.09
peerfectly 527.26
peering 395.07 413.33 583.24
peerless 382.23 588.25
peerlesses 493.21
peers 540.22 624.10
peer's 340.36
peersons 060.25
pees 119.35
peese 050.05
Peeter 616.09
peethrolio 280.24
peeve 220.05
peever 154.17
peeves 304.F4
peevish 345.10
peewee 011.10 017.20
peg 199.26 362.20 413.02 577.16 586.12
Peg 436.10 579.17
Peganeen 331.10
Pegeen 490.32
pegged 072.27 149.07
pegger 584.06
Pegger 091.01
Pegger's 092.06
pegging 026.36 504.36
peggot 537.01
peggy 291.05 496.19
Peggy 212.07
peggylees 508.19
peg-of-my-heart 290.03
pegs 163.17
peh 296.28
peihos 205.32
Peingpeong 058.24
peins 055.30
Peins 594.15
peint 155.23
peirce 556.35
peisth 091.04
Peiwei 321.34
peixies 316.17
Pekin 507.28
Pekoe 506.35
pelaged 358.10
pelagiarist 182.03
Pelagiarist 525.07
Pelagios 538.36
Pelah 077.25
peleja 325.11
pelf 520.14
pelfalittle 010.34
pelhaps 130.35
pelican 359.01
Pelican 197.19
pelium 128.35
pell 284.10
pellet 283.F3
pellets 019.03 128.12
pellmale 430.22
pellmell 547.02
pellover 325.12
pellow 617.10
pellucid 108.02
Pelman 369.28
Pelmit 559.05
pelotting 102.16
Pelouta 567.35
pelt 074.13
pelted 015.29 089.04
pelting 172.14 471.21
peltries 548.26
peltry 391.36
pelts 145.01
pelves 551.13
pelvic 608.23
peme 350.18
pemmer 481.36
pemmican 120.11
Pemmican's 197.27
pemp 403.04
pen 118.24 182.03 262.27 276.07 278.19 301.11 302.21 303.02 412.32 433.08 460.19
Pen 306.18
penal 045.10 090.36
penals 188.32 465.05
penalty 061.09
Penalty 373.32
penance 240.14 355.14 515.01
penancies 147.17
pence 013.02 098.14 521.06 589.03
Penceless 210.22
penceloid 359.09
penchant 270.17
Pencho 349.02
pencilled 093.25
Pencylmania 228.19
pendant 281.07
pendencies 054.33
Pender's 210.08

pending 061.09 275.F2 443.11 499.01
pending 349.07
pene 349.01 357.10
Penelope 212.10
penelopean 123.04
peneplain 594.23
penetrant 417.01
Penetrators 008.05
pengapung 313.30
pengeneepy 275.F1
pengeypigses 313.16
penic 156.03
peniloose 581.01
penincular 315.30
peningsworths 548.23
penisills 566.09
penisolate 003.06
Penisole's 622.10
penitent 457.03 569.33
penitential 605.23
Penman 125.23
penman's 483.02
penmark 606.26
Penmark 301.F5
penmarks 421.18
penmight 212.18
penn 013.28
Penn 019.32
penname 182.32
pennant 298.07
penned 093.25 232.17
pennis 495.13
penny 054.32 200.27 210.34 273.F5 456.06 603.05
Penny 307.02
pennyatimer 472.21
pennyawealth 288.F1
pennydirts 025.02
Pennyfair 226.25
pennyfares 080.34
pennyladders 479.27
pennylotts 203.06
pennysilvers 241.02
penparing 364.05
penproduct 108.31
pens 061.36
Pens 617.22
pensamientos 443.15
penscrusher 150.05
Pensée 403.14
pensible 152.30
pensile 173.10
pensilled 553.11
pensils 261.10
pension 024.17 211.13 387.29 412.29 443.32 545.04
Pension 181.05
pensionee 301.19
pensioners 504.31
Pensive 082.20
penstock 305.26
penstroke 115.07
pent 240.11 577.25
pentacosts 624.34
pentapolitan 565.04
pentecostal 099.21
pentecostitis 130.09
penteplenty 211.07
pentiadpair 152.35
pentschanjeuchy 004.25
pentschmyaso 339.06
penultimatum 424.26
penumbra 115.23
penumbrella 462.21
Peny-Knox-Gore 606.19
Penzance 501.19
Peocchia 471.03
Peonia 415.02
peony 445.16 571.17
peoplades 134.05
peoplade's 069.28
people 014.13 042.25 110.05 122.29 128.12 174.01 174.36 221.21 240.34 288.28 312.34 428.02 471.35 472.35 533.30 560.23 621.28 627.24
People 057.14
Peopler 104.15
peoples 229.32 278.22 619.09
people's 033.27 085.19
peopling 140.12 525.18
pep 282.03 294.F1 563.28
Pep 308.17 405.14
pepeace 345.12
Pepep 590.04
pepet 601.28
pepette 143.31 147.29
Pepette 232.25 413.24
pepettes 272.F4
Pepigi 575.29 576.08
Pepigi's 576.06
Pepinregn 568.34
pepped 587.07
pepper 197.24 406.16 412.14
peppered 536.23
peppering 460.06
pepperpot 209.11
Peppers 214.16
Peppt 144.17
Peppybeg 173.26
peppydecked 379.25
pepst 541.15
pept 134.06
per 020.20 031.23 079.10 126.05 142.02 142.02 182.24 187.13 210.03 233.25 308.03 388.06 389.03 390.11 390.22 484.33 488.26 529.02 558.15 577.20 577.23 606.26 619.04
per 287.27 443.13
Per 081.07 535.19 613.03
peragrine 014.28
perals 434.06
perambulatrix 364.04
perambulaups 576.20
perce 626.25
Perce 491.25
perceivable 353.26
perceived 100.32 470.02
Perce-Oreille 175.28
percepted 368.36
perception 364.22
perch 031.02 068.14 476.05 492.26 554.04
perchance 141.17 395.28 403.24 516.22
perched 120.19
perches 189.13 450.07
perchin 136.30
perchypole 369.19
Percorello 134.19
percussors 541.11
Percy 235.29 352.10
Percy 440.09
perdition 068.16 282.03
Perdition 250.26
perdrix 447.28
perdunamento 220.21
pere 360.07
père 462.01
Père 184.34
Père 124.34
pereat 610.16
Peredos 610.34
peregrinantibus 398.16
peregrine 282.L3
Peregrine 398.15 398.15
peregrines 484.29
perennious 057.22
perensempry 364.24
perfect 043.34 115.08 143.35 174.36 247.11 269.05 270.07 293.23 389.19 417.24 424.23 439.26 443.09 458.35 493.29 527.12 533.02 549.12 597.31 605.36
Perfect 222.19 568.29
perfection 026.01 109.09 227.19 277.25 279.F05 431.34 529.03
perfectly 113.24 458.06
perfectpeace 364.20
perfectportioned 602.03
perfects 181.25
Perfedes 343.09
perfidly 395.20
perforated 448.12
perforations 124.23
perforce 575.28
performance 032.30 032.32
performed 026.19 318.23
performer 434.35
performers 495.25
performing 109.18
perfrances 478.19
perfumance 219.05
perfume 095.23 109.26 234.24 237.06 280.25
perfumed 138.09
Perfume's 437.17
perfumios 430.27
perfyddye 480.12
pergaman 303.23
perhaps 032.02 058.36 109.16 122.33 150.02 150.06 177.16 186.10 269.07 411.34 413.18 511.04 519.09 519.23 523.10 563.22 573.35 620.11
Perhaps 519.26 523.19 563.23
perhapsing 597.20
perharps 089.33
perhelps 309.08
Perhelps 238.19
perhips 237.35
perhopes 154.03
perhops 415.17 443.23
perhumps 602.24
peri 011.09
Pericles 306.L2
periculosus 466.31
periglus 327.13
perigrime 392.19
perihelygangs 015.05
perikopendolous 339.13
peril 323.26
perilous 037.05 186.05
perils 202.08 576.25
perilwhitened 394.35
perimutter 298.28

perinanthean 613.17
period 030.04 108.32 164.15 200.02 533.26 599.15
periodically 522.17
periodicity 577.21
Periodicity 308.L2
periods 362.29
periparolysed 612.19
peripatetic 298.L3
peripateting 266.06
periphery 298.L3
periplic 123.22
peripulator 313.33
Peris 616.11
perish 138.15 452.02
perished 049.14 289.03 343.30 549.26
perishers 265.20 347.25
Perisian 143.36
periwhelker 515.04
periwig 246.07
periwinkle 393.19
perizomatis 185.16
Perjantaj 325.11
perked 371.35
Perkin 039.04
Perkodhuskurunbarggruauyagokgorlayorgromgremmitghundhurthrumathunaradidillifaititillibumullunukkunun 023.05
perks 413.36
perkumiary 511.17
Perlanthroa's 601.22
perlection 094.10
permanent 037.13 575.28
Permanent 153.02
permeated 498.09
permettant 228.10
permienting 162.14
permish 187.12
permission 032.31 251.13
permit 409.10 414.07 501.10 616.27
permitted 008.05 041.05
permitting 113.24 564.07
Permitting 483.35
permutandies 284.12
Pernicious 467.34
perofficies 358.15
perorate 425.19
perorhaps 062.25
Perousse 439.35
perpendicular 060.25
Perpending 187.18
perpepperpot 499.12
Perperp 298.24
perpersonal 509.35
perperusual 368.13
perpetrified 023.30
perpetual 115.16 573.04
Perpetual 222.19
perpetually 532.17 606.01
perpetuation 550.03
perplagued 539.11
perplex 123.17
perplexedly 090.35
perplexing 516.28
perporteroguing 595.20
Perrichon 254.14
perroqtriques 515.33
perry 288.22 367.20
persan 286.08
persecussion 125.16
persecuted 391.15
persecutorum 051.31
Persee 497.27
perseguired 092.01
persen 324.19
persence 596.11
persent 370.05 618.36
Perseoroyal 358.20
persequestellates 107.18
perseverance 097.18
pershan 280.15
Pershawn 449.15
pershoon 141.25
persianly 183.10
persians 532.02
Persia's 583.14
persicks 038.11
Persic-Uraliens 162.12
persins 048.16
persisted 076.20 599.11
persistence 143.11
person 060.25 078.36 085.29 087.09 089.06 099.25 110.21 118.21 122.30 122.31 122.31 125.11 161.06 165.33 186.03 187.29 215.25 251.31 268.18 268.20 278.15 280.12 332.07 365.02 405.09 413.08 413.19 432.18 433.26 468.09 484.05 486.20 490.09 527.33 532.20 572.35 606.28
person 354.08
Person 071.31
persona 242.13
personably 618.22
personage 534.23
personal 109.26 115.09 120.17 167.02 359.02 431.02 511.15 598.01
personalities 107.24 498.33
personality 038.27 144.23 166.24 247.09
personally 558.04
personeel 584.33
personer 476.13
personnalitey 461.04
persons 123.30 220.36 223.36 373.30 374.35 476.19 478.29 529.08 617.09
perspectable 362.35
perspire 437.14
perspirer 059.33
perspiring 429.14
Persse 044.14 044.24 419.24
Perssed 106.05
perssian 357.09
Perssiasterssias 339.18
persuade 356.02
pert 043.08 327.03
pertained 355.12 547.06
perthanow 366.12
pertimes 489.22
perts 363.04 620.34
Pertsymiss 186.36
perturbing 136.22
perty 157.30 600.32
peruke 560.25
perus 317.01
perused 116.05
peruser 115.13
peruses 543.29
perusienne 021.17
perusiveness 614.23
perusual 516.09
Peruvian 253.01
pervenche 281.06
Pervenche 615.03
Pervenche 028.27
pervergined 238.23
pervert 164.32
pervert's 174.36
Pervinca 223.07 580.17
pervinciveness 281.14
pervious 321.01
pervoys 296.02
pescies 451.11
pesciolines 245.11
pesco 230.06
pesition 390.32
pesk 524.31
peso 234.05
pessim 149.36
Pessim 106.13
pessname 561.10
pessovered 553.08
pest 039.14 099.04 190.03 199.08 558.15 587.27
pestered 015.06 545.35
pesternost 596.10
pestituting 616.17
pet 096.22 138.04 147.29 220.05 232.10 248.09 431.34 441.17 447.29 457.25 459.25 587.22 588.07 626.26
pet 352.28
Pet 337.22
Pet 071.35
petalliferentes 601.16
Petault 118.28
Pete 026.05
peteet 019.02
Pete-over-Meer 205.34
peter 398.14
Peter 040.16 043.09 065.15 085.05 210.22 212.02 212.03 438.19 449.16
Peter 104.15
Peterborough 442.11
peternatural 451.17
peterpacked 355.02
Peters 152.14 159.23
Peters 106.20
Peter's 277.10 520.14 580.04
peterwright 269.08
petery 013.02 288.F6
petit 262.F4
Petitbois 440.12
Petite 210.10
Petite 157.33
petition 422.19
petitionists 312.27
petitions 543.07
petnames 561.36
petpubblicities 368.13
Petra 264.12 264.14
Petrard 497.08
Petricksburg 326.25
Petrie 350.27
Petries 481.35
petrifake 077.01
Petrificationibus 610.03
Petrin 135.10
petriote's 228.07
petrock 203.31
petrolling 323.31

petroperfractus 041.06
Petrus 161.26 407.15
petrusu 053.15
Pets 106.04
petsybluse 261.02
pette 143.32
petted 352.04 439.14
pettedcoat 497.32
petter 079.23 241.35 451.22
pettest 079.23 145.08 458.04
petticoats 466.33
Petticoat's 561.31
petties 087.29
pettiest 009.36
pettigo 279.F12
pettikilt 611.36
pettipickles 133.20
Pettit 372.11
pettitily 191.19
petto 504.18
petty 008.25 021.17 231.03 332.31 336.24 361.15 406.19 454.36 612.16
Petty 186.19
pettybonny 124.27
pettycourts 545.30
Pettyfib's 210.31
pettythicks 176.22
pettyvaughan 609.02
petulance 120.04
petunia 434.18
petween 432.09
peu 274.L2
Peucchia 471.04
Peurelachasse 076.36
peurls 549.20
peut-être 041.36
pew 061.09 273.16 283.03 283.03 283.04
pewcape 533.09
pewmillieu 552.28 552.28
pews 120.01
pewter 199.19
Pewter 307.26
pewterers 312.36
pewterpint 558.01
pewtewr 593.17
pewty 058.35
pewtyflushed 058.36
Pfaf 601.03
pfan 296.22 596.32
pfander 481.34
pfann 538.27
Pfarrer 161.27
pfath 599.04
pfeife 464.20
Pferdinamd 535.09
pfiat 034.07 034.07
pfierce 344.26
Pfif 600.30
pfife 077.14 411.11
pfinish 596.31
pfooi 125.22
pfoor 282.31 282.31
pfor 596.31
pfortner 531.25
pfot 333.34
pftjschute 003.19
pfuffpfaffing 529.30
pfuit 033.34 033.34
pfun 596.31
pfunded 599.05
pfunder 481.34
pfurty 285.F3
Ph. 151.33 (Ph. Dr's)
phace 012.09
Phailinx 346.35
Phaiton 110.10
phaked 264.19
phalanx 470.04
Phall 004.15
phallopharos 076.34
Phallusaphist 072.14
phantastic 182.04
phantastichal 470.18
phanthares 565.19
phantom 184.08 264.19 327.25
phantomweight 039.13
pharahead 292.19
pharaoph 129.36
Pharaops 625.03
pharce 004.17
pharoah 062.20
Pharoah 387.26 580.12
pharoph 452.20
pharphar 215.01
pharrer 578.06
phase 285.F5
phases 254.27 358.03
phassionable 396.25
phatrisight 167.10
phausdheen 412.09
phaymix 331.02
phaynix 473.16
pheasant 569.23
pheasants 449.18
Phelan 370.21
phelinine 268.18
Phelps 067.26
phemous 167.24
Phenecian 221.32
Phenice-Bruerie 038.04
Phenicia 068.29 576.28
Phenician 197.31
Phenitia 085.20
pher 278.F1
phew 474.12
Phew 010.24
phewit 042.04
phewn 412.09
Phibb 569.08
Phibbs 187.20
Phibia's 601.21
phie 059.20
phifie 004.28
Phig 169.23
Phil 050.33 093.33 444.08
philadelphians 572.25
Philadespoinis 165.28
philadolphus 167.09
philanthropicks 173.18
philanthropist 544.12
philim 264.19
philioquus 156.17
philip 160.27
Philip's 420.29
Phill 006.08
phillippy 009.01
Phillipsburgs 497.19
phillohippuc 140.13
Philly 038.35 142.28
Phillyps 067.22
philomel 248.02
Philomela 307.L1
philomelas 237.36
Philomena 212.12
philophosy 119.04
philopotamus 449.32
philosopher 047.01
philosophism 163.17
Philpot 210.30
philtred 189.05
Philuppe 542.09
Phin 044.11
Phineal 346.12
Phineas 029.05
Phishlin 050.33
Phiss 587.24
phiz 146.11 363.17
Phiz 420.09
phiz-à-phiz 153.21
phizes 580.08
phizz 067.27
phlegmish 397.24
phlegms 089.10
Phlenxty 593.04
Phoebe 147.14
Phoebe 200.10
Phoebe's 583.19
Phoebus 431.36
Phoenican 608.32
Phoenis 590.05
phoenish 004.17 322.20
phoenished 130.11
phoenix 055.28 088.24 128.35 136.35 265.08 332.31 406.10 553.25
Phoenix 205.25 283.F3 321.16 382.04 587.25 621.01
pholk 264.20
pholly 050.33
phone 502.33
Phone 346.12
'phone 275.16
phonemanon 258.22
phoney 418.03 464.22 533.30
phonio 016.07
phono 452.12
phonoscopically 449.01
Phook 379.16
phooka 194.36
phophiar 343.17
phopho 475.01
Phopho 475.12
Phornix 080.06
phospherine 583.13
phosphor 475.15
Phosphoron 603.36
phost 409.06
phot 345.26
Photoflashing 583.15
photognomist 336.34
photography 277.25
photoist 111.26
photophoric 472.17
photoplay 516.35
photoprismic 611.13
photoreflection 611.16
photos 465.15
photosensition 123.12
photoslope 349.10
photure 233.02
phrase 036.08 041.05 055.08 117.36 118.01 128.06 423.16
phraseology 073.03
phrases 120.23 121.06 256.19
phthat 198.17
phthin 417.06
phthir 417.06

phullupsuppy 417.15
phumeral's 346.13
phunkel 502.33
phwhat 198.17
phwhtphwht 141.34
phwinshogue 182.34
Phwum 412.06
Phyllis 060.04
Phylliscitations 491.30
phyllisophies 435.10
physical 035.23 098.09
physically 341.35
physician 191.16
physicians 173.16
physicking 437.12
physics 543.25
physiog 412.16
pia 518.33
pia 178.17
Pia 027.16
Piabelle 610.21
pialabellars 243.07
pian 200.35
pianage 450.23
pianissime 038.31
piano 278.F3 437.28 544.19 618.16
pianoback 517.22
pianutunar 327.21
Piaras 310.11
piawn 377.14
pibe 221.29
pibered 037.33
pibrook 427.11
picalava 595.27
picaresqueness 486.34
piccaninnies 175.33
piccions 248.05
Piccolina 210.10
piccolo 054.17
pice 256.31 604.03
Picea 160.01
picious 527.33
pick 080.19 083.30 112.08 152.03 194.13 207.09 208.03 220.05 248.36 278.12 288.06 337.27 360.06 376.21 424.07 447.34 456.01 459.03 468.11 490.18 500.35 548.13
pick 273.L3 418.20
Pickardstown 262.21
picked 020.25 022.27 084.06 086.13 093.02 162.12 210.26 255.20 272.11 326.03 376.08
Picked 104.15
Pickedmeup 106.20
Picker 616.09
pickersup 039.03
picket 010.07 291.19
pickets 350.17
picking 011.12 324.04 443.22 452.13 507.26
Picking 300.F1
pickings 183.30 534.11
pickle 029.07 153.19 316.17 508.24 524.28
pickled 580.29
pickledhoopy 054.31
pickles 334.20 508.26
pickneck 141.35
pickninnig 292.19
pickopeck 416.17
pickpackpanel 575.35
pickpocket 282.15
pickpocketpoint 282.15
pickpocketprod 282.16
pickpocketpromise 282.16
pickpocketpumb 282.15
pickpockets 183.31
pickpuckparty 524.35
picks 115.17 143.02
picksticked 424.20
pickts 204.07 565.35
picky-pocky 082.14
picnic 094.02 261.14
picnic 399.24
Picta 043.30
pictail 521.11
pictograph 220.11
pictor 164.04
pictorial 284.28 284.29 284.30
pictorials 544.09
picture 011.36 079.27 318.09 405.03 428.24 530.08 559.11 617.22
Picture 106.04 165.15
pictures 221.18 242.07 243.01 330.23 388.31 565.06
Picturescu 053.02
picturesque 440.11
Picturshirts 518.21
Picuchet 302.10
piddle 007.27
piddyawhick 346.22
piddysnip 312.14
pidgeons 515.24
pidgin 374.35 611.05
pidginfella 611.27
pidgins' 463.28
pie 067.22 145.31 197.27 252.27 363.04 375.02 441.17 450.16
Pie 296.09
piebald 554.06
piebold 250.36 273.27
piece 016.31 033.10 098.26 150.07 161.09 213.05 313.07 346.19 361.04 397.18 458.01 509.35 524.08 545.36 564.13 565.23 609.36 609.36
Piece 275.F4
piecebag 102.16
pieces 164.23 172.08 543.07 560.06
pied 395.04
pied 338.11
Pied 012.36
Pieder 220.20
piedigrotts 513.14
piedish 464.09
piedom 508.24
piejaw 188.11
pieman 408.20
Pieman 202.14
piena 200.35
pienofarte 162.04
pier 063.28
pierce 038.34 208.09 251.14 333.22 333.28 390.05
Pierce 447.23
pierced 084.34 124.01 130.32 548.36
pierceful 222.32
piercers 133.11
piercey 482.04 482.04 482.04
Piercey 482.04
piercing 281.F3
Pierre 219.12
pierrotettes 594.34
Pierrse 420.24
piers 266.04 332.27 372.08
Piers 496.15
Piers' 593.09
piersified 044.09
Piessporter 038.05
pietad 128.20
pietaring 202.11
Pieter 550.31
Pieter's 117.24
pietrous 159.04
piety 188.20 470.31
pife 341.17
piff 012.11 074.15 282.30 282.30
Piff 341.16 518.17
piffle 576.06
pifflicative 282.L3
pig 064.08 086.14 143.35 176.29 241.09 273.16 359.22 415.35 438.26 460.10 463.01 595.11
Pig 420.10 420.11 482.05
PIG 303.R3
pigaleen 143.35
pigdirt 069.22
pigdish 422.17
Pige 272.L1
pigeegeeses 089.34
pigeon 082.13 337.01 426.16 569.23
pigeoness 186.27
pigeonheim 129.23
pigeonhouse 197.32 444.24
pigeons 010.36 136.29 147.22 239.31 480.03
pigeon's 458.21
pigeons-in-a-pie 407.29
pigeonstealer 522.36
pigeony 584.04
Pigeschoolies 100.06
pigey 485.30 485.31
Pigeys 101.09
pigfellow 245.02
pigger 200.13
piggiesknees 552.22
pigglywiggly 438.07
piggotry 099.19
piggots 349.03
Piggott's 043.32
piggy 015.17 496.18
piggytails 435.24
pigheaded 517.05
pigiron 210.13
pigmaid 015.30
pigmyland 253.11
pignatties 432.15
pignpugn 243.07
pigotted 133.15
Pigott's 282.F4
pigpin 331.12
pigs 119.07 170.20 511.18 619.11
pig's 025.12 212.05 362.01 410.16
Pig's 517.15
pigs' 051.30
pigses 313.22
pigskin 395.35 603.20
pigsking's 122.19

pigstenes 538.32
pigstickularly 087.09
pigstrough 373.18
pigtaiI 232.36
pigtail 082.21 128.14
Pigtarial 106.11
pigtorial 584.36
pigttetails 609.04
pike 008.15 064.24 134.16
450.16 623.14
Pike 025.28 420.11
pikebailer 031.27
piked 321.32
pikehead 600.19
pikeopened 022.33
pikes 031.02
piketurns 570.04
pikey 086.26
Pikey 300.F1
Pilax 156.05
pilch 492.25
Pilcomayo 197.35
pile 130.04 211.05 380.35
624.30
piled 004.27 548.26
piledrivers 585.15
pilend 200.19
pilerinnager's 312.27
piles 128.35 496.14
pilgarlick 413.13
pilger's 248.13
pilgrim 234.20 390.24
pilgrimage 051.29 472.17
pilgrimst 220.35
pilipili 209.11
Pill 031.28
pillaged 579.30
pillale 145.12
pillar 016.04 289.03 422.30
pillarbosom 471.07
pillarbox 066.27 442.33
pillarposterns 235.22
pillary 322.32
pillasleep 556.33
pilled 369.15
pilleoled 152.23
pillfaces 078.27
pillgrimace 423.08
pillings 169.24
Pillools 373.28
pillory 016.03
pillow 024.30 057.34 211.09
328.23 445.30 526.02 603.13
pillowed 040.19
pillowing 366.15
pillowscone 006.24
Pills 156.28
pilluls 128.36
piloter 539.36
pilscrummage 305.33
pilsener 313.14
pilsens 492.18
piltdowns 010.30
pilzenpie 037.32
pim 232.15 307.F3
Pim 043.09
pimp 051.17 279.F18 457.13
pimpadoors 351.34
pimparnell 564.28
pimpim 333.09
Pimpimp 106.20 106.21
Pimpim's 533.33
pimple 346.32
pimpled 273.14
Pimploco 135.08
pimps 135.03
Pim's 548.26
pin 205.10 208.09 282.26
282.30 443.29 466.02 474.14
pinafore 584.16
pinafrond 021.33
pinch 064.22 128.13 257.22
269.25 397.21 419.31
pinchably 417.21
Pinchapoppapoff 461.15
pinched 423.02
pinchgut 568.22
pinching 350.26 449.22
pinchme 465.18
Pinck 032.02
pinctured 160.08
pine 014.32 102.28 301.12
571.09
Pine 221.29
pineapple 170.30
pinebarren 053.16
pinecorns 505.05
pinefully 158.04
pines 151.18 159.35
pineshrouded 546.01
pinetacotta 160.07
ping 189.23 233.28 233.28
541.24
Ping 233.28
pinge 396.20
pingers 355.01
pinginapoke 359.26
pinging 231.11
pingping 035.23
Pingpong 213.18
pings 327.24
Pingster's 550.13
pinguind 577.27
pining 154.17 626.12
pink 043.28 059.27 083.07
127.25 185.12 236.05 248.36
277.25 310.27 337.22 367.05
367.06 367.06 368.11 512.04
544.32 559.16 567.09 570.25
574.25 614.15
Pink 367.05
Pinkadindy 353.28
pinked 461.05
pinkee 550.11
pinker 053.10
Pinkingtone's 184.23
pinkman 514.32
pinkpoker 340.04
pinkprophets 029.16
pinks 115.15
pink's 268.F5
pinksir's 099.16
pinkun's 128.12
pinkwilliams 575.15
pinky 215.20 567.07
pinmarks 238.01
pinnacle 122.10
pinnacle's 070.13
pinnance 342.02
pinnatrate 310.09
pinners 034.20
pinnigay 511.17
pinny 204.31
pinnyfore 226.25
pinnyweight 007.25
Pinpernelly 445.11
pinpin 598.18
pins 210.11 333.25
pinsel 425.18
pinslers 492.30
pint 260.06 305.17 405.33
438.22 492.17 511.19 514.32
pintacostecas 152.27
pinter 320.19
Pinter's 092.07
pints 356.14 508.02
Piobald 071.29
pioghs 350.17
pioja 389.03
piop 425.36
piopadey 470.07
piotersbarq 549.24
Pioupioureich 181.04
pioupious 335.36
pious 032.31 034.14 110.36
185.27 240.33 244.36 356.29
440.08 486.20 544.16 557.12
573.25
Pious 014.09 280.28 486.20
piously 182.02 605.13
Piowtor 497.28
pip 232.09 274.F3 310.09
314.25 314.25 314.25 517.25
563.07 588.06
Pip 459.25 540.14
pipe 035.11 051.33 137.27
270.06 335.10 450.19 520.11
603.21 607.08 616.05 619.27
pipe 355.01
Pipe 602.24
piped 025.10 043.34 205.32
540.14
pipelines 310.05
Pipep 502.09
piper 418.16
Piper 472.09
Piper 346.15
pipers 023.31 277.23
pipes 188.27 198.01 379.16
pipetta 147.33
Pipetta 470.21
pipette 374.11 571.17
Pipette 276.F6 500.23 500.25
500.32 500.32
pipettishly 563.05
Pipetto 470.21
piping 371.05 385.10 615.09
Piping 340.33
Pipitch 540.14
pipkin 086.06
Pipkin 372.09
pipless 121.19
pipos 054.17
pippa 055.16
pippap 301.07
pippappoff 337.01
pippin's 506.25
pippive 282.32
pipple 538.13
pipples 537.30
pippup 624.09
pippy 146.33
pips 153.13
piquant 123.36
piquante 061.16
pique 344.02
piquéd 124.10
piractical 337.23
pirates 463.21

Pirce 491.25
pire 244.03
pirigrim 600.35
pirlypettes 080.35
pirmanocturne 328.17
pirryphlickathims 199.35
piscines 127.35
pisciolinnies 494.10
Piscisvendolor 408.36
Piscium 600.06
piscivore 171.08
piscman 061.24
pish 189.01
Pisk 297.06
pisness 534.21
pison 212.24
pisononse 039.14
pisoved 548.10
pispigliando 038.14
piss 185.23
Pissasphaltium 157.02
pist 099.05
pistania 206.31
pistany 287.13
pistil 237.03
pistol 063.04
pit 033.09 053.31 222.01 594.29
Pit 033.12
Pit 106.07
pitch 068.14 070.28 093.04 283.02 360.03 443.09 584.03
pitch 274.L4
Pitch 104.15
pitchbatch 162.31
pitchblack 385.06
Pitchcap 278.L1
pitcher 210.34 233.01 531.15 598.21
Pitcher 515.35
pitchers 438.13
pitchies 415.07
pitchin 136.31
pitchin 346.18
pitching 139.12
pitchur 587.14
piteous 174.19
piteousness 363.24
pitfallen 049.30
pith 399.33
pithecoid 443.23
pithy 351.09
pities 562.08 564.28
pitiless 251.10
pitly 076.12
pitounette 143.32
pitpat 020.22
pitre 291.25
Pitre 192.13
Pitre-le-Pore-in 135.10
pits 262.F2 615.10
pitschobed 339.05
pitssched 254.01
Pitsy 342.16
pitted 361.15
pitter 588.22
pittites 427.29
pitts 032.11 545.35
pitty 244.20 361.14
pittycoat 043.20
pity 047.13 175.02 211.07 304.23 381.15 427.24 458.24 464.05 549.27 570.27 570.29 585.12 627.06
Pity 459.24 535.27 535.28 535.34
Pitymount 541.13
pity-prompted 060.02
più 292.12
pius 156.20
pive 282.30 282.30 282.31 282.31 282.32
Pivorandbowl 351.14
pivotal 030.06
pivotism 164.03
PIX 304.R2
pixes 086.09
pixillated 421.33
pixylighting 011.12
pixy's 583.33
piz 327.14
pizdrool 287.31
pizzicagnoling 092.19
Pla 297.17
plab 057.03
plabbaside 331.17
plabs 312.33
placator 534.05
place 019.20 029.20 032.01 034.10 043.16 061.33 069.21 085.14 089.01 099.26 110.06 110.09 110.20 118.21 128.26 137.07 146.14 159.21 172.05 181.20 182.03 188.12 190.21 194.36 215.10 215.25 239.31 247.24 247.25 257.15 260.06 278.15 292.30 307.F4 335.09 336.22 355.14 356.34 368.19 374.35 386.20 390.26 421.24 430.17 432.18 433.27 434.27 436.07 458.01 458.02 462.29 467.23 472.33 475.27 476.06 478.36 479.02 479.06 490.10 490.23 503.10 503.18 504.10 514.36 515.25 520.04 522.22 546.24 565.07 570.13 570.30 571.04 571.10 577.25 586.02 586.21 596.28 598.01 599.15 600.33 609.36 621.31 623.13
place 350.04
Place 041.32 132.22 141.01 306.17 306.18 317.29 420.30 497.12 568.06
Placeat 104.22
placed 042.14 062.32 358.29 364.21 422.01
placefined 537.15
placehider 110.30
placehunter 585.23
placelike 609.02
places 056.09 129.28 196.14 264.15 331.18 495.16 532.36 537.26 617.09
places 341.23 350.04
place's 012.32
placewheres 056.33
placeyear 346.26
placid 067.35
placing 486.14
plads 265.14
plage 017.27 483.29
plage 201.18
plagiast 577.32
plague 174.02 212.24 243.23
plagueburrow 479.24
plaguepurple 109.11
plagues 131.12 465.34
Plagues 071.35
plaguiest 577.33
plaid 030.24
plaidboy 027.09
plain 014.31 030.20 048.02 050.11 059.27 079.01 086.15 086.34 109.20 113.05 124.19 141.12 174.06 181.12 189.24 205.03 261.19 265.29 297.24 303.30 328.14 347.03 414.10 427.21 453.21 462.23 541.28 564.28 577.26 579.21 606.31
Plain 623.18
plaine 017.19
plainer 120.07
plaining 148.36
plainly 057.19 081.12 122.22 390.24 407.08 429.05
plainly 107.06
plainplanned 614.24
plains 064.17
plaint 093.23 385.29
plaintiff 080.04
plaintiff's 182.22
plais 495.01
plaise 199.20 623.15
plaised 381.21
plaising 264.29
plait 290.23
plaît 281.05
plaited 207.02
plak 113.14
plan 108.10 206.07 206.08 274.04 275.F4 361.33 515.27 585.23 604.15
Plan 190.12
Plan 071.27
planckton 477.25
plane 124.11 128.03 139.23 152.01 160.06 296.29 394.34 604.04
planed 439.12
planemetrically 429.10
planet 412.17
planets 583.17
planet's 042.15
plangorpound 056.06
plank 128.04 192.15
planked 311.32
plankgang 478.16
planko 012.24
plankraft 301.23
plankrieg 162.09
planks 314.06
planned 061.31
planner's 165.10
planning 374.25 543.28
plansiman 057.03
plant 147.20 293.10 305.26 451.30 544.33
plantage 332.11
plantagenets 504.02
plantagonist 516.24
plantainous 470.20
Plantarum 503.35
plantation 280.05
planted 031.31 135.05 279.F24 553.18 579.29
planteon 613.18
planter 025.22 600.32
planters 577.33

plantitude 505.05
plants 279.F03
plant's 165.10
plantsown 090.08
planturous 133.07
planty 519.25
planxty 397.05 439.15
Plaom 179.09
plap 296.22
plaps 470.08
plase 093.05 166.01
plasfh 463.18
plash 202.32
plasheous 332.23
plaster 048.04 133.35 253.15
plastic 263.12
platauplain 236.24
plate 009.31 056.19 113.05 137.26 302.04 417.15 456.06 579.11 580.30
Plate 039.06 198.14
plateful 142.07
plateglass 589.30
plates 150.03 286.18 356.31 510.22 625.07
platform 128.04 456.28
platinism 164.11
platinum 192.17
Plato 307.L1
Platonic 292.30 622.36
platoonic 348.08
Platsch 562.15
platschpails 101.27
platteau 199.26
platter 038.02 615.09
platterboys 367.02
platterplate 006.32
plattonem 257.11
platzed 539.20
plauded 550.03
plaudered 269.05
plaudits 043.34
plause 093.24
plausible 019.21 299.26
plawshus 581.22
play 013.30 024.01 032.32 056.01 058.33 069.14 128.16 128.16 144.12 163.05 175.31 175.33 175.35 197.16 225.07 234.16 237.19 240.20 257.31 261.F1 280.32 304.12 337.22 361.01 366.19 407.01 414.25 419.24 433.13 438.07 444.34 449.26 450.34 476.34 477.25 509.31 517.03 521.16 538.34 604.20 625.03
Play 009.24 525.28 526.18 559.29 569.29
Play 176.02
playable 041.23
playaboy's 584.17
playact 426.33
playactrix 526.33
playajest 577.32
playboyish 183.04
played 060.19 149.01 202.25 219.13 284.13 496.20 589.19
played 418.16
Played 105.01
PLAYED 281.R1
player 461.29
players 024.36 043.06 048.10 219.07 350.26
playfair 233.12
playfilly 562.01
playful 124.25
playgue 378.20
playguehouse 435.02
Playhouse 219.02
playing 012.23 027.06 064.03 073.13 077.10 088.30 095.04 096.33 169.22 184.16 197.22 220.23 327.28 354.32 362.32 385.11 393.34 416.36 430.09 434.08 444.26 500.02 504.24 555.11 560.05 582.23 586.11 589.07
playing 341.04
Playing 375.29 522.15
plays 108.27 112.17 127.31 139.12 253.06 309.05 347.15 371.26 396.04 445.08 488.27 488.27 488.28 502.23
playtennis 470.20
Playup 554.09
plea 151.33 163.14
pleace 113.34 617.20
Pleace 349.25
pleacing 055.31
plead 102.18
pleaded 034.20 127.27
pleaders 256.08
pleading 172.33 587.16
pleads 151.33 607.34
pleas 091.19 310.26 367.05 367.06 367.06
pleasable 512.12
pleasant 032.17 111.23 135.18 174.31 339.15 540.04
Pleasant 252.07
pleasantly 164.08
pleasantries 455.23
pleasantry 344.18
please 018.18 019.02 019.10 035.15 037.25 080.36 087.06 096.15 111.32 119.07 124.04 124.05 124.05 141.24 146.32 147.09 159.19 160.25 161.05 166.02 174.13 174.20 224.15 232.18 272.13 274.F3 343.08 368.02 373.32 385.23 398.07 403.19 412.15 423.16 434.01 434.32 446.07 453.35 458.09 458.16 458.18 485.30 495.32 501.07 502.21 506.27 523.11 528.36 535.28 560.16 560.17 564.02 582.34 585.13 585.19 588.25 595.09 609.06 609.07 609.08 617.16
please 200.07 349.26
Please 145.10 232.18 272.12 560.16 571.01
pleasebusiness 146.22
pleased 030.17 083.16 085.19 088.36 134.25 154.04 236.03 418.09 464.35 489.24 553.17 584.29 608.17 620.23 624.21
pleasegoodjesusalem 192.35
pleasekindly 239.01
pleasemarm 624.19
Pleasend 042.10
pleasesir 612.07
pleasestir 263.23
pleasethee 332.16
pleaseyour 568.15
pleashadure 554.07
Pleasie 485.32
pleasing 170.27 526.32 527.09
pleasons 357.10
pleastoseen 165.26
pleasurad 016.11
pleasure 127.22 127.22 131.15 149.23 268.05 324.32 445.10 522.25 616.07
pleasures 189.07 444.24
pleated 207.02
pleathes 265.19
pleating 257.04
pleats 297.08
pleatze 350.19
Pleaze 543.17
pleb 175.03
plebeia 085.13
plebeians 386.29
plebiscites 523.05
plebmatically 129.19
plebs 312.33
plebsed 485.10
Plece 278.24
pled 134.03 336.08
pledge 025.14 035.14 043.15 192.11 206.18 310.28 311.32 326.14 405.11 588.27
pledge 354.19
Pledge 307.06
pledged 094.07 131.21 495.22 544.12
pledges 078.20 444.25 562.30 624.35
pleding 327.13
pledjures 496.01
pleece 368.20
plein 023.36 333.27 541.22
Plein 567.35
pleissful 200.31
pleisure 619.01
plelthy 028.03
plemyums 590.11
plenary 445.08
Plenge 105.01
pleninsula 135.18
plenished 128.24
Plentifolks 567.31
plentihorns 451.07
plentitude 241.07
plenty 025.19 026.33 135.24 308.20 311.35 316.07 362.30 443.16 465.08 498.17 505.06 549.32 612.05
Plenty 502.01
Plenty 440.10
plentymuch 485.34 612.15
plentyprime 279.F18
plenxty 143.05
ples 372.03
plesently 595.07
plethora 006.16
plethorace 616.26
plethoron 579.15
pletoras 542.02
pleures 011.25
plexus 227.30 448.33
pliche 406.04
plicyman 057.03
plied 317.20 481.06 606.32
plied 348.31
plies 129.02 567.29
pliestrycook 486.17
plieth 282.04

plight 066.22 094.07 149.01 318.34 416.19
plighter's 514.19
plightforlifer 444.11
plighty 229.09
plikaplak 562.15
plikplak 562.03 562.03
plimsoles 397.17
plinary 319.07
Pline 281.04
plinkity 178.24
plinnyflowers 354.26
Pliny 255.18 255.18
plipping 396.31
P.L.M. 413.14 (poor late Mrs)
plobbicides 331.17
plodding 521.09
plodge 318.27
plods 231.14 396.18
plodsfoot 015.31
plomansch 085.25
plonk 178.24
plonkyplonk 609.33
Plooney 615.02
ploose 617.03
plop 279.04
Plop 396.33
plores 011.33
ploring 064.17
ploshmat 562.01
plosively 419.20
plostures 317.35
plot 119.32 235.16 374.25 465.32 558.36
Plot 104.15
PLOT 303.R3
plotch 364.26
plotlets 539.24
plotsch 081.02
plotsome 312.18
plotting 582.35
plotty 076.18
plough 030.15 121.17 134.15
ploughboy's 208.06
ploughed 137.15 279.F13
ploughfields 208.06
ploung 225.17
plouse 338.04
plousiman 057.03
plover 383.16 478.36
plovery 140.23
plow 336.29 452.16
plower 318.13
Plowp 072.09
plowshure 549.27
plubs 312.33
plucher 482.12
pluck 081.19 178.13 215.08
Pluck 015.22
plucked 158.35
plucketed 117.07
pluckily 253.16
plucking 425.01 504.34
pluckless 146.17
plucks 086.09
pluds 231.14
plug 243.21 359.15
plugchewing 209.01
plugg 081.30
Plugg 099.21
plugged 035.25 396.28
pluggy 053.25
pluggy 345.06
Pluhurabelle 201.35
pluie 158.24
pluk 053.24 053.24
plultibust 358.27
plultiply 405.01
plum 493.07
plumages 367.22
Plumb 617.02
plumbate 541.24
plumbing 319.19
plumbs 006.17
plumbsily 149.29
plume 204.11
plume 229.03
Plume 177.30
plumed 231.13 288.F5
plumeflights 119.15
plumes 180.09 183.32 233.16
plumodrole 043.18
plump 109.20 167.21
plumpchake 446.10
Plumpduffs 302.F1
plumped 288.F5 549.31
Plumped 319.15
plumper 201.06
plumpers 272.L3
plumpest 170.27
plumpkins 353.27
plumply 164.17
plumps 129.19
plumptylump 363.24
plumpudding 170.36
plums 451.06
plumsized 084.11
plumsucked 123.24
plumyumnietcies 348.22
Plundehowse 525.22
plunder 081.21 209.12
plundered 118.36 579.30
plunderpussy 011.13
plunders 188.12
plundersundered 596.03
plunge 584.17
plunged 203.23
Plunger 486.09
plunges 539.18
plunging 066.22
plunk 043.13
Plunk 495.20
Plunkett 127.19
pluplu 265.F4
plurabelle 553.26
Plurabelle's 215.24
Plurabilities 104.02
plurable 264.02
plural 488.17
plurators 215.25
pluribie 290.24
plurielled 224.25
plurity 568.05
plus 030.24 084.11 115.15 315.05 385.16 396.18 435.09 497.09 551.19
plus 283.L1 340.27 405.32
pluse 328.35 412.31
plush 561.30
plushfeverfraus 603.19
plushkwadded 516.09
plusible 138.09
plusieurs 281.09
plusneeborn 547.05
plusquebelle 327.06
plussed 607.31
Plussiboots 415.03
pluterpromptly 255.29
plutherotested 187.17
plutherplethoric 104.17
Plutonic 292.30
plutonically 267.09
plutorpopular 078.12
plutous 269.27
pluvaville 297.25
Pluviabilla 548.06
pluviali 185.15
pluvious 451.36
pluxty 566.28
pluzz 407.30
ply 262.27 399.32 625.21
plyable 388.07
Plyfire 439.35
plying 525.34
Plymouth 389.01
p.m. 100.17
pneu 458.21
pneuma 124.16
pneumantics 172.20
pneumax 156.14
pneumodipsics 151.30
pneumonia 434.20
pnomoneya 313.12
pnum 476.35
po 622.07
Po 453.22
Po 105.07
P.O. 421.07 (Post Office)
poach 450.02 623.02
poached 016.36 380.24
poaching 209.14
poachmistress 412.23
pobalclock 068.30
pobbel 334.24 454.35
Pobiedo 219.12
poblesse 567.26
Pocahontas 559.32
Pocahonteuse 106.16
pocchino 054.18
poce 261.F4
pock 523.28 538.14
pocked 029.07
pocket 050.30 161.10 279.F33 516.18 579.11
pocketanchoredcheck 537.15
pocketbook 131.02 136.19
pocketcoat 030.22
pocketed 255.20
pocketmouth 054.35
pockets 093.02 323.17 428.24 484.18 507.26 529.28 580.35
pocketside 208.21
pockle 617.08
pocks 538.14
poco 456.08
Pod 412.31
podatus 121.27
podding 617.20
poddle 016.21 208.30
Poddle 106.05
poddlebridges 600.08
poddy 478.22
Poddy 361.15
Poder 220.20
podestril 542.17
Podex 185.03 398.02
Podomkin 333.04
podrida 092.02
Podushka 333.28

poele 059.32
poenis 596.06
Poe's 534.21
poestcher 345.17
poesther 429.18
poestries 145.24
poesy 091.03
poet 048.22 279.F23 445.32 515.34 539.06 619.31
poeta 482.32
poeter 372.04
poetesser 232.13
poetics 413.12
poetographies 242.19
poetries 435.26
poetry 230.24 377.17 523.24
Poetry 307.11
poet's 265.28
poetscalds 425.24
Poffpoff 012.12
Poggadovies 184.31
poghue 068.12 083.33 384.34 395.24
Poghue 376.21 376.21 376.21
poghuing 022.25 385.32 385.32 388.23
poghyogh 037.22
pogne 344.23
pognency 343.01
Pogue 588.29
poh 173.22
pohlmann's 278.F3
poi 295.32 295.32
poi 540.12
poignings 143.19
poignt 160.32
Poindejenk 179.28
poinds 295.30
poing 204.12
poingt 050.02
point 012.31 025.20 033.08 060.17 084.35 098.21 114.21 120.28 162.17 194.32 249.28 287.14 288.13 296.10 313.19 321.07 322.31 363.01 385.30 411.23 414.10 433.15 434.18 436.20 437.03 437.04 437.09 478.07 482.33 511.16 513.19 522.06 559.21 565.01 567.04 567.07 575.11 586.22 587.04 587.23 588.07
point 350.11
Point 267.F1 580.34
pointblank 179.02
Pointcarried 304.05
pointed 036.17 124.08 407.23
pointedly 063.05
pointefox 242.35
Pointer 289.21
pointers 057.01
pointing 055.16 097.12 163.26 374.15 419.20 566.34
pointing 340.04
Pointing 331.01
pointopointing 181.24
points 034.24 085.28 114.07 114.09 133.34 193.29 330.14 373.24
points 419.01
pointsins 599.21
pointstand 426.24
poirette 235.34
poise 282.07 493.29
poised 520.33
poison 174.02 209.07 283.32 331.18 484.27 582.05
poisonal 230.20
poisoned 133.05 480.16
poisoner 463.13
poisoning 048.05 492.16
Poisonivy 186.13
Poisse 177.12
poissission 245.13
poissons 451.06
pojr 343.19
pokar 606.33
poke 095.01 273.15 296.29 461.23 548.13 613.28
Poke 490.18
poked 083.30 320.17
pokehole 339.02
poker 224.15 229.18 261.F1
pokers 078.13
pokes 066.23 246.10
pokeway 315.34
pokeys 542.22
poking 188.32 568.36
pokker 326.22
Pol 330.05
Poland 130.30
polar 177.33 602.30
POLAR 271.R1
polarbeeber 087.22
polarised 092.10 164.02
polcat 513.13
polder 330.22
polders 549.19
poldier 073.17
pole 024.34 194.08 284.05 350.20 451.05 492.26 566.35
Pole 086.12
poleaxe 053.32
polecad 341.01
polecat 181.23
poled 393.12
poleetness 543.01
poleetsfurcers 565.04
polemarch 380.12
polemypolity's 133.18
polentay 240.16
polepost 013.28
polerpasse 128.25
poles 189.13 328.08
poletop 244.03
police 113.24 137.19 300.01 443.04 524.06 530.04 583.24 618.20
Police 306.25
policeman 145.22 562.18 580.07
policeman's 085.34
policepolice 113.25
policist 590.05
policy 539.08
poligone 231.30
Polikoff's 339.15
πόλιν 269.L2
polis 023.15 128.22
Polis 072.16
polise 113.36
polished 072.31 497.35
polisignstunter 370.30
poliss 281.F2
Polistaman 202.15
polite 413.20 599.21 618.35
politeness 190.11
politic 165.27
political 108.30 150.20
POLITICAL 272.R1
politicoecomedy 540.26
politics 306.14
politish 084.35
politymester 324.20
polk 236.16
polkar 331.11
polkas 418.14
Polkingtone 144.30
poll 088.16 277.10 284.F1 568.14 580.11 622.02 622.31
Poll 147.13
Pollabella 619.16
pollard 537.29
Polldoody 479.06
polled 551.35
Polled 159.04
pollen 238.35
pollex 340.28
pollititians 173.16
Pollock 229.31
Pollockses' 028.06
pollsies 221.08
pollute 186.21
pollution 237.23
Pollux 431.36
Pollux 307.L1
polly 323.07
polly 270.L1
Polly 440.28 562.14
pollyfool 015.14
pollygameous 241.05
pollylogue 470.09
pollynooties 209.31
pollysigh 586.28
pollyvoulley 346.18
pollywollies 508.19
Polo 567.35
polog 607.21
polombos 120.02
polony 621.13
polosh 137.29
polped 396.32
polps 153.13
polster 526.02
polt 130.35
Polthergeistkotzdond-herhoploits 187.15
polthronechair 423.07
poltri 247.09
poltronage 342.13
poly 495.16
Polycarp 254.09 600.05
polyfizzyboisterous 547.23
polygluttural 117.13
polyhedron 107.08
Polymop 222.12
Polynesional 106.09
pom 527.31 586.12
pome 080.22 080.22
pomefructs 019.15
pomelo 253.24
Pomeranzia 038.11
Pomeroy 027.26 290.F5
pomme 020.29 184.28
pommes 504.33
pommettes 207.10
pomoeria 249.16
Pomona 062.34
pomp 077.24 135.03 624.14
Pompe 153.17
Pompei 329.25

Pompeius 307.L1
Pompery 064.15
pompey 568.24
pompifically 155.08
Pompkey 568.25
pompom 349.23
pompommy 609.33
pompoms 167.17
pomposity 282.L3
pomps 537.04 602.22
pomp's 625.10
pompship 343.29
pon 004.27 056.15 096.04 279.04 420.14 480.02 582.28
'pon 524.09
ponch 257.23
poncho 381.15
poncif 154.12
poncks 032.03
pond 278.10 511.17
pondant 546.07
pondered 261.10 454.25 619.26
pondering 043.12
pondest 526.29
pond's 301.F1
Pondups 616.35
pondus 035.35 559.24
pondus 277.L6
ponenter 480.10
poneys 285.13
pong 233.28 327.25
ponging 519.17
Pongo 609.35
ponk 369.23
pons 553.21
pont 493.29
Pont 578.25
pontdelounges 321.34
ponte 178.24
ponted 580.01
ponteen 410.14
pontiff 198.12
Pontiffs 307.17
pontiff's 089.35
Pontifical 514.27
pontificate 544.23
pontification 569.16
pontificator 139.17
pontine 332.28
Pontius 156.05
pontofacts 532.09
pontofert 350.05
Pontoffbellek 412.10
poo 144.34 282.30 282.31 563.07
Poo 144.19 546.26
poodle 269.F1
Poof 439.15
poog 492.12
poohoo 162.27
poohoor 224.36
poohpooher 498.22
Pook 338.32
pookal 313.35
pookas 102.15
pool 007.07 073.17 135.14 188.23 213.36 264.F2 328.01 330.21 338.14 365.29 486.31 490.32 525.35 600.05 600.05
Pool 096.19 174.28 546.34
Poolaulwoman 054.04
Poolbeg 046.18 215.01
Poolblack 035.16
poolermates 526.36
pooles 164.04
pooley 584.12
pooleypooley 206.28
Poolland 390.35
poolp 442.31
pools 194.36 204.18
poop 084.06 416.32
poopahead 560.27
poopery 388.21
pooping 496.20
Poopinheavin 220.34
poopishers 370.34
poopive 282.32
poor 039.20 047.13 048.19 049.02 062.17 068.16 078.29 084.08 111.15 114.32 117.21 138.15 148.33 159.01 161.24 161.24 200.03 208.31 210.02 210.10 214.06 220.22 223.28 224.09 224.17 240.01 240.03 290.06 290.07 290.09 293.02 321.03 322.11 371.36 380.11 380.24 380.33 381.16 386.13 387.14 387.15 387.28 388.36 390.20 391.04 391.14 391.15 391.23 391.25 392.07 392.10 392.19 393.27 395.12 396.27 397.02 397.15 397.21 397.26 405.06 408.10 413.12 427.34 429.04 431.20 434.15 440.24 442.17 448.30 453.03 453.28 459.05 460.08 462.13 462.15 463.20 465.22 469.29 486.14 488.29 489.06 495.35 527.04 535.27 535.29 535.34 536.07 537.11 555.12 605.07 609.06
Poor 009.32 049.15 155.12 200.15 226.04 391.04 393.05 412.24 421.04 446.24 488.11 534.05 536.08 565.29 583.03
pooraroon 620.05
poorblond 273.27
poorboir 392.16
poorchase 443.30
poorest 151.20
poorhouse 392.26
Pooridiocal 106.11
poorin 300.30
pooripathete 226.06
poorish 432.12
poorjoist 113.36
poorliness 243.08
poorloves 625.24
poorly 048.22
poormen 566.02
pooro 529.30
Poorparents 175.09
poors 187.02 333.31 375.09 498.33
Poors 373.01
poorters 069.26
poorusers 060.27
Poosycomb 391.23
poot 395.28
poother 200.06
poots 368.20
pootsch 519.03
poour 291.04
pooveroo 416.13
pop 039.16 197.24 211.21 223.10 310.35 332.13 457.22
Pop 269.28
Popapreta 179.19
popcorks 381.10
pope 419.22 458.05 500.18 580.29
Pope 078.28 078.28
popeling 133.20
popers 303.09
popes 277.F1 343.30
Popes 151.15
pope's 618.04
Pope's 448.17
popespriestpower 188.07
popetithes 326.06
popetry 466.11
Popey 349.19
popeye 013.30
popeyed 189.10
popguns 065.11
popiular 351.12
poplar 100.13 248.29 523.24 535.04
Poplar 369.10
poplarest 599.26
poplin 042.33 211.17
Poplinstown 539.24
popo 427.07 532.30
Popofetts 106.24
popoporportiums 343.18
Poposht 441.06
poposterously 153.25
Popottes 366.01
poppa 331.01
Poppa 280.17
Poppagenua 513.20
Poppakork 497.28
Poppamore 173.22
Poppea 572.36
popped 330.15
Popper 370.03
poppies 476.20
popping 567.28
Poppolin 104.15
Poppop 569.25
poppos 288.F4
poppy 365.12 445.16 448.20
Poppy 102.25
poppyheads 084.17
Poppypap's 025.05
poppyrossies 351.13
pops 352.21
popsoused 339.34
populace 032.17 045.14
popular 026.28 061.15 190.25 194.28 305.21 404.25
popularly 123.23
Population 436.10
populators 524.32
populo 089.05
populose 609.02
Populus 160.13
popwilled 155.32
popynose 009.20
por 054.17 214.06 339.23
porage 395.29
porca 009.36
Porca 463.06
porchway 177.22
porcoghastly 178.30
porcupig's 535.20
pore 612.18
Pore 141.27 145.19
porecourts 005.36
poring 189.31 515.24

pork 039.17 326.33 411.36 433.11 617.12
porkbarrel 212.23
porkego 566.26 566.26
porker 304.13 368.11
Porker 071.12
porkers 091.07
porkodirto 368.11
porkograso 038.03
porks 141.31
pork's 462.35
porktroop 057.15
porlarbaar 370.27
Pornter 570.15
Porphyrious 264.F3
porphyroid 100.17
porple 392.20
porpoise 427.21 437.30 623.14
porpor 200.04
porporates 185.10
porpus 076.13
porridge 442.21 489.16
porridgers 409.20
porrish 280.L2
porsenal 083.08
Porsons 018.22
port 076.16 094.32 135.29 328.08 328.22 371.13 480.13 587.17 613.32
port 231.06
Porta 205.27
portable 082.06 414.11 605.08
portal 054.10 614.33
portals 258.29
portar 406.10
Portarlington's 406.02
portavorous 089.16
portcullised 127.36
porte 551.35 603.30
Porteleau 553.14
portemanteau 240.36
portent 546.10
Portentos 104.23
porter 022.29 122.10 135.07 136.04 138.32 187.16 260.06 510.24 511.19 530.12 560.08
Porter 560.24 560.26 561.03
Porter 072.03 106.32
porterblack 187.17
portereens 563.24
Porterfeud 091.15
Porterfillyers 371.01
porterfull 016.04
porterhouse 204.09 405.23
porterpease 021.18 022.06
porters 142.17 219.06 609.33
Porters 560.22
Porterscout 388.15
Porterstown 276.L5
porteryark 624.15
portey 039.10
Porthergill 104.18
porthery 023.10
portion 487.35
portions 222.14
Portiuncula 306.24
portlifowlium 083.31
Portlund 602.17
portly 043.08
portnoysers 323.08
porto 133.14
Porto 560.31
Portobello 027.26 134.18 290.F5
portocall 316.28
portocallie 054.16
portogal 114.25
portraits 182.19
portraiture 165.17
portreeve 547.17
portrifaction 078.21
portrout 059.08
Portsymasser 186.35
Portterand's 088.33
portugal's 463.19
porty 051.24
porumptly 338.15
Porvos 484.32
porzy 334.04
po's 236.30
posably 236.35
pose 157.35 191.12 265.14 361.04 372.04 435.05 520.14
Pose 267.F2 303.02
Posed 092.13
poseproem 528.16
poser 147.20 476.23
Poser 093.14
poses 254.28
posh 151.34 329.29 584.08
Posh 315.33
Poshbott 340.31
Posht 099.35 454.06
Poshtapengha 377.27
poshup 158.30
Posidonius 080.28
posied 552.27
posited 574.04
Positing 164.04
position 124.12 166.35 363.28 529.18 559.21 564.01 582.29 590.22 608.09 617.09
positions 359.33 466.03
Positions 274.06
positive 108.30
positively 111.28 421.28 446.09 448.27 468.23 488.17
Positively 180.32
posque 067.32
posquiflor 561.20
poss 021.18 022.05 022.29 412.26
Poss 466.30
possabled 397.25
posse 471.23
possess 057.16 189.17 532.30 573.20
possessed 050.16 108.13 181.13 398.23 450.36
possessing 411.02 483.30 616.13
possession 063.18 378.21
possetpot 294.31
possible 110.11 145.31 173.19 240.30 298.28 530.34 599.13 612.22 614.10
possibles 110.15
possibly 052.32 065.16 069.27 098.23 107.10 110.16 118.24 386.34 409.31 415.30 420.02 442.17 595.36
possing 051.02
posspots 258.16
possum 096.34 191.12
possumbotts 622.11
post 166.21 181.34 190.03 237.20 289.05 298.05 340.33 348.09 364.06 404.07 422.12 428.15 430.20 446.28 462.22 470.26 483.13 484.10 514.29 579.11 583.23 617.23
Post 145.23 206.11 211.31 278.13 307.02 404.07
Post 071.36
postages 456.29
postal 066.10 485.36
postallion 279.F28
postanulengro 472.22
postbillers 373.23
postboys 587.06
Postboy's 039.36
postcard 388.31
postcards 027.32
postchased 405.01
postconditional 270.01
POSTCREATE 262.R2
postcreated 605.08
postea 185.18
posted 034.03 232.17
postequities 438.14
poster 027.18 336.22 554.01
posteriors 075.24
posterity 096.35
postern 099.16 127.09 305.27 493.32 538.15
posterwise 483.03
postexilic 472.34
postface 582.20
posth 556.36
posthaste 456.24
posthastem 238.02
postheen 092.21
Posthorn 482.19
posthumious 563.04
posthumour's 316.34
posthumust 422.14
postilium 453.36
postillion 279.F28
postleadeny 348.05
postlots 036.13
postlove 406.35
postlude 426.33
postludium 469.29
postman 488.19
postman's 027.07
Postman's 176.07
postmantuam 113.02
Postmartem 455.11
posto 430.10
postoboy 043.17
postoffice 567.02
postoomany 408.13
postoppage 369.34
postoral 374.17
postpaid 101.25
Postpone 579.14
postponed 051.22
postposition 178.04
postproneauntisquattor 019.27
postprophetical 011.30
postpuberal 037.01
Postreintroducing 246.36
posts 460.21
post's 028.17
postscrapped 370.10
postscrapt 124.32
postscript 042.09 122.21
Postscript 393.31
postulate 369.30
postulation 392.22
Postumus 377.09

postvortex 150.07
postwartem 263.11
posuit 185.20
posy 278.24 604.03
pot 025.07 038.01 118.24 136.17 138.03 142.05 160.15 198.13 227.09 291.F7 380.25 385.14 414.29 451.05 524.27 612.20 615.09
Pot 279.04
Pot 104.22
potably 118.15
Potanasty 444.29
Potapheu's 193.20
potapot 531.24
potatorings 208.11
potators 521.04
potatowards 240.36
potatums 549.31
potched 184.18
potchtatos 323.17
pote 056.22
poteen 056.26 125.22 451.01
poteentubbs 077.30
potent 053.05 060.21 186.05 419.23 492.35
potential 115.21 304.08 487.03
potheen 085.26
pother 303.15 594.31
potherbs 190.06
potholed 031.06
pothook 066.15 119.29
pothooks 181.13 280.16
potients 466.06
potifex 345.29
potion 397.18
potlids 041.11
potlood 425.28
potmother 011.09
Potollomuck 254.22
pots 078.12 144.32
pots 346.15
potstill 246.10
Potstille 105.23
Pott 220.07
pottage 037.31 167.22 289.05 466.25 487.16 542.30
pottagebake 414.09
potted 550.14
potter 240.22
Potter 134.06 274.F3
potters 201.22
potter's 618.33
Potterton's 602.15
pottery 111.23 503.05 543.07
potting 622.06
pottish 393.11
pottle 180.20
pottled 138.32
pottleproud 255.26
pottles 267.F5
Potts 073.08
potty 072.23
pou 107.22
Pou 415.26
pouch 024.32 066.25 430.30
pouder 147.32
poudies 540.36
Poudre 012.36
pouffed 315.16
poul 038.28
poule 201.01
Poule 192.13
Poulebec 369.29
Poulepinter 482.20
poules 117.24
Poulichinello 043.23
poulit 256.08
poulsen 326.26
poulterer 435.28
poultice 302.04
poultriest 112.05
poultry 187.13
Poultry 184.16
poultryhouse 371.13
poultryyard 589.28
pouly 322.12
Poum 568.13
pounautique 315.34
pounce 114.21 282.08
pouncefoot 367.05
pound 190.06 192.17 309.23 406.01 499.26 511.13 566.01 579.17
pound 398.32
pounderin 089.25
pounds 322.14 521.06 579.30 589.03
pounds 398.34
poupeep 435.25
pour 027.29 067.09 141.36 357.05 360.01 372.06 617.25
pour 081.29
Pour 613.08
Pourable 325.05
pouradosus 610.16
pouralittle 010.32
pourbox 165.31
pourch 209.29
poured 042.18 042.24 324.17 560.19 580.10
pourer 320.20
pouring 373.26 438.13 469.31
Pouringrainia 031.25
Pouringtoher 571.20
pouriose 015.36
Pourmeerme 409.17
Pournter 570.19
Pournterfamilias 570.20
Pouropourim 245.36
pourporteral 099.04
Pourquoi 479.28
pourquose 018.31
pours 134.19 137.34
poursuivant 005.07
Poursuivant 498.12
poursuive 175.19
poussepousse 008.07
pousseypram 008.07
pout 248.10
pouters 027.18
Poutresbourg 162.30
pouts 214.15
Pouts 461.02
pouved 117.10
Pov 051.13
Povar 339.05
poverty 192.10
povotogesus 316.28
powder 114.21 193.07 233.19 440.27
Powder 210.31
Powell 376.22
power 056.11 076.15 092.08 098.26 140.34 213.31 242.12 298.12 303.04 323.27 347.05 409.36 425.12 441.28 491.24 569.35 616.30
power 345.19 399.18
Power 317.31 346.20 521.22
powered 436.03
powerful 605.18
powers 087.10 089.05 266.14 299.27 321.01 484.23 488.08 495.13
Power's 205.25 495.04
powlver 550.18
powther 272.L3
Powther 349.23
powwows 011.10
pox 523.28
Poynter 622.27
Pozor 100.05
pozzo 181.12
pp 314.20
pp. 123.19 (pages)
p.p. 467.33
P.P. 432.07 (parish priest)
P. P. 536.06 (P. P. Quemby)
P.P, 498.11 (Antepummelites P.P,)
ppenmark 189.06
P.P.M. 131.03 (postage prepaid in money)
P.P.O. 388.20 (Notre Dame 1132 P.P.O.)
pppease 571.21
ppppfff 116.33
P.Q.R.S. 484.22
pra 228.26
prace 350.19
practicable 559.04
practical 033.03 142.21 269.13
practically 088.11
practice 116.29 283.10
practices 537.16
practise 573.25
Practise 579.22
practised 083.33
practising 085.06 432.23 572.24
praddies 351.07
pragma 056.31
praharfeast 541.24
prain 522.29
prairial 407.01
prairie 019.14
prairmakers 059.18
prais 141.36
praise 088.33 141.06 227.26 235.19 240.20 430.18 571.12
praised 411.13
praisegad 485.05
praisegood 085.17
praisers 029.33 386.35
praises 211.06 305.30 472.24
praising 526.32
praisonal 485.05
praktice 353.01
pram 166.12 328.03
pramaxle 214.24
prame 141.06
prance 186.36 303.F2 513.13
prancer 445.14
Prancess 312.22
pranjapansies 059.14
prank 398.35
pranked 223.33
pranklings 139.26

prankquean 021.15 021.15 021.26 022.02 022.11 022.13 022.27 023.12
pranks 068.22 095.05 337.22 340.11 394.28
Pranksome 508.28
pranzipal 405.32
prapsposterus 016.03
prater 142.12 551.15
pratey 515.35
pratician 593.17
praties 056.26 069.30 327.02 406.11
Pratiland 124.25
pratschkats 101.26
prattle 337.09
prattlepate 173.11
prattly 470.09
pratyusers 593.17
prava 052.15
pravacy 328.17
praverbs 242.12
Pravidance 147.17
praviloge 605.07
Pravities 050.10
prawn 249.01 395.11
prawns 261.06
praxis 458.35
pray 079.21 115.06 168.12 188.19 188.19 188.20 256.01 301.06 311.30 375.25 382.16 434.33 447.14 466.22 467.04 472.32 482.18 528.12 530.32 568.06 569.13 571.19 579.21 585.12 604.31 615.15 626.26
Pray 172.36 336.11 585.12
prayce 361.32
praydews 504.30
prayed 075.16 089.15 132.26 178.31 363.24 415.34
prayer 122.08 222.04 231.25 235.01 307.F9 398.12 482.23 530.35 605.22
prayers 214.19 454.28 569.13
Prayfulness 601.29 601.29
prayhasd 333.28
praying 149.02 292.09 325.28 438.17 444.16 453.14
prayings 403.11
Praypaid 590.11
praypuffs 234.24
prays 287.01 558.08 623.30
prayses 222.29
prayshyous 350.16
Pray-your-Prayers 258.35
praze 398.27
P.R.C.R.L.L. 378.09 (PerCe o'ReiLLy)
preach 168.03 483.08
preached 116.26
Preacher 493.36
preaches 225.06
preaching 242.11 432.23 467.09 579.22
preachybook 611.25
preadaminant 617.23
preadamite 530.28
preaggravated 358.27
prealably 394.20
preambler 429.04
prearranged 107.33
prease 350.18
preast 281.L4
preature 465.34
PREAUSTERIC 266.R1
prebeing 488.19
prebellic 537.18
prebendary 043.12
precedent 285.F2 585.27 614.34
precedings 603.25
preceedings 352.18
precentor 060.32
precentors 026.21
precincts 294.20
precious 095.24 143.31 148.09 317.36 457.35 460.19 461.07 500.25 500.28 571.21
preciousest 146.31
precipitate 604.18
precipitation 182.15 324.28 551.19
precise 164.09 179.15 290.05
precised 311.28
precisely 164.25 368.16
precisely 353.30
Precisely 514.21
precisingly 365.17
precluded 466.33
precondamned 418.30
precoxious 052.14
PRECREATE 262.R2
precreated 605.05
Precurser 506.06
predamanant 076.02
predicable 269.13
predicament 131.12
Predicament 308.L2
predictable 192.33
predicted 324.26
predikants 138.27
prediseased 423.27
pree 240.11 282.31 282.31 336.10 513.13
preealittle 010.32
preechup 318.19
preelectric 380.12
preeminent 380.20 504.15
preempson 537.36
preen 268.05
preesses 232.06
preester 094.36
prefaced 119.15
prefacies 347.21
prefall 030.15
prefer 148.03 165.21 272.14 562.04
preference 447.26
preferment 291.F5
preferred 141.19 170.26 476.24
preferring 109.20 488.33
prefers 098.30
prefixed 214.04
prefurred 141.22
pregnant 438.11
pregross 284.22
prehend 223.25
prehistoric 385.18 477.36
Prehistoric 059.15
preholder 529.34
prejuice 405.36
prelaps 497.08
prelates 102.15 440.11
prelimbs 431.14
prelove 406.35
premature 189.28
premier 062.25 595.10
premier 430.22
premises 028.36 042.08 046.05 066.32 181.09 256.08 422.08
premisses 381.35
premitially 409.34
Premver 110.23
prenanciation 089.26
prence 289.02
prender 541.10
Prenderguest 124.15
Prendregast 144.06
prenticeserving 533.07
prentis' 422.20
prentisses 510.11
Prepare 530.17
prepared 050.03 093.09 412.31 469.33 495.12
Prepatrickularly 316.05
prepensing 345.04
prepestered 178.03
preplays 374.07
prepoposal 575.32
preposing 345.05
preposition 595.25
prepositus 228.34
prepossessing 115.32
prepostered 101.25
preposterose 582.02
preposterous 033.32 189.21 356.35
preposters 190.32
Prepostoral 086.21
prepping 274.30
preprocession 156.08
prepronominal 120.09
preprosperousness 308.21
preprotestant 534.16
preprovided 614.30
prepueratory 274.30
prepurgatory 161.23 446.36
prerepeated 081.33
prés 142.12
presainted 304.22
presaw 075.10
Presbutt-in-the-North 569.05
presbyoperian 294.01
Presbys 210.27
presbyterian 391.29
prescriptions 419.30
preseeding 275.F4
presence 036.28 116.21 165.16 224.04 290.10 413.20 564.25 623.10
presends 572.19
presenile 078.01
present 076.21 077.24 081.08 082.34 108.26 111.13 115.32 170.08 173.31 186.01 188.30 269.30 304.08 314.21 389.17 389.18 389.19 407.32 422.17 477.16 496.36 507.31 524.17 566.21 567.32 570.26 595.27 599.27 613.13 618.11
present 341.35
Present 303.L3
Presentacion 528.19
presentation 431.30 556.04
PRESENTATION 272.R1
presented 035.35 163.21 561.32
presentiment 597.27
presenting 107.11
presention 505.36

presently 048.09 323.29 453.30 456.24 537.06 582.02
presentment 341.18
presents 011.30 025.01 092.23 183.31 221.31 241.04 254.08 284.26 289.23 363.31 364.07 458.15 563.37
presents 355.02
Presepeprosapia 265.22
Preservative 097.18
Preservativation 184.16
Preserved 055.18
preshoes 237.08
presidency 229.33
presquesm'ile 056.28
press 123.07 229.08 275.26 284.F3 360.06 374.32 379.06 379.06 550.03
Press 379.06 503.35
pressance 347.36
pressant 221.17
pressantly 295.29
pressdom 440.01
pressed 015.02 057.28 092.14 136.15 499.26 551.10 607.17
presses 387.36
pressing 151.03 155.18 446.22 624.29
presspassim 050.24
pressure 121.25 557.25
pressures 310.35
presswritten 438.18
prest 225.11 256.04
presta 207.24
prestatute 117.35
Prestissima 256.04
Prestopher 484.32
prestreet 097.21
presuaded 078.17
presumption 267.F3
presumptively 137.15
presumptuably 417.35
presurely 455.17
presurnames 030.03
pretells 017.03
pretend 169.02 249.34 546.22
pretendant 013.11
pretended 067.20
pretenders 252.15
pretending 198.25
pretends 573.19
preter 160.30
preteridentified 615.05
preterite 563.22
preteriti 287.20
preteriting 143.08
preterpost 600.17
pretext 069.22 161.32
preties 031.24
pretinately 055.09
pretonsions 511.17
pretti 225.33
prettier 471.07
prettiest 145.27 508.26
prettilees 008.04
prettily 079.21 337.09
Prettimaid 247.34
prettish 351.07
prettly 470.09
pretty 011.32 114.10 188.05 191.31 210.31 220.04 267.10 289.26 361.14 384.25 386.15 391.36 395.26 407.07 446.05 459.25 508.24 524.14 537.13 548.24 556.16 557.21 564.27 588.35
Pretty 443.15 625.24
Pretty 106.14
prettydotes 269.06
Prettyplume 318.12
prettypretty 159.14
pretumbling 013.18
prevailend 288.24
prevailing 568.30
prevened 551.12
prevenient 585.09
prevent 069.24
prevented 426.31
preventing 395.21
previdence 062.07
Previdence 325.02
previous 039.30 079.06 167.28 356.23 448.05
previously 479.23
prevision 107.25
prexactly 177.32
prey 080.21 379.08 582.32
preyed 231.06
preyers 351.25
preying 228.03 350.25
prhose 423.16
prhyse 375.34
Priam 006.23
priamed 240.36
priamite 513.20
priapic 115.32
priars 438.17
priccoping 554.03
price 089.23 101.13 189.22 264.22 279.04 302.03 425.19 439.28 444.21 458.28 500.27 500.28 500.30 500.30 516.23 521.07 537.13 571.12 579.20
price 418.21
Price 071.14
priced 432.12
priceless 458.06 461.20 500.32
pricelist 535.08
prich 249.35
pricing 406.35
prick 248.05 576.26 615.27
pricked 083.06
pricker 019.17
pricket 014.32
pricket's 014.33
pricking 061.36 090.12 149.01 452.12
prickled 291.27
prickly 570.27
pricoxity 224.36
pride 017.30 139.17 145.13 210.17 250.31 297.30 309.06 355.13 406.25 422.15 422.20 452.25 563.11 577.16
Pride 017.30 296.05 620.06
pridejealice 344.32
pridely 366.14
Pridewin 171.35
prie 058.26 058.28
priers 196.21
Priers 375.18
priest 026.06 038.26 058.05 086.19 086.34 204.04 227.09 458.04 510.34
Priest 326.24
Priest 440.02
priesterrite 301.03
priesters 492.33
priestess 360.25
priestessd 234.15
priesthunters 386.36
priestly 039.01
priest-mayor-king-merchant 447.15
priesto 289.17
priestomes 613.04
priest's 605.07
Priest's 176.17
priesty 466.21
prifixes 162.13
prig 089.15 173.08 563.26
Prigged 053.06
prigging 163.10
priggish 041.27
prigs 279.F17
pril 110.23
prim 101.35 288.06 327.16
prima 241.21
Prima 289.29
primace 604.22
primafairy 478.32
primal 263.20 286.20 606.10
Primamère 548.28
Primanouriture 300.L1
primapatriock 531.33
primarily 038.19
primarose 556.17
primary 085.06 286.05
primas 155.21
Primas 014.12 014.13
primates 229.01
Primatially 569.17
prime 069.17 161.15 212.19 248.03 360.04 385.14 405.14 439.11 451.01 558.02 577.04 605.18
primed 367.22 427.31 539.05 580.29
primelads 210.04
primer 020.08 623.32
Primer 269.F4
primerose 361.22
primers 440.23
primes 483.21 550.12
primesigned 024.28
primeum 356.11
primeval 599.09
Primewer 041.35
primilibatory 604.08
primises 497.24
primitive 405.03
PRIMITIVE 267.R1
primkissies 340.11
primmafore's 453.03
primomobilisk 163.21
Primrose 039.36 553.06
primtim's 227.17
Primum 185.14
Primus 512.27
prince 089.06 099.24 135.12 138.10 143.07 254.35 278.26 373.15 422.15 460.12 463.36 549.07
Prince 236.03 571.20
princeable 626.27
princeliest 474.10
princeps 164.01
princer 363.04
princes 242.26 566.20

princesome 239.29
princess 091.06 148.08 183.32 243.30
princesse 157.32
princest 254.06 387.19
princhе 618.06
principalest 612.20
principality 518.05 605.17
principals 266.16
principel 089.06
principeza 497.32
principial 121.18 163.25
PRINCIPIUM 286.R2
principles 035.22 550.33
PRINCIPLES 271.R1
principot 408.11
Prine 129.26
pringlpik 011.10
prink 340.11 425.24
prinkips 234.20
print 120.36 132.13 180.17 334.32 407.08 532.08
printed 043.25 456.31
printink 187.18
prints 020.11 280.22 387.20
prior 069.35 486.36
priority 501.13
priorly 607.02
priors 422.36
Prisca 494.11
prisckly 467.32
prise 054.21
prised 064.04
prisent 498.31
Prisky 513.20
prisme 287.10
prismic 235.24
prison 364.26 543.27
prisonals 363.32
prisonce 536.24
prisoned 472.09
prisoner 085.31 100.25
Prisoner 499.30
prisonpotstill 463.34
prispast 292.11
prisscess 396.08
Prisson 176.02
pristmoss 141.05
pristopher 120.02
Pritchards 044.08
Pritchards 176.02
prities 137.11
pritt 337.28
pritticoaxes 546.16
prittle 021.04
Prittlewell 503.35
pritty 242.17 502.14
priv 136.32
privace 138.19
privacy 586.04
private 058.32 059.28 066.05 069.04 098.18 130.10 177.19 181.17 196.16 225.06 235.21 336.22 438.15 438.21 459.20 529.11 533.08 544.05 582.33 613.34 616.07
Private 534.32
Private 295.L1
privatear 327.36
privately 043.25
privates 239.20 289.21 523.35 587.34
Privates 107.06
privation 551.21
prive 351.20
prives 614.16
privet 412.27
privileged 605.32 616.13
privily 571.26
privious 338.06
Privius 390.23
privy 179.10
privy-sealed 448.29
privysuckatary 177.19
prize 017.30 036.13 057.04 092.15 111.06 170.07 251.34 257.22 327.29 344.21 433.33 485.20 532.33 556.12
prize 418.21
Prize 280.24
prized 340.28
prizelestly 237.08
pro 057.36 136.17 183.26 514.22 529.04 552.03
pro 056.03 122.09 190.17 211.14 518.05
Pro 523.21 540.13
Pro 521.10
proach 297.14
probable 052.32 432.26 612.23
probably 069.26 076.34 104.17 107.11 110.17 110.20 120.16 152.04 417.36 442.21 557.31 595.35
PROBAPOSSIBLE 262.R1
Probe 286.20
probed 606.21
probenopubblicoes 371.24
prober's 476.12
probiverbal 060.32
problem 032.32 135.26 149.17 150.18
Problem 286.19
problematical 524.25
pro-Brother 193.21
probscenium 180.03
proceded 111.10 605.28
Proceding 412.29
proceed 067.07 448.04
proceeded 073.18 253.23
proceeding 149.14
proceedings 157.30 443.11 610.02
proceeds 431.28
procent 240.28
process 063.32 165.31 182.03 230.31 497.03 515.15 609.31 614.31
processes 414.28
processingly 607.29
processly 358.05
processus 550.02 304.L3
procisely 177.33
proclaim 030.08 155.10 603.36
Procne 307.L1
proconverted 220.30
Procreated 605.04
procul 255.15
PROCUL 286.R4
proculs 384.18
procurator 572.19
procuratress 352.13
procure 545.06 573.07
procured 447.36
procuring 115.23
prod 470.02
prodder 520.20
prodection 285.F2
prodestind 328.10
prodesting 577.33
prodestung 126.22
prodgering 559.36
prodigal 210.17
prodigence 190.22
prodigits 414.05
Prodooce 087.31
prodooced 035.27
prodromarith 030.04
prods 231.13
produce 185.29 222.16 569.31
produced 230.18 493.11
producer 219.07 255.27
Producer 577.15
producers 497.01
Produces 303.L3
producing 484.11
product 254.04 518.16
production 359.23 419.31 422.06
products 163.34
prof 606.27
profane 087.07 335.30
profanian 277.F7
profeen 562.32
proferring 504.30
proferring 345.29
professed 290.20
profession 618.30
professional 042.34
profèssionally 124.10
professor 459.30
Professor 150.15 151.11 151.32 161.02 165.27
profetised 520.29
proffer 223.21 575.31
profferred 441.35
profile 489.27
profit 068.28 109.02 181.17 275.21 582.10
profiteered 585.06
profiteers 448.23
proforhim 240.14
proformly 342.28
profound 099.23 107.12
profoundly 476.21
profoundth 158.16
profund 452.18
profundis 075.18
profundust 535.29
profused 301.F3 334.09
profusedly 015.23
profusely 544.02 564.07
profusional 141.24
profusive 006.16
progeniem 078.12
progeny 188.35
programme 220.25 446.34 531.27
progress 236.26 473.21 567.20 625.13
PROGRESS 272.R1
progromme 443.08
Prohibition 453.14
prohibitive 019.15
projectilised 353.28
projector 576.18
prole 039.05
PROLEGOMENA 262.R1
prolegs 155.28
proletarian 575.05
prolettas 340.18

proliferate 078.09
PROLIFERATE 279.R1
prolling 546.36
prolonged 041.31 600.19
prom 200.01
promenade 408.12 579.07
promethean 585.11
Prometheus 297.L2 307.L1
prominence 564.12
prominent 438.27
prominently 037.26
promiscious 066.04
promisck 323.11
Promiscuous 560.01
promise 062.13 110.23 209.15 249.13 442.14 443.16 546.20
Promise 297.L2
promised 225.32 519.32 521.12
promisefuller 562.11
promises 005.28 038.21 183.32 440.13 535.11
promishles 590.12
promising 433.27
promisk 421.01
promissly 361.09
promisus 238.15
prommer 033.12
promnentory 623.06
promonitory 317.31
promontory 506.19
Promoter 210.35
promotes 437.20
prompollen 418.19
prompt 309.08 397.21 404.16 475.29 558.36 623.32
Prompt 319.16
Promptboxer 049.30
prompter's 179.36 435.20
Promptings 221.22
promptitude 529.03
promptly 150.15 417.05
Promptly 589.25
Prompty 287.13
promulgate 092.36
promulgating 156.09
pronaose 228.28
prong 249.16
pronged 124.03
prongs 090.12 628.05
pronolan 490.15
prononsable 478.19
pronouncable 478.11
pronounced 118.27 287.14 420.02
pronouncing 351.23
pronuminally 490.08
prooboor 491.32
proof 147.32 160.10 316.07 316.07 364.01 431.16
proofpiece 533.07
proofpositive 084.20
Prooshious 008.10 008.11 008.13 008.14
prootha 521.03
prop 309.08 404.16 536.15 626.13
propagana 080.20
Propagandi 289.02
propagate 112.14
propaguting 078.12
propaired 413.01
proparly 602.34
propastored 094.13
PROPE 286.R4
propecies 153.02
propel 335.15
propelled 049.25
Propellopalombarouter 314.11
propencil 311.10
propendiculous 493.10
propennies 546.28
propenomen 059.15
proper 062.21 067.14 076.17 078.33 099.31 149.31 166.27 214.17 269.14 270.17 288.12 290.13 379.27 391.10 405.09 410.33 433.01 441.36 464.15 546.08 557.23 600.33 604.05 623.06
Proper 085.20 307.26
properer 276.02
properismenon 059.16
properly 108.20 121.21 175.03 363.32 421.27 436.15 455.28 524.02 589.25
propertied 556.27
properties 221.26
Properties 295.L1
property 465.32 492.27 558.36 576.05 600.01
prophecies 409.28 412.02
prophessised 520.14
prophet 033.33 050.06 307.F2
prophetarum 550.02
prophetethis 367.32
prophets 305.01
prophetting 480.07
prophitable 240.32
propogandering 059.22
proportions 443.23
proposed 060.05 410.29 575.25
proposer 572.19
proposing 606.09
propositions 572.22
propounde 378.24
propounded 220.30
propped 142.05 429.18
propper 162.13 279.F06
propprior 358.09
proprecession 156.08
propredicted 427.31
proprey 519.04
proprietary 574.06
proprietor 194.09
proprietoress 406.05
propriety 108.12
proprium 251.05
proprium 185.19
props 559.15 578.24 608.24
propsperups 230.35
proptably 619.10
propter 605.21
pros 404.16
pro's 117.15
prosator 185.14
proscribed 436.10
Proscription 301.L3
prose 488.24
Proserpronette 267.11
Prosession 379.05
Prosim 334.18
prosit 334.18
prosodes 268.19
prosodite 190.35
prosp 136.32
prospect 252.08 362.34 442.12 541.02
Prospect 476.11
prospector 137.31
Prospector 455.20 576.18
prospects 139.16
prosperousness 428.11
prosplodes 249.15
Prost 424.09
prostability 189.07
prostalutes 285.29
Prostatates 350.15
prostatution 365.17
prostitating 235.02
prostituent 386.22
prostituta 115.15
prostitute 116.16 551.14
prostrandvorous 417.11
prostrated 006.15
prostratingwards 484.04
prosy 185.17
protect 074.04
protected 185.30
Protector 255.16 569.15
protectors 318.25
proteiform 107.08
protem 076.21
protemptible 497.35
protended 056.12
protest 085.16 534.09 534.28 536.30
protestant 530.28
Protestant 071.21
protestants 456.03
protested 575.08
protesting 091.17
prothetic 041.30
proto 476.03
protohistory 169.21
protonotorious 604.22
protoparent's 121.08
protoprostitute 186.27
protosyndic 031.19
protown 097.21
proud 023.17 057.09 060.09 144.28 168.03 264.02 278.F7 318.01 324.04 464.36 578.20 583.07 618.26
Proud 012.25
proudest 248.05 427.23
proudly 093.04
Proudpurse 620.05
proudseye 007.36
Prouf 303.14
prouts 482.31
provaunce 256.29
prove 093.05 150.15 155.18 311.29 432.28 437.22 437.34 443.13 462.13 532.24 533.14 595.26
proved 084.25 127.27 134.20 155.29 161.01 446.05 529.31
provencial 144.10
provenciale 478.20
provencials 230.05
proverb 390.27
proverbial 110.12
proviant 037.34
provide 316.24
provided 045.31 462.23 574.16 613.31
Provideforsacrifice 571.32
providence 069.28 404.22

providencer's 337.05
providential 075.23 107.31 514.31 599.13
providentiality 362.31
providentially 222.01
providing 484.13
provim 356.15
province 134.15 297.30 529.36
provincial's 447.12
proving 117.20
Provision 297.L2
provisionally 478.13
provocative 187.31 251.31
provocatives 052.02
provoke 034.29
provoked 124.09 488.10
provoking 488.09
provokingly 052.02
provorted 022.16
provost 005.22 534.13
prow 029.24 062.36 198.07
prowed 316.02
prowes 548.11
prowess 283.21
prowl 340.18 435.29 589.15
prowlabouts 222.24
proxenete 198.17 198.22
Proxenete 198.17
proxtended 476.07
proxy 391.20 462.16 537.08
prr 502.09
Prronto 353.19
Prszss 105.10
Pruda 212.06
prudals 228.11
prude 269.04
prudencies' 075.23
prudentials 539.12
prudentiaproven 099.23
prudently 119.13
prudity 325.08
prue 337.27
prumisceous 386.24
prumpted 466.22
prumptly 003.20
prune 247.36
prunella 206.35
Prunella 435.19
prunktqueen 250.29
prunty 228.20
Pruny-Quetch 550.32
prural 138.08
pruriel 269.04
pruriest 241.05
prurities 436.22
prusshing 539.30
prussic 305.14
prussyattes 359.07
pruth 209.17
pry 011.18 188.08 279.F17
prying 438.10
pryperfect 165.32
prytty 020.32
p.s. 042.08
P.S. 406.20 619.17 (Post Scriptum)
psadatepholomy 389.17
psalm 242.30
psalmen 167.16
psalmodied 470.13
psalmsobbing 525.21
Psalmtimes 506.13
psalmum 185.21
psalter 125.07
psalty 456.04
pschange 346.29
Pschla 415.26
Pschtt 360.26
pscore 285.F3
pseudoed 177.21
pseudojocax 063.30
pseudoselves 576.33
pseudostylic 181.36
pseudowaiter 155.01
psexpeans 242.30
Pshaw 303.07
Psich 499.12
psing 167.16
Psing 242.30
Psk 469.08
psoakoonaloose 522.34
psocoldlogical 396.14
psourdonome 332.32
psuckofumbers 340.26
psumpship 040.12
psyche 416.06
psychic 129.03
psychical 439.33 482.17
psychoanolised 522.32
psychological 109.13
psychomorers 476.14
psychophannies 340.25
psychosinology 486.13
psychous 536.05
pszinging 415.14
pszozlers 415.14
Pszths 424.01
P.T. 288.17 (P.T. Publikums)
ptah 411.11 590.19
ptchjelasys 417.23
ptee 019.01
ptellomey 198.02
pthuck 037.30
pthwndxrclzp 284.14
P.t.l.o.a.t.o. 286.03 (plates to lick one and turn over)
Ptolemy 540.07
Ptollmens 013.11
Ptolomei 529.34
ptossis 437.09
ptover 280.20
ptpt 413.22
Ptuh 415.26
pu 459.03 533.03
Pu 144.18 593.23
Puard 184.31
pub 098.29 136.33 371.13 624.16
Pub 602.24
pubably 608.23
pubbel 556.26
pubblicam 262.29
pubchat 586.01
public 030.23 070.29 076.14 077.21 085.14 085.16 113.23 140.10 150.29 166.06 181.16 182.01 186.12 194.09 196.16 313.02 338.04 404.21 423.22 507.08 524.01 529.11 532.15 539.09 564.36
public 276.L4
publication 292.07 534.17
publicity 356.23
publicked 160.20
publickers 412.35
publicking 229.08
publicly 112.23 133.29 166.23 573.19
publicranks 329.31
publics 239.20 320.06 415.20
publikiss 066.06
Publikums 288.17
publikumst 593.17
Publin 315.24
publish 620.21
published 034.22
Publius 336.22
Publocation 071.16
pubpal 443.30
pubs 134.02 578.24
pub's 334.24
Pubwirth 340.34
puce 414.32
pucelle 029.08
pucieboots 531.22
puck 227.29 278.13 326.03 369.29 563.26
Puckaun 210.35
pucker 068.16
puckerooed 604.03
puckers 496.20
pucket 037.30
pucking 231.21
PUCKING 304.R3
pucktricker's 425.30
pud 365.27 445.12
pudd 548.05
pudden 038.22 363.17
puddenpadded 120.10
puddigood 590.20
puddin 424.12
pudding 138.29 164.17 375.02 441.15 550.14 566.04
puddings 437.21
puddinstone 017.06
puddle 007.27
puddled 393.32
Puddlefoot 071.26
Puddlin 287.05
puddy 137.01
Puddyrick 053.30
puddywhack 289.17
puddywhackback 064.25
puddywhuck 353.17
pudendascope 115.30
puder 128.12
pudge 617.14
Pudge 210.14
pudgies 426.14
pudging 286.F5
pudny 320.09
pudor 023.33
pudore 185.15
puds 220.14
pueblos 568.21
pueblows 422.30
Puella 061.16
Puellywally 061.25
puer 407.14
Puer 483.21
puerile 188.29 290.F4
puerity 237.25
puertos 536.16
Puetrie 178.17
puetry 509.35
puett 614.16
puff 012.11 023.33 074.14 146.07 194.05 282.30

282.30 282.31 282.31
282.32 439.15 509.29
Puff 438.19 518.18
Puffedly 419.32
puffers 183.12
puffiing 252.02
puffing 095.16 136.22 200.18
609.25
puffins' 463.28
Pufflovah 207.09
puffout 536.16
puffpuff 210.14 341.16
puffpuff 349.23
Puffpuff 071.29
puffs 333.32
puffumed 236.02
Puffut 156.34
Pugases 231.21
puggaree 052.24
puggatory 266.L1
Pugger 350.06
puggy 446.12
Pughglasspanelfitted 076.11
pughs 349.03
pugilant 148.35
pugiliser 426.07
pugnate 354.19
pugnaxities 090.06
pugnoplangent 394.36
Puh 182.28
puhim 144.35
Puhl 297.18
puir 013.25 163.09
Puirée 579.05
puisne 055.12
puisny 477.22
puissant 546.03
pujealousties 350.15
pukers 250.11
Pukka 010.17
pukkaleens 326.11
Pukkaru 010.17
Pukkelsen 316.01 319.23
pukny 350.22
pulbuties 340.32
pulcherman 434.35
pulchers 339.14
pulchrabelled 627.28
pulchrum's 384.18
pulcinellis 220.21
puler 596.25
Pules 166.20
Pulex 418.23
pulexes 438.22
pulfers 276.L1
pulga 389.03
pulicy-pulicy 414.26
puling 112.04
pull 034.33 100.32 132.14
144.18 173.09 206.23
253.16 266.F4 296.25
332.12 392.19 440.28
446.33 468.13 482.15
520.08 568.14
Pull 248.18 525.29
Pull 105.28
Pulla 262.F4
Pullabella 512.10
pulladeftkiss 418.22
pullar 328.01
pullars 540.24
pulldoors 434.30
Pulldown 420.25
pulled 021.15 064.33 084.23
129.33 160.20 287.31 330.25
362.02 429.03
pulled 350.11
pullet 361.15 465.24
pulleter 537.20
pulletneck 146.30
pullets 256.02 367.22
pulley 311.26
pulling 093.12 179.18 618.17
pulling 354.03
pullit 396.05
pullll 456.12
pullon 381.12
pullover 074.12
pullovers 268.F4
pulls 079.27 187.18 373.35
375.33 594.26
pulltomine 615.24
pulluponeasyan 008.20
pullupped 310.33
pullwoman 055.19
pullyirragun 352.14
pulmonary 172.13
pulp 323.14 475.12
pulpably 187.02
pulpbox 439.31
pulper 281.F2
pulpic 185.02
pulpicly 458.36
pulpit 050.22
pulpitbarrel 472.04
pulpititions 276.F1
pulpous 396.24
pulsans 185.18
pulse 214.24 428.16
pulses 349.11
pulshandjupeyjade 261.01
pulu 089.29
pulverised 555.23
pulversporochs 343.27
puma 332.13
Pumar's 263.F1
pumbs 243.22
pumkik 236.17
pumme 230.36
pummel 289.12
pump 135.04 370.30
pump 355.01
Pump 040.04 049.10
pumpadears 545.25
pumped 126.21 292.F1 369.13
pumpernickel 406.06
Pumpey 350.07
pumpim 010.16
pumping 046.27 374.06
pumpkel 408.20
pumpkin 094.17
pumpkins 577.26
pumproom 101.26
pumps 098.25 323.02 363.31
pumpt 164.11
Pumpusmugnus 484.35
pun 278.19 326.03
Pun 307.02 307.03
Punc 612.16
punch 116.23 368.26 514.33
Punch 255.26 514.13 620.23
Punch 176.06
punchbowl 582.06
punched 022.14
puncheon 373.20 455.02
Puncheon 069.33
Punchestime 194.25
punchey 334.20
punchpoll 227.22
Punchus 092.36
Punct 017.23 222.26
pùnct 124.11
puncta 041.19
punctilious 039.19
punctual 100.16
punctuation 123.33
punctum 296.03
puncture 299.20
punctured 124.01
pundit-the-next-best-king 505.27
Pung 097.30
pungataries 352.36
pungent 544.03
punic 090.36
Punic 123.25
punical 032.06
punished 320.36
punishments 584.20
punk 277.25 488.27 488.27
488.28 512.07
Punk 367.07 488.26
Punkah's 297.18
Punked 302.04
punkt 556.24
punman 517.18
Punman 093.13
punned 013.02
punnermine 519.03
punns 239.35
punplays 233.19
puns 078.13 183.22 295.04
punsil 098.30
punster 467.29
punt 191.36 206.21 537.29
589.12
Punt 263.F2
punting 423.17
Punting 376.19
puntlost 374.11
puntomine 587.08
puntpole 547.22
Punt's 437.17
punxit 180.12
puny 209.23 270.30 434.18
567.34 627.24
punzy 334.04
pup 235.29
pupal 287.31
pupa-pupa 414.25
pupil 431.34
pupils 152.08 251.30
pupilteacher's 279.F04
pupilteachertaut 292.24
puppadums 303.18
Puppaps 510.09
puppаring 516.28
puppetry 219.07
Puppette 014.08
puppyhood 563.29
pups 480.19
puptised 091.33
Pupublick 105.23
pupuls 542.18
pupup 534.17
pur 243.08
pura 518.33
pura 178.17
Purabelle 610.21
puraduxed 611.19

puraputhry 597.15
purate 301.19
purcell's 412.22
Purcell's 516.24
purchase 365.03 545.04
purchypatch 031.23
purdah 221.13 274.20
pure 026.01 034.24 095.25 095.34 121.09 160.09 164.15 175.31 183.04 191.14 204.12 232.04 233.33 237.25 237.25 240.28 280.28 287.F4 290.22 328.01 385.21 395.26 409.11 431.09 446.10 454.16 460.02 465.23 486.26 533.03 556.04 576.06 581.30 608.04 612.13
Pure 173.17 222.19 299.F3 474.01
Purebelle 027.16
pured 326.05
pureede 099.30
purefusion 222.02
purely 078.30 107.10 108.29 149.21 241.25 431.11 514.31 522.07
Purely 486.26
purer 407.14
puresplutterall 262.16
purest 036.33 043.32 063.29 107.19 385.26
puresuet 441.14
purfect 181.02
purgad 379.33
purgations 432.27
purgatory 177.04
purge 355.13 422.08 582.29 618.15
Purge 080.07
Purged 071.29
purification 446.28
puritan 475.11
puritas 031.23
purity 188.24 529.03
puritysnooper 254.21
purk 012.24
purling 199.12
purliteasy 153.07
purly 236.21
purmanant 596.05
Puropeus 014.09
Purpalume 433.01
purple 082.03 243.30
purplesome 577.27
purports 341.25
purpose 041.30 069.21 069.26 108.18 152.08 179.04 185.05 306.05
purposely 082.08 085.35 151.26
purposes 032.31 357.34
purposeth 389.16
purpular 039.12
purpurando 504.17
purr 295.05 561.09
purringly 234.21
pursaccoutred 594.14
purscent 181.23
purse 072.35 072.35 392.32 422.20 474.11
pursebroken 168.03
purseproud 446.03
purses 242.14
Purses 580.30
pursewinded 450.07
purseyful 043.35
Pursonally 449.04
purssia 224.02
pursuance 524.06 616.15
pursuant 267.09
pursue 055.25 165.12 376.24
pursued 176.27 413.30
pursueded 603.17
pursues 146.10
pursuing 139.03
pursuit 534.25
PURSUIT 266.R1
pursuited 092.02
pursuiting 300.27
pursuits 084.35
pursuive 232.03
pursunk 329.09
Pursy 243.34
pursyfurse 072.35
Pursyriley 482.05
purtagh 314.30
Purtsymessus 186.36
purty 139.23 224.28 264.28
Purty 513.06
purtybusses 432.20
purups 357.09
purveys 083.11
purview 228.27
PURVIEW 272.R1
purvious 606.16
purvulent 160.05
pusched 423.34
puseyporcious 510.33
push 094.32 202.16 236.17 278.F5 465.09 474.13 520.09 606.26
Push 202.15
pushed 313.17 357.11 552.11
pushers 540.25
pushkalsson 323.16
pushpull 314.19
pushpygyddyum 414.26
puss 329.04 517.17 553.27 553.28
pussas 086.10
pusshies 079.30
pussiness 461.13
pusspull 317.04
pussy 278.06 435.24 561.09 561.10
Pussy 561.35
pussycorners 555.11
pussyfoot 553.28
pussyfours 043.29
pussykitties 090.14
pussypussy 011.13
pust 099.06
pustules 189.33
put 027.34 029.18 029.32 031.07 051.24 069.21 072.36 090.29 090.34 094.12 098.03 098.15 098.16 101.13 124.24 131.13 133.26 136.16 142.04 149.28 150.02 152.24 172.18 188.03 196.20 202.21 205.16 245.34 246.02 252.25 272.22 274.31 277.F1 288.18 289.22 315.22 319.23 320.10 325.36 332.02 364.10 380.24 391.07 410.01 420.01 421.35 422.19 424.02 439.21 440.14 446.31 453.10 468.24 491.34 495.14 506.01 509.21 518.11 520.16 522.01 538.34 546.27 560.09 566.13 615.26
put 262.L2 345.16 347.34
Put 434.19 435.16 466.06 487.05
Put 032.24 176.01
puta 274.23
putaway 237.15
Putawayo 509.24
putch 284.F1
puteters 111.01
Putor 093.21
putrenised 520.07
puts 026.02 151.32 265.F2 445.32 588.01
puts 338.16
Putsch 378.19
Putshameyu 565.15
putt 443.31
puttagonnianne 512.18
puttees 030.24
Putterick 187.18
putther 355.02
puttih 351.29
putting 066.02 095.24 241.32 279.F04 394.05 422.11 483.15 490.12
putting 349.29
Putting 169.08 455.29
Putting 107.05
putty 210.34 379.21
putty 201.07
Putzemdown 542.08
putzpolish 141.14
puwsuance 061.09
puxy 083.33
Puzt 603.05
puzzle 210.11
puzzler 475.04
puzzles 364.07
puzzling 136.21
puzzly 275.L1
Puzzly 275.L1
puzzo 181.11
puzzonal 183.07
P.V. 420.31 (pax vobiscum?)
pwan 233.28
pwopwo 523.05
pygmyhop 268.29
pyjamas 176.26
Pykemhyme 379.36
Pylax 092.36
Pynix 534.12
pyramidous 553.10
pyre 024.33 128.35 209.31 265.09 322.23 466.09 516.15
pyrolyphics 570.06
pyrraknees 199.21
pyrress 244.18
Pyrrha 179.10
Pyrrha 548.28
Pyrrhine 548.28
pyrrhique 020.32
pyth 007.14
Pythagorean 116.30
pzz 244.17

Q. 508.23 (P. and Q.)
q.e.d. 182.21 (quod erat demonstrandum)
Qith 358.22
Q. P. 369.10 (Mr Q. P. Dieudonney)

qq 314.19
qua 336.21 395.12 419.13 438.27 486.36 507.33
quack 466.05 579.10
quackchancers 342.31
quacker's 129.13
quackfriar 191.01
quacking 487.01
quacknostrum 085.11
quad 112.06 306.13 397.15 413.23
Quad 057.24
quadra 467.30
quadrangle 608.24
quadrant 127.06 517.26
quadrifoil 124.21
Quadrigue 486.03
quadriliberal 477.19
quadrilled 015.09
quadrilles 513.33
quadroons 522.34
quadrumane 123.16
quadrupede 325.31
quae 287.25 496.36
Quaedam 101.09
quaff 139.22
quaff'd 122.12
quaffoff 007.13
quaggy 197.26
Quai 135.23 434.15
Quaidy 460.26
quail 244.30
quailed 154.09
quailless 547.21
quailsmeathes 595.17
quainance 012.18
Quaine 508.28
quaint 036.08 208.24 474.21
quaintaquilties 508.19
quaintesttest 050.18
quaintlymine 010.29
quaith 447.35
quake 275.L4
Quake 593.14
Quake 497.01
quaked 549.08
quakers 170.09 395.12
quaker's 070.18 085.11
quaking 395.24
quaky 018.30
qual 580.13
qualis 150.10 167.05
Qualis 150.14
qualities 382.07
quality 133.32 149.29 219.04 278.01 394.28
qualm 016.30
quamquam 531.24
quandary 303.26
quando 188.09
Quando 502.15
quandour 151.35
quant 416.13
quantities 382.07
quantity 171.30 185.30 278.01 485.14 559.14
Quantity 083.22 270.02
quantly 167.06
quantum 149.35 167.07 594.14
Quantum 508.06
Quanty 224.28
Quaouauh 004.03
Qu'appelle 197.08
quaqueduxed 243.33
quaram 368.26
quaran's 297.32
quarantee 255.13
quare 215.13 303.26
Quare 089.27
quareold 581.09
quarify 179.15
quarks 383.01
quarrel 119.06 281.20 475.19
quarreler 179.05
Quarrellary 298.18
quarrels 580.22
quarry 194.08
Quarry 023.19
quart 618.14
Quarta 101.09
quartan 555.08
Quartandwds 262.L3
quartebuck 384.01
quarter 100.14 157.15 205.27 529.06 544.06
quarterbrass 008.19
quarterbrother 537.21
quarterings 476.34
quartermasters 477.13
quarters 036.05 054.26 172.08 475.07
Quarters 068.15
quartet 513.29
quartetto 325.10
quartos 300.30
Quartos 428.19
quarts 283.04
Quartus 153.32
quary 132.32
Quary 442.19
Quas 155.21
quashed 183.22
quasi 543.30
quasi-begin 056.28
quasicontribusodalitarian's 099.36
quasimodo 248.01
quatrain 122.11
quatren 290.09
quatsch 296.02
Quatsch 520.27
quatyouare 476.13
quatz 086.03
qu'autour 281.07
quay 205.08 406.26
Quay 172.15
Quayhowth 129.24
quaysirs 540.23
quazzyverzing 359.07
que 184.19 281.08 281.09 291.24
quean 068.22 245.28 269.21 328.31 348.34
queans 128.17
Queasisanos 183.01
queasithin' 056.28
queasy 198.35 319.14
queck 579.10
Queck 491.25
queckqueck 270.14
Qued 299.03
quee 492.19
queeleetlecree 395.32
queemswellth 238.32
queen 050.20 068.22 083.23 135.01 157.35 208.33 223.24 240.17 312.22 360.13 405.27 488.02 497.32 567.13
queen 399.04
Queen 387.24 495.28 548.02
Queena 377.19
queenbee 590.28
queendim 157.29
queendom 241.22
Queeniee 147.13
queenly 392.20 556.12
queenoveire 028.01
queens 132.10 379.18 394.28 417.25 446.25
queen's 101.24 289.05 465.27 560.01
Queen's 219.16 385.13 388.26 521.35 553.24
queensh 578.36
queensmaids 504.21
queer 018.30 027.31 083.32 096.07 148.18 208.30 215.12 260.F2 319.14 463.12 583.05
Queer 620.19
queerest 241.22
queering 252.01
queery 512.33 545.06
Quef 298.05
Queh 389.30
quelled 563.36
Quemby 536.06
quemdam 220.33
quemquem 186.22
quench 300.31
queque 180.01
quer 294.31
quercuss 128.02
querfixing 260.12
queries 101.05
queriest 313.31
querqcut 517.26
querrshnorrt 067.15
query 061.05 123.36 442.19
queskins 528.36
quest 003.21 178.21 221.04 250.28 269.20 360.13 508.25 562.31
Questa 061.16
questies 098.34
questing 199.01
question 031.33 043.13 059.19 084.33 093.26 149.15 150.10 160.36 166.03 266.F4 280.14 356.14 370.01 476.32 487.25 515.20 574.10
questioned 060.12 396.32 616.36
questions 436.12 438.11 587.22
questuan 239.06
questuants 508.19
questure 602.18
questy 109.01
queth 049.11
queue 560.06
Queue 105.02
queue's 454.35
quhare 016.01
quhimper 149.04
quhiskers 117.07
qui 459.03 594.15
qui 185.21 496.36
Qui 571.31 594.14
Qui 086.29 419.12 496.36
quiat 263.L3
quibus 188.09

quicely 368.17
quick 019.17 035.26 038.09 062.18 100.35 134.04 193.29 206.08 239.05 265.03 274.F1 304.07 312.13 318.03 395.35 432.16 482.26 563.36 579.09 583.05 583.30 595.02
Quick 208.01 260.08 279.F08 414.13 491.25 567.28 583.25
Quick 106.36 275.L4
quickamerries 508.20
Quickdoctor 227.05
quicked 226.24
quicken 275.15
Quicken 361.07
quickenbole 504.25
quickened 469.15
quickenly 295.19
Quickenough 620.19
quickenshoon 014.04
quicker 442.13 472.12 487.01 512.14
quickest 433.26
quickfeller 285.07
quicklimers 174.28
quicklingly 571.17
quicklining 319.13
Quicklow 175.03
quickly 153.14 428.26 471.28
quickmarch 282.26
quickquack 469.09
quickquid 161.02
quickrich 474.07
quicks 270.14 508.25
Quicks 298.04
quickscribbler 122.02
quickset 553.18
quicksilver 271.F5
quicksilversong 138.02
quicktime 560.09
quickturned 457.29
quicquid 188.08
quid 019.34 128.14 456.09
quid 521.11 526.12
Quid 625.07
quidam 033.35
quiddus 465.18
quies 128.22
quiescence 314.19
quiescents 386.18
quiet 027.22 037.19 052.09 098.02 101.24 135.36 206.24 225.06 246.03 358.02 408.02 518.12 586.29 626.23 627.09
Quiet 244.28
quieter 571.27
quietly 109.03 120.18 153.16 545.19 556.17
quietude 036.10
quill 108.02 300.31 525.29
quillbone 229.30
quilled 182.10
quills 183.21
quilt 076.30 380.26 559.13
Quilty 212.07
quims 283.04
Quin 305.20
quincecunct 206.35
Quinceys 285.F6
quincidence 299.08
quinconcentrum 463.21
quine 254.31
quinet 117.11
Quink 495.18
Quinn 221.25 562.27
quinnigan 496.36
Quinnigan's 497.01
quinnyfears 389.23
quinquegintarian 111.06
quinquisecular 462.34
quintacasas 549.03
Quintus 100.16 153.33
quip 440.07
quiproquo 432.05
quips 463.08
quipu 412.28
quiqui 117.11
quirasses 343.22
quire 440.07
quiritary 036.10
quirk 208.01
quiry 475.19
quis 255.35
Quis 496.36 524.15
quiso 174.14
quisquiquock 126.06
quisquis 301.23
quistoquill 419.21
quit 073.01 196.07 228.21 411.09 456.36 462.19 470.35 562.30
quit 418.32
quite 019.03 019.11 036.06 048.20 061.04 073.01 078.16 099.36 109.07 112.25 119.35 119.36 120.03 153.25 154.21 161.26 162.07 166.04 167.26 172.07 174.12 183.06 201.36 205.20 234.21 253.20 315.19 334.16 378.34 412.32 419.29 426.08 441.27 515.15 533.12 536.07 537.27 540.30 544.08 563.11 565.02 570.34 581.33 596.20 596.27 598.08 619.10
Quite 017.17
quitesomely 612.28
quitewhite 008.03
quith 149.04
quits 134.04 276.12
quitting 255.09
quitybus 040.32
Quivapieno 182.30
quiverlipe 578.21
quivers 477.25
quivvy 494.17
Quiztune 110.14
quizzed 019.34
quizzers 198.35
quizzing 124.36 522.25
qum 233.32
Quo 546.02
quobus 513.29
quod 019.35
quod 185.19 263.L3
Quodestnunc 609.24
quodlibet 287.26
Quodlibus 013.27
quoffs 610.19
Quoint 299.08
Quoiquoiquoiquoiquoi-quoiquoiq 195.06
quoit 053.23
quoite 061.16
quoites 374.10
Quok 294.14
quoke 595.02
quokes 275.L4
quolm 623.25
quomodo 188.09
Quonda 502.15
quondam 033.34 252.35
quoniam 033.36 484.13 484.14 611.10
Quoniam 414.10
quonian 144.30
quopriquos 055.16
Quoq 258.04
quoram 443.01
quorum 312.35 475.31
Quos 389.30
quosh 487.13
quoshe 260.F1
quostas 342.10
quot 129.27
quot 496.36
quotad 463.32
quotal 042.27
quotation 108.34
quotatoes 183.22
quote 395.18
Quote 154.21
quoted 123.11
quoth 412.21
quoths 302.01
quotidients 254.04
quotients 281.20
quoties 098.34
quoties 188.09
quoting 534.12
Quotius 385.14
quound 603.31
quovis 163.15
Quuck 466.04
quum 186.22
Q.V. 420.28 (quod vide)
Qvic 202.21
qvinne 062.10
qwaternions 138.02
Qweer 413.29
qwehrmin 343.22
qyous 472.06

R 226.30 (R is Rubretta)
R. 464.03 (David R. Crozier) 541.04 (R. Thursitt)
ra 415.11 415.11 415.12 415.12
raabed 210.02
raabers 579.14
raabraabs 491.14
raaven 136.13
rab 075.21
Rab 248.35
Rabbin 537.09
Rabbinsohn 243.31
rabbit 206.15 569.23
rabbited 409.20
rabble 206.01
rabies 523.29
Rabworc 086.13
race 033.22 061.28 063.12 080.16 099.22 116.30 167.25 285.07 330.16 352.25 441.03 514.36 547.26 566.01 566.01 583.08 600.11
race 201.19
Race 341.20 342.32
racecourseful 194.26
raced 097.09 356.09

racenight 039.33
racer 108.06
racerider 481.30
racers 288.F5
races 017.24 035.05 236.26 253.07 437.03
racesround 277.04
racey 606.35
Rachel 221.12
Rachel's 580.05
racing 341.29
racings 117.22
racist 465.30
rack 130.05
racketeer 355.17
Racketeers 019.19
rackushant 338.02
racky 114.25
racy 213.03 327.31 465.30
raday 348.35
radden 445.17
raddled 120.14
Raddy 521.31
radient 267.23
radients 256.30
radification 369.06
radio 380.16
radiolumin 265.27
radiooscillating 108.24
radiose 579.10
Radium 222.18
Radlumps 374.06
radmachrees 286.14
Radouga 248.35
rael 093.05
raffant 298.04
Raffaroo 521.32
raffle 179.33
Raffle 262.L4
rafflement 302.27
raffles 050.26
raffling 447.03
raft 212.25 547.15 605.21
rafted 605.15
rag 114.22 220.22 407.35
Ragamuffin 290.F5
ragamufflers 516.07
Ragazza 436.06
ragbags 384.27
rage 073.13 176.21 180.23 199.23 511.15 559.24
raged 148.35
Rageous 139.21
rages 227.21
Raggiant 132.01
raging 228.30 516.25
ragingoos 493.30
Raglan 132.21
raglanrock 339.10
raglar 064.03
ragman 543.31
ragnar 019.04
ragnowrock 416.36
Ragonar 169.04
rags 061.13 151.17 214.26 453.11
Rags 619.19
ragsups 241.28
ragtimed 236.23
ragwords 478.09
Raheniacs 497.20
Raheny 142.15
rahilly 174.29
rahjahn 388.33
Rahli 497.27
Rahoulas 062.05
raid 194.25 225.09 347.27 364.08 524.35
Raid 024.20
raiders 006.18
raiding 350.30 482.32 622.28
raign 312.12
raigning 339.27
railchairs 528.35
railing 205.32 390.05 577.35
railings 235.23
raille 175.26
railway 445.02
railwaybrain 444.03
railways 059.36
Raimbrandt 176.18
raiment 548.22
rain 021.22 021.22 021.22 021.31 021.31 022.09 022.09 022.09 081.21 099.03 136.05 329.35 351.25 365.19 387.20 428.24 437.35 501.34 519.32 568.11 588.22 621.09 627.11 627.13
Rain 074.18 255.12
rainborne 285.15
rainbow 079.08 102.27 613.24
rainbowed 133.31
rainbowl 107.12
rainbowpeel 475.13
Raincoats 107.07
raindrips 074.17
Raindrum 503.01
raine 086.06
rained 108.05 596.35
rainelag 542.05
rainfall 134.30
raining 022.18 022.18 090.08 390.22
rainkiss 446.16
Rainmaker 087.06
rainproof 461.05
rains 057.01 174.23 237.30
rainstones 279.02
rainwater 390.21
rainy 192.33 204.18
rainydraining 372.18
rainyhidden 081.09
raise 047.29 249.21 436.35 478.06
Raise 348.27
raised 057.01 065.01 138.21 367.21 431.29 541.05 579.28
raisin 130.16
raising 186.34 209.36 385.10
raisins 154.31 183.13
rake 024.36 211.18 428.24 516.04 560.05
rakehelly 283.10
rakes 349.13
Rakes 199.28
Ralli 447.24
rallthesameagain 094.27
rally 352.10 362.02 446.27 515.25 519.17 593.03 593.03 593.04 593.04
Ralph 613.21
ram 028.36 208.04 256.07 396.15 490.04 624.14
Ramasbatham 018.29
ramble 506.13 506.14 506.14
rambler 267.28
ramblers 381.06 470.05
rambles 041.36
rambling 200.06 244.24 481.15
Rambling 355.18
rameschecckles 452.21
ramify 083.08
Ramitdown's 063.25
rammed 580.05
ramming 247.06
ramp 078.21 078.21 078.21 226.28 252.05 407.08 519.17
rampaging 530.15
rampant 448.19 599.07
rampante 473.19
rampart 099.29
ramping 015.36 314.12 436.04
Ramrod 435.13
ramsblares 256.11
ramsbutter 350.23
ramshead 486.21
ramskew 323.18
ramskin 020.05
ran 014.02 020.28 094.06 171.04 208.14 209.30 268.F6 398.11 398.20 439.09 466.19 466.21 539.21 543.04 622.17
rancer 484.19
rancers 394.09
rancher 568.02
rancid 182.17
rancing 204.30 370.33
rancoon 256.26
rand 186.29 250.24
random 028.36 405.09 583.06
Random 381.11
Randy 329.01
Ranelagh 481.35
rang 072.26 177.09 360.22
range 179.03 181.24 229.12 518.15
ranger 168.04
rangers 375.10
Rangers 438.15 451.14
Rangers' 587.25
ranges 613.22
ranging 042.29 310.07
rangled 019.05
ranjymad 010.09
rank 019.04 176.25 613.25
Rank 105.16
ranked 541.26
ranks 274.02 469.26
ranky 514.05
rann 044.07 044.07 044.07 044.16 044.16 044.16 045.27 046.25 046.26 363.05 363.05 451.15 580.33
ranns 044.17 045.27
Ran's 316.20
ransom 538.35
ransomed 580.35
rant 133.13 519.18
rantandog 446.13
ranted 132.12
ranter-go-round 550.27
Rantinroarin 372.31
Rantipoll 193.20
Raoul 372.09
rap 243.03 315.07 341.02 444.21
Rapax 158.29

rape 277.F2 364.25 511.33 525.34
Rape 500.17 611.02
raped 197.21 542.29
rapes 423.25
Rapes 072.10
rapidly 068.04 068.04 154.19
rapidshooting 194.34
rapier 224.32
rapin 333.17
rapparitions 507.06
rappe 196.24
raps 130.17 182.32 455.14
rapsods 043.34
rapt 020.10 542.34
raptist 328.28
raptivity 246.19
rare 009.12 080.31 183.08 235.26 406.02 441.18 544.24 553.13 606.14
rared 019.14
rarefied 318.02
rarely 120.34 316.20 472.27 545.01 560.33
Rarely 306.F7
rarer 312.25 472.04
rarerust 430.06
rares 373.09
rarevalent 050.22
rariest 121.16
rarumominum 154.02
ras 348.27
Ras 256.09
rascals 042.07
rasch 594.17
Rasche 222.10
Rased 623.36
rash 199.22 306.F4 443.08
rasher 352.22
rashest 441.03
rashness 136.16
rasing 363.10
raskly 233.34
raskolly 156.10
rasky 351.36
raspberries 438.10
raspberry 529.02
raspings 095.31
Rassamble 338.27
rassembled 538.27
rassembling 373.14
rassias 596.12
rassociations 348.05
rasstling 625.15
rast 102.04
rat 037.36 197.04
Ratatuohy 342.24
rate 070.32 163.24 172.12 229.27 429.11 583.06
rated 126.05 132.11
ratepayer 086.27
rates 113.07 273.03 542.17
Rates 145.31
rath 016.27 340.16 532.12
Rathanga 497.11
rathe 292.02
Ratheny 129.24
rather 082.31 114.03 128.16 131.06 131.29 177.17 181.28 222.35 232.25 242.15 281.29 408.12 408.24 413.33 414.16 421.24 440.35 454.22 479.23 502.06 571.19 586.10
Rathfinn 377.22
Rathgar 497.11
Rathgarries 619.06
Rathgreany 620.11
rathmine 215.11
rathure's 394.10
ratification 245.31
ratified 083.34
rating 061.13 095.35
ratio 151.02
ratiocination 109.04
ration 496.14
rational 551.29
rationed 133.04
rations 159.25 296.04
ratkins 241.25
rats 134.17 180.26 378.21
Rats 154.07
rats' 446.27
ratshause 535.17
Ratskillers 231.33
rattan 553.03
rattanfowl 066.35
rattattatter 456.36
ratties 488.35
Rattigan's 426.35
rattillary 378.09
rattle 210.10 231.01 392.28 445.31
rattlemaking 467.09
Rattler 072.06
rattles 303.F2 353.13
rattlin 011.19
rattling 531.09 618.30
ratty 458.06
raucking 294.19
raucously 097.35
raugh 070.12
raughty 582.21
Raum 353.29
raumybult 416.03
rave 041.14
raven 062.04 189.33 315.35 480.01
Raven 521.13 521.17
ravenfed 097.14
ravenindove 354.28
ravening 357.16
ravenostonnoriously 300.18
ravenous 068.26
ravens 136.30
Ravens 266.F3 539.35
ravery 338.31
ravin 008.34 238.25
raving 465.19
ravings 335.29
ravishment 362.30
ravisht 014.08
raw 083.29 111.01 111.01 311.32 323.05 529.03 587.29
rawcawcaw 413.35
rawdownhams 093.08
rawhoney 017.13
rawjaws 493.09
rawkneepudsfrowse 526.25
rawl 049.14
rawlawdy 343.21
rawlies 133.11
rawly 037.32 626.25
Rawmeash 260.F1
rawmeots 350.22
rawny 437.18
rawrecruitioners 351.06
Rawrogerum 290.F3
rawshorn 335.20
rawside 301.27
rawsucked 407.17
Rawth 499.33
rawther 174.29
raxacraxian 099.28
ray 267.13 274.06 530.08 595.09
Rayburn 387.35
rayheallach 099.27
rayingbogeys 304.09
Rayiny 007.26
rays 411.28
rays 339.01
Raystown 097.07
raze 278.21 322.19
razed 314.16 338.31
Razed 421.11
razing 552.20
Razzkias 081.34
razzledar 065.13
razzledazzlingly 339.19
R.C. 443.24 (R.C. Toc H) 520.35
R. C. 306.F3 (Roman Catholic)
re 130.14 481.21
re 366.17 575.09
R. E. 466.33 (Mr R. E. Meehan)
reach 072.20 084.32 112.21 167.20 210.02 616.33 622.30 626.07
Reach 621.24
reached 138.06 547.13
Reacher 319.20
reaches 101.29 482.33
reaching 018.29
reachly 162.22
reachy 561.01
reactions 159.21
read 008.31 030.10 031.36 033.14 094.10 122.32 145.18 147.13 179.26 189.04 191.34 220.24 258.31 298.07 300.16 305.01 356.26 374.04 375.18 397.27 419.18 430.20 431.04 466.13 467.34 468.20 523.11 566.35 626.18
Read 167.26 604.06
Read 071.17
readable 048.17
Reade 197.06
reader 120.13
readers 112.36 551.31 573.35
Reade's 063.02
readily 470.31
readiness 131.25
reading 028.20 055.33 062.26 099.13 127.20 127.23 146.22 161.23 162.11 166.11 185.10 205.20 212.33 229.30 356.19 452.08 454.05 490.04 543.25 544.09 623.20
reading 176.08
Reading 030.11
readings 020.15
readjustment 150.34
reads 079.36 138.15 312.31
ready 188.22 271.04 408.30 471.16
Ready 246.19
readyeyes 298.14
readymade 381.14

readymaid 276.F2
readyos 231.34
readypresent 333.11
readyrainroof 612.03
real 062.26 064.27 083.22 099.27 129.15 161.15 166.07 191.22 292.20 413.20 446.36 455.26 483.22 616.15 619.13
Real 207.12 260.F3 376.12 536.05
Real 303.L3
realise 113.01 487.13 487.18 561.29
realising 035.21 398.12
realisinus 357.09
realithy 503.04
reality 149.27 181.35 241.35 611.21
really 050.15 061.05 072.31 118.31 148.23 149.35 179.15 181.36 206.16 224.32 262.10 386.14 386.15 391.34 392.07 396.19 427.06 459.18 460.10 464.18 507.34 509.11 516.11 524.01 555.03 557.21 562.33 597.35 615.15
Really 013.01
really's 090.30
realm 415.36
realtar 560.13
reamalgamate 575.27
reamalgamerge 049.36
reams 178.05 619.18
reanouncing 365.01
reap 451.07
reaper 457.09
Reaping 106.06
reappears 434.35
rear 014.24 042.09 242.07 312.11 488.30 566.01
reared 129.05 135.04 188.16 420.14 579.28
rearin 450.07
rearing 021.01 229.02
rearrexes 610.04
rearrived 003.05
rears 047.11
reason 042.12 087.10 150.19 158.31 178.05 189.30 212.17 247.05 263.27 380.19 423.26 423.32 438.34 610.28
reasonable 010.29 483.12
reasonabler's 411.16
reasons 007.29 064.35 150.20 150.22 293.06 347.24 495.08
reassemble 213.17
reassuranced 378.03
reassured 151.01
reassuring 108.19
reat 300.12
'reathed 142.36
reawlity 292.31
rebald 364.01
rebellious 437.05
rebelliumtending 287.29
rebels 171.07
reberthing 062.07
rebmemer 445.13
rebollions 151.14
rebolutions 346.08
reborn 304.27
rebuke 494.32
reburns 614.08
rebus 012.34 523.20
Rebus 104.14
rebustly 368.17
rebuttal 097.19
recall 035.18 073.25 116.12 367.11 431.31
Recall 530.21
recalled 098.17
recalling 122.05 610.36
recalls 294.27
recant 212.32 520.29
recapture 082.02
recausing 483.01
receassing 607.25
receded 599.10 605.31
receding 472.17
receipts 447.03
receive 414.11 568.23 603.08
received 034.36 037.06 181.28 483.32 543.22 574.24 604.30
receiver 412.23
receives 076.05 614.33
recensors 134.35
recent 150.06 220.29 312.25 495.29 534.30 595.35
recently 150.24 174.23
receptacles 439.28
recepticle 055.31
reception 535.24
receptionated 370.18
receptoretentive 070.36
Rechabites 546.01
recherché 149.24
rechristien 201.35
recidivist 107.10
recipe 456.10
recipimus 456.10
reciping 343.31 543.06
recipis 089.22
reciprocities 304.L3
recirculation 003.02
recital 174.04 533.14
recitatandas 468.01
recitating 620.23
recitativer 409.04
recite 411.16
reciting 182.19 282.24
reck 271.12
reckan 283.23
recken 253.29 303.29
reckitts 212.27
reckless 411.03
Recknar 313.15
recknitz 208.35
reckoneyes 465.03
reclam 546.22
reclined 130.06 165.03 450.09
reclined 284.L2
Reclined 619.27
recluse 606.09
recognisances 261.20
recognise 082.17
recognition 063.05
recoil 160.35 348.08
Recoil 466.08
recolcitrantament 371.23
recollect 357.24 409.04 502.11
Recollect 434.06
recollection 278.08 445.29
recombination 614.35
recommence 444.15
recommend 533.06
recommended 525.04
recommending 163.30
recommends 089.26
recompile 566.14
recompounded 253.35
reconciled 174.33 209.25
reconcilement 080.17
reconjungation 143.13
reconnoistre 081.34
reconnoitre 455.04
reconnoitring 072.29
reconstituted 355.01
reconstitution 596.09
reconstricted 036.09
reconstruct 515.22
recoopering 059.05
record 034.01 473.13
recorded 031.34 033.24 061.33
Recorder 536.31
Recordership 475.27
records 189.35 416.23 561.35
recorporated 228.20
Recount 496.17
recoup 577.20
recourse 049.35 230.24
Recourser 481.02
recoursers 452.23
recourses 143.12
recoursing 322.36
recover 611.12 611.26
recovered 220.28
recovering 344.19
recovery 165.03
recreated 606.07
recreation 142.25
Recreation 306.22
recreuter 364.19
recriution 491.35
recrossed 060.35
recruit 140.30
recruited 405.29
recrutched 579.32
recte 543.17
recti 581.18
rectiline 073.32
recting 112.35
recto 123.36
rector 126.10
Rectory 291.18
recur 271.08
recurrent 124.21
recurrently 254.25 287.28
recurs 481.10
recursed 029.09
recusant 519.34
recycling 099.05
red 009.04 031.25 039.33 043.25 062.19 116.07 120.14 127.26 135.06 144.24 182.06 203.26 242.19 252.33 267.14 268.F6 279.F30 304.07 387.27 387.30 391.30 396.10 404.25 412.14 438.10 451.21 463.24 464.20 469.03 522.04 530.09 531.08 584.02
red 286.L2 383.12
Red 029.15 235.13 330.14
redaction 036.11
redbanked 277.F7
Redbreast 211.27
redcedera 160.05
redcoatliar 264.F3
redcocks 022.03
redcolumnists 438.18

redcrossed 084.20
redd 058.31
redden 536.18
reddinghats 551.08
reddled 324.06
reddr 184.07
reddy 421.06
rede 018.06 018.18 201.01 201.28 283.22 324.06 418.06
redecant 240.13
redeeming 041.30
redelivered 048.06
redemption 036.25
reder 249.14
redfellows 450.06
redferns 548.25
redflammelwaving 101.17
red-Fox 511.09
redhand 085.12
redhandedly 122.08
Redhead 471.14
redheaded 095.20
redhot 231.32
redipnominated 088.20
Redismembers 008.06
redissolusingness 143.14
redistribution 219.07
Rediviva 490.26
redivivus 050.15
redletter 050.31
redletterday 456.34
redmaids 543.21
redmass 483.13
redminers 027.16
Redmond 552.11
redneck 297.17
redoform 624.20
redonda 179.12
redoubt 541.21
redoubtedly 356.01
redpublicans 053.28
redress 489.22 514.17 617.18
redressed 232.20
redritualhoods 033.01
reds 207.10
redshank 411.33
redshanks 386.29
Redshanks 500.10
Redspot 582.31
redtangles 298.25
redtettetterday 490.27
redthorn 015.03
redtom 021.31
Redu 540.21
reduce 442.30 622.04
reduced 165.36 166.07 420.04 499.03
reducing 189.35
reductions 453.08
redugout 351.06
redwoodtree 030.14
reeboos 066.05
reechoable 253.27
reed 385.06 398.30 433.09 442.34
Reed 094.06
reedery 244.28
reedles 239.36
reeds 158.07 364.21 408.29
reeducation 097.18
reedy 198.25
reef 006.07
Reef 056.07
Reefer 323.10
reeform 072.25
reek 427.11 437.18
reeked 183.08
reeker 490.10
reekeries' 536.09
reekierags 007.24
reekignites 334.10
reeks 129.27 602.16
Reeks 092.26
reekwaterbeckers 077.30
reeky 173.27
reel 064.25 064.26 064.26 174.04 288.08 513.23
reeled 134.09
reeling 186.25 205.32 374.17
reelly 512.20 512.20
reelway 236.23
reely 445.07 527.25
reemyround 381.30
reen 519.24
Reenter 321.34
reeraw 111.01
reere 540.31
reestablishment 304.L3
reeve 408.22
Reeve 197.01 197.01
reexchange 471.06
reexplosion 078.04
refaced 052.26
refection 455.09 504.33
referacting 345.32
referee's 498.35
reference 039.28 524.08
references 444.01
referend 061.28
Referent 526.18
refergee's 379.32
Referinn 328.26
referring 507.31
Referring 617.34
refers 115.34
refined 167.02 531.16
reflected 157.18 159.06 334.06
reflecting 186.03 385.25
reflection 037.13 157.24 220.09 423.17
reflections 271.08 460.25 536.14
reflects 492.15
refleshmeant 082.10
reflexes 467.03 623.01
reflexives 268.25
refloat 160.04
reflotation 589.29
refluction 299.18
refond 457.16
reform 045.16 045.17 523.13 552.21
Reform 509.28
reformatory 147.15
reformed 361.04 544.12 619.09
reformee 059.28
reformication 333.30
reforms 150.17
refractions 256.31
refraining 151.26
refrains 044.10
refrangible 150.34
refrects 612.16
refresh 542.36
refreshed 055.10
refreshment 191.08
refreskment 129.29
refresqued 088.29
refuge 062.01 555.21
refugee 587.18
re'furloined 419.29
refuse 193.25 543.33
refused 172.20
Refuseleers 058.23
refutation 374.29
regain 228.22
regaining 318.07
regal 381.21 619.18
regale 184.24
Regalia 551.24
regally 068.22 231.12 455.27
Regally 013.02
Regal's 587.08
regard 303.10 570.36
regarders 034.16
regarding 359.06
regardless 516.05
regards 059.14 358.06 406.33 452.24 461.31 510.10 523.35 546.03
regards 355.03
regatta 397.33
regattable 051.07
regatta's 051.22
regatts 366.10
regeneration 284.21 606.11
regenerations 600.09
regent 374.29
regents 090.07
regginbrow 003.14
Regias 497.05
regicide 162.01
Regies 577.15
regifugium 051.31
regime 116.08
regimentation 551.17
Reginald 342.33
Reginia 391.01
region 026.14
regional 038.02
regionals 253.11
regional's 482.16
regions 009.12 166.20
region's 471.19
register 397.13 450.28
registered 414.12 574.05
registers 451.05
Registower 364.21
reglar 130.05
reglimmed 075.09
reglow 349.07
regn 607.25
Regn 213.09
regnans 056.36
regnumrockery 388.34
regressive 099.18
regret 155.10 406.14 422.34
regretfully 575.08
regrettable 299.31 524.03
regrettitude 098.15
regrouped 129.12
regul 397.34
regular 026.34 086.17 108.06 181.32 411.17 411.33 544.22
Regular 307.26
regularly 129.12 437.17
regulationing 524.05
regulect 340.13
regums 233.17
regurgitation 558.03

rehad 231.25
rehearsal 407.28 617.16
rehearse 326.02
rehearsed 055.16
rehearsing 477.09
Rehmoose 236.19
rehorsing 315.16
rehr 207.07
reicherout 533.32
Reich's 553.35
reidey 314.03
Reid's 052.04
reign 231.33 335.02 415.36
reignbeau's 203.27
reignbolt's 590.10
reigner 312.17
reignladen 503.34
reigns 129.28 258.01
Reilly 347.08 581.07
Reilly-Parsons 026.32
Reillys 381.14
Reims 209.25
rein 355.17
Reincorporated 387.36
reine 064.16 068.21
Reinebeau 548.28
reinebelle 527.30
reinethst 531.13
Reinette 373.22
reinforced 430.17
reining 332.15
reins 028.13 533.10
reinsure 428.12
reinvented 077.05
reinworms 059.12
reire 329.28
reise 025.32
reiseines 497.31
reiter 315.13
reiz 210.28
reized 279.F22 542.01
Rejaneyjailey 064.19
rejected 232.23
rejection 252.28
rejoice 456.19 464.36
rejoicement 071.06
rejuvenated 041.13 112.20
rekindle 027.13
rekindling 083.04
relate 283.22
related 181.17
relation 240.27 326.14
relations 283.12 427.21 579.31
relative 115.27 412.04 436.17
relatively 479.26
relatives 525.08
relaxable 183.32
relay 035.23 533.29
relayed 405.01
relays 471.16
release 253.14 363.32 495.31
released 048.04 222.33
releasing 491.13
relentless 156.35
relevution 338.06
relic 435.22
relics 087.32 091.05 411.04
Relics 578.05
relicts 625.12
Relicts 104.07
relief 125.18 163.14 409.20
444.01 476.33 543.27 564.10
574.24 595.03
reliefed 541.24
Relieve 106.30
relieved 032.23
relieving 357.34
relights 244.03
religion 089.13 447.25 530.28
Religion 071.22
religions 326.22
religion's 045.16
religious 031.22 045.17 124.12
Religious 602.25
relique 111.22
relish 455.33
relished 037.35
reliterately 431.32
relix 340.15
Relle 580.30
relly 373.30
relogion's 317.02
reloose 224.35
reloy 517.30
reluctant 523.08
reluctingly 092.04
Rely 435.22
relying 156.33 530.19
remain 113.32 150.20 238.15
485.14 485.15 489.07 489.26
remainder 454.35
remainders 098.16
remained 034.02 052.02
remaining 483.29
remains 013.10 047.25 110.30
124.31 509.35 590.02 617.27
remark 110.19 419.28 463.29
493.13
remarkable 127.35 532.35
Remarkable 086.32
remarkably 123.35
remarked 031.24
remarketable 533.31
remarking 149.20 370.09
remarklable 240.27
remarks 181.24 431.02
remarriment 062.07
remarry 197.16
remarxing 083.15
remassed 358.13
reme 098.32
remedy 558.13
remember 027.14 087.04 094.33
108.08 114.26 133.27 144.20
148.27 193.11 201.31 254.24
279.F25 338.33 380.30 391.19
430.03 432.02 468.34 483.05
489.15 501.16 614.20 614.22
617.08 621.09 622.17 625.29
Remember 230.35 367.11 434.14
440.26 617.26 623.09 623.16
626.08
Remember 508.05
rememberance 039.03
remembered 069.31 255.08
279.F04 315.29 409.09 484.25
rememberem 604.16
remembering 024.29 474.23
remembers 050.22 075.01 245.06
remembore 387.17 390.34 392.11
remembored 384.35 388.18
remembrance 305.28 318.07
484.28
remembrances 589.35
remembrancetie 144.24
remembrandts 403.10
rementious 159.34
remere 493.12
remesmer 360.24
remews 134.17
reminants 069.19
remind 144.27 190.17 370.13
489.29 493.12 570.11 600.02
628.07
reminded 064.12
reminder 262.F7 283.11
reminding 120.32 320.36
reminds 013.06 387.14 390.15
397.07 505.30
reminiscence 119.13
reminiscensitive 230.26
remittances 428.25
remnance 220.33
remnants 027.36
remoltked 333.13
remonstrance 367.03
remonstrancers 012.14
Remonstrant 525.07
remote 056.21
remoter 595.36
remotest 064.11
Remounting 504.14
remounts 505.31
removal 529.08 544.05
remove 191.11 531.29
Remove 456.13
Remove 071.16
removed 066.31 091.02 162.05
314.02 314.05 483.34 544.07
579.34 617.27
Removed 420.29
removing 165.33
remumb 608.22
remumble 295.04
remure 493.13
Remus 442.08 525.34
renascenent 596.04
renations 358.03
Renborumba 351.05
render 357.36 541.10
rendered 403.23 573.22 575.14
rendering 573.09 584.35
renders 485.04
rending 170.24
Rendningrocks 258.01
rendypresent 036.19
Renée 269.F2
reneemed 363.13
renew 226.17
reneweller 594.01
renewmurature 344.17
renns 039.14
renounce 139.27
renounced 096.36
Renove 579.10
renownsable 581.05
renownse 243.21
Renshaw 132.10
rent 047.11 086.31 221.32
450.02 544.23 586.17
Rent 339.28
rental 069.17
Renter 106.26
renting 088.26
rents 085.33
Rents 273.03
renulited 395.33
renumber 328.20
reoccur 481.16

rep 027.19 136.32 303.22
repairs 492.24
Reparatrices 618.15
reparteed 186.33
repassed 584.35
repassing 546.11
repastful 406.26
repastures 193.06
repeals 585.25
repeat 240.33 317.29 328.09 378.23 511.26 521.28
Repeat 045.25
repeated 037.14 170.30 179.29 409.33
repeater 052.06
repeating 384.16 388.32 389.15 389.36 394.06 397.07 398.08 481.31 499.22
repeation 110.07
repeats 294.28
Repeers 421.03
repelled 430.12
repent 539.15
repentance 128.21
repented 423.23
repents 441.36 573.32
repepulation 362.04
repersuaded 123.09
repetition 055.29
repetitions 120.16
repippinghim 298.25
replaceable 585.10
replaced 236.25
replacing 446.08
Replay 560.06
replenquished 381.34
replete 356.31 499.24
repleted 345.20
replied 061.21 067.24 082.31 409.11 410.24 410.31 411.25 413.32 419.20 421.21 422.24 424.17 424.26 425.09 454.25
replique 542.24
reply 060.09 167.28 519.31
replyin 035.26
repopulate 188.35
report 098.02 123.25 129.15
report 342.33
reported 084.12 137.18 530.18
reporter 602.17
reporterage 070.05
reporters 191.19
reports 358.11
repose 027.23 452.20 545.35 586.03
Repose 028.33
reposing 404.02
reposiveness 408.15
reppe 196.11
repreaches 274.11
repreaching 029.25
reprehensible 573.17
representation 509.01
representative 042.22 221.03
Represented 176.07
represents 119.19
repressed 190.33
reprimed 052.06
reproaches 274.07
reprobare 163.04
reprobate 557.27
reprodictive 298.17
reproducing 342.21
reproof 418.20
reproved 155.36
reproving 431.05
reptiles 616.16
reptile's 289.25
reptrograd 351.27
republican 393.23
republican's 090.05
republicly 305.14
republished 123.27
repulsed 135.25
repulsing 469.36
repunked 131.15
repurchasing 596.30
repure 492.36
reputation 069.04 356.28 532.25
reputed 545.06
reputedly 368.18
request 032.30 051.23 055.33 091.02 207.13 257.32 391.20 537.17 575.20
requested 421.15 585.36
requests 108.30
requiesce 017.26
requiestress 262.15
required 290.10 495.31
requirements 599.28
requisites 066.34
requisted 238.15
rer 234.29
rere 030.16 109.33 214.22 326.26 363.30 475.30 492.25
Rere 442.08
rereally 490.17
reredos 018.29
reredoss 228.28
rerembrandtsers 054.02
rereres 113.08
rererise 053.13
reres 225.29
rereway 564.03
rerising 277.14
reromembered 371.11
reroused 055.11
rescension 410.36
rescue 311.17
rescued 098.23
Rescues 302.L2
rescune 500.04
research 595.25
resemblance 081.23
resemble 135.33 460.34
resembled 174.24
reserve 573.24
reserves 574.21
reserving 575.33
reshockle 541.21
reshottus 352.25
reside 235.12
residence 111.33 187.22 457.01 560.13 564.15
residents 100.32
residenze 539.20
resides 558.14
residuance 367.24
residue 253.22
resignation 056.17
resigned 068.13 098.16 574.08
resin 478.10 505.01 564.20
resipiency 100.15
resistance 140.17 316.04
resistant 072.19
resiteroomed 052.07
resk 408.04
resnored 040.05
resolde 538.08
resolution 076.17
resolved 150.23
resonance 360.03
Respassers 594.14
respeaktoble 351.31
respecks 207.13
respect 436.25 464.01 557.30
Respect 495.32 579.14
respectability 544.11 544.32 545.07
respectable 037.25 060.24 169.03 436.17 543.23 543.26 543.28 543.30 543.32 543.35 544.03 544.06 544.15 544.19 544.21 544.27 545.03 545.11 545.11 545.11 624.08
Respectable 270.11
respectableness 362.23
respectables 351.28
respectably 545.12
respected 545.11
respectfulness 587.12
respecting 266.22 312.32 566.32
respective 222.15
respectively 124.05 222.08 523.35 585.07
respects 298.10 358.30 523.36
respectsful 072.17
resplendent 611.23
respond 072.18
responded 123.35 414.14 461.33
response 115.10 307.F9
responsed 059.21
responsen 601.10
responses 140.14
responsible 580.03
Responsif 494.36
respunchable 029.35
respund 214.08
ressembling 181.11
rest 025.26 102.21 118.32 133.31 148.20 197.25 245.01 250.12 253.21 293.F2 381.07 407.28 429.20 442.16 453.20 475.23 527.04 549.07 585.34 607.36 622.23
rest 284.L2 340.19
Rest 295.15 472.05 543.13 595.29
restage 607.07
restant 284.26 429.18
restart 382.14
restaure 434.05
reste 540.16
rested 619.33
Resterant 602.18
restfully 061.05
resting 058.34 483.31 491.31 511.18 544.33
restings 041.18
restore 552.21
restrained 214.14 568.21
restraint 071.01 121.30
rests 424.30 582.27
resty 597.26
restyours 034.30
result 077.17
resulted 345.22
results 222.15 614.05
resume 517.04

ribberrobber 021.08
ribbeunuch 332.19
ribbings 250.04
ribble 198.25
ribbon 265.24 503.24
Ribboncake 340.27
ribboned 588.35
Ribbonmen 071.23
ribbons 028.13 082.21 120.06 434.21 548.10
Ribeiro 340.06
ribroast 455.31
ribs 140.16 180.11 350.24 432.09 475.16 490.18 580.35
R.I.C. 221.27 (Royal Irish Constabulary)
rice 086.35 225.31 314.33 404.29 485.26
Rice 420.30
ricecourse 423.30
riceplummy 405.34
rices 016.35
riceypeasy 406.03
rich 014.04 078.06 107.20 189.15 406.15 441.18 462.03 479.07 527.14 550.10 570.15 622.33
richer 042.13
riches 252.23 328.35 375.09 566.02 589.05
richestore 390.12
richlier 357.17
Richman's 515.04
richmond 207.06
Richmond 375.21
Richmound 420.23
richmounded 542.04
richt 231.27
richtly 252.23
richview 284.F3
Rick 134.11
ricka 199.34
rickets 209.33 293.05
rickissime 227.10
rickwards 230.22
rickyshaws 553.36
Rico 584.28
ricocoursing 609.14
ricorder 210.03
ricordo 513.17
Ricqueracqbrimbillyjicquey-jocqjolicass 254.15
rid 084.01 613.25
R.I.D. 325.01
riddle 170.04 324.06
riddles 219.22
riddlesneek's 516.06
riddletight 622.28
ride 304.12 328.13 334.26 373.28
ride 103.03
Rideau 551.06
rider 204.11 313.11
riders 567.27
Riders 346.06
rides 128.15 355.17 564.25
ridesiddle 342.16
Ridewheeling 437.04
ridge 447.29 475.22 532.13
ridiculisation 149.27
ridiculous 112.20 445.27
riding 041.21 095.35 102.13 140.19 199.33 214.12 491.35 498.03
ridingpin 419.23
ridings 078.19
Ridley's 049.18
ridottos 541.20
ridy 043.11
Riesengebirger 133.06
Riesengeborg 005.06
rieses 199.24
rifal's 352.18
rife 411.10
riffa 298.04
rifing 374.29
rifle 321.02
riflers 238.32
Rifles 451.13
rifles' 330.08
riflings 364.33
rifocillation 266.16
rifuge 552.06
rigadoons 236.23
Rigagnolina 225.15
rigardas 566.26
right 009.30 035.25 065.10 067.01 067.15 068.20 085.18 096.23 097.04 112.12 112.31 120.03 133.03 158.12 166.35 169.15 180.10 183.29 186.26 187.25 190.20 193.03 197.01 197.33 204.28 208.04 210.36 233.36 239.19 250.20 273.F6 296.14 296.14 296.17 312.28 314.23 335.09 355.08 371.18 376.16 378.18 381.10 384.09 387.16 393.23 397.04 398.21 407.02 411.13 428.15 432.29 435.07 435.17 442.13 454.21 479.15 496.34 508.34 510.34 519.13 520.22 521.22 530.25 548.17 554.07 558.12 564.12 578.12 581.05 586.19 586.20 586.33 588.13 606.16 622.23 624.31
right 345.20 354.08 399.18
Right 019.04 228.24 379.34 526.10
rightabout 371.23
rightbold 383.17
rightcame 067.04
rightdainty 409.12
rightdown 108.05 424.35
rightgorong 019.05
righthand 289.10
rightheaded 121.22
righting 422.34 490.29
rightjingbangshot 396.01
rightly 124.14 171.21 201.28 476.31 537.27
rightoway 093.14 585.32
rightrare 606.31
rights 035.04 082.25 089.20 132.04 141.22 144.18 318.07 457.12 573.16 576.35 584.20 584.36
Rights 175.30
RIGHTS 268.R1
rigidly 457.06
rigmarole 174.04
rignewreck 416.36
rigorists 397.36
rigout 312.15
rigs 553.20 619.18
Riland's 323.26
rile 142.36
Riley 495.17
Riley 342.17
rill 023.17 104.03
rillarry 314.19
rillies 527.28
rillringlets 194.31
Rillstrill 175.23
rim 391.31 494.12
rima 200.33
rime 154.31 496.14
rimepress 043.25
rimes 478.10
rimey 502.30
rimimirim 016.28
rimrim 553.24 553.24
Rina 373.22
rinbus 319.05
rince 484.19
rincers' 604.06
rincing 624.19
rindless 183.13
ring 024.33 025.30 058.13 072.20 131.16 147.19 147.19 167.32 197.27 205.01 226.25 239.36 246.13 249.21 355.26 415.19 441.21 494.10 500.04 566.18 569.04 580.26 621.34
Ring 225.30 536.09 590.27
Ring 176.02
ringarosary 459.02
ringasend 585.09
ringbarrow 479.34
ringcampf 498.26
ringdove 085.17
ringeysingey 583.31
ringing 074.11 239.26 279.02 319.05 515.02
ringleaders 497.33
ringless 566.18
ringrang 268.02
ringring 393.26
ringround 314.24
rings 015.04 033.32 138.09 304.09 458.32 534.19
Ringsend 083.20 547.19
ringsengd 328.25 328.25
ringside 466.07
Ringsingsund's 601.26
ringsome 003.14
ringsoundinly 225.02
ringstresse 547.32
rink 510.15 554.07
rinks 351.16
rinn 153.06
rinnaway 009.35
rinnerung 300.16
rinning 009.28
rinse 614.05
Rinse 205.13
rinsed 219.06
Rinseky 497.28
rinsings 245.33 614.05
rintrospection 445.29
rinunciniation 537.03
Rinvention 602.26
Rio 232.36
riot 118.29 256.36 510.22
riots 015.36 027.17 042.18 209.33 514.28
Rip 304.01 466.13

Riparia 211.10
ripe 034.29 162.36 212.16 451.07
ripecherry 251.20
ripely 474.07
riper 050.31
ripest 532.30
ripidarapidarpad 234.19
ripidian 071.03
ripis 287.28
ripostes 126.08
ripper 466.13
rippest 466.13
ripping 277.F2 558.23
rippling 474.07
rippripplying 360.22
riputed 492.36
ripy 395.33
rise 004.16 004.35 005.19 011.36 012.31 053.09 056.13 062.15 068.28 078.07 126.11 146.03 153.04 278.19 293.20 368.29 432.04 525.30 589.17
rise 346.17
Rise 074.03 114.19 200.35 437.05 553.06 619.25 619.28
Rise 104.08 105.22
risen 191.36 407.24 609.20
riser 440.04
rises 240.05 249.08 335.33 434.34
risible 419.03
risicide 161.17
rising 035.24 053.15 143.19 213.24 318.29 354.34 368.08 382.10 388.17 424.36 478.35 517.31 575.10 583.36 628.05
rising 399.25
Rising 105.05
risings 593.23 598.13
risingsoon 312.08
risirvition 434.20
risk 145.22 197.19 238.16
RISK 304.R3
risking 579.04
risky 351.35 433.17
rison 146.05
risorted 314.17
rispondas 052.15
Riss 340.35
risurging 596.06
risy 597.26
rite 167.33 279.F25 283.22 392.22 606.13
ritehand 027.04
rittlerattle 607.11
ritual 036.10 335.05
ritzies 619.18
rival 084.07 132.10 174.28 186.30 574.28
rivalibus 287.28
rivalry 541.20
rivals 143.21 208.14
Rivapool 266.03
rive 266.F3
rived 473.09
riven 622.02
river 085.01 110.01 139.28 148.19 153.10 159.10 159.16 188.06 213.09 288.F3 399.31 410.11 467.22 470.24 514.25 540.07 577.12 586.12 600.08 602.21 605.12 605.13
River 173.17
River 222.13
Rivera 536.01
riverend 203.18
riverflags 207.03
river-frock 444.28
rivering 216.04
riverpaard 139.32
riverpool 017.07
riverrun 003.01
rivers 277.03
riverside 264.23 450.02
rivets 140.17
Rivière 289.26
riviers 586.23
rivierside 547.18
rivishy 580.14
rivisible 284.08
Rivor 312.09
rivulets 209.30
rivulverblott 538.31
Rix 378.13
rizing 363.10
rizo 206.15
Rizzies 454.21
R.M.D. 404.30 (Royal Mail, Dublin and Ready Money Down)
R.N. 528.28 (2 R.N. — Radio Belfast)
rng 569.04 569.05
Rng 569.04 569.05
roach 079.10
roache 596.18
road 032.01 070.15 085.10 127.01 244.24 246.25 283.F2 287.05 371.35 441.32 452.21 467.34 471.21 521.35 564.10 566.15 578.01 584.06 586.33 623.24
road 346.17
Road 080.33 100.13 132.21 235.13 291.18 390.09 397.14 436.24 447.16 506.24 618.22
roade 197.35
roads 024.18 200.19 372.21 530.15 566.01
roadside 031.31 160.15
roadstaff 035.07
roadsterds 254.35
roalls 315.01
roam 026.16 103.08
Roamaloose 236.19
roamed 250.24
Roamer 553.35
roamers 576.34
roamer's 586.25
roamin 489.16
roaming 153.23 347.31
roammerin 332.14
roar 214.35 330.08
roaratorios 041.28
roaring 188.11 264.04 542.06 581.07 626.24
Roaring 087.17 212.02
roars 046.18 514.05 533.33
roarses 040.13
roarum 017.09
roary 023.27
roaryboaryellas 327.32
roast 317.01
roasted 249.12 362.03
roastering 341.29
roastery 406.05
roasties 531.09
Roastin 231.33
roat 160.15
rob 192.25 594.33
robbage 151.34
robbed 168.09 516.21
Robber 185.01
robberer 583.28
robberers 032.09
robbers 507.25
robbing 440.27 453.18
robblemint 424.36
robby 245.09
robe 200.02 427.19
robecca 203.04
robed 068.23
robenhauses 154.08
roberoyed 546.18
robes 339.28
Robidson 199.29
robins 504.35 619.24
Robinson 065.15
robinsongs 238.29
Robinson's 480.32
Robman 519.26
Robort 086.07
robost 622.29
robot 219.23
Robroost 537.09
robulous 012.34
robur 112.35
Roby 156.27
Roche 034.09 041.04 290.F5 449.16
Rochelle 371.33 466.25
rochelly 073.23
roches 129.35
rock 064.03 088.26 193.25 254.19 289.03 567.01 580.07 600.31
Rock 221.32 426.04 497.14
rockabeddy 472.02
Rockabill 104.06
rockaby 582.24
Rockaby 278.L4
rockbound 007.01
rockbysuckerassousy-oceanal 384.03
rockcoach 415.10
rockcrystal 084.29
rockcut 551.31
rockdove 577.17
rocked 227.21 505.17
rockelose 472.07
rocker 211.35
rockers 372.20
rockery 355.17 464.30
Rockery 220.34
rockies 198.31
rocking 014.34 081.36
rockingglass 193.16
Rocknarrag 221.23
Rockquiem 499.11
rockrogn 353.21
rocks 003.07 005.14 019.04 073.09 073.33 170.24 190.32 194.31
Rocks 043.07
rock's 606.13
rocksdrops 244.23
Rockyfellow 129.21

rod 076.28 131.14 250.25 305.18 307.F1 365.27 436.22 553.01
Rod 444.30
rodants 435.36
rode 580.06
Rode 369.11
rodeo 445.09 469.34
Roder 228.24
Roderick 129.11 129.11 129.11 380.12 380.33 381.11 381.25
Roderick's 539.01
rodes 563.13
Rodey 510.26
rodger 177.36
rodies 551.14
Rodiron's 141.03
rodmen's 098.22
rodolling 389.27
rods 405.12
rody 028.36
roe 039.09 314.12
Roe 277.F4 394.18 397.36
Roebuckdom 090.26
roebucks 070.12
Roebuck's 142.12
roedeer 500.12
roedshields 328.35
roeheavy 170.28
roehorn 414.07
roes 096.02
Roe's 122.12 543.33
roesthy 577.13
roeverand 130.08
Roga 602.12
Roga's 602.13 604.02
rogated 542.23
rogation 447.19
roger 066.21
Roger 373.15
Rogers 363.08 481.16
Rogerson 211.16
Roggers 413.25
rogister 439.26
rognarised 089.17
Rogua 604.18
rogue 359.20 372.28 522.11
Rogue 588.28
Roguenaar 360.17
Roguenor 313.15
rogues 096.03 176.24 355.16 595.16
Rogues 105.19
rogues' 219.23 438.34
roguesreckning 258.01
roguing 022.25
Roh 130.13
Rohan 212.11 251.34
roi 131.09
rok 124.07
Rolaf's 301.30
Roland 056.15
Rolando 279.F14
Rolando's 385.35
Rolantlossly 610.07
role 205.29 389.08
Rôle 298.L1
Rolf 263.15
roll 007.36 019.04 045.02 064.25 074.05 074.05 149.14 175.02 328.21 372.26 385.36 389.08 398.19 495.16
roll 044.26
rolland 353.15
rollcky 623.24
rolle 614.06
rolled 172.16 231.30 329.18 362.07 389.09 426.34 517.14 580.03 615.21
roller 315.12 441.33
rollets 458.32
rollicking 140.20 355.16 381.11
rolling 326.31 428.11 451.20 510.24 565.32
rollingpin 441.17
Rollo 389.08 443.21
Rolloraped 330.20
rollorrish 378.09
Rollo's 619.17
rollpins 531.07
rolls 107.21 299.24 385.35 540.03
rollsrights 005.30
rolltoproyal 097.13
rolly 221.08
rollyon 291.22
rolvever 352.09
roly 621.13
rolypoly 304.14
rolywholyover 597.03
rom 391.31
Roma 487.22
Roma 445.13
romads 070.02
Romain 302.25
roman 027.02 043.12 467.34 486.02
Roman 050.24 091.35 307.17 388.32 389.26 390.17 409.19 419.22 530.11
romana 287.21
romance 239.21
romance's 395.30
romanche 199.34
romanitis 151.10
romano 389.19
romanos 564.09
romanoverum 361.32
romantic 151.17
romantical 413.35
Romas 209.25
rombombonant 053.01
rome 098.31 465.35
Rome 129.26 298.33 374.19
romekeepers 006.04
romena 518.24
romence 404.14
Romeo 081.10 152.21 463.08 481.16
Romeopullupalleaps 303.02
Romeoreszk 200.09
romeruled 185.05
Rome's 299.31
romescot 159.19
Romeune 144.14
Romiolo 531.21
rommanychiel 472.22
romp 164.15 407.07 562.13
rompan 440.04
rompant 374.13
rompers 271.05
romping 441.03 532.31
rompride 226.29
romps 355.17
Romps 222.13
romptyhompty 341.32
Romulo 122.09
Romunculus 525.33
ronaldses 117.20
Ronayne 373.22
rond 533.23
rondel 222.34
rondinelles 359.29
Roneo 391.21
roner 426.04
Roner 373.22
Roners 327.12
rong 167.32
ronged 416.23
roo 244.10 244.10
Roob 382.05
roober 328.01
rood 250.24 450.07 564.23
roods 189.13
roof 006.06 136.16 249.07 341.02 544.23 609.13
roof 338.06
Roof 530.20
Roofloss 420.27
roofs 165.33 625.20
roofstaff 567.10
rooftree 025.13
roohish 250.11
roohms 538.12
rooked 369.14
rookeries 139.31
rooking 529.30
rooking 347.36
rooks 189.34
Rooks 017.09
rooksacht 137.31
rookwards 547.24
rookworst 077.32
rool 405.20
rooly 520.32
room 033.12 094.25 099.20 114.24 115.23 125.20 179.36 201.31 328.16 421.31 560.06 565.19 589.29
room 264.L2
Room 153.23 533.12 560.05
Room 072.01
rooma 345.17
roome 017.10
roomiest 456.27
rooming 097.12
rooms 245.31 561.02 619.18
roomwhorld 100.29
roomy 443.27
Roomyeck 139.36
roomyo 326.13
roon 521.35
rooshiamarodnimad 509.13
rooshian 509.07
Rooshious 009.18
Rooskayman 089.07
roosky 335.24
roost 436.16 621.14
rooster 489.36
rooster 383.09
rooster's 220.22
root 065.01 096.31 130.14 145.31 173.09 213.13 411.13 424.17 545.36 564.30
Rooters 421.32
Rootha 521.03
rooths 084.03
rootie 040.22
rootles 030.15

roots 055.29 083.11 272.09 478.11 505.04
roovers 566.31
rope 133.02 372.05
roped 142.23 330.19
ropeloop 333.28
Ropemakers 310.15
ropen 377.08
ropes 446.26
Ropes 072.06
Roping 475.31
Ropper 611.01
ropy 395.33
roranyellgreenlindigan 611.06
Rore 159.01
Rorke 373.30
rorosily 239.36
rory 003.13
ros 339.08
ros 314.34
Rosa 032.11 093.27 264.24
Rosairette's 376.07
rosan 528.06
rosaring 147.19
Rosasharon 034.29
Rosbif 171.01
roscan 042.11
roscians 339.11
Roscranna's 329.17
rose 014.18 043.27 044.04 052.09 081.32 096.01 101.07 122.25 126.24 130.30 140.26 142.36 249.26 264.F3 277.16 290.01 304.02 421.16 441.16 473.16 476.33 477.24 502.07 588.35
Rose 092.18 205.24 223.06 236.08 267.F1 485.12 495.24
roseaced 231.20
rosebuds 583.21 583.22
Rosecarmon 526.28
rosecrumpler 395.16
rosed 317.32
rosegarden 597.15
roselixion 346.13
Rosemiry 444.29
rosengorge 563.31
Rosensharonals 620.04
Roseoogreedy 133.07
Rosepetalletted 562.02
Roseraie 235.13
Rosered 064.27
roserude 143.25
roses 094.36 267.28 321.32 463.09
rosescenery 359.33
roseschelle 179.32
rosetop 144.01
rosetted 551.30
roseway 470.18
roshashanaral 340.27
Rosimund's 245.18
rosin 137.27
Rosina 609.11
rosing 346.20 363.10 517.32
rosinost 594.18
Rosocale 250.27
rosolun 351.09
ross 247.20
Ross 340.35
Rossa 212.04
Rosse 391.30
rossecullinans 286.14
rossies 095.04 285.F3 327.16
rossum 240.16
rossy 122.16 250.03 465.30
Rossya 463.24
rost 530.34
roster 235.14
rosy 021.15 028.24 182.11 569.33
rosyposy 430.22
rot 133.12 145.01 180.25
Rot 003.12 422.09
rota 057.33 282.25 466.19
Rota 466.19 466.21
rotables 127.01
Rotacist 496.34
rotary 312.31
rotary 304.L3
rotatorattlers 604.15
rote 167.33 335.05 366.31 590.07
rotgut 381.32
roth 176.23
Rother 204.28
rothgardes 541.26
rothmere's 540.25
rothole 370.20
rotorious 047.08
rotproof 077.17
Rots 154.13
Rotshield 129.20
rotten 045.08 079.30 173.26 535.20
rotter 090.26 369.14
rotter's 138.35
rotty 054.13
rotundarinking 205.33
rotundaties 542.28
roturns 018.05
roude 534.20
roudery 340.02
Roué 497.22
Rouen 283.F2
rouge 122.15 124.28
rouged 372.06
rougey 260.18
rough 019.05 043.25 077.15 228.08 254.29 407.29 464.08
Rough 263.15
roughly 087.36
roughnow 347.02
roughshod 118.06
roughty 196.24
roulade 165.01
roumanschy 243.16
round 006.19 012.34 015.04 019.18 025.31 027.07 028.06 029.13 043.21 055.23 065.02 067.13 073.24 090.07 092.19 095.35 098.32 119.14 132.01 137.01 137.09 138.21 142.16 143.20 143.23 147.23 159.20 161.26 173.18 194.35 198.33 205.32 205.34 206.35 208.20 225.30 226.21 226.29 236.17 237.14 239.07 250.04 252.29 255.32 255.33 255.34 255.34 255.35 255.36 257.26 266.11 279.F25 285.F4 291.F3 294.11 304.09 306.02 309.07 315.19 319.05 319.07 323.31 326.28 330.35 331.23 351.16 377.10 381.10 381.11 388.19 389.03 389.08 389.09 393.33 394.08 397.12 406.02 416.27 416.28 416.28 428.21 435.17 438.09 442.36 449.26 452.22 452.22 453.10 453.26 454.21 455.20 459.18 461.09 462.12 466.04 469.16 471.15 482.11 488.06 497.02 498.24 498.26 498.29 510.34 513.12 513.22 514.05 515.25 521.08 523.24 532.32 534.19 541.26 548.05 559.23 562.13 580.29 583.17 585.03 601.17 607.15 613.12 620.34 621.16 622.05 626.12
round 176.18 341.04 346.06 383.06 399.06
Round 541.31
Round 123.26
roundabout 146.07
roundagain 252.30
rounded 157.33 214.01
roundered 162.22
rounders 504.15
roundhead 004.34
roundhered 465.17
roundhouse 356.05
rounding 405.19 578.15 623.36
roundish 602.01 602.03
roundlings 441.34
roundly 226.35
Roundpoint 260.15
rounds 119.13 456.25 586.01
Rounds 590.30
roundsabouts 328.10
roundshows 292.06
roundtableturning 285.03
Roundthehead 006.34
roundtheworlder 007.36
roundup 388.34 446.27
roundward 017.18
roundwood 542.05
roung 487.16
Rountown 497.11
rouse 064.12 139.25 152.01 436.36
roused 580.09
rouseruction 499.01
rousing 365.07
roust 224.07
rouster 371.28
rout 226.29 343.07 355.16 570.31
route 321.13 381.04 440.05 578.29 602.29 625.14
Route 329.30
routes 041.18 580.33
routs 310.13
rovely 365.23
roven 276.F2
rover 197.31 327.27
Rover 375.21
Roverend 341.26
roving 429.20
rovinghamilton 300.27
rovining 358.04
Rovy 228.24
row 116.28 174.06 202.23 292.F3 320.07 449.21 497.31 543.36
Row 042.30 551.06
rowantree 588.31
rowdey 484.20
rowdinoisy 053.17
Rowdiose 324.18

rowdownan 258.04
rowdy 009.22 087.05
rowed 131.11 203.13
rowers 272.12
rowler 484.19
Rowley 376.31
Rowleys 330.14
Rowlin's 602.11
rowly 485.16
rowmish 072.24
Rowntrees 544.35
rows 304.F4
rowsary 072.25
rox 019.05
Roxana 212.11
Roxy 513.21
Roy 541.21
roya 199.34
royal 009.35 068.22 086.01
151.29 187.13 194.06 208.18
248.01 260.F3 275.15 348.15
381.07 381.11 404.30 428.15
448.20 450.15 545.16 564.35
566.20 567.10 570.02 577.10
625.04
Royal 037.20 420.28 455.26
536.15
Royal 032.33
royalirish 608.25
royally 162.28 305.14
Royally 013.02
royals 220.31
royalty 030.16 245.29
royde 284.01
Royenne 388.07
royghal 099.27
Royloy 378.09
royol 287.05
Roy's 062.31
royss 205.29
roysters 407.01
royt 603.03
rpdrpd 234.21
rpnice 346.29
R.Q. 125.01
rrreke 208.24
rrrr 122.06
Rrrwwwkkkrrr 378.07
ru 558.29
ruad 052.04 309.16 324.06
Ruadagara's 601.24
Ruadh 083.19
ruah 038.29
rub 174.09 358.34 395.11
505.03
rubbages 017.04 079.31
rubbed 043.30 086.09 094.11
rubbeling 552.10
rubber 160.19
rubberend 144.30
rubberised 035.10
rubbers 175.34
rubberskin 610.31
rubbing 039.25 196.17 203.34
313.34 421.22
Rubbinsen 594.11
rubbinthe 142.06
rubble 207.06
rube 328.01
ruber 224.03 568.02
Rubeus 160.08
Rubiconstein 211.16
rubicund 007.16
rubiend 038.34
rubinen 249.07
rubiny 379.24 413.34
rubmelucky 315.15
Rubretta 226.31
rubric 122.08 605.23
rubricated 520.34
rubrickredd 020.08
rubrics 432.30
Rubrilla 492.13
rubsh 261.L2
Ruby 156.26 440.28 494.04
rubyjets 122.11
Rubyjuby 379.16
ruching 416.35
ruck 225.09 281.26 511.33
rucks 337.34
rucksunck 621.06
R.U.C's 529.27 (Royal Ulster
Constabulary's)
ructified 313.08
ructiongetherall 346.12
ructions 080.15
Ructions 192.02
rudacist 090.26
rudd 023.01 582.28
rudden 378.08
rudder 135.23
ruddertail 539.19
rudderup 139.25
ruddery 624.05
ruddiness 087.28
ruddist 256.09
ruddled 030.24 403.08
ruddocks 346.03
ruddy 122.16 348.35 421.34
541.13
Ruddy 368.32 559.24
ruddyberry 027.16
ruddycheeks 493.08
rude 023.03 080.28 100.27
136.36 167.03 185.11 277.F2
283.20 307.F1 325.27 392.06
rudely 122.09
rudeman 344.15
ruderic 285.F3
rudes 352.01
rudess 112.35
Rudge 292.F1
rudhe 356.18
rudimental 366.07
rudrik 369.18
rudskin 220.15
rudy 386.02
rue 017.25 226.11 226.11
226.11 279.F11 433.36 558.30
577.30
Rue 060.01 227.14 444.12
Rueandredful 348.14
rueckenased 344.35
rued 068.31 515.02
ruelles 279.F31
ruely 536.12
Ruemember 488.18
rueroot 130.25
ruffin 366.23
Ruffle 467.06
ruffles 552.19
ruffo 247.10
ruffs 623.20
rufthandling 384.26
ruful 198.35
Rufus 122.17
rug 466.27
rugaby 449.35
rugby 518.01
ruggedness 404.18
ruggering 174.32
Ruggers' 616.33
rugilant 148.35
rugiments 350.34
rugs 244.17
rugular 610.10
ruhm 243.11
Ruhm 281.23
ruhmuhrmuhr 017.23
ruhring 198.04
ruin 039.34 381.17 472.15
566.01
Ruin 072.09
ruinating 064.18
ruinboon 612.20
ruind 247.16
ruined 271.16
ruines 281.07
Ruines 289.26
ruing 579.04
ruings 139.27
ruining 099.03
ruins 279.F28 414.03
Ruins 518.06
Ruiny 007.25
rule 129.25 142.36 156.04
283.20 355.17 389.08 414.09
581.17
ruled 114.07 142.23 575.32
ruler 133.03
rules 082.02 371.18 529.28
ruling 553.01
Rullo 389.08
rum 117.25 256.06 256.06
321.24 334.20 493.13
Rum 069.33 359.16
Ruman 518.22
rumanescu 484.29
rumba 309.07
rumble 041.14 045.02
rum-ble 044.26
rumbledown 207.06
rumbler's 086.30
Rumbling 590.29
rumblions 581.31
rumer 097.15
rumilie 445.34
ruminating 022.23
Rumjar 341.06
rummest 383.09
Rumnant 611.24
rumnants 323.21
rumour 583.17
rumours 028.24
Rumoury 096.07
Rump 127.33
rumpart 324.20
rumpffkorpff 250.04
Rumpty 099.20
rumpumplikun 370.24
rumpus 433.16
rums 058.15
run 012.03 084.03 097.01
097.07 104.03 109.19 113.20
114.03 114.08 145.36 153.23
167.25 212.24 214.25 225.10
232.27 236.04 283.F3 288.F3
312.05 432.28 444.07 447.31
449.08 451.33 460.15 471.11

472.33 475.30 544.17 584.09 604.01 604.15
run 201.15
Run 283.F3 373.25
runabout 059.25 441.21
runagate 197.35
runalittle 010.32
runameat 566.14
runaway 227.11 462.17
runaways 620.29 620.30
runbag 313.25
runced 371.04
runcure 613.25
rund 239.36 320.22
rundreisers 055.23
runes 018.05 067.20 279.F19 479.34 571.08
runfields 039.02
rung 056.15 165.12 268.03
Runn 179.11
Runnel 013.34
runner 030.17
runners 352.06
runneth 540.07
runnind 285.04
running 032.32 102.04 194.23 209.25 247.05 257.03 368.03 445.20 447.09 553.31
Runningwater 469.14
runnymede 525.19
runs 133.21 150.05 247.01 275.22 348.07
Runtable's 387.36
runtoer 624.09
runway 579.04
ruodmark 244.14
ruoulls 133.20
rupeds 397.16
rupee 492.36
ruperts 241.31
rupestric 081.13
Rupprecht 088.22
ruptures 533.32
rural 038.35 173.04 471.35
rurale 154.11
rurally 090.31
rure 156.03 332.34
Rure 152.26 551.24
ruric 309.10
ruridecanal 484.28
Rurie 254.02
ruru 036.25
ruse 142.36 227.17 368.29
Ruse 596.34
rush 018.28 034.30 123.34 335.14 471.16 626.24 628.04
Rush 015.02 497.11 526.06 616.33
Rush 105.22
rushers 292.03
rushes 278.10 376.35 441.04 460.24
rushfrail 567.29
rushgreen 208.18
rushing 430.20 430.21
rushirishis 322.02
rushlit 004.19
rushroads 589.04
rushy 034.20 067.31
rushyears 122.02
rusin's 290.F7
rusinurbean 040.07
rusish 492.09
russ 199.22
Russers 340.35
russets 059.02
Russian 101.20
russians 461.14
russicruxian 155.28
Russkakruscam 352.33
Russky 253.03
russuates 349.20
rust 003.23 247.22 348.09 392.27
rusten 393.34
rustic 564.26
rustics 130.17
rustle 202.31
rustlings 095.31
rusty 146.11 410.09
rut 279.F31 478.14
rut 340.14
Rut 097.12
rutches 297.31
rute 284.14 606.31
rutene 340.05
ruth 058.31 255.12 596.21
Ruth 147.13 192.28 257.21
rutilanced 349.15
Rutland 042.36 148.08 437.05
ruts 129.20
Rutsch 314.12
ruttengenerously 350.06
Rutter 088.21 593.06
rutterdamrotter 017.15
rutterman 314.12
Ruttledges 072.04
Rutty 525.04 537.10
ruttymaid 525.13
ruvidubb 178.02
ruz 136.13 204.02 557.04
ruze 411.30
Ryall 227.29
Ryan 077.14 288.F6
rybald 177.12
ryce 329.22
rye 379.26
ryehouse 312.17
ryuoll 456.25

s 333.01 333.02 339.30 339.30
S 571.30
S 565.26 565.28
S. 083.03 (J. J. and S.)
351.14 (S. Pivorandbowl)
369.08 (S. Bruno's)
378.19 (S. Megan's)
512.11 (S. Sabina's)
523.16 (S. Samson)
569.05 (S. Presbutt-in-the-North)
569.05 (S. Mark Underloop)
569.06 (S. Lorenz-by-the-Toolechest)
569.06 (S. Nicholas Myre)
569.07 (S. Gardener)
569.07 (S. George-le-Greek)
569.07 (S. Barclay Moitered)
569.08 (S. Phibb)
569.09 (S. Jude-at-Gate)
569.09 (S. Weslen-on-the-Row)
569.10 (S. Molyneux Without)
569.10 (S. Mary Stillamaries)
601.21 (S. Wilhelmina's)
601.21 (S. Gardenia's)
601.21 (S. Phibia's)
601.21 (S. Veslandrua's)
601.22 (S. Clarinda's)
601.22 (S. Immecula's)
601.22 (S. Dolores Delphin's)
601.22 (S. Perlanthroa's)
601.23 (S. Errands Gay's)
601.23 (S. Eddaminiva's)
601.23 (S. Rhodamena's)
601.23 (S. Ruadagara's)
601.24 (S. Drimicumtra's)
601.24 (S. Una Vestity's)
601.24 (S. Mintargisia's)
601.25 (S. Misha-La-Valse's)
601.25 (S. Churstry's)
601.25 (S. Clouonaskieym's)
601.25 (S. Bellavistura's)
601.26 (S. Santamonta's)
601.26 (S. Ringsingsund's)
601.26 (S. Heddadin Drade's)
601.27 (S. Glacianivia's)
601.27 (S. Waidafrira's)
601.27 (S. Thomassabbess's)
601.28 (S. Loellisotoelles)
's 352.12
sa 478.23
saack 011.35
saale 196.15
Saaleddies 263.18
Saara 210.30
saarasplace 571.24
Saas 209.11
sabaothsopolettes 343.24
sabaous 180.07
sabbatarian 229.19
sabbath 030.14 410.32 530.09 551.27
sabboath 021.25
sabboes 011.34
sabboth 054.29
Sabbus 388.09
sabby 420.16
sabcunsciously 394.31
sabes 023.30
sabez 054.14
Sabina's 512.11
sabines 265.11
sable 199.18 441.21 546.06 599.07 606.05
sabotag 409.29
sabre 223.19 353.09
Sabrine 197.21
sac 167.34
sacco 210.01
Sacer 168.13
Sachsen 175.12
sack 061.12 087.16 112.08 301.29 371.31 374.21 428.22 432.33
sackcloth 577.31
sackclothed 421.36
Sacked 479.32
sackend 138.33 340.36
Sackerson 530.22
sacking 116.35
Sacks 536.11 536.11
Sacksoun 015.35
Sackville-Lawry 514.24
sackvulle 014.03

sacral 433.28
sacral 303.L1
sacrament 606.10
sacramental 440.21
sacré 081.29 462.01
sacred 025.13 100.25 158.29 167.28 268.F1 356.24 425.36 495.13 516.25
Sacred 089.02 454.34
sacredhaunt 326.24
sacreligion 365.03
sacrestanes 173.17
sacret 537.33
sacreur 081.29
sacrifice 305.F1 444.20
sacrilege 573.03
sacrilegious 081.24
sacristary's 564.15
sacristy 511.09
sad 042.09 178.02 281.F3 318.21 336.15 346.21 357.05 357.05 366.36 398.29 488.31 556.10 571.12 627.36 628.01
Sadam 496.21
sadcontras 156.10
Saddenly 363.13
sadder 055.20 315.35
sadderday 390.06
saddishness 182.07
saddle 030.21 061.20 081.14 137.02 469.07
saddlebag 406.10
sadfaced 533.09
sadfellow 301.18
sadisfaction 445.08
sadly 549.27 566.18
sadurn's 137.09
sael 326.19
saelior 594.34
saelir 326.16
safe 014.27 039.01 064.04 112.15 155.14 199.26 208.22 228.25 356.29 446.24 449.12 449.26 489.11 540.27 613.01 623.03
safe 418.13
safeathomely 078.01
safely 033.15 093.13 415.33 498.08 584.30
safer 565.34
safety 114.09 220.12 297.26
Safetyfirst 006.02
saffrocake 172.20
saffron 203.24 611.36
Saffron 455.07
saffronbreathing 550.17
safras 234.28
saft 075.17 197.11 327.10 600.05
safter 512.14
saïty 412.28
sag 491.02
S.A.G. 066.17 (Saint Anthony Guide)
saga 048.17 394.27
sagacity 111.33 132.30
Sagart 485.01
sagasand 374.36
sagasfide 313.11
sagd 311.21 315.21 316.33 316.36 317.01 317.04 317.04 319.23 319.27 319.30 320.01 320.02 320.05 320.06 320.08 320.09 320.11 320.12 320.14
sage 053.09 613.16 616.22
sageness 482.22
sager 612.23
sages 059.23 389.01
saggard 555.13 555.15
saggarth 098.16
saggarts 135.36
saggind 342.34
sagging 600.27
Sagittariastrion 600.06
Sagittarius 343.01
sago 248.01
Sago 279.F25
sagobean 523.19
sagon 275.09
Sagos 551.04
sah 421.29
sahara 060.14
Sahara 127.26 336.15
Sahara 104.21
sahatsong 110.24
sahib 054.13 121.19 302.03
Sahib 492.23
sahibs 497.31
sahul 415.25
sahuls 026.14
said said
saida 418.17
saidaside 059.04
saidn't 279.F07
sail 135.23 139.04 220.31 244.26 433.33 479.28
sailalloyd 373.04
sailcloth 182.33
sailder 620.07
saildior 256.27
sailed 320.35 382.27 480.10
sailend 312.06
sailer 311.02
sailing 420.15
saillils 338.21
sailor 031.11 124.32 279.F23 606.35
Sailor's 267.L2
sailorsuits 377.11
sails 288.16
sailsmanship 325.17
sailspread 453.24
Saindua 561.19
Sainge 110.06
saint 053.08 247.20 350.31 423.31 427.28 460.05 520.34 612.24 613.16
Saint 031.25 034.28 039.09 040.36 041.24 041.33 044.06 056.08 081.11 088.23 135.19 147.10 153.01 186.13 211.26 223.20 236.08 240.21 243.27 252.07 252.11 274.12 291.01 292.05 307.22 326.25 336.35 343.05 359.34 388.13 388.14 390.01 405.24 409.07 420.19 422.29 430.02 442.36 449.14 449.27 457.02 484.11 487.36 488.05 523.08 530.10 550.13 556.03 556.03 564.32 606.04 616.34
Saint 341.27
Sainta 471.05
Sainte 147.26
sainted 237.29 264.26
Sainted 141.03
Saintette 556.07
saintity 110.34
saintly 341.29
saintomichael 621.02
saints 062.18 210.14 264.31 288.16 388.36 440.22 520.16 532.13
Saints 175.05
sair 011.34 416.04 416.05
sairey's 570.29
sais 155.17
saise 208.01
saith 013.20 026.18 042.04 145.06 263.22
Saith 104.10
sake 014.23 027.08 038.32 070.30 078.26 080.19 081.21 094.32 096.24 102.08 133.18 184.13 187.03 198.22 235.04 252.20 253.15 377.31 384.15 389.11 393.03 395.24 397.23 447.08 528.02 531.26 535.25 561.28 590.18
sake 271.L4
SAKE 300.R1
sakellaries 156.15
sakes 442.10
sakes 418.13
Saki 317.02
saksalaisance 327.24
sal 358.20
salaam 067.25
salaames 497.33
salaciters 608.17
salacities 115.12
salade 285.F6
Salam 360.27
salamagunnded 323.27
Salaman 116.01
salamander 531.30
Salamangra 009.13
Salamoss 161.27
Salamsalaim 245.01
salandmon 279.F22
salary 306.F3
Salary 072.01
salat 235.01
salaum 360.27
salb 292.27
salders' 379.08
sale 444.22 498.35 574.06 606.36
Salem 481.22
Salemita 471.05
salemly 512.35
sales 141.30 446.28
Sales 212.15
salés 142.12
salesladies' 616.15
salesman 045.31
salestrimmer 323.14
salg 262.F2
salices 526.32
salient 084.35
salig 028.05
salilakriyamu 601.03
saling 428.08
saliva 037.25
salivarium 286.21
sall 013.22 013.23 291.06
Sall 144.34 532.11

sallemn 599.12
sallies 160.13 359.18 491.23
sallow 051.01 571.08
sallowfoul 512.25
sallowlass 559.34
sally 019.29 076.27 272.10 281.21 364.30
Sally 204.15 249.35 293.F2
sallybright 011.17
Sallynoggin 195.01
sallysfashion 446.06
Sallysill 609.12
salm 163.03
salmen 264.17
salmenbog 531.03
salmo 525.12
salmofarious 079.32
salmon 028.35 041.27 079.11 132.35 170.27 337.10 460.28
Salmon 025.14 141.03 174.28
salmoner 525.21
salmonkelt's 169.19
Salmonpapered 559.02
salmons 569.26
Salmonson 297.03
Salmosalar 007.16
salmospotspeckled 208.12
salms 360.27
salomon 198.04
salon 453.12 497.15
Salong 579.24
saloom 323.27
saloon 141.28 372.11 395.10 511.24
saloons 550.24
Saloos 008.14
saloot 333.12
salor 202.14
sals 198.11
salsedine 536.23
salt 050.34 110.02 137.35 167.20 168.08 256.28 279.F23 363.17 393.02 454.24 483.24 507.34
salt 201.19 260.L3 345.30
Salt 261.F2
Saltarella 627.05
salters 312.36
salthorse 365.33
saltings 017.20
saltire 546.09
saltklesters 571.36
saltlea 081.17
Saltmartin 419.08
saltpetre 566.03
salts 036.01
Salts 596.36
saltsick 628.04
Saltus 543.19
saltwater 290.17 386.19 387.17 392.16
salty 028.28 395.11 524.32
saltymar 329.04
saltz 261.25
saluate 520.11
salubrate 343.28
salubrated 305.03
salus 427.29
salutable 244.18
salutamt 237.12
salutary 454.18 598.04
salutat 167.24
salute 026.09 084.14 519.31
Salutem 413.04
saluting 037.10
salvadged 459.08
salvage 498.22
salvation 026.18 091.32
Salvation 552.15
Salvation 104.06
Salvatorious 538.03
salve 012.34 107.22 223.02 301.F1 314.24 409.31 594.04
Salved 421.06
salvines 495.36
salving 363.31
Salvo 228.35
salvocean 623.29
salvy 305.29
sam 524.09
Sam 049.21 065.08 087.10 185.08 210.26 408.22 467.18
Sam 341.35
sama 625.27
Samael 342.05
Saman 387.31
Samaritan 556.06
sambat 493.02
samblind 379.20
sambre 198.34
same 005.29 006.30 008.17 009.34 010.12 014.26 018.05 018.19 019.19 021.25 026.25 026.29 028.25 032.20 034.22 035.12 035.29 037.06 037.16 041.15 050.30 065.36 068.09 070.08 070.23 073.36 077.12 081.30 082.10 082.11 083.33 091.18 094.34 108.18 109.32 126.19 129.14 134.17 147.36 149.17 150.05 150.13 150.18 150.22 161.10 161.10 167.02 168.08 168.08 168.09 168.09 173.19 175.33 190.24 190.35 198.20 213.33 226.17 240.24 240.25 242.07 255.34 263.01 263.16 272.25 285.08 287.30 288.24 291.25 313.20 315.06 324.31 325.20 335.25 352.03 359.11 359.12 369.34 370.17 376.26 380.10 398.03 420.04 422.24 433.04 436.31 452.25 457.36 463.16 471.29 477.36 478.29 481.10 481.13 485.30 486.21 491.05 492.14 495.35 508.24 515.23 518.03 518.35 527.01 527.32 538.08 545.02 558.03 578.27 589.33 606.28 609.36 611.36 612.06 612.10 616.19 625.11 625.17
same 354.08
Same 300.22 322.25 487.29 611.10
Sameas 483.04
sameold 615.06
sameplace 489.10
samers 021.32
sames 177.34 331.04
Sames 106.34
samesake 028.35
samething 284.08
sametime 611.08
sametimes 365.14
samewhere 347.10
samhar 242.20
samilikes 576.33
samite 108.25
sammarc 253.12
sammel 586.22
sammenlivers 100.30
Sammon 362.06
Sammons 069.34
Sammon's 557.36
sammy 335.08
Sammy 222.36 466.10
Samoanesia 428.02
samoans 603.19
samp 340.23
sampam 178.17
samped 315.13
samph 360.17
samphire 601.11
sample 112.04 304.24 322.07 606.26
Sample 523.01 523.01
samples 082.28 624.30
samply 491.03
sampood 206.30
Sampson's 431.12
Samson 523.16
Samson 307.L1
samtalaisy 173.15
samuraised 354.24
Samyouwill 093.34
San 050.18 302.32 317.02 347.16
sanced 569.27
Sancta 154.28
sancti 398.31
sanction 482.02 529.06
sanctsons 498.13
sanctuaries 230.17
sanctuary 026.26 359.36 442.26
Sanctus 570.32
sand 114.21 317.13 350.31 526.02
sandbag 455.20
sandbath 129.13
Sanders 413.05
Sandgate 329.21
sandhurst 162.08
Sandhyas 593.01 593.01 593.01
sands 132.21 189.14 415.22 446.01 548.03
Sands 067.18 241.30
sandsteen 529.02
sandy 200.14 369.14 490.18
Sandy 491.01 492.01 492.02
sane 039.01 129.15 155.16 370.13
sanes 557.03
sang 060.30 110.23 178.20 329.15 330.08 383.15 469.25 618.24
Sangannon's 297.F3
sangasongue 244.07
sanger 254.33
sangles 390.14
Sanglorians 004.07
sangnificant 357.15
Sangnifying 515.08
sangs 200.12
sangty 222.23
sanguine 220.11 448.33
sanguish 231.16
sangwidges 142.01
sanit 060.16
sanitational 150.17
sanity 154.04

sank 129.05 175.03 191.36 408.03 473.16
sanked 275.F5
sankeyed 533.20
sankh 202.32
sankt 549.24
Sankya 060.19
sann 339.02
sans 040.22 040.22 307.F3 417.34 483.14
Sans 372.06
sansa 464.11
sanscreed 215.26
sansfamillias 398.11
sansheneul 119.25
sant 277.F6
Sant 041.02 243.34 498.03
Santa 209.23 264.24 307.16
Santalto 247.20
Santamonta's 601.26
santillants 155.25
Santos 455.36
santoys 058.32
santry 343.32
Santry 142.15 310.13
santryman 014.13
Sants 613.06
Saom 179.09
saon 213.15
saoul 569.24
saouls 499.17
Saozon 411.30
sap 035.26 143.19 511.33 595.31
sap 344.02
sapientiam 287.25
sapo 415.05
sappertillery 530.18
sapphire 459.01 494.05 549.18
Sappho 307.L1
Sapphrageta 542.19
saps 434.02
sapstaff 512.14
saptimber 450.12
sar 214.30 339.06
Sar 172.02
Saras 600.05
Sara's 254.12 567.03
sarch 012.10
sarchent 596.28
sarchnaktiers 156.12
sard 365.35
Sardanapalus 182.18
Sarday 192.19
sardinish 035.35
Sare 293.17
Sare 106.28
Sarga 294.L1
sari 333.20
saries 432.22
Sarmon 615.18
sarra 624.14
s'arrested 223.21
sarsencruxer 516.31
Sarterday 460.29
sarthin 203.09
sartor's 314.17
sartunly 448.32
Sarum 552.01
sarve 456.13 468.27
Sarver 606.13
sas 130.17
sash 244.25 387.05
sashes 080.35 542.34
sass 552.29
sassad 378.22
sassage 240.01
sassed 322.21
sassenacher 350.24
sassers 433.26
Sassondale 609.16
Sassqueehenna 594.30
sassy 459.11
sastra 061.20
sat 033.04 075.16 127.33 155.29 171.24 279.F27 334.25 355.26 435.26 439.13 557.19 606.06
Sat 342.29
Satadays 280.07
Satan 559.12
Satanly 232.23
Satan's 184.36
Satarn's 494.10
satchel 152.14 267.11
satchels 385.11
sate 008.07 153.24 276.13 330.13 343.10 382.19 549.29 550.21 606.06
sated 034.06 057.25 417.14
sathinous 505.08
satieties 435.31
satiety 229.07
satin 032.26 324.03 445.11
satin 349.09
satinfines 238.17
satins 012.23
Satis 269.20
satisfaction 172.29 575.26
satisfactorily 123.28
satisfied 099.35 134.23
Satisfied 420.27
satisfies 468.07
satisfunction 341.25
satisfy 049.16 224.28
saton 302.12
satoniseels 344.09
Sators 230.28
satrap 476.22
satraps 154.13
sats 355.25 355.27
satt 153.24
sattin 162.15
satuation 319.35
saturated 612.13
Saturday 530.01
Saturday 399.25
Saturnalia 097.33
Saturnay 366.15
Saturnights 602.22
saturnine 264.05
Saturn's 090.17
satyr 088.15
Satyrdaysboost 583.19
Satyr's 415.14
sauce 186.16 249.34 440.19 452.07
sauce 274.L2
Sauce 164.22
saucepan 292.13
saucerdotes 440.22
saucicissters 096.13
saucily 123.27
saucy 246.14 562.13
Saucy 147.14
Sauer 485.03
Saul 306.L2
saule 159.05
saulely 131.11
sault 199.14
saultering 627.05
saults 107.15 359.17
saum 249.22
saumon 139.03
saumone 538.20
saunces 064.24
SAUNDERSON 221.06
saunds 295.12
saunter 093.35 437.06
sauntering 202.28
Saunter's 534.20
Saur 344.33
sausage 544.28
sausages 616.22
sausepander 531.05
Sauss 376.14
saussyskins 324.12
sauterelles 253.07
sautril 568.12
Sauvage 106.16
sauve 331.33
Sauvequipeu 222.10
Sauzerelly 531.22
sava 205.22
savage 063.34 191.11 573.06
savagery 114.13 573.13
savaliged 350.35
save 004.07 012.05 018.04 030.20 051.20 070.01 120.34 132.09 165.07 186.22 215.08 215.29 215.34 235.15 239.26 245.14 254.08 255.14 318.04 325.29 374.14 403.24 456.10 487.26 499.15 516.16 517.20 527.23 573.14 579.36
save 418.21
Save 208.02 319.16 628.05
savebeck 372.15
saved 094.03 096.34 117.10 288.14 298.F2 321.06 321.27 359.06 412.35 463.20 484.20 561.03 622.09
saves 273.04
savest 314.20
saviles 353.09
saving 030.13 240.32 289.23 311.30 321.19 362.18 445.12 552.17 612.26
Saving 276.L4
savings 084.30
Savings 105.33
savingsbook 412.33
saviored 146.24
saviour 483.23
saviourise 255.17
savioury 456.06
savium 610.08
savohole 398.27
Savourain 059.30
savouries 128.30
savouring 430.28 533.01
savours 079.07 240.17
savuneer 243.25
savuto 205.22
savvy 485.31 611.20
saw 029.10 050.27 058.06 088.10 098.16 100.15 112.02 129.26 198.03 207.35 208.29 208.32 209.04 213.06 213.15 237.07 241.20 249.26 313.10

320.30 322.08 338.26 359.06 416.04 466.20 470.24 495.28 504.08 511.03 514.16 518.03 563.23 581.25 581.25 586.09 604.01 604.01
saw 200.12
Saw 023.11 046.15 046.16
Sawabs 351.32
sawdust 245.31 441.05 468.33 557.08
sawl 014.03
sawlogs 242.29
sawn 608.22
Sawy 200.19
sawyer 132.36 173.29 549.25
Sawyer 211.28
Sawyer 104.10
sawyery 580.04
Sawyest 608.21
sax 403.02
Saxenslyke 600.24
saxo 016.07
Saxolooter 379.08
Saxon 088.22 304.18
saxonlootie 058.24
Saxons 085.25
Saxontannery 495.27
saxopeeler 441.33
saxum 281.L4
saxums 565.35
saxy 492.14
say 005.27 007.26 013.10 015.21 018.33 019.27 025.28 050.34 053.27 057.10 067.33 067.33 081.35 082.08 086.28 087.24 089.08 109.17 112.29 114.01 114.30 115.11 115.36 121.01 123.33 125.12 130.21 136.10 136.11 149.36 151.09 158.33 160.13 160.22 161.21 162.29 163.11 164.16 165.08 166.34 168.12 180.31 181.36 183.09 188.28 190.14 192.25 193.12 193.17 199.25 200.22 201.28 207.31 208.05 208.31 208.34 213.31 224.30 233.13 234.36 240.30 241.01 241.08 247.01 253.11 254.29 258.10 269.31 272.F2 277.19 279.F06 288.05 289.21 289.30 290.20 297.16 304.06 321.02 329.26 335.21 339.23 341.01 346.19 357.16 358.29 361.10 362.14 366.11 366.16 370.25 371.08 371.09 371.09 371.20 371.32 372.27 373.11 374.11 380.13 382.08 387.03 390.20 391.28 392.01 392.22 394.35 395.07 395.21 398.12 405.15 407.09 410.06 410.26 412.13 412.30 412.31 413.36 414.06 419.31 421.15 421.29 422.13 424.15 429.11 436.13 439.06 439.27 439.29 441.29 442.19 443.34 447.35 448.02 451.28 456.09 459.02 459.11 459.12 459.25 460.14 460.31 463.15 466.31 472.26 476.30 477.01 479.30 480.11 481.24 483.17 484.06 484.12 487.08 490.33 493.26 501.24 505.27 507.16 507.34 511.25 512.30 515.02 516.23 516.34 520.13 521.11 522.26 523.31 525.15 526.03 527.17 532.24 538.18 539.16 540.23 546.30 555.06 555.06 558.34 565.08 570.18 571.01 581.25 581.29 587.35 595.07 597.35 597.35 597.35 599.35 606.35 611.27 612.04 612.17 613.16 623.04 623.10
say 399.15
Say 107.36 115.03 226.30 244.25 292.F2 317.20 339.23 480.03 559.21 581.24 597.36 604.01
saycalling 336.05
sayd 311.23 311.25 316.11 316.26 316.31 317.05 317.07 317.15 317.17 325.18 325.20 325.21 325.21 325.26 325.27 325.30 325.31 326.06 326.07 326.07 326.08 326.09 326.12 326.13 326.14 326.26 326.28 326.32 326.35 328.03 328.07 328.13 328.18 328.18 356.06
sayed 299.10 489.20
sayeme 568.15
sayest 518.23
sayeth 493.31
sayfohrt 313.04
saying 015.23 022.05 025.22 049.14 077.13 082.21 099.23 122.30 171.05 174.05 232.19 256.24 304.26 335.25 335.32 335.36 376.34 380.06 384.09 384.16 391.21 396.13 432.08 439.25 452.28 507.20 516.10 594.10 619.10 621.19 625.12
saying 349.35
Saying 321.25 368.04 623.14
sayings 220.24
Sayings 036.12
sayld 325.25
sayle 311.28
sayman's 095.15
says 012.05 012.06 022.06 028.32 045.19 049.18 053.24 054.20 057.08 057.09 057.09 057.10 080.23 095.23 112.03 141.04 145.05 150.30 185.23 233.14 260.06 326.32 337.15 359.15 437.22 458.33 459.11 459.11 468.05 468.29 477.06 479.30 480.16 494.30 494.30 495.14 495.18 512.28 520.01 520.01 520.02 524.11 524.25 524.29 524.30 524.33 524.36 526.20 557.27 558.20 588.03 588.06 588.07 627.32
says 399.25
Says 238.22 262.F6 337.25
saysaith 377.03
saysangs 548.34
saywhen 489.30 533.34 533.34
saywint 201.20
Sayyessik 346.23
sazd 311.30 312.15 313.07 322.17 322.18 322.35 323.01 323.04 323.06 323.08 323.09 323.16 323.17
sazed 389.27
sbogom 347.02
sbrogue 581.16
sbuffing 222.26
Scaald 324.17
scabie 576.01
scabsteethshilt 529.31
scaffold 568.35 621.29
scaffolding 314.02
scainted 600.22
scald 455.36 456.01
Scaldbrothar's 099.13
scaldbrother 223.19
scalded 320.13 586.21
Scaldhead 376.24
scalding 026.07 115.04 389.32
scalds 189.32
scale 064.07 132.25 134.09 134.30 151.34 282.30
Scale 624.11
scales 190.18 579.02
scaliger 491.28
scaligerance 524.31
scaling 255.31
scallop 081.11 207.27
Scally 172.35
scalp 037.11 205.34 590.26
scalpjaggers 497.06
scaly 177.11 464.11 477.25
Scamander 214.30
scamp 470.32
scamper 080.34
scampitle 046.19
scamps 356.07
scamptail 320.25
scampulars 011.20
scan 254.08
scanagain 451.26
scand 623.26
scandal 028.17 465.02 483.06
scandal 342.08
scandalisang 188.21
Scandalknivery 510.28
scandaller 614.29
scandalmongers 514.01
scandalmunkers 095.34
scandalous 385.31 388.23
Scandiknavery 047.21
scandleloose 343.24
scanning 349.14
Scant 582.14
scanty 305.23 305.24
Scape 329.36
scaper 480.02
Scapolopolos 064.31
scapulars 183.18
Scapulars 376.05
scarab 415.25
scarce 100.30 132.25 380.27 598.07 627.09
scarcely 033.15
scare 024.31 446.11 490.35
scarecrown 237.24
scared 202.06
scaremakers 052.14
scareoff 141.09
scares 078.23 224.18 280.03 345.30
scareyss 292.24
scarf 198.36 253.27 306.01 559.14
scargore 535.15
scarlad 562.10
scarlet 185.11 205.08 497.07 536.23 564.28
scarlett 339.12
scarred 134.30
scarsely 356.22

scat 325.18
scatab 538.11
scatchophily 190.34
scatological 483.36
scats 451.16
Scatter 594.01
Scatterbrains' 099.34
scattered 388.11 545.34
scatterguns 031.19
scattering 226.22 343.06
scatterings 609.36
scatterling 508.03
scattery 086.24
scaurs 317.29
scavengers 080.05 080.05
scavenging 079.34
scayence 608.03
sceaunonsceau 229.33
scedar 171.11
scenatas 353.28
scene 007.15 013.03 034.10 036.15 055.10 073.01 088.25 138.21 140.24 255.29 280.01 314.15 350.28 458.06 531.12 559.01 560.04 580.16
scene 342.21
Scene 222.17 558.35
sceneries 570.30
Scenery 087.33
scenes 028.22 053.01 222.11 385.19 453.02
scenic 560.13 602.27
scenically 370.09
scenictutors 372.12
scenities 061.01
Scenography 510.13
scenopegia 613.09
scent 097.01 204.34 235.05 250.32 420.30 525.10
Scent 138.26
Scenta 434.23
scentaminted 440.19
scentaurs 032.03
scentbreeched 012.22
scented 176.28 407.19 587.34
scentpainted 095.16
scents 319.02 498.30
scents 343.14
Scents 480.33
sceptre 455.16
sceptre's 277.L3
schall 223.27
schalter 511.30
schamer 192.08
schamlooking 467.10
Schams 093.21
schappsteckers 514.08
scharlot 352.06
Schaum 509.11
schayns 342.29
schedule 274.04 442.12 524.04 558.16
Scheekspair 191.02
Schein 266.08
scheining 528.22 613.10
scheldt 206.26
schelling 416.04
Schelm 369.27
schemado 240.07
scheme 309.07 515.07
Scheme 307.09
schemed 309.16
schemes 045.13
schemes 073.15
scheming 563.33
schenkt 133.29
schenkusmore 096.24
scherinsheiner 221.10
scherts 299.01
scherzarade 051.04
schi 243.06
Schi 243.06
schicker 181.04
schillings 036.13
schinker 464.10
schismacy 585.26
schismatical 572.33
schisthematic 424.36
Schiumdinebbia 324.27
schizmatics 440.25
Schizophrenesis 123.18
schkrepz 343.22
schlang 289.19
schlangder 270.15
schlice 007.18
schlimninging 607.24
schlook 007.18
schlucefinis 228.14
schlymartin 377.10
schmallkalled 083.35
schnapsack 350.34
schneezed 417.22
Schoen 603.04
schola 151.09
scholar 489.26
scholarch 031.21
scholard 215.26
Scholarina 241.08
scholarist's 341.29
Scholarland 135.19
scholars 043.07 388.36 427.34 447.07
scholars' 041.11
scholiast 121.35
Scholium 299.01
schoo 487.34
school 026.34 080.34 151.08 178.19 250.33 362.08 423.34 483.23 524.20 548.33 601.13 620.12
schoolbelt 027.06
schoolboy 614.29
schoolcolours 466.27
schooler 193.19 393.33
schoolfilly 101.16
schoolgirl 226.33
schoolgirl's 183.25 407.07
schooling 223.33 312.02 557.18
schoolmam 478.33
Schoolmaster's 055.01
schools 459.13 525.05
schoolteacher 166.21
schoon 350.33 391.09
schooner 029.23
schoonmasters 395.06
schoppinhour 414.33
Schore 266.08
schortest 230.10
Schott 149.19 149.24 161.23 161.33 514.27
Schottenboum 116.06
Schottenhof 538.32
Schottenly 514.09
schouwburgst 257.31
schouws 578.13
schpirrt 343.21
schratt 556.35
schraying 513.14
schreis 058.09
schritt 556.35
Schtinkenkot 163.06
schtschupnistling 114.06
Schtschuptar 343.21
Schue 452.07
schulder 035.13
Schulds 602.24
schurtiness 298.33
schurts 064.18
schwalby 542.21
schwants 113.12
schwearmood 292.23
Schweden 220.25
Schweeps's 556.36
schwemmy 229.04
Schwipps 146.12
Schwitzer's 176.35
schwrites 113.12 113.14 113.15 113.15 113.16
schystimatically 157.22
sciat 163.03
scielo 244.25
science 038.35 227.23 230.22 394.35 440.19 505.27 579.07
sciencium 415.16
Scieoula 626.13
scilicet 611.11
scimitar 341.15
scimmianised 344.08
Scioccara 471.03
scissions 618.14
scissymaidies 192.02
sciupiones 293.08
sclaiming 315.19
scoel 467.25
scoff 467.16
scoffed 406.17
scoffin 353.06
scoffing 005.22
Scoffynosey 257.14
scolastica 431.23
scolded 561.30
scolderymeid 239.18
scones 131.10
scoop 334.23 480.13 492.11
scoopchina's 343.15
scooped 321.26
scooping 408.02
scoot 177.35
scooter 191.21
scoppialamina 183.01
scorbutic 136.11 136.11
scorch 584.04
scorched 232.14
scorchers 433.02
scorchhouse 454.33
scorching 354.27
Scorching 196.15
score 020.15 068.31 092.13 135.20 161.29 222.03 429.08 449.01 543.05 558.06 623.05
Score 205.22
scorenning 330.23
scores 256.30
scoretaking 052.14
scorn 199.25 515.07
scorns 459.12
scotch 289.19 537.29
Scotch 066.11 108.15 422.06 487.15

scotched 210.27
scotchem 366.27
scotcher 008.23
scotchlove 093.32
scotfree 093.03
Scotia 043.30
Scotia's 407.21
Scotic 412.24
scotobrit 387.05
scotographically 412.03
scotsmost 404.21
Scott 211.29
scotty 521.11
scoula 220.19
scoulas 314.35
scourched 531.10
scoured 205.26
scourge 101.11 251.02
scouse 441.09
scout 227.20 343.20
scouting 274.27
scouts 534.24
Scouts 220.03
scoutsch 204.06
scouturn 128.05
scow 134.30 317.08
scowegian 016.06
scowpow 375.05
S.C.R. 256.32 (South Circular Road)
scrab 219.03
scrabbled 182.13
scrag 300.32
scraggy 003.05
scrant 026.27
scrap 118.33 194.24 466.27
scrape 514.16
Scrape 579.13
scraped 122.22
scrapheaped 098.17
scrapie 040.22
scrapin 371.23
scraping 012.33
Scrapp 514.35
scraps 356.25 543.30
scrapy 173.27
scratch 051.06 211.12 336.18 370.02 412.32 415.04
Scratch 227.28
scratched 182.13
scratching 111.07
Scratching 623.31
scratchman 393.01
scrawl 122.35
scrawled 135.34 615.10
scrawling 020.21
scream 314.14 469.04 604.16
Screamer 374.10
screaming 087.29 206.15 363.06
screams 239.32 253.27
screech 547.35
screeching 354.28
screeder 320.04
screen 134.28 167.12 314.24
screen 349.08
Screen 134.10
screendoll 577.16
screeneth 348.27
screw 296.F2 437.02
screwed 549.36 624.01
screwing 161.32
scribae 185.22
scribblative 189.10
scribble 419.31 606.19
scribbledehobbles 275.22
scribe 108.04 108.04
scribeall 442.33
scribenery 229.07
scribentis 185.22
scribicide 014.21
scribings 615.10
scrimm 314.13
scrimmaging 428.06
scriobbled 182.13
scripchewer 412.04
scripes 158.17
scripple 301.10
scrips 623.32
script 123.33 124.22
scriptsigns 118.28
scriptural 172.34
scripture 107.08 121.21 254.27
Scripture 537.26
scriptured 356.25
scripturereader 067.12
scroll 014.18 278.03 433.16
scrope 302.21
scroucely 227.20
scrounger 172.36
scrub 206.27 321.33 551.11
scrubbed 220.18
scrubbing 157.15
scrubbs 579.34
scrublady 181.22
scruboak 210.29
scrubs 278.03
scruff 178.04
scruffer 178.04
scrufferumurraimost 178.04
scrum 427.22
Scrum 375.21
scrumala 298.04
scrumptious 180.08 384.21
scruples 240.07 428.06 466.08
scruting 426.22
scrutinising 119.12
scudi 054.12
scudo 243.34
scuffeldfallen 355.27
scuffold 014.25
Scuitsman 391.04
scuity 602.28
sculled 203.13
Scullerymaid's 181.17
sculling 391.18
scullion 555.21
scullions 129.02
scullion's 305.30
scullogues 398.03
sculpting 121.26
scum 180.19 322.05 517.02
scumhead 299.F2
scummy 443.36
scup 345.24
scupper 320.30
scuppers 133.08
scurface 496.11
scurve 133.03
scurves 376.15
scurvy 137.28
scusascmerul 518.23
Scuse 016.05
scut 176.26
scutfrank 405.23
scuts 619.11
Scuts 245.28
scutschum 005.08
Scutterer 340.01
Scutticules 518.22
scutties 197.33
scuttle 453.24
Scuttle 072.01
scutt's 352.01
scye 327.34
scygthe 341.10
Sczlanthas 351.14
'Sdense 048.01
Sdops 074.19
Sdrats 332.32
se 212.36 281.05 281.10
Se 301.16
S. E. 354.16 (S. E. Morehampton)
sea 003.04 005.23 023.12 028.15 040.12 050.35 086.15 102.07 116.15 138.05 179.32 202.24 204.25 223.13 234.31 268.F6 288.F4 318.34 320.29 326.10 362.11 383.17 384.04 386.05 387.27 387.27 387.30 388.30 388.30 398.16 407.18 413.13 420.30 424.11 442.15 470.35 480.04 485.13 540.08 544.31 549.21 579.29 593.05 599.35 626.07
sea 352.17
Sea 037.18 231.10 241.29 338.14 492.10 626.07
seaarm 275.17
Seabeastius' 104.06
seaborn 387.12
seaborne 469.15
seachest 328.20
seafire 245.08
Seaforths 039.22
seagoer 233.11 367.20
seagull 383.16 424.10
Seagull's 026.31
seahags 627.26
Seahawk 383.16
seakale 261.06
seakings 049.10
seal 148.03 212.23 324.09 397.32 545.16
Sealand 111.01 257.36
sealed 062.27 094.08 337.14
sealer's 317.07
sealevel 463.05
sealiest 507.35
sealingwax 404.23
sealring 357.12
seals 349.20
sealskers 626.19
sealump 332.17
Sealy 370.21
seam 078.10 078.10 297.08 508.03
seaman's 306.F6
Seamen 540.36
seamer 613.32
seamist 237.06
seamless 475.13
seams 127.09
Sean 093.29 220.11 427.27
seanad 372.11 454.35
seapan 559.10
Seapoint 129.24 594.34
search 005.18 042.33 114.05 127.20 157.30 157.30 186.33

223.12 292.18 490.13 511.07 546.32 604.31 626.17
Search 269.23 421.02 532.02
searchall's 550.19
searchers 534.25
searclhers 298.15
Searingsand 137.17
seas 085.02 219.16 327.06 331.35 493.31 547.24
Seas 187.19
seasant 315.13
sease 136.03
seasea 547.24
Seaserpents 493.10
seasick 210.20
seasickabed 392.06
seasiders 056.04
seasilt 628.04
season 037.35 229.34 432.26 446.22 502.31
seasoners 236.27
Season's 579.23
seaswans 383.15
seat 075.16 085.14 137.30 295.25 316.18 356.35 435.31 439.13 445.35 540.03
Seat 361.06
seated 061.14 120.31 166.02 249.18
seater 336.03
seath 365.36
seats 370.26 466.07 564.17 582.34
seatuition 385.30
seavens 541.01
seaventy 541.01
seawall 254.02
seaweeds 469.17
sebaiscopal 365.09
Sebastion 536.01
sec 017.17
Sec 610.20
seccles 416.23
secede 462.28
seceded 156.10 540.02
secession 129.18 487.03
secheressa 204.01
Secilas 526.35
Seckersen 530.21
Seckesign 530.20
seckhem 571.02
seclusion 476.16
second 005.08 013.12 022.26 028.16 038.05 052.35 062.30 069.13 090.01 101.10 119.24 133.34 161.05 170.10 268.20 269.02 287.10 291.14 308.03 312.14 320.18 336.27 406.08 406.15 438.29 455.12 458.01 459.35 466.25 519.12 520.29 536.26 536.29 546.04 551.22 564.01 620.03
second 346.03
secondary 038.27 166.21
secondbest 121.32
secondclass 419.34
secondmonth 037.15
secondnamed 326.27
seconds 516.17
seconds 353.30
second's 130.30
secondsnipped 317.24
secondtonone 126.10
secrecy 586.04
secred 009.10 416.07
Secremented 082.03
secrest 023.19
secret 038.14 043.26 147.27 150.20 182.34 193.17 194.19 273.F7 293.F2 368.24 368.27 425.16 434.26 452.18 525.15 560.30 587.22 599.26 615.14
Secret 360.16 374.35 435.31 515.12
Secret 038.34
secretairslidingdraws 511.29
secretary 040.16 369.25
secretely 543.10
secretions 192.22
secretly 079.12
secrets 407.21
secs 247.06
sectary 166.18
section 061.09 524.05 558.16 602.27
sections 042.23 042.23
sects 550.33
secular 004.17 066.06 081.08 178.18 228.11
seculi 512.36
Secumbe 230.20
secund 360.04
secunding 153.01
secundis 287.23
Securely 263.27
securelysealing 603.11
SECURES 306.R1
Securest 593.13
security 514.30 545.01
Securius 513.01
securus 096.33
sed 140.05 263.L3
sedan 469.35
sedans 554.03
sedated 554.03
seddled 030.09
Seddoms 060.06
sedentarity 072.18
sedentes 287.21
sedeq 025.24
sedge 007.21 213.06
sedges 209.07 526.05
SEDIMENT 300.R1
sedimental 171.18
sedon 340.36
sedown 492.20
sedro 439.06
seduce 573.05
seduced 345.05
seducente 166.23
seducing 191.17
seducint 366.23
sedulous 466.21
see 006.12 006.32 006.32 007.20 012.20 012.25 013.14 017.18 018.34 021.02 028.20 032.02 033.11 050.24 052.35 062.36 066.24 068.02 069.11 082.27 082.35 085.29 087.11 091.24 112.02 113.32 114.23 115.17 121.22 123.07 124.32 134.28 136.27 137.22 138.23 139.02 144.36 146.28 147.08 148.09 148.14 150.30 151.26 152.29 154.03 156.33 158.05 158.13 158.30 164.27 165.05 172.27 174.13 178.36 178.36 178.36 188.04 189.04 193.16 201.02 201.02 208.35 209.30 213.07 215.04 220.11 225.02 226.12 237.07 239.12 244.26 247.18 248.15 248.18 249.02 250.28 250.33 261.24 265.F5 267.01 267.F1 270.27 271.07 273.F2 275.F4 285.27 292.14 294.02 295.11 296.31 298.02 298.02 298.04 299.07 300.28 302.F1 317.13 321.19 321.25 330.23 332.22 338.09 356.30 358.01 358.11 366.16 367.30 368.30 374.29 375.08 375.35 377.12 377.33 379.09 385.16 390.21 393.31 394.12 395.13 411.32 422.31 423.12 425.15 429.10 435.02 436.31 438.32 445.26 446.07 448.06 450.20 452.14 453.19 453.24 454.23 456.25 458.23 461.20 461.35 461.36 461.36 464.05 464.15 466.08 467.19 468.19 472.07 472.23 475.20 478.01 479.31 479.32 479.35 480.24 482.29 483.16 486.16 486.17 489.08 490.11 491.08 492.24 493.02 495.32 503.08 505.25 520.10 525.27 530.01 534.10 535.01 540.16 542.26 548.21 548.22 550.03 551.07 556.35 557.04 562.18 562.27 563.08 563.19 563.19 564.10 564.33 566.21 566.25 566.34 567.07 571.15 582.17 583.03 583.15 584.01 587.03 590.24 597.02 609.20 618.16 620.01 621.29 621.29 622.01 624.10 627.35 628.04
see 104.20 271.L4 341.23 342.08 345.06 345.11 345.23 355.04 383.05
See 017.16 019.12 054.01 059.32 167.28 171.02 291.F6 299.20 304.F1 340.32 374.09 411.32 435.25 445.03 448.09 484.29 499.10 499.11 535.15 572.11 594.13 599.04
See 106.13
seeable 609.20
seeboy 010.14 010.15 010.19
seecut 612.14
seed 130.17 144.10 250.29 314.12 496.12
Seed 231.23
Seed 176.15
seedfather 055.08
seedfruit 135.31
seeds 235.21 296.01 593.20
Seeds 447.36
seedsmanchap 221.34
seedy 183.23
seegn 580.17
seeheeing 299.14
seein 052.34 557.08
seeing 029.10 150.01 169.21 184.05 193.10 229.28 239.12 281.F4 304.09 344.12 356.33 362.06 408.09 422.06 468.16
seeingscraft 162.30

seek 005.25 102.04 128.23
215.06 264.08 266.27 267.01
277.26 301.F1 389.36 451.26
539.17 540.34 607.14
Seek 228.06 372.35 372.35
372.36 373.01 373.02 373.02
373.03 373.04 593.05
seekalarum 081.08
seeker 189.28 364.28 496.33
Seekersenn 586.28
Seekeryseeks 231.36
Seekhem 571.02
seeking 028.25 142.35 144.11
359.36 363.25 444.01 475.24
seekings 602.01
Seekit 415.34 454.35
seeklet 248.26
seeklets 491.13
seekness 062.07
seeks 032.03 161.22
Seeks 223.25
seel 297.03
seeleib 505.08
seeless 468.25
seelord 325.16
seem 053.02 062.26 065.35
066.19 114.09 143.26 143.27
177.33 337.23 379.06 404.02
479.25 537.28 562.21 595.21
623.01
ſeem 238.07
seemaultaneously 161.12
seemed 040.09 052.30 097.27
247.17 283.29 313.18 411.26
430.02 509.18 575.31
seemetery 017.36
seemeth 015.34
seeming 143.27 312.23 331.04
seemingly 034.06 083.15
seemingsuch 612.25
seemly 496.29
seems 035.36 121.24 121.30
169.11 179.15 285.09 292.02
515.17 516.34 527.01 622.13
seems 341.03
seemsame 161.22
seemself 114.23 143.26
seemy 455.18
Seemyease 235.30
seen 003.14 007.32 013.01
028.01 037.04 047.18 052.19
100.12 113.33 114.23 132.13
141.35 153.18 155.15 165.13
179.24 233.18 244.23 247.32
329.27 329.36 341.14 343.34
352.04 378.08 382.13 389.14
431.06 464.26 465.06 469.18
478.26 478.29 516.07 530.08
534.26 544.31 559.33 562.34
566.23 568.02 568.12 587.05
600.21 603.21 604.29 616.19
620.14 623.01 626.20 627.27
628.09
seen 176.16 262.L2
Seen 106.24
seene 052.36
seenheard 061.29
seenso 145.01
seep 027.07 354.29 601.06
Seeple 007.28
seepoint 588.15
seepy 207.13
seequeerscenes 556.24
seer 108.04 174.12 611.20
seers 342.04 342.04
seer's 096.28
sees 245.33 323.34 327.25
416.30 603.26 625.36
sees 340.27
see's 308.02
seesaw 004.33 508.27
seesers 150.09
seesidling 294.21
seethe 239.31
seethes 251.14
seethic 310.28
Seeworthy 599.21
see-you-Sunday 089.14
seeyu 527.27
seeze 408.19
segment 405.34
segn 540.36
segnall 607.14
segnet 377.28
segund 288.09 315.22
segur 233.31
sehdass 511.30
sehehet 398.27
sehm 620.16
Sehyoh 339.02
seidens 279.F13
Seidlitz 272.L3
seifety 205.10
seight 369.19 595.36
seigneur 290.14
seilling 521.35
seim 215.23
Sein 277.18
seiners' 477.12
seinn 042.11 042.12
seinsed 241.16
Seints 214.31
Seir 073.04
seitseman 285.19
seize 247.31 328.33 586.33
627.29
seized 038.26 063.18 152.24
356.22 367.21
Seized 420.36
seizer 549.25
Seizer 271.03
seizes 027.04
seizing 096.31
sekketh 418.06
selary 413.01
seldomer 031.27
seldomers 263.01
select 076.15 448.02 522.14
selected 124.23
selection 539.21
selections 032.35 117.28
selene 192.30
Selene 244.26
selenely 513.01
selenium 323.25
self 084.21 126.22 174.16
183.03 184.06 184.11 263.09
277.21 302.05 344.17 358.36
429.14 465.31 483.29 485.01
489.25
self 304.L1
selfabyss 040.23
selfchuruls 303.24
selfcolours 237.04
selfdenying 073.02
selfdom 395.01
selfevitant 186.33
selfhide 359.03
selfinterest 589.08
selfless 395.02
selfloud 267.17
selfmade 252.26
selfpenned 489.33
selfraising 188.30
selfreizing 265.07
selfrespect 188.21
selfrespecting 033.19
selfridgeousness 137.34
selfrighting 471.05
selfs 235.02
selfsame 124.23 581.33
selfseeker 438.03
selfsounder 121.26
selfsownseedlings 160.10
selfstretches 014.31
selfsufficiencer 240.14
selfthought 147.09
selftinted 403.07
selfwilling 191.17
Selina 212.06
seling 565.31
sell 115.25 137.29 148.11
162.33 248.26 254.11 268.F1
316.33 500.30
Sell 018.07 374.20 571.13
579.20
sellable 598.04
sellaboutes 566.09
sellafella 311.27
selldear 161.13
selled 363.27
selleries 346.09
selling 068.05 086.27 243.24
394.20
Selling 578.23
Sellius 161.25
sellpriceget 616.11
sells 386.25 440.13
selluc 253.12
selm 254.31
selmon 625.16
selo 340.16
Selskar 028.26
selt 537.07
Selvae 147.07
selvage 553.08
selve 356.11
selver 226.25 314.24 497.35
Selver 104.09
selveran 019.02
Selverbergen 310.04
selverbourne 371.33
Selvertunes 299.23
selves 075.09 086.18 112.25
238.09 300.28
selvischdischdienence 357.25
sem 419.24
Sem 170.15 249.18 286.30
semagen 162.28
semantics 173.32
sembal 408.20
semblance 220.32 574.30
semblant 250.06
sembles 563.36
semeliminal 337.09
semenal 296.04
semenoyous 156.12
semetomyplace 114.18
semi 513.17

semicolonials 152.16
semicoloured 463.14
semicupiose 290.04
semidemented 179.25
semidemihemispheres 508.21
semidetached 545.01
semifinal 123.03
semination 130.17
semiological 465.12
semiope 562.26
semiprivately 050.28
semisemitic 191.02
semisigns ,56.23
semisized 170.19
semisubconscious 172.30
semiswoon 474.11
semitary 085.09 594.08
Semiunconscience 123.21
Semmi 258.11
semmingly 057.18
Sempatrick's 035.24
semper 107.34
semper 167.34
semperal 342.08
sempereternal 274.14
Semperexcommunicambi-
ambisumers 155.04
semperidentity 582.15
Semperkelly's 032.29
semplgawn 426.10
semposed 066.19
Sempronius 128.15
sempry 241.33
sempstress 577.31
sems 228.15
Semus 168.14
sen 361.03 538.30
Sen 488.07
senaffed 037.33
senate 388.36 513.30
senators 474.21
Sencapetulo 054.34
Senchus 397.31 398.23
send 092.22 165.05 229.03
235.19 237.18 238.07
304.17 350.35 375.04
379.25 440.25 443.19
472.13 479.21 520.19
Send 244.34 500.13 621.07
Send 440.20
Sendai 196.19
Sendday's 005.11
sendee 598.09
sendence 615.02
sender 488.23
Sender 421.10
Senders 369.28 389.36
sending 079.32 234.24 367.23
446.03
sendor 379.03
sendred 207.11
sends 003.20 127.16 128.09
458.15
Send-us-pray 213.19
seneschals 566.08
senest 242.06
sengaggeng 240.10
sengentide 577.29
sengers 603.10
Sengs 610.22
senhor 054.13
senior 090.36 397.11 440.17
463.32 574.16
Senior 387.25 477.20 569.32
569.32
Senior 212.34 212.35
senken 029.06
sennacassia 612.15
Sennacherib 150.16
senne 213.15
Sennet 219.13
sennight 598.32
senny 603.16
Senonnevero 353.09
sens 358.21
sensation 018.26
Sensation 147.03
sensationseeking 121.03
sense 013.01 032.18 033.15
096.32 109.12 109.15 112.12
117.36 124.02 170.01 191.17
193.35 272.22 292.28 325.04
454.05 481.23 490.05 505.31
522.29 612.29
sense 345.27 419.06
Sense 199.35
sensed 057.13 268.F6 519.02
senses 020.01 092.16 385.20
394.31 424.30 476.29
senses 348.29
Senses 105.31
sensesound 121.15
sensibility 189.06
sensible 037.04 089.12
sensitivas 238.09
sensitive 185.07 450.35
sensory 107.15
sent 034.22 045.09 068.15
235.21 467.30 472.25 483.11
496.30 496.31 516.21 542.36
543.04
Sent 071.33
sentas 268.03
sentby 458.29
sentence 129.08 149.32 288.04
558.17
Sentence 106.13
sentenced 057.36 120.12
sentenced 175.09
sentiment 192.22
sentry 343.32
seomen 331.29
seoosoon 595.08
separabits 255.35
separate 585.24
separated 109.29 109.33 124.28
544.25 614.34
sepiascraped 182.32
sept 173.24 187.20 398.03
552.03
SEPT 267.R1
septain 284.06
septicoloured 611.06
septuncial 179.22
septuor 549.09
septuply 078.18
sepulchres 028.28
Sepulchre's 343.05
sepulture 254.28 599.13
sequansewn 208.17
sequence 066.07 359.31 576.21
sequenced 134.10
sequencias 484.34
sequent 252.29 270.27
sequentiality 110.15
sequestering 556.27
Sequin 372.11
Sequoia 126.12
ser 182.21 624.08
Ser 272.27 499.10 499.10
serafim 498.33
seralcellars 545.27
seraphic 606.10
seraph's 471.24
Serbonian 539.25
sere 336.15
serebanmaids 126.19
serendipitist 191.03
serene 154.19 171.25 385.26
452.24 454.31 596.33
Serenemost 568.31
Sereth 469.14
serf 340.24 499.16
serf's 333.13
serge 511.05
Serge 131.08 322.17
sergeant 618.31
sergeantmajor's 331.02
Sergo 186.33
serial 028.26 118.10 320.33
532.33
serially 522.12
serical 512.02
series 107.33 285.21 286.08
443.36 575.17
seriolcosmically 263.24
serious 029.34 395.14 468.10
522.09 544.14
seriously 100.31 114.14 586.18
seriousness 072.30 084.21 523.07
seriph 182.10
sermo 152.07
sermon 324.27 432.09
sermons 471.19
Serni 111.06
serostaatarean 310.08
serpe 486.21
serpent 089.32 494.10
serpenthyme 206.34
serpentine 121.20
Serpentine 080.06
Serpentine 303.L1
serpents 540.01
serpumstances 297.07
servance 125.10 598.36
servant 174.11 449.14 574.08
604.27
servants 233.17 235.12 544.29
servation 351.33
serve 164.22 188.19 188.19
309.23 325.25 340.24 543.29
552.13
serve 106.01
served 040.24 183.16 221.05
285.F6 424.12 492.35 533.02
Serven 048.14
servent 321.24 605.15
server 063.32 233.17 432.34
serves 272.15 314.22 360.36
594.33
serve's 141.15
service 159.36 389.03 408.14
446.28 472.27 529.12 544.33
575.03 576.30 604.16 616.36
Service 306.20 413.04
Service 304.L1
services 575.14
servile 411.03
serving 068.09 467.36

Servious 082.03
serwishes 585.06
ses 441.18
Sesama 302.L2
sesameseed 095.15
sese 185.16 287.26
seses 488.08
sesquipedalia 116.30
sess 316.18
sessions 529.07 557.13
sester 458.10
sesthers 003.12
sesuos 511.11
set 022.07 052.21 122.26 126.07 128.32 131.13 134.10 135.23 137.24 138.01 139.01 152.28 152.31 178.24 190.26 203.16 220.17 223.15 229.27 247.07 250.30 258.30 270.17 292.26 297.03 308.02 318.19 324.15 324.15 327.32 335.05 358.17 363.04 382.14 426.03 440.14 456.15 469.35 476.10 493.21 530.13 542.22 559.02 568.35 614.17 623.28
set 348.33
Set 106.27
setalite 583.14
Setanik 338.23
setdown 004.17
Seter 153.24
seth 287.12
sethulose 029.28
setisfire 234.24
Seton's 441.04
setrapped 344.26
sets 312.03
Sets 313.04
set's 324.15
sett 198.34 241.11 499.19
sette-and-forte 404.26
setting 040.22 041.35 079.28 090.02 094.24 096.28 114.26 278.F2 394.02 529.23 567.05 616.27
settings 264.05
settle 154.22
settled 181.06 549.29 599.17
settlement 392.21 575.27
settles 115.28
settles 106.15
setton 601.18
setts 061.14
seu 601.30
Seudodanto 047.19
seufsighed 058.17
Seumas 211.04 219.22
seusan 327.30
Seval 339.15
sevelty 616.09
seven 010.35 026.06 045.15 066.14 084.04 123.06 129.22 194.25 215.15 215.16 215.17 219.16 242.05 285.05 290.08 291.F2 312.06 316.16 325.28 355.25 356.05 377.02 379.14 386.32 415.04 423.23 424.30 438.23 492.25 525.17 552.16 558.19 579.33 589.20 605.29 605.32 612.34 622.11
seven 274.L3
Seven 026.09 059.01 248.35 469.04 541.01
Seven 106.31
sevenal 126.19
Sevenchurches 059.16
sevencoloured's 277.01
sevendialled 551.32
sevenfold 605.30
Sevenheavens 446.01
sevenhued 611.06
sevenpence 083.02
sevenply 474.24
sevens 012.21 158.22 162.34 386.33
sevenscore 101.16
sevenspan 178.24
seventeenyearold 060.23
seventh 061.36 098.08 100.16 173.28 494.29 529.04 605.26 611.20
Seventh 153.33
seventies 054.08
seventip 562.09
seventyseventh 053.03
sever 348.02 451.29
several 012.30 036.06 040.18 050.30 061.03 066.01 082.07 098.23 283.15 283.16 313.16 330.03 382.07 518.16 537.26 573.20 605.29 611.17 614.05
Several 432.33
severalittle 010.33
severalled 367.27
severalls 230.17
severally 574.32 605.32
severalty 398.04
severe 082.15 279.F11
severn 199.10
Sevilla 223.06
sew 312.16 322.08 374.14 545.34
sewer 016.05 320.14
sewerful 179.33
sewers 004.14
sewery 207.13
sewing 028.07 453.07
Sewing 275.F1
sewingmachine 626.15
sewn 340.02
sex 048.02 060.14 123.08 178.21 200.31 250.01 268.02 354.28 364.24 436.17
Sex 106.29
Sexaloitez 213.19
Sexcaliber 008.36
Sexencentaurnary 535.04
sexes 283.08
Sexe-Weiman-Eitelnaky 151.11
sexfutter 384.28
sexmosaic 107.13
sexname 575.06
sexon 388.31
Sexophonologistic 123.18
Sexsex 291.26 535.04
sexth 186.14 484.07
sextiffits 420.26
sextnoon 605.30
sexton 416.13 511.08
Sexton 230.11
sextones 148.08
sextum 281.L4
sextuple 611.23
Sexuagesima 298.27
sexular 492.32
sey 486.26
sez 095.18 095.18
Sez 125.23
sfidare 068.17
Sft 621.08
sfumastelliacinous 157.32
sgocciolated 054.33
sgunners 349.15
Sgunoshooto 160.29
sh 148.04
Sh 146.32 148.04 193.27 193.28 453.22
S. H. 489.30 (S. H. Devitt)
Shaam 580.18
shabbty 025.02
shack 069.17
shackle 397.17
shackled 426.20
Shackleton 317.15 541.22
Shackleton's 392.33
shack's 468.33
Shackvulle 626.11
shad 537.01
shadda 197.23
shaddo 404.13
shade 134.32 179.05 189.33 242.18 251.16 279.F16 620.28
shader 255.02
shades 145.33 158.07 226.13 262.F5 594.15 607.14 621.23
shadow 042.19 057.32 357.16 462.21 465.25 487.14 565.14 588.15 626.25
shadow 354.09
Shadow 495.24
shadowed 377.28 474.02
shadowers 060.21
shadows 215.09 281.17 281.18 518.03 580.27 583.14 603.18
Shadows 221.21
shadowstealers 560.23
shady 060.20 564.25
shadyside 585.29
shaell 601.30
shaft 068.29 597.24
shafts 053.11 546.09
shag 470.34 619.01
shaggspick 177.32
shaggy 133.04
shagsome 566.33
shahrryar 357.19
shaik 275.F5
shains 550.10
shake 006.09 015.26 036.20 200.24 242.15 251.21 273.09 280.35 347.24 415.06 435.28 451.24 473.22 531.25 595.05
Shake 209.14 248.23 273.F1
shakeagain 143.21
shakeahand 096.23
shakealose 143.22
shakedown 040.25
Shakefork 274.L4
Shakeletin 393.01
shaken 508.01
shaken 354.15
shakenin 566.11
shakers 174.09
shakes 365.06
Shakeshands 028.04
shakespill 161.31
shakeup 514.19
Shakhisbeard 177.32

shaking 021.36 172.22 184.07 194.31 232.34 395.25 505.11 546.09
shaking 342.29
shall Shall
shallave 225.14
Shallburn 377.07
Shalldoll 141.05
shallots 550.15
shallow 552.26
shallshee 508.27
shallto 187.01
Shallwelaugh 037.28
Shallwesigh 037.28
shally 360.23
Shalmanesir 150.16
shalt 023.12 239.12 332.15 360.23 433.22 433.22 433.23
shalthow 341.16
sham 170.25 170.25 323.34 415.23 478.21 518.21
Sham 170.24
'sham 351.26
shamanah 075.14
shambe 622.07
shambles 335.09
shame 060.05 094.12 148.12 202.33 257.20 275.20 361.23 375.13 414.32 425.22 445.16 468.19 582.10 600.31 618.10
shame 526.14
Shame 307.17 534.32 618.10
shamebred 164.15
shamed 075.11 539.18
shamefaced 461.26
shamefieth 488.02
shameleast 227.34
shamelessly 124.17
shamelessness 182.14
shamemaid 212.17
shames 615.35
Shames 093.21 534.32
shamewaugh 465.08
shamiana 182.01
Shamman 192.23
shamming 065.29
shammy 206.10
shammyrag 612.25
Shamonous 425.06
Shamous 425.06
shampain 407.31
shampaying 138.31
shamrock 124.21
Shamrogueshire 472.01
shams 014.34
shamshemshowman 530.03
Shamus 534.33 564.32 604.18
Shamwork 613.10
Shanahan 027.14
Shanator 475.23 475.24
Shanavan 372.30
Shand 141.06
Shandeepen 141.06
Shandon 393.27
shandy 021.21 588.12
shandymound 323.02
Shane 461.25
Shane's 080.32
shanghai 398.28
shanghaied 485.24
shank 501.08
shanks 538.28 578.01
shanksaxle 144.33
Shanks's 471.21
Shannon 211.09
Shannons 213.34
Shan-Shim-Schung 483.04
shantey 330.08
shantungs 240.30
shanty 305.23 305.23 305.24
shantyqueer 584.21
Shanvocht 048.03
shao 322.04
shap 595.32
shape 042.05 050.36 082.16 087.27 096.22 240.34 327.26 375.35 387.25 405.10 434.30 487.13 617.33
Shape 225.29
shapekeeper 123.24
shapeless 509.07
shapely 290.02 602.04
Shaper 184.09
shapes 024.30 464.26 589.24
Shapesphere 295.04
shapewrucked 155.09
shapings 128.11
shapner 098.30
Sharadan's 184.24
shard 548.31
share 029.06 065.08 137.16 365.22 366.09 432.02 476.29
Share 579.16
shared 408.20 446.32
shared 341.21
sharee 198.19
shareholders 582.08
sharepusher 491.26
shares 189.27 543.25 545.02
Shares 361.05
sharestutterers 027.35
sharing 182.15 447.03 468.33 544.01
shark 558.18
Sharkey 307.20
sharks 312.18
Sharks 393.11
sharkskin 053.21
sharm 619.31
sharmeng 427.14
sharming 427.14
sharp 130.26 212.29 219.01 248.06 450.34 604.01
sharped 080.21
sharpen 006.23
sharping 566.09
sharpnel 341.03
sharps 098.11
sharpshape 563.02
shartclaths 491.19
shartshort 360.20
Shasser's 494.20
shat 093.18 192.02 288.27
Shattamovick 354.01
shattat 366.30
Shatten 370.34
shatter 512.35 595.31
shatterday 301.21
shatton 612.33
shatz 451.16
Shaughnessy's 623.22
Shaughraun 289.24
Shaum 364.08 483.03
Shaun 094.12 126.04 206.11 215.35 216.01 216.02 404.07 404.07 405.02 405.07 405.09 407.13 407.28 409.08 409.11 409.33 410.20 410.24 410.28 410.31 411.23 411.25 412.13 413.30 413.32 414.14 414.16 419.20 420.17 420.18 420.19 421.15 421.21 422.19 422.24 424.14 424.17 424.24 424.26 425.07 425.09 426.01 427.19 442.22 533.34
Shaun 526.14
Shaunathaun 462.08
shaunti 408.34 408.34
Shaunti 408.33
shaunty 312.30
shauted 249.34
Shauvesourishe 221.33
Shavarsanjivana 597.19
shave 149.07 240.34 330.16 380.27
shaved 464.08 529.32
shaven 543.27
shavers 041.08
shavers' 377.11
shaving 146.29
shavings 444.29
shaw 041.08 112.34
Shaw 263.07 378.24
Shawe 193.18
shawhs 497.30
shawl 007.32 117.01 144.04 213.29
shawlders 621.12
shawls 393.16
shaws 331.21
Shaws 257.12
shay 603.12
Shay 308.10
shayest 565.08
shaym 092.28
shays 453.21 554.01
shayshaun 092.32
she she She She
Shea 378.25
Sheames 177.30
sheap 172.09
shearing 604.34
shearingtime 204.14
sheath 198.03 332.32
Sheawolving 049.28
sheba 198.03
shebby 005.16 577.09
shebears 522.15
shebeen 068.21
shebi 029.26
shecook 136.14
shed 027.36 128.21 201.36 257.14 312.34 415.35 423.04 434.14
she'd 050.28 079.23 079.24 198.23 199.15 199.27 203.01 206.06 210.01 331.08 441.16 494.24
She'd 199.30
shedders 365.23
shede 231.08
Shedlock 165.32
shedropping 581.19
shee 006.13 009.07 009.07 068.21 143.30 288.09 395.15 395.15 395.25 395.25 603.12
Shee 009.07 248.02 290.01 290.05 409.02 536.36
sheegg 450.01

sheek 614.06
sheeks 275.F5
Sheem 188.05 580.18
sheemen's 094.36
sheenflare 344.24
sheeny 626.25
sheep 043.06 069.17 194.13 227.12 240.35 301.06 372.13 412.34
sheepcopers 229.09
sheepfolds 563.09
sheeples 342.07
sheep's 319.32 449.28
sheeps' 148.10
Sheepshopp 305.05
sheepside 035.13
sheepskeer 344.06
sheepskin 182.11
sheepskins 156.19
sheer 463.34 614.15
Sheeres 328.14
sheerest 461.06
Sheeroskouro 317.33
sheeshea 092.31
sheet 103.09 111.09 139.01 532.03
Sheet 105.13
sheets 077.28 133.08 179.29 213.24 315.14 395.14 491.32 530.09 546.01 575.21
sheets 340.15
sheew 061.07
Sheflower 609.11 609.11
shegulf 547.32
shehind 222.36
Shehohem 188.18
shehusbands 390.20
Sheidam 250.07
sheik 494.22
Sheila 451.23
Sheila 176.03
Sheilmartin 354.16
shekleton's 512.28
shelenk 008.06
shell 012.12 210.36 357.36 469.17 594.03 621.04
she'll 012.09 012.10 201.36 226.10 226.14 226.18 271.15 328.30 588.07 627.07
she'll 399.07
She'll 027.12 027.32 271.14
shellalite 350.28
shellback 561.16
shellborn 134.19
Shellburn 421.04
shellies 231.12
shelling 234.04
shellings 305.F1
shellmarble 207.07
shells 131.23 548.33
shells 399.05
Shelltoss 338.21
shellyholders 450.10
sheltafocal 117.14
sheltar 421.21 542.14
shelter 159.36 487.31
sheltered 359.33
shelterer 562.11
sheltering 060.20
sheltershock 008.30
Shelvling 315.32
shem 249.28
Shem 094.11 125.23 169.01 170.22 170.25 177.23 179.06 182.17 187.34 193.28 212.18 215.35 216.02 420.17 420.18 423.15
Shem 526.14
Shemans 397.31
shemblable 489.28
shemeries 187.35
Shemese 425.03
Shemish 423.01
Shemites 552.09
shemletters 419.19
Shemlockup 180.06
shemming 190.33
Shemmy 169.20
shemozzle 177.05
Shem's 169.11
Shemsen 533.34
Shemuel 464.13
Shemus 169.01 211.31
Shen 003.13
shenker 365.21
shenstone 332.13
shentre 227.22
Sheofon 083.08
sheol 078.10 078.10 083.08
sheolmastress 228.17
Sheols 177.10
sheopards 396.17
Shep 453.15
shepe 373.13
sheperdress 239.09
Shepherd 540.27
Shepperd 552.11
shepullamealahmalong 485.33
sheraph 226.20
Sheridan's 213.01 545.35
sherif 029.17
sheriff 046.07
sheriffsby 540.20
sherious 570.25
Sherlook 534.31
Sherratt 380.02
Sherratt's 380.02
sherries 058.15
sherrigoldies 256.12
sherriness 097.16
Sherry 625.01
shertwaists 434.20
Shervorum 465.05
Shervos 464.07
shes 238.27
Shes 241.26
she's she's She's
sheshe 570.25
shesses 051.17
shessock 272.F4
shester 413.06
shestnuts 183.24
shet 318.21 324.15
shetters 363.09
Shettledore-Juxta-Mare 051.23
sheutseuyes 244.32
sheverin 140.18
shevering 478.31
shewed 549.32
shewing 112.36
Shewolf 026.12
shey'll 092.30
shibboleth 267.21
shick 342.07
shide 029.27
shied 510.23
shield 480.32 624.21
shieldfails 344.25
shieldplated 077.09
shields 514.36
shieling 159.01
shieling 280.L2
shielings 520.14
Shieling's 526.33
shielsome 526.34
shiff 428.21
shift 284.F4 293.03 293.03 315.07 413.06 446.32 583.06
shifting 092.29 253.25
Shifting 560.04
shiftless 551.14
shifts 089.30 213.27 289.12 333.21 355.29
shifty 328.06
Shikespower 047.19
Shilkanbeard 532.08
shill 294.02
shillelagh 114.12
Shillelagh 361.20
shilling 049.04 219.04
shillings 438.22 465.24 520.12
shillipen 172.02
shillto 187.01
shillum 281.L4
Shim 225.14 424.08
Shimach 228.15
Shimar 010.06 010.18
shimars 339.15
shiminey 583.33
shimmer 284.29
shimmering 092.29 194.16
shimmers 157.08 528.21
shimmershake 222.35
shimmeryshaking 336.28
shimmy 015.25 148.34 208.13
Shimmyrag's 366.21
shimps 320.14
shims 393.15 531.18
shimwhir 346.26
shin 148.34 258.28 513.24 517.18 595.05
shin 172.02
Shin 010.06 010.18
Shina 231.09
shinar 320.03
shindies 499.21
shindy 621.36
shine 068.28 094.11 117.05 130.22 202.30 206.07 222.24 284.28 385.28 517.17 559.28
shiner 200.28
shines 065.09 215.06 320.03 436.28
Shinfine 346.27
shingeller 468.09
shinging 409.02
shingles 391.26
Shing-Yung-Thing 231.09
shining 004.12 092.28 186.15 385.11 502.12 519.21
shinings 427.10
shinkhams 041.14
shinkly 342.29
shinkobread 199.19
shinner 149.07 455.04
shinners 465.18
shinners' 552.06
shins 210.11 443.16 505.04

shinshanks 315.35
Shinshin 336.20 336.20
Shinshone 152.36
shintoed 539.11
shiny 055.15 179.06 271.F5 551.25
shiorts 295.F1
ship 063.25 084.36 210.20 291.02 323.02 370.35 382.27 383.20 479.30 480.07
Ship 323.04 460.08
shipalone 062.04
shipchild 579.01
shipfolds 325.31
Ship-le-Zoyd 370.29
shiply 315.09
shipman's 255.30
shipmen 026.23
shipped 367.21
shipping 097.24
shippings 547.35
ships 325.18 363.23 394.15
Ships 460.08
ship's 311.21 311.23 311.36 313.09
shipshaped 128.06
shipshep's 313.18
shipside 577.30
shipsteam 171.35
shire 502.32 528.30 548.29 578.36
shire 201.13
shirked 341.29
shirker 530.23
shirkers 051.11
shirking 190.28
Shirksends 028.02
shiroskuro 612.18
shirt 027.11 033.07 045.25 082.22 085.34 089.30 196.11 211.27 247.28 292.11 305.15 335.32 368.32 381.13 436.33 437.26 446.31 463.22 512.04 560.25 619.34
shirt 383.05
shirtness 166.09
shirtplisse 578.08
shirts 098.21 183.18 228.10 355.29
shirtsails 493.01
shirvant 200.18
shit 179.06
shitateyar 319.27
Shite 142.07
Shitric 532.08
shittery 352.28
shittim 301.24
Shiva 080.24
shiver 188.24 237.32 274.09
shivered 099.14
shiverer 110.24
shivering 178.31 526.05 578.01
Shivering 507.35
shivery 597.24
Shize 006.13
shjelties 554.06
shkewers 344.29
shleeps 244.35
Shlicksher 280.10
Shlicksheruthr 280.27
shllwe 234.25
Shlossh 349.16
shnout 179.06
Shoal 202.05
shoaled 320.30
shoals 264.17
Shoan 603.04
shock 112.27 241.30 357.36 393.09
Shock 377.07
shocked 072.22 126.22 346.20 464.25 538.28
shocking 136.22 385.31 391.25 393.35
Shocking 090.29
shockings 144.21
shocks 233.09
Shockt 308.11
shod 288.27
shoddied 319.03
shoddy 164.23
shoddyshoes 226.24
shoe 013.25 024.23 183.34 275.F2
Shoe 441.23 565.19 565.30
shoebard 133.27
Shoebenacaddie 200.23
shoeblacks 386.29
shoed 255.36
shoehanded 255.01
shoehandschiner 333.04
shoeheel 404.33
shoeing 135.03 181.20
shoeings 368.31
shoenumber 533.05
shoepisser 451.36
shoes 063.35 137.28 267.26 450.03 459.16 489.22 530.26
shoesets 011.23
shoeshines 069.13
shoeshoes 622.10
shoestring 121.08 451.33
shoeweek 144.24
shome 225.14 231.04 336.09
shomers 034.16
shone 075.11 212.18 280.31 528.21
Shone 441.23
Shonny 377.27
shoo 262.13
shoodov 069.13
shooing 482.19
shook 128.17 148.34 170.31 176.30 314.32 322.11 373.13 412.14 471.32
shookatnaratatattar 339.18
shookerloft 243.28
shool 364.09
shoolbred 127.11
shoolerim 112.07
shoolthers 252.01
Shoom 565.30
Shoon 603.04
shoos 011.18
shooshooe 417.34
shoot 063.03 179.06 198.03 262.F5 311.27 337.01 438.20 508.32
Shoot 473.17 610.33
shooters 241.29
shoother 371.26
shooting 065.11 274.27 475.15 505.05 524.23
shootings 616.07
shootmaker 320.17
shoots 125.01 316.35 354.34 372.05 475.12
shootsle 316.35
shootsmen 538.32
shootst 626.05
shop 023.05 026.30 167.32 437.18 540.16 560.16 560.17
shop 350.06
Shop 029.01 560.16 560.16
shopahoyden 255.31
Shopalist 006.33
shopes 280.21
shopgirls 504.22
Shopkeeper 539.06
shopkeepers 128.16
shopkeepers' 183.26
shoply 315.09
shopper 161.24 372.05
Shops 106.04
shop's 317.06
Shopshup 244.06
shopsoiled 550.23
Shop-Sowry 221.34
shopswindow 448.01
shore 003.01 312.18 479.10 494.33
shored 098.06
shores 012.10 132.20
Shores 175.25
shorn 089.17 250.05
Shorn 454.07
shorp 617.27
shorpshoopers 352.26
short 003.04 003.19 026.33 046.07 049.21 050.07 062.23 110.26 120.24 122.02 169.01 171.34 177.13 194.28 198.02 224.02 241.01 291.07 315.07 328.06 426.19 440.22 489.22 515.20
short 201.17
Short 525.07
shortartempa 178.02
Shortbred 235.32
shortcake 550.13
shortened 121.36
shorter 122.21
shortfingeredness 031.16
shortfront 009.04
shorth 434.33
shorties 494.33
shortiest 419.15
shortlegged 012.26
shortly 067.33 150.21 292.07 429.01 536.02 562.28 617.26
shorts 437.11 614.14
shortshins 015.31
Shortts 269.F4
shortusians 451.24
shorty 039.19 172.28
Shorty 039.18 212.02 523.23 524.07 524.10
shossafat 051.17
shot 023.05 032.09 040.32 062.32 128.17 132.21 169.09 198.30 231.10 234.04 260.06 315.11 319.03 341.06 451.28 585.13 590.10
shote 342.19
Shotland 510.13
shotly 609.19
shots 137.01
Shotshrift 494.20

shotted 171.32
shou 542.02
shoul 149.08
should should Should Should
shouldbe 155.24
shoulden 364.27
shoulder 053.08 053.08 134.05 146.25 169.15 211.32 398.10 436.33
shoulder 343.14
shoulderblades 033.06
shouldered 446.17 580.31
shoulderedboy's 336.04
shouldering 260.11
shoulders 174.09 324.02 530.26 559.33
shouldhavebeen 042.19
shouldier 322.03
shouldn't 459.25
Shouldrups 157.10
shouldst 563.32
shoulthern 404.20
shourter 320.19
Shousapinas 223.02
shout 042.11 101.05 305.26 493.33
Shout 420.27
shouted 412.14 521.29
shouter 446.33
shouters 329.15
shouting 060.12 181.02 612.33
shoutmost 006.18
shouts 112.04 442.04 542.06
shouts 352.28
shove 047.02 336.10 374.24 431.26
shoved 390.02
shovel 210.34
shovelled 127.05
Shovellyvans 495.02
shover 166.17
shoviality 006.19
shoving 354.30 364.35
show 004.25 008.03 032.35 040.12 056.15 062.28 086.07 112.35 118.33 128.11 163.08 179.06 197.15 200.24 205.09 205.19 221.16 228.09 233.10 233.10 242.23 291.F5 303.04 315.17 326.29 330.35 347.24 364.11 377.21 424.33 425.09 441.22 441.23 442.22 443.14 460.09 514.03 523.06 529.36 540.32 561.17 561.27 566.33 566.34 570.02 570.33 582.28 600.27 604.20 607.29 611.07 611.34 625.05
show 418.14
Show 077.28 283.32 441.22 441.23 448.09 468.15
showchest 426.11
showdows 355.30
showed 025.21 123.33 208.15 257.05 288.21 360.29 423.32 431.16 493.10 523.34 606.25 611.22
showen 224.22 224.27
shower 011.03 127.26 144.03 228.09 237.32 277.15 297.05 453.31 490.30
showeradown 088.32
showered 183.16
showering 125.19
showerly 621.09
showerproof 182.16
showers 051.02 108.04 213.20
showery 063.09
showeryweather 447.32
showing 093.04 191.28 222.17 257.23 365.31 463.03 531.17 589.24 606.30
showing 342.22 342.25
Showing 334.25
Showing 107.06
showings 151.33
showlaced 340.30
showlots 225.36
showly 252.22
showm 029.04
Show'm 092.13
showman's 463.02
shown 107.13 163.33 260.F3 585.13 611.18 617.22
Shown 420.35
showne 551.26
Showpanza 234.06
showplace 600.30
showrs 601.35
shows 114.13 127.33 128.20 129.21 133.16 134.20 162.12 299.24 376.20 382.11 565.14 616.22
show's 114.30
Show's 346.11
showshadows 546.23
showshallow 153.06
show-the-flag 496.04
showthers 029.06
Showting 116.06
shoy 465.07 467.12
shraking 541.18
shrapnel 035.28
shrecks 090.11
shrewd 273.11
shricked 138.34
shrieking 090.10
shrievalty 063.15
shrill 594.29
shrillgleescreaming 383.15
shrimpnet 471.26
shrine 051.19 601.32
shrineshriver 341.27
shrinked 527.27
shrinking 238.09 524.23
shrinks 298.33
shrivering 240.05
shriving 532.03
shroonk 015.31
shroplifter 273.11
Shrove 227.31
shrub 043.08 505.21
shrubbery 538.34
shrubrubs 420.08
Shrubsher 280.16
Shrubsheruthr 280.19
shrug 225.03
Shruggers' 181.05
shrunk 199.21
shsh 358.12
Shsh 036.20
Shshsh 148.16
Shshshsh 148.32
Sht 144.17
shtemp 064.01
shubladey's 511.27
shuck 026.14 199.22 338.02 612.34
Shuck 466.15 466.16
Shucks 535.17
shudder 358.05 487.04
shudders 238.07 504.07
shuddersome 179.24
shuffering 223.01
shuffle 026.01 273.09 286.12
Shufflebotham 315.04
shuffled 409.22
shufflers 051.08
shuffling 606.29
shuft 413.06
shugon 535.20
Shuhorn 556.36
shuit 620.04
shuk 288.27 413.11
shukar 357.02
shulder 207.19
shuler's 514.19
Shuley 049.06
Shultroj 160.31
shummering 342.07
Shumpum 345.23
shun 249.28 540.14
Shun 093.13
Shunadure 475.27
Shunders 413.06
sh'undn't 279.F05
shunned 337.33
shunner 415.24
shunning 579.03
Shunny 057.05 475.29
shunshema 098.04
shunt 419.24 454.33 454.33
Shunt 454.33
shunted 272.26
shunter 336.09 446.33
shur 425.02
shure 333.15
Shurenoff 354.05
shurts 023.09
Shusies-with-her-Soles-Up 531.22
shut 023.05 101.04 130.19 161.24 316.20 335.13 570.02
shut 341.34
Shut 021.20 022.06 324.15
Shut 105.21
SHUT 182.32
Shuter 265.F5
Shutmup 355.08
shutter 023.05 352.25 513.01
Shutter 420.29
shuttered 102.01
shuttinshure 371.17
shuttle 277.23
shuttm 352.14
shuttoned 022.34
Shuvlin 169.23
Shvr 497.23
shy 094.11 133.15 171.34 179.06 190.24 202.27 242.16 248.17 287.F1 411.27 439.33 450.02 459.26
Shy 147.01
shyasian 564.35
shyblumes 548.04
shyfaun 015.21
shylight 358.01
shylit 222.36
shyly 252.21
shyme 124.27

shypull 300.13
Shyr 198.09
Shysweet 582.27
si 160.30 230.17 568.09 607.18
SI 305.R1
sia 160.30
Siam 108.26
Siamanish 425.16
siamixed 066.20
siang 244.35
siangchang 119.24
Sianta 471.05
Siar 089.28
Sibernia 297.05
Sibernian 567.35
sibi 185.25
sibicidal 040.31
sibspecious 374.08
sibspeeches 096.30
sibster 465.17
sibsubstitute 028.35
sibsuction 221.03
sibylline 031.36
sic 076.07 124.12 610.16
sic 368.14
SIC 260.R2
siccar 586.30
sicckumed 314.34
sich 006.25
sick 024.22 045.15 068.21 120.20 171.16 252.35 289.14 420.24 432.33 482.30 543.24
Sick 156.05
SICK 300.R1
Sickamoor's 281.20
sickamours 460.23
sickcylinder 179.34
sickenagiaour 305.03
sicker 054.24 076.08 442.28 535.17
Sickerson 471.30 530.21
Sickfish 072.11
sickle 457.10
sickle 341.10
sickles 457.10
sickle's 360.24
sickling 243.23
sickly 459.08 512.25
sicknells 324.28
sickself 426.13
sics 247.05
sicsecs 356.15
Sicut 601.16
sid 202.23
Sid 059.07 410.36
siddle 432.21
side 003.05 012.15 016.23 017.11 029.04 031.15 042.32 042.32 049.12 050.27 053.12 061.35 071.03 078.31 086.28 130.07 139.19 155.14 161.20 167.11 180.10 209.20 212.27 212.29 214.02 228.25 230.04 255.28 257.09 264.F3 270.04 324.07 338.18 338.27 354.30 359.06 359.34 375.22 404.16 406.03 433.28 444.09 449.27 455.18 466.14 470.29 474.03 497.22 516.06 558.07 559.15 589.11 597.11 597.11 625.35 625.35
side 343.18
Side 250.11 559.21
sidecurls 280.36
sideeye 431.08
sideline 513.30
siden 240.08
sideofthe 142.06
sideposts 064.10
Sideral 604.12
siderbrass 511.30
sidereal 035.33 426.24
Sideria 078.11
siderodromites 160.21
sides 060.34 078.26 150.35 336.03 392.01 505.05 536.29 540.04 614.20
sideslipped 204.15
sidesmen 567.21
sidesplit 511.21
sidesplitting 454.08
sidetracks 080.01
sidewaist 236.36
sidewheel 040.29
sidewiseopen 474.09
Siding 070.05
sidled 209.19
Sidlesham 030.07
sidleshomed 098.05
Sidome 582.30
sidster 500.21
sidulcis 209.35
sie 430.20
sie 540.11
sieck 416.13
siecken 009.05
siècle 192.14
siege 061.25 301.27 545.28
sieger 352.25
Sieger 281.23
siegewin 539.27
Siegfield 106.12
siegings 073.24
sieguldson 371.06
sieme 243.16
siemens 245.08
sierrah 481.18
Sierre 159.05
siesta 433.07 501.10
sieur 523.15
sieve 199.23
sieves 411.05
sieze 482.35
sifadda 232.28
Sifted 440.19
Sig 399.09
sigarius 076.07
sigen 319.28
Sigerson 608.10
sigeth 503.28
sigh 007.08 011.25 093.27 124.27 149.06 158.06 173.08 194.19 203.19 213.16 278.11 280.33 449.19 512.26
Sigh 546.02
sighdid 006.14
sighed 157.36 158.05 172.15 405.28 454.24 509.22 576.10
sigheds 299.01
sighin 202.20
sighing 384.04 571.23
Sighing 470.16
sighings 095.32
sighinspirer 395.17
sighs 144.21 179.27 184.01 366.24 620.17
sighs 418.29
sight 012.16 091.24 122.24 159.35 175.04 199.06 200.26 224.24 239.12 242.23 247.20 269.02 280.01 289.F1 347.06 361.05 397.04 430.06 433.35 449.21 471.28 520.29 520.30 566.28 575.14 628.02
sights 011.36 215.09 469.20
sightsee 205.04
sightseeing 237.16
sigilposted 075.04
Sigismond 537.08
sigla 032.14 119.19
sign 036.24 091.31 091.35 111.19 114.36 115.06 119.17 121.08 122.35 200.21 207.16 234.13 245.35 249.16 316.25 317.11 326.06 356.25 357.14 391.19 405.19 406.30 454.06 471.12 483.29 486.28 490.29 490.30 514.16 527.15
Sign 378.13
signal 078.22 625.15
signal 341.03
signalling 248.06 321.12
signation 241.21
signature 115.08 181.15 484.13
Signature 302.L2
signed 112.30 168.08 337.13 350.29 463.05 529.13 574.15 601.35
signed 071.22
Signed 307.05 480.13
signet 357.14
signics 223.04
significance 487.09
SIGNIFICANCE 276.R1
significantly 088.09
significat 148.17
signifies 116.09
signifieth 283.20
signify 478.12
Signifying 599.09
signing 035.14 111.21 302.18
signlore 036.17
Signorina 164.30
signory 017.22
signs 018.18 019.33 028.28 117.13 123.33 143.23 275.09 281.22 374.09 393.02 597.10 625.02
Signs 608.26
signum 044.03
Signur's 243.16
Sigurd 608.10
Sigurdsen 429.19
sihl 200.24
Siker 237.31
Sikiang 199.19
siktyten 029.26
Silanse 228.17
silbils 424.33
silbings 491.04
Silder 187.19
silence 013.03 031.32 075.18 083.04 098.02 115.25 193.11 203.21 230.23 235.07 280.30 337.17 382.14 393.35 452.20 476.08 557.12 565.15 570.03 627.10

Silence 061.01 074.09 378.32
SILENCE 501.06
silenced 421.36 467.20 594.36
silent 073.29 100.03 123.35
133.01 183.27 244.30 454.27
473.22 482.23 524.22 568.09
602.12
silent 345.19
Silent 014.06
Silent 176.08
silentiousness 427.33
silentioussuemeant 062.03
silentium 044.04
silents 267.17 548.34
Silents 334.31
silentsailing 556.01
silenzioso 147.35
silex 023.20
silfrich 497.36
siligirl 200.19
silipses 156.13
silk 108.24 128.11 133.08
148.30 204.35 321.10 354.32
395.11 504.28 545.04
silkclad 134.24
silke 061.11
Silkebjorg 163.30
silken 154.10
silkettes 457.23
silkhouatted 056.07
silkily 577.31
silkinlaine 034.23
silks 528.19
Silks 508.29
silkskin 445.05
silktrick 221.34
silky 458.27
Silkyshag 016.34
sillarsalt 570.36
Sillayass 231.18
sillieries 346.11
sillied 094.03
silliver 200.28
sillonise 056.16
Sillume 244.26
silly 253.09 562.14
silly 159.18
sillybilly 416.08
sillying 076.29
sillymottocraft 623.19
sillypost 200.22
Sillysall 609.12
Silurian 051.29
silvamoonlake 202.28
silvanes 495.36
Silvapais 113.11
silve 619.30
silver 028.30 031.07 164.26
244.25 280.31 291.02 406.05
433.32 477.25 522.19 549.29
Silver 134.10
silvered 548.23
silvering 275.11 580.21
silvernetss 366.11
silverymonnblue 399.05
silvestrious 388.26
Silvoo 561.30
silvoor 009.31
silvry 140.27
silvy 148.08
sim 162.27
Sim 305.05 408.21 620.15
Simba 203.32
simbum 253.13
simian 192.22
similar 056.18 433.04 476.22
515.10 545.02 616.03
Similar 353.28
similarly 031.09 107.30
similies 601.16
similitude 404.12
simmence 367.13
simmering 247.14 556.33
simon 408.20
Simon 142.27
simoniac 573.31
simp 200.21
Simpatica 212.11
simper 149.06 290.23
Simper 065.05
Simpers 282.F2
Simperspreach 299.22
simplasailormade 232.34
simple 052.11 065.27 167.09
174.02 204.13 230.30 260.16
304.03 337.27 514.01 572.23
625.06
simpled 273.15
Simples 291.F8
simpletop 299.15
simplex 493.24
simplicissime 488.03
simpliciter 487.33
simplicity 411.12
simpling 318.15
simply 056.02 065.29 067.22
144.14 193.23 203.22 224.34
241.25 249.34 430.28 458.30
459.13 493.09 527.29 588.06
616.18 617.17 619.06
Simply 017.03 337.15 459.09
491.03 503.07 527.15
simplysoley 598.19
simpringly 451.31
Simpson's 043.07
simself 460.11
simulchronic 182.12
simules 250.04
simultaneous 131.31 546.22
simultaneously 109.34
simwhat 245.10
sin 005.14 011.26 048.16
149.09 196.18 233.05 289.10
298.22 339.22 378.21 385.10
467.25 527.28 577.05 580.20
sin 353.01
Sin 094.18 234.06
Sin 176.14
sina 198.16
Sinbads 327.25
since 003.23 018.18 025.09
026.04 027.26 029.26 032.33
050.14 051.04 052.10 063.25
077.12 078.30 087.19 112.25
113.31 119.22 121.21 122.12
122.29 146.24 151.34 157.02
173.15 180.28 188.01 193.34
196.13 204.03 214.23 223.17
229.23 236.24 243.13 246.16
246.27 249.03 251.28 251.36
253.04 253.07 253.23 263.20
296.21 297.10 298.25 300.02
327.26 329.36 331.27 333.21
335.02 359.02 362.05 363.22
367.15 376.01 376.17 397.24
409.21 410.17 419.35 421.16
431.18 456.33 458.12 461.09
465.06 467.20 468.07 479.20
479.23 496.27 505.10 507.03
508.27 528.30 530.08 532.17
539.17 544.23 553.07 562.16
570.21 574.05 584.30 593.10
595.24 598.04 615.02 621.19
622.14 622.14 623.22
since 625.13
Since 014.35 117.16 236.19
279.05 307.05 346.18 396.21
420.36 574.25 588.28 590.18
614.09 621.02
Since 418.27 418.29
sincerely 503.19 562.36
sincerestly 379.27
sinctifying 417.35
sincuries 290.08
Sindat 256.26
sindays 432.33
sindbook 229.32
sindeade 363.20
sinder's 532.03
sinduced 004.09
Sindy 491.01
sindybuck 412.35
sine 113.06
sine 185.15 287.20
sinegear 609.01
sinelab 234.08
sinequam 163.23
sinews 133.16
sinewy 559.32
sinfintins 624.18
sinflowed 481.09
Sinflowed 481.09
sinflute 590.01
sinfly 267.F3
sing 011.16 058.13 129.07
131.19 164.34 187.19 190.30
226.19 236.10 236.15 249.25
252.29 279.F32 294.30 334.21
366.36 398.04 398.17 409.14
415.18 432.29 438.12 489.33
528.10 528.10 571.01 625.16
sing 419.06
Sing 209.35 224.16 328.24
338.32 349.04 419.23 441.21
528.09 569.23
Singabed 256.33
Singabob 094.33
singachamer 556.15
Singalingalying 267.07
singaloo 359.19
singalow 488.11
singame 469.22
singasong 485.31
singasongapiccolo 450.19
singe 466.21
singelearum 488.11
singen 065.36 603.10
singer 164.32 164.35 467.32
singers 626.14
singimari 203.24
singin 253.12
singing 042.14 234.34 240.09
276.04 304.30 373.34 390.24
397.10 453.24 466.19 492.09
548.03 586.26
Singing 296.18
singingsing 280.06
single 063.17 119.21 137.35
201.22 202.14 290.20 362.26

388.24 420.02 472.27 534.30 604.13
Single 579.09
Singlebarrelled 286.F4
singlebiassed 168.07
singlehanded 087.16
singleminded 042.22 124.07
Singlemonth 236.10
singlette 329.02
singorgeous 492.34
singoutfeller 257.07
Singpantry's 007.10
sings 135.35 163.03 385.24 487.24
Sings 304.F5
singsigns 138.07
singsing 116.01 601.18
singthee 442.25
singtime 104.02
Singty 222.23
singular 187.30 488.16 523.22 547.33
singularly 153.24
singulfied 306.06
singult 159.13
singulvalvulous 310.04
Sinior 533.16
sinister 300.26 384.26 463.02 546.08
sinistrant 233.16
sinistrogyric 120.27
sinistrous 197.01
Sinjon 274.02
sinjoro 160.32
sink 007.13 061.17 120.13 296.F3 311.02 317.03 450.36 560.04 560.05 560.06 628.10
Sink 145.04 301.24 373.07 373.07
sinkalarum 178.18
Sinkasink 373.07
sinkathink 342.28
Sinkathinks 342.26
sinker 305.18 463.20
sinking 108.13 140.26 224.25
sinks 131.02 336.30 517.32
sinks 260.L3
sinkts 432.36
sinned 204.36 523.09 547.03
Sinned 420.24
sinner 314.18 607.04
Sinner 192.13 192.13
sinnerettes 457.22 587.24
sinners 532.14
sinner's 184.23
sinnfinners 036.26
sinning 050.23 523.09
sinningstone 564.30
sinns 330.18
Sinobiled 263.F4
sinople 546.10
sins 062.21 069.04 147.18 188.25 307.F3 314.25 357.29 494.31
sinscript 421.18
sinse 083.12 239.02 338.02
sinses 227.31
sinsin 116.18 116.18
sinsinsinning 505.09
sinsitives 527.27
sint 335.27
sintalks 269.03
sinted 482.22
sintry 343.32
sinuorivals 348.30
sinus 374.33
Sinya 348.34
siocur 011.18
siomen's 549.18
siouler's 208.25
sip 009.17 095.24 368.25
Sip 510.30
Siparioramoci 468.20
siphonopterous 417.01
sippahsedly 366.23
sipped 124.33
sipper 052.12
sipping 443.29
sips 227.04
sir 020.20 024.16 024.28 025.08 026.34 027.34 036.24 043.18 067.23 085.03 087.31 090.21 112.12 122.15 145.17 153.35 180.04 191.14 224.28 273.F7 300.F2 346.29 374.27 381.09 430.07 466.30 477.08 478.02 489.36 504.15 506.19 520.10 522.03 522.20 522.22 522.26 525.29 528.03 528.36 532.04 532.06 563.12 564.32 568.25 578.16 590.21 613.25
Sir 003.04 040.35 040.35 096.07 096.07 293.F2 329.05 366.05 420.36 570.19 590.06
Sir 104.09
Siranouche 338.24
sirch 416.14
Sirdarthar 347.09
sire 053.28 089.21 128.35 234.13 255.12 375.21 442.09 502.31 596.12
sire 486.05
Sire 271.03 549.34 566.29 568.34
sired 547.23
Sireland 428.07
sirens 050.24
sires 342.21
Siresultan 612.09
sirious 426.24
Siriusly 513.01
sirphilip 088.31
sirr 516.15
sirrebob 245.27
Sirrherr 541.13
sis 184.02 431.29 489.16
Sis 448.34
sisars 162.01
Siseule 104.10
sish 080.35
Sish 587.19
siskinder 469.23
siss 019.29 158.06
sissastones 493.11
sissastrides 564.36
sissed 314.31
sissers 250.08
Sissibis 452.08
sissy 094.11 335.08
Sissy 441.18
sissymusses 154.08
sisteen 157.08
sister 014.33 053.10 086.27 165.14 220.09 384.22 393.17 394.24 431.15 439.14 442.17 459.18 556.05 605.36 621.17
Sister 210.24 235.30 391.33 431.21 439.26
sisterhood 059.18
sisterin 007.32
sister-in-love 067.36
sisterisle 051.25
sisters 032.07 188.22 362.25 393.22 447.01 508.23 544.30 579.33
Sisters 248.35 386.24 386.24
sisters' 183.27
Sisters' 092.24
Sistersen 186.19
sisterwands 407.22
sistra 468.35
sit 057.05 059.32 135.07 181.30 206.22 207.30 229.26 232.24 268.13 297.28 304.13 324.02 360.34 374.14 434.32 449.26 470.03 499.23 499.27 623.24
Sit 093.31
sitbom 256.27
site 005.25 007.35 041.34 090.13 108.04 338.18 541.36 601.16 623.29
Site 420.27
sitinins 494.22
sitisfactuary 084.15
sititout 071.01
Sitric's 012.32
sits 057.25 141.17 226.04 544.25 618.28
sitta 625.27
sittang 198.34
sittem 131.11
sitter 578.29
Sitterdag-Zindeh-Munaday 205.16
sitthing 256.27
sitting 025.12 094.19 147.07 153.34 166.10 190.36 296.15 392.21 407.07 445.33 453.09 484.10 492.29 509.06 559.26 562.01
sitting 201.07
sitton 012.22
Sittons 058.35
situate 086.34
situation 037.04 385.26
situations 529.14
situm 287.22
Sitys 117.19
Siuccherillina 471.03
sive 189.19
siven 495.08
sivispacem 087.14
six 014.22 047.12 082.12 082.27 084.26 086.30 122.14 138.29 140.09 162.34 179.08 236.03 264.22 264.23 273.F7 335.01 336.07 438.22 446.19 478.09 478.09 490.21 529.07 550.34 558.18 589.22
Six 213.27 248.32 291.F2
Six 359.24
sixdigitarian 362.01
sixes 012.21 054.07 158.22
sixpence 069.18
sixpenny 191.01
sixpennyhapennies 549.36
sixponce 568.13
sixt 619.28
Sixt 347.18

sixth 062.27 423.07
Sixth 153.33
sixtine 430.31
sixton 552.23
sixtric 313.24
Sixtus 153.33
sixtusks 234.13
sixty 059.33 128.32 135.05 265.27 405.12 410.33
Sixty 007.33
sixtyfives 055.14
sixtyfour 559.35
sixtysix 211.17
sixtysixth 497.26
sixuous 297.22
sizars 551.29
size 072.27 136.24 166.04 314.34 452.15 509.28 616.20 628.03
sizes 024.30 464.26
sizing 479.28
sizzled 531.14
sizzleroads 577.28
S. J. 440.10 (S. J. Finn's)
sjuddenly 441.24
skald 056.22
skalded 551.04
Skaldignavia 254.33
skall 074.01 074.04 364.14 548.01
Skam 093.21
skand 223.33 310.30
Skand 157.16
skaping 353.26
skarlot 060.04
skarp 233.33
skat 539.35
skate 525.36
skating 131.06
skattering 243.18
skatterlings 073.34
skattert 345.18
skeep 313.05
skeepsbrow 535.16
skeer 561.01
skeezy 466.09
Skekels 150.17
Skelly 390.07
skelp 445.07
skelterfugue 121.28
skelts 227.05
skeowsha 215.12
skephumble 503.16
Skerretts 044.08
skerries 316.12
Skerry 376.26
Skertsiraizde 032.08
sketched 052.35
skettle 329.12
skew 494.02
skewbald 554.06
skewer 267.F5
Skewered 303.11
ski 413.14
skib 329.12 508.17
skibber 315.14
Skibbereen 315.34
Skibbering's 302.13
Skibereen 210.19
skibluh 240.33
skid 525.35
skiddystars 090.08
skidoo 077.27 503.16
skidoos 273.12
skiff 228.08
Skiffstrait 481.06
skilful 099.22
skill 024.03
skillet 397.22 531.13
skillfilledfelon 355.27
skilllies 089.19
skillmistress 571.07
skillmustered 149.08
Skilly 229.14
skillyton 422.09
Skim 440.05
skimiskes 347.05
skimmelk 262.22
skimming 142.01
skimperskamper 353.33
skimpies 513.14
skin 184.08 413.21 464.11 510.16
Skin 105.31
skinful 344.17
skinners 312.35
Skinner's 043.03 532.32
skins 200.01 317.22 569.34
skinside 507.06
skinsyg 550.17
skintighs 373.27
skip 377.10 437.16
Skip 271.F2
skipgod 488.22
skippies 328.13
skips 560.11
skirl 335.10
skirling 035.29
skirp 513.15
skirriless 495.03
skirt 040.09 065.06 199.13 208.25
skirtaskortas 247.29
skirtmishes 022.30
skirtmisshes 021.19
skirts 027.14 194.27 315.16 439.01 522.09
skirtsleeves 067.31
skittered 370.06
skittering 243.17 273.22
Skittish 577.22
skittled 187.01
skittles 341.13
Skivinis 536.31
skivis 347.35
skivs 540.36
skivvies 130.18
sknow 287.04
sknows 305.20 333.15
Skokholme 279.F27
skol 198.20
skolar 326.29
skole 265.06
Skole 265.06
skoll 224.20
skool 308.F2
skoopgoods 346.25
skorned 410.08
skorth 434.33
Skotia 164.05
skould 056.14
Skowood 257.12
skreek 474.21
skrene 443.35
skreve 141.20
skrevened 182.14
skrimmhandsker 607.05
Skrivenitch 423.15
Skud 010.36
skuld 091.24 539.35
Skulkasloot 610.14
skulksman 616.21
skull 017.18 025.22 169.11 310.30 374.28 464.09
skullabogue 528.37
skullhullows 613.20
skumring 056.08
skunk 462.36
Skunk 136.15 365.22
Skunkinabory 323.20
skunner 205.21
sky 011.02 110.05 226.19 235.08 238.30 494.12 541.06 594.01 599.35 620.27
sky 383.04
skybuddies 309.20
skyerscape 004.36
skyfold 613.02
skygrey 475.31
skyhighdeed 461.08
skyless 331.01
skysign 004.13
skyterrier 424.04
skyup 014.34
slaaps 007.28
slab 077.25 170.35 600.26
slack 438.25
slackerd 516.01
slackfoot 427.01
slackly 190.28
slacks 443.27
slade 165.36
slag 453.23
slags 141.08
slagt 500.17
Slain 011.28
slaine 609.34
slake 311.16 319.12
slaking 015.33
slalpers 314.35
slam 577.08
slammocks 358.34
Slander 034.12
slanderising 463.29
slander's 102.17
slaney 206.24
slang 207.18
slanger 494.26
slanguage 421.17
slangwhangers 174.08
slant 113.31
Slant 336.20
slanty 305.24
slap 148.06 565.23 565.23 595.31
slapbang 550.26
slapmamma 461.17
slapottleslup 371.04
slapped 148.06
slappin 486.30
slapping 279.F28 507.09
slaps 138.18
slapse 291.25
slapstick 473.13
slashed 545.31
Slasher 099.25
slashers 178.14
Slash-the-Pill 283.F3
slataper's 542.33

Slatbowel 161.27
slate 052.26 279.F01 445.20 542.33 589.31
slated 116.33
slatepencil 211.12
Slater's 511.04
slates 385.11
slatters 616.09
slauchterday 539.28
slaughed 326.36
slaughter 087.16
slaughterer 255.01
slaunga 072.29
slaunter 315.25
slaunty 311.01
slav 159.30
Slavansky 355.11
Slavar 355.11
slave 290.F7 316.29 569.36 572.29 580.26
slave 354.07
Slave 494.23
slaved 081.04
slaver 480.02
slaves 446.33
Slaves 255.14
slavey 333.05 351.22 375.30 589.09
slavey's 137.28
slavish 260.16
Slavocrates 328.12
Slavos 424.01
slay 191.32
Slayer 203.32
slaying 559.11
sleap 277.13
sled 310.36
sledding 426.25
sledgy 099.05
slee 230.19 577.35 603.13
Slee 571.30
sleek 065.06 141.02
sleeking 541.30
sleekysilk 271.F5
sleep 041.06 074.18 170.18 189.29 192.19 192.20 199.12 241.09 248.19 249.02 259.04 305.23 375.05 393.35 397.28 403.05 408.08 429.22 445.22 473.24 475.28 481.07 551.02 562.24 563.02 563.10 576.10 578.09 597.02 608.33 608.34 617.29
Sleep 114.19 280.34
Sleep 106.14
sleeped 373.02
sleeper 310.10 597.26
sleeping 054.05 074.18 088.08 350.29 389.02 540.17 556.14 556.22 620.36
sleepingchambers 566.07
sleepingtop 499.25
sleepish 143.06
sleepless 589.24
sleepper 295.10
sleeproom 562.17
sleeps 012.05 561.08 583.10
Sleeps 072.05
sleeptalking 459.05
sleepth 555.01 555.02
sleepy 027.30 132.08 252.21
sleepytalking 327.21
sleet 380.31
sleeting 274.26
sleets 416.35
sleetshowers 552.35
sleety 566.17
sleeve 169.13 295.18 311.33 440.28
sleevemongrel 441.32
sleever 352.15
sleeves 042.10 196.08 531.17
sleighding 006.02
slender 255.36 430.27 602.01 602.02
slepp 495.15
slepped 299.10
slept 039.32 041.06 087.03 278.F5 619.25
slettering 114.18
sleuth 597.24
sleuts 442.35
slew 080.24
Slew 565.17
slewd 203.32
slewed 289.09
slice 170.35 455.30
sliced 178.15
slicing 078.34
slick 473.12
Slick 376.31
slicker 208.02
slickers 444.33
slickfoot 426.36
slickly 237.36
slickstick 094.02
slid 182.05
slidder 381.03
slide 195.03 311.01 367.21 595.36
slidepage 300.14
sliders 579.04
slides 248.09 325.22
sliding 274.26 288.F4 357.20
sliduant 100.11
slies 094.18
sliggymaglooral 381.30
slight 247.22
Slight 144.02
slightly 038.31 073.03 237.35
Sligo's 141.02
slim 202.27 596.32
Slim 446.27
slime 209.32
slimed 338.24
slimes 615.34
slimmer 430.27
slims 140.26
sling 622.19
Sling 338.22
slingslang 486.14
slink 233.29
slinking 343.13
slip 043.24 108.28 122.05 200.21 202.27 279.F12 433.31 473.08 563.10 627.35
Slip 080.31 377.08 435.18
slipashod 426.36
slipny 187.01
slipped 182.02 278.F5 420.06 599.07
slipper 122.05 201.33 224.30 267.F6
slippering 271.F5
slippers 394.11
slippery 178.10 604.29
Slippery 341.35
slipping 038.12 077.09 093.26 195.01 328.23 477.23 579.04
slippy 377.34
slips 042.29 073.19 227.03 584.13
Slips 105.19
slipt 139.18
Slipver 342.16
slit 190.04 267.11
slithe 057.26
slitheryscales 526.01
slits 465.20
slitsucked 016.03
slittering 114.17
Slivenamond 503.32
sliving 322.20 557.08
slob 316.35 426.11
Slobabogue 350.29
slobodens 541.26
slobs 600.26
slobs 201.18
sloe 568.04
slog 346.28 543.03
Slog 500.17
slogan 141.28 593.14
slogan 272.L3
slogging 583.27
sloghard 415.32
slogo 577.35
slomtime 228.34
sloo 603.13
slooching 342.01
sloomutren 377.10
Sloomysides 399.09
sloop 379.30
slooped 621.20
sloopers 288.F4
slooping 394.11
sloops 510.28
sloot 204.16
sloothering 195.03
slop 026.30 178.25 214.17 437.23
Slop 556.32
slopbang 356.32
slope 122.35 318.27
slopely 600.01
sloper 335.11
sloper's 291.26
sloping 279.F28
slopingforward 037.02
slopper 492.27
slopperish 051.03
sloppery 311.01
sloppily 221.05
slopping 538.04
Sloppy 107.06
Slops 620.32
slosh 267.F5
Slot 176.03
slots 404.24 500.12 526.16
slouch 040.21 073.19 322.11
slough 546.08
sloughchange 239.04
sloughed 098.05
sloughing 188.22
slove 253.04
slovenly 543.34
slow 097.28 165.04 181.35 186.04 206.26 274.F1 318.21 383.20 391.09 492.16 582.05 598.12

Slow 045.14 056.30
slowback 332.36
slowcut 056.22
slowe 264.F2 480.36
slowguard 579.12
slowjaneska 333.05
slowly 173.33 186.01 215.10
slowrolling 190.31
slowspiers 174.28
sloy 431.04
sloze 348.08
sluaghter 500.17
slub 552.26
Sluce 600.14
sludge 447.09
sludgehummer's 439.23
sludgenose 334.28
slug 424.27 616.05
sluggered 416.20
slugger's 436.19
Sluice 297.17
slum 446.27
slumber 040.14 064.12 256.34 428.16
Slumber 321.18
slumbersomely 429.22
slumbred 541.30
slumbring 608.16
slumbwhere 580.15
Slumdom 307.17
slummy 051.18
slump 130.31 438.21 619.33
slumped 382.26
slumper 394.04
slumply 600.01
slums 209.33 589.05
Slupa 319.18
sluppery 626.12
slur 214.30
slush 448.07
slushmincepies 210.21
slusky 620.33
slut 024.23 620.33
Slutningsbane 304.04
sluts 495.23
Sluts 107.06
Slutsend 503.14
Slutsgartern 532.22
Sluttery's 181.18
sly 065.22 130.18 154.02 195.01 363.03 519.36 595.16 627.04
slygrogging 381.36
Slyly 428.08
Slynagollow 580.34
Slyne's 548.27
Slypatrick 051.08
Sm 624.25
Smacchiavelluti 251.26
smack 444.22
Smack 060.32
smacked 170.31 201.32 383.18
smag 407.04
smal 017.32
small 014.04 038.16 039.22 040.15 042.08 048.20 068.03 069.18 189.06 368.09 462.29 488.32 627.19 627.20
small 270.L1
Small 046.01 124.35 559.12
Small 072.09
smallclothes 465.09
smaller 052.32 119.19 122.21
smallest 533.05
smallfox 159.28
smallnice 384.25
smalls 329.02 417.20 542.32 597.27
smark 601.36
smarket 298.06
smart 081.27 300.04 405.15 431.03 445.07 453.35 559.34
smart 338.05
smarter 163.18 303.24 445.14
smartest 232.35
smartly 322.21
smarts 028.21
smash 435.35
smashed 214.24
smashers 026.36
smashing 276.F2
Smatterafact 183.07
smear 143.36 283.32
smearbread 124.13
smeared 178.09
smearsassage 595.11
smeeching 583.04
smell 087.12 142.32 171.10 181.10 197.31 204.33 323.10 331.29 393.01 423.19 484.01 562.28
smell 275.L1 355.04
Smell 305.F3
smellar 444.13
smelled 147.32
smellful 582.17
smelling 142.32 368.10 430.26
smellpex 263.08
smells 250.25 299.F3 495.04 535.32
smells 201.17
smellsniffing 237.17
smelly 192.24
smelt 117.25 138.22 153.05 462.29
smeltingworks 614.31
smeoil 603.01
Smerrnion 129.23
Smertz 499.08
Smeth 106.16
smetterling 417.04
smeyle 426.15
smickers 173.32
smilabit 288.05
smile 020.19 052.33 056.31 114.02 142.32 166.02 227.26 227.26 234.17 238.27 318.02 337.23 426.06 427.36 430.23 433.22 460.29 509.26 523.23 532.34
smile 339.25
Smile 055.02 624.25
smiled 031.13 087.01 157.34 192.30 329.16
smiledown 029.11
smiles 207.35 280.08 562.27 610.09
smileyseller 101.23
smiling 142.32 176.22 203.35 238.10 375.33 448.26
smiling 271.L3
Smiling 223.17
smilingly 430.26
smily 240.33
sminkysticks 556.30
Smirching 435.02
smirk 583.04
smirking 028.05
Smirky 360.08
smirte 262.F1
Smirtsch 499.07
smith 576.36
Smith 048.12 372.11 468.10
Smith 263.L2
smithereen 079.33 589.30
smithereens 238.29
Smith-Jones-Orbison 302.23
Smith's 504.26
Smithwick 481.21
smoake 143.30
smock 396.09
Smock 147.32
smockname 186.28
Smocks 105.27
smog 593.06
smoiling 411.25
smoke 328.11 337.13 362.01 469.28 536.20 559.12 577.12 578.18
Smoke 319.31
smokeblushes 064.26
smoked 035.34
smokeless 436.04
smoker 190.27 221.36
smokers 433.17
smokes 128.19
smoke's 100.15
smokewallet 053.21
smoking 127.21 127.23 130.36 334.09 609.26
smokingstump 557.29
smolking 417.12 607.08
smolking 347.36
smolt 170.28
smolten 007.17
smolty 524.29
smooking 320.06 343.24
smooky 583.33
smooltroon 604.15
Smoos 621.25
smooth 012.03 279.F01 464.02 604.13
smoothen 101.07
smoothing 203.34 604.36
smoothing 348.32
smoothpick 141.10
smorfi 247.09
smorregos 407.02
smother 200.03 473.17 502.22
smothered 296.22 470.27
smotthermock 378.27
smthngs 349.27
Smucky 100.05
Smud 594.11
Smug 140.03
smuggled 581.07
smuggler 247.30
smuggling 436.07
smuggy 552.21
smuggy 430.16
smugpipe 241.14
smugs 345.15 446.19
smuked 089.09
smukking 294.20
smukklers 327.01
smuling 550.29
smut 113.14 183.15 207.08 586.02
Smuth 434.36

smutsick 538.31
smutsy 370.33
smutt 517.13
smutter 066.25
smuttering 245.04
smuttyflesks 141.08
Smyly 209.33
Smyth 552.12
Smythe 178.22
Smythe-Smythes 166.16
snaachtha 502.04
snack 406.09
snae 622.02
snaeffell 552.35
snaggletooth's 462.13
snags 206.05
snailcharmer 465.20
snake 019.12 036.07 132.16 271.F5 587.23
Snake 107.03
snaked's 564.34
snakedst-tu-naughsy 505.07
Snakeeye 534.27
snakelet 145.11
snakepit 385.17
snakes 210.26 239.04 422.06 464.08 494.15
Snakeshead 212.13
snaking 288.F4
snakk 233.33
snakked 597.36
snakkest 560.35
snakking 436.12
snaky 020.33
sname 490.12
snap 098.19 148.14 171.31 332.01
Snap 379.08 445.04
snapograph 522.21
snapped 336.33 363.03
snapper 341.06
snapping 583.18
snappings 095.32
snappy 060.13 144.27
snaps 063.08 183.11
snare 500.01
snarsty 315.23
snatch 627.30
snatched 589.14
snatchvote 582.03
sneak 351.01 617.20
sneakers 034.01
Sneakers 615.28 618.05
sneaking 009.01 463.06
sneaks 019.13
snee 205.21
sneers 042.36
sneeze 012.33
sneezed 051.28
sneezing 110.33
sneezturmdrappen 346.29
sneither 315.07
snevel 037.35
snewwesner 372.16
Snf 625.17
sniff 134.35 513.13
sniff 345.10
sniffbox 563.32
sniffed 038.07 095.19
sniffer 594.28
Sniffer 189.28
sniffers 465.20
Sniffey 181.25
sniffling 453.05
snifflynosed 152.09
sniffnomers 235.29
Sniffpox 060.33
sniggering 229.08
snigs 616.17
snip 469.31
Snip 332.01 445.03
snipehitting 042.35
snipers 320.36 449.29
snipery 066.02
snipes 199.03
snivelled 231.30
snob 050.30 161.32
snobbing 535.29
snobbishly 037.31
snobsic 056.22
snoo 266.07
snoodrift 503.32
snoody 332.01
snook 471.18
Snooker 493.14
snooks 507.19
snooping 006.03
snoores 007.28
snoores 345.11
snoozer 174.03
snore 017.10 064.05 392.12
snore 399.13
snores 213.30 430.12
snoring 024.23 448.26 504.25 544.07
snorler 037.12
snorres 257.36
snorring 578.02
Snorryson's 551.04
snorsted 326.21
snorth 318.35
snose 231.31
snot 171.27 183.29
snots 494.32
snout 594.28
snoutsnooded 547.14
snouty 204.29
snow 128.20 134.32 307.F5 380.31 428.23 468.12 502.02 507.01 570.06 578.04 588.19 588.19
snowbox 503.02
snowdon 205.21
snowdrift 535.30
snowdrop 265.L1
snowly 607.25
snows 320.29 416.32 433.02
Snowtown 622.34
Snowwhite 064.27
snowybrusted 462.10
snowycrested 044.01
snub 484.11
snubnosed 107.11
snuff 495.09
snuff 345.10
snuffbuchs 545.23
snuffchests 077.29
snuffdrab 208.25
snuffed 295.08
snuffers' 212.30
snuffing 603.27
Snuffler 260.F1
snug 046.05 276.F5 372.11 454.32 463.31 587.08
snug 201.17
snugged 368.36
snugger 565.36
snuggest 350.30
snuggily 406.18
snugging 625.11
snugglers 548.08
Snugsborough 503.14
so so So So
Soa 484.32
Soak 171.35
soaked 085.31
Soakersoon 566.10
soaking 214.25 320.30
soaky 052.05
soakye 542.22
soalken 342.06
soamheis 425.22
soampling 323.14
soan 200.13
soandso 432.10 441.22 482.34
soandsuch 108.28 517.30
Soangso 004.28
soap 021.28 093.27 180.06 212.24
soapbox 469.30
soaped 220.17
soaps 138.17
soapstone 140.27
Soapy 305.F3
soar 152.01 423.24 505.17
soard 222.22
soared 136.34 360.28
soarem 469.22
soaring 458.13
soay 200.13
sob 269.11 353.16 486.01
Sobaiter 339.09
sobarkar 339.09
sobbed 171.15
sobber 353.03
sobbing 384.04
Sobbos 388.09
Sobeast 245.02
sober 029.34 059.25 214.18 289.15 313.09 510.36 510.36
sobered 072.33
soberer 489.29
soberiquiet 506.17
soboostius 468.04
sobralasolas 014.08
sobranjewomen 054.08
sobrat 563.07
sobre 353.09
Sobriety 542.09
sobrine 230.32
Sobrinos 488.29
sobs 140.18 166.14 282.01 288.F1 408.21
Sobs 006.14
sobsconcious 377.28
sobstuff 232.24
socalled 167.05 380.15 596.19
soccage 539.23
soccered 093.13
socerdatal 607.06
socerine 230.33
Soch 497.13
sociable 040.28
social 107.32 114.23 116.08 156.35 163.34 415.31 446.28
socialights 032.09
socialist 524.25
socializing 498.20
socially 599.15

socianist 132.19
sociationist 144.05
societate 142.08
societies 362.29 540.25
society 050.23 073.32 125.03 302.29 381.19 423.36 577.13
Society 173.17 412.25 608.10
socioscientific 112.11
sock 087.16 359.19 581.06
SOCK 300.R1
sockboule 366.09
sockdologer 091.15
Sockerson 370.30
sockets 224.13
Sockeye 069.34
socks 128.10 468.25 507.07 578.09 584.16
socks 201.15
Socks 193.19
sockson 371.16
socolled 152.26
Socrates 306.L2
socried 506.26
soculums 346.24
sod 019.28 047.21 111.31 172.20 194.27 224.07 324.14 408.08 430.13 521.19 549.08 582.25 596.02 600.14
Sod 415.15
sodalists 366.09
sodalites 241.35
sodality 050.20
sodden 134.05 192.26 246.10 368.27
soddenly 514.27
soddenment 065.34
soddering 582.22
soddy 264.F1 299.F1 360.17
sodemd 052.05
sodhe 356.18
sodias 604.09
Sodom 188.23
sodouscheock 524.24
sods 173.21
Sod's 004.06
sodullas 468.11
soe 317.18
Soe 597.01
soed 041.26
Soesown 535.02
soeurs 351.29
soever 099.22 242.29 600.25 618.25
soevers 598.01
sof 360.06
sofa 268.14 362.31 618.16
sofacover 394.01
sofarfully 156.15
sofas 433.16
sofer 114.26
Soferim 118.18
soffiacated 534.28
soffran 625.30
soffsoaping 045.31
soft 004.14 021.23 053.18 068.08 114.22 122.02 134.23 138.17 140.23 202.27 215.28 254.30 338.24 407.27 410.33 426.10 433.28 446.16 462.25 512.30 528.23 548.20 563.37 628.08
Soft 619.20
softball 114.27
softbodied 413.31
softboiled 336.31
softclad 134.19
soften 052.06
softest 621.08
softing 376.35
softly 407.20 442.31 482.03 571.18
Softly 624.21
Softly 427.05
softmissives 237.13
softness 146.26
softnoising 476.36
softnosed 035.25 115.13
softongue's 037.21
softrolling 404.22
softsidesaddled 554.04
softsies 058.17
softspoken 477.13
softzing 158.06
Sogermon 222.09
soggert 174.25
soggy 491.36
sogns 596.08
sogs 613.06
Sohan 212.12
sohns 314.28
soho 426.04
sohohold 478.30
sohole 036.30
soide 053.23
Soideric 378.13
soiedisante 461.24
soil 017.05 079.16 108.06 168.02 327.28 465.30 606.28 614.16 624.03
soild 025.18
soilday 338.18
soiled 067.36
Soiled 421.08
soilers 325.24
sojer 142.09
sojestiveness 222.32
sojournemus 264.15
sokaparlour 157.17
soke 442.10
sokeman 034.28
sokolist 491.06
sol 057.26 331.14
Sol 253.09
sola 189.19 314.34
Sola 102.15
solafides 337.06
solans 384.01
Solans 094.27
solar 611.17
solarly 512.35
solarsystemised 263.24
solas 596.07
solascarf 030.23
solase 470.07
Solasistras 090.02
solation 284.18
solation 338.08
solb 292.27
solbing 491.04
sold 081.14 148.11 197.26 235.28 238.13 382.13 500.21 500.22 571.11
Sold 434.17 500.21
Sold 072.06 102.31
soldats 520.18
solde 226.07
solder 317.07 317.22
Soldi 280.23
soldier 366.07
Soldier 619.17
soldier-author-batman 162.06
soldiered 049.07
soldiering 399.12
soldierry 344.02
soldiers 058.24 338.04
soldier's 536.23
soldies 563.31
soldpewter 167.21
soldpowder 393.22
soldr 362.10
Soldru's 124.30
soldthere 161.13
Soldwoter 247.23
sole 051.35 092.09 167.36 206.32 229.35 243.10 286.21 392.21 425.12 454.01 488.17
Sole 565.13 568.29
solely 052.29 075.05 109.12 363.01 458.31 509.21
solem 158.29
solemenly 126.16
solemn 036.20 067.21 409.04 570.03 606.06
solemnly 049.31
Solemonities 188.25
solemonly 337.10
solence 052.36 602.14
soleness 624.11
soles 404.21
solfa 268.14
solfanelly 450.10
solgier 073.17
solicates 604.09
solicit 572.30
solicited 144.31
solicitor 369.26 618.06
solicitous 618.18
solicitresses 090.16
solid 003.20 094.03 183.21 396.10 599.11
Solidan's 355.21
solidbowel 462.13
solied 367.29
solitar 443.01
solitary 072.18 193.08 422.06
solitires 567.34
solittle 030.01
solitude 337.14 454.18
Solitude 246.35
soliven 546.02
soll 340.32
Soll 044.13 549.01 549.01
sollecited 356.05
sollemn 599.12
sollicitor's 270.05
Sollis 219.12
sollow 426.16
solly 011.35 248.13
sollyeye 129.14
Solman 451.11
solo 165.06 424.07
Solo 469.21
Solo 496.13
solod 394.35
solom 363.18
solomn 577.08
solomnones 288.14
Solomon 176.08 307.L1
Solon 307.L1

solone 469.21
solong 469.21
solongas 239.05
solongopatom 344.30
solons 476.14
Soloscar 580.18
solotions 166.27
soloweys 330.08
solowly 337.26
solphereens 009.25
solphia 450.18
Solsking 607.28
solstitial 082.10
soluble 299.F3
solus 189.19
solution 170.23 284.18 590.22
solve 012.33 459.03 619.30
Solve 504.13
solvent 345.32 578.30
solver 146.21 305.22
solving 085.22
Solvitur 409.29
soly 610.09
Solyma 471.05
Solyman's 542.28
Som 620.15
somany 593.05
Somany 094.27
somatophage 171.03
sombogger 204.21
sombren 327.06
sombrer 473.20
sombring 271.11
somday 481.07
some Some Some SOME
someathome's 116.20
somebalt 620.07
somebodies 486.19
somebody 107.30 118.12 220.16 442.31 616.06
Somebody 293.F2 411.34
somebody's 248.25
somebooby 146.06
somebrey 620.09
someday 119.31
Someday 457.19
Somedivide 019.18
Somehards 016.13
somehow 040.27 118.11 523.03
Somehow-at-Sea 291.26
somehows 310.09
Somehows 107.18
somekat 184.31
somekid 562.34
somelam 562.35
somenwhat 598.08
someof 369.21
someone 061.25 464.08 483.07 536.26 602.07 616.06
Someone 202.13
somepart 403.18
someplace 065.22 488.20
somepooliom 156.16
somepotreek 012.22
Somer's 502.29
somersault 295.21
somersautch 517.29
somes 607.20
someseat 353.31
something 083.01 107.32 134.36 172.25 220.15 357.06 394.03 439.26 457.25 459.24 472.14 475.25 476.20 496.29 515.10 519.29 522.26 530.05 539.13 560.22 575.21 598.17 602.06 606.16 606.35 621.32 623.05 627.11
Something 293.F2 307.F5 454.08
somethink 083.14
sometime 097.21 319.35 372.07 427.34 543.24
Sometime 224.11 413.04 624.03
sometimes 027.09 108.34 113.27 121.09 193.33 357.35 359.05 537.21 544.19 575.15
Sometimes 482.22
sometypes 267.19
somewan's 477.09
somewhat 364.27 404.09 563.14
somewhatly 368.18
somewhave 501.21
somewhawre 292.32
somewhere 021.25 022.12 040.29 118.08 118.11 146.33 223.35 230.18 562.34 565.15 570.26 624.04
Somewhere 014.16 469.06
somewherise 602.07
somewhile 347.10
somewhit 448.34
somewho 404.10
somewhot 345.30
somewhure 186.28
somewhys 445.32
Somewind 448.30
somewome 298.19
somewords 369.28
Sommboddy 415.17
somme 593.08
sommerfool 415.27
sommerlad 331.26
Sommers 453.16
sommething 208.24
somnbomnet 176.36
Somndoze 219.05
somnia 193.30
somnione 293.07
Somnionia 594.08
somniorum 193.30
somnolulutent 076.30
somour 067.10
somrother 345.10
Som's 563.32
Somular 017.09
somun 163.03
somwom 346.26
son 032.04 047.21 053.25 054.13 068.11 070.34 082.36 109.06 125.02 125.03 125.05 164.11 169.14 173.13 182.34 184.06 189.18 194.21 209.15 214.27 226.09 228.04 231.18 234.12 286.31 289.10 297.05 302.12 313.35 317.14 326.15 375.17 379.09 420.17 429.03 440.15 443.21 479.11 500.33 501.24 507.34 523.16 530.10 543.16 543.29 570.22 602.12 614.31
son 301.17 526.15
Son 088.15 094.18 328.04
Son 349.21
sonce 352.16
song 028.17 093.29 129.08 135.35 172.15 189.23 190.30 236.10 251.11 294.18 344.05 351.11 359.32 360.14 383.15 391.27 414.14 543.09 571.11 617.32
song 419.06
Song 126.05 414.14
songbird 412.07
songdom 251.36
songs 433.17 442.25 510.33
Songs 222.06
songslide 570.02
Songster 472.09
songster's 041.30
songtoms 015.14
sonht 214.19
sonhusband 627.01
Sonias 528.25
Sonly 565.29
sonnamonk 145.34
Sonne 593.08
sonnenrounders 312.06
sonneplace 568.09
sonner 607.04
sonnies 194.24 365.33
sonnur 317.15
sonny 188.34 335.08
sonogog 136.01
sononward 071.09
sonora 200.14
sonority 461.33
sonorous 230.23
sons 014.11 014.12 019.28 019.28 125.03 210.04 216.02 344.36 426.30 469.03 498.28 544.30 570.23 584.31 589.10 621.10
Sons 028.32 141.19 382.04
Sons 072.07
son's 475.23
sonsepun 251.05
sonson's 053.33
sont 281.09 281.10 281.11
son-to-be 325.15
Sonyavitches 348.34
son-yet-sun 090.01
soo 427.24 599.04
Sooftly 333.04
sooit 205.30
sookadoodling 622.05
soolth 311.34
soomone 594.09
soomonelses 594.10
soon 004.16 019.01 032.02 043.26 046.06 056.12 068.03 091.01 094.32 111.16 123.14 140.29 140.29 174.11 198.02 201.26 207.18 209.04 231.25 256.17 275.F3 280.21 298.03 302.02 325.07 347.23 369.36 374.23 378.20 429.12 437.34 442.17 442.22 458.25 463.09 467.32 502.18 502.18 556.20 562.19 568.12 572.03 577.19 583.16 586.20 604.12 606.35 607.27 607.27 608.18 608.18 615.17
Soon 245.19 268.07 572.17
soonas 241.11
sooner 009.18 095.24 171.05 343.34 460.15
Sooner 089.07 440.32
soonly 308.02
Soons 256.14
soontobe 052.35

soorce 209.14
soorcelossness 023.19
soord 354.30 539.29
Soord 238.31
soords 090.10
soorkabatcha 052.22 604.03
soort 016.01 366.33
soorts 326.36
soot 119.34 232.05 277.01 559.03
Soot 251.27 311.23 494.14
sooth 018.07 024.12 117.25 240.30 251.14 353.03 368.25 509.18 539.14
Soothbys 557.02
soothe 447.05
sootheesinger 366.25
soother 093.24
Soother 373.01
soothing 203.25
Soothinly 363.13
soottee 025.03
sooty 143.05 193.05
sootynemm 420.05
sop 068.21 246.10
sope 318.20
sopes 578.23
soph 189.01
sophister 551.29
sophology 149.20
sophsterliness 354.18
Sophy 031.16 155.26
Sophy-Key-Po 009.34
sophykussens 413.20
sopjack 489.12
sopor 261.15
sopped 498.19
sopper 326.32
soppisuppon 233.34
soppositorily 406.19
sopprused 345.08
soppyhat 267.F6
soprannated 441.12
soprano 222.07
soptimost 234.13
sor 153.23 378.23
Soracer 008.12
sorafim 344.25
sord 352.09 379.21
Sordid 049.21
sordidly 522.05
sordomutics 117.14
sore 005.29 047.13 109.13 120.28 189.32 210.03 239.32 274.18 336.23 459.23 484.04 485.09 517.07 534.26 620.31
sored 549.27
soredbohmend 505.34
soreen 600.21
sorefister 551.29
sorefoot 426.36
soreful 527.10
sorellies 454.28
sorely 087.09 423.11 431.24
sorensplit 596.31
sorepaws 468.32
sorer 063.34
Sorer 053.26
sores 025.24
soresen's 370.24
sorestate 242.01
Sorestost 069.15
soreunder 232.19
sorey 229.29
Sorge 189.18
sorgues 200.17
sorgy 392.16
Sorley 499.22
soroquise 425.15
sororal 461.33
Sorority 181.18
Soros 601.33
sorowbrate 518.22
sorra 381.32
sorracer 336.04
sorraday 436.27
sorrafool 301.15
sorrasims 148.21
sorratelling 367.15
sorrel 080.03
sorrelwood 611.34
Sorrento 246.24 497.14
sorrogate 149.29
sorrors 230.11
sorrow 061.35 127.26 135.22 213.06 620.31
sorrowful 549.12 571.13
sorrowmon 344.05
sorrows 387.18
sorry 144.36 146.26 173.09 185.18 208.27 236.01 280.12 389.32 391.34 457.34 461.12 507.16 508.08 509.10 509.11 509.14 527.04 571.23 581.24 581.25 581.25 590.04
sorry 338.12
Sorry 469.24 533.36
Sors 299.L2
sort 008.07 042.02 042.05 066.02 066.03 070.13 089.14 097.19 109.03 114.27 123.34 159.15 159.36 171.16 188.33 200.26 214.17 247.33 269.14 313.17 382.19 437.29 470.02 474.24 507.08 596.18 627.24
Sorte 608.29
sorter 602.31
sorters 412.26
SORTES 281.R2
sorth 539.14
sorting 540.28
sortofficially 606.19
sort-of-nineknived 162.05
sorts 051.10 051.11 111.29 127.10 379.31 411.03 464.26 625.05
Sorts' 329.31
sos 184.02 232.29
S.O.S. 387.23 (1132 S.O.S.)
sosannsos 127.19
sosay 601.12
sose 538.30
soseptuple 343.18
sosie 003.12
sosiety 459.10
soso 301.17 571.23
Soso 144.12
Sososopky 471.01
soss 316.18
sosson 232.28
sossy 459.11
Sostituda 271.F4
sostressed 067.23
sosuch 317.28
soswhitchoverswetch 293.08
Sosy 459.10
sot 037.31 597.21
Sot 074.13 324.14 496.07
sotchyouroff 346.11
Soteric 393.08
sothisfeige 014.02
sotiric 288.18
sotisfiction 161.02 452.06
soto 261.F4
sot's 114.23
Sot's 147.05
Sots' 041.32
sotspot 286.F5
sotten 324.32
sottovoxed 313.18
soturning 415.09
Sotyr 254.23
souaves 287.31
souber 353.03
souch 187.06
Souchong 115.04
souckar 362.15
Soude 184.29
soufered 454.24
souff' 204.02
soufflosion 184.30
souffrant 241.07
souffsouff 117.18
souftsiezed 162.07
souftwister 567.30
sough 264.11 407.20
soughed 223.30
sought 015.16 040.02 087.15 097.22 300.23 311.10 395.18
sought 342.27 418.29
soughts 440.24
soul 034.18 038.28 129.36 144.16 145.26 165.18 178.31 188.17 230.23 231.28 235.07 285.F5 293.02 298.F2 329.18 380.24 394.24 423.28 472.26 533.03 538.13 571.13 622.21
soul 280.L4 345.13
soulard's 292.23
soulcontracted 182.34
sould 264.20 359.26 362.19
souldrer 202.14
soulfisher 118.35
soulleries 346.10
soullfriede 376.36
soully 114.01
soulnetzer 234.15
Soulpetre 059.17
souls 024.34 043.15 246.08 378.31 410.08 579.13 579.30 627.19
souls' 476.33
Soulsbury 541.29
soulskin 377.28
soulsurgery 536.06
soulths 370.31
soun 343.23 620.16
sound 013.01 017.35 109.15 112.12 158.12 179.17 204.16 204.21 242.27 256.23 257.26 266.18 279.F25 335.18 350.32 360.03 485.23 486.20 518.35 522.29 586.33 597.02 598.04 612.29 619.21
soundconducting 183.09
sounddance 378.29
sounder 163.18
soundest 096.32
soundhearing 237.17

soundigged 141.24
soundings 501.12
soundlessly 054.05
soundly 093.13 507.09
soundpicture 570.14
sounds 074.10 107.19 117.12 136.36 169.24 210.23 309.23 319.01 499.27 515.11 562.02
Sounds 106.30
soundsense 121.15 138.07
soundwaves 023.26
soup 026.31 133.14 210.08 437.23 520.08
soup 280.L2
soupay 406.14
souped 058.29
Souper 131.04
souperhore 549.14
soupirs 453.12
Soupmeagre 456.11
soupplate 265.F2
souprette 531.16
soups 079.07 177.25
Soup's 356.15
souptumbling 404.35
souptureen 394.02
sour 143.29 154.25 171.18 368.21 485.10 574.31
source 181.20
sourceress 251.12
sources 030.05
sourd 353.14
Sourdamapplers 146.13
Sourdanapplous 254.23
Sourdanian 221.32
sourdine 150.03
sourdsite 597.12
soured 317.03
sourface 050.10
souriantes 130.01
sourir 234.18
Sourire 548.28
sours 036.01
souse 186.16 246.10
soused 316.31 453.05
sousenugh 596.14
souser 117.30
sousers 519.34
Souslevin 222.08
sousoucie 308.24
souspirs 058.09
Soussex 524.15
sousy 173.01
Sousymoust 232.07
soutane 115.17
soute 288.15
south 035.31 398.09 482.28 547.21
South 078.26 306.16 482.29 559.05
Southby 534.15
southdowner 083.24
southeast 051.30
southenly 011.01
southerly 520.30
southern 042.28 471.12
southerwestern 203.03
southfolk's 215.25
Southron 034.13
southsates 209.08
southside 095.09
Southwalk 578.30
soutstuffs 167.19
souvenir 027.32 037.18 210.02
souwest 447.21
souwester 085.34
Souwouyou 252.03
sov 561.08
soveal 419.04
sovereign 013.02 374.28 495.22 504.19
sovran 455.07
sovvy 607.22
sow 091.06 130.05 199.25 215.10 250.29 297.21 448.11 490.31 490.33
sow 176.15
Sow 262.19
sowage 545.34
Sowan 077.04
sowansopper 356.17
sowarmly 430.20
sowasso 517.21
sowbelly 557.11
sowell 533.04
Sower 072.10
sowerpacers 542.11
sowesthow 254.16
sowheel 093.36
sowill 366.28
sowing 451.06
sowiveall 145.27
sowlofabishospastored 612.08
sowls 593.20
sowman's 169.14
sowmmonay 184.30
sowns 333.29
sowriegueuxers 361.36
sows 321.29
Sowsceptre 230.28
sowsealist 072.23
sowsieved 155.13
sowtay 184.30
sowterkins 311.23
sowwhite 451.20
Sowyer 372.06
soxangloves 022.35
soy 485.13
soybeans 140.31
soye 512.01
soze 345.08
sozh 199.25
sozzle 456.21
spa 129.15 565.33
space 052.08 109.22 143.06 152.18 152.18 154.25 155.06 160.36 163.32 169.07 223.23 254.27 254.27 394.10 425.12 429.12 462.31 558.33
space 163.20
space-element 164.33
spacemaker 247.02
spaces 415.28 416.05 416.06 504.14 594.03
spacest 419.07
spache 303.08
Spache 181.03
spaciaman 425.32
Spacies 600.03
spaciosing 470.19
spaciosum 425.32
spacious 150.36
spadeaway 582.22
Spadebeard 480.12
spadefuls 405.30
Spaight 318.12
Spaign 447.28
Spain 213.34
Spainien 539.14
spake 052.12 268.23 338.23 363.25 595.02
Spake 479.33
spalniel's 350.30
spalpeens 032.16
span 067.29 163.18 266.05 273.04
span 277.L1
spancelled 475.08
spanglers 151.09 521.01
spanich 233.35
spaniel 194.08
spaniels 030.19
spanish 300.17 463.35
Spanish 141.01 144.13
spanishing 477.26
spank 627.04
spanking 494.25
spanks 437.32
spanning 255.32
spans 403.06
sparable 404.21
sparanto 419.13
spare 042.20 052.08 068.05 148.20 211.06 436.33
spare 341.34
Spare 042.20 489.23 559.13
spared 396.28 472.11 589.28
sparefours 202.01
sparematically 296.26
sparepennies 546.27
spareshins 314.26
sparing 102.02
sparingly 061.35 079.36
spark 322.20 330.02 330.03 396.28 473.18
spark 383.11
sparker 435.17
sparkers' 524.05
Sparkes 376.23
sparkle 132.30
sparkling 451.25 462.11
Sparkling 236.05
sparks 594.20
Sparks 098.04
spark's 232.33
Sparks' 199.35
sparksown 274.23
Sparrem 575.30
Sparro 353.21
sparrownotes 135.35
Sparrow's 548.27
sparse 086.01
Spartacus 116.11
spas 211.24
spasms 434.29
Spasms 391.28
spasoakers 097.20
spass 417.25
spasso 152.29
spat 037.23 297.05 350.32 377.13 470.28 515.03 572.05
spatched 473.09
spate 198.19 198.19
spates 134.08
spathe 613.17
spatial 358.05 417.12
spatialist 149.19
spatiality 172.09
spattees 011.20

spatters 209.26
spatton 464.11
spawife 242.36
spawn 324.05
Spawning 525.16
spawnish 596.13
spch 023.04
spck 023.04
speach 349.26
speachin 485.12
speafing 619.20
speagle 248.06
speak 018.08 038.20 062.22 102.29 130.18 141.33 145.24 148.23 162.36 195.05 261.28 299.29 328.07 334.16 338.23 367.04 374.34 436.21 468.17 472.23 477.08 481.19 490.30 527.33 533.12 534.24 560.22 561.17 588.23 596.22 625.29
Speak 100.35 225.20 306.23 410.23 496.34
speakable 150.26
speakeasy 553.26
speakee 485.29
speaker 174.09 309.19 459.28
speaketh 593.24
speaking 108.20 115.11 122.29 122.30 161.05 268.20 388.30 388.35 389.18 479.27 535.26 618.23
speaking 263.L1
speaks 013.03 061.22
spear 131.25 485.19
speared 131.14
spearhead 549.03
spearing 244.04 541.06
spearlight 450.14
spearspid 594.21
spearway 078.14
special 032.30 067.11 096.32 140.31 184.01 277.F1 423.14 458.29
species 112.14 160.10 574.17
specific 151.27 501.21
specification 245.32
specious 153.17 293.18
specis 209.12
speckled 035.32 403.21
speckled 383.06
specks 102.12 251.16
specs 039.27
spect 537.32
spectacle 179.25 609.21
spectacularly 241.06
spectacurum 611.14
spectantes 287.22
spectracular 349.17
spectral 056.17
spectrem 318.33 498.31
spectrescope 230.01
specturesque 427.33
speculative 050.13
sped 191.15 568.13
speece 616.27
speech 038.17 072.22 137.36 140.27 143.04 173.35 174.10 183.15 233.18 237.06 318.28 355.09 378.32 469.30 507.21 515.12 620.34
speechform 149.29
speeching 611.10 611.11
speechreading 568.31
speechsalver's 345.20
speed 118.30 373.10 448.17 471.35
speedhount 232.28
speediest 191.09
speeds 429.12
speedwell 080.03 458.14
speel 274.14 303.F1
speer 267.04
Spegulo 052.14
spekin 533.06
spell 020.14 043.16 047.28 089.19 097.25 123.01 145.19 458.14
Spell 275.24
spellbinder 278.09
spelled 118.27
speller 191.30
spelling 026.35 620.35
Spelling 307.25
spellings 571.07
spells 094.13 248.28 373.27 479.18 503.24 571.05
spelt 496.19
Spence 350.27
spend 053.25
spend 418.21
spending 281.F4
Spendlove's 625.08
spends 273.04
spendthrifts 253.08
spent 408.04
spent 339.25
spentacles 397.35
spenth 102.25
speople 141.05
speranza 211.24
Speranza 297.F1
spermin 525.23
sperrits 234.02
spetial 154.35
spew 530.30
spewing 421.27
spey 209.17
spezzata 152.31
sphanished 473.20
sphere 280.31 298.28 503.05
spheres 426.25
sphericity 151.03
Spheropneumaticus 484.30
sphinxish 324.07
sphoenix 473.18
Sphygmomanometer 608.10
spiane 158.11
spice 165.05 251.14 263.F2 365.33 456.20
Spice 292.06
spicer 025.23
spiceries 550.09
spices 316.29 504.28
spick 515.03 572.05
spick 277.L1
Spickinusand 326.20
spickle 050.08
spickness 279.F17
spick's 334.01
spickspan 613.24
Spickspookspokesman 427.32
Spickspuk 250.10
spictre 299.05
spider 108.15 244.27 352.24 481.05
spidsiest 297.09
spied 197.29
spier 023.35
spies 573.03
spight 111.01
spigotty 016.06
spike 100.15
spikes 338.23
spikesman 517.12
spiking 535.15
spill 094.12 145.20 570.28
Spill 560.05
spilled 420.33
spilleth 267.11
spillicans 283.02
spilling 328.24 461.03 508.33
Spillitshops 355.31
spills 540.26
Spilltears 060.01
spillway 204.16 255.11
spilt 183.24 461.35
spin 127.14 163.18 203.05 270.22 318.10 562.09
spinach 346.03
spinado 550.27
spinasses 611.36
spindle 031.15 615.28
spindler 131.18
spindlers 375.22
spindlesong 336.14
spindthrift 335.34
spine 279.F10 409.17
spinister 465.06
spink 627.04
spinned 541.30
Spinner's 414.32
spinney 244.27 450.21
spinning 021.06 442.15
spinooze 414.16
spinosis 150.08
spins 330.12
Spinshesses 241.03
Spinsters 307.07
spint 416.16
Spira 485.19
spirally 121.24
spirals' 300.27
spiration 157.29
spires 287.18 541.06
spiriduous 482.02
spirit 092.09 129.36 265.10 287.18 389.16 472.32 484.31 536.01 610.27
spirits 027.24 082.09 177.18 289.F2 312.29 348.11 394.10 436.21 456.19 495.04 555.23
spirit's 220.25
spiritual 191.16 191.26
Spirituosen 256.07
spirituous 371.01
spiritus 194.06
Spirituttu 406.20
spirt 271.12 473.18
spirts 439.22
Spish 287.F3
Spissially 113.16
spit 158.30 230.02 297.19 311.31 350.32 362.18 381.07 453.05 464.11 484.28 516.28 612.04
spitch 432.25
spite 158.33 168.04 269.08 288.26 358.07 562.30 579.07
spitefired 539.11

spiter 287.F1 417.24
spites 476.15
spitfire 330.03
spits 183.24 410.13
spitter 270.19
spitting 022.25 084.03 178.29 250.09 586.01
spittinspite 519.05
spittish 152.22
spittle 025.01 209.27 354.30
spittoons 038.10
spittyful 240.05
Spitz 207.21
spizzing 417.26
splabashing 431.16
spladher 454.14
Splanck 505.28
splane 369.02
splash 172.15 460.28
Splash 060.29
splattering 470.08
spleen 553.28
spleen 303.L1
splendid 429.17
Splendid 140.04
splendidly 461.18
splendorous 347.17
splendour 568.29
Splesh 460.28
splet 365.06
Spletel 140.04
splication 369.02
spliced 197.13
splinters 009.23
splish 072.35
spliss 296.F2
split 161.32 171.06 228.05 229.20 271.21 308.03 323.08 333.25 377.12 438.06 461.36 467.02 519.35 553.28
Split 247.31
splitpuck 445.15
splits 349.13
splitten 253.34
splodher 454.14
splosh 488.28
spluched 172.25
spluiced 316.09
splume 072.36
splunderdly 357.02
splunthers 352.09
splurge 179.30
splutter 472.24
spluttered 114.24 120.04
spoeking 323.36
spoen 240.22
spofforth 583.32
spoil 097.25 122.18 208.10 436.32 451.23 579.16
spoil 343.18
spoilcurate 221.10
spoiled 011.18 131.14 138.04 177.15 209.28 211.21 547.08
spoileds 273.12
spoilfives 202.01
spoils 124.32
spoke 021.17 050.08 055.33 574.11
spoken 108.36 122.31 258.20 268.19 268.21 433.06 532.11
Spoken 044.08 250.10 303.13
spokes 225.19 247.04 447.04
spokesman 294.09 517.13
spoking 240.28
spolish 038.02
spond 214.08
spondaneously 414.01
spondee 282.L2
sponge 381.17 516.26
sponged 220.17
spongelets 542.22
sponges 035.02
sponiard's 180.11
sponsar 229.22
sponse 451.21
sponsibility 189.06
sponsor 133.10
Sponsor 531.27
sponsorship 326.28
spont 414.08
spontaneous 110.29
spontaneously 034.21
sponthesite 597.14
spoof 048.01
spookeerie 307.F2
spooker 178.06
Spooksbury 442.07
spooky 266.05
spool 341.04
spoon 144.09 190.07 211.15 242.12 269.28 286.F5 331.01 334.02 334.02 385.29
spoonfind 449.09
spoon-me-spondees 139.20
spoons 115.15 246.14
spoor 475.24
spooring 027.24
spoorlessly 050.11 427.06
spoors 251.07
spoorwaggen 141.17
spoorway 078.14
sporran 099.11
sport 371.18 448.25 450.25 472.14 623.05
sported 208.13 404.27
sporten 455.31
sporticolorissimo 240.15
sporting 067.11 185.09 375.24
sportive 437.16
sports 126.15 279.06 550.25
sports 342.33
Sports 306.25
Sport's 051.21
sporty 312.17
Spose 361.09
sposhialiste 240.03
spot 010.31 016.36 062.31 081.13 129.17 143.17 144.35 172.04 198.23 215.05 251.27 252.26 297.26 435.13 451.25 501.14 594.13 609.21 624.24
spotch 600.16
spotless 132.31
spotlight 506.27
Spotlight 560.04
spots 124.23 302.F1
spotted 139.32
Spotted 436.23
spottprice 290.25
spouse 043.04 215.22 327.02 355.32
spousefounderess 244.18
spout 068.30 111.22 168.04
spouting 087.36
S.P.Q.R.ish 229.07
SPQueaRking 455.28
sprack 080.20
spraining 384.18 386.10
sprakin 485.13
sprang 541.06
sprangflowers 059.11
sprankled 224.13
sprat 431.13
spratties 524.28
sprawling 549.28
spray 319.14 598.14
Spraygun 349.12
Spreach 378.32
spread 098.24 158.28 213.21 213.22 214.16 491.08 553.04
Spread 213.22 213.23
spreadeagle 482.15
Spreadeagles 106.22
spreading 025.09 477.11 477.19
spree 192.19 198.05 319.15
spreed's 058.11
sprids 007.09 552.13
sprig 238.10 248.29 329.25 458.13
Sprig 161.28
spring 078.15 165.25 172.07 194.30 196.23 279.F17 301.25 321.31 395.14 627.32
spring 342.25
Spring 264.25 271.12 365.34
Spring 293.L2
springapartings 095.33
springfalls 607.24
springing 295.19 328.30 524.22
springs 318.29 460.28 556.09
springside 443.28
springsides 507.07
springwell 571.02
springy 604.29
sprink 141.11
sprinkled 213.25
sprinkling 524.23 588.22 616.17
sprint 627.05
sprise 606.36
sprit 363.17
sprite 431.09 564.27
spritties 234.18
sprizzling 207.15
sprog 161.28
sprogue 507.22
sprogues 083.13
sproke 407.09
sprout 455.21
sprouting 466.08
sprouts 475.33 542.09
sprowled 004.11
sprowly 617.19
sprsnwtch 349.27
spruce 365.32
sprue 523.29
sprung 279.F17
Sprung 293.L2
sprungen 502.08
spry 274.15 337.28 627.04
spry 383.11
Spry 301.01
spt 227.09
spuckertuck 037.29
spucks 378.27
spud 083.29
spudds 102.12
spudfully 542.01
spuds 372.25 466.28 475.10
spuds's 122.18

spuitwyne 078.20
spuk 323.36 417.01
Spuke 281.L3
spuking 178.07
spume 324.05
spumy 017.10
spun 137.36 143.24 321.03
574.29 620.35
spunish 548.08
spunk 525.23
spunn 157.08
spur 204.13 469.07
spurios 161.09
spurious 049.09 186.34
spurk 346.32
spurring 035.21
spurs 008.18
spurt 232.01 532.36
spurtfire 117.17
spurtle 330.03
spurtles 330.03
spurts 118.30 234.17 415.05
spurts 342.34
sputabout 043.36
sputing 222.26
sputsbargain 312.25
spy 010.01 010.31 101.22
530.29 588.04
spyballs 247.21
spyre 473.18
spy's 238.30
squabbles 454.36
squad 133.10 152.09 438.28
squad 343.13
squads 122.24
squak 151.22
Squalchman 390.36
Squall 469.18
squalled 320.30
squalls 444.13
squalor 282.02
squamous 462.17
squandered 193.01
square 185.35 186.12 285.F4
460.09 475.05 486.15 543.04
560.10 584.15
Square 086.35 095.36 260.10
SQUARE 302.R2
squarecuts 051.07
squarer 429.14
Squarish 368.30
Squarr 139.36
squash 386.10
Squash 390.32
squat 245.29
squaton 413.19
squatquit 551.26
squats 139.07 366.10
squatting 397.12
squattor 019.26
squawfish 484.36
squeak 049.04
squeaked 424.06
squeal 228.06
squealed 180.05
squealing 422.36 444.14
squeals 150.35
squeam 331.08
squeer 151.15
Squeer 384.10
squeeze 514.32
squeezed 138.04 171.17
squeezer 142.09
squeezers 531.12
squeezing 512.06
squelch 392.36 424.06
squibs 211.21
squidself 186.06
squiggling 245.11
squince 180.25
Squintina 567.29
squire 570.15
Squire 456.30
Squiremade 504.02
squirmside 444.28
squirrels 157.14
squirt 249.01
squirted 626.15
squirtscreened 186.07
squisious 144.15
squitting 438.13
squool 426.05
Sr 279.F06 (Senior)
Sraid 543.17
Sraughter 008.17
Sree 546.27
sreeked 200.01
srumpas 160.31
S.S. 060.32 (S.S. Smack)
098.07 (S.S. Finlandia)
292.29 (Eating S.S. collar)
S. S. 550.07 (S. S. Paudraic's)
ssan 124.08
Sss 019.12
st 339.30 339.30
St 048.11 (Hilton St Just)
053.31 (St Tomach's)
406.24 (St Jilian's)
528.06 (St Audiens)
St. 220.03 (St. Bride's)
221.01 (St. Patricius')
Sta 086.29
stab 087.16 349.02
stabat 594.14 594.15
Stabimobilism 308.L2
stable 060.04 107.30 141.21
211.33 335.12
stablecert 610.17
stablecloth 039.06
stablecrashers 341.20
stabled 355.24
stablelads 465.15
stables 293.07 320.15
stabletalk 120.23
stabling 323.35
stabmarooned 549.22
stabs 124.02
stabulary 156.26
Stacey's 028.31
stackle 368.32
stacks 137.31
stade 446.18
stadion 471.16
staff 306.01 474.03 544.29
Staff 593.06
staffet 469.07
Staffetta 462.05
Staffs 272.31
stag 042.06 447.19
Stag 622.29
stage 049.29 059.05 073.24
078.03 147.01 164.07 181.01
335.05 408.28 456.14 468.23
619.09
staged 032.10
Stagemanager's 558.36
stager 509.18
stages 066.14 509.17
stagetolets 221.23
stagey 058.34
staggered 187.07
staggerhorned 590.28
staggering 451.20
staggerjuice 521.12
stagnant 204.17
staidy 545.32
stail 350.01
stain 111.20 141.32 382.12
stainedglasses 463.14
stainks 371.01
stains 085.33 196.18
stains 339.20
Stainusless 237.11
stair 580.23
staircase 131.17 498.04 543.31
560.09
staired 616.29
staires 489.02
stairrods 520.05
stairs 527.09 530.35 560.05
Stairs 105.06
stake 433.14 451.19 563.03
Stakelum 212.06
stakes 514.05
staking 373.19
stakkers 413.16
stale 009.18 142.04 183.24
292.20 396.23 423.24 444.03
540.24 598.21
stalemating 560.11
stalement 313.18
stalks 121.02 460.11
stall 317.09
stalled 355.24
stalls 033.10 207.16
staly 198.06
stambles 423.24
stambuling 033.36
stammer 252.36 467.19 511.08
stammpunct 309.04
stamoror 547.25
Stamp 437.21
stamped 109.07 391.21 470.29
stampforth 009.16
stamping 179.36 263.05
stamps 211.31 382.12
stanch 084.22
stand 036.24 052.22 054.27
067.14 135.08 160.09 166.28
169.08 169.16 187.32 200.18
328.32 408.31 447.34 478.36
506.29 523.17 538.35 566.12
575.09 609.36 613.33 620.01
623.13 626.22
Stand 012.24 187.28 325.05
359.30 501.07 614.15
standard 137.26 529.17 539.19
567.10
standbuild 099.08
Standerd 439.36
Standerson 413.14
Standfast 210.28
Standfest 275.08
standing 033.12 036.14 093.01
242.30 393.36 413.14 449.20
451.26 483.22 516.27 557.20
568.08 616.18
Standing 306.22 504.05
Standing 176.12

standings 476.09
standpoint 587.15
stands 116.17 119.21 119.21
121.04 127.07 129.08 138.04
184.04 245.36 490.10 568.16
585.27
standup 174.06
Stane 042.27
staneglass 609.15
Staneybatter 291.11
stanidsglass 277.F5
stank 175.04 455.15
stanks 111.03
stanserstanded 594.24
stanth 251.04
staot 348.04
stap 595.32
staple 004.34
Staple 077.23
Staplering 262.20
staples 536.09
star 155.20 317.06
341.15 461.02 471.09
511.28
Star 028.23
starabouts 155.25
starboard 517.36
starch 029.28 204.32
starchamber 475.18
starchart 096.28
starchboxsitting 053.31
starck 007.31
stardaft 439.10
stardust 184.23
stare 264.11 334.24 368.34
507.02 626.25
staregaze 382.17
stareotypopticus 611.25
starer 319.33
stares 403.12
starey 503.05
starfort 246.04
stargapers 339.19
staring 582.19
stark 053.16 133.01 145.19
566.34
stark 354.03
starkened 381.21
starland 244.24
starlight 495.13
Starlin 272.27
starling 070.16
Starloe 382.30
starmenagerie 476.25
Starn 303.06
starnly 454.21
starr 211.01
Starr 549.35
starre 349.21
starring 143.22
starryk 274.24
starrymisty 539.21
stars 004.12 005.21 065.11
065.13 134.15 144.08 160.22
246.13 248.13 385.28 602.30
Stars 059.02 185.31
starshootings 022.12
starspangled 404.27
start 032.25 050.03 111.35
148.16 163.26 181.29 222.03
327.19 336.18 369.21 398.08
471.11 529.30 621.35 624.16
Start 227.28
started 021.31 022.17 064.17
200.08 516.36 531.23 589.30
starting 122.28 454.14 594.36
604.13
Starting 019.22
startling 136.22
Startnaked 264.F1
startraps 579.03
starts 136.19 437.03 606.30
622.31
starved 040.23
starves 265.L2
starving 083.06 196.15 544.32
Starving 488.27
starvision 364.17
state 039.32 049.25 052.26
117.34 119.20 127.33 149.36
160.02 171.07 251.09 406.19
438.17 483.31 495.21 509.21
599.17 604.23
stated 034.03 036.05 087.02
162.28 434.36
statement 063.21 079.36 492.14
519.30
statements 033.19
states 043.29 143.08
States 130.28
statesmen 272.25
static 309.22 499.34
staties 552.01
station 429.23 476.05 480.08
557.30
stationary 488.05
stationery 185.05 412.27
stations 041.21
Stator 179.11
statue 041.35 214.11 386.22
statuemen 471.28
statues 058.19 386.25 495.31
statuesques 553.12
statuesquo 181.34
Statulina 561.09
stature 334.18 357.31
statute 558.13
statutes 322.33
statutory 220.36
staub 565.11
staun 423.24
staunch 061.32 534.14 568.17
Stauter 490.20
stave 135.35 457.06
stavekirks 552.04
staveling 466.17
staves 427.02
stavrotides 482.10
stay 032.04 035.07 075.07
176.31 177.27 187.21 199.20
226.10 244.11 244.28 250.12
274.F1 366.16 404.15 427.16
449.13 485.04 497.17 528.29
564.31 566.18 586.35 597.19
608.36
stay 159.18
Stay 005.18 334.22 434.13
stayed 030.21 627.10
stayer 427.28
stayers 469.24
staying 014.36 325.36 540.22
stayne 420.12
staynish 199.17
stays 132.16 208.14 232.21
299.15 333.20 433.24 564.27
569.03 570.08 619.12
staystale 509.35
Ste 048.12 (Ivanne Ste Austelle)
stead 128.28 283.31
steaded 211.18
steadied 356.08
steadiest 575.31
steadily 438.01
steady 006.22 119.32 144.18
306.10 306.10 306.10 306.11
544.08 560.10
steady 342.06
Steady 058.09 306.10
Steadyon 625.21
steak 091.23 405.35 406.02
406.10 406.16
steaked 595.11
steal 011.30 091.10
117.01 180.29 243.12
580.21
steal 349.35
Steal 303.05
stealdily 349.18
Stealer 570.35
stealing 052.31 093.26
steals 167.15 507.05
stealth 137.22
steam 294.F3 512.21
Steam 176.18
steamadories 395.09
steamin 453.14
steamships 395.05
steamy 395.08
steatopygic 522.31
Steck 534.35
steed 262.22 362.13 621.31
steel 366.06 529.25
Steel-the-Poghue 600.32
steelwhite 563.16
steeming 531.09
steep 026.24 135.01
Steep 347.04
Steepbell 141.05
steeping 196.13
steeplechange 289.07
Steeplepoy's 328.27
steerage 323.35
steered 551.23
steerner 602.30
stehs 251.10
stehts 139.08
steifel 301.18
stein 536.20
stele 068.29 460.17
stell 232.11
stellar 449.03 511.28
stellas 177.10 427.10 551.30
stella's 257.02
stem 216.03 240.17
stemming 169.03
Stemming 565.13
stems 571.06
Stena 608.16
stench 436.25
'Stench 017.31
stenchions 343.07
Stene 247.04
stenk 059.20
stenoggers 476.14
stenorious 454.09
step 020.08 112.21 199.02
210.26 232.18 282.F4 370.13
441.01 560.10 614.16 616.30
step 349.09

Step 252.31 252.31 421.12 621.04
stepchildren 576.32
Stephens 300.F2
Steploajazzyma 102.15
steplonger 191.05
stepmarm 587.10
Stepney's 578.36
steppebrodhar's 070.26
stepped 152.25 465.06 491.34
steppes 204.03 339.30
stepping 332.10
steppingstone 262.20
steppit 554.06
stepplease 272.14
steps 249.22 362.25 436.03 447.34 467.34 529.26 542.16 618.32
Steps 068.14
Steps 105.30
stepschuler 482.17
stepshore 051.31
stepsons 127.01
stepstones 481.27
steptojazyma's 578.22
stepwalker 472.21
stercore 185.24
stercus 185.19
stereo 504.10
sterling 398.32
sterlings 236.24
stern 036.35 066.21 110.07 282.07 291.F4
sternbooard 077.06
sternely 004.21
sternes 199.07
sterneward 256.14
sternish 454.22
sternly 123.09 292.30 486.28
sternwheel's 027.36
sterres 624.09
Stessa's 104.08
stetched 315.03
Stetson 054.32
Steving's 550.06
stew 038.24 190.09 268.15
Stew 268.14
stewardesses 384.23
stewards 041.36
Stewart 227.29
stewed 192.07 404.36
stewhard 455.34
steyne 305.29 505.21
stheal 461.13
sthers 471.12
sthings 379.17
sthore 412.25
stiar 599.06
stick 007.31 081.32 084.36 086.04 091.31 130.01 223.08 225.19 253.12 331.12 374.21 622.32
stick 277.L3
Stick 435.19
sticker 566.10
sticking 069.27 332.31 441.11 507.14
stick-in-the-block 583.26
sticklered 132.04
stickme 296.03
stick-pass-on 474.04
sticks 111.03
sticksword 236.05
stickup 315.17 512.04
stickyback 183.11 470.29
stickypots 257.16
stiff 006.22 062.22 082.08 211.18 214.18 289.15 296.30 379.18 461.23 462.05 534.14
stiffen 442.33
stiffstaff 191.36
stiffstarched 556.07
stiffstuffs 434.24
stigmataphoron 606.27
stigmy 193.17
stil 075.05
stile 191.01 250.05 347.13
stiles 116.33 147.08 505.22
still 004.03 005.14 007.20 015.20 019.32 020.02 025.34 031.29 031.31 034.36 035.12 035.17 043.08 043.35 049.02 052.07 054.07 055.20 061.31 069.11 076.20 082.23 084.35 098.32 100.35 101.28 107.35 124.34 125.21 136.19 137.19 138.03 138.27 146.10 148.03 150.33 154.15 156.22 158.15 158.16 162.31 164.35 168.12 169.02 170.13 170.13 170.17 170.18 172.06 173.15 188.29 193.29 194.03 207.30 221.04 235.19 242.29 244.28 249.09 256.33 262.22 265.01 265.09 265.F2 267.28 274.06 276.23 288.28 291.14 313.16 317.36 332.04 350.32 360.03 362.32 367.24 372.07 378.17 380.19 390.22 393.07 398.22 399.31 415.22 419.18 425.07 429.13 429.15 430.03 434.32 440.03 448.35 454.23 460.25 466.10 467.01 472.28 482.32 486.26 489.07 496.32 513.03 533.26 536.22 536.22 538.04 556.06 556.06 556.18 558.05 558.06 558.11 565.16 575.06 585.17 596.04 597.31 602.10 604.17 607.07 607.22 608.27 608.36 613.33 619.19 620.11 620.30 622.20 625.08 625.17 625.27 626.19 626.21 628.07
still 346.09 347.36 348.29 349.18
Still 114.02 226.12 251.21 296.16 374.06 425.04 426.13 452.22 501.21 510.05 527.10 527.35 561.01 563.37 568.15 621.11 626.16
Still 164.20
Stilla 028.23 526.23
Stillamaries 569.10
stillandbut 581.33
stillandbutallyouknow 581.27
stilled 551.28 556.20
stiller 399.31
stilleth 597.31
Stillhead 355.06
stilling 052.36 318.10
stilller 503.04
stillness 403.05
still's 276.22
stillstand 588.05
stillstream 486.23
stillstumms 347.11
stilstand 058.31
stilts 204.03 236.26
stiltstunts 347.13
stimm 239.19
stimmering 236.29
stimmstammer 272.F4
stimulants 042.04
stincking 092.16
stinger 317.01
stings 256.36 604.36
stink 214.30 606.27
stinkend 079.30
stinker 617.10
stinkers 210.03 455.15
stinking 237.26 482.26
stinkingplaster 101.24
stinkmakers 342.09
stinkpotthered 050.04
stinks 033.16 250.26 318.32
stinksome 183.06
stint 025.01
stipple 182.18
stir 158.06 178.13 255.04 462.08 577.36
stirabout 246.14
stirabouter 070.25
stircus 319.06
stirkiss 557.03
stirpes 287.23
stirred 549.09
stirring 529.10
stirrup 272.21
Stirrup 040.02
stirs 222.33 244.27
stirs 345.11
stissas 347.28
stitch 028.07 180.02
Stitch 106.02
stitcher 495.07
stitchimesnider 320.04
Stitchioner's 106.12
stitchless 451.31
stivers 313.30
Stll 502.11
stlongfella 082.13
stoan 287.19
stoane 187.19
stoatters 596.27
stoccan 345.17
stock 051.07 085.01 137.19 322.09 471.19 510.17 536.14 539.30 547.23 574.28 594.18 619.35
stockangt 495.09
stockend 154.34
stockfisch 056.25
stockies 459.08
stocking 257.24
stockinger's 548.22
stockings 128.11 208.12 226.24
Stockins 503.15
stockknob 241.24
stockpot 251.05 406.01
stocks 128.12
stod 056.14 346.27
stoddard 584.01
stodge 284.L1
Stodge 071.34
stohong 230.36
stoke 177.01 214.09
stoker 089.01
Stokes 619.32
stole 176.29 288.F4 396.23 403.05 565.14

stolemines 539.13
stolen 181.14 240.08 375.27 434.05
stolentelling 424.35
stoles 441.21
stolidly 163.20
stoliolum 117.11
stolp 312.01
Stolp 312.01
Stolterforth 537.08
stomach 093.09 163.34 169.17 184.03 323.18 410.16 462.27 579.22
Stomach 106.07
stomachs 022.23
stomebathred 467.15
stomewhere 145.04
stomicker 199.21
stommick 097.29
stone 014.32 025.31 040.19 064.33 065.01 073.34 077.24 080.29 084.31 091.12 091.31 094.05 135.04 153.23 153.24 159.04 213.03 216.01 216.04 230.26 259.02 259.02 259.02 259.02 259.02 265.01 283.18 312.21 357.26 376.14 376.15 497.22 518.10 560.36 563.21
Stone 106.36
stonebread 566.03
stonecold 211.32
stoned 194.26 205.35
stonefest 552.05
stonegloss 609.15
stonehead 132.12
stonehinged 069.15
stonengens 005.31
stones 072.27 103.09 131.22 136.35 183.20 213.24 224.06 259.02 466.35 506.36 537.01 605.01
stones 350.04
Stones 306.23
stonestepping 178.23
Stonewall 010.02
stonewalls 291.19
stoney 044.09 242.23
Stoney 552.12
stoniness 267.26
stonker 612.34
stony 553.29
stonybroke 040.15
stoo 339.30
stood 036.05 038.18 042.05 102.07 130.26 133.36 157.19 178.05 202.18 322.18 335.30 405.11 413.13 454.23 525.33 538.36 587.06
Stood 106.28
stooderin 437.31
stook 004.23
stool 278.F2 394.08
stoolball 129.29
stooleazy 343.27
stools 161.35 210.30 476.31 544.21
stoop 018.18 019.02 019.10 077.16 077.16 232.18 238.30
Stoop 018.17 144.13
stooping 008.23
stoops 170.14 361.03
stoopt 339.30
stop 021.23 021.24 022.10 022.10 068.18 118.14 124.04 124.05 124.05 124.05 171.10 203.22 205.14 205.14 229.02 232.30 272.12 274.06 300.09 300.10 379.06 379.06 379.06 390.12 411.06 411.06 411.06 445.19 451.12 457.08 462.20 495.31 565.34 609.07 609.07
stop 341.08 433.19
Stop 021.23 022.10 088.01 232.19 232.24 252.31 272.09 282.F4 373.18 379.05 421.13 421.13 421.14 421.14 577.36
Stop 032.23
stopandgo 449.22
stopes 444.08
stopgap 455.19
stopped 245.11 426.19 476.09
Stopped 105.24
stopping 069.35 453.08
stoppress 588.33
stops 170.06 294.04 298.25 468.12 540.16
Stops 105.31
stopsign 155.26
stop-that-war 577.06
store 009.18 046.03 051.36 063.17 257.08 266.02 271.F2 425.02 550.14
storehundred 126.06
storehuse 240.29
storen 132.11
stores 025.03 253.18 594.19
Stores 616.35 616.36
storey 536.26
Storey 219.21
Storiella 267.07
stories 005.29 183.11 368.35 427.23
storik's 177.26
stork 325.06
Stork 197.19
Stork 106.18
storks 255.09
storm 232.34 527.30
stormcrested 468.30
stormed 167.22
stormies 627.31
Stormount 028.22
stormtrooping 344.23
storridge 614.12
storstore 326.23
stortch 443.25
storthingboys 054.09
storting 553.32
story 012.03 028.26 035.01 055.02 063.31 091.06 113.18 115.36 135.35 173.19 174.01 206.21 225.05 319.33 325.19 335.01 344.20 352.03 364.03 369.22 374.36 374.36 479.07 481.11 486.01 519.08 530.20 562.34 564.05 564.21 597.16 616.04
story 418.28
Story 106.14
storyaboot 336.17
storyan 028.02 028.03
storybooks 219.24
storybouts 427.31
storyplace 625.06
storywalkering 361.32
stoties 186.22
stotter 096.31
stottered 006.09
stotterer 337.18
stoub 063.33
stoup 310.29
stour 199.24
stourbridge 184.12
stout 009.18 052.06 139.09 159.12 208.14 254.03 369.13 382.04 382.27 391.13 411.02 453.05 471.36 498.17 574.31
Stout 443.30 619.32
Stoutgirth 150.11
stoutlier 570.17
stoutstamping 603.11
stow 065.05 257.15 503.21
stowed 098.06 313.30
stowing 556.26
Stowlaway 370.36
stoytness 537.17
stp 186.27
stphruck 190.02
straat 491.09
strabismal 189.08
straddle 102.13
strafe 451.04
strafe 344.09
straggled 589.23
stragglers 520.07
straggles 340.13
straight 036.21 054.28 113.26 171.23 444.15 461.21 480.06 487.25 542.16 564.10 596.32
Straight 310.12 620.01
straightaway 109.19
straightcut 156.29 236.36
straightened 330.14
straightforward 174.06
straights 279.F28 393.30
straightwalking 603.11
strain 129.05 214.02 373.09
strainbearer 585.07
strained 543.25 579.31
strainger 531.12
straining 479.04
strains 038.34 043.31
strait 183.34 207.23 252.25 340.32 420.28 512.15
straith 617.36
straits 300.F4 539.22
strait's 583.04
strake 012.25 377.29
straks 315.23
stralegy 008.32
Strame 104.10
stramens 502.30
Stranaslang 338.22
Strand 327.23 534.27
strande 277.L3
stranded 182.24
strandlooper 110.31
strandweys 315.30
strang 276.22
strangbones 343.04
strange 039.32 053.32 066.12 121.20 131.29 283.22 351.02 539.23
strangely 083.07 107.11 110.25 507.21
Strangely 279.02

stranger 051.31 109.32 191.06 213.33 247.11 443.09 488.34 563.11 564.09 597.04
strangerous 625.05
strangest 470.22
Strangest 307.12
strangewrote 419.18
strangfort 577.33
strangle 145.26
Strangler 534.27
strangling 339.31
Straorbinaire 295.17
strap 229.03
straphanger 444.19
strapping 396.07 510.07
straps 356.25
strassarab 117.15
strate 110.33 549.15
Strate 242.24 294.F1
Strategos 307.L1
Strathlyffe 387.09
stratified 181.06
stratum 076.05
strauches 595.04
strave 569.34
straw 035.12 049.29 085.34 131.17 192.26 192.36 393.25 434.17
Straw 176.15
strawberry 064.28 435.21 559.06
strawbirry 207.10
strawcamel 368.32
strawng 004.10
strawnummical 494.01
straws 073.10
straxstraightcuts 576.20
stray 178.20 214.36 268.03 270.28 431.02 431.27 438.06 453.27 620.30
strayed 236.23 292.16
strayedline 294.02
strays 499.33
streak 027.11 164.26 274.13 351.08
streaking 174.30
streaks 580.21
streaky 618.07
stream 003.07 007.22 057.11 153.03 153.10 159.10 332.23 460.21 565.31 602.13
Stream 105.07
streamer 567.13
streameress 326.10
streamers 208.08
streamfish 595.10
streaming 501.27
streamlet 057.11
streamline 560.30
streams 131.22 139.24
stream's 297.23
streamsbecoming 597.08
Streamstress 324.33
streamy 131.28
Streat 169.23
streelwarkers 243.22
street 045.09 053.29 118.21 129.16 155.26 253.06 253.07 291.17 330.12 363.04 386.21 388.27 443.10 459.18 469.10 545.28 553.05 583.15 603.22
Street 006.02 034.09 043.01 044.06 058.26 083.22 086.29 098.24 134.20 248.33 351.32 405.28 461.07 482.19 488.05 490.20 492.23 507.27 516.28 518.06 529.16 529.35 538.22 557.36
Street 072.02 105.32
streetdoor 098.13
streetfleets 005.32
Streetpetres 420.35
streets 099.05 131.05 135.20 147.05
Streets 447.14
stremmis 536.11
strenfy 426.07
streng 547.31
strenghth 093.36
strenging 376.12
strengly 011.29
strength 335.20 405.30 459.29 557.33 587.13 598.24
strengthen 027.24
strenth 102.25
stress 129.05 468.20
strest 351.18
stretch 276.F5 475.09 486.36 495.13 556.27 568.01 598.24
stretched 109.27
stretcher 319.28
stretchers 448.16
stretching 487.14
strete 110.34
stretes 372.21
strew 226.10 566.03 566.17
strewed 131.26 427.10
strewing 447.15 504.25
strick 339.31
stricken 094.05
stricker 512.15
stricly 119.08
strict 327.36 432.06 487.27 504.17 524.03
Strict 364.31
strictest 586.04
strictly 100.28 109.24 459.19 575.12 585.36
stride 190.30 204.17 473.19 625.22
strident 236.20
strides 622.08
striding 411.31
stridulocelerious 611.29
strife 038.09 541.34
strifestirrer 561.34
Stright 245.22
strike 083.06 087.09 131.20 209.22 252.22 304.06 409.34 448.27 501.17 547.35
strike 201.13
Strike 306.F2 440.15 491.15
strikes 067.04 069.12 328.11
strikest 537.31
striking 053.20 087.11 207.15 316.03 414.35 507.21
strikingly 425.05
string 466.24
stringamejip 458.27
stringbag 221.30
Stringstly 615.32
strip 009.28 229.18 240.25 441.02 461.21 521.13 537.33 586.03
Strip 527.09
stripe 135.06 135.06 316.30 322.22
striped 131.29 445.01
stripes 210.14
striplings 589.24
stripny 187.01
stripped 068.01 564.24
stripping 086.05 151.25 526.23
strips 212.32 451.03
stripture 293.F2
striving 060.28
stroka 073.12
stroke 035.29 188.33 206.23 444.17 482.26 511.06
strokes 123.06 303.05
strokest 454.19
stroll 069.28 245.19 416.27 416.28
strollagain 416.28
strollers 213.27
strolling 479.08 479.08
strombolist 128.18
strombolo 494.17
strond 547.20
strong 016.08 027.36 032.33 059.26 116.19 210.09 275.08 366.18 367.25 376.12 424.24 428.09 433.15 439.21 441.27 454.17 456.09 473.12 483.04 523.13 570.16 573.29 576.15 605.35 625.09
Strong 079.27 079.33
strongbow 547.30
strongbowed 288.15
strongbowth 311.15
strongbox 082.24
strongday 138.17
stronger 279.F35 336.20
strongers 058.16
strongholes 167.13
strongleholder 371.02
strongly 443.03 447.35 502.07 538.05 627.12
strongsmelling 134.25
strongsround 275.18
strongth 023.03
strop 322.21
strove 090.36 171.08
stroves 340.13
strow 112.34
strown 152.27 245.31
strubbely 020.25
Strubry 604.17
struck 035.19 052.29 080.04 083.27 090.23 101.15 101.20 101.21 131.11 159.12 176.29 233.19 393.08 444.18 506.34 523.24 541.12 580.07 580.16
struck 175.14 339.31
strucklers 132.09
structure 615.06
strues 282.28
struggle 086.29 515.21
struggled 081.35
struggling 189.17 518.04
Struggling 545.24
strulldeburgghers 623.23
strumans 203.24
strumpers 556.30
strumpet 530.14
strung 005.08
strungled 339.32
strupithump 006.04
strut 197.02 245.19 296.F2
strutforit 413.18

struts 236.20
Strutt 626.11
strutting 543.19
Strutting 278.F7
struxk 004.22
stuarts 498.01
stub 365.27 598.21
stubbled 026.06
stucckomuck 091.01
stuccstill 153.20
stuck 050.07 082.18 082.23
208.19 225.19 317.35 411.10
430.12 441.11 503.30
stucks 247.04
stud 194.26 234.10 300.32
studbook 443.24
studd 583.36
studding 037.23 220.31
studenly 344.09
student 180.36 544.14
students 151.29
studiavimus 306.11
studied 408.36
studience 427.31
studiert 304.20
studies 368.35
studiorium 266.13
Studiosus 193.13
studious 121.28
Studium 123.18
studvaast 552.08
study 089.29 114.31 128.28
181.14 347.23 489.33
studying 037.22
'stuesday's 407.31
stuesser 460.32
stuff 177.30 182.17 320.23
338.23 366.30 405.13 453.35
465.07 496.25
Stuff 320.23
stuffed 406.18 617.20
stuffel 327.15
stuffering 078.03
stuffing 170.36
stuffstuff 096.11 145.24
stugging 013.12
stulpled 223.12
stult 200.15
stultitiam 510.05
stumble 114.08 114.09 173.04
328.11
stumblebum 351.36
stumbled 030.21
stumbledown 481.27
Stumblestone 210.29
stumbletumbling 598.08
stumbling 197.26
stummer 016.17
stummi 243.07
stummock 355.30
stummung 187.03
stump 027.35 112.05 376.06
456.35 537.12
Stump 497.01
stumpen 366.29
stumpling 183.20
stumps 129.33 583.35
stumpstampaded 043.23
stumuk 599.20
stun 016.17 098.04
stune 466.36
stunk 181.26
stunned's 080.10
Stunner 370.23
stunning 083.24
stunt 369.22
stunts 624.16
stunts 282.L1
stupefaction 604.33
stupendous 066.08
stupidest 458.11
stuping 196.13
stupor 261.15
stuprifying 437.28
sturdy 551.13 596.33
sture 371.17
sturgeone 450.15
sturgeons 569.27
sturk 017.14
sturm 335.17 335.18 335.19
Sturm 300.L2
stutter 197.05
Stutterers' 531.35
Stuttering 004.18
stutters 139.09
Stuttertub 538.34
Stuttutistics 616.22
stuumplecheats 322.02
Stuyvesant 550.31
sty 086.28
styearcases 416.22
style 036.09 055.15 108.02
347.13 377.06 397.30 422.21
432.17 442.34 443.33 445.33
459.15 575.29 606.27 614.16
Style 093.31
styles 181.15
Styles 307.19
stylish 121.32
stylled 236.33
stylo 186.15
styve 130.05
suaged 457.07
suam 185.17
suant 446.23
suas 185.19
Suasusupo 428.01
suavium 122.32
sub 337.17
sub 185.20
subconscious 173.32
subdiaconal 605.21
subdolence 573.23
subdominal 451.01
Subdue 214.31
subhuman 090.27
subject 085.07 110.17 155.18
164.17 165.30 280.09 522.10
545.28 605.16
subjected 062.24
subjects 041.24 151.02 394.24
subjunct 496.24
subjunctions 269.03
subjunctive 468.09
sublation 369.06
subleties 550.12
subligate 508.22
sublimate 515.16
sublimated 299.L1
sublimation 185.36
sublime 112.21 445.27 452.14
456.02
sublime 419.07
Sublime 517.10
Sublime 072.02
sublimer 551.35
subliminal 247.08
Sublissimime 612.12
sublumbunate 607.21
submarine 587.17
submerged 363.21
submerger 232.32
submission 154.31
submit 573.32
subnesciousness 224.17
subordinating 164.33
suborned 530.09
suborner 290.26
subpenas 438.29
subpencilled 066.16
subporters 372.09
subred 590.08
subrises 370.24
subs 596.12
subscribers 544.02
subscription 414.05
Subsec. 061.09
subsections 532.34
subsequent 149.31 614.35
subsequently 085.26
subsequious 291.08
subsidity 410.11
subsisting 582.15
subsquashed 155.13
substance 040.06 220.32
substantively 412.11
substintuation 055.35
substisuit 487.11
substittles 314.26
substituted 487.02
substitutionally 031.06
substrance 597.07
substrate 163.24
subtaile 270.15
Subtend 297.06
subterranean 098.06
subtler 080.12 516.35
subtlety 186.34
subtractional 150.33
suburb 205.24
suburban 575.20
suburbanites 382.01
Suburbia 309.09
suburbiaurealis 332.34
suburb's 230.04
suburrs 454.30
subustioned 228.33
suc 368.14
Suc 610.19
succar 137.01
succeeded 321.18
succeeding 228.18 437.34
succers' 524.05
succes 156.36
success 462.28
successful 515.15
Successful 306.19
successfully 159.24 404.31 474.06
523.32
successfulness 341.32
successive 005.15 036.11
595.27
successivecoloured 126.19
successively 080.11
successor 311.24
succo 054.13
Succoth 013.28
succuba 530.33
succumb 492.35 530.33

such 003.19 010.29 029.06 030.06 032.21 033.18 034.06 034.27 036.29 037.27 037.28 042.26 059.13 060.08 063.04 063.11 063.11 063.11 063.12 069.07 070.12 072.18 077.22 080.13 082.33 087.09 090.23 093.07 096.26 096.33 101.23 102.05 104.16 110.33 115.26 115.29 117.06 120.31 122.27 124.14 140.22 143.15 150.25 157.13 160.11 160.19 164.18 169.22 169.22 172.17 172.36 177.15 180.31 185.01 187.17 190.16 190.16 190.16 190.16 223.16 230.25 233.09 234.35 243.19 247.17 249.36 251.05 252.19 268.26 272.24 290.15 291.03 300.16 319.35 364.03 366.04 379.26 380.19 382.01 396.08 396.08 408.12 408.29 409.05 410.29 411.35 420.25 421.18 425.33 426.07 429.20 444.20 447.24 447.25 448.28 453.19 460.16 461.19 472.27 475.33 478.16 481.11 483.17 484.10 505.08 528.15 532.29 533.01 533.14 538.06 538.24 546.21 548.25 553.17 557.27 558.22 567.05 568.05 570.15 580.24 581.33 583.14 585.09 586.22 588.30 588.30 589.13 599.33 600.27 603.03 610.09 616.16 618.32 622.08
such 176.14 340.06 345.04 418.10
Such 090.29 114.11 144.13 202.22 241.31 280.09 332.10 506.04 507.24 512.07 524.36 535.17 537.33 569.34 585.27 597.22
suchanevver 077.01
sucharow 346.11
suchaway 360.31
suchawhy 360.32
Suchcaughtawan 197.36
suches 077.36
suchess 229.33 538.06
suchky 253.04
Suchman's 150.10
Sucho 199.29
suchurban 139.16
suck 053.25 088.32 096.24 136.02 149.06 198.27 322.08 381.30 423.20 480.14
suck 270.L1
Suck 485.07 485.08
suckabolly 472.02
suckage 079.12
suckbut 252.35
sucked 193.34
sucker 114.27 424.28
suckers 023.30
suckersome 511.20
suckets 508.01
sucking 042.31 245.18 456.32
suckingstaff 235.36
Suckit 415.35
suckle 277.F1 480.14
suckled 463.15
suckling 086.18 287.19 403.17
suckmouth 394.22
suckpump 366.10
sucks 133.19
suctions 385.12
suda 213.04
sudden 120.04 253.29 589.22
suddenly 109.25 110.06 289.30 454.20 454.21
Suddenly 514.07
suddles 021.28
suddly 566.28
Sudds 215.17
Sudlow 032.10 434.08
sudly 345.10
sudsevers 202.02
sue 019.29 437.31 446.06 508.31
Sue 135.08 146.11 210.25 513.06
sued 313.34 454.19
Sued 301.F1
Suenders 330.01
sues 130.18 567.30
suessiest 234.18
suet 086.02
Suetonia 271.07
suety 213.26
sù''fàç'e' 124.11
suffer 145.15 445.18 585.18
Suffer 301.03
sufferant 433.08
suffered 033.17
suffered 273.L3
suffering 043.10 120.13 488.16 557.31
Suffering 068.24 093.30 094.28
sufficiently 109.07 417.36
suffix 481.24
Suffoclose 047.19
suffragate 439.35
Suffrogate 242.24
suffusion 100.23
sufter 037.21
sugans 286.F5
sugar 029.28 092.20 334.23 380.27 496.30 587.30
sugarloaf 208.07
Sugarloaf 521.13
sugars 107.15
Sugars 616.12
sugarstick 485.08
sugarstuck 214.15
sugay 608.20
sugerly 277.F5
suggest 082.35 188.05 479.24 482.21 483.02 506.29 615.35
suggested 078.36 160.03 422.22 573.14
suggesting 058.30 100.34 421.17
suggestion 033.18 033.31 049.17 053.05 121.07 165.20 445.09 511.19
suggestions 546.36
suggestive 109.26 115.29 165.24
sugjugation 525.04
sui 570.36
suicidal 100.10
suicide 462.36
Suid 387.02
suigar 405.35
suil 180.25
Suilful 512.25
suing 574.08 575.28
suir 203.09 387.30
suirland 446.25
suirsite's 319.06
suis 269.20
Suiss 129.34
suistersees 538.25
suit 029.32 035.04 059.22 115.17 182.26 269.F2 311.22 317.22 322.17 324.12 326.24 363.15 404.20 441.02 443.27 515.34 534.19 609.06 624.29
Suit 063.16
suitable 107.27
suitably 320.36
suitcases 192.07
suitclover 286.15
suite 041.16 295.32 324.30 395.20 432.02 433.31 436.04
suite 344.12
suiterkins 301.F1
suits 006.07 296.19 474.19 521.29
suivied 197.33
sukand 052.35
Sukceded 105.30
suke 540.11
suked 363.18
sukes 606.32
sukes 418.13
sukinsin 437.29
Sukkot 612.15
sukry 199.19
Suksumkale 296.F3
sula 209.35
Sulch 419.04
sulfeit 086.02
Sulfer 537.30
sulhan 034.06
sulk 396.20
sulken 342.06
Sulken 535.16
sulkers 315.28
Sulkinbored 393.08
sulks 133.20 256.33 508.29
sulky 210.08
Sulla 573.06 573.13 573.31
sullemn 416.05 599.12
sullen 310.35
sullenly 086.36
sulleries 346.10
Sulleyman 495.07
sullibrated 379.07
sullied 205.17
Sullivan 093.30
Sullivani 573.07 573.13
sullivans 058.10 142.26
sullivan's 581.04
Sullivence 602.26
sulliver 021.28
Sully 212.03 435.29 495.01 558.12 558.14 618.08 618.29
Sullygan 622.23
sullyport 200.21
sulph 222.25 415.06
Sulphate 184.29
sulphur 174.16 261.26 565.33
sulphuring 352.36
sulpicious 254.08
Sultamont 416.16
Sultan 266.F1
sultana 497.30
Sulten 317.15
sultrup 014.18
sultry 030.14 063.08
Sulvans 616.11

sum 014.19 014.26 283.03 304.31 336.34 423.32 514.04 519.02 606.28
sumbad 548.14
sumbsuch 608.22
sumday 436.27
Summ 231.23
summan 007.18 241.02
summarily 390.19
summat 524.25
summe 153.31
summed 271.02 316.05 509.19
summer 034.29 132.20 284.30 326.30 397.31 473.05
Summerhill 012.28 265.F2
Summerian 504.06
summers 135.31
summersaulting 115.15
summersultryngs 380.31
summerwint 607.24
summery 319.10 414.33
summing 558.10
summiramies 553.11
summit 032.34 139.08 222.11 471.09 624.11
summock 061.17
summon 362.06
Summon 141.28
summone 546.15
Summoner 049.23
summoneth 553.33
summonorother 255.05
summonses 471.24
summour 371.15
summum 603.30
summus 313.25
summwer 327.20
sumns 280.04
sumonserving 078.07
sumphoty 341.08
sumptuous 046.05 451.23
sumthelot 019.18
sumtim 527.28
sumtotal 450.36
sumus 168.14 551.13
sun 130.22 136.05 162.15 202.30 208.10 263.27 320.29 355.27 473.16 494.27 503.23 504.36 513.12 524.25 609.20 612.30
Sun 063.24
sunbeam 131.29
sunblistered 181.08
sunbonnet 040.09
sunbubble 607.32
Sunburst 071.15
sunksters 371.01
sunctioned 531.02
Sunda 350.33
Sundaclouths 295.07
Sundae 235.34
sundance 615.02
sundawn 138.36
Sunday 102.15 176.20 276.27 304.F1 493.02 544.28 556.02 556.05
Sunday'll 398.34
sundays 039.25
Sundays 045.15
sunder 020.17 405.35 468.21
sundering 156.01
sunders 526.14
sundew 130.25
sundises 289.08
sundown 203.26
sundowner 083.28
sundry 147.25
sundust 601.02
Sundy 227.31
sundyechosies 007.24
sunface 089.32
Sunfella's 096.02
sunflawered 350.11
sunflower 470.07 509.21
sung 018.03 025.29 104.02 175.32 276.08 338.02 355.08 432.30
sung 399.13
sunhat 242.14
sunk 171.13
sunkenness 068.30
sunkentrunk 371.03
sunkin 478.14
sunksundered 349.15
sunless 211.30
sunlife 517.20
sunlight 544.35
sunlike 594.11
sunlit 578.23
Sunnuntaj 325.11
sunny 012.15 456.11
sunny 348.30
Sunny 211.06 249.18 305.05
sunnybank 264.23
sunnyroom 417.14
sunpictorsbosk 351.24
suns 135.24 355.25 355.26 409.28 493.28
sun's 469.04
sunsaw 011.26
sunseeker 110.30
sunset 127.26 191.27
Sunshat 009.02
sunshine 056.19 504.06
sunsick 452.35
Sunsink 359.36
sunsmidnought 543.12
sunsoonshine 603.02
sunsunsuns 415.22
sunt 484.07 603.32
sunt 179.02
suntime 083.09 576.31
suntimes 133.19
sunto 540.17
suntry 343.32 539.16
sunup 428.18
sunuppers 537.11
sunward 473.19
suomease 329.02
suora 528.16 528.17
Suora 346.05
sup 124.33 227.04
Sup 121.35
suparior 404.18
super 183.27 290.25 538.08 564.19 605.15
super 287.22
Superabit 625.07
superb 452.26 545.29
superbers 467.35
superbly 154.12
supercargo 220.33
Supercharger 133.22
superciliouslooking 120.18
supercrowd 042.22
supereminent 381.16
superexuberabundancy 612.05
superfetated 252.17
Superfetation 308.L2
superficies 041.19
superfine 128.14 570.23
superflowvius 526.25
superimposed 165.25
Superior 181.31
Superlative 276.L5
supernatently 524.20
supernoctural 598.17
supernumerary 499.20
superpbosition 299.08
superscribed 066.16
superseding 304.L1
supershielded 309.17
supershillelagh 025.15
supersocks 160.20
superstation 533.32
superstituettes 378.12
suphead 344.26
supine 468.07
supped 037.30 560.34
supper 028.19 052.12 152.22 215.18 235.33 380.15 385.01 389.06 434.04
supperaape 221.07
supperfishies 524.31
suppers 283.08
suppertide 037.18
supplant 414.23
supplied 039.35 061.02
suppliesdemands 369.02
suppline 366.03
supply 008.08 066.34 575.10
Supply 307.10
support 036.07 072.28 284.F3
supporters 087.27 220.27
suppose 149.12 149.13 424.24 448.02 474.13 489.17
Suppose 242.27
supposed 280.26
supposedly 063.12 179.05
supposing 118.09
supposing 338.12
Supposing 523.33
supposingly 544.28
supposition 572.32
suppoted 232.22
Suppotes 105.20
Suppoutre 337.18
suppoxed 090.25
suppraise 356.19
supprecate 569.18
suppressed 280.12 356.20
suppressions 515.16
Suppwose 337.16
suppy 161.25
supra 004.27
suprasonic 123.12
supreem 605.16
supreme 035.22 037.33 173.08 461.31 564.13
supremely 576.05
supremest 154.12 610.09
suprime 343.29
supstairs 560.11
suqeez 296.03
sur 340.35
sur 280.L4 281.06
Sur 238.31 551.02 594.01
Sur 072.03
surabanded 494.28

Surager 492.21
surcease 129.08
surceases 454.31
surch 187.06
surcingle 030.23
surcoat 559.09 567.30
surd 016.20 284.14
surdity 538.18
surdout 343.13
surdumutual 530.10
sure 007.25 012.17 013.08
020.36 027.12 027.34 029.17
040.32 088.08 088.11 088.28
091.10 096.06 096.17 099.35
118.31 122.35 140.21 147.13
172.16 174.14 177.25 215.13
239.08 248.03 251.27 253.24
262.F7 279.F07 282.09 312.35
317.13 331.08 336.22 337.24
365.25 365.25 368.27 379.07
381.30 384.12 384.12 386.12
390.30 392.02 392.06 392.18
395.30 395.31 397.07 404.14
407.16 426.10 428.15 442.11
444.36 451.05 452.05 452.30
455.19 455.23 458.11 462.22
472.12 481.17 483.26 490.03
503.31 511.06 512.35 513.01
514.19 515.30 524.33 539.35
540.28 558.30 581.08 590.04
596.32 601.01 615.09 623.33
626.10 626.15
sure 383.03 418.15
Sure 024.17 089.33 095.11
198.26 198.27 301.06 365.24
422.27 422.28 434.21 454.04
463.33 465.14 478.36 496.03
502.13 515.26 521.34 526.22
526.28 595.21 604.11
Sure 383.02
surefoot 426.36
surelier 118.19
surely 039.12 063.03 115.01
258.14 294.16 546.22 623.21
Surey 361.05
surf 363.25
surface 404.01 605.16 624.02
surfacemen 208.36
surfaces 151.02
surfed 198.04
surfered 312.04
surfers 354.11
surfriding 399.04
surge 327.05
surgence 017.25
surgent 341.15
surgents 494.12
surgeon 492.22
Surgeon 443.19
surgeonet 088.32
surgeons 263.12
surging 380.28
surking 606.31
Surley 499.24
surly 110.04
Surly 329.16
surmounted 013.24
surname 108.21
suroptimist 069.16
Surpacker 375.15
surpassed 465.01 490.21
surpleased 222.09
surplice 204.31 279.F35
surpliced 404.28
surplus 381.32
Surplus 145.30
surpraise 493.36
surprends 582.17
surprise 093.10 438.21 509.25
surprised 082.32 423.31 490.34
608.09 618.16
surprises 165.30
surprisingly 109.28 176.19
surprize 306.04
surr 181.02
Surrection 593.02
surrender 068.13
surrented 130.34
surrounded 476.23 546.19 568.20
surrounding 110.32 412.34
surssurhummed 015.15
sursumcordial 581.13
surtaxed 582.11
Surtopical 090.27
surtout 052.25
surtout 399.14
surtouts 546.16
surtrusty 031.26
surveice 349.25
survey 109.29 540.13
surveyed 032.22
surview 285.26
surviva 614.11
survive 446.07
surviving 138.34
sus 155.04
suscepto 185.15
suscribers 523.31
suso 011.16
suspect 166.20 509.08
suspectable 362.23 362.27
suspected 086.33 124.14 145.04
172.12
suspecting 286.26
suspendeats 211.27
suspended 422.01
Suspended 106.13
ſuſpens 238.08
suspensive 143.08
suspices 094.26
suspicion 374.09 483.05 540.32
suspicioning 040.22
suspicious 062.28
suspiciously 436.19
suspired 407.19
Susquehanna 212.06
Sussumcordials 453.26
Sustain 454.18
Sustainer 005.18
sustaining 049.20
Sustains 302.L1
susu 345.19
susuing 116.01
susuria 209.35
Susy 562.14
sutchenson 315.30
sutor 326.27
Sutt 241.11
sutton 017.11 587.23
Sutton 533.30
suttonly 315.29
Suttonstone 371.30
suulen 534.33
Suvarn 594.01
suzannes 552.20
suzerain 313.14
Suzy's 435.15
Svadesia 594.04
svalves 311.17 311.17
Svap 595.30
Svapnasvap 597.04
svarewords 436.12
Sveasmeas 607.20
svend 345.31
svertgleam 099.16
svig 132.34
svo 317.02
S.V.P. 495.32 (s'il vous plaît)
svvollovving 394.06
swaaber 485.24
swab 203.05
swabsister 566.10
Swabspays 181.05
Swad 071.26
swaddled 444.10
swaddles 471.33
swaddlum 027.28
swaggelers 321.31
swaggerest 626.10
swaggering 543.20
swaggers 028.21
swags 615.27
swagstruck 279.F30
swains 202.09
swales 199.23
swallen 325.26
swallow 031.13 279.F07
swallowall 033.08
swallowed 416.21
swallower 199.02
swallowing 166.13 177.03 521.05
swallows 319.11
swallowship 139.04
swallying 406.12
swam 136.08
swamp 171.01 213.02 600.26
swamped 027.26
swamplight 024.01
swampstakers 514.30
swan 063.35 171.04 423.22
600.31
swanchen's 548.33
swanee 581.06
swank 053.22 137.03 197.06
257.14 279.F29 589.12
swanker 317.12
swankies 438.32
swanks 498.01
swankysuits 626.09
Swann 410.03
swannbeams 127.15
swanns 516.18
Swanny 289.02
swan's 226.05
swansgrace 577.03
swansruff 208.19
swansway 450.05 465.35
swanwater 248.23
swap 446.19
swapsons 206.11
swapstick 342.31
swaradeed 312.02
swaradid 021.24 022.11
swaran 131.22
sward 250.35
swarded 007.30
sware 083.07 264.12 264.13
434.13
swarm 124.26 496.33

swarming 417.14 420.12
swarms 135.36
swarns 238.33
swart 014.03 097.06 511.22
Swarthants 250.05
swarthy 137.03 550.19
swarwords 501.13
swash 211.36 381.14
swashing 520.06
swathed 545.31 604.07
swathings 498.29
swatmenotting 507.14
swatting 173.11
sway 355.19
sway 354.11
swayed 404.15 496.33 615.03
Swayed 072.07
swayful 244.27
swayin 395.17
swaying 377.36 524.23 602.05
Swayn 326.36
sways 580.27
swaystick 569.19
Sweainey 391.33
swealth 408.01
swear 091.08 144.36 147.25 148.03 148.21 206.18 277.F5 357.12 357.15 421.28 425.36 460.35 462.12 462.12 487.17 518.03 518.08 520.28 520.32
Swear 440.08
swearin 521.01
swearing 148.21 329.32 519.23 524.17
swears 065.07
swearsome 134.25
sweat 014.04 300.31 475.01 539.36 563.19 615.23
Sweatagore 037.02
sweatandswear 053.33
sweated 024.04
Sweatenburgs 552.16
sweatful 030.22
sweating 214.26
Sweating 612.33
sweatoslaves 309.12
sweatyfunnyadams 065.05
Swed 137.07
Swede 082.03 387.19 517.05
swedhe 356.18
swee 094.15 094.15
swee 340.19
sweeatovular 156.15
sweecheeriode 359.19
sweeden 211.03
sweeds 141.12 557.28
Sweeney's 424.27
sweenyswinging 504.23
sweep 127.13 530.12
sweepacheeping 622.05
sweeper 311.14
sweeping 453.08
sweepplaces 533.22
sweeps 025.26 387.33 586.09
Sweeps 618.11
sweepsake 603.14
sweepstakes 447.03
sweepstakings 387.10
sweept 347.30
Sweepyard 413.04
swees 154.30
Swees 617.36
sweestureens 170.04
sweet 015.02 023.11 041.07 064.35 065.20 068.07 080.18 116.23 143.33 145.17 147.30 158.01 160.04 160.17 166.10 203.20 237.11 263.29 279.F32 279.F36 280.05 291.06 300.11 302.14 312.23 379.28 406.11 413.14 422.21 431.19 433.08 443.08 449.30 457.29 471.36 472.07 477.33 494.02 524.01 552.22 561.10 561.13 563.17 568.11 588.01 622.01 627.08 627.08
sweet 267.L1 399.03 418.14
Sweet 046.12 143.01 208.27 248.23 273.F4 460.10 466.35
Sweet 164.19
sweetempered 190.01
sweeten 018.26
sweetened 446.19
sweeter 116.12
sweetest 617.32
sweeth 340.18
sweetharp 224.16
sweetheart 328.21 619.17
sweetheartedly 579.06
sweetish 590.20
sweetishsad 360.02
sweetissest 148.05
sweetly 562.28
sweetmeat 428.01
sweetmeats 306.03
sweetmoztheart 360.12
sweetness 145.13 276.F6 528.01 615.33
sweetpea 392.25
sweets 036.01 128.30 563.03
Sweetsome 265.06
Sweetstaker 237.34
sweetster 598.13
Sweetstore 176.06
sweetthings 625.24
sweetwhome 138.30
sweetworded 376.20
sweety 225.20 527.21
sweetykins 148.04
swell 026.15 121.24 127.04 154.18 171.29 405.21 434.19 606.33 626.11
Swell 040.01
swellaw 449.04
swelled 441.26
swelling 180.01
swellish 053.23
swells 578.24
swelt 324.03
swensewn 372.16
swept 549.21
swering 557.12
swerve 003.01
swete 017.24
sweynhearts 254.03
Swhipt 303.06
swift 036.35 066.21 165.02 198.03 282.08 359.36 449.03 450.06 467.27 486.26 596.33
Swifte 101.08
swifter 454.20
swiftly 004.23 256.13
Swiftpatrick 564.32
swift's 568.30
Swift's 294.16
swiftshut 292.24
swigamore 241.21
swigged 424.27
swigswag 597.21
Swikey 187.02
swill 319.25
swills 569.24
swilly 211.36
swiltersland 488.30
swim 120.13 204.27
swimborne 041.07
swimford 296.F3
swimmed 251.30
swimmies 326.34
swimming 215.09
Swimming 627.03
swimminpull 377.35
swimmyease 408.27
swimp 230.09
swimswamswum 007.01
swin 188.23
swine 576.26
Swine 173.06
swinespepper 550.11
swiney 092.15
Swiney 261.L1
swing 226.20 443.09 548.34
Swing 262.L1
swinge 279.F29
swingingging 234.35
swinglowswaying 100.21
swinglyswanglers 371.03
swings 235.23
Swingy 516.05
swinking 361.33
swiping 250.06 347.29
Swiping 058.14
swirl 451.25
swirls 212.27
swish 501.12
Swish 106.07
swishawish 012.22
swishbarque 620.35
swished 319.32
swishing 070.03
swishingsight 345.35
Swiss 183.30
swisstart 454.03
switch 138.13 235.33
Switch 403.17
switchbackward 381.03
switched 498.25
switchedupes 423.20
switcheries 554.08
switches 028.30
switches 338.35
swithin 433.35
Swithin's 034.28
Swithun's 178.08
swits 462.30
swittvitles 116.01
Switz 093.06
swobber 141.19
swobbing 070.04
swolf 199.03
swollen 111.36 571.22
swollup 018.03
swoo 094.15
swoolth 034.19
swoon 278.F4
swooner 331.07
swooning 145.20
swooped 028.15
swooren 348.14

swoors 163.25
swooth 340.18
swoothead 474.12
swop 016.08 242.33
Swop 423.18
swopsib 568.12
sword 051.05 056.11 152.31 211.30 442.16 498.26
sword 349.30
Sword 306.19
Swordmeat 490.20
swords 116.15
Swords 266.F2
swordsed 142.27
swordswallower 150.04
swore 067.13 206.04 316.08 590.05
sworming 019.13
sworn 038.33 475.18
swp 406.12 406.12
swrine 173.19
swuck 230.09
swuith 240.17
swum 552.36
swumped 328.20 451.29
swung 209.19
swure 228.04
sybarate 451.32
Sybil 501.13 501.14
Sybil 399.04
sybilette 267.20
sycamode 533.17
sycamore 024.31 397.23
sycamores 384.01 388.24
Syce 094.06
Sycomore 095.21
sycomores 203.21 555.08
sycopanties 094.16
Syd 595.33
syddenly 553.31
Sydney 060.27 489.31
syf 418.26
syg 317.18
sygnus 423.21
Sygstryggs 077.13
Sykos 115.21
sylb 292.27
sylble 129.08
syllabelles 061.06
syllable 267.21
syllables 108.20 140.08
syllabub 097.17
sylp 594.12
sylph 531.29
Sylphling 495.05
Sylvae 360.13
sylvan 016.31 522.17
Sylvanus 570.32
Sylvester 473.03
Sylvia 061.01
Sylviacola 133.15
sylvias 337.17
sylvious 564.25
sylvup 225.16
symaphy 522.33
symbathos 159.27
symbolising 031.22
symethew 253.12
symibellically 292.25
Symmonds 310.14
sympathisers 060.01
sympatrico 464.16
symperise 226.07
symphony 409.10
symphysis 092.10
sympol 612.29
Sympoly 242.16
symposium's 211.24
sympowdhericks 618.15
synamite 291.03
Synamite 494.33
synchronisms 290.07
syncopanc 349.10
syncopation 109.05
syndic 542.16
Synds 310.03
syne 051.16 238.13 274.05 384.17 393.16 398.26
synerethetise 156.14
syngagyng 244.07
syngeing 549.03
synnbildising 332.28
synnotts 352.13
synodals 156.16
Synodius 487.36
synopticals 394.05
Synopticked 367.17
synthetic 185.07 612.25
synthetical 596.33
syphon 060.03
Syringa 492.23
syringe 188.30
syrop 494.21
syrup 026.32 211.24 432.01
sysentangled 161.13
system 026.11 077.04 100.33 161.07 161.08 288.F3 309.19 355.26 458.24 494.10
System 306.30
systematically 507.08
systems 429.12
systomy 597.21
sytty 020.19
syung 267.08
szabad 054.18
Szasas 172.23
szed 322.35 325.17
Szerday's 088.14
szeszame 333.01
szewched 265.F5
Szpaszpas 101.27
Szpissmas 101.28
szszuszchee 333.05
szumbath 129.28

t 333.01
T 013.24 (T. Totities) 235.28 486.15
't 037.20
ta 244.09
ta 491.19
T. A. 077.02 (T. A. Birkett)
Taaffe 320.23 582.08
taal 076.08 247.01
Taal 105.09
taart 407.04
taarts 535.16
taas 209.12
Taawhaar 613.05
tab 099.12
tabard 099.12 265.23
tabarine 027.20
Tabarins 360.26
tabbage 555.19
tabell 326.01
tabernacles 534.25
tabinet 043.04 533.10
Tabitha 235.30
table 073.03 124.10 127.21 127.23 143.36 266.11 304.30 374.05 381.11 462.24 498.24 513.36 531.06 544.18 559.12 626.12
tableau 065.06
Tableau 590.23
tabled 312.22
tableknife 050.29
tablelights 038.06
tablenapkins 405.31
tabler 456.14
Tabler 559.30
tables 026.35 094.26 268.09 283.13 389.03
tablesheet 585.31
tablestoane 594.22
tablotts 458.23
Taboccoo 427.13
Taborneccles 613.09
tabouretcushion 028.06
Taboutot 372.10
tabrets 559.10
tabs 219.24
tabu 435.30
tabular 167.23
tabularasing 050.12
tac 009.15
Taceate 604.19
taces 559.10
tache 111.20 599.20
tachie 194.31
tacit 099.02
tacitempust 457.32
Taciturn 017.03
tackle 166.29 281.20 315.15 439.04 460.04
tackling 417.30
tact 037.04 410.24 576.02
tactic 202.13
tactile 478.27
tactilifully 457.28
tactily 430.30
tactlessly 092.27
tacto 165.34
Tad 273.F8 481.20
taddy 628.08
taeorns 236.30
taerts 079.08
Taff 211.15 211.15
TAFF 338.05 338.15 339.18 339.31 340.13 340.25 341.08 342.33 344.01 345.04 345.16 346.14 347.34 348.29 352.16 352.35 353.33 354.07
taffetaffe 012.23
Taffyd 034.17
Taft 277.11
tag 037.14 114.30 315.26 351.17
Tag 590.29
tager 322.21
tagus 208.02
Taharan 380.21
Taif 318.23
tail 010.11 010.20 065.10 117.31 167.15 177.26 180.24 196.19 208.25 233.03 285.11 324.05 381.28 436.36 455.23 465.30 466.13 479.09 490.35 510.03 530.20 627.04

tail 383.13
Tail 156.07
tailcoat 190.26
tailed 123.06
tailend 050.04
tailibout 229.25
taillas 547.21
tailliur 067.14
tailor 129.06 297.29 440.30
Tailor 043.17
tailorless 329.02
tailors 315.11 324.14 529.15
tailor's 028.07 099.12
Tailor's 385.33
Tailors' 510.14
tailoscrupp 010.13
tailour 594.36
tails 119.36 120.01 272.06 396.18
tailsie 096.35
Tailte 083.23
tailtottom 344.17
tailturn 386.27
Tailwaggers 262.L4
tailwords 288.03
tailyup 498.06
taincture 286.05
taint 581.32
taintily 236.22
Taiocebo 043.23
Taiptope 512.20
tairor 070.20
Taishantyland 131.35
taiyor 312.03
tak 273.18 376.13
Tak 142.07 340.10 534.02
takable 243.03
take 005.19 012.19 024.16 025.36 036.24 051.33 067.07 068.23 079.20 079.23 080.31 091.05 091.31 096.20 102.21 113.31 115.14 119.27 137.08 141.02 142.34 145.06 146.03 152.11 152.13 159.21 164.30 166.01 167.25 167.27 170.05 178.26 186.09 189.27 193.05 228.08 238.06 259.05 272.17 287.05 292.10 294.06 304.11 313.24 334.05 351.24 397.19 412.20 414.13 425.07 425.33 431.23 438.05 439.27 443.08 447.32 448.01 455.11 456.34 459.12 469.08 469.22 470.03 477.17 478.01 483.02 487.05 495.34 506.30 513.27 515.13 516.13 516.16 525.10 526.07 528.05 528.35 531.11 534.11 540.08 547.13 562.30 563.35 564.30 571.08 582.28 586.02 595.31 612.17 616.16 619.32 621.05 621.11 621.33 623.09 623.14 623.20
take 399.15
Take 065.05 206.23 251.17 268.22 317.26 318.03 322.01 344.07 393.06 408.33 420.26 454.02 464.04 465.22 465.35 528.20 563.35 565.23 594.13 598.15 599.23 628.14
Take 032.23
TAKE 282.R1
takecups 345.27
takee 082.13
taken 025.34 050.09 066.29 076.24 082.28 103.09 109.35 110.20 119.35 120.01 121.13 125.20 139.03 163.29 190.18 219.06 221.31 278.F3 290.F1 298.08 315.19 333.12 336.34 366.18 423.32 433.07 436.15 523.34 570.16 618.32
takenplace 504.12
taker 497.27
takes 113.21 129.28 149.05 150.28 171.03 175.29 203.10 213.13 213.36 232.31 244.28 293.21 331.07 428.20 510.03 544.13 564.01 625.28
takes 342.35
takestock 418.34
takeyourhandaways 496.06
takin 292.20
taking 012.19 014.25 040.28 043.15 048.13 068.04 085.14 142.34 167.19 171.34 191.07 284.15 358.33 379.03 392.27 422.24 435.02 441.36 442.07 459.26 491.27 516.08 527.33 529.36 530.03 539.20 587.11 589.07 603.21 605.27 621.27
Takiya 471.03
Taks 619.33
Tal 056.34
Talbot 447.13
talc 538.04
tale 040.07 041.36 044.09 113.18 197.27 209.17 212.21 215.35 323.23 335.05 335.27 336.09 358.17 366.28 425.02 448.24 483.03 486.01 541.28 607.01 626.18
talebearer 325.18
taledold 563.27
taler 317.27
talerman 319.08
tales 053.05 247.03 275.24 330.12 431.31 431.32 440.18 522.05 522.05 545.26
Tales 359.24
taletold 453.18
taletub 272.18
taling 213.12
talis 150.10 167.05 167.05
Talis 149.34 150.01 150.01 150.04 150.04 150.05 150.05 150.13 150.13
tality 149.30
talk 012.03 028.11 057.34 091.13 094.27 113.26 130.19 191.26 215.32 215.34 225.18 360.35 459.14 561.36 597.19 624.10
Talk 171.29 238.22 378.36 462.26 480.36 494.04
talka 315.31
talkatalka 117.19
talked 059.26 150.24 153.06 465.19
talker 378.31
talker-go-bragk 438.16
talkeycook 394.07
talkin 379.07 478.24
talking 025.12 028.02 289.18 387.11 424.29 452.07 472.12 482.25 522.26 523.05 527.10 562.16 596.20 602.31
Talking 285.F1
talkingto 187.34
Talkingtree 564.30
talks 333.36 441.32 459.13 562.02 618.35
talktapes 196.08
tall 024.02 (o' tall) 062.28 063.10 233.01 283.02 321.10 344.13 366.28 386.17 387.03 519.18 545.26 554.02 554.02 604.28 609.36 620.01
Tallaght 083.19 334.33
Tallaght's 194.35
talled 319.33
talledged 545.14
taller 126.11 336.02 522.08
Tallhell 525.06
tallin 015.25
talling 520.36
tallmidy 469.02
tallonkindles 549.03
tallow 136.09 398.11
tallows 498.26
tallowscoop 008.35 009.34
talls 059.07 579.03
talltale 510.29
tallworts 564.20
tally 019.18 437.27
Tallyhaugh 622.27
tallyhos 467.36
talonts 606.30
Talop's 241.15
talor 375.34
talus 539.26
Talviland 176.27
tam 055.15
Tam 015.26 034.17 276.21 379.34 481.36
Tamagnum 404.26
Tamal 598.19
Tamas-Rajas-Sattvas 294.L2
tambaldam 258.21
tambarins 415.09
tambourine 248.09
tambre 209.36
tame 350.30 425.25
Tame 146.11
tamelised 110.11
Tames 424.03
tamileasy 173.15
Tamlane 550.30
tammany 442.03
tammar 200.31
tamming 622.07
tammit 338.25
tammy 241.25 315.25
Tammy 510.10
Tamor 255.04
Tamotimo's 599.23
tampting 015.26
tamquam 300.32
tams 130.17
Tams 028.24
Tamstar 187.22
tamtam 608.32
tamtammers 027.20
Tamuz 013.26
tan 046.15 055.15 208.17 288.15 445.22 480.04 619.33 626.22
Tanah 351.22
tanapanny 588.18
tanbark 423.29

Tancred 337.35
tandem 284.27 395.06
Tandem 486.05
tanderest 594.18
tandsel 534.09
Tandy 516.31
tang 598.04 621.13
Tang 623.13
tangerine 180.09
tangle 476.03
tangled 152.10 239.08
tanglesome 024.26
tango 248.01
Tangos 574.05 574.20
tangotricks 444.27
tangue 485.22
tank 098.07 129.06 359.11
Tank 105.16
tankard 035.34
Tankardstown 097.04 097.08
tankar's 317.07
tanker's 351.26
tanks 584.32
tankus 527.28
tankyou 009.31
tanned 240.23
Tanneiry 312.09
tannenyou 553.03
tanner 182.23 294.30
Tanner 071.28
tannoboom 564.22
tanny 603.05
tanquam 586.29
tans 176.25
tanssia 325.10
tansy 226.10
Tansy 164.22
tantae 287.23
tantamount 108.33
Tan-Taylour 511.29
tante's 439.13
tanto 521.10
tantoncle's 250.13
tantoo 416.13
Tantris 486.07
tantrist 571.07
tantrums 189.05 490.24 595.15
tantum 167.06
tantumising 149.35
tanyouhide 093.08
taon 415.08
taotsey 242.26
tap 006.24 083.30 239.24 265.23 319.09 444.26 531.31 598.04
Tap 058.23
Tapaa 427.09
tapatagain 058.23
tape 079.23 311.31 393.25
Tape 322.08
tapegarters 436.01
taper 207.15 527.22
tapers 549.05
taper's 115.04
tapette 079.23
tapizo 160.30
tappanasbullocks 611.26
tappany 611.04
tapped 036.13 168.09
tapping 505.01
tappropinquish 612.24
tappyhands 470.08
tapting 202.11
tar 085.24 409.14 505.02
Tar 385.33
Tara 375.24 535.08
tarabom 007.34 007.34
tarabooming 173.21
tarabred 411.22
taradition 151.20
tarafs 365.17
tarandtan 027.09
Taranta 513.12
Tarar 329.35
Tarara 247.28
Tarararat 267.F6
tararulled 552.29
Tara's 491.26
taratoryism 359.03
tardest 517.29
tardeynois 154.09
tare 118.34 426.15 509.26
tare 341.22
tares 110.09 190.21 198.29 598.19
tarf 625.18
target 321.03
targum 112.07
tarikies 356.17
tark 581.10
tarkeels 152.32
Tark's 239.01
tarn 079.08 599.22
Tarn 201.03
tarned 177.02
tarnelly 431.17
tarnished 226.05
tarnpike 132.32
tarns 331.20
Tarpeia 167.18
Tarpey 214.34 384.11 390.13 475.28 476.26 519.31 520.08
Tarpeyan 526.30
Tarpey's 405.05
Tarpinacci 368.33
tarpitch 232.01
tarpon 136.27
tarponturboy 362.08
tarr 232.36
Tarra 319.25
tarrable 520.02
tarrant's 583.29
tarrapoulling 320.03
Tarra's 009.21
tarrascone 227.35
tarred 549.15
tarriers' 182.15
tarries 336.09
Tarriestinus 157.02
tarrk 034.01
tarry 228.22 291.07 428.09
Tarry 043.17
tarrying 579.29
tar's 443.27
tart 247.18 302.14
Tart 059.14
tartagliano 478.19
tartallaght 478.12
tartan 130.24
tartanelle 583.03
tartar 341.12
Tartar 514.24
Tartaran 227.35
tartars 135.24 238.22
tartatortoise 233.34
tartlets 430.25
tartly 322.21
tarts 116.23
Tarty 519.33
tasbooks 256.18
tasing 342.35
task 525.11
Taskmaster's 036.27
tasks 263.21
Tass 489.09 593.06
tassed 322.21
tassie 461.30
tassing 043.08
tastarin 227.35
taste 079.22 087.12 109.16 166.33 177.26 212.25 334.36 456.04 485.09 548.23 621.12
tastefully 221.24
tastefully 349.08
tastelessly 092.27
tastes 413.12 431.03
tastes 355.05
tastily 285.F6
tasting 319.09
tasty 603.06
tastytasting 237.17
Tasyam 601.03
tata 057.28
Tatcho 068.34
Tate 295.08
tathair 273.F8
tatoovatted 346.03
tattached 562.21
tattat 623.35
tattered 180.17
Tattersull 516.06
tatterytail 097.26
tattle 235.32 597.09
tattled 545.26
tattlepage 212.34
tattling 244.01
Taub 105.09
Taubiestimm 546.29
Taubling 007.06
tauch 021.29
taucht 441.15
tauftauf 003.10
taught 025.05 060.17 131.05 147.31 157.31 163.05 544.19 585.12
taughter 127.02
taughters 543.15
taughtropes 301.01
taughts 527.02
Taulked 106.29
Taunt 361.10
taunts 247.35 613.07
Taurrible 138.17
Taurus 466.31
taut 133.08 315.25
taut 349.09
tautaubapptossed 080.07
tautaulogically 006.30
tauth 336.28
tautologically 119.21
tauttung 612.08
tav 132.17
tavarn 599.22
tavern 265.23 521.17
Tavern 205.25 229.15
tavern's 368.24
taw 097.26
t.a.W. 289.14 (the at Wickerworks)

tawe 199.26
Tawfulsdreck 068.21
tawn 311.06 540.21
tawney 068.35
tawny 100.20 549.28 571.08
taws 349.01
Tax 420.22
taxed 132.11
taxes 273.03
taxing 525.12
taxis 070.28
taxpayers 182.35
tay 012.16 102.20 110.11 117.30 199.18 331.02 371.31 603.06 621.14
Tay 145.05 603.05
tayboil 026.07
taying 392.09
tayle 007.11
tayler 311.26
tayleren 311.24
taylight 328.23
taylorised 356.10
taylor's 061.28
Taylor's 365.33
taylz 524.24
tays 137.08
taytotally 181.21 330.06
T.B. 172.13 (tuberculosis)
T. C. 495.12 (T. C. King)
TCD 424.11 (Trinity College, Dublin)
tch 111.20
Tch 297.17
T.C.H. 131.04
Tcheetchee 244.20
t. d. 317.01 (til Dennis)
T.D.S. 131.03 (<u>Ter</u> <u>Die</u> <u>Sumerdum</u>)
te 075.09 077.22 335.19 335.20
<u>te</u> 167.24
tea 050.18 056.26 116.24 119.30 247.14 260.03 299.F3 369.32 382.07 392.32 440.21 449.13 496.28 507.12 578.22 585.31
Tea 260.02 302.09 406.28
Teac 139.30
teacakes 460.32
teacan 247.14
teach 146.15 239.23 361.06 444.26 579.25
<u>Teach</u> 418.14
teachet 484.22
teaching 166.18 389.14 620.34
teachings 431.28
<u>Teachings</u> 123.21
teachit 242.32
Teague 210.20 281.F2 337.30
teak 076.11
Teak 607.03
Teakortairer 343.09
teal 165.21
tealeaves 449.33
tealer 325.16
tealofts 255.08
<u>Team</u> 176.02
teamdiggingharrow 600.13
teams 174.28
teamwork 546.15
Teangtaggle 287.F4
teangue 260.F1
Teapotty 247.15 247.15
teapucs 236.31
teaput 221.13
tear 028.29 082.22 159.13 159.13 319.31 365.33 375.32 445.04 457.21 509.26 525.30 568.13 607.15 625.31
tearfs 346.21
teargarten 075.01
tearing 205.11 256.17 582.02
tearly 489.31
Tear-nan-Ogre 479.02
tearorne 210.31
tears 022.16 054.20 116.36 145.19 148.11 158.21 159.11 159.13 178.12 183.24 184.23 212.18 225.32 230.24 254.17 276.06 282.01 381.21 413.17 463.10 470.06 500.33 563.05
Tears 421.10
tearsday 301.20
tearsheet 022.01
tearsilver 426.09
teartoretorning 256.17
tearts 051.36
teary 007.05
tea's 308.02
tease 068.17 068.17 068.17 270.16 330.04 461.13 607.15
Teaseforhim 246.34
teasel 130.25
teaser 111.27 561.04
teasers 284.16
teasesong 203.30
teasetime 191.28
teashop 177.36
teasily 068.01
teasim 234.25
teasing 200.16
<u>teasing</u> 433.19
teaspilled 305.04
teaspoonspill 534.09
teastain 111.20
teasy 112.30
Teasy 212.08 527.09
teatables 616.23
teat-a-teat 432.11
teath 270.F2
teatime 170.26
<u>Teatime</u> 071.17
teatimes 603.18
teatimestained 114.29
teatoastally 038.23
teats 222.27
teawidow 545.04
teaze 550.20
Techertim 210.15
technologically 164.16
tect 552.14
<u>tectu</u> 165.35
<u>tectucs</u> 418.34
Ted 034.17
Teddy 142.27 587.09
teddybearlined 208.17
teddyfy 191.23
Tee 006.28
TEE 305.R1
Teek 151.23
teel 007.05
teem 519.25
teeming 471.25
Teems 215.22
teen 440.29 626.09
teenes 227.12
teens 430.11 556.07
teerm 478.11
tees 542.14
teeth 007.13 041.31 075.20 101.36 134.06 149.01 183.36 210.32 288.07 397.22 437.24 508.01 517.16
teething 563.04
teeths 020.25 084.03 271.F1
teetootomtotalitarian 260.02
teetotum 489.17
Teewiley 355.30
Teffia 604.04
<u>teffs</u> 349.11
tefnute 570.36
teggs 351.03
tegmen 249.15
Tegmine-sub-Fagi 403.09
tegolhuts 416.35
tegotetabsolvers 004.09
Teheresiann 538.02
teign 201.21
<u>teilweisioned</u> 345.35
<u>teilwrmans</u> 323.19
teiney 594.21
teint 559.28
teit 478.23
Tek 142.05
Tekkles 373.03
tel 227.34
teldtold 597.08
<u>teleframe</u> 349.09
telekinesis 198.21
telemac 176.36
TELEOLOGICUM 264.R1
telepath 460.21
telephone 118.13
telephony 052.18
telescope 178.28
telescopes 295.12
telesmell 095.12
telesphorously 154.07
televisible 265.11
television 150.33 254.22
Television 052.18
Televox 546.29
Telewisher 489.21
tell 010.26 020.23 023.31 035.01 035.18 036.33 051.12 053.08 055.02 067.24 082.13 083.16 083.25 089.22 089.23 089.24 092.30 094.19 094.19 094.19 098.28 101.02 101.20 113.12 114.27 115.25 117.06 117.19 127.06 148.10 148.26 149.12 154.03 154.36 164.25 173.14 190.10 190.14 193.04 193.13 193.14 196.02 198.14 201.21 202.07 204.33 206.14 207.30 213.33 214.05 214.20 216.03 216.03 226.30 234.32 239.23 240.24 240.25 242.26 263.F4 269.12 276.23 277.18 286.30 289.27 344.20 352.14 353.12 364.02 366.28 366.36 374.01 374.34 380.32 381.27 391.35 412.20 414.07 423.04 423.27 427.26 436.06 442.28 451.10 451.27 452.06 452.32 452.33 454.28 456.14 459.23 459.36 460.22 464.34 465.12 476.20 476.31 485.18 489.23 499.22 499.34 507.17 508.09

509.13 510.03 515.27 520.11 521.04 526.11 529.14 532.29 533.30 536.26 537.02 539.04 539.15 541.28 556.16 564.02 570.09 598.24 599.36 600.32 622.16 625.05
tell 200.10 200.10
Tell 148.02 196.05 196.05 198.18 198.28 198.28 200.10 200.10 200.33 201.21 202.07 206.08 216.01 216.03 307.14 338.09 343.08 452.32 479.22 483.13 501.02 507.25 521.35 535.27 560.22 602.09
Tell 071.36 107.04
tellabout 361.08
tellafun 086.14
Tellaman 584.31
tellas 101.02
tellavicious 349.28
Telle 597.36
telled 315.35
teller 310.30 319.24 424.14
Telleth 505.19
tellforth's 552.26
Tellibly 303.F1
telling 007.05 073.01 170.05 179.29 213.12 312.22 389.36 395.02 410.28 410.35 426.22 431.30 475.26 493.02 510.09 516.11 519.34 524.15 565.35 586.35 586.35 624.32
telling 341.26
Telling 176.11
Tellmastoly 485.31
tellmastory 397.07
Tell-No-Tailors' 006.03
tells 068.32 129.06 221.12 244.07 279.F19 305.01 380.04 480.08 524.18 557.36 589.19 623.05
tells 341.31 350.13
tellt 560.24 561.12
telltale 183.11 233.01 550.25
Telltale 268.L1
telltuss 338.22
tellurem 513.02
tellus 101.02
tellusit 331.06
telluspeep 275.L2
tellyhows 335.01
Telmetale 216.03
tem 056.34
tem 056.03
Tem 088.35 379.34
t'embarass 418.24
tembledim 258.21
tembo 209.11
Temorah 087.08
Temoram 593.13
temp 424.01
Temp 196.22
temperance 063.19
temperasoleon 596.26
temperate 452.36
temperature 134.31 491.27
tempest 471.24
templar 486.16
temple 155.04 244.06 288.21 391.12 398.14 486.15
Temple 122.12
templeogues 553.12
temple's 562.10
Templetombmount 192.35
tempo 369.24
tempor 164.35
temporal 155.11 163.14 164.36
temporalities 484.18
temporarily 150.31
temporibus 251.29
temporiser 154.26
tempory 231.17
Tempos 468.29
temps 281.04
tempt 142.34 204.08
Tempt 610.18
temptated 089.01
temptation 238.14 311.13
Temptation 436.11
temptations 573.11
temptatrix 079.18
tempted 392.04 457.06
temptiness 434.24
tempting 069.28 142.33
tempt-in-twos 245.19
temptive 477.18
temptoed 150.03
temse 448.28
temtem 608.31
temts 250.14
ten 020.15 035.31 051.34 070.29 073.20 082.14 101.34 119.07 121.28 131.36 189.22 207.32 213.27 255.31 255.31 262.29 283.21 288.06 403.02 432.26 458.26 464.35 589.19
Ten 278.18 284.16
Ten 105.04
tenacity 082.24
tenant 428.25
tencents 242.04
tencho 146.21
tend 224.15
'tend 191.22
tendency 298.26 439.21 492.31
tender 145.17 160.13 280.11
tenderbolts 140.17
tendered 574.14
Tenderest 456.03
tenderfoot 186.24
tenderloined 115.13
tenderly 573.01
tenderosed 336.27
tenderumstouchings 237.18
tendrolly 368.17
tends 349.09
tendulcis 541.32
teneat 610.06
ténèbres 179.27
tenebrous 122.22 281.02
tenemants 414.06
tenenure 539.33
tenitorial 082.25
tenk 396.27
Tenman's 187.22
tenners 282.27
tennis 214.27 361.10 366.10
Tennis 452.09
tennises 059.33
tenor 035.32
tenorist 048.21
tenpound 082.26
tenpounten 211.20
tense 186.01 269.09 598.29 599.14
tenspan 547.29
tent 362.13 566.10
tentacles 394.13
tentement 538.10
Tenter 339.16
tenters 133.34
tentes 613.06
tenth 543.35 615.32
tentpegs 113.19
tents 244.05
tents 274.L3 342.06
tenuacity 053.17
tenuit 515.09
tenyerdfuul 088.19
tenzones 246.33
Teobaldo 553.13
teom 412.18
Teomeo 238.35
tep 273.20
Tep 595.18
teppling 534.30
ter 022.18 294.10 557.09
Tera 326.14
terce 360.04 546.08
Terce 619.27
tercentenary 386.36
Teresa 155.26
Teresa 491.16
term 082.06 098.15 124.02 124.22 151.04 452.19
term 418.24
terminal 114.30
terminals 552.01
terminus 576.19
Terminus 456.26
terms 234.22 246.27 283.08 390.23 452.22 519.20
termtraders 581.15
ternatrine 326.15
ternitary 416.25
terooly 534.08
terpary 390.23
Terra 261.F2
Terrace 351.29
terraces 544.26
terracook 020.06
Terracotta 481.32
Terracussa 119.02
Terracuta 240.19
terram 185.14
terranean 120.29
terrars 314.35
terrarum 096.33
Terrecuite 133.30
Terrefin 279.F24
terrerumbled 258.23
terrestrial 263.28 388.23
Terreterry's 531.34
terrian 185.28
terrible 072.31 291.02 451.36 549.11
terrible 381.23
terriblitall 461.14
terribly 144.36 459.18 464.05 516.11 560.32
terricious 114.29
terricolous 018.29
terrier 132.17 144.33
Terrierpuppy 262.L4
terriers 567.24
terrified 243.05
terrine 080.23
Terriss 105.35
territorials 147.05

terroirs 602.15
terror 022.32 062.25 116.08 545.10
Terror 261.26
TERROREM 306.R1
terrorgammons 433.02
Terrors 420.28
terrorum 076.08
terroth 343.08
Terry 210.34 366.21 484.33
Terry 071.22
terse 124.22
Terse 058.32
tersey 322.17
Tersse 322.18
Tertia 057.32
tertianly 090.29
tertium 526.12
tertius 465.18
terug 578.32
Terziis 111.06
tesseract 100.35
test 207.30
testament 073.32 083.23
testcase 582.12
teste 584.10
tested 132.34 368.25
testers 170.02
testey 538.15
testies 098.34 332.12
testificates 525.04
testifighter 092.04
testify 539.02
testimonials 524.36
testimonies 034.23
testimony 173.30
testis 087.34
testymonicals 463.03
tesura 327.05
tet 328.33
tet-at-tet 567.09
tete 004.22
tether 262.20 528.26
tethera 457.13
tethered 020.04
tetigists 575.19
teto-dous 230.12
tetrachiric 123.16
tetradomational 614.27
tetrahedrally 477.01
tetranoxst 555.10
tetraturn 295.20
tetters 180.26
tetties 416.35
Teufleuf 240.24
teviots 206.30
tew 295.30 538.21
texas 026.15
Texas 274.F3
text 120.15
Tez 202.22
tezzily 417.06
th' 147.25 226.34 238.08
tha 141.34 328.29 328.29
tha 491.19 491.19
thaas 555.01
Thacolicus 193.21
thadark 622.15
Thaddeus 246.18 456.30
th'adult' rous 146.10
Thady 281.F2
Thaet 601.30
thah 522.21
thair's 177.25
thak 054.19
thalassocrats 367.25
thalk 461.28
Thallasee 324.09
tham 114.19
Tham 318.16
Thamamahalla 362.22
thamas 598.15
thames 199.01
than than
THan 298.13
tHaN 298.13
thanacestross 018.03
thane 316.05
Thane 593.10
thangas 015.12
thank 037.29 094.31 116.09 123.04 142.35 155.14 194.02 204.31 214.35 235.09 366.04 370.12 384.12 385.31 387.31 390.18 423.13 458.20 570.16 617.06
Thank 366.05 540.29
thankeaven 059.21
thanked 037.05 258.28 344.18 370.11
thankful 118.32 406.21 560.21
thankfully 085.17 460.02
thanking 142.35 377.30
thanks 039.10 086.22 091.27 093.15 144.34 174.31 190.20 191.03 244.29 262.07 273.F6 273.F8 302.05 304.27 395.18 413.01 456.02 458.25 489.09 489.25 543.13 574.25 584.30 585.10 590.06 598.15 615.14 619.03
thanks 345.21
Thanks 143.32 304.05 373.28 585.05
thanksalot 582.03
Thanksbeer 518.34
thanksbetogiving 380.09
thankskissing 061.21
thankstum 598.15
thankyou 111.14
thankyouful 599.21
thans 141.17
tharctic 519.19
Thargam 296.F3
tharr 130.04
thartytwo 389.25
thash 366.29
thass 479.09
thassbawls 520.05
that that That That
thatch 322.01
thatch 121.11
Thatcher's 318.17
thatchment 139.30
that'd 451.04
that'd 201.14
That'd 510.09
thathens 519.19
th'athlate 462.28
thatjolly 093.34
Thatll 533.36
that'll 029.12 375.27 456.34
That'll 442.34 468.14 625.13
That'll 383.12
thats 158.29 230.03 451.16
Thats 611.33
that's that's That's That's
thatseme's 511.04
thatt 034.08
thatthack 348.31
Thaunaton 499.09
Thaurd 319.20
thaurity 358.28
thausig 265.26
thauthor 452.10
th'avignue 226.34
thaw 035.15 054.14 205.22
Thaw 205.22 424.35
thawe 626.26
thawed 015.15
thawght 141.32 556.34
Thawland 579.28
thaws 184.02
Thawt 095.17
thay 453.12 461.29
thaya 213.21
thayin 395.18
the the The The THE
the 020.18 247.18 251.18 251.19 257.27 334.30 343.36 396.22 396.22 598.10 628.16
The 598.09
thea 229.26
theabild 159.31
theactrisscalls 363.28
theagues 622.24
Theagues 176.13
thealmostfere 067.10
theare 462.14
theas 613.22
Theas 277.L5
theated 461.28
theater 098.11
Theatre 268.16
theatrocrat 029.15
Theban 134.35
theck 423.11
thee thee Thee Thee
theeadjure 594.05
theeckleaves 608.26
theem 265.18
theemeeng 395.02
theerose 248.02
theer's 137.05
thees 223.09 259.03 354.28 607.19
theese 496.19
theetime 548.32
theeuponthus 394.29
theeward 267.05
theft 039.17
their their Their Their THEIR
theirinn 604.08
theirn 538.26
theirs 013.19 068.33 069.11 075.07 087.10 157.29 224.25 224.36 234.10 251.04 352.11 357.29 472.33 513.35 551.08 553.17 582.14 599.02
theirs 175.19
Theirs 200.04 318.26 324.18 563.28
their's 004.10 253.24
theirspot 582.14
Thej 236.13
thel 236.13
thelemontary 422.28
thelitest 320.07
Thelma 147.15

thelon 202.22
them them Them Them
theme 037.05 491.05
themes 159.22 223.08
Themes 614.08
themis 167.25
themise 138.10
Themistletocles 392.24
Themistocles 307.L1
themodius 528.23
th'Empyre 289.10
thems 357.32
thems 353.07
them's 625.19
themself 384.34
themselse 003.07
themselves 008.04 013.31 014.12 015.19 056.02 060.35 076.16 096.04 109.14 161.13 180.04 182.08 189.18 208.07 222.16 290.04 298.18 314.31 322.29 380.36 394.06 397.14 417.09 426.32 460.24 474.17 475.03 475.20 476.14 476.30 513.32 524.20 564.26 569.31 577.20 582.06 585.35 589.26 609.14 611.22
themselves 346.02
themses 101.04
then then Then
thenabouts 069.24
Thenanow 311.13
thence 120.01 298.11 477.21 586.13
thender 335.11
theng 333.02
thenked 487.07
then'll 250.14
then-on-sea 539.24
thenown 595.34
Then's 598.28
thentimes 101.15
Theo 439.19
Theoatre 587.08
theobalder 263.05
theobibbous 140.13
Theoccupant 348.14
Theocritus 307.L1
theodicy 419.29
theogamyjig 332.24
theogonies 353.01
theologies 358.27
theology 189.04
theoperil 223.28
Theophil 163.25
Theophrastius 484.30
theopot 242.15
theorbe 360.05
theorbo 472.08
theoric 308.L2
theorics 149.28
theories 030.05 076.10
theory 073.31 149.35 163.24 163.36 595.19
theosophagusted 610.01
ther 061.20 334.22
there there There There
thereabouts 506.25
thereanswer 604.07
thereass 538.32
therebeneath 249.09
therebetween 561.25
thereby 076.06 143.15 186.02 189.09 258.30 544.04 605.34
Therecocta 134.18
thered 371.14
There'd 451.26
therefor 226.08
therefore 013.20 174.24 321.02 488.01 566.30 576.04
Therefore 064.35
thereinafter 492.35
thereinofter 378.30
thereinofter 345.28
thereinunder 093.04
there'll 012.14 354.26 436.13 532.04 626.19
there'll 399.02
There'll 028.27 626.19
therenow 555.07
thereof 020.18 069.22 183.09 363.31 503.28 536.20
thereon 613.02
thereopen 363.34
thereout 227.19
thereover 160.28
theres 318.26 373.21 541.20 621.17
Theres 345.30
there's there's There's There's
theresomere 627.05
theresweep 533.22
Thereswhere 514.10
thereto 026.09 187.07
theretofore 605.34
therety 347.04
thereunto 552.26
thereup 571.05
therever 110.10
therewhere's 012.15
Therewith 048.04
Therewithal 564.25
therinunder 438.28
thermidor 406.36
thermites 057.12
thermos 071.02
therrble 628.05
thes 222.09
Thesaurus 503.34
these these These These
th'estrange 017.33
thet 206.25 620.07
thetheatron 596.01
th'ether 452.13
thette 199.08
theumperom's 070.25
thews 364.05
they they They They
they'd 139.26 193.14 212.23 375.18 454.12 622.33
they'd 104.23
theygottheres 311.04
they'll 279.F18 368.28 446.20 525.36 620.06
They'll 582.13 627.35
theyre 301.F2
they're 027.12 054.01 065.01 147.21 204.34 205.09 226.33 246.33 248.32 251.20 279.F16 368.27 376.36 436.08 569.31 600.25 622.01 622.02 625.12 627.35
they're 209.09
They're 147.09 227.27 500.02 578.32 621.19 622.09
theys 368.34
theystood 555.07
they've 135.08 348.36 506.25 527.28 617.13 621.32
They've 204.35 234.36 377.35
thg 515.06
Thi 607.19
thick 023.04 039.22 099.31 123.02 160.29 189.13 242.08 296.20 322.09 325.34 404.20 438.07 463.17 502.18 536.13 583.32 596.20
Thick 213.09 256.35
Thickathigh 277.F6
thicked 084.36
thickens 348.09
thicker 130.32 215.09 266.08 406.29
thickerthanwater 070.26
thicket 580.15
thicketloch 248.23
thick-in-thews 129.33
thicklish 038.17
thickly 171.30 266.29
thickness 475.05
thicks 618.08
thicksets 087.30
thickshut 419.27
thickuns 424.19
thicville 541.35
thides 366.29
thief 372.31 436.21 541.31
Thief 117.01
Thieve 497.22
thieves 173.28
thieves' 057.34 410.36
thievesdayte 325.06
thieving 487.34
thigging 015.13
thigh 319.32 417.18 569.22 596.20
thighne 102.01
thighs 089.31 613.22
thight 240.09 461.27
THIGHTHIGHTTICKELLY-THIGH 305.R1
Thik 019.06
thikke 506.04
thildish 461.28
thim 073.07 215.33
Thim 507.02
thimble 129.07
Thimble 268.15
thimblecasket 561.16
thimbles 059.06 500.02
thime 114.01
thimes 327.09 614.08
thin 009.03 068.08 099.31 126.05 202.27 236.13 236.13 256.35 408.24 409.01 436.02 463.17 564.19 587.02
Thin 236.13 236.13
Thin 106.24
Thinathews 277.F6
thinconvenience 520.06
thine 235.03 235.09 266.29 271.F4 275.25 408.24 412.08 454.02 458.20 527.16 602.12
Thine 140.06 450.33
thiner 117.01
thine-to-mine 283.10
thing 006.30 016.18 018.16 025.06 029.17 037.27 041.06

051.21 067.32 069.16 082.33 087.08 087.11 107.36 108.08 113.05 118.07 118.21 120.08 125.04 150.13 159.15 165.01 167.18 172.35 181.13 190.10 191.28 202.15 202.27 212.26 215.24 223.09 224.16 247.33 252.25 253.08 269.26 278.15 334.20 334.21 336.16 395.26 396.21 411.26 411.35 418.09 419.23 423.14 438.02 451.34 452.05 452.21 452.26 454.26 470.22 470.29 484.27 490.09 521.09 521.34 527.07 528.15 536.07 560.07 574.23 611.26 612.01 612.07 612.17 612.31 612.31 612.31 627.05
thing 350.14
Thing 058.01 242.23 313.14 536.31
thingabib 620.22
thingabolls 543.08
thingabossers 088.29
thingajarry 333.02
Thingamuddy's 423.34
Thingavalla 460.32
Thingavalley 328.27
Thingcrooklyexineverypasture-sixdixlikencehimaroundher-sthemaggerbykinkinkankan-withdownmindlookingated 113.09
thingdom 333.31
thingdome 018.21
thinghowe 076.14
thinglike 608.22
Thingman 346.25
things 013.20 026.21 049.03 066.03 066.33 108.09 119.05 119.09 154.35 160.17 178.22 188.04 232.25 237.01 248.14 270.11 275.03 275.04 275.19 276.23 296.F5 305.06 306.F7 316.24 328.07 328.32 332.29 337.11 374.35 398.25 425.32 441.10 447.02 471.25 516.33 522.12 533.13 547.06 550.08 597.04 625.05 627.23
Things 536.31 540.13
thing's 015.33 599.31
thingsumanything 417.26
think 012.16 061.25 099.14 108.13 132.19 142.33 144.05 145.21 149.10 149.11 173.02 173.14 180.32 181.14 187.05 191.03 199.09 222.05 236.05 250.30 253.02 264.F2 268.F4 270.F3 291.13 294.30 296.02 296.15 303.24 318.04 326.36 343.09 343.19 343.20 345.14 361.23 361.33 365.03 373.19 381.08 387.15 392.34 409.23 423.14 427.35 431.10 442.20 442.20 443.03 445.21 445.28 447.22 448.32 457.20 458.09 458.22 460.16 469.08 471.22 476.18 483.28 484.27 485.08 494.28 510.36 511.01 518.13 519.18 519.27 519.29 521.15 522.28 532.15 539.05 539.10 542.12 558.11 560.35 561.28 562.22 570.11 570.15 586.09 615.21 620.06
think 350.05 383.10
Think 088.01 154.06 206.03 343.09 379.11 442.20 487.04 528.19 579.22
thinkamalinks 613.19
thinkamuddles 409.18
thinkards 312.31
thinkaviking 609.19
thinkers 124.24
thinker's 224.04
Thinker's 409.21
thinking 043.17 100.24 142.33 146.28 148.15 214.14 268.04 279.F03 316.26 393.15 410.10 412.02 412.25 422.09 428.04 452.10 467.22 469.27 482.24 487.07 625.31
Thinking 491.08 627.13
thinkingthings 379.14
thinkinthou 054.14
thinkled 487.11
thinkling 154.30 256.04
thinkly 342.29
thinks 118.15 133.05 146.09 234.23 267.F5 319.18 319.20 328.07 336.26 436.03 583.07 621.28
Thinks 071.18
thinkyou 232.17
thins 160.29
thinskin 169.19
thinthin 615.31
Thinthin 615.31
thinwhins 419.01
third 022.21 039.09 064.14 122.31 133.12 157.30 165.04 170.10 187.29 197.19 268.18 433.02 444.21 486.11 522.27 567.16 605.23
Third 582.29
thirdly 552.21
thirds 040.10 288.10
thirdst 311.16
thirst 187.23 381.27 516.25
Thirst 302.09 317.05
thirstay 006.14
thirsthy 405.33
thirstuns 389.24
thirsty 100.17 517.30
thirt 284.16 291.06
thirteens 248.32
thirtieth 119.25
thirtunine 133.17
thirty 070.33 073.10 077.06 156.02 246.03 444.12 497.09 517.29 574.26
thirty 338.05
Thirty 274.12 307.18
thirtybobandninepenny 396.18
thirtynine 573.20 574.27 596.08
thirtyseven 255.32 255.33
thirtytwo 036.17 120.25 123.06 182.23 256.22 388.12 448.03
this this This This
thisa 535.13
Thisafter 568.30
thisahere 523.32
thise 372.08
thisens 334.16
thishis 356.11
thisorder 540.19
this's 530.31
Thistake 352.12
thistle 433.35 587.27
Thistle 378.18
THISTLE 303.R3
thistlewords 169.22
Thisutter 598.19
thiswis 612.18
thisworlders 251.09
thit 366.29
Thit 106.15
thithaways 114.16
thither 158.25
Thnkyou 533.36
tho 265.18 265.18
tho' 238.08 366.20
Tho' 271.F5
Tho' 105.03
Thoath 254.02
thockits 037.30
thofthinking 162.23
thogged 487.07
thoh 398.21
thoil 019.06
thokkurs 326.22
Thok's 046.21
thole 134.02 541.23
Tholedoth 230.26
tholes 597.17
thollstall 539.22
Tholomew's 140.01
tholse 077.10
Thom 090.26 215.33 506.28 507.01 507.34
Thom 176.0I 176.01
Thomars 543.17
Thomar's 090.26
Thomassabbess's 601.27
thome 461.28
thomethinks 149.03
thomistically 510.18
thoms 575.36
Thom's 534.27
thon 031.10 334.32 354.34 415.31 568.17
Thon 011.05
thonder 314.29
Thonderbalt 106.15
Thonderman 176.01
thong 224.35 396.31
thongs 015.29 192.17
Thon's 011.03 011.04 011.04 582.32
thonther 365.22
thonthorstrok 018.16
thoo 601.11 601.11
Thoorsday 086.11
thoose 617.04
thor 154.23 198.29 279.F26 311.06
thord 138.33
Thord 532.09
thore 053.26
thore's 310.20
thorgtfulldt 537.04
Thoris 090.26
thorizon 494.09
Thorker 132.18
Thorkill's 051.16
thorly 609.26
Thormendoso 312.08
thorn 019.06
Thorne's 192.11
Thorneycroft 552.13
thorngarth 281.02
thorns 256.04 264.28

Thornton 063.06
thorntree 083.08 277.17
thornwood 246.04
thorny 274.L3
thornyborn 506.26
Thornycraft 510.10
thorough 048.17 178.08 541.35
thoroughbass 565.22
thoroughfare 140.12
thoroughgoing 141.01
thoroughly 138.28 229.34 544.15
thoroughpaste 190.34
Thorp 004.27
thorpes 331.21
Thorpetersen 310.03
thorpeto 077.07
Thorror 626.28
Thor's 424.22
Thorsman 568.17
Thorstan's 543.16
thorstyites 137.24
Thortig 283.01
thortin 378.12
Thortytoe 073.15
thorush 360.16
Thos 090.26
those those Those
th'osirian 350.25
thot 049.31
thother 224.33
th'other 452.13
thothfolly 415.28
thots 597.25
Thot's 485.36
thou Thou Thou
Thouat's 206.25
thoud 457.31
thouest 601.12
though though Though
thought 024.08 029.19 061.06 067.29 068.24 072.24 088.10 100.25 126.16 144.19 146.18 146.18 148.16 153.05 158.15 162.21 171.34 174.30 183.08 186.17 188.08 191.35 192.01 192.01 198.23 202.32 211.04 225.18 231.11 231.15 291.F4 299.30 303.F1 332.33 337.17 343.33 369.26 378.32 415.16 416.29 429.16 431.19 454.05 454.12 487.04 487.08 487.14 519.27 526.22 571.11 596.10 600.24 603.05 622.24 627.21 627.23
thoughtful 159.03 464.16
thoughtfully 584.34
thoughtless 238.36
thoughts 052.34 147.20 288.10 298.32 311.16 428.05 446.03 528.20 531.31 549.30 561.32 565.03
thoughtsam 292.14
thoughtsendyures 295.03
thoughy 370.04
thougths 251.17
thoult 516.23
Thounawahallya 056.07
thounce 262.L2
thousand 005.28 041.33 051.04 064.34 081.04 119.14 156.19 156.21 159.11 174.23 188.36 192.17 210.05 305.10 326.15 357.18 404.36 412.26 412.27 413.23 519.07 535.28 564.19 604.25 617.04 627.15
Thousand 412.24
Thousand 342.15
thousandfirst 254.19
thousands 135.20 297.10 438.24 505.06
thousand's 325.07
thousandtimes 338.02
t'house 077.28
thousendsthee 628.14
thout 479.28
Thou-who-thou-art 418.07
thow 023.24 023.24
thracks 019.20
thrain 484.04
thraitor 019.07
thrall 145.32
thranes 513.26
thrash 203.05
thrate 374.05
thread 063.26 205.08
threading 579.03
Threadneedles 551.33
threads 245.10
threadworm 437.14
threadworms 121.19
threaspanning 248.27
threat 598.26
threatens 127.16 573.05
threathy 320.22
threaties 329.32
threats 070.12
threbled 330.06
three 008.21 008.30 011.01 019.21 020.15 022.29 022.34 029.07 042.33 043.14 043.18 051.15 058.24 061.27 065.27 065.34 066.30 075.17 078.19 081.28 082.07 088.27 094.17 095.11 101.23 108.20 113.14 117.23 122.21 122.24 122.26 126.08 127.13 127.35 128.17 128.31 129.03 131.02 131.32 134.31 137.01 139.02 141.14 144.17 151.25 156.02 161.30 173.26 179.29 180.09 193.07 201.28 202.18 203.13 211.17 222.29 228.09 236.12 238.26 241.29 246.15 252.12 253.20 254.03 264.05 264.21 284.17 284.23 290.06 305.F1 312.28 314.12 315.11 319.11 322.26 322.28 329.15 332.03 337.04 337.20 348.21 351.07 351.26 360.29 362.25 362.33 367.08 373.02 376.25 376.26 379.36 380.29 384.33 386.03 386.32 387.13 396.26 410.34 423.21 438.22 442.04 444.12 463.03 465.05 465.24 474.18 474.19 480.03 481.10 499.17 506.04 514.12 519.31 520.12 520.14 521.07 526.16 529.15 529.24 535.32 537.30 538.14 539.18 541.29 546.15 549.21 558.01 558.14 558.16 572.25 586.23 587.06 589.08 589.32 596.16 606.14 608.06 612.26 616.10 620.05 623.02
three 342.23 526.13
Three 144.02 373.23 377.11 436.05 478.29 494.26 514.11 521.31 525.31 584.10 608.34 611.01 626.26
Three 105.31 383.01 526.13
THREE 166.17 305.R1
threeabreasted 365.15
threeece 594.32
threed 196.10
threedraw 178.27
threefaced 132.12
threefoiled 010.08
threefurts 415.05
threehandled 285.13
threehandshighs 272.22
threehatted 089.31
threehundred 444.12
threeingles 297.27
threelegged 019.22 331.08
threelungged 426.05
threepartite 405.31
threepence 544.26
threeplexes 133.30
threequickenthrees 377.11
threes 057.19 158.21 328.07 379.05 386.32
Threes 176.05 281.L2
three's 020.24 279.F02 317.29
threescore 264.21
threescoreten 079.10
threespawn 358.12
threestar 424.34
threestory 367.15
threeth 525.31
threetop 152.34
threft 335.33
threi 616.09
threne 094.14
threnning 058.18
threshold 311.14 418.05
threw 110.29 134.04 146.12 146.29 294.08 313.22 315.14
threwed 231.29 506.25
thrice 131.36 247.08 250.28 417.33 424.14 483.31 515.29 562.08
Thrice 618.10
thricetold 317.27
THRICKY 305.R1
thrie 041.18
thried 196.10 328.19
thries 129.22
Thrift 307.09
thrilldriver 395.16
thrilled 166.12
thrilling 331.07
thrilljoy 486.08
thrillme 148.02
thrills 279.F02
thripthongue 477.28
thritytwo 516.17
throat 086.33 180.20 254.29 381.26 425.27 454.11 520.12 598.26 611.08
throat 303.L1
throats 152.24 292.10 317.28
throatyfrogs 394.21
throb 395.17
throbbing 020.02
throbbst 626.05
throes 427.20
throman 378.05
throne 120.28 279.F11 382.26 534.24
throne 277.L3

throng 178.14
thronguards 361.19
thronsaale 551.05
Throsends 478.03
throstles 449.19
throte 374.06
throth 410.36 511.12
throttle 319.03 457.33
throttled 540.15
Throu 565.08
throug 178.27
through through Through Through THROUGH
throughandthoroughly 220.30
throughers 450.26
throughlove 370.04
throughout 020.15 033.30 066.06 121.02 143.09 335.21 532.10
throughsighty 611.32
throust 395.36
throuth 151.22
throw 040.30 091.31 172.19 203.30 226.10 240.19 273.10 341.16 357.05 387.18 388.01 458.32 489.12 495.05 511.23 547.20 612.34
Throw 212.24 214.16
throwen 230.35
thrower 507.32
throwing 304.26 377.24 385.17
Throwing 200.29 424.04
thrown 015.07 033.07 049.17 049.18 172.32 366.04 406.04
thrownfullvner 348.14
throws 050.33 433.21 435.27
Throws 122.13
throw's 357.26
Thrst 497.23
thru' 501.04
Thrubedore 411.29
thrue 483.36
thruely 372.18
thrufahrts 085.09
thruming 381.19
thrummings 041.21
thruppenny 190.19 485.17
thrush 491.26
Thrushday 520.17
thrushes 323.22
Thrushes 223.17
thrushes' 586.26
thrusshed 366.33
thrust 019.07 050.03 155.12 252.04 435.14
Thrust 251.06
Thrust 104.24
thrusty 365.33
thruth 493.24
thruths 288.03
Thrydacianmad 577.01
thrysting 388.06
Thsight 262.L2
thts 302.26
thuartpeatrick 003.10
thubulbs 354.01
thuch 023.24 023.24
thuck 019.06
thuckflues 416.33
thud 363.25
thud 342.14
Thud 221.20 612.36
thudderdown 295.14
thuddysickend 084.32
thuds 598.30
thug 240.12 495.03 618.29
Thug 212.03
Thugg 485.11
Thuggeries 540.31
thuggery 177.35
thugogmagog 222.14
thugs 015.13
thum 213.16
thumb 073.16 227.11 338.29 625.16
thumbed 547.32
thumbnail 452.12
thumbprint 114.31
thumbs 067.05 169.17 282.27 426.28
thumbshow 507.23
thumbtonosery 253.28
thumfool's 019.06
thump 285.06 295.14
thump 352.28
thumping 454.29 612.34
thumpsday 301.21
Thumpsem 155.33
thumpty 550.36
thuncle's 586.31
thund 607.25 607.26
thunder 005.15 052.31 057.15 127.16 152.01 209.12 262.12 294.26 454.22
Thunder 184.06 491.34
Thunder 071.33 175.10
Thunderation 245.26
thunderburst 362.30
thundercloud 246.07
thunder'd 299.12
thundered 506.07
Thundereth 062.14
thundering 095.16 167.22
thunderous 035.31 509.09
thunders 409.29
thundersday 005.13
Thundersday 514.22
thundersheet 503.02
thunderslog 581.16
Thunderweather 464.10
Thundery 194.14
thunk 504.12
thunkhard 049.29
thunkum 422.27
Thunner 565.17
thunpledrum 162.03
Thuoni 499.08
thur 300.30
thurd 314.29
Thurdsday 491.27
thurever 202.12
thurifex 449.15
thurily 465.10
thurkells 091.09
thurkmen 348.21
Thurnston 038.35
thurrible 477.21
Thursitt 541.04
Thursmen's 080.14
thurso 203.33
thurst 319.34 599.06
Thurston's 053.14
thurteen 378.22
thurum 006.05 006.05
thus 031.06 033.11 060.01 061.21 073.23 115.03 123.07 125.05 166.23 190.20 319.07 320.34 321.06 366.13 368.24 370.24 390.27 415.08 426.27 499.02 578.10 604.31 610.14
Thus 014.35 023.14 057.16 058.32 104.05 163.12 262.05 313.29 330.12 406.28 546.23 595.33
thusengaged 351.22
thusly 286.30
thut 337.34
Thuthud 373.15
thuthunder 378.07
thwackaway 434.26
thwackers 561.04
thwacks 019.20
thwaites 331.20
thwarted 188.36
thwarters 145.20
thwealthy 438.24
thwuck 434.26
thy thy Thy Thy
thyacinths 092.16
thylike 427.17
thyme 020.24 430.29 612.07
Thyme 161.28 236.27
Thymes 501.19
thyne 593.04
thynne 584.33
Thyrston's 326.35
thyself 242.32 266.29
ti 147.18 607.17 607.17 607.22 607.22
ti. . 501.05 (time)
tiara 205.33 387.03
Tiara 131.09
Tib 028.05
tibbes 424.29
Tibble's 236.08
Tibbs 117.19
tibby 603.05
Tiberia 424.09
Tiberias 115.11
Tiberiast 123.30
tiberiously 119.16
tibertine's 211.05
tic 009.15 180.22
ticements 239.08
tich 465.29
Tichiami 289.29
tick 119.23 615.29
tick 418.25
Tick 139.29 322.05 517.31
Tickell 386.26
ticker 097.12 559.15
ticket 050.26 424.10
tickets 543.22
Tickets 262.L4
tickey 527.01 538.15
tickeyes 043.09
tickle 050.13 076.28 123.29 180.24 198.12 315.15 319.13 598.14
Tickle 598.14
tickled 145.30 384.31 584.02
tickler 166.29
tickles 021.29
tickleticks 290.07
ticklets 238.02
tickling 417.29
ticklish 468.18
tickly 144.34
tick's 026.15
ticktacking 396.27

tictacs 009.06
tid 628.12
tidal 206.13
tiddle 141.09
tiddywink 023.34
tide 029.21 170.06 244.14 316.17 320.35 365.35 415.19 426.20
tide 103.01
tides 261.05 312.10
Tides 123.26
tidetable 579.24
tidies 459.10
tiding 547.16
tidings 194.23 472.19 483.09 551.15
Tidingtown 202.09 202.10
tidled 297.31
Tids 371.25
tidy 543.22
tie 099.11 213.26 328.09 443.28 458.27 527.02
TIE 305.R1
Tieckle 018.20
tied 434.22 452.16 480.23 577.27
tief 312.01
Tiemore 378.20
tiempor 317.03
Tiens 486.18
tiercely 253.19
Tierney 091.08 091.09
tiers 590.30 590.30
Tiers 590.30
ties 183.19 611.01
tiff 334.15
tiffin 229.26
Tiffpuff 509.28
Tiffsdays 221.06
tifftaff 338.12
Tifftiff 102.28
tig 322.21 351.17
tigara 599.06
tiger 465.36
Tiger 445.13
tigernack 577.02
tigerwood 035.07
Tiggers 246.32
tigh 607.17 607.17
Tighe 369.30 408.23
tight 117.33 176.30 208.23 250.04 296.15 334.16 377.17 431.03 436.24 445.22 455.12 584.32
Tight 462.05
Tight 071.17 106.22
tightening 627.01
tighteousness 005.18
tightly 562.21
tightmark 262.F1
tights 012.23 315.15 366.04 423.02 551.08 589.25
tightsqueezed 462.10
tighttaught 235.23
tighty 223.09 531.23
tigris 202.34
tigtag 364.30
Tik 141.33 376.05
Tikkak 534.03
Tiktak 534.03
til 013.22 312.08 316.36 320.22 326.18 546.15 577.29 596.08
til 104.10 537.10
tilar 202.14
tilburys 554.02
tile 127.06 240.35 415.35
tiler 023.11
tileries 552.14
tiler's 626.09
tilhavet 202.10
till till Till Till TILL
tillalaric 336.12
tillamie 584.31
tillbag 257.19
tillfellthey 370.32
tillgive 434.14
Tillia 160.01
tillicately 525.02
tillies 212.21
Tilling 007.05
tillstead 547.06
tillsteyne 056.14
tilltold 316.01
Tilltop 624.11
tillusk 338.17
tilly 026.03 498.26
Tilly 385.33
tillycramp 556.36
tilt 197.30 290.F2 315.25 462.09 560.14
Tiltass 512.35
tilted 311.01
tilth 024.03
tiltop 420.12 560.12
tiltyard 064.01
Tilvido 409.30
tilyet 191.06
tim 019.27 385.10 481.31
Tim 015.26 331.11 390.13 598.27
Tim 342.03
Timb 139.10
timber 039.13 235.16 575.19 604.28
timberman 080.26
timbers 274.09
timbertar 328.30
timblespoon 038.20
timbrelfill 295.F2
timbreman 414.04
timbuy 561.04
Timcoves 039.14
time 003.09 005.19 010.25 014.07 021.05 021.33 023.24 026.11 028.30 032.21 033.04 033.26 033.36 035.17 035.34 036.09 037.06 039.30 041.21 045.07 049.04 051.16 052.08 063.20 064.22 065.24 068.04 069.35 072.24 075.13 077.12 078.31 079.12 080.06 081.30 081.36 087.12 088.36 091.13 095.35 096.23 101.10 102.05 107.09 109.22 109.31 109.33 112.17 112.18 116.07 118.08 118.23 118.26 121.29 124.11 125.05 125.06 130.36 131.24 134.28 134.29 137.20 141.15 143.05 149.23 151.21 154.16 159.06 161.10 163.21 163.34 167.02 167.20 170.05 170.29 172.11 172.14 172.29 173.11 173.19 177.07 182.06 196.13 197.15 199.15 202.31 203.16 206.25 223.23 224.01 224.34 227.36 232.31 234.14 237.05 238.05 238.18 244.09 244.32 247.23 248.31 250.14 251.09 253.07 254.27 254.27 259.04 264.F3 267.15 267.F5 272.24 274.21 275.F2 277.24 286.17 288.14 289.09 290.01 290.05 290.08 300.10 303.31 307.F5 310.25 327.15 329.10 333.32 334.06 335.25 339.16 343.26 347.01 348.18 350.22 356.16 356.16 358.05 363.01 366.04 370.32 376.26 378.18 379.32 380.14 380.18 384.36 387.30 389.17 390.34 392.08 392.26 393.07 394.07 394.10 397.09 397.36 405.22 407.03 409.07 409.13 411.04 412.15 412.30 415.24 417.08 422.24 423.27 425.08 425.13 427.35 430.08 431.23 431.26 431.35 432.16 438.07 438.24 442.12 443.20 445.14 446.31 448.04 448.32 449.01 449.05 451.08 453.30 453.33 454.29 457.21 460.34 462.31 467.33 468.25 469.12 472.35 473.08 473.13 474.08 475.27 476.32 477.16 477.28 482.24 484.22 484.27 485.32 493.08 503.10 505.10 507.04 507.06 513.03 517.25 517.31 522.34 526.02 526.24 527.06 531.24 540.31 547.12 555.11 558.23 559.17 567.28 570.21 577.20 577.20 579.17 581.29 582.19 583.07 586.22 599.14 603.15 611.09 611.10 615.15 616.17 616.21 620.15 621.10 621.26 621.27 621.32 622.16 626.21 626.24 627.13 627.21
time 073.16 419.08
Time 051.33 088.01 221.17 319.08 546.24 620.15 622.21
Time 176.11 415.15
Timeagen 415.15
timeblinged 612.21
timecoloured 029.20
time-factor 164.34
timefield 475.24
timekiller 247.02
timelag 347.20
timelike 609.02
timemarching 323.31
timentrousnest 241.10
Time-o'-Thay 599.03
timepates 272.23
timeplace 080.13 416.24
timers 327.31
times 012.13 026.09 053.34 065.08 069.03 079.14 092.22 102.11 104.05 117.04 120.12 129.36 145.21 150.01 153.12 155.30 156.02 167.23 185.09 186.29 191.14 193.07 214.08 215.23 225.11 227.10 252.23 263.17 279.F03 284.11 289.F6 292.16 305.10 312.11 353.15 356.27 359.25 361.30 386.07 386.07 386.08 386.08 386.08 387.18 413.11 421.18 426.26 427.04 440.29 445.27 453.01 474.23 481.10 487.13 498.01 500.14 507.23 514.12 518.17

519.07 521.12 526.01 526.01 537.18 555.03 575.01 580.24 584.24 589.25 605.29 605.31 605.32 626.03 626.26
Times 307.11 600.02
Times 275.L3
Time's 455.29
timespiece 052.07
timesported 056.03
timetable 405.10
timetetters 396.27
Timgle 588.23
timid 094.14 258.02 565.12
timidy 252.19
timing 013.31
timkin 328.05
Timm 093.35
timmersome 356.34
Timmotty 379.34
timmtomm 406.17
Timmy 027.01
Timmycan 015.26
timocracy 291.08
timoneer 197.33
Timor 231.10
Timoth 342.05
Timothy 258.35 274.11
Timour 136.21
timpan 206.02
timped 015.26
Timple 244.06
timpul 621.34
Tim's 622.07
Timsons 617.13
timtits 505.01
timtom 463.01
timtomtum 519.10
timus 428.25
tin 012.05 067.13 150.35 197.20 262.29 283.02 321.29 371.04 563.31
Tina-bat-Talur 327.04
Tinbullet 193.21
tincelles 226.04
tinckler's 405.06
tincoverdull 359.12
tinct 244.13
tinctunc 278.L1
tincture 182.09
Tincurs 338.25
tinder 093.26
tinder 347.34
tinders 010.18
Tindertarten 191.21
ting 147.18 294.24 294.25 294.25 294.25 624.31
tingaling 569.12
tinge 474.07
tinged 612.13
tinger 624.31
tingle 439.29
tingled 152.10
tingling 239.08 288.03
tingmount 053.06
Tingsomingenting 414.34 416.27
tingtingtaggle 419.15
tingtumtingling 231.02
tingued 601.31
tink 359.11 532.29
Tinker 202.14
tinkers 151.09 495.01
tinker's 210.06 363.05
tinkle 227.06
tinkledinkledelled 346.26
tinkling 532.28
tinkt 560.14
tinktact 418.34
Tinktink 102.14
tinkyou 009.31
tinned 170.27
tinner 243.16
tinnteack 063.36
tinny 257.09 449.13
tinpanned 082.34
tinpinnypan 466.02
tins 077.08
tin's 433.21
tinsammon 228.36
tinsel 551.09 559.03
tint 244.13 386.01
tintacks 183.20
tintanambulating 497.35
Tintangle 232.21
tintin 235.32
Tintin 235.32
tintingface 563.15
tintingfast 020.08
Tintinued 359.27
tinto 208.13
tints 247.34
tiny 009.05 057.28 114.05 201.21 209.24 395.18 435.04 621.21
Tiny 244.01 304.19
tiomor 342.35
tionnor 242.20
tip 083.30 111.26 239.24 338.26 444.07 444.26 449.24 455.11 531.31
Tip 008.08 008.11 008.15 008.16 008.21 008.36 009.30 010.07 010.11 010.21 079.23 111.30 112.02 113.30 115.01 273.21 303.05 599.23 599.23 599.23
Tipatonguing 584.03
tipbids 101.05
tipherairy 584.31
tipidities 242.17
Tipknock 530.33
tiplady 585.01
tipmast 504.23
tipoo 302.02
tipp 610.07
Tipp 342.30 342.30
tipped 193.20 291.08
Tipped 105.10
Tipperaw 110.36
tippers 027.33 448.23
tippertaps 594.35
tipperuhry 082.03
tippits 172.32
tipple 317.03
Tipple 359.16
tippled 136.18
Tipple's 026.30
tippling 006.08 462.20
tippoty 054.12
Tippoty 054.12
tippy 065.32
tips 053.22 134.09 411.05 570.33
Tipsey 008.29
tipside 205.28
tipstaff 035.27
tipster 039.19
tipsy 194.29
tipsyloon 534.17
tiptapped 138.19
tipting 202.11
tiptip 481.31
Tiptip 079.27
Tiptiptip 079.34
tiptition 561.22
tiptoe 467.31
Tiptop 176.06
Tiptoptap 319.09
tiptoptippy 065.32
tiptupt 277.11
tire 502.32
tired 158.22 386.03 397.09 464.22 578.24 585.35
tireless 407.21
Tiresias 307.L1
tiresome 396.15 396.15 396.16 396.17
tireton 224.27
Tireton 224.27
tirewoman 572.27
tiring 013.08
tirnitys 240.20
tiroirs 511.27
tirra 359.28
Tirry 206.19
Tirtangel 594.04
tis 116.36 116.36 143.18
Tis 287.16 293.23 565.14
'tis 'Tis
Tisdall 468.28
tishy 232.31
Tisn't 202.35
'Tisraely 027.01
tiss 461.30
Tiss 588.35
tissle 465.30
tissue 070.12 144.03 237.04 499.19
tissuepaper 139.02
tissues 590.09
Tista 198.27
tistress 486.20
tisturb 378.20
tit 017.34 017.34
Tit 501.05
titaning 583.17
titelittle 342.16
Titentung 512.11
Titep 237.27
titfortotalled 542.32
tithe 012.19 212.20 410.15 627.14
titheman 057.06
tithes 273.03 574.09
tithing 541.09
tities 527.28
titillation 557.24
Titius 128.15
title 099.18 119.19 137.10 139.29 231.01 290.28 408.12 501.02 575.06
Title 500.13 500.13
titled 165.15 544.20
titleroll 134.09
Titley 607.17
titranicht 555.10
tits 199.07 236.34 528.16
t.i.t.s. 179.32 (that is to say)
Titteretto 435.08
tittering 215.29

TITTERITOT 305.R1
tittertit 225.01
tittery 097.26
titties 272.07
titting 327.22
Tittit 501.02
tittivits 374.04
tittle 036.33 318.09 331.12
tittlebits 416.18
tittlehouse 017.34
tittles 212.34 379.29
tittletell 597.08
tittlies 282.13
tittup 576.27
titty 327.08
Titubante 403.09
titular 432.20
titulars 134.11 222.15
Titus 070.14
Tivel 008.28
Tix 568.13
tixtim 534.17
tizzer 286.22
Tizzy 457.27
tluly 533.06
T. M. 221.27 (T. M. Finnegan)
T.N.T. 077.05 (trinitrotoluene)
to to To To TO
toad 154.02 464.19 506.01
toadcavites 571.36
toadhauntered 293.F2
Toadlebens 339.21
Toaro 136.14
toarsely 150.12
toasc 199.17
toast 164.24 586.36
toasted 362.03
toaster 050.18
toastface 531.08
toastified 382.02
toastingforks 090.11
toastingfourch 408.33
toastmaster 462.02
toastworthy 347.18
tob 344.30 344.30 344.30
Tob 090.03
Tobaccos 435.30
tobaggon 141.11
tobarrow 455.13
tobay 315.32
Tobecontinued's 626.18
tobies 406.25
Tobkids 067.11
toboggan 084.06
Toboggan 369.08
toboggan's 435.30
Tobolosk 162.15
Toboo 225.08
Toborrow 455.12
tobtomtowley 534.18
toburrow 455.13
tobuy 172.06
toby 211.12
toccatootletoo 461.27
Toc H 443.24 (Talbot House)
tocher 520.14 557.10 557.11
tochters 584.32
tocoming 274.14
tocsin 255.07
tod 505.23
Tod 505.23
Tod 261.L1
todas 144.13
todate 294.28 598.23
today 076.23 102.28 107.23
125.21 135.24 169.07 257.01
322.16 472.29 486.27 488.27
570.11 620.12
Today 275.25
Today's 614.21
toddle 236.04
toddler 166.16
toddy 321.24 619.33
todie 060.28 408.22
todie 381.23
todo 095.05 257.01
todos 598.02
tods 283.14
todue 381.23 381.24
toe 020.34 075.17 226.21
226.21 379.34 485.09 562.09
Toe 421.09 469.27
tóecap 518.09
toed 181.03
toeing 317.18
Toemaas 101.09
toenail 085.02
toes 151.21 169.19 180.26
234.12
toe's 468.26
Toesforhim 246.34
toesis 415.12
toethpicks 025.16
toetippit 207.34
toewards 120.22
tofatufa 606.36
toff 315.32 346.35
toffee 127.24
Toffeelips 441.12
Toffee's 534.21
Toffeethief 010.01
toffette 413.19
Toffey 249.29
toffiness 338.12
Toffler 606.29
toffs 011.25 440.30
toff's 536.14
tofftoff 065.31
Toft 277.11
tofts 331.21
tog 220.14 311.33
toga 242.25
Toga 112.30
togather 453.16
togatherthem 015.02
Togatogtug 351.17
togery 277.F2
together 028.07 032.25 092.35
112.23 124.26 169.09 181.29
188.23 244.32 279.F08 329.15
348.21 361.04 375.36 384.09
434.22 435.34 436.25 438.01
465.15 470.08 475.18 492.26
495.17 517.14 557.05 611.15
Together 044.14
togethered 396.24
togethergush 581.27
togethering 601.31
togged 240.35
togglejoints 199.22
togive 560.34
toglieresti 307.F7
togodder 155.27
toground 332.12
togs 520.21
togutter 332.12 517.14
toh 014.30
tohp 593.24
toil 282.02 354.36 448.21
599.30
toiled 324.05
toileries 348.22
toilermaster 613.32
toilers 325.24
toilet 395.10 395.16
toilettes 191.26
toiling 199.02
toils 245.01 539.34
Tok 141.30
tokay 172.24
Tokaya 471.03
toke 157.24
token 037.06 219.06 313.24
487.36 541.12 586.27 608.26
token 419.02
tokens 315.06
tokens 354.21
Tolan 601.34
Tolbris 545.20 545.21 545.21
told 005.29 018.19 029.01
030.12 035.32 052.13 059.27
094.05 117.12 145.14 149.13
149.25 179.05 213.11 215.35
227.08 229.36 263.23 275.F5
283.30 287.03 313.10 336.14
347.20 358.18 363.21 426.22
467.03 468.28 476.15 478.08
479.22 491.12 504.12 510.20
515.26 519.30 519.34 539.13
563.09 572.27 587.34 621.26
623.27
Told 466.11
tolder 317.07
toldteld 597.08
tole 117.31
Tolearis 255.15
Toler 127.07 326.01
tolerably 516.08
tolerant 163.15
toleration 557.27
tolfoklokken 353.15
tolk 317.07 332.10
Tolka 528.13
Tolka 201.18
Tolkaheim 052.09
tolkan 599.09
tolkar 503.17
tolkatiff 016.06
tolkies 541.18
tolkshap 499.21
toll 004.08 004.08 007.05
024.02 (o' toll)
127.01 132.14 266.05 334.07
427.23
Toll 052.25 221.29
tollacre 567.35
Tollacre 567.34
tolled 275.24
toller 035.32 082.04 121.36
372.03
tollerday 016.05
tollerloon 320.09
Tollertone 512.11
tollgate 044.06
tolling 403.22
tolloll 065.17
Tolloll 525.05
Tollollall 547.11
tolls 388.14

toloseher 279.F09
Tolv 403.02
tolvmaans 549.10
tolvtubular 309.14
tom 172.28 284.15 338.26 363.12 385.10 579.17
tom 525.24
Tom 027.01 039.16 039.28 057.24 094.02 142.28 212.02 258.36 390.13 436.11 588.23 597.30
Tomach's 053.31
tomahawks 505.01
toman 034.31
to-maronite's 470.14
tomarry 324.33
Tomar's 068.31
tomashunders 229.21
tomaster 279.F09
tomate 423.30
Tomatoes 285.F6
tomauranna 102.28
Tomazeus 504.19
tomb 020.03 246.09 329.23 343.04 597.06
tomb 346.16
Tomb 139.10 572.02
tombaldoom 258.21
tombaut 280.L4
tombed 017.29
Tombigby 210.15
tombing 026.23
tombles 005.03
tombours 510.19
tombs 503.26
Tombs 329.22
tombshape 265.03
tombstone 113.34 392.24
tombucky 234.32
Tombuys 358.33
tome 014.29 191.21 325.34
Tome 439.35
tomeadow 315.33
tomellow 060.29
Tomes 155.22
tomestone 253.34
tomiatskuns 350.26
tomirror 408.19
tomiss 279.F09
tomkeys 347.10
tomkin 326.30
Tomkins 067.24
Tomley 265.F5
Tommany 106.08
tommelise 244.30
Tommeylommey's 093.03
tommix 058.24
tommuck 344.35
Tommy 331.12 481.32 526.08
Tommy 071.35
tomollow 565.21
Tomorrha's 141.35
tomorrow 042.02 205.03 275.25 304.15 305.32 309.15 374.04 486.27 488.27 567.16 570.12 573.24 575.28 579.19 587.13 611.12 611.25
tomorrowmorn 558.17
tomorrows 280.06
tomorrow's 614.21
tomorry 408.22
tomory 172.24
Tomothy 617.12
tompip 178.27
tompull 290.03
toms 196.22
tom's 584.07
Tomsky 509.05
tomtartarum 317.04
tomthick 291.07
tomthumb 412.06
Tomtinker 342.03
tomtittot 260.02
tomtompions 151.18
tomtummy's 019.04
ton 035.31 126.17 278.19
Tonans 504.19
tonay 102.28
tondo 247.09
tondur 332.21
tone 090.01 166.08 200.13 365.11 454.27 552.08
Tone 572.15
tonearts 560.34
tonedeafs 522.28
tonehall 165.09
tones 012.30 031.09
tong 177.05
tonging 519.16
tongs 286.23 392.29
tongser's 442.03
tongue 015.18 036.32 068.32 083.16 087.32 089.25 122.33 127.29 138.20 146.28 152.11 169.16 180.19 227.07 248.20 270.18 288.07 361.07 381.32 385.17 406.13 425.27 440.28 444.23 457.32 467.14 479.03 489.23 499.21 518.09
Tongue 206.25
tongueopener 345.27
tonguer 536.08
tongues 054.06 083.11 281.16 292.17 315.04
tongues 340.04
tonguesed 381.20
tonguespitz 569.01
Toni 323.32
tonic 193.09
tonigh 126.02
tonight 202.35 425.27 570.08 618.06
tonights 320.16
Tonnerre 009.23
tonnerwatter 368.07
Tonnoburkes 106.06
tonnowatters 070.09
tonobloom 564.23
tonobrass 609.28
tons 408.06 451.21 459.34
Tons 266.07
tonsils 459.09
tonsor's 234.11
tonsure 043.12
tont 378.21
tonuant 035.31
tonuout 258.04
tony 006.07 435.04
too too Too
tooath 015.05
toobally 305.14
Toobiassed 580.08
Toobliqueme 445.34
tooblue 328.09
toock 423.10
toockled 363.18
toodooing 050.08
toofarback 004.19
toogasser 232.04
took 022.08 026.32 046.02 059.22 059.26 060.34 061.33 062.23 068.04 079.01 090.03 093.10 110.21 114.01 128.26 132.34 133.09 134.15 153.04 170.22 180.28 193.19 213.16 245.26 246.28 283.24 290.F6 305.17 316.08 327.27 331.27 338.29 347.23 352.07 379.32 380.25 416.27 416.28 416.28 423.12 429.10 438.24 480.25 491.12 493.01 504.10 504.10 515.25 549.27 556.03 589.03 604.28 617.05
tooken 484.17
tool 035.16 201.27
toole 024.01 (a' toole)
Toole 468.28
Toolers 617.13
Toole's 405.24
tooletom 496.20
Tooley 053.29 529.16
tools 544.11 572.02
toolth 311.34
toombs 532.28
toomcracks 011.04
toomellow 346.12
Toomey 526.08
toomourn 011.14
toomuch 388.14
toomuchness 122.36
toon 117.32
toone 486.06
to-one 189.24
toonigh 011.13
toooldaisymen 524.11
toop 396.18
toork 359.02
toos 068.17
toosammenstucked 036.10
toosday 617.21
toot 457.21 457.22 457.22 490.26
Toot 490.26 490.26 512.34
tootal 006.28
toot-a-toot 147.03
tooth 066.02 101.34 183.36 247.17 353.09 456.04 506.25 534.08 541.20 571.35
toothbrush 443.25
Toothbrush 176.16
toothick 233.01
toothmick 005.19
toothsake 300.13
toothsome 183.30 227.35
tootle 253.17
tootlepick 410.24
tootlers 510.18 (o' tootlers)
tootling 433.17
tootoo 238.17 427.28
Tootoo 485.35
tootoological 468.08
tootorribleday 381.24
tootpettypout 268.13
tootrue 355.21
toots 225.02
Toot's 331.33
tootwoly 396.34
tootyfay 384.30
toowards 078.31

toowhoom 613.04
top 010.20 022.15 047.02 081.16 082.03 094.05 131.17 163.18 163.21 222.23 248.11 296.18 314.17 322.03 338.26 380.21 397.11 417.06 423.24 510.07 530.35 531.30 594.18 609.25 615.20
Top 240.35 303.13 370.16 410.35 595.18
topaia 595.26
topantically 034.02
topazolites 549.17
topcoated 448.07
tope 615.01
Tope 020.13
toped 083.29
topee 030.23
topers 322.27 386.04 549.05
toper's 381.11
Toper's 004.27
topes 136.18
Tophat 513.10
topheavy 335.35
topheetuck 225.09
Tophet 108.26
tophole 220.13 451.09
topical 599.23
topiocal 275.08
topkats 347.30
toplots 333.36
topmast 351.15
topmorning 041.14
topnoted 439.19
topper 220.26
topperairy 131.05
Topphole 342.31
topping 053.22 405.21 444.07
toppingshaun 558.23
toppitt 039.13
topple 068.18 321.29
toppled 136.19 471.10
topplefouls 120.31
topples 068.17
toppling 484.09
tops 476.34
topsawyer's 003.07
topsawys 374.34
topside 311.26 355.29 611.04 611.27
Topside 485.31
topsirturvy 275.14
Topsman 167.18
topsowyer 299.28
topsquall 180.05
Toptic 419.25
toptip 313.26 321.34
toptypsical 020.15
tora 603.34
Toragh 029.17
toran 245.10
toray 151.24
Torba's 125.09
torc 529.33
torch 244.04
torchbearing 221.07
torched 319.11
torchlight 145.36
torchlit 178.14
torchpriest 080.26
tore 094.06 132.21 372.25
torgantruce 083.35
Torkenwhite 374.06
tormentors 579.03
torn 054.35 058.07 085.35 158.35 286.10 307.F5 458.01
tornaments 227.21
toroidal 331.23
torpentine 478.13
torpid 530.24
torporature 597.32
Torquells 493.20
torquinions 467.35
Torrenation 366.27
torrific 396.34
torrifried 060.21
torroar 057.08
tors 519.22 541.06
torse 165.18 607.33
Torsker 106.05
torskmester 271.04
torso 291.15
Torsos 106.01
Torstaj 325.10
Tortoiseshell 479.04
Tortor 105.25
torts 241.07
tortuours 548.30
Tortur 136.21
tortures 557.31
tory 042.28 087.26 143.12
Tory 359.26
Tory 105.26 175.25
Tory's 024.31
torytale 020.23
to's 244.20
tosdays 408.19
tosend 070.08 230.13
tosh 419.32
Tosh 060.22
Toshowus 057.20
toside 010.35
tosorrow 563.37
tospite 086.23
toss 051.35 130.15 202.06 444.10 584.07
Toss 379.12
tossed 122.10 157.32 417.05 526.33
tossed 399.20
tosser 485.10
Tosser 027.01
tosset 563.12
Tossforhim 246.35
tossing 040.25 431.36 471.23
Tossmania 416.30
tosspot 221.13
tossup 466.03
tosty 603.06
tot 091.28 114.05 129.28 236.34 333.27 444.10 542.14
Tot 232.15
total 058.12
totalage 343.16
totalisating 029.33
totality 079.12
Totalled 597.08
totalling 497.08
totam 397.32
totamulier 166.26
totchty 284.17
totem 480.31
Totem 481.04
totems 086.23
toten 389.33
totether 413.27
tother 143.19
tother's 570.13
tothink 056.31
toth's 570.13
totients 281.19
Toties 098.34
Totities 013.24
Totius 385.14
toto 150.18 537.17
totomptation 362.04
totouches 594.21
tots 039.33 075.03
totstittywinktosser 359.12
totter 251.11
tottered 354.09
totterer 290.16
totters 180.26
totties 272.07
Totties 105.34
tottinghim 284.F2
totty 365.12
Totty 125.11 327.07
Totty 281.L2
tottydean 413.10
totum 287.25
Totumcalmum 026.18
Totumvir 585.24
tou 358.22
touch 022.16 115.09 138.36 182.06 191.35 226.05 233.10 239.24 290.25 301.25 327.10 375.30 397.20 435.18 441.14 444.07 447.06 455.16 463.33 472.08 517.22 532.22 562.21
touch 355.05
Touch 441.22 507.13
touchant 359.15
Toucheaterre 019.14
touched 054.30 237.28
touched 350.01
toucher 056.10 242.18 251.29
Toucher 506.28 507.33
touches 273.13
touchin 039.24 072.22
touching 034.24 042.03 052.36 119.13 172.32 351.21 432.27 446.04 463.24 478.07 484.12 524.03 524.11
Touching 587.25
touchline 398.09
touchman 327.23
Touchole 008.26
toucht 090.15
touchwood 332.12
touchy 037.05
touf 446.18 446.18
tough 202.30 225.21 279.F34 337.35
Tough 249.29
Toughertrees 022.24
toughnecks 169.02
toughs 272.07
Toughtough 468.08
toughts 342.03
toughturf 145.07
toulong 531.18
touloosies 531.18
Toumaria 228.34
Toumbalo 347.26
toun 540.26 577.29
Toun 481.14
tour 335.29 409.31 523.32 578.33 580.17

tour 353.34
Tourable 132.18
tourabout 142.10
touraloup 108.27
tourch 027.13
tourers 032.29
touring 609.01
tourist 076.35
Tourlemonde 021.27
tourments 230.13
Tournay 087.08
tourned 116.14
tournedos 416.34
tournesoled 236.35
tourneyold 383.23
tournintaxes 005.32
tourrible 344.13
tourtoun 227.35
tous 370.24
Toussaint's 455.05
tout 129.06 327.16 327.16
369.13
tout 081.28
touters 351.34
toutes 237.36
touthena 602.30
touting 453.16
Toutou 449.10
Tout's 419.02
tout-tait 528.14
tow 026.15 317.20 494.18
551.22 623.13
toward 042.35 292.02 357.28
566.24
towards 031.16 032.34 036.18
056.12 098.20 135.11 146.31
268.25 307.14 321.12 324.25
326.15 442.23 448.04 483.31
504.14 551.20 575.31 598.24
605.28
towards 338.06 340.05 343.02
352.19
towawd 523.04
towel 389.35 534.27
towelhat 584.15
towelling 291.25
tower 077.10 264.30 380.16
466.33 566.20
Tower 450.16 464.32 467.16
481.36 534.35
towerable 224.12
towerds 313.34
towerettes 077.19
towers 127.15 354.27
towertop 087.29
towhead 040.25
Towhere 224.08
towhorse 137.28
town 023.35 027.19 056.35
063.18 065.18 076.16 084.35
132.26 139.07 172.05 191.26
214.29 224.07 295.17 298.F3
356.35 372.02 411.24 427.03
443.21 447.30 508.27 570.08
Town 071.23
towned 569.19
towney's 586.28
townland 015.02
townlands 496.08
townmajor 442.06
towns 138.05 448.12
town's 516.04
townsends 283.15
township 137.22
township's 075.12 095.12
townside 356.34
townsmen 540.26
Towntoquest 279.08
towooerds 237.01
Towy 215.11
toxis 304.17
toy 404.26 548.31 628.09
toyast 184.31
toying 392.09
toyler 311.06
toyms 602.36
tra 051.17
Trabezond 165.22
trace 034.36 230.36 272.20
traced 080.12 114.08
tracemarks 127.34
tracers 129.22
traces 203.03 510.23
tracing 107.10
track 028.29 203.04 437.16
Track 471.27
tracked 404.18
tracking 600.12
tracks 026.16
tractive 234.16
trade 012.30 047.20 076.35
130.33 316.29 330.04 537.13
tradefully 538.03
trademark 108.22
trader 198.06 331.24
Trader 072.09
Trader's 387.35
tradertory 132.19
tradesmanmarked 547.33
tradesmen 545.01
tradesmen's 134.29
tradewinds 095.03
trading 317.08
tradition 474.04 510.22
TRADITION 268.R1
traditional 094.26 388.22
traduced 283.06
Traduced 275.F6
traemen 551.13
traffic 448.08
tragedoes 343.22
tragic 171.15
tragoady 005.13
traidor 378.05
trail 037.12 119.14 234.16
244.23 447.34
trailed 208.26 552.17
trailers 304.16
trailing 093.03 227.12 323.15
475.25 479.21
trailmost 052.20
train 102.09 604.14
Train 105.09
trained 247.33
trainer's 583.25
traines 513.26
trainful 497.08
training 322.19
Trainity 315.02
trainsfolk 537.19
traipsing 476.03
trait 114.32
Traitey 440.02
traitor 569.36
Traitor 117.02
Traitor's 471.27
traits 107.29
Traits 105.26
tram 447.32
tramaline 040.30
tramestrack 081.07
tramity 327.08
tramp 093.30 142.11 340.23
trampatrampatramp 613.02
tramped 404.18
trample 433.13
Trampleasure 609.11
tramplers 567.18
trampthickets 428.26
trams 595.13
tramsitus 415.04
tramsported 452.14
tramtokens 194.31
tramtrees 005.31
trancedone 374.03
trancefixureashone 613.09
Trancenania 531.34
trancepearances 548.25
tranched 569.27
trancitive 594.03
trancoped 043.22
Tranquilla 569.14
Tranquille 244.28
transaccidentated 186.03
transcripped 617.23
Transformation 222.17
transformed 349.06
transfusiasm 425.15
transfusion 252.19
transgression 189.03
transhibernian 055.20
transhipt 111.09
transit 448.09
translace 233.09
Translate 573.33
translated 606.03
translatentic 311.21
translation 152.12
Translout 281.F2
transluding 419.24
transmaried 050.11
transmitted 604.30 614.36
Transname 145.21
Transocean 100.01
transom 100.23
transparent 434.22
transparents 230.33
transparingly 063.09
transpiciously 173.02
transpires 049.12
Transports' 066.08
Transton 393.31
transtuled 050.17
transubstantiation 557.29
trap 065.34 210.21 332.02
544.10
trapadour 224.25
trappaza 257.04
trapper 088.17
trapping 083.02
traps 027.33
Traroe 405.20
trars 065.20
trash 046.06 420.03
trashold 228.30
traublers 354.29
traumaturgid 496.24
Traumcondraws 420.33
traums 081.16

traumscrapt 623.36
travail 190.21
travailled 137.16
travaillings 344.34
travalled 569.19
travel 469.10 620.13
traveller 156.30
Traveller 056.20
travellers 584.31
travellers' 433.17
travelling 118.23 476.12
Travelling 307.10
travellingself 358.13
travels 173.03 544.31
Travener's 054.22
traverse 492.14 540.05
traversé 281.11
traverses 349.15
traversing 474.22
trawlers 382.21
tray 403.04
trayful 430.24
traylogged 608.23
tr'c'stle 018.06
tre 134.09
treachers 075.07
treacla 568.33
treacle 048.04 474.10
Treacle 039.16 039.28 212.02
treacling 419.15
treacly 544.25
Treaclyshortcake 379.04
tread 145.13 280.29 473.11 602.31
tread 383.12
treading 584.18
treadmill 494.24
treadspath 594.27
Treamplasurin 370.18
treasauro 462.22
treason 581.32
treasure 024.33 146.32 278.17 430.15 440.34
treasures 454.04
treasuried 146.27
treasuring 172.29
treat 032.26 178.19 317.08 424.07 507.29 521.20
treated 174.24 618.20
treatment 232.07 429.07
treats 092.22
treattening 361.10
treatyng 083.36
treble 474.10 589.06
Treble 490.20
trebly 267.17
Tredcastles 414.04
tree 031.31 135.05 137.27 152.02 194.15 259.01 259.01 259.01 259.01 259.01 271.28 340.08 376.07 430.04 469.17 503.30 505.27 522.17 535.31 535.32 556.19 564.21 588.35 607.06
tree 350.02
Tree 063.23 221.31
Tree 106.36
treebark 279.01
treeblock 080.30
treecoloured 339.12
treed 230.35
treefellers 420.08 506.16
treegrown 252.18
treeing 368.15
treeleaves 427.02
Treely 090.31
treemanangel 505.33
treen 587.02
treepartied 087.35
treepes 243.24
treepurty 012.24
treerack 227.20
trees 103.10 136.34 235.16 259.01 361.02 505.16 505.16 571.06 588.29 588.32
Trees 030.01
tree's 381.02
treeshade 058.21
treeskooner 332.02
Treestam 104.10
treestem 424.28
treestirm 621.36
Treestone 113.19
treeth 044.09 505.19
Treetown 266.03
treetrene 230.26
trefling 478.25
trefoils 599.07
trefoll 526.22
trein 077.35
trek 478.14
trekant 559.27
trektalk 172.30
trelawney 091.18
Trem 588.32
trema 601.28
tremble 148.34 565.06
trembles 565.11
trembling 549.08
tremblingly 035.17
tremblotting 565.09
trembly 232.33
trembold 588.33
tremendous 430.21
tremors 188.23
tremours 194.14
tremylose 185.28
tren 172.01
trench 529.27
trencher 602.36
trend 614.21
trenned 486.27
trent 200.34 327.09
trentene 092.12
trepas 499.05
treple 465.23
tresdobremient 348.03
trespass 087.21 532.19 587.30
trespassers 128.34
trespasses 587.28 615.36
trespassing 059.35 081.02 160.36 270.F3 439.02
tress 183.29 480.04
tresses 199.36 241.14
Tresses 102.32
trestles 560.12
trestraversed 416.31
Trestrine 279.F24
treu 050.19
treubleu 076.32
treuson 575.34
Trevi's 192.12
trews 320.26
trewsershins 507.14
trey 350.24
T. R. H. 539.32 (Their Royal Highnesses)
Tri 100.06 308.07
triad 052.13
triagonal 297.24
trial 242.14 558.26 606.25
trianforan 123.24
triangle 278.L1
triangular 019.13
triat 357.03
tribal 132.32
tribalbalbutience 309.02
tribe 240.12
tribes 093.36 552.14 563.13
tribluts 385.14
triboos 011.02
tribunal 093.03
tribunals 057.33
tribune 053.20
Tribune 375.24
tribune's 198.33 313.23
tribute 042.14 133.28 277.24 313.23 364.22 541.10
tributes 497.28
Tricarême 184.32
Trichepatte 228.06
triching 436.05
trick 330.04 376.31 476.17 538.34
trickkikant 297.09
trickle 096.15 096.15 096.15 172.27 204.23 327.14
trickled 319.31
tricklesome 295.30
tricklies 126.14
Trickpat 487.23
tricks 046.06 060.19 283.04 361.02 627.18
Tricks 398.18
Tricks 282.L1
tricksome 589.02
Trickspissers 503.29
tricky 007.03
tricolour 503.24
tricoloured 054.31
tricuspidal 273.28
tridont 547.22
triduum 097.33 517.35
tried 035.06 057.36 087.09 157.19 157.20 157.31 275.21 316.22 374.19 511.33 557.15 579.35
Tried 378.12 420.21
Tried 107.05
triel 238.31
tries 026.01 082.15 128.25 183.14
trieste 301.16 301.16
trieved 094.07
trifid 281.16
trifle 109.25 120.18 223.22 318.08 441.34
trifles 463.35
triflets 341.34
trifling 086.18
trifoaled 485.24
trifoliorum 326.08
trifolium 425.20
triforium 326.08
trifulgurayous 422.30
trifum 326.07
trig 311.19
triga 469.34

trigamies 300.26
trigemelimen 271.13
trigger 468.15
triggity 352.28
trightyright 419.02
t'rigolect 234.26
trihump 022.28
trike 108.05
trilbits 285.F1
trilibies 548.29
trilingual 099.34
triliteral 505.04
trilithon 119.17
trilled 250.01
trillion 120.12
trillitter 286.22
trills 202.01
trillt 189.23
trilustriously 483.22
trim 120.03 408.09 557.09
trimmed 600.23
trimming 327.08
trimmings 376.07
Trina 212.12
Trinathan 478.26
trine 546.17
tringers 349.01
trinidads 492.30
trinies 513.26
trinitarian 388.36
Trinitatis 240.10
trinity 014.34 135.12 180.09 215.26 389.04 548.12
Trinity 257.12 326.04 386.22 467.30
trink 016.30 321.29
Trink 345.24
trinkettoes 215.13
trio 042.01 169.14
Triom 013.26
Trion 105.33
Trionfante 305.15
trip 009.29 009.30 027.33 210.20 226.19 332.01 428.27 443.33
Trip 440.21
tripartite 486.28
tripe 480.22
tripeness 612.17
tripenniferry 485.02
triperforator 303.22
tripertight 465.14
tripes 265.L2
Tripier 167.26
tripiezite 086.02
triple 128.22 205.33 595.25
Triple 486.04
triplehydrad 036.07
triplepatlockt 069.25
triplescreen 137.26
triplets 530.06
triplewon 008.15
tripods 286.24
tripos 452.10
tripped 117.16 159.16 236.22 301.F3
trippertrice 312.20
trippetytrappety 332.15
trippiery 020.33
tripping 205.04 315.14 499.05 578.17
trippings 453.25
trippiza 257.04
Tripple 106.33
trippudiating 513.22
trippy 009.29
triptych 486.32
triptychal 031.22
tripulations 094.13
tripupcables 077.09
triput 387.34
tris 278.25
tris 499.30
Tris 022.29
Tris 499.30
triscastellated 551.31
trisexnone 331.15
trishagion 605.14
Trishagion 305.L2
Trisolanisans 384.32
triss 096.15
Triss 467.07 588.29
trissed 550.01
Trisseme 353.02
trisspass 363.26
trist 230.13 299.01
Tristan 159.32 398.29
tristar 288.22
triste 571.14
tristended 169.20
tristian 022.17
tristich 481.10
tristiest 234.03
tristinguish 066.29
Tristior 158.01
Tristis 158.01
Tristissimus 158.01
tristitiae 185.20
tristitone 092.07
Tristopher 021.12 021.21
Tristram 003.04 211.26
Trists 513.26
tristurned 100.28
tristy 521.22
tristys 449.07
Tristy's 383.11
trit 158.14
tritan 547.23
trite 120.03
Trite 061.27
tritons 531.30
Tritonville 203.13 585.02
tritt 337.19
triump 244.35 281.F1
triumph 066.28 433.08
Triumphanes 153.29
triumphant 493.31 593.24
Triumphants' 066.09
triumphs 549.32
triumphs 342.22
triune 422.26 605.14
triv 306.12
trivets 117.34
Trivett 377.17
trivials 581.23
triweekly 099.34
Trix 147.14
trixiestrail 578.17
triz 412.10
troad 389.24
trochees 007.03
trod 408.08
Troia 448.11
Troia 086.29
Trojan 381.31
trokes 598.30
Trolldedroll 324.01
trolled 383.17
trolling 454.13
trollop 409.06
trolls 531.30
trolly 129.02 606.18
trombsathletic 319.26
trompateers 553.36
trompe 023.26 224.20
trompes 023.27
tronf 136.32
trons 148.22
troop 273.25
troopers 510.05
troopertwos 588.18
trooping 329.28 360.20
troopsers 319.22
trootabout 113.12
trooth 107.16
Trop 169.05
tropadores 288.02
trope 410.05
tropeful 466.10
trophies 262.24 450.14
tropic 026.12 568.29
tropical 073.15 426.23
Tropical 211.29
troping 237.02
tropped 034.06
troppers 510.04
Troppler 048.15
tropps 484.04
trosstpassers 345.28
trost 454.03
troster 050.19
trot 200.17 279.F20 456.01 583.11 583.12 594.34
Trot 440.17
troterella 059.36
troth 015.23 135.11 214.06 229.09 279.F34 325.08 351.30 453.28 473.13
TROTHBLOWERS 303.R2
Trothed 486.27
trots 318.09
trotsy 208.30
trotters 445.05 553.29
trotthers 319.29
trotting 144.24
trotty 141.01
trou 510.20
troubadouring 173.04
troublant 005.07
trouble 033.31 134.04 134.07 214.10 220.28 233.15 425.08 425.33 441.30 444.10 450.22 458.29 459.16 616.35 617.05 620.13
trouble 267.L2 267.L2
Trouble 267.L2
troublebedded 245.30
troubled 546.17
troubles 138.02 453.13 627.14
Troubles 294.19
troubleth 057.06
troublin 201.19
troublous 581.01
trouchorous 148.19
trou-de-dentelle 265.L1
trouders 311.29
trough 253.21
Trough 104.07
troup 250.30

troupe 049.20
troupkers 350.26
trousend 268.26
trousers 061.25 065.21 177.07 491.35 544.24 559.08
trousers 383.06
trousertree 521.07
trousseau 065.15
trousseaurs 144.22
trout 028.04 079.08 239.08 449.33 495.09 621.12
troutbeck 076.26 578.21
trouters 126.13
trouth 410.11 459.23
troutlet 170.28
troutling 007.21
trouts 569.26
Trouvas 370.08
trouvay 478.21
trouved 110.33 201.01
trouveller 286.F2
trouz 413.29
Trovatarovitch 341.09
trovatellas 366.23
trovatore 301.17
trove 430.15
trover 471.14
trow 061.33 226.14 480.02 567.21 603.11
trowed 362.06
trowel 004.30
trowelling 572.05
trowers 598.03
trowlers 447.19
trowswers 085.35
troy 225.04
troykakyls 567.34
Troysirs 011.36
truant 042.32 277.17
truants 505.06
Truants 255.28
truanttrulls 552.10
truath 015.25
truce 011.15 122.09 336.19 336.19 336.19 337.10 501.12 588.19
truce 349.16
trucers 587.18
truck 358.10 598.30
Truckeys' 282.L2
trudged 606.18
trudgers 375.34
trudging 202.28
true 004.10 012.15 035.01 040.30 047.28 061.32 068.13 081.15 085.35 091.26 093.17 096.27 115.08 124.06 125.17 145.18 159.36 165.07 166.01 172.18 178.34 187.33 190.20 193.26 209.17 224.02 232.04 240.35 247.13 264.31 310.28 352.11 355.34 356.03 370.04 396.10 417.24 431.20 434.20 442.10 450.24 459.19 465.18 472.21 473.03 473.06 490.10 490.16 498.25 500.25 503.20 505.25 505.26 521.16 523.10 535.28 557.14 565.07 567.08 576.19 587.19 590.08 590.20 602.31 605.09 611.21 617.07
true 418.30
True 019.31 146.04 242.21 500.25 501.04 570.14 570.14
True 107.02
trueart 199.19
trueblues 542.03
truefalluses 506.18
truemen 553.32
trueprattight 265.09
trues 127.03 611.22
true's 478.25
truesirs 324.19
truesome 560.35
truest 109.15 328.08
true'tis 152.02
truetoflesh 481.30
truetoned 063.20
true-to-type 139.29
truetotypes 454.13
truetowife 011.29
trueveres 289.27
truffles 174.34
truh 378.06
truies 088.12
Truiga 074.09
trulley 498.06 577.14
trullopes 520.25
trulls 134.33
trulock 340.07
truly 032.25 041.31 061.05 076.05 081.19 138.08 165.18 326.15 359.01 386.14 429.09 452.05 457.19 461.36 489.26 490.30 621.17
Truly 224.10 517.01
Trulytruly 517.21
trumble 341.09
trumblers 283.13
trumbly 583.31
trump 286.13 476.17 528.35
trumpadour 439.09
trumpered 584.01
trumpers 251.33
trumpery 046.06
trumpet 068.24 470.28
trumpeted 261.06
trumpeting 093.30
Trumpets 622.06
trumple 016.27
trumps 122.18
trunchein 530.19
trundler 255.10
trundletrikes 284.24
trundling 583.25
trunk 373.17 601.32
trunkles 296.27
trunks 068.09 315.15 389.18 544.32
trunk's 299.18
trunktarge 325.29
trurally 357.34
truss 226.18 315.16 433.34
trust 027.31 112.14 235.14 270.F3 363.24 379.27 447.32 459.31 487.05 550.33 602.30
Trust 228.20 460.14 530.29
Trustan 383.18
trusted 232.08
trustee 574.07 574.08 574.12 575.29
trusthee 574.24
trustin 394.24
trusting 038.20
trusty 037.12 574.21
trustyman 480.03
truth 027.02 036.33 061.35 096.27 120.04 169.08 174.12 293.02 318.23 355.36 368.26 391.35 452.04 490.16 521.05 539.15 556.16 614.21
Truth 033.32
Truth 305.L1
truthbosh 348.32
truthful 113.18 424.14
truthfully 083.25 411.14 452.06
truths 160.24 396.31
Truths 107.04
trutted 584.01
trwth 132.05
try 067.09 177.24 188.32 225.33 247.34 255.17 291.21 361.09 367.12 435.19 436.29 456.12 456.15 456.29 465.29 467.21 517.17
Try 285.F5 627.07
Try 105.09
trying 006.14 040.33 063.32 065.19 081.34 086.04 110.36 150.09 172.34 181.01 283.31 288.07 291.22 296.13 372.35 372.36 373.01 373.03 373.05 434.09 443.30 487.07 487.11 530.26
tryomphal 590.10
tryon 179.33 320.18 422.26 590.09
tryone 422.26
tryonforit 271.05
tryracy 348.27
tryst 119.30 226.14 486.07 491.12 571.18
tryst 486.04
trystfully 317.36
trysting 146.07 189.05 290.02 571.10
tsay-fong 325.14
tschaina 243.15
tschemes 288.02
Tschitt 499.09
tse 423.04 423.04
tsei-foun 325.14
tseu 322.12
tsifengtse 299.26
tsin 057.03 057.03 057.04
Tsin 057.03
tsing 485.28
Tsing 485.28
tsingirillies' 351.12
tsinglontseng 611.30
tsmell 344.26
tso 124.07
tsukisaki 233.34
T. T. 369.11 (Mr T. T. Erchdeakin) 432.06
ttittshe 469.01
ttoo 113.15
ttou 565.06
ttrinch 009.19
ttt 515.05 515.06
tu 461.30
tu 104.11 155.17 155.30 291.24
Tu 407.15
tuae 412.09
tuam 589.07
Tuam 141.02
Tuami 211.10

Tuan 346.28
Tuatha 381.06
tub 004.22 162.15 212.21 262.F3 378.26
tuba 412.08
tubalence 338.17
tubas 327.16
tubatubtub 290.21
tubb 048.17 354.36
tubbathaltar 606.02
Tubber 438.13
tubberbunnies 430.36
Tubbernacul 584.31
tubbernuckles 507.11
tubble 334.06
tubbloids 219.18
Tubbournigglers 244.06
tube 082.19 319.13 535.26
tubenny 041.20
tuberclerosies 541.36
tubes 302.F3 396.16
Tubetube 407.22
tublin 335.28
tubote 066.30
tubous 613.36
tubshead 439.10
tubsuit 188.29
tubtail 333.23
tubthumper 108.17
tubtime 562.07
tubular 084.02 463.17
tuck 004.29 109.11 130.14 407.02 441.32 603.14
Tuck 196.08 565.36 585.31 614.14
tucked 083.30 168.10 315.26
tucker 568.18
tucking 332.34
tuckish 530.36
tuckt 624.17
tucsada 518.25
Tucurlugh 479.06
tud 423.04
Tudor 307.14 498.02
Tuesday 520.03
Tuesy 388.04
tuff 291.24 291.24
Tuff 349.07
tuffbettle 369.01
tufnut 624.17
tuft 099.11 234.12 559.28
tuft 342.27
tufted 564.15
tug 175.30 249.20 253.25 272.20 310.31 409.12
Tugbag 491.06
Tugged 385.33
tuggerfunnies 431.01
Tuggers 246.33
tuggling 013.17
tugowards 584.33
tugs 323.03 551.23
Tugurios-in-Newrobe 155.05
Tuhal 329.16
tuk 413.11 504.12
Tuk 142.02
Tukurias-in-Ashies 155.05
tulipbeds 526.06
tulipies 146.07
tulippied 331.08
Tulko 125.04
Tullafilmagh 324.10
Tullagrove 284.05
Tullbutt 262.F6
Tulliver 464.13
Tulloch-Turnbull 171.31
Tully 526.30
tullying 467.36
Tullymongan 099.26
tululy 089.36
tum 007.05 052.23 413.02
Tum 578.06
tumass 093.09
Tumbarumba 596.11
tumble 154.33 331.07 415.22 444.09 461.31 612.17
tumbled 117.29 314.36 429.22
Tumbleheaver 352.15
tumbler 228.08 559.14
tumblerbunks 041.07
tumblerfuls 386.09
tumblerous 088.20
tumblers 127.21 127.22 510.23 567.20
tumbles 388.04
tumbletantaliser 174.21
tumbling 470.23 475.33 580.22 624.33
Tumblin-on-the-Leafy 174.26
tumbluponing 484.02
tumbo 209.11
tumbril 556.23
tumbty 496.07
tumbuldum 258.20
tumescinquinance 240.08
tummed 541.31
tummel 201.02
tummelumpsk 323.28
Tummer 071.16
tummlipplads 570.04
tummy 492.34 603.06
Tummy 257.13 262.F6
tummy's 227.22
tumpel 175.17
tumple 520.09
Tumplen 607.30
tumptytumtoes 003.21
tumstull 240.09
tumtim 415.18 419.15
tumtum 234.33
tumtum 231.05
tumtytum 180.26
tumulous 261.18
tumult 316.23
Tumult 184.06
Tumulty 261.19
tumulum 056.34
tun 421.18 602.11
tunc 453.19 504.11
Tunc 611.04
Tunc 122.23
tunc's 298.07
tunder 227.06
tune 148.34 408.23 450.27 452.16 467.32 483.06
Tune 197.36 408.23 500.35
Tune 071.32
tuned 310.04 351.15
tunepiped 371.35
tunes 116.14 437.28 541.33
tunf 353.16
tung 158.14
Tung 623.12
tunga 185.11
tungs 599.09
Tung-Toyd 123.20
tunic 093.03
tunics 247.29
tunies 533.16
tuning 319.23
tunnel 208.21
Tunnelly's 435.34
tunnels 432.15
tunnibelly 113.36
tunnilclefft 583.35
tunning 560.14
tunnybladders 090.12
tunnygulls 595.14
Tunpother 364.26
Tuns 479.12
tunshep 532.13
tuntapster 245.32
tuodore 504.21
Tuohalls 077.02
Tuomush 008.26
tuone 314.28 314.28
Tuonisonian 048.23
tup 595.09
Tupling 481.14
tupped 238.20
tuppeny 465.23
Tuppeter 372.06
tupps 533.35
turb 111.31
turban 029.27
turbane 029.22
turbary 213.07
turbid 108.02
turbot 316.30
Turbot 516.27
Turcafiera 479.15
Turco 132.29
turdenskaulds 228.36
ture 089.35
tureens 304.F4
turf 117.17 225.21 235.32 294.26 327.31 356.23 408.09 602.31 625.17 625.18
Turf 071.33
turfbrown 194.22
turfentide 206.34
turfeycork 310.34
turffers 342.03
turfing 518.15
turfish 281.F2
turfkish 347.36
turfs 510.19
turfsod 056.24
turftussle 610.35
turfur 039.15
turfwoman 012.11 575.05
turfy 559.28
turgid 136.27
turgos 205.29
turisses 553.11
turk 080.10 366.19
Turk 098.10 181.22 520.02
turkay 510.08
turkery 118.22
turkest 442.33
turkey 113.26 464.29
Turkey 043.08 266.F1
Turkey 176.15
turkeycockeys 493.14
turkeys 316.23
Turkey's 248.20
turkeythighs 548.20
turkies 483.08
turkish 144.14

Turkish 235.17
turkiss 215.21
turkling 586.30
turly 090.29
turlyhyde 549.31
turmbing 357.21
turmoil 130.17
turn 024.24 032.17 034.07 052.19 069.05 076.12 093.08 097.11 099.02 109.35 118.09 122.25 129.36 132.25 139.16 172.13 205.31 242.19 265.F2 286.18 316.29 317.20 328.06 369.32 410.17 410.21 443.20 445.26 448.04 449.09 449.28 456.13 502.07 528.28 530.11 582.07 583.11 597.10 625.34 625.35
turn 342.17
Turn 248.07 251.26 428.09 466.09
turnabouts 469.02
Turnagain 248.33
turncoats 323.12
turned 031.16 079.34 111.12 123.14 130.24 139.05 181.19 207.18 322.06 372.17 428.24 433.29 448.35 461.02 463.22 470.31 499.02 527.32 530.08 546.31 575.03 579.29 579.34 587.14 600.14
turnedabout 164.13
turner 390.06
turning 013.29 026.35 083.36 109.17 114.16 114.16 152.36 154.19 179.29 262.29 280.19 334.34 364.34 426.26 453.11 564.13 627.02
Turning 251.23
turnintaxis 554.01
turniphudded 517.07
turnips 190.04
turnips 276.L1
turnkeyed 542.28 594.34
turnkeys 456.32
Turnlemeem 022.14
turnover 012.16
turnovers 385.16
turnpaht 018.32
turnpike 031.01
Turnpike 293.13
turnpiker 031.27
turns 019.18 031.27 136.05 138.27 328.02 589.23 594.33 627.18
turnspite 231.33
turnstone 479.18
turnupon 473.11
turnups 404.31
turpi 185.24
turpidump 364.29
turpissimas 573.30
turpiter 573.20
turpitude 522.14
turps 523.28
turquewashed 235.08
turquin 278.F7
turquo-indaco 284.28
turrace 199.31
turreted 099.19
turrible 205.29
turridur's 060.31
turrified 053.35
turrises 265.11
turruns 557.09
turs 320.22
Turtey 220.20
turtle 118.24
turtled 363.25
turtles 393.11
turtle's 404.34
turtling 253.10
turtlings 061.02
turturs 491.14
turty 007.06
turv 071.10
turves 014.01
turvku 294.19
tusk 349.30
Tuskar 025.26
tusker 245.01
Tuskland 427.22
tuskpick 071.03
tussing 222.26
tussle 082.04 134.33
tussocks 053.10 428.26
tussy 550.20
tustard 555.19
Tut 102.22
tute 287.25
tutor 248.16 251.22 458.03
tutores 126.24
Tut's 291.04
tutti 369.24
tutties 417.19
tuttifrutties 497.10
Tuttu 486.14
tuttut 242.18
Tuttut's 029.28
Tutty 335.29 367.10
tutu 145.01 337.19 491.13
tutu 397.33
Tutu 052.03
tutus 113.08 113.09
tutute 117.15
tuum 283.L1
tuvavnr 054.15
Tuwarceathay 490.28
tuxedo 033.07
tvigate 564.35
Tvistown 197.09
twa 059.34 541.29
twaddle 369.36
twadgedy 061.07
twain 143.18 246.27 295.31 431.35
twain 418.25
Twainbeonerflsh 571.29
twainly 267.18
twainty 242.18
twalegged 285.13
twalette 344.12
twalf 248.21
twang 425.30
twanged 205.33
twangty 364.05
twas 541.29
'twas 004.34 029.16 273.20 290.26 293.12 334.02 404.10 404.12 404.13 435.23 530.26 548.13 589.22
'Twas 006.23 039.14 097.29 248.30 251.27 467.30 511.23
'Twastold 246.22
twattering 037.17
twawsers 276.F1
tway 346.27 468.30
twee 246.15 337.16
tweedledeedumms 258.24
tween 203.12
tweendecks 511.25
tweeny-dawn-of-all-works 041.09
tweet 009.16
twelffinger 437.13
twelfth 119.24 375.11 508.06 607.06
Twelfth 364.03
twelfths 378.33
twelve 025.30 035.33 111.08 126.06 147.05 170.02 194.29 210.22 213.28 284.18 376.14 376.15 389.03 403.04 408.34 427.34 443.12 497.22 511.13 517.29 524.21 544.18 551.33 557.14 566.12 573.06 573.13 575.35 617.24
Twelve 167.23 283.F1
Twelve 071.31 105.35
twelvechamber 063.15
twelve-eyed 335.01
twelvemile 009.16
twelvemonthsmind 460.30
twelvemonthsminding 280.08
twelvepins 006.01
twelvepodestalled 513.35
twelves 353.30
twenny 177.27
twennysixandsixpenny 396.17
twent 284.16
twentieth 119.26
twenty 102.11 130.27 147.07 207.32 264.22 413.23 436.22 438.24 457.01 463.03 556.04 558.22
Twenty 105.03
twentyaid 469.30
twentyeight 283.F1 617.24
twentyfour 221.30 405.22
twenty-four 087.15
twentyfourthly 123.03
twentyg 075.04
twentylot 586.24
twentynine 234.34 255.33 289.12 327.35 430.01 595.07
Twentynine 105.25
Twentynines 249.36
twentysecond 134.12
twentythree 255.34
twentytun 582.35
twentytwo 404.24 412.26 412.27
'twere 116.13 403.20 403.24 557.21
'Twere 330.07 538.10
twhisking 427.19
twice 066.23 127.13 190.24 193.06 214.25 289.08 389.33 405.27 455.34 467.27 487.09 487.33
Twice 250.27 433.22
twiceaday 066.04
twicedated 210.36
twicedhecame 288.14
twicenightly 027.19
twicer 485.24
twicetook 625.01
twick 460.28
Twick 460.28
twickly 467.27
twicycled 416.30

twiddledeedees 258.24
twig 023.25 240.23 248.29 467.10 621.30
twigged 209.06
twigs 235.32 361.02
twigst 252.19
twilette 525.03
twilight 397.29 460.29
twilight 399.25
twill 519.01
'twill 238.06 408.22 456.13 460.25 468.26 556.21
'Twill 346.29 452.33 568.29
Twillby 075.15 075.15
twilled 232.14 314.32
twilling 029.08
twillingsons 583.11
twills 202.01
twim 436.11
twimbs 354.24
twiminds 188.14
Twimjim 211.06
twin 029.22 063.02 116.24 177.21 188.30 238.28 408.20 546.16 597.13
twine 232.14 257.17 468.12
twined 426.10 450.16 563.01
twinedlights 015.02
twinestraines 528.17
twineties 436.01
twinfreer 162.09
twinge 444.03
twinge 344.08
twinger 375.18
twinges 278.F4
twingling 279.F33
twinglings 222.34
twings 460.29
twingty 364.04
twiniceynurseys 134.08
twinkle 065.10 460.28
twinklers 486.25
twinkletinkle 295.F2
twinkling 022.27 291.F4 426.34
twinklins 101.29
twinkly 148.13
twinky 312.21
twinminsters 552.03
twinn 469.01
twinned 491.31
twinngling 620.15
twinning 562.19
twinnt 292.30
twins 418.25
Twins 215.28
twinsbed 555.07
twinsome 161.30
twinsomer 234.07
twinstreams 528.17
twintomine 223.09
twintriodic 310.04
twinx 524.24
twirlers 459.35
twisk 205.10
twist 066.21 483.02 583.05 616.05
twisted 183.20 475.17
twisters 361.06
twisty 505.11
twit 065.10
twitch 463.16 587.27
twitchbells 222.34
Twitchbratschballs 072.02
twitches 301.22
twithcherous 088.18
twitter 193.14
twitterings 095.31
twitterlitter 037.17
twittersky 600.23
twittwin 360.02
twittynice 450.18
twixt 171.18 192.20 203.12
'twixt 087.36
twixtytwins 286.F4
two 008.03 011.36 012.20 017.24 021.11 022.05 029.08 031.17 031.19 032.11 034.20 039.06 039.14 040.31 043.06 043.14 051.14 052.03 052.08 057.04 060.15 060.29 061.22 061.23 065.23 065.26 065.26 065.28 065.30 065.30 070.33 073.10 078.26 082.07 084.26 085.12 086.17 087.17 088.25 089.30 090.16 094.15 094.36 102.11 108.04 117.23 117.34 119.23 120.36 122.27 122.30 124.22 124.26 124.26 127.35 128.17 129.03 131.01 131.08 138.22 140.08 140.25 145.36 151.28 160.03 161.19 163.09 165.13 169.17 169.18 182.25 187.12 188.10 192.02 194.26 196.10 197.30 199.30 200.03 200.27 200.31 201.01 203.14 204.02 207.12 207.36 208.15 210.29 211.02 211.20 214.05 224.33 236.12 238.01 241.28 242.14 249.22 251.22 256.05 264.04 265.20 265.25 265.25 265.F2 270.26 274.12 284.22 285.23 285.24 289.27 297.13 311.04 314.11 316.04 316.09 322.25 325.24 327.08 331.07 333.10 358.32 362.25 367.05 367.08 373.01 374.31 375.10 375.10 379.15 379.16 384.33 384.33 385.15 385.15 387.13 389.33 391.32 392.32 393.21 396.26 397.12 397.12 397.27 403.02 408.03 410.34 411.07 413.22 415.05 420.07 422.16 422.35 425.19 432.11 440.13 442.06 442.26 446.10 457.02 457.21 461.02 462.33 463.17 466.28 475.21 480.01 483.08 488.03 488.27 488.28 489.19 489.24 490.04 490.14 491.13 497.09 497.33 497.34 503.15 507.05 508.31 508.32 510.18 510.18 519.11 519.35 522.07 522.09 522.14 526.23 527.19 527.24 529.12 530.02 532.34 535.32 536.29 537.29 538.14 544.16 544.26 546.05 546.16 551.30 557.17 558.01 558.16 559.01 559.06 561.01 561.05 561.30 562.21 563.23 565.23 566.19 569.31 569.34 570.23 572.25 574.03 580.12 583.07 584.10 587.26 588.11 588.21 589.28 589.33 596.16 597.10 608.05 608.07 612.26 616.11 617.02 619.11 620.18 620.20 622.10 622.27 625.28 626.09 626.14
two 201.14 209.08 338.05 341.08 418.30
Two 014.11 019.21 089.03 204.05 246.35 302.27 307.06 374.21 375.09 379.15 413.29 494.33 560.06 567.06 588.35 590.24 608.33 610.36 620.16 628.05
Two 105.23 105.31 106.21 275.L2
TWO 166.16 305.R1
twoatalk 066.20
twobar 208.21
twobble 319.13
twobirds 562.17
twobis 562.17
twobreasttorc 612.02
twoce 594.31 594.32
twoddle 006.28
twoe 110.14
Twoedged 497.08
twoel 594.09
twofeller 299.29 303.31
twofold 288.03 490.16
Twofold 305.L1
twofootlarge 272.22
twofromthirty 093.12
twohandled 530.29
twohangled 615.19
twoheaded 276.L1
twoinns 111.17
twolips 015.01
twolve 076.02
twolves 479.14
twomaries 126.18
Twomass 341.24
twomesh 221.34
twomeys 252.20
Twomeys 313.26
Twonderful 295.16
twone 003.12
twoo 442.03
twoodstool 040.23
twoohoo 449.25
twooned 396.24
twoport 318.13
tworthree 345.10
twos 057.19 158.21 285.25 285.25 445.01 468.12 585.10
Twos 176.04 281.L2
two's 020.24
twosday 457.19
twosides 484.14
twosingwoolow 360.03
twosome 188.14
twotime 611.28
Twotongue 385.04
twotoosent 438.24
twotoothed 539.36
twould 518.35
'twould 024.25 139.19 199.30
'Twould 024.24 027.21 620.30
twoways 087.22
Twoways 442.11
two-we 189.24
twowsers 276.F1
twum 348.22
Twwinns 330.30
twy 312.21 312.21 361.22 438.05
Twy 022.05
twyly 610.14
twylyd 331.28

twyst 424.06
tyan 457.13
Tyburn 504.24
Tycho 260.10
tyddlesly 583.35
tye 315.32
Tyeburn 540.15
tyghting 379.05
tyke 431.12 617.31
tyke's 528.33
Tykingfest 086.13
tyled 183.05
tyler 328.10
tympan 310.11
tyne 211.17
tynpan 224.19
tynwalled 262.F3
tyon 313.24
t'yous 091.27
type 037.01 109.02 124.03
151.06 172.18 179.13 309.17
443.24 615.01
types 120.36 136.18 162.09
166.05 419.26
Typette 478.03 478.27
typmanzelles 470.32
typtap 430.11
typtopies 020.13
typureely 406.21
typus 115.31
Typus 020.13
tyr 344.03
Tyrannous 071.17
Tyrants 162.01
tyre 584.13
tyred 394.16
Tyre-nan-Og 091.25
tyrent 498.01
tyres 359.13
Tyrian 249.08
Tyro 151.23 603.34
tyron 163.09
tyrondynamon 163.30
Tyrone's 049.07
tyronte 569.35
Tyrrel 060.09
Tyrrhanees 330.09
tyrs 053.12
Tys 215.22
tysk 316.05
Tyskminister 037.08
Tytonyhands 265.21

u 037.21 302.25
U 235.28 (I sold U)
251.32 299.F3
U 106.25
Uachet 494.15
Ualu 004.02 004.03 004.03
UaRhuamhaighaudhlug 310.11
ubanjees 205.32
Ubeleeft 150.09
Uberking 611.33
Ubermeerschall 133.21
ubi 188.08
Ubi 167.33
UBI 260.R1
ubideintia 610.07
ubidience 605.29
Ubipop 540.14
ubivence 356.12
Ublanium 013.34
Uck 466.21
Udamnor 499.09
uddahveddahs 085.03
udder 160.29 322.09
Uden 537.30
Udi 504.21
Udite 504.20
U'Dunnell's 007.12
ueber 299.10
ufer 214.08 214.08
uff 268.27
Uganda 545.09
uge 567.21 567.21
uggamyg 116.32
ugged 004.29
ugh 590.19
Ugh 249.27 249.27 320.22
ugliest 079.15
ugly 453.07
Uglymand 317.28
Ugol 297.F2
ugola 513.08
Uh 340.17
uhindred 330.33
uhrweckers 615.16
uhu 285.12
uhud 285.12
Uian 148.22
uila 427.06
Uisgye 497.23
uitlander 581.03
Ukalepe 229.13
ukonnen 323.26
ukukuings 095.32
Uladh 078.27
Ulaf 567.18
Ulcer 389.05
ulcers 521.25 529.27
Uldfadar 182.18
ulemamen 054.08
Ulerin's 194.14
Ulick 337.36
Ulikah's 434.29
Ulissabon 442.09
Ulitzas 551.33
Ulivengrene 329.06
Uliv's 550.18
Ulla 214.07
Ullahbluh 339.02
Ullhodturdenweirmudgaard-
gringnirurdrmolnirfenrir-
lukkilokkibaugimandodrrerin-
surtkrinmgernrackina-
rockar 424.20
ullo 185.15
Ulloverum 610.06
Ulm 293.14
Ulma 100.36 264.12 264.13
ulmost 460.16
Ulo 243.24
ulstar 520.34
Ulster 451.13 498.11
Ulster 398.33
ulstra 283.L1
ulstramarines 225.05
ulstravoliance 316.02
Ulstria 270.L4
ult 110.09
ultimate 134.01 605.04
ultimatehim 589.35
ultimately 482.31
ultimendly 029.35
Ultimogeniture 300.L1
ultitude 325.35
Ultonian 385.13
ultra 515.14
ultradungs 343.29
Ultramare 433.01
ultramontane 478.31
ultraviolent 590.08
ultravirulence 425.35
ululation 006.17
ulvertones 318.33
Ulvos 565.05 565.05
ulvy 058.05
ulykkhean 123.16
um 013.24 037.05 057.12
304.30 414.13 506.12 563.07
Umartir 499.09
umbas 214.07
umbedimbt 059.32
Umbellas 106.32
umber 248.01 588.20 601.06
umberella 530.29
umberolum 338.07
umbique 183.14
umbloom 467.11
umbozzle 352.30
umbr 620.01
umbracing 537.06
umbraged 354.09
umbrageous 380.15
umbrance 220.32
umbrasive 362.17
umbrella 052.27 159.35 182.15
309.17 573.36
umbrella 277.L3
Umbrella 098.24
Umbrian 024.20
umbrilla-parasoul 569.20
umbris 513.02
umbroglia 284.04
umclaused 569.14
umdescribables 298.32
umfullth 155.28
umgyrdle 548.17
U.M.I. 446.08 (you are my and
you are me)
umnder 595.24
umniverse 410.17
umoroso 269.L1
ump 447.21
Ump 516.15
Umphrey 032.15
umphrohibited 085.09
umpire 174.07 337.02
umpires 497.29
umpple 184.14
umprincipiant 594.02
umproar 273.26
umprumptu 093.14
Umpthump 376.10
umpty 295.24
umptydum 567.12
umptyums 345.18
umque 389.29
ums 415.18
umscene 017.15
Umsturdum 352.24
umsummables 417.09
umto 461.03
umvolosy 200.15
umwalloped 324.29
umzemlianess 352.18
un 039.22 053.22 098.23
un 081.29 199.29 383.04
'un 418.18

una 061.01
Una 094.12 147.14 212.12 267.25 576.06 601.24
unable 611.19
unaccompanied 544.15
unaccountably 086.03
unacumque 605.32
unadulterated 445.35
unadulteratous 363.34
unadulterous 161.17
unaided 475.36
unanimously 032.27
unappalled 452.23
unasyllabled 183.15
unaveiling 503.26
unbalanced 174.17
unbeaten 161.16
Unbeknownst 445.26
unbespokables 496.31
unbeurrable 162.02
unbewised 378.30
unbiassed 491.33
unblest 563.13
unbloody 423.15
unbluffingly 116.01
unborn 164.35
unbottled 575.13
unbox 287.11
unbracing 581.18
unbridalled 298.30
unbrodhel 445.06
unbroken 419.01
unbrookable 123.32
unbu.. 341.02 (unbuttoned)
Unbuild 624.07
unbulging 310.27
uncained 059.10
uncarable 041.01
uncertain 031.09 084.05 100.33 185.30 558.03
UNCERTAINTY 282.R4
unchanging 167.28
uncharted 254.18
Uncken 348.23
unclaimed 472.29
Unclaimed 421.02
uncle 466.30
Uncle 442.08 496.02 608.07 622.07
Uncle 278.L2
Unclean 237.21
uncle-in-law 284.F4
uncles 521.26
uncle's 043.16
unclish 376.16
unclose 023.11
unclothed 539.03
unclouthed 366.15
uncoil 121.24
uncomeoutable 367.32
uncommon 523.23
uncommons 380.07
uncomparisoned 152.05
uncompetite 325.04
unconcerned 221.10
uncondemnatory 090.35
unconditional 163.23
unconnected 121.18
unconnouth 227.27
unconscionable 266.30
unconsciounce 623.25
unconsciously 153.03 173.33
uncontrollable 011.33 032.07
Uncontrollable 184.15
uncounthest 365.18
uncouple 577.18
uncouth 239.35
uncouthrement 113.01
uncover 096.28
Uncovers 602.24
uncreepingly 445.36
uncrown 169.13
uncrowned 289.30
unctuous 113.36 476.23
uncustomarily 138.09
uncut 544.16
und 018.21 270.31
Und 163.06
unda 007.26
Undante 269.L1
undaring 368.35
undated 589.25
unde 287.22 478.16
Unde 089.27
UNDE 260.R1
undeceived 174.04
undecidedly 542.20
undecimmed 497.09
undefallen 233.33
undeleted 183.36
undemonstrative 115.27
under under Under UNDER
underages 544.25
Underbund 324.13
underclothed 441.05
underdown 394.03
undered 483.27
underfed 572.01
Underfifteen 529.09
underfoot 433.13
undergang 376.11
undergroands 481.15
underground 076.33 113.32 128.09
underhand 504.27
underheerd 160.26
underhold 141.14
undering 349.32
underlacking 289.11
underlayers 572.05
underlinen 097.24
underlings 193.01
underlinings 121.20
Underloop 569.05
undermined 579.32
undernearth 610.04
underneed 357.32
underpants 206.27
underrails 041.21
underreared 038.28
underrupt 368.04
Undershift 147.26
undersiding 581.17
undersized 559.29
underslung 188.27
understamens 236.35
understamp 456.28
understand 161.33 180.11 435.28 436.18 437.13 444.30 445.11 445.15 451.35 453.05 457.26 458.28 459.22 459.31 460.31 465.26 496.05 522.06 526.25 558.34 595.22
understand 399.22
Understand 307.21 412.20
understanding 266.19 606.01
understandings 152.04 271.F4
Understandings 175.27
understands 627.15
Understeady 432.22
understood 041.06 104.17 124.04 163.22 222.14 621.23
understouttered 272.21
Understrumped 421.07
understudium 486.08
Understudy 271.F4
undertake 537.16
underthaner 335.26
undertoken 613.30
Underwetter 009.27
underwhere 365.11
underwittingly 124.15
underwood 360.15
Underwood 526.23
Underwoods 248.28
underworld 147.27
underworp 302.17
undesendas 612.11
undesignful 426.12
undesirable 517.03 562.30
undesirables 243.19
Undetrigesima 433.03
undeveiled 075.05
undevelopmented 279.F06
undfamiliar 427.21
undher 364.29
undification 209.02
Undiform 222.13
undilligence 187.16
undines 547.08
undiscernibles 050.01
undishcovery 326.31
undisides 008.32
undistributed 164.06
undivided 110.13 292.31
undo 208.16 288.07 361.29 569.02
Undo 011.28
undoing 437.34 509.27
undone 025.20 058.01 075.06 094.09
undoubted 060.18
undoubtedly 118.15
Undoubtedly 425.09
undraped 435.14
undress 004.35 115.10 441.30
undresses 102.32
Unds 302.26
undths 158.16
undulant 041.07 468.30
undullable 391.06
Undy 023.20
undyeing 527.23
unearly 135.31
uneasy 040.14
unegoistically 488.16
unelgible 482.21
unemancipated 081.04
unencumbered 545.18
unend 598.07
unenglish 160.22
unerr 555.22
unethical 487.27
uneven 104.03 517.33
unevented 517.34
unexpected 120.27
unexpectedly 110.28
unexpectednesses 067.34
unfacts 057.16

unfallable 153.26
unfashionable 120.35
unfeigned 075.19
unfettered 118.02 567.05
unfillable 131.10 492.26
unfilleted 474.07
unfilthed 111.32
unfitting 127.04
unfoiled 354.22
unfold 075.23
unfolded 186.01
unfolden 608.28
unforgettable 058.20
unfortunate 090.17
unfortunates 544.13
Unfortunates 421.09
unfriended 056.21
unfriends 391.35
unfrillfrocked 191.01
Unfru-Chikda-Uru-Wukru 024.07
unfruitful 421.28
unfurl 019.26
ung 361.17
Ung 054.18
ungainly 121.25
Unge 267.L3
ungeborn 370.07
ungiven 355.06
ungkerls 314.31
ungles 288.06
unglish 609.15
unglucksarsoon 344.01
Ungodly 261.L3
ungoing 331.04
ungraceful 414.24
ungreekable 181.22
unguam 095.27
ungue 162.29
unguents 550.18
unguest 135.19
unguished 288.17
Ungulant 157.04
UNGUMPTIOUS 308.R2
unhappiness 189.10
unhappitents 258.22
unhappy 257.02
unheading 548.35
unheardth 231.22
unheavenly 185.29
unhemmed 104.03
unherd 223.01
unhesitent 133.14
Unhindered 507.22
unhomy 396.12
unhook 133.34
unhume 097.24
uniates 043.13
Unic 291.01
Unica 267.25
unicorn 462.20
Unicorns 622.25
unicum 156.25
unification 610.23
uniform 123.10 324.10 579.14
uniformication 529.07
uniformly 612.13
unify 142.19
unimperatived 176.25
unimportant 381.05
uninational 348.32
uninformed 414.07
uninsured 544.12
unintentionally 163.29
uninterruptedly 405.07
unintiristid 538.03
unintoxicated 089.08
uniomargrits 249.12
union 240.20 446.29 585.25
Union 077.23
unionism 133.15
unionist's 066.11
Unionjok 155.16
unions 566.03
Unions' 066.09
unique 422.15
Unique 105.36
unirish 290.28
unisingular 251.32
uniswoon 060.11
unit 049.13
unitarian 389.11
unitate 298.13
unite 584.34 585.25
united 043.29 132.33 161.26 398.11 446.17 488.33 560.28
United 130.28 181.17 185.31 325.05
unitedly 181.19
Uniteds' 066.08
uniter 446.08
unitred 320.15
unity 604.32
Unity 101.08 176.20
unium 317.29
uniun 162.26
univalse 054.23
Univarsity 287.30
universal 117.13 293.17 388.12 388.28 447.28 606.08
UNIVERSAL 260.R3
universalisation 032.21
Universally 045.31
Universary 389.11
universe 170.04 263.26 440.36 585.03 624.19
universe 419.03
university 124.01 173.13
Unjoint 569.21
unjoyable 529.36
unkalified 005.16
Unkel 228.17
unknowable 062.32
unknown 026.21 079.17 096.29 110.30 179.04 239.30 380.23
Unknun 353.15
unlace 569.23
unlatched 244.30
unlawful 144.31
unlawfully 084.33
unleavenweight 019.24
unleckylike 438.26
unless 161.12 165.35 252.23 410.03 410.14 441.15 458.29 476.06 501.26 579.11 586.31
Unless 519.28 619.25 620.14
unletched 459.26
unleventh 517.33
unlicensed 086.14
unlifting 363.33
unlike 039.12 177.33
Unlikelihud 021.24
unlimited 046.07
unlist 350.34
unlitness 404.12
unlitten 259.03
unlivable 186.03
unlodgeable 420.23
unlookedfor 108.32
unloosed 183.34
unloud 601.28
unlucalised 087.18
unlucky 307.F7
unmanner 033.18
unmansionables 052.26
unmask 590.24
unmatchemable 508.26
Unmentionability 107.07
unmentionable 300.03
Unmentionable 420.04
unmentionablest 320.12
unmerried 226.18
unmesh 267.13
unminted 170.08
unmistaken 123.30
unmitigated 067.19
unmixed 092.26
unmoved 430.14
Unn 283.01
unnamed 378.10
unnatural 504.33 572.24
unnecessarily 515.14
unnecessary 120.15 411.03
unner 538.35
unnerstunned 378.22
unniversiries 551.28
unnoticed 470.21
unnotions 614.17
unnumerose 158.11
uno 134.09
unobserved 092.22
unoculated 541.27
unpackyoulloups 526.18
unpardonable 562.36
unparishable 130.05
unpassible 298.18
unpeppeppediment 463.11
unperceable 616.32
unpious 303.25
unpleasant 072.26
unpop 451.24
unpreoccupied 558.04
unpro 408.12
unprobables 609.05
unpurdonable 537.36
unquestionable 183.23 495.25
unquiring 003.21
unraidy 204.10
unravel 422.20
unrawil 361.33
unreadable 179.26
unreformed 352.02
unregendered 581.16
unrelieved 510.04
unremarkably 368.17
unremitting 342.04
unremuneranded 171.32
unrescued 100.10
unrested 026.17
unripe 532.23
uns 050.02 235.28 306.04 415.16 548.04
uns 383.05 383.06
unsaid 293.18
unsatt 248.06
unschoold 237.13
unseen 158.36 194.18 403.22
unselfish 426.13
unselves 368.16
unsheathed 546.09

unsheathing 340.30
unsheckled 354.07
unshent 267.26
unshrinkable 173.36
unshrinkables 417.13
Unsightbared 156.35
unsightliness 131.19
unskilled 164.32
unskimmed 205.30
unsleeping 451.10
unsmiling 115.22
unsolicited 070.13 173.30
unspeechably 238.36
unstant 143.08
unsteaden 533.35
unsteadily 513.33
unstoppable 128.01
unstrict 295.22
unsuccessfully 545.08
Unsure 500.19
unsuspectingly 174.25
unswer 037.21
unt 338.17
untaken 490.16
untamed 196.23
untellable 227.36
unterdrugged 266.31
untergone 223.29
unterlinnen 577.29
Unterwealth 078.10
unthanks 119.34
unthinkables 417.13
unthinking 068.32
unthowsent 597.05
untidled 070.16
untie 133.34
Untie 202.20
until 004.33 006.20 014.11 074.18 116.22 160.07 163.31 174.03 181.17 200.36 219.01 219.18 220.15 230.11 248.09 272.24 336.14 365.02 380.26 409.08 443.17 448.28 548.20
Until 621.10
untill 321.28
untillably 275.05
untired 229.17
untirely 059.13
untireties 597.07
untiring 092.21
untisintus 611.24
untitled 104.04
Untius 092.35
unto 032.05 034.06 063.27 073.33 073.35 077.24 111.15 158.09 190.01 232.08 234.27 258.11 258.23 264.12 264.13 283.14 318.25 325.26 332.13 363.23 393.17 395.32 458.20 466.22 493.28 528.16 528.21 542.12 543.14 547.06 561.22 594.08 600.18 608.31 617.07
Unto 421.01
Untouchable 237.24
untoupon 595.04
untranscended 429.17
untrue 462.14
untrustworthily 057.18
untruth 169.09 459.36
untuoning 353.17
Unuchorn 157.03
Unum 013.24
unused 069.29 183.20
unusuable 324.29
unveilable 050.09
unvuloped 378.35
unwachsibles 483.19
unwards 325.09
unwary 107.26
unwashable 575.15
unwashed 049.22 191.11
unwatched 435.31
unwhisperably 182.28
unwhorsed 137.17
unwill 318.35
unwillingly 488.08
unwisdom 439.13
unwished 049.22
unwishful 035.24
unwithstandable 253.30
unwordy 408.10
Unworthy 071.21
uov 407.17
uoves 184.29
up up Up Up
upalepsy 232.30
upandinsweeps 123.08
upandown 125.14 524.34
Upanishadem 303.13
upann 538.32
upastairs 362.33
upat 013.34
upborne 383.20
upcloses 221.22
updipdripping 029.25
upers 394.31
upfallen 363.33
Upfellbowm 505.29
upfielded 449.34
upfrom 426.20
Upgo 338.32
upheavals 184.03
upheld 354.08
uphere 222.31
uphill 202.16
uphills 546.32
upholder 313.03
upholding 321.04 476.11
upholdsterer 296.F1
upin 060.35 094.24
upinandoutdown 612.14
upindown 065.32
up-in-Leal-Ulster 482.29
upinto 331.13 474.14
Upjack 487.04
upjock 007.35
upjump 010.16
Upkingbilly 053.36
upkurts 366.27
upleave 352.03
uplifted 054.31
uplon 318.04
Uplouderamain 257.33
Uplouderamainagain 258.19
upmeyant 455.20
upom 153.27
upon upon
ùpon 124.11
upong 015.19
upout 596.22
upover 140.24
upown 005.20
upp 614.14
upped 530.27
upper 062.22 101.29 262.03 484.31 578.31 589.18
upper 346.33
Upper 533.12 602.20
Uppercrust 078.11
upperon 600.29
upperotic 439.25
uppershoes 608.25
upperstairs 461.18
upperturnity 366.21
upping 548.34
uppish 484.14
upplaws 132.15
uppletoned 323.30
Upploud 257.30
upponnus 607.35
uppum 279.F27
Uppygard 609.17
uprecht 239.19
upreized 547.22
upright 067.01 135.27 261.23 396.04 429.21 483.23 486.15 518.24 575.35 583.01
Upright 536.33
uprighted 427.06
uprighter 362.16
uprights 183.10
uprip 179.08
uproar 150.25
uproor 006.06
uproose 448.18
ups 239.16 353.19
upsadaisying 363.03
upseek 075.11
upservatory 551.25
upset 183.20 215.07 499.26
upshoot 014.24 261.14
upshotdown 441.33
upsidedown 373.34
upsidown 119.28
upsiduxit 060.33
upsits 127.17
upsittuponable 284.26
upsomdowns 049.24
Upsome 239.09
upstairs 561.02
upstanded 004.35
upstheres 109.19
upstored 333.11
upsturts 266.13
upsydown 512.01
upt 412.32
uptaking 538.29
uptenable 397.33
Upterputty 068.28
upthe 234.32
uptheaires 354.01
upthecountrylifer 356.34
upthrow 492.02
uptied 094.08 315.04
uptoputty 612.32
upturned 439.10
upturnpikepointandplace 003.22
Upu 425.08
Upwap 018.36
upwards 040.34 444.04
upwithem 282.17
upyourhealthing 077.31
ur 102.07 507.22
Ur 241.31
Ural 494.16
Urania 583.16
uration 269.F3
urb 481.17 598.28
urban 154.20 601.05

Urban 539.32
urbanious 277.08
urbanorb 589.06
urbes 076.07
urbiandorbic 096.36
URBIS 306.R1
urbjunk 624.24
Urbs 551.24
urchins 025.30 152.09
urdlesh 338.21
urge 115.32 149.21 167.07
394.32 442.20 486.35 572.30
urged 187.06
URGES 267.R1
Urgothland 197.09
uri 102.07
uria 102.07
urinal 407.17
Urinia 171.28
Urloughmoor 577.14
urned 024.05
urns 077.29
urogynal 619.02
Urovivla 061.36
Urp 016.26
urqurd 233.32
urs 535.03
Urse's 097.05
urssian 352.01
Ursulinka 471.31
Ursussen 353.12
urthing 426.19
Uru 136.11
uruseye 252.16
urutteration 284.21
us us Us US
usage 458.09
uscertain 609.35
use 019.01 039.23 061.34
066.01 081.24 108.02 114.12
130.16 143.36 152.07 161.35
163.21 191.27 230.36 236.28
247.05 277.F1 292.08 421.16
425.06 464.03 472.12 482.13
520.24 523.08 525.03 527.13
Use 087.32 581.15
U.S.E. 070.01
used used Used
usedn't 200.20
usedtowobble 510.28
useful 077.21 089.16 398.09
Useful 129.26
usefully 164.28
usefulness 551.21
usemake 433.27
uses 125.13 333.16 567.09
Uses 306.30
usetensiles 053.18
useth 036.31
ushere 052.16
ushered 206.35
Usherette 267.12
using 060.25 280.24 544.29
usking 198.35
Uskybeak 157.06
Usolde 383.18
uspart 626.31
Usquadmala 184.28
Usque 497.23 499.31 499.31
499.32
Usqueadbaugham 024.14
usquebauched 319.04
usquiluteral 297.27
Ussa 214.07
usses 019.29 354.33
ussies 101.04
Ussur 353.12
Usted 054.13
usual 038.10 038.13 039.29
060.28 061.15 077.25 089.16
109.03 111.21 115.14 178.21
186.32 236.27 378.16 405.16
435.09 436.14 443.23 456.25
516.11 530.12
usually 059.25 081.32
usuals 031.23
usucapture 035.29
usupped 426.06
Usurp 016.27
usylessly 179.26
ut 292.12
ut 163.03 440.12 524.15
Ut 610.16
Utem 223.36
utensilise 447.01
utensils 381.34
Uteralterance 293.L1
uterim 187.36
utharas 113.07
U' Thule 235.19
uti 185.16
utile 549.30
utilised 166.23
Utilitarios 078.11
utility 049.20
utmost 190.11
utmostfear 505.06
utpiam 611.25
utskut 233.32
uttentions 166.29
utter 117.12 181.16 551.21
561.30
uttered 174.11 420.18
utterer 016.15
uttering 432.12 617.19
utterly 053.33 097.22 110.19
120.27 174.03 292.06 408.04
458.20
Utterly 538.12
uttermosts 353.25
utterrock 606.32
uus 120.32
uval 466.32
Uval 140.03
uves 184.29
Uvuloid 157.05
Uwayoei 267.20
uxpiration 058.08
uxter 324.03
uxuriously 451.32
uyes 241.11
uym 446.03

v 162.36 333.01
v 576.03 576.06
v̄. 123.17
v. 147.06
V̄ 284.F4 (V for wadlock)
333.02
458.33 (Vespatilla)
V. 544.36 (V. de V's)
546.03 (lord V. king)
Va 473.17
vaal 110.09 199.10
vaast 338.14
vacancies 530.07
vacant 173.09 498.07
Vacant 421.11
vacants 143.05
vacation 411.01
vacillant 439.31
vacticanated 152.23
vacuum 151.07 188.17
vadnhammaggs 352.05
Vae 292.01
Vaersegood 346.23
vagrant 294.F2
vague 608.01
vaguely 273.F6
vagurin 625.34
vaguum 136.34
Vah 594.01
vailed 606.04
vain 015.12 251.18 457.09
486.26 556.14 577.24 623.18
vainly 172.33
Vainly 097.21
vain's 146.09
vainyvain 076.26
vair 575.16
vairy 456.12
Vakingfar 310.10
Val 210.18 439.17
valdesombre 343.16
vale 210.31 264.25 428.10
600.07
Vale 156.25 203.26 305.28
420.25
valed 318.29
valency 616.13
valentine 020.34
Valentine 249.04
valentino 458.02
Valentino's 289.28
vales 023.23
valet 271.L3
valeter 184.11
valetotum 038.25
Valgur 256.22
valiance 038.01
valiantine 439.17
valing 469.18
valinnteerily 364.06
Valkir 099.16
valkirry 068.15
valkyrienne 220.05
vall 553.22
vallad 493.03
valle 074.02
Vallee 158.19
Valles 147.07
valleties 625.07
valley 093.06 427.05 501.30
504.16 564.26
valleylow 319.01
valleys 022.27
Valleytemple 602.22
vallsall 231.07
vallums 478.12
Valorem's 342.11
valour 165.07 325.13
vals 528.23
valsed 248.12
valsehood 291.20
Valsinggiddyrex 281.F1
Valtivar 331.26
valuable 386.23
valuation 041.34
valuations 256.31

value 069.17 069.18 172.09 442.16 574.20
Value 307.24
valued 364.06 524.13
values 111.29 123.14 235.14 590.15
values 355.05
valure 478.23
valuse 283.10
vam 623.16
vamp 246.22 246.22 246.22
Vamp 559.05
vampared 551.02
vampas 611.04
vampire 411.31
vamps 435.36
Vamps 071.32
vampsybobsy 611.26
van 021.10 021.22 021.32 023.14 054.04 056.21 100.31 238.24 314.23 365.28 414.04 435.29 530.20 607.08
van 111.12
Van 225.26
Van 491.16
Vance 211.32
vanced 539.19
vanessance 177.17
vanessas 107.18
vanesshed 427.07
vanessy 003.12
vanfloats 530.23
vanhaty 178.03
Vanhomrigh's 174.26
Vanhungrig 406.30
Vania 239.14 239.14
Vanias 239.15
vanilla 248.01
Vanilla 460.33
vanillas 347.28
Vaniorum 239.15
Vanisha 461.02
vanished 131.23 337.08
vanishing 449.04
Vanissas 295.02
Vanissy 449.04
Vanistatums 295.02
vanitty 212.32
vanity 143.36 449.04
Vanity 434.24
vannflaum 364.28
vantads 601.14
vantage 290.12
vanvan 598.18
vapid 435.16
vapour 157.23
var 200.11 360.18
var 050.05
Vardant 600.33
vardar 202.16
variables 582.16
Variagated 310.15
Varian 221.12
variance 156.16
varians 211.19
Varian's 451.17
variant 120.17
Variants' 380.01 380.02
variations 221.19
varicoarse 214.24
varied 038.31
variety 042.03 099.28 123.28 237.06 456.14
Varina 101.08
various 173.32 173.35 181.15 254.27 254.28 381.34 532.36 533.10 575.18 598.08
variously 118.26 129.12
varlet 136.13 335.08
varmints 024.32
varnashed 339.11
varnish 412.11
varsatile 468.02
varses 301.10
varsus 272.31
Vartman 599.04
vartryproof 290.19
Vartryville 205.26
varuations 619.04
vary 324.01 519.14
Vary 519.14
varying 252.16
vas 185.19
Vasa 255.16
vaseline 182.28
vases 077.30 189.21
Vasileff's 049.13
vassal 316.29
vassals 398.03
vassal's 030.20
vast 512.15
vastelend 335.12
vaster 355.29
vastly 539.15 547.03
vat 130.12
Vatandcan 139.34
vatars 599.05
vatercan 339.35
vaticanned 210.27
vaticination 142.19
vaticum 309.21
vats 082.07
Vatucum 243.31
vauce 312.05
Vaughan 482.18
vaulsies 236.20
vault 552.08
vaulting 123.08
vaultybrain 159.25
vaunt 102.13 118.03 226.02
Vauntandonlieme 485.18
vaunty 274.29
vaux 439.17
Vauxhall 058.33
vauxhalls 550.35
Vayuns 597.25
V.B.D. 131.03
V.D. 529.25 (Hansen, Morfydd and O'Dyar, V.D.)
ve 247.31
veal 406.18 556.33
vealar 424.26
vear 343.35
Vechers 509.03
vecious 481.29
vective 581.03
vector 490.01
vectorious 298.14
Vedette 577.16
Vedi 540.12
Vee 072.10
veek 288.F4
veen 562.32
veer 312.11
veered 247.31
veereyed 344.23
veerious 373.30
veetoes 152.33
veg 455.30
vegateareans 518.13
vegetable 423.28
Vegetable 295.L1
vegetables 145.09 192.07 503.06
vegetal 611.15
vegetarian 465.21
Vehement 501.19
vehicles 133.13
vehicule 135.27
vehmen's 581.02
veil 238.17 527.23 556.03 556.11 562.10
Veil 020.34
veilch 403.15
veilchen 403.15
veilde 403.15
veiled 139.01
Veiled 156.32
veils 290.F6 318.18
vein 553.01 614.33
veines 577.04
veiniality 463.11
veino 510.06
veins 214.24 275.22 300.31 475.14
veiny 264.14
veirying 324.28
Vela 147.14
velamina 611.13
veldt 422.32 543.14
velediction 077.25
velican 331.25
velicity 154.34
Velivision 610.35
velivole 275.18
velkommen 553.34
velktingeling 419.12
vellatooth 303.03
velleid 610.14
Vellentam 238.25
vellicar 385.12
Vellicate 563.35
velligoolapnow 348.16
vellum 179.31 568.32
vellumes 155.27
vellumtomes 595.22
velly 166.31
velnerate 167.30
velnere 314.34
velocipede 089.24
velociter 185.22
velos 247.02
velour 478.22
veloutypads 230.30
velut 313.20
velvet 242.06 321.11
velveteens 067.28
velvetthighs 061.23
Vely 299.25
ven 317.14
vend 167.29
venders 090.05
vendettative 187.31
vendoror 374.20
venerable 077.02 605.27 605.33
Venerable 439.17 489.14
venerated 124.17 182.01 381.31
venerections 356.33
Veneris 551.34
venersderg 203.20

vengeance 019.07 112.19 581.03
venia 185.15
venials 562.36
Venice 105.01
venicey 232.11
Venis 113.21
venison 034.25
venisoon 003.10
venitas 038.25
venite 287.20
venom 101.24
venoussas 471.08
venstra 561.01
vented 415.27
venter 100.27
ventholes 221.30
ventilated 004.09
ventitillated 288.F4
ventrifugal 605.17
Ventriliquorst 105.20
ventriloquent 056.05
ventruquulence 360.21
ventura 207.26
venture 245.19 272.15 341.14
ventured 099.33 509.23
ventures 131.01
Ventures 106.21
venturous 498.33
venue 582.05
Venus 299.L1 435.03
venuse 281.L1
Venuses 079.18
venuson 093.17
venusstas 413.29
venuvarities 355.36
vepers 569.18
ver 158.07
Ver 222.11
Vera 449.10
verawife 532.18
Verb 594.02
verba 121.09
verbage 183.13
verbal 036.09 515.15
verbally 523.10
verbanned 537.28
verbaten 037.15
verbe 279.F09
verbed 486.09
verbiage 121.03
verbigracious 037.13
verbigratiagrading 611.29
verbish 413.10
verbivocovisual 341.18
verbos 116.16
verbs 016.08 432.19
verbumsaps 585.18
Vercingetorix 088.22
verdant 612.03
verdants 530.23
verdhure's 110.10
verdict 093.01
verdidads 432.30
verdigrass 007.30
verdigrassy 231.07
verdigrease 412.33
Verdons 004.04
Verdor 099.29
verdure 412.11
Vere 280.17 300.14
verg 468.08
Verg 093.21
verge 040.23 166.15 244.14 474.08
Vergemout 354.17
verges 395.22
vergin 553.01
vergitabale 357.34
Vergobretas 048.07
Vergognese 435.08
veribally 410.10
veriblest 334.02
Vericus 373.24
veridust 568.02
veriest 410.36
verikerfully 536.17
verilatest 440.01
verile 439.36
verily 238.03
Verily 546.24 546.24
Verily 341.26
veripatetic 417.32
veritable 033.02
veritably 289.04
veriters 607.02
veritiny 527.17
Veritotem 255.14
veritues 510.06
verity 607.02
Verity 434.25
verjuice 412.17
vermelhion 352.17
Vermicelli 199.29
vermicular 082.12
vermillion 144.29
vermin 239.17
vermincelly 548.17
verminous 462.27 544.25
vernacular 265.F2
Verney 160.08
Vernon 093.31
Vernons 498.25
vero 301.17
Veronica's 204.30
veronique 458.14
verry 527.25 565.10
Verschwindibus 270.L3
Verse 293.L2
verses 443.11
versets 343.35
versicle 596.30
versingrhetorish 346.19
version 030.10 031.21 038.31
verso 123.34
verst 566.35
versts 081.15 081.15
versus 378.19 447.18
verswaysed 298.23
vert 005.06 034.25 213.20 270.16
verted 483.33
Vertex 293.L2
verts 178.12
verumvirum 166.26
Veruno 569.31
vervain 597.34
verve 279.F10 577.03
verveine 250.23
very very Very Very
veryman 534.14
verypetpurpose 614.34
verysoon 055.06
verytableland 010.34
veryveryvery 280.25
vesamong 177.11
vesdre 204.32
vesh 525.20
Veslandrua's 601.21
vesles 201.23
Vespasian 132.18
Vespatilla 414.25 417.19 417.30
Vespatilla 418.15
vesper 606.04
vespers 276.11
Vespertiliabitur 276.11
vespertine 177.11
vespian 484.17
vespreys' 146.09
vessel 232.35
vessels 189.21
vesta 012.09
Vesta 526.30
vestacoat 242.34
vestal 023.35
vestalite 440.32
vestas 183.16 536.18
vested 546.06
vestee 447.33
vestiges 602.26
vestimentivorous 227.35
vestin 250.31
vesting 578.33
Vestity's 601.24
vestments 451.01
Vestrae 104.22
Vestray 026.07
vestry 552.36
vesy 162.25
vet 114.22 201.23 234.02
vetals 599.07
vetchvine 209.20
Vetera 078.27
Veto 267.23
vetriol 101.24
Vetus 267.22
Veuve 556.09
vexed 059.19 490.02
vhat 567.01
vhespers 038.14
vi 052.15 160.31 414.14
vi 566.26
via 129.16 170.26 478.14 567.01 577.23
via 042.26 098.05 426.35
Via 052.15
viability 081.01
vialact 604.14
vialds 164.17
viands 239.31
viasses 183.13
vibroverberates 249.15
vic 062.06
Vicar 084.19
Vicarage 291.18
vicariously 506.28
vicar's 596.20
vice 172.03 176.23 183.26 288.01 434.36 506.33 513.12
vicefather 480.26
viceflayer 050.21
vicefreegal 033.30
viceheid 251.15
viceking's 018.13
vicemversem 384.27
vicereeking 438.28
viceregal 032.36
vicereine's 209.34
vicereversing 227.19

vicerine 388.33
vices 160.26
viceuvious 570.05
viceversa 063.03
Viceversounding 355.10
vicewise 286.29
V.I.C.5.6. 495.31
vich 375.33
vicinals 081.01
vicious 098.19
Vickar 255.27
Vickar's 495.17
Vickers 330.13
vicking 279.F21
vickyvicky 527.16
vico 417.06
Vico 260.15 452.21 497.13
vicociclometer 614.27
Vi-Cocoa 026.31
Vico's 246.25
vicous 134.16
vics 082.27
Victa 558.28
victar 349.25
victim 165.19 490.02
victimisedly 472.20
victims 241.33
victis 596.06
victolios 082.12
victor 610.35
Victor 179.11 211.18
victored 490.02
Victoria 568.06
victorias 351.01
Victorias 598.06
victorienne 057.28
victories 329.14
victorihoarse 472.20
victory 454.17 500.06
Victory 094.36 188.27
Victrolia 105.14
Victuallers 067.18
victualler's 618.10
victuum 364.33
vicus 003.02
Vicus 551.34
vide 296.02
Vide 493.26 493.26
videbis 113.30
videvide 416.16
vidim 297.F2
vidnis 597.19
Vidu 566.26
vidual 079.28
vie 279.F09 279.F10
vied 247.19 509.23
Vielo 209.34
vienne 209.34
vierge 203.29
viersified 044.09
Vieus 293.12
view 006.30 007.36 019.26 059.26 059.36 085.28 114.15 136.36 143.10 226.03 226.34 264.27 270.25 392.26 410.03 432.22 515.23 540.08 559.21 564.01 564.08 573.02 582.30 587.04 588.07 590.23 606.14 618.15
view 418.35
View 097.02 369.10
viewed 470.10
Viewed 440.02
viewmarc 249.03
views 060.35 127.24 421.29
Views 106.28
viewsed 593.09
Viggynette 600.12
vigil 189.29 434.14 519.02
vigilance 034.04
vigilant 439.32
vigilantes 078.19
viginity 279.F15
vignettes 440.22
vignettiennes 356.36
vignetto 493.30
vigor 614.09
vigorously 421.22
viisi 285.20
vike 241.09
Vike 044.10
vikelegal 131.22
Vikens 331.20
Viker 622.08
Vikeroy 100.05
vikid 527.05
viking 046.13 265.F2
vikings 030.09
vikissy 433.04
Vikloe 290.24 375.33
Vikloefells 626.18
Vikramadityationists 493.12
viktaurious 353.12
viktrae 537.10
vil 430.13
vild 263.19
vilde 209.20
vile 033.17 530.05
viled 130.23
vilest 042.15 435.16
vilities 354.05
vility 354.05
vill 128.08 330.08 503.29
villa 347.26 543.16
Villa 519.33
village 043.28 043.29 119.27 141.11 174.25 176.28 253.31 362.01
villagettes 008.03
villain 137.07 460.05
Villain 122.17
villain's 086.30
villapleach 034.31
villas 139.06 553.20
villa's 582.36
villayets 365.16
ville 130.23 190.21 264.30
Ville 102.19
villeins 545.14
Villem 387.19
villen 578.03
villes 281.08
ville's 006.04
villities 625.07
Villumses 242.01
vim 623.16
vimvital 036.03
vin 619.34
vinagerette 548.18
vinars 038.25
vincentian 038.26
vincibles 232.26
Vinctis 292.01
vindicat 076.07
vindicative 053.14
vindicatively 269.31
Vindner 072.10
vine 005.11 117.23 358.17
vinebranch 604.04
vinedress 212.17
vinegar 005.11
vinegarth 542.12
Vineland 213.35
vinery 581.11
vines 140.25
vineshanky's 229.04
vinesmelling 093.08
vinesregent's 564.13
vineyard 553.18
vineyards 462.03
vinnage 381.04
vinting 351.30
vintivat 596.18
vintner 139.34 318.20 580.24
vinvin 437.11 437.11 598.18
Viola 223.07
violaceous 612.11
violast 231.20
violates 207.11
violating 529.17
violence 068.36 097.21 174.24
violens 285.F6
violent 097.31 183.02 449.05
violents 461.17
violer 003.04
violet 023.02 403.22 481.35 606.04
violetian 203.29
Violet's 143.26
viper 210.27
Viper's 435.16
Vipra 596.29
viragos 432.11
virchow 537.05
vires 515.14
virevlies 199.36
virgated 115.26
virgil 270.25
virgilances 569.16
virgils 618.02
virgin 115.19 192.04 408.08 454.17 513.27 572.23 602.13
virginelles 561.25
virginial 365.09
VIRGINIANAE 281.R2
Virginia's 304.25
virginity 573.14
virgins 250.23
virgin's 342.27
Virgin's 206.06
virgins' 183.27
Virgintiquinque 134.13
virginwhite 433.03
virgitarian 171.03
Virgo 026.13
viricordo 215.23
virid 227.21
viridable 059.11
viridities 014.33
viriditude 612.23
viridorefulvid 284.30
viridosus 234.08
virility 291.23
virilvigtoury 395.36
viritas 518.31
virtual 107.26
virtually 426.07
virtue 020.09 133.32 142.17 427.26 434.05 539.03

Virtue 255.14
virtues 518.05 605.25
virtuoser 287.01
virtus 546.19
virulence 097.21
virumque 389.19
virus 321.06
virvir 357.34
viry 527.05
visa 210.27
visage 275.12 286.F3
visanvrerssas 173.25
visavis 053.07
visceral 437.09
vise 352.05 352.06
viseversion 349.07
vish 525.20
visibilities 608.01
visibility 048.01 051.04
visible 227.23 494.09
visibly 034.24 171.30 430.14 504.08
vision 109.20 179.31 405.13 486.32 611.32
Vision 566.28
visional 042.21
visionbuilders 191.34
visit 041.31 108.04 172.06 194.27 565.34 588.09
Visit 307.01
Visit 104.19
visitated 156.32
visitation 251.02
visitations 340.28
visited 124.15 244.14 533.10 572.33 602.17
Visitez 540.10
visiting 029.23 334.35 367.12
visitor 070.13
Visits 105.02
vispirine 257.02
vista 264.24 485.06
Vista 289.29
vistule 199.27
visualises 525.01
visuals 097.30
visus 183.14
vitae 084.05 160.14
Vitalba 600.22
Vitale 221.22
vitalmines 456.20
vitals 385.17 608.16
vitaltone 309.19
vitandist 424.05
Vitavite 308.01
vitch 437.30
Viteilius 573.28
Vitellius 573.08
Vitellius 307.L1
vitellusit 406.14
viterberated 157.01
vites 523.17
vitiated 150.23
vitious 141.09
vitricus 230.34
vitroils 603.35
Vitruvius 255.20
vittles 242.12
vituperation 097.22
vitupetards 371.02
viv 243.29
Viv 331.26
Viv 028.27
vivant 065.07
vivarious 165.10
vivat 610.16
vivaviz 587.22
vive 419.13
Vive 286.L1
vivelyonview 018.29
vivers 199.23
vives 351.16 548.01
Vivi 209.34
vivid 395.29
vividence 366.03
viviparam 185.14
viviparous 242.28
vivisuture 253.34
vivle 110.17
vivlical 183.13
vivvy 264.F1
vixendevolment 578.34
vixens 479.21
vixen's 403.20
vizago 052.15
Vjenaskayas 348.23
Vjeras 348.23
vlls 258.02
Vlossyhair 265.21
Vnost 552.12
voax 039.15
vocable 118.27
vocabulary 086.01
vocal 407.34
vocality 052.11
vocational 447.07
vocative 122.03
voce 407.13
voce 185.22
Vociferagitant 355.10
vociferated 404.07
vociferatings 032.22
vodashouts 502.20
vodavalls 580.01
vode's 367.34
voes 245.17 245.17
vogalstones 224.19
vogt 077.14
Vogt 054.05
vogue 398.17 617.36
voguener 577.13
Vogul 162.16
voi 068.26
voice 004.11 048.21 073.14 095.16 132.27 154.28 192.10 194.19 247.06 318.33 363.09 404.08 407.13 409.11 435.04 435.20 466.36 472.05 487.21 487.22 492.01 515.28 565.15 602.12 604.02 608.18 624.05
Voice 306.20
voicebox 397.11
voiced 051.27 058.27 438.33 470.05 523.09
voices 454.30 487.04 571.25
voicey 200.08
voiceyversy 453.17
voicical 450.24
voicies 601.18
void 100.27 229.27 469.11 515.14
voida 415.34
voided 135.34
voids 037.09 367.33
voil 528.22
voina 518.31
voise 016.23 407.14 448.34
voixehumanar 441.26
Voking's 157.17
vokseburst 444.15
Vol 051.13
vol. 123.19 (volume)
Volans 488.15 558.18
volant 024.05
volantine 020.34
volants 418.31
Volapucky 116.31
volatile 396.29
volatiles 038.25
Volatilis 161.26
volcano 410.11
volcanoes 319.07
volens 271.20
volgar 211.13
volhvuns 609.24
volimetangere 509.33
volkar 352.17
vollapluck 034.32
vollayed 072.29
volleyball 157.07
volleyholleydoodlem 379.12
volleying 581.03
Vologue 088.26
volomundo 416.16
volp 480.28 480.28
volponism 097.14
volses 435.10
volt 118.06
voltapuke 040.05
volted 549.16
volts 285.18 285.18 285.18 285.19 285.19 285.19 285.20 285.20 285.20 285.20 285.21
voluant 339.29
voluble 435.06
volucrine 112.12
volume 048.05
volumed 328.11
volumen 610.16
volumes 145.19 151.02 574.11
volumes 419.05
volumnitatis 412.09
voluntarily 605.06
voluntary 572.28 612.01
voluntears 116.12
volunteer 050.15
volunteers 441.34
volunteers' 580.30
volupkabulary 419.12
volupty 396.29
volve 270.25
volvular 492.33
vom 623.16
vomit 089.17
vomitives 448.15
von 021.34 022.09 022.19 022.22 022.31 150.05 249.20 279.F24 365.28 413.15 460.26 535.02
Von 293.12
vonderbilt 543.11
vongn 553.34
Vonn 352.24
Voolykins' 250.31
voon 365.28
voos 114.25
vop 578.17
vopiscus 193.31
vorasioused 416.24

Vortex 293.L2
vortically 297.12
Vortigern 565.12
vos 269.20
vosch 416.14
vosellina 154.29
vote 044.10 142.19 146.15 407.13
Vote 572.06
voted 166.22
voter 551.36 551.36
Voter 551.36
voterloost 376.08
voters 510.27
voteseeker 448.26
voting 076.16
votre 478.20
Votre 428.16
Vott 345.09
voucher 126.24 574.16
voucherfors 029.17
vouchers 545.22 574.10
Vouchsafe 424.15 570.14
vouchu 484.29
voult 403.16
voulzievalsshie 578.16
vous 058.26 058.28
Vous 478.19
Vousdem 439.17
Vousden 050.15
Voutre 009.14
Vowclose's 203.26
vowed 385.21 563.20
vowelglide 486.07
vowelise 360.06
vowelthreaded 061.06
vows 065.07 276.F4 563.12
vowts 243.36
vox 250.23
voxes 142.19
voyaging 323.06
voyantly 248.25
voyce 536.22
voylets 261.02
voyoulence 432.31
voyous 485.11
V.P.H. 099.13 (cf. 284.F4 286.L1)
vrayedevraye 253.33
vremiament 155.30
vryboily 534.01
V's 544.36 (V. de V's)
V.S. 492.21 (veterinary surgeon)
Vuggybarney 200.06
Vuggy's 106.26
vuice 182.23
vuile 360.18
vuk 480.31 480.31 480.32 480.32
vulcanite 334.09
vulcano 089.28
vulcanology 494.07
vulcans 079.18
Vulcuum 514.12
vulganized 481.14
vulgar 119.26 384.36
Vulgariano 181.14
Vulgaris 418.25
vulgo 573.04
vulgovarioveneral 098.18
vulgure 289.F1
Vulking 626.27
Vulnerable 206.06
vulser 248.12
vulsyvolsy 378.31
vultures 435.29
Vulturuvarnar 512.08
Vulva 482.07 482.07 482.07 482.08
vulve 297.27
Vuncouverers 088.27
vuncular 230.31
vund 378.30
vuol 456.08
vuotar 393.13
vuoxens 383.24
Vurry 521.03
vursus 272.31
Vux 160.13
V.V.C. 489.03
vvollusslleepp 368.19
vying 178.22
Vyler 277.F4

W 226.32 (W waters)
Waaaaaa 297.17
waaded 178.15
waader 331.27
waag 197.26
waage 098.32
Waal 209.03
waalworth 004.35
waapreesing 088.26
Waarft 332.19
waast 017.28
wabbash 210.01
wabblin 520.25
wabsanti 005.22
Wacht 076.23 372.31
Wachtman 556.23
wackering 320.26
wad 017.08
Wadding 377.15 573.26
waddled 277.F7
Waddlewurst 494.17
Waddlings 024.20
waddphez 535.01
Wade 204.07
waders 537.19
wades 309.05
wading 589.29
wadlock 284.F4
wadmel 181.28
wafers 183.34
waft 232.29 427.12
wag 098.29 149.13 172.35 413.35 489.21 496.15
wage 324.31 450.34
waged 547.07
wageearner 543.27
wage-of-battle 469.26
wager 377.26
wager 354.07
wages 273.03
wagged 354.23
wagger 315.26 449.24
waggerful 253.10
waggery 079.02
wagging 619.07
waggling 010.13
waggonhorchers 339.18
waggonways 553.29
waggonwobblers 604.17
waggy 301.15
waging 316.34
waglugs 595.16
wagon 461.01
wagoner 230.12
wagoners 540.24
wagrant 010.29
wags 167.03
wagsfools 595.12
wagtail 377.14 582.11
Waherlow 105.30
Waidafrira's 601.27
waif 547.04 579.01
waifstrays 138.15
wail 006.36 017.20 138.35 180.21 232.13 360.13 419.14 469.21 470.12 470.14 472.01 474.01 474.06
Wail 011.02
wailful 433.30
wailing 148.35 491.32
Wailingtone's 542.04
wailsday 301.21
wailth 091.28
Wain 426.25
waist 018.36 028.31 251.15
waistbands 065.02
waistcoat 024.29
waistcoats 183.35
waistend 058.35
waistfully 164.07
waistress 255.33
waists 394.15
wait 051.22 074.18 122.17 142.34 170.06 257.17 325.36 327.18 380.32 397.21 405.25 450.33 453.29 457.08 460.31 465.10 489.02 507.17 620.28 620.31 620.31
Wait 147.09 215.03 232.05 279.F17 374.16 375.04 525.10 571.34 572.07
waitawhishts 345.11
waited 387.19
waither 594.32
waiting 028.08 034.07 102.23 116.21 142.34 147.07 177.01 205.15 207.16 227.04 235.28 276.01 317.19 392.33 424.09 567.29 609.22 609.23
waiting 201.08
waitresses 587.26
waits 379.22 422.16 601.36
Waits 130.10
waityoumaywantme 070.17
waived 194.32
Waives 105.02
Waiwhou 202.12
wake 006.15 007.03 024.10 043.17 055.07 074.01 075.07 117.06 154.10 192.20 194.29 238.22 262.15 309.07 351.36 357.35 375.08 394.15 427.29 436.32 453.03 478.35 481.08 496.15 510.16 514.20 546.01 578.01 585.20 608.28
wake 201.11 399.13 418.23
Wake 024.14 221.26 359.27 607.16
Wake 415.15
waked 102.02 139.10 496.35 625.33
waken 276.18 562.23 584.13
Wakenupriseandprove 571.32
waker 587.01

wakes 326.12 362.20 382.25 608.30 608.32
Wakeschrift 205.17
wakeswalks 455.05
waking 229.22 333.29
Waking 222.19
wald 386.07 478.10
Wald 622.25
waldalure 359.34
Waldemar 317.17
waldmanns 345.04
waldy 540.34
Wales 447.17
Walhalloo 541.22 541.22 541.22
walk 021.27 022.13 042.31 081.03 085.10 091.14 114.08 130.07 131.29 172.03 235.33 237.30 241.09 246.34 287.F1 294.F3 323.34 394.08 410.33 411.06 445.02 448.22 449.09 472.07 520.01 546.01 551.34 553.17 567.20 570.29 580.27 621.33
Walk 017.17 182.31 214.03 241.03 261.F2 390.16 405.14 429.06 473.23
walked 018.24 098.20 127.32 135.19 152.35 153.28 234.06 441.07 534.26
Walker 210.13 376.30 394.12 473.03 476.04 526.18 555.12
Walkie 485.32
walking 024.17 030.19 058.25 152.20 197.04 200.19 202.22 317.18 411.03 427.28 449.06 505.16
Walking 176.09
walkner 170.18
walks 194.24 487.31 618.18
wall 006.09 007.32 013.15 026.24 059.35 069.06 069.07 069.07 079.34 090.22 116.18 118.20 124.06 139.13 182.16 233.02 294.02 334.24 347.10 347.32 392.26 437.10 444.09 464.22 469.10 481.28 497.25 528.32 544.04 544.21 552.20 553.24 559.04 559.05 560.04 587.15 598.22
wall 278.L4
Wall 044.13 045.04 045.05 095.14 101.18 379.11 496.07 542.04 560.04
Wall 044.27 044.28 175.20 176.04
Wallaby 601.34
wallat's 153.30
walled 163.27 316.13
walleds 289.F6
Wallenstein 032.29
Walleslee 133.21
wallet 306.01 474.03
wallets 348.31
wallfloored 269.09
Wallhall 609.18
wallhall's 005.30
wallhole 069.07
wallies 497.13
Wallinstone 008.01
Wallisey 312.29
wallop 445.25
Wallop 196.16
wallops 020.27 087.19
wallopy 165.20
Wallor 181.03
wallow 192.24 257.18
wallowed 132.01
wallowing 319.25
wallowing 341.12
Wallowme 204.07
wallpapered 461.19
Wallpurgies 530.31
wallruse 324.09
walls 027.06 071.02 156.03 183.09 249.06 266.20 273.01 449.19 507.01 559.02
wallstrait 003.17
wally 333.09
Wally 211.11
walnut 405.25
Walpurgas 229.16
walrus 031.13 071.03
Walsall 378.19
walsh 318.19
walshbrushup 340.03
Walt 061.19 076.27
walters 064.20 064.20 373.06 373.06
Walther 141.19
walts 320.10
Walty 508.15
waltz 282.F4
Waltz 078.32
Waltzer 473.04
waltzers 245.22
waltzing 239.28 475.11
waltzywembling 507.10
walve 349.12
wamb 346.16
wambles 339.01
Wamen 167.31
wampun 548.31
wamth 348.25
wan 006.07 092.26 139.13 182.34 201.29 333.27 386.21 479.15 556.31 557.08 579.33
Wan 072.04 072.05 072.05 105.04
wana 335.20 335.20
wanamade 138.07
wand 245.23 321.04 405.01 478.10 586.34
Wanda 147.14
wandelingswight 077.36
wanden 243.20
wandercursus 318.10
wanderducken 323.01
wandered 589.21
wanderful 059.13
wandering 043.02 144.22 335.12 446.09 469.03 508.07
wanderlad'll 374.03
wanderlook 312.30
wanderloot 354.23
wanderness 318.17
wanders 265.16
wandervogl 419.14
wanderwards 598.05
wandler 606.31
wandly 368.08
Wandrer 377.13
wandret 299.17
wands 552.04
wandshift 369.20
waned 186.08
Wang 270.F2
wangfish 098.22
wangh 351.21
wangles 390.14
wanhope 154.33
wanigel 300.05
wanings 379.25
wanked 464.22
wankyrious 565.03
wann 516.18 516.18
wanna 138.08
wannot 167.16
Wans 021.18
wan's 304.01
Wanst 372.04
Wanstable 485.24
want 024.32 042.09 068.24 075.12 078.33 101.02 139.12 148.06 151.10 159.31 161.05 196.03 198.14 201.21 209.13 213.18 222.10 238.02 238.18 247.24 275.17 278.14 278.18 336.02 337.32 337.32 337.32 362.29 405.23 453.03 453.25 454.34 456.17 457.30 461.20 478.32 489.08 489.08 515.21 522.19 522.33 522.35 570.23 570.26 570.30 598.22 617.18 620.01
want 201.05
Want 300.01 301.25 364.10
Want 418.30
wantanajocky 331.24
wanted 020.30 082.22 085.05 110.02 135.07 150.21 191.19 314.06 366.04 382.06 424.02 496.18 516.30 564.29 616.31
Wanted 125.10
Wanterlond 618.22
wanthingthats 221.14
wanting 516.15 516.29 623.30
wantingly 164.05
wantnot 160.28
wanton 162.16 243.20 251.06 334.05 620.25
wants 043.21 050.33 065.14 143.19 147.05 278.02 306.F1 378.21 409.34 422.17 442.31 443.21 458.30 466.17 521.21 523.32
Wants 072.07
wanxed 358.25
waount 446.02
wapentake 030.09
wappents 339.10
wappin 588.05
wapping 347.13 510.25
wappon 566.22
wapt 034.24
war 003.06 008.32 027.32 031.10 049.05 094.07 094.35 098.34 101.07 142.30 142.31 151.36 178.25 184.01 228.13 243.08 258.12 279.06 279.06 301.02 330.30 348.25 426.18 499.29 518.19 518.31 570.12 620.23
war' 064.04
wararrow 043.21
warbl 597.29
warbler 360.14
warblers' 449.19
warbling 056.27
warbly 200.11

warcheekeepy 275.F1
Warchester 446.31
warclothes 337.11
warcry 352.27
ward 022.20 080.27 352.07 476.10 615.01
Ward 212.07
Wardeb 526.20
warden 132.36 429.19
Warden 495.12
warder 373.33
Warders 446.31
warderworks 067.09
wardha 212.20
wardmotes 132.24
wardorse 383.21
wardrobe 033.07 065.14 077.20
wards 285.23 425.13 527.13 550.22
ward's 442.25
wardsmoats 005.33
ware 155.02 252.02 261.03 281.16 360.27 373.24 416.07 450.29 464.04 469.21 525.32 542.13 576.36 614.16
Ware 060.29 102.22 315.33 480.21
wareabouts 255.07
warehouse 498.30
wares 013.34 433.03
Ware's 572.32
Warewolff 225.08
warfare 177.05 491.32 516.35
warful 594.12
Warful 340.09
Warhorror 091.30
waring 534.18
wark 351.36
wark 383.10
warken 263.18
warld 345.31 608.34
warlessed 021.22
warlord 025.27
warm 010.25 021.36 027.24 122.02 186.30 265.23 434.02 502.19 528.13 578.09 627.18
warmas 468.11
warmblooded 033.22
warmed 423.30
warmen 596.07
warmer 355.32
Warmer 324.25
warmest 356.33
warmet 594.10
warmin 471.32
warming 052.22 101.31 441.27 588.13
warming 209.09
warmingpan 211.11
warmly 124.13 525.04
warmth 566.05
warmwooed 579.33
warn 328.11 359.18 461.32 494.35 573.28
warnder 049.06
warned 203.36
warnerforth's 245.08
Warneung 503.28
warning 006.07 115.12 121.08 292.11 339.09 430.04 439.20 517.10 530.27 604.24
warnings 321.12
warns 020.10
warn't 509.32
warnward 379.02
warp 211.17
warped 183.08
warping 497.03
warpon 615.19
warr 366.32
warrant 057.17 359.08
warranto 546.02
Warre 539.27
Warre 175.13
warred 247.29 271.23
Warren 574.04
warrent 625.10
warried 125.16
warring 107.31
warriors 034.04 277.F3
warrior's 176.35
warrs 531.05
warry 316.34 365.08
wars 014.09 119.02 270.31 289.F6 301.30 323.13 473.08 588.11
Wars 440.10
war's 246.03
War's 330.30
warsail 588.17
warschouw 541.23
warsheet 131.20
warson 350.33
warst 365.08
wart 138.07
wartar 341.12 610.20
Wartar 610.20
warthes 206.33
warthog 269.12
war-to-end 178.25
wartrews 008.21
wartrey 126.21
wartrophy 083.14
warts 051.18
Warum 479.36
warwhetswut 272.05
warwife 101.18
warwon 612.11
wary 244.01 449.34
was was Was Was
wasbut 231.13
wasch 336.12
wasching 064.20
wash 083.18 127.24 162.18 197.34 247.23 265.F1 272.23 290.20 459.09 507.30 509.01 526.07
Wash 156.28 196.07
washable 268.F7 574.25
washawash 290.21
washed 021.27 046.12 196.14 570.32
Washed 358.23
washemeskad 207.24
washer 023.34
Washerwoman 176.08
washerwomen's 183.25
washes 135.06 272.F3
washing 208.14 214.17 380.29 443.28
washing 201.14
Washing 107.01
Washington 032.29
washingtones 434.22
washleather 557.28
washout 174.08
Washte 373.05
washtout 578.23
washup 628.11
washwives 281.01
washy 616.31
Washywatchywataywatashy 484.26
wasistas 514.10
wasnottobe 085.22
was'nt 380.17
wasn't 096.12 204.04 204.04 496.07 516.15
Wasn't 279.F26
Wasn't 106.22
waspering 414.29
wassailbowl 131.23
wassailhorn 091.27
Wassaily 005.05
wassand 359.07
wassarnap 129.29
Wasserbourne 198.08
wasseres 601.06
wasserguss 492.24
wassing 595.08
wast 152.18 152.19 488.36 617.31
was't 570.10
waste 019.32 114.20 141.10 151.21 158.10 185.08 300.29 309.13 555.22
Waste 494.14 578.30
wasted 075.14
wastended 320.17
Wastenot 418.30
wastepacket 058.35
waster 178.12 523.05
wasterpaperbaskel 194.13
wasters 041.09
wastersways 153.23
wastes 035.31 064.01
waste's 112.26
wasteward 235.07
Wastewindy 549.15
wasting 100.20 411.31
Wasting 499.29
wastobe 062.11
wastohavebeen 076.33
Wasut 203.08
wat 061.18 508.15
Wat 227.29
Watacooshy 484.26
watarcrass 491.19
watch 034.04 035.19 076.28 137.05 154.16 186.20 215.08 220.26 245.16 302.15 355.31 449.36 464.25 469.28 506.30 542.15 623.29
Watch 295.22 438.15 465.35 499.29 607.12
watchcraft 468.24
watched 110.05 319.35 366.08 509.02
watcher 508.35 510.08
watchers 403.24 476.11
watches 151.13 517.36
watchful 075.07
watchhouse 084.18
watching 028.06 057.26 166.20 398.23 505.02 508.35 509.02 509.03 509.04 531.14
watchyoumaycodding 346.24
water 004.23 024.31 046.27 049.12 050.34 071.09 098.24 100.01 130.33 136.06 137.01

141.11 146.29 196.12 212.25 213.07 235.25 254.11 264.16 280.34 318.01 319.25 326.34 361.35 364.20 365.10 381.18 386.11 390.22 391.17 415.34 419.22 450.14 451.15 461.01 463.20 466.09 521.19 521.19 525.03 526.21 540.06 541.33 559.15 571.09 586.34 605.30 605.33 605.34 606.01 606.04 606.12 620.19
Water 316.25 521.19 546.33 551.24 586.05
Water 105.24
waterbaby 198.08
waterboy 228.31
waterburies 290.06
waterbury 035.28
Waterclocks 177.28
watercloth 022.25
watercourses 605.19
wateredge 569.17
Waterfood 071.22
Waterford 031.20
waterfowls 595.12
watergasp 190.22
waterglucks 200.08
watergood 492.24
Waterhose's 088.01
Waterhouse's 213.16
watering 386.04 393.01
wateringplatz 447.21
waterleg 210.15
Waterloo 176.10
waterloogged 428.20
waterloose 008.02
waterlows 202.17
Waterman 104.13
watermark 112.32
watermen 447.11
waterproof 380.34
waterroses 548.24
waters 025.34 056.18 076.29 076.29 080.25 096.14 098.22 103.11 116.19 140.21 166.19 192.01 215.31 215.31 215.34 216.04 216.04 226.32 230.14 297.20 305.29 312.04 312.04 334.36 372.35 446.14 458.16 460.25 462.04 462.05 526.09 526.09 588.23 599.26 605.12
waters 399.07
Waters 342.25
water's 469.04
watersheads 496.23
waterside 363.21
watersilts 021.06
waterstichystuff 252.26
watertap 544.16
waterungspillfull 124.24
waterwag 144.33
waterweed 207.03
waterworkers 585.16
waterworld 367.26
watery 078.19 452.30
watford 483.30
wath 134.30 495.23
wather 371.07 371.20 371.31 372.26 373.10
wathy 616.31
Watkins 587.20
Watling 042.26 134.20
Watllwewhistlem 469.25
watsch 004.22
Watsch 525.02
watsy 475.35
Watsy 245.33
wattarfalls 383.23
watter 594.10
watthour 310.25
wattle 332.11
wattling 328.03
wattsismade 321.09
wauking 597.12
wauks 545.29
wauld 336.10
waulholler 348.10
wave 018.02 023.27 023.27 023.28 023.28 062.04 132.08 331.24 442.12 510.32 596.06 602.29
Wave 094.06 280.19
Wave 104.07
wavebrink 547.20
waved 058.06 470.35
waveleaplights 571.01
waveney 209.18
waverings 222.34
waves 046.12 101.30 139.20 159.34 232.11 256.23 267.13 331.35 384.06 384.08 390.16 424.29 431.16 620.35 624.03
Waves 373.08
waveslength 394.17
wavetrap 287.F1
waving 087.28 275.12 526.05 588.30
wavus 203.31
wavy 028.33 208.17 475.25
wax 193.03 238.31 537.04
waxedup 270.10
waxen 115.04 251.23
waxened 583.29
waxenwench 029.24
waxes 057.20 335.18 468.11
waxing 010.09
waxwork 206.36
waxworks 113.22
waxy 618.11
way 004.19 006.35 008.09 010.22 016.04 024.18 028.25 030.11 047.02 048.20 051.28 062.30 063.19 065.08 070.23 072.27 080.30 080.32 081.04 082.35 084.12 091.29 095.06 110.08 110.18 110.31 119.06 121.09 124.19 129.12 130.19 137.21 148.14 163.35 164.21 164.31 183.02 186.26 190.10 190.36 200.26 205.31 206.22 209.05 211.04 212.30 215.10 215.11 226.34 230.10 233.08 239.30 245.21 248.28 252.02 254.12 254.22 267.27 275.04 278.25 279.F06 283.31 287.F4 288.22 299.F3 303.01 303.03 303.30 317.23 318.30 323.35 328.03 331.15 333.09 335.25 337.27 340.32 341.17 345.01 354.23 367.26 367.26 367.26 367.27 381.03 381.15 384.15 386.12 386.33 387.08 390.31 393.33 394.02 399.33 406.12 407.19 411.26 414.08 422.21 425.04 427.03 427.35 427.36 429.15 431.10 431.10 431.16 432.09 432.29 435.05 435.25 436.08 436.15 442.22 442.23 445.10 445.12 446.26 447.29 449.08 451.15 453.23 455.30 459.20 460.35 461.03 464.02 464.16 466.15 474.20 475.19 475.32 476.09 476.30 477.02 477.22 477.24 477.27 477.29 482.26 487.20 490.03 490.27 501.14 505.26 507.08 509.33 516.21 521.15 522.10 522.15 527.18 527.20 530.17 532.32 536.08 544.27 555.14 555.18 556.12 557.33 567.09 571.08 577.35 578.18 579.02 582.25 583.27 584.22 585.12 589.04 594.05 604.35 620.11 620.28 623.21 623.21 628.15
way 342.22 343.01
Way 303.03 447.29 448.18 490.03 497.12 525.31 588.08
Way 106.16 176.15
waybashwards 202.22
wayed 256.24
wayfared 042.26
wayfarre 102.21
waylaid 138.13
Waylayer 062.35
wayleft 580.01
waynward 351.08
ways 022.08 028.29 040.26 123.31 143.11 152.30 157.31 200.31 203.04 227.13 227.13 257.03 282.29 285.29 316.12 320.06 405.08 412.02 445.06 446.02 458.05 460.26 473.02 503.01 506.23 538.25 546.32 552.15 587.21 595.07 606.18
ways 399.27
Ways 105.23
wayseeds 545.33
wayve 371.28
wayward 238.05
waywayway 194.25
waywords 369.01
waz 004.14
Wazwollenzee 321.12
WC 066.18 (West Central)
W.D. 448.11
W.D.'s 071.19 (W.D.'s Grace)
we we We We
wea 626.03
weak 016.08 093.36 148.35 276.22 396.12 437.10 577.01 579.09 608.30
Weak 411.06
Weakear 568.26
weaken 368.19
weaker 079.33 467.28
weakly 424.14
weakminded 544.28
weakness 270.08
weaks 138.16
weal 242.21 363.19 497.14 579.17
weal 418.34
weald 080.13 564.24
Weald 366.34
wealker 603.15
we-all-hang-together 048.23
weals 563.32
wealth 264.F2 530.34 579.16 589.13

wealthes 064.04
wealthshowever 253.08
wealthwards 324.31
wealthy 236.12 530.09
weam 238.28
wean 562.29
weaned 542.10
weaner 470.24
weanling 234.18
weapon 084.05 134.15 248.15
weaponright 539.20
weapons 277.F3 602.10
weaponswap 518.17
weapt 149.04
wear 060.17 063.17 146.15
191.27 224.27 246.18 291.F3
315.03 357.08 404.17 435.21
537.33 578.08
Wear 378.32
weard 375.35
weare 319.28 319.28
weared 487.21
wearers 181.27
weariness 276.01
wearing 085.33 109.22 166.06
226.14 253.20 351.03 374.26
411.24 447.33 453.09 508.03
511.27
Wearing 516.08
wearrier 350.33
wears 116.36 194.28 206.33
363.08 536.22 544.24
wearsense 075.03
weary 093.33 202.22 542.11
556.21 628.01
Weary 222.19
wearywide 152.18
wearywilly 056.22
weastinghome 372.17
weat 225.12
weather 010.29 085.19 113.23
189.17 335.12 369.35 480.07
502.18 579.23
weatherbitten 255.06
weathered 357.30
weatherest 568.30
weathereye 437.26
weathering 070.32
weatherings 117.27
weather's 024.25
weatherside 476.05
weavers 313.01
weaver's 043.18 211.18
web 131.18
webbeth 481.05
webgoods 255.08
webley 082.16
Webster 036.11 479.30
Weck 537.34
wecker 375.19
wecking 158.23
wed 377.17 556.21 562.03
595.06
wed 383.12
we'd 149.10 298.03 347.22
360.25 620.10
We'd 201.24
wedded 284.F4 585.22
weddens 088.15
wedding 024.13 093.36 111.14
135.11 436.31 508.06 511.02
578.33
Wedding 222.18
Wedding 104.09
weddingtown 625.35
wedge 297.23 436.03 436.08
wedgeword 072.18
wedhe 356.18
wedlock 548.05
Wedlock 071.28
Wedmore 391.27
Wednesbury 062.28
wednessmorn 376.11
weds 549.28 560.30
wedst 330.29
wee 006.31 056.16 057.13
057.13 069.30 114.23 117.34
149.08 156.32 170.18 197.18
212.25 244.10 247.18 259.03
312.14 351.08 354.34 360.34
416.04 446.04 477.03 483.24
523.27 576.15 578.32 619.15
wee 103.06 340.19 354.09
Wee 054.18 156.31 360.34
weed 245.24 254.19 294.F2
433.36 448.20
weedeen 365.32
weedhearted 240.22
weeds 209.05 282.F1
Weeds 447.36
weedulicet 042.32
weedwastewoldwevild 613.21
weedwayedwold 612.29
weedy 199.07
Weedy 526.05
week 045.15 070.02 124.17
145.28 180.30 190.17 209.04
351.02 393.16 410.34 608.30
week 399.16
Week 307.19
Week 105.21 106.16
weekday 112.25
weekend 051.36 129.28
weekenders 124.36
weeklings 242.06
weekly 042.03 151.16 544.08
Weekly 439.36
weekreations 585.01
weeks 339.14 457.19 550.23
Weeks 246.01
week's 517.32
weel 448.07
Weel 044.13
weeming 277.04
weeniequeenie 577.02
weeny 102.18 335.21
weenybeenyveenyteeny 021.01
weenywhite 621.31
weep 029.11 093.27 142.32
145.12 158.23 192.23 226.01
230.25 389.20 494.14
weepbig 188.24
weeper 434.16
weeper's 556.11
weepful 361.06
Weepin 518.11
weeping 075.21 142.32 160.01
162.26 207.04 257.01 303.08
347.11 380.25 462.07 505.16
505.30 558.24 590.03
weeping 418.12
Weeping 563.32
Weeping 106.06
Weepon 344.05
weeponder 344.05
weeps 470.05 562.06
Weeps 418.01
weerpovy 333.14
weeseed 625.24
weeshywashy 199.17
weet 009.16
weeter 354.34
weeting 223.36
weevils 024.06
weevily 381.10
weevilybolly 516.10
weewahrwificle 493.19
weewee 598.34
weflected 523.02
wefting 318.32
weg 241.10 249.20 257.19
315.23
weggin 278.F7
wegschicked 541.21
weh 159.17
Weh 408.15
Weh 159.17
wehicul 490.03
Wehpen 388.03
wehr 518.32
wehrmuth 348.13
wehrn 317.21
Weib 267.20
weibduck 138.34
weibes 098.01
weidowwehls 526.32
weigh 074.16
weighed 064.33 126.16 208.22
282.19 407.05 457.07
weighing 255.31
weighs 132.26
weight 138.35 155.19 199.33
304.06 332.19 344.34 396.09
408.06 426.31 482.15 539.34
583.24 621.33
weightier 013.28
weightiness 156.34
weighting 228.30
weights 207.27 289.01
weighty 589.09
Weighty 105.04
Weih 465.07
Wei-Ling-Taou 081.34
weiners 470.25
weir 429.06 626.07
weird 017.14 112.25 199.05
281.02 423.27 562.28 627.29
weird 342.11
weirdest 152.29
weirdly 204.24
weirdst 287.L1
weirs 194.34
Weir's 140.02
Weisingchetaoli 609.10
Weissduwasland 479.29
weisswassh 282.22
weitoheito 338.35
weke 617.17
wel 536.25
welcome 176.22 235.31 245.25
305.10 321.05 382.10 404.36
422.24 464.19 567.11
Welcome 071.22
welcomed 493.03
weld 587.15
Welhell 552.16
welholden 077.22
Welikin's 106.17
welkim 588.17

welkins 131.16
Welkins 178.11
welkinstuck 157.11
Welks 557.02
well 003.21 006.32 011.03 013.13 032.20 033.08 041.09 049.16 053.25 063.09 063.09 081.30 083.03 089.02 089.34 095.12 095.13 111.11 111.11 111.16 111.16 111.28 111.28 115.36 117.06 126.14 135.15 148.06 155.29 158.02 161.33 188.31 191.15 193.16 196.16 196.22 201.35 204.28 205.03 206.18 207.31 214.17 220.17 222.05 237.36 239.11 245.18 248.13 253.16 257.15 257.19 267.21 272.15 275.25 279.F21 280.10 291.28 299.21 299.21 299.21 313.10 313.28 314.23 317.36 330.26 344.06 355.08 364.27 364.30 364.35 364.36 368.08 369.05 369.25 369.30 370.25 379.26 381.08 381.24 386.01 386.12 390.30 390.34 391.25 391.27 392.01 392.04 406.08 410.21 413.12 417.30 422.04 424.29 425.05 428.14 431.30 434.36 437.26 438.14 438.32 439.33 440.36 442.22 443.22 444.23 444.23 449.20 449.22 454.18 454.28 454.28 455.30 459.22 461.35 463.01 465.10 472.15 480.11 480.16 480.21 484.17 508.36 511.21 513.30 521.04 523.15 542.15 551.07 551.10 553.08 561.17 564.36 565.08 567.21 572.15 578.12 578.19 584.35 584.36 585.02 585.07 585.08 585.10 585.13 606.01 606.29 609.26 615.15 617.05 617.10 619.36 625.34
well 344.04 345.06 350.06
Well 006.30 015.22 060.08 066.22 094.27 096.23 096.25 096.26 111.26 111.30 145.05 154.25 155.03 196.04 196.06 198.02 198.27 198.28 200.28 201.25 203.17 205.16 206.09 206.22 208.34 209.18 212.28 213.11 262.09 273.F6 280.13 280.20 286.30 296.15 299.21 302.07 372.28 374.19 377.13 408.09 411.27 420.36 422.23 427.17 452.34 455.30 457.05 462.01 468.23 481.22 484.15 492.14 501.19 503.19 505.36 508.07 508.32 510.31 515.27 536.28 570.11 578.19 584.34 598.11 615.13 617.17 617.30 618.35 619.06
we'll we'll We'll
Welland 205.03
wellasdays 041.01
wellasits 331.06
Wellaslayers 337.21
wellbelavered 448.13
wellbooming 565.05
wellbred 352.17
Wellcrom 625.07
welldressed 037.27 407.04
welled 181.11
Welled 328.26
wellesday 058.29
welleslays 041.01
wellesleyan 510.22
wellfired 514.07
wellformed 134.26
wellheld 584.19
wellinformed 123.19
welling 168.04
wellingbreast 277.06
Wellinghof 541.21
wellings 209.33
Wellingthund 335.18
Wellington 085.10 567.02
Wellingtonia 126.12
wellingtonorseher 203.07
wellingtons 460.01 529.33
Wellington's 286.11
Wellinton's 047.07
wellknown 060.27 321.09 503.08 575.19
wellmade 320.11
wellmeant 515.13
wellmet 447.30 488.33
wellnigh 050.03 097.22
wellnourished 355.24
wellprovided 404.22
wells 579.24
Wells 079.23
wellsowells 578.19
wellstocked 603.19
welltass 338.22
wellteached 413.08
wellth 551.07
welluminated 461.18
wellwarmed 040.02
wellwilled 246.30
wellwillworth 357.03
wellwishers 099.31 172.33
wellworth 398.23 541.06
wellworthseeing 127.35
welly 361.14
wellyoumaycallher 396.07
Welsey 377.13
Welsfusel 412.34
Welsh 008.05 033.26 390.15
welsher 322.08 480.12
Welsher 590.13
Welshers 372.14
Welshman 390.13
Welshrabbit 559.28
welshtbreton 491.32
welt 336.28 454.02
weltall 416.03
welted 404.20
Welter 324.24
weltering 064.20
weltingtoms 176.21
Weltington 371.36
weltr 597.29
wen 290.20
wench 200.30 408.21 553.26
Wench 175.14
wenchalows 333.01
Wenchcraft 269.F4
wenche 388.06
wenchen 243.20
wenches 351.11
wenches' 129.13
wenchful 562.05
wenchman 323.10
wenchyoumaycuddler 608.25
wend 203.04 227.13 267.27 267.27 278.21 416.14 502.01 517.06 562.31 580.13
Wendawanda 199.12
wendelled 581.10
wenden 243.20
wenderer 245.24
wending 619.24
wendowed 351.10
wends 314.35 595.02
wensum 200.19
went 003.08 014.14 015.13 019.35 021.26 022.13 026.04 037.09 043.21 060.06 060.36 067.18 070.31 074.10 080.33 094.07 095.27 098.01 118.26 126.13 128.22 136.22 138.20 139.01 139.32 150.19 164.12 174.05 178.23 196.06 204.06 205.23 206.12 213.23 214.01 226.34 227.13 234.19 242.24 250.32 267.27 286.F1 301.10 329.20 335.07 351.11 351.35 352.02 370.20 380.21 380.26 381.09 391.30 414.09 416.27 423.36 424.06 424.15 427.15 431.01 444.34 467.15 469.16 474.01 488.30 496.29 508.28 516.22 519.04 545.01 549.24 556.25 556.35 557.04 574.34 579.02 605.10 623.06 626.29
went 525.23
Went 105.34
wented 223.35
weothers 238.26
wepowtew 061.06 523.02
wept 034.24 247.17 547.08
Werbungsap 269.20
werden 263.19
were were Were
we're 025.24 093.11 172.24 214.07 215.15 237.33 239.06 239.08 271.29 272.01 293.22 294.F5 295.11 336.23 378.12 378.28 396.13 408.14 446.20 455.17 464.03 496.28 500.35 512.21 569.25 582.14
we're 201.15
We're 304.28 379.35 408.26 463.17 584.08
We're 103.05
werenighn 358.28
weren't 160.18 335.24 368.21 451.19 497.04 521.10
Wereupunder 081.11
werfed 580.04
Werra 208.02
wert 241.08 538.10
Wery 102.18
wes 563.35
we's 530.32
weser 209.22
weslarias 482.11
Weslen-on-the-Row 569.09
Wesleyan 086.33
west 003.21 065.08 066.33 070.14 077.03 085.15 095.20 140.32 442.12 457.20 473.22 479.02
West 274.13 523.25
West 105.07
westasleep 449.35
westborders 474.18
weste 162.17

west-east 114.05
Westend 292.06
wester 600.17
westering 315.27
western 183.04 398.09
Western 604.26
westerness 021.22
westerneyes 537.11
westernmost 178.29
westfrom 605.10
westhinks 116.13
westinders 541.33
westlandmore 553.30
westminstrel 454.09
Westmunster 131.10
westnass 502.06
Weston 534.16
Westreeve-Astagob 503.14
Westwicklow 277.16
wesways 005.22
wesz 516.04
wet 012.16 019.14 024.21 051.03 060.03 061.18 117.18 195.01 196.18 198.06 277.15 277.F3 394.03 397.13 420.16 436.30 463.10 506.21 585.31 618.28
wet 399.21 525.24
Wet 092.07 433.35
Wet 106.16
we't 366.16
wetbed 188.01
wetford 133.28
Weth 316.09
Wethen 471.35
Wetherly 445.32
wethers 604.34
wetmenots 588.09
wetsend 372.34
wetsments 323.10
Wett 610.20
wetted 140.21
wetter 039.14 178.30 347.07
wetterhand 121.22
wettest 390.25
wetting 260.17 314.33 416.10 461.18 620.22
wettings 409.29
Wettingstone 550.31
we've 026.33 054.02 147.16 267.F6 287.F3 334.32 619.11
We've 251.36 306.12 338.01 621.04
We've 071.11
wevey 041.23
wewere 055.15
Wexford-Atelier 531.15
Wexterford's 549.18
wextward 245.08
weys 283.14
whaal 325.31 415.07
whaanever 077.14
whaas 555.01
whaboggeryin 305.33
whack 122.18 444.08
whackawhacks 335.19
whacked 434.11 577.27
whacker 467.28
whackfolthediddlers 042.01
whacking 084.27
whackling 612.16
whad 314.30
Whad 141.08
Whaddingtun 140.01
whaet 601.30
whafft 015.10
Whagta 233.36
Whahat 522.24
whake 519.04
Whake 595.03
whale 015.24 135.29 311.33
Whalebones 434.25
whaled 307.F2
whaler 469.16 589.12
Whales 241.28
whale's 120.11 197.36
whalf 350.25
whaling 078.03
whalk 245.12
Whalley 536.33
Whallfisk 013.34
whallhoarding 365.16
whallrhosmightiadd 056.07
wham 493.17
wha'm 174.13
Whambers 562.13
whang 122.13 122.15 122.16 122.17 122.18 520.25
whang 341.05
Whangpoos 297.F5
whant 603.32
whapping 533.17
wharabahts 379.07
Wharall 354.01
wharf 580.05
wharfore 208.35
Wharnow 213.30
wharom 547.06
Wharrem 576.07
Wharton's 012.23
wharves 330.12
whas 304.20
whase 007.11
Whase 007.09 007.10
Whastle 072.09
what what What What
what' 143.29
whatabout 057.10
whatall 476.23
Whatalose 246.27
whatarcurss 225.12 225.13
Whatarwelter 012.09
Whatbetween 367.01
whate 387.25
whateither 355.36
whatever 066.18 109.10 144.08 145.02 157.27 184.12 196.09 211.36 260.F1 269.05 320.17 359.14 368.05 370.01 370.03 381.32 396.23 440.36 455.22 503.22 508.07 571.20 598.17
whatever 399.26 540.09
Whatever 146.01 563.15
Whateveryournameis 479.12
whatfor 256.26 282.11
Whath 068.25
whather 239.20
whatholoosed 113.20
whathough 117.19
Whatif 007.23
whatinthe 142.06
whatlk 347.07
what'll 046.32 277.09 439.24
What'll 623.14
whatmore 377.03
whatnot 236.28
whats 187.06
what's 034.10 188.12 235.15 270.F2 306.F5 321.22 354.33 415.16 424.35 432.29 447.04 454.23 460.30 461.10 465.07 519.36 604.20 604.21
What's 214.10 225.11 272.F1 411.36 441.05 450.30 531.20
What's 176.11
whatsintime 432.33
whatsthats 019.17
Whatthough 315.17
whattinghim 346.28
whatwar 351.24
whatwidth 340.25
whatyouknow 362.14
whatyoulike 298.11
whatyoumacormack 450.25
whaves 463.32
whawa 066.24
Whawe 180.31
Whawk 215.30
whay 167.08
Whaytehayte's 342.22
wheat 075.10 076.35 134.27 521.19 536.06 590.06 616.10
Wheat 501.08
Wheatacre 257.21
wheatears 550.26
Wheatears 071.11
wheaten 244.22
wheateny 379.26
wheater 026.08
wheathers 396.25
Wheatley's 443.29
Wheatstone's 013.16
wheckfoolthenairyans 360.08
whee 297.F5
wheedle 110.36 466.17
wheedling 181.08
wheel 069.05 213.04 260.08 382.22 415.07 496.10 519.18 520.24 566.22 617.07
wheel 341.05
Wheel 405.24
wheelbarrow 079.26
wheeled 055.27 393.33
wheelhouse 276.25
wheels 006.29 247.03 454.21
wheepingcaugh 511.14
wheer 416.14 417.07
wheer's 137.06
wheesindonk 230.12
wheeze 188.33 273.23 297.02 351.07
wheil 070.03
wheile 356.13
whele 370.32
whelk 208.28
whelks 321.15
whelldselse 239.34
whelp 192.12 516.29
whem 348.26 493.16
when when When When WHEN
whenabouts 555.03 558.33
whenas 037.21 130.14 292.24 557.13 607.12
Whenastcleeps 614.12
whenat 608.29
whenby 535.05
whence 011.02 062.05 090.01 101.14 247.26 369.35 576.20 594.24

Whence 051.03 260.08 267.08 594.13
whenceforward 243.04
Whencehislaws 539.29
Whene'er 562.27
whenever 088.09 239.07 324.06 373.21 468.28 521.36 544.12 573.22 583.34
Whenin 356.16
Whenn 062.34
when's 194.11
When's 448.14
whensday 457.20
whenso 289.22
whenyouheard 362.15
wher 547.02
Wherapool 300.09
<u>whercabroads</u> 419.02
<u>where where</u> Where <u>Where</u>
<u>whereaballoons</u> 274.28
whereabouts 108.25 203.14
whereafter 326.17
whereafters 095.29
whereagainwhen 513.31
whereamid 606.04
Whereapon 617.03
whereas 036.03 051.01 091.05 092.33 268.09 372.08 377.25 487.27 524.01 557.15 611.19
Whereas 092.12 616.16
whereat 040.12 161.18 284.08 605.28
wherebejubers 394.32
wherebus 239.30
whereby 055.34 423.32 493.23 515.16
whered 044.18
wherefore 005.18 582.02
Wherefore 053.27 100.24 264.12 470.12 542.15
wherein 107.19 130.16 265.29 363.33 589.28
Wherein 016.21 194.03
whereinbourne 367.29
whereinn 600.07
<u>whereis</u> 338.34
<u>Where-is-he</u> 211.36
wherend 187.05
whereof 557.30 605.17 605.25
<u>Whereof</u> 231.06
<u>whereoft</u> 445.33
Whereofter 313.14
whereom 356.13
whereon 090.36 473.24 553.32 605.18
whereoneafter 093.01
whereopum 153.26
where's 149.28 204.31 204.32 244.20 275.25 316.35 319.21 403.19 430.35 432.32 433.26 472.12
<u>where's</u> 418.14
<u>Where's</u> 299.16 301.02 448.10 464.25 528.18 530.17
wheresoever 036.31 476.09
wherethen 603.25
wheretwin 004.34
whereupon 082.21 115.18 574.21 605.21
whereuponce 382.20
whereupont 607.30
wherever 124.21 173.21 205.25 467.36 469.07 532.10
whereverafter 606.07
wherewithin 551.26
wherewithouts 541.05
whereyouwot 362.15
Wherfor 545.14
wherry 029.22 138.11 153.36
Wherry 307.F2
wherth 599.03
Whervolk 565.06
whesen 461.26
whet 042.23 311.19 332.31 556.26 563.28 603.24
Whet 360.29
wheth 139.30
whether 031.07 083.13 088.05 089.09 100.01 101.03 101.04 113.28 114.31 120.29 174.19 178.34 187.05 226.01 239.20 271.13 292.22 359.13 382.03 412.11 502.12 522.06 523.06 532.12 546.12 582.13 586.17
Whether 088.11 090.24 606.20
whethered 603.18
whethertheywere 081.33
whets 018.25
<u>whetwadth</u> 340.25
whew 576.09 576.09
whewwhew 576.09
whey 167.07 395.01 441.05
wheywhingingly 171.15
which <u>which</u> Which <u>Which</u>
Whichcroft 139.33
whicher 588.17
whiches 321.25
whichever 358.32 455.07
Whichus 614.12
Whicker 434.11
Whiddington 052.10
whide 300.F4
whiff 015.10 181.23
whiffat 414.13
whig 042.28
<u>Whigger</u> 071.10
whiggissimus 079.03
Whiggler 284.25
whiggy 153.36
whight 358.23
whights 143.11
Whigs 359.26
whig's 020.23
whilask 362.11
whilde 040.13
while <u>while</u> While <u>While</u>
<u>whileas</u> 054.32
whiled 260.14
whilehot 322.05
whilepaper 416.21
whiles 143.15 163.26 191.06 234.18 326.35 328.19 363.30 449.02 474.08 536.13 548.07
<u>whiles</u> 346.15 419.01
Whilesd 325.12
whilest 257.08 288.04 383.19
while'twas 406.17
whileupon 313.10
whiling 224.13
whilk 097.19 370.26 390.23
whilko 102.27
whillbarrow 015.24
whilom 292.21 310.29 336.34 380.21 574.36
Whilp 622.26
whilst 015.22 110.36 114.29 238.16 251.30 357.20 385.28 437.35 445.31 477.27 558.21
Whilst 149.29 371.19
whilstly 269.09
whim 271.17 416.08 493.17
whimbrel 017.20
whimmering 505.07
Whimper 410.30
whimpered 154.32
whimpering 173.05 547.17
whimpers 094.04
whims 102.27
whimsicalissimo 473.04
whimsoever 239.19
whimwhim 331.30 331.30
whine 154.15 183.33
whinealittle 010.33
whines 024.13
whingeywilly 232.24
whinging 192.31
whinn 469.01
whinninaird 541.32
whins 261.04
whip 053.14 554.09
<u>whipedoff's</u> 345.26
whiplooplashes 119.12
whippers 532.27
whipping 222.26
whippingtop 210.32
whipples 331.05
whippoor 449.31
whippy 525.27
whips 363.23 384.33 626.06
whipt 417.22
whirl 220.28
whirled 582.20
whirligig 119.14
whirligigmagees 027.20
whirling 184.06
whirlwind 133.12
whirlworlds 017.29
whirr 261.04
whirrld 147.22
WHIS 293.R1
whish 407.11 407.11 457.30 597.36
Whish 628.13
whished 469.24
whishing 587.12
whisht 018.09 557.11
Whisht 193.12 366.34 441.06 477.10 478.35
<u>Whisht</u> 105.19
<u>whishtful</u> 333.34
whisk 326.34 627.04
Whisk 531.18 531.19 531.20
whiskcoat 404.25
whisked 431.33
whiskerbristle 071.03
whiskered 585.23
whiskers 490.18
whiskery 139.08
whisking 168.03
whisklyng 516.07
Whiskway 510.33
whiskwigs 083.05
whisky 506.35
whisp 158.06
whisper 059.05 139.19 193.14 282.F4 313.17 457.30
whispered 069.04 281.17 435.03
Whisperer 096.10

whisperers 615.30
whispering 121.14 374.26 431.06
whispers 127.16 220.26
whisping 148.01 384.32
whisple 412.21
whispring 024.10
whisprit 291.20
whispy 600.32
whiss 148.26 297.F5
whissle 060.04
Whist 560.12
whisth 292.30
whistle 150.12 223.11 316.10 406.12 490.35 540.15 576.07
WHISTLE 303.R3
whistled 049.01
whistlers 626.13
whistlewhirling 192.34
whistling 049.01 372.31 407.01
Whiston's 359.23
whit 084.27 513.25 536.25
Whitby 587.11
whitch 221.14 546.35
whitchly 226.01
white 008.17 010.02 010.11 010.12 027.13 033.23 041.13 043.26 063.26 066.20 066.20 077.19 080.03 084.19 096.01 097.05 101.14 112.20 116.07 126.20 128.20 133.25 135.06 135.22 148.28 169.08 171.24 176.24 184.07 205.18 247.32 252.34 270.F2 277.14 290.20 347.01 379.33 413.28 438.09 439.07 439.32 441.06 441.15 448.13 459.17 463.04 463.24 486.24 488.30 491.32 494.28 500.12 501.28 504.36 508.33 536.14 538.13 559.33 564.05 567.24 571.16 577.04 600.23 600.28 622.02 623.09
white 032.23 344.11
White 029.15 269.F4 334.15 403.06 447.18 482.05
White 106.02 106.07 107.01 433.18
Whitebeaver 160.16
whiteboys 385.09
Whiteboys 329.25
whitecaps 502.34
whiteclad 605.06
whitehat 322.01
Whitehead 311.24
Whitehed 535.21
whitehorse 132.12
whitehorsed 075.15
Whitehowth 535.26
Whiteknees 302.14
Whiteleg 372.14
whiteley 127.12
whiteliveried 241.28
whitelock 031.15 596.26
whiteluke 529.20
whitemalt 037.34
Whiteman 263.09
whitemost 234.09
whiten 210.32
whiteness 148.30 364.01
whitening 071.01 442.14
whiteoath 535.27
whiteopen 234.07
whitepot 538.35
whiter 527.20
whites 049.07 184.18 542.26 557.12
Whiteside 095.15
whitesides 352.04
whitespread 628.10
Whitest 501.29
whitestone 005.17
whitethorn 015.03 556.19
whiteyoumightcallimbs 238.30
whither 034.20 062.01 089.09 100.01 224.18 356.11 359.35 488.02 576.21
Whither 594.12
whithered 260.14
whitherout 607.26
whithpeh 138.10
Whithr 599.04
Whitlock 098.25
Whitmore 377.03
whitness 241.36
whitside 204.24
whittlewit 108.06
Whitweekend 099.17
whizz 347.16
whizzcrash 356.32
whizzer 178.20
whizzling 416.34
who who Who Who WHO
whoa 467.10
Whoa 016.16
Whoah 480.36
whoahoa 366.16
whoak 411.06
whoalike 358.29
Whoam 562.10
Whoan 272.20
whoasever 362.18
Whoat 016.16
whoe 360.05
whoel 169.12
whoer 588.18
whoever 037.09 050.07 122.32 212.04 396.23 619.02
whoēver's 050.34
Whoevery 460.16
whoewaxed 490.01
Whofe 572.16
Whoforyou 076.31
whofoundland 412.04
whogave 413.15
Whogoesthere 455.19
whoishe 499.35 499.35 499.35 499.36 499.36
Whoishe 499.35 499.35
Who-is-silvier 211.35
whol 312.19
wholawidey 625.25
whole 006.12 010.19 023.02 023.15 024.33 025.10 026.10 033.06 048.19 053.25 064.09 069.05 072.33 078.03 079.19 080.34 084.10 084.13 086.02 086.28 090.21 090.22 092.01 097.20 117.36 118.01 130.31 135.29 137.22 147.03 148.28 150.16 173.19 174.16 176.33 177.09 179.11 187.05 204.19 222.14 229.09 230.19 238.12 241.27 248.12 283.05 283.20 287.16 288.12 289.15 292.22 295.23 312.04 315.07 318.09 322.18 322.19 324.15 334.23 348.15 350.22 355.33 364.26 366.33 381.35 385.30 387.10 389.33 396.22 406.34 415.20 423.14 431.12 431.34 434.22 436.04 440.35 447.10 451.02 455.09 475.06 480.31 489.04 492.04 496.10 509.32 510.17 512.01 515.27 519.02 519.04 520.12 521.08 523.30 530.18 535.11 536.28 543.23 545.22 553.08 570.18 575.27 581.28 585.03 596.11 599.29 601.19 602.07 616.17 625.36
whole 343.15
Whole 207.25
Whole 175.07
wholeabelongd 323.20
wholeabuelish 452.34
wholebeit 356.23
wholeborough 162.30
wholeborrow 017.04
wholebroader 051.19
wholed 137.36 336.04 563.32
wholedam's 043.20
wholefallows 229.19
wholehail 552.35
whole-heartedly 150.28
wholehog 228.18
Wholehunting 373.20
wholemole 614.27
wholenosing 365.16
wholes 375.08
whole's 125.02 340.36
whole's 419.02
wholesole 238.27
wholesome 163.36 181.13 540.04
wholeswiping 537.17
wholetime 570.07
wholetrouz 413.30
wholewife 533.04
who'll 205.04 270.28 291.12 439.25 441.19 448.17 448.17 460.12 583.21
Who'll 273.F5 448.18 626.17
wholly 070.02 077.16 155.16 264.F3 326.11 424.33 551.29
Wholly 231.16 307.04
whollyisland 111.18
whollymost 271.F5
wholst 346.26
wholume 048.19
Wholyphamous 073.09
wholyway 242.24
whom Whom
whomafter 589.25
whomamong 605.06
whome 138.30 296.31 332.27 379.03
whomever 078.36
whomin 484.05
whomsoever 413.32 551.16
whomto 356.24
whoo 297.F5
Whoo 439.20
whool 415.07 617.07
Whooley 368.29
whoonearth 155.29
whoop 024.14 232.30 454.13
Whoopee 246.01
Whooper 368.29
whooping 423.26
whooping 383.05
whoopsabout 331.17
whoosh 457.24

Whooth 007.30
whoo-whoo 149.27
whoozebecome 240.06
Whope 572.17
whopes 308.F2
whoppers 170.31
whopping 423.27
Whor 349.01
whorable 438.17
Whore 241.33
Whore 105.34
whores 130.06 200.29
whores' 183.27
whorl 006.24 150.13 225.31 415.08
whorled 272.04
whorly 242.23
Whorort 139.33
whorse 084.27 610.02
whorship 547.27
whorts 221.15
who's 117.07 192.31 376.35 448.26 626.32
Whosaw 535.13
whose whose Whose
Whose 518.10 (Whose B. Dunn)
whosebefore 095.29
whosekeeping 422.14
whosepants 319.32
Whoses 147.19
whosethere 019.17
whoso 116.17
whosoever 426.02
whosold 606.21
whoson 369.21
whoss 347.16
whot 135.07 222.09 459.36
whotes 184.18
whother 618.25
whotwaterwottle 176.36
whou 135.06
whould 513.13
whouse 221.15
whowasit 142.05
whowghowho 291.04
Whowham 147.34
whowho 409.27
whowitswhy 272.06
whowl 284.19
whowle 309.22
Whoyteboyce 004.05
whud 342.14
whuebra 202.13
whugamore 132.19
whuit 597.36
whuite 388.16
whulerusspower 248.21
whulesalesolde 326.23
whumember 493.17
whuon 202.23
Whure 478.25
Whur's 478.24
Whu's 478.23 480.18 480.18 500.03
whuskle 556.27
why why Why Why WHY
whyacinthinous 118.28
Whyafter 614.24
whybe 052.35
whydidtha 019.06
Whydoyoucallme 479.13
whye 372.04
whyed 317.27
whyfe 350.14
Whyfor 239.26 309.11
Whyfore 379.22
whyi 006.13
Whyle 607.22
whyre 115.19
whys 424.17
Why's 150.10
whyse 297.03
Whysht 018.10
Whyte 064.21 223.17
whyterobe 139.04
wi 170.18 525.06
wi' 140.18
wibfrufrocksfull 236.12
wick 046.19 390.05 583.32 608.30 625.17
Wick 358.23 499.13
wicked 022.05 022.06 060.08 070.32 088.27 248.28 390.29 459.36
wickeday 219.04
Wickedgapers 366.02
wickeding 310.29
wickedy 583.34
Wickenlow 203.01
wicker 108.23
wickerchurchwardens 116.27
wickered 014.01
wickerpotluck 210.05
wickerworker 559.06
Wickerworks 288.28
Wickerymandy 200.07
wicket 072.28 532.18 589.24
wick-in-her 583.31
wickle 585.30
wicklowpattern 029.23
wickred 527.25
wicks 435.19
wick's 083.06
wickser 311.11
Wid 017.08
widamost 449.28
widdars 009.21
Widdas 577.22
widders 243.36
widdershins 470.36 511.01
widdle 620.23
widdy 387.33
wide 008.21 010.21 035.08 036.22 058.27 099.15 135.21 147.05 212.30 254.35 352.15 429.06 505.05 548.29 577.27 583.16 583.33 614.14
Wide 271.29
Wide 106.01
wideawake 242.05
wideheaded 472.05
wideheight 418.08
widely 389.14
widelysigned 543.06
widens 250.32
wider 070.07 115.21 341.13 376.02
widerembrace 471.06
widerproof 155.29
WIDERURGES 267.R1
widest 356.28 443.14 585.03
Widger 039.11 610.36
widming 616.04
widness 316.04
widnight 391.33
widnows 340.14
widow 079.27 214.26 227.06 284.F4 380.31 544.10 556.09 580.29
Widow 079.33
widowed 088.03
widower 313.11 375.26 618.25
widowers 387.17 390.14
widowpeace 101.18
widows 500.10 567.28
widows' 183.26
widowshood 461.06
widowt 102.02
width 056.27 058.14 245.20 323.22 336.04 376.02 566.15 578.08
Wiederherstellung 296.L1
wieds 426.21
wiege 098.32
wield 091.27
wielded 157.02
wielderfight 003.06
Wieldhelm 574.15
wiening 546.31
wiesel 197.04
wife 020.27 029.07 050.06 066.23 116.03 193.20 248.22 336.26 362.13 373.26 455.04 495.33 514.23 530.13 543.34 544.21 572.27 572.33 573.30 618.04 618.04
wife 340.13
Wife 167.29
Wife 072.07 175.08
wifebetter 356.09
wifely 581.17
wi'fennel 037.36
wife's 116.03 116.04 255.26 312.16 320.23
wiffey 527.11
wiffeyducky 577.01
wiffriends 444.35
wifish 511.14
wifukie 532.30
wig 051.06 150.29 193.13 204.24 390.36 559.25 576.15 587.31
Wigan's 551.03
wigeared 414.36
wigger 315.26
wiggle 112.01
wigglewaggle 526.16
wiggly 204.14 622.32
wiggywiggywagtail 302.07
wight 102.18 407.05 559.27
wigs 092.35
wigwarming 553.26
wigworms 282.13
Wijn 256.07
wik 196.13
wikeawades 608.34
wiking 338.30
Wikingson 241.18
wil 357.27
wilby 017.21
wilcomer 317.10
wild 022.11 039.29 044.01 049.05 071.04 092.31 094.07 160.02 184.20 243.20 250.33 281.03 331.35 363.22 378.04 384.02 403.13 419.24 430.29 451.06 461.07 463.10 475.10 476.01

476.01 492.10 525.32
526.21 536.34 540.28
556.18 589.23 627.26
627.27 627.28
Wild 052.10 229.01
Wild 106.01
Wildairs' 210.25
wildbroom 056.24
wildcaps 383.19
wilde 041.09 069.03 081.17
Wilde 307.20
Wildemanns 358.23
wildering 244.33
wildes 510.11
wildeshaweshowe 256.13
wildest 034.26 157.02
wildewide 098.02
wildfire 350.35
wildfires 090.09
wildflier's 446.18
wildgaze 197.14
wildgoup's 185.06
Wildhare 227.04
wildr 597.29
wildrose 210.10
Wildrose 229.11
wilds 186.15 246.22
Wilds 497.13 503.34
wild's 269.11
wildsbillow 160.19
wildth 549.26
Wildu 053.02
wildwood's 556.17
wildwoods' 282.F1
wildworewolf's 244.10
wildy 566.32
wile 142.36 282.28
wile 345.17
wilelife 113.03
wiles 149.09 223.03 227.02
596.07 615.33
Wiles 303.07
wiley 332.09
wilfrid's 449.08
wilfulness 281.17
Wilhelmina's 601.21
Wilkins 464.19
wilkinses 090.11
wilkling 269.12
will will Will Will
will 141.20 250.27 251.06
260.04 391.30 411.11 467.04
545.14
Will 044.13 051.12 146.11
337.21 532.11 575.29 596.36
Will 175.19
willbe 236.28 364.04
willbedone 328.36
Willbeforce 126.20
willed 523.03 545.15
Willed 272.04
willesly 273.26
Willest 250.03
willfully 238.06
willhap 425.27
William 031.14 440.03 507.35
543.17
Williams 277.F4
Williamstown 615.20
Williamswoodsmenufactors 027.17
Willie 351.12
willing 036.24 224.05
277.06
Willingdone 008.10 008.16 008.17
008.33 008.34 008.35 009.03
009.07 009.09 009.09 009.11
009.14 009.15 009.23 009.26
009.34 010.01 010.02 010.04
010.07 010.10 010.12 010.13
010.16 010.17
Willingdone's 009.11
willingly 092.14
willings 302.F2
willingsons 097.34
willingtoned 334.13
willmate 350.35
Will-of-the-Wisp 211.02
willow 207.04 278.08 361.08
Willow 583.28
Willowm 160.02
willowy 098.35 333.14
willpip 314.25
wills 004.01 079.24 608.27
Willses 577.21
willside 239.29
willy 223.03 360.23 449.31
Willy 610.36
willynully 582.08
willyum 581.21
wilnaynilnay 339.33
Wilsh 160.27 160.28
wilt 015.21 015.23 255.05
325.25 516.22
Wilt 076.27 512.12 512.12
512.13
wilted 225.36
wilting 450.12 559.03
wilts 251.15
Wiltsh 327.22
wily 233.12
Wilysly 137.11
wimdop 101.04
wimman 012.03
Wimmegame's 375.16
wimmering 098.01
wimn 443.16
wimpled 273.15
wimwim 101.08
Wimwim 101.07
win 051.34 079.24 117.06
327.08 358.19 362.21 433.14
462.03 489.03 528.34 556.21
584.07
Win 088.36 473.21
winblowing 519.22
Wince 303.32
winced 198.13
winceywencky 097.27
winches 578.23
wind 013.29 019.34 023.14
080.27 083.05 091.27 097.10
112.35 136.05 137.27 143.33
149.09 179.29 180.21 194.06
226.05 228.10 232.29 258.06
271.27 276.14 282.F1 315.15
333.18 335.12 363.23 365.19
372.19 380.04 380.08 391.17
393.33 428.20 443.07 471.21
476.02 518.07 528.03 578.01
587.02 603.27 619.22 626.04
Wind 094.05 324.25
Wind 176.01
windaborne 561.20
windaug 198.23
windbag 273.23
windbags 621.06
windblasted 194.14
winde 374.29
winded 408.04
Winden 243.20
Windermere 212.36
windeth 264.18
windfall 023.34
windfoot 131.25
windhame 415.29
windies 010.28
windiest 288.24
windigo 267.16
windigut 171.17
winding 024.19 046.07 077.28
206.30 405.08 428.15
windingly 080.26
windmachine 503.02
windopes 586.31
window 026.30 043.14 051.35
121.04 127.34 249.16 327.22
358.01 456.35 559.04 586.05
window 399.13
windowcurtains 543.31
windowdisks 055.22
windower's 024.09
windows 135.21 235.26 395.08
395.11 552.27 609.14
window's 282.F1
windowsill 490.33
windr 597.28
windrush 208.22
winds 043.27 157.31 376.33
383.20 503.18 565.31
wind's 010.30 477.06
Windsewer 420.24
windstill 274.25
windstorming 203.03
windswidths 394.16
windtor 551.01
windtreetop 331.05
Windup 092.06
windward 471.24 602.05
windwards 315.23
windwarrd 524.19
windwhistling 506.22
windy 056.29 437.05 565.04
588.32
wine 056.27 117.20 179.34
265.23 273.F4 326.28 362.19
406.22 434.29 498.01
Wine 177.28
wineact 587.35
winebakers 290.27
wined 351.11
wineglasses 183.21
Winehouse 014.14
wineless 053.04
wineman 382.25
wine's 170.13
wineshop 042.24
wineskin 187.08
winesour 037.34
winespilth 381.09
Winestain 149.28
winetavern 536.21
wineupon 410.14
winevat 171.25
winevatswaterway 512.05
wing 040.28 255.13 377.13
457.19
wing 275.L2
winged 185.05 359.35 624.31
winged 418.26

wingh 351.21
winging 383.16 519.17
wingless 285.05
wingrests 077.06
wings 455.21 469.09 469.31 628.10
wingsets 262.23
wingtywish 364.13
wingweary 232.29
Wingwong 361.14
wink 005.21 073.25 074.08 193.20 273.F3 310.29 583.35
winked 408.21
winkel 255.23
winken 130.07
winker 273.25
winkers 495.22
winker's 514.20
winkies 561.34
winking 145.02 148.14 588.36 595.08
winking 383.13
winkle 199.11
winklering 413.34
winkles 297.13 321.15
winks 028.18 053.09 116.17 162.27
Wink's 249.04
winksome 327.26
winky 328.05
Winkyland 435.25
Winland 469.11
winn 347.14
Winne 610.22
winner 170.09 379.11
Winner 427.30
winnerful 265.15 265.15
winners 523.15
winneth 369.20
winnie 327.08
Winnie 020.35 227.14 279.F22
winning 191.17 201.24 249.04 309.05 325.36
Winning 527.20
winninger 366.07
Winning's 503.15
Winnowing 105.13
winny 257.09
Winny 039.11 610.36
winpower 117.20
wins 273.16 285.10 358.32 473.03
Wins 361.01
winsome 157.31
winsor 341.23
Winsure 227.02
winter 028.08 057.30 097.12 326.29
winter 399.13
winterlong 603.09
wintermantle 242.35
winters 065.01 423.23
winter's 201.11
Winterwater's 187.19
Winthrop's 502.29
winxed 358.25
wious 189.01
wip 465.08
wipe 019.11 144.03 178.06 426.14 434.16 443.10
Wipe 304.F3
wipealittle 010.33
wiped 227.31
wipehalf 534.29
wipenmeselps 612.24
wipers 204.30
wipethemdry 578.19
wipin 336.30
wipin'fampiny 046.19
wiping 042.10 150.11 303.09 314.33 578.32
Wippingham 019.15
wirbl 597.29
wire 289.09 488.28 502.33
wired 223.34
wireless 449.29 489.36 557.15
wires 135.35
Wires 098.14
Wirrgeling 088.33
wiry 328.05
wis 021.02 158.04 622.31
wischandtugs 064.19
wisden's 584.16
wisdom 114.20 162.23 231.11 462.11 606.06 611.20
Wisdom's 526.15
wise 031.07 033.04 099.22 123.02 210.34 237.19 251.06 253.07 262.18 281.F3 322.12 368.28 427.32 491.04 513.35 560.24 568.27 576.23 607.03 625.16
wiseable 016.24
wiseableness 472.03
wiseacre's 480.34
wisechairmanlooking 416.07
wisecrackers 033.16
wisefolly 321.03
wiseheads 405.04
wisehight 368.24
Wisely 595.18
wiser 164.33
wisest 426.33 493.12
wish 011.14 053.32 056.10 059.30 109.28 144.21 154.16 160.14 200.30 202.34 203.29 244.16 278.16 325.06 372.14 441.16 446.14 452.29 453.01 457.09 457.09 469.36 495.34 517.27 562.08 596.35 612.04 616.28 617.32 620.27
Wish 203.29
Wish 104.24
wisha 019.05
Wisha 019.05 427.35 477.05
Wisha 399.15
wishawishawish 381.29
wished 053.29 223.36 335.28 432.33
wishening 386.06
wisher 446.14
wisherwife 066.16
wishes 147.20 181.27 197.15 413.24 573.04
wisheths 346.05
wishful 255.33
wishing 073.17 075.13 245.18 308.19 582.04
wishmarks 251.17
wisht 617.31 626.34
wishtas 327.23
Wishwashwhose 614.03
wishwish 092.31
wishy 616.31
wishyoumaycull 223.14
wishywashy 191.36
wising 054.36
wisness 204.22
wisp 111.32 404.15
wispful 568.12
wispywaspy 548.24
Wissixy 524.26
wist 160.28 204.25 261.03 416.15
Wist 160.28
wisteria 248.01
wistfultone 248.07
wit 021.16 061.30 255.26 398.20 521.17 620.29
witch 251.11 468.35
witchawubbles 079.31
witchbefooled 337.03
witching 509.04
Witchman 245.16
Witchywithcy 175.14
with with With With WITH
Withal 358.20
Withasly 226.28
wi'that 499.20
withd 168.07
Withdraw 585.26
withdrawn 595.19
withdrew 080.25
withdrewers 546.06
withdwellers 036.30
withe 553.35
Wither 004.29
withering 473.02
withers 386.33 550.26
Withers 176.02
withes 331.21
withim 388.05
within 041.33 075.14 085.02 087.07 093.12 119.06 122.10 139.01 152.18 154.01 182.05 215.02 228.04 229.12 244.19 247.03 288.20 328.30 344.13 368.24 415.17 433.05 436.10 475.34 476.34 500.03 522.05 556.14 563.11 579.28 625.30
Within 541.04
withins 520.16
withnot 578.31
Withought 261.13
withould 344.32
without 026.20 034.30 041.03 070.33 085.16 089.19 122.11 125.04 149.05 149.21 160.10 173.07 174.05 174.10 176.28 193.27 198.26 233.15 272.04 272.04 276.05 302.17 302.21 330.31 333.09 351.20 365.10 368.13 369.33 379.02 405.14 405.18 405.36 420.05 421.16 432.24 432.24 441.36 444.17 455.17 471.28 473.06 490.25 491.13 492.13 504.17 512.21 514.29 522.35 526.12 551.19 557.25 558.08 559.07 559.14 566.21 566.22 575.12 582.21 585.34 596.23 596.23 598.19
without 341.32 345.12 354.18
Without 330.31 569.10
Without 106.03 383.13
withouten 256.08 598.02
withsay 318.18
withswillers 171.20
witht 380.31
withumpronouceable 479.09

Withun 604.07
Withworkers 495.11
withyin 419.14
witless 247.22
witness 054.24 073.29 086.33 089.02 089.08 314.04 515.21 522.27 575.20 617.28
witnesses 029.11 375.02
wits 018.25 279.F36 440.01 545.35
wit's 061.17 185.07
witsends 170.13
witt 139.30
witter 022.04
wittest 022.28
wittiest 170.16
witting 272.04
wittold 505.32
wittol's 417.23
witty 041.23 120.03 377.14 588.36
Wittyngtom 341.31
Wit-upon-Crutches 209.07
witween 458.01
witwee's 457.36
wiv 587.31 588.05
wivable 579.25
wive 142.36 215.15 318.04
wives 183.26 363.10 364.35 438.22 540.36
Wives 034.30
Wives 106.31
WIVES 300.R1
wives' 079.19
wivewards 581.10
wivvy 028.33
wi'Wolf 444.32
wixy 010.07
wi'yer 122.14 525.27
wiz 357.33
wiz 352.35
wizening 271.29
wizzard 017.28
wizzend 521.17
W.K. 503.12 (wellknown kikkinmidden)
W. K. 369.11 (Mr W. K. Ferris-Fender)
W. K. O. O. 013.14
wnt 427.16 (went)
wo 506.13
Wo 506.13
woa 128.23
woabling 452.01
woad 227.21
wobban 013.26
wobble 309.22
wobbles 300.27
Wobbleton 372.14
wobblewers 019.11
wobblish 615.26
wobiling 403.10
Wod 365.26
woden 082.16
wodes 126.03
wodhalooing 324.18
wodhar 130.04
Wodin 535.05
wodkar 063.06
wody 348.12
woe 011.07 094.16 135.23 168.03 194.11 194.12 273.08 275.27 320.16 471.31 526.20
Woe 103.07 321.15 499.08 506.15 506.15 526.20
woebecanned 007.17
woeblots 225.36
woed 388.06
Woefear 226.06
woemaid 149.09
Woeman's 022.08
woent 164.07
Woermann 610.22
Woes 379.10
woesoever 576.19
woewoewoe 194.24
Woff 593.06
woful 281.21 503.22
Woful 503.21
Woh 499.08
wohl 058.13 312.25 536.36
wohld 593.03
wohl's 330.28
wohly 349.19
Wohn 139.36
wohned 152.18
Wohntbedarft 221.33
woice 153.36 240.06
woid 378.29 596.21
woiney 518.21
woke 580.32 615.22
woken 461.27
wokenp 064.05
wokinbetts 242.05
woking 368.09 491.34 608.30
wokklebout 242.15
woksed 358.26
wol 244.22
Wolafs 319.27
wold 336.17 450.29 505.02 549.25
Wold 257.24
Woldomar 255.16
wolds 503.21
wold's 248.24
wolf 202.24 323.34 462.26
Wolf 480.04
wolfbone 052.19
Wolfgang 480.36
Wolfhound 480.04
wolfling 516.21
wolfsbelly 080.13
wolfwise 480.28
wolk 351.36 609.31
wolken 588.20
Wolkencap 023.21
wolkenic 240.26
wolkingology 387.12
Wolkmans 616.25
woll 379.21
wollan 376.05
wollies 337.24
Wollinstown 309.16
wollops 349.30
wollpimsolff 353.17
wollsey 578.07
wolly 225.20
Wolossay's 492.10
wolp 406.06
Wolsey 049.08
Wolsherwomens 287.L1
Wolsley 292.F3
Wolverhampton 442.09
wolvertones 565.05
wolves 099.14 479.13
wolvesfoot 550.21
wolving 318.33
wom 610.18
woman 020.33 028.03 056.27 058.29 079.09 090.23 108.31 112.20 146.16 158.25 158.32 194.02 206.21 207.34 211.23 214.16 220.23 227.10 242.26 243.30 246.12 270.26 274.19 283.F1 309.21 336.12 386.09 392.36 397.01 403.15 411.09 413.09 423.20 438.03 445.12 448.10 454.20 466.05 466.15 468.06 486.12 495.35 511.14 511.23 539.35 547.05 564.07 575.07 576.02 576.27 579.34 599.35
Woman 083.19 145.29 389.15 390.32 496.09 526.20 559.20 559.26
Woman 107.03 177.28 213.02 292.06
WOMAN 266.R1
womanage 270.10
womanahoussy 578.32
womanhid 069.02
womanish 584.20
womankind 128.19
womanly 038.14 537.33
womans 369.20
woman's 040.20 509.27 544.04 622.04
Woman's 559.08 559.10 582.31 617.35
womans' 511.23
woman't 505.08
womb 143.21 193.33
Womb 293.L1
wombful 483.18
Wombwell 060.22 529.01
wome 201.24
women 016.05 101.01 133.10 134.24 173.06 189.14 375.36 532.33 548.26
womenlong 462.03
Womensch 318.27
womhoods 375.09
womit 492.03
Wommany 600.30
womn 465.28
womth 348.25
won 036.21 051.33 117.21 128.18 137.32 144.09 151.24 180.13 214.28 304.01 325.07 327.08 337.34 358.32 361.02 398.20 408.27 412.27 529.24 536.36 621.11
Won 469.27
wonced 198.14
wonday 481.08
wonder 046.01 143.34 196.14 212.23 215.04 235.25 251.15 277.F1 281.02 290.F6 291.07 327.07 333.01 375.35 379.16 475.03 491.13 517.32
wonder 201.14
Wonder 248.34
Wonder 071.14
wonderdecker 620.07
wondered 101.01 146.29 454.23
wonderful 194.33 252.06 295.15 381.26 446.02 458.31 518.11 556.09
Wonderful 071.14

wonderfully 084.10
wondering 138.01 274.18 417.06 439.21 507.32 508.06
Wondering 229.14
wonderland's 374.03
Wonderlawn's 270.20
wonderlost 363.23
wonderlust 576.21
wondern 013.33
wondernest 318.17
wonders 265.15
wonderstruck 057.15
wonderwearlds 147.28
wonderwomen 395.31
wondr 597.29
wone 017.19
Wone 265.23
wonet 292.12
wonged 366.32
wonks 595.08
wonna 240.02
wonner 246.15
wonnerful 265.16
wons 273.16 614.18
wonsome 157.31
wonst 597.05
wont 101.12 239.30 251.06 263.F2 278.19 300.17 431.31
won't 025.01 027.35 146.23 201.31 215.34 233.13 248.26 254.24 271.16 368.29 391.29 424.16 435.05 436.28 445.20 457.15 458.19 459.12 467.12 468.15 487.26 487.33 495.31 576.08 621.05 621.09 624.23 624.23
won't 399.11 399.15
Won't 047.16 488.32
Won't 071.36
wonted 372.13
Wonted 499.31
wonterers 355.33
wontnat 487.21
wonts 004.01
woo 046.31 079.24 133.25 133.25 148.30 264.18 462.03 556.21
wood 070.27 080.03 080.28 098.26 098.35 200.02 301.24 320.10 335.33 354.23 362.22 453.15 503.36 561.03 574.01 588.33 599.27
Wood 068.31 223.20 348.21
Woodbine 351.12
woodbines 587.07
woodcut 043.25
woodcuts 580.04
woodcutter 356.36
wooden 016.33 413.36
Woodenbeard 467.15
Woodenhenge 596.13
woodensdays 565.05
woodfires 404.06
Woodin 503.28
woodint 303.21
woodlessness 055.28
woodmann 042.20
woodpiles 011.21
woods 074.10 076.25 112.04 359.18 478.34 556.17 619.23
wood's 586.23
woodtoogooder 602.09
woodwards 034.15
woodwordings 280.04
woodworld 189.24
woody 449.31 504.22
woodyshoes 008.19
wooed 189.23 251.19 325.30 366.34
wooeds 290.18
wooer 246.30
woof 211.18 455.21
Woohoo 046.32
wooing 132.08
wook 593.14
woold 225.19
woolf 223.03
woolfell 305.12
woolied 511.32
woolies 180.32 404.22
Woolington 568.19
woollem 138.32
woollen 042.33
woollied 334.26
woollies 373.16
woolly 028.06 039.29 133.25 381.26
woolly's 454.11
woolpalls 621.15
wools 248.22
wools 353.33
woolsark 493.20
woolseley 017.11
woolselywellesly 052.27
Woolsley 337.21
Wooluvs 479.15
Woolwhite's 078.32
Woolwichleagues 347.09
Woolworth's 072.14
wooly 223.03
Wooly 508.15
woolywags 092.20
woom 465.08
wooman 170.14
Wooming 603.01
Woooooon 436.05
woops 177.33
woor 414.03
woos 351.11 619.15
Woos 330.31
Woose 104.24
Woovil 369.12
wooving 318.32
woowoo 036.23
Woowoo 082.31
Woowoolfe 467.15
wop 167.01 243.34
Woppington 210.25
wops 513.13
wopsy 348.31
wor 379.11
wor 433.20
worbbling 270.F2
word 009.10 020.14 036.08 049.23 080.28 083.10 093.25 115.01 115.07 115.12 118.01 120.05 136.36 146.27 149.34 165.08 167.29 172.30 173.02 174.11 180.30 186.06 189.29 206.20 238.12 243.30 249.04 249.06 249.13 251.19 252.27 266.F2 267.16 283.30 284.21 289.16 300.11 317.11 325.36 367.17 379.07 385.05 405.11 422.10 424.23 424.35 454.26 463.13 467.28 476.01 477.13 487.05 507.22 538.06 545.16 551.16 578.14 593.22 596.31 606.21 614.21 615.01 619.22
Word 167.28
Word 175.12
wordchary 225.02
wordcraft 356.36
worded 115.06
worden 223.27
worder 483.16
Wordherfhull 624.23
wordless 223.34
wordloosed 219.16
wordpainter 087.13
wordpress 020.09
words 014.14 037.16 052.32 062.32 072.28 098.26 098.35 108.36 114.08 121.13 128.06 164.18 167.33 174.10 184.26 188.25 258.02 279.F07 287.F3 292.20 299.F3 421.18 421.23 422.21 424.33 425.29 432.10 432.17 458.07 460.26 469.29 480.25 482.34 486.09 506.30 516.32 531.32 536.25 542.21 597.10 598.23 600.20 611.11 611.28
words 345.19
Words 074.16 433.07
word's 168.01
wordsharping 422.02
wordth 056.27
wordworth's 539.05
wordwounder 075.19
wordybook 530.19
wore 050.26 113.17 162.33 204.24 208.06 234.18 269.21 317.30 372.26 416.06 420.07 487.11 556.08 625.32
wore 201.07
woren't 366.16
worf 174.02
work 026.23 035.31 081.03 246.09 287.F4 327.30 366.19 409.34 410.30 410.33 411.03 411.06 425.10 425.29 446.28 467.18 518.12 543.25 543.36 625.13
Work 473.21
worked 048.23 191.33 221.19 310.02 507.22
worked 284.L1
Worked 590.27
worker 113.34
workers 011.15
working 140.17 149.34 333.24 446.34 560.04 571.35
workings 615.14
Workings 489.13
workingstacks 006.01
workit 548.14
workman 098.25
works 014.05 095.03 226.12 356.22 440.16 524.04
workship 289.07
world 006.12 018.19 019.35 023.10 028.29 032.10 042.12 042.13 042.16 052.08 055.09 064.25 064.26 064.26 067.02 067.26 075.21 079.19 083.12 088.06 091.25 091.25 091.25 098.35 111.08 139.01 140.11 140.11 140.12 140.13 147.27

156.20 160.17 174.20 183.04 186.07 189.10 194.24 200.30 205.08 229.17 230.35 234.06 237.14 239.22 244.13 252.26 257.24 263.F1 274.F4 275.06 281.25 288.F2 289.21 290.02 314.21 335.21 348.36 356.11 360.33 363.23 375.36 381.15 384.36 385.07 387.36 391.24 397.24 417.10 426.11 431.19 452.30 469.11 485.23 499.33 505.12 510.16 526.21 532.10 546.31 564.12 576.23 589.04 593.03 597.29 600.02 608.28 611.13 611.18 617.33 624.01 625.25
world 345.35
World 028.20 222.20 285.27 341.20 342.32
World 105.29 107.03 175.07
worldins 364.28
worldrenownced 341.19
worldroom 100.29
worlds 158.10 412.02 422.16 530.03 619.11
world's 012.02 123.36 275.27 278.13 278.16
worldstage's 033.03
worldwide 419.07
worldwise 314.25
worldwithout 244.01
worldwright 014.19
worm 037.14 082.06 193.08 435.23
Wormans' 387.21
wormcasket 415.01
wormd 354.22
wormingpen 610.32
wormquashed 379.10
worms 026.07 183.29 540.01
Worms 175.09
worn 107.21
Worndown 489.22
Worns 619.19
Worn't 348.02
worold 255.18 441.19
worrawarrawurms 225.13
worrid 467.07
worried 108.10
worrier 596.11
worries 273.08 393.25 580.26
worrild 258.21
worry 097.02
Worry 202.19
worrybound 590.03
worrying 620.13
worryld 059.10
worse 079.32 092.36 166.19 176.31 203.05 233.11 269.F1 341.13 380.26 425.06 468.07 488.24 542.19
Worse 283.28 438.16
worship 186.30
Worship 045.09 391.32
worshipful 024.08 264.32
worshipful 201.15
worshipfuls 089.22
worships 092.23
worst 183.03 204.14 232.05 331.02 482.12 581.07
Worst 072.14
worsted 517.19
worstered 320.16
wort 102.20
worth 073.26 111.26 121.01 158.02 165.30 172.22 179.35 199.08 209.14 209.16 230.25 246.15 246.32 248.13 317.26 413.23 458.28 474.23 475.21 581.08
wortha 419.32
Worther 028.31
worthies 241.30 467.12 550.01
worthily 596.34
worths 527.34
worthy 029.19 032.21 163.19 448.21 557.26
worts 378.24
wortsampler 305.10
wos 444.30 444.30
wosen 337.16
woshup 154.18
wot 062.23 255.10 336.36 420.14 420.15
wot's 061.18
wotty 120.03
wouest 153.27
would would Would
wouldbe 042.13 060.16 531.31 566.17
wouldbewas 595.35
would-do 434.35
wouldmanspare 077.16
Wouldndom 409.01
wouldnt 360.23
wouldn't 065.03 066.35 073.11 088.34 113.21 140.28 144.17 148.13 207.17 207.22 283.24 297.28 384.13 385.23 393.34 411.30 437.24 450.02 451.10 490.33 491.36 509.25 517.27 520.35 620.26
wouldntstop 221.06
wouldower 587.10
wouldpay 028.32
woulds 396.19
would-to-the-large 576.24
woule 481.29
wound 129.10 222.16 247.23 319.24 548.33
woundabout 242.05
wounded 232.12 278.25
Wounderworker 008.35
woundid 072.22
wounds 124.03
wounted 361.25
woup 506.22
wove 207.01 552.04
woven 292.21
wovens 375.35
woves 330.12
wowhere 054.03
wowow 378.33
woxen 375.19
woyld 535.28
woylde 588.03
W.P. 086.34 (P.W.= Parnell Witness)
Wrack 498.24
wrackt 058.31
wraimy 347.07
wraith 414.03
wrake 557.06
Wramawitch 027.28
wrang 508.02
wranglers 266.21
wrap 273.08
wrapped 150.31
wrapper 511.36
wrasted 122.08
wrastle 586.01
wrath 058.31 076.31 443.07
wrathbereaved 085.17
wrathfloods 070.31
wrathmindsers 541.26
wrath's 251.08
wraughther 379.21
wrd 515.05
wready 266.22
wreak 387.20
wreaking 069.36
wreath 556.08
wreathe 251.08 613.24
wreathed 303.15
wreathing 336.27 387.34
wreck 084.29
Wreck 229.14 290.F5 306.27
wrecker 327.27
wrecks 545.23 579.09
wreek 518.09
wren 265.10 504.03
Wren 278.12
Wreneagle 383.04
wrenn 364.30
Wrenns 431.13
wresterected 099.30
wrestled 227.30
wrestles 220.13
wrestless 143.21
wretch 148.16 390.02 483.17 563.04
wretched 123.23 231.14
wretch's 063.21 171.22
wreuter 495.02
Wrhps 626.04
wriggle 356.12
wriggled 204.17
wriggles 118.30
wriggling 435.35
Wriggling 616.16
wriggolo 524.35
wright 301.07 466.15 597.11
Wright 327.26
wrigular 291.28
wrily 485.16
wring 466.15 550.26
Wring 213.19 213.20
wringing 022.02 149.02
wringle's 454.02
Wringlings 367.31
wringwrowdy 266.21
wrinkle 319.05
wrinkles 051.18 465.19
wrinkling 403.08
wrinklings 208.10
wrinkly 555.22
wripped 546.16
wrists 196.17 426.20
wristsends 336.29
writ 177.23 201.01 306.13
writchad 138.33
write 055.09 115.01 181.30 229.26 256.30 278.18 279.F05 296.18 302.23 369.28 431.29 441.17 447.10 458.18 460.18 490.25 563.15
Write 301.F5 447.06
writer 114.33 476.21
Writer 413.04

writer's 121.25
writes 227.10 255.18
writhefully 229.27
writher 291.28
writing 019.36 027.10 114.16 114.17 118.19 125.07 146.22 184.09 229.02 229.30 278.14 362.28 391.20 418.03 420.04 482.31 492.28 494.20 625.13
Writing 413.26
Writing 176.06
writings 303.19 487.36
writress 038.30
written 066.14 066.18 107.09 118.33 169.08 175.32 252.27 337.13 368.03 369.16 420.17 484.31 544.02
wrocked 463.31
wroght 595.19
wrong 028.04 090.29 093.15 096.08 151.09 159.01 160.23 163.11 169.15 170.22 171.36 190.36 202.34 202.35 231.34 256.24 270.F2 299.14 309.17 322.08 330.15 351.35 384.29 388.24 391.25 393.26 411.35 434.33 442.20 466.15 477.06 508.16 511.07 527.06 527.34 627.07
wrongcountered 186.24
wronged 243.02 489.07 597.11
wrongheaded 120.36
wronglings 367.31
Wrongly 420.33
wrongstoryshortener 017.03
wrongtaken 586.32
wrongwards 567.03
wrote 013.21 014.14 094.06 107.36 118.13 118.14 118.14 122.33 127.09 185.35 374.30 413.17 624.04
wroth 003.12 058.31
Wroth 058.30
wrothing 589.27
wrothschields 010.35
wrottel 183.07
wrought 137.26 252.14 563.09 575.21
wrunes 019.36
wrung 471.33
wrusty 196.17
wryghtly 319.06
wrynecky 480.23
wthth 349.27
Wu 590.13
wubblin 139.13
wubbling 198.24
Wucherer 422.34
wuck 257.18 584.22
wuckened 295.14
wud 183.08
wuddle 257.18
w'udn't 279.F06
wugger 079.02
wuke 320.22
wukeleen 335.22
wulderment 449.02
Wulf 385.17 385.17
Wullingthund 335.17
Wulv 535.15
Wulverulverlord 074.04
wumble 314.36
wumblin 555.14
wumping 268.11
wumps 363.31
wumpumtum 273.08
wun 303.21
wunder 084.10
wunk 074.08
wunkum 422.26
wupper 206.31
wurld 498.24
Wurm 270.F2
wurming 084.30
wurms 163.10
wurrums 019.12
wurst 245.02
wurstmeats 129.01
wush 290.17
wustworts 265.27
wutan 325.31
Wutt 610.19
W.W. 040.03 (Block W.W.)
W. W. 039.02
Wwalshe's 495.27
W.X.Y.Z. 484.22
wych 235.19
Wyer 398.02
wyerye 200.33
Wyes 600.30
Wykinloeflare 549.18
Wymmingtown 339.26
wynd 552.17
wyndabouts 206.05
wynds 552.16
Wynns 440.09
Wynn's 137.05 609.15
wyst 203.15
wyvern 100.20

X 138.05 421.10 530.08 (X ray)
X. 334.04
Xanthos 235.09 235.09 235.09
Xaroshie 091.36
Xavier 212.14
Xenia 147.14
Xenophon 308.L1
Xero 574.12
xmell 397.21
xooxox 456.23
xoxxoxo 456.23
xray 248.01
Xristos 342.18
X.W.C.A. 141.18
xxoxoxxoxxx 456.23
X.X.X.X. 458.03
X Y Z 443.24

y 464.06
Y 138.05 226.31 (Y is for Yilla) 351.17 364.27 421.10 477.31 (Yawn)
Y. 334.04
ya 270.30 270.30
Ya 051.16 483.22
Yaa 348.01
yaar 415.32
yaars 593.10
Yad 605.04
yaggy 302.08
yaghags 296.19
yaghoodurt 387.10
yahoomen 553.33
yahoort 205.30
Yahooth 310.17
yahrds 243.01
yak 233.32
Yakov 201.34
Yales 346.07
yallah 233.32
yallow 577.26
yam 253.24 481.35 604.23 604.23
Yaman 386.36
yambing 386.05
yampyam 178.15
yamsayore 292.17
yan 457.12
Yan 246.31
Yang 109.06
yangsee's 213.36
yangsheepslang 299.25
yangster 130.15
yank 228.07
yankered 312.05
yanks 194.27
Yanks 543.05
Yankskilling 618.26
yaours 305.03
yaourth 424.13
yap 466.02
yaping 201.07
yappanoise 090.27
yapyazzard 016.09
Yarak 491.20
yarcht 335.29
yard 026.33 142.06 182.24 369.19 374.25 389.25 520.15 567.04
Yard 124.08 523.18
yardalong 029.03
Yardly's 156.28
yards 165.08 475.05
yards' 544.17
yardscullion's 239.19
Yardstated 097.35
yare 331.29 556.35
Yare 200.16
y'are 499.20 525.08
Y'are 525.08
yarn 320.35 444.35 598.22
yarns 091.21 620.35
yarn's 345.16
yarnspinners 050.19
Yarrah 258.09
Yasas 596.34
Yash 240.01 240.02
Yasha 240.01 240.02
Yass 343.19
Yass 071.11
Yastsar 353.09
yat 276.22
yateman 225.18
Yates 027.27 534.15 557.02
yaung 253.28 253.29
yav 478.11
yaw 009.04 009.04
Yaw 009.04
yawash 233.32
yawers 446.09
Yawhawaw 619.34
yawn 097.29 200.15
Yawn 474.01 474.11 476.19 477.27
yawned 407.28
yawning 028.05 056.03 086.36
yawpens 364.15

yaws 156.19
yayas 101.19 101.19
yayis 199.16
ybbs 578.17
ycho 180.25
ycholerd 370.33
yclept 254.07
Ydwalla 088.23
ye ye Ye Ye
yea 019.28 136.10 153.30
153.31 170.20 258.15 279.F16
320.28 425.02 540.16 619.30
Yea 032.01 201.34 368.34
yeager 446.09
Yealand 130.08
yeamen 536.28
year 013.36 112.10 116.13
118.09 121.28 131.27 143.01
190.16 192.17 202.17 234.24
279.F16 284.27 302.F2 380.27
387.23 388.19 391.02 430.03
440.14 445.21 467.02 512.36
517.34 539.28
Year 015.08 015.09
yeards 624.16
yearin 362.22 362.23
yearing 375.14
yearl 391.07
yearletter 137.24
yearlings 292.31 558.22
yearlyng 069.17 069.18
yearn 269.11
yearning 091.21 239.02
yearns 620.36
years 004.26 014.35 018.04
029.26 034.04 047.12 058.03
069.20 073.21 086.16 108.16
108.16 118.11 124.31 132.01
133.17 142.03 167.31 199.10
214.04 228.24 230.13 231.19
231.19 235.10 238.20 242.07
246.12 274.29 302.24 318.15
321.22 323.13 347.04 347.10
380.14 390.19 426.23 437.35
439.03 453.31 477.23 479.26
483.15 497.06 519.08 519.09
519.23 519.23 535.30 547.12
574.28 602.29 625.30 625.30
627.15
years 103.05
year's 142.16 397.30
years' 021.26 022.13
yearschaums 050.30
yeas 312.25
Yeasome 613.04
yeassymgnays 256.13
yeast 578.04
Yeast 135.10
yeastcake 563.29
yeasterloaves 598.20
yeastwind 558.18
yeastyday 004.21
yeat 170.16
Yed 073.28 626.20
yeddonot 535.09
Yee 606.12
yeeklings 068.35
yees 283.27
yeg 330.07
yeggs 076.06 285.04
yeggyyolk 404.29
yeh 408.15 611.11
yeigh 584.22 584.22
yeladst 130.03
yell 230.36
ye'll 140.15 140.18 367.13
446.26
yella 434.06
yellachters 092.02
yellagreen 171.16
yellan 023.01
yellavs 338.21
yelled 197.11
Yellin 180.06
Yelling 329.16
Yellman's 485.29
yellow 164.26 175.36 267.14
288.F2 470.26 538.09
577.26
Yellow 071.10
yellowatty 089.12
yellowed 110.10
yellowhorse 360.30
Yellowhouse 503.14
yellowmeat 594.32
Yellownan's 184.22
yellows 551.09
yellowstone 430.06
yellup 338.15
yelp 375.15 445.17
Yem 246.31
yemploy 464.04
yen 449.25
yenkelmen 370.07
Yennessy 212.01
yeoman's 567.04
Yeomansland 265.02
yeomen 500.10
yep 427.15 512.10
Yep 145.27
yer 031.10 101.10 140.16
140.18 140.19 408.19
500.01
yerds 492.25
Yerds 493.26
yere 237.31 598.32
yerked 432.08
yerking 567.36
Yerra 095.07 477.04
Yerra 399.09
yers 408.20
yerself 301.08
yerthere 282.28
yes Yes
yesayenolly 368.18
Yesche 506.17
yese 365.24
yeses 184.02 184.02 184.02
yesplease 248.02
Yesses 560.17
yessis 349.35
yest 597.11
yester 318.07
yesterday 042.06 112.10 521.10
yesterdicks 126.18
yestereve 429.12
yestern 007.15
yesters 280.07
Yestersdays 054.03
yesterselves 473.11
yesterweek 488.06
Yesther 069.14
Yesthers 624.25
yestoday 570.12
yestreen 527.30
yestures 267.09
yet yet Yet
yetaghain 344.28
yeth 143.01 265.18
yetheredayth 346.22
Yet's 250.14
yetst 590.19
Yetstoslay 087.08
Ye've 528.36
yew 023.36 098.36 254.11
361.07 469.27
yewleaved 339.28
yewleaves 460.24
yews 232.13 362.17
yeye 294.01
yez 465.12
ygathering 010.32
Yggdrasselmann 088.23
Yggely 267.19
yhdeksan 285.18
Yhesters 624.25
Yia 344.07
Yid 485.08
yidd 318.07
yield 025.07 194.06 573.09
573.12
yielded 564.20
yielding 229.28 573.19
yields 057.02 075.10
yif 091.09
yilks 184.18
Yilla 226.31
yillow 577.26
yimissy 234.26
Yinko 329.01
yiou 446.02
Yip 258.09 451.16
Yipyip 466.01
yirely 119.25
Yirls 346.08
yismik 234.26
Yiss 398.17
yit 138.08
yiu 322.04
yiz 008.10
yksi 285.21
yksitoista 285.18
yldist 135.18
ylifted 569.19
ymashkt 547.14
Ymen 092.22
yo 424.22
yoats 041.09
Yod 485.05
yoe 223.11
yoe 484.36
yoelamb 091.32
yoeureeke 230.01
yogacoga 341.08
yogpriest 601.01
yoh 007.28
Yoh 007.27
yohou 490.13
Yoick's 209.04
yok 155.16
Yokan 203.15 531.35
yoke 030.21 137.32 318.10
469.36
yoke 486.03
yokels 041.08
Yokeoff 531.35
Yoking 270.03
yokohahat 482.11
yolks 184.18

yon 031.06 264.30 317.35 403.12 453.30 456.12 472.16 524.25 539.27 569.22
Yon 244.13 615.17
yond 244.03 590.21
yonder 153.09 215.35 216.01 267.14 564.26 587.17
yonderworld 593.23
yondest 292.02
yondmist 007.30
yonks 308.22
Yonne 214.13
yonsides 556.24
yonther 617.32
yontide 081.17
yoors 593.10
Yopp 372.10
yor 101.09
yord 229.01 388.02
yore 015.20 036.07 053.30 142.30 279.03 385.19 393.36 446.02 461.09
Yore 359.24
yorehunderts 054.25
Yorek 190.19 283.15
yores 156.21 377.29 435.24
Yorick 465.32
York 095.02 534.02 576.22
Yorke 485.12
yorkers 583.36
York's 071.12
yorn 314.32
Yoruyume 231.10
yose 365.24
yosters 277.F7
you you You You
youd 258.03 360.24
you'd You'd You'd
youdled 236.21
youdly 419.03
yougander 428.10
yougendtougend 247.07
Youghal 582.26
youghta 568.33
youhou 585.04
you-know-what-I've-come-about-I-saw-your-act 255.25
youlasses 130.03
youlk 613.11
you'll You'll You'll
youlldied 308.17
youllow 427.18
youman 036.06
young 006.29 012.02 012.03 014.32 042.29 056.17 064.16 082.20 092.21 112.32 126.23 130.30 134.24 161.29 166.04 167.32 169.20 173.05 182.22 183.25 191.16 202.27 232.28 237.11 242.16 242.18 251.12 279.F35 288.16 292.10 366.07 371.07 398.22 405.13 430.31 447.11 454.29 458.03 462.08 472.36 472.36 482.17 491.08 528.23 529.05 529.08 542.27 542.27 542.27 546.05 582.23 587.20 596.25 607.15 619.14 621.15
young 352.22 383.11
Young 307.06
youngdammers 572.02
youngend 533.26
younger 082.11 102.01 609.11
Younger 255.18
youngers 024.12
younger's 627.06
youngest 166.01 472.36 609.12
youngfree 318.09
youngfries 572.04
youngheaded 136.25
younging 336.26
youngling 237.29
youngly 224.22
youngs 242.16
youngsters 362.32 529.36
youngsteys 538.25
youngthings 373.27
younker 162.33
younkers 134.22 431.35
youpoorapps 595.20
your your Your Your YOUR
you'r 455.07
youre 434.32
you're you're You're You're YOU'RE
youreups 300.F2
Yourishman 463.26
yourll 456.25
yourn 538.01
yours 054.03 064.35 066.16 146.30 156.22 170.23 173.07 190.27 191.12 239.11 239.14 283.F1 321.22 327.13 395.20 454.06 460.02 481.14 515.22 515.28 522.02 522.33 594.15 621.36 623.33 624.03
Yours 113.17 485.04
yourself 024.18 096.17 145.09 154.10 187.36 188.02 188.18 190.15 192.31 238.35 272.F2 286.06 302.F3 312.10 322.09 350.19 356.10 379.19 380.13 396.05 397.08 405.25 411.36 425.06 437.28 439.27 444.20 445.21 447.36 457.15 464.23 465.01 465.09 480.23 480.28 485.08 496.25 505.26 506.29 515.19 518.18 522.31 525.02 565.01
yourself 418.35
yoursell 300.05
yourselves 098.36 370.17 465.33
yourshelves 425.05
yous 011.35 037.29 093.05 408.14 453.03 462.01 484.02 499.16 521.04 535.03 535.24 541.14 593.09 613.34
yous 266.L1
you's 316.33 344.31
yoush 174.13
youssilves 337.25
youstead 010.19
youth 006.23 031.05 078.34 092.16 144.29 191.19 224.28 253.06 371.18 410.29 432.17 621.30
youth 338.11
youthel 314.32
youthfood 231.06
youthful 134.23 375.06 532.20
youthfully 283.F1
youthlit's 270.23
youthrib 318.25
youths 020.30
youthsy 092.29
youtou 585.04
you've You've
youwasit 142.05
youyou 588.24
youyouth 194.04
yow 156.19
yowling 192.09
yoxen 018.32
yr 334.19
yr 497.23
Yran 493.13
Yreland 605.04
yrish 605.05
ys 393.30 393.30
Ys 527.01 570.12
Ysamasy 493.07
Ysat 598.28
Yseen 299.19
ysendt 332.29
Yshgafiena 605.19
Yshgafiuna 605.20
Ysit 075.11
ysland 605.04
yslanding 605.20
Ysle 605.17
yslet 605.20
ysletshore 605.28
Ysnod 325.14
Ysold 113.19
Yssel 198.13
Yssia 605.12
yst 203.15
Ysut 580.18
yu 477.35 478.25 478.31 478.32 481.05 520.27 520.29 520.35 522.01 522.02 535.22
Yubeti 088.28
Yuddanfest 082.36
yude 171.01
Yuinness 212.01
Yuke 071.35
Yul 245.06
yulding 469.16
Yule 334.33 549.13
Yule 508.05
yules 295.05
Yuletide 082.36
yulone 117.10
yulp 323.16
Yuly 070.03 082.28
yum 065.21 590.11
Yun 477.03
yunder 057.15
yung 115.22
Yung 100.06
yungfries 170.06
Yuni 082.28
yunk 388.01
yunker 464.21
yuonkle's 467.14
yup 425.02
yup 343.15
Yup 258.09 512.11
yur 477.35 478.24 478.32 499.21 519.21 519.21 520.28 521.01 521.22 521.23
Yurap 010.17
yurning 143.29
yurrup 338.16
yurself 499.22
Yus 379.21
yuss 475.34
Yussive 262.F1
Yutah 016.10

yuthner 007.29
Yva 147.14
Yverdown 559.13
Yverzone 407.18
Yves 147.11 291.01 523.08
Y.W.C.A. 391.02

z 333.03
Z 138.06 421.10
zabs 578.17
Zachary 580.08
zackbutts 552.28
zag 330.21
zahur 349.04
zakbag 206.09
Zambosy 207.16
zango 233.31
zany 179.25
Zaravence 340.34
Zassnoch 049.04
zassy 186.16
Zastwoking 310.17
zawhen 231.15
zay 068.27 068.27
Zay 068.27
zaynith 038.03
zaza 248.02
zazimas 186.16
zdrst 091.36
zeal 101.25 288.18 472.26 576.20
Zeal 082.04
Zealand 171.02
zealot 165.21
zealous 161.21 232.22 269.18
zed 123.04
Zee 028.29
zeebs 480.31
zeed 167.08
Zeehere 403.11
zeemliangly 415.24
Zeepyzoepy 075.08
zees 051.28 283.27
zeit 415.26
Zeit's 078.07
zeloso 144.12
zelots 543.19
ZELOTYPIA 264.R1
zembliance 317.33
Zemzem 105.07
Zenaphiah 492.18
Zenith 494.13
Zentral 069.36
zentrum 256.29
zephiroth 029.13
zephyr 404.27
zephyros 479.08
zero 164.10 403.20
Zerobubble 536.32
Zerogh 107.22
zeroic 284.10
zeroine 261.24
Zerothruster 281.L3
Zessid's 034.31
zest 560.34
Zetland 544.01
Zeus 269.18 524.30
Zeuts 414.36
zezera 568.32
Zezere 214.31
zhanyzhonies 101.28
zhooken 170.17
Zid 334.04
ziel 529.24
ziff 610.07
zig 330.21
Zigzag 105.07
Zijnzijn 075.08 075.08
zimalayars 502.05
zimmer 069.32
zimmerminnes 349.04
zimzim 048.16 048.16
Zin 500.29 500.31
Zingara 068.09
Zingari 112.07
zingaway 581.10
zingo 233.31
zingzang 020.22
zinnzabar 182.09
Zinzin 500.05 500.05 500.09 500.20 500.26 500.34 500.34 501.01
Ziod 571.12
Zip 176.14
zipclasped 232.12
zipher 283.04
zipping 449.25
zirkuvs 323.19
zitas 285.03
zitherer 048.15
zitterings 222.33
zitty 250.12
zivios 548.01
zma 318.06
zmear 170.16
'Zmorde 018.01
znigznaks 288.18
Znore 266.07
zo 170.17 214.19 318.06
Zoans 057.07
zoantholitic 611.14
zober 536.21
zodisfaction 512.07
zoedone 479.08
zogzag 111.08
Zokrahsing 230.26
zole 034.32
Zolfanerole 439.35
zolfor 183.01
zollgebordened 580.02
zone 135.32 439.03 478.06
zones 328.08
zoo 047.04 093.18 263.F1 525.20
Zoo 244.17
Zoo 104.20
zoo-doo-you-doo 065.30
zoohoohoom 488.14
zoom 029.13 150.12
zoomed 541.32
zooming 451.09
zoomorphology 127.13
zoopark 564.06
zoot 370.14
Zoot 321.30
zooteac 056.23
zootzaks 077.31
zoravarn 243.10
Zosimus 567.30
Zot 110.14 345.08
zotnyzor 343.19
zouave 048.10
zounds 499.27
zouz 241.28
Zovotrimaserovmer-avmerouvian 113.04
zozimus 063.32
zozzymusses 154.08
zswound 214.10
zuccherikissings 446.11
zuckers 241.03
zug 249.20
zuggurat 100.19
Zulma 147.14
zulu 340.17
zulugical 165.21
Zuma 339.33
Zumbock 276.13
Zumschloss 368.22
Zundas 240.18
zurichschicken 070.08
Zusan 212.08
zvesdals 234.15
zwarthy 199.07
Z.W.C.U. 141.18
Zweep 391.06 391.06
Zweispaltung 296.L1
zwelf 524.30
zwilling 187.33
zwivvel 157.12
zyngarettes 351.12

NUMBERS

1 126.10 358.36
10 143.29
1001 492.23
1014 420.25 (1014 d)
106 159.33
11 095.14 148.33 574.26
1132 013.33 (1132 A.D.) 014.11 (1132 A.D.) 119.26 310.03 387.23 388.20 388.26 389.13 391.02 397.30 420.20 (1132 A.D.) 420.23 (1132 a)
11.32 348.32
1169 389.13 391.02
12 168.13 420.23 421.11
13 420.21 421.11
1542 528.30
17.67 072.21
1768 391.02
17:69 275.17
18 242.16 242.16
1885 061.10

2 093.33 (Op. 2) 123.19 139.15 248.33 358.36 420.33 528.28 574.26 575.06
22.5 618.13
28 157.16
29 064.35 420.19
2bis 436.24

3 139.29 248.33 359.01 420.31
31 420.20 421.11
32 061.09 069.33 095.14
39 607.32

4 140.08 359.04
432 119.26 486.02
4.32 290.05 (4.32 M.P.) 462.35 618.13
49 410.15

5 141.08 359.06 508.02

50-50 269.L1 (M. 50-50)
555 123.19
566 013.36 (566 A.D.)
014.07 (566 A.D.)
5688 150.28

6 141.28 359.09
60 421.03

7 142.08 420.35
73 508.02

8 142.30 420.28 618.13
81 174.26 242.10

9 143.03
92 420.24
965 420.26
'98 038.04

II 061.10 121.34
II 342.24

III 121.34 169.23 261.F2
IV 121.34
XI 121.34
XVII 121.35
xxiv 123.19
XXX 121.35
MDCXC 121.35

SYMBOLS AND MONEY EXPRESSIONS

ш 006.32
Ǝ 036.17
Musical setting of the "Ballad" 044
11/- 070.01
—— 072.09 072.09
——' 072.11
A . . . . !
? . . . . O! 094.21
H_2CE_3 095.12
& 111.11 111.15 111.16 111.16
ꟽ 119.17
Δ 119.19
⊣ 121.03
⊢ 121.07
→ 124.08
Λ 124.09
= 124.10 286.02
&c. 163.22 306.15
3/9 166.08
C_3 211.29
ꓶ 266.22
Bar of music 272.L2
∞ 284.11 (infinity)
nCr 284.26 (North Circular Road)
mPm 285.15
∵ 292.11 (because)
∴ 292.12 (therefore)
Geometrical figure 293
Earwicker family symbols 299.F4
Line drawings 308
9d. 420.22
H_2O 495.26

SYLLABIFICATIONS

à 281.12
aar 370.27
aarse 301.02
abahts 379.07
abal 186.10
abala 600.10
aballoons 274.28
abanded 494.28
abashing 431.16
abawlers 497.05
abbess 289.26
abbess's 601.27
abbeycliath 237.33
abecedarian 198.20
abed 051.13 156.34 180.19 254.34 256.33 392.06 544.30 600.08
abeddy 472.02
abel 224.10 362.05 470.27 579.18
abell 326.01
abella 368.12 512.10 512.10 619.16
abellars 243.07
abelle 201.35 553.26 571.15 610.21 610.21
abelled 627.28
abelles 061.06 192.25
abelle's 215.24
abelli's 182.20
abellous 539.29
abells 569.12
abellum 040.28
abelongd 323.20
abetts 095.22
abey 541.17
abgut 490.14
abib 620.22
abil 513.25 513.25
abiliter 392.36
abilities 104.02 240.20
ability 597.28
abill 104.06
abilla 333.30 548.06
abilling 450.29
ablebodied 160.34
abled 397.25 409.26
ablen 072.34
abler 071.13
ablest 063.29 320.12 375.36
aboardshoops 077.28
abobs 414.05
aboc 456.22
abogue 350.29 528.37
abolls 543.08
abolly 472.02
aboo 054.01 304.12 580.15
aboot 336.17
aboots 288.25
abortan- 257.27
abory 323.20
abote 297.09
abound 338.34
abount 202.04
abouter 070.25 101.03
aboutes 566.09
abouties 496.33
abouts 010.26 069.24 108.25 155.25 203.14 206.05 222.24 255.07 328.10 469.02 506.25 555.03 558.33
abouts 355.03
aboutwoman 151.06
above 468.13
abrack 495.23
abrac's 274.12
abrigies 110.23
abroad 066.07 202.29 417.20
abroads 333.15
abroads 419.02
abroad's 115.28
abrog 549.01
abrupth 242.19
absanti 005.22
absolvers 004.09
abub 097.17
abuelish 452.34
abule 066.30
abundancy 612.05
abundantly 088.07
abusies 568.04
abyss 040.23
acarry's 492.19
accanponied 607.32
accent 180.35
accents 087.03 344.25
accessible 159.33
accidentated 186.03
accompanied 544.15
accord 415.18
accorde 222.02
accountably 086.03
accoutred 594.14
ace 295.26
aced 231.20
acer 008.12
acerution 107.19
aces 575.36
acessory 237.36
acestross 018.03
acettera 339.36
ach 090.31
ach- 332.05
achamer 556.15
achan 398.16
achap 237.15
achapel-Asitalukin 110.08
ache 127.31 294.F1 302.28 362.20 423.17
acheeping 622.05
acher 350.24
acheronistic 202.35
achers 579.33
aches 225.11 270.09
achet 494.15
achord 284.03
ach's 053.31
acht 137.31
achthercuss 054.04
acinous 157.32
aciodes 450.19
acities 115.12
ack 408.32
acks 222.11
ackterickstícks 149.22
acola 133.15
acooshy 484.26
acosagh- 414.19
acosta 172.22
acostecas 152.27
acosts 624.34
acotta 160.07
acqbrim- 254.15
acqmirage 470.20
acre 080.07 111.02 257.21 320.33 390.01 559.10 567.34 567.35
acreedoed 515.25
acreena 376.34
acre's 480.34
across 470.35
acrwatter 135.06
act 255.25 414.19 426.33 587.35
actacurs 518.22
actical 337.23
acticals 388.31
acticors 048.07
acticuls 617.14
acting 009.05 157.12 345.32
actinism 611.31
action 036.11 310.36 332.30
action 274.L2
actionable 048.18
actions 159.21

active 300.20
actogram 165.23
actoristic 334.07
actors- 314.08
actrisscalls 363.28
actrix 526.33
acts 192.23
acumen 415.04
acuminal 055.29
acuminamoyas 201.30
<u>acumque</u> 605.32
<u>ad</u> 016.11 128.20 463.32
adam 019.30 040.34 067.23 180.16 221.13 469.20 485.32 496.21 514.23 532.06
adama 224.29 224.30
adamanvantora 598.33
adamaud 451.03
adameen 021.06
adaminant 617.23
adamised 080.01
adamite 530.28
adammangut 214.19
adams 065.05
adam's 057.20 436.07
adamson 187.35
adapolam 396.09
adar 326.26 358.20 358.20
adarthella 151.20
<u>adbaugham</u> 024.14
<u>add</u> 056.07
adda 232.28
addem 538.25
addendance 358.35
adder 311.16
<u>addios</u> 348.01
adeils 236.29
adelfian 073.18
adelphians 572.25
adem 034.31
adey 470.07
adieu 580.17
adim 560.19
adimply 097.26
adin 073.35 601.26
<u>adindy</u> 353.28
adipates 163.31
adition 151.20
adjure 594.05
adjustables 236.28
adjustment 150.34
admiral 567.22
ado 240.07 464.02 485.21 504.35 550.27
adolphus 167.09
adomina 471.03
adonine 158.01
a-Donk 614.29
adont 338.21
Adoo 227.33 290.09
adoodling 622.05
adoor 107.36
adoors 351.34
adoory 377.02
adore-günneral 352.23
adores 288.02
adories 395.09
adorion 398.18
adorn 395.10
adornaments 291.12
adoro 263.F3
adory 395.10 395.22
ados 178.26
adour 224.25 439.09
adouring 173.04
adovies 184.31
adown 010.28 010.28 088.32 456.26
adowns 509.34
a-dreams 597.20
adrope 089.19
ads 244.15 299.30 302.17
adulterated 445.35
adulteratous 363.34
adulterous 161.17
adult'rous 146.10
adumped 590.01
adums 303.18
aduna 623.28
adunderry 323.21
adure 475.27 554.07
adventure 138.31 231.10
advice 432.18
adye 313.18
aeblen-Balkley 326.25
aehe 206.15
aeorns 236.30
aerial 274.32
aering 332.20
aetther 077.15
afact 183.07
afar 513.16
afear 318.05
afesh 256.25
affair 505.32
affed 037.33
affianced 061.19
affica 463.06
afid 595.03
afield 100.19
afire 621.03
afore 584.16
aforitch 069.12
a-four 430.03
afraida 272.03
afras 234.28
afrond 021.33
aftara 343.33
after 049.35 053.07 093.01 326.17 446.23 492.35 512.14 533.04 568.30 589.25 606.07 612.02 614.24
aftercheeks 463.11
afters 095.29 130.20
afts 133.30
agaba 276.09
agad 258.03
agadye 313.18
agains 333.11
again's 006.14 093.35
against 178.01
agait 051.13
agakhroustioun 396.19
agam 093.15
<u>agamated</u> 308.L2
agana 080.20
agandi 289.02
agany 506.28
agar 423.18 464.11
agara's 601.24
agar's 102.08
agate 197.35
age 053.03 079.12 115.31 151.34 183.13 223.08 243.27 296.12 270.10 324.18 329.23 332.11 355.29 395.29 410.13 450.23 491.08 510.12 534.23 541.09 541.19 545.34 555.19 559.31 564.16 607.07
<u>age</u> 342.13 343.16
agearries 529.26
aged 018.15 358.10 390.14
<u>aged</u> 354.09
<u>ageg</u> 169.14
agen 162.28
<u>agen</u> 415.15
ager's 312.27
ages 008.04 017.04 079.31 241.03 456.29 544.25
<u>ages</u> 298.L1
aggeng 240.10
agglomeratively 186.10
aggravated 358.27
aggs 352.05
agh 310.12
aghain 344.28
aghbally 014.09
agheall- 332.05
agin 503.11
agios 538.36
agitant 355.10
aglionic 513.17
agnian 389.22
agnone 225.15
agog 222.14
<u>agog</u> 071.26
agogue 477.21
agolance 265.08
agon 337.28
agonising 260.10
agonist 516.24
agonistic 040.14
AGONISTIC 275.R1
agonnianne 512.18
agonoser's 290.21
agoras 155.32
agore 037.02
agos 432.11
agrass 482.09
agreed 574.32
agreeing 574.33
agreement 574.33
agreening 607.24
agrees 214.22 323.18
agunnded 323.27
agusaria 117.04
ahahn 205.29
ahanahanahana 554.10
aharan 380.21
ahars 241.27
ahbella 585.24
ahbluh 339.02
ahead 234.27 426.23 494.24 560.27
aheads 288.17
ahem 421.19
ahim 060.05 374.35 611.08 612.03
ahmalong 485.33
ahn 128.26
<u>ahnsy</u> 105.14
ahnthenth 608.24
ahnung 378.36
ahoy 285.14 285.14 285.14
ahoyaway 285.14
ahoyden 255.31
ahs 202.36 205.02 593.22
<u>ahs</u> 339.25
ahur 349.04 359.17

Ahuri 165.28
ahurling 455.01
ahurries 214.03
aichon 230.24
aid 469.30
aidafrira's 601.27
aided 475.36
aiding 098.23 348.11
aidor 378.05
aill's 235.16
aimd 315.30
aims 113.11 282.06
aindua 561.19
ainey 391.33
ainoy 212.14
aint 191.13
air 004.10 011.34 022.36 044.01 045.16 416.04 416.05 462.10 577.10
airafall 140.25
airain 338.26
aircanny 408.16
aird 541.32
aire 295.17 423.03
aired 413.01
aires 065.04 256.20 354.01 564.18
airette's 376.07
airey's 570.29
airial 407.01
airioes 326.18
airity 606.22
airmaid 352.08
airmaidens 601.08
airmakers 059.18
airs 052.12
air's 069.08 177.25
airs' 210.25
airslidingdraws 511.29
airy 131.05 505.14 584.31 620.12 621.06
airyans 360.08
aisance 327.24
aise 343.01
aisies 284.12
aisigheds 387.21
aisy 173.15 176.22
aisymen 524.11
aitoikon 416.12
aizurely 427.01
ajar 305.F2
ajarry 333.02
ajeams 399.34
akelly 463.02
akes 350.20
akey- 582.32
akiltic 326.09
akins 355.22
akroid- 257.27
akruscam 352.33
aks 292.30 315.23
aksically 178.06
aktiers 156.12
alaam 067.25
alaames 497.33
alabellars 243.07
alaciters 608.17
alacities 115.12
aladin 073.35
alah 084.11
alahmalong 485.33
alaisance 327.24
alaisy 173.15
alamangra 009.13
alamina 183.01
alanars 594.05
alang 148.23
alanna 100.07
alantic's 336.27
alaric 336.12
alarum 081.08 178.18
alas 077.35
alast 551.01
alawd 341.30
alba 600.22
albania 114.25
albarnstone 280.31
albe 459.27
alce 613.27
alded 324.28
aldermann 503.10
aldses 117.20
ale 031.12 145.12 296.26 405.19 581.18
aleak 058.25
aleau 383.21
a-leaves 551.12
alectralyse 067.08
aleekie 210.08
aleen 143.35
aleesh 192.26
alehus 294.16
alelouh 258.03
alend 546.33
alewd 325.08
alf 248.21
algaceous 613.18
algia 228.25 314.36
algiabrown 286.01
alice 344.32
alice 105.17
alices 526.32
alicious 421.04
alick 158.04 456.08
aliens 162.12
alignments 120.16
alike 167.19 358.29 551.29
alimpaloop 302.24
aline 040.30
aling 569.12
alingalying 267.07
alist 006.33
Alister 370.21
alite 350.28 440.32 583.14
alites 241.35
alitey 461.04
alive 162.18 293.20 500.02
alively 273.20
alivline 178.05
alizzy's 111.06
alla 520.03
allagamated 308.L2
allah 233.32
allahbath 417.27
allasee 324.09
allchoractors- 314.08
alled 256.12
allehs 550.12
alley 291.04 532.32
alley 105.27
allin 228.04
all-Muslim 068.12
allow 577.26
allowme 204.07
alloyd 373.04
allpersuasions 537.03
alls 113.27 351.22
all's 550.19
allthatsortofthing 178.05
allthesameagain 094.27
alltitude 004.33
alltolled 376.13
alltraumconductor 378.09
alluck- 378.09
allums 478.12
allusaphist 072.14
alluvial 213.32
allwho 015.11
ally 035.23 038.23 430.10
allyedimseldamsels 432.21
allymedears' 328.20
allyoum 295.12
allyous 271.03 334.17
almanesir 150.16
almostfere 067.10
aloan 624.07
aloe 359.33
aloft 340.30
aloid 471.12
aloitez 213.19
alolosis 054.32
alomon 198.04
alone 062.04 236.09 236.10 237.03 418.01 588.05
aloner 032.36
along 029.03 103.11 312.27 485.33 579.24
aloora- 615.08
alors 025.10
alot 325.08 410.11 582.03
aloud 077.29
Alouette's 450.16
alow 265.12 488.11
alowre 496.13
alows 333.01
alpasplace 081.15
alpeens 032.16
alpers 314.35
alpheson 089.34
alppling 007.02
als 005.01
alsoletto 281.19
altar 344.27 560.13 606.02
altarshoming 470.15 470.17
altated 505.14
altay 376.30
alter 568.32
alterance 293.L1
alterand 569.09
altered 201.09
alters 312.36
alterum 572.19
altheouse 338.20
altid 326.21
altin 457.31
altitude 040.32
altivar 331.26
alto 247.20
altomeetim 336.09
alton 248.22 569.28
Alton 572.36
altons 019.09
altxebec 323.04
alty 398.04
aludination 372.24
alumballando 409.29
alumbus 484.32
alure 359.34 478.23
aluse 283.10

alusi 290.19
aluvu 594.23
alviland 176.27
always 458.09
alway's 141.02
alying 267.07
ama 267.F4
amaba 267.F4
amabapa 267.F4
amagoaded 180.03
amain 257.33
amainagain 258.19
amalgamate 575.27
amalgamerge 049.36
amalinks 613.19
amam 331.17
aman 103.08 202.15 256.25 303.23 386.36 387.31 425.32 584.31 598.34
aman 354.10
aman- 414.19
amanant 076.02
amanded 326.23
amanessy 505.24
amanish 425.16
amantanai 595.20
amantaya 498.15
amanvantora 598.33
amaraca 255.15
ama's 204.05 253.28
amassofmancynaves 370.15
amasy 493.07
amater 560.28
amatory 357.22
amatt 560.25
amazon 199.13
ambat 493.02
amber 100.12
ambiambisumers 155.04
ambing 386.05
amble 338.27
ambler 429.04
ambles 423.24 494.32
amblings 582.05
ambolator 490.03
ambre 198.34
ambulating 497.35
ambulatrix 364.04
ambulaups 576.20
ambuling 033.36
am-Bummel 191.10
ambye 600.30
amen 014.20 054.08 167.31 240.06 536.28
amena's 601.23
amens 502.30
amento 220.21
amere 583.12
ameron 561.24
amerries 508.20
ameyu 565.15
ami 211.10
amic 102.05
amica 254.16
amid 357.07 606.04
amie 584.31
amientos 443.15
amies 300.26 553.11
amieson 126.05
amin 311.02
amina 183.01
aminal 244.13
amine 531.21
aminous 288.19
aminted 440.19
amintul 064.25
aminx 261.01
amis 240.06
amisas 233.30
amman 205.30 267.18 568.32
ammangut 214.19
ammen 454.13
amn 514.23 538.33
amnesically 251.04
amnesty 570.07
amnisia 158.10
amo 212.36 212.36
amoci 468.20
amockame 542.13
amon 163.30
amond 503.32
among 177.11 605.06
amoor 292.01
amoore 069.06
amoor's 059.02 281.20
amor 231.28 247.27 499.11
amorate 092.27
amore 024.31 132.19 173.22 241.21 338.19 397.23 600.11
amores 003.04 384.01 388.24
amoror 547.25
amorous 040.14
amors 551.10
amorse 313.11
amount 108.33 359.12 380.12
amour 335.07
amourfully 158.27
amourie 493.36
amourneen's 428.08
amours 250.16 593.08 460.23
amp 123.15
ampared 551.02
amphilius 596.18
amphions 222.07
amphyre 137.24
amplin 593.24
ampling 323.14
amplum 198.21
amplus 099.33
ampulars 011.20
amt 237.12
amy 063.12
amybows 011.12
amyg 116.32
amy's 576.04
ana 055.05 080.20 182.01 212.11 309.14 331.25 351.30 417.12 497.30 583.09 597.19
ana 184.19 287.21
anabal 186.10
anadoon 543.30
anagh 284.06
anah 075.14 358.19
anajocky 331.24
anal 611.13
anamaraca 255.15
anambulating 497.35
ananas 170.20
ananima 456.27
anaral 375.24
anars 594.05
anas 360.09 570.12 601.14
anausteriums 387.14
ancee 202.21
ancee 105.14
anchoredcheek 537.15
ancients 498.34
andas 468.01
Andean 106.08
andeatar 406.07
ander 581.33
anderducken 323.01
anderson 413.14
andesias 542.31
andew 501.34
andeyn 525.28
andies 284.12 535.33
andine 542.08
anding 484.07
andiums 269.10
andivis 468.10
ando 092.19 232.31
andoilish 466.23
an-Doras 073.26
andoria 369.25
andraves 363.07
andredful 348.14
andreian 318.11
andros 203.13
andrum 124.36
andsel 534.09
andser 600.12
andswear 053.33
andump 223.04
andurk 055.21
andwds 262.L3
andywhank 064.07
anelang's 353.31
anevver 077.01
anew 623.16
anforan 123.24
angaluvu 594.23
angel 222.22 505.33 551.15 594.04
angelical 040.07 407.15 605.11
angelines 161.01
angelion 223.19
angelist 391.33
angelo 230.03
angels 628.10
angiolesque 081.23
anglage 275.F6
anglas 485.12
angle 050.27 165.13 190.32 534.36 608.24
angle 278.L1
angled 416.09 615.19
anglers 151.09 521.01
angles 298.25 390.14 390.14
anglian 042.28
angling 347.12
angoly 611.30
angonamed 361.21
angorpound 056.06
angso 004.28
angster 130.15
angt 495.09
angtaggle 287.F4
angtennas 414.26
angue 260.F1
angular 019.13 286.21
ani 049.19 237.30
ania 185.31 504.24
ania's 339.14 549.16
anigel 300.05
anights 015.20 283.26
anik 338.23
anima 456.27
animalism 127.14

animation 087.34 143.08
animously 032.27
aniuvia 627.27
anjeuchy 004.25
ankered 312.05
ankle 286.20
anknee 211.28
ann 012.06 293.22 312.01
503.23 516.18 516.18 538.02
538.32
anna 030.22 100.07 102.28
138.08 270.04 275.14 294.29
406.28 551.06
annah 138.23 377.19 477.05
Annah 038.30
annalism 254.26
annas 071.12
anna's 076.24 329.17
annaship 354.19
annated 441.12
annaulinn 264.28
anne 512.18
annes 350.22 391.05 552.20
annians 277.05
annies 452.27
annity 042.14
annlueamoore 069.06
anno 330.06 348.19
anno 182.20
Anno 246.32
annon's 297.F3
anno's 123.32 373.16
annoy 009.06 162.16
annsos 127.19
annual 142.25
annuar- 332.05
annus 151.32
anny 370.21 455.09 455.10
455.10 586.31 588.18
anoaning 628.03
anoch 502.01
anoff 116.32
anolised 522.32
anon 171.12 183.07 258.22
338.03
anoobs 550.35
anorder 374.16
anos 183.01
another 040.03
anouet 408.04
anouncing 365.01
anov 038.22
ansen 053.04
anserstanded 594.24
anson 138.12
answa 023.20 023.20
answer 287.02 604.07
ansyfett 531.07
ant 408.35
anta 513.12
antaglionic 513.17
antagonist 516.24
antaj 325.11
antanai 595.20
antar 243.15
antarchy 167.06
antas 598.06
antaya 498.15
antes 611.28
anthean 613.17
anthemlander 609.32
antholitic 611.14
anthos 235.09 235.09 235.09
anthroa's 601.22
anthrope 071.32
anthropicks 173.18
anthropist 544.12
anthus 092.13
anti 237.26
antibus 398.16
antic 379.31 615.04
antically 034.02
antics 172.20 173.32 441.28
450.27
antifloures 256.09
antig's 055.27
antlament 614.02
antlets 567.31
antlossly 610.07
antonio 483.17
antora 598.33
antram 553.32
ants 343.23 435.36
anulengro 472.22
anungopovengreskey 056.36
anus 163.17
anus 440.13
anuweir 448.31
anxiety 087.06
anymous 435.31
anymphs 548.02
anymus 423.02
anything 417.26
anywhere 072.19
anza 558.28
anzanzangan 389.01
anzas 598.06
anzer 558.27
anzussch 488.07
aorbinaire 295.17
aotre 473.17
aowl 240.12
aozaozing 407.18
apalla 316.21
aparang 345.05
apartings 095.33
apartita 412.29
aparts 238.26
ape 221.07
ape 271.L4
apee 058.25 583.29
apeer 019.31
apengha 377.27
a-pennies 313.16
aperon 011.34
apex 297.14
apheu's 193.20
aphist 072.14
à-phiz 153.21
aphoron 606.27
apic 115.32
apiccolo 450.19
a-pie 407.29
apinas 223.02
aping 505.08
a-pipe 220.26
apnow 348.16
apolam 396.09
apologise 151.07
apommenites 498.10
apon 617.03
apoppapoff 461.15
apose 332.07
aposed 118.30
Aposteln 569.08
appainted 090.16
appaled 427.07
appalled 452.23
apparitions 507.06
appealed 452.22
appear 615.17
appearance 186.12 483.10
appeared 050.08
appears 434.35
appel 078.20 314.33 483.15
appelle 197.08
appladdy- 044.20
apple 121.11 126.17 167.15
170.30 246.29
applepied 276.F5
applers 146.13
apples 271.24
applications 026.36
applicom 262.28
applous 254.23
appointed 286.28
appointing 437.22
appointments 107.33
appropriating 108.36
apricus 161.26
April 035.03
aproariose 121.27
apron 297.11
aptotously 157.21
aptz 571.28
aqueduxed 243.33
aquillia's 204.07
aquilties 508.19
aquintaism 245.12
arab 117.15
arahast 114.04
araks 491.18
aran 131.22
arancitrone 132.28
arancy 102.25
aranta 513.12
aranth 561.21
ararat 267.F6
aras 010.16 310.11
arasing 050.12
arber 065.32
arbitrary 099.09
arbs 219.11
arc 269.24
arceathay 490.28
arcenlads 075.08
arcenors 096.35
arceson 423.01
arch 020.29 030.20 031.21
074.11 188.16 188.16 188.16
203.04 249.31 364.07 392.20
581.05 612.27 612.27 612.28
archal 075.14
archas 062.21
arched 156.29 273.04
arches 203.27
Archet 222.02
archialisation 181.07
archic 080.25
archicism 525.10
archies 298.L2
arching 167.12
archistically 072.16
architect- 005.01
archly 412.28
archology 388.29
arch's 532.01
archt 335.29
archy 077.18 167.06 447.33

arck 007.31
arcolepts 395.08
arcosis 475.10
arctic 519.19
Arcy 587.04
ardargoos 347.14
arden's 242.33
ardi 185.21
ardin 245.14
ardor 374.16
ards 191.33
area 198.08
arean 310.08
arearing 466.11
arenias 263.F2
arestary 280.L1
arestive 554.01
Arezzo's 260.13
arge 599.18
argisia's 601.24
argobawlers 005.31
argogalenu 184.13
argoos 347.14
argul 327.18
argumends 245.10
arhodes 208.26
aria 117.04
arial 613.36
arial 106.11
arias 387.13 482.11 553.16
ariastrion 600.06
ariaumaurius 113.04
arina 101.08
arios 078.11
aris 202.18
arised 089.17 092.12
arith 030.04
ark 153.27 409.35 468.29 493.20 547.26 581.08 590.02 624.15
arka 198.05
arkery 577.34
arks 369.20
arksky 034.03
arktic 339.21
arlik 254.30
arlington's 406.02
arly 602.34
arm 027.04 186.35 275.17 291.22 530.17
armament 494.03
armanize 466.25
armed 507.12 557.23
armes 426.14
arming 549.11
armon 615.18
arms 608.17
arms 353.35
arnall 108.18
arnell 564.28
arnels 241.32
aroe 405.20
aroma 143.03
arome 155.05
aron 582.20
aroon 015.04 620.05
arosary 459.02
arose 302.27 556.17
arouma 209.18
aroun 004.32
around 010.30 033.36 039.21 269.05 355.09 613.23
around- 314.08
aroundhers- 113.09
arounds 261.F1
aroundside 612.14
arow 346.11
arra 091.04
arrah 258.09
arranged 107.33
arranging 438.03
arras 320.18 388.01
array 341.22
arres 101.29
arrested 223.21
arrests 349.33
arrexes 610.04
arries 529.26
arrived 003.05
Arrosa 207.15
arrow 043.21
arrowa 209.19
arrums 566.16
ars 009.21 061.27 065.20 162.01 332.08 543.17 551.29 593.10 599.05 606.33 617.03
arse 008.17 008.21 010.02 010.11 010.13 010.21 027.01 046.20 340.24 371.22
arsely 150.12 356.22
arsencruxer 516.31
arses 040.13 301.10
arsey 333.08
arshes 182.27
arskield 567.19
arsky 013.22
arson 350.33
arss 251.11 602.23
arst 537.10
arsty 395.02
arsus 272.31
arsy 543.20
art 088.23 199.19 253.04 324.20 418.07 485.01
artars 135.24
arted 013.27 150.12
artempa 178.02
arters 558.22
arte's 251.28
artful 121.27 378.33
arthar 347.09
arthella 151.20
arther 618.30
arthin 203.09
arthur 375.08
arthy 091.13
artiest 616.02
artir 499.09
artistic 182.19
artman 599.04
arto 247.10
artpeatrick 003.10
artryproof 290.19
artryville 205.26
arts 460.17 560.34
art's 531.11
artsky 338.09
arty 160.08 303.13 390.10 453.04
Arty 463.22
artyly 547.04
arum 017.09 081.08 178.18 317.04 479.36 485.26 552.01
arum 503.35
arum- 314.08
arumominum 154.02
arums 445.17 566.13 566.14 566.15
arundser 078.16
arx 285.09 347.02
arxaquy 388.29
aryman 390.31
asa 325.17
asach 595.03
asagam 093.15
asaloppics 386.06
asama 596.24
asas 172.23 596.34
asay 263.L4
asc 199.17
ascene 331.30
ascent 538.33
asch 491.15
ascircles 228.13
ascmerul 518.23
ascu 064.32
asend 585.09
ash 240.01 240.02 260.F1 359.11
asha 240.01 240.02
ashanaral 340.27
ashaw 527.08
ashaws 098.13
ashe 246.14 485.33
ashed 061.18
Ashies 155.05
ashkt 547.14
ashod 426.36
ashone 613.09
ashore 469.06
ashunders 229.21
asia 489.10
asia 105.26
asiada 054.17
asian 166.32 564.35 610.12
asianised 191.04
aside 059.04 082.14 331.17
asider 418.02
asies 463.30
asioused 416.24
asis 112.26 470.15 470.17 470.19
Asitalukin 110.08
asits 331.06
ask 362.11
askayas 348.23
asker's 404.27
askew- 257.27
askieym's 601.25
askivvymenassed 492.06
askortas 247.29
aslang 338.22
aslayers 337.21
asleep 397.16 449.35 476.22 556.33
asloop 562.16
asloot 610.14
aspects 208.11
asperaguss 448.17
asphaltium 157.02
asphault 581.30
aspirated 251.31
aspis 405.26
asporation 257.25 463.21
asprewl 437.11
aspsed 426.33
ass 006.21 067.19 093.09 096.01 141.34 174.15 231.18 254.15 260.18 323.21 343.19

373.29 380.25 423.18 479.09 495.15 512.35 538.32 555.11 581.22 625.27
ass 071.11 342.10 418.24
assa 398.15
assa 280.L1
assabbess's 601.27
assamble 338.27
ass-and-pair 522.19
assbawls 520.05
assed 110.18 492.06 491.33 543.12 580.08
assemble 213.17
assembled 498.27 538.27
assembling 358.33
assent 037.22
assents 575.35
asserted 357.31
asses 153.36 183.13 343.22 611.36
assession 198.17
assias 596.12
assinated 241.02
assing 457.30 607.25
assity 353.25
asso 517.21
assoboundbewilsothou-toosezit 154.33
associations 348.05
assocrats 367.25
assorted 503.09
assousyoceanal 384.03
asstling 625.15
assumed 086.12
assundrian 439.34
assuranced 378.03
assured 151.01 235.25
assurers 608.17
assures 356.20
assuring 108.19
ast 364.29 493.35
Astagob 503.14
astarin 227.35
astartey 091.14
astcleeps 614.12
asteamadorion 398.18
aster 279.F09 455.14
astered 098.12
astering 341.29
asterssias 339.18
astery 406.05
asthmatic 366.23
astomosically 615.05
astones 493.11
astra 061.20 061.20
astrides 564.36
astronomy 449.11
astrool 622.13
astrophear 222.12
astsar 353.09
asunder 546.12
asundery 339.25
asure 162.14
atakia 450.11
atalk 066.20
atall 073.09
ate 604.19
Atelier 531.15
atellye 492.07
atentions 241.05
aterre 019.14 504.24
ateskippey 076.19
ateyar 319.27
Atha-Cliath 420.20
atharept 250.27
athaun 462.08
athay 490.28
atheis 522.30
athem's 588.16
athens 519.19
atheristic 357.13
atheses 309.08
athews 277.F6
athic 072.14
athicus 602.27
athigh 277.F6
athims 199.35
athirst 052.06
athlate 462.28
athletic 319.26
athome 457.35
athomely 078.01
athome's 111.11 116.20
athor 525.15
atic 062.02
atica 212.11
atick 268.08
atkin 081.18
atkins 241.25
atmas 243.27
atnaratatattar 339.18
atom 296.06
atoux- 414.19
atre 059.09 587.08
atrus 558.27
atsee 297.18
atskuns 350.26
atta-Belle 139.35
attached 562.21
atta-Cleath 057.31
attendance 604.20
attention 099.09 434.28
attes 359.07
atthack 348.31
atthoms 312.07
attic 178.17
attics 545.27
attilad 251.01
attillary 378.09
attracted 099.09
attrapped 372.01
atullagh- 332.05
atullepleats 530.27
au 541.19
auberg 333.35
Auberge 124.34
aubes 208.11
Auborne 495.18
auburnea's 381.04
auctors 413.07
Audeons-behind-Wardborg 569.11
audi 152.14
audibble 016.18
audience 533.31
audio 134.06
aug 198.23
aughacleeagh 310.12
aughacleeaghbally 014.09
aught 224.31 315.06
aughts 327.06
auguration 099.26
auking 597.12
auks 545.29
auld 152.26 213.04 336.10
aulds 228.36
aulinn 264.28
ault 118.28 581.30
aultaneously 161.12
aulwoman 054.04
aum 249.22 360.27 364.28 509.11 600.36
aumon 139.03
aumone 538.20
aums 050.30
aum's 364.08
aumunt 008.25
aun 042.12 094.30 126.12 210.35 268.F6 325.14 407.04 573.33
aunelegants 353.27
auner 568.06
auning 041.22
aunstown 291.10
aunt 031.16 224.03 229.04 364.23 373.32 384.30
aunter 069.27
aunties 435.01
auntisquattor 019.27
aunts 284.F5
aunty 359.28 407.06 429.01 539.06
auntyjogging 053.07
auplain 236.24
aura 345.02
auran's 060.33
aura's 327.15
aurealis 332.34
aurealised 085.32
aurious 353.12
aurnary 535.04
auro 462.22
aurore 587.01
aurousians 344.33
aurs 032.03 272.10 595.16
auru 335.16
aururu 335.16
aurwatteur 078.05
Auscullpth 532.09
ausland's 116.21
auspices 332.14
auspices 100.18
auspiciously 049.13
AUSTERIC 266.R1
austeriums 387.14
autamed 277.L5
autel 462.01
author 452.10 533.29
author-batman 162.06
autour 281.07
auwatter 578.19
auwck 133.01
ava 073.36
avala 178.33
avalla 460.32
avalley 328.27
avalls 580.01
avalonche 028.09
avar 172.11 213.09
avaster 024.19
ave 225.14
aveiling 503.26
avent 527.22
avera 255.14
averan 146.08
averas 009.36
averred 343.30
aves 288.16
avez 478.20
avicks 101.33

avico 179.19
avignue 226.34
avik 185.34
aviking 609.19
avin 316.32
avis 053.07 435.18
avitches 348.34
aviz 587.22
avogue 100.08
avore 393.29
avorous 089.16
avourneens 290.24
avrotides 482.10
avvents 604.12
awades 608.34
awahallya 056.07
awaited 041.28
awake 041.15 242.05 476.11
a'war 436.13
awards 018.32
awares 371.26
awash 233.32 290.21
away 009.35 039.08 062.19
109.19 197.06 208.22 227.05
227.11 237.15 285.14 360.31
369.09 370.36 432.17 434.26
462.17 493.25 581.10 582.22
awayo 509.24
awayo 353.29
aways 028.23 114.16 114.17
496.06 548.16 620.29 620.30
awd 523.04
awe 626.26
awed 015.15
aweens 241.26
awer 151.23
awers 446.09
awes 135.09
awful 159.30 432.13
awght 141.32 556.34
awghurs 008.25
awl 237.06 322.02
awl 342.06
awland 579.28
awlanmore 050.23
awlity 292.31
awmbroke 074.15
awn 006.26 068.06 139.36
303.21 377.14 443.02 498.14
awn- 003.15
awndest 503.33
awnroc 388.02
awns 605.01
awpens 364.15
awry 514.24
awsers 276.F1
awyggla 048.16
awys 374.34
ax 063.30 092.36 156.05
156.14 192.03 369.15
ax 158.29
axacraxian 099.28
axarksky 034.03
axe 053.32 229.23 323.04
407.24
axes 344.24 516.05
axion 604.15
axis 458.35
axity 179.14
axle 116.33 144.33 214.24
axled 359.23
axodias 498.04
axters 393.32
aya 471.03
ayearn 379.23
ayenolly 368.18
ayir 323.30
ayis 199.16
ayman 025.32
ayne 373.22
azalles 075.03
azar 389.32
azillahs 102.03
azolites 549.17
aztecs 242.11
azul 494.05

ba 267.F4 335.03
baad's 104.18
baar 370.27
bab 258.12
babbaun 126.12
babe 066.30 378.03
babies 584.14
babipibambuli 306.F5
bably 608.23
babobed 040.02
babogue 350.29
babs 314.30
baby 198.08
bac 054.16
baccio 045.28
bach 346.22
back 004.19 009.12 023.31
057.25 060.13 064.25 067.29
084.03 108.01 134.11 144.07
160.21 183.11 204.25 238.05
289.F3 294.28 309.02 322.20
324.19 332.36 381.01 385.06
386.09 389.04 412.21 426.22
470.29 498.04 510.27 517.22
561.16 564.07 579.05 586.17
backagain 114.19
backcrook 127.17
backed 492.29 608.24
backers 530.02
backs 066.13 222.11
back's 321.08
backshattered 137.13
backward 381.03
backy 011.11
bad 054.18 211.23 240.16
268.19 534.10 548.14
bad- 003.15
badah 609.32
baddend 541.27
badgered 097.06
badiah 531.11
badies 228.36
badkessy 471.02
badory 395.22
badour 462.26
badouring 173.04
bads 327.25 541.14
badtomm 006.11
baffle 610.30
baft 137.23 508.02
baft 123.21
bag 067.09 102.16 206.09
207.18 221.30 232.12 257.19
273.23 313.25 377.08 390.16
398.30 406.10 444.20 455.20
491.06 514.34
bag 350.11
bagbone 567.06
bage 410.13
baggers 560.23
baggon 141.11
baggy 011.11
bags 026.01 064.35 095.14
252.02 337.11 384.27 430.31
616.14 621.06
bagwindburster 359.13
bahi-Ahuri 165.28
baht 093.20
bahts 379.07
bailer 031.27
bailey 127.06
bailis 540.20
bain 499.31
baiscopal 365.09
baiter 339.09
bake 414.09 453.06
baked 139.11
bakelly 463.02
bakers 290.27
bakks 034.08
bakuk 116.32
bal 132.06 186.09 186.10
408.20
bala 600.10
balanars 594.05
balanced 174.17
balant 338.17
balbalbutience 309.02
bald 065.03 177.12 364.01
525.18 554.06 554.06
bald 071.29
baldam 258.21
balder 263.05
baldo 553.13
baldoom 258.21
balds 423.18
bale 357.34
baleau 383.21
balee 013.12 305.19
baleine 175.16
balistics 004.05
balk 054.30
Balkally 612.32
Balkley 326.25
ball 079.16 083.27 114.27
129.29 157.07 316.23 317.13
339.10 541.19 557.10 584.23
ballacks 315.28
ballah 317.12
ballando 409.29
ballds 075.17
balled 232.15
ballem 277.F1
baller's 262.L1
balloon 322.07
balloons 274.28
balls 112.15 247.21 231.21
406.34 416.23 463.17 502.20
523.12
balls 072.02
bally 305.14 410.10 440.25
460.12 612.15
bally 350.12
ballyed 323.16
balm 558.35
balmed 078.06
balmy 578.21
balo 347.26
balong 103.11
baloo 180.28
baloosing 607.10
balots 324.14

balsemate 499.01
balt 620.07
balt 106.15
Baltic 320.21
bam 046.10
bamb 251.18
bambombumb 341.06
bambuli 306.F5
bambum 273.L4
ban 013.26 031.12
ban-Annah 038.30
banborn 055.10
band 062.10 146.20 226.18
banded 494.28
bandiment 497.05
bands 065.02 393.16
bane 029.22 162.21 304.04
bang 304.F1 356.32 469.35 550.26
banger 071.35
bangers 390.12
banging 140.16
bangoist 364.32
bangshot 396.01
banjees 205.32
bank 264.23 526.01 547.30
banked 277.F7
bankment 547.18
banks 006.34 055.04
bankum 445.34
banmaids 126.19
banman 344.06
banned 247.30 537.28
banners 084.13
bans 460.22
banson 138.12
banter 082.15
baothsopolettes 343.24
bapa 267.F4
bapptossed 080.07
baptist 388.14
baptistae 287.24
bar 055.32 070.29 086.08 113.03 132.24 208.21 358.30 497.29
baraced 354.17
barass 418.24
barate 451.32
barative 140.33
bar-atta-Cleath 057.31
barb 169.04 480.24
barbar 120.34
barbarorum 555.24
barbarous 171.16
barbarus 157.27
barbebeway 348.36
bard 099.12 133.27 197.28 265.23 422.13
bardfields 010.34
bardin 245.14
bare 030.01 312.06
bare 163.04
bared 156.35
barg- 023.05
bargain 312.25
baric 133.04
barihams 518.28
barine 027.20
barins 360.26 415.09
bariste 009.35
barium 049.10
bark 279.01 329.06 382.28 423.29 446.30
Bark 211.02
barkar 339.09
barke's 378.36
barm's 531.10
barnaur-Jaggarnath 342.13
barney 200.06
barnies 584.14
barnstone 280.31
baroom 052.25
baroon 316.09
baropolis 181.06
barouter 314.11
barq 549.24
barque 620.35
barrack 327.24
barred 411.02 481.18
barrel 138.18 212.23 351.03 439.12 444.15 472.04
barrelled 286.F4
barren 053.16
barrett 171.14
barrow 015.24 079.26 244.34 455.13 479.34
barrows 595.23
bars 437.07
bart 105.14
barumba 596.11
baryntos 187.21
bas 214.07
basco 329.01
base 154.12
bash 210.01
bashap 491.19
bashaws 098.13
bashes 336.33
bashing 431.16
bashwards 202.22
basiant 347.35
basis 304.L2
bask 102.17
baskel 194.13
bass 295.01 565.22
basses 351.14
bast 016.09
bastion 536.01
basund 494.35
bat 084.04 171.09 493.02
bata 102.19
batarian 229.19
batch 162.31
batcha 052.22 604.03
baten 037.15
bath 129.13 129.28 198.05 290.13 312.06 417.27
bathaltar 606.02
batham 018.29
bathos 159.27
bathred 467.15
baths 188.26 284.04 333.36
bathtub 606.02 606.07
batiste 117.12
batman 162.06
batoom 006.10
batos 512.22
batrus 558.27
batta- 044.20
bat-Talur 327.04
battaring 326.16
battell 479.25
batter 080.02 291.11
battersbid 515.30
battle 176.31 221.18 469.26
battled 272.28 403.06
battle's 093.16
bau 466.01 481.20
bauched 319.04
baugham 024.14
baugi- 424.20
baumblatt 150.27
baun 126.12
baurnus 240.21
baush 091.28
baut 280.L4
baw 494.29
bawdy 095.07 095.07
bawl 039.23 147.04
Bawler 382.22
bawlers 005.31 497.05
bawls 284.19 520.05
bawlveldts 032.27
baw's 176.36
bax 330.21
bay 208.03 313.26 315.32 386.24 464.35
baybohm 029.02
bayre 333.34
bays 550.24
bayse 602.15
baysse 464.21
bayyates 303.07
bazounded 552.28
bazzlement 375.26
beacons 358.25
beadle 511.09
beak 157.06
beaks 416.10
bealbe 459.27
beam 054.01 091.18 131.29 237.14
beamer 508.03
beams 127.15 566.05
bean 040.07 357.06 523.19
beans 140.31
bear 014.35 132.32 275.F3 481.24 614.07
beard 086.18 177.32 464.12 467.15 480.12 532.08
bearded 387.08
bearer 115.18 325.18 511.21 585.07
bearians 285.L3
bearing 186.15 221.07 426.29
bearlined 208.17
bears 522.15 572.06
beast 245.02
beastius' 104.06
beat 151.18
beat 255.15
beaten 161.16
beater 553.02
beaters 542.30
beatha 384.09
beats 403.05
beau 527.29
beau 548.28
beaubel 146.17
beau's 203.27
beaver 160.16
beaverbrooker 072.10
bebeway 348.36
bec 323.04 369.29
becanned 007.17
becca 203.04
becca's 483.19
bechers 130.15
bechronickled 380.08

bechos- 414.19
beck 076.26 232.16 372.15 578.21 609.16
becked 064.31
beckers 077.30
become 240.06
becoming 597.08
becontinued's 626.18
bed 005.20 018.18 040.02 051.13 156.34 180.19 188.01 254.34 256.33 332.17 339.05 376.35 392.06 441.29 457.28 541.36 544.30 555.07 565.36 600.08 619.07
bedarft 221.33
bedded 245.30
bedder 252.12 253.09
beddum 200.23
beddy 243.06 472.02 616.01
be-dee 437.07
bedicate 379.19
bedimbt 059.32
bedinous 414.36
bedone 328.36
bedore 411.29
beds 526.06
bee 387.24 590.28
beeber 087.22
beef 190.05
beeforeness 419.04
beehivehut 605.24
beejee 234.31
beems 258.35
beencleaned 091.17
beenyveenyteeny 021.01
beer 084.36 518.34 614.07 617.21
beeron 563.12
bees 146.17
bees 398.34
beestsch 571.28
beetons 437.24
befooled 337.03
beforce 126.20
before 095.29
before-Wicked 434.10
beg 046.18 173.26 215.01 248.34 262.F7 398.29
begeneses 350.31
beggar 070.34 135.13
beggars 510.19
beggfuss 041.13
begin 056.28
begs 430.34
begunne 104.12
behaved 464.33
behavers 520.18
behinder 379.24
behind-Wall 434.10
behind-Wardborg 569.11
beina 221.25
beit 125.02 305.11
beit 342.04
bejibbers 187.11
Bejorumsen 529.16
bejubers 394.32
bekka 471.02
beknownst 445.26
bel 005.23 071.03 146.17 210.12 210.12 337.08 538.10 556.01 556.05 556.16 562.03 595.06
belavered 448.13
beleaved 625.30
beleeft 150.09
beli 120.14
belief 484.15
belief-stakes 170.33
believing 301.04 468.16
belimned 357.29
beling 552.10
belise 068.29
belisk 335.33 567.01
beliza 328.36
Belkelly 611.27
Belkelly-Balkally 612.32
bell 059.35 073.10 121.36 141.05 245.25 278.11 311.18 324.25 326.01 343.03 434.25 604.11
bell 346.33 491.16
bella 209.24 279.F31 368.12 512.10 512.10 512.10 566.23 585.24 619.16
bellars 243.07
bellas 106.32
belle 027.16 201.35 327.06 527.30 553.26 556.07 571.15 610.21 610.21
Belle 139.35 246.20
Belle 540.10
belled 152.23 420.25 551.12 618.34 627.28
belledem 545.29
bellek 412.10
belles 061.06 192.25 237.08
belle's 215.24
bellic 537.18
bellically 292.25
belliching 407.32
bellied 245.30
bellies 142.02 233.25
belliney 432.21
belling 031.32 518.19 567.36
bellis 446.07
belli's 182.20
bellished 386.01
bello 027.26 134.18 290.F5
bellous 539.29
bellow 383.22
bells 007.02 022.31 028.28 208.27 222.34 282.F1 361.22 371.12 566.18 569.12
bellulo 052.14
bellum 040.28
belly 080.13 095.36 113.36 206.36 270.F2 393.18 485.32 557.11
bellye 568.23
belly's 137.12
belong 569.03
belongd 323.20
belonghead 611.33
belovers 520.19
belovs 468.13
below 239.33 569.03
belowstard 607.26
belowther 266.10
belpaese 129.27
bels 169.14
belt 027.06 534.19 559.09
beltye 138.23
belums 323.15
belus 594.23
ben 395.12
benacaddie 200.23
benboss 013.24
bend 364.36 578.20
benders 130.02
bends 102.06
bene 606.13
beneath 249.09
beneaus 527.28
ben-Edar 030.11
beneros 346.04
bening 349.31
Benn 375.32
benny 041.20 041.20
benopubblicoes 371.24
benses 504.29
beold 015.32
beonerflsh 571.29
ber 271.19
berated 157.01
berates 249.15
berds 152.17
berd's 381.23
bereared 492.27
bereaved 085.17
berella 530.29
berg 037.01 151.13 333.35
berge 328.16
berged 056.26
bergen 310.04
berginiste 163.19
berillas 373.21
beriquiet 506.17
berkhelm 273.28
bern 202.20
bernabohore 245.13
berolum 338.07
berra 568.17
berried 264.26
berries 130.14 376.28 438.10 504.33
berrimates 535.33
berrow 391.14
berry 027.16 041.25 064.28 066.17 228.18 310.29 430.25 435.21 444.28 529.02 544.17 559.06 566.04
berryeke 221.33
berry's 342.15
bert 088.21 274.29 388.29
berth 004.32
berthing 062.07
berths 598.06
bertine's 211.05
berty 233.18
berutters 241.26
besendean 494.19
beshottered 352.30
besides 431.18 523.24
beson 578.31
bespokables 496.31
best 121.32 173.11 253.01 277.20 414.33 536.21
bestas 352.35
bestic 038.11
best-king 505.27
bestopoulos 424.07
besty 191.17
besume 371.22
bet 278.01
betasselled 474.08
Beth 290.06
bethey 412.25
bethizzdryel 241.27
beths 302.F1

beti 088.28
betogiving 380.09
betothem 053.15
bett 208.20 495.25 595.07
bette 209.14
better 298.03 356.09
betters 107.09
betther 234.29
bettised 192.36
bettle 369.01
betts 095.22 242.05
bettyelsas 444.31
bettyformed 183.13
between 250.35 367.01
_561.25
beugled 284.19
beurrable 162.02
beurry 461.02
bewas 595.35
beway 348.36
bewilsothoutoosezit 154.33
bewised 378.30
bey 406.33 484.23 541.17
bey 346.05
beycliath 237.33
beyond 570.01
beyron 357.02
bey's 558.02
beyth 533.08
bez 017.36
bezigues 350.20
bezond 165.22
bezzled 589.32
bhar 080.14
bhing 273.22
bhour 484.29
bhoy 624.23
bhrakonton 508.12
bhramsa 481.18
biad 254.16
bianca 342.09
biassed 168.07 491.33 580.08
bib 620.22
bibber 423.05
bibbous 140.13
bibis 300.17
bibles 539.02
bibs 203.19
bid 108.02 515.30
bidden 011.29
biddy 021.09
bideintia 610.07
bidience 605.29
bids 101.05
bidson 199.29
biduubled 583.27
biedo 219.12
biels 116.28
bierd 332.22
biered 560.20
bierhome 181.06
bies 006.02 100.14
bif 171.01
big 091.11 188.24 398.30
bigby 210.15
bigenesis 240.13
biger 613.11
biggar 015.30
bigpipey 130.36
bigs 099.11
bijance 389.03
biking 437.06
bil 337.19 513.25 513.25
bilashings 211.07
bild 159.31 588.33
bilder 077.03 377.26
bildin 546.17
bildising 332.28
biled 263.F4
bilee 205.07
bileejeu 329.30
bilei 031.20
bilette 267.20
bilettes 073.35
bilibum 194.18
bilibus 466.32
bilily 164.02
biling 403.10
biliter 392.36
biliter 154.22
bilker 037.35 111.21 296.07
bill 115.28
bill 104.06
billa 333.30 548.06
billers 373.23
billey 238.04
billing 450.29
billow 160.19
bills 414.28
billsilly 015.18
billy 021.09 053.36 075.15
416.08
billy- 254.15
biloroman 084.15
bils 424.27 424.33
bil's 116.13
bilt 543.11
bin 019.12 370.09
bind 093.18
binder 278.09
binding 143.14
bine 351.12
bines 587.07
bing 553.18
bings 491.04
bins 409.02 625.23
bin's 181.17
bio 230.16
biogenselman 173.13
biography 413.31
bipibambuli 306.F5
bique 183.14
bird 010.32 010.34 039.21
098.36 256.26 412.07 451.16
476.01 534.36 595.33
birdies 416.12
birds 147.07 180.28 388.25
438.35 527.26 562.17
bird's 496.31
birdy 505.17
birg 012.36
birger 133.06
birk 553.03
birry 207.10
bis 066.25 228.26 419.32
436.24 452.08 514.22 562.17
bis 113.30
BIS 306.R1
bishing 041.11
bishkis 568.19
bishop 392.14
bishopric 134.29
bishospastored 612.08
bison 302.23
bisses 475.35
bisumers 155.04
bit 019.02 061.19 223.04
266.26 247.09 288.05 312.14
469.01 498.22 547.01 557.03
559.34 561.24
bit 625.07
bitered 059.15
biters 111.04
bites 263.F1
bits 255.35 285.F1 334.04
416.18 570.29
bitsch 141.23
bitten 255.06 303.16
bix- 414.19
biyas 114.28
blabbers 042.04
blabstard 241.29
blachk 503.23
black 006.01 016.29 035.16
114.10 187.17 301.06 385.06
405.36 447.05 451.15 457.18
583.22
black 398.32
blackblobs 339.21
blacked 429.21
blacks 129.32 221.22 386.29
Blacks 409.23
blacksliding 405.09
blad 056.25
bladders 090.12
blade 063.02 222.29
blades 033.06
blagrogger- 582.32
blah 340.12
blaimend 074.15
Blakes 409.23
blancer 049.22
blanes 135.28
blanium 013.34
blank 179.02 474.14
blankered 612.22
blares 256.11
blaseed 237.19
blasey 485.13
blasst 071.18
blast 219.17 471.13
blasted 194.14
blasting 416.35
blasts 504.31
blatt 150.27
blawn 139.36
blaze 021.17 540.29
bleak 316.22
bleakest 365.18
bled 397.25
bleeding 370.23
bleege 277.12
bleen 023.01
bleh 300.18
blemm'as 182.21
blend 614.32
blenn 066.18
bless 087.03 443.05
blesse 567.26
blest 063.29 320.12 334.02
375.36 563.13
bleu 076.32
bleus 157.26
blick 290.22
blid 140.27
blin 328.03 447.23
blind 119.31 379.20
blinged 612.21
blinkers 612.21

blinly 347.35
bliqueme 445.34
blissed 107.16
blistered 181.08
blitzbolted 078.07
blive 481.25
blizzered 416.20
blobs 339.21
block 080.30 277.02 583.26
blocks 072.36
bloddy 324.11
blond 273.27 429.19
blong 013.04
blonker 611.34
blonovi's 230.15
blood 049.27 169.19 171.32 292.09
blooded 033.22 170.33
blooder 378.11
bloodheartened 577.07
bloody 070.25 423.15
bloom 467.11 564.23
bloon 389.27
blos 568.21
bloshblothe 280.33
bloss 237.12
blothe 280.33
blots 225.36
blott 538.31
blotting 565.09
blotts 458.23
blow 407.05 517.08
blower 227.32
blowers 270.13
BLOWERS 303.R2
blowing 476.01 519.22
blown 059.35 422.04 461.34
blows 049.26 422.30
blow's 552.19
blu 180.12
blubber 329.11
blue 063.16 142.10 171.17 226.32 253.36 328.09
blue 399.05
blueboltered- 378.09
blues 542.03
blue's 556.10
bluffed 084.09
bluffer 590.20
bluffingly 116.01
bluh 240.33 339.02
blume 267.29
blumes 548.04
blunt 116.02
bluse 261.02
blushes 064.26
blushing 357.32
bluts 385.14
bly 283.28
bo 050.16 336.02
boababbaun 126.12
boabaybohm 029.02
boam 558.15
board 159.32 180.36 374.15 451.03 469.18 517.36 517.36 551.28 582.07
board 349.08
boarder 358.20
boards 058.33 098.06 262.25 375.06
boardshoops 077.28
boaryellas 327.32
boassity 353.25
boat 065.30 131.02 136.20 139.34 215.01 321.14 418.05 479.31
boat 104.16
boath 021.25
bob 005.02 094.33 245.27 270.27 590.17
bobandninepenny 396.18
bobbies 113.36
bobbis 334.04
bobed 040.02
bobo 622.23
bobs 414.05 540.29
bobs 189.19
bobsy 611.26
bobus 352.11
boc 456.22
boccoo 427.13
boche 388.21
bock 037.06 095.02 276.13 310.28
bocker 442.09
bockers 098.21
bocks 222.28
bock's 189.07 292.05
bocroticon 614.28
bod 116.32
boddy 415.17
boddylwatcher 026.17
bode 040.17
boden 466.22
bodens 541.26
bodied 160.34 413.31
bodies 486.19
bodoff 370.17
body 063.16 088.14 107.30 118.12 160.07 220.16 289.15 293.F2 309.16 329.18 411.34 438.16 442.31 482.25 597.21 616.06
body's 101.13 248.25 361.12 521.24
boel 437.08
boes 011.34
bog 376.03 398.30 531.03 556.25
boge 036.16
bogen 464.30
bogeys 304.09
boggaleesh 192.26
boggan 084.06 369.08
boggan's 435.30
bogger 204.21
boggeryin 305.33
bogom 347.02
bogue 350.29 528.37
boh 078.32
boher 373.05
bohm 029.02 055.28
bohmend 505.34
bohore 245.13
boi 201.25
boiassed 110.18
boil 026.07 231.13 604.24
boiled 336.31
boily 534.01
boir 392.16
bois 440.12
boisterous 547.23
boites 235.24
boits 211.28
bok 129.23 379.17
boko 051.17
bokovskva 498.15
bolator 490.03
bold 053.14 091.11 250.36 273.27 315.03 383.17 451.17 474.15 588.33 606.18 615.06
bolder 309.13
boldy's 361.12
bole 451.07 504.25 596.21
boles 303.19
boleshqvick 302.18
boleth 267.21
bolgs 381.05
bolier 317.15
bolist 128.18
bollags 541.18
bollions 151.14
bolls 543.08
bolly 321.15 472.02 516.10
bolo 494.17
bolosk 162.15
bols 376.27
bolster 577.12
bolted 078.07
boltered- 378.09
bolts 135.25 140.17
bolt's 590.10
bolum 154.18
bolus 118.04
bom 007.34 007.34 256.27
bom 103.02 103.02 103.04 103.04
bomasum 097.15
bomb 424.18 588.20
bombom 552.29
bombomboom 103.02 103.04
bombonant 053.01
bombs 304.16
bombumb 341.06
bommers 258.34
bomnet 176.36
bon 442.09
βον 269.L2
bonant 053.01
bond 510.35
bonds 617.07
bone 036.32 052.19 085.08 177.21 192.29 193.29 221.23 229.30 249.07 330.34 347.12 425.01 550.10 567.06 603.23
bone 565.26
bonegorer 255.15
bones 016.03 031.25 122.08 343.04 387.33 391.32 434.25 504.25 569.03
bong 245.26
bongusta 438.02
bonian 539.25
bonnet 040.09
bonny 124.27
bons 542.22
boo 054.01 191.35 225.08 304.12 373.25 464.07 580.15
booard 077.06
boob 442.36 580.14
boobied 416.03
boobrawbees 146.17
booby 146.06
bood 104.18
boof 609.16
booh 372.30
book 018.17 131.02 136.19 229.32 380.24 412.33 422.15 443.24 460.20 530.19 611.25

book 275.L4
bookers 549.04
bookisonester 177.14
bookpage 428.16
books 219.24 256.18
boom 564.22
boom 103.02 103.04
boomaround 613.23
booming 173.21 565.05
boon 029.11 181.25 556.29 612.20
booned 323.33
boor 491.32 585.34
boormistress 023.29
boors 552.20
boor's 487.12 615.33
boos 011.02 066.05 154.11
boose 052.24 140.33 488.11 590.19
boosh 240.24 586.26
booshkees 417.12
boosoloom 012.13
boost 583.19
boosting 320.06
boostius 468.04
boosycough 095.08
boot 336.17
booth 394.27
bootle 315.22
boots 026.10 035.10 126.13 210.16 288.25 415.03 466.34 467.01 531.22
boots' 469.08
boove 110.17
boowood 239.01
boozelem 515.28
bor 398.27
boracum 442.08
borad 492.22
bordened 580.02
border 025.10
borders 474.18
bordunates 156.11
bore 387.17 390.34 392.11 396.36
borealic 487.01
bored 384.35 388.18 393.08
boren 525.21
borg 005.06 012.35 310.03 316.13 529.21 569.11 582.21
borg 072.12
borgenthor 246.06
borgey 327.30
borines 533.15
borised 310.18
born 055.10 059.18 084.29 114.12 134.19 137.14 159.24 164.35 178.10 194.12 210.04 304.27 370.07 387.12 506.26 547.05 585.18
borne 041.07 285.15 383.20 469.15 495.18 561.20
borneccles 613.09
borned 530.09
borner 290.26
boroff 340.20
borough 029.35 057.35 132.22 162.30 260.12 340.34 442.11 503.14
borougham 104.20
borough-the-Less 569.14
borre 248.17
borre's 415.32
borro 095.18
borrow 017.04 455.12
borry 333.33
borry 105.08
bort 086.07
bortan- 257.27
borumba 351.05
bory 323.20
bos 019.31 112.31 148.20 319.20 388.09 409.16
bose 287.19 623.17
bosed 345.34
bosh 051.36
bosh 348.32
boshicksal 283.L2
bosition 299.08
bosk 351.24
bosolom 180.27
bosom 170.35 180.12 471.07
bosomheaving 189.25
boss 013.24 020.08 052.24 273.23 415.17 442.27 442.27 485.33
bossed 012.28 574.25
bossers 088.29
bossities 493.22
bost 622.29
bosuned 313.04
bosy 207.16
bot 219.23 316.30 447.13 516.27
botag 409.29
botch 010.18
botchum 610.11
bote 066.30 297.09 458.16
both 054.29 258.34 542.23
botham 315.04
bothed 230.02
bothy's 354.15
botinesque 512.18
botipacco 069.36
botomia 318.25
bott 340.31
bottes 023.01
bottle 095.27 182.31 263.24 458.18 569.25
bottled 140.33 382.03 575.13
bottom 164.29 390.36
bottomed 110.26
botts 622.11
bouch 169.21
boucqs 206.12
bough 236.21
boughnoon 470.15
bought 115.25 415.17
boule 366.09
boulees 087.05
boulotts 625.25
boum 116.06
bound 007.01 055.27 064.33 243.05 292.26 317.06 323.32 439.15 461.23 525.01 560.01 590.03
bound 104.16 338.34
boundbewilsothoutoosezit 154.33
boundin 110.03
bounding 190.31
bount 202.04
bour 091.14 135.02 171.27
bourd 178.28
bourg 162.30
bourine 248.09
bourne 198.08 268.16 367.29 371.33
bournes 365.34
bournigglers 244.06
bouscher 156.35
boused 158.04
bout 229.25 242.15
boutbarrows 595.23
boutcheries 350.16
bouties 496.33
boutot 372.10
bouts 155.25 163.23 298.16 427.31
bouve 333.20
bovo 234.01
bow 079.08 102.27 376.31 381.13 403.06 442.27 547.30 576.27 613.24
bowbreak 546.23
bowcrural 557.17
bowed 133.31 270.16 288.15
bowel 161.27 462.13
bower 450.16
bowl 060.14 107.12 131.23 351.14 582.06
bowls 080.11 389.28
bowm 505.29
bown 397.20
bowpeel 475.13
bows 011.12 304.28
bowth 311.15
bowyers 312.36
box 022.22 066.27 082.24 091.26 098.12 122.13 165.31 207.10 276.25 287.11 299.18 326.36 393.28 397.11 439.31 442.33 469.30 503.02 562.14 563.32 618.12
boxer 049.30 142.11
boxers 575.08
boxes 077.11 122.26 165.21
boxsitting 053.31
boy 010.14 010.15 010.19 027.09 043.17 051.33 142.09 152.13 159.21 177.36 228.31 237.15 242.08 245.04 277.23 344.29 362.08 363.14 372.29 377.13 410.29 417.17 439.30 442.05 443.11 451.27 453.16 466.29 488.21 530.21 559.30 563.26 614.29
boyce 004.05
boyes 435.15
boyish 183.04
boyne 041.26 211.34
boyo 329.17
boys 033.09 054.09 094.01 129.13 179.08 205.28 209.30 266.18 291.11 329.25 363.06 367.02 369.07 385.09 385.09 526.17 529.24 543.09 587.06
boys 349.26
boy's 039.36 041.12 208.06 336.04 471.32 584.17 620.22
boys' 555.17
boyum 258.34
bozzle 352.30
bozzy 040.07
bra 202.13
brace 220.15 316.09 328.30 388.05 471.06
brace 106.32
braced 244.29

bracing 537.06 581.18
brack 495.23
bracken 005.23 319.04
brac's 274.12
braged 354.09
brageous 380.15
braggat 060.12
braggin 022.35
bragh 303.14
braghs 330.09
bragk 438.16
brags 360.17
brain 159.25 444.03
brains' 099.34
braios 497.24
braithers 052.11
bralasolas 014.08
brance 220.32
branch 029.03 604.04
branching 123.08
brand 068.19 311.30 484.13
484.34 582.31
brandt 176.18 176.18
brandtsers 054.02
brandy's 155.36
branjewomen 054.08
brant 198.31
brars 270.24
bras 467.05 550.35
brasilian 442.14
brass 008.19 373.29 511.30
609.28
brassador-at-Large 472.10
brasses 041.11
brassured 235.25
brasterd 320.07
brasures 550.24
brat 555.20 563.07
brate 518.22
brathairs 052.12
brathran 252.04
bratschballs 072.02
brattlefield 609.34
brattons 152.05
braves 246.33
brawbees 146.17
brawl 338.03
brawler 144.05
brawn 590.25
bray 340.01
brdsz 105.11
bread 124.13 199.19 317.01
416.18 550.25 566.03
breads 310.22
break 160.35 546.23
break 353.31
breaker 054.30 107.31
breakfastbringer 473.23
breakical 293.16
breaking 164.23
breakingly 182.21
breamstone 225.22
breast 211.27 277.06
breasted 365.15
breasttorc 612.02
breathing 550.17
brecht 539.30
breciades 534.02
brecky 534.19
bred 127.11 164.15 235.32
411.22 541.30 590.08
bred 352.17
breds 152.16
Bree 375.32
breech 182.24
breeched 012.22
breeches 389.35 539.02
breen 087.31
Breen's 056.32
breighten 537.11
brella 462.21
bremient 348.03
bren 327.06
bretas 048.07
bretellated 227.36
breton 491.32
brets 559.10
brett 542.34
brew 138.01 283.24 419.27
brewer 104.12
brewery 015.35
brewham 097.16
brey 265.01 333.08 620.09
breyhambrey 317.10
breys 553.06
briania's 339.14
briannus 151.32
bribaddies 228.36
brick 552.05
bricken 086.24
brickredd 020.08
bricks 042.32
bridalled 298.30
bride 013.27 022.26 203.02
500.21 500.22 500.22 500.27
500.27 500.30 501.03 561.16
576.06
bride 399.03
brides 566.16
brides' 548.03
bridge 063.14 097.22 129.09
136.30 184.12 306.25
bridged 547.25
bridges 600.08
bridging 305.08
bridian 263.13
Brien 070.07 270.31 370.21
385.15
briertree 588.31
bries 127.36
briggan 399.14
briggans 530.12
bright 011.17 211.33
brighteners 524.28
brigid 404.35
brigies 110.23
Brigstow 537.24
brill 015.36
brilla 492.23
brilla-parasoul 569.20
brimbilly- 254.15
brin 346.15
brine 013.26 043.22 197.21
230.32
bring 271.11 608.16
bringer 473.23
brink 547.20
brink 342.25
brinos 488.29
brinus 134.06
Briny 095.04
bris 545.20 545.21 545.21
bris 513.02
brises 370.24
brist 443.19
bristle 071.03
brit 387.05
british 403.23
bro 160.30 188.27
bro 155.04
broaching 324.36
broad 066.07 202.29 417.20
broader 051.19
broads 419.02
broad's 115.28
broddy 234.06
brodhar's 070.26
brodhel 445.06
broed 378.34
brog 549.01
broggt 600.12
broglia 284.04
brogue 313.23 343.31 581.16
brogued 444.05
bröke 022.36 040.15 074.15
092.02 373.29 420.33 541.25
broken 168.03 191.27
broken 419.01
broking 041.29
brolly 315.20
bromette 022.20
brondas 243.16
bronn- 003.15
bronne 352.21
bronry 440.05
bronses 573.21
bronze 242.34
brooch 413.15
brood 129.10 248.35
brooda 078.17
brook 142.12 427.11 514.25
537.35 563.26
brookable 123.32
brooker 072.10
brool 005.34
broom 056.24
broomirish 600.33
brooms 403.11
brooth 243.13
broren 199.34
brose 520.36 529.01 608.20
brose 201.15
brot 163.06 163.06
broth 398.02 482.05
brothar's 099.13
brothelly 436.14
brother 066.26 168.07 223.19
489.28 537.21
Brother 193.21
brothers 301.F2
brother's 585.29
brothred 404.29
brotto 425.20
brou's 148.19
brow 003.14 006.25 012.08
093.25 183.30 535.16
browed 264.06
brown 194.22 243.25 286.01
424.36
browns 020.02
brows 371.03 394.23
browth 121.33
browtobayse 602.15
brthirhd 310.15
bru 490.26
bruch 323.09
bruck 499.33
Brueller 150.15
Bruerie 038.04

Bruin's 128.25
bruised 021.35
Bruiser 376.09
bruk 073.13
Brullo 151.11
brum 009.27 134.08 134.08
brume 336.15
brundt 318.31
brune 352.22
bruno 488.08
brupth 242.19
brush 443.25
brush 176.16
brushup 340.03
bruskblunt 116.02
brusted 462.10
brute 255.13
bruws 228.34
Bryan 376.08
bryf 418.27
Bryony 450.32
bub 029.35 097.17
bubble 536.32 607.32
bubblye 526.09
bubhub 239.33
bubly 384.29
bucca 369.26
buccinate 156.12
buccio 045.28
buccus 118.16
buch 103.08
buchin 568.28
buchs 545.23
buck 344.16 384.01 412.35 469.11
buckdom 090.26
bucked 535.08
bucker 139.06
bucketnozzler 024.35
buckets 005.03 372.18
buckle 214.05
bucklenoosers 319.29
bucks 070.12
buck's 142.12
bucky 234.32
bud 024.01
buddies 309.20 415.19
budds 450.18
buddy 021.08 346.25
budja 056.34
budmonth 553.23
buds 161.29 459.03 583.21 583.22
budvispa 596.29
buelish 452.34
buff 022.35 336.19
buffing 222.26
bug 186.21 326.22 475.20 582.10
bugga 095.18
bugger 496.03
bugled 589.32
bugs 015.06 540.35
buia 424.10
build 099.08 624.07
builders 191.34
building 015.07 274.11
built 063.15 071.02 394.17 489.14
buiting 433.20
bukividdy 327.34
buktu 288.23
bukujibun 484.26
bul 136.08
bulance 084.02
bulbs 354.01 531.08 557.12
bulbul 355.10
buldum 258.20
bule 066.30 242.34
buless 050.36
bulger 132.29
bulging 310.27
buli 306.F5
buling 033.36
bulissa 256.33
buljoynted 310.31
bull 171.31
buller 584.08
bullet 193.21
bullies 322.33
bullished 356.30
bullocks 611.26
bulls 547.35
bully 021.07 025.33 490.35
bully's 587.07
bulose 475.14
bulous 004.30
bult 416.03
bulumbumus 598.05
bum 065.28 155.32 177.14 194.18 253.13 351.36 598.34
bum 273.L4 506.31
bumb 341.06
bumbose 623.17
bume 340.23
Bummel 191.10
bumn 617.36
bumper 087.01
bum's 535.10
bumsaps 585.18
bumul- 023.05
bumus 598.05
bun 294.F4 484.26 531.17
bunate 607.21
bunckley 224.36
bund 324.13
bunda 577.15
bung 098.10 235.05
bungsap 269.20
bunk 267.F6
Bunk 258.36
bunking 388.20
bunks 041.07
bunkum 316.14
bunnies 430.36
buns 308.F2
buny 232.05
buone 368.13
buoyant 415.01
bur 112.35 386.21
burdy 378.05
burenda 232.03
burg 261.16 326.25
burg- 090.31
burgghers 623.23
burgh 018.23 057.36 384.17 487.09 560.07
burgher 265.13 578.35
burghers 543.19
burgs 497.19 552.16
burg's 453.33
burgst 257.31
burial 614.32
buries 113.34 290.06
burk 005.35
burkes 106.06
burlygrowth 558.20
burn 013.26 059.17 102.07 134.29 171.14 265.07 280.27 377.07 387.35 421.04 504.24 540.15 552.22
burnea's 381.04 396.01
burner 369.08
burnes 549.04
burnia 275.05
burns 009.25 614.08
burnt 139.23 384.28
burntress 137.23
burnum 509.24
burnums 450.31
burra 393.26
burrow 005.35 147.26 455.13 479.24 577.14
burrs 454.30
Burrus-Caseous 167.04
burry 214.32
burst 091.03 362.30 444.15 614.32
burst 071.15
burster 359.13
bursts 066.19 295.F1
burt 339.06 598.07
bury 035.28 062.28 080.33 132.36 193.15 237.05 297.20 372.17 374.28 442.07 541.29
burys 554.02
bury's 578.26
bus 013.11 040.32 251.01 449.15 489.06 598.34
buses 409.15
bush 012.08 087.35
bushe 586.11
bushed 034.33 085.03 285.17 470.04
busheers 163.12
bushes 007.35 542.35
bushi 561.32
bushing 431.17
bushure 201.20
busies 568.04
business 146.22
busked 546.10
busker 040.21
busodalitarian's 099.36
busqued 038.03
buss 147.30 291.14 327.18
busses 006.01 432.20
bust 075.04 156.10 165.28 358.27
bust 106.33
busted 600.19
buster 535.09
bustered 324.01
bustioned 228.33
bustly 368.17
Bustonly 135.13
buth 561.08
butience 309.02
buties 131.20 340.32
buts 612.12
butt 023.32 160.02 262.F6 415.18 435.33
buttal 097.19
butter 350.23 388.19
butterbust 165.28
butterbust 106.33
butting 142.18
butt-in-the-North 569.05
button 391.34 607.35

buttons 061.22
butts 396.35 434.25 552.28
butus 121.10
buwel's 366.20
buy 077.29 172.06 247.18 537.23 561.04
buys 358.33
buzz 534.04
buzzled 234.03
bworn 597.18
bye 225.34 382.29 409.11 454.03 454.04 500.22 600.30
byg 339.11
byl 532.25
bylike 171.13
byoperian 294.01
byrdes 348.34
bys 210.27 557.02 595.01
byscuttlings 095.33
bysuckerassousyoceanal 384.03
byte 073.16

caald 324.17
cabbis 612.02
cabby 487.10
cabe 033.02
Cabe 200.03
cable 158.10
cables 077.09
cacacanotioun 354.21
cacaon 179.12
cacians 160.12
caco 233.27
cad 003.11 341.01 518.12
cadabra 184.26
cadas 152.27
caddie 200.23
cadendecads 601.14
cadenus 055.30
cadilly 577.05
cadont 338.21
cads 601.14
caecated 076.36
caetera 514.20
caeterorum 514.20
caffin- 414.19
cafiera 479.15
cage 539.23
caged 329.13 600.36
cagnoling 092.19
cahlike 153.32
caill's 235.16
cain 303.32
cained 059.10
cainnin 391.33
caires 065.04
cairn 479.34
cake 172.20 175.29 239.01 379.04 550.13 563.29
cake 340.27
cakeache 294.F1
cakes 370.01 460.32
calamitumbling 514.11
calava 595.27
calced 448.30
calds 425.24
cale 250.27
calfe 476.26
caliber 008.36
call 035.18 073.25 116.12 316.28 367.11 431.31 450.19 494.06 530.21
called 098.17 167.05 380.15 596.19 621.27
callem 094.34
callering 070.20
callher 396.07
callie 054.16
callimbs 238.30
calling 122.05 336.05 543.09 610.36
callme 479.13
calls 294.27 337.10 363.28
callzie 383.17
calm 556.22
calmum 026.18
caloured 205.08
calpable 363.32
calves 229.15
cam 262.29 352.33 550.20
came 067.04 288.14
camel 020.01 368.32
camellated 285.21
cameramen 435.09
cameyou-e'enso 065.31
camination 497.02
caminous 288.19
camode 533.17
camomilla 492.13
campaigning 356.31
campassed 543.12
campf 498.26
campness 470.19
can-again 451.19
canal 484.28
cancancacacanotioun 354.21
candeater 406.07
candees 057.19 182.08
candle 188.34
candled 025.26
candleloose 343.24
cane-Law 324.22
cane-Lee 324.22
canesian 123.27
canicans 497.18
caninnies 175.33
cann 089.10
canned 007.17 210.27
Cannell 392.30
Cannochar 348.19
cannon 174.22
canny 408.16
canotioun 354.21
canponied 607.32
cans 019.16 283.02 289.05
can's 531.26
cant 212.32 240.13 359.19 520.29 553.15
cantenue 347.22
canting 498.21
cantle 379.23
cantos 381.18
cants 156.05
caon 179.12
cap 023.21 185.35 198.32 247.19 257.06 321.10 406.14 415.07 495.30 518.09 541.12 559.20 567.07 583.05
cap 278.L1
capable 108.35 186.33
capacity 576.02
cape 004.36 317.36 533.09
Caper 415.10
capes 562.05
capetulo 054.34
capiture 537.23
capnoise 168.11
capped 448.14 481.30 532.34
cappellas 527.01
capron 026.12
caps 383.19 502.34
cap's 306.F2
capturable 058.22
capture 035.29 082.02
car 137.01 210.19 385.12 434.27 580.18 615.21
cara 471.03
carable 041.01
caraborg 316.13
Carbery 194.02
carbry 144.05
carcarcaract 414.19
card 228.23 388.31
cards 027.32
care 330.07 433.06
carefully 122.22
carême 184.32
carete 206.14
carett 501.04
cargo 220.33
caries 228.02
carine 268.18
carlows 129.01
carmon 526.28
carnadined 079.03
carnate 292.15 596.04
carnations 308.19 600.09
carnons 276.L1
caro 409.14
carott 390.25
carp 254.09 539.26 600.05
carras 320.18
carried 304.05
carry 494.34
carry's 492.19
cars 192.06
carshal's 536.21
cart 079.26 434.31
carthy 137.02
Carthy's 200.35 381.02
cartilaged 437.08
cartys 027.25
cas 129.06 152.27
casandrum 124.36
casas 549.03
case 131.17 356.23 498.04 543.31 560.09 576.30 582.12
Caseous 167.04
cases 192.07 416.22 544.26
caseus 163.15
cash 149.17
cashl- 414.19
casket 415.01 561.16 578.07
casques 431.03
cass 254.15
cassel 376.32
cassia 612.15
cassidy 087.15
cassing 206.01
cast 060.31 120.14 314.26 364.33 449.02 534.34 567.20
caste 237.21
castellated 551.31
caster 108.22
casters 388.07
castle 379.01 471.16
castles 414.04
castrum 567.36

casts 128.30 307.25 318.15
casualisation 076.07
casually 005.25
cat 089.24 148.17 181.23 240.11 388.03 393.13 445.19 513.13
catch 206.33 328.16
catcher 461.15
catered 219.06
Cathayan-Euxine 263.13
catootletoo 461.27
cattls 386.35
catura 291.F6
caugh 511.14
caught 329.13
caughtawan 197.36
caught-emerod's 063.18
caughtscheaf 612.25
cauld 152.26 213.04
cault 385.03
caulture 569.35
caur 577.17
caurs 317.29
cause 536.24
caused 176.30 332.27
causes 596.25
causing 483.01
caust 419.09 424.08
caustum 185.25
cautelousness 111.20
cautious 034.26
cavated 605.26 605.27 605.33
cavement 596.28
caving 508.21
cavites 571.36
cawber 131.16
cawcaw 413.35
Cawley 025.36
Cawley's 392.08
Cawthelock 587.30
cayence 608.03
cease 118.04 129.08
ceases 454.31
ceassing 607.25
ceathay 490.28
cebo 043.23
cecity 236.30
cedar 171.11
ceded 105.30
cedera 160.05
cedras 235.17
cedron 171.11
celcism 082.31
celebrated 470.06
celerious 611.29
celery 586.27
cell 086.05
cellar 410.13
cellars 545.27
cellas 615.02
celles 226.04
celles' 227.18
cellies 012.28 250.12
cellory 308.03
cells 017.06
cellular 116.11
celsius 597.31
celticocommediant 033.03
cemt 262.01
cenatas 353.28
cended 222.35
cendiarist 426.02
cendiary 424.31
cene 137.17
cenors 096.35
cens 013.29 483.21
cense 207.01 235.17 378.33
censed 179.10 336.35 412.14 536.19
censitive 230.26
censive 465.12
censor 136.17
censors 134.35
censtrobed 263.06
census 523.30
cent 240.28
centaurnary 535.04
centaurs 032.03
centenary 386.36
centian 038.26
centime 123.15
centor 060.32
centors 026.21
centre 106.36
centric 310.07 605.16 606.03
centrum 463.21
cents 242.04
cephalous 310.06
ceps 164.01
ceptered 290.01
cera 568.32
cerfs 113.11
ceritis 096.02
cert 610.17
certain 022.17 031.09 084.05 100.33 185.30 558.03 609.35
certain 340.26
CERTAINTY 282.R4
certinelazily 121.24
certitude 178.32
cerution 107.19
cess 433.05
cessantlament 614.02
cessas 327.24
cessed 492.05
cessers 600.24
cessory 237.36
cesters 348.28
cestuish 115.12
cetera 071.07 127.22 127.22
ceterogenious 595.23
ceterus 379.31
cettera 339.36
chace 335.10 553.23
chad 138.33 565.10
chaf 274.01
chafers 435.35
chaff 089.36 240.15 444.29
chafts 133.30
chaina 243.15
chainted 237.11
chair 251.22 423.07 493.05
chairch 358.27
chairmanlooking 416.07
chairs 357.06 528.35
chake 446.10
chalk 233.35
chamber 063.15 475.18
chambers 566.07
chambre 182.09
chamed 502.28
chamer 556.15
champ 077.19
chamtur 496.26
chan 284.08
chance 141.17 363.29 395.28 403.24 516.22
chance 345.22
chancers 342.31
chang 119.24
change 239.04 252.10 289.07 346.29 464.20 491.07 538.08 574.24 575.11 577.12
change 106.18
changeability 308.L2
changed 083.32
changing 042.36 167.28 394.18
chankata 024.23
chantedly 461.33
chantement 028.08
chanting 543.08
chap 221.34 237.15
chap 349.18
chapel 374.31 571.18
chapel-Asitalukin 110.08
Chapelle 080.36 334.36
chaplain 564.32
chapper 439.30
chappy 357.05
chaps 370.27
charge 313.20
charged 040.16 529.14 586.05
charger 133.22
charmer 290.16 465.20
charming 561.13
chart 096.28
charted 254.18
chary 225.02
chas 030.14
chasa 160.06
chase 443.30
chased 405.01
chasing 475.28
chasm 229.24
chasse 076.36
chasser 228.14
chat 586.01
chats 494.25
chaun 419.17
chaup 209.31
chaw 303.21
cheaf 612.25
cheap 300.F3 406.36 574.13 574.22
cheats 322.02
check 016.08 537.15
chedolche 302.22
chee 209.22 333.05 474.10
cheekeepy 275.F1
cheeks 041.11 463.11 493.08
cheeky 376.20
cheena 616.12
cheep 357.03
cheeping 622.05
cheeriode 359.19
cheetchee 244.20
chef 058.20
cheirst 308.F1
chekes 390.09
chemical 167.06
chen 209.34 531.06
chen's 548.33
chepes 077.29
chepps 067.17
chept 347.12
chequer 375.20
chequered 091.30
cher 345.17
cherché 149.24
cherib 150.16

cherikissings 446.11
cherrily 031.30
cherry 251.20
chert 613.30
chess 588.28
chessvan 013.27
chest 328.20 426.11 596.06
chested 109.03
chester 390.18 446.31 448.14
chests 077.29
chestviousness 156.14
chetaoli 609.10
chevre 276.13
chevuole 089.06
chew 233.33
chewer 412.04
chewing 209.01 587.31
chick 565.21
chicked 541.21
chicken 070.08
chicker 423.19
chid 340.02
chief 024.33 033.06 127.10 251.29 392.14 483.18
Chief 219.13
chiefmaker 206.07
chiefs 213.27
chiel 472.22
chievmiss 020.31
chiff 350.07
Chikda-Uru-Wukru 024.07
child 555.16 579.01
child 481.02
children 576.32
Children 102.29
childs 244.09 244.10
child's 167.08
chill 099.12
chill's 248.11
chily 565.20
chimbers 369.08
chime 026.28 051.32
chimings 360.11
chimple 282.14
chin 039.24 072.22 136.30 136.31 219.20 257.21 447.19 465.28 568.28 601.32
chin 346.18
china's 343.15
chind's 252.05
chine 495.23
chinello 043.23
chingarri 180.14
chin-grin 082.12
chinly 344.16
chino 054.18
chip 329.01
chiric 123.16
Chirruta 204.12
chitt 499.09
chiu 209.23
chjelasys 417.23
chlocracy 484.32
choating 404.07
chob 357.03
choff 495.09
choid- 135.16
cholerd 370.33
chonal 277.02
chone 277.01
chong 115.04 299.F3
chonry 482.12
choo 348.19
chooks 009.16
choor 608.21
chop 241.36 311.24
chopchap 304.F2
choractors- 314.08
chord 013.18 284.03
choreal 145.25
choredcheck 537.15
choristic 234.20
chorn 157.03
chorous 148.19
choses 291.12
chosies 007.24
chouc 035.08
chough 249.30
chow 474.10 537.05
christ 569.15
christian 114.11
christien 201.35
chromatic 611.06
chromatokreening 392.28
chronic 182.12
chronickled 380.08
chronism 393.20 515.11
chronisms 290.07
chrost 331.14
chthumpered 360.09
chu 466.04 480.04 480.05 484.29
chub 342.19
chubby 461.24
chucha 027.20
chuckers 310.32
chuff 352.34
chuffuous 131.34
chugger's 379.03
chullard 392.15
chum 005.08
chummin- 314.08
chums 051.15
chun 220.19
chuna 346.15
chup 318.19
chur 587.14
church 082.19 431.25 533.27
churches 059.16
church's 546.21
churchwardens 116.27
churls 381.33
churuls 303.24
chute 003.19 200.05
chutes 616.26
chysm 282.25
cicero 152.10
ciclist 145.11
ciclometer 614.27
ciel 504.24
cielo 244.25
cientotrigintadue 054.12
cif 154.12
cilier 335.18
ciliouslooking 120.18
cilled 093.25
cimmed 497.09
cimoroon 207.25
cinct 297.21
cinctis 185.15
cincts 294.20
cindgemeinded 252.16
cingk 550.35
cingle 030.23
cinssies 603.28
cint 366.23
cinta 615.03
cinthinous 118.28 281.14
ciolated 054.33
cionator 154.07
cioppachew 233.33
ciphered 118.01
circensor 136.17
circle 132.13 505.13
circles 228.13
circling 209.24
circulars 295.31
circulingly 055.27
cirrhonimbant 599.25
cis 568.10
cisamica 254.16
cisprinks 537.05
cissions 618.14
cississies 526.34
cissous 449.15
cissters 096.13
cissymaidies 192.02
cistral 109.19
citadel 073.24
citas 610.08
citations 491.30
cited 356.05
CitEncy 421.23
citendency 305.09
citers 608.17
cites 523.05
cities 115.12 368.13 473.20
citrantament 371.23
citron 575.16
citrone 132.28
cits 368.19
city 049.17 053.17 094.18 100.34 107.24 108.28 111.33 132.30 151.03 151.06 154.25 187.07 356.23 411.12 424.34 494.22 541.27 576.02
city 072.11
CITY 286.R3
civicise 446.35
civily 055.13
cizism 231.27
clack 423.05 469.10
clacking 256.06
clacks 595.33
clad 110.24 134.19 134.24 392.29 605.06
claim 030.08 129.22 155.10 603.36
claimed 421.02 472.29 574.13
claiming 093.19 315.19
claination 603.23
clam 546.22
clamazzione 173.15
clammitation 153.25
clamoured 100.02
clan 484.23
claney 083.24
clangavore 393.29
clangle 456.22
clapadad 347.27
clappers 614.13
claret 411.14
clasped 232.12
class 125.13 294.08 359.12 395.13 396.11 419.34 444.04 451.34 459.04
classed 089.16
classical 179.23
clastics 447.34

clates 049.14
claths 491.19
clatter 147.21
claused 569.14
clava 170.33
claver 352.23
clavers 285.25
claws 491.07
clay 314.21 569.07
clean 237.21 448.10
cleaned 091.17
Cleath 057.31
cleay 212.15
clee 210.19 498.12
cleeagh 310.12
cleeaghbally 014.09
cleeath 539.17
cleeps 614.12
cleeva 134.01
clefft 583.35
clefield's 381.14
cleivka 341.09
clept 254.07
clerk 382.13
clerks 312.36
clerosies 541.36
Clery 385.07
Clery's 386.20
clete 013.30 279.07
cletus 155.34
clever 426.03
cliath 237.33
Cliath 420.20
cliaver 159.30
clid 302.12
cliffs 010.36
cling 153.26
clip 210.22
clish 376.16
clitties 284.23
clived 481.13
cloak 016.34 155.02 567.18
cloaked 339.29
clock 068.30 087.15 219.01
406.09 427.34 449.24 517.25
519.31 531.24 558.18 617.21
clocks 177.28
cloded 356.07
clog 127.07
clogypst 364.18
cloke 553.14
cloose 617.04
clord 362.09
close 023.11 047.19 102.14
207.32 545.30
closed 063.27 411.18 450.21
586.17
closed 072.06
closes 221.22
close's 203.26
closet 551.25
closhant 552.24
closing 484.11
closure 605.24
cloted 026.10
cloth 022.25 039.06 182.33
456.14 536.30 577.31
clothe 543.14
clothed 421.36 441.05 539.03
550.29
clother 549.33
clothes 064.02 337.11 465.09
clothesed 355.19
cloths 537.15 569.01
clotted 097.16
cloud 246.07 296.27 480.26
590.17
clouded 277.15
Clouds 018.23 519.07
clouted 049.26
clouthed 366.15
clouths 295.07
clover 286.15
club 197.07 205.06 436.29
528.07
clubber 335.13
clucking 256.06
clud 456.23
cludded 155.09
clused 157.12
clusium 084.15
clutch 572.02
clzp 284.14
coach 415.10
coal 411.32 411.32
coalman's 326.10
coarse 214.24
coastedself 321.06
coat 024.29 030.22 043.06
043.20 150.28 190.26 193.19
242.34 391.14 404.17 404.25
451.02 497.32 559.09 567.30
coated 448.07
coatliar 264.F3
coats 183.35 289.19 323.12
407.36 466.33
coats 107.07
coat's 561.31
coaxed 192.08
coaxes 546.16
cobely 294.12
cock 031.18 044.02 051.22
136.14 447.12 468.30 538.22
cockeys 493.14
cocks 022.03 245.03 303.F2
cock's 329.26
cockstown 097.04
Cocoa 026.31
cocommediant 033.03
cocopotl 294.24
cocoursing 609.14
cocta 134.18
cod 578.08
codden 326.34
codding 346.24
coded 232.26
codedition 512.17
codeignus 624.26
coel 467.25
coffin 353.06
coffin- 414.19
coffing 005.22
coffynosey 257.14
coga 341.08
coghamade 089.30
cognisances 261.20
cognise 082.17
cognition 063.05
cognits 283.27
coh 040.05
cohaired 275.01
coherend 242.15
coherently 040.05
coho 040.05
cohoran 020.09
coid 443.23
coil 121.24 160.35 348.08
466.08
coincidences 597.01
cokes 232.01
cola 133.15 237.12 382.05
colacion 528.20
colanius 118.13
colar 516.35
colarinas 361.28
colation 417.27
colcitrantament 371.23
cold 211.32 265.03 290.15
382.12 502.09 578.23
colded 561.30
colderymeid 239.18
coldlogical 396.14
colepts 395.08
colicus 193.21
colina 210.10
coline's 226.15
collaborators 118.25
collakill 060.08
collect 357.24 409.04 434.06
502.11
collection 278.08 445.29
colled 152.26
college 389.09
collin 533.33
collion 538.29 538.30 538.33
collogher 540.09 540.11 540.12
collogher-la-Belle 540.10
colohour 176.10
colombs 335.28
Colonel 317.30 600.17
colonials 152.16
colons 374.09
colopulation 557.17
colorissimo 240.15
colour 503.24
coloured 029.20 054.31 126.19
339.12 434.08 463.14 611.06
611.35
coloured's 277.01
colours 237.04 466.27
colous 018.29 173.16
colout 286.F5
col's 302.03
coltous 348.03
colum 298.31
columnists 438.18
com 262.28
comayo 197.35
comb 391.23 422.25
combating 597.17
combe 235.16 254.35
combination 614.35
combs 022.04 152.28
come 238.32 240.06
280.07 448.32 567.24
623.01
come 344.12
come- 255.25
comed 369.18 372.01
comedy 425.24 540.26
comeoutable 367.32
comer 317.10
comeraid 036.20
comers 142.16
comes 276.F2
comeshare 191.18
come-union 227.30
comic 580.25
Comic 222.07

coming 022.31 194.22 264.10 274.14 602.19
comitated 280.29
commediant 033.03
commence 444.15
commend 356.27 533.06
commended 525.04
commending 163.30
commends 089.26
commers 322.26
commincio 432.04
commixtion 347.22
common 041.04 276.24 435.33 523.23
commons 380.07
communicables 087.19
communicambiambisumers 155.04
communicated 181.35
commuter's 056.01
comologosis 341.30
comondation 382.19
comore 095.21
comores 203.21 555.08
comoss 409.12
comparisoned 152.05
compass 480.26
compatabilily 164.02
compatibly 085.27 533.05
competite 325.04
compile 566.14
complete 560.07
completet 119.14
complimentary 613.11
complishies 349.34
composition 614.34
compounded 253.35
computables 367.31
con 352.02 363.17 614.28
concentrum 463.21
conception 444.11
concerned 221.10
conche 390.17
conchoid- 135.16
concordia 054.10
concrete 077.17
condamned 418.30
condemnatory 090.35
conditional 163.23 270.01
conditionally 326.08
conditioned 521.24
condra's 293.F1
condraws 420.33
condriac 181.35
conducting 183.09
conductor 378.09
cone 297.11 297.11 403.08
conee 003.07 140.35
cones 131.10
coney's 449.08
confounder 323.06
confusalem 355.11
conjungation 143.13
Conn 376.01
connected 121.18
connection 228.17
connections 348.06
Connee 549.28
connell 070.29
Connell 081.09 386.22 507.26 580.31
connell's 310.28
Connell's 382.05
conner 319.04
Conner 317.31
connerman 141.25
connmuns 521.28
connoistre 081.34
Connor 271.01
connouth 227.27
cononnulstria 229.17
Conor 380.12 380.33 381.25
conoscope 349.18
conscience 123.21
conscionable 266.30
consciounce 623.25
conscious 072.30 173.32 377.28
consciously 153.03 173.33 174.01 300.25
consciousness 421.22
consistency 192.32
consorted 239.28
constein 211.16
constituted 355.01
constitution 596.09
constricted 036.09
constrictor 085.18
construct 515.22
contaminated 292.15
content 407.34
contigruity 607.20
continent 388.05
continue 537.16
continued's 626.18
continuous 501.22
contracted 182.34
contras 156.10
contribusodalitarian's 099.36
controllable 011.33 032.07 184.15
conundrums 506.03
convenience 520.06
convenient 172.25
convention's 516.29
conversioning 512.16
converted 220.30
convulsing 231.16
coo 245.18 427.13
coocoon 483.35
cook 020.06 136.14 214.23 394.07 486.17
cooker 323.13
Cooks 456.31
cook's 551.04
cool 006.13 006.13
Cool 139.14
coole 569.23
coolsha 626.35
coombe 243.23 334.35
coombs 542.03
coon 256.26 483.35 519.03
coon's 499.13
coon's 105.21
coop 405.21
coopering 059.05
coops 537.23
coor 414.06
Coort 376.01
coose 018.33
cooshy 484.26
coover 141.15
cop 338.32
copal 365.09
copanc 349.10
cope-acurly 140.19
coped 043.22
copers 229.09
coping 554.03
copious 137.30
copodium 334.03
copolos 368.33
copotl 294.24
copper's 480.17
copper's 338.35
cops 428.27
coque 575.16
cor 228.21
corant 328.25
corawman 242.13
cordation 142.25
corde 222.02
corded 482.35
corder 210.03
cordia 054.10
cordial 260.F2 313.07 581.13
cordials 453.26
cordo 215.23 513.17
core 185.24
coree 584.30
corello 134.19
cores 432.31
corico 584.27
coricori 623.01
cork 310.34
corks 381.10
Cormacan 463.22
cormack 450.25
Cormack 137.02
Cormick 376.01
corn 348.11 462.20
Cornel 607.29
corneltree 588.31
corner 577.08
corners 555.11
cornies 102.11
cornish 151.19
corns 505.05 622.25
coronate 250.35
coroners 602.16
corot 266.23
corpolous 541.25
corporate 580.23
corporated 108.15 228.20 332.14
corpse 509.32
corrall 285.F2
corrier 367.32
corruption 062.18
cors 048.07
cors 344.10
corsaired 600.11
corss 056.03
cosagh- 414.19
cosmic 394.32
cosmically 263.24
cosmos 613.12
cost 510.26
costa 172.22
costal 099.21
costant 567.21
costecas 152.27
costello 072.05
costitis 130.09
costive 027.10
costs 624.34
cosycasket 578.07
cot 159.19 227.03 242.33
cotes 129.22 232.13
coth 013.28
Cothraige 054.14
cots 111.26
cotta 160.07 481.32

cottch 439.04
cotted 185.04 496.03
cotten 434.05
cotther 275.09
cotton 612.31
cottoncrezy 009.08
cotts 543.21
cott's 529.31
cou 054.15
couch 597.17
couched 542.28
cough 095.08 397.24
coughawhooping 128.10
coula 220.19
coulas 314.35
Couley 242.36
coulored 443.34
count 496.17
counted 575.11
countenanced 537.03
counter 321.28
countered 186.24
counthest 365.18
counting 282.29
country 293.F1
countrylifer 356.34
coup 099.30 577.20
coup 105.28
couple 577.18 613.10
coupling 614.30
coups 300.17
courched 531.10
couriered 471.15
course 049.35 230.24 237.23 423.30
courseful 194.26
courser 481.02
coursers 452.23
courses 143.12 605.19
coursing 322.36 609.14
court 236.22
courting 009.07 094.28
courts 005.36 030.23 089.17 545.30
cousien 162.14
cousin 055.17 313.09 422.17
cout 060.30
couth 239.35
couthrement 113.01
coutred 594.14
coutsch 204.06
couverers 088.27
covan 597.15
cover 096.28 394.01 577.18 611.12 611.26
coverdull 359.12
covered 220.28 291.16
covering 344.19
covers 602.24
covert 564.03
covery 326.31
coves 039.14
cow 134.30 228.32 317.08
cow 105.26
cowards 276.F1
cowding 061.07
cowegian 016.06
Cowell 607.04
cowls 456.16
cowmoney 416.17
cowpow 375.05
cox 124.36 234.17
coxious 052.14
coxity 224.36
coy 226.28
coys 469.26
crackcruck 426.05
cracker 304.F1
crackers 026.30 033.16
cracking 076.05 143.13 376.09
cracks 011.04
craft 120.25 162.30 241.23 269.F4 356.36 468.24 483.11 510.10 604.13 623.19
crag 300.32
crake 493.32
cramation 342.19
cramp 556.36
crank 424.10
cranks 329.31
cranna's 329.17
craptions 364.19
cras 534.34
crash 356.32 382.19
crashers 341.20
crass 152.08
crass 491.19
crat 397.26
crates 328.12
craw 341.18
crawl 074.14
Crawl 617.11
Crawls 618.01
craxian 099.28
crazemazed 389.27
crazyaztecs 242.11
cream 236.04 527.13
creaminated 366.17
creaming 383.15
creas 345.02
creasious 277.F2
create 604.27
CREATE 262.R2 262.R2
created 484.19 605.04 605.05 605.08 605.35 606.07
creates 088.09
creating 282.28
creation 142.25 306.22 581.28
creator 551.07
cred 337.35
credible 155.03 301.04 425.21
credit 033.24
cree 395.32
creed 215.26
creeder 320.04
creedoed 515.25
creena 376.34
creepers 006.05
creepingly 445.36
creke 285.F5
cremuncted 227.32
creppy- 044.20
crescence 138.06
crescendied 492.07
crescent 276.F3
cressing 288.03
crested 044.01 468.30
crezy 009.08
Crian 087.18
cribibis 300.17
cried 506.26
crimed 078.32
crimsoned 180.02
cripped 617.23
criticos 551.31
critus 307.L1
crockeries 443.25
croft 139.33 552.13
crom 625.07
cromforemost 362.05
Cronione 415.21
crook 066.15 127.17
crookers 245.08
crookly- 113.09
crooks 155.17
crooksman 556.27
croom 156.06
crooned 043.32
cropfs 306.02
cross 412.36
crossed 060.35 084.20 120.19
croticon 614.28
crotty- 044.20
croucely 227.20
crow 133.22 360.04
crowd 042.22
crowded 543.22
crown 169.13 237.24 329.29
crowned 289.30
crucer 480.25
cruciated 137.13 192.18
cruck 426.05
crude 358.06
crum 050.13
crumbling 415.21
crumbs 430.29
crumines 613.17
crumpler 395.16
crums 449.36 563.24
crupp 010.13
crural 557.17
crusha 262.15
crusher 150.05
crust 018.31 078.11
crusted 038.07
crutched 579.32
Crutches 209.07
cruwell 022.14
crux 173.02
cruxer 516.31
cruxian 155.28
crween 587.13
cry 068.20 143.17 475.08 494.06
cry 352.27
cryphul 242.30
cryptogam 546.13
crystal 084.29
c'stle 018.06 018.06 018.06
cu 484.29
cub 516.16
cuba 530.33
cubation 112.21 397.34
cubone 221.23
cuccia's 561.24
cuchet 302.10
cuddle 379.20 391.03
cuddler 608.25
cue 380.10
cuffs 149.02 542.13
cuish 090.34
cuite 133.30
cuitsman 391.04
cuity 602.28
cul 397.32 490.03 584.31
cul 255.15
CUL 286.R4
cula 306.24 494.09
cula 122.21 440.02

culacticors 048.07
culapuloids 540.33
cular 023.01 082.12 230.31 265.F2 315.30
cularly 004.31
cula's 601.22
culated 541.27
culates 349.17
culdus 137.24
cule 070.06 097.15 135.27
culeads 128.36
culeneous 570.17
cules 018.11 037.11 518.22
cules 353.26
cules' 081.03
culingly 055.27
culink 166.26
culisation 149.27
culising 352.27
cull 223.14
Cullagh 622.04
cullaghmore 025.31
culled 203.13
cullen 141.35
cullerymaid's 181.17
cullinans 286.14
culling 092.26 391.18
cullion 555.21
cullions 129.02
cullion's 239.19 305.30
cullised 127.36
cullogues 398.03
cullpth 532.09
cullus 248.16
culmination 232.08
culone 132.15
culos 016.04
culos 113.30
culosity 173.34
culossed 492.05
culosus 466.31 466.31
culous 112.20 229.32 410.16 445.27 493.10
culously 088.13 097.14
culpatory 056.15
culpting 121.26
culpuration 368.12
culs 384.18 617.14
cult 303.F1
cultads 302.17
cultural 086.20 405.11
culture 164.25
culum 264.07
culums 346.24 553.30
culus 525.33
culusts 367.14
cum 156.25 228.22 243.31 309.21 442.08
cum 089.27
cumbe 230.20
cumbered 545.18
cumbre 279.F27
cum-Enheritance 264.09
Cumhal 243.14
cuminamoyas 201.30
cumo 198.02
cumque 605.32
cums 234.34 542.30
cumtra's 601.24
cumuddher-in-chaff 240.15
cumul 375.29
cumule 198.34
cunct 206.35 497.10
cund 007.16 360.04
cundenances 382.02
cunding 153.01
cundis 287.23
cunditate 185.24
cundus 574.12 574.12 574.12
cune 500.04
cuniar 019.03
cuniarity 241.05
Cunnuc 378.13
cunsciously 394.31
cuoniams 278.04
cup 004.11 138.29 237.01 261.25 321.16 334.10 345.24 450.31 561.12 561.14 616.20
cupassit 167.33
cupement 151.19
cupes 349.32
cupiose 290.04
cupiscent 432.10
cupper 276.09 320.30 330.09
cuppered 155.28
cuppers 133.08
cupping 171.08
cups 144.09 145.14 232.35 321.15 433.25 568.14 616.23
cups 345.27
cups' 355.12
cupth's 516.19
cur 011.18 602.23
cura 164.30
curable 041.01
curables 197.25
curacy 143.07
curate 221.10
curator 572.19
curatress 352.13
curbs 303.19
cure 014.25 389.06 545.06 550.18 573.07 613.25
cured 447.36 541.27
curedent 184.23
curers 422.03
cures 011.20
curface 496.11
curies 290.08
curing 115.23
curiosited 449.01
curious 363.28
curious 484.36
curius 513.01
curling 345.26
curls 024.30 280.36
curlugh 479.06
curly 140.19
curra 214.21
curraghed 322.19
currals 234.15
currant 460.33
curred 380.05
current 124.21
currently 254.25 287.28
curs 338.25 518.22
cursed 029.09
cursekissed 078.33
curser 506.06
cursing 516.19
cursioned 324.31
curss 225.12 225.13
curst 311.36
cursus 318.10
curtains 543.31
curum 611.14
curus 096.33
curve 133.03
curverself 540.33
curves 376.15
curvy 137.28
cus 319.06 373.24
cus 185.19
cusado 485.21
cusagh- 414.19
cusant 519.34
cusascmerul 518.23
cuse 016.05
cushiccups' 355.12
cushion 028.06
cushla 480.23
cushla 399.18
cushy 556.32
cuspidal 273.28
cuss 054.04 128.02 174.16 407.17
cus's 056.01
cussa 119.02
cussed 324.24 526.27
cusses 435.35
cussion 125.16
cussors 541.11
cusst 275.19
custard 475.15
customarily 138.09
cut 043.25 056.22 076.19 156.29 176.26 236.36 240.34 517.26 544.16 551.31 571.06 612.14
cut 601.16
cuta 240.19
cut-dean 550.27
cuterre 541.35
cutes 607.22
cutey 484.07
cutfrank 405.23
cuts 051.07 245.28 284.02 460.09 572.04 576.20 580.04 619.11
cutschum 005.08
cuttas 541.17
cutted 496.03
cutter 356.36 492.15
cutterer 340.01
cutticules 518.22
cutties 197.33
cuttle 453.24
cuttle 072.01
cutt's 352.01
cwmwladed 590.16
cycled 416.30
cycles 208.09 310.07 375.13
cyclical 605.04
cyclicling 153.26
cycling 099.05
cydlac 203.26
cye 327.34
cygthe 341.10
cylinder 179.34
cylmania 228.19
Cymric-Helleniky 263.14
cynical 610.14
cynicism 353.08
cyphyllicks 525.08
cysts 613.20
czlanthas 351.14

da 007.26 031.18 037.22 054.17 058.09 135.31 139.32

147.12 147.12 147.14 158.02
160.30 172.31 179.12 197.23
199.12 200.31 204.10 204.10
212.06 213.04 221.28 224.02
228.10 232.03 232.28 234.05
239.10 271.F4 272.02 272.02
272.03 348.35 350.33 388.11
415.34 416.25 434.07 445.32
466.19 466.21 469.34 470.01
470.36 470.36 477.22 478.13
478.13 481.21 502.15 518.06
518.25 521.06 527.27 528.12
545.09
da 092.02 466.20
dable 053.04
dabout 057.25 539.25
daces 575.36
dach 254.28
dacianmad 577.01
dacist 090.26
daclouths 295.07
dactylism 522.07
dad 020.31 286.04 347.27
435.01 590.21
daddy 016.01 306.03
daddy- 332.05
dadge 485.13
dadin 601.26
dads 432.30 492.30
dad's 439.13 486.01
dae 235.34
daew 597.31
Daffy 084.14
daft 439.10
dag 186.21 199.04 453.13
531.01
dagad 009.26
dagh- 044.20
dags 096.09 413.10 484.14
dag-Zindeh-Munaday 205.16
dah 524.36
dahm 205.31
dahveddahs 085.03
dai 196.19 532.31
daign 153.15
daily 136.26
dailyones 058.11
daims 113.11
daintee 102.32
daintily 254.31
dainty 238.03 409.12
dairy 505.14
daisers 035.17
daisies 242.17
daisying 363.03
daisymen 524.11
dal 317.33
dal- 003.15
dale 007.02 609.16 620.21
dale 342.07
dales 553.35
dale's 209.06
dalesaga 220.24
Daley 048.13
dalgan 091.08
dalgoland 388.19
dalicence 040.27
dalisks 335.33
dalisque 226.32
dalkin 201.26
dall 468.28 587.32
dalled 256.12 298.30
dally 200.20 406.01
dalough 062.35 248.30
dalough-le-vert 605.11
dals 234.15 611.17
dam 033.34 033.35 111.03
142.22 220.33 250.07 252.35
254.25 255.22 258.21
dam 346.16 471.34
dama 450.32
daman- 414.19
damanant 076.02
damanu 364.33
damanvantora 598.33
damapplers 146.13
damble 226.17
dame 530.33
dames 015.17 194.28 509.24
damestough 485.16
daminant 617.23
damines 451.03
daminiva's 601.23
dammangut 214.19
dammers 572.02
dammum 515.09
damn 252.34 326.32
damn- 414.19
damnbut 381.25
damned 421.02
damned 418.30
damnor 499.09
damo 212.36 212.36
damoiseau 230.14
damors 551.10
damp 201.06
dampster 319.16
damrotter 017.15
dams 069.10 351.31
dam's 043.20
damsels 432.21
dan 056.14 420.26 602.28
danapalus 182.18
danapplous 254.23
danars 387.11
dance 249.11 358.35 378.29
465.23 615.02
danced 109.06
dances 342.12
dancy 282.F4
dandgunne 025.23
dandle 328.31
dando 232.31
dandyline 535.01
danelang's 353.31
daneously 414.01
danes 389.10
dane's 438.14
danfest 082.36
dang 185.31
danger 168.05
danian 221.32
Daniel 625.12
danified 133.28
dankje 150.11
dann 012.06
danser 513.16
danseuses 098.12
dansked 330.34
dante 269.L1
dantic 510.03
danto 047.19
daphne 406.25
dapodopudupedding 599.08
dapolam 396.09
dappel 078.20
dar 065.13 202.16 326.26
dar 341.29
darapidarpad 234.19
dard 389.25
dardi 185.21
dare 068.17 202.31 436.31
516.06
darean 205.05
dared 480.20
daredonit 353.11
darft 221.33
dargoos 347.14
dariaty 345.29
daries 241.29 443.31
darimus 432.30
daring 368.35
daris 202.18
dark 203.25 622.15
darkery 231.14
darnel 094.31
darner 108.17
darpad 234.19
darri 180.13
dar's 597.01
dart 206.18
darthar 347.09
darthella 151.20
darty 160.08
dary 181.07 303.26 581.27
dary 071.16
dascircles 228.13
dasguesched 232.33
dash 233.17
dasher 051.14
dasherisher 176.11
dashouts 502.20
dass 511.30
dasson 248.04
dat 256.26
datal 607.06
date 267.02 294.28 598.23
601.36
dated 210.36 589.25
datepholomy 389.17
dates 088.25
daties 542.28
dating 256.22
dats 520.18
dattle 353.11
datus 121.27
daublin 373.19
daucher 498.14
daugghter 444.26
daughter 389.10
daunelegants 353.27
dauner 568.06
da-Uru-Wukru 024.07
davalls 580.01
daw 196.17 360.04
daweens 241.26
dawl 322.02
dawn 006.26 099.01 138.36
dawn-of-all-works 041.09
dawpeehole 120.31
daws 141.18
daw's 276.06
day 004.21 005.10 005.13
005.24 016.05 027.11 035.04
042.06 050.32 058.05 058.29
059.11 059.19 066.03 066.04
069.28 070.26 076.23 079.10
086.11 089.14 089.18 102.15
102.28 107.23 110.28 112.10

112.25 119.31 125.21 129.13
135.24 138.17 145.01 169.07
176.20 182.26 192.19 194.11
205.16 209.28 211.16 219.04
233.36 257.01 264.04 275.25
276.27 278.22 284.29 294.04
294.F4 301.20 301.20 301.21
301.21 301.21 301.21 304.F1
322.16 337.28 338.18 338.18
347.01 348.35 378.20 390.06
407.08 433.07 433.12 434.17
436.27 436.27 455.05 455.24
456.34 457.19 457.19 457.19
457.20 460.19 460.29 472.29
481.07 481.07 481.08 485.06
486.27 488.27 489.35 490.27
491.27 493.02 497.27 502.13
513.12 514.22 517.31 520.03
520.17 521.10 530.01 539.28
544.28 547.33 556.02 556.05
556.08 570.09 570.11 570.12
596.16 602.20 613.08 617.21
620.12
day 353.07 381.24 399.21 399.25
daybrandy's 155.36
dayde 538.20
dayed 415.14
dayevil 423.28
daying 389.21
day'll 398.34
daylooking 109.07
dayne 333.23
daynism 350.12
days 039.25 041.01 045.15
054.03 069.10 089.18 101.15
127.25 133.18 221.06 240.29
280.07 282.27 408.19 432.33
470.17 473.09 542.33 547.28
553.15 553.16 561.06 565.05
615.25
days 104.12
day's 005.11 088.14 117.05
407.29 407.31 487.34 506.10
540.33 573.02 588.34 614.21
daysboost 583.19
daysed 617.29
dayte 325.06
dayterrorised 184.08
dayth 346.22
daze 562.16
dazmy 492.32
dazzle 113.01
dazzlingly 339.19
Dea 210.14
deacon 055.17
deaconess 209.06
deaconesses 366.24
deaconry 254.06
dead 488.20 505.21 560.18
deade 363.20
deaf 329.27
deafdom 236.30
deafs 522.28
deakin 369.11
deal 280.26 384.24 585.17
dealing 333.10
dealings 077.21
deams 293.12
dean 413.10 494.19 550.27
deaned 291.F4
deanupper 501.32
dear 013.27 013.27 060.31
062.01 146.19 161.13 492.16
dearment 571.04
dears 348.07 395.34 538.19
545.25
dears' 328.20
deary 005.26
Dea's 059.23
deatar 406.07
deave 476.21
Deavis 041.04
deb 526.20
debble- 332.05
deblank 253.34
deboko 051.17
deburgghers 623.23
decads 601.14
decanal 484.28
decanesian 123.27
decant 240.13
deceived 174.04
decencies 494.04
decency 436.01
dechious 578.20
decidedly 542.20
decimmed 497.09
decimoroon 207.25
de-citron 575.16
decked 261.02 379.25
decker 620.07
decks 511.25
declan 484.23
decores 432.31
decorous 608.09
decorum 092.05
decoy 226.28
decoys 603.29
dectural 165.09
ded 418.06 551.02
deddoh 340.31
de-dentelle 265.L1
dedit 153.28
deditioned 484.24
dedroll 324.01
dedye 340.31
dee 210.01 437.07 452.28
598.09
dee 342.29
deece 375.03
deed 140.14 185.31 312.02
315.31 424.05 461.08
deedees 258.24
deedumms 258.24
deedust 055.03
deekchimple 282.14
deen 095.17 365.32
deenen 564.35
deep 381.10 470.06
deepen 141.06
deer 500.12
deeth 079.17
deevin 264.28
defallen 233.33
deftkiss 418.22
defyne 510.10
degarius 498.03
deh-Munaday 205.16
dehobbles 275.22
dehooly's 440.15
dehorn 428.15
dehowse 525.22
deiculosus 466.31
deignus 624.26
deils 236.29
deintia 610.07
deism 162.23
dejenk 179.28
deksan 285.18 285.19
del 207.26
delaries 004.03
Delawarr 212.04
delays 577.24
deleted 183.36
deleure 064.19
delfian 073.18
delibile 185.25
delig 265.10
delikato 566.26
deliond 361.23
delivered 048.06
dell 270.21 360.33
dell 276.L2
della 349.21
delled 346.26
delling 562.26
dells 549.32
delly 089.18
deloire 207.11
delond 626.28
delonde 609.17
delounges 321.34
delph 403.11
delphians 572.25
delusk 576.03
dem 439.17 545.29 624.08
demaer 317.18
demands 369.02
demd 052.05
demean 494.31
demeanour 035.06 189.26
dememdes 542.24
demented 179.25
demia's 263.11
demicolons 374.09
demihemispheres 508.21
demmed 239.33
demmed 353.08
demon 455.27
demonstrative 115.27
dems 278.F7
demuredemeanour 189.26
den 046.02 050.15 102.24
167.35 255.31 260.18 407.20
436.03 516.19 541.13 541.16
den 350.02
den- 424.20
dency 305.04
dend 239.34 541.27
dendecads 601.14
dendron 042.20 588.32
dene 553.22
denen- 003.15
deney 284.F1
deneys 350.23
DENIES 308.R2
denname 276.F1
dens 088.15 504.34 517.22
den's 030.02 282.25 584.16
dense 048.01
density 350.12
denskaulds 228.36
dent 184.23 484.09
dentaccia 180.15
dentament 253.19
dentated 186.03
dentelle 265.L1
dentifide 051.05
dention 593.16

dentity 049.36
denture 524.17
denus 413.27
denying 073.02
denzando 226.30
denze 539.20
deosy 396.31
deoturanian 289.20
dependence 118.02 500.14
dependent 129.24 510.24
depict 039.09
depondant 602.17
deq 025.24
derg 203.20
derivative 084.16
dermann 503.10
derodromites 160.21
derry 058.36 210.04 323.21
dersh 617.12
derts 394.18
descendanced 109.06
descent 068.20
describables 298.32
descript 121.09
desedo 351.05
desendas 612.11
desia 594.04
desias 542.31
designful 426.12
desirable 456.30 517.03 562.30
desirables 243.19
desmally 566.12
desombre 343.16
despoinis 165.28
destained 341.05
destind 328.10
desting 577.33
destinies 092.11 497.04
destril 542.17
destung 126.22
detached 079.06 545.01
detic 114.15
detrigesima 433.03
deurscodeignus 624.26
deus 246.18 326.03 456.30
deus 341.24
deveide 340.21
deveiled 075.05
developmented 279.F06
dever 341.35
devere 266.10
devil 194.15 281.F3
deville 294.18
devolment 578.34
devoting 408.18
devraye 253.33
dew 040.17 130.25 244.29 501.34 582.11 598.22
dewed 061.08
dewing 463.09
dews 504.30 556.18
dewstaned 128.02
dewy 600.06
dextrous 107.11
dey 470.07
deyled 570.34
deyn 525.28
deys 387.35
deztious 339.05
dhoo's 371.33
dhreamdhrue 320.21
dhrift 418.07
dhrue 320.21 378.28
di 345.23
diabbled 239.33
diabolum 074.08
diaconal 605.21
dialled 551.32
dialler 309.14
diamondise 428.11
diaptotously 157.21
dibble 016.18
dibblon 362.02
dicat 569.21
dich 132.36
dick 469.23
dicks 126.18 241.09
dicky 178.28
dict 391.11
dicted 167.23 458.03
dictic 524.33
diction 060.21 077.25 155.08
dictions 269.F3 439.06
dictive 298.17 612.09
dictus 569.21
didact 050.36
didads 432.30
diddle 493.20
diddlers 042.01
diddy 257.21
didilli- 023.05
didtha 019.06
die 004.05 060.28 200.23 276.26 295.01 295.01 408.22 409.30 472.21 550.28 613.03
die 381.23 546.11
died 159.12 308.17 319.03 470.13 555.15
diedow 455.14
diejestings 536.07
dienence 357.25
dierry 344.02
dies 263.18 284.12 314.13 325.07 350.33 351.07 354.25 379.28 435.05 459.10 468.30 499.21 535.33 540.36 554.02 563.31
dies 341.11
diest 622.10
dieuw 221.11
different 601.15
dification 209.02
diform 222.13
dig 324.33 425.35
digged 141.24
digger 189.28
digging 121.32
diggingharrow 600.13
dighsayman 323.03
dights 498.32
digitarian 362.01
digits 414.05
dignavia 254.33
digrotts 513.14
digs 006.25 069.32 228.35
dik 057.32
diken's 440.01
diketsflaskers 556.30
dillain 219.20
dilli- 023.05
dillies 336.29 475.09
dilligence 187.16
dillongi 519.08
dilly 577.05
diluvial 047.04
diluvious 014.16
dim 019.22 157.29 258.21 297.F2 395.01 560.19
dimadim 552.25
dimatzi 234.01
dimbt 059.32
dimdim 552.25
dime 161.04 610.11
diminy 475.02 475.16
dimissional 395.01
dimmansions 367.27
dimply 097.26
dimseldamsels 432.21
din 050.05 069.10 073.35 088.21 151.31 229.33 236.10 262.11 311.32 407.27 546.17 548.06 601.26
dinah's 250.31
dinburgh 487.09
dindy 353.28
dine 536.23 542.08
dinebbia 324.27
dinelles 359.29
dinernes 100.06
dines 547.08
dine's 039.34
ding 006.02 310.29
dinhole 581.20
dinkledelled 346.26
dinly 225.02
dinogues 601.31
dinpotty 059.12
dins 327.19 415.13
din's 108.27
dint 303.21
dints 080.11
diochesse 171.25
dior 256.27
dios 348.01
diose 163.26
dipdripping 029.25
dipitist 191.03
dipnominated 088.20
dipsics 151.30
dirt 069.22
dirto 368.11
dirts 025.02
disante 461.24
discernibles 050.01
dischdienence 357.25
dischord 013.18
discriminatingly 369.27
diseased 423.27
dises 289.08
diseut 236.20
dish 031.24 210.22 229.14 243.15 422.17 461.28 464.09 607.09
dishaw 131.08
dishcovery 326.31
dishdrudge 221.14
dished 224.34
dishing 462.02
dishness 182.07
dishsized 111.08
disides 008.32
disimally 006.16
disk 086.35
disks 055.22
dismembers 008.06
dismic 298.28
dispute 309.10
dissolusingness 143.14
distance 457.24

distributed 164.06
distributer 530.10
distribution 219.07
dit 006.08
ditchies 241.01
ditheroe's 221.31
dities 242.17
dittery 410.02
ditty 411.29
dityationists 493.12
divide 019.18
divided 110.13 292.31
divil 050.02
divirdual 396.20
divis 468.10
divisibles 472.30
diviva 490.26
divivus 050.15
divvy 331.24
dix- 113.09
dixed 248.30
dizzled 234.02
dizzying 203.27
dmmrng 258.02
doaty 094.30
dobahs 388.18
doblins' 600.23
doboits 211.28
dobrass 373.29
dobremient 348.03
dock 098.31 329.08 378.16
docks 034.09 491.07
docks 346.03
dock's 533.11
docktor 241.15
docta 134.18
doctor 227.05 553.33
dodr- 424.20
doer 532.04
doeren- 257.27
doff 123.24 363.26 370.17
doff's 329.23
doff's 345.26
dog 030.24 179.04 446.13
dogged 492.06
dogs 096.36 312.32 385.34
doh 340.31
doilish 466.23
doilskins 370.35
doily 083.15
dokondylon 056.13
dolche 302.22
dold 563.27
dole 144.10
dolence 573.23
dolenes 609.04
doll 141.05 527.24 577.16
Dollett 290.09
dolling 389.27
dolls 249.01
dolmagtog 246.05
dologer 091.15
dolon 349.20
dolor 408.36 445.18
dolphing 300.28 555.20
dolphinglad 563.26
dolphos 093.33
dolphted 234.35
dolphus 167.09
dom 090.26 101.27 110.04 130.29 188.16 188.23 236.30 241.22 244.34 251.36 307.17 330.29 333.31 373.15 395.01 409.01 424.33 440.01 508.24 564.34 568.33 594.06
domain 600.10
domar 255.16
domational 614.27
dome 018.21 147.26 155.15 213.31 379.15 582.30
domedaries 443.31
domer 031.27 319.06
domers 263.01
domina 471.03
dominal 451.01
dominant 014.17
domite 072.11
domkin 333.04
Domnally 420.28
domnation 362.03
domodary 181.07
doms 060.06 361.23
dom's 239.34
don 201.36 481.21
donagh 490.06
donational 128.28
donche 255.23
donda 179.12
dondering 623.24
dondher- 187.15
donell 553.12
dong 333.18
donia 241.30
donit 353.11
donius 080.28
donk 230.12
Donk 614.29
donnance 184.19
donnay 478.26
Donnell 087.12
Donner 087.32
donney 369.10
Donogh 106.02
donome 332.32
Donoshough 349.19
donot 535.09
dons 004.04
dont 338.21 547.22
dontelleries 205.02
dontos 244.35
doo 010.06 010.09 010.14 077.27 079.21 144.12 227.33 503.16 584.22
dooce 087.31
dooced 035.27
dood 185.31
doodle 244.33 258.05 376.24 404.28
doodled 332.05
doodlem 379.12
doodling 622.05
doodman 339.29
doodoo 149.08
doody 479.06
dooing 050.08
dook 340.20
dooleyoon 107.19
doolins 372.16
doom 258.21 343.26 552.25 613.03
doompsy 373.06
doon 461.13 472.06 543.30
doons 094.03 236.23
dooped 326.24
door 054.11 098.13 107.36 110.30 146.36 257.13 579.12
door 071.13
doored 369.14
doorknockers 445.31
doors 351.34 385.27 434.30
doory 377.02
doos 273.12
doosh 258.05
doosled 331.33
dootsch 070.04
doo-you-doo 065.30
dop 101.04
dopes 586.31
dops 074.19
dopudupedding 599.08
dor 099.29 189.14 332.08 332.13 333.08 378.05 379.03 406.36 477.34 538.31 560.03
dor 041.05
dora 434.07
Doras 073.26
dorboys 266.18
dore 093.06 411.29 504.21
dore 185.15
dorefulvid 284.30
dore-Juxta-Mare 051.23
dores 288.02
dorf 071.33
doria 369.25
dories 395.09
dorion 398.18
dorme 245.02
doro 263.F3
doror 374.20
dorozone 321.23
dorp 383.23
dorse 383.21
dorus 255.21
dory 395.10 395.22
dos 018.29 172.35 178.26 325.33 416.34 433.02 465.13 598.02 610.34
dose 351.17
doses 077.30
dosian 187.07
doso 312.08
doss 228.28
dostay 058.11
dosus 234.08 610.16
dotary 013.20
dotes 269.06 440.22
doth 230.26
dotonates 353.23
dotted 121.16
dottos 541.20
douasoys 059.01
doubray 340.01
doubt 541.21
doubted 060.18
doubtedly 118.15 356.01 425.09
doubting 468.15
doucks 456.15
doueen 005.23
douga 248.35
dougal 482.09
Dougal 214.36 475.30
Dougall 384.14 386.06 389.18
doughall 588.29
douiro 327.04
douix 200.22
doun 252.32
dour 224.25 238.35 439.09 462.26
dour 151.35

douring 173.04
dours 360.30
dous 230.12
douscheock 524.24
dout 343.13
dov 069.13
dove 085.17 354.28 577.17
dovely 327.35
dovers 370.31
dovies 184.31
dovites 048.24
dow 455.14
Dowd 089.13 439.20
dowdy 333.26
do-wells 544.29
dower 587.10
dower'd 371.18
dowern 427.18
downan 258.04
downdillies 475.09
downdivvy 331.24
downdummies 530.03
downe 506.24
downer 083.24 083.28
downes 549.04
downhams 093.08
Down-in-Easia 482.29
downmind- 113.09
downs 010.30 049.24 509.34
down's 063.25
dows 355.30
dowth 116.15
doxy 225.21
doygle 142.15
doyle 017.13
Doyles 048.13
doyoucallem 094.34
doyoucallme 479.13
do-you-do 035.16
doze 219.05
dozy 061.03 429.22
drab 208.25
draft 598.05
drag 565.18
dragger 126.04
dragon 577.01
draining 372.18
drainit 414.13
drake 486.13
drama 050.06 517.02
dranse 199.10
drap 073.17
draped 435.14
draper's 040.15
draping 509.22
drappen 346.29
drasselmann 088.23
drats 332.32
drave 539.29
draves 363.07
draw 178.27 585.26
drawee 575.14
drawer 266.30
drawers 575.18
drawn 419.32 595.19
draws 328.05 420.33 511.29
drawsing 379.04
drazzles 504.35
dreach 090.34
dread 329.09 347.19
dreadfilled 019.24
dreads 243.01
dream 228.13
dreama 079.28
dreamed 551.11
dreams 366.14 597.20
dream's 219.05
Dream's 061.04
dreamsed 615.24
dreamt 075.05 307.12
drear 209.20
drearies 042.35
dreck 068.21
dree 600.20
dregs 129.01
dreisers 055.23
dreme 342.30
drengs 343.11
dress 004.35 102.12 115.10 157.08 159.09 212.17 239.09 246.18 297.01 331.09 360.35 384.31 441.30 455.05 489.22 514.17 529.32 529.33 560.27 617.18
dressed 037.27 232.20 407.04 441.05
dresses 586.13
dresses 102.32
drew 080.25
drewers 546.06
drick 126.05
drift 503.32 535.30 598.05
drifting 100.33
drin 498.33
dring 511.31
drinker 107.32
drinking 096.03
drinks 277.04
drinn 052.27
drinny 028.12
drip 023.22
dripping 029.25 089.01
drips 074.17
drive 449.08
driver 059.25 395.16
drivers 585.15
drix 447.28
drizzle 552.35
drock 541.02
drole 043.18
droll 121.17 276.01 324.01
drolleries 507.16
drolling 449.35
drolly 368.17
dromadary 581.27
dromadary 071.16
dromarith 030.04
dromed 032.31
dromites 160.21
dromus 451.11
drone 074.14
drool 287.31
droops 626.17
drop 265.L1
dropdrap 073.17
drope 089.19
dropper 494.24
dropping 208.36 581.19
droppings 564.31
drops 235.05 244.23
drowsay 597.23
droyd 282.20
drst 091.36
drua's 601.21
drud 220.21
drudge 221.14
druff 037.11
drugged 266.31
druid 611.05
drum 051.34 085.22 124.36 162.03 178.01 240.27 288.22 356.19 503.01 531.09 553.03
drum 345.12
drum- 314.08
drummers 497.17
drums 135.31 506.03
drund 597.05
drunkard's 125.02
drunks 263.04
drups 157.10
dru's 124.30
dry 147.25 469.27 578.19
dryel 241.27
dry's 177.04
du 198.18 540.21
dua 561.19
dual 186.04 396.20 528.24
DUAL 282.R1
dualman 442.27
Duane 365.25
dub 072.34 553.27 625.36
dubb 178.02
dubblandaddy- 332.05
dubility 607.03
dublins 087.30
Duc 073.26
ducabimus 306.12
ducare 433.06
ducators 408.02
duced 128.09
ducente 166.23
ducint 366.23
duck 135.26 138.34
ducked 294.14 471.18
ducken 323.01
duckling 070.23
ducks 358.29 553.22
ducky 577.01
ductor 492.22
ducts 152.28
ducus 211.16
dud 294.17
due 054.12 604.17
due 381.23 381.24
duepoise 407.06
dues 338.20
duff 469.21
Duff 313.34
duffs 302.F1
dugalius 573.08 573.28
dugout 351.06
duke 335.30
dukiboi 201.25
dukon 071.35
dulceydovely 327.35
dulcis 209.35 541.32
dulibnium 310.07
dulicet 042.32
dull 359.12
dullable 391.06
dullas 468.11
dullescence 054.35
dulligence 531.02
dullin 309.13
dulls 351.25
dulocelerious 611.29
dulsily 031.24

dum 020.19 033.35 089.33
200.23 258.20 296.06 352.24
567.12
duman 593.07
duman's 593.07
dumb 619.01
dumbdrummers 497.17
dumbones 387.33
dumbtoit 078.33
dumenos 174.19
duments 127.04
dumic 497.15
dummies 530.03
dumms 258.24
dump 080.06 223.04 332.17
364.29 615.12
dump- 314.08
dumped 118.22 590.01
dums 303.18
dum's 273.01
dumutual 530.10
dun 083.29 586.19
duna 094.31 623.28
dunamento 220.21
dunan- 257.27
duncing 310.13
duncle 211.29
dundarri 180.13
dunder 370.33
dunderry 323.21
dune 079.15
dung 004.27 004.27 100.05
185.32
dung 273.L3
Dungaschiff 350.07
dunglecks 416.11
dungs 343.29
duniforms 344.10
Dunnell's 007.12
Dunnochoo 348.19
dunphyville'll 375.05
duolcis 568.10
dupe 252.34
dupedding 599.08
dupes 423.20
dupoider 169.18
dur 165.07 332.21
durately 038.07
durbar-atta-Cleath 057.31
durby 448.14
durd 023.04
dure 475.27 554.07
during 368.35
durk 055.21
duroy 085.33
durras- 257.27
dur's 060.31
durses 127.28
durst 347.09
durt 387.10
durty 196.15
durumchuff 352.34
dushka 333.28
dusk 419.21
dust 018.04 055.03 108.25
184.23 245.31 314.16 441.05
447.13 468.33 535.29 557.08
568.02 601.02
dustand 492.17
duty 235.11
duubled 583.27
duum 097.33 517.35
duwasland 479.29
dux 252.20 425.20
duxed 243.33 611.19
duxit 060.33
d'weh 470.13
dwell 036.28
dwellers 036.30
dwellingness 488.02
dwindle 122.35
d'woe 470.13
Dwyer 116.16 446.31 602.14
dyall 325.25
Dyar 529.25
dydos 433.02
dydowdy 333.26
dye 305.F1 313.18 340.31
480.12
dyed 492.05
dyedo 527.17
dyeing 527.23
dyfy 191.23
dyhips 214.21
dying 055.23 171.17
dyk 325.32
dyke 470.04
Dyke 008.27
dykers 181.04
dylly 357.21
dylon 056.13
dyn 593.03
dynamon 163.30
dynamonologos 194.16
dyng 214.09 359.33
dyr 321.25
dzey 347.08

each 228.35 576.30
each 048.14 349.26
eachbird 098.36
eachin 485.12
eachother 389.07
eagen 415.15
eager 446.09
eagle 024.29 248.06 482.15
eagle 383.04
eagles 106.22
eal 525.29
eanupper 501.32
ear 009.24 014.35 038.23
182.20 222.12 327.36 425.16
492.16 568.26
earcases 416.22
eareans 518.13
eared 156.23 414.36
earfaceman 429.20
earhoure 587.01
earin 362.22 362.23
earing 375.14 466.11
earis 255.15
eark 409.35
earl 391.07
earlds 147.28
early 135.31 164.02 502.16
502.16 502.16 502.16
earner 543.27
earnity 133.31
ears 011.24 148.04 321.22
477.23 550.26
ears 071.11 176.13
earsy 314.27
earth 155.29 410.16 531.13
571.15
earth's 068.34
earum 488.11
earwicked 539.04
eary 343.32
ease 016.06 057.25 235.30
237.35 329.02 365.29 408.27
576.24 595.32
ease 339.01
easechapel 571.18
eased 266.30 423.27
eases 361.05 571.11
Easia 482.29
easily 068.01
east 051.30 114.05 135.10
245.02 447.20 578.04
east 418.29
eastcake 563.29
easter 091.17
easterloaves 598.20
easts 030.07
eastwind 558.18
eastyday 004.21
easy 040.14 123.16 153.07
173.15 553.26
easyan 008.20
easyosey 584.11
eat 610.06
eat 418.15
eater 150.02 192.33 334.12
eaters 542.30
eathay 490.28
eating 061.15 432.11
eats 211.27 530.27
eau 015.18 199.26 383.21
553.14
eavesdroppings 564.31
eazy 343.27
ebbed 374.08
ebbia 324.27
ebbiated 029.29
ebolutions 346.08
ebriated 429.23
eccles 416.23 613.09
ech 237.20 377.03
echo 584.34
echoable 253.27
echolowing 510.26
eck 139.36
eckenased 344.35
Ecluse 520.19
ecomedy 540.26
ectheion 539.03
ecting 284.01
ecumans 369.24
edams 351.31
Edar 030.11
edd 540.33
eddies 263.18
edeosy 396.31
edge 007.21 569.17
edged 497.08 545.14 550.25
edged 338.11
edges 478.34
edgment 344.08
edible 016.23 088.06 422.26
594.32
edicted 458.03
edition 512.17
editioned 484.24
edor 053.04
education 097.18
Education 307.03
edward 088.31
eedypuss 445.23
eehew 399.29 399.29 399.29

eel 584.33
eeled 335.06
eels 344.09
Eels 450.06
een 527.30
e'en 049.24
e'enso 065.31
e'er 562.27
eer'd 485.27
eers 337.25
eese 071.04
eeser 565.10
effects 483.01
effectual 118.28
effia 604.04
effible 183.14
efficient 284.12
EFTAY'S 308.R1
eg 032.03 330.07
egans 358.23
egg 081.23 192.32 382.11
450.01
eggbetter 298.03
eggfuss 041.13
eggs 076.06 184.32 285.04
333.33 351.03
eggyyolk 404.29
Eglise 184.27
ego 096.20 131.26
ego 566.26 566.26
egoases 576.33
egobragh 303.14
egoist 488.21
egoistically 488.16
egoric 336.36
egos 307.L1
egypt 104.22
Egyptian 130.30
ehe 206.15
ehmen's 581.02
ehrmin 343.22
eider 209.22
eifel 301.18
eiffel 314.01
eight 283.F1 617.24
eightened 243.06
eilish 063.06
eire 028.01 280.01
eirinn 604.08
eirn 538.26
eiro 340.06
eiry 312.09
eirying 324.28
eison 146.16
Eitelnaky 151.11
either 355.36 566.10
eithne 394.26
eke 221.33 602.21
ekellous 099.20
ekkles 373.03
elated 484.08
elbaw 494.29
eldster 318.31
electric 380.12
electrick 322.31
elegants 353.27
elegy 077.26
element 164.33
elemontary 422.28
eletion 279.04
elevution 338.06
elf 170.17 524.30
elgany 334.08
elgia 243.29
elgible 482.21
elia 525.14
elias 266.01 340.22
eligum 296.F3
elijiacks 156.26
eliminal 337.09
eliric 513.32
elitest 320.07
elixion 346.13
elixtrolysis 163.31
el-Jovan 472.15
elks' 243.01
ell 360.33
ella 133.02 173.11 178.27
206.35 435.19 549.19 618.04
622.03 627.05
ella 349.21
ellas 327.32 527.01 615.02
ella's 205.11
ellbo 336.02
elle 290.02 528.08 528.09
563.05
ellene- 219.17
eller 468.09
elles 113.11 226.22 253.07
279.F31 339.16 359.29 365.28
462.07 512.16 545.25 601.28
617.23
elles 281.07
elli 084.36
Elligut 365.26
ellis 220.21
ellisotoelles 601.28
ellman's 485.29
ells 549.32
elly 525.16 531.22
elopment 394.10
elsas 444.31
else 003.07 239.34 260.05
282.05 503.22
elsers 371.34
elses 594.10
elsesbody 329.18
elsk 233.33
elskar 028.26
elsy 398.18
elta 076.21
Elta 221.13
eluct 374.12
eluctable 184.08
eluctably 120.32
elure 560.27
elv 199.05
elves 551.13
elysiums 379.17
emancipated 081.04
emani 237.30
embal 408.20
embarass 418.24
embaurnus 240.21
embellishing 119.16
emberable 608.31
emberer 201.10
emberried 264.26
embers 024.11
emble 343.03
embrace 471.06
embria 494.13
embs 087.07
embulger 132.29
emdown 542.08
Emeratic-Hebridian 263.13
emerod's 063.18
eminent 380.20 381.16 504.15
emita 471.05
emitter 317.34
emma 092.25 133.36
emman's 202.20
emm'as 182.21
emorous 158.11
empered 190.01
employ 464.04
empor 317.03
emposed 066.19
empson 537.36
empson's 245.24
emptied 313.21
empties 549.22
emptiness 434.24
empty 319.36 372.19 386.08
Empyre 289.10
emt 262.01
emvowelled 515.12
enactment 222.16
enbowls 389.28
encore 003.04
encumbered 545.18
Ency 421.23
end 019.31 023.10 038.34
042.10 050.04 051.36 051.36
058.35 070.08 074.15 079.30
083.20 084.32 099.17 129.28
138.18 138.33 144.30 153.22
154.34 178.25 187.05 199.02
200.19 203.18 230.13 239.34
239.35 242.15 248.15 268.26
269.17 288.24 291.01 312.06
312.32 320.23 327.02 327.23
332.01 335.12 340.36 372.34
434.34 503.14 505.34 508.18
510.20 521.17 533.26 535.15
535.30 541.27 547.19 585.09
586.27 598.07 600.36 614.04
617.07
end 292.06 341.26 342.35
end- 257.27
enda 232.03 331.26
endally 406.01
endas 488.06
endascope 115.30
endbookers 549.04
endean 494.19
endeavour 624.35
endecads 601.14
endecate 273.17
ended 003.11 169.20 284.19
320.17 357.29 413.33
enden 608.29
endency 305.09
ender 335.11
enders 124.36 330.01
ender's 126.16
endet 420.19
endevolment 578.34
endgiddyex 066.12
Endicoth 277.F4
endifine 051.06
ending 276.11 298.05
endissimest 154.06
endly 029.35
endmacht 240.13
endor 379.03
endowed 351.10
ends 020.16 028.02 102.06
170.13 202.19 283.15 324.35

336.29 376.14 452.34 478.03 478.05 505.06 548.27 585.16 593.13
endsea 428.21
endsthee 628.14
endth 310.21
endtougend 247.07
endyures 295.03
enfant 244.35 545.36
enfichue 268.13
eng 333.02
engaged 306.F3 351.22
engals 601.10
engd 328.25 328.25
engens 005.31
engien 146.20
engine 337.20
englisches 532.10
english 160.22
engorge 563.31
Enheritance 264.09
enked 487.07
enkelmen 370.07
en-la-Valle 380.09
ennia 473.01
ennious 057.22
enough 380.22 620.19
ensempry 364.24
entangled 161.13
ente 105.25
enter 321.34
entide 577.29
enties 336.32
entitled 571.28
entrousnest 241.10
ents 331.12
enugh 596.14
enzando 226.30
eofhome 133.17
eoggs 178.33
eon 613.18
eorns 236.30
Epée 329.30
epi 611.18
epiphanal 611.13
epistemion 116.31
epistle 108.24
epiwor 611.22
equal 017.35
equin 372.11
equinade 455.28
equined 607.33
equities 438.14
equoia 126.12
equother 336.24
era 457.13
era- 314.08
eragusaria 117.04
eras 009.36 009.36 595.28
era's 623.07
eratic-Hebridian 263.13
erdebble- 332.05
erden 350.02
erdes 315.21
erdulous 568.03
ere 237.31 487.21 598.32 613.23 627.05
erebus 239.30
erecordant 450.28
erect 153.28 155.23 600.14
erected 099.30
erecting 284.01
erections 356.33
erendth 310.21
eres 601.06
erescaper 228.29
erethetise 156.14
eretyred 395.06
erges 022.32
ergic 349.07
ergical 338.11
ergs 533.22
eric 004.32 285.F3 378.13 393.08
erically 185.29
erick 478.28 498.23
ericks' 024.22
erie 038.04
erik 320.28
erils 434.07
erim 112.07
erin 007.32 089.25 140.18 332.14 437.31
erin 338.36
eriN 226.31
erin- 424.20
ering 244.25 453.06 478.31
erin's 194.14
erinsheiner 221.10
erintly 485.26
erinunder 438.28
eriodendron 042.20
erio-Miletians 309.11
erios 540.35
eris 551.34
erish 608.19
erk 582.29
erkegaard 246.01
erl 268.F3
erlehome-upon-Eskur 220.35
erls 450.17 536.19
ern 184.17 621.05
erne 382.28
ernest 532.06
erogamy 537.26
erogenal 616.20
erol 619.36
erotic 439.25
eroticisms 614.35
erotundity 055.36
erovmeravmerouvian 113.04
err 555.22
erred 343.30
errig 353.31
errin 587.02
errin 525.21
errinsilde 391.16
errors 545.13
errstaffs 178.23
erse 273.28 530.19 534.18 607.11
ersegood 346.23
erssas 173.25
erssias 339.18
erst 283.07
erther 499.07
erthings 368.20
eruction 499.01
erung 300.16
eruption 612.23
erxeses 286.08
eryin 305.33
erz 577.22
erzherr 289.09
escalating 005.01
escapading 388.03
escape 053.01
escaper 228.29
Escaut 203.21
escence 054.35
esche 506.17
esias 542.31
Eskur 220.35
esolde 538.08
esparation 257.26
esperanto 582.08
esperation 257.25
esperons 245.23
espertieu 289.22
esprit 267.F3
esprot 354.07
essance 066.14 177.17
esse 295.26
essel 559.06
essence 378.08
essiest 234.18
essive 162.19
establishment 304.L3
estady 598.11
estarolies 368.11
estcher 345.17
ester 210.35 413.06 458.10
esterrado 289.22
Esterre 052.29
esterrite 301.03
estfar 476.04
esther 069.14 429.18
esthers 003.12 624.25
esther's 427.01
esthetic 173.18
estimated 125.21
estnunc 609.24
estrange 017.33
estries 145.24
estuan 239.06
estuants 508.19
estumation 204.02
esture 602.18
eternal 274.14
ether 325.30 452.13 462.34
etheredayth 346.22
etherich 054.03
ethetise 156.14
ethical 109.21 487.27
ethics 038.36
etiams 384.27
etnass 094.01
être 041.36
ettna 212.10
eturnally 298.17
eturningties 582.20
euchoristic 234.20
euclidius 155.32
eugh 308.02
euhumorisation 331.31
eung 503.28
eunuch 332.19
eupanepi 611.18
euphraties 199.14
eure 064.19
eureeke 230.01
euresponsor 542.25
European 037.26
europeans 519.01
eux 102.12
Euxine 263.13
euyes 244.32
eval 599.09
evar 203.36

evay 322.04
eve 037.16 214.01 429.12 513.25
evelo 039.07
even 104.03 136.28 283.F1 380.14 475.33 502.04 517.33
evener 325.01
evented 517.34
ever 036.31 048.08 077.14 078.36 099.22 110.10 158.14 202.12 206.08 239.19 242.29 242.31 253.08 362.18 364.23 413.32 426.02 426.03 455.22 461.11 476.09 508.33 551.16 576.19 600.25 613.20 618.25
<u>ever</u> 341.35 342.12
everafter 606.07
evero 353.09
evers 202.02 598.01
ever's 050.34 362.18
every 460.16
every- 113.09
everyournameis 479.12
evidence 062.07 325.02
evil 194.15 423.28 538.12
evild 613.21
evils 024.06
evily 381.10
evilybolly 516.10
evitant 186.33
evolment 578.34
evre 273.12
evver 077.01
ewality 523.04
ewer 041.35
ewere 055.15
ewers 019.11 550.19
ewill 620.27
ewr 593.17
ex 066.12
exactly 177.32 515.22
exagoras 155.32
exampling 356.14
exanimation 087.34
excellsiored 553.15
excessible 285.28
exchange 471.06
Exchange 135.10
excommunicambiam-bisumers 155.04
excretory 175.31
executive 042.08
exegesis 511.16
exelcy 521.04
exhaustible 160.04
exilic 472.34
exinction 083.25
exinevery- 113.09
existence 366.02
existent 526.12
exmouth 177.25
exojesus 296.10
exousthaustible 091.27
expected 120.27 324.27
expectedly 110.28
expectednesses 067.34
expensive 170.27
explosion 078.04
expressibles 357.28
exshellsis 154.35
extensive 356.28
extremity 464.23
exuberabundancy 612.05
eyar 319.27
eydes 035.02
eydge 506.26
eye 007.36 010.21 013.30 069.34 129.14 169.12 183.17 252.16 273.F3 294.01 329.10 344.05 347.08 408.26 423.07 431.08 437.26 534.27 564.07
eyeare 414.12
eyed 088.15 134.26 189.10 214.25 249.03 327.29 335.01 344.23 361.36 434.28 480.10 533.20 534.18 590.02 609.05
eyedeal 384.24
eyeing 209.01
eyeld 148.33
eyeoneyesed 323.29
eyes 011.06 025.03 043.09 074.06 235.24 257.23 298.14 310.29 398.18 404.14 465.03 493.05 537.11
<u>eyes</u> 176.13 344.12 418.31
eyesed 323.29
eyeyed 444.16
eyria 255.10
eyrieglenn 553.22
eyss 292.24
eyus 074.06

fabishospastored 612.08
fabulation 558.01
fac 524.30
face 003.14 030.21 046.20 050.10 089.32 095.04 159.15 207.19 315.09 357.23 363.21 370.25 404.01 442.30 496.11 531.08 550.29 563.15 577.11 582.20 605.16 624.02
<u>face</u> 071.12 071.15
<u>fàç'e'</u> 124.11
faced 050.21 052.26 076.01 081.13 119.15 120.36 132.12 359.28 461.26 533.09
facedness 091.18
faceman 429.20
facemen 208.36
facepacket 492.20
faces 078.27 151.02 356.06 493.06 589.23
<u>faces</u> 352.19
facey 279.F08
facies 337.06 347.21 380.03
fact 183.07 404.32 474.05
<u>fact</u> 341.12
faction 078.21 445.08 512.07 604.33
factness 123.10
factor 164.34 380.11
factors 027.17 127.16
facts 057.16 110.01 156.09 532.09
factuary 084.15
fadar 182.18
fadar's 597.01
fadda 232.28
fadder 496.26
faddle 323.08
fadher 180.35
faf 601.03
faffing 529.30
fag 180.22
Fagi 403.09
fahrts 085.09
<u>faiate</u> 180.12
<u>fail</u> 244.06
fails 344.25
fair 134.27 226.25 233.12 360.05 472.22 515.27
fairance 504.18
fairioriboos 154.11
fairs 129.21
fairy 478.32 621.06
faitititilli- 023.05
faitly 090.19
fake 077.01
falia 465.32
falidebankum 445.34
fall 023.34 030.15 078.08 088.02 090.06 134.30 140.25 197.30 225.36 257.29 273.10 570.06
<u>fall</u> 348.04
<u>fallable</u> 153.26
fallar 029.07
falled 149.04 258.14
fallen 017.27 049.03 049.30 191.27 233.33 355.27 363.33 426.13
fallhim 251.11
fallible 100.15 201.33
falling 417.13 535.33
fallows 229.19
falls 383.23 503.15 607.24
fallther- 332.05
falluses 506.18
fally 053.24 329.28
<u>fal's</u> 352.18
famado 492.22
famatios 059.34
fame 619.13
famed 085.25 132.23 173.22 545.03
familiar 427.21
familias 389.15 391.10 570.20
familla 434.11
famillias 395.15 398.11
family 611.09
famous 098.18 229.15
fampiny 046.19
fams 621.26
fan 080.27 262.22 296.22 596.32
fance 538.30
fanciers 438.35
fancy 292.20
fand 167.19
fander 481.34
fanelly 450.10
fanerole 439.35
<u>fanetes</u> 565.28
fang 418.08 494.20 563.31
fanian 277.F7
fann 538.27
fannfawners 309.09
fant 599.06
fanti 260.09
fantulus 166.22
fanu 213.01
fanunian 265.04
fany 230.20
far 058.31 096.05 102.07 139.06 176.32 234.28 310.10 407.14 476.04 513.16 581.31 589.10
farafield 100.19
farback 004.19

farder 378.25
fare 130.09 140.12 177.05 209.04 491.32 516.35 518.02
fared 042.26
fares 080.34
farforth 581.28
farfrom 565.32
farfully 156.15
faring 026.04
farings 241.03
farious 079.32
farlane 100.03 180.10
Farlane 210.10
farm 183.04 257.05 524.20
farnham 090.24
faroo 521.32
farover 613.08
farre 102.21
farreating 432.11
farreation 390.11
farred 278.26
Farrell 212.13 516.31
farrer 161.27
farsts 613.23
farte 162.04
farther 057.04 414.35
farthers 281.F1
farthring 202.02
fartodays 622.15
farts 453.12
fas 031.36 443.13
fashion 227.08 446.06
fashionable 120.35
fashioned 194.33 276.F2
fassa 398.15
fast 020.08 046.13 210.28 434.31
fas-Taem 311.12
fastbringer 473.23
fastened 208.16
fasting 584.28
fat 035.10 051.17 087.10 414.13 483.25
fatal 084.20
fatas 005.15
fatch'd 014.28
fates 131.04
fath 596.07 599.04
father 015.08 033.04 045.13 055.08 094.33 095.20 191.34 206.02 215.14 234.11 246.06 266.F2 313.09 325.18 382.18 431.18 480.26 482.01 560.26
fathers 585.14
father's 070.28 099.12
fathom 362.08
fat's 533.28
fatufa 606.36
faulter 334.12
faulters 355.35
faun 015.21
faust 160.27
favour 364.06
fawkes 574.36
fawners 309.09
fax 260.12
fay 224.29 321.05 384.30
fayette 026.16
Faynix 139.35
fazzio 345.23
feald 602.15
fear 226.06 279.01 318.05 403.10 439.07 492.27 505.06
feared 475.03
fears 389.23
Fearsome 227.32
fearsome's 294.13
feartonights 622.15
feasance 532.19
feast 147.16 261.21 357.17 380.10 528.06 541.24
feater 334.12
feather 355.12 577.06
featured 602.02 602.05
features 577.11
fecalties 366.20
fect 532.29
fed 037.30 097.14 185.10 375.33 449.32 456.24 572.01 580.04
fed-ben-Edar 030.11
fedes 343.09 597.16
fee 418.02
feed 333.06
feeding 209.01 337.05
feeds 336.13
feel 290.15 420.13 420.13 510.33
feelbelong 569.03
feeled 335.06
feelingfit 431.01
feen 562.32
feerd 497.16
feet 279.08 422.09
feets 545.30
feife 464.20
feige 014.02
feigned 075.19
feit 453.28
felde 184.28
feldfallen 355.27
feld's 108.15
feldt 585.22
felicitous 537.14
fell 119.10 238.14 305.12 350.21 541.15 552.35 558.28
fella 082.13 311.27 374.34 611.27 611.27
fellas 611.10
fella's 096.02
fellay 395.19
fellbowm 505.29
feller 247.23 257.07 285.07 299.29 303.31
fellers 420.08 506.16
fellfoss 202.32
fello 174.14
fellors 221.12
fellow 039.32 129.21 191.19 245.02 301.18 350.35 422.11 447.30
fellows 148.24 450.06
fellow's 205.33 261.F2 410.04
fellows' 056.35
fells 316.31 380.04 626.18
fellsed 373.14
fellthey 370.32
felon 355.27
felt 163.09 290.14
feme 092.24
fender 069.32
Fender 369.12
fendi 131.08
fendy 222.23
fengtse 299.26
fennel 037.36
fenrir- 424.20
feofhome 133.17
fer 027.03 193.04 250.34 354.32 512.07
feral 120.10
ferall 013.15 111.15
ferant 035.11
fercings 364.08
ferdinamd 535.09
fere 067.10
ferended 284.19
ferentes 601.16
ferer 365.01
fergee's 379.32
fergs 233.21
fericiously 182.05
fermentated 537.18
fermont 183.05
fermoy- 257.27
fernhim 074.17
ferns 519.06 548.25
feros 497.23
ferreters 055.13
ferry 485.02 580.12
fers 183.16
fersenless 415.33
fert 350.05
ferteed 345.25
ferus 136.08
fesh 256.25 459.07
fesstiydt 510.32
fesswise 546.07
fest 082.36 086.13 275.08 388.04 552.05 563.30
festa 104.04
fester 600.11
festoons 106.34
festouned 256.09
fests 541.16
fet 440.24
fetated 252.17
fetation 308.L2
fetched 473.13
fête 186.12
fetor 119.10
fett 531.07
fetta 462.05
fettered 118.02 411.15 567.05
fettering 475.10
fetts 106.24
feu 436.02
feud 058.35 091.15
feuersteyn 225.24
feuille 191.18
feverfraus 603.19
few 244.08 570.35 607.02
Fewney 622.05
fex 136.18 449.15
fex 185.14 345.29
fey 501.10
fff 116.33
fhull 624.23
fianced 433.05
fianxed 235.22
fiat 034.07 034.07
fiat 613.14
fib's 210.31
fication 209.02
fichue 268.13
ficking 300.25
fickle 310.10
ficle 493.19

fiction 161.02 185.03 192.19 452.06 574.34
fictional 261.17
ficules 018.11
fid 281.16
fidalicence 040.27
fidare 068.17
fide 051.05 157.25 178.18 313.11 480.09 485.20
fidel 520.13
fidelities 572.23
fidels 589.34
fides 087.03 141.13 337.06
fidly 395.20
fie 004.28
field 077.08 080.08 100.19 360.12 475.24 553.19 609.34
field 106.12
fieldchaplain 564.32
fielded 449.34
fields 010.34 039.02 043.02 174.27 203.06 208.06
Fields 569.08
field's 381.14
fiena 605.19
fiend 055.06
fiendship 542.18
fier 128.19 378.24
fiera 479.15
fierce 344.26
fieries 501.26
fif 600.30
fife 077.14 411.11
fiffty 208.26
fifif 284.15
fifteen 529.09
Figgis 550.32
fighs 588.10
fight 003.06 464.27
fighter 092.04
fighting 453.03
figure 602.27
figured 596.29
fijjiz 347.19
fild 273.L3
filicial 613.18
filips 463.36
fill 295.F2
fillable 131.10 492.26
fill'd 122.13
filled 019.24 101.23 248.24 310.26 417.27 481.08
filledfelon 355.27
filler 324.26 338.27
fillers 475.11
filles 434.28
filleted 474.07
filling 042.21
filly 101.16 395.20 562.01
fillyers 371.01
filmagh 324.10
filming 398.25
filmsies 279.F14
filmung 375.01
fils 374.24
filthed 111.32
filthyheat 492.29
fim 498.33
fin 279.F24 366.23 376.17
final 123.03
find 449.09
findention 593.16
finders 585.16
finding 261.07
findth 153.34
fine 051.06 128.14 188.07 346.27 426.31 547.25 570.23
fined 537.15
finely 389.16
fines 238.17
finesof 289.05
fing 018.35 226.26
fing 341.11
fingee 018.34
finger 067.29 246.08 437.13
fingeredness 031.16
fings 238.17 455.33
finibility 245.12
finis 228.14
finish 596.31
finishing 543.29
finisissimalls 298.30
finister 228.28
finitatively 613.35
finite 037.04 127.04 505.24
finitely 180.07
finn 377.22
finnan's 578.06
finners 036.26
finnisk-en-la-Valle 380.09
finns 099.15
Finns 330.17
fino 541.04
finpot 356.03
fins 483.27
fintins 624.18
fir 352.27
fire 003.09 029.07 046.06 117.17 234.24 245.08 330.03 350.35 409.23 439.35 514.09 542.26 552.27 594.21 621.03
firearms 353.35
fired 005.26 405.35 514.07 514.27 539.11 589.24
fires 052.19 090.09 304.22 404.06 501.25 581.14
fire's 013.36
firessence 378.08
firmierity 291.F8
firmly 520.32
first 003.24 006.02 254.19 413.16 450.34 452.20 539.03
firts 521.01
fisch 056.25
fisck 198.09
fish 098.22 221.07 281.F2 312.02 511.14 546.18 595.10
fish 072.11 484.36
fisher 118.35
fishfellows' 056.35
fishies 524.31
fishing 173.36
fisht 621.12
fishy 480.16
fisk 013.34
fissi 356.09
fist 534.19
fister 551.29
fit 339.04 431.01 501.26
fit 339.26 512.36
fits 420.26
fit's 194.17
fitted 076.11
fitting 052.31 127.04
fitzhuorson 529.20
fiuna 605.20
fives 055.14 202.01
fivest 596.16
fix 102.13 465.26 551.28
fixed 214.04 545.16
fixes 162.13
fixing 260.12
fixioners 377.24
fixureashone 613.09
fizzing 060.24
fizzyboisterous 547.23
fjaell 057.14
flaa 129.30
flag 339.13 463.22 496.04
flaged 494.21
Flagonan 027.25
flags 207.03
flaherty 520.30
flai- 054.15
flake 041.20 561.19
flakes 017.28 502.35 570.06
flame 301.05
flammabilis 232.03
flamme 084.34
flammed 080.24
flammelwaving 101.17
flamtry 348.35
Flanagan 210.20
flank 561.02
flap 452.04
flapper 266.31
flare 344.24 549.18 610.03
flash 210.32 246.08
flashing 583.15
flaskers 556.30
flaum 364.28
flauwing 397.01
flavoured 111.34 444.22 556.15
flawered 350.11
flawforms 596.24
flayer 050.21
flea 417.03
fleckled 602.04
flected 120.21
flecting 605.29
flections 411.18
flee 129.30
fleeced 578.10
fleeter 377.27
fleetfoot 128.04
fleets 005.32
Flemmings 542.23
flesh 186.05 481.30
fleshed 271.F4
fleshmeant 082.10
flesks 141.08
flexibly 454.06
flexions 519.35
flexuous 124.06
flicksrent 298.15
flier's 446.18
flies 118.32
flights 119.15 324.36
flights-the-charmer 290.16
flinarsky 013.22
fling 478.25
flingent 142.18
flinging 011.11
flinsborg 582.21
flirts 418.32
float 065.29 160.04
floats 530.23
flod 209.30
floe 017.22

flood 118.12
flooded 126.24 589.27
floods 070.31
floored 269.09
flooring 577.34
flor 561.20
florated 088.17
flord 336.13
flore 364.14
flosion 184.30
flotation 589.29
flounce 221.11
floures 256.09
flow 042.20 174.20
flowed 481.09 481.09
flower 212.16 237.31 409.14 459.35 470.07 509.21 609.11 609.11
flowering 406.24
flowerleaf 121.10
flowers 014.36 059.11 354.26
flowing 117.03
flown 405.36
flowret 360.30
flowrets 254.36
flowvius 526.25
floyeds 536.23
flsh 571.29
fluction 299.18
Fluctuary 080.29
flue 185.21
fluent 605.19
flues 416.33
fluh 037.20
fluke 023.25
flung 419.11
Flure 389.07
flushed 058.36
flute 007.03 590.01
fluthered 063.27
flutter 117.14 121.05
flutter-afraida 272.03
fluvia 107.17
fluvious 182.11
fluvium 095.16
flux 567.13
fly 232.11 244.27 267.F3 291.F4 458.17 528.28
flyer 534.36
foaled 485.24
foaptz 571.28
fobsed 408.19
focal 117.14
focillation 266.16
foco 231.32
fodder 242.10
foderacies 349.34
fodren 326.24
fodt 339.34
foederated 537.18
foedted 137.14
foefom 007.09
foes 487.10 571.35
fog 048.02
fogg 607.31
fogged 536.19
foh 353.14
fohrt 313.04
foil 124.21 359.35
foiled 010.08 354.22
foils 599.07
foje 160.31 160.31
foklokken 353.15
fold 014.25 043.31 075.23 288.03 375.35 462.35 490.16 527.22 605.30 613.02
fold 305.L1
folded 186.01 359.32
folden 608.28
foldingmorn 571.32
folds 325.31 563.09
foliorum 326.08
folium 425.20
folk 283.14 537.19
folker 038.15
folks 567.31
folk's 215.25
foll 526.22
followable 325.35
folly 157.07 279.F12 321.03 415.28
folly 625.06
folthediddlers 042.01
fom 007.09
fond 212.18 457.16 477.30
fonder 328.04
fondler 612.09
fong 325.14
food 437.20
food 071.22 231.06
fooi 125.22
fool 015.14 299.16 301.15 415.27
fool 175.17
fool- 314.08
fooled 337.03
fooling 584.18
fools 595.12 613.28
fool's 019.06
foolthenairyans 360.08
foor 282.31 282.31
foost 070.15
foot 008.15 015.31 128.04 128.13 131.25 186.24 199.16 204.06 222.31 330.33 367.05 426.36 426.36 426.36 427.01 433.13 444.05 457.11 550.21 553.28
foot 071.26 175.17
footed 120.07 160.19
footed 341.21
footlarge 272.22
footlers 029.10
foots 469.24
forabit 019.02
forall 018.35 458.22
foran 123.24
forasti 512.27
forator 303.22
force 126.20 461.06 484.02 575.28
forced 430.17
ford 014.05 031.20 086.11 133.28 182.26 296.F3 483.30 547.17 576.26 583.12
ford 353.23
Ford 512.31
ford-Atelier 531.15
ford-on-Mudway 393.09
fordrock 541.02
ford's 549.18
fore 005.18 013.20 014.31 053.27 064.35 091.07 100.24 130.02 160.33 174.24 208.35 226.25 250.17 264.12 319.19 321.02 326.22 332.20 372.13 378.17 379.22 470.12 488.01 537.04 542.15 566.30 576.04 582.02 584.16 587.16 587.35 594.29 605.34
forefather 033.04
forefelt 163.09
foregoing 599.33
forehand 253.14 576.23
foremost 362.05
foreness 419.04
fore's 453.03
foretime 108.22 478.04
foretombed 586.30
forget 147.01 231.24
forgettable 058.20
forgetting 231.24
for-giggle 377.19
forgilhisjurylegs 060.11
forgiven 490.24
forhers 547.29
forhim 010.19 098.36 240.14 246.34 246.34 246.35
forhold 365.03
forit 271.05 413.18
foritch 069.12
forium 326.08
fork 087.14
fork 274.L4
forks 090.11
fork's 028.04
forlake 348.04
forlifer 444.11
form 018.25 045.16 045.17 072.25 099.19 107.08 122.20 123.10 128.04 149.29 158.10 198.25 222.13 229.08 324.10 413.31 456.28 462.07 509.28 523.13 552.21 579.14 623.17 624.20
formal 357.27
formally 056.27
formation 137.34 222.17 374.26 509.28 599.17
formatory 147.15
formed 123.19 134.26 183.13 352.02 361.04 414.07 544.12 619.09
formed 349.06
formee 059.28
former 334.12
formication 333.30 529.07
formly 612.13
formly 342.28
forms 150.17 596.24
forms 344.10
fornax 319.34
fornobody 292.14
forownly 235.27
fors 029.17
forsacrifice 571.32
forsaken 183.18
forseeking 346.31
forsight 417.23
fort 246.04 567.25 577.33
forte 404.26
forted 340.23
forter 548.12
fortes 595.14
forth 009.16 073.18 441.12 473.10 537.08 570.21 581.28 583.32
forths 039.22 343.33
forth's 245.08 552.26 575.11

fortner 531.25
fortotalled 542.32
fortumble 417.14
fortunate 090.17
fortunates 421.09 544.13
fortune 113.32 357.23 476.02 566.34
fortunes 492.28
forty 068.19
forus 460.27 465.09 505.33
forvell 626.33
forward 037.02 174.06 243.04
foryou 076.31 148.01
foskerfusker 178.36
foss 202.32
fostered 042.07
fosters 368.04
Fosti 048.19
fot 333.34
fottafutt 599.08
fou 197.25
fought 086.26
foukou 320.05
foul 183.15 212.19 512.25 515.26 520.25
foul- 090.31
foule 602.32
fouler 197.08
fouling 206.33
fouls 120.31
foulties 357.04
foun 325.14
founder 121.27 323.06
founderess 244.18
foundland 412.04
four 022.23 087.15 221.30 250.12 393.22 405.22 430.03 517.30 559.35 581.22
four 353.35
fourch 408.33
fours 043.29 202.01
fourthly 123.03
fowl 066.35 586.21
fowlium 083.31
fowls 595.12
fox 030.18 159.28 242.35 293.F2 360.11
Fox 511.09
foxed 087.22
foxphiz 307.F7
fox's 245.09
fractions 256.31
fractured 310.10 466.12
fractus 041.06
fragate 439.35
fraida 272.03
frail 567.29
fram 317.09
frame 349.09
framed 022.36 241.18
frances 478.19
franchisable 024.27
franchised 548.19
frangible 150.34
frank 405.23
franka 343.28
frantic 297.32
fraternitisers 608.06
fraud's 460.20
fraudurers 173.17
fraus 603.19
frays 090.07
free 017.19 093.03 152.12 173.07 204.19 236.31 239.22 276.F2 318.09 387.35 439.08
free-Down-in-Easia 482.29
freegal 033.30
freer 162.09
french 296.F1 392.15
frenchllatin 495.27
frength 341.11
fresh 542.36
freshed 055.10
freshenall 619.15
freshment 191.08
freshpainted 452.19
freskment 129.29
fresqued 088.29
fressor 124.15
frey 356.17 550.02 582.26
friar 191.01
friars 048.03
friaryfamily 611.09
fria's 430.24
frich 497.36
frichunfoldingmorn 571.32
frids 019.09
frie 023.20
frieclub 436.29
fried 060.21
friede 376.36
friend 289.23
friended 056.21
friendly 076.04
friends 391.35 444.35 460.18
fries 097.03 170.06 572.04
frieze 327.01
fright 423.17
frightened 521.24
frighthisdualman 442.27
frillfrocked 191.01
frinch 008.11 008.13 486.17
frira's 601.27
frish 098.24 264.06
frisking 572.04
frock 444.28 467.11
frocked 166.15 191.01
frockies 431.03
frocksfull 236.12
frogate 242.24
frogs 121.05 394.21
fromthirty 093.12
frond 021.33 609.12
front 009.04 055.10 204.25 339.07 415.28
fronted 280.23
fronts 369.04
froraids 316.03
frost 338.31
frothdizzying 203.27
frow 486.06
frowned 555.22
frow's 119.10
frowse 526.25
fru-Chikda-Uru-Wukru 024.07
fructs 019.15
fructuosities 348.33
frue 370.04
frufrocksfull 236.12
fruice 171.18
fruit 135.31 194.12 428.01 495.24
fruitful 421.28
fruityfrond 609.12
frumpishly 242.19
fru's 245.33
frutties 497.10
fry 035.14 446.12
ftjschute 003.19
fu 396.36
fubling 346.01
fuchs 574.04
fudgist 323.23
fuffpfaffing 529.30
fug 354.32
fugal 605.17
fuggading 350.05
fugium 051.31
fugle 011.09
fugue 121.28
fuit 017.32 033.34 033.34
fukie 532.30
fulgurayous 422.30
full 011.29 016.04 124.24 152.26 229.30 231.09 236.12 286.31 415.06 494.36 512.09
full 342.16 348.04
fulldt 537.04
fulled 590.13
fuller 562.11
fullness 224.10
fulls 350.34
fullth 155.28
fullvner 348.14
fulvid 284.30
fum 326.07
fumance 219.05
fumastelliacinous 157.32
fumbed 482.21
fumbers 340.26
fume 333.16 542.22 624.24
fumed 236.02 320.25
fumios 430.27
fummed 370.28
fun 060.34 086.14 203.31 596.31 607.16
function 341.25
fund 452.18
funded 599.05
funder 481.34 596.03
fundum 229.21
fundust 535.29
funkfires 581.14
funnies 431.01
funnyadams 065.05
funx 035.09
fuoco 387.03
fur 039.15 215.19
furcers 565.04
furcht 481.09
furioted 138.28
furking 302.15
furl 019.26
furloined 419.29
furred 141.22
furse 072.35
furst 238.24
furters 332.08 533.15
further 288.F7
furto 070.05
furts 415.05
furty 285.F3
furwards 357.36
furz 294.23
fused 156.31 542.11 605.34
fusel 412.34
fuseleers 058.23
fuseries 431.13

fush 525.31
fusiasm 425.15
fusing 242.16
fusion 100.23 222.02 252.19 432.14 542.11
fusionism 117.33
fusker 178.36
fuson 019.19
fuss 041.13 430.22
fussed 078.21 193.21 513.31
fussion 353.25
fustigation 150.07
fut 156.34
futt 599.08
futter 384.28
futthered 322.10
fuul 088.19
fuxes 249.02
fuyant 502.35
fyd 034.17
fydd 529.25
fyddye 480.12
fyn 418.27
fyne 510.10
fysis 329.34
fyx 200.05

gaar 370.27
gaard 246.01
gaard- 424.20
gaars 221.15
gab 490.08
gaba 276.09
gabawlers 497.05
gabblers 540.24
gabet 577.17
gabollags 541.18
gaby 449.35
gaceous 613.18
gad 009.26 024.07 180.04 202.05 258.03 379.33 485.05 612.32
gad 346.33
gadag 186.21
gaddy 195.03
gade 551.34
gading 350.05
gado 464.02
gadovies 184.31
gadye 313.18
gaff 522.22
gaffe 268.12
gafiena 605.19
gafiuna 605.20
gag 363.36
gage 577.05
gageflavoured 556.15
gageg 169.14
gaggeng 240.10
gagnolina 225.15
gagyng 244.07
gain 228.22 343.09
gaining 318.07
gainly 121.25
gains 241.33
gain's 434.15
gainus 361.03
gait 051.13
gaiterd 320.07
gal 033.30 114.25 297.F2
gala 233.36 475.02 475.13
gale 022.10 184.24 406.24 469.15
galenes 453.19
galenu 184.13
gales 468.14 562.12
galia 551.24
gall 021.23 176.20 384.14 386.06 389.18 480.34 500.04
galla 520.03
gallaghers 090.10
gallant 168.10 620.07
gallian 138.11
gallians 106.17
galls 215.14 326.08
gall's 405.06 496.18
gallus 484.35
galowre 496.13
gals 601.10
gal's 040.25 463.19
galstones 224.19
galuvu 594.23
gam 093.15 261.27 296.F3 546.13
gam 346.17
gaman 256.25 303.23
gamated 308.L2
gamb 346.17
gambols 012.27
game 373.26 445.34 569.17 569.25 614.18
gameous 241.05
game's 375.16
gamies 300.26
gamma 120.34
gammoner 560.11
gammons 433.02
gamore 132.19
gams 075.02
gamyg 116.32
gamyjig 332.24
gan 199.18 389.01 622.23
gan- 332.05
gana 080.20
ganas 570.12
ganasanavitch 278.23
ganda 545.09
gander 428.10
gandering 059.22
gandi 289.02
gandy 276.17
gang 376.11 466.29 478.16 480.36 560.14
gangd 127.28
ganger 490.17
gangers 540.24
ganger's 126.15
ganglions 571.36
gangs 015.05 032.27 068.31
gangsted 496.15
gannon's 297.F3
gans 286.F5
ganson 530.31
gansum- 314.08
gantast 319.26
gantogyres 596.23
gants 398.15
gap 037.08 455.19
gapemonides 007.16
gapers 366.02
gapers 339.19
gapo 202.07
gar 497.11
gara 068.09
gara's 601.24
Garath 622.04
garced 338.13
gard 555.13 555.15 609.17
gardaddy 306.03
garden 062.19 597.15
gardener 133.06
gardens 617.22
gardes 541.26
gardien 483.25
gards 210.04 579.12
gardsmanlake 599.19
garee 052.24
garettes 351.12
gargley 234.31
gargoh 245.14
gari 112.07
gari's 408.26
garius 498.03
garius 076.07
garlick 413.13
garmenteries 181.29
garments 311.30
garnath 342.13
garri 180.14
garries 619.06
garry 346.24
Garry 526.24
gar's 102.08
garseen 615.31
gart 485.01
garten 075.01 253.31
gartern 532.22
garters 011.22 436.01
garth 098.16 281.02 542.12 580.11
garths 435.07
garts 135.36
gas 036.13 160.30 171.35 176.31 229.16 239.05 485.29 494.23 496.13 511.21 556.29
gas 423.33
gasand 374.36
gaschiff 350.07
gases 231.21
gasp 190.22
gasps 568.07
gass 555.11
gassed 020.31
gasser 232.04
gassy 207.26
gast 144.06
gasta 099.09
gasti 423.33
gastulus 532.12
gat 060.12
gate 044.06 069.21 128.34 149.29 149.32 197.35 234.01 242.24 329.31 337.10 337.10 373.25 439.35 508.22 564.35 625.35
gate 105.26
Gate 569.09
gated 113.09 115.26 310.15
gatem 506.10
gates 004.06 249.07 612.24
gath 286.06
gather 453.16 548.13
gathered 587.29
gathering 010.32
gatherthem 015.02
gathumbs 337.25
gatogtug 351.17
gats 497.08
gatts 366.10

gaul 237.18
gaulgalls 326.08
gauzements 159.08
gave 413.15
gawn 426.10
gaws 548.24
gay 020.26 054.23 273.17 451.30 511.17 578.22 608.20
gayle 360.02
gayment 236.30
gaze 009.05 084.12 197.14 382.17 548.03
gazed 069.12
gazelle 238.36
gazer 143.26 193.12 471.09
gean 361.11
geant 319.12
gear 429.08 609.01
gearls 626.03
gearries 529.26
gebirger 133.06
gebordened 580.02
geborg 005.06
geborn 370.07
geds 241.27
gee 006.32 018.34 231.14 588.02
geegeeses 089.34
geela 407.18
geena 354.15
geequanee 072.08
geering 372.20
gees 027.20 166.01
gee's 379.32
geese 446.19
geeses 089.34
geg 054.23 169.14
gegst 272.17
gehaven 100.07
gein 316.19 374.24
geing 549.03
geist- 187.15
gel 300.05
gelaut 484.09
geld 084.04
gelegenaitoikon 416.12
gelert 177.22
geling 088.33
geller 468.09
gelly 231.13
gels 015.14 359.32 567.33 587.26 601.01
gem 456.22 542.27 542.27 542.27 566.06 586.30
gemble 343.03
gemeinded 252.16
gemelimen 271.13
gemout 354.17
gemyeyes 025.03
genal 431.35
genating 004.36
genation 251.17
genations 018.20 018.20
gend 533.26
gendered 137.14 581.16
gendtougend 247.07
general 567.22
generand 372.06 604.23
generation 284.21 331.31 606.11
generations 600.09
generously 350.06
geners 267.17
geneses 350.31
genesis 240.13
GENETIC 275.R1
genets 504.02
genever 406.20
geng 240.10
genically 436.09
geniem 078.12
genious 154.20 595.23
geniture 300.L1
genius 034.14
genral 243.10
genselman 173.13
genses 488.35
gent 024.26 281.24 374.29 496.10 523.22
gentide 577.29
gentilisation 031.33
gentilmensкy 034.18
gentius 464.16
gently 537.19
gents 090.07
genua 513.20
genuinas 209.32
genuine 087.28
GENUINE 279.R1
geolettes 440.20
ger 352.10
gerd's 444.21
gerenal 338.19
gerend 584.28
gerent 566.21 566.24 574.33
GERILAG 305.R1
gerl 268.F3
gerls 450.17
germon 222.09
gern 565.12 565.12
gern- 424.20
gerotty 498.17
gerre 272.29
gesima 298.27 433.03
gest 489.11
gestern 407.30
gestfudgist 323.23
gesumy 234.12
gesus 316.28
get 243.03 433.33 616.11
geta 542.19
getherall 346.12
gethered 396.24
gethergush 581.27
gethering 601.31
getherum 186.25
getorix 088.22
gets 467.27 507.09 597.09
getter 451.04
getting 373.26
geyboren 525.21
geyed 015.03
geyer 042.15
geylywayled 331.32
ghal 099.27
ghalian 564.30
gharagh- 003.15
ghastly 178.30
gheall- 332.05
Ghimley 290.07
ghirs 241.32
ghistan 493.02
ghost 353.03
ghosted 136.07 494.03
Ghoul 354.06
ghoulish 615.04
ghowho 291.04
ghundhurth- 023.05
ghurs 008.25
ghurutty 493.13
giants 067.07
giaour 068.18 305.03
gibbets 420.21
gickers 046.21 046.22
gidding 346.09
giddy 132.20
giddyculling 092.26
giddyex 066.12
giddyrex 281.F1
gieling 322.03
gien 272.29
gift 187.10
gift 418.20
gifting 246.28
giftness 498.27
gig 119.14
gigasta 081.05
gigmagees 027.20
gild 549.32
giles 416.32
gilhisjurylegs 060.11
gill 588.32
gill 104.18
gills 012.21 215.14
gilt 127.34
gimandodr- 424.20
gin 004.01 207.29 228.21 292.10 292.17 320.15 327.36 386.26 487.29 543.17 548.32
ginbottle 458.18
ginbrow 003.14
ginds 431.04
gine 529.22
gineral 292.F1
giness 184.17
ging 617.17
ginger 022.34
gingoos 493.30
gink 294.02
gink's 285.L2
gins 012.26 376.23
gintadue 054.12
gintarian 111.06
gintiquinque 134.13
giography 234.12
giol 143.33
giolesque 081.23
gionds 277.22
girillies' 351.12
girl 092.25 200.19 226.33 532.20
girlies 094.01
girlified 329.17
girls 054.09 367.01 504.22 601.13
girls 105.10
girl's 183.25 407.07
girond 209.18
girth 150.11
gist 214.12 323.23
gistanters 357.05
gists 575.19
git 029.08
gitabale 357.34
gits 093.05
give 434.14 560.34
given 077.27
given 355.06
giver 545.32
giver 345.28

givers 057.17
giving 380.09
glaa 265.F4
glad 258.28 563.26
glaggagglomeratively 186.10
glam 506.29
glances 405.20
glands 451.04
gland's 595.10
glaning 221.19
glarying 339.19
glas 075.16 142.14 485.12
502.35 550.24
glas 625.13
glass 084.29 100.23 101.29
167.20 193.16 247.36 252.07
277.F5 408.24 415.28 455.16
460.21 486.24 589.30 609.15
glasses 031.17 183.21 386.16
387.06 463.14
glasspanelfitted 076.11
glassy 208.09
glatteraglutt 349.12
gleam 099.16
glee 182.08
gleement 348.13
gleescreaming 383.15
glenn 553.22
glens 602.15
glen's 142.13
gless 074.15
glibly 079.18
glibtograbakelly 463.02
glide 486.07
glie 584.09
glik 578.36
glim 434.13
glimmed 075.09
glims 141.15
glin 087.26 092.04
glint's 006.35
glionic 513.17
glish 609.15
glo 202.22 528.23
glodynamonologos 194.16
gloe-Noremen 309.11
glom 533.22
gloo 207.33
gloomering 565.02
glooral 381.30
gloot 290.18 478.34
gloovah 369.19
glores 286.31
glorians 004.07
gloriously 063.22
glosia 525.08
gloss 609.15
glossary 423.09
glossies 497.19
glotte's 532.22
glove 374.12
gloves 022.35
gloving 144.28
glow 585.05
glow 349.07
glow's 245.08
Gluckin 180.08
glucks 200.08
glucksarsoon 344.01
glugs 595.16
glus 198.33 327.13
glut 612.13
glutables 151.28
glutt 349.12
glutton 240.27
gluttural 117.13
glyph 122.07
glyphy's 595.07
glyptics 419.19
gmard 371.22
gnaceous 186.13
gnacio 228.11
gnates 115.33
gnavia 254.33
gnawns 605.01
gnays 256.13
gneses 411.29
gniagnian 389.22
gnir 221.09
gnirurdr- 424.20
gnobs 274.F2
gnols 223.03
gnomen 030.03
gnomes 283.27
gnomist 336.34
gnone 225.15
gnoscere 287.27
gnosible-edible 088.06
GNOSIS 262.R2
gnysthy 239.22
go 014.16 060.19 096.20
163.09 208.13 279.F12 281.F3
338.32 441.29 449.22 552.23
567.24 570.29 577.35
goad 097.23 624.17
goad 346.34
goaded 180.03
goading 203.28
goady 005.13
goak 005.07
goak's 339.04
goalgaceous 613.18
goalucrey 358.09
goarchicism 525.10
goat 035.13 215.27 240.34
353.02 596.01
goaters 522.16
gob 047.03 232.32 463.01
466.34 467.18 503.14
gobawlers 005.31
gobbleus 157.26
goblin 039.21
gobragh 303.14
go-bragk 438.16
gobretas 048.07
gobrew 283.24
gocciolated 054.33
god 046.24 079.21 091.28
111.03 488.22
godden 625.18
godden 339.24
godder 155.27
godlap 344.02
godly 261.L3
godoo 079.21
godparents 189.01
gods 004.01 004.01 005.33
289.16
goeasy 123.16
goer 233.11 367.20 587.36
goers 086.33 381.36
goes 007.27 007.27 303.11
goesthere 455.19
gog 006.19 006.19 025.23
136.01 366.26
gogagog 071.26
gogalenu 184.13
gogmagog 222.14
gognese 435.08
gogran 396.16
go-gully 499.04
gogusty 035.03
goh 245.14
going 042.36 141.01 264.10
292.29 331.04 599.33
going 294.L1
go-jumpy 332.24
gok- 023.05
goknob 344.14
gol 297.F2
gola 513.08
goland 388.19
gold 075.10 127.34 179.34
214.02 289.06 561.21
goldell 360.33
goldies 256.12
golds 211.03
golect 234.26
golhuts 416.35
goll 512.01
Goll 370.22
golla 485.33
gollow 580.34
Golly 395.03
gology 387.12
goloo 131.35
golorum 498.19
golosh 346.02
gom 347.02
gomaister 568.17
gomery 058.26 543.28
gomeryite 525.07
gomery's 426.11
gomuster 393.08
gon 019.15 371.36 535.20
593.10 621.25
gonamed 361.21
gonblack 016.29
gondola 447.32
gondoom 343.26
gone 021.05 223.29 231.30
265.03 310.18 336.06 385.03
386.07 547.34
goneahead 426.23
gones 012.29 263.17
gong 026.27 029.24
gongty 366.32
gonies 353.01
gonnianne 512.18
gono 085.05
gonoch 498.23
gons 167.07 613.11
gony 102.07
goo 276.15
good 021.30 085.17 346.23
369.08 492.24 500.19 590.20
goodchob 357.03
gooder 358.16 602.09
gooding 379.22
goodjesusalem 192.35
Goodman 212.09
goods 255.08 346.25
gool 371.22
goolapnow 348.16
gooms 456.15
goont 327.29
goontangues 541.34
goos 347.14 493.30
goose 026.05

Gooseberry's 342.15
goosip 623.03
goothoyou 471.02
gopark 051.20
gopatom 344.30
gopovengreskey 056.36
gor 613.28
gora 062.16
goraumd 309.24
gorballyed 323.16
gore 037.02 535.15 553.07
Gore 606.19
gored 339.29
gorer 255.15
gorge 378.23 563.31
gorgeous 492.34
goric 336.36
gories 397.25
gorios 454.15
gorladns 353.19
gorlay- 023.05
gorman 236.24
gorod 565.21
goromboassity 353.25
gorong 019.05
gorool 165.21
goround 525.17
go-round 550.27
gorpound 056.06
gorridgorballyed 323.16
gorror 423.16
gor's 102.08
gorude 240.18
gory 303.13
gos 187.01 205.29 316.35 407.02
gos 307.L1 345.20
gosmotherthemselves 353.27
gosongingon 274.24
gosterfosters 368.04
got 338.30 537.01
gotangos 019.05
gotenente 228.27
gotetabsolvers 004.09
goth 626.28
gothic 120.22 263.10
gothland 197.09
gotisters 137.08
gotstrade 602.21
gott 188.31 240.35 346.22
gotted 133.15
gotter 612.31
gotter 349.32
gotthened 345.34
gottheres 311.04
gottom 582.01
gott's 043.32 282.F4
gotty 531.17
gotty's 071.12
goturny 309.23
goul 277.03
gould 479.05
goup's 185.06
gourge 049.34
gout 180.07 312.15 351.06
goutfeller 257.07
gouts 358.04
gow 478.18
gowe 207.24
gown 297.03
goyed 456.01
grab 332.15
grabakelly 463.02
grabbed 498.05
grace 057.23 220.02 227.23 391.02 413.03 434.21 468.32 530.28 577.03
grace 260.L1
graceful 414.24
gracious 037.13
grad 351.27 491.35
gradation 557.23
graddagh- 044.20
grade 108.02
gradia 534.22
grading 611.29
grafiend 055.06
graible 301.F4
grain 197.28
graine 019.23
grained 026.34 088.16
grainia 031.25
gram 165.23 430.11 609.10
gram 399.09
grammatical 307.F7
GRAMMATON 286.R1
gran 396.16
grand 191.34
granda 160.30
grandgosterfosters 368.04
grandhotelled 017.33
grandyoulikethems 535.12
granes 004.04
grange 057.09
grantit 004.35
grapce 489.04
graph 007.15 220.11 226.01 226.01 438.19 467.33 488.24 522.21
grapher 472.09
graphers 121.11
graphically 292.28 412.03
graphice 604.19
graphies 242.19
graphique 339.23
graphs 032.13
graphy 120.22 275.F2 277.25 476.33 482.17 510.13
graso 038.03
grass 007.30 207.02 482.09 494.19
grassy 231.07
grate 253.17 387.19 460.26
gratiagrading 611.29
gratises 409.26
grau 247.35
gravated 063.07
graved 560.18
gravius 572.30 572.33 573.02 573.05 573.15
gravure 013.07
gravy 171.01
graw 377.04 494.26 511.02 511.07
gray 101.35 214.33 585.20
grayer 186.08
greany 620.11
grease 412.33
greasing 399.23
greasymost 156.17
greawis 552.02
greb 068.25
gred 029.01
gree 086.14
Gree 488.36
greedy 133.07 373.14
greef 565.13
Greek 569.07
greekable 181.22
green 032.29 086.35 101.36 171.16 208.18 443.36 471.13 611.34
greenable 609.01
greening 607.24
greenlindigan 611.06
greenold 186.08
greenst 346.04
grees 397.12
greest 514.28
greeth 243.03
greget 343.15
Gregor 520.04 520.10
gremmit- 023.05
grene 228.08 397.35
grene 329.06
greon 279.F32
greskey 056.36
gressulations 234.21
Grete-by-the-Exchange 135.10
gretta 067.31
grettitude 098.15
greven 622.20
grewnworsteds 611.35
grey 014.34 288.28 475.31 583.18
greyned 603.35
greys 603.18
gri 193.17
gridando 093.20
grieff 536.12
grievy 227.06
Griffith-Moynihan 307.09
grig 406.30 464.28
grim 093.29 244.21 448.24 455.13 483.33 600.35
grimace 423.08
grime 392.19
grims 348.05
grimst 220.35
grin 082.12 139.01
grinantibus 398.16
grind 128.08
grine 014.28 398.15 398.15
grine 282.L3
grines 484.29
gringnir- 424.20
gripe 141.21
gripment 084.16
gripper 535.13
grips 183.32
gris 202.34
grish 351.08
gristly 170.34
grits 249.12
gro 171.29
groamlius 322.34
groands 481.15
grobgrab 332.15
grocer 437.17
Groevener 325.01
grog 006.19
grogging 381.36
grom- 023.05
gromme 443.08
groom 040.02 362.09
gross 284.22 556.25
grossest 425.15
grotts 513.14

ground 076.33 113.32 128.09 128.31 161.34 332.12 494.24 546.11
grouped 129.12
grove 284.05
groved 265.01
grovemazes 221.20
growback 389.04
growdnyk's 102.19
grown 006.31 036.18 056.12 170.30 252.18 407.13 478.14
growth 128.20 558.20
gru 540.21
gruau- 023.05
grubs 245.26
grudged 534.22
gruggy 418.19
grunch 342.17 342.17
grund 223.31
grung 576.31
grunter 423.33
grunting 273.20
guage 323.05 466.32 478.09
guall 073.14
guam 095.27 095.28
guard 084.34 232.30 260.06 371.34 579.12
guardargoos 347.14
guarded 464.12
guardiant 151.20
guardise 005.17
guardism 180.32
guardness 357.18
guards 361.19
guard's 093.06
guchuna 346.15
gude 626.06
guds 073.06 275.10
guels 206.14
guents 550.18
guepe 417.22
guere 233.30
guerre 233.30 339.23
guerrig 353.31
guesched 232.33
guesed 381.20
guest 063.22 124.15 135.19 325.17
gueuxers 361.36
gugoothoyou 471.02
gugulp 613.22
guidd 366.12
guides 363.09
guidous 427.13
guile 071.19
guind 577.27
guines 088.20
Guiney's 381.19
guinnengs 129.10
guinnsis 421.26
guin's 285.L2
guired 092.01
guise 414.16 532.27
guished 288.17
gul 201.22 327.18 397.34
gul 162.16
gula 162.12
gulant 157.04
gular 610.10
gulash 287.F4
guldson 371.06
guled 341.11
gulf 547.32
gulfied 306.06
gull 383.16 424.10
gulls 595.14
gull's 026.31
gully 499.04 518.09
gulp 190.18 613.22
gulphia 320.20
gult 159.13
gultonia 343.01
gulvalvulous 310.04
gum 112.07 126.12 422.28 526.26 590.24
GUMPTIOUS 308.R2
gums 233.17
gumtreeumption 191.13
gun 336.06 350.32 352.14
gun 349.12
gund 288.09 315.22
gunitals 525.05
gunn 008.14
gunnded 323.27
gunne 025.23
gunne 104.12
gunneral 352.23
gunners 349.15
gunoshooto 160.29
guns 031.19 065.11 173.22 177.09 552.28
gur 233.31 256.22
gurat 100.19
gurayous 422.30
gurd 608.10
gurdsen 429.19
gurdy 231.15
gureen 279.03
gures 282.11
gures 352.29
gurgitation 558.03
gurin 625.34
gurios-in-Newrobe 155.05
gurr 351.30
gurtha 403.12 403.13
gus 058.15 265.06 378.19 489.17 515.30
gusaria 117.04
gush 178.12 581.27
guss 326.05 362.16 448.17 492.24
gust 616.16
gusta 438.02
gusted 610.01
gustered 212.33
gustissimost 104.06
gusty 035.03
gut 022.36 171.17 214.19 365.26 381.32 455.10 455.10 455.11 490.14 507.10 548.15 568.22
gutfulls 350.34
guting 078.12
guts 319.12
gut's 491.06
gutstract 346.33
gutter 332.12 517.14
guy 119.32 339.21 528.26 598.33
gyddyum 414.26
gye 497.23
gyings 256.31
gynal 619.02
gyndelse 282.05
gynes 613.35
gyng 244.07
gypst 364.18
gyrdle 548.17
gyres 596.23
gyric 120.27
gyt 186.28
gyttens 239.23

H 443.24
haab 312.19
haar 362.31 613.05
haared 468.36
haba 418.17
habit 545.18 624.08
habit 350.04
habitands 062.16
habitation 550.30
habited 421.08
habiting 602.22
hach 100.07 329.33
hack 190.06
hacknolan 303.F3
hacks 005.31
hade 329.04
hadure 554.07
haendel 054.27
hafts 133.30
hag 492.11
hagal 107.36
hagar 530.34
hagen 328.22
Haggans 299.23
hagion 605.14
hagion 305.L2
hagionous 520.33
hags 296.19 340.08 627.26
hague-Marengo 223.16
hahat 482.11
hahing 600.07
hahn 110.21 205.29
hahnthenth 608.24
hahs 183.14
hai- 054.15
haighaudhlug 310.11
hail 552.35 558.19
hailed 234.27 417.10
hailey 329.36
hain 344.28
haincold 578.23
hainodaisies 242.17
hair 108.23 166.15 183.18 265.21 273.F8 323.03 475.15 527.21
haire 423.03
haired 147.35 220.12 265.19 275.01 609.03
hairs 444.27
hair's 177.25
haitch 443.01
hake 240.18 446.10
hal 243.14 329.16 582.26
haled 311.08
haleine 156.36
hales 461.21
halething 029.16
half 100.19 161.11 533.34 534.29
halft 247.06
halian 564.30
hall 058.33 117.16 165.09 408.26 458.02 588.09 609.18
halla 362.22
halley 536.33
hallfisk 013.34

hallhoarding 365.16
hallo 485.22
halloo 541.22 541.22 541.22
halloon 323.25
hallowed 587.14
hallrhosmightiadd 056.07
halls 077.02 125.13 550.35
hall's 005.30
hallya 056.07
halooing 324.18
halpence 338.28
hals 557.10
halted 121.07 241.32
halter 511.30
halters 054.25
haltshealing 611.28
halves 540.32
ham 018.29 019.15 030.07
040.11 088.21 090.24 095.09
097.16 123.08 147.34 277.F4
284.F4 284.F4 315.04 318.21
369.12 387.28 388.21 393.05
397.18 422.18 422.26 434.12
492.23 493.17 570.19
ham 071.21
ha'm 174.13
hambers 562.13
hambrey 317.10
hame 098.08 319.30 326.18
415.29 616.04
hamer 192.08
hamerat 127.31
hamieson 126.05
hamilton 300.27
hamlooking 467.10
hammaggs 352.05
hamme 351.16
hammers 033.09
hammlet 418.17
Hammud's 156.22
hammyum 613.12
hamnk 365.21
hampton 442.09
hampton 354.16
hams 041.14 058.30 093.08
093.21 208.31 286.29 455.07
518.28
ham's 039.17 584.02
hamsk 481.24
han 016.01 027.14 034.06
147.30 212.12 616.03
hanagan 417.31
hanahanahana 554.10
hanaral 375.24
hanced 460.30
hand 027.04 042.09 052.25
085.04 085.12 096.23 121.22
168.06 177.31 240.10 246.23
253.14 271.11 289.10 321.27
369.02 371.25 435.08 467.13
495.02 504.27 534.20 572.06
576.23
handaways 496.06
handbaddend 541.27
handed 087.16 255.01
handedly 122.08
hander 276.02
handled 285.13 530.29
handler 444.21
handler 072.13
handling 384.26
hands 028.04 080.14 137.25
194.05 265.21 286.13
304.01 330.33 430.21
470.08
handschiner 333.04
handshighs 272.22
handsker 607.05
handsy 621.21
handy 612.01
hanees 330.09
hanga 497.11
hangas 015.12
hangd 391.08
hanged 049.26
hanger 114.22 444.19
hangled 615.19
hangs 224.08
hang-together 048.23
hann 446.01
hanna 212.06
hannes 391.05
hanno's 123.32
hans 343.25
hanshrub 588.31
hant 129.17 603.32
hantes 502.10
hants 250.05
hanyzhonies 101.28
hao 233.24
haohao 233.26
haoul 499.18
hap 022.33 395.27 404.11
425.27 514.22
hape 008.17
ha'pence 046.18
hapennies 549.36
hapes 313.32
hapje 257.02
hapnot 110.07
happiness 189.10
happing 533.17
happitents 258.22
happluddy- 044.20
happsteckers 514.08
happy 110.07 111.29 131.15
257.02 556.19
haps 062.25 130.35
hapsing 597.20
har 080.14 130.04 242.20
464.31 492.26 549.28
har 346.14
Hara 049.03 580.32
harabahts 379.07
harall 354.01
haran 380.21
haras 113.07
hard 012.36 034.08 049.29
276.12 322.11 415.32 455.34
464.18
hardened 087.34
harding 273.23
hards 016.13 443.05
hard's 109.21 412.05
hare 016.01 227.04
harem 331.19
hare's 335.29
harfeast 541.24
harican 489.20
hariwallahs 609.33
hark 500.04
harksome 080.26
harlot 352.06
harma 093.22
harmonious 109.23 188.26
harom 547.06
harp 066.29 224.16 466.18
harps 089.33
harrem 576.07
harrods 127.11 159.15
harrow 600.13
hart 275.14
harters 008.19
hart's 541.03
hasd 333.28
hase 491.18
hash 075.20 366.29
hassten- 414.19
hast 114.04
hast 349.19
hastcold 265.03
haste 317.20 456.24
hastem 238.02
hastern 598.10
hasting 371.11
hastle 072.09
hat 008.16 009.02 041.02
059.06 242.14 255.12 267.F6
322.01 351.18 415.32 482.11
513.10 522.24 567.01 584.15
hatchery 201.25
hater 408 11
hates 551.35
hatmas 243.27
hatoux- 414.19
hats 085.30 551.08
hatsong 110.24
hattaras 010.16
hatted 089.31 265.F2
hatton 539.02
haty 178.03
haubeen 568.28
haudhlug 310.11
haugh 622.27
hault 581.30
haun 364.19 419.17
haunaton 499.09
haunt 224.03 326.24 368.07
hauntered 293.F2
haunts 595.15
haurd 319.20
hause 535.17
haused 533.18
hauses 154.08
hausig 265.26
hausthible 091.27
hav 324.30
havebeen 042.19 052.29 076.33
havemiseries 288.25
haven 060.22 100.07 143.10
244.29 478.16
haves 463.32
havet 202.10
haveyous 068.20
haw 202.04 450.05 520.20
hawa 066.24
hawaw 619.34
hawe 180.31
haweshowe 256.13
hawk 215.30 383.16
hawks 505.01
hawl 315.16
hawn 443.02
hawrd 023.28
hay 167.08
haymix 331.02
haynix 473.16
hayns 342.29
haytehayte's 342.22

haza 176.27
hazar 389.32
hazards 615.07
hazelwood 372.15
hazi 056.11 521.22
hazometron 559.24
hazs 177.20
hazy 111.24
hazyheld 625.26
head 003.20 004.30 004.34 006.34 015.31 020.16 029.24 031.10 040.25 119.29 131.13 132.12 143.20 178.34 204.01 212.13 229.32 234.27 241.20 254.12 262.F6 274.04 274.08 275.13 292.19 299.F2 311.24 316.24 339.02 344.26 349.02 373.33 376.24 415.03 426.08 426.23 439.10 450.06 452.15 471.14 474.12 482.23 486.21 490.15 494.24 511.24 525.28 538.34 549.03 560.27 582.26 589.06 589.15 600.19 611.33
head 355.06
headed 047.01 095.20 120.36 121.22 127.01 136.25 152.09 381.35 472.05 513.07 517.05
headed 276.L1
heading 548.35
headoromanscing 327.11
heads 084.17 236.33 288.17 405.04 407.36 496.23 581.12
head's 190.02 233.16
heaheahear 466.25
heal 011.23 461.13
healian 023.11
healing 204.03 611.28
heall- 332.05
heallach 099.27
health 622.28
healthing 077.31
healths 280.13
healy 608.08
hean 123.16 583.17
heap 057.13 124.24 307.23
heaped 098.17
heaps 102.24
hear 222.12 237.12 337.26 466.25 486.30 584.36
heard 017.15 038.27 061.29 121.36 362.15 562.24
heardth 231.22
hearing 237.17
hearingly 096.30
hearingness 581.31
hears 023.26
hearsilvar 467.35
heart 290.03 328.21 336.34 360.12 407.24 536.10 539.15 619.17
Heart 143.02
hearted 171.01 240.22 560.28 608.18
heartedly 150.28 579.06
heartened 535.19 577.07
heartened 354.13
heartening 189.26
hearthed 602.16
hearts 254.03 563.29
heartzed 331.23
heartzyheat 102.19
heasts 367.32
heat 102.19 364.17 492.29
heated 415.19 461.28
heathen 549.07
heatherous 129.14
heavals 184.03
heaven 469.30 590.08
heavenly 185.29
heavens 446.01
heaver 352.15
heavin 220.34
heaving 189.25 190.31 353.16
heavy 170.28 335.35 587.10
hebeau 527.29
heber 604.04
hebited 224.11
Hebridian 263.13
hebus 286.F1
hecame 288.14
heck 423.11
heckhocks 130.20
hed 535.21
heda 469.34 478.13
hedarhoad 081.09
hedars 566.11
hedge 475.10
hedonum 610.06
hedrally 477.01
hedron 107.08
heds 547.34
hed's 229.36
hee 123.02 628.14
heed- 023.28
heeding 397.22
heehewheehew 399.29
heeing 299.14
heel 093.36 319.03 404.33 410.32
heeldy 230.12
heeling 021.12
heelless 081.22
heels 009.29
heem 404.26
heen 200.18
heerd 160.26 538.29
hees 029.12
heetuck 225.09
Hefferns 519.06
heid 251.15
heifer 614.01
height 132.22 418.08 606.02
heighten 336.08
heil 070.03
heild 326.05
heile 356.13
heim 052.09 129.23 533.18
heirn 538.26
heis 425.22
heiss 347.34
heist 299.14
heito 338.35
hekarry 207.24
hel 445.06 586.18
held 480.20 584.19 586.26 625.26
held 354.08
helic 091.35
helizod 452.11
hell 525.06 552.16
hella 151.20
helldselse 239.34
helled 292.18
Helleniky 263.14
hellows 569.25
hellt 077.27
helly 283.10
helm 273.28 574.15
helmina's 601.21
helot 019.18
help 010.13 130.20 157.13 192.12 516.29
helps 067.26 238.19 309.08
help's 181.18
helsson 124.29
helv 262.F1
helygangs 015.05
hem 003.13 115.14 147.11 188.18 193.09 348.26 374.04 421.19 484.36 493.16 514.29 571.02 571.02 571.25
hemans 397.31
hemeand 170.10
hemey 246.18
hemispheres 508.21
hemmed 104.03 320.14
hemons 059.28
hemoth 007.14
hemp 317.28
hems 183.14
hem's 318.05
hemuth 244.36
hen 393.23 578.20
hena 602.30
henceforward 243.04
hended 438.01
hends 343.25
heneul 119.25
henge 596.13
hengist 214.12
henguts 319.12
heniacs 497.20
henna 594.30
henning 234.19
hennyhindyou 272.19
hens 038.22 478.15
hent 388.05
henter's 381.13
hentleman 010.18
heol 228.33
heorebukujibun 484.26
heory 163.25
heouse 338.20
herairy 584.31
herapool 300.09
herb 005.23
herbal 478.09
herbour 171.27
herbs 190.06
hercabroads 419.02
herculossed 492.05
herd 223.01 540.27
herdoff 363.26
hered 445.31 465.17
heredayth 346.22
herenow 394.34
herers 617.18
herfhull 624.23
herhead 426.08
hericks 618.15
hering 017.24 354.24 354.25 354.25 444.17 525.20
heringcan 518.18
heringpot 020.07
herlehome-upon-Eskur 220.35
herlynt 232.13
herman 392.15
hernabreen 087.31
hernapark 321.08

herr 289.09 541.13
herra 326.26
herrn 272.25
herry's 584.01
hers 143.16 298.15 408.27 414.30 543.19 547.29 608.10
hers- 113.09
herself 526.29
her-Soles-Up 531.22
hersson 319.29
herstellung 296.L1
heruthr 280.19 280.27
hervolk 565.06
hery 051.17 557.04
hesitant 542.24
hesitent 133.14
hespers 038.14
hessock 272.F4
hessvan 013.27
hest 313.14 365.18
hester 413.06
hesters 624.25
het 064.01 108.26 398.27
hets 182.13
hett 355.31
heu 058.18
heuman 214.22
heure 346.07
he-used-to 291.03
hew 010.24 399.29 399.29 399.29 474.12
hewas 079.03
hewersoftened 077.32
hewheehew 399.29
hewit 042.04
hewn 412.09
heying 347.31
hi 206.15
hian 090.28
hib 607.32
hibbert 388.29
hibeline 071.26
hibernian 055.20
hibernskers 497.06
hiberring 504.30
hibilley 238.04
hibisces 349.20
hibitance 348.16
hibitating 437.14
hible 091.27
hiboh 078.32
hibow 442.27
hiccups' 355.12
hicked 049.27
hicksal 283.L2
hid 069.02
hidarhoda 434.07
hidden 081.09 284.25
hide 019.08 081.10 093.08 127.26 300.F4 340.11 359.03 403.14 483.31 583.21
hider 110.30
hides 366.29
hidin 486.30
hids 342.26
hie 059.20
hiem 277.15
hifie 004.28
hig 169.23
high 097.01 319.30 408.07 451.22 547.21 582.29
highdeed 461.08
higher 451.22
higherland 392.31
highest 080.20 104.04 451.22
highs 134.31 272.22
hight 358.23 358.24 368.24 425.31
hightful 497.24
hights 143.11
hike 603.16
hil 131.28
hill 012.27 012.27 012.28 012.28 012.29 022.19 050.30 132.22 202.16 265.F2 288.12 360.34 415.09 474.22 506.02 529.24 568.22 607.27
hillbarrow 015.24
hillhead 003.20
hilloupa 339.32
hills 044.08 448.04 546.32
hilly 174.29
hilp 622.26
hilt 529.31
himaroundhers- 113.09
himba 257.04
himbelling 567.36
himel 120.26
himper 149.04
hims 005.16 199.35 535.11
hind 222.36 295.06 564.08
hind 350.15
hindered 507.22
hinding 285.F5
hindred 330.33
hinds 146.08
hind's 252.05
hinduce 289.06
hindyou 272.19
hinee 182.12
hinees 016.31
hinerstones 207.07
hing 261.F4 273.22 607.08
hinged 069.15
hingeywilly 232.24
hinis 272.27
hink 608.22
hinn 469.01
hinninaird 541.32
hinnon 078.09
hino 054.18
hinsky 064.31
hint 340.23
hion 352.17
hiornal 228.33
hippuc 140.13
hips 214.21 237.35
hir 568.16
hired 359.03
hirk 182.12
hirondella 359.28 359.28
hirr 492.17
hirring 007.19
hirs 241.32
hisbeard 177.32
hish 250.11
hiskers 117.07
hislaws 539.29
hisn 442.30
hiss 148.26 297.F5
hissle 060.04
hist 343.34
histan 493.02
histenency 146.34
histhest 269.19
histhy 623.10
historic 059.15 385.18 477.36
historicold 382.12
history 169.21
hisway 577.23
hithim 358.36
hititahiti 337.29
hito 054.33
hitting 042.35
hive 561.07
hivehut 605.24
hiven 315.22
Hiver 548.29
hiviour 430.19
hlug 310.11
ho 058.16 058.16 117.16 206.16 244.09 328.25 352.23 352.26 431.32
hoa 366.16
hoad 081.09
hoak 411.06
hoangoly 611.30
hoarding 365.16
hoarse 472.20
hoasts 551.03
hoats 051.15 081.30
hoatstory 051.13
hob 097.03 359.17
hobbilies 005.32
hobbis 511.28
hobbles 275.22
hobbyhorsical 434.07
hobix- 414.19
hoch 025.25
hock 311.33
hockery 160.13
hockits 037.30
hocks 130.20
hod- 424.20
hoda 135.31 348.35 434.07 478.13
hodagrey 583.18
hodamena's 601.23
hodammum 515.09
hoda's 569.33
hodatantarums 445.17
hodes 208.26
hodge 266.01
hodie 546.11
hodomantic 241.08
hoe 039.17 360.05 379.36
hoebok 129.23
hoel 169.12
hoer 588.18
hoesed 178.01
hoewaxed 490.01
hof 253.32 538.32 541.21
hofe 572.16
hoffer 087.16
hog 228.18 269.12
hogan 388.17
hogfulled 590.13
hogged 487.07
hoh 054.28
hohem 188.18
hoho 590.04
hohold 478.30
hohs 352.29
hoiled 324.17
hoist 268.F4
hoken 360.08
hokeypoo 256.02
hokkurs 326.22
hol 312.19

holan 341.24
holawidey 625.25
hold 076.02 133.18 141.14 143.17 228.30 242.05 278.F7 281.24 311.14 352.24 365.03 377.02 418.05 438.20 478.30 544.07
holden 077.22 234.36
holden 340.26
holder 313.03 313.03 320.05 371.02 517.09 529.34
holders 366.05 450.10 488.04 574.19 582.08
holding 321.04 476.11 489.20
holdings 616.14
holdit 535.06
holdpp 571.29
holds 025.10 181.12
holdsterer 296.F1
hole 008.26 036.30 046.21 069.07 070.19 120.31 134.02 163.01 178.29 194.18 201.23 220.13 278.03 323.06 339.02 342.31 351.18 370.20 386.03 398.27 428.13 434.09 447.02 451.09 464.13 521.08 541.23 581.20
hole 350.11
holeborough 162.30
holeborrow 017.04
holed 031.06 137.36 336.04 563.32
holedoth 230.26
holemole 614.27
holenosing 365.16
holes 015.09 167.13 221.30 241.12 375.08 549.05 597.17
holler 348.10
Hollerins 291.11
holleydoodlem 379.12
hollow 319.01
holly 050.33 070.02 077.16 155.16 231.16 264.F3 307.04 326.11 424.33 551.29
hollyisland 111.18
hollymost 271.F5
holm 132.33 139.33 331.36
holma's 517.19
holme 279.F27
holme 341.19
holomew's 140.01
holse 077.10
holson 332.08
holst 346.26
holster's 276.F5
holy 352.22 416.19
holyphamous 073.09
holyway 242.24
hom 338.22 459.24
homatism 241.25
homba 165.22 257.04
hombulus 286.F1
home 022.21 041.17 074.06 074.07 181.06 133.17 138.30 138.30 215.32 225.14 231.04 244.10 296.31 332.27 336.09 372.17 379.03 382.20 382.26 388.13 434.03 446.35 457.35 461.28 473.05 531.13 602.33
homeans 333.15
homed 098.05
homely 078.01
homers 034.16
homes 286.F1
home's 111.11 116.20 363.22
homethinks 149.03
home-upon-Eskur 220.35
homiah 032.01
homing 470.15 470.17
homme 365.04
homme's 106.12
hompty 341.32
homrigh's 174.26
homy 396.12
hon 126.05 213.08
honagyan 334.11
honal 277.02
hond 462.21
hone 176.27 190.30 210.32 277.01 353.18 460.17
honest 572.21
honey 017.13
honeybeaverbrooker 072.10
hong 230.36
honies 101.28
honnda 481.21
honochie 228.01
honoured 073.36
honours 552.30
hontas 559.32
hony 133.02
hoo 046.32 162.27 297.F5 439.20 449.25
hoochee 209.22
hood 012.33 029.29 059.18 163.05 188.10 235.16 251.10 270.08 291.20 298.12 329.09 351.29 362.21 452.06 461.06 492.08 563.29 571.14
hooded 588.16
hoods 033.01 375.09 375.09
hood's 227.34 403.22 483.05
hoodurt 387.10
hooed 230.21
hoof 386.18
hoohoo 379.13
hoohoom 488.14
hoohoor- 003.15
hook 066.15 119.29 133.34 228.30 379.16 601.35
hooka 194.36
hooken 170.17
hooks 181.13 280.16
hool 415.07 617.07
hoola 329.17
hoolagh 128.33
hoolags 498.10
hooley 368.29
hooley 340.20
Hooley 125.04
Hooligan 593.12
hools 377.34
hooly 100.07 520.33 608.08
hooly's 440.15
hoom 318.06 488.14
hoomen 553.33
hoomeo 485.34
hoon 301.05 593.18
hoon 273.L1
hoonearth 155.29
hoop 197.27 454.13
hooper 368.29
hooping 423.26
hooping 383.05
hoops 450.35
hoopsabout 331.17
hoopy 054.31
hoor 224.36
hoor- 003.15
hooric 555.10
hoort 205.30
hooru 016.26
hoo's 371.33 439.20
hoose 617.04
hoosh 457.24
hoot 092.06
hoot 354.18
hootch 485.35
hooth 007.30 310.17
hooting 263.04
hooved 049.27
hoo-whoo 149.27
hoozebecome 240.06
hop 268.29 612.35
hope 010.02 154.33 236.07 572.17
hoper 414.21 414.22 416.08 417.03 417.22 417.33
hoper 418.11 418.12
hopes 154.03 308.F2
hoploits 187.15
hopparray 341.22
hopper 307.16
hopperminded 041.12
hoppers 170.31 257.05
hoppers 105.28
hopping 194.34 423.27
hops 415.17 443.23
hor 054.13 349.01 365.05 377.25
horable 438.17
horace 325.13 616.26
horanghoangoly 611.30
horason 347.03
horc 018.34
horchers 339.18
hord 243.34
horde 243.10 285.F3
hore 020.36 046.22 197.21 229.12 245.13 397.05 481.26 504.22 549.14
horehounds 531.25
horizon 494.09
horn 084.08 091.27 118.23 157.03 245.01 274.07 316.15 414.07 428.15 479.35 482.19 556.36 563.06
horned 112.22 590.28
horners 589.32
horning 500.13
horns 008.31 451.07 528.28
horn's 204.21
horror 091.30 311.25 626.28
horrors 019.25
horse 084.27 121.23 132.12 137.28 221.18 360.30 365.33 370.23 413.07 521.12 522.16 610.02
horsebroth 482.05
horsed 075.15 137.17
horseluggars- 023.28
horship 547.27
horsical 434.07
horsing 315.16
horsman 568.17
horush 360.16
horwan 352.34
hos 205.32 231.28 322.30 322.30 467.36

hose 239.10 423.16
hosens 133.16
hosepants 319.32
hose's 088.01
hosililesvienne 348.36
hosmightiadd 056.07
hoss 347.16
hosses 397.22
hosso-Keevers 310.17
hoss's 443.29
host 396.24 409.06
host 345.29
hosters 219.08
hosting 501.32
hostmark 473.09
hosts 314.22
hoststown 329.25
hostus 532.04
hostwhite 214.15
hot 135.07 140.04 222.09 231.32 322.05 406.20 459.36
hot 345.26
hotelled 017.33
hotes 184.18
hother 618.25
hotwaterwottle 176.36
hoty 341.08
hou 135.06 202.12 490.13 585.04
houatted 056.07
houche 462.07
hough 349.19
houghted 018.02
houker 415.06
houl 024.15
houlas 062.05
hould 513.13
hoult 105.12
houly 057.06
houma 020.17
houn 108.17
houn- 003.15
hound 480.04
hound 343.15
hounding 352.20
hounds 531.25
hounin's 035.32
hount 232.28
hour 221.01 310.25 364.24 414.33 484.29
hour 176.10
houraised 262.25
houre 587.01
hours 117.29 238.17 429.08
hourter 320.19
house 005.14 014.14 017.34 021.10 021.13 030.16 042.24 043.19 054.27 057.34 077.28 084.18 108.19 139.32 151.01 177.13 179.18 179.35 184.13 186.31 197.32 204.09 219.02 220.35 221.15 256.34 271.06 274.22 276.25 289.18 312.17 319.23 319.30 353.13 356.05 362.34 371.13 377.05 390.04 392.26 395.29 405.23 409.22 427.04 427.36 428.08 435.02 444.24 454.33 481.29 498.30 503.14 523.26 545.03 597.14
house 354.17 345.19
househumper 107.34
houses 039.31 116.34 416.36 537.01
house's 137.21 213.16
housh 059.20
housie 575.26
houssy 578.32
hout 033.36
hove 012.36
hoved 383.15
hovens 324.29
hoves 278.11
hove's 403.16
howe 076.14 256.13 365.11
howffse 538.16
howghowho 291.04
howham 147.34
howiatrees 259.06
howitswhy 272.06
howl 284.19 567.36
howle 309.22
howley 608.09
howling 547.21
howls 116.29
howlsballs 231.21
howmuch 414.11
hows 107.18 282.18 310.09 335.01
howse 525.22
howth 129.24 448.18 535.26
howwhen 394.29
hoy 054.26 077.06 285.14 285.14 285.14 377.27 460.27 624.23
hoyaway 285.14
hoyden 255.31
hoykling 384.05
hoyle 323.02
hoyteboyce 004.05
hrift 418.07
hrone 417.11
hronehflord 336.13
hroneroom 498.07
hropes 349.11
hu 285.12
huam 452.35 499.10
huamhaighaudhlug 310.11
hub 239.33
hubadah 609.32
hud 021.24 186.08 285.12 312.03
hud 342.14
huddart 206.18
hudded 517.07
hue 182.08
huebra 202.13
hued 043.20 167.10 223.30 234.26 288.F5 336.12 411.24 602.04 611.06
huest 240.03 414.08
hugamore 132.19
hugewhite 350.10
hugging 384.21
Huggins 519.05
hugh 325.32
Hugh 382.22
hugon 535.20
hugugoothoyou 471.02
hui 281.04
huise 091.04
huit 597.36 620.04
huite 388.16
huith 091.04
huk 288.27 413.11
hukar 357.02
hul 415.25 415.32
hulation 058.08
hulerusspower 248.21
hulesalesolde 326.23
hulic 603.30
hulked 049.27
hull 370.34 624.23
hullows 613.20
hullpulthebell 245.25
hulme 130.24
hulments 624.28
huls 026.14
hum 613.04 618.14
human 090.27 619.19
humanar 441.26
humanasant 084.05
humationary 077.33
humberland 387.09
humble 503.16
hume 097.24
humed 032.13
humember 493.17
humious 563.04
humispheure 346.07
hummed 015.15
hummer-Phett 355.31
hummer's 439.23
humming 198.01 549.20
hummour 331.33
humnk 365.21
humorisation 331.31
humour's 316.34
hump 006.04 022.28 358.24
humper 107.34
humph 328.34
humpledan 420.26
humps 602.24
humpta- 314.08
humpty 550.36
hums 281.L4
humust 422.14
hun 201.24 244.32 254.03 254.26
hunara- 023.05
hund 339.07 607.25 607.26
hunderts 054.25
hundhurth- 023.05
hundread 347.19
hundred 126.06 133.17 444.12
hunds' 548.15
hunerhinerstones 207.07
hung 058.04 228.16 295.18
hung 200.12
hungrig 406.30
hungry 288.28
hunigan's 006.20
hunkered 274.L3
hunkn 553.34
huns 127.13 610.03
hunt 320.11 332.04
hunter 107.14 576.25 585.23
hunters 283.25 386.36 497.07
hunting 124.27 373.20
huntus 622.27
huon 202.23
huoni 499.08
huorson 529.20
huoys 491.36
hur 300.30 349.04 351.32 359.17
hurabelle 201.35
hurd 314.29

hurdles 570.05
hurdlestown 203.07
hurdsday 491.27
hure 457.15 478.25
hure's 110.10
hurever 202.12
huri 165.28
hurifex 449.15
hurily 465.10
hurling 455.01
hurrible 477.21
hurries 214.03
hurrish 607.20
Hurry 008.27
hurs 234.28
hur's 478.24
hurst 162.08 351.29
hurteen 378.22
hurth- 023.05
hurtiness 298.33
hurts 064.18
hus 267.05 294.16 320.11 351.24 464.32 581.22 585.11 604.07
hu's 478.23 480.18 480.18 500.03
hus- 023.05
husband 627.01
husbands 390.20
huse 240.29
husen 337.11
hush 628.12
huskle 556.27
hustorily 323.35
hut 392.31 605.24
hut 043.23
hutian 375.24
huts 416.35
hutton 549.04
hvuns 609.24
hyacinthinous 118.28
hyacinths 092.16
hyas 593.01 593.01 593.01
hyber 464.10
hyde 549.31
hydrad 036.07
hydrants 182.36
Hyens 291.10
hygiecynicism 353.08
hyllygully 518.09
hyme 206.34 379.36
hymful 536.16
hymn 015.13
hyms 183.15
hynte 224.03
hyr 326.02
hyrs 348.11
hyse 375.34
HYSTERIC 266.R1
hyttel 338.08

iberia 424.09
iberian 078.25
iberias 115.11
iberiast 123.30
iberiously 119.16
ibernia 297.05
ibernian 567.35
ibiliter 154.22
ibis 452.08
ibisces 349.20
iboe 359.36
iboh 078.32
ibow 442.27
ice 502.18
iching 407.32
ichthyan 007.20
icical 450.24
icon 614.28
icori 623.01
icycled 416.30
id 026.17 072.22
idens 347.06
identified 615.05
identity 582.15
ides 366.29
idim 297.F2
idiocal 106.11
idiotically 615.05
idnis 597.19
idsglass 277.F5
iectiones 185.19
igen 332.04 332.04
ighevisien 423.05
ignacian 153.21
ignites 334.10
iivdluaritzas 572.15
ikan 197.29
ikin 032.06 113.08
ikke 221.28 506.04
ikon 279.F12
ikos 252.15
ilands 348.16
ild 155.24 410.09
ilde 391.16
ildies 325.28
ildish 461.28
ile 056.28
ilex 023.20
ilium 453.36
ilks 184.18
ill 493.03 499.08 588.32 589.15
illas 430.36
illi- 023.05 023.05
illicately 525.02
illicit 385.25
illium 062.11
ills 124.14 414.28
illsilly 015.18
illume 244.26
im 156.27 186.14 224.02
image 053.03
imbeina 221.25
imesnider 320.04
imitable 441.14
immanence 394.33
immence 367.13
impellant 486.35
imperatived 176.25
important 381.05
imposed 165.25
impudent 469.24
imsolff 308.F2 353.17
inaboss 485.33
inadays 542.33
inafter 049.35 446.23
inaire 295.17
inall 154.05 242.31
inandoutdown 612.14
in-a-pie 407.29
inapoke 359.26
inardor 374.16
inaring 087.05
inat 323.28
inausland's 116.21
inbeddy 243.06
inbetts 242.05
inbond 510.35
inbored 393.08
inbottle 458.18
inbourne 367.29
incarnate 596.04
incarnated 535.36
incest 254.06 387.19
inch 293.15 362.09
incidance 049.36
incidence 299.08
incidences 597.01
incident 060.23
incidental 109.28
inckers 617.02
incline 478.20
inconvenience 520.06
incorporated 387.36
incular 315.30
incurred 380.05
ind 285.04
ind 342.34
indaco 284.28
indeade 363.20
indergored 339.29
inderivative 084.16
indernees 234.19
inders 541.33
indians 483.08
indicat 076.07
indicative 053.14
indicatively 269.31
indies 010.28 499.21
indiest 288.24
indigan 403.13 611.06
indigo 267.16
indigut 171.17
indonche 255.23
indonk 230.12
indove 354.28
indown 065.32
indrias 219.11
indring 511.31
indrinny 028.12
inds 431.04
induce 289.06
induced 004.09
indwards 371.36
infected 436.15
infinite 505.24
inforced 430.17
informed 123.19 414.07
infrowned 555.22
ingated 113.09
ingcomed 369.18
ingelbrett 542.34
ingels 359.32
ingenting 414.34 416.27
ingerls 450.17
ingles 297.27
inglish 275.F6
ingorgeous 492.34
ingulfied 306.06
ingult 159.13
inhanced 460.30
inhand 052.25 467.13 572.06
in-hand 168.06
inhands 286.13
inhaven 143.10
inheavin 220.34
in-her 583.31
inholder 320.05

inishmhan 616.03
iniumin- 278.04
injills 141.09
injon 274.02
injoro 160.32
ink 166.26 187.18 294.02
425.24 441.13
inker 357.11
inklers 419.26
inkling 154.30 256.04
inkus 081.22 322.30
inlaine 034.23
inland 469.11
inlandia 098.07
in-laugh 312.13
in-law 021.14 284.F4 323.15
436.16 545.05
in-laws' 183.28
inlay's 506.09
in-Leal-Ulster 482.29
in-lieu 139.29 220.22
in-load 448.15
in-louth 049.15
in-love 067.36
inluminatedhave 278.04
inmidden 503.08
inn 052.27 264.28 328.02
328.26 347.14 469.01 482.07
600.07 604.08
Inn 512.34
innager's 312.27
inne 610.22
inned 374.14 491.31
innes 025.27
in-Newrobe 155.05
innghis 024.35
inngling 620.15
inning 562.19
innoculises 394.30
inns 111.17 330.30
inn's 372.29
innt 292.30
innteerily 364.06
innturns 539.31
inoilia 456.03 456.03
inpot 356.03
inpotty 059.12
inquinance 240.08
inregn 568.34
insacks 035.09
insee 600.13
insiduously 580.19
insight 551.34
insistence 354.14
inspirer 395.17
instone 008.01
instushes 346.02
instye 305.06
insure 428.12
insured 333.06 544.12
insweeps 123.08
intaxes 005.32
intaxication 447.29
intaxis 554.01
intentional 151.08
intentionally 163.29
interest 589.08
interestingly 179.12
intermutuomergent 055.11
interruptedly 405.07
inthe 142.06 142.06
in-the 300.F4
in-Thews 129.33
inthou 054.14
intimate 495.25
intime 432.33
intiristid 538.03
intona 617.06
intoxicated 089.08
introducing 246.36
introspection 445.29
intuation 055.35
intus 611.24
inunder 017.32
inurney 264.L2
inusand 326.20
invasive 072.17
inveils 541.30
invented 077.05
invention 602.26
in-waders 089.22
in-wait 007.35
inwhitepaddynger 612.18
inworms 059.12
IO 305.R1 305.R1
iodrama 050.06
iodreama 079.28
ion 206.11 398.18
ions 222.07 248.05 328.08
380.23 581.31
iouker 183.33
ipathete 226.06
ipso 488.09
iraizde 032.08
ire 488.26
ired 005.30 068.10
ireland 428.07
ireling's 270.30
irely 119.25
iremonger 584.05
ireton 224.27 224.27
irgland's 595.10
iric 513.32
iries 551.28
irigate 601.33
iris 186.28
irish 126.24 290.28 309.24
347.08 427.03 600.33 608.25
Irish 322.02
irishblooder 378.11
irisher 092.18
irishis 322.02
irland 446.25
irls 346.08
iron 210.13
iron's 141.03
irragun 352.14
irrara 497.04
irrgeling 088.33
irse-made-earsy 314.27
Isaac 227.33
ised 087.18 565.33
iseels 344.09
iseut 236.20
ishguss 326.05
ishmhan 616.03
isht 320.05
isis 305.21 470.16 470.18
470.20
island 111.18 525.30
isle 017.18 051.25 463.31
514.26 529.20 578.25
islender 378.11
isles 254.33
isliness 148.36
ismade 321.09
ismenon 059.16
ismion 326.33
isolate 003.06
isold 607.31
isonester 177.14
isonian 048.23
isoot 487.32
isotoelles 601.28
ispiration 257.25
issa 256.33
issabon 442.09
is-silvier 211.35
ist 293.01
istas 514.10
ists 280.27
iswhatis 223.27
itachapel-Asitalukin 110.08
italian 151.08
italukin 110.08
itas 060.16 119.11
itch 069.12 376.19 423.15
529.16
itcherous 181.08
iter 315.13
iterum 247.17
ither 325.13
ithyphallic 481.04
itinerant 594.07
itsch 141.23 247.27
itself 123.27
Ituc 237.29
ivanhoesed 178.01
iva's 601.23
ivdluaritzas 572.15
iveagh 408.28
ivel 008.28
ivelyonview 018.29
ivengrene 329.06
iver 013.17
iverever 242.31
ivis 468.10
ivor 295.02
ivory 502.02
ivy 186.13
ivying 199.36
ixion 346.13
ixtion 343.18
izago 052.15
ized 429.24 545.33
izing 498.20
izod 032.16 062.35 096.08
101.11 178.09 324.04 452.11
izod 107.05
izzdryel 241.27
izzed 550.36
izzer 286.22
izzier 471.07
izzier's 408.23
izzledazzle 113.01
izzy 073.07 200.31 373.27
457.27 538.22
izzy 399.11
izzyboy 530.21

ja 056.34 389.03 532.18
532.18 537.24
jab 498.16
jab 342.14
jacent 036.15
jaciulations 089.10
jack 171.17 177.24 422.33
487.04 489.12 528.36
jacking 581.11

jackmartins 007.04
jacobs 188.28
jacob's 089.15
jacques 335.34
jaculate 338.27
jade 261.01
jaell 261.03
jaer 284.F4
jagd 055.16
Jaggarnath 342.13
jagged 180.18 339.12
jaggers 497.06
jagmartin 086.02
jahn 388.33
jahoo 609.18
jahs 282.24 282.24
jailey 064.19
jakers 469.11
jakes 463.09 547.22
jallisuus 325.11 325.12
jalmar 284.F4
jambe 422.33
jambo 199.20
jambras 550.35
jamja 537.24
jams 193.35
janaral 492.29
janeska 333.05
janeyjailey 064.19
jankeltian 311.22
jantaj 325.11
japansies 059.14
jappy 054.23
jar 026.18 088.20 305.F2 341.06
jarry 333.02
jars 621.15
jaunties 233.23
jaw 125.19 188.11 256.19
jawbreakical 293.16
jaws 300.13 493.09
jazyma's 578.22
jazzyma 102.15
jealice 344.32
jealousties 350.15
jeams 399.34
ject 608.08
jected 232.23 321.06
jectilised 353.28
jection 221.36 252.28
jective 412.13
jector 576.18
jee 234.31
jeean 546.18
jees 205.32
jelasys 417.23
jeld 136.13
jell 006.36
jelly 170.34 486.18
jellybies 006.02
jelties 554.06
jem 242.33
jemsums 325.17
jenaskayas 348.23
jenk 179.28
jeras 348.23
jerichol 470.18
jermine 289.10
jerries 064.23
Jerusalem 105.06
jest 577.32
jester 338.12
jester's 073.14
jestings 536.07
jestiveness 222.32
jestky 335.02
jesus 296.10
jesusalem 192.35
jets 122.11
jetties 358.24
jeu 329.30
jeuchy 004.25
jeunerate 422.08
jevin 563.37
jew 250.07 250.07
jiacks 156.26
jibbers 187.11
jibed 317.30
jibun 484.26
jibway 134.14
jicquey- 254.15
jiff 501.10
jig 146.02 332.24 479.14
jigs 302.04
jills 141.09
jim 211.06
jimboed 238.18
jine 224.03
jingbangshot 396.01
jiniks 439.33
jinks 094.29
jinksky 513.11
jinpalast 597.13
jip 458.27
jist 258.04
jivana 597.19
jo 397.11 398.04 476.32
Jobber 178.22
jobbers 368.28
jocax 063.30
jock 007.35
jocky 331.24 383.24
jocqjolicass 254.15
joculated 129.10
joe 003.12
jog 414.22
jogging 053.07
john 060.31
johns 268.07
johnson 440.08
Johnson 377.32
joimt 231.31
joined 584.30
joineth 533.24
joining 060.08
joins 185.28
joint 108.14 569.21
jointed 104.05
joints 199.22
joist 113.36
jok 155.16
joke 071.18
joked 320.23
jolicass 254.15
jolking 094.04
jolly 093.34
jombyourselves 465.10
jon 255.13 274.02 471.14
jones 275.F5 576.36
Jones-Orbison 302.23
joni 609.08
jons 207.30
jook 329.29
jord 006.36
jorg 163.30 343.36
jorgn 124.29
jorn 622.06
joro 160.32
jorum 290.F3
jorumsen 529.16
jos 238.33 526.17
joss 611.05
jourd'hui 281.04
Journal 531.36
journed 585.27
journemus 264.15
Jovan 472.15
jowl 222.31
joy 045.10 045.11 245.21 460.09 486.08 583.17
joyable 529.36
joyed 068.02
joymt 534.18
Joynes 370.21
joynted 027.02 244.29 310.31
joys 357.18 428.20 466.18 587.06
joytsch 485.13
jschute 003.19
ju 352.28
jube 231.18 444.22
jubers 394.32
jubes 273.17 396.34
jublian 340.06
juby 379.16
juddenly 441.24
jugation 525.04
jugers 057.18
jugging 351.10
juggles 557.05
juice 261.F3 405.36 412.17 521.12
ju-jaw 256.19
juliennes 553.17
july 203.20
jumbo 359.04
jump 010.16
jumpy 332.24
jun 008.29
junct 496.24 573.20
junction 078.35 251.12 575.04 595.25
junctions 269.03
junctive 468.09
junctive 305.L1
junctively 524.19
junctor 125.07
jungation 143.13
junk 624.24
jupers 279.F22
jupeyjade 261.01
jure 594.05 617.10
jured 595.36
jures 496.01
jurious 234.29
jurylegs 060.11
justilloosing 180.03
justled 092.06
jute 110.26
jutes 067.17
Juxta-Mare 051.23
jypt 198.01

kaans 387.02
kaart 538.08
kabatcha 052.22 604.03
kabbis 456.07
kabulary 419.12
kack 531.25

kad 207.24
kadoodling 622.05
kaffier 059.29
kah 246.05
kak 137.12 534.03
kakould 171.10
kakruscam 352.33
kakyls 567.34
kale 261.06 296.F3
kalepe 229.13
kalified 005.16
kalled 083.35
kally 612.32
kalsson 323.16
kalus 480.20
kam 446.03
kan 053.24 206.02
kanbeard 532.08
kand 052.35
kandcropfs 306.02
kanek 258.17
kang 457.08
kankan- 113.09
kannan 028.19
kannonkabbis 456.07
kansakroid- 257.27
kant 297.09 414.22 432.32 559.27
kanter 561.02
kants 077.22 138.27
kants' 064.13
kapak- 257.27
kaparka 178.33
kapuk 257.27
karakter 098.09
karoff 049.03
karry 207.24
kars 365.17
kart 377.33
karthy 091.13
karu 010.17
kase 282.09
kasm 533.24
kat 184.31 197.10 354.26
kata 024.23 024.23
kating 078.24
katnaratatattar 339.18
kats 101.26 347.15 347.30 366.08
katsch 296.24
kattershin 333.07
kature 085.33
kavicks 101.33
kawn- 003.15
kay 172.24 510.08
Kay 282.23
kaya 471.03
kayas 348.23
kaylands 595.26
kayman 089.07
kaysure 063.04
keamic 102.05
kean 197.29
keaven 059.21
kedoer- 257.27
kee 485.29
keeamore 338.19
Keef-Rosses 310.16
keels 152.32
keen 210.19 321.34 565.19 620.24
keep 313.05
keeper 123.24 129.31 376.10 377.01 438.30 443.04 539.06
keepers 006.04 128.16 142.24
Keepers 370.08
keepers' 183.26
keeping 422.14
keeping 345.20
keepy 275.F1
kees 417.12
keet's 197.21
Keevers 310.17
keevna 331.25
keg 367.11
kehley 090.28
kek 033.24
kekkle 372.15
kel 228.17 408.20
kelled 324.13
kellous 099.20
kells 091.09
kelly 011.23 361.16 390.07 463.02 611.05 611.27
kelly-Balkally 612.32
kelly-on-the-Flure 389.07
kelly's 032.29
KELLYTHIGH 305.R1
kelt 413.01
keltian 311.22
kelts 227.05
kelt's 169.19
kempt 013.08
ken 348.23 588.20
kencap 023.21
kenend 248.15
kenic 240.26
Kenna's 589.18
kenner 321.01
kenny 142.04
kens 331.20
keptive 541.02
kerbrose 608.20
kerfully 536.17
kerks 005.33
kerl 462.17
kerls 314.31
kernwindup 090.08
kerretts 004.08
kerries 082.22 316.12 577.25
kerry 038.22 073.31 076.24 376.26
kers 350.26
kersse 322.09
kery 385.09
keses 280.03
kessy 471.02
keth 418.06
kettle 329.12
kewdy- 257.27
kewers 344.29
key 008.08 020.25 040.29 043.08 056.36 100.29 113.26 146.15 187.02 266.F1 306.09 315.22 317.05 317.05 337.29 368.10 368.14 416.06 422.07 464.29 516.20 527.01 533.08 538.15 568.25 568.26 602.34 616.11
key 176.15
key- 582.32
keycockeys 493.14
keyed 542.28 594.34
keyes 043.09
keygels 567.33
Key-Po 009.34
keypoo 256.02
keys 087.25 285.14 316.23 347.10 456.32 460.02 552.09
keys 106.11
key's 248.20
keys' 282.L2
keythighs 548.20
keyvilla 609.18
khean 123.16
Khorwan 352.34
khroustioun 396.19
kiang 199.19
kiboi 201.25
kick 375.04 423.10
kick 344.09
kicked 067.19
kicks 370.02
kid 441.09 527.05 562.34
kidimatzi 234.01
kidmass 215.21
kids 067.11
kiel 027.23
kiel 307.L1
kien 468.03
kies 587.27
kiest 502.24
kik 236.17
kikant 297.09
kil 175.05 412.36
kill 060.08 255.13 347.21 589.15
killer 122.26 247.02 430.33
killers 231.33
killer's 409.28
killing 008.23 618.26
kill's 051.16
killy-Belkelly 611.27
killy-Belkelly-Balkally 612.32
kilt 414.07 611.36
kiltic 326.09
kilty 057.09
kim 588.17 598.20
kimbo 249.23
kimono 214.11
kims 373.34
kin 011.34 017.02 020.05 032.06 039.04 051.15 053.21 079.20 081.18 086.06 094.17 102.09 102.09 110.08 113.08 166.08 169.19 180.08 182.11 184.08 187.08 201.26 205.18 207.14 220.15 229.30 240.30 253.16 253.31 257.22 262.24 268.15 290.F7 292.20 295.F1 311.07 326.30 328.05 329.04 333.04 346.28 367.33 369.11 369.28 372.09 377.28 379.07 381.36 387.28 395.35 413.21 414.04 420.09 428.03 429.17 445.05 446.05 464.11 464.19 478.14 478.24 485.13 507.28 510.16 533.06 537.35 537.35 550.15 552.36 565.13 575.25 576.15 576.28 578.16 581.22 603.20 610.31 621.25 627.23
kin 105.31 345.17
kinamucks 465.33
kinaton 235.27
kinatonetically 614.30
kinatown 484.16
kinbetts 242.05

kind 096.30 117.17 128.19 270.F4 297.F4 465.31 585.34 596.05
kind 268.L4
kinder 469.23
kindle 027.13
kindles 549.03
kindling 083.04 117.17
kindly 239.01
kinerny 264.L2 264.L2
kinesis 198.21
king 011.01 025.29 046.13 092.16 111.08 187.11 198.35 231.12 251.35 265.F2 270.03 279.F21 302.15 310.17 314.01 333.21 338.30 359.25 368.09 375.34 416.10 449.32 452.11 452.27 455.28 476.35 491.34 495.20 510.18 534.31 606.31 607.28 608.30 611.33 626.27
kingbilly 053.36
kingfar 310.10
kingfest 086.13
kinghorn 563.06
king-merchant 447.15
kingology 387.12
kingr 326.07
kings 030.09 049.10 316.27 436.11 603.29
king's 018.13 070.19 122.19 157.17
kingson 241.18
kingtone 144.30
kinguette 032.11
kinias 256.21
kinish 465.31
kinkinkankan- 113.09
kinloeflare 549.18
kinmidden 503.08
kinotons 005.32
kins 026.02 026.02 034.09 067.24 131.16 148.04 156.19 178.11 200.01 213.28 222.13 241.25 301.F1 311.23 317.22 320.26 324.12 355.22 364.28 365.12 370.35 397.28 405.31 464.19 500.02 528.36 569.34 577.26 582.19 587.20 588.18 596.17 600.23
kins 281.L2 353.27
kin's 334.35 578.33
kin's 106.17
kins' 250.31 485.21
kinsback 322.20
kinscum's 534.33
kinses 008.06 090.11 125.11
kinsin 437.29
kinson 043.10
kinstool 559.07
kinstuck 157.11
kinurney 264.L2
kinwhose 276.F4
kiosk 597.13
kipper 144.07
kippers 257.05
kips 234.20
kir 099.16
kirk 326.25
kirks 552.04
kirry 068.15
kis 568.19
kish 144.14 235.17 564.09
kish 347.36 424.03
kishabrack 495.23
kished 527.31
Kishgmard 371.22
kishouse 139.32
kiss 015.16 062.31 066.06 096.05 203.35 215.21 446.16 523.14 533.20 557.03
kiss 418.22
kissed 078.33 156.17
kisses 111.17
kisses 105.32
kissies 340.11
kissime 227.10
kissing 061.21 300.15 436.09
kissings 446.11
kissy 433.04
kit 055.07 415.34 454.35 548.14
kites 484.20
kitties 090.14
kittle 160.27
kitty 361.16
kivinis 536.31
kivis 347.35
kivs 540.36
kivvies 130.18
kiya 471.03
kkkrrr 378.07
klakka- 044.20
klaska- 044.20
klatscha- 044.20
klaus 155.31 155.31
klesters 571.36
kley 361.25 447.24
kleydoodle 258.05
kling 199.35 269.12 289.10 586.30
klings 068.35
kloe 290.24 375.33
kloefells 626.18
klokken 353.15
klopatz- 044.20
kloth 542.34
knaver 505.34
knavery 047.21
knaving 091.11
knee 067.23 211.28 230.05
knee 346.02
kneed 075.21 091.34
kneeghed 241.24
kneeghs 393.29
Kneels 291.10
kneepudsfrowse 526.25
knees 023.20 026.35 199.21 302.14 330.34 409.16 461.24 552.22 554.06
knell 388.34
knells 324.28
kneze 102.13
knickers 208.15
knie 194.28
knife 050.29 455.31
knight 126.18
knights 381.33
knived 162.05
knivery 510.28
knob 241.24 344.14 559.09
knobs 157.12 378.01
knock 447.15 530.33
knockers 445.31
knocker's 091.34
knolan 303.F3
knoll 499.23 552.23
knot 361.10
knots 162.10 202.20 225.36 302.F2 541.14
know 224.18 246.24 287.04 362.14 366.06 581.27
know- 255.25
knowable 062.32
known 026.21 060.27 079.17 091.28 096.29 110.30 123.22 179.04 239.30 321.09 380.23 503.08 575.19 596.10 616.30
knownst 445.26
knows 305.20 333.15
Knox-Gore 606.19
knuckledownedgment 344.08
knucks 467.30
knun 353.15
knut 512.16
ko 051.17 214.10 416.16
kock- 090.31
kockles 623.08
kodeboko 051.17
kodhus- 023.05
koe 506.35
koff's 339.15
kohahat 482.11
koiffed 339.11
kok's 008.20
kolist 491.06
kom 205.27
kome 182.23
kommen 553.34
komuck 091.01
kon- 044.20
kondylon 056.13
kong 119.25
kongsby- 582.32
konn- 003.15
konnen 323.26
kont 286.26
konton 508.12
K.O.O. 013.14
kook 295.F1
kooken 170.16
kookin 550.15
kool 533.26
kop 417.33
kopendolous 339.13
kopfgoknob 344.14
kopfs 272.16
kopp 078.05
kork 497.28
korked 176.30
korpff 250.04
korran 177.09
kors 622.24
kortas 247.29
kosmikon 468.21
kosouso 345.24
kost 320.09
kot 044.20 612.15
kot 163.06
koto 233.35
kotzdondher- 187.15
kould 171.10
kount 178.32
kov 201.34
kovskva 498.15
kowchaff 089.36
kox 567.24
Kraal 186.19
kraft 301.23
krahsing 230.26

kramadityationists 493.12
krass 323.21
krat 199.34
krauts 550.11
kraval 366.20
Kraw 284.F4
kraydoubray 340.01
kreations 585.01
kreator 411.15
kreening 392.28
krel 597.32
krepz 343.22
krieg 162.09
krieged 539.11
kring 279.05
krinm- 424.20
kriyamu 601.03
kroid- 257.27
Kroon-Kraal 186.19
kropper 331.16
kruscam 352.33
kry 093.13
ku 241.22 294.19
kuays 535.07
kubine 284.F4
kuffs 339.12
kujibun 484.26
kuk 116.32
kuki 245.02
kukuings 095.32
kulon 258.10 258.14 258.18
kum 027.10 422.26
kumed 314.34
kumiary 511.17
kums 288.17
kumst 593.17
kun 370.24
Kundred 376.02
kung 457.07
kunun 023.05
kupot 424.07
kur 220.35
kurat 056.19
kurias-in-Ashies 155.05
kurios 261.25
kurs 326.22
kurts 366.27
kurun- 023.05
kus 081.22
kushk 203.35
kusky 070.30
kussens 393.32 413.20
kut 233.32
kuvs 323.19
kwadded 516.09
kwart 291.22
kweeny 519.11
kyls 567.34
kyrienne 220.05
kyrious 565.03
kysh 084.16

là 332.18
laa 129.30 265.F4
laam 067.25
laames 497.33
laaming 566.09
lab 234.08 599.18
labashing 431.16
labella 209.24
labellars 243.07
la-Belle 246.20
la-Belle 540.10
labells 569.12
labials 465.26
lable 240.27
λαβον 269.L2
labour 436.20
laboured 489.31
labouring 006.23
laburt 339.06
lac 203.26 461.19
lace 207.05 233.09 235.34
387.04 569.23
laced 340.30
lacey 043.33
lach 099.27 596.14
la-Chapelle 080.36 334.36
lachasse 076.36
lache 165.14
lachers 502.14
lachk 503.23
lachsen 532.11
lachters 092.02
lachus 004.04
lachy 155.34 341.17
laciters 608.17
lacities 115.12
lack 166.30 285.01 428.22
lacking 289.11
lacks 315.28
lact 604.14
lad 051.08 219.22 231.29
251.01 251.01 331.26 343.08
442.24 493.03 496.11 548.10
562.10 563.26 593.15
ladaew 597.31
ladays 069.10 615.25
ladd 141.08
ladders 479.27
laddin 407.27
laddy- 044.20
lade 617.24
laded 291.05
laden 503.34 586.36
lader's 334.33
lades 134.05
lade's 069.28
ladey's 511.27
ladh 078.27
ladher 454.14
ladies 054.11 348.22 361.24
386.15 492.34 569.02
ladies' 616.15
ladim 560.19
ladin 073.35
lad'll 374.03
ladns 353.19
l-a-dreams 597.20
lads 075.08 210.04 465.15
467.25 570.04
ladst 130.03
lady 018.07 181.22 229.09
229.10 301.11 318.04 528.24
585.01 598.33
lady's 537.32
laender 382.28
laeugh 005.05
laf 567.18
lag 347.20 542.05
LAG 305.R1
lage 229.10
lagh 128.33 334.13
lagh- 332.05
lags 043.02 498.10 541.18
laguerre 233.30
lah 235.07
lahat 389.23
lahbluh 339.02
lahn 128.26
laid 138.13 177.21 239.03
285.F6 311.12 499.31
laidills 124.14
laiding 348.11
laids 438.23
laine 034.23
lained 247.19
lairy 040.30
laisance 327.24
laisy 173.15
lake 202.28 599.19
lake 348.04
lakriyamu 601.03
lala 026.13 450.26
lalah 067.33
lalahs 523.16
laling 483.24
lall 547.11
lalooly 595.17
lam 347.21 363.18 562.35
lamam 331.17
lamaya 627.03
lamb 065.07 091.32 223.01
lambe's 440.18
lambs 009.28
lamb's 178.13
lame 438.23
lament 189.34 614.02
lamie 584.31
lamina 183.01
laming 542.04
lammocks 358.34
lamode 221.24
lamore 600.11
lamos 327.33
lamourie 493.36
lamours 250.16
lamp 327.05 559.36 613.01
lamplight 438.30
lamps 305.F3
lan 327.19 536.35
lana 351.30
lanars 594.05
lance 059.07 084.02 265.08
562.32
lance 350.13
lanced 349.15
lancer 049.22
lancey 360.34
lanchonry 482.12
lancinant 597.24
lancollin 533.33
land 010.34 013.05 015.02
021.16 025.28 040.19 042.25
042.36 056.15 061.02 062.25
067.25 070.06 073.02 074.05
078.13 078.13 081.17 088.30
111.01 124.25 130.08 130.30
131.35 135.19 139.20 148.08
156.30 169.24 171.02 176.27
187.28 197.09 205.03 213.35
215.22 235.11 244.24 245.16
253.11 257.01 257.36 264.31
265.02 276.F7 295.19 311.05
313.19 318.32 320.28 323.20
335.07 337.34 340.24 347.11
352.09 353.15 359.26 359.35
378.06 387.09 388.19 390.35
392.31 392.34 403.18 412.04

427.22 428.07 435.25 437.05 446.25 446.25 469.11 479.29 480.10 488.30 510.13 525.30 528.18 544.01 547.16 548.01 548.01 553.30 579.28 582.25 583.20 589.22 599.23 601.35 605.04 605.04 615.28
land 440.21
landaddy- 332.05
landbut 581.33
landbutallyouknow 581.27
lande 157.36 158.11
lander 057.32 141.22 432.36 487.31 513.12 581.03 609.32
landers 040.34 228.07 398.05
landhar 492.26
landia 098.07
landine's 039.34
landing 539.18 605.20
landiskippy 011.10
landman's 521.07
landmon 279.F22
landmore 553.30
lando 279.F14 570.03
lando 409.29
lando's 385.35
landrua's 601.21
lands 097.03 290.18 348.16 385.09 455.08 474.18 496.08 542.02 595.26 600.35 604.24
land's 014.31 116.21 129.27 171.06 199.18 203.03 213.35 288.13 300.29 304.21 323.26 374.03 406.13 595.10
landsland 391.15
landsmen 311.01
land-West 514.24
landy 064.03
lane 051.08 100.03 180.10 210.10 287.30 373.25 390.04 491.15 550.30 568.22
laner 412.36
lanes 135.28
lanes' 354.33
laney 043.33 083.24 084.08 206.24
lang 148.23 289.19 338.22 547.33
langavore 393.29
langder 270.15
langing 445.10
lang-lang 054.15
langlast 006.26
lang's 353.31
langthis 232.32
language 421.17
lanisans 384.32
lanium 013.34
lanius 118.13
lanna 270.04
lannah 377.19 477.05
lannensis 600.29
lanner 100.06
lannludder 370.28
lanns 229.03 626.06
lanny 370.21
lanse 228.17
lansiman 057.03
lanst 601.05
lantern's 197.26
lanthas 351.14
Lanthern 010.27
lanthroa's 601.22
lantic's 336.27
lantlossly 610.07
lanus 163.24
lanver 422.02
lap 325.08 378.02 404.25 437.36
lap 344.02
lapaloosa 254.23
lapidating 544.13
lapluck 034.32
lapnow 348.16
lapping 057.11
laps 497.08
lapse 418.33
lapsing 333.06
lapucky 116.31
lapuloids 540.33
lard 215.26 433.35
larded 472.31
lard's 292.23
large 017.32 272.22 576.24
Large 472.10
larged 069.16 622.33
largement 310.06
laries 004.03 156.15
larinas 361.28
lariohoot 092.06
larion 361.30
laroo 450.06
larry 314.19
laryrook 184.16
las 547.21
lase 470.07
lasee 324.09
lash 287.F4
lashe 246.14
lashes 119.12
lashings 211.07
lasolas 014.08
lass 136.25 159.30 179.12 293.22 407.27 415.28 559.34
lassal 128.32
lasses 025.21 130.03 295.27
lassies 607.15
lasso 423.02
lassocrats 367.25
lassoed 426.27
last 006.26 186.11 231.20 304.21 527.35 551.01
last 354.03
lastered 543.10
lastics 447.34
lasting 220.29 499.02
last's 132.03
lastus 325.10
lat 030.10
latavala 178.33
latched 244.30
late 003.06 035.11 083.27 462.28
latentic 311.21
later 043.20 170.32 558.10
laterally 323.29
laterelly 337.04
laters 390.01
later's 533.23
latest 440.01
latetolove 472.19
latiginous 475.17
latin 467.14 495.27 596.25
latin- 219.17
latine 444.36
latinenties 336.32
LATIO 305.R1
lation 369.06
latria 157.19
lattary 350.27
latter 382.13 619.03
lattin 519.16
lauchterday 539.28
laud 032.27 172.19
lauded 550.03
laudered 269.05
lauding 234.21
laudits 043.34
laugh 037.28 084.32 312.13 532.08
laughed 326.36 492.04 554.08
laughing 283.18 361.18
laugh's 079.35
laughsed 580.07
laughter 062.06 087.16
laughterer 255.01
laum 360.27
laun 268.F6
launched 162.31
launds 614.08
launic 266.24
launstown 291.10
laups 576.20
laura's 327.15
lause 093.24
laut 484.09 609.10
lav 010.35
lava 595.27
laval 628.06
la-Valle 380.09
La-Valse's 601.25
lavant 285.16
lavaster 024.19
lave 225.14 244.04 290.03 439.32 564.21 621.24
laveras 009.36
lavered 448.13
laves 013.19 499.26
lavia 600.05
lavicious 349.28
lavs 338.21
law 021.14 083.34 169.04 203.17 284.F4 323.15 333.19 436.16 449.04 464.34 511.15 515.13 536.29 545.05 553.22
Law 324.22
lawd 490.04
lawd 341.30
lawdy 343.21
lawer 151.23
lawforms 596.24
lawful 144.31
lawfully 084.33
lawghurs 008.25
lawn 139.36 498.14
lawnd-via-Brigstow 537.24
lawney 091.18
lawnroc 388.02
lawn's 270.20
lawrie 550.31
lawrs 141.14
Lawry 514.24
laws 132.15 310.25 524.04 539.29 589.34
laws' 183.28
lawsey 064.13
lawshus 581.22
lawyer 374.20
lax 092.36 100.13 156.05

laxable 183.32
laxarksky 034.03
laxes 516.05
lay 035.23 315.05 351.32 357.03 395.19 492.14 510.14 510.15 533.29
laya 329.32
layars 502.05
layass 231.18
layed 072.29 405.01
layer 062.35
layers 043.03 165.26 337.21 572.05
layer's 056.11
layman 472.03
layor- 023.05
lays 041.01 471.16 577.24
lay's 506.09
laze 548.31
lazilee 232.35
lazily 121.24
lazy 214.20 360.07
le 528.14
lea 081.17
lead 547.15
leaded 144.06
leadeny 348.05
leader 214.11
leaders 497.33
leads 128.36
leaf 121.10 153.15 271.F5 407.24
leaffs 421.12
leaflong 470.25
Leafy 174.26
leagh 557.11
league 224.23 378.28 540.02
leagues 347.09
leak 058.25
leaking 042.10
leal 339.31
Leal-Ulster 482.29
lean 025.27 032.15 132.29 550.08
leans 291.21
leap 079.12 242.02 277.13 547.16
leaper 203.07
leaplights 571.01
leaps 303.02
learies 370.19
learis 255.15
learning 252.05 389.04
lears 176.13
learum 488.11
leary 243.29 566.36
Leary 043.21
leas 434.36
lease 534.22
leasely 232.20
leash 461.23 613.08
leashing 623.02
leass 141.34
least 227.34 237.04
leather 557.28
leathury 536.11 536.11
leau 383.21 553.14
leave 289.01 352.03 610.05 610.05
leaved 055.27 124.20 140.34 243.13 265.04 339.28 448.36 600.36 625.30
leavely 296.31
leavenweight 019.24
leaves 121.05 275.11 336.15 389.20 427.02 449.33 460.24 551.12 580.19 608.26
leaves 106.25
leavest 624.22
leavos 470.19
leay 212.15
lebens 339.21
lebone 192.29 550.10
lebuone 368.13
lech 061.14
lecherskithers' 323.18
lechheight 132.22
lecited 356.05
leckman 337.06
lecks 343.31 416.11
lecktuals 161.06
leckylike 438.26
lect 234.26
lection 094.10
lectium 153.30
lectralyse 067.08
lectual 268.28
led 011.21 124.19 223.12 405.34 495.36 588.25
ledan 420.26
ledar 065.13
ledas 279.F27
ledd 540.33
leddies 263.18
ledeosy 396.31
ledes 054.11
ledged 338.11
ledges 072.04
ledhropes 349.11
le-Duc 073.26
lee 129.30 133.21 232.35
Lee 324.22
leeft 150.09
leege 277.12
leek 568.27 623.26
leekie 210.08
leeks 449.33 550.10
leem 577.22
leeme 351.20
leems 619.26
leen 143.35 476.28
leeng 549.13
leep 397.16 476.22
leep 345.11
leeps 244.35
leepy 426.18
leer 051.07
leers 193.17
lees 008.04 356.11 508.19
Lees 330.17
leesh 192.26 229.17
leet 272.08
leetlecree 395.32
leetness 543.01
leetsfurcers 565.04
leff 081.35
leff's 049.13
lefft 583.35
leffy 332.28
left 054.11 510.35 580.01
lefts 357.21
leg 011.06 210.15 337.30 361.25 372.14 478.35 613.29
legal 131.22
legallooking 518.15
legels 587.26
legged 012.26 019.22 123.01 167.10 285.13 331.08
legger 166.17
legibelling 031.32
legible 119.15 421.34 482.21
legions 228.32
legitimate 543.35 572.31
legobrew 283.24
LEGOMENA 262.R1
legoturny 309.23
le-Greek 569.07
legs 059.09 060.11 155.28 188.29 225.09 233.02 251.18 256.36 284.02 316.32 351.20 498.03 522.16 582.22 594.28 607.20
legs 341.28
legsonder 310.16
legtium 550.06
leib 505.08
leich 037.01
leid 610.14
leid 151.19
leigh 257.17
leiney 295.F1
leinster 381.16
leish 335.17
leison 146.16
leisure 619.01
leize 018.02
leja 325.11
lekar 301.01
lelouh 258.03
lem 138.32
lemagne 280.28
lemamen 054.08
leman 485.07
lemanden 467.27
lemaney 423.04
lemans 243.28
lemeem 022.14
lemenly 126.16
lements 252.05
lemerched 412.10
lemm'as 182.21
lemon 331.17
lemonde 021.27
lemonities 188.25
lemonly 337.10
lemontary 422.28
lems 567.16
lemyums 590.11
lena 057.32 211.08
lenasmole 223.17
lend 200.19 239.35 288.24 312.06 335.12 546.33
lender 378.11
lenders 204.22 229.03 551.02
lender's 126.16
lends 593.13
lendsea 428.21
lene 164.31
lenes 609.04
lengro 472.22
length 146.04 166.18 394.17
leninsula 135.18
lenk 008.06
lenn 066.18 553.22
lens 271.20
lensed 113.28
lenta 099.09
lentam 238.25
lentay 240.16

lentous 611.29
lenu 184.13
leogos 349.22
leoled 152.23
leon 136.27 367.20 388.16 596.26
leosus 161.25
leotorium 503.05
leotto 251.25
lep 464.29 525.10
lepe 229.13
le-Pore-in 135.10
lepot 559.15
lepsy 232.30
lept 115.30
lepts 395.08
lesh 338.21
lesias 553.21
les-Pains 213.18
Less 569.14
lesse 203.08 277.11
lessk 361.13
lest 419.35 585.08 619.36
lest 339.25 354.03
lested 299.16
lestrine 407.14
lesvienne 348.36
letched 459.26
letheometry 370.13
lething 029.16
letin 393.01
letlitter 073.29
LETRISTICKS 281.R1
lets 221.23 224.12
lett 339.12
letta 087.23 157.08 157.17 159.05 159.06 329.35 422.33 561.11
lettas 340.18
letter 050.31 060.10 080.14 097.32 137.24 397.29 459.23
LETTER 308.16
letterday 456.34
lettered 424.23
lettering 114.18
letters 183.11 419.19 430.24
lettes 193.23
lettle 198.22
letto 281.18 281.19
lettres 534.21
leuds 283.24
leuf 240.24
leur 058.26
leure 064.19
leutey 493.21
leutheriodendron 042.20
levante 228.10
leveens 201.27
level 463.05
leven 388.12
leventh 517.33
levers 370.35
le-vert 605.11
levin 222.08 299.12
levoila 388.22
levution 338.06
lewd 203.32 325.08
lewder 323.09
lewed 289.09 531.14
lewis 352.14
lews 489.07
lex 023.20 083.09 169.03 571.08
lex 340.28 418.23 493.24
lexes 133.30 438.22
lexis 073.25
lextronite 349.14
ley 201.35 312.29
leyan 510.22
leyden 585.16
leyg 130.21
leypoe 427.27
leys 106.08
leyves 608.28
le-Zoyd 370.29
lezza 211.14
lezzo 281.19 336.24
lhee 628.14
li- 054.15
liablous 186.23
liaks 292.30
liando 038.14
lianess 568.04
lianess 352.18
liangly 415.24
liar 264.F3 606.30
liar's 008.20
libany 489.32
libatory 604.08
libbrium 599.18
libellous 048.18
liberal 477.19
liberated 342.34
libet 287.26
libies 548.29
libnium 310.07
libout 229.25
librated 379.07
librine 043.22
libris 477.23
libum 194.18
libus 013.27
lic 260.F1
licately 525.02
lice 007.18 344.32
licence 032.03 040.27
licensed 086.14
licet 042.32
lichinello 043.23
liciated 486.34
licious 421.04 528.17
licit 029.01
licitor's 270.05
lick 126.21 158.04 166.30 225.09 292.10 337.36 409.12 413.13 416.15 456.08 461.14 537.33
lick 105.23
lickathims 199.35
licked 160.20 470.29
licker 117.26
lickers 412.35
lickers' 056.36
lickey 422.07
licking 140.20 229.08 355.16 381.11
lickmaam's 277.F1
licks 525.08
lick's 485.01
licksher 280.10
licksheruthr 280.27
licky 392.25
lico 110.31
lic-on-you 174.15
licterate 336.31
lictuous 128.29
licyman 057.03
licy-pulicy 414.26
lid 140.27
lidebankum 445.34
li-di 345.23
lids 041.11 234.16 248.16
lie 357.08 430.31 445.34 534.10 584.09
lied 257.06 289.04 303.20 324.02 367.29 387.09 470.14 552.10 601.20
liefd 077.21
liefest 562.07
liefing 361.18
liegia 207.12
liek 409.24
lieme 485.18
liens 422.32
lienyouger 548.20
lieras 361.19
liers 540.23
lies 006.35 089.19 096.06 100.06 126.14 138.11 251.30 293.F1 364.10 368.11 437.17 441.26 462.11 525.02 601.16 618.07
liesemoutioun 354.20
liessian 151.22
liest 384.24
lietry 291.12
lieu 139.29 220.22
lievtonant 338.19
liewithhers 143.16
lif 318.24
life 113.03 150.33 261.19 407.20 517.20 589.22
life 338.06
lifeboat 065.30
lifer 356.34 444.11
liffe 210.18
liffey 054.24
liffi 159.12
liffic 576.36
liffious 317.32
lift 318.06 361.18 495.08
lifted 054.31 569.19
lifter 273.11
lifters 130.01
lifting 363.33
liftle 504.14
lig 028.05 265.10 502.17
ligant 014.04
ligate 508.22
ligere 163.04
liggymaglooral 381.30
light 003.13 004.33 011.17 020.20 024.01 030.13 064.06 100.23 131.28 145.36 147.25 190.33 208.28 224.12 236.02 266.13 320.26 321.18 328.23 358.01 378.17 383.20 397.29 417.07 425.21 427.16 438.30 441.16 449.07 450.12 450.14 460.29 495.13 495.14 498.25 506.27 544.35 560.04 587.03
light 399.25
lighted 135.30
lightful 291.25
lighting 011.12
lights 015.02 032.09 032.26 038.06 095.24 134.18 135.20 244.03 260.F3 475.10 492.09 571.01

light's 091.18 626.34
ligible 356.21
lign 296.27
lignol 338.21
ligns 364.03
liguchuna 346.15
ligue 256.36
ligum 296.F3
lihud 021.24
lik 254.30 578.36
likah's 434.29
liked 057.20 174.05 434.12 437.01
likeevna 331.25
likelihud 021.24
liken 050.06
likence- 113.09
likeness 033.29
likes 163.12 576.33
likethems 535.12
likevice 085.16
liking 483.19
likin's 106.17
likos 252.15
likun 370.24
lilakriyamu 601.03
lilesvienne 348.36
liletter 459.23
lils 338.21
lilts 112.33
lilty 373.34
lim 337.26
liman 594.34
limb 358.15 447.33
limbeina 221.25
limbinated 131.32
limbraves 246.33
limbs 238.30 337.26 431.14 537.29 559.36
lime 013.14 032.11
limed 506.07
limen 271.13
li-meng 338.26
liment 163.02
limentation 209.03
limers 174.28
limes 553.10
liminal 247.08 337.09
LIMINAL 276.R1
limitator 334.15
limited 046.07
limn 443.16
limned 357.29
limninging 607.24
limonde 327.25
limoney 344.21
limony 192.32
limpaloop 302.24
limpsests 182.02
lin 353.33
lina 210.10 304.19
linarsky 013.22
lina's 430.36
linda 445.32
linder 408.34
lindigan 611.06
line 008.30 031.36 040.30 073.32 088.17 178.05 186.07 202.08 212.22 223.32 294.02 398.09 447.01 513.30 535.01 548.29 555.14 560.30 582.32
line 071.26
linear 279.04
lined 007.20 140.29 156.20 208.17
linen 097.24 198.36
lines 161.01 235.23 245.11 252.15 299.19 310.05 380.17 587.26 595.14
liness 354.18
ling 395.19 419.12 538.31 569.12
lingalying 267.07
linger 475.22
linger 346.32
lingerer 192.05
lingt 242.08
Ling-Taou 081.34
lingua 117.14
lingual 099.34 122.32 392.24 424.02
lining 275.01 319.13
linings 121.20
lini's 531.21
link 166.26
linka 471.31
linkity 178.24
links 567.36 613.19
linn 264.28
linnates 345.28
linnen 577.29
linnies 494.10
linns 076.25
linnteerily 364.06
linnyflowers 354.26
lino 052.16
linoise 226.05
linorum 264.07
linos 042.30
linsh 243.25
linx 346.35
lio 488.10
liodraping 509.22
liom 156.16
lion 223.19 380.10 555.21
liond 361.23
lionial 488.31
lionic 513.17
lionized 483.22
lionola 488.09
lions 129.02 571.36 581.31
lion's 305.30
lior 594.34
liorten 315.32
lios 240.33
lip 069.34 170.29 326.35 377.26 397.19 539.24 558.22 597.12
lipe 578.21
liped 559.23
lipos 207.09
lipped 609.04
lipplads 570.04
lips 006.26 015.01 171.18 276.F6 441.12 442.15 455.01 463.36 511.31 533.02 577.26 603.02
lipses 156.13
liqueme 445.34
liquitudinis 100.34
liquorst 105.20
lire 488.26
lired 005.30
liric 513.32
lisa 304.03
lisato 255.01
lisha's 351.23
lisks 550.11
lisle 578.25
lisotoelles 601.28
lisp 254.13
lisp 105.11
lispering 580.19
liss 281.F2 296.F2
lissa 212.09 256.33
lissabon 442.09
lissciously 414.30
lisse 578.08
lissimime 612.12
lisslesoughts 379.15
list 006.33 072.23 192.01 350.34 491.06 524.25 535.08
listaman 202.15
listed 049.07
listen 237.09
listening 384.20
lister 546.04
listing 503.30
listingness 355.05
listings 414.29
listletomine 023.28
lists 009.28 113.27
list's 051.27
lit 004.19 053.16 083.27 178.14 222.36 226.27 241.13 256.08 494.02 578.23
lite 350.28 440.32 583.14
liteasy 153.07
lited 395.33
liter 247.02
literal 505.04
literately 431.32
literative 023.09
lites 241.35 549.17
litest 320.07
litey 461.04
lith 053.15 242.28 539.01
lithe 057.26
lithon 119.17
lithostroton 073.30
liths 594.22
lithual 512.16
lithy 503.04
lititians 173.16
litmious 184.36
litness 404.12
litopucos 011.14
litre 265.21
lit's 270.23
litten 259.03
litten's 528.04
litter 037.17 073.29 286.22 420.35
litterettes 284.15
litteris 512.17
litties 284.23
little 007.26 010.27 010.32 010.32 010.32 010.32 010.33 010.33 010.33 010.33 010.33 010.33 010.34 010.34 019.03 030.01 111.33 144.13 492.08 526.34
little 342.16
littled 358.07
littleme 446.02
littlers 083.35
littlesons 019.28
littoral 286.19
litz 182.07 421.27

litz 272.L3
litzas 551.33
liuia 236.17
liuto 043.33
liur 067.14
livable 186.03
livans 006.15
live 038.02 041.27 083.05 092.21 139.19 162.18 227.14 279.F21 293.20 311.22 316.14 395.17 481.25 500.02 525.29 533.27 538.21 551.22 612.10
lived 235.31 481.13 534.26
livehunkered 274.L3
lively 273.20
liven 546.02
liven 341.20
livenamond 503.32
livened 357.28 564.17
livengrene 329.06
livening 468.21
liventh 032.31
liver 021.28 200.28 211.03 334.15 464.13 499.28 620.13
liverian 381.18
liveried 241.28 358.23
livers 073.33 100.30
liverside 563.01
lives 019.08 138.25 272.F4 335.28 462.31 538.11 617.15
livetion 160.11
livial 213.32
livid 432.31
liviero 456.10
living 104.01 283.17 532.14 532.16 597.07
livisciously 437.04
livline 178.05
liv's 550.18
livver 097.30
lixion 346.13
liza 291.14
lizabeliza 328.36
lizards 101.25
liziies 114.05
lizod 452.11
lizzy's 111.06
llatin 495.27
lloyd 373.04
lo 202.22
load 006.27 193.01 199.23 448.15
loads 525.23
loaf 134.27 208.07 521.13
loafen 378.23
loafonwashed 159.27
loafs 498.07
loajazzyma 102.15
loan 624.07
loaner 520.09
loaves 598.20
lob 437.06
lobbicides 331.17
lobe 419.21 551.25 599.18
lobobo 622.23
located 189.30
location 071.16
locative 162.19
locaust 419.09
loch 248.23
lochlannensis 600.29
loch-Turnbull 171.31
lock 031.15 031.24 039.05 073.31 098.25 160.12 165.32 229.31 230.10 279.F02 284.F4 368.15 409.13 474.02 531.24 548.05 584.03 587.28 587.30 596.26 616.02
lock 071.28 340.07
locked 268.02 450.31 552.22
lockers 524.29
locks 256.36 337.31 566.29 615.23
locks 418.22
lockses' 028.06
lockstown 097.07
lockt 014.07 069.25
lockup 180.06
locky 151.24
loco 135.08
locous 295.01
locus 254.20
locution 155.08
locutioning 381.18
locutionist 072.16
locutor 177.19
locutory 575.04
lod 394.35
loddledome 379.15
lode 097.31 215.08 223.08
loded 356.07
lodgeable 420.23
lodgeries 607.07
lodher 454.14
lodotonates 353.23
loe 290.24 375.33 382.30
loefells 626.18
loeflare 549.18
loer 151.31
lofa 045.03
lofabishospastored 612.08
loffs 026.04
loft 017.28 031.01 191.16 204.19 243.28 361.18 506.02 569.19
loft 340.30
loftfan 262.22
loftical 005.01
lofts 255.08
log 073.07 077.13 154.23 581.16 607.21
logass 555.11
loge 128.01 583.04 605.07
loged 091.09
loger 091.15
logged 344.14 608.23
loggedlike 297.28
loggers 019.19
logging 151.17
logic 073.01 474.05
logical 109.13 134.34 220.30 310.21 373.21 396.14 465.12 468.08 483.36
logically 006.30 119.21 164.16 612.19
LOGICUM 264.R1
logion's 317.02
logistic 123.18
logium 410.04
logos 194.16
logosis 341.30
logs 242.29 461.20
logue 327.03 470.09
logues 398.03
lohn 324.16
lohned 049.06
lohs 019.31
loid 359.09 471.12
loider 336.24
loids 540.33
loined 115.13 419.29
loire 207.11 419.12
lois 086.07
loitez 213.19
loits 187.15
loits 272.L4
lok 051.16
lokbloon 389.27
lokki- 424.20
loky 368.10
lold 117.10
loll 065.17 525.05
lollall 547.11
loly 089.35
lom 363.18
lomansch 085.25
lombarouter 314.11
lombos 120.02
lombs 335.28
lomdree 600.20
lome 256.11
lommey's 093.03
lomn 577.08
lomnones 288.14
lomon 198.04
lon 318.04
lona 211.07
lonche 028.09
lond 261.F2 294.04 618.22 626.28
londe 609.17
lone 007.28 017.33 062.04 117.10 215.33 237.03 361.19 450.28 469.21 498.12 520.18 581.34
lonely 092.25 152.19
lones 113.06 378.23 603.26
lone's 161.03
lonettes 273.18
lonety 598.18
long 007.01 013.04 029.03 081.31 102.28 111.33 173.19 184.07 188.03 269.F4 296.04 312.27 315.32 363.11 371.33 415.32 461.12 462.03 469.21 470.25 473.12 485.33 518.10 531.18 579.24 585.29 587.36 603.09
longas 239.05
longd 323.20
longe 406.03
longed 041.31 600.19
longement 132.03
longer 191.05
longfella 082.13
longi 519.08
longing 495.23
longlegs 498.03
longopatom 344.30
longs 545.24 567.01
long's 071.35
longsidethat 612.10
longst 085.09
lonian 417.12
lonians 381.05
lonts 606.30

lontseng 611.30
loo 046.33 073.05 131.35 200.36 359.19 541.22 541.22 541.22
loo 176.10
lood 425.28
looderamaun- 314.08
loof 274.26 476.07 623.19
loofer's 395.34
loofliest 265.29
loogged 428.20
loogions 509.34
looing 324.18
look 007.18 021.18 022.05 022.29 059.18 130.33 162.36 182.20 312.30 324.33 534.31 544.29 556.23 570.32
look 418.35
looked 542.15
lookedfor 108.32
looker 191.25
lookers 125.09 355.24
looking 061.04 092.25 095.14 109.07 111.19 120.18 128.06 153.03 289.11 416.05 416.07 442.02 467.10 518.15 589.23
lookingated 113.09
lookly 404.32
lookond 520.27
loola 475.02 475.14
lools 373.28
looly 178.16 595.17
loom 012.13 323.27 329.26 385.29
loomenos 615.08
loon 320.09 327.33 370.14 389.27 534.17
loonade 513.21
looney 331.12 624.24
loonik 432.20
Looniys 464.07
loons 094.35 131.29
loop 295.32 302.24 325.09 333.28 379.30 394.14 562.16 569.05 597.20
looped 423.06 621.20
looper 110.31 327.01
loopers 288.F4
looping 394.11
loopings 551.01
looplashes 119.12
loops 510.28 557.02
looral 381.30
looralooraloomenos 615.08
loos 008.14 443.36
loosa 254.23 494.25
loose 008.02 029.03 224.35 236.19 314.26 343.24 498.23 522.34 581.01 617.04
loosed 113.20 183.34 219.16
loosely 413.27
loosh 064.28
looshoo- 257.27
loosies 531.18
loosing 180.03 607.10
loost 376.08
loosus 625.22
loot 146.17 204.16 290.18 333.12 354.23 478.34 610.14
looter 379.08
loothering 195.02 195.03
lootie 058.24
looting 359.16
lootly 372.34
loover 093.07
looves 434.06
lop 029.03 058.04 063.32 232.34 420.27 496.36
lopalombarouter 314.11
lope 359.14
loped 099.19 324.29 378.35
loper 048.15
loper's 457.14
lopes 520.25 622.09
lopocattls 386.35
lopon 443.06
lopos 107.14
loppics 386.06
lopping 039.35
lops 584.13
lops 349.30
lop's 241.15
lopulos 306.10
lopysius 155.31
loquent 283.08
loquohy 290.F6
lora 458.14
lord 025.27 074.04 097.24 135.08 135.09 141.24 254.36 316.06 325.16 336.13 355.25 362.09 565.12
lord 106.33
lorded 472.30
lord's 541.09
lore 036.17 539.24
lores 011.33
lore's 480.06
lorians 004.07
loring 064.17
lorium 410.04
lors 010.03 025.10
lors 290.18
losby 244.07
lose 029.28 143.22 185.28 246.27 360.25 472.07 475.14 488.35 609.02
loseher 279.F09
loser 512.18
loserem 304.31
losh 137.29
losh 346.02
losha 106.23
loshmat 562.01
losk 162.15
losobuth 561.08
loss 018.22 318.18 366.03 410.04 420.27 548.35
lossa 551.35 551.35
lossay's 492.10
lossegg 129.14
losses 261.12
lossh 349.16
lossies 497.19
lossly 610.07
lossness 023.19
lossyhair 265.21
lost 118.07 238.29 239.03 363.23 374.11 596.10
loster 265.02
lostures 317.35
losy 200.15
lot 019.18 063.22 143.07 165.21 325.08 410.11 582.03 586.24
lote 531.17
loth 542.34
lothe 254.14
lothe 105.12
lotions 166.27
lots 036.13 225.36 324.14 333.36 534.19 550.15 596.12
lotsphilots 062.16
lottery 359.16
lottes 181.29
lotte's 532.22
lotticism 374.13
lotting 102.16
lotto 281.19
lotts 203.06 458.23 625.25
lottylike 101.03
lotwashipper 408.35
loud 077.29 180.34 257.30 267.17 305.26 440.08 441.25 522.26 601.28
louderamain 257.33
louderamainagain 258.19
loud's 353.16
lough 039.09 062.35 248.30
loughed 023.29 418.03
lough-le-vert 605.11
Loughlin 106.07
Loughlins 049.33
loughmoor 577.14
louh 258.03
Louis 246.17
loung 225.17
lounges 321.34
loup 108.27 547.16
loupa 339.32
loups 526.18
lour 234.20
louse 338.04
loused 175.03
louset 323.04
lousiman 057.03
lousmei 068.18
lousom 338.34
lousties 350.15
lousy 301.08
lout 010.04 281.F2 286.F5 314.29
louta 567.35
louth 049.15
lovah 207.09
lovar's 540.31
lovar's 294.18
love 021.09 022.24 067.36 093.32 159.14 253.04 288.10 289.04 300.28 325.30 328.07 338.31 370.04 406.35 406.35 472.19 486.22
loved 132.24 296.23 410.26 413.25 448.11 488.04 524.06 533.28 619.03
loven 220.21
lover 056.15 074.12 224.14 294.27 299.09 301.F3 325.12 356.09 383.16 478.36 485.20 620.14
lovers 268.F4 520.19
lover's 567.08
loverum 610.06
lovery 140.23
loves 004.09 205.18 530.15 625.24
love's 625.08
loving 030.18 144.28 438.02
lovis 388.08
lovs 468.13

lov's 532.22
lovving 394.06
low 023.16 032.10 141.24
153.18 175.03 203.01 203.18
214.30 265.12 277.16 290.24
296.27 301.F4 316.03 319.01
336.29 360.03 379.10 427.18
434.08 452.16 488.11 553.20
569.24 617.10
low 105.30 199.28
lowed 007.33
lower 064.10 318.13
lower's 364.04
lowes 343.17
lowing 154.35 175.04 510.26
lowlane 491.15
lowlap 437.36
lowly 337.26
lowm 160.02
lowman's 334.36
lown 333.14
lowp 072.09
lowpattern 029.23
lowre 313.05 496.13
lowrings 338.28
lows 168.02 202.17 297.02
333.01 470.30
lows 346.31
low's 538.29 549.18
lowshure 549.27
lowswaying 100.21
lowther 266.10
loy 378.09 431.04 517.30
loyd 373.04 616.01
loydhaired 609.03
loyd's 590.05
loyiss 453.26
loyrge 533.35
loze 348.08
luaritzas 572.15
lubberate 300.23
lubber's 173.09
lubdead 488.20
lubejubes 396.34
luber 157.01
lubrate 343.28
lubrated 305.03
luc 253.12
lucalised 087.18
lucanized 545.33
luccia 157.24
lucefinis 228.14
lucens 234.08
lucid 108.02
luck 034.32 210.05 417.07
luck- 378.09
lucks 200.08
lucksarsoon 344.01
lucky 055.28 307.F7 315.15
417.10 502.12
lucre 200.20
lucrey 358.09
lucrine 112.12
lucrum 050.13
lucrumines 613.17
luct 374.12
luctingly 092.04
luction 162.13
lucylamp 327.05
lud 153.24
ludd 331.09
ludder 370.28
luddy- 044.20
lude 426.33
ludillongi 519.08
ludination 372.24
luding 419.24 507.28
ludin's 108.27
ludium 469.29
lueamoore 069.06
luego 470.33
luffer 590.20
lug 310.11
luggars- 023.28
lugged 343.27
lugh 479.06
lughurutty 493.13
lugical 165.21
lugs 180.24 449.20 595.16
luhy 340.06
Luinn 328.02
luir 458.34
luius 484.11
lujo 397.11 398.04 476.32
lujorum 290.F3
luka 609.07
lukajoni 609.08
luke 529.20
lukin 110.08
lukkilokki- 424.20
lulia 083.34 083.34
lull 246.03
lulled 078.04
lullu 353.28
lulo 052.14
luls 128.36
lulutent 076.30
luly 089.36 533.06
lum 056.34
lumballando 409.29
lumbs 319.17
lumbumus 598.05
lumbunate 607.21
lumbus 484.32
lume 244.26 433.01
lumen 255.19 610.16
lumes 155.27
lumin 265.27
luminated 461.18
luminatedhave 278.04
luminatured 568.34
luminous 155.20
lummmm 595.19
lump 323.23 332.17 332.17
363.24 613.01
lumpfleeter 377.27
lumphantes 502.10
lumply 595.19
lumps 374.06 380.07
lumpsk 323.28
lums 478.12
lumses 242.01
lun 351.09
luna 627.30
lunch 240.32 406.09
lund 069.08 602.17
lunder 102.10 578.22
lung 057.14 155.24 331.25
lungged 426.05
lunkenend 248.15
lunn 370.28
lunthers 352.09
lunuk- 023.05
luono 081.33
lup 397.19
lupa 550.15
lupalleaps 303.02
lupe 325.30
lupkabulary 419.12
luponing 484.02
luppe 542.09
lupped 310.33
lupping 395.06
lupsuppy 417.15
lupsus 005.27
lupty 396.29
lure 359.34 478.23 560.27
lured 548.11
lurem 513.02
lure's 061.04
lurning 222.25
lusch 406.06
luscious 148.01 482.05
luse 261.02 283.10
lusi 290.19
lusk 338.17 576.03
lust 077.31 107.13 576.21
lusting 222.30
lustre 528.19
lustred 349.15
lustrelike 032.26
lustriously 483.22
lusts 367.14 444.25
lusty 508.29
lut 479.13
lutent 076.30
luteral 297.27
lutor 387.13
luve 208.25
luvey 297.22
luvia 107.17 546.35 547.05
585.32
luvial 047.04 080.25 213.32
404.01
luvii 287.25
luvious 014.16 182.11
luvium 095.16 251.02
luvs 479.15
luv's 315.13
luvu 594.23
luwed 319.12
lux 431.36
lux 307.L1
luxes 429.17
luxiously 038.04
luxty 566.28
lwd 482.13
lycopodium 334.03
lyd 331.28
lyffe 387.09
lyg 471.31
lying 267.07
lyingplace 262.F1
lyke 413.07 600.24
lykeses 280.03
lykkhean 123.16
lylac 461.19
lylaw 511.15
lymp 167.22 261.11
lympiading 084.31
lyn 044.11 062.34
lyng 069.17 069.18 516.07
lynn 248.07
Lynn 148.36
lynt 232.13
lyon 273.27
lyonview 018.29
lyovyover 350.06
Lyph 355.32

lyphics 570.06
lyputtana 583.09
lyrical 452.03 615.04
lys 057.28 155.25 359.32
lys 354.14
lysaloe 359.33
lyst 186.11
lysus 196.21
lyt 237.09 615.24
lytl 105.10
lytrical 415.01
lyzettes 237.02

ma 020.17 033.18 050.06 056.31 069.14 079.28 092.25 093.22 093.22 098.04 100.36 102.15 115.32 120.34 124.16 130.05 133.36 135.27 143.03 147.14 147.15 195.04 200.33 205.31 224.29 224.30 241.21 256.04 260.F1 261.F2 264.12 264.13 268.24 273.02 289.29 290.27 290.27 297.30 298.27 306.F1 306.F1 307.04 318.06 332.13 348.11 376.01 380.25 389.15 395.23 426.03 433.03 450.32 456.27 461.17 471.05 474.05 487.22 502.36 517.02 517.25 562.06 568.01 578.05 580.20 586.07 595.27 596.24 598.12 601.28 602.13 619.16 621.08 621.09 625.27
ma 085.13 121.09 268.L3 302.L2 339.33 345.17 445.13
maam's 277.F1
maans 549.10
maas 101.09
maasch 491.15
mable 508.26
mac 176.36 329.18 559.35
macan 463.22
macarett 501.04
macchiavelluti 251.26
mace 568.30 604.22
mach 228.15
machine 503.02 626.15
machrees 286.14
macht 240.13
machus' 100.16
mack 137.02 358.21 450.25
mackenzies 065.12
macks 019.09
macmacmac- 332.05
macmahonitch 529.16
macolacion 528.20
macormack 450.25
macoulored 443.34
macrees 343.11
macrobius 255.20
macron 318.09
macsaint 267.F1
maculacy 247.28
maculate 045.14
maculatus 191.13
mad 010.09 038.14 103.08 158.03 190.32 291.24 374.22 473.07 509.13 577.01
madam 019.30
made 084.28 089.30 138.07 184.04 192.27 230.34 232.34 252.26 320.11 321.09 357.30 381.14 432.24 454.36 504.02 561.26 581.17 581.36
made-earsy 314.27
mades 239.10
made's 008.32 464.06
madethemology 374.17
madhawn 443.02
madityationists 493.12
mado 240.07
madomina 471.03
madories 395.09
madorion 398.18
madoro 263.F3
madory 395.10
mads 070.02 386.28 410.32
madst 086.18
maer 317.18 444.32
mag 407.04
magandy 276.17
magareen 376.18
magd 436.12 540.22
mage 053.03 072.20 507.02 543.21
magees 027.20
magellan 512.05
magen 162.28
mages 486.34
mage's 142.13
maggerby- 113.09
maggin 337.18
maggs 352.05
magh 054.19 324.10 381.22
maglooral 381.30
magna 625.26
magnage 450.23
magne 280.28
magnetic 497.16
magnian 352.11
magnom 020.07
magnum 404.26
magoaded 180.03
magog 222.14
magreeth 243.03
magtog 246.05
magula 162.12
magunnded 323.27
mah 032.04 374.22
maher 221.23
Mahon 099.28
mahonitch 529.16
mahs 346.05
mai 471.01
maid 014.33 015.30 138.08 148.24 149.09 164.08 212.17 247.34 257.01 276.F2 352.08 364.03 390.31 428.08 433.28 525.13
maid 433.19
maidens 601.08
maidesses 011.31
maidies 192.02
maids 126.19 181.10 504.21 514.26 526.23 543.21
maids 104.21
maid's 059.36 181.17
maids' 066.13 183.25 229.14
maierians 345.01
mail 240.12 364.05 457.02 471.26 563.16 565.32
Mailey 220.11
mailia 410.23
maimed 489.31
maimthem 504.31
main 024.06 081.08 224.34 257.33 302.25 346.27 469.25 473.25 527.21
main 352.21
mainagain 258.19
maining 239.34
maintalish 296.L1
maios 553.16
maires 256.20
maisigheds 387.21
maister 568.17
major 029.02 442.06 572.21
major's 331.02
mak 212.13 498.16
make 197.10 278.12 433.27
maked 551.11
makenoise 031.21
maker 060.27 087.06 126.10 206.07 247.02 301.04 317.23 320.17 618.30
makers 052.14 059.18 310.15 585.15
makers 342.09
maker's 335.11 583.28
making 124.29 192.36 467.09
makor 342.28
makt 547.14
mal 233.32 251.36 289.11 334.15 599.05
mala 184.28 298.04
malaid 285.F6
male 430.22 485.26 577.01 581.18 594.31 617.25
malelouh 258.03
malency 318.02
malhill 132.22
malice 021.21 488.16
malicked 470.29
malinks 613.19
mall 389.07 581.15
mallards 080.09
mallkalled 083.35
mallow 575.17
malls 298.30
mallt 240.29
malong 485.33
mals 005.01
mals 341.04
malster 062.03
malt 021.35 037.34 086.06
mam 331.17 478.33 491.29 528.10
mama 586.07
mamahalla 362.22
mamen 054.08
mamma 461.17
mammy's 626.27
mana 184.19 287.21
manage 270.10
manager's 558.36
managh 284.06
manahoussy 578.32
manangel 505.33
mance 310.22
manchap 221.34
manche 199.34
manclatter 147.21
mancowls 456.16
mancy 051.35 117.33 228.20 281.14
mancynaves 370.15
mand 235.29 317.28 325.22 366.26 403.12 435.28 514.02

manded 326.23
manden 467.27
mandodr- 424.20
mandovites 048.24
mandrite 496.08
mandy 200.07
mane 123.16 179.21 230.33 310.20
manescu 484.29
manesir 150.16
manessy 505.24
manet 272.05
maney 207.25 423.04
mange 494.21
manged 164.28
mangra 009.13
mangut 214.19
mani 237.30
mania 228.19 416.30 480.21 521.32
maniac 471.14
manian 261.15
manic 263.10
manish 425.16
manisht 320.05
manitis 151.10
manize 466.25
manlake 599.19
manlooking 416.07
manmarked 547.33
manmaun 614.17
mann 042.20 048.10 066.32 071.08 088.23 129.16 250.19 250.21 328.26 356.02 503.10 578.11 578.11 610.22
mann 071.34
manner 033.18
Mannigan's 523.18
mannity 042.14
manns 358.23
manns 345.04
mann's 278.F3
mannstown 243.26
manny 455.09 455.10 455.10
mano 389.19
manocturne 328.17
manometer 608.10
manon 258.22 338.03
manonger 108.18
manorum 543.16
manos 564.09
manovers 570.05
manoverum 361.32
manox 512.04
manright 546.20
mansbell 278.11
mansboxer 142.11
mansch 085.25
manschy 243.16
manse 528.09
manseprated 239.21
mansfluh 037.20
mansionables 052.26
mansioned 265.04
mansions 367.27
mansland 265.02
manspare 077.16
manstongue 355.24
manstown 047.22
manswold 073.28
mant 615.32
mant 353.06
mantanai 595.20
mantarchy 167.06
mantaya 498.15
manteau 240.36
manted 601.05
manths 421.34
manti 237.26
mantic 241.08 284.27
mantics 172.20
mantitions 571.22
mantle 024.09 242.35
mantled 125.02
mantrue 403.22
mants 414.06
mantuam 113.02
manu 364.33
man-up-in-the-Sky 543.29
manvantora 598.33
manvir 465.07
manx 085.36
many 094.27 131.08 171.19 355.22 408.13 442.03 593.05 600.30
many 106.08
manychiel 472.22
manyeth 274.20
manygoround 525.17
manyness 122.36
manything 417.26
manzelles 470.32
map 042.15 287.14
mar 010.06 010.18 317.17 319.34 329.04
Mara 040.16 122.16 122.19 460.17
Mara 270.L2
maraca 255.15
maranth 561.21
marazalles 075.03
marble 207.07
marc 249.03 253.12
march 282.26 380.12
marchands 352.26
marchers 469.12
marching 210.15 323.31
mard 345.13 371.22
mare 279.F09 433.01 576.28 583.09
Mare 051.23
marea 198.08 244.14
maree 186.25
marellous 180.10
Marengo 223.16
marginable 004.19
margrits 249.12
mari 203.24
maria 228.34
marian 177.02
maried 050.11
maries 126.18 435.30 569.10
marilla 184.20
marine 587.17
marines 225.05
mario 450.24
Mario 407.16
Marios 243.35
mark 009.32 017.01 108.22 110.19 112.32 114.32 137.25 189.06 192.21 222.03 244.14 262.F1 301.F5 419.28 421.29 430.06 463.29 473.09 493.13 529.35 533.35 567.12 601.36 606.26
markable 086.32 127.35 532.35
markably 123.35 368.17
marked 031.24 547.33 581.21
marken 126.23
market 298.06 316.30
marketable 533.31
marking 149.20 370.09
marklable 240.27
marks 066.01 080.10 127.34 161.08 181.24 238.01 251.17 283.23 421.18 431.02
mark's 553.23
marly 242.02
marm 291.22 587.10 624.19
maro 499.07
marodnimad 509.13
maronite's 470.14
maroon 015.04
marooned 549.22
marpoorter 327.33
marqueza 328.14
marriage 210.12
married 176.13
marriedad 020.31
marriment 062.07
marry 197.16 324.33
mars 339.15 540.15
marsch 332.18
marshal 099.24
marshy 017.08
martem 455.11
martial 149.07
martin 086.02 377.10
martin 354.16 419.08
martins 007.04 392.03 467.33
martir 499.09
maru 609.07
maruluka 609.07
marulukajoni 609.08
marxing 083.15
mary 389.13
maryllis 609.12
mas 091.05 092.30 101.28 176.26 182.24 186.16 209.25 211.04 219.22 243.27 281.01 296.01 301.F5 328.21 374.10 421.02 460.35 483.35 556.05 577.32 598.15
mas 573.30
ma's 166.16 204.05 253.28 268.17 517.19 578.22
maserovmeravmerouvian 113.04
mash 466.12
mashed 110.14
mashkt 547.14
masiada 054.17
masine 294.25
mask 131.12 590.24
masker's 404.27
masks 221.27
masque 603.03
mass 093.09 111.29 125.01 197.15 215.21 238.21 413.24 483.13
mass 341.24
massed 023.16 332.26 358.13
masser 186.35
massing 457.30
massofmancynaves 370.15
mast 248.31 351.15 504.23 590.15
master 004.04 035.30 237.13 251.28 279.F09 337.18 358.18 360.36 462.02 479.29 560.29

568.35 587.33 596.18 613.32 624.11
master-in-chief 127.10
masters 186.36 385.35 394.17 395.06 477.13
master's 036.27 055.01 305.31
mastoly 485.31
mastory 397.07
mastress 228.17
masts 407.20
masy 493.07
mat 137.04 198.13 262.F4 524.25 562.01
mata 135.16
mataphoron 606.27
matchemable 508.26
mate 125.08 134.01 232.19 243.32 350.35 387.23 417.20 423.30 461.24 487.13 499.01 523.23 548.07 575.27 577.04 605.04
mate 072.15
mated 308.L2
matehim 589.35
mately 482.31
mater 297.01 560.28
materialities 394.32
mates 049.19 055.04 229.01 526.36 535.33
matetam 336.09
matha 329.14
mathematical 394.31
mather 296.21
mathes 595.17
mathunara- 023.05
matically 129.19 296.26
matick 268.08
mating 560.11
mato 499.07
matoysed 133.26
matron 086.19 257.05
matt 415.13 560.25
matter 258.33 478.17
matterafact 183.07
matterpoetic 468.10
mature 189.28 425.31
matures 239.11
matzi 234.01
maud 451.03
mauderman 596.14
maukins 365.12
maul 292.27 317.16
mauling 186.23
maultaneously 161.12
maun 479.35 614.17
mauns- 314.08
maunt 384.30
mauranna 102.28
maurius 113.04
maw 146.04
mawm 193.30
mawther 146.05
max 342.02
maxodias 498.04
may 352.10 471.01
maya 627.03
mayability 597.28
maycallher 396.07
maycodding 346.24
maycuddler 608.25
maycull 223.14
mayers' 364.26
mayne 363.08
maynoother 371.26
mayo 197.35
mayor 138.24
mayor-king-merchant 447.15
mayres 379.05
may's 227.17 374.07
maywantme 070.17
maze 411.08
mazed 389.27
mazes 221.20
mazeus 504.19
mazia 627.28
maziful 104.01
meade 286.07 568.22
meadow 315.33
meads 558.19
meagre 456.11
meal 017.16 301.28 397.33 457.04 582.16
mealahmalong 485.33
mealers 545.27
mealian 347.10
mealine 008.30
meals 283.23
mealturn 621.14
meaminning 267.03
mean 049.05 339.09 444.05 448.33 494.31 538.18
meand 170.10
meandine 542.08
meaning 077.26
meanium 113.03
meanour 189.26
means 285.27 333.15 465.11 522.08
meansuniumgetherum 186.25
meant 062.03 082.10 318.31 515.13 535.18
meant 231.08
meantry 286.L4
meants 318.26
mear 372.02
meas 607.20
mease 329.02
meash 260.F1
meat 211.23 242.25 428.01 490.20 566.14 594.32
meated 498.09
meathes 595.17
meats 129.01 306.03 550.14
meby 611.04 611.26
mecarott 390.25
mecula's 601.22
med 199.09 372.01
medallised 551.32
mede 269.18 525.19 583.11
medears' 328.20
mediant 033.03
mediata 228.23
medy 503.17
mee 099.31 205.31 628.14
meeching 583.04
meem 022.14
meena 585.24
meeng 395.02
Meer 205.34
meerme 409.17
meerschall 133.21
meet 238.06 259.06
meet 339.24
meethes 595.17
meetim 336.09
meeting 051.10
meffible 183.14
meg 086.19 199.21
meggs 333.33
Meghisthest 269.19
mei 068.18 529.34
meid 239.18
meidagad 009.26
mein 330.24
meinded 252.16
meining 267.03
meising 417.28
meister 191.35
mejig 146.02 479.14
mejip 458.27
meknot 361.10
mel 181.28 201.02 248.02 451.07 539.22 541.31 586.22
mela 235.32 236.06
mela 307.L1
melakins 355.22
melas 237.36
meleg 011.06
melhion 352.17
meliamurphies 293.10
melimen 271.13
melise 244.30
melittle 111.33
melk 262.22 425.09
mell 323.01 547.02
mellar 444.13
mella's 354.26
melle 560.01 563.05
mellian 443.10
mellow 060.29
mellow 346.12
mells 019.08
mellt 436.18
melo 253.24
melode 223.08
melodious 184.15
melong 111.33
melosophopancreates 088.09
meltingmoult 241.24
meltingworks 614.31
melucky 315.15
melumpsk 323.28
mem 518.33
member 488.18 493.17 493.27
members 008.06 557.15
memdes 542.24
meme 054.16
memer 445.13
memorial 600.26
memormee 628.14
mems 235.05
mena 212.12 518.24
menagerie 476.25
menag's 334.25
menal 296.04 352.01
mena's 601.23
menassed 492.06
mend 074.15 505.34 510.20
mended 440.35
mendly 029.35
mendoso 312.08
mends 245.10 326.02 548.27
mene 439.14 440.35
meneck's 334.25
mened 075.20
menen 285.18
menessy 513.31
menfichue 268.13
meng 338.26 414.28 427.14

mengro 171.29
mengst 476.20 505.16
mengst 123.21
menial 321.23 345.01
menie 244.05
meniere 075.03
mening 625.26
menlivers 100.30
menn 503.10
meno 572.16
menon 059.16 116.33
menos 615.08
menos 174.19
menot 215.08
menots 389.02 588.09
menotting 507.14
me-nought 227.16
menoyous 156.12
mens 013.11 232.07 245.08 325.16 351.23 502.30 621.35 628.06
mens 185.17
mens' 528.33
mensch 318.27 397.23
mensch 161.03
mensesness 241.11
mensipater 342.26
mensky 034.18
mensy 344.30
ment 025.16
menta 613.18
mental 035.22 171.18 366.07 440.21 452.03
mentalist 072.21
mentally 056.13 115.33 149.32
mentalness 543.07
menti 062.26
mentially 610.01
mentically 394.14
mentionability 107.07
mentionable 300.03 420.04
mentionablest 320.12
mentioned 299.06
mentious 159.34
mentivorous 227.35
mento 220.21
mentoed 545.24
mentrousnest 241.10
menuensoes 425.18
menufactors 027.17
meo 238.35 485.34
me-o'er-the-hazy 111.24
meoil 603.01
me-ondenees 139.21
meots 350.22
mequick 215.07
meramybows 011.12
meravmerouvian 113.04
merchant 447.15
merched 412.10
mercies 349.25
mercy 534.13
mercyonhurs 234.28
mere 243.05 493.12 583.12 627.05
mere 212.36
mère 256.20
mère 548.28
mere's 540.25
merge 017.24 049.36
mergeant 318.34
merged 363.21
mergent 055.11
merger 232.32
merges 310.24 428.17
mergreen 032.29
merian 504.07
merically 185.29
mericle 326.31
meridian 430.04
meries 348.07
merigas 171.35
merin 332.14
meritus 392.14
mermauderman 596.14
mernians 376.12
merollingeyes 011.06
meroughgorude 240.18
merouvian 113.04
merried 226.18
merriers 619.28
merries 312.28 508.20
merrnion 129.23
merry 378.33 488.32 588.17
mers 498.29
mer's 476.07
mertime 085.36
merul 518.23
merzial 069.35
mes 504.28
meselles 339.16
meselps 612.24
meses 452.34
mesh 221.34 267.13 546.04
meskad 207.24
mesmer 360.24
mesnider 320.04
mess 091.35 237.07 364.35 534.01 613.25 619.05
messe 236.07 596.02
messed 310.25
messerag 239.07
messer's 530.32
messican 105.36
messus 186.36
mest 154.06
mester 004.18 271.04 283.F2 324.20 607.30
mestoon 572.17
met 417.21 447.30 488.33 518.10 594.10
metale 216.03
metallikos 252.15
metangere 509.33
meteering 407.02
meter 386.05 608.10 614.27
meters 235.17
meth 106.16
methers 135.05
methew 253.12
methyst 245.07
metic 431.34
metical 286.23
metoloves 004.09
metomyplace 114.18
metre 194.09
metrically 429.10
metron 559.24
metrum 036.14
mettant 228.10
mettle 359.04
metusolum 378.15
metuus 514.23
meum 356.11
meune 144.14
meup 106.20
meus 185.04
mew 541.15
mewetma 297.30
mews 134.17
mew's 140.01
mey 246.18 366.27 526.08
meyant 455.20
meyle 426.15
meys 252.20 313.26
meyu 565.15
miad 575.09
mic 102.05
mica 254.16
mical 494.01
mice 215.32
micha 234.01
michael 279.F34 459.02 621.02
Michael 382.12
michael's 090.10
Michael's 600.18
michal 340.21
micheal 011.23
mick 005.19 097.29 358.21 376.01
micker 199.21
mickers 173.32
mick's 520.01
micumtra's 601.24
mid 357.01 357.07 357.07 561.26 606.04
middelism 344.22
midden 503.08
middle 253.31 468.26 605.12
middles 077.31
midgets 306.13
midins 415.13
midlands 474.18
midnought 543.12
midor 406.36
midships 605.14
midwhiches 353.25
midy 469.02
mienious 296.08
miens 549.31
mienting 162.14
mientos 443.15
mieras 009.36
mig 458.17
might 210.36 212.18
mightcallimbs 238.30
mightiadd 056.07
mightily 263.25
mighty 128.03 562.33
mighty 383.04
miherculossed 492.05
mihi 213.07
mik 234.26
mike 116.23
miknie 194.28
mikon 468.21
mile 009.16 553.05
miles' 350.21
Miletians 309.11
milia 427.25
miliafamilias 389.15
miliar 237.35
milias 081.06
milibatory 604.08
milie 445.34
milikan 318.15
milintary 338.20
miliours 345.02
militery 166.04

militiaman 354.10
milits' 567.11
milk 624.32
milkcars 192.06
mill 494.24 531.10
milla 211.08 211.08 211.08
434.11 492.13
millafoulties 357.04
millah 521.15
millas 350.21
millers 084.01
millersfolly 625.06
millian 129.16
millierly 414.34
millieu 552.28 552.28
million 144.29
millor 614.13
mills 316.11 577.21
milt 277.F5
mim 267.02 353.15
mime 180.04 599.36 612.12
mimirim 016.28
mimus 219.09
min 024.34 078.27 139.28
253.35 283.13 343.22 372.23
383.24 484.05
mina 183.01 611.13
mina 153.02
mina- 314.08 314.08 314.08
minamoyas 201.30
minar- 003.15
mina's 601.21
minbass 295.01
mincepies 210.21
mind 070.35 329.35 379.26
460.30 552.24
mind- 113.09
minded 018.17 033.29 041.12
042.22 099.32 124.07 160.33
427.33 464.17 544.28 576.24
minding 280.08 528.08
minds 188.14
mind's 339.01
mindsers 541.26
mindwaiting 377.20
mine 010.29 023.28 077.04
093.14 167.03 194.04 215.11
223.09 283.10 301.11 361.01
519.03 531.21 587.08 615.24
mine 105.12
mined 141.25 170.11 579.32
mineers 112.33
miners 027.16
minerva 061.01
mines 450.11 451.03 456.20
539.13 613.17
mine-sub-Fagi 403.09
ming 481.12 521.01
mingled 345.01 363.26
minglement 092.28
mingst 462.04
minies 453.26
minister 037.08
ministers 597.34
ministrants 492.16
minium- 278.04
miniva's 601.23
minivorous 128.07
minnes 349.04
minning 267.03
minopalmular 613.18
minpull 377.35
minsters 552.03
minstrel 454.09
mint 235.36 424.36 440.23
minted 170.08 440.19
mints 024.32
mintul 064.25
minussed 609.30
minx 261.01
minxed 130.11
minxt 222.32
mio 416.18 416.18
miolo 531.21
miracles 427.23
mirage 470.20
miramies 553.11
mirching 435.02
mire 226.24
mirican 132.02
mirim 016.28
mirks 078.08
mirror 408.19 582.20
mirth 074.10
miry 444.29
misas 233.30
misceous 386.24
miscious 066.04
misck 323.11
mise 356.12
miselves 487.18
miseries 288.25
misery 202.03
mish 072.24 187.12 414.32
mished 251.12
mishes 022.30
mishles 590.12
misk 421.01
miskes 347.05
misola 348.31
misole 267.15
miss 006.15 020.31 145.06
186.36 186.36 237.07 245.34
279.F09 624.06
miss 278.L2
MISS 305.R1
missage 298.07
missem 364.02
misses 381.35
misshes 021.19
missies 075.08
missing 042.36 119.31
mission 049.35 545.12
missional 395.01
missives 237.13
missly 361.09
missy 145.07 234.26
mist 007.30 131.26 237.06
477.30
mistaken 123.30
misthued 167.10
mistletocles 392.24
mistocles 307.L1
mistor 050.23
mistress 023.29 412.23 571.07
misty 539.21
misunderstanding 118.25
misus 238.15
mit 492.03 559.05
mita 471.05
mitas 119.11
mite 203.18 291.03 494.33
513.20
mite 072.11 349.13
mites 057.12
mite's 119.11
mither 325.13
mitially 409.34
mitiate 535.03
mitigated 067.19
mittal 479.20
mittalman 529.08
mittences 599.12
mitting 232.10
mittled 428.07
mix 058.24 331.02 433.23
mixed 066.20 092.26 194.04
mixtion 347.22
mo 253.35
moaned 430.13
moanesia 428.02
moaning 041.22
moans 603.19
moats 005.33
mobbed 501.12
mobile 152.25 163.20 483.24
mobilisk 163.21
mobilism 308.L2
moboil 448.29
mobus 407.27
moci 468.20
mock 061.17 355.30 358.21
378.27 411.19 423.01 622.19
mockame 542.13
mockical 515.16
mocking 205.28
mocks 235.23 358.34
mocks 105.27
mod 137.03
mode 221.24 409.11 533.17
modicum 362.31
modied 470.13
modius 003.02 528.23
modo 248.01
modo 188.09
modst 085.30
modus 034.18 157.26
moe 007.15 353.14
moecklenburg- 090.31
moeria 249.16
moes 460.17
mohn 377.31
moi 046.18
moil 130.17
moiseau 230.14
moisselle 230.15
moist 044.01 627.03
mok 102.25 125.19 247.06
498.15
mokst 518.33
mole 129.04 223.17 242.31
614.27
molking 347.36
mollient 409.25 607.02
Mollies 106.34
mollow 565.21
molly 360.28 450.25
molnir- 424.20
molon 155.36
molten 007.17
moltked 333.13
molus 467.35
moment 082.34
momilla 492.13
mominous 543.06
mominum 154.02
momorphemy 599.18
mon 013.20 017.21 064.04
051.33 077.07 094.14 119.17

175.33 198.04 205.11 236.08 262.F1 271.20 279.F22 318.06 488.04 526.28 534.14 615.18 625.16
mon 261.L1 416.12
mona 062.34 498.18
monary 172.13
monay 184.30
mon-Carbery 194.02
mond 118.05 207.06 375.21 503.32 537.08 552.11
mondations 340.09
monde 021.27 327.25 438.30 519.05
monders 497.31
monder's 234.12
mondhued 288.F5
monds 134.07 310.14 343.05
mond's 391.18
mone 274.25 538.20 546.15 594.09
monelses 594.10
monence 337.04
mones 285.29
monetised 574.29
money 140.28 302.05 344.21 416.17 423.30 489.11
moneya 313.12
moneys 595.15
mong 396.06 478.23
mongan 099.26
mongan- 332.05
mongded 418.06
mongepadenopie 179.34
monger 144.30 584.05
mongers 514.01
mongled 345.01
mongrel 441.32
mongs 064.14
monheber 604.04
moniac 573.31
monian 184.36 387.18
monicals 463.03
monides 007.16
monies 456.21
monimoss 545.32
monite 403.17
monities 188.25
monitory 317.31
monk 145.34
monker 610.32
monknounest 269.26
monkst 609.30
monkynous 417.15
monkysh 084.16
monnblue 399.05
monolith 539.01
monologos 194.16
monorother 255.05
mons 059.28
mon's 199.01 433.04
mont 012.35 264.16 375.27 386.20 390.29 416.16
montane 478.31
montary 422.28
monta's 601.26
Monte 202.09
month 037.15 236.10 553.23 553.23
months 542.32
month's 329.19
monthsmind 460.30
monthsminding 280.08
monthst 015.34
montory 506.19
mony 172.11 250.36 451.12 462.06
monymh 490.13
mood 125.06 292.23 590.16
moodmined 141.25
mood's 369.31
mook 231.07
mooking 320.06 343.24
mookse 153.21
mooky 583.33
mooltroon 604.15
moolwashable 577.07
moomeining 267.03
moon 059.01 167.34 233.34 280.07 329.19 375.12 395.09 557.09
moondag 453.13
mooners 395.13
mooney 219.19
moonger 340.20
moonium 377.15
moonlake 202.28
moon's 201.10
moor 086.09 211.26 292.01 577.14
moore 069.06 609.03
moors 012.27
moor's 059.02 281.20
moos 621.25
moose 236.19
moose 053.18
moosed 158.03
mooster 576.18
mooth 054.25 595.01
mop 222.12 531.23
mophilust 107.13
mor 055.03 098.33 148.31 231.10 331.25 487.23 499.11
mor 342.35
morafamilla 434.11
morah 087.08
moral 084.04 572.34
moralities 145.26
moralizing 434.01
moram 593.13
morate 092.27
morde 018.01
mordhar 099.25
more 024.16 024.31 025.31 041.33 049.11 050.23 057.26 073.11 084.05 095.21 096.24 129.30 132.19 148.31 173.22 180.01 197.17 238.06 241.21 288.10 314.15 315.35 336.16 338.19 377.03 377.03 378.20 391.27 397.23 438.10 439.12 473.07 491.11 504.35 553.30 583.11 585.05 585.22 586.36 600.11 608.12
more 399.28
moreans 015.05
morefussed 513.31
moreland 553.30
morers 476.14
mores 003.04 203.21 384.01 388.24 555.08 626.01
more's 475.07
moret 350.05
morfi 247.09
morg 020.07
morgans 547.34
morial 009.34
morica 562.31
moricas 395.35
morinthorrorumble 353.24
mork 479.32
morken 378.14
mormee 628.14
mormo 253.35
morn 347.04 376.11 558.17 571.32
morn 346.12
morning 041.14
morniser 242.13
moroon 207.25
moror 547.25
moroso 269.L1
morphemy 599.18
morphology 127.13
MORPHOMUTATION 281.R1
morphoseous 190.31
morphysed 434.32
morregos 407.02
morrha's 141.35
morrow 244.34 380.22 568.24
morrows 280.06
morrow's 614.21
morry 408.22
mor's 236.09
morse 313.11
mortal 152.34
mortal 105.17
mortial 349.02
Morum 460.18
mory 148.31 172.24
mos 034.02
mosa 549.14
mosaic 107.13
moses 047.19 585.22
mosing 569.02
moslattary 350.27
mosophy 134.14
moss 141.05 161.27 409.12 545.32 550.21
mossive 031.32
most 006.18 009.16 014.19 050.17 052.20 056.03 058.14 066.32 118.36 126.10 130.03 151.01 154.32 156.17 167.25 178.04 178.29 187.09 190.11 194.03 194.19 234.09 234.13 246.28 248.32 271.F5 278.23 292.04 326.34 358.11 362.05 404.21 407.25 407.36 413.32 417.04 422.14 424.08 434.19 445.16 449.28 450.35 460.16 470.17 526.18 547.04 567.31 568.31 570.02 576.31 590.15 605.11
most 072.14
mostfear 505.06
mostfere 067.10
mostinmust 394.30
mosts 353.25
mot 021.14 396.06
motch 415.13
mote 128.19 484.21
moted 172.31
moter 331.27
motes 132.24
moth 007.14 244.36 587.21
moth 342.05
mother 011.09 125.12 149.23 167.32 187.24 200.03 242.25

253.02 253.02 253.03 299.10 439.08 449.36 473.17 502.22 545.09 560.28
mothered 296.22 470.27
mothers 083.17 585.14
mother's 253.03 479.01
mothers' 183.27 183.28 183.28
motherthemselves 353.27
mothy 258.35 274.11 617.12
motion 365.27 436.36
motthermock 378.27
mottocraft 623.19
motty 379.34
mou 144.35 314.22
moud 010.08
mould 206.34 582.10
moulded 186.02
mouldered 143.14
mouldy 382.15
moult 241.24
mound 008.05 111.34 135.09 323.02 386.20 420.23 464.26
MOUND 276.R1
mounded 542.04 588.19
mount 028.22 053.06 108.33 192.35 247.34 359.12 380.12 541.13 580.22 588.15 623.23
mountain 019.32 129.04
mountains 243.05
mounted 013.24
mounting 504.14
mountjoy 460.09
mountof 470.16
mounts 505.31
mount's 375.23
mour 023.08 331.33
moures 102.27
mourfully 158.27
mourican's 447.06
mourmeant 231.08
mourn 011.14
mourneen's 428.08
mourning 247.18
moury 096.07
moury 104.10
mouse 120.06 553.02
mouselles 113.11
mousin 107.23
moust 232.07
mout 007.16
mout 354.17
mouth 054.35 131.18 177.25 245.23 263.02 364.15 389.01 394.22 437.20 493.07 578.25
mouth 071.19 525.25
mouthed 429.18
mouther 224.10 424.19
moutherhibbert 388.29
mouthing 329.33
mouths 367.34
mouth's 510.04
mouthst 519.21
moutioun 354.20
mov 411.18
movable 117.35
move 191.11 404.10 456.13 531.29
move 071.16
moved 066.31 091.02 162.05 314.02 314.05 420.29 430.14 483.34 544.07 579.34 617.27
moves 499.11
movick 354.01
moving 165.33
movingth 274.20
movs 499.11
mow 068.05
mown 557.19
mow's 579.01
moxed 438.29
moy- 257.27
moyas 201.30
moyers 539.07
Moyly 095.03
Moynihan 307.09
moyno 609.24
moztheart 360.12
muccumul 375.29
much 171.19 261.29 388.14 414.11 484.16 485.34 495.20 612.15
much 349.33 350.02
muchers 381.07
muchness 122.36
muck 091.01 254.22 344.35 386.33 456.27
muck 072.08
mucks 465.33
muckst 449.35
mucky 100.05
mud 006.05 068.14 228.33 420.08 552.05 594.11
mudder 496.26
muddher-in-chaff 240.15
muddles 409.18
muddymuzzle 352.29
muddy's 423.34
mudgaard- 424.20
mudicate 536.04
mud's 156.22
mudst 332.26
Mudway 393.09
muee 291.28
muehler 213.02
muffin 290.F5
mufflers 516.07
mugee 588.02
muggies 342.02
Muggli 123.11
mugglian 123.21
mugnus 484.35
muhrmuhr 017.23
Muhun 254.03
muid 306.28
Muirk 622.05
muirries 081.28
muk 599.20
muk 349.23
muked 089.09
mukking 294.20
mukklers 327.01
mulanchonry 482.12
mular 017.09 613.18
mulberryeke 221.33
Mulcnory 397.36
mule 073.35 198.34 525.31
muled 133.30 234.25
mules 250.04
mulette 230.07
mulier 166.26
mulikick 344.09
muling 550.29
mulion 380.10
mulium 498.30
mullagh 390.09
mullah 292.F3
mullas 319.08
mullium 613.25
mullun- 023.05
mulo 122.09
mult 184.06 316.23
multeemiously 285.10
multy 215.25 261.19
muluation 593.15
muluius 484.11
mulum 056.34
mum 026.18 279.F34 279.F34 279.F34 302.16 416.02 491.28 603.30
mum 515.09
mumb 608.22
mumble 295.04
mumina- 314.08
mummer 029.26
mummers 356.06
mummur 604.11
mummy 547.04
mun 014.36 136.01 163.03 534.11 538.23
Munaday 205.16
munconomnulstria 229.17
muncted 227.32
munculus 525.33
mund 088.23 253.05 256.11 514.02
mundher 092.09
mundo 416.16
munds 105.02
mund's 245.18 469.16
mundson 325.22
mune 244.26
muneranded 171.32
mung 057.14 187.03 258.16 375.01
munites 497.20
munkers 095.34
muns 047.08 521.28
munster 131.10
munt 008.25
mup 355.08
mur 100.18
murabi 139.25
murables 197.25
muraised 354.24
murals 579.31
murature 344.17
murdherers 617.18
mure 013.10 493.13
muredemeanour 189.26
muristic 594.28
murk 143.07 404.10
murket 378.08
murl 437.31
murphies 293.10
murphyc 031.35
murraimost 178.04
murrlubejubes 396.34
murrmal 251.36
Murty 472.15
muscles 015.32
muse 272.F3
muser 612.01
musers 032.10
mush 008.26
musical 365.08
musin 539.16
musk 267.28
Muslim 068.12
musong 595.04

musses 154.08
muster 393.08
mustered 149.08
mustering 364.09
mustimus 108.12
mustwhomust 223.27
mut 450.17 593.21
mutandies 284.12
mutant 361.20
mutating 460.12
MUTATION 281.R1
mutative 036.32
mutativeness 112.12
mutch 143.29
mute 016.14
muter's 056.01
muth 244.36 348.13 434.36
muthisthy 623.10
muth's 042.27
mutic's 117.14
mutose 314.21
mutras 080.24
mutren 377.10
mut's 277.L2
mutt 517.13
mutter 066.25 298.28
muttering 245.04
muttony 241.16
muttyflesks 141.08
mutual 530.10
mutualism 308.L2
mutuomergent 055.11
muzd 163.02 425.28
muzement 125.13
muzzle 352.29
myaso 339.06
mybows 011.12
mycapnoise 168.11
myeyes 025.03
myg 116.32
mygdaleine 094.16
mygdaloid 183.12
myhead 229.32
myjig 332.24
mylaya 329.32
mylose 185.28
mymy 162.25
myn 130.21 326.19 367.10
625.02
myn 342.20
myng 295.08
mynn 584.14
myplace 114.18
mypolity's 133.18
myriameliamurphies 293.10
myriams 265.22
myround 381.30
mysell 585.07
mysterion 301.18
mystic 293.18
mystsprinkled 153.27
mysty 155.24
myth 581.24
mythey 331.09
mythical 354.10
mytic 147.08

naachtha 502.04
naady's 253.16
naar 360.17
naarse 301.02
naas 344.29
nabeatha 384.09
nabohore 245.13
nabortan- 257.27
nabory 323.20
nabraggat 060.12
nabudja 056.34
nacaddie 200.23
naccus 159.28
nacerution 107.19
nacestross 018.03
nach 090.31
nachan 398.16
nacht 047.28 339.05 451.14
528.29
nachy 392.04
nacies 340.29
nack 577.02
nacked 505.34
nacking 302.F1
nackskey 602.34
nacles 534.25
nacosagh- 414.19
nacow 228.32
nacrusha 262.15
nacuddle 391.03
nacul 584.31
nad 202.26
nados 178.26
nage 082.19 239.13 381.04
555.19
nager's 312.27
naggin 548.32
nagging 583.09
naggs 548.23
naggy 026.03
nagin 503.11
nagollow 580.34
nags 069.11
nag's 334.25
nail 024.15 085.02 115.05
452.12
nailed 288.06 329.24
nails 283.18
nairyans 360.08
naisies 284.12
naked 206.30 264.F1
naked's 564.34
nakedst-tu-naughsy 505.07
nakes 019.08
nakked 597.36
naks 288.18
naktiers 156.12
naky 151.11
nalitey 461.04
nall 088.24 607.14 619.15
nalls 351.22
nally 449.04
naluhy 340.06
nam 024.15 163.01 237.26
nama 267.F4 502.36
namaba 267.F4
namabapa 267.F4
namagoaded 180.03
namaraca 255.15
namd 535.09
name 032.18 094.34 108.21
145.21 177.22 182.32 186.28
244.08 261.F3 276.F1 358.07
408.18 414.03 441.29 485.05
490.12 506.01 515.25 561.10
561.13 567.14 575.06
named 046.01 059.16 100.20
326.27 361.21 378.10
nameis 479.12
nameron 561.24
names 029.31 030.03 098.27
201.32 234.22 468.13 561.36
595.34
namesh 546.04
name-Turricum 228.22
namon 163.30
namond 503.32
na-Murty 472.15
nan 246.21 246.21 258.04
284.15 393.10 466.29
nana 469.21
nance 220.33
nanciation 089.26
nand 332.16
nands 288.16
nane 613.30
naned 041.17
nangonamed 361.21
nania 531.34
nanno 182.20
nan-Og 091.25
nan-Ogre 479.02
nan's 184.22 299.16 578.06
nanters 552.06
nantes 485.11
nanthean 613.17
nanya 578.21
nanymous 435.31
naose 228.28
nap 129.29
napalus 182.18
nape 371.03
naping 505.08
napkins 405.31
na-poghue 384.34 385.22
na-Poghue 388.25
na-Poghue's 203.36
na-pogue 385.03
napoke 359.26
napoppsky 404.24
napped 021.21 595.35
nappers 556.29
napping 336.25
napplous 254.23
naps 256.20
napsack 350.34
naquillia's 204.07
nara- 023.05
naratatattar 339.18
narch's 532.01
nard 177.18
nardor 374.16
nared 551.35
narks 369.20
narld 345.30
narlybird 010.32 010.34
narrag 221.23
narsty 315.23
nasant 084.05
nascenent 596.04
nased 344.35
nashed 339.11
naskieym's 601.25
nass 094.01 502.06 549.34
607.25 625.27
nassed 492.06
nasty 444.29 503.07 556.29
nat 140.02 160.04 487.21
494.06
natal 091.23
natality 447.08
natan 227.20

natbe 599.19
nate 296.29 350.33 593.08
nate 354.19
natently 524.20
nates 115.33 165.16
nates 353.23
nath 342.13
nathan 478.26
nathaun 462.08
nathere 081.16
nathor 525.15
nation 023.02 026.19 036.22 058.08 068.34 130.17 142.19 241.21 352.26 366.27 414.08 505.12 557.33
national 128.28 284.13 448.14
national 348.32
nations 351.26 358.03 361.01
natively 088.07
natives 274.F2
nativomentally 149.32
nator 154.07
nats 314.35 347.06
natsching 222.27
natties 432.15
natullagh- 332.05
natural 128.27 240.14 451.17 504.33 572.24
natured 568.34
natut 395.23
naughsy 505.07
naughties 537.08
naulinn 264.28
nauning 041.22
naur-Jaggarnath 342.13
naut 242.07
nautic 530.18
nautique 315.34
naver 505.34 520.26
naves 370.15
navia 254.33
nawns 605.01
naw's 430.36
nax 319.34
naxities 090.06
nay 087.08 102.28 184.30 366.15
nayance 233.29
nayed 061.34
nayman 025.32
naynilnay 339.33
nays 043.30 256.13
naze 398.30
neadher 560.18
neal 442.05
neal 346.12
nealey 071.36
nean 481.13
neans 546.18
neant 254.20
néants 131.09
near 026.07 095.30 416.04
nearly 135.31
nearth 610.04
neash 359.11
neath 318.17 503.13
neathere 081.16
nebbia 324.27
neber 209.07
necessarily 515.14
necessary 120.15 411.03
necies 377.16
neck 039.10 056.24 136.26 141.35 146.30 162.10 297.17 581.12
necked 152.09
necks 169.02
neck's 334.25
necky 480.23
nects 416.11
ned 054.05 300.06 498.20
neeborn 547.05
need 075.21 079.16 201.03 357.32 580.31 602.03
needis 433.36
needles 551.33
neeghed 241.24
neeghs 393.29
neel 584.33
neemed 363.13
neen 232.06 376.01
neepers 196.18
neepy 275.F1
nees 139.21
neesgnobs 274.F2
neess 187.17 376.10
negand 573.31
negation 306.L1
negnousioum 397.27
negreon 279.F32
nehmon 416.12
neighbour 193.27
Neill 495.27
nein 029.32
neir 486.35
neirist 397.02
neiss 556.28
neither 101.06 230.09 315.07
nek 258.17
nel 341.03
nell 379.10 553.12 564.28
nella 173.11 184.32 206.35 291.F6 435.19
nella 303.L1
nelle 351.32 583.03
nelles 359.29
nelli 084.36
nellic 326.13
nellis 220.21
nello 043.23
nells 324.28
nelly 224.30 431.17 445.11 450.10 584.17
nelly's 151.07 435.34
nemanon 258.22
nemberable 608.31
nemm 420.05
nemorous 158.11
nence 313.30
nenny- 090.31
nenter 480.10
nenties 336.32
nentory 623.06
nepos 389.28 392.18
nes 468.12
nesans 076.22
nesciousness 224.17
nesional 106.09
neska 333.05
ness 019.07
nesse 547.06
nessessity 613.27
nessised 261.F1
nessive 162.19
nesst 363.07
nest 011.15 065.09 070.03 177.17 234.10 241.10 241.13 242.06 290.22 318.17 333.27 441.01 527.03 535.19 561.31 576.28 627.30
nest 342.09
nestegg 081.23
nester 177.14
nests 450.33 450.33
net 043.04 088.32 176.36 219.13 292.12 377.28 381.13 471.26 533.10
nets 384.02
netss 366.11
nett 176.03
nette 143.32
nettes 538.22
netto 493.30
netzer 234.15
netzeveil 208.10
neul 119.25
Neva 205.34
nevel 037.35
never 077.14 406.20
nevero 353.09
nevver 077.01
new 143.03 182.25 215.23 226.14 226.17 315.29 460.36 471.10 529.05 534.02 594.15 620.02 623.16
new 201.05
newality 523.04
newburgher 265.13
neweller 594.01
newgnawns 605.01
newmurature 344.17
newreck 416.36
Newrobe 155.05
news 254.10 277.18
new't 075.12
newwail 022.12
newwesner 372.16
nexandreian 318.11
next 290.15 302.19 580.28 598.14
next-best-king 505.27
ney 010.15 010.15 010.15
neya 313.12
neze 102.13
niagnian 389.22
niatwantyng 499.05
nibblers 572.01
nic 017.14
nican 287.F4
nice 019.07 346.29 384.25 450.18 471.04
nice-Bruerie 038.04
niceynurseys 134.08
niche 007.15
nicholas' 090.11
nicht 555.10
nichts 219.02 409.21
nick 240.02 363.19 457.36 478.26
nickally 430.10
nickburns 009.25
nickel 406.06
nickerbocker 442.09
nickerbockers 098.21
nickered 192.31
nickers 492.25
nickin 102.09 102.09
nicking 314.01 314.01 531.28

nickknaver 505.34
nickknots 162.10
nickle 104.08
nickled 380.08
nicks 027.06 527.20
nick's 434.21
nickt 508.33
nicky 158.35
nics 223.04
nid 607.18
nider 320.04
nidsglass 277.F5
niece 038.09 532.24
niejinksky 513.11
Niell 550.31
niel's 350.30
nietcies 348.22
nig 292.19 607.18
nigel 300.05
nigglers 244.06
nigh 011.13 050.03 097.22 126.02
nighn 358.28
night 017.33 039.33 053.19 089.16 100.22 126.18 136.27 153.34 170.07 192.19 202.35 245.32 378.11 381.27 391.33 396.31 425.27 427.10 452.26 470.07 480.09 505.24 510.07 520.16 562.29 570.08 598.32 618.06 623.15
night 071.15 201.13 399.23
nighted 241.22 489.31 615.15
nighter 071.10
nighters 618.24
nighth 450.17
nighting 095.21
nightlamp 559.36
nightly 027.19 142.24
nightmayers' 364.26
nights 015.20 283.26 320.16 325.09 335.26 357.24 365.31 446.05 453.32 489.35 602.22
night's 012.04 041.14 225.17 403.20 497.32
nightsmore 608.12
nigznaks 288.18
nihilisation 353.22
nik 228.07 338.23 432.20
nikan 197.29
nikin 032.06
niks 439.33
nild 042.26
nilnay 339.33
nim 539.19
nimad 509.13
nimancy 117.33
nimbant 599.25
nimiissilehims 005.16
nims 564.21
nin 391.33 566.11
nin 277.L2
nincstricken 599.28
nine 133.17 150.25 155.06 158.01 234.34 255.33 264.05 268.18 289.12 327.35 430.01 534.12 573.20 574.27 595.07 596.08 618.24
nine 105.25
ninecyhandsy 621.21
ninehalf 533.34
nineknived 162.05
ninelives 462.31
ninepenny 396.18
nines 249.36
nine's 285.27
ninnies 175.33
ninnig 292.19
ninny 166.25
nins 494.22
nints 351.32
ninuinn's 372.29
nip 045.08
nipped 317.24
nippers 485.36
nir 221.09 319.07
nirfen- 424.20
nirilles 346.20
nirps 027.09
nirur- 424.20
nis 174.30 174.30
nisch 325.12
nisgels 601.01
nisills 566.09
nisonian 048.23
niss's 289.13
nist 132.19 256.24 298.08
nistling 114.06
nisty 207.28
nit 268.13 315.03 416.15 611.18
nital 486.15
nition 614.17
nits 018.25 227.06 283.27 416.29
nittrick 353.14
nitys 240.20
nitz 208.35
nitza 228.07
niuvia 627.27
nive 545.22
nivers 267.06
niveses 141.16
nivia's 601.27
nix 023.16 049.13 080.06 116.18 139.35 473.16 534.12
nixed 311.26
noaning 628.03
noarch 612.27 612.27 612.28
noark 468.29
noball 339.10
nobble 074.11
nobby 550.09
nobiled 263.F4
nobkerries 082.22
noble's 548.16
nobli 064.30
nobloom 564.23
nobody 292.14
nobrass 609.28
nobs 157.12 274.08 274.F2 448.23
nob's 491.21
nobsic 056.22
noburkes 106.06
noc 578.10
noccovitch 159.28
noch 049.04 476.06 498.23 502.01
nochar 348.19
nochs 328.10 357.30
nock 507.36
nockmeggs 333.33
nocksters 081.28
nockturn 064.16
noctural 598.17
nocturne 328.17
noculises 394.30
nod 325.14
nodals 156.16
node 374.07
nodius 487.36
nods 112.34
noedler 204.09
noel 440.17
noff 354.05
noget 243.03
nogg 556.34
noggers 476.14 572.03
noggin 195.01
nogging 557.05
nogh 106.02
noight 412.06
noilia 456.03 456.03
noirs 128.08
nois 154.09
noise 031.21 090.27 168.11 226.05 535.23
noised 258.21
noiser 530.36
noisers 350.15
noising 476.36
noisy 053.17
noko 214.10
nolan 303.F3 490.15
noleum 391.21
nolina 225.15
nolised 522.32
noll 076.26 267.06 422.32 476.06
nolleges 623.32
nolly 368.18
nollyrock 010.31
nolulutent 076.30
nom 450.04
nome 153.20 158.10 230.34 332.32 451.21 533.22
nomeans 285.27
nomen 059.15 206.03 241.21
nomeo- 596.14
nomer 562.04
nomering 122.06
nomers 235.29
nomes 098.27 243.05 552.10
nomial 156.02
nomian 172.17
nomic 599.17
nomina 098.27
nominal 120.09
nominated 088.20
nominous 331.22
nomoneya 313.12
non 201.21 201.21
nonem 513.08
nones 179.02
nonest 411.29
nong 343.23
Nonhanno's 123.32
nonia 437.30
nonna 433.04
nonnevero 353.09
nonnulstria 229.17
nononously 367.35
nonsable 478.19
nonsceau 229.33
nonse 039.14
nonthedubblan- 332.05
nonymay's 374.07
nonymos 034.02

nonymoses 047.19
noo 144.12 266.07 525.27
noobs 550.35
noodle 065.24 065.26 065.32
noodrift 503.32
noody 332.01
noof 623.20
nook 184.17
nooks 235.23
nook's 212.33
noon 030.14 050.32 070.33 079.20 187.05 228.04 309.15 460.29 470.15 605.30
noose 568.20
nooser 329.05
noosers 319.29
noosh 456.26
nooter 325.23
nooth 553.13
noother 370.34 371.26
nooties 209.31
nootvindict 370.32
nopfs 052.27
nopie 179.34
nopolies 357.30
nops 356.07
nopubblicoes 371.24
nor 313.15
nore 266.07 273.12 359.03
Noremen 309.11
nork 378.06
normal 034.28
normally 538.28
normanous 360.33
noromacron 318.09
norres 257.36
norring 578.02
norrt 067.15
norryson's 551.04
norseher 203.07
norsted 326.21
north 318.35
North 569.05
norval 570.01
nos 250.27 456.23
nose 009.20 073.08 125.20 231.31 334.28 540.35 549.13
nosed 032.12 035.25 107.11 115.13 152.09 254.01 498.13
nosegates 612.24
noser's 290.21
nosery 253.28
noses 157.25
nose's 182.04
nosey 257.14
nosing 365.16
nost 552.12 594.18 596.10
noster 031.07
nostrilled 115.26
nostrum 085.11
No-Tailors' 006.03
notch 037.03 353.19 534.01
notcheralled 348.33
notcracking 143.13
note 363.09
noted 439.19
notes 021.03 135.35
nothel 485.31
notherum 609.09
noticed 470.21
notions 614.17
notioun 354.21
notknow 224.18
notorious 604.22
nots 162.10 231.35 245.10 288.07 358.02 579.16 599.14
nots 295.L2
not's 377.18
nott 107.20
nottes 350.29
notting 144.23 507.14
nottobe 085.22
notts 352.13 580.01
notty 021.07
nouceable 479.09
nouche 338.24
nought 227.16 389.05 543.12
nouit- 044.20
noukan's 245.05
noun 104.16
nounest 269.26
noupes 158.18
nourished 355.24
nouriture 300.L1
nourrice 081.29
nous 417.15
nousioum 397.27
noussas 471.08
nout 179.06 353.14
nouth 227.27
noutso 245.01
nov 038.22
nove 579.10
novel 054.21
novene 291.28
noviacion 230.16
novio 230.16
novi's 230.15
nowatters 070.09
nowhood 329.09
Nowlan 176.20
nowling 442.05
nowme 446.26
nown 595.34
nownced 341.19
nownsable 581.05
nownse 243.21
nows 274.F2
nows 340.14
nowse 453.17
nox 567.01 596.20
nox 342.02
nox-atta-Belle 139.35
noximost 422.14
noxious 085.28
noxst 555.10
noyato 339.03
noyous 156.12
noys 349.26
noysers 323.08
noze 392.06
nozzler 024.35
nrk 621.20
nuala 559.33
nuar- 332.05
nuarration 205.14
nubble 181.11
nubial 386.04
nubierhome 181.06
nubies' 066.37
nuboyes 435.15
nubulocirrhonimbant 599.25
nuc 378.13
nucane-Law 324.22
nucane-Lee 324.22
nuchorn 157.03
nuckles 507.11
nud 345.30 600.11
nude 359.10
nufleshed 271.F4
nug 607.18
nugh 596.14
nuh 620.16
nuhulation 058.08
nuinette 540.34
nuinn's 372.29
nuit 469.01
nuit 515.09
nuitants' 043.10
nuk 003.15
nukkunun 023.05
nulengro 472.22
nulinorum 264.07
nulited 395.33
nulls 318.32
nullused 161.36
nully 582.08
nulstria 229.17
num 420.20 476.35
numagula 162.12
numantic 615.04
number 234.34 318.30 325.14 328.20 533.05
numbers 286.17
numerary 499.20
numerose 158.11
numina 098.27
numinally 490.08
nummical 494.01
numque 389.28
nun 023.05 099.07 353.15 431.30
nunc 609.24
nunch 127.31
nuncies 373.12
nuncing 409.27
nunciniation 537.03
nuncs 407.32
nundurumchuff 352.34
nune 569.07
nungopovengreskey 056.36
nuns 177.08
nunsense 245.21
nunska 585.22
nuntaj 325.11
nuorivals 348.30
nuova 230.15
nupciacion 528.19
nuphars 075.01
nur 317.15
nur's 243.16
nurse 147.21
nurseys 134.08
nursfjaell 057.14
nusand 326.20
nushka 207.08
nusstas 413.29
nut 221.06 376.09 376.09 390.31 405.25 453.16 517.07 520.23 587.10 624.17
nute 570.36
nuts 125.20 162.25 183.24 285.03 613.22
nut's 084.23 622.10
nut's 341.31
nutshedell 276.L2
nutted 377.18
nutunar 327.21
nuweir 448.31

nuzz 571.28
nuzza 573.01
nyas 193.14
nychts 247.03
nyckle 602.33
nyk's 102.19
nymh 490.13
nymphs 548.02
nyss 318.35
nyzor 343.19

oaf 134.27
oak 005.07 210.29 411.06 446.13 460.24
oaked 601.02
oakgravy 171.01
oak's 339.04
oaptz 571.28
oaro 136.14
oarsely 150.12
oasts 551.03
oat 016.16
oath 006.33 254.02 535.27
oaths 116.28
oatre 587.08
oats 041.09 051.15 081.30
oatstory 051.13
obangoist 364.32
ober 186.14
obiling 403.10
objibway 134.14
obli 064.30
oblige 567.26
Oblong's 266.06
obobo 622.23
oboes 006.36 455.26
oboroff 340.20
oboy 043.17
obscure 247.34 431.32
observed 092.22
obstaclant 345.21
obstant 485.01
obulus 219.14
oc 578.10
ocale 250.27
occidents 288.11
occupant 348.14
occupation 344.21
occupied 558.04
occur 481.16
occurs 391.13
ocean 100.01 623.29
oceanal 384.03
ocelating 165.13
ocident 059.09
ockles 623.08
ocular 068.01 235.25
oculars 587.07
oculated 541.27
oculises 394.30
ocur 011.18
odd 380.14
oddities 275.F5
odeboko 051.17
odeontic 151.34
odes 268.19
odeztious 339.05
odias 498.04
odin 503.28 535.05
odint 303.21
odiotiosities 222.02
odious 184.15
odiousness 159.31
odite 190.35
odities 614.02
odius 487.36
odore 504.21
odorers 459.27
odories 025.04
odorous 412.07
odorus 032.12 255.21
oedler 204.09
oelanders 398.05
oer 624.09
oermann 610.22
o'er-the-hazy 111.24
oevre 164.18
ofa 045.03
offbellek 412.10
offensive 078.30
offer 415.13
offered 620.16
offers 183.34
office 567.02
officially 606.19
officies 358.15
offs 465.06
off's 345.26
ofhids 342.26
ofman 019.17
ofoaptz 571.28
ofsen 142.06
oft 277.11 316.21 394.18 445.33
ofter 313.14 378.30
ofter 345.28
oftfun 607.16
oftlhee 628.14
oftly 333.04
ofts 331.21
ofty 114.23
ofumbers 340.26
Og 091.25
ogam 223.04
ogblagrogger- 582.32
oggs 178.33
ogonies 353.01
Ogre 479.02
ogreedy 133.07
ogrefright 423.17
ogues 553.12
ohigh 373.07
ohlstery 271.F3
oider 336.24
oikon 416.12
oiks 242.02
oil 019.06 130.17 390.02 393.08 440.25 448.29 603.01
oilable 153.27
oilboys 543.09
oiled 004.31 324.17
oilia 456.03 456.03
oiling 411.25
oilish 466.23
oils 564.20 603.35
oilskins 370.35
oily 083.15 138.25 534.01
oinabrathran 252.04
oiney 518.21
oiseau 230.14
oista 285.17 285.18
oistre 081.34
oisy 198.12
okbloon 389.27
olafs 319.27
olaf's 301.30
olando 570.03
olave 244.04
old 009.11 014.25 015.32 060.23 075.20 110.16 113.19 117.10 186.08 225.19 228.30 242.05 255.18 257.24 310.16 311.14 326.17 336.17 337.01 352.24 383.23 411.01 418.05 441.19 450.29 478.30 505.02 505.32 549.25 553.26 563.27 581.09 590.14 606.21 607.31 615.06
oldaisymen 524.11
oldandairy 505.14
oldbethizzdryel 241.27
olde 265.13 383.18
oldell 360.33
olden 102.24 234.36
older 517.09
olders 372.34
oldfashioned 276.F2
oldhyms 183.15
oldies 563.31
oldkarakter 098.09
oldloom 385.29
oldomar 255.16
oldorboys 266.18
oldpewter 167.21
oldpowder 393.22
oldry 005.06
olds 503.21
old's 248.24
ole 008.26
olearis 255.15
oleon 596.26
olevante 228.10
olf 201.34
olfa 268.14
olfanelly 450.10
olfoklokken 353.15
olgar 211.13
olgian 242.06
olgier 073.17
olgor 613.28
oliolum 117.11
oll 065.17 525.05
ollall 547.11
ollo 254.25
ollogass 555.11
ollomuck 254.22
olmagtog 246.05
ololy 089.35
olosha 106.23
olothe 254.14
ols 182.22
olvever 352.09
olyhagionous 520.33
om 059.20 079.36 088.36 100.23 153.27 156.16 179.09 179.09 187.21 188.23 253.23 285.F4 292.21 310.29 330.29 333.34 336.34 344.30 347.02 356.13 356.32 363.18 365.26 365.26 380.21 412.18 471.32 475.21 508.24 547.06 564.34 574.36 582.01 589.07 606.15
om 013.26 106.03
oma 207.34
oman 034.31
omar 255.16
omar's 068.31
omatic 055.36
ombarouter 314.11

omber 373.02
ombition 366.29
ombonant 053.01
ombos 120.02
ombre 222.32
ombren 327.06
ombrer 473.20
ombres 312.09 529.24
ombres 285.L3
ombring 271.11
omdree 600.20
omelet 586.18
omelette 059.31
omen 331.29
omenously 353.06
omen's 549.18
omeo 238.35
o'-me-soul 225.01 225.01
omfrie 023.20
omichael 621.02
ominous 543.06 552.24 560.17 613.28
ominum 154.02
omise 356.12
omkin 290.F7
omnes 497.10
omnibus 099.10
omnis 314.34
omnones 288.14
omnosunt 258.02
omomiom 285.15
omorous 112.29
omphal 590.10
omphrey 032.14
omphreyld 031.08
omport 549.22
oms 361.23 621.01
om's 070.25
om-Trent 531.03
omyn 326.19
onabraggat 060.12
onadimply 097.26
onage 596.01
onages 241.03
onan 027.25
onans 504.19
onaskieym's 601.25
onced 198.14
onchepps 067.17
onchin 447.19
oncle's 250.13
ond 294.04 520.27
onde 609.17
ondenees 139.21
onder 310.16
ondes 327.21
ondo 247.09
ondolone's 161.03
onds 277.22
ondur 332.21
oneafter 093.01
oneire 280.01
onerflsh 571.29
ones 058.11 611.12 611.17
one's 183.02 190.33
one's 176.09
onester 177.14
oneyesed 323.29
onger 108.18
ongered 357.14
ongster 186.31
onguardiant 151.20
onhurs 234.28
oniseels 344.09
onisonian 048.23
onkle's 467.14
onlieme 485.18
ono 362.32
ons 113.06 613.11
onsample 397.32
onthiance 296.20
onton 349.31
Onton 611.20
onts 606.30
onus 607.35
onward 071.09
onwashed 159.27
oof 623.20
oogged 428.20
oogy 492.11
oola 475.02 475.14
oopanadoon 543.30
oosing 607.10
oosoon 595.08
oosus 625.22
ooth 323.04
ooze 414.16
oozebecome 240.06
oozers 156.13
ope 562.26
opean 598.15
opeck 416.17
oped 244.15 378.35
open 165.05 234.07 363.34 377.08 419.14 474.09 518.36
opends 324.35
opened 022.33
opener 345.27
openhaven 478.16
opening 060.29
opent 612.06
oper 343.23
operation 568.20 604.24
operian 294.01
operous 057.33
opes 520.25 586.31
opeus 014.09
oph 129.36 452.20
ophenguts 319.12
ophilias 110.11
opia 545.10
opie 179.34
opon 443.06
oponhurrish 607.20
opper 454.01
opper's 268.12
opposides 382.16
ops 625.03
opter 546.07
opterous 417.01
optic 419.25
OPTICAL 272.R1
optically 055.22
opticals 394.05
opticked 367.17
optics 139.16
opticus 611.25
optimist 069.16
optimost 234.13
option 449.17
optysia 174.19
opum 153.26
op-Zoom 073.26
ora 514.22 623.27
oracles 617.25
oraculous 229.32
orage 539.22
oral 346.35
oram 481.16
orange 208.15 450.09
oranyellgreenlindigan 611.06
orate 425.19
orayellers 416.34
orb 589.06
orba's 125.09
orbe 360.05
orbean 357.06
orbic 096.36
orbinaire 295.17
Orbison 302.23
orbo 472.08
orbtracktors 221.20
orcure 389.06
orded 286.F3
ordenwater 117.04
order 126.09 374.16 540.19
ordinal 157.27
ordinary 144.16 176.21 263.F4 408.13 516.34
ordinately 437.36
ordinating 164.33
ordination 551.17
ordunates 156.11
ore 292.17
orebukujibun 484.26
orefulvid 284.30
Oreille 175.28
oreiller 572.23
oreilles 102.12
oreland 446.25
orellies 454.28
orelump 613.01
organson 530.31
organtruce 083.35
orgean 312.05
orgels 015.14
orgeyborgey 327.30
orgilhisjurylegs 060.11
orglin 087.26
orgues 200.17
orgy 392.16
orhaps 062.25
orheuman 214.22
oricori 623.01
originally 169.02 314.16
orioles 119.15
orion 398.18
oriose 016.01
orium 410.04
ork 378.06
orkenwhite 374.06
orkus 373.12
orl 130.33
orlandes 564.23
orme 245.02
ormillor 614.13
ornaments 227.21 291.12
orne 210.31
orns 236.30
oro 263.F3
oromacron 318.09
oronage 596.01
orong 019.05
orother 255.05
oroyal 358.20
orpentine 478.13
orphan 060.07
orpound 056.06
orreor 254.13

orreor 105.11
orrish 378.09
orrong 098.10
orror 423.16
orsay 405.05
orscape 143.28
orse 383.21
ort 086.07 139.33
ortemporate 082.17
orthoducts 152.28
orthree 345.10
orts 069.09 076.17 120.31 221.15 295.F1
orwall 621.19
orwombanborn 055.10
os 231.34
osa 246.10
oscan 042.11
oscians 339.11
oscillating 108.24
oscuro 107.29
osey 584.11
osiosus 437.33
osirian 350.25
osiriously 470.13
oskouro 317.33
oskuro 612.18
osomines 450.11
ossassinated 241.02
ossed 415.11
ossianusheen 267.19
ossiphysing 277.L5
ost 594.18 622.29
osters 277.F7
otchy 344.10
o'-Thay 599.03
othel 485.31
other 142.11 143.19 187.24 224.33 238.25 252.16 255.05 300.05 336.24 389.07 452.13 527.29
others 238.26
other's 546.16 570.13
otherum 609.09
othink 056.31
otiosities 222.02
otitubes 158.36
otomise 356.12
otther 275.09
ottheres 311.04
otto 251.25
ottos 541.20
otuli 180.14
otus 285.L1
ouch 535.21
oud 010.08
oughal 582.26
oughta 568.33
ouiro 327.04
oukan's 245.05
ould 072.34 171.10 344.32 348.17 362.19
oulish 518.35
ounce 541.07 623.25
ounce 262.L2
ourishman 463.26
ourmony 462.06
ouroines 348.29
ours 107.22 146.16 250.17 251.27 305.03 318.22 345.02 360.30
our's 155.14
ourth 424.13
ouse 338.20 597.14
oused 617.29
oust 414.01
ousthausthible 091.27
outdown 612.14
outen 256.08 598.02
outer 314.11
outermost 194.19
outers 603.19
outerthus 414.12
outfeller 257.07
outing 513.35
outs 358.04 509.33
ov 407.17
oved 548.10
oveire 028.01
ovelance 350.13
oven 220.21 339.04 365.13
ovence 268.10
ovene 291.28 528.01
ovened 603.35
ovengreskey 056.36
ovens 324.29
over 003.04 012.16 013.18 056.15 066.06 074.12 140.24 160.28 206.35 224.14 280.20 294.27 299.09 301.F3 325.12 353.16 388.17 443.02 451.34 455.08 597.03 601.01 607.10 613.08 620.14
over 350.06
overboard 159.32
overca 230.31
overed 553.08
overing 609.34
over-Meer 205.34
overs 268.F4 370.31 385.16 567.12 570.05
overseer 409.35
overswetch 293.08
overture 243.11
overum 361.32 610.06
oves 184.29 601.02
ovna 049.08
ovos 133.35
ovular 156.15
ovyover 350.06
o'-war 046.15 046.16
o-wars 133.17
oway 093.14 585.32
owe 207.24
owed 154.07
owelsy 444.11
ower 587.10
owered 370.19
owl 074.16 240.12 284.19 361.16
owlding 142.03
owldmoutherhibbert 388.29
owle 309.22
owler 585.02
owlted 181.19
owm 160.02
own 005.20 090.08 119.28 125.14 156.13 197.05 208.18 274.23 313.05 333.14 351.05 381.03 429.21 456.05 481.12 524.34 557.19 565.21 595.34
owner 529.34
ownly 235.27
owno 569.32
own's 205.09
ownself 447.10
o'women 436.13
owsha 215.12
owt 102.02
owth 116.15
ox 019.05 055.03 456.23 456.23 456.23 456.23 456.23 456.23 456.23 512.04 567.24
ox 308.L2 525.12
oxana 212.11
oxe 594.29
oxen 018.32 375.19
oxenetic 175.31
oxens 383.24
oxer 602.35
oxis 304.17
oxity 179.14
oxodised 183.33
oxside 128.10
oxtended 476.07
oxy 513.21
oyato 339.03
oyghal 099.27
oygle 142.15
oyld 535.28
oylde 588.03
oyloy 378.09
Oyly 279.F21 574.01
oyol 287.05
oysters 407.01
ozone 321.23 542.07

pa 055.16 094.13 129.15 147.13 178.02 207.29 221.29 267.F4 268.26 280.17 311.27 319.18 331.01 414.25 426.17 464.11 485.30 497.12 550.15 565.33 596.29 611.19
pa 339.32 412.29 606.05
pa- 054.15
Pa- 054.15 054.15
paa 427.09
paard 139.32
pac 487.31
pacco 069.36
pace 618.07
pacem 087.14
Pacem 212.04
pacers 542.11
pack 324.13
packed 355.02
packer 375.15
packet 058.35 492.20
packpanel 575.35
packyoulloups 526.18
pact 133.13
pacts 470.36
pad 234.19 595.22
padatback 289.F3
padded 120.10
paddyfair 472.22
paddynger 612.18
paded 043.23
padenopie 179.34
padey 470.07
padge 285.06
padoors 351.34
pads 230.30 246.31
padums 303.18
paese 129.27
pagallus 484.35
pagana 080.20
pagandi 289.02

page 206.01 212.34 300.14 369.34 428.16
pagemonite 403.17
pagenua 513.20
paging 530.15
pagodlap 344.02
pagods 005.33
pah 306.07 588.24
paht 018.32
paid 101.25 590.11
pails 101.27 250.09
pain 328.36 407.31
Pains 213.18
pain's 553.36
painted 090.16 095.16 452.19 504.34
painter 087.13
paintime 365.07
pair 059.34 152.35 191.02 462.10 522.19 606.23
paired 413.01
pairently 081.36
pairs 238.01 492.24
pais 113.11
pak- 257.27
pakork 497.28
pal 320.12 337.08 365.09 443.30 446.24
pal 175.17
palace 552.23
palast 597.13
paled 427.07
paleogos 349.22
palepsy 232.30
palisoot 487.32
pall 432.13 528.21 549.05
palla 316.21
palleaps 303.02
palled 452.23 506.09
pallid 109.10
palls 621.15
palm 407.23
palmover 601.01
palmular 613.18
palniel's 350.30
palombarouter 314.11
paloosa 254.23
palpabuat 113.30
palpabunt 023.25
palpeens 032.16
pals 441.12
palsive 386.29
paltar 344.27
paltry 022.26
palume 433.01
palus 182.18
pam 178.17
pamore 173.22
pamound 464.26
pan 151.14 206.02 211.11 224.19 292.13 310.11 423.09 435.27 440.04 466.02 486.18 559.10 562.14 581.09
panasbullocks 611.26
panc 349.10
pancian 488.32
pancreates 088.09
pander 531.05
pane 235.33
panel 575.35
panelfitted 076.11
panelled 529.06
panepi 611.18
pang 231.17
pangle 190.32
pani 182.28
panies 234.16
panishadem 303.13
panks 600.24
pann 538.32
panned 082.34 493.22
panny 588.18
panoff 116.32
panquost 388.28
pansies 059.14
pant 374.13
panters 609.13
pantically 034.02
panties 094.16
panting 394.36
pantry's 007.10
pants 042.31 206.27 319.32
panungopovengreskey 056.36
panwor 611.19
pany 611.04
panza 234.06
panzussch 488.07
pap 301.07
papar 065.12 065.19
papaveri's 172.01
paper 111.09 127.20 127.23 139.02 416.21 419.29 457.34
paperbaskel 194.13
papered 461.19 559.02
papoff 461.15
papoosiesobjibway 134.14
papparrass- 332.05
papple 126.17
pappoff 337.01
papreta 179.19
paps 480.14 510.09 583.22
pap's 025.05
par 208.13 210.13
parable 404.21
parading 327.16
paralleled 286.F4
paralysed 177.05
param 185.14
parang 345.05
paranto 419.13
paraparnelligoes 303.11
parasoul 569.20
paratrices 618.15
parcenors 096.35
pard 028.22 276.12
pardon 445.17
pardonable 562.36
pards 396.17
pared 170.15 551.02
parent 434.22
parentations 600.09
parents 189.01 230.33
parents 175.09
parent's 121.08
paria 211.10
parient 336.31
parile 283.22
paring 364.05 516.28
parior 404.18
parioramoci 468.20
parishable 130.05
parisien 151.09
park 051.20 321.08 524.06 564.06
parka 178.33
parkment 364.07
park's 245.17
parlour 157.17
parly 602.34
parnell 564.28
parnelligoes 303.11
parolysed 612.19
paroxemete 132.03
parque 359.35
parr 003.17
parr- 332.05
parrently 081.22
Parsons 026.32
part 091.19 324.20 403.18 405.06 569.20 626.31 626.32
parte 334.09
parted 087.21
parteed 186.33
parthenopes 542.21
particular 602.07 613.33
partied 087.35
parting 454.26
partings 095.33
partite 405.31 486.28
Partland 067.25
partner 580.26
partners 488.05
partnuzz 571.28
partridge 301.30
parts 238.26 252.30 373.17 414.27
party 413.08 524.35
parvious 377.13
pas 052.14 095.23 101.27 160.31 211.24 403.16 499.05 594.06 611.04 619.34
pa's 280.18
pasafello 174.14
pass 087.21 203.02 363.26 532.19 587.30
passable 499.19
passe 128.25
passed 465.01 489.21 490.21 584.35
passers 128.34 594.14
passers 345.28
passes 407.35 564.21 587.28 615.36
passia 527.07
passible 298.18
passible 340.05
passim 050.24
passing 059.35 081.02 160.36 270.F3 439.02 546.11
passit 167.33
pass-on 474.04
passos 272.05
past 041.29 151.22 292.11
past- 090.31
paste 190.34
pastful 406.26
pastored 094.13 612.08
pasture- 113.09
pastures 193.06
paszpas 101.27
pat 013.34 020.22 284.24 327.29 487.23
patagain 058.23
patap- 090.31
patch 009.03 009.03 031.23 559.13
patched 473.09 596.31
pate 173.11
pateers 553.36

patently 085.32
pater 081.05 342.26
pater's 104.20
pates 272.23
patetic 417.32
patetic 298.L3
pateting 266.06
path 022.08 460.21 594.27
pathe 613.17
pathete 226.06
paths 488.26
patica 212.11
patkin 081.18
patlockt 069.25
patom 344.30
patonguing 584.03
patria 271.L2
patriate 100.10 490.16 602.34
patrician 166.34
patrick 031.31 051.08 091.06
394.12 404.35 564.32
patricks 133.27
patrick's 026.22 035.24 508.23
patrickularly 316.05
patrico 464.16
patriock 531.33
pats 436.02
patstrophied 612.19
patte 228.06
pattees 011.20
pattern 029.23
patup- 090.31
patz- 044.20
paulettes 208.18
pauling 131.12
paulmurphyc 031.35
pauper's 422.15
pavin 316.32
paw 100.21 110.03 587.32
621.21
pawn 339.27
paws 468.32
PAX-BELLUM 281.R1
pay 028.32 221.29 406.14
payer 086.27
payers 182.35
paying 138.31
payns 533.20
pays 181.05 392.07
paza 257.04
pe 120.09
pea 392.25 572.36
peace 101.18 301.F1 364.17
364.20 503.13
peace 345.12
peach 349.26
peachin 485.12
peachment 220.29
peachum 235.21
peafing 619.20
peahahn 205.29
peal 004.07 141.12 335.11
pealance 338.11
pealed 452.22
pealling 527.26
peals 253.28 585.25
pean 598.15
peans 242.30
pear 340.10
pearances 548.25
pearant 490.07
peard 353.14
pearl 561.15
pease 021.18 022.06 417.07
571.21 573.12
peased 319.24
peasement 610.27
peasy 406.03
peation 110.07
peatrick 003.10
pebble 620.19
pebbles 072.33
pecies 153.02
peck 416.17
pecked 492.09
pecks 207.13
ped 559.23
pedalia 116.30
pedariaty 345.29
pedding 599.08
peddlars 347.27
pede 089.24 325.31 446.01
pedemics 539.36
pediment 463.11
pediments 596.23
peds 343.32 397.16
pee 030.23 058.25 246.01
248.18 386.26 387.06 492.36
583.29
peecuffs 542.13
peeds 416.33
peegeequanee 072.08
peehole 120.31
peehouses 416.36
peel 110.29 274.14 303.F1
475.13 508.29
peeler 441.33
peelers 522.16
peels 569.04
peep 227.12 435.25 624.09
peep 275.L2
peeped 508.27
peepers 389.26
peer 019.31 257.20 267.04
337.36
peers 421.03 570.22
peer's 145.24
pees 134.35
peg 208.22 210.25
pegia 613.09
pegs 113.19
peh 138.10
pekin 533.06
pel 397.19
pel 175.17
pelago 605.05
pelago's 029.23
pelhullpulthebell 245.25
pelicans 601.34
pelick 020.34
pellas 527.01
pelled 606.32
pelles 545.25
pelling 518.20
pellopalombarouter 314.11
pelting 004.04
pelts 344.15
peltsion 518.23
pelure 560.27
pen 077.20 321.20 359.01
377.08 388.03 563.06 610.32
pen 141.06 172.02 342.26
penal 398.07
penas 438.29
pence 046.18 069.18 069.18
083.02 142.01 161.22 165.31
321.25 338.28 350.27 413.36
425.14 544.26 586.23
pence 141.07 266.L1
penced 348.18
pencil 056.12 211.12 311.10
pencilled 066.16
pencils 504.27
pendeats 211.27
pendements 515.33
pendent 602.20
pendiculous 493.10
pending 187.18 279.F18
pendolous 339.13
peners 193.02
penetrablum 178.30
penetrativeness 308.L2
penger 294.F1
pengha 377.27
penhelp 010.13
pening 067.16
penmark 189.06
penmeselps 612.24
penned 489.33
pennies 011.21 313.16 546.27
546.28 549.36
penniferry 485.02
penny 099.14 190.19 191.01
208.21 351.21 396.17 396.18
485.17
pennyhapennies 549.36
penomen 059.15
penpack 324.13
pens 364.15
pensing 345.04
penstake 137.32
pent 612.06
pentacles 397.35
pentake 030.09
penth 102.25
pentices 315.18
pentings 492.30
pents 339.10
peny 465.23
peong 058.24
people 141.05
pep 494.15 502.09 540.14
peppeppediment 463.11
pepper 292.07 550.11
peppercast 120.14
pepperpot 499.12
peppers 607.34
peprosapia 265.22
peptic 050.21
peptist 453.15
pepulation 362.04
per 179.14
perca 067.36 444.36
perceable 616.32
perd 483.21 552.11
perdition 455.06
perfect 165.32 468.09 489.34
perfectible 122.35
perfection 109.09 428.07
perfectly 033.22 582.31
perforator 303.22
perfractus 041.06
peributts 396.35
peried 345.21
peril 223.28
perise 226.07
perismenon 059.16
permanent 101.30
permeable 152.24

pernelly 445.11
perom's 070.25
peron 600.29
perrytiff 493.03
persaturals 341.30
perse 117.15
persite 581.19
personal 135.26 509.35
personating 086.08 490.15
Person's 123.25
perssly 240.10
persuaded 123.09
persuasions 537.03
pert 487.11
pertheloss 318.18
pertieu 289.22
pertillery 530.18
perts 241.31
perups 230.35
perusual 368.13
pervious 348.06
perwhis 121.12
perybally 460.12
peschyites 365.09
pest 131.13 150.27
pestered 098.13 178.03
pestric 081.13
peswch- 414.19
pet 043.13 133.08 361.09 449.31 449.31 461.35 601.28
petalletted 562.02
petally 605.15
petards 371.02
petbackagain 114.19
peter 372.06
peter's 426.21
petersen 310.03
petiginous 189.32
petite 325.04
petition 492.28
petitioning 356.07
peto 077.07
petpurpose 614.34
petre 059.17 566.03
petres 420.35
petriark 153.27
petrified 023.30
pets 266.05 279.F18 436.02 491.22 583.18
petsi 276.F4
petta 470.21
petta 147.33
pette 014.08 079.23 096.14 143.31 147.29 232.25 248.19 276.F6 374.11 413.24 478.03 478.27 500.23 500.25 500.32 500.32 571.17
pettes 080.35 272.F4 531.19
pettishly 563.05
petto 470.21
pettypout 268.13
petulo 054.34
petus 268.24
pety 015.26
peu 222.10
peupresiosity 132.03
peus 014.09
pew 442.35 520.05
pewter 167.21
pex 263.08
pexojesus 296.10
peza 497.32
pezzata 152.31
pfaffing 529.30
pfff 116.33
pforter 548.12
phage 171.03
phagusted 610.01
phalines 595.14
phallic 481.04
phalna- 257.27
phamous 073.09
phanes 013.16
phanished 473.20
phannd 129.17
phannies 340.25
phantes 502.10
phanypes 626.05
phar 325.26
pharey 046.30
pharos 076.34
pharospasmockical 515.16
phars 075.01
phasia 122.04
phault 581.30
Phelim's 072.04
pheph 125.17
phere 295.04
pheres 062.21
phessised 520.14
Phett 355.31
pheu's 193.20
phex 415.28
phez 535.01
phiar 343.17
phight 425.31
phil 163.25
phile 358.12
philias 110.11
philim 590.17
philip 088.31
philius 596.18
philomos 123.14
philos 606.05
philots 062.16
phils 115.12
phires 553.10
phiz 051.01 307.F7
phlegmatised 394.21
phlickathims 199.35
phobe 035.02 358.12
phobes 076.23
phobian 478.32
phoebia 415.10
phoenix 473.18
phoggs 005.32
pholomy 389.17
phon 308.L1
phone 013.16 118.13 462.16
phonethics 038.36
phoney 388.08
phonia 446.30
phoniaksically 178.06
phonious 123.12
phonise 515.11
phonium 533.17
phono- 135.16
phonoised 258.21
phonologistic 123.18
phony 052.18
phor 475.15
phoric 472.17
phoron 603.36 606.27
phorously 154.07
phos 536.19
phosically 319.34
phosis 107.13
phosy 119.04
photorejected 251.07
photy 341.08
phrastius 484.30
phrenesis 123.18
phreum 077.34
phro 140.05
phrohibited 085.09
phruck 190.02
phthisis 305.21
phudded 517.07
phul 348.05
phullopopulace 342.18
phumble 503.16
phumeral 369.33
phyl 080.22
phyllicks 525.08
phyre 137.24
phyrious 264.F3
phyroid 100.17
physicians 116.27
physicking 156.11
physis 092.10
pialamina 183.01
piam 611.25
piam 287.27
piane 158.11
piano 176.33
piastered 098.12
pibambuli 306.F5
pic 039.02 115.32
piccolo 450.19
pick 071.03 141.10 177.32 410.24
picked 364.36
picker 312.16
pickers 538.21
pickle 050.08
pickles 133.20
picks 025.16 173.18
pickthalamorous 040.14
picolas 423.35
pics 386.06
pict 039.09
pictified 230.32
pictorsbosk 351.24
pictre 299.05
picture 570.14
pidarapidarpad 234.19
pidarpad 234.19
pidgeonlover 485.20
pidian 071.03
pidities 242.17
pidumic 497.15
pidump 364.29
pie 037.32 179.34 296.26 407.29
piece 033.03 052.07 131.33 161.11 209.27 328.16 455.26 533.07 559.11 590.11 619.02
pied 276.F5 331.08
pieno 182.30
pierce 512.24
piercing 474.12
pierre 614.03
pies 088.25 210.21 450.05 513.14
piety 206.20
piezite 086.02
pifer 136.17
pig 176.03
pigeons 029.10

piggle 285.08
pigi 575.29 576.08
pigi's 576.06
pigliando 038.14
pigotty 016.06
pig's 535.20
pig's 072.14
pigses 313.16
pik 011.10
pike 031.01 132.32 293.13
pikepointandplace 003.22
piker 031.27
pikes 286.15
pil 497.13
pilagian 387.05
piles 011.21
pill 161.31 448.15
Pill 283.F3
pillar 033.23 063.29
pilled 230.05
pillerindernees 234.19
pillsation 095.01
pils 480.33
pilt 535.24
pim 010.16
pimsolff 353.17
pin 060.35 094.24 148.22
211.12 212.08 266.F2 331.12
336.30 370.08 419.23 441.17
486.30 491.06 561.32 588.05
pinacci 368.33
pinandoutdown 612.14
pinas 223.02
pindhrue 378.28
pindown 065.32
pine 287.16 553.25 624.25
pineal 115.31
pines 510.34
pin'fampiny 046.19
pinghim 298.25
pinhour 414.33
pinjars 621.15
pinny 437.18
pinnypan 466.02
pinregn 568.34
pins 006.01 014.22 113.02
144.17 193.08 312.21 531.07
549.36 559.20
pin's 506.25
pint 558.01
pinter 482.20
pintheochromatokreening 392.28
pinto 331.13 474.14
piny 046.19
pionia 348.30
pious 303.25
pip 178.27 314.25 314.25
314.26
pipe 220.26 231.31 237.15
241.14 315.24
piped 371.35
pipes 243.21 499.29
pipey 130.36
pippinghim 298.25
pirine 257.02
pirrt 343.21
pis 405.26
piscus 193.31
pishers 370.34
pissated 179.25
pisser 451.36
pissers 503.29
pissially 113.16
pissimas 573.30
pissing 302.06
pissmas 101.28
pistic 536.05
pistol 228.33
pistola 117.27
pistolear 038.23
pisuppon 233.34
pit 033.01 077.27 207.34
211.22 247.32 385.17 427.34
554.06
pita 067.33
pitally 444.28
pitch 009.12 232.01 540.14
566.03
pitchback 009.12
pitched 121.16 179.22
piter 183.13 390.22
piter 342.14 573.20
pithump 006.04
pititions 276.F1
pitle 046.19
pitout 506.32
pits 172.32 544.14
pitschens 038.22
pitt 039.13
pittles 040.36
piular 351.12
pive 282.32 282.32
piwor 611.22
piza 257.04
pizo 160.30
pizzles 411.15
pkon- 044.20
pkot 044.20
plabashing 431.16
place 003.22 052.10 065.22
080.13 081.15 114.18 134.32
231.24 262.F1 362.34 416.24
481.21 488.20 489.10 504.08
504.09 504.12 527.06 548.33
568.09 571.24 600.30 612.08
624.34 625.06
place 418.11
placeable 585.10
placed 079.13 090.03 236.25
placement 599.10
places 127.11 533.22
placing 446.08
pladdy- 044.20
plades 134.05
plade's 069.28
pladher 454.14
plads 570.04
plagued 539.11
plaid 227.22
plain 036.15 236.24 594.23
plaina 158.19
plak 562.03 562.03 562.15
plan 060.30 079.29
planadas 553.12
planck 505.28
plane 369.02
plangent 394.36
planned 489.34 614.24
plantad 564.22
planters 025.19
planting 579.33
plantz 542.01
plapping 057.11
plasm 133.24
plaster 101.24
plastered 181.08
plasters 152.26
plasurin 370.18
plate 006.32 119.03 182.33
265.F2 284.25 486.29
plate 104.11
plated 077.09
plates 231.24
platts 559.24
platz 447.21
plaud 032.27 172.19
play 095.21 283.05 484.18
501.11 516.35 521.33 560.06
569.34 589.27
play 293.L1
players' 056.35
playn 609.15
plays 233.19 374.07
pleaced 292.04
pleach 034.31
pleaches 553.11
pleas 422.29
pleasant 072.26
please 248.02 256.26 270.23
272.14 461.19
pleased 222.09
pleasely 232.20
pleasure 609.11
pleats 530.27
plegs 607.20
plenquished 381.34
plenty 211.07
plethoric 104.17
plex 149.30
plexes 133.30
plexious 421.34
plexus 114.33
pleyurs 224.22
plic 123.22
plie 430.31
plin 593.24
plique 148.17
plisse 578.08
plodes 249.15
plodher 454.14
ploits 272.L4
plompervious 348.06
plon 141.05 318.04
plore 557.34
ploser 512.18
plosition 419.11
plosium 589.36
plot 135.17 284.07
plother 142.11
plots 033.17 124.29 368.09
plotsch 343.28
plotting 624.12
ploud 257.30
pluched 172.25
pluck 034.32
plucking 084.06
pluddy- 044.20
plug 428.12
plumbs 041.20
plume 072.36 318.12
plumes 026.10
plummy 405.34
plunderdly 357.02
plunderer 326.09
plunthers 352.09
plurabel 224.10
plural 297.21
plus 099.33 145.30 381.32
plush 474.14 516.27

plussed 410.10 586.24
plussedly 156.09
plussing 475.04
plutor 387.13
pluvium 251.02
ply 320.01 405.01 474.24
530.16
pneumaticus 484.30
pnice 346.29
po 192.03
Po 009.34
poblican 172.23
pocattls 386.35
pocket 035.27 282.15
pocketpoint 282.15
pocketprod 282.16
pocketpromise 282.16
pocketpumb 282.15
pockets 183.31
pocking 572.03
pocky 082.14
poclogypst 364.18
pod 078.05
podch 620.32
podded 498.32
podestalled 513.35
podium 334.03
podium-am-Bummel 191.10
podopudupedding 599.08
podorme 245.02
pods 286.24 484.02
podvas 343.34
poe 427.27
poet 177.21
poetic 468.10
POETIC 308.R2
poetryck 393.10
poff 337.01 461.15
pofforth 583.32
poghue 384.34 385.22
Poghue 388.25 600.32
Poghue's 203.36
pogreasymost 156.17
pogue 303.04 385.03
pohlstery 271.F3
poider 169.18
poinis 165.28
point 038.03 129.24 134.32
149.18 260.15 282.15 355.14
367.30 468.17 482.34 576.19
583.34 587.15 588.15 594.34
pointandplace 003.22
pointed 550.30
pointing 181.24
pointlex 083.09
poise 206.24 362.08 407.06
427.21 437.30 623.14
poise 277.L6
poison 101.22
poisoned 339.33
poke 359.26
poker 493.10 558.30
poker 340.04
pokery 113.26
poking 240.28
pol 612.29
polam 396.09
polamos 327.33
pole 044.04 160.07 249.26
358.34 369.19 390.11 503.33
547.22 622.30
polendom 101.27
poleon 388.16
poleriding 589.01
poles 421.32
polettes 343.24 623.17
poli 111.18 230.16
poliarchialisation 181.07
polies 357.30
polin 104.15
polis 024.18 128.03 181.06
222.07 318.24 335.07 345.02
594.08
polish 038.02 141.14
politan 080.01 306.25 524.02
530.16 543.01 565.04
polite 309.10
politely 192.26 540.01
politos 316.15
polity's 133.18
polkaloops 557.02
poll 053.10 057.17 167.13
193.20 227.22 242.04 524.17
pollard 350.10
polled 435.12
polled 176.07
pollen 418.19
pollocks 418.22
polloosa 494.25
pollyon 273.27
polodotonates 353.23
polonians 616.24
polootly 372.34
polopocattls 386.35
pol's 155.19
poluono 081.33
poly 242.16 304.14
polygon 339.35
polylogic 474.05
polypools 302.32
pom 153.27
pommenites 498.10
pommy 609.33
pompounded 036.02
pomuk 349.23
pon 186.13 344.05 443.06
ponce 382.20 568.13
pond 098.20 214.08 244.14
328.19
pondage 271.02
pondaneously 414.01
pondant 602.17
pondas 052.15
pondee 457.28
pondee 282.L2
pondees 139.20
ponder 344.05
pondful 110.32
ponds 238.34
pond's 018.02
pondy 430.05
pone 579.14
poned 051.22 569.26
ponence 277.02
pong 015.19 213.18 231.10
ponhurrish 607.20
poniard's 180.11
ponied 607.32
poning 484.02
ponism 097.14
ponnus 607.35
ponse 167.29
ponsif 494.36
ponskneed 075.21
pont 135.17 607.30
pon-the-Baltic 320.21
ponthus 394.29
pontify 097.23
poo 256.02 276.17 302.02
389.29 561.32
pood 206.30
poods 416.34
poof 048.01
poofool- 314.08
pool 017.07 085.15 088.34
224.17 266.03 300.09 311.31
448.13
pooliom 156.16
pools 302.32
poomark 533.35
poor 074.13 340.11 449.31
poorapps 595.20
poorter 327.33
pooser 379.13
poosiesobjibway 134.14
poostles 617.05
poosts 221.32
pootsies 077.32
pop 013.30 067.22 451.24
540.14 565.20 565.20
popaw 587.32
popees 422.02
pophanypes 626.05
popo 214.28 319.21
popodorme 245.02
popolamos 327.33
poposal 575.32
popotamuns 047.08
poppapoff 461.15
poppopcuddle 379.20
poppsky 404.24
pops 234.36 304.23
popticus 611.25
populace 342.18
popular 078.12
populate 188.35
populipater 081.05
porates 185.10
porcious 510.33
Pore-in 135.10
porello 172.23
poreoozers 156.13
pores 367.25
pork 407.19 407.19
porn 120.09
porna- 090.31
porochs 343.27
porportiums 343.18
pors 313.19
port 025.05 133.21 166.32
200.21 318.13 407.21 407.21
471.36 549.22 579.22
ported 452.14 536.02
portent 464.07
porter 038.05
porter- 257.27
porterage 070.05
porteral 099.04
porteroguing 595.20
porterous 560.31
porters 191.19 221.03 372.09
porth 578.27
portion 397.18
portioned 602.03
portiums 343.18
ports 187.07 386.26 497.26
ports 341.25
ports' 066.08
porty 338.20

pos 054.17 144.05 288.F4 365.19 553.21
posal 575.32
posale 149.17
posant 549.34
poscals 446.36
pose 332.07 361.09 417.28 618.01
posed 066.19 118.30 276.07
poses 348.24
poshialiste 240.03
posht 441.06
posing 345.05
position 111.07 178.04 419.30 533.11 572.32 589.17 595.25
positions 572.22
positive 084.20
posito 185.25
positoed 498.35
positorily 406.19
pository 415.33
positus 228.34
posopher 365.05
posophia 394.19
poss 297.F5 382.20 495.06
possels 411.16
possessing 115.32
possette 484.33
possible 110.19 175.05 417.32 617.08
POSSIBLE 262.R1
possive 162.19
post 013.28 036.05 077.05 090.06 178.09 193.18 200.22 364.06 422.03 600.17
postdating 256.22
posted 075.04
posteln 569.08
poster 325.10 533.16
postered 101.25
posterioprismically 612.19
posteriorious 083.11
posteriorly 343.16
posterns 235.22
posterose 582.02
posterous 033.32 189.21 356.35
posterously 153.25
posters 190.32
posterus 016.03
postes 126.08
postila 449.11
postolopolos 134.22
postolopulos 306.10
postoral 086.21
posts 064.10 183.10 541.07
postulance 483.30
postumia 607.09
postures 182.02
posy 430.22
pot 020.07 031.03 093.32 117.18 152.11 194.08 209.11 210.30 221.13 242.15 251.05 294.31 305.27 329.08 356.03 406.01 408.11 424.07 494.34 496.19 499.12 538.35 559.15 582.14 593.23
pot 071.23 262.L2
potacarry's 492.19
potamians 437.25
potamuns 047.08
potamus 064.17 210.35 449.32
pote 337.24
poted 232.22
potent 573.22
potentem 185.14
potes 105.20
pother 364.26
potion 310.36
potl 294.24
potluck 210.05
potomac 559.35
potreek 012.22
potria 243.29
pots 192.29 219.06 257.16 258.16 616.12
potsi 276.F4
potstill 463.34
pottes 366.01
potthered 050.04
pottleslup 371.04
potty 059.12 247.15 247.15
poty 054.12 054.12
poulling 320.03
poulos 424.07
pound 056.06 082.26
pounde 378.24
pounded 036.02 220.30 253.35
pounten 211.20
pour 043.34 174.23
pouree 236.15 236.15 236.16 236.17
pourers 112.24
poused 548.11
pousing 344.16
pout 268.13 288.09 596.22
poutre 337.18
povengreskey 056.36
pover 140.24
povernment 273.06
povy 333.14
pow 015.27 375.05 535.31
powder 393.22
powdered 190.01
powdhericks 618.15
power 008.36 047.19 117.20 178.27 188.07 248.21 274.10 410.25 459.33 521.24 576.26
powered 426.09 557.30
powers 387.11
pown 005.20
pows 363.20
powtew 061.06 523.02
powtherplother 142.11
pox 045.29 060.33
poxed 090.25
poxtelating 581.13
poxy 386.31
poxyomenously 353.06
poyride 105.35
poy's 328.27
pracing 365.35
practices 050.28
praise 356.19 493.36
praised 536.25
praisiate 337.23
praisiation 041.28
pram 008.07
prate's 334.01
prattight 265.09
pray 213.19 561.20 598.14
prayer 244.36
prayers 081.27
Prayers 258.35
Prayins 291.10
preach 299.22 378.32
preaches 274.11
preaching 029.25 292.09
precate 569.18
precession 156.08
precht 088.22
precisely 057.16
precurious 363.28
predicted 427.31
preem 605.16
preesing 088.26
pregnable 411.33
preints 105.18
prencisses 365.28
prendered 285.28
prends 582.17
preoccupied 558.04
prescriptible 085.07
presence 108.33 499.28
present 036.19 151.21 333.11 526.12
presentation 509.01
presented 176.07
presents 119.19
preserved 533.04
presiosity 132.03
press 020.09 043.25 356.21 548.02 588.33
pressed 190.33
pressgangs 068.31
pressible 470.31
pressible 568.16
pressiom 278.F2
pression 115.24
pressus 470.16
prestuberian 381.14
preta 179.19
prette 531.16
previousday's 407.29
prey 441.07 519.04 585.32
preys' 146.09
prezzion 064.31
priams 131.08
prican 350.21
price 290.25 530.01
price 072.04
priceget 616.11
pricers 375.25
pricus 161.26
pride 226.29
pried 101.22
priest 080.26 483.13 601.01
priestpower 188.07
priest's 122.07
prig 365.32
prik's 538.15
prime 279.F18 343.29
primed 052.06
primor's 273.02
primustimus 108.12
prince 139.35 416.13
principially 483.20
principiant 594.02
prines 504.26
prinks 537.05
prinse 137.16
print 114.31
prints 080.10
prior 358.09
priori 343.18
prioric 083.11
priquos 055.16
prise 606.36
prise 419.01
priseandprove 571.32

prising 532.26
prismic 611.13
prismically 612.19
prisoms 127.03
priss 197.35
prissis 460.23
priss's 525.34
prit 291.20
pritties 234.18
private 040.16
privately 050.28
privates 351.27
privet 363.30
prize 306.04
prizzling 207.15
pro 408.12
proariose 121.27
probable 110.12 110.12 110.15 499.19 538.05 617.09
probables 609.05
probare 163.04
probate 557.27
probro 188.27
procession 156.08
proctor 366.23
prod 282.16
prodictive 298.17
produce 283.13
producing 342.21
product 108.31 546.15
proem 528.16
professional 456.29
profound 058.09
profundity 394.31
prog 161.28
progressive 614.31
progue 053.27 507.22
progues 083.13
proham 570.19
prohome 074.06 074.07
proise 318.05
promifazzio 345.23
promise 282.16
prompted 060.02
promptly 255.29
promptued 171.09
proneauntisquattor 019.27
pronette 267.11
prong 370.01
pronius 128.15
pronominal 120.09
pronouceable 479.09
proof 077.17 155.29 165.32 182.16 290.19 380.34 461.05 527.19 548.21 616.32
proof 418.20
proofment 603.03
proper 096.14 131.33 269.F3 384.29 387.07 391.24 395.15
properable 538.12
properial 484.20
properies 278.05
properly 337.22
proper's 422.20
property 617.35
propheticals 011.30
prophets 029.16
propinquans 185.16
propinquish 612.24
propos 433.17
proprevious day's 407.29
propriety 034.15
proquo 432.05
proresurrectionism 483.10
prosapia 265.22
prosperousness 308.21
prossable 609.06
prostitute 186.27
prosts 347.11
protestant 534.16
protos 498.04
proud 255.26 446.03
provable 530.34
prove 571.32
proved 155.36
proven 099.23
provided 404.22 614.30
providence 012.01
provincial 377.23
proving 431.05
provocative 162.20
provoker 466.22
prowl 139.31
prowled 004.11
prowly 617.19
proxemetely 295.31
prue 523.29
prumptu 093.14
prused 345.08
prusshers 608.10
prussians 135.16
pry 241.33
psing 476.03
psjute 110.26
pst 395.36
psychidically 041.05
pterous 417.01
ptit 054.16
pu 412.28 425.08
pubber 594.18
pubblicities 368.13
pubblicoes 371.24
puberal 037.01
publican 393.23
publicans 053.28
publican's 090.05
publick 105.23
publicly 305.14
published 123.27
puck 445.15
puck- 090.31
puckalips 455.01
Puckins 376.01
puckparty 524.35
pucks 371.12
pucky 116.31
pucos 011.14
pucs 236.31
puddels 621.13
pudding 170.36
puddingpodded 498.32
PUDENIES 308.R2
pudiating 513.22
puds 477.11
pudsfrowse 526.25
pudupedding 599.08
pueratory 274.30
puff 509.28
puffs 038.30 065.11 234.24
puggers 613.27
pugn 243.07
pugnable 152.24
puitwyne 078.20
puk 113.13 257.27
pukan 037.32
puke 040.05 040.05
puke 281.L3
puking 178.07
pul 621.34
pulator 313.33
pulence 126.16
pulent 282.22
pulenta 099.09
pull 290.03 300.13 314.19 317.04 377.35 441.15 552.10
pull 338.15 418.33
pullajibed 317.30
pullamealahmalong 485.33
pullar 177.03
pullcelery 586.27
pulled 488.22
puller 241.09
pulley 492.23
pullupalleaps 303.02
puloids 540.33
puls 542.18
pulsed 135.25 501.20
pulsing 434.28 469.36
PULSIVENESS 286.R4
pulthebell 245.25
pum 153.26 279.F27 345.23
pumb 282.15
pummelites 498.10
pump 366.10
pumplikun 370.24
pumstances 297.07
pumtum 273.08
pun 224.36 251.05 301.13 548.31
punchable 029.35
punchers 386.30
punct 309.04
pund 214.08 329.07
punded 310.05
punder 081.11
pung 072.33 313.30
punge 050.04
punish 548.08
punked 131.15
punkment 536.03
punn 157.08
punsch 594.35
punters 439.33
punto 619.34
punts 541.01
pup 355.30 624.09
pupcables 077.09
puppy 262.L4
pupus 007.08
pur 329.02
purando 504.17
puration 368.12
Purcell 187.18
purchasing 596.30
purdonable 537.36
pure 024.24 204.13 492.36
pureely 406.21
pures 234.30
purgas 229.16
purgative 356.30
purgatory 161.23 446.36
purgers' 556.28
purgies 530.31
purk 346.32
purl 443.34
purple 109.11 111.02
purpoise 362.08
purpose 614.34
purr 597.16

purring 035.21
purse 042.30 620.05
pursuant 594.28
purty 012.24
purudo 289.22
purus 557.06
pus 007.08 020.13 115.31 128.36 198.29
pusher 491.26
pusmugnus 484.35
puss 445.23 516.29 597.16
pusse 416.15
pussy 011.13 028.10
pust 457.32
put 016.20 221.13 387.34
putabout 043.36
puthry 597.15
putiliser 092.24
puting 222.26
putred 350.17
putsbargain 312.25
puttana 583.09
puttanach 090.31
putty 068.28 612.32
puzzler's 326.11
pyam 178.15
pygard 609.17
pygic 522.31
pygyddyum 414.26
pyl 607.34
pynghome 602.33
pyr 020.10
pyre 289.10 439.34 473.18
pyre's 354.27
pyroy 568.34
pyrs 157.28
pyrus 121.02
pysian 005.23
pysius 155.31
pyssinia 318.32

qcut 517.26
qeez 296.03
qiq 029.18
quack 221.09 469.09
quackeringly 542.23
quacks 099.02
quadmala 184.28
quailing 552.22
quain 141.22
quake 133.12 144.33
qualifications 529.07
quam 163.23 300.32 586.29
quammythical 354.10
quanee 072.08
quanne 606.30
quansewn 208.17
quantities 447.03
quantity 114.25
quara 557.01
quart 139.07
quarters 051.32 202.16 285.F5 410.04 498.04 559.32
quashed 379.10
quatsch 270.L1
queadbaugham 024.14
queam 331.08
quean 021.15 021.15 021.26 022.02 022.11 022.13 022.27 023.12
quean's 102.10
queathed 579.32
queehenna 594.30
queen 207.36 250.29 508.26
queenie 577.02
queenies 234.13
queens 154.12
queer 151.15 384.10 420.22 584.21
queers 357.08
queerscenes 556.24
queesh 287.F4
queesthers 476.36
queets 487.27
queezit 412.08
quells 493.20
quenchers 178.03
queracq- 254.15
quest 279.08
questellates 107.18
questionable 183.23 495.25
Quetch 550.32
queue 019.24
queue 151.10
queues 280.18
quey- 254.15
queytuitte 609.17
quick 215.07 280.32 537.31
quickenthrees 377.11
quickyessed 365.11
quid 234.17
quid 161.02 188.08
quidance 465.23
quidself 186.06
quiem 499.11
quiet 137.06 506.17
quil 238.10
quill 419.21
Quillad 219.22
quiller's 050.09
quillia's 204.07
quilocus 254.20
quilt 556.16
quilties 508.19
quiluteral 297.27
quin 278.F7 372.11
quinance 240.08
quince 180.25
quinions 467.35
quinn 048.15
quinonthiance 296.20
quinque 134.13
quintaism 245.12
quintina 567.29
quipeu 222.10
quiquock 126.06
quire 205.22
quires 229.31
quiring 003.21
quirt 376.04
quished 490.01
quisitive 505.09
quissimam 287.23
quisted 238.15
quists 167.36
quit 551.26
Quite 088.14
quitting 438.13
quiviry 208.07
quo 181.34
quo 432.05
quock 126.06
quodoboits 211.28
quohy 290.F6
quoi 479.28
quoia 126.12
quointance 145.10
quorst 105.20
quos 055.16
quose 018.31
quost 388.28
quother 336.24
quou 151.29
quovis 484.34
qurd 233.32
quuliar 606.30
quuntly 357.14
qvick 302.18
qwind 360.36

ra 561.01
raab 018.13
raabhraab 072.13
raape 221.07
raascal 323.32
raatched 541.17
rab 237.16
rabahts 379.07
rabbit 366.18 559.28
rabelowther 266.10
rabi 139.25
rable 545.12
race 051.25 089.32 199.31 350.19 616.26
raced 354.17
racer 008.12 336.04
rachknell 388.34
racies 349.34
racing 365.35
raciously 285.02
rack 080.20 227.20 327.24 498.24
rackinarockar 424.20
rack-on-Sharon 526.28
racks 015.36 019.20
rackt 058.31
racles 617.25
racy 348.27
rad 114.05 491.35
raddy 335.15
rade 051.04
rads 299.30
raely 027.01
rafel 049.23
rafferteed 345.25
raft 301.23
rag 010.15 221.23 239.07 565.18 612.25
ragadye 313.18
ragan 395.36 504.14
raganisations 086.21
ragate 439.35
rage 048.04 196.24 243.27 395.28 395.29 514.04 602.25 607.21
rage 340.28
raged 339.28 369.01
raged 354.09
ragedy 425.24
rageehouse 108.19
ragel 552.25
rageous 380.15
rager 492.21
rager's 434.04
rages 011.19 061.31 544.25 613.29
ragetopeace 364.17
ragheall- 332.05
raging 320.25

ragious 143.25
ragorridgorballyed 323.16
rags 007.24 267.10 583.01
rag's 366.21
Rah 237.28
rahast 114.04
rahsing 230.26
raid 036.20 543.17
raidd's 344.07
raider 619.30
raiders 387.02
raidor 378.05
raids 316.03
raidy 204.10
raie 235.13
raignghistan 493.02
rail 097.23
railian 060.27
rails 041.21
raimost 178.04
raimy 347.07
rain 059.30 313.14 320.31 338.26 484.04 500.35 570.05
raine 019.23 210.33
rainer 324.08
raines 528.17
rainia 031.25
rainit 414.13
rainroof 612.03
raised 262.25 354.24 536.25
raising 188.30
raisonal 485.05
raith 414.03
raizde 032.08
Rajas-Sattvas 294.L2
rake 012.25 377.29 448.10 557.06
rakin 485.13
raking 541.18
raks 315.23
raks 491.18
raky 368.10 368.14
rale 154.11
ralereality 289.04
ralia 353.24
raliens 162.12
rall 354.01
rally 090.31 220.15 277.04 420.03
ram 089.05 112.22 156.02 211.12 228.15 262.F4 344.31 553.32 568.19 593.13 609.22
ram 481.16 586.05
rama 602.13
ramadityationists 493.12
ramater 560.28
ramawitch 027.28
rambling 624.14
rame 104.10
ramens 502.30
ramies 553.11
ramny 335.36
ramoci 468.20
rams 315.21 316.11 343.30 445.24
ram's 532.32
ramsa 481.18
ramy 063.12
ramybows 011.12
ran 019.02 037.23 131.22 137.08 144.18 146.08 152.36 177.09 323.22 358.21 380.21 390.10 455.07 491.36 493.13 594.25
rancia 226.31
rancita 572.36
rancitrone 132.28
rancos 386.30
rancy 102.25
rand 113.08 130.08 372.06 432.09 601.02
randbowl 351.14
randed 171.32
RANDES 276.R1
randiums 269.10
randoms 358.03
rand's 088.33
ranes 513.26
rang 268.02 508.02
Rangans 030.01
rangaparang 345.05
ranged 107.33 203.27
ranger 372.12
ranghoangoly 611.30
ranging 596.08
rangle 608.24
ranglers 266.21
rangoontangues 541.34
rang's 096.23
rani 049.19
rania 185.31 504.24 583.16
rankastank 344.26
ranke 420.36
ranked 246.25
rankled 224.13
Rann 372.32
rannies 493.06
ranoch 502.01
rans 087.25 595.22
ransy 453.09
rant 026.27
ranta 513.12
ranyellgreenlindigan 611.06
ranzia 038.11
rap 010.17 273.08 310.20 476.22
rape 623.16
raped 330.20 435.14
rapest 508.23
rapidarpad 234.19
rapoblican 172.23
rapped 150.31 344.26
rapper 361.27 511.36
rapps 595.20
raps 154.13 184.26
rapurl 443.34
rara 209.21 214.06 255.15 497.04 497.04
rarder 113.09
rare 606.31
Rarelys 354.14
raschil 358.28
rasesheorebukujibun 484.26
rash 439.07
rashers 497.34
rashning 338.08
rasing 050.12
rasioused 416.24
raskelled 324.13
rasound 315.23
rassannuar- 332.05
rasselmann 088.23
rasted 122.08
rasticandeatar 406.07
rastle 586.01
rat 033.16 100.19 127.31
ratar 059.24
ratatattar 339.18
rate 092.27 097.23 374.05 451.32 497.21
rated 157.01
rateers 379.36
rathon 254.33
ratiocination 142.17
ration 143.13 205.14 269.F3 356.24
rational 020.01 432.07
rations 270.03 620.24
rats 332.32 536.33 615.16
ratt 380.02 556.35
ratted 097.02
rattle 607.11
rattlefield 609.34
rattlers 604.15
rattling 356.32
ratt's 380.02
ratty 209.10
rauch 157.28
rauches 595.04
raughter 008.17
raughther 379.21
raumd 309.24
raun 042.12 289.24
raval 366.20
ravar 172.11 213.09
ravarn 243.10
rave 569.34
raved 062.02 097.17 164.28
ravel 422.20
raves 246.33 363.07
ravmerouvian 113.04
ravyingly 416.07
raw 110.36 111.01 152.10 553.03
raw 491.19
rawbees 146.17
rawil 361.33
rawman 242.13
rawnummical 494.01
raxes 296.04
ray 026.07 101.35 151.24 246.26 248.01 372.28
ray 341.22
rayce 361.32
rayed 208.35 493.28
rayedevraye 253.33
raying 513.14
rayous 422.30
razalles 075.03
raze 398.27
razzias 338.22
reach 090.34 378.32
reached 523.14
reachesly 541.08
reaching 110.05 292.09
read 425.05
readable 179.26
reader 067.12
readers 091.17
reading 270.29 568.31
ready 266.22 523.14 602.33
reagh 129.24
reak 387.20
reaking 069.36
real 035.33 145.25 331.19 406.36 426.24 568.20
real 353.29
REAL 262.R1

realic 487.01
realis 332.34
realised 085.32
reality 289.04
really 490.17
ream 440.07
reamdhrue 320.21
ream's 219.05
reaper 555.10
rear 182.20 209.20
rearance 162.10
reared 038.28 492.27
rearing 466.11
rears 140.32
reations 585.01
reb 068.25
rebelling 518.19
rebob 245.27
reborn 059.18
rebukujibun 484.26
recapturable 058.22
rechaun 419.17
recht 088.22 239.19
recirculation 003.02
reck 416.36
recklessness 435.11
reckning 258.01
recknocksters 081.28
reckons 524.18
recks 090.11
recordant 450.28
recordation 142.25
recreating 282.28
recruitioners 351.06
recting 284.01
rectus 101.13
red 029.01 064.27 189.05 207.11 214.23 319.25 320.15 337.35 376.02 380.03 404.29 407.12 439.36 467.15 483.27 517.11 527.25 590.08
red- 378.09
redas 052.15
redd 020.08
redent 484.09
redful 348.14
redman 590.22
redonnance 184.19
reds 132.05 189.11
red's 277.01
redt's 406.09
ree 052.24 100.08 150.02 373.25 546.27 584.30
reece 594.32
reed 196.10 566.36
reede 099.30
reed's 058.11
reek 012.22 314.23 518.09
reeke 230.01
reeked 200.01
reekeransy 453.09
reeking 438.28
reeksmen 053.26
reel 489.35
reels 414.35
reelwarkers 243.22
reely 406.21
reem 143.25 605.16
reen 214.13
reeponskneed 075.21
reesh 467.05 467.05 467.11
reesing 088.26
reeta 091.22
reether 093.32
reetsar 612.06
reeve 547.17
reeve-Astagob 503.14
reflection 611.16
reformed 352.02
regal 032.36 332.26
rege 132.29
regendered 581.16
regent's 564.13
regionary 533.08
reglias 256.03
regn 568.34
regnation 224.14
regular 179.03
regularshaped 134.25
regulorum 133.36
rehmoose 053.18
rehoot 354.18
rei 616.09
reich 138.32 181.04
Reid 313.34
reider 209.22
reign 013.02 374.28 495.22 504.19
reigner 385.32
reille 175.28
reillental 357.18
reilles 270.16
Reilly 044.14 044.24 616.01
Reilly's 071.25
reils 482.04
reinausland's 116.21
reine's 209.34
reinette 471.01
reinettes 348.22
reintroducing 246.36
reisers 055.23
reized 547.22
reizing 265.07
rejected 251.07
rek 190.19 283.15
reke 208.24 602.21
rel 310.27
rel 105.11 105.11
reland 352.09 359.26
relations 557.17
relevance 249.24
relevant 511.04
relieved 510.04
religion 365.03
rell 294.23
rella 627.05
relli 243.34
rello 134.19
relode 097.31
remarkably 368.17
remberg 151.13
remberried 264.26
rembrace 471.06
rembrandtsers 054.02
remembers 557.15
remiament 155.30
remitting 342.04
remmis 536.11
removable 117.35
remuneranded 171.32
remus 398.12 489.06
Remus 122.09
remyhead 229.32
renal 338.19
rend 051.36 144.30 187.05 203.18
rend 341.26
rendally 406.01
renderguest 124.15
rendipitist 191.03
rendissimest 154.06
rendregast 144.06
rene 228.08 397.35
renews 254.10
renfy 426.07 426.07
rengistanters 357.05
rening 330.25
rening 267.L3
renis 335.16 335.16
renn 364.30
renning 058.18 330.23
renns 431.13
renore 359.03
renownced 341.19
rent 298.15 498.01
rented 130.34 372.08
rents 576.27
reny 455.08
reor 254.13
reor 105.11
repeated 081.33
reperible 057.18
reppelling 518.20
repressible 470.31
rept 250.27
rerden 350.02
rere 487.21 613.23
rered 107.21
reretonbiking 437.06
reretyred 395.06
rerin- 424.20
rerotundity 055.36
rerssas 173.25
res 196.18
rescued 100.10
respect 188.21
respecting 033.19
respectively 119.26
respects 460.09
respondent 314.03
responsor 542.25
ressy 176.06
rest 023.19 279.08 351.18 388.02 548.09 599.26
rest 418.27
restanes 173.17
restary 280.L1
rested 026.17 223.21
restedness 055.25
rester 257.24
resterected 099.30
resti 307.F7
restians 565.01
restive 554.01
restless 143.21
restocrank 424.10
rests 077.06 132.23 357.11
rests 349.33
resurrectionism 483.10
reszk 200.09
retane 228.28 557.22
retas 048.07
retentive 070.36
retombed 586.30
retonbiking 437.06
retter 365.09
retto 435.08
retts 044.08
retyred 395.06

reuter 364.19 495.02
rev 203.14
revalent 050.22
revatov 505.26
reverend 511.07
reversing 227.19
reviews 541.25
revolitionary 234.11
rex 281.F1
rexes 610.04
rexes 305.L1
rey 422.27
reydes 035.02
reys 311.35 541.15 557.02
rhanees 330.09
rhatty 209.10
rhea 513.22
rhetorish 346.19
rheuman 214.22
rhine 548.28
rhinerstones 207.07
rhoad 081.09
rhoda 434.07
rhodes 208.26
rhose 423.16
rhosmightiadd 056.07
rhoun- 003.15
Rhuamhaighaudhlug 310.11
rhyse 375.34
rhythmytic 147.08
ria 495.34
riaumaurius 113.04
rib 318.25
ribadies 228.36
ribarbebeway 348.36
ribboned 147.23
ribnob's 491.21
riboos 154.11
ribouts 298.16
ribs 038.31
ric 532.08
ricals 302.06
rice 227.14 442.36
rich 054.03 070.01 095.25 101.11 136.15 474.07
riched 076.25
richon 254.14
richschicken 070.08
richudes 340.26
rick 003.10 030.09 048.05 053.30 126.05 129.11 129.11 129.11 183.23 187.18 380.12 380.33 381.11 381.25 444.36 465.32 478.28 486.02 530.21
ricked 067.18 138.34 410.21
rickredd 020.08
ricks 027.02 595.12 618.15
rick's 361.03 531.15 539.01
ricks' 024.22
ricksburg 326.25
rickson's 055.35
ricksticks 149.22
rico 464.16 584.27
riconcilible 434.20
ricordo 215.23
ricori 623.01
ric's 012.32
ricy 205.16
rid 232.15 262.F3 467.07
rida 092.02
ridden 110.31 553.36
riddle 274.02
riddon 219.20
ride 226.29 265.15
ride 105.35
ridecanal 484.28
rider 481.30
riders 581.19
rides 548.12
ridge 084.07 442.21 469.18 489.16 614.12
ridge 281.L4
ridgeousness 137.34
ridgers 409.20
ridge's 344.07
ridgorballyed 323.16
ridhirring 007.19
ridicynical 610.14
ridiminy 475.02 475.16
riding 589.01
riding 399.04
ridinghim 524.21
ridinghued 411.24
ridiocal 106.11
rids 007.09 552.13
riegueuxers 361.36
riel 552.27 609.20
rielising 613.15
riendo 220.19
riesh 070.04
riesk 320.13
riff 205.23
riffs 006.17 539.28
rifrif 532.20
rift 418.07
rifty 025.34
rig 114.24 406.30 464.28 513.05 535.02 565.18 623.17
rig 353.31
rigal 201.25
rigger 335.13
riggolo 524.35
righ 021.13
righevisien 423.05
righ's 174.26
right 065.25 067.01 083.07 090.33 098.19 118.16 135.27 153.11 185.30 191.22 245.22 261.23 297.13 300.32 301.07 327.26 333.24 395.27 396.04 429.21 466.15 483.23 486.15 487.14 518.24 527.24 536.33 537.27 539.20 546.20 575.35 583.01 597.11
rightdown 120.32
righted 427.06
righter 362.16
righting 471.05
rightofoaptz 571.28
rights 005.30 183.10
rightyright 419.02
rigidly 162.28
rigolect 234.26
rigular 291.28
rik 369.18
rikaans 387.02
rikawitch 437.29
rike 462.29
riki 317.02
rikissings 446.11
rik's 177.26 538.15
ril 347.01
rile 283.22
riley 482.05
rileys 467.29
rill 081.14 493.03
rillas 373.21
rillass 159.30
rilles 346.20
rillies' 351.12
rily 485.16
rim 112.07 187.36 224.02 245.36 247.22 529.15
rimaserovmeravmerouvian 113.04
rime 343.29 392.19
rimiknie 194.28
rimis 418.05
rinarr 254.21
rind 232.16
rindwards 371.36
rine 388.33
rines 504.26
rinfrowned 555.22
ring 007.19 022.10 056.08 058.19 087.05 122.06 143.22 147.19 198.12 202.02 202.11 213.19 213.20 244.25 244.33 251.23 262.20 279.05 288.F6 289.F6 320.28 332.20 357.12 390.04 391.01 395.23 413.34 462.17 465.27 466.11 466.15 504.30 511.31 550.26
ringaar 370.27
ringarouma 209.18
ringarung 210.03
ringdo 431.32
ringers 349.01
ringing 022.02 149.02 348.10
ringle's 454.02
ringlets 194.31
ringlings 367.31
ringmaries 435.30
ringnesses 279.F05
ringnettes 538.22
ringnir- 424.20
ringroam 126.20
rings 118.05 208.11 222.34 272.20 287.10 338.28 388.25 428.12 467.09 524.26
ringsand 137.17
ringstroms 004.06
ringwrowdy 266.21
rinka 102.26
rinking 205.33
rinn 052.27
rinnager's 312.27
rinned 319.26
rinny 028.12
rino 607.01
rinos 488.29
rinsers' 321.02
rinuzza 573.01
riock 531.33
rioled 310.27
riolopos 107.14
riorts 069.09
riosmas 091.05
rioted 138.28
riote's 228.07
riou 257.07
rip 039.11 179.08
ripa-Chirruta 204.12
ripe 291.11 532.23
ripped 546.16
ripple 076.30
ripthongue 477.28
rique 133.02
rir- 424.20
rira's 601.27

ris 396.03
risation 352.19
rise 053.13 226.07 255.17 493.28 543.12 602.07
riseandprove 571.32
rised 089.17 092.12 318.34 356.10
riser 154.26
rises 265.11 370.24 493.28
rish 280.L2
rishe 104.09
rishis 322.02
rishnyas 193.14
rising 277.14 347.29 463.29 505.14
risings 449.28
risk 582.04
risks 426.32
risky 347.17 513.20
rison 235.06
risons 191.09 552.07
rispondee 457.28
riss 197.35 230.32
riss 105.35
risses 553.11
rissis 460.23
riss's 525.34
ristid 538.03
ristocras 534.34
risus 440.07
rit 256.08
ritch 074.13 548.35
ritchad 138.33
rite 062.03 171.04 274.10 301.03 303.22
rithmatic 537.36
rities 137.11
rits 234.02
ritt 337.28 551.08
ritticoaxes 546.16
ritualhoods 033.01
ritza 469.14
ritzas 572.15
riubicundenances 382.02
riuolate 035.11
rivaliste 161.20
rivals 348.30
river 013.17 059.25
riverever 242.31
rivering 240.05
rives 449.30
rivett 377.17
rivor 295.02
rix 088.22 447.28
riz 412.10
R.L.L. 378.09
ro 422.09
road 030.18 097.23 389.24 471.26
roads 119.28 475.03 577.28 589.04
roam 126.20
roands 481.15
roar 010.35 057.08 150.25 273.26 442.34 488.13
roarin 372.31
roariose 121.27
Roarke 099.33
roa's 601.22
roast 455.31
roaster 421.31
rob 583.09
robber 021.08
robberating 082.24
robbst 626.05
robe 033.07 065.14 077.20 139.04 155.05 586.04
robed 263.06
robing 238.16
robinson 434.12
robius 255.20
roc 388.02
Roche 294.22
rock 010.31 083.20 124.21 203.31 339.10 416.36 502.35 541.02 579.02 606.32 611.02
rockar 424.20
rocked 463.31
rockery 388.34
rocks 005.35 258.01 326.01
rockses' 491.32
rocured 541.27
rod 435.13 565.21
rode 613.22
rodicule 070.06
rodies 341.11
rodities 614.02
rodnimad 509.13
rodromites 160.21
rods 159.15 355.19 456.16 520.05
rod's 063.18 536.35
roe 087.02 405.20
roes 146.24
roe's 221.31
rogarius 572.19
rogate 149.29 149.32 242.24
rogbones 016.03
rogenal 616.20
roger 554.03 554.03
rogerum 290.F3
rogger- 582.32
roght 595.19
rogn 353.21
rogue 053.27 507.22 581.16
rogues 083.13 547.01
rogueshire 472.01
roguing 595.20
rogynal 619.02
roh 585.04
rohgin 228.21
roid 100.17
roidverj- 257.27
roines 348.29
rokes 598.30
rokorran 177.09
rokse 158.16
rol 619.36
rol 340.19
rola 618.22
rold 255.18 441.19
role 174.04 439.35 445.32
rolebone 550.10
rolics 452.01
rolies 368.11
rolio 280.24
roll 134.09 276.01 324.01 461.16 601.16
rollanes' 354.33
rolleries 507.16
rolling 190.31 404.22 449.35 454.13
rollingeyes 011.06
rolly 368.17
rolum 338.07
rom 059.20 243.33
roma 143.03
romacron 318.09
romain 469.25
romaios 553.16
romal 346.04
roman 084.15 288.24 378.05
romancy 228.20
romans 582.33
romanscing 327.11
romarith 030.04
romatose 427.11
romboassity 353.25
rome 095.06 155.05 444.09
romelodious 184.15
romembered 371.11
romor 055.03
rompers 510.20
rom's 070.25
romst 339.14
ronage 596.01
ronals 620.04
rondas 243.16
rondo 239.27
rone 212.04 348.26
ronehflord 336.13
roneroom 498.07
ronesen 023.19
rong 019.05 098.10 267.13 370.01
ronged 203.27
rongwith 407.04
ronn- 003.15 003.15
ronne 352.21
ronry 440.05
ronses 573.21
ronte 569.35
ronthiarn 296.23
roo 416.13 450.06 521.32
roocyphyllicks 525.08
rooed 604.03
roof 101.17 612.03
roofs 006.06 543.13
rook 184.16 427.11
rooky 040.30
rool 165.21
rooly 534.08
room 008.09 008.10 010.22 040.02 041.16 052.25 079.25 100.29 101.26 137.29 156.06 159.22 265.F2 315.18 319.27 396.11 417.14 492.17 498.07 557.08 559.01 562.17 613.03 618.27 627.09
room 105.04
roomed 052.07
roomer 069.32
rooms 198.33 278.F4 362.33 625.19
roomsniffer 142.10
roon 207.25 311.17 316.09 620.05
rooned 355.19
roonk 015.31
roont 012.22
roor 006.06
roose 299.11 448.18
roosers 280.L3
rooshoos 084.02
roost 537.09
roostokrat 199.34
root 053.23 130.25 169.18 321.35
rooth 231.11

roots 138.14 285.12 303.20
rootsch 222.12
roow 625.19
rope 208.19 376.30
ropeahahn 205.29
ropes 009.19 301.01
ropes 349.11
ropodvas 343.34
ropos 513.21
roposophia 394.19
rops 343.10
rop's 502.29
roqtriques 515.33
rort 139.33
rorty 516.19
ros 346.04
rosa 207.15
rosary 459.02
rosas 561.19
rose 015.01 039.36 158.11
210.10 229.11 248.02 302.27
324.04 361.22 362.16 407.17
433.11 520.36 553.06 556.17
582.02 608.20
rosed 336.27
rosends 478.03
roses 127.08 498.23 548.24
roseshoew 159.28
rosies 541.36
rosily 239.36
rosmas 301.F5
roso 269.L1 588.12
ross 018.03 290.F1
ross 342.18
rossbucked 535.08
rosser 480.12
rossers 246.27
Rosses 310.16
rossies 351.13
rosspower 008.36
rossy 094.30
rosts 347.11
rosy 093.07
rot 266.23
rote 374.06
roth 003.12 029.13 058.30
058.31 343.08 410.36 511.12
rothagenuine 087.28
rother 255.05
rother 345.10
rothery 405.27
rothing 589.27
rothschields 010.35
rotsky 294.18
rotted 078.36 467.13
rottel 183.07
rotter 017.15
rotto 425.20
rotts 513.14
rotty 498.17
rotundity 055.36
rotundo 295.24
rou 107.20 352.31
rouchy 344.32
rough 037.02 330.16
roughbread 317.01
roughgorude 240.18
rough's 341.27
roukaparka 178.33
rouma 209.18
roun 011.18
round 039.21 084.24 096.14
171.08 275.18 277.04 314.24
381.30 386.35 417.28 525.17
550.27 552.09 613.23 618.15
round- 314.08
roundabout 448.04
roundabrupth 242.19
rounders 312.06
roundisements 536.10
rouns 358.28
rount 406.13
rountown 142.13
roused 055.11
rousers 319.26
rousians 344.33
rousse 154.23 439.35
rousseau 065.15
rousseaurs 144.22
roust 395.36
rout 463.30 533.32
routed 371.33
router 314.11
routers 603.19
routes 457.23
routh 151.22
routiknow 366.06
routs 153.22
rouvian 113.04
rouw 413.15
rov 136.08
rover 013.18 613.08
r'over 003.04
roves 340.13
rovgods 289.16
rovivla 061.36
rovmeravmerouvian 113.04
row 112.34 327.10 425.19
427.03 541.17 617.16
row 346.11
Row 569.09
rowa 209.19
rowbrate 518.22
rowd 527.03
rowdy 266.21
rowen 230.35
rowkas 516.10
rowmon 344.05
rown 152.27 245.31
roy 027.26 085.33 100.05
208.20 290.F5 568.34
royal 097.13 353.18 358.20
royd 282.20
royed 546.18
royt 500.24
rst 091.36
ru 010.17 327.17 335.16
ruad 599.05
ruads 344.18
ruah 428.15
ruarso 054.17
rua's 601.21
ruations 619.04
rubbely 020.25
rubber 069.36 497.29
rubberation 575.13
rubdish 229.14
ruberuption 612.23
rubescent 055.29
rubordolor 445.18
rubry 604.17
rubs 420.08
rubsher 280.16
rubsheruthr 280.19
rubyat 247.03
ruchially 533.28
ruck 190.02
ruckard 376.32
rucked 155.09
ruction 499.01
ructive 300.24
rud 406.21
rudd 338.09
rudder 379.20
ruddy 274.03
rude 143.25 240.18
rue 291.03 320.21 378.28
523.29 558.29
rueme 541.17
ruerunts 053.34
rues 282.28 344.29
ruff 037.11 208.19
ruffled 243.18
rug 126.20 578.32
rugitate 057.27
ruhry 082.03
ruimadhreamdhrue 320.21
ruin's 128.25
ruiven 078.24
ruke 560.25
rul 518.23
ruled 185.05
rulentous 611.29
ruler 547.23
rulldeburgghers 623.23
rulled 552.29
ruly 332.07
rum 006.05 006.05 009.27
134.08 134.08 240.28 295.25
476.12 610.06
rum 163.03
rum- 314.08
rumane 123.16
rumans 203.24
rumathunara- 023.05
rumba 351.05 596.11
rumbas 513.16
rumber 339.31
rumbian 346.06
rumble 353.24
rumbled 258.23
rumchuff 352.34
rumd 006.06
rumed 345.18
rumeny 010.03
ruminate 167.07
rumominum 154.02
rump 590.03
rumpas 160.31
rumped 421.07
rumpers 556.30
rumping 386.35
rumptly 338.15
rums 019.12 221.26 566.14
566.16
rum's 316.19
rumstouchings 237.18
rumurraimost 178.04
rumvirum 166.26
run 003.01 136.20 386.30 465.17
run- 023.05
runa 210.31 613.34
rund 223.31 597.05
rundgirond 209.18
rundo 158.07
rundser 078.16
runes 019.36
rung 210.03 230.23 300.16
310.08 471.33 576.31

rungspillfull 124.24
runi's 407.33
runner 076.19 337.01
runo 569.31
runs 557.09 594.30
runts 053.34
rup 014.18 249.14
<u>rup</u> 338.16
rupee 442.25
rups 157.10 357.09
rupt 024.22 368.04
ruption 332.26
rural 138.08
rurally 357.34
rurd- 424.20
ruru 335.16
rusalaming 542.04
ruscam 352.33
ruse 324.09 619.29
<u>rused</u> 339.24 345.08
<u>ruseye</u> 252.16
rush 029.21 207.03 208.22 353.12 360.16 366.11
rush-Irish 322.02
rusias 256.21
rusing 347.29
russhed 366.33
russheying 347.31
russhing 539.30
russhius 494.19
russpower 248.21
rust 357.06 430.06
rusted 420.31
rusty 196.17
rut 229.34
ruta 204.12
rution 107.19
rutteration 284.21
rutters 241.26
rutty 493.13
ruuts 230.34
ru-Wukru 024.07
ruysh 005.16
ruyume 231.10
Ryan's 185.25
ryar 357.19
ryboily 534.01
ryd 537.31
rydacianmad 577.01
rye 137.31 200.33 525.16
ryely 498.19
ryghtly 319.06
ryk 274.24 314.23
<u>ryllies</u> 268.L1
<u>Ryne</u> 372.32
rynecky 480.23
ryng 282.21
ryssia 329.20

saacles 058.04
saale 551.05
sabil 513.25
sable 478.19 581.05
sabon 442.09
saboobrawbees 146.17
sabosuned 313.04
saboth 542.23
sabouties 496.33
sabouts 328.10
sabuss 147.30
sach 284.F4 595.03
sache 178.35
sacht 137.31
sack 011.19 206.10 240.21 311.29 350.34
sacke 550.30
sackin 368.31
sacks 035.09
sackvilles 375.12
sacre 080.07 111.02 320.33 390.01
sacreedoed 515.25
sacrifice 571.32
sad 360.02 378.22 496.13 580.18 588.17
sada 518.25
sadaisying 363.03
sadam 485.32 532.06
sadatepholomy 389.17
saddled 554.04
saddlelonglegs 498.03
sadoor 107.36
sadrawsing 379.04
saduck 135.26
sadventure 138.31
safe 082.02 424.15 570.14
saffron 560.27
saga 220.24
sagam 093.15
sagar 423.18
sagastions 369.27
sage 119.05 240.01 595.11
sagt 535.19
sahur 359.17
saide 542.25
saigneur 243.31
sail 588.17
sailbowl 131.23
sailhorn 091.27
sailing 556.01
sailormade 232.34
sailoshe 095.06
sails 493.01
saily 005.05
saint 267.F1
sainted 304.22
saint's 455.05
saith 377.03
sake 007.08 028.35 043.36 130.29 145.33 279.09 300.13 359.04 453.28 561.14 603.14 617.06
<u>sake</u> 418.22
sakely 313.33
sake-me-nought 227.16
sakenly 368.17
sakes 350.20 498.02
saki 233.34
sakiltic 326.09
saking 021.08
sakroid- 257.27
salaim 245.01
salaisance 327.24
salamer- 596.14
salaming 542.04
salap 325.08
salar 007.16
sale 149.17
salemdo 368.09
salesolde 326.23
salewd 325.08
saline 471.12
salittle 010.33
sall 154.05 378.19 609.12
<u>sall</u> 231.07
<u>salliesemoutioun</u> 354.20
sally 383.22 449.26
sallycopodium 334.03
salmodied 470.13
saloaner 520.09
saloner 032.36
salooner 337.33 625.11
saloop 325.09
saloppics 386.06
salor 529.19
salot 325.08
salt 331.30 373.17 484.05 570.36
saltarshoming 470.15 470.17
salter 512.02
salty 456.04
<u>salver's</u> 345.20
<u>salves</u> 352.36
sam 292.14 292.16
sama 130.05 596.24
<u>sama</u> 302.L2
samasy 493.07
same 092.08 124.23 161.22 356.14 581.33 619.13
sameagain 094.27
samed 489.18
samelike 612.02
sameseed 095.15
samientos 443.15
sammen 454.13
sammenstucked 036.10
sammih- 044.20
sammon 228.36
samong 177.11
sample 397.32
sampler 305.10
samples 280.23
<u>samples</u> 342.08
<u>san</u> 124.08 285.19 286.08 470.33
sanavitch 278.23
<u>sance</u> 347.36
sancta 380.03
sand 137.17 326.20 359.07 374.36 432.18
sandalled 241.15
sandraves 363.07
sandrum 124.36
sands 122.01 567.02
sane 173.34
saned 209.33 245.09
sang 188.21 328.06 346.22 534.11
sanger 609.19
sangs 548.34 586.27
sanguineous 572.26
sanjivana 597.19
sannsos 127.19
sannuar- 332.05
sanos 183.01
<u>sans</u> 185.18
sant 221.17 315.13
sante 212.10
santee 198.16
santes 611.28
santi 005.22
santly 295.29
sanvrerssas 173.25
sap 269.20
sapastip- 090.31
<u>saphist</u> 072.14
sapia 265.22
sapper 338.18
saps 585.18

sap's 264.03
sar 344.16 612.06
sarab 117.15
saras 060.20
sarch 203.04
sarching 167.12
sark 493.20 547.26
sarlik 254.30
sarnap 129.29
sarsoon 344.01
sart 088.23
sassage 595.11
sassents 575.35
sastones 493.11
sastrides 564.36
sat 598.28
sate 590.13
sated 452.09
sates 209.08
satiated 314.33
saties 112.36
sato 255.01
sator 185.14
satt 248.06
Sattvas 294.L2
saturals 341.30
saturas 379.31
saturncast 449.02
satz 518.18
sauce 272.17
sauciations 413.18
saucyetiams 384.27
sault 295.21
saulting 115.15
saunderstaid 363.36
saup 414.17
sauro 462.22
sautch 517.29
save 017.17 234.27
saved 097.17
saving 585.15
savolo 068.19
saw 004.33 011.26 075.10
210.11 362.14 407.11 508.27
535.13 542.16 596.30
saw- 255.25
sawyer's 003.07
sawys 374.34
saxle 144.33
saxters 393.32
say 036.04 192.33 318.18
405.05 431.35 597.23
601.12
say 263.L4
saybaysse 464.21
saydighsayman 323.03
sayenolly 368.18
sayers 108.29
say-fong 325.14
saying 246.11
sayman 323.03
sayore 292.17
says 438.36
say's 492.10
sayto 223.27
say-ugh 407.30
scabby 487.10
scad 003.11
scalds 425.24
scales 526.01
scalon 550.16
scan 042.11
scap 185.35
scape 004.36 053.01 143.28
595.04
scar 580.18
scare 374.29
scarems 102.25
scarf 030.23
scarp 539.26
scatch 206.33
scaur 577.17
scayed 156.20
scemed 404.09
scenary 609.03
scene 017.15 067.10 185.30
194.18 321.21 331.30 413.11
523.34 553.24
scenery 359.33
scenes 358.04 556.24
scenest 535.19
scenium 180.03
scens 194.16
scent 165.10 181.23 330.07
432.10 502.06
scent 348.29
scenting 294.23
scents 279.F29 527.29
scents 386.18
scepistic 536.04
scepto 185.15
sceptre 230.28
sceptres 032.03
schaft 505.35
schaina 243.15
schal 254.03
schall 133.21
schalled 132.24
schals 566.08
schange 346.29
schanjeuchy 004.25
schaums 050.30
schaundize 210.02
schaup 209.31
scheaf 612.25
scheckles 452.21
schelle 179.32
schemes 288.02 364.05
scheock 524.24
schical 417.09
schicked 541.21
schicken 070.08
schicker 423.19
schields 010.35
schiff 350.07
schiner 333.04
schitt 499.09
schla 415.26
schloss 368.22
schluss 095.28 139.33
schoof 386.18
school 051.11 327.08 430.02
562.13
schoold 237.13
schoolhorse 413.07
schoolies 100.06
schott 482.14
schotten 138.13
schouw 541.23
schrift 205.17
schtt 360.26
schuft 012.09
schuler 482.17
schum- 314.08
Schung 483.04
schupnistling 114.06
schuptar 343.21
schuss 221.23
schute 003.19
schwindibus 270.L3
scides 008.35
scientific 112.11
scindgemeinded 252.16
scint 563.16
scion 333.21
scissan 298.26
scissor 388.23
scissors 563.02
sciusgardaddy 306.03
scodeignus 624.26
scone 006.24 227.35
scoop 008.35 009.34
scoor 414.06
scopal 365.09
scopalian 559.26
scope 115.30 127.35 150.32
178.28 230.01 431.14 449.34
scope 275.L2 341.23 349.18
scopes 295.12
scophonious 123.12
scopically 449.01
scoping 484.23
score 101.16 170.01 264.21
285.F3 346.24 580.06
scoreten 079.10
scorta- 090.31
scot 159.19
scoups 300.17
scouse 467.17
scout 388.15
scowl 223.18
scranna's 329.17
scraped 182.32
scrapped 370.10
scrappers 049.28
scrapt 124.32 623.36
scraptions 364.19
scrat 397.26
scratching 391.10
scraw 341.18
screaming 383.15
screed 215.26
screen 131.19 137.26
screened 186.07
screw 085.35 523.31
screwed 491.10
screwments 043.32
screwn 576.20
scribbler 122.02
scribe 179.23
scribed 066.16 099.18 496.05
scribers 523.31 544.02
scripped 617.23
scrips 156.05
script 042.09 122.21 219.17
294.10 374.03 393.31 421.18
scriptible 085.07
scription 414.05
scrubbers 550.19
scrummage 305.33
scrums 449.36 563.24
scruple 541.08
scrupp 010.13
scrween 587.13
scu 053.02
sculdus 137.24
scullion's 239.19
scullpth 532.09
scums 542.30

scum's 534.33
scumuddher-in-chaff 240.15
scuppered 155.28
scupth's 516.19
scure 326.17
scurrals 234.15
scut 076.19
scutch 163.08
scuts 284.02
scuttling 470.22
scuttlings 095.33
scutum 133.09
scyown 351.05
scythe 415.01
se 299.26 423.04 423.04
sea 029.24 094.25 143.21 317.24 317.24 428.21 447.25 456.32 495.04 539.24
Sea 291.26
seaboard 582.07
seaboob 580.14
seach 576.30
seal 454.27
sealed 448.29
sealing 015.09 603.11
sealist 072.23
sean 139.22
seania 593.05
sear 328.33
search 595.25
searfaceman 429.20
seas 130.33 584.09
seaseilers 319.21
seat 384.22 577.28 600.21
seat 353.31
seated 108.01 430.05 559.07
sec. 061.09
secants 298.24
secluded 503.29
second 134.12
secrandable 596.09
secration 557.35
secs 152.35 356.15
sectarian 358.08
section 253.34
sections 532.34
sect's 523.34
sectualism 524.12 524.36
sectuous 029.30
secular 462.34
secure 022.17
securers 366.28
secussion 125.16
sedd 361.23
sedents 284.22
sedes 552.07
sedine 536.23
see 205.04 239.05 296.F1 297.18 324.09 360.31 495.03 497.27 531.33 558.34 600.13
seech 259.03
seed 004.31 095.15 237.19 271.13 452.32 475.29 625.24
seeding 275.F4
seedlings 160.10
seedo 564.04
seeds 545.33
seehim 129.09
seeing 075.13 127.35 157.21 179.01 237.16
seeingetherich 054.03
seek 075.11 444.35 479.34
seeked 418.28
seeker 110.30 438.03 448.26 548.14
seeking 121.03
seeking 346.31
seeks 231.36 462.10
seekwenchers 284.23
seels 373.29
seels 344.09
seem 567.35
seemim 353.15
seen 029.09 029.19 068.33 158.36 165.26 194.18 299.19 403.22 615.31
seep 366.14
seepeepers 389.26
seer 409.35 493.30 550.34 612.16
seer 340.13
sees 015.15 538.25
see's 213.36
seesaw 375.31
seesee 386.35
sef 557.05
seguired 092.01
seher 203.07
sehn 245.23
seht 593.23
sei-foun 325.14
seigneur 184.30
seilers 319.21
seines 497.31
seized 574.05
seky 497.28
sel 184.10 425.18 534.09 618.02
sel 105.15
seleep 345.11
self 003.20 020.21 032.07 036.35 073.21 101.19 114.23 114.31 140.34 143.26 161.01 168.01 171.04 186.06 187.04 193.31 242.32 261.07 266.29 288.08 301.08 313.33 321.06 329.19 358.13 384.34 395.02 426.13 447.10 460.11 499.22 540.33 557.01 611.21 627.06
selfish 238.28 426.13
selforelump 613.01
selfs 234.10 298.27
selfsake 617.06
selfwhose 439.21
seling 315.31
sell 014.03 185.01 300.05 537.25 581.06 585.07
sella 133.02 549.19 618.04 622.03
sellas 151.31
sella's 205.11
selle 230.15
seller 101.23 467.15
sellers 312.35
selles 113.11 339.16 352.31
sellina 154.29
sells 554.03
sellus 478.08
selman's 422.16
selp 333.13
selps 612.24
sels 604.25
selse 003.07 239.34 503.22
selt 051.30
selv 199.05
selved 156.25
selver 028.11
selves 098.36 101.22 368.16 370.17 465.33 473.11 487.18 547.24 576.33 607.19
selving 608.05
selx 444.18
sem 155.33 384.28
seman 285.19
sembling 181.11
sembria 494.13
sembulger 132.29
seme 353.02
semen 181.01
seme's 511.04
semidemicolons 374.09
seminating 425.11
semitic 191.02
semma 133.36
semmih- 044.20
semple 254.01
sempry 364.24
sen 142.06 155.33 324.19 378.25 488.15
senal 083.08
senaps 256.20
sence 538.30 596.11
send 024.09 024.10 042.10 070.08 070.09 083.20 230.13 268.26 269.17 291.01 320.23 326.28 327.02 335.27 350.28 372.34 434.34 503.14 535.15 547.19 585.09 614.04 617.07
sendas 612.11
sendean 494.19
sendee 228.22 458.10
sends 028.02 170.13 283.15 336.29 478.03 478.05 505.06 572.19 610.28
sendsthee 628.14
sendt 332.29
sendyures 295.03
seng 611.30
sengd 328.25 328.25
senic 499.05
senile 078.01
senless 415.33
senn 586.28
sens 162.18 228.32 322.32 492.18
sen's 621.19
sensation 616.25
sense 056.28 075.03 121.15 138.07 147.06 229.36 245.21 326.21 373.18 378.06 391.11 422.06 614.14
sensed 499.25
sensible 291.23
sensical 487.28
sensing 352.16
sensition 123.12
sent 321.15 321.23 370.05 438.24 578.14 597.05 618.36
sentant 313.33
sentience 600.22
seoggs 178.33
separable 032.07
sepeprosapia 265.22
sephyring 418.29
seprated 239.21
septuple 343.18
sequestellates 107.18
sequient 422.21
sequious 291.08

ser 600.12
sercizism 231.27
seres 601.06
serf 240.11
series 113.02
serk 582.29
serovmeravmerouvian 113.04
serpents 493.10
serpronette 267.11
serum 240.28
servaged 267.18
servant 097.34
servants 034.19 432.06
servatory 551.25
serve 366.11
served 171.13
servent 364.19
servicemajor 572.21
serving 078.07 533.07
seses 463.30
sess 461.09
sessel 559.06
session 379.05
sest 148.05
set 078.25 127.26 180.29 183.20 191.27 214.13 215.07 223.35 277.F7 434.06 447.28 499.26 505.13 553.18 563.12
seth 036.31
setl 199.01
sets 011.23 059.02 087.30 262.23 480.12 553.10 583.19
sette 559.28
setter's 141.19
setting 076.02
setton 239.05
sett's 529.17
setty 562.07
seu 322.12
seuladed 291.05
seule 104.10
seuls 315.19
seuyes 244.32
sevelised 254.01
seven 255.32 255.33 620.04
seventh 053.03
sever 362.18
severalation 523.22
severs 202.02
sewed 507.07
sewer 420.24
sewn 208.17 372.16
sex 125.17 523.28 524.15
sexed 525.08
sexelcy 521.04
sexes 564.11
sexnone 331.15
sexonism 363.35
sexpeans 242.30
sextine 364.11
sexual 120.35 522.30
sexuous 175.31
sexycle 115.16
sey 312.29
seyes 310.29 398.18 404.14
sezit 154.33
sha 215.12
shaap 539.31
shack 309.22
shade 058.21
shadem 303.13
shades 445.04
shadows 546.23
shadure 554.07
shaft 241.13
shag 016.34 492.11
shaire 423.03
shake 222.35
shaker 107.31 159.19 254.32 285.F4 447.31
shakey 535.11
shaking 336.28
shallassoboundbewilso-thoutoosezit 154.33
shallehs 550.12
shallow 153.06
shal's 536.21
sham 030.07
shambles 061.14 494.32 538.22
shame 241.14 481.26 481.26
Shame 182.30
shameyu 565.15
shams 286.29
shan 280.15 344.22
shanagan 417.31
shanaral 340.27
shandjupeyjade 261.01
shands 028.04
shane 489.27
Shane 437.33
shaned 534.30
shank 411.33
shanks 315.35 386.29 500.10
shanky's 229.04
shant 338.02
shantyland 131.35
shap 499.21
shape 229.21 265.03 313.27 448.23 471.25 474.02 563.02 608.29
shaped 128.06 134.25 373.13 502.19 529.21
shapen 015.30
shaper 339.36
shapes 313.32 565.07
share 018.31 191.18
shared 603.13
shark 193.05 500.04
sharon 034.29
Sharon 526.28
sharonals 620.04
sharping 422.02
shat 009.02
shats 085.30
shattaras 010.16
shattered 137.13
shaun 092.32 558.23
Shaun 211.31
shaw 131.08 132.10 132.10 132.10 303.07 366.34 527.08
shaweshowe 256.13
shawn 449.15
shaws 098.13 553.36
shea 092.31
Shea 182.30
shead 212.13 241.20 439.10
sheads 496.23
shealing 611.28
shealth 622.28
shean 123.25
sheat 364.17
sheathed 546.09
sheathing 340.30
sheaven 469.30
shebeau 527.29
sheckled 354.07
shed 023.27
shed 071.24
shedell 276.L2
shee 052.21 062.09 192.30 306.17 316.21 347.15 475.02 486.33 508.27 574.34
sheeba 468.36
sheels 009.29
sheen 267.19 284.30 389.27
Sheen 223.18
sheens 164.22
sheep 133.25
sheepslang 299.25
sheers 163.12
shees 029.12 348.17 612.33
shee's 581.09
sheet 022.01 131.20 180.12 503.02 585.31
sheetbaths 188.26
sheets 116.26 220.31 603.08
shein 387.05
sheiner 221.10
shekarry 207.24
shell 407.23 479.04
shelled 292.18
shells 183.12 420.15 435.19
shellsis 154.35
shelp 157.13
shelves 373.13 425.05
Shem 421.25
shema 098.04
shemeskad 207.24
shemist 185.35
shemp 317.28
shemshowman 530.03
shen 332.36
sheneul 119.25
shent 267.26
sheorebukujibun 484.26
sheory 163.25
shep 532.13
shep's 313.18
shere 052.16
shert 352.05
sherwomens 287.L1
shesses 241.03
sheying 347.31
sheyls 089.18
shiamarodnimad 509.13
shian 509.07
shibilley 238.04
shicksal 283.L2
shie 091.36 578.16
shied 095.18
shield 129.20 223.29
shielded 309.17
shielder's 590.25
shields 328.35
shiffle 371.28
shift 147.26 325.21 369.20 603.14
shighs 272.22
shill 415.09
shillelagh 025.15
shilling 255.30
shilt 529.31
shim 029.33 199.13
shimmy 173.27
Shim-Schung 483.04
shin 333.07 482.16 585.08
shine 056.19 138.31 439.08 440.31 504.06 603.02
Shine 437.33

shines 069.13
shiningem 586.30
shins 015.31 314.26 428.14 470.36 507.14 511.01
shiny 073.21
ship 023.13 027.23 040.12 042.07 045.09 053.31 090.36 118.03 123.16 129.25 137.22 139.04 174.35 186.30 193.32 289.07 312.16 325.17 326.28 332.23 343.29 344.13 390.35 391.10 391.32 428.19 433.11 472.09 475.27 492.36 542.18 545.07 547.25 547.27 558.26 575.28 583.21
ship 354.19 419.06
shipful 024.08 264.32
shipful 201.15
shipfuls 089.22
ships 092.23 147.04 219.10 311.08 395.05 587.18 605.14 606.13 625.04
ship's 075.12 095.12
shipt 111.09
shipwracked 275.18
shire 197.10 406.03 472.01
shirt 251.13 387.05 404.27
shirts 518.21
shis 054.18
shleep 435.26
shnorrt 067.15
shock 008.30 353.21
shockle 541.21
shod 118.06 426.36
shoe 063.22 447.17
shoes 008.19 226.24 237.08 270.24 288.12 595.23 608.25
shoew 159.28
shogue's 037.34
shoh 353.05
shomed 098.05
shoming 470.15 470.17
shone 152.36 613.09
shoo- 257.27
shoob 010.09
shooe 417.34
shook 601.35
shoon 014.04 141.25
shoopers 352.26
shoops 077.28
shoos 084.02
shoot 014.24 261.14
shooter's 056.04
shooting 194.34
shootings 022.12
shooto 160.29
shoots 237.02 366.20
shop 042.24 046.03 130.33 177.36 322.27 332.24 338.24 516.28
shopp 305.05
shoppard 276.12
shoppers 105.28
shops 355.31
shop's 158.30
shore 026.14 051.31 232.20 264.17 390.16 469.06 605.28 623.30
shored 197.18 370.36
shorn 335.20
short 360.20
shortcake 379.04
shorten 479.17
shortener 017.03
shossers 146.13
shot 058.23 171.14 274.17 288.20 396.01 426.35 524.34
shotbackshattered 137.13
shotdown 441.33
shots 037.23 221.22 464.30
shott 524.14 524.16
shotten 420.35
shottered 352.30
shottus 352.25
shough 349.19
shouker 415.06
shouldered 136.25
shoulders 490.15
shous 536.13
shouse 428.08
shouses 537.01
shouters 356.06 378.26
shouts 502.20
shoveller 013.08
show 120.07 163.13 246.23 386.27 507.23 559.18
showe 256.13
showers 552.35
showever 253.08
showman 530.03
shows 292.06 443.35
showus 057.20
shriek 141.13
shrift 494.20
shrine 559.07
shrinkable 173.36
shrinkables 417.13
shriver 341.27
shrouded 546.01
shrub 588.31
shuam 452.35
shuffle 041.17 371.28
shunders 229.21
shunds' 548.15
shune 100.05
shunned 489.18
Shunny 475.29
shup 154.18 158.30 244.06
shure 058.20 371.17 464.02 549.27
shure 201.20
shus 320.11 581.22
shut 292.24 395.29 419.27
shuts 388.33
shy 234.04 424.09 484.26 484.26 624.24
shyous 350.16
shyshooter's 056.04
si 285.21
si- 054.15
siarch 188.16
sib 568.12
sibby 465.31
sibellies 233.25
sibis 452.08
sibles 483.19
sic 056.22
Siccaries 228.02
sich 499.12
sick 155.30 193.02 210.20 235.22 452.35 489.20 538.31 570.02 628.04
sickabed 392.06
sickend 084.32
sickers 321.31 373.31
sicking 156.11 437.12
sickners 530.02
sicks 038.11
sics 151.30
sic-Uraliens 162.12
sid 026.17
siddle 342.16
side 010.11 010.35 019.12 031.03 031.31 035.13 042.25 059.04 070.20 073.05 079.07 082.14 090.07 095.09 095.15 102.09 114.06 127.03 128.10 134.01 135.32 138.01 153.16 160.15 204.24 205.26 205.28 208.21 230.03 239.29 264.23 301.27 301.29 311.03 311.26 314.32 315.10 331.17 355.29 356.34 363.21 394.27 405.05 428.24 443.28 444.28 450.02 456.17 466.07 476.05 485.31 486.33 486.33 507.06 521.28 533.05 547.18 551.23 557.36 562.23 563.01 564.22 565.23 574.34 577.30 578.01 585.29 596.04 605.28 611.04 611.22 611.27 612.14
side 071.11 106.03 201.05
sidedown 373.34
sidemissing 119.31
sider 418.02 610.18
sideration 451.36
siders 056.04 141.10 497.10
sider's 442.23
sides 007.34 008.32 035.09 041.03 141.10 352.04 362.05 370.26 375.24 382.16 384.28 463.33 484.14 507.07 507.10 556.24 568.26
sides 359.24 399.09
sidesaddled 554.04
sidesofme 499.26
sidethat 612.07 612.10
siding 483.25 581.17
sidity 410.11
sidled 315.05
sidling 294.21
sidonius 080.28
sidown 119.28
sid's 034.31
sidus 615.23
siduxit 060.33
siegates 004.06
sieged 075.05 127.13 352.25
sieuresponsor 542.25
sieved 155.13
siezed 162.07
sif 512.13
sifengtse 299.26
sifings 238.17
siftly 018.08
sigh 037.28 586.28 601.08
sighed 058.17 261.24
sigheds 387.21
sighosa 246.10
sighs 230.28 502.19 571.21
sight 075.13 167.10 249.02 392.27 405.23 417.23 540.33 551.34 569.21
sight 262.L2 345.35
sightbared 156.35
sighted 031.04 079.03 143.09 600.13
sighting 437.05
sightliness 131.19

sights 100.05 352.32
sighty 611.32
sigirls 105.10
sign 004.13 155.26 182.07 407.23 530.20
signation 056.17
signed 024.28 068.13 098.16 261.06 543.06 574.08
signeur 569.20
signi 412.08
signing 498.12
signore 575.29
signs 056.23 080.11 118.28 138.07 369.01
signstunter 370.30
sihkes 202.01
sik 346.23 437.32
sikal 237.30
sikants' 064.13
sikin 113.08
silde 391.16
silehims 005.16
silencers 143.16
silene 019.11
silf 497.36
sililesvienne 348.36
silk 271.F5
sill 161.28 490.33 538.14 609.12
silled 553.11
sillies 537.35
sillos 302.16
sills 566.09
silly 015.18 229.28 435.07
silt 628.04
silts 021.06
silvar 467.35
silver 138.20 271.F5 426.09
silvers 241.02
silversong 138.02
silves 337.25
silvier 211.35
sily 149.29 172.27
sim 029.33 234.25 334.18 354.31 354.31
siman 057.03
sime 227.10 588.06
similar 358.03 484.34
simple 561.09
sims 148.21
simulant 298.10
simulating 384.34
sin 018.21 057.03 057.03 057.03 057.04 107.23 116.18 255.07 368.21 437.29 459.15 478.10 505.01 539.16 564.20
sinbal 420.12
sinbond 510.35
since 499.25
sinclose 545.30
sind 212.20
sindensity 350.12
sindonk 230.12
sine 046.20 238.25 294.25
sinent 337.08
sines 207.12 532.21
sing 158.08 158.08 167.16 186.01 230.26 242.30 251.10 298.26 299.02 333.06 371.34 379.04 390.06 426.28 476.03 485.28 485.28 597.20
sing 345.12
singchetaoli 609.10
singer 366.25
singey 583.31
singgiddyrex 281.F1
singglass 247.36
singing 513.34
singirillies' 351.12
singlass 084.29 460.21
singlontseng 611.30
singrhetorish 346.19
sings 245.33 614.05
singsund's 601.26
singular 251.32
singwoolow 360.03
sinia 318.32
sink 359.36 373.07 518.01
Sink 531.21
sinky 326.12
sinn 528.08
sinnantes 485.11
sinnturns 539.31
sinology 486.13
sinost 594.18
sins 048.16 110.05 499.25 599.21
sin's 290.F7
sinster 051.18
sintime 432.33
sintus 611.24
sinuously 294.31
sinurbean 040.07
sinus 357.09
sion 326.18 518.23
siop's 422.22
sioused 416.24
sip 623.03
siph 213.29
siphono- 135.16
siphysing 277.L5
sipiences 261.19
sippated 026.31
sippus 038.16
sir 150.16 481.14 612.07
siraizde 032.08
sire 019.30 068.11 493.31 510.29
sire 105.29
siries 551.28
sirrs 355.28
sirs 011.36 324.19 540.23
sir's 099.16
sirt 388.03
sirturvy 275.14
sirvition 434.20
sis 155.16 178.01 395.32 415.12 522.33
sis 349.35
sise 230.13
sish 492.09
sisliffi 159.12
sismade 321.09
Sissers 375.25
sissies 526.34
sissimalls 298.30
sissimost 014.19
sission 245.13
sistas 514.10
sister 566.10
sistershood 351.29
sistorous 155.07
sistras 090.02
sit 075.11 318.06 331.06 334.18
sitalukin 110.08
sitaraw 152.10
sitas 060.16
site 240.28 581.19 597.12 597.14
sitease 576.24
sited 449.01
sitensies 187.30
siteroomed 052.07
siters 387.13
sites 228.31 589.33
site's 319.06
sithin' 056.28
sitoista 285.17 285.18
sits 127.17 186.09 324.14 331.06
sits 106.23
sitslike 152.19
sitt 541.04
sitter 390.36
sitteth 546.22
sitting 053.31
sittuponable 284.26
situs 415.04
six 211.17 443.22
sixandsixpenny 396.17
sixcoloured 611.35
sixdix- 113.09
sixing 048.13
sixpenny 396.17
sixth 497.26
sixths 149.12
sixy 524.26
size 333.20 529.29
size 106.14
sized 059.08 084.11 111.08 123.26 170.19 255.29 457.16 548.09 559.29 602.02 602.05
sizer 418.05
sizinned 374.14
skad 207.24
Skaerer-Sissers 375.25
skaffier 059.29
skakruscam 352.33
skamper 353.33
skan 606.15
skance 204.20
skatchairch 358.27
skate 200.04
skaulds 228.36
skawn- 003.15
skayas 348.23
skayman 089.07
skede 551.24
skeeamore 338.19
skeer 344.06
skelled 324.13
sker 607.05
skerelks' 243.01
skery 385.09
skew 323.18 583.31
skewdy- 257.27
skewerer 055.21
skey 602.34
skhwindel 426.27
skib 549.34
skied 157.11
skield 567.19
skieym's 601.25
skilk 133.33
skilled 164.32
skillers 231.33
skilling 008.23 618.26
skimmed 205.30

skin 016.24 020.05 051.15 053.21 166.08 169.19 182.11 187.08 220.15 229.30 240.30 253.16 262.24 295.F1 367.33 377.28 395.35 429.17 445.05 552.36 565.13 603.20 610.31 621.25
sking's 122.19
skinned 609.04
skins 156.19 320.26 324.12 370.35 528.36
skip 464.35 502.36
skippers 257.05
skippey 076.19
skipping 579.05
skippy 011.10
skips 232.10
skirt 335.09
skirt 200.12
skirts 558.36
skite 453.21
skithers' 323.18
skittle 160.27
skivee 192.21
skivvymenassed 492.06
skleydoodle 258.05
skons 370.33
skool 533.26
skooner 332.02
skortas 247.29
skouro 317.33
skull 384.01
skulled 498.14
skuns 350.26
skuro 612.18
skut 233.32
sky 006.27 013.22 034.03 034.18 060.11 064.31 070.30 185.11 253.03 256.33 303.01 335.24 338.09 340.02 355.11 360.16 404.24 442.11 509.05 513.11 524.35 600.23
sky 294.18
Sky 543.29
skybaush 091.28
skybeak 157.06
skydrear 209.20
skykorked 176.30
slaap 398.14
slachsen 532.11
sland 440.21
slands 097.03
slang 299.25 338.22 486.14
slanging 209.01 445.10
slant 316.32 608.24
slapping 276.02
slaps 370.27
slaters 390.01
slats 206.35
slattary 350.27
slaughter 062.06
slaund 614.08
slav- 219.17
slaved 478.15
slaves 137.33 309.12
slavoff 219.14
slay 087.08 357.03
slayers 337.21
slayer's 056.11
slays 041.01
sleap 547.16
sledhropes 349.11
slee 133.21
sleems 619.26
sleep 037.18 064.01 074.02 397.16 411.07 411.07 449.35 476.22 556.33
sleeping 157.14 451.10
sleeps 116.20
sleeve 289.27 411.26
sleeves 067.31 161.30
sleeves 343.13
sleeveside 562.23
sleuth 033.31
slewder 323.09
sleyan 510.22
sleyg 130.21
slF 230.22
slibris 477.23
slick 225.09
slide 570.02
sliding 405.09
slidingdraws 511.29
slight 383.20
slim 497.30
slim-all-Muslim 068.12
slimed 506.07
sling 230.29
slinger 506.18 520.22
slip 326.35 377.26 597.12
slipped 204.15
slipping 310.05
slips 171.18 442.15 577.26
sliving 597.07
slleepp 368.19
slo 553.32
sloddledome 379.15
sloes 571.17 583.22
slog 073.07 581.16
slogging 151.17
sloop 562.16 597.20
slooped 423.06
sloot 610.14
slop 363.29
slope 349.10
sloper 248.10
slops 583.36
slosby 244.07
slots 596.12
slought 329.06
sloup 547.16
slowlap 437.36
slu 595.21
slucylamp 327.05
slumbered 007.20
slump 332.17
slung 188.27 331.25
slup 371.04
sly 137.11 226.28
slyder 505.07
slyke 413.07 600.24
small 323.06 490.04 581.15
Smashall 516.05
smather 296.21
smathes 595.17
smeathes 595.17
smeethes 595.17
smell 095.12 344.26
smeller 182.17
smelling 093.08 134.25
smellt 436.18
smellygut 455.10
smellyspatterygut 455.11
smid 357.01
sm'ile 056.28
smiled 555.18
smiles 015.11
smiling 115.22
smillers 084.01
smith 043.05 148.32 184.15 228.05 304.F4
smith 342.08
smitt 197.11
smoke 013.22
smoker 200.12
smokes 350.26
smoking 586.01
smothered 191.25
smotherthemselves 353.27
smuck 386.33
snake 100.11 139.31
snapped 021.21
snarers 208.12
snark 353.11
snatcher 125.21 445.03
sneek's 516.06
snider 320.04
sniffer 142.10
sniffing 237.17
snip 045.08 312.14
snipped 317.24
snoch 476.06
snod 325.14
snolleges 623.32
snoo 144.12
snooded 547.14
snooper 254.21
snor 236.28
snored 040.05
snots 358.02
snottobe 085.22
snoutso 245.01
snuff 124.35
snuh 620.16
soaken 405.35
soakers 097.20 604.08
soaking 438.19
soakoonaloose 522.34
soaping 045.31
soars 266.09
sobaric 133.04
sobbers 364.23
sobbing 525.21
sober 186.14
sobordunates 156.11
soboundbewilso-thoutoosezit 154.33
socale 250.27
soccurs 391.13
sociately 224.23
sock 272.F4
socks 053.10 160.20 428.26
soclever 426.03
socoldlogical 396.14
socrats 367.25
sod 056.24 444.34
sodaintily 254.31
sodalism 352.20
sodalitarian's 099.36
sods 043.34 289.04
sod's 087.29
soep 240.22
soes 349.28
soeurses 432.23
soever 036.31 158.14 239.19 364.23 413.32 426.02 476.09 551.16 576.19 613.20
soever 342.12
soever's 362.18

sof 289.05
sofacts 156.09
sofairy 621.06
sofarforth 581.28
soff 552.18
sofia 552.07
sofrichunfoldingmorn 571.32
soft 531.08
softened 077.32
softfun 607.16
softlhee 628.14
sogar 497.12
sogerraider 619.30
sohame 326.18
sohito 054.33
sohn 243.31
soid 035.21
soil 544.07
soild 336.30
soiled 550.23
soiling 146.08
soilman 071.14
soirs 219.11
sokey 315.22
sokushk 203.35
sol 108.27 525.16 568.07
solabella 209.24
solade 289.28
solamisola 384.31
solance 562.32
solanisans 384.32
solas 014.08
solate 003.06
solation 228.07
sold 113.19 337.01 606.21 607.31
solde 326.23 383.18 500.25 538.08
soldereds 356.04
sole 238.27 267.15 365.07
soled 236.35
solem 124.35
solent 609.02
soleon 596.26
solering 462.17
soles 397.17 486.20 607.31
sole's 622.10
soleself 329.19
Soles-Up 531.22
soletto 281.18 281.19
soley 598.19
solff 308.F2 353.17
solicited 070.13 173.30
solies 006.35
soliloquisingly 063.20
solis 228.12
sollation 581.13
sollieras 361.19
solock 584.03
solom 180.27
solookly 404.32
soloom 012.13
soloosely 413.27
solt 394.30
soluded 081.12
solum 378.15
solun 351.09
solusingness 143.14
solution 076.17 147.17 362.30
solved 150.23
som 100.23
somation 339.28
sombre 343.16
sombred 570.07
sombres 312.09
somdowns 049.24
Somebody 088.14
somedever 341.35
somendeavour 624.35
someness 023.14 152.19 534.32
somer 234.07 477.18
somere 627.05
somes 008.04
some's 432.35
somewhere 433.10
somines 450.11
somingenting 414.34 416.27
sommation 432.14
somnia 120.14
somnia 193.29
somst 364.25
son 025.04 043.10 053.33 054.32 058.32 065.15 076.17 087.28 089.34 093.17 113.34 124.29 126.05 133.22 138.12 146.16 149.20 163.26 187.35 211.16 212.24 232.28 235.06 241.18 242.01 248.04 252.36 297.03 302.23 303.30 315.30 319.29 323.16 325.22 326.30 332.08 347.03 348.18 350.33 369.21 370.30 371.06 371.16 377.25 377.32 382.04 384.28 387.04 410.26 413.14 422.30 423.01 434.12 440.08 446.30 466.24 471.30 482.01 483.20 483.20 523.16 529.20 529.30 530.21 530.22 530.31 532.01 537.36 568.03 568.28 574.02 575.34 578.31 585.06 608.10
son 176.02 199.29 307.L1
SON 221.06
sonally 449.04
sonbound 461.23
sonce 536.24
sondale 609.16
sonder 310.16
sone 209.35
song 056.05 110.24 138.02 203.30 204.13 231.29 276.19 336.14 390.24 450.21 462.03 485.31 595.04
songapiccolo 450.19
songbook 380.24
songebook 460.20
songer 405.07
songingon 274.24
songs 238.29 457.29
songue 244.07
sonia 542.01
sonian 048.23
sonic 123.12
sonius 267.06
sonne 201.04
sonority 062.04
sons 018.22 019.28 019.28 026.32 060.25 089.34 097.34 127.01 129.35 156.04 191.09 192.04 197.24 206.11 215.35 223.05 229.23 257.36 305.17 333.16 357.10 451.06 498.13 552.07 583.11 617.13
sons 175.21
son's 043.07 053.33 055.35 063.02 245.24 245.24 252.36 252.36 252.36 374.02 431.12 479.11 480.32 551.04
son's 123.25 123.26 359.27
sons' 476.04
sonse 614.14
soo 478.20
sooks 344.27
soon 003.10 055.06 286.24 300.04 312.08 318.28 473.18 566.10 595.08
soon 344.01
soonerite 171.04
soonome 158.10
soons 606.29
soon's 394.28
soonshine 603.02
soops 491.06
soort 043.35
soot 411.22 487.32
sooth 188.13
sop 377.34 423.10 569.30
sop 307.L1
sope's 290.12
soph 261.23
sophagusted 610.01
sophat 255.12
sophenguts 319.12
sopher 047.01 365.05
sophia 394.19
sophies 435.10
sophism 163.17
sophopancreates 088.09
sophy 134.14
sopky 471.01
sopolettes 343.24
sopotomac 559.35
sopper 063.01 356.17
sopper's 268.12
sorcelled 476.29
sorceration 608.02
sore 107.23 304.05 320.12 473.20 580.34
sores 256.21 397.26
Sorgmann 578.11
sorily 447.07
sorley 408.25
sorrow 563.37
sort 186.32 219.12 540.01
sortail 444.17
sorted 314.17
sortofthing 178.05
sos 255.33
so's 368.14 488.24
sosiftly 018.08
sosing 426.28
sossianusheen 267.19
sot 223.11
sothoutoosezit 154.33
sotoelles 601.28
sotorisation 352.19
sotted 028.20
soucie 308.24
soud 553.30
sought 409.08 512.30
soughts 379.15
soul 225.01 225.01 474.02 569.20
souling 302.L1
souls 243.06 623.28
soult 010.14 222.27
soumeselles 339.16
soun 015.35
sound 121.15 315.23 323.27

sounder 121.26
sounding 355.10
soundinly 225.02
soundscript 219.17
souns 230.03
soup 246.31 428.01
soupcans 289.05
souper 393.12
sour 037.34
sourd 464.13
sourdly 430.14
sourdonome 332.32
sourer 457.14
sourishe 221.33
soused 339.34
sousedovers 370.31
sousiated 151.29
souso 345.24
sousyoceanal 384.03
sout 007.29
south 114.03
souwea 552.02
soved 548.10
sovereign 221.07
sovitz 514.30
sow 021.20
sowarries 263.F2
sowearit 331.15
sowells 578.19
sower 593.20
sowl 361.16
sown 090.08 197.05 274.23 381.03 535.02
sownseedlings 160.10
Sowry 221.34
sowyer 299.28
sox 525.12
soys 059.01
space 015.18 115.07 455.29
Space 124.12
spacem 087.14
Spain 050.20
spain's 553.36
spake 014.20
spaking 066.15
spaltung 296.L1
span 178.24 251.16 547.29 613.24
spangled 404.27
spanned 004.13
spanners 534.31
spanning 248.27
spano-Cathayan-Euxine 263.13
spanquost 388.28
sparation 257.26
spare 077.16
sparingly 063.09
spart 626.32
spasmockical 515.16
spass 363.26
spastored 612.08
spat 329.12
spatterygut 455.11
spawn 339.27 358.12
speak 456.26
speaking 267.08 355.35 486.08
speaktoble 351.31
spear 152.33 340.10
specious 296.28 374.08
speckled 208.12 362.15
specks 207.13
specs 191.32
spectrum 329.36
speds 343.32
speech 100.28 273.19 484.02
speechably 238.36
speeches 096.30
speed 600.14
speels 569.04
speer 257.20
speer's 145.24
spell 238.03
spellers 112.06
spellor 179.30
spells 257.34
spell's 343.08
spelly 552.27
spendeats 211.27
spenking 186.11
ſpens 238.08
spent 563.06
spera 497.15
sperations 105.30
spertieu 289.22
sperups 230.35
spew 520.05
sphere 239.34 295.04 453.22
spheres 508.21
spheure 346.07
sphex 415.28
sphores 081.25
spices 094.26 477.16
spicially 440.19
spick 177.32
spid 594.21
spidal 273.28
spied 375.31
spiels 393.35
spiers 174.28
spies 088.25
spil 497.13
spill 156.03 161.31 448.15 534.09
spilled 230.05 305.04 526.30 563.05
spillerindernees 234.19
spillfull 124.24
spillouts 156.13
spills 356.14
spillsation 095.01
spils 480.33
spilt 535.24
spilth 381.09
spin 491.06
spindhrift 418.07
spinne 417.24
spinners 050.19
spinning 431.31
spins 499.24
spintheochromatokreening 392.28
spionia 348.30
spiration 257.25
spired 407.19
spirer 395.17
spires 049.12
spirine 257.02
spirs 058.09
spis 405.26
spissated 179.25
spissers 503.29
spissing 302.06
spit 033.01
spite 086.23 231.33 519.05
spiterebbed 374.08
spitters 616.23
spittles 040.36
spitz 569.01
split 511.21 596.31
splits 237.23
splitting 454.08
splodes 249.15
splush 474.14
splutterall 262.16
spoil 102.21
spoiled 038.25
spoiler 201.10
spokables 496.31
spoken 477.13
spoken 175.16
spokes 085.36
spokesman 427.32
spoking 322.01
spond 328.19
spondas 052.15
spondee 457.28
spondees 139.20
spondful 110.32
sponds 238.34
spond's 018.02
spondy 430.05
sponging 440.07
sponsor 542.25
spookspokesman 427.32
spoon 038.20 445.19
spoonspill 534.09
spoor 340.11
sporation 257.25 463.21
sport- 257.27
sported 056.03 452.14
sports 386.26
sports' 066.08
spos 144.05
spot 135.17 221.13 286.F5 498.32 582.14 582.31
spot 349.14
spots 021.27
spotspeckled 208.12
spotted 477.19
spousals 129.03
spoused 503.18
spousing 605.08
sprate's 334.01
sprawl 476.19
spray 561.20
spreach 299.22
spread 365.31 453.24 559.06 628.10
spreak 536.02
sprezzion 064.31
sprig 365.32
spring 024.10
springlike 535.02
sprinkled 153.27
sprinkler 180.34
sprinks 537.05
sprit 291.20
sprogue 053.27
sprout 030.08
sprung 023.30 162.14 600.18
spuk 250.10
spund 214.08 329.07
spur 124.17
spurt 050.03
spurudo 289.22
spurus 557.06
spy 139.26 237.03
spyneedis 433.36
squadmala 184.28
squall 180.05

squammythical 354.10
squara 557.01
square 363.24
squashed 155.13
squatters 344.19
squattor 019.26 019.27
squeadbaugham 024.14
squeer 420.22
squeesh 287.F4
squeezed 462.10
squeezer 376.20
squibezigues 350.20
squilocus 254.20
squiluteral 297.27
squire 205.22 485.21
squirial 550.24
squodoboits 211.28
squoro 102.16
staatarean 310.08
stab 493.23
stability 189.07
stable 010.17 485.24
stably 523.27 618.32
stabulish 429.19
stack 279.F12
stacks 006.01
stad 602.35
staff 035.07 035.27 191.36 235.36 366.19 479.27 512.14 567.10 571.05
staffs 178.23
stag 577.17
stage 610.35
stages 346.32
stage's 033.03
staid 363.36
stails 393.11
stain 111.20 141.24 149.28 546.01
stained 114.29 341.05
stainer 489.17
stainers 312.36
stairs 362.33 373.09 461.18 556.34 560.11 561.02
stake 137.32 352.12 441.06 537.22
staker 237.34
stakers 514.30
stakes 170.33 447.03
stakings 387.10
stale 126.11 509.35 624.27
stalk 131.13 236.34 307.F1 504.19
stall 512.05 539.22
stalled 088.19 513.35
stallings 123.18
stallion 279.F28
stalutes 285.29
stam 104.10
staman 202.15
stamens 236.35
stamite 594.05
stammer 272.F4
stamp 302.28 456.28
stampaded 043.23
stamping 603.11
stan 246.18 485.06 493.02
stances 297.07
stancias 350.16
stand 017.14 058.31 070.11 165.17 230.27 426.24 434.13 444.30 489.02 492.17 588.05 616.30
standable 253.30
standed 004.35 594.24
standing 061.11 100.09 100.21 171.21 184.01 240.31 347.30 429.15 530.08
standing 106.35
standingly 141.21
stands 173.34
stane 021.05 552.30
staned 011.22 128.02
stanes 173.17 462.25
stangs 553.36
stank 344.26 548.08
stan's 543.16
stant 143.08
stanters 357.05
staple 253.34
star 176.20 187.22 194.14 288.22 352.33 424.34 520.34
star 271.L1 287.08
starched 556.07
starching 033.08
stard 241.29 607.26
starde 312.08
stare 361.32 389.05 461.22 465.33
starin 227.35
stark 615.25
starolies 368.11
starr 069.14
starred 040.21 467.29 563.25
stars 090.08 157.09 159.08
start 382.14
started 232.12
startey 091.14
starts 337.21
stary 280.L1 338.35
stas 413.29
stase 603.35
statates 350.15
state 242.01 439.36 478.12
stated 070.06 097.35
statics 151.30
station 533.32
stationed 515.01
statums 295.02
statute 117.35
statution 365.17
staunton 534.35
stay 006.14 058.11
staying 312.15
stead 010.19 547.06
stead 430.15
steaden 533.35
steadily 053.07 513.33
steady 432.22
stealer 522.36
stealers 560.23
steam 171.35
steamadorion 398.18
stears 219.03
steckers 514.08
sted 026.26 054.13 326.21 496.15 593.12
steds 611.35
steed 598.04
steen 169.18 529.02
steer 550.08 598.05
stef 366.31
steil 097.05
steilend 335.12
stein 032.29 211.16
stein's 136.31
steinsong 231.29
steirs 533.17
stell 548.07
stella 101.08 278.F3
stellates 107.18
stellatria 157.19
stelle 048.12
stelles 365.28
stelliacinous 157.32
stellos 471.08
stellous 132.13
stellung 296.L1
stem 424.28
stem 167.34
stempting 356.20
stench 061.13 450.07
stenes 538.32
stenton 135.25
stents 337.21
step 016.02 166.07 455.19 456.36
steppen 077.20
steppers 399.18
stepping 178.23 386.31
steps 141.18 157.15 475.25
ster 318.31 327.13 528.12
sterdamp 138.24
sterds 254.35
sterelles 462.07
stereways 153.22
stering 467.29
sterliness 354.18
stern 407.30 560.25 598.10
sternis 596.07
sternmost 407.36
steroprotos 498.04
sterpet 133.08
sterr 069.14
sterssias 339.18
stessa 278.F3
stewte 236.28
steyn 225.24
steyne 056.14 075.14
steys 538.25
stiak 162.15
sticandeatar 406.07
stich 481.10
stichystuff 252.26
stick 035.35 094.02 170.11 242.09 336.24 473.13 485.08 535.07 569.19
stick 342.31
sticked 424.20
sticks 149.22 556.30
STICKS 281.R1
stickularly 087.09
stiesed 363.12
stif 456.24
stiff 100.15 264.F1 366.19 374.19 413.29 534.34
stift 321.04
stil 237.03
stila 449.11
stiles 586.26
still 153.20 246.10 274.25 463.34
still 175.21
stille 482.07
stille 105.23
stillery 371.25
stillone 581.34
stilts 414.23
stimm 546.29

sting 577.33
stings 303.26 406.34 406.34
stink 183.06
stinks 163.09
stintuation 055.35
stiom 296.02
stipital 436.01
stipple 015.35 093.25
stips 351.16
stir 246.13 263.23 311.10
stir 271.L1
stirdames 509.24
stirm 621.36
stirrer 561.34
stirring 508.22
stirrup 245.36
stisuit 487.11
stitating 235.02
stitone 092.07
stittywinktosser 359.12
stituettes 378.12
stoane 594.22
stock 050.05 305.26 533.35
stock 346.14 418.34
stocked 603.19
stodds 370.23
stoear 539.01
stoel 251.22
stoels 350.23
stoff 359.11
stoffs 161.16
stohns 502.20
stoker 145.32
stol 353.34
stold 411.01
stoll 133.29
stollo 254.25
stoly 485.31
stom 346.16
stomach 192.22
stomata 135.16
stomes 416.33 613.04
stomoses 585.22
stomy 597.21 597.21
stone 005.17 008.01 017.06 031.32 036.18 041.35 063.28 068.30 077.34 079.29 100.13 100.26 113.19 113.34 123.14 132.01 140.27 141.15 146.34 182.31 192.35 210.29 221.34 225.22 253.34 262.20 276.F3 280.31 293.14 331.04 332.13 334.06 370.34 371.30 392.24 430.06 479.18 503.26 539.03 550.31 564.30 568.23
stone 037.24 176.08 481.01
stoneaged 018.15
stonebelly 393.18
stoneburg 261.16
stoned 128.02
stones 081.06 207.07 224.19 279.02 322.33 375.31 481.27 493.11 504.32
stone's 013.16 170.32
stonnoriously 300.18
stood 555.07
stool 040.23 130.06 229.29 358.36 443.29 559.07
stoole 352.03
stooloo 343.16
stools 373.28
stoomerries 312.28
stoon 127.15 572.17
stop 144.01 144.01 221.06 375.27 475.14
stophere 452.01
stoppable 128.01
stoppage 369.34
stoppers 152.16
stopressible 568.16
stops 422.13
stord 163.22
store 326.23 327.05 390.12 552.21 556.33
store 176.06
stored 333.11
storeen 528.32
storey 452.16
storied 544.36
stories 017.27 068.07
storily 323.35
storm 086.20
storming 203.03
storms 339.13 392.28
storrap 310.20
storsioms 320.04
story 051.13 367.15 397.07
story 280.L1
storyshortener 017.03
stost 069.15
stost's 514.11
stote 540.17
stoun 624.27
stouned 256.09
stout 038.36 412.36
stout 099.04
stouters 329.31
stoutsalliesemoutioun 354.20
stouttered 272.21
stoutuent 537.22
stow 537.24
stowelsy 444.11
stract 346.33
strade 602.21
strades 495.30
strafes 443.12
straightcuts 576.20
straines 528.17
strait 003.17 083.36 481.06
strandvorous 417.11
strange 017.33
Strap 070.12
strape 623.16
straps 106.23
stras 324.29
strass 178.29 556.25
strate 163.24
straw 589.36
stray 472.13 506.21
straylians 321.09
strays 138.15
stream 058.25 427.12 486.23 547.31
stream 175.21
stream-Auborne 495.18
streamed 407.11
streaming 148.27
streams 074.14 526.29 528.17
streeds 553.35
street 097.21
strella 178.27
streme 432.31
strength 120.24
strenth 359.17
stress 228.17 255.33 262.15 324.33 326.10 486.20 577.31
stresse 547.32
stressed 067.23
stretched 033.05 054.30
stretcheds 600.18
stretches 014.31
strete 132.06
strew 395.01
strey's 064.06
stricken 599.28
strict 156.29 295.22
stride 023.18 208.23 429.02
strides 564.36
striking 199.04
stril 542.17
strill 175.23
strilling 276.20
string 121.08 451.33 533.09
string 345.22
strion 600.06
strip 233.06
strip- 090.31
stripe 208.16
stripes 504.31
stripperous 232.28
stritch 162.32
strode 356.04
strok 018.16
stroke 115.07 303.27
stroki 221.09
strollajerries 064.23
stroms 004.06
strong 626.02
strool 622.13
stroom 319.27 613.03
strophear 222.12
strophied 612.19
stross 018.03
stroton 073.30
strow 617.16
strucceleen 132.15
struce 613.12
struces 108.12
struck 057.15 126.07 155.24 261.26 279.F30
strum- 314.08
strumpa- 090.31
strumped 421.07
strums 362.33
strung 087.28
struss 128.26
stryggs 077.13
stuards 017.25
stuarine 549.20
stubs 157.28
stuck 035.36 036.16 085.11 157.11 214.15
stuckacqmirage 470.20
stucked 036.10
stucks 460.02
studded 208.06
studium 486.08
study 271.F4
stuff 007.13 232.24 252.26
stufffostered 042.07
stuffinaches 225.11
stuffs 167.19 170.26 434.24
stull 240.09
stullt 353.18
stum 598.15
stumbling 514.05 560.10
stumms 347.11
stump 070.17 544.09 557.29
stun 376.04

stundished 187.03
stung 085.18 126.22 135.09
stungwashed 342.13
stunned 378.22
stuns 389.24
stunshed 448.06
stunter 370.30
stuntonopolies 357.30
stunts 347.13
stup 020.13
sturdum 352.24
stureens 170.04
sturk 346.07
sturn- 314.08
sturping 457.12
sturs 317.12
sturts 266.13
stushes 346.02
stuskers 459.06
stutterers 027.35
sty 155.24 171.25 328.19 395.02
stye 305.06
stylic 181.36
styx 206.04
suahealing 204.03
suary 341.28
suates 349.20
subconscious 072.30
sub-Fagi 403.09
substantiation 557.29
substitute 028.35
sucapture 035.29
successfully 545.08
such 108.28 317.28 442.05 517.30 534.23 608.22 612.25
suchhewas 079.03
suckatary 177.19
sucked 016.03 123.24 407.17
sucker 010.19 417.17
suckerassousyoceanal 384.03
suckle 504.36
suckler 587.19 588.04
suckling 329.20
suckofumbers 340.26
sucks 452.01
suction 221.03
sue 336.13
sueded 603.17
suemeant 062.03
suessmein 330.24
suet 185.04 441.14
suetude 484.03
suetudinous 472.19
suffering 070.36 253.32 473.01
sufferings 184.01
sufficiencer 240.14
sufficient 409.25
sufficiently 125.21
sugger 141.34
suies 228.03
suing 116.01
suit 188.29 487.11 613.31
suited 092.02
suiter 070.21
suiting 300.27
suits 377.11 626.09
suivant 005.07 498.12
suive 232.03
suive 175.19
sukisaki 233.34
sul 510.25
sulant 484.15
sulinka 471.31
sull 516.06
sullied 525.03
sulphido- 596.14
sultan 612.09
sultantly 542.29
sultryngs 380.31
sulummmm 595.19
sulumply 595.19
sum 097.15 097.15 200.19 240.16 245.27 270.02
sumanything 417.26
sumbling 514.06
sumcordial 581.13
sumcordials 453.26
sume 371.22
sumer 152.21
sumers 155.04
sumkale 296.F3
summables 417.09
summed 336.35
summer 199.13 501.16
sumpship 040.12
sumptinome 153.20
sums 325.17
sumumina- 314.08
sun 090.01 117.04
sunck 621.06
sund 494.35
Sunday 089.14
sunder 213.16 328.08 546.12
sundered 136.07 596.03
sundered 349.15
sundery 339.25
sundrian 439.34
sund's 601.26
sundurst 347.09
sune 234.28
sung 350.08 352.17
suni 338.14
sunk 329.09
sunkener 241.24
sunt 258.02
suos 511.11
sup 009.17 039.03 265.F2 377.33 446.09 466.03 563.24 583.33
super 041.05
supo 428.01
supped 426.06
supper 360.36
suppers 087.23 147.16 564.18
supplier 135.28
suppon 233.34
supposed 424.25
suppy 417.15
sups 241.28
sur 353.12
sura 327.05
surad 016.11
sure 021.30 024.16 043.12 054.08 063.04 070.03 146.10 162.14 227.02 234.13 346.34 364.14 373.19 378.06 428.12 459.25 500.19 550.03 551.01
sured 235.25 252.22
surely 455.17
surers 608.17
sures 356.20
surfaced 081.13
surgent 287.23
surgery 536.06
surging 596.06
surhummed 015.15
suria 209.35
surnames 030.03
surrectioned 352.13
surt- 424.20
suspectingly 174.25
sussen 353.12
susupo 428.01
sut 203.08 333.34 580.18
sute 391.20
suture 253.34
suus 325.11 325.12
swab 245.34
swag 597.21
swagginline 582.32
swain 289.25
swain's 248.21
swallawer 151.23
swallower 150.04
swamswum 007.01
swanglers 371.03
swans 383.15
swap 518.17
sward 279.F30 404.02
swarmer 365.14
swarn 397.13
swathed 547.14
swatter 270.07
sway 284.F5 371.21 371.21 450.05 465.35 493.11
swaying 100.21
sways 005.22 153.23
swaysed 298.23
swear 053.33
sweat 025.15
Sweat 102.30
sweeeep 041.29
sweep 141.28 533.22
sweepers 006.05
sweeps 123.08
sweest 431.33
sweet 170.07 357.24 398.12 561.21 582.27
sweetened 533.19
sweetheartening 189.26
sweetstown 358.08
swell 040.01 150.31
swells 336.27
swellth 238.32
swelly 365.30
swer 037.21
swerks 221.09
swers 085.35 257.35
swetch 293.08
swhere 514.10
swhitchoverswetch 293.08
swibe 547.28
swill 150.30
swillers 171.20
swim 170.36
swin 404.19
swinging 404.19 417.25 504.23
swinish 535.20
swipe 281.F2
swiping 537.17
swise 279.F21
swold 073.28
swolle 070.07
swoon 060.11 474.11
sword 236.05
swords 178.04
swore 193.33
swormarose 302.27

swound 214.10
swuards' 026.31
swum 007.01
swundled 598.03
swut 272.05
sychomorers 476.14
syclitties 284.23
sycomb 391.23
sydown 512.01
syg 010.05 550.17
sygth 290.10
syllabled 183.15
syllables 190.35 306.26
sylph 416.14
symbles 608.23
symgnays 256.13
symples 338.25
syn 354.33
syndic 031.19
syne 112.08
sys 620.26
syseas 584.09
syskins 324.12
systemised 263.24
systems 148.18
szinging 415.14
szonese 347.09
szoppy 560.27
szozlers 415.14
szths 424.01

tab 467.31
tabadtomm 006.11
tabale 357.34
taballs 406.34
tabatoom 006.10
taberra 569.17
table 033.02 060.04 083.15 107.30 141.21 169.02 211.33 335.12 367.32 405.10 485.24 579.24
tablecert 610.17
tablecloth 039.06
tablecrashers 341.20
tabled 355.24
tablelads 465.15
tableland 010.34
tables 127.01 293.07 320.15 580.06 581.04 616.23
table's 387.36
tabletalk 120.23
tableturning 285.03
tabling 323.35
tably 619.10
tabout 113.12
tabulish 429.19
tac 089.35 270.14
taceas 213.30
tache 127.31
tached 562.21
tack 279.F12 315.19 602.10
tacking 396.27
tackle 368.32
tacks 183.20
tacooshy 484.26
tacotta 160.07
tacs 009.06
tact 087.14
tact 418.34
tacularly 004.31
tad 128.20 463.32
tades 553.21
tads 244.15 601.14
Taem 311.12
taen 136.36
taenk 317.26
taey 512.21 512.21
taff 035.27 366.19 512.14
taff 338.12
tafocal 117.14
tag 066.04 364.30 409.29 577.17
taggle 287.F4 419.15
tagliano 478.19
taglionic 513.17
tagore 037.02
tah 411.11 590.19
tahelv 262.F1
tahiti 337.29
taiI 232.36
tail 082.21 097.26 128.14 133.14 294.09 302.07 320.25 333.23 377.14 397.32 436.26 444.17 521.11 539.19 564.03 582.11
tail 105.16 350.01
taile 270.15
tailed 003.19 121.10 236.16
tailing 492.30
tailment 353.04 543.03
tailor 255.30
Tailors' 006.03
tails 018.27 054.34 393.11 435.24 436.30 545.29 609.04
taim 367.30
taimns 355.28
tain 284.06
taine 292.F2
tainted 127.27
tairer 343.09
tait 528.14
taj 325.10 325.11 325.11
tak 534.03
takam- 003.15
takatsch 296.24
take 030.09 062.10 097.25 352.12 537.16
taken 123.30 292.02 490.16 586.32
taker 237.34
takes 447.03
takia 450.11
taking 052.14 261.05 389.12 484.01 538.29 625.09 627.04
takings 387.10
tal 006.28
talaclamoured 100.02
talaisy 173.15
talamesse 236.07
tale 018.22 019.25 020.23 038.10 126.11 183.11 216.03 221.22 233.01 396.23 423.24 509.35 510.29 550.25 624.27
tale 268.L1
tale-a-treat-in-itself 123.27
taled 003.17
tales 220.13 224.08
taliessian 151.22
taliote 504.18
talish 296.L1
tality 580.13
talk 037.21 066.20 120.23 172.30 236.34 261.28 307.F1 420.30 504.19
talkers 032.08
talkin 414.04
talking 327.21 438.08 459.05 566.11
talks 121.02 269.03 460.11
tall 073.09 416.03 461.14 476.23 512.05
tallaght 478.12
talled 550.14 597.08
taller 417.16
talling 497.08
tallyouknow 581.27
talone 418.01
talook 059.18
Talur 327.04
tam 238.25 333.25 336.09 594.12
tam 104.10 397.32
tamai 471.01
tamed 196.23
tamed 277.L5
tamoror 547.25
tamovick 354.01
tamplin 593.24
tams 485.03
tamulier 166.26
tamuns 047.08
tan 025.09 027.09 227.20 260.17 274.09 343.10 352.32 359.05 463.35 485.06 602.18
tan- 257.27
tanach 090.31
tanai 595.20
tanajocky 331.24
tanambulating 497.35
tance 388.15
tancy 016.30
tand 005.28
tandog 446.13
tane 228.28 557.22
tang 198.34
tangel 594.04
tangere 509.33
tangincies 298.24
tangle 232.21 465.03
tangled 161.13
tangles 298.25
tango 534.11
tangos 019.05
tangs 553.36
tangues 541.34
tanik 338.23
taning 583.17
tanned 441.33
tannery 495.27
tan's 187.08
tansy 026.35
tantaliser 174.21
tantarums 445.17
tanth 251.04 266.23
tantini 238.23
tantitempoli 230.16
tantivy 359.29
tanto 419.13
tanzies 379.07
taoli 609.10
Taou 081.34
tap 319.09 430.11 544.16
tap- 090.31
tapengha 377.27
taper's 542.33
tapes 196.08
tapet 461.35
taph 420.11
tapped 138.19 318.29

tapper 070.22
tappers 480.09
tapping 381.09
taps 594.35
tapster 245.32
tar 059.24 288.22 328.30 341.12 341.12 343.21 393.13 406.07 406.07 560.13 610.20 610.20
tar 277.L4 339.18
tara 343.33
tarcrass 491.19
tarcurss 225.12 225.13
tarde 312.08
tares 135.21
tarf 016.22
tarfalls 383.23
targe 325.29
targisia's 601.24
targumends 245.10
tarial 106.11
tarin 227.35
taring 202.11
tarmined 170.11
tarn 303.06
tarnly 454.21
tarn's 494.10
tarosexual 120.35
tarr 211.01 549.35
tarre 349.21
tarriffs 539.28
tarring 143.22
tarryk 274.24
tarrymisty 539.21
tars 135.24 358.21
tarshes 182.27
tart 454.03
tartarum 317.04
tartempa 178.02
tarten 191.21
tartenment 534.08
tartery 346.01
tarums 445.17
tary 350.27
tas 060.16 160.31 514.10
tashees 348.17
tashie 403.11
tashy 484.26
tass 338.22 512.35
tasselled 474.08
taste 083.17 409.13
tat 057.07 366.30
tata 495.10
tatapadatback 289.F3
tatapapaveri's 172.01
tatating 242.14
tatattar 339.18
tatches 288.F7
tate 142.08
taterre 504.24
tateyar 319.27
tatias 256.21
tatorattlers 604.15
tatortoise 233.34
tats 540.29
tattar 339.18
tattatter 456.36
tatums 295.02
tatuohy 342.24
taub 565.11
taught 153.31 235.23
taun 423.24
taunties 435.01
taunton 534.35
tauplain 236.24
taure 434.05
taurious 353.12
taurnary 535.04
taurus 118.13
taut 292.24
tauter 490.20
tauwero 199.23
tavala 178.33
tavern 536.21
taw 090.01
tawneymen 361.24
tax 097.22 099.11
taxed 582.11
taxerxes 337.36
taxes 005.32
taxication 447.29
taxis 235.18 554.01
tay 006.14 184.30 240.16 376.30 406.28
tay 262.L2
taya 498.15
Taylour 511.29
tayn 295.F1
tayne 420.12
taynish 199.17
tays 435.12
TAY'S 308.R1
taywatashy 484.26
tchjelasys 417.23
tchouc 035.08
tea 062.16
teac 056.23
teached 413.08
teacher 038.35 166.21 184.35
teacher's 279.F04
teachertaut 292.24
teack 063.36
team 171.35 511.02
teamadorion 398.18
tear 159.16 327.36
teareans 518.13
tears 015.09 060.01 116.12 219.03 562.30
tease 576.24
teased 266.30
teasing 276.F1 437.36
teasy 153.07
teavvents 603.28
techt 076.36
teckers 514.08
tectis 364.21
ted 054.13
tee 019.01 025.03 300.25
tee 102.31
teed 345.25
teedee 342.29
teeming 531.09
teemiously 285.10
teen 219.15 219.15 379.28
teen-a-lax 100.13
teened 174.29
teeny 021.01 298.27 457.36 533.19
teerily 364.06
tees 011.20
teet 019.02
teethshilt 529.31
tegos 307.L1
tegument 186.01
teilend 335.12
teilius 573.28
tel 508.17
telating 581.13
teld 597.08
tell 073.12 258.15 258.15 597.08
tellable 227.36
tellarias 387.13
tellecktuals 161.06
teller 123.23 415.25
telleries 205.02
tellers 135.04
tellible 016.33
telling 288.08 367.15 424.35
tellius 573.08
tellius 307.L1
tellmeknot 361.10
tellomey 198.02
tells 017.03
tellus 252.15 527.01
tellusit 406.14
tellye 492.07
tels 540.21
tem 076.21 131.11 223.35 223.36 224.01 224.03 224.07 263.11 306.07 459.27 480.31 506.10 618.24
tem 481.04
temp 064.01 175.01
tempa 178.02
temper 553.02
temperance 178.35
temperate 542.12
tempered 167.27 190.01 426.06
tempestuous 143.16
tempibles 175.01
temple 602.22
tempoli 230.16
temporal 303.L1
temporate 082.17
tempore 606.09
temporised 137.18
temptable 352.01
tempter 154.06
temptible 497.35
tempting 356.20
temption 155.13
tempust 457.32
tems 086.23
tems 353.29
tem's 456.28
ten 029.26 079.10 241.18 315.32 318.15 389.33 392.05 414.04
ten 349.31
ten- 414.19 414.19
tenable 397.33
TENACITY 286.R3
tenante 281.L1
tenant-Groevener 325.01
tences 599.12
tench 524.30
tency 016.26
tend 297.06
tended 056.12 169.20 320.17 413.33 476.07
tendency 305.09
tender 399.17
tendered 392.09
tending 287.29
tends 448.10
tened 567.28
tenency 146.34
tenente 228.27

tenes 538.32
tennis 470.20
tense 097.26 296.F4
tense 418.33
tensies 187.30
tensiles 053.18
tensilise 447.01
tent 076.30
tented 317.31
tentended 413.33
tenters 058.32
tentical 016.36
tents 258.22 337.21
tentsed 348.12
tentung 512.11
tenue 347.22
tep 237.27 237.27
tepholomy 389.17
terand's 088.33
terds 254.35
termed 536.12
termentdags 413.10
tern 355.21
ternish 454.22
ternitay 406.28
terny 397.16
terpet 133.08
terputty 068.28
terra 601.33
terrado 289.22
terranean 098.06
terre 019.14 033.12 504.24
541.35
terre 175.11
terred 189.16
terrier 424.04
terrorised 184.08
terry's 531.34
tersees 538.25
terssias 339.18
tert 345.18
terum 572.19
tery 166.36
terza 212.12
teself 187.04
tessa 278.F3
tessa's 104.08
tesser 232.13
test 022.28 050.18 230.10
tested 187.17
testicle 413.17
testificated 438.30
testions 301.30
testudinous 609.14
tet 119.14
tetabsolvers 004.09
tetails 609.04
teter 423.18
teters 111.01
tether 413.27
tetry 060.20
tetterday 490.27
tetters 396.27
tettes 594.34
tettetterday 490.27
teuto- 219.17
tew 061.06 523.02
teyar 319.27
tha 019.06 475.02 502.04
thaab 312.19
thabala 600.10
thack 348.31
thah 240.06
thair 273.F8
thalamorous 040.14
thalamou 314.22
thalians 569.29
thall 117.16
thallacamellated 285.21
thalltale 019.25
thaner 335.26
thanga 497.11
thanks 119.34 239.22 316.10
thanor 184.18
thanow 366.12
thanwater 070.26
thaokan- 257.27
thar 599.07
tharas 113.07
thares 565.19
thargogalenu 184.13
tharhea 513.22
thats 019.17 221.14
thaun 454.09 462.08
thausthible 091.27
thay 490.28
Thay 599.03
Thaya 294.L2
thayan-Euxine 263.13
theaires 354.01
theal 461.13
theatre 033.10
theatron 596.01
theayter 214.14
thebell 245.25
thedocks 491.07
theecease 118.04
theen 082.09
theeng 395.02
theesinger 366.25
theg 032.04
theleast 237.04
thelemew 541.15
theless 581.36
thelest 619.36
thelizod 452.11
thella 151.20
thelock 587.30
theloss 318.18
thelot 019.18
themagger- 113.09
themall 389.07
thematic 424.36
theme 177.02
themerically 185.29
themology 374.17
themore 180.01 238.06 314.15
thems 474.24 535.12
thems 272.L4
themselves 353.27
thena 602.30
thenairyans 360.08
thends 343.25
thene 115.30
thened 345.34
theners 326.13
thenth 608.24
theochromatokreening 392.28
theology 341.28
theometry 370.13
theomime 180.04
THEOSIS 286.R2
theouse 338.20
thepot 093.32
therapper 361.27
thercuss 054.04
therdebble- 332.05
thered 134.22
therem 231.13
thergarmenteries 181.29
thergeist- 187.15
thergills 215.14
therich 054.03
thermore 288.10
thern 357.32
therootsch 222.12
thers 135.05 252.01 471.12
thesameagain 094.27
theses 309.08
thesious 266.L1
thesis 298.L3
THESIS 282.R1
thesite 597.14
thetta 569.14
thew 253.12
theway 063.01
theways 602.31
thews 129.33 277.F6
thewsyass 260.18
theye 344.05
thiance 296.20
thiarn 296.23
thible 091.27
thick 170.33 199.12 233.01
291.07
thicket 112.05
thickets 428.26
thicks 176.22
thief 010.01 459.33
thievious 271.05
thigh 277.F6
thighs 061.23 548.20
thim 232.17 388.05
thin 203.09 417.06 463.27
thin' 056.28
thing 058.02 077.31 133.35
178.05 207.22 208.24 231.22
253.08 256.27 284.08 295.28
359.25 415.22 426.19 455.22
541.09 561.04 627.33
Thing 231.09
thingboys 054.09
thingling 395.19
things 338.17 368.20 373.27
379.14 379.17 556.28 598.01
599.01 599.35 625.24
thing's 026.25
thingthats 221.14
think 056.31 083.14 162.21
570.27
think 342.28
thinkables 417.13
thinked 343.25
thinker 107.32
thinkful 543.13
thinking 068.32 162.23
thinks 116.13 149.03 242.04
556.13
thinks 342.26
thinly 363.13
thir 417.06
thirhd 310.15
thirst 052.06
thirties 494.33
thirty 093.12
thisfeige 014.02
thisis 305.21
thisishis 177.33
thisment 434.29

thisthy 623.10
Thither 452.27
thithering 216.04
thngs 349.27
thoid 029.15
thold 242.05
tholder 517.09
thole 201.23 370.20
tholed 535.02
tholobruised 021.35
tholoman's 100.04
tholomas 352.05
tholoosed 113.20
tholy 416.19
thom 278.F2
thomanew 623.16
thome's 116.20
thoms 312.07
thon 009.33 119.17 254.33
thone 190.30 353.18
thong 424.34
thongue 117.15 477.28
thongues 511.31
thoothoo 623.10
thor 009.05 148.17 246.06 300.19 452.10 525.15
thora 006.16
thorace 616.26
thorc 018.34
thore 197.21 397.05 412.25
thoreths 601.08
thoric 104.17
thoricks 027.02
thoring 181.12
thorn 015.03 015.03 114.11 556.19
thorn 338.35
thorndene 553.22
thorne 321.04
thorns 057.23 135.02 160.06 204.20 549.02
thoron 579.15
thoroughly 220.30
thorpe 081.21 291.19 541.25
thorrorty 516.19
thorrorumble 353.24
thors 036.35 578.34
thorstrok 018.16
thos 231.28 494.06
thouducks 358.29
thoudux 252.20
though 117.19 315.17 426.18
thought 022.07 080.16 147.09 258.32 261.13 316.31 359.02 403.18 404.04 405.07 475.32
thoughtfully 342.34
thould 344.32
thow 254.16 341.16
thowsent 597.05
thoyou 471.02
threaded 061.06
threateningly 246.06
three 255.34
three 345.10
threes 245.19
threnated 542.18
threw 356.02
threwer 064.14
thrick 486.02
thrift 335.34
thrifts 253.08
thrig 565.18
thrill 515.28
thrills 450.11
thro 092.01 310.09
throa's 601.22
throat 091.11 183.19 279.F33
throats 128.09
throes 616.32
throlio 280.24
thronechair 423.07
throned 606.03
thronosed 032.12
throposophia 394.19
throproise 318.05
throp's 502.29
throughwards 594.19
throw 492.02
throwers 192.30
thrown 504.32 570.36
throws 240.16
thrush 385.02
thrushes 384.03
thrust 574.24
thrusted 356.29
thruster 281.L3
thuck 037.30
thud 373.15
thudders 510.01
thuds 156.15
thug 344.04
thule 321.08
Thule 235.19
thulic 603.30
thumb 412.06
thumbs 337.25
thump 006.04 376.10 385.15
thumper 108.17
thumpered 360.09
thumpronouceable 479.09
thun 604.07
thunara- 023.05
thund 335.17 335.18
thunder 078.05 378.07
thundered 547.28
thunn- 003.15
thur 004.29 349.05 487.20
thurd 156.33
thure 529.23
thurf 388.17
thurin 335.35
thuris 594.02
thurminous 429.02
thurnstock 346.14
thurnuk 003.15
thur's 523.14
thury 536.11 536.11
thwacker 594.19
thwart 564.24
thwartships 311.08
thwndxrclzp 284.14
thyan 485.10
thyme 206.34
thyme's 090.07
thyrs 348.11
thys 354.32
tic 419.25
tice 164.31
tich 481.10
tick 176.35 268.08 378.18
ticked 367.17
TICKELLYTHIGH 305.R1
ticker 308.04
tickles 437.31
TICKS 281.R1
ticktating 243.08
tid 326.21 498.32 538.03
tide 034.22 037.18 081.17 082.36 206.34 453.36 577.29
tide 165.02
tider 626.02
tides 011.13 365.14 482.10 502.23
tide's 097.03
tidled 070.16
tie 133.34 144.24 202.20
tied 094.08 279.F23 315.04 563.18
tiered 194.27
tiers 156.12
ties 019.09 027.28 031.24 112.36 117.18 133.04 233.23 432.15 436.01 496.33 510.31 517.33 548.24 582.20 597.07
ties' 577.34
tiesed 363.12
tieu 289.22
tiff 016.06 366.19 493.03
tiffed 548.16
tiffits 420.26
tig 283.01 356.15
tigern 565.12
tighs 373.27
tight 265.09 441.08 465.14 622.28
tig's 055.27
til 170.21 237.03 310.29 549.13 625.23
tilely 299.25
tiles 586.26
tilifully 457.28
till 302.02 321.28
tilla 194.22
tillably 275.05
tillery 530.18
tilli- 023.05
tilmensky 034.18
tils 138.14
tim 210.15 284.09 301.24 336.09 415.18 419.15 527.28 534.17
timaney 207.25
timber 450.12
time 007.21 032.28 052.01 083.09 083.17 085.36 088.34 097.21 099.35 104.02 108.22 123.15 130.35 137.15 137.36 170.26 191.28 192.06 194.25 204.14 209.05 211.22 224.11 228.34 230.19 239.16 290.17 314.31 319.10 319.35 323.30 325.30 365.07 368.34 372.07 390.06 395.34 413.04 427.13 427.34 432.33 444.25 455.31 478.04 496.29 528.05 543.24 548.32 550.34 557.31 560.09 562.07 570.07 571.36 576.31 610.35 611.08 611.28 612.21 624.03
time 071.17 349.06
timed 236.23
timendly 029.35
timer 472.21
timers 398.24
timer's 037.15
times 027.09 101.15 108.34 113.27 121.09 133.19 193.33 254.22 263.17 338.02 357.35 359.05 361.26 365.14 384.08

462.24 463.12 482.22 489.22 506.13 537.21 544.19 557.32 566.02 575.15 593.08 603.18
time's 064.36 348.27
timestained 114.29
timid 093.17
timier 105.11
timm 546.29
timogeniture 300.L1
timologies 101.17
timominous 613.28
timo's 599.23
tim's 227.17
timus 108.12
tin 008.18 117.30 162.15 362.09 378.12 393.01 457.31 500.35 519.16 596.25
tin 350.09 350.09 350.09 350.09
tinas 059.12
tinbeddy 243.06
tincking 092.16
tincts 599.20
tinders 541.33
tinenties 336.32
tines 601.13 601.13
ting 376.18 553.32
tingeling 419.12
tingface 563.15
tingfast 020.08
tings 113.03 250.08
tini 238.23
tinins 494.22
tinju 352.28
tinker 342.03
tinkle 295.F2
tinkus 322.30
tinroarin 372.31
tins 421.36 533.06 540.31 624.18
tinsion 371.24
tint 334.24
tinted 403.07
tinties 552.24
tinuation 558.12
tinued 067.16
tinus 157.02
tiny 323.11 527.17
tip 313.26 321.34 562.09
tip- 005.01 090.31
tipacco 069.36
tipaltar 344.27
tipoll 193.20
tipper 483.19
tippit 207.34
tipple 015.35 093.25
tippy 065.32
tipreaching 292.09
tipsypote 337.24
tir 499.09
tired 229.17
tirely 059.13
tirenis 335.16 335.16
tires 567.34
tireties 597.07
tiring 092.21
tiringly 261.17
tiristid 538.03
tiro 536.21
tisfactuary 084.15
tisintus 611.24
tissues 048.18
tistag 066.04
tit 004.35 054.16 225.01 346.35 372.11
titat 057.07
titempoli 230.16
tites 427.29
tithes 326.06
titians 173.16
tities 013.24
titillated 288.F4
titilli- 023.05
titily 191.19
titiptitop- 005.01
TITITITILATIO 305.R1
title 440.08
titled 104.04
titles 567.14
titoff 524.29
titone 092.07
titout 071.01
tits 505.01
titties 093.19
tittles 314.26
tittot 260.02
tittshe 469.01
tittywinktosser 359.12
tituitary 037.01
tity's 601.24
tivits 374.04
tiydt 510.32
tjschute 003.19
toarted 150.12
toastally 038.23
toastrool 622.13
tob 445.13
tobe 052.35 062.11 085.22 229.33
to-be 325.15
tobechronickled 380.08
tobedder 253.09
toble 351.31
tobodoff 370.17
toby 423.33
toccan 345.17
tod 571.14
today 455.24 513.12 570.12
todays 622.15
todds 370.23
tods 283.29
tody 533.36
toe 073.15 147.23 265.17 286.20 423.33 467.31
toed 150.03 498.35 539.11 545.24
toel 251.22
toelles 601.28
toels 350.23
toer 624.09
toes 003.21 015.31 152.33 215.13 393.30
toff 359.11 524.29
toffbellek 412.10
tofficially 606.19
toffs 161.16
toff's 119.02
toflesh 481.30
toft 394.18
tofty 114.23
tog 246.05
togesus 316.28
together 048.23 109.20 155.31 155.36 181.20 380.08 425.34 438.18 451.23 470.23 484.24 509.14 523.13 533.18 574.34
togiving 380.09
togotter 349.32
tograbakelly 463.02
togs 071.24
togtug 351.17
toher 571.20
tohong 230.36
toikon 416.12
toiled 546.06
toils 564.20
toista 285.17 285.18
toit 078.33
tojazyma's 578.22
tokan 296.24
token 350.18 613.30
tokens 194.31
tokinatown 484.16
tol 258.07 258.10
told 189.31 246.22 247.02 316.01 317.27 396.23 411.01 453.18 505.32 596.04 597.08
tole 603.30
tolets 221.23
toletta 329.35
tolios 082.12
tolk 130.21 390.24
toll 133.29
tolled 376.13
tollmens 013.11
tollomuck 254.22
tolomei 529.34
tolonely 152.19
tolove 472.19
toloves 004.09
tol's 417.23
tom 021.31 048.18 088.36 122.07 163.19 252.35 296.06 333.34 333.34 344.17 344.30 463.01 496.20 561.04 582.01
tom 341.31 346.16
tomake 240.16
tomance 310.22
tomata 135.16
tomate 417.20
tomatetam 336.09
tomb 366.32
tombed 586.30
tombmount 192.35
tomebathred 467.15
tomed 367.30
tomeet 238.06
tomeetim 336.09
tomercies 349.25
tomes 416.33 595.22 613.04
tometusolum 378.15
tomewhere 145.04
tomia 318.25
tomichael 621.02
tomicker 199.21
tomind 329.35
tomine 023.28 167.03 223.09 361.01 587.08 615.24
to-mine 283.10
tomise 356.12
tomkin 290.F7
tomm 006.11 406.17
tommick 097.29
tomomiom 285.15
tomophilust 107.13
tomosically 615.05
tomptation 362.04
toms 015.14 176.21 455.17 534.02 598.21

tomtotalitarian 260.02
tomtowley 534.18
tomtum 519.10
tomy 597.21
tomyplace 114.18
ton 294.22 541.03 569.28 612.33
ton 508.12
tona 617.06
tonant 338.19
tonant-Cornel 607.29
tonates 353.23
tonbiking 437.06
toncle's 250.13
tondus 273.L4
tone 062.09 092.07 144.30 158.35 248.07 276.F3 309.19 312.21 372.28 404.04 512.11 536.32 573.34
toned 063.20 070.07 323.30 334.13 548.05
tonem 257.11
tonement 568.09
tones 138.01 148.08 299.22 318.33 434.22 565.05
tone's 184.23 542.04
tonetically 614.30
tong's 058.10
tongue 355.24 385.04
tongues 223.28 404.06
tongue's 037.21
tonguing 584.03
tonia 126.12
tonia 343.01
tonian 385.13
tonights 622.15
tonner- 003.15
tonnerwetter 585.11
tonnoriously 300.18
tonobble 074.11
tonone 126.10
tonorseher 203.07
tonosery 253.28
tonoze 392.06
tons 351.04
tonsions 511.17
tonsure 364.14
tonuation 284.20
tonyhands 265.21
too 416.13
toogooder 358.16 602.09
toohoohoor- 003.15
took 063.29 432.18 625.01
tool 130.06
toolatetolove 472.19
Toole 433.05 557.07
Toolechest 569.06
toolers 005.03
tooles 138.26
tooloo 343.16
tools 373.28
toolyrical 452.03
toom 006.10
toomany 408.13
toomanyness 122.36
toomerries 312.28
toon 127.15 572.17
toory- 257.27
toosent 438.24
toosezit 154.33
tooth 177.26 242.08 303.03
toothdmand 403.12
toothed 387.08 539.36
tooth's 462.13
tootletoo 461.27
tootomtotalitarian 260.02
toovatted 346.03
top 005.02 031.02 063.29 087.29 144.01 144.01 152.34 210.32 244.03 299.15 315.32 320.27 331.05 376.25 420.12 423.33 449.23 475.20 483.19 499.25 560.12 624.11
top 176.06
top- 005.01
tope 512.20
topeace 364.17
topical 090.27
topically 415.29
topies 020.13
topointing 181.24
topoof- 314.08
topoxy 386.31
topped 033.09
topper 435.12
toppled 549.34
toproyal 097.13
tops 118.19 193.15 422.13 532.35
top's 266.11
toptap 319.09
toptippy 065.32
toputty 612.32
tor 497.28 551.01
tora 598.33
toras 542.02
torattlers 604.15
torc 612.02
tores 126.24
torest 279.08
toretorning 256.17
torey 452.16
torial 584.36
tories 384.02
torik's 177.26
torios 041.28
torix 088.22
tork 353.11
torn 537.10
torning 256.17
toros 325.34
torrap 310.20
torreor 254.13
torreor 105.11
torribleday 381.24
tors 221.20
torsed 010.36
torsioms 320.04
tortoise 233.34
tory 132.19 274.30 317.31 357.22 506.19 530.11 599.16 623.06
tory 266.L1
toryism 162.06 359.03
toryum 153.26
toseen 165.26
tosend 070.09
toslay 087.08
toss 338.21
tossed 080.07
tossem- 414.19
tosser 359.12 520.13
tossic 187.02
tossis 437.09
tosst 108.05 624.02
tost 069.15
Tosti 309.19
tost's 514.11
tot 193.02 260.02 372.10
TOT 305.R1
total 450.36
totalies 110.17
totalitarian 260.02
totalled 542.32
totaller 417.16
totally 181.21 330.06
tote 540.17
totem 255.14 516.24
totem 071.31
tothem 053.15
toties 186.22
totoryum 153.26
totously 157.21
tots 588.35
totte 609.17
totter 096.31
tottered 006.09
totterer 337.18
tottom 344.17
totum 038.25 426.21 489.17
totype 324.01
to-type 139.29
totypes 454.13
tou 565.06 585.04
toub 063.33
touch 171.02 174.10 465.27
touchable 237.24
touche 067.36
touched 120.10
touches 594.21
touche's 450.36
touching 509.05
touchings 237.18
touchups 171.27
touchy 552.04
tougend 247.07
tough 485.16
toumers 497.18
toun 023.12 227.35 624.27
tounette 143.32
toup 310.29
toupon 595.04
tour 199.24
tourbridge 184.12
tourf 086.10
tourious 340.01
touristing 055.24
tourne 143.30
tourneys 472.34
tous 286.13
tout 052.25 071.01 134.26 141.08 152.27 211.35 286.13 412.36 506.32 578.23
tout 099.04 399.14
toutcas 129.06
touts 272.27 546.16
toutsalliesemoutioun 354.20
toux- 414.19
tover 280.20
towards 084.30 240.36
towel 513.33 559.07
towelsy 444.11
tower 100.17 237.22 364.21
towerly 004.36
toweyt 583.30
towhom 369.12
towife 011.29
towing 550.28
towley 534.18

town 047.22 071.07 078.18 097.04 097.04 097.07 097.07 097.08 097.09 097.10 097.10 097.21 129.24 142.13 142.14 152.28 197.09 202.09 202.10 203.07 235.36 243.26 262.21 266.03 270.13 274.30 288.11 291.10 309.16 329.25 339.26 358.08 390.03 462.24 462.28 481.28 484.16 497.11 507.35 523.12 539.24 582.33 607.34 615.20 622.34 622.34 622.34 622.34 622.35 625.25 625.35
town 276.L5 383.06
townian 167.10
town's 015.01 265.28
towntonobble 074.11
towobble 510.28
Toyd 123.20
toyds 531.05
toys 058.32
toysed 133.26
toytness 537.17
trace 552.09
track 081.07 577.23
tracks 080.01
tracktors 221.20
tract 346.33
tractable 477.20
tractional 150.33
trade 532.25 602.21
traders 581.15
trades 495.30
traduced 607.05
trae 537.10
traente 105.25
tragedy 425.24
trail 578.17
train 122.11
trained 567.33
trained 348.29
trainer 106.09
traines 528.17
tram 553.32
trame 104.10
tramens 502.30
trammed 567.33
trance 060.03 240.29 397.28 423.06 597.07
tranicht 555.10
transcended 429.17
trants 407.05
trap 033.32 047.09 084.34 287.F1 465.21 476.22
trape 623.16
trapped 344.26 372.01
trappety 332.15
trapping 031.08
traps 030.04 154.13 184.26 579.03
traps 106.23
traumconductor 378.09
traverse 609.14
traversed 416.31
traversers 538.06
traxity 391.07
tray 026.07 459.22 503.07
Traynor 370.22
treachesly 541.08
treat 169.23
treated 364.16 575.30
treating 322.29
treat-in-itself 123.27
treats 021.03 141.12
treck 240.17
tree 025.13 025.30 030.14 055.27 062.34 083.08 088.02 100.11 146.34 159.04 180.22 184.14 191.18 247.04 274.15 277.17 291.06 371.30 420.11 439.11 492.09 503.13 503.30 521.07 564.30 588.30 588.31 588.31 588.31
tree 176.08
treeatic 062.02
trees 005.31 022.24 202.30 244.02 259.06 280.30 504.21 544.35
treetop 331.05
treeumption 191.13
treeyou 009.13
treffender 069.32
trell 081.14
trella 178.27
trelly 534.09
tremmis 536.11
tren 290.09
trench 572.05
trench 344.09
trenched 357.33
trene 230.26
trenfy 426.07
trennty 228.24
trenous 603.18
Trent 531.03
trenth 102.25 359.17
treox 055.03
trepidation 338.29
trepider 467.05
trepifide 157.25
tress 038.30 137.23 189.25 228.17 255.33 262.15 324.33 326.10 352.13 370.05 486.20 577.31
tresse 547.32
tressed 067.23
tresses 090.16 587.26
tresson 585.06
trest 351.18
trettanth 266.23
treu 459.21
trews 008.21
trey 126.21
treying 533.16
tri 247.09
triad 167.04
trial 466.28
tribe 341.25
tributed 371.12
tributes 220.20
tric 313.24 532.08
trice 227.14 312.20
trick 003.10 180.05 221.34 288.22 322.31 353.14 486.07 577.08
trick 339.31
trickee 165.06
tricker's 425.30
trickery 579.06
tricks 060.06 437.01 444.27
trick's 361.03
tricksburg 326.25
tricksling 230.29
trickster 423.06
trickularly 316.05
trickx 211.33
tric's 012.32
tricus 230.34
trie 178.17
trieatedly 302.24
tried 178.09 534.35
tries 027.29 145.24 235.28 365.02 435.26 481.35 548.26 549.33 609.03
trigesima 433.03
trigesumy 234.12
trigger 335.13 540.30
trigintadue 054.12
trikes 284.24
tril 542.17 568.12
trill 081.14
trill 175.23
trilled 115.26
trilling 276.20
trilly 096.04
trimaserovmeravmerouvian 113.04
trimmer 323.14
trin 068.35
trinch 009.19
trine 326.15
triodic 310.04
trion 600.06
tripes 303.F1 504.31
triques 515.33
tris 486.07
trispissing 302.06
triss 230.32
trisscalls 363.28
trist 571.07
TRISTICKS 281.R1
tritch 162.32
trite 607.02
trix 526.33
trixy 269.31
tro 437.33
trodantic 510.03
trodden 056.24
trodding 151.10
trodontos 244.35
trofio 169.23
troj 160.31
trol 340.19
trolling 323.31
trollops 582.34 603.28
trompit 247.32
tron 468.36
tronage 342.13
tronning 347.31
troon 604.15
troop 057.15
troopers 223.11
trooping 344.23
troosers 280.L3
trope 461.09 533.02 561.20 610.36
trope 265.L1
tropes 009.19 301.01
trophied 612.19
trophy 083.14
tropic 252.21
tropical 349.06
tropolis 594.08
trorsehim 570.33
trossers 246.27
trot 469.03
troth 162.33
troton 073.30
trottel 229.18
trotter 475.31

trotting 180.18
troubles 192.16
trough 373.18
trousnest 241.10
troussy 588.07
trout 059.08
trouvetout 211.35
trouz 413.30
trovarr- 003.15
trovent 425.28
trow 326.22
troyed 538.07
tru 114.27
trubbely 020.25
trubry 604.17
truce 083.35 424.20 613.12
truces 108.12
truck 279.F30
truck- 378.09
tructed 284.15
true 063.10 355.21 403.22
459.20 459.21 462.14
trues 191.14 282.28
truewith 598.34
truis 247.10
truism 604.33
trulls 552.10
trumans 203.24
trumeny 010.03
trumpers 556.30
trumpet 530.14
trumpets 179.22
trumtrum- 314.08
trunk 371.03
trunner 337.01
trup 014.18
trupithump 006.04
truquulence 360.21
truser 082.18
truss 128.26
trust 483.10 529.05
trustworthily 057.18
trusty 031.26
truth 169.09 459.36
try 052.05 053.12 060.20
099.19 161.22 230.05 253.29
291.12 305.07 343.32 343.32
348.35 391.36 466.11 494.25
509.35 535.18 539.16 552.36
try 286.L4
tryck 393.10
trycook 486.17
tryggs 077.13
trygods 004.01
trying 442.25
tryk 425.28
tryngs 380.31
tryproof 290.19
tryville 205.26
tsar 353.09
tschanjeuchy 004.25
tse 299.26
tseng 611.30
tsey 242.25 242.26
tu 288.23
tub 272.18 312.25 358.22
538.34 542.05 606.02 606.07
tubante 403.09
tubbs 077.30
tube 036.36 566.35
tuber 481.28
tuberian 381.14
tubes 158.36 542.06
tubruskblunt 116.02
tubular 309.14
tuck 225.09
tuck 037.29
tucked 036.10
tucks 460.02
tucs 418.34
tudor 093.08
tuesday's 407.31
tuesser 460.32
tufa 606.36
tuffel 327.15
tug 351.17
tugging 013.12
tugs 064.19
tuh 415.26
tuition 385.30
tuitte 609.17
tul 064.25
tulass 179.12
tuled 050.17
tules 276.23 348.06
tuli 180.14
Tuli 228.25
tull 240.09
tullagh- 332.05
tullepleats 530.27
tum 012.05 167.06 271.12
273.08 296.03 394.30 462.25
462.26 489.17 519.10 541.28
598.15
tum 281.L4 287.22 287.25
tumble 417.14
tumbling 013.18 404.35 514.05
514.11 560.10 598.08
tumbulumbumus 598.05
tumcalmum 026.18
tumising 149.35
tummer 016.17
tummi 243.07
tummock 355.30
tumms 347.11
tummung 187.03
tummy's 019.04
tumn 178.30
tums 295.02 549.31
tumtingling 231.02
tumtoes 003.21
tumtumpty 106.20
tumuk 599.20
tumuled 133.30
tumvir 585.24
tun 006.33 140.01 376.04
582.35
tunar 327.21
tu-naughsy 505.07
tunc 290.23
tunc 278.L1
tundarinking 205.33
tundaties 542.28
tundished 187.03
tundity 190.02
tundo 295.24
tune 110.14 222.06 426.25
466.36 581.07
tunes 299.23
tung 512.11 612.08
tungpelick 020.34
tungs 240.30
tunly 448.32
tunmighty 128.03
tunshed 448.06
tuohy 342.24
tuoning 353.17
tuonn- 003.15
tup 020.13 242.24 415.34
415.35 576.27
tup- 090.31
tuponable 284.26
tupped 547.29
tupt 277.11
tur 136.21 496.26
tura 291.F6
turanian 289.20
turb 378.20
turbaned 353.06
turboy 362.08
turden- 424.20
tureen 394.02
tureens 170.04
turf 017.09 145.07
turgid 496.24
turing 371.15
turk 017.14
turk 346.07
turkish 051.27
turmdrappen 346.29
turn 017.03 064.16 128.05
295.20 386.27 621.14
turn 354.19
Turnbull 171.31
turne 328.17
turned 091.16 100.28 254.14
439.10 457.29
turning 285.03 415.09
turnity 366.21
turnpikepointandplace 003.22
turns 018.05 369.03 539.31
570.04 606.18
turn's 470.13
turnup 314.08
turny 309.23
turping 457.12
Turricum 228.22
turted 093.07
turtled 005.17
turtls 624.26
turuvarnar 512.08
turvy 275.14
tuse 062.11
tuskers 459.06
tusks 234.13
tuss 338.22
tussem- 414.19
tussle 610.35
tut 395.23
tutors 372.12
tutory 220.36
tuttutistics 616.22
tututu 406.20
tuvisky 187.08
tving 325.20
twaimen 279.F23
twain 287.13
twantyng 499.05
'twas 404.11 406.17
tweed 210.30
tween 184.07 355.30 432.09
458.01 570.24 600.06
tweenly 247.30
twides 360.05
twin 004.34 360.02
twine 259.07
twined 488.03
twink 426.32
twinklers 131.28

urr's 454.30
urself 499.22
urssia 224.02
urther 206.09
Uru-Wukru 024.07
usand 326.20
usaphist 072.14
use 062.11 289.F4 328.34
used 161.36 173.36 344.30
used 339.24
used-to 291.03
users 060.27 593.17
uses 070.12
usheen 267.19
usians 451.24
usit 331.06
usk 338.17
usless 237.11
usmore 096.24
uspeep 275.L2
uspical 345.29
us-pray 213.19
uspurudo 289.22
usses 075.22
usshers 608.10
ussin 116.18
usslleepp 368.19
usuable 324.29
usual 368.13 516.09 516.32
usucapiture 537.23
ut 203.08 313.20 580.18
ut 601.16
utah 016.10
utan 325.31
uthr 280.19 280.27
utmost 006.18
utter 598.19
utteration 284.21

vaast 552.08
vace 138.19
vacuan 362.25
vad 088.29 611.21
vaded 247.08
vadesia 594.04
vadged 459.08
vague 577.23
vailend 288.24
vailing 568.30
vain 597.34
vaipar 208.13
vairn 327.12
vakon 394.26
val 140.03 466.32 628.06
vala 178.33
valch 241.12
vale 457.11 502.27 581.19
valent 050.22 164.03
valet 320.15
valeurised 543.02
valike 348.03
valise 345.11
valla 460.32
vallator 139.18
Valle 380.09
valled 569.19
valley 215.10 328.27
valleys 015.03
valls 580.01
vallupped 339.09
valoos 443.36
valse 054.23
Valse's 601.25
valsshie 578.16
valvered 518.17
valves 311.17 311.17
valvulous 310.04
van 007.04 013.27 031.21 197.20 372.30 436.29 602.28
vana 597.19
vanas 601.14
vanashed 061.18
vanda 037.22
vander 331.27
vandets 198.11
vane 536.18
vanes 005.31 495.36
vanger 328.27
vans 006.15 007.04 495.02
vansky 355.11
vant 200.18
vantonoze 392.06
vantora 598.33
vantry 150.21
vap 595.30
vapieno 182.30
vapnasvap 597.04
var 331.26
vara 191.10 621.11
varewords 436.12
vargraine 019.23
vari 213.20
variable 033.05
variant 431.06
various 165.10
varioveneral 098.18
varities 355.36
varminus 008.28
varn 243.10 594.01 599.22
varnan 333.10
varnar 512.08
varome 155.05
varos 541.36
varr- 003.15
var's 294.18
varsanjivana 597.19
varsity 287.30
varters 011.02
varts 203.11 317.16
vary 327.28
vas 238.09 343.34
vasable 594.33
vases 598.12
vast 481.15
vaster 024.19
vat 171.25 213.08 302.01 485.10 596.18 610.16
vatswaterway 512.05
vatted 346.03
vatter 361.21
vaughan 609.02
vaughther 326.07
vaun 138.17
vaunce 256.29
vauncement 608.03
vavnr 054.15
vay 478.21
vaynience 024.02
V.C. 489.03
veal 419.04
vealive 162.18
vealled 602.23
veasmeas 607.20
veautays 435.12
vebereared 492.27
vectuals 405.36
veddahs 085.03
veegickers 046.21 046.22
veens 201.27
veenyteeny 021.01
veer 112.26
veeture 409.17
vegnue 448.17
veice 349.25
veide 340.21
veil 208.10
veilable 050.09
veiled 075.05 360.35 375.29
veiling 220.33 503.26
veiloped 244.15
veils 541.30
vein 020.02 212.16
veine 250.23
veins 571.36
vel 382.28
vel 471.34
veldts 032.27
veletta 087.23 561.11
veling 613.30
vell 626.33
velluti 251.26
velo 039.07
velsache 178.35
velsion 285.F3
veluir 458.34
velyonview 018.29
vemmarea 244.14
vena 191.10
venal 126.19
vena's 619.29
vence 268.10
vend 345.31
vendolor 408.36
vene 291.28 528.01
vened 066.31 551.12 603.35
venements 564.33
veneral 098.18
vener's 054.22
venge 178.22
venient 585.09
venirs 302.F2
venomoloped 099.19
vens 426.21
vent 425.28 527.22
vents 603.28 604.12
ventyres 051.14
venue 625.06
ver 093.20 110.10 110.23 139.28 157.16 327.32 422.02 550.18 595.24
ver 342.16
vera 255.14
verand 130.08
veras 009.36
verb 390.27
verbal 060.32
verberates 249.15
verberration 143.13
verbial 110.12
verbs 242.12
verca 230.31
verdown 559.13
vere 266.10 492.16
veres 289.27
vere's 227.16
vergined 238.23
verging 055.04
vergin's 028.27
verin 140.18

vering 478.31
veri's 172.01
verj- 257.27
verleaved 448.36
verleffy 332.28
vermer 416.31
vern 100.20
vernal 300.07
verness 035.10
vernetss 366.11
vernikan 197.29
vero 353.09
verol 619.36
veroo 416.13
verred 343.30
vers 282.26
versa 063.03
versarian 535.14
versary 493.05
verse 231.02 288.01 410.17 492.14 540.05
versé 281.11
versed 416.31
versem 384.27
verses 349.15
vershen 332.36
versified 061.31
versing 227.19 474.22
version 349.07
versiries 551.28
versounding 355.10
versus 167.34
versy 453.17
vert 604.05 605.11
vertgleam 099.16
vertones 318.33
verum 361.32 610.06
veryburies 113.34
veryone 209.27
verzing 359.07
verzone 407.18
vesant 550.31
vesdals 234.15
vesser 534.20
vested 132.09
vestment 341.14
vet 202.10
vett 377.17
vever 352.09
vewtheless 061.07 523.03
vey 313.19
viabilla 548.06
via-Brigstow 537.24
vibrational 394.03
vic 202.21
vice 085.16
vicer 322.04
vices 051.29 141.20 266.15 356.07 390.32
vicies 534.15
vicious 349.28
vick 188.05 302.18 354.01
vicking 463.28
vicks 101.33
vico 215.23
vics 610.08
vicuum's 473.06
vid 284.30
viddy 327.34
vide 043.24 212.17 247.31 320.08 568.02
vidence 366.03
vider 455.07
vidfinns 099.15
vidies 222.27
vido 409.30
vidubb 178.02
vied 197.33 541.16
vieng 595.21
vienne 348.36
view 018.29 228.27 284.F3 285.26 420.26 447.20 504.16
VIEW 272.R1
viewable 403.23
viewed 296.01 329.16
views 541.25
viewscope 449.34
vig 132.34
vigate 564.35
vigheds 547.34
vignue 226.34
vigsen 616.03
vigtoury 395.36
viikko 325.10
vik 185.34
viking 609.19
vikkeen 565.19
vikkingr 326.07
vil 535.15
vild 613.21
vile 411.03
vile 354.12
viles 353.09
viliouker 183.33
vilky 621.21
villa 223.06 388.22 609.17 609.18
villainous 077.03
ville 043.26 061.21 153.18 203.13 205.26 235.18 294.18 297.25 310.20 420.21 503.17 541.35 552.12 585.02
villed 553.26
ville-Lawry 514.24
ville'll 375.05
villes 375.12
vilous 117.19
vim 356.15
vin 021.06 264.28 299.12 316.32 538.24 622.35
vin 106.26
vinca 223.07 580.17
vinciveness 281.14
vind 250.03 608.23
vindict 370.32
vine 209.20 212.31
vines 495.36
ving 325.20
vingite 491.07
vings 235.03
vining 358.04
vinis 536.31
vinne 062.10
vinne 267.L3
vinnes 124.30
vinophobe 358.12
vinsible 367.25
vinsibles 527.12
vinxed 090.06
viny 333.36
violated 285.02
violent 518.02 590.08
viparam 185.14
viparated 004.24
viparous 242.28
vir 465.07 585.24
virdual 396.20
virens 088.02
virgin 376.35
virs 230.34
virtue 318.05
virulence 425.35
virum 166.26
viry 208.07
vis 250.01 403.14 435.18 504.16
vis 347.35
vischdischdienence 357.25
vishy 580.14
visible 081.01 158.28 265.11 284.08 546.29
visible-gnosible-edible 088.06
visibly 504.09
visien 423.05
vision 052.18 107.25 150.33 254.22 364.17 610.35 626.28
visit 078.10
visky 187.08
visors 316.02
vispa 596.29
vispacem 087.14
visper 460.07
vistown 197.09
vistura's 601.25
visual 341.18
vit 339.04
vit 496.36
vital 036.03
vitalised 448.16
vitally 354.05
vitch 049.08 159.28 207.08 278.23 341.09 368.33 498.02
vitches 348.34
vitellines 252.15
vitem 510.34
vitles 116.01
vito 513.17
vits 374.04
vitz 514.30
viva 490.26 614.11
vivla 061.36
vivorous 613.19
vivus 050.15
vixen 603.29
viz 587.22
vlies 199.36
vnr 054.15
vrention 424.20
vrerssas 173.25
vrouw 413.15
vo 317.02
voca 203.15
vocacaon 179.12
vocal 466.35
vocation 056.05 178.18 305.28
vocht 048.03
vocnas 537.06
voco 032.24
vocovisual 341.18
voeh 029.04
vogels 113.16
vogl 419.14
vogue 100.08
voh 313.31
voice 003.09 439.19
voiced 225.02 623.08
void 475.13
voila 388.22
voiled 546.06

voinabrathran 252.04
voising 186.01
voke 286.16
vol 262.F2 388.03
volations 350.31
vold 326.17
vole 275.18
volent 450.11
voles 627.32
voletta 157.08 157.17 159.05 159.06
voliance 316.02
volitionary 234.11
volk 565.06
vollovving 394.06
vollusslleepp 368.19
volment 578.34
volo 068.19
volo 466.19
voloh 466.27
volosy 200.15
volscian 151.10
volsy 378.31
volted 284.09
voluation 073.32
volucanized 545.33
voluccia 157.24
volucrum 050.13
volucrumines 613.17
voluptary 358.02
volving 080.12
volvuli 292.16
volvulis 292.19
vomony 172.11
vond 244.31
voo 561.30
voodawpeehole 120.31
voopf 177.31
voor 009.31
vor 276.14
vora 623.27
vorage 539.22
vorandbowl 351.14
vore 171.08 393.29
vorous 089.16
vorted 022.16
vortex 150.07
vos 484.32 565.05 565.05
vote 582.03
voto 413.36
votogesus 316.28
votrimaserovmerav-merouvian 113.04
vouces 243.35
voucha 466.20
voulley 346.18
voused 340.22
vovae 505.13
vow 065.23
vowals 249.13
vowal's 412.30
vowdeed 424.05
vowelled 515.12
vowels 023.36
vowtion 072.24
vowtried 534.35
vox 546.29
voxed 313.18
voyd 072.11
voyelles 116.28
voyous 116.28
voys 296.02
vu 594.23
vucant 553.15
vulent 160.05
vulle 014.03 626.11
vulnerable 404.25
vulnerably 077.02
vuloid 157.05
vulon 148.18
vuloped 378.35
vulse 255.24
vult 057.32
vulteeny 298.27
vultures 138.34
vulve 314.20
vulverblott 538.31
vulverher 060.07
vums 261.14
vunculusts 367.14
vuneer 243.25
vuns 609.24
vuole 089.06
vup 225.16
vurdy 038.15
vurdyburdy 378.05
vurite 347.36
vus 230.29
vuto 205.22
vyhum 618.14
vyingly 416.07

wa 059.34 541.29
waaber 485.24
waad 018.14
wab 203.05
wabeg 248.34
wabs 351.32
wabsister 566.10
wabspays 181.05
wache 423.17
wachsibles 483.19
wacka 079.05
wackaway 434.26
wacker 594.19
wackers 561.04
wacks 019.20
wad 071.26
wadded 516.09
waddle 369.36
waddled 444.10
waddles 471.33
waddlum 027.28
waddyng 214.09
wader 581.03
waders 089.22
wades 608.34
wadgedy 061.07
wador 189.14
wadth 340.25
wag 144.33 274.17 423.03 597.21
wage 247.05 338.20 545.34
wagering 098.33
wagers 312.26
waggelers 321.31
waggen 141.17
waggerest 626.10
waggering 543.20
waggers 028.21
waggers 262.L4
wagginline 582.32
waggle 526.16
wags 092.20 243.17 615.27
wagstruck 279.F30
wagtail 302.07
wahallya 056.07
wahrwificle 493.19
wail 021.25 022.12 081.30 344.25 345.14
wailable 228.24
wailed 590.16
wailing 194.01 474.11
waimen 279.F23
wain 276.26 287.13 289.25 452.36
waindhoo's 371.33
wainers 313.01
wain's 248.21
waist 236.36
waists 434.20
wait 007.35
waited 041.28 364.20
waiter 155.01
waites 331.20
waiting 122.25 377.20
wake 174.33 242.05 311.16 393.25 473.23 510.16
wake 349.25 350.01
waked 560.15
wakemiherculossed 492.05
waken 255.05 576.12
wakening 597.26
waker 059.27 619.12
wakers 351.25
waker's 173.09 581.06
wakes 321.17
walby 542.21
walch 338.09
wald 264.27
wale 077.09 133.33
wales 040.10 199.23 242.33
walf 248.21
walk 578.30
walker 110.36 472.21
walkering 361.32
walking 086.25 121.17 603.11
walks 455.05
wall 003.19 010.02 013.07 033.08 051.12 088.21 108.01 135.01 135.16 254.02 299.09 419.16 581.09 621.19
wall 261.L3
Wall 434.10
walla 088.23
wallahs 609.33
wallawer 151.23
walldabout 539.25
walled 262.F3 518.33
wallen 325.26
wallet 053.21
walley 105.27
wallis-West 157.34
wallon 152.06
walloner 152.06
walloped 324.29
wallow 398.17
walls 262.24 291.19 448.08 589.30
Walls 153.01
wally 061.25
wallying 406.12
walshe's 495.27
walther 519.24
walt'zaround 010.30
waltzer 443.21
wan 046.01 077.04 152.06 173.29 197.36 201.29 201.30

208.25 233.28 233.28 322.06 352.34 498.13
wand 141.30 195.05
wanda 199.12
wandcoat 391.14
wanderbaffle 610.30
wands 407.22
wandshe 556.35
wanee 581.06
wang 130.35
wangle 041.03
wanglers 371.03
wanights 015.20
wanker 520.06
wanorder 374.16
wanouet 408.04
wans 557.09
wan's 477.09
wansopper 356.17
wanst 346.33
wanstairs 556.34
wanting 112.21
wantme 070.17
wants 113.12
wantyng 499.05
wap 018.36
war 046.15 046.16 351.24 370.32 403.04 436.13 577.06
waradeed 312.02
waradid 021.24 022.11
waran 131.22
warceathay 490.28
ward 077.19 394.35 471.13
Wardborg 569.11
warden 515.35 544.08
wardens 116.27 555.07
warden's 242.33
wards 240.36 553.31 594.19
ware 066.31 182.09 420.19 548.20
wareke 602.21
wares 371.26
warfees 494.28
wark 544.21
warkers 243.22
warmed 040.02
warmer 365.14 423.15
warming 553.26
warmly 430.20
warn 397.13
warns 238.33
warp 066.29 140.02
warr 212.04
warrawurms 225.13
warrd 524.19
warred 421.05
warries 263.F2
wars 133.17
wart 291.22
wartem 263.11
warthy 199.07
warts 296.19
warwords 501.13
wary 107.26
wary 342.33
wash 133.08 192.16 211.36 233.32 319.25 381.14 529.18 550.33
washable 575.15 577.07
washed 013.06 049.22 050.29 159.27 191.11 235.08
washed 342.13
washing 520.06
washipper 408.35
washwhose 614.03
washy 191.36 199.17
wasland 479.29
waspy 548.24
wassh 282.22
wasso 517.21
waster 203.03
wastewoldwevild 613.21
wasti 056.33
wasty 080.26
wat 538.04
watashy 484.26
wataywatashy 484.26
watch 576.30
watched 435.31
watcher 026.17
watchwise 119.18
watchwomen 379.33
watchywataywatashy 484.26
water 070.26 117.04 171.13 173.30 205.26 206.31 211.10 248.23 290.17 386.19 387.17 390.21 392.16 420.07 469.14 534.04
waterbeckers 077.30
waterloover 093.07
waternions 138.02
waters 084.30
water's 187.19
waterway 512.05
waterwottle 176.36
wather 600.08
watmenotting 507.14
watschers 105.33
watter 135.06 270.07 368.07 578.19
wattering 037.17
watters 070.09
watteur 078.05
watties 315.21
watts 490.24
watty 089.12
waugh 465.08
waul- 314.08
waurs 272.10
wave 023.13
Wave 248.08
waved 204.23
waves 023.26 460.25 471.23
waving 101.17
wawd 523.04
wawsers 276.F1
wawy 061.10
wax 025.06 141.31 184.20 404.23
waxed 490.01
waxing 261.L3
way 009.35 021.08 022.28 022.33 031.06 039.08 040.18 043.26 043.27 043.28 062.19 063.19 078.14 078.14 080.02 085.21 093.14 109.19 134.14 140.36 153.30 177.22 178.10 178.31 197.06 198.32 202.12 204.16 206.26 208.22 209.21 227.05 227.11 236.23 237.15 242.24 255.11 260.13 281.22 284.F5 285.14 302.14 315.34 321.14 334.34 343.07 346.27 348.36 355.19 360.31 369.09 370.36 371.21 371.21 391.19 432.17 434.26 445.02 448.05 449.14 450.05 462.17 465.35 468.30 470.18 473.05 478.15 493.11 493.25 510.33 512.05 535.10 535.10 543.30 544.03 544.30 564.03 565.21 565.36 577.23 579.04 581.10 582.22 582.29 585.32 604.12 605.16 607.12
way 338.07
waybrain 444.03
wayed 421.07
wayedwold 612.29
wayferer 365.01
wayhoist 268.F4
wayin 395.17
wayled 331.32
waymen 546.36
wayn 326.36
wayo 509.24
wayo 353.29
wayoei 267.20
ways 005.22 005.22 012.01 028.23 059.36 087.22 113.06 114.16 114.17 117.16 140.20 153.22 153.23 219.20 244.27 288.05 289.16 310.08 318.19 410.08 435.35 442.11 458.23 484.25 496.06 548.16 553.29 576.19 576.34 595.14 602.31 620.29 620.30
waysed 298.23
wds 262.L3
wea 552.02
weainey 391.33
weak 126.07
weaker 421.12
weal 225.30
wealing 345.14
wealth 078.10 288.F1 408.01 449.18
wealthy 438.24
weam 601.17
weamy 337.16
weand 464.01
wear 115.11 448.29
weareagain 455.25
wearied 543.01
wearit 331.15
wearlds 147.28
wearmood 292.23
weary 232.29
weather 447.32 464.10
weatness 061.07
webbed 544.23
webcrusted 038.07
webs 214.16
weck 552.02
weckers 615.16
wed 137.07
wedder 283.L2
wedding 325.27
weddyng 327.32
wedge 073.01
wedge 339.01
wedhe 356.18
wednoget 243.03
wedoff 123.24
wedown 380.35
wee 011.10 017.20 094.15 094.15 246.15 337.16
wee 340.19
weeatovular 156.15
weed 013.23 207.03 512.25

weeden 211.03
weeds 141.12 469.17 527.03 557.28
weeeep 041.29
weeger's 311.09 312.02
week 144.24 488.06
week 106.31
weekend 099.17
weeker 593.03
weekly 099.34
weeks 063.08
week's 393.13 565.14
ween 587.13
weens 241.26
weeny 519.11
weep 391.06 391.06
weepers 006.05
weeps's 556.36
weept 347.30
weer 413.29
wees 154.30 617.36
wee's 457.36
weest 431.33
weestureens 170.04
weet 302.F2
weg 046.04 086.26
wegian 046.23 049.28
weh 470.13 513.07
wehls 526.32
wehr 131.07
wehrmin 343.22
wei 321.34
weigh 312.05 372.13
weighed 417.34
weight 007.25 019.24 039.13 046.30 390.08
Weiman-Eitelnaky 151.11
weir 448.31
weir- 424.20
weisioned 345.35
weissed 378.24
wel 513.33 549.34
welaugh 037.28
welf 524.30
welglass 408.24
welietry 291.12
well 022.14 036.28 038.07 039.08 040.01 040.32 060.22 080.03 085.18 093.34 130.11 150.31 172.03 212.33 225.30 246.24 376.22 458.14 468.28 469.19 472.13 492.18 500.06 503.35 512.17 521.35 529.01 533.04 571.02 607.04
well 201.13
welled 116.32
wellens 371.28
weller 594.01
wellesly 052.27
wells 053.36 236.02 351.01 544.29
well's 068.15 080.07 260.F1
wellswendows 382.11
wellth 238.32
welly 009.02 250.13 365.30
wellys 151.32
wels 313.25
wel's 366.20
welshian 618.34
welter 012.09
welton 038.09
wembling 507.10
wemmy 229.04
wemwednoget 243.03
wen 073.36 322.06 372.28 389.31 406.11 586.21
wench 029.24 334.29
wenchers 284.23
wencky 097.27
wendolenes 609.04
wendows 382.11
wenger's 445.36
wenk 105.10
wenn 433.06
wensteil 097.05
went 284.16
wept 498.33 549.21
werds 313.34
wering 557.12
werks 221.09
wero 199.23
wesigh 037.28
wesner 372.16
west 447.21
West 157.34 514.24
wester 042.29 085.34
western 203.03
westhow 254.16
wet 076.18 298.22 452.31
wetch 293.08
wetma 297.30
wetter 009.27 585.11
wevild 613.21
wewhistlem 469.25
wey 277.F4
weynhearts 254.03
weys 315.30 330.08
weyt 583.30
weywomen 542.36
whaar 613.05
whack 289.17
whack- 332.05
whackback 064.25
whackers 042.31
whair 108.23
whaling 285.F4
whalmed 356.35
wham 147.34 387.28
whangers 174.08
whank 064.07
whare's 335.29
whatis 223.27
whatly 368.18
whatmay 230.17
whave 501.21
whawre 292.32
whealian 023.11
wheedler 119.30
wheedling 415.02
wheel 040.29 058.03 059.06 093.36 286.17 319.03 410.32
wheeling 186.02 437.04 614.27
wheel's 027.36
wheezian 067.13
whelker 515.04
whelmed 381.17
whelp 441.31
whemoe 007.15
whencewithersoever 613.20
wheres 056.33 084.07 283.25 477.33
wheres 349.29
where's 012.15
whergs 533.22
wherise 602.07
whetswut 272.05
whey 558.02
whiches 353.25
whick 346.22
whig 021.01 301.08
whigg 360.32
whiggern 511.02
whiggs 175.25
whilome 345.16
whingingly 171.15
whins 419.01
whipper 496.12
whippit 077.27
whipt 303.06
whir 346.26
whirling 192.34
whis 121.12
whishts 345.11
whisk 050.12
whiskered 558.15
whisking 427.19
whisks 436.22
whisperably 182.28
whistle 556.15
whistle 342.20
whistlem 469.25
whistling 506.22
whit 448.34
whitchoverswetch 293.08
white 007.14 008.03 064.27 086.11 121.22 136.05 137.21 187.02 214.15 235.06 241.14 374.06 380.03 433.03 451.20 510.30 563.16 569.19 596.32 621.31
white 350.10
whitened 394.35
whitepaddynger 612.18
white's 078.32
whits 088.28
whiz 180.06
whole 247.07
wholyover 597.03
whom 369.12
whome 138.30
whomight 230.17
whomust 223.27
whoom 613.04
whooping 128.10
whora- 090.31
whore 154.21 229.12
whores 418.22
whorld 100.29
whorse 137.28
whorsed 137.17
whose 276.F4 439.21 614.03
whot 345.30
whou 202.12
whoyle 323.02
whtphwht 141.34
whu 076.32
whuck 353.17
whugger 360.32
whura- 090.31
whure 186.28 457.15
whys 445.32
whyse 369.34
wibe 547.28
wich 352.12
wichleagues 347.09
wick 006.33 031.27 126.04 134.16 243.19 261.F2 460.28 460.28 481.21
wicked 539.04

Wicked 434.10
wicker 517.25
wickerkishabrack 495.23
wickers 030.07
wicking 086.17
wicklow 277.16
wickly 467.27
wicks 135.14
wickweck 552.02
wid 367.29
wide 013.34 098.02 152.18 171.24 228.08 584.15
wide 419.07
wides 360.05
widey 625.25
widge 538.03
widgeon 329.11
widges 142.01
widow 545.04
width 340.25
widths 394.16
wielder 056.11
wife 011.29 020.29 066.16 101.18 242.36 451.29 532.15 532.18 533.04 627.02
wife's 117.06
wificle 493.19
wig 017.34 023.25 164.29 240.23 246.07 248.29 467.10 578.04 621.30 625.02
wigamore 241.21
wigged 209.06 424.27
wigger 031.28 491.30
wigger's 070.21 579.25
wiggly 438.07
wight 077.36 262.11 310.26
wigs 047.16 047.17 079.16 083.05 221.28 235.32 243.17 361.02 552.21
wigst 252.19
wigswag 597.21
wijk 361.21
wike 596.06
wikey 187.02
wik's 550.18
wild 319.04
wildebeestsch 571.28
wilderblissed 107.16
wiley 355.30
wiliam 347.32
wille 609.18
willed 155.32 232.14 246.30 297.07 314.32
williams 575.15
willing 029.08 187.33 191.17
willingly 488.08
willingsons 583.11
wills 202.01
willth 593.12
willworth 357.03
willy 056.22 232.24
wilshsuni 338.14
wilsothoutoosezit 154.33
wiltersland 488.30
wim 436.11
wimbs 354.24
wiminds 188.14
wimjim 211.06
wimminpull 377.35
wimp 230.09
win 029.22 063.02 116.24 177.21 184.35 188.30 238.28 360.02 397.06 398.06 404.19 408.20 539.27 546.16 597.13
win 171.35
wince 624.26
wind 133.12 281.F2 360.36 428.13 448.30 534.04 558.18
windaws 141.18
windburster 359.13
winded 292.13 450.07
windel 426.27
windibus 270.L3
window 118.18 448.01
window'd 291.09
winds 095.03
winds' 006.36
windup 090.08
windy 549.15
wine 232.14 257.17 428.01 468.12 510.19
wined 426.10 450.16 563.01
winedlights 015.02
winestraines 528.17
wineties 436.01
winfreer 162.09
wing 121.21 252.28 397.01 505.17
winga 499.10
winger's 028.15
winging 367.33
winglyswanglers 371.03
wings 460.29 576.14
wingty 364.04
wink 023.34 198.15 426.32
winker 174.19 320.27
winking 333.29 361.33
winkle 078.22 393.19
winks 341.15
winktosser 359.12
winminsters 552.03
winn 469.01
winned 491.31
winngling 620.15
winning 055.07 562.19
winns 330.30
winnt 292.30
wins 215.28 286.F4
wins 418.25
winsbed 555.07
winsome 161.30
winsomer 234.07
winst 518.21
winstreams 528.17
wint 607.24
wint 201.20
winter 110.22 502.02
winters 580.06
winter's 209.05
wintomine 223.09
wintriodic 310.04
winx 524.24
wipe 281.F2
wiped 120.10
wiping 058.14 250.06 347.29
wipps 146.12
wire 169.04
wirth 340.34
wis 552.02 612.18
wisdom 439.13
wise 013.32 019.20 056.20 078.30 084.24 113.06 118.27 119.18 146.28 235.02 253.05 263.19 278.07 279.F21 281.22 286.29 314.25 405.19 411.04 413.30 437.25 439.01 480.28 483.03 483.18 519.34 525.11 546.07 547.03 558.06 563.30 596.25
wise 352.20
WISE 293.R1
wised 225.05 298.23 378.30
wiseopen 474.09
wiser 253.09
wish 364.13 501.12
wish 106.07
wishawish 012.22
wishbarque 620.35
wished 049.22 319.32 553.20
wishegoths 148.20
wisher 489.21
wishers 099.31 172.33
wishers' 414.02
wishes 585.06
wishful 035.24
wishing 070.03
wishingsight 345.35
Wisp 211.02
wistel 406.11
wit 065.10 108.06
witch 027.28 437.29 463.16 587.27
witchbells 222.34
witchbratschballs 072.02
witcheries 554.08
witches 301.22
witching 220.07
witdnessed 413.23
wite 066.17
withal 564.25
withcherous 088.18
withcy 175.14
withdownmind- 113.09
withem 282.17
withersoever 613.20
withhers 143.16
with-her-Soles-Up 531.22
within 238.28 433.35 551.26
within's 034.28
without 238.27 244.01
without-his-Walls 153.01
withouts 541.05
without-word 468.06
withstandable 253.30
withstanding 061.11 100.09 171.21 240.31 347.30 429.15
withstempting 356.20
withstumbling 560.10
with-Sweat 102.30
withun's 178.08
witing 054.35
witless 515.30
witness 005.14
witnessed 254.10
wits 273.25 462.30
witswhy 272.06
witt 135.29
witthered 134.22
wittingly 124.15
witts 015.24
witt's 279.F27
wittvitles 116.01
wittwin 360.02
wittynice 450.18
witz 093.06
witzer 011.24
witzer's 176.35
wiveall 145.27

wives 128.27 128.32 281.01 588.36
wivvel 157.12
wixed 333.22
wo 483.15 483.15 601.08 611.24
woah 474.15
wobble 319.13 510.28
wobblers 604.17
woce 594.31 594.32
woch 318.22
wocky 612.12
woddle 006.28
wodedook 340.20
woe 470.13
wog 430.23
wogen's 241.18
woh 115.17
woking 310.17 368.13
wold 073.28 110.16 588.34 612.29
woldwevild 613.21
wolf 026.12 199.03
Wolf 444.32
wolff 225.08
wolf's 244.10
wolldy 019.11
wolle 070.07
wollenzee 321.12
wollies 508.19
wolve 076.02
wolves 479.14
wolving 049.28
wom 346.26 475.21
woman 012.11 054.04 055.19 101.32 151.06 327.03 396.05 572.27 575.05
woman 165.16 176.08
womanly 067.24
wombanborn 055.10
wome 298.19
women 054.08 087.27 180.01 379.33 395.31 436.13 542.36 581.18
womens 287.L1
women's 183.25
won 008.15 601.03 612.11
wonder 388.02
wonderful 295.16
wondering 336.16
wonderment 300.19
wonders 564.16
wone 003.12 213.15
wong 361.14
wonton 349.31
woo 094.15 442.03
wood 035.07 080.08 135.13 136.33 169.05 211.05 239.01 246.04 257.12 265.17 293.13 332.12 360.15 372.15 526.23 542.05 611.34
wood 277.L2
woods 244.01 248.28 337.19 374.28
wood's 157.16 450.33 556.17 578.30
woods' 282.F1
woodsmenufactors 027.17
woodstool 040.23
woodtree 030.14
wooed 579.33
wooerds 237.01
woohoo 449.25
woolfe 467.15
woolow 360.03
woolth 034.19
wooned 396.24
wooren 348.14
woorledes 054.11
woors 163.25
woos 420.31
wooth 340.18
woothead 474.12
wopwo 523.05
wor 611.19 611.22
worc 086.13
word 051.05 056.11 072.18 129.08 152.31 211.30 227.23 236.05 262.07 306.19 390.20 441.36 442.16 468.06 487.12 498.26 561.27
word 349.30
worded 021.20 077.25 376.20
wording 022.06
wordings 280.04
wordmeat 490.20
words 073.19 100.28 116.15 169.22 178.04 266.F2 279.F21 288.03 369.01 369.28 436.12 478.09 487.32 501.13 569.28 624.18
wordsed 142.27
wordswallower 150.04
wordy 408.10
wore 234.09
worefore 326.22
worewolf's 244.10
work 012.01 189.22 191.11 206.36 224.26 358.04 397.10 502.17 546.15 550.12 613.10
work 104.20
worked 553.09
worker 008.35 080.08 559.06
workers 495.11 585.16
working 441.24 603.10
works 041.09 067.09 113.22 288.28 614.31 618.02
world 102.08 117.27 147.27 189.24 367.26 385.04 431.31 463.16 593.23
worlder 077.36
worlders 251.09
worlds 017.29
world's 318.14 571.35
worm 099.01 437.14 492.25 509.29
wormarose 302.27
worming 019.13
worms 059.12 078.08 121.19 282.13
worn 013.10 110.17 183.18 596.36 597.18 614.14
worp 302.17
worse 416.10
worship 433.11
worsoever 364.23
worst 077.32
worsteds 611.35
wort 490.18
worth 004.35 019.11 057.35 137.34 137.35 288.F1 357.03 398.23 458.23 541.06
worthies 127.18
worthily 057.18 547.15
worths 363.06 548.23 548.25
worth's 539.05
worth's 072.14
worthseeing 127.35
worthy 244.18 347.18 599.21
worthy 071.21
worts 265.27 564.20
wose 337.16
wot 362.15
woter 247.23
wottle 176.36
woulds 339.16
wound 214.10 226.05
wounder 075.19
wouyou 252.03
wows 011.10
wowsers 276.F1
wracked 275.18
wray 068.31
wreak 545.23
wreathed 234.14
wreck 416.36
wrench 070.24
wright 014.19 269.08 560.09
wrine 173.19
wring 470.14
wristed 532.27
writemen 059.27
writer 063.10 439.10
writes 113.12 113.14 113.15 113.15 113.16
writhy 231.13
writing 135.15 464.22
written 280.02 438.18
wrmans 323.19
wrng 349.27
wrong 190.12 606.31
wrote 419.18
wrowdy 266.21
wrucked 155.09
wuards' 026.31
wubbles 079.31
wuck 230.09 434.26
wug 349.11
wuggers 031.11
wuggly 027.32
wugs 485.21
wuith 240.17
Wukru 024.07
wulf 088.22
wum 348.22 412.06
wumped 328.20 451.29
wumpty 374.34
wunga 499.10
wurly 257.18
wurms 225.13
wurst 494.17
wut 272.05
wwwkkkrrr 378.07
wy 601.08
wyd 091.19
wyfyn 418.27
wyggla 048.16
wyll 464.06
wyly 610.14
wylyd 331.28
wympty 314.16 314.16
wyne 078.20 088.21
wys 202.15 374.34

xamplus 099.33
xebec 323.04
xenetic 175.31
xerxes 337.36
ximious 505.14

yaard 201.31
yagok- 023.05
yahzade 032.08
yall 227.29 325.25
yam 055.03 178.16 455.23 601.03
yama's 253.28
yamnyam 306.F5
yam's 455.23
yan 077.14 288.F6
yana 055.05
yand 601.14
yangs 276.F2
yank 191.04
yant 215.01 308.19 327.21 455.20
yaplaina 158.19
yar 215.02
yard 064.01 068.08 191.06 221.15 413.04 455.01 467.24 553.18 589.29 621.35
yard 213.01
yards 462.03
yark 624.15
yas 593.01 593.01 593.01
yashmakt 547.14
yass 231.18
yat 322.22 365.35
yatants 598.25
yates 303.07
yattes 359.07
yavitches 348.34
yawnd 511.17
yazzard 016.09
y-Benn 375.32
y-Bree 375.32
year 113.35 346.26
yearcases 416.22
yeare 414.12
yearn 364.10 379.23
yearold 060.23
years 040.10 122.02
year's 212.31 327.07 569.13
yearspray 561.20
yeborn 585.18
yechosies 007.24
yeck 139.36
yedimseldamsels 432.21
yedo 527.17
yegut 455.10
yeh 085.31 085.31 553.35
yeind 160.28
ye-landsmen 311.01
yellas 327.32
yellers 416.34
yellgreenlindigan 611.06
yelp 141.13 141.13
yemn 330.07
yenesmeal 301.28
yer 066.19 122.14 132.36 173.29 211.28 299.28 372.06 525.27 549.25
yer 104.10
yerdfuul 088.19
yerear 182.20
yers 371.01
yer's 003.07
yery 580.04
yesed 323.29
yeses 604.22
yesesyeses 604.22
yesmellygut 455.10
yesmellyspatterygut 455.11
yessed 061.34 365.11
yessha 105.20
yessik 346.23
yessoyess 488.19
yest 331.23 608.21
yets 365.16 608.21
yet-sun 090.01
yeux 102.12
yin 305.33 419.14
yina 561.19
yind 007.33
yir 553.04 553.04 553.04
yirragun 352.14
yis 199.16
yiss 453.26
ylium 152.36
yo 197.18 256.19 326.13
yoe 073.22
yoei 267.20
yogh 037.22
yoh 339.02
yoking 343.27
yolk 404.29
yon 079.20 136.27 291.22 313.24 313.29 625.21
yone's 176.09
yor 312.03
yore 292.17
york 569.18
yorn 392.12
youblong 013.04
youcallem 094.34
youcallme 479.13
yougono 085.05
youlikethems 535.12
youlloups 526.18
youm 295.12
youmacormack 450.25
youmaycallher 396.07
youmaycodding 346.24
youmaycuddler 608.25
youmaycull 223.14
youmaywantme 070.17
youmeant 318.31
youmightcallimbs 238.30
younger 548.20
youngs 595.11
yourselftoastrool 622.13
yourselves 465.10
yous 068.20 091.27 120.28 156.12 271.03 334.17 350.16 412.13 430.34 472.06 485.11
youst 414.01
youth 194.04
yow 534.02
ysied 607.14
ysle 517.22
ysled 605.20
yu 499.19 519.18 521.01 527.27 565.15
yue 549.20
yum 055.03 153.26 186.14 208.27 414.26 581.21 613.12
yumba 198.11
yume 231.10
yumnietcies 348.22
yums 089.03 590.11
yums 345.18
yung 267.08
Yung-Thing 231.09
yuns 597.25
yuoll 456.25
yup 498.06
yures 295.03

zabad 054.18
zabar 182.09
zaccio 435.09
zade 032.08
zag 111.08
zag 105.07
zago 052.15
zaks 077.31
zalles 075.03
zalond 261.F2
zame 333.01
zang 020.22
zanies 236.29
zannes 552.20
zanzangan 389.01
zanzarity 415.26
zaozaozing 407.18
zarity 415.26
zaround 010.30
zasas 172.23
zava 073.36
zay 337.07
zed 322.35 325.17
zee 321.12
zekiel 027.23
zekiel 307.L1
zelf 170.17
zelles 470.32
zemdown 542.08
zemlianess 352.18
zend 521.17
zend- 219.17
zeone 241.19
zerain 313.14
zerday's 088.14
zerszonese 347.09
zerum 344.31
zeszame 333.01
zette 578.36
zeus 504.19
zewched 265.F5
ziehowffse 538.16
ziel 335.13
zienius 483.32
zievalsshie 578.16
zigues 350.20
zild 410.09
zillahs 102.03
zinahurries 214.03
zinascu 064.32
Zindeh-Munaday 205.16
zinging 415.14
zinned 374.14
zion 064.31
zit 154.33
zite 086.02
zither 360.01
zitr 171.11
zitround 171.08
zlanthas 351.14
zoepy 075.08
zoic 101.15
zolites 549.17
zom 162.19
zomatis 185.16
zond 165.22
zone 407.18
zones 246.33
zonese 347.09
Zoom 073.26
zoor 244.19

zooys- 257.27
zoppy 560.27
zor 343.19
zosius 483.32
zoug 438.08
zounded 552.28
zoupgan 199.18
zour 199.14
zourikawitch 437.29
zouts 301.28
zouzalem 258.08
Zoyd 370.29
zozlers 415.14
zpaszpas 101.27
zpissmas 101.28
zucker 071.20
zuland 156.30
zulblu 180.12
zumbath 129.28
zumpher 278.F1
zum's 494.35
zurnying 362.33
zussch 488.07
zuszchee 333.05

NUMBERS

5.6. 495.31

OVERTONES

aback 037.06 315.19
abandon 198.26
abate 364.20
abbey 167.18
abdicate 379.19
abdominal 451.01
abecedarian 494.19
abed 095.22
abeyance 073.15
abjure 585.27
ablative 268.22
ablebodied 416.03
ablution 424.19 606.24
aboard 267.F6
abominable 181.11
abomination 026.19 561.28
aboriginal 314.16
aboulia 255.28
abound 577.15
abrasive 362.17
abroad 129.10
abscess 525.08
absence 432.25 552.07
absent 005.22
absentee 198.16 228.22
absentminded 018.17 252.16 272.13 464.17
absit 318.06
absolute 325.08 325.08 325.08 325.09 527.13 575.05 595.19 595.21 609.02
absolutely 090.20 161.17 341.31 372.34 404.32 413.27 502.24 595.19
absolution 147.17 228.07 322.32
abstain 141.24 546.01
abstract 378.32
absurdity 538.18
absurdly 430.14
abuse 034.33 040.23 070.12 345.34
academy 425.24
accent 144.10 527.29
accessible 285.28
accidence 269.14
accidentally 589.22
acclamation 153.25
accommodation 382.19
accompany 356.31 607.32
accomplish 587.32
accomplishment 349.34
according 061.07 094.28 180.05 184.23 236.36
account 178.32 180.05 414.22
accoutrement 113.01 507.11
accumulate 198.34 590.16
accurate 056.19 242.03 601.33
accurately 189.31
accursed 600.11
ache 184.13 233.01 296.12
achieve 466.30
acid 167.21 450.20
acknowledge 303.F3
acknowledgment 344.08
acolyte 158.03 490.04
aconite 158.03
acorn 151.19
acoustic 180.05
acquaintance 145.10 296.20 417.08 514.17
acquiesce 037.22 365.11
acre 579.33 625.20
Acropolis 167.13 541.25
across 056.03 173.02
acrostic 206.04
action 272.11 344.22 362.10 365.10 603.29
actionable 042.15 419.33
actor 241.01
actress 363.28 526.33
actual 143.07
acutely 189.31
adamite 072.11
adapt 320.04
add 334.15
addition 063.01
address 420.23 568.31
adieu 073.22 158.20 158.20 244.29 250.07 250.07 409.30 570.04 598.14 613.03
adjacent 036.15
adjourn 585.27
adjust 180.03 460.10
adjutant 598.25
admiral 105.17 326.26 553.13
admire 539.07
admission 545.12
admit 222.15 545.08
admonish 080.24
adolescent 054.35
adopt 234.35 284.F4
adorable 562.33
adore 249.01 368.34
advance 225.02 539.19
advancement 608.03
adventure 051.14 100.06
advertisement 181.33 434.29
advice 390.32 506.33
advocate 256.08
aerate 061.15
aerial 407.01 613.36
aeronautic 530.18
aesthete 343.17
aether 053.04 098.03 349.05 452.13
afar 003.09 294.23
affect 248.26
affidavit 451.19
affix 235.22
affliction 297.29
afford 512.31
affray 090.07
afield 602.15
afraid 011.06 172.21 279.F30 497.17
African 191.04 350.21 387.02 489.27
aftereffect 483.01
afternoon 017.16 079.20 099.34 127.31 183.07 232.18 280.07 346.12 461.13 568.30
afterwards 416.10
agape 190.18 317.36 417.22
Agapemonite 007.16 407.17 481.36 498.10
age 344.34 505.17 617.17
aggregate 343.15
aghast 343.34
aglow 528.23
agnomen 206.03 241.21
agnostic 170.11
agony 353.01
agreeable 609.01
agreement 084.16 348.13
agricultural 086.20 173.16
ahead 538.29
ahem 359.22 359.22 458.10
aide-de-camp 348.02
ail 179.31 381.28
aim 329.05
aimlessly 562.16
air 053.04 231.30 238.05 256.13 256.23 280.19 358.21 360.28 425.16 483.29 556.35 565.17
airiest 269.05
airily 057.22
airship 625.04
airy 052.20 521.03
aisle 179.31
aitch 005.09 337.07 376.19 537.34 581.19
alarm 426.14 566.13

alas 159.05 166.30 203.08 226.06 359.32 359.33 548.35 626.34 628.15
albatross 137.23
albeit 054.01 305.11 356.23
Albigensian 240.13 350.31
album 535.10
alchemist 185.35
alcoholic 393.02
alderman 197.24 325.13 358.26 365.30 593.07 593.07
ale 007.12 423.12
Alexandrian 318.11 439.34
algebraical 293.16
alias 086.07 240.33 434.36 575.24
alibi 225.34
alight 583.14
aliquant 283.08
alkaline 167.19 393.02
allege 617.31
allegedly 086.14
allegory 336.36
alleluia 083.34 083.34 236.17 304.31 456.03 456.04
Allhallows 019.25 304.F5
alliance 242.34
alliterative 023.09
allotheism 309.08
allow 251.27 305.26 333.14
Allsouls 304.F5 329.31 359.26 368.14 488.24
allspice 455.29
allude 108.27 234.21 507.28 507.28
alluvial 080.25
almanack 334.25 512.04
almighty 009.26 011.23 017.08 104.01 155.24 279.F34 331.09 365.01 469.02 562.33
almond 118.05
almondtree 600.20
almoner 497.31
aloft 243.28 476.07
alone 049.06 224.16 311.17 324.16 325.14 327.33 333.14 413.28 450.28 520.18 531.13 601.15 628.15
along 191.22 399.31 407.04 414.22 628.15
aloof 628.15
aloud 341.30 448.27 490.04 601.28
alphabet 018.18 019.02 183.13 208.20 483.19 553.02 568.32 619.07
alpine 017.34
altar 434.17 452.03 596.34 603.14
alter 331.03 336.33 350.15 359.23 483.30
altitude 004.33 325.35
altogether 155.36 232.04 349.32 358.16 523.13
aluminium 113.03 309.23
amalgamate 285.21
amanuensis 425.18
amateur 239.11
amaze 364.13 552.17
ambassador 472.10
amber 527.29 588.20
ambidextrous 423.06
ambition 366.29
ambivalent 518.02
ambush 007.35 156.35 230.02 356.30 357.32 470.04 542.35 546.10
amen 007.08 015.29 024.06 069.11 080.19 081.08 092.22 110.21 139.28 147.11 193.30 213.21 222.24 224.07 226.35 235.05 237.26 239.21 243.02 244.26 279.F26 279.F34 279.F34 279.F34 311.02 317.09 333.31 353.04 360.07 365.26 374.04 377.31 389.28 397.23 406.22 416.02 419.10 422.18 427.08 439.14 444.05 448.33 457.04 458.10 461.32 473.25 484.36 495.33 495.33 495.33 495.33 518.33 528.10 538.17 538.18 612.30 620.09
amenity 513.31 530.36
American 132.02 318.15 355.22 362.31 387.02 447.06 489.20
amethyst 153.27
amid 014.33 044.01 085.30 086.18 096.32 222.32 231.07 332.26 339.24 449.35 462.04
amnesty 513.31
amorous 112.29 269.L1
amount 505.31
ampere 551.02
ampersand 241.15
amulet 230.07
amuse 107.23 158.03 417.28
amusement 125.13 341.26
anachronistic 202.35
anaesthetic 435.06
anagram 093.29
analyse 522.32
analysis 115.22 280.03
analyst 095.27 395.04
anastomosis 585.22
anathema 588.16
anatomy 154.11 241.16 356.12 504.30
ancestor 096.34 600.24
ancestral 109.19
anchor 030.07 098.06 225.10 312.05 321.11 329.09 375.03 457.07 457.07 467.33 599.20 599.20
anchorite 548.12
ancient 243.11 324.08 355.23 419.24 536.32 538.12
anciently 005.13
anemone 274.25
anent 123.21
anew 614.09 620.16 627.27
anfractuosity 348.33
angel 063.26 075.19 143.33 158.35 183.07 223.03 226.22 227.18 230.25 416.32 457.32 470.30 498.34 512.23 519.01 534.18 552.25 596.14 601.10 604.10 607.22
angel-in-chief 239.29
angelus 068.18
anger 158.35 318.35 351.30 538.05
angle 346.18
Anglo-Indian 106.08
Anglo-Norman 386.28
Anglo-Saxon 363.35 532.11
angrily 120.22
angry 101.36 317.16 343.15 411.11 520.22
anguish 265.20 288.17 346.34 490.01
animal 244.13 294.F5
animation 568.04
aniseed 222.26 271.13
ankle 051.15 207.01 480.17 495.09 521.26
anklet 224.12
annalist 395.04
annihilate 597.24
annihilation 058.08 353.22
anniversary 389.11 493.05 551.28
announce 409.27 445.26
annoy 148.05 339.03 342.28 349.26 460.36 533.36
annoyance 233.29
annual 127.14
annunciation 528.19
anoint 492.34 548.03
anon 143.15 431.30 569.07
anonymous 112.29 423.02 435.31 495.02 543.06 563.17
anonymously 367.35 617.30
another 077.01 101.06 125.12 165.10 209.07 280.09 375.08 581.33
answer 005.25 019.30 023.20 023.21 037.21 089.27 105.14 105.14 105.15 152.01 156.21 173.05 181.34 199.01 202.20 202.21 224.04 257.35 286.20 340.33 446.09 458.29 470.14 521.17 528.36 534.09 558.27 558.28 596.01 598.06 598.06 600.12 600.13
ant 087.23 158.16 268.11 331.15 338.17 339.36 418.09 418.09 418.09 515.36 579.12
antagonist 174.17
antecedent 284.22
antediluvian 310.07 585.32
antenna 414.26 537.08
anthem 153.27 326.16 588.16
anthropoid 318.05
anthropomorphic 031.35
Antichrist 308.F1 346.04
antichristian 114.11
antinomian 167.03 184.36
anti-Parnellite 498.10 542.21
antipodes 422.02 489.10
antithesis 177.33 266.L1 305.21
antler 263.F1
anus 457.12 463.03
anvil 310.20 420.21
anxious 113.36 565.03
anybody 070.25 234.06 444.31
anyone 046.01 176.09 213.15 464.01 475.21 596.36
anything 207.22 222.26 251.10 271.13 368.21 426.19 505.17
anywhere 448.31 602.20
aorist 514.36
apart 328.08 487.11
aperitif 493.03
apex 353.06
aphrodisiac 203.27
apocalypse 006.26 364.18 455.01 526.18 557.02 626.05
apologise 317.30
apology 607.21

apostle 126.06 326.11 411.16 446.36
apostrophe 612.19
apothecary 492.19
appall 527.26
appalling 131.12
apparel 351.03
apparent 336.31 490.07
apparently 014.16 081.22 081.36 085.32
apparition 600.09
appartment 451.32
appeal 004.07 167.35 335.11 339.22 441.33 508.29 528.21 606.32
appear 023.26 026.25 222.31 292.08 337.36 448.17 512.24 570.22
appearance 162.10 315.18 338.11
appendage 271.02
appetitic 524.33
applaud 136.03 257.30 257.33 258.19 347.27
applause 093.24 132.15
apple 005.30 028.19 078.20 106.24 170.16 184.14 186.10 201.33 254.23 314.33 338.14 406.09 483.15 504.24 505.29 584.02
applepie 287.16 298.01
appletree 088.02 184.14
applicable 004.32
apply 008.08
appointment 536.03
appraise 547.22
appreciate 227.26 271.F5 337.23 534.02
appreciation 041.28
apprehend 223.25
apprentice 270.06 365.28 422.20 533.07
approach 297.14 324.36
approximate 132.03
approximately 295.31 353.06
apricot 350.21 489.27 556.14
April 015.36 110.23
apron 011.34 570.19 600.29
apropos 188.27 523.05
apse 552.07 571.29
apt 208.04
aquatint 599.20
aqueduct 128.09 243.33 471.18 553.22
aquiline 088.17
Arab 491.14
Arabian 346.06 433.18
Araby 187.11 190.30 234.31
arc 230.07 244.26 281.F1
arch 547.29
archangel 498.34
archbishop 491.19
archdeacon 369.11 440.01
archduchess 171.25 171.27 209.06
archipelago 601.34
architectural 165.09
ardour 360.30
area 164.34 513.22
arena 394.34
areopagus 005.33
argument 008.25 305.13
aright 090.33
arise 053.13 104.09 210.28 237.19 493.28 496.23 610.04 619.29 626.06
aristocrat 199.34 367.25 424.10 534.34
arithmetic 147.08 268.08 293.18 431.34 537.36
ark 223.02 321.27 335.29 347.02 490.23 527.22
arm 345.16 445.24 454.03 511.18 566.13 612.33
Armenian 038.11 069.11 113.03 181.23 190.25 296.08 321.23 345.01 352.11 530.36
armistice 011.13 351.16
armour 335.07 353.20 361.14 595.16 623.15
army 279.F11
aroint 406.13
aroma 209.18
around 012.22 015.04 055.27 107.36 209.18 226.05 355.19 386.35 439.15 521.35
arouse 055.11
arrah 204.31 428.15
arraign 203.27
arrange 203.27 246.25 528.05 596.08
arrangement 219.05
arrear 107.21 140.32
arrest 420.31 532.27
arrival 348.30
arrogant 395.36
arrow 138.14 434.04 626.06
arrowroot 130.13 231.11 285.12
arse 020.26 088.17 088.19 098.07 110.18 116.02 122.06 122.07 127.18 127.19 154.18 164.13 175.11 184.01 214.09 221.15 231.30 241.15 241.32 241.33 251.11 268.L4 275.F5 281.F1 299.24 301.02 315.01 317.34 326.10 328.10 330.14 344.34 352.12 352.29 357.15 364.29 371.25 375.19 421.23 453.09 457.02 487.33 489.09 490.05 514.34 534.18 547.29 583.02 602.23 612.35 617.03 618.23
arsehole 561.06
art 531.01 599.05
arteriosclerosis 498.23
Arthurian 387.32
artichoke 390.09
artillery 070.31 378.09 530.18
Aryan 215.27 316.04 508.02 525.06
ascension 410.36 600.22
ascent 252.29
ascertain 444.17 609.35
ash 004.15 055.30 141.32 244.25 320.08 460.24 542.34 588.28 588.28
ashamed 143.34 373.13 489.18 489.18 502.28 506.07
ashore 197.21 527.08
ashtree 503.30
Asian 191.04
Asiatic 072.14 242.11
ask 064.32 083.29 113.08 197.17 198.35 199.27 202.15 224.31 240.34 256.25 270.14 326.16 356.25 417.04 436.11 451.14 518.23 561.01 572.17
asleep 041.29 139.18 192.20 345.11 368.20 377.26 383.20 394.15 398.14 423.06 435.26 473.08 473.24 597.12
aslumber 570.07
aspect 415.28
aspen 417.24
asphalt 032.27 285.F5 520.05 581.30
aspic 084.03
aspiration 105.30 157.29
aspirin 257.02
ass 088.19
assail 146.08 486.20
assassinate 241.02 357.31 488.26
assault 331.30
asscart 377.33
assegai 004.06
assemble 514.06 563.36
assiduous 220.04
assignation 241.21
assistance 469.31
assistant 608.06 608.06
assize 162.01
associate 151.29 314.33
association 146.14 384.04 384.27 413.18 608.02
assuage 457.07
assume 234.28
assumption 295.24
assure 162.14 442.16
Assyrian 350.25
astern 450.07
asthma 130.05
astonish 018.15 187.03 448.06
astound 624.27
astral 050.10
astride 279.F27
astrolabe 551.25
astrologer 064.23 601.34
astrology 008.32
astronomical 494.01
astrosphere 222.12
astute 236.28
asylum 152.36
ataxia 304.17
atheist 167.10
athlete 279.07 462.28
athwart 139.07 291.22
atlas 531.31
atman 481.23
atmosphere 067.10 452.01 505.06
atoll 004.08 004.08
atom 284.15 313.12 333.25 353.22 353.29 367.30 598.21
atomic 615.06
atone 603.30
atonement 568.09
atrocity 391.07
attack 097.22 270.14 348.31 450.11
attain 367.30
attainder 188.07
attend 297.06 491.02 542.12
attendance 358.35
attention 100.05 166.29 241.05 364.12 364.14
attic 353.13
attire 319.27 359.03

attraction 391.07
auburn 174.31 174.31 244.33 280.31 336.15 499.31 617.36
auctioneer 028.32
audible 053.04
auditor 444.26
aught 004.14
August 353.03
auld 484.21
aunt 071.35 340.33 395.05 508.27
aunt-sally 346.09 346.10 346.10 346.10
aunty 147.17 293.19
aura 032.04
aurora 327.32 416.34
auspice 071.13 094.26 477.16
Australian 060.27 321.09 488.20 601.34
author 052.17 071.23 148.17 229.07 397.34 510.30
authority 358.28 516.19
autocrat 434.31
automatic 303.19
autosuggestion 369.27
autumn 065.02 178.30 251.04 271.10 271.12 617.36
available 050.09 228.24
avalanche 028.09 162.31 240.32 406.09
avarice 143.07 189.15
avenge 055.04
avenue 226.34 448.17 549.20 582.05
average 524.32 539.22
avert 213.20
avesta 012.09
avoirdupois 206.24 277.L6 407.06
avowtrie 412.30 424.05 534.35
avuncular 230.30
awake 024.14 055.07 192.20 320.22 325.36 357.35 469.04 510.16 560.15 596.06 608.34
awaken 170.18 255.05
awakener 537.06
aware 281.16
away 093.15 115.17 247.05 330.29 460.35 506.21 536.08 628.15
awful 004.36 281.21 304.28 322.08 340.09 348.05 361.13 369.12 419.32 594.12
awfully 329.28 458.17 619.32
awkward 233.32
awl 403.16
awry 137.31 266.04
axe 486.28 486.32 486.32 583.02
axiom 285.29 296.02
aye 280.04 532.14 532.14
azure 180.12 387.32 515.30

babe 023.30 551.09
babel 015.12 064.11 118.18 199.31 254.17 258.12 344.28 354.27 384.29 467.16 523.32 532.25 536.08 624.09
baboon 029.02
baby 104.07 278.L4 284.L3 300.17 423.05 472.02 565.21
Babylonian 417.12
bachelor 010.03 064.32 221.12 315.01 356.09 516.04 543.02 548.11
back 073.21 143.03 232.16 320.08 320.22 323.23 323.28 338.36 350.01 350.12 365.13 415.10 415.11 421.14 422.07 433.21 446.33 446.33 490.04 507.15 526.30 535.08 540.21 549.16 549.16 620.35
backbone 085.08
backlooking 128.06
backnumber 286.17
backroom 059.20
backseat 356.35 590.13
backside 007.34 010.11 071.11 090.07 106.03 153.16 201.05 249.02 352.32 370.26
backslide 405.10
backstump 070.17
backwards 018.32 202.22 230.22 244.01 339.16 374.28 487.32 624.18
bacon 007.10 041.13 059.20 161.31 199.17 205.19 257.15 257.19 257.22 318.21 320.29 339.04 363.17 382.11 405.33 406.15 456.22 603.01
bad 054.22 304.17 379.17 444.26 532.24
badly 337.32 337.32 361.25 444.18
badman 337.03
badtempered 167.27 360.09
bag 012.35 035.10 099.11 118.35 173.26 221.35 227.30 237.16 344.11
baggage 539.21
bagpipes 007.34 286.15
bailey 295.F1 540.20
bailiff 421.12
bairn 363.12
bake 603.06
baker 335.06 435.09
balance 313.21 338.17 506.08
balcony 240.18
bald 250.36 273.22
baldaquin 154.12
balderdash 233.17
baldric 390.08
balk 215.32 215.33
ball 056.01 058.12 073.08 082.29 091.14 101.17 125.13 273.02 309.22 317.19 337.35 389.28 445.24 512.09 557.12 616.14
ballad 175.27 253.21 493.03 495.03 593.15
ballast 390.03
ballbearing 186.15 285.L3
ballocks 180.24 337.30 611.27
balloon 389.27
bally 159.30 285.25 295.F1 352.23
ballyhoo 263.04
Baltic 187.02
bamboo 239.01
bamboozle 180.27
banana 071.12 100.07 145.35 170.20 199.20
banbury 333.33
band 320.10 582.31 598.03
bandbox 330.21
bandolier 073.17
bane 052.19 499.31
bang 008.12
banish 528.04
bank 040.19 055.07 060.10 127.28 232.02 274.02 338.36 420.34 520.26 538.28 615.26
bankclerk 510.21
bankrobber 510.20
bankrupt 049.32 266.23 590.03
banquet 038.06 397.06
banshee 316.21 409.02 581.09
bantamweight 039.13
banter 204.03
baptise 080.07 091.33 192.36 276.F1 326.06 339.34 363.12 537.08
baptist 453.15
bar 032.36 248.35 270.24 337.33 470.34
barbarian 071.30 285.L3
barbarous 241.26
barber 087.22 106.31 261.L1
bard 060.10 352.32 593.04
bare 437.08 516.14
barefaced 160.19 373.14
barely 017.13 287.19
bargain 070.27
barge 371.22
baritone 180.08 254.33 536.32 562.03
bark 060.14 132.33 197.28 443.16 542.19
barley 073.26 239.32 270.26 362.03 363.35 365.32 436.12 453.06 472.02 553.20 602.16
barleycorn 598.36
barmaid 387.21 526.23
barman 040.24 051.33 523.31
barmbrack 274.12 531.10
barn 211.21 275.F6 513.09
barndance 330.34
barometer 331.27
baron 107.36 339.27
barony 265.20
barrack 005.35 366.20
barrel 071.26 085.02 088.31 266.10 348.04
barren 365.19
barrow 391.14 479.25
barter 372.07
base 203.34
basement 365.10 535.18
basemetal 359.04
baseness 378.16
bashful 543.02
basin 207.19
bask 556.33
basket 121.05 141.10 194.13 277.F7 549.34 614.15
basketchair 358.27
bass 129.11 131.08 141.15 311.17 442.08
bastard 241.29 315.21 586.15 593.12 603.34
bat 160.02 284.04 464.28
bate 389.31
bath 478.13 493.02 548.14
bathe 178.15
batter 242.23 320.29 467.15
battery 358.12
battle 016.20 023.22 073.12 130.13 140.33 246.27 246.33

337.34 354.33 372.07 380.16 385.15 479.25 518.21
battleaxe 516.05
battledore 390.16
battlefield 010.08 310.26 609.34
battleline 235.23
battler 497.20
bauble 579.10
baulk 100.28
bawl 622.24
bay 029.22 342.23 374.16 374.18
bayonet 568.21
beach 168.03 360.28 442.13 537.30
beachsuit 613.31
bead 411.17 548.30
beadle 373.23 549.32
beadsman 258.34
beaker 077.30
beam 225.22 245.07 285.10 348.26 348.26
beamend 505.34
bean 239.32 463.35
beanstalk 126.11 307.F1 504.19 615.25 624.10
bear 087.21 087.22 132.05 247.22 268.16 328.02 364.01 366.14 370.27 437.08 468.32
beard 068.27 332.22 352.32 373.29 393.08 560.20
bearer 604.28
bearing 287.10
bearings 321.13
bearskin 200.01
beast 038.11 191.17 286.24 367.32 406.34 406.34 487.17 532.35 560.20
beastly 096.34 100.01
beat 089.32 154.24 180.31 231.23 376.09 521.19
beater 356.09
beatific 452.19
beatitude 158.36
beautiful 011.29 058.36 106.18 227.07 268.14 396.36 603.15
beautifully 395.20
beautify 262.F6
beauty 058.35 122.09 162.35 220.07 227.28 235.36 291.F7 300.22 374.19 391.34 487.16 560.20
beautyparlour 454.19
beautyspot 220.07 291.F7 534.24 600.16
beaver 052.24
beckon 222.36 603.01
become 373.26
bed 095.22 121.32 221.07 255.24 262.F7 262.F7 262.F7 262.F7 262.F7 297.32 345.15 395.22 461.30 526.08 595.08 597.16 598.22
bedad 353.11
bedamned 239.33
bedazzle 234.02 234.03 474.08
bedboard 349.08
bedevil 050.02 239.33 583.27
Bedouin 241.26
bedroom 245.30
bee 124.27 307.F1 416.10 540.16
beech 503.33
beef 171.01
beefsteak 170.33
beeftea 308.R1 421.09
beehive 315.22 561.07
beeline 262.F1
beer 006.24 070.16 077.29 087.22 130.12 181.06 256.07 315.22 348.04 496.29 518.21
beetle 354.33
beetroot 094.30
before 250.12
beforeness 419.04
befuddle 323.08
beg 106.25 359.22 570.25 607.18
begad 286.04 366.12 590.21
beget 241.27
beggar 015.30 241.27
beggarmaid 269.23
beggarman 494.36
begin 262.19 279.F17 282.05 292.08 311.31 345.25 346.09 377.11 523.07
beginning 056.20 129.10 239.23 271.23 282.05 378.29 487.20
begone 111.03 240.06
begorra 423.16 485.33 520.03
begrime 078.32
begum 564.19
behaviour 068.20 430.19
behead 397.22
behemoth 244.36 367.34
behest 367.32
behind 295.06
behold 012.36 015.32 053.14 058.04 143.17 239.10 278.11 326.05 336.15 382.20 408.24 412.01 451.17 500.33 625.26
belch 224.13 412.07
belfry 053.12
Belgian 239.32 376.04
belie 088.13
believe 092.21 106.25 145.26 153.17 155.06 155.06 243.13 289.01 289.04 289.04 299.12 324.19 325.30 351.20 361.13 409.24 439.32 476.21 481.25 534.22 534.26 541.24 562.12 610.05 610.05 625.30
believer 352.15 520.19 520.19
belike 409.24 412.10 449.33 469.02
belittle 048.04
bell 032.03 072.16 244.15 284.19 299.F1 349.01 463.17 568.14 568.14 594.23
belladonna 450.32 585.24
belles-lettres 281.R1
bellicose 018.33
bellow 154.07 154.35 617.10
bellows 289.14 486.32 486.32
belly 323.16
bellyache 302.28
bellyful 350.21
beloved 488.20 489.31
belt 346.15 492.36
bend 491.12
beneath 450.17
benediction 310.36
benefaction 185.03
benefice 380.03
beneficence 302.07
benefit 339.26 453.18
benevolent 450.11
benighted 018.02
bequeath 336.24
bereave 228.12 243.13 243.18
beriberi 376.28 542.01
Berlitz 467.25
berry 025.33 142.03
berserk 582.29
beseech 454.27 576.30
beside 261.24
besides 301.28
bespeak 066.15
bespectacled 386.16
best 020.35 106.33 165.28 225.11 286.L3 311.25 329.11 334.02 356.26 382.20 434.26 452.21 480.24 485.23 531.05 533.36 539.12 560.20 597.05
bestman 511.02
bestseller 123.23
bet 088.36 451.02
betake 350.18
bethink 153.31 422.09
betide 360.05 563.18
betimes 489.22
betray 068.31 493.28
betrayal 466.28
better 093.24 106.33 165.28 167.21 203.04 234.29 241.35 242.23 252.12 298.22 314.18 356.22 374.29 422.25 429.13 467.33 493.04 506.03 533.36 540.32
betterment 440.23
beverage 289.23
beware 060.29 244.01 278.07 315.33 464.04 576.35
biassed 110.18
Bible 110.17 280.L1 523.32
bibulous 280.L1 549.32
bicker 118.05
bickerer 252.16
bicycle 058.04 115.16 284.23 295.31 416.30 450.24 567.33
bid 415.23
big 225.36 241.09 245.02 334.16 339.11 420.10 420.11 484.09 491.35
bigamy 537.26
bigger 208.01 324.27
bigotry 099.19
bigotted 133.15
bile 288.26
bill 188.07
billet 344.27
billiards 589.07
billow 366.15
billposter 373.23
billygoat 197.07 466.34 467.01
bimetallist 344.22 551.32
bind 233.06 323.33
binge 612.21
binocular 394.30
binomial 285.27
biography 423.17
birch 503.33
bird 007.36 037.17 070.16 079.30 095.36 105.11 169.05 180.07 256.06 296.07 309.04 348.34 363.05 364.31 381.23 450.18 465.28 609.04
birdseye 504.16
birth 062.07 199.02 330.28

birthday 027.11 035.04 059.11 484.14 497.27
birthplace 231.24
birthright 190.12 300.32
biscuit 166.14 284.02 433.20 542.30
bisect 284.02 564.11
bisexualism 524.12 524.36
bishop 089.08 130.33 158.30 158.30 177.36 190.19 241.36 302.01 374.16 435.11 491.20 606.13
bismuth 577.04
bit 101.05 124.07 172.32 255.26 407.04
bitch 112.05 209.15 251.11 278.23 314.28 322.05 340.02 348.34 360.03 362.10 369.21 437.30 540.14 543.10 586.15
bite 005.30 211.29 250.08 291.06 354.35 433.20 542.19
biter 291.06
bitterly 138.35
bitters 498.09
black 017.24 093.04 162.31 176.24 207.18 219.24 220.13 229.27 247.31 286.15 290.22 294.28 316.22 316.27 340.15 344.12 365.18 387.20 410.09 492.15 503.23 510.19 515.33 528.06 550.20 563.13 563.13 563.15 563.15 563.31 601.05 626.22
blackball 232.15
blackbird 010.34 450.18
blackcurrant 141.35
blackeyed 327.29
blackguard 135.03 260.06 347.14 361.19
blackmail 069.02
blackmailer 545.27
bladder 197.05 224.19 408.27
bland 312.28
blank 093.04 333.21 350.11 355.07 617.01
blanket 503.03 578.10
blarney 381.22 472.06
blaspheme 320.25
blasphemous 167.14 167.14
blast 241.29 299.16 303.24 304.13 340.08 593.12
blather 022.09 077.15 354.18 408.27 479.18 488.18
blatherskite 200.04
blaze 056.09 372.10
bleareyed 590.02
bleat 022.09
bleed 255.18 305.05 499.30 553.07 587.16 593.12 608.10
blend 321.24
bless 071.18 156.27 262.F6 318.30 325.32 335.27 352.35 392.20 398.20 416.20 441.07 442.32 451.28 452.25 562.25
blind 076.36 093.04 098.03 098.04 098.04 156.20
blindman 467.17 508.17
blissful 235.04
blithe 202.25
blitz 563.23
blizzard 318.30
bloke 609.04
blood 070.26 122.14 130.34 221.20 288.26 341.33 347.06 378.04 553.07 614.11
bloodorange 241.03 405.33
bloodstained 341.05
bloodstone 011.22
bloodstream 074.14
bloody 014.20 016.09 031.11 034.09 039.26 053.25 063.34 070.26 073.06 076.18 081.26 081.27 081.30 081.30 090.31 253.16 263.09 303.27 305.F1 323.04 323.04 338.09 345.06 345.25 350.06 351.34 352.29 403.12 425.13 436.27 448.27 448.28 448.33 491.28 511.21 553.08 553.08 593.03
bloom 203.10 245.07 267.29 453.13
blooming 078.27
blossom 069.03 204.08 535.33
blotting 101.20
blouse 261.02 265.F5
blow 112.35 234.32 237.19 241.04 351.13 351.30 537.24
blue 023.01 029.02 037.18 043.27 076.32 095.04 106.31 176.23 180.12 240.33 267.15 267.15 277.F4 320.28 323.04 327.32 339.28 344.12 384.28 385.35 403.12 432.31 457.18 537.24 540.29 543.21 555.10 587.27 593.03 596.21 611.06
bluebeard 332.22 560.20
bluebell 282.F1 361.22 626.19
bluecold 213.04
blueeyed 534.18
bluenose 453.17 540.35
blueribbon 219.20
bluestocking 368.31
bluff 346.25 467.17 508.17
blunder 388.25
blunderbuss 327.18 600.19
blush 279.F01 299.17 431.17
boaconstrictor 180.35
boar 245.13
board 007.09 025.10 058.11 077.06 321.28 539.20 557.15
boardinghouse 186.31
boast 140.10
boasthard 315.21
boatsong 352.17
bobtail 105.16
bodily 343.27 425.18
bodkin 079.20 268.15 446.05
body 040.07 300.22 300.23 416.03 547.27 602.27
bodyguard 093.06
bodysnatcher 026.17
Boer 491.32
bog 347.20 510.19
bogus 075.02
Bohemian 032.35 333.15
boil 034.11 044.08 049.15 137.01 151.14 164.11 456.23
boilingpoint 513.18 575.11
bold 093.35 139.11 188.33 299.12 303.05 336.04 366.10 380.28 390.08 469.14 555.21 600.27 626.02
bolero 034.33
bollweevil 516.10 613.21
boloney 360.23
bolshevik 302.18
bolster 526.02
bolt 106.15
bomb 506.18
bombardier 317.15
bombast 320.06
bomber 341.27
bonbon 542.22
bondman 346.28
bone 055.05 058.15 268.16 308.F2 353.07 397.20 590.20
bonfire 439.34 501.26
bonnet 020.28 136.28 176.36 372.19 494.25
bonny 177.36 363.19 520.26 520.26 586.14 586.14
boohoo 162.27
book 013.30 091.06 094.29 098.12 111.32 134.36 156.06 206.12 210.06 255.21 264.06 288.23 309.03 336.17 347.20 351.24 375.16 427.32 445.07 485.06 516.25 537.31 597.06
bookmaker 618.30
boon 498.16
boot 023.01 141.15 288.20 332.35 332.35 332.35 332.35 368.20 388.19 443.31 480.30 568.19 599.07 599.08 599.08 599.08 622.11
bootlegger 019.19 166.17
booze 158.04 257.21
boozy 448.36
bordel 029.01
border 081.32
bore 248.17 297.31 415.32 595.20
borealis 327.32 416.34
born 120.09 263.19 321.08 339.34 352.16 365.05 392.12 617.25
borrow 011.17 275.06 375.28 491.19 512.24 538.08 541.17 565.36 578.26 602.17 625.19
Borsalino 032.36 520.09 625.11
Borstal 353.34 391.09 504.26 512.05 624.33
bosky 614.15
bosom 012.13 079.36 204.08 231.08 338.34 345.33 348.07 371.02 449.16 449.22 471.32 535.33 579.01
boss 141.15 257.21 311.17 442.08 608.15
bosun 371.02 389.31
botanic 622.36
both 281.01
bother 156.23 248.32 303.15 343.20 444.17 594.31
botheration 528.31
Botree 503.13
bottle 016.20 016.21 029.01 071.03 085.01 093.16 129.11 130.13 138.32 170.30 176.31 177.01 180.20 198.22 245.32 255.26 267.F5 283.F1 315.22 328.22 348.04 348.07 352.30 371.04 419.26 565.11 578.22 610.30
bottlewasher 026.17 105.33
bottom 048.18 061.26 085.01 163.19 278.F2 281.F2 296.06 316.18 333.34 340.09 350.14

366.32 369.12 445.13 564.34 594.12
boudoir 207.11
bough 265.F5 447.23 447.24
boulder 136.35
bounce 370.30 370.35
bounder 296.29 543.04
boundless 157.25
bouquet 531.12 614.15
bourne 471.30
bow 322.36 423.22 434.04 568.22 618.23 626.06
bowel 515.12
bower 228.12 266.16
bowl 151.23 160.01 161.27 164.27 265.23 341.13 362.19 441.28 462.13 469.14 559.25
bowlful 464.21
bowling 072.32
bowlinggreen 517.09
bowman 226.07
bowsprit 197.35 525.34
box 225.21 330.21 337.19 537.31 542.29 545.23
boxer 090.02 266.26
boxingmatch 415.13
boy 011.08 011.08 105.35 201.25 245.04 245.05 245.20 247.18 252.23 281.F2 318.11 328.29 331.18 358.33 366.34 377.27 380.28 392.16 415.01 422.29 431.20 491.36 541.17 562.24 606.13 610.12 624.23
boyfriend 273.L1
boyg 416.19
boyishness 565.13
braces 446.33 559.10
brain 074.13 104.13 187.26 463.20 522.29 594.01
brake 295.F1
branch 265.F5
brand 232.28 417.12
Brandenburger 265.13
brandish 009.34 224.34 382.02 462.02
brass 627.20
brat 431.13
brave 338.28
bravo 313.31
bray 020.26 246.26 620.09
braze 531.08
brazen 301.02
breach 323.11
bread 023.34 024.05 165.10 198.06 225.12 225.12 225.13 237.32 261.13 287.31 291.06 356.18 378.34 408.01 411.19 483.24 531.01 542.34 597.16 603.08 608.10 621.14
breadcrumb 563.24
breadth 318.11
break 070.04 070.04 090.24 124.07 141.34 159.17 199.07 232.02 247.06 372.25 416.15 422.07 538.28 562.16
breakfast 012.14 041.13 121.34 124.09 131.04 252.30 320.09 338.31 343.33 359.28 413.16 434.31 453.12 528.06 563.30 575.11 608.20 613.23 621.12
breakwater 420.07
breast 044.01 148.30 320.07 462.10 537.09
breath 165.10 324.03 344.19 389.31 439.16 452.25 578.31
breathe 056.32 075.04 228.12 410.02 420.04 452.25 482.03 590.25
breeches 044.08 106.09 126.10 176.02 225.06 234.09 265.F5 317.23 440.30 442.13 534.19 613.31
breed 168.08 317.01 411.22 452.25
breeks 199.07
breeze 241.20 407.17
Brehon 059.28
brevity 222.27
brewer 425.31
brewery 038.04
briar 450.32 450.32
brick 106.06 266.04 352.05
bridal 445.06
bride 239.28 286.L3 309.06 310.16 312.07 367.28 389.31 422.15 465.05 502.09 622.03
bridegroom 189.27 362.09
bridesmaid 514.26
bridge 058.10 110.23 136.23 136.24 239.35 274.32 389.35 447.17 514.26
brief 143.30 276.10 396.29
brigade 348.25 349.10
brigadier-general 329.05 352.23
bright 055.04 436.28
brighten 242.27 448.18 537.11
brighter 324.34
brightest 563.17
brightly 207.16
brightness 223.06
brilliant 059.30
brimstone 505.33
brine 051.29 110.02 148.19 310.15 366.15 502.09 595.05
bring 224.31 230.23 278.L5 310.08 328.25 339.19 542.27 624.32
brisk 575.10
briskly 467.32
British 228.19 351.07 362.10
Briton 152.05 313.31 491.33
brittle 328.22
broach 127.14 213.33 239.35
broad 006.26 237.22 288.08 378.34 483.24
broadcast 311.36 510.26 526.27 567.20
broader 324.34
brogue 083.13 329.21 507.22
broil 184.17
broke 164.23 230.36 347.21
bronchitis 536.13
bronze 483.09 536.09 578.04
brood 590.25
broth 243.13 318.11
brothel 328.22 368.19
brother 022.02 052.11 052.12 070.27 099.13 170.04 191.20 198.19 234.04 252.04 252.14 276.F2 296.23 303.15 305.16 325.26 404.29 408.25 423.36 425.30 427.19 459.22 464.24 468.03 469.26 483.21 488.18 488.18 489.16 489.30 511.11 520.20 561.16 598.12 620.16
brother-in-law 153.18 312.13
brotherly 436.14 439.27
brougham 284.F4
brow 198.07 228.34 324.04 336.29 340.18 389.28 548.11
brown 050.23 130.34 153.07 187.24 249.01 344.12 418.31 522.34
browse 602.15
bruiser 266.26 596.15
brush 012.08 348.32 491.26
brushup 318.19
brute 292.F2 596.15
brutestrength 359.17
bubble 164.11 181.11 224.12 626.19
bubblebath 290.13
bubbleglass 359.12
buccal 562.25
buccaneer 323.01
buck 094.29 379.17 622.29
buckeroo 604.03
bucket 059.07 296.30 393.13 397.06 531.12
buckle 208.11 314.32 471.22 536.15
bucko 011.14
buff 467.17 508.17
buffalo 118.07
bug 297.07
bugger 007.24 068.16 079.02 081.26 081.27 095.18 111.32 114.26 119.30 134.04 139.06 141.22 186.20 186.21 204.22 303.27 350.06 444.14 496.20 533.28 542.26 542.35 556.25 563.14 613.27
bugle 284.20 320.19 562.27 567.23 626.19
build 080.28 369.15 416.03 450.24 509.33 511.34 543.11
builder 062.08 077.03 111.21 296.07 309.13 377.26
bulbul 384.29
bulge 224.13 239.32 299.19 563.14
bulgine 299.19 316.19 529.22
bull 006.35 519.08 541.16 553.31
bullet 238.32 344.28 346.20 625.25
bulletin 060.28
bulletproof 616.32
bullfighter 566.10
bullfinch 486.17
bullion 313.29 393.12 575.11 595.11
bullock 189.07 368.10 368.15
bullring 534.19
bullseye 408.26
bulrush 029.21 494.19
bum 046.09 550.04 594.13 600.27
bumblebee 416.10
bumbo 338.27
bump 205.06 618.17
bumper 468.27
bumpkin 353.27
bun 183.22
bunch 292.03 511.30
bundle 320.19 349.32
bungalow 496.13 624.07
bunkum 422.26
buoy 377.27 491.36

burden 292.28 580.02
burgeon 275.F5
burglar 141.14 197.19
burgomaster 004.18 062.03 191.35 393.08 568.17 576.18 607.30 624.11
burial 415.31
burly 257.18
burn 289.13 318.31 437.01 455.02 578.28 586.11
burnie 525.36
burnous 215.20
burrow 422.32
burst 089.09 197.35 224.18 509.30 512.05
bury 421.06 578.26 613.30
busby 339.11 516.09
busconductor 553.33
bush 070.21 189.18 240.24 305.25 305.25
bushman 594.23
business 026.35 070.03 117.21 117.21 174.30 174.30 321.20 330.34 363.07 367.02 378.16 406.34 406.34 450.33 450.33 497.24 534.21 535.17 549.35 565.22 580.28 601.01 618.19 618.36
busman 129.13 353.07
buss 124.27
bust 291.14
bustle 102.10 578.22
busy 238.34
busybody 040.07
butcher 064.18 242.03 338.09 600.29
butler 166.17 242.03 385.15
butter 124.13 161.19 163.03 225.12 225.13 225.13 237.32 287.31 397.18 425.09 444.17 483.24
buttercup 428.27 433.25
butterfly 262.13 293.F1
butterscotch 163.08
buttock 025.25 176.35 311.33 431.07
button 011.19 291.F4 341.02 498.35 508.04 548.05
buttonhole 320.05 350.11 464.13
buttress 433.11
buxom 266.01 606.15
buy 025.18 416.18
byandby 297.14
bye 161.14 161.14 249.30 295.32 295.32 432.08 432.08 433.20 433.20 521.36
byebye 146.33 354.31
byelaw 310.25 374.20 594.28
bygone 016.29 263.18 275.L3 285.28 348.11 390.20 621.01 621.01

cabbage 034.08 071.35 390.12 419.32 456.07 456.08 456.23 475.35 555.19 568.28 612.02
cabin 384.23 622.07
cabler 060.29
cabman 542.14
cack 137.12
cackle 279.F25 372.15 511.11 585.30
cactus 590.19
caddy 350.33
cadger 498.13
Cadillac 516.05
cagehouse 533.18
cajole 092.19
cake 011.24 116.22 146.08 149.06 170.16 236.17 280.16 333.35 365.02 423.12 446.10 448.07 617.25
calabash 051.36 240.24
calcium 035.02
calculate 004.32
calendar 341.29 347.02 432.36 492.26 513.12 578.22
calico 516.16
calicular 516.35
caliph 426.13
caliphate 533.28
calisthenic 499.05
call 083.36 112.35 151.15 152.26 164.34 198.07 267.L1 320.13 327.20 337.17 338.23 346.24 346.25 360.13 360.14 414.34 415.29 495.18 495.19 502.11 502.18 506.06 534.01 551.35 596.32 622.01
callboy 543.09
calm 354.32 363.18 378.05 623.25
calory 365.36
camel 104.21 120.26 275.05 320.26 323.28 334.15 344.09 590.07
camouflage 339.13 463.22
camp 491.07
campaign 162.08 539.32
Canadian 287.F3
canal 525.18 548.04
cancan 006.21 006.21 113.10 316.13
cancel 373.29
candidate 498.32
candle 276.10 276.23 302.03 356.19 379.23 463.34 557.04
candlelight 020.20
candlemas 236.07
candy 406.07
candy-sucker 241.03
cane 028.19 516.23
cannibal 004.05 339.10 362.05
cannon 028.19 334.26 334.26 391.33
cannonball 339.10
canoe 065.32
canon 334.26 334.26 451.14
cant 077.22 120.31
cantankerous 463.13
cantharides 415.09
canton 496.09 548.04
canvasser 534.20
cap 056.24 221.29 232.33 257.28 257.28 283.02 334.10 403.08 510.34
capability 263.29
capable 305.11 310.12 363.32
caparison 152.05
caper 475.35
capital 131.02 369.32 369.36 548.17
capon 075.21 233.03 316.34 319.18 569.26
Capricorn 026.12
capsize 260.04
captain 023.11 060.30 082.29 187.08 295.F1 311.09 311.27 312.02 316.34 319.18 320.25 322.25 323.13 343.10 352.32 360.19 362.09 371.15 511.02 540.18 587.05
captivity 246.19
captor 568.33
capuchin 447.19
car 339.14 340.08 577.34
caramel 354.32
carapace 416.15
caravan 031.21 333.10 602.28
caraway 276.26
carawayseed 625.24
card 076.20 374.05
cardinal 185.10 282.20 282.20 282.21 282.22 282.23 440.09 484.19 600.34
care 177.09 351.25 421.08
careful 515.36
carefully 289.11 374.33 536.17
carelessness 111.20
caress 292.24
cargo 245.14
caricature 085.33 291.F6 302.31 602.23
carman 237.22
Carmelite 211.29 338.06
Carolingian 087.28
carousal 406.15
carriage 351.11
carrier 349.12 515.24
carrot 207.25 390.25 501.04
carry 158.36 183.19 207.24 350.33 372.28
cart 164.17 377.33 538.08 594.29 610.17
Carthaginian 087.28
cartridge 011.19
caryatid 158.36
case 149.33 187.03 341.23 557.03
casement 387.23 548.07
cashmere 226.24
cask 176.30
cassock 311.29
cassowary 263.F2
cast 199.24 311.36 324.24 332.27 510.26
caster 279.F23
castle 037.22 128.17 376.32 381.22 388.07
cat 008.08 040.11 089.35 101.27 120.02 151.14 177.07 184.31 197.10 197.10 212.07 252.34 322.22 333.07 335.19 335.19 341.01 344.11 347.30 394.28 415.32 452.05 511.32 539.35
catacomb 542.03
catalogue 440.04
cataract 414.20 600.14
catastaltic 366.23
catastrophe 222.12 504.31
catch 009.31 012.16 019.16 031.10 106.24 311.22 358.02 450.24 461.01 465.28 494.34 531.20 601.32
catch-as-catch-can 614.33
caterpillar 063.29 241.09 350.10
catgut 507.10 548.15
catheter 357.13

catholic 027.02 091.35 158.04 239.21 310.36 344.15 347.31 370.36 409.12 440.04 485.01 486.02 519.26 603.30 611.07 611.10 611.24
catkin 465.31
cat-o'-nine-tails 462.31
catty 147.12 531.15
caul 495.18 578.10
cauldron 151.13
cauliflower 409.14 612.02
cause 269.29 319.29 322.09 378.15 378.15 615.27
causeway 227.05 284.F5 343.07 391.19 478.15 503.01
cautel 230.10
cavalier 162.22 234.03
cavalry 370.07
cave 108.27 512.22
cavehouse 177.20
cavern 132.02
cease 229.22 488.08
cedar 235.17 244.05 511.30 558.35
ceilidhe 372.14 372.15
ceiling 155.24
celebrate 011.17 305.03 305.08 343.04 343.28 345.28 379.07 421.19 422.04 484.13 518.22
celebrity 535.33
celery 346.09 346.10 346.10 346.11
celibacy 191.17
cellar 279.F23 570.36
cellular 516.35
celluloid 373.04
Celt 390.07 413.01 537.07
Celtic 237.20 311.22 344.12 492.09
cemetery 017.36 085.09 594.08
censor 440.11
centipede 063.02
central 069.36
centre 183.29 227.22 256.29 437.06
century 230.17 290.08 535.05
cereal 545.27
cert 011.27
certain 017.11 162.15 203.09 284.06 365.07 371.17 449.03 481.20
certainly 109.25 110.06 232.23 234.31 363.13 363.13 448.32 514.07 514.27 522.05 553.31
cess 449.24
cesspool 338.15
chaff 551.03
chain 213.05 342.29 371.12 542.10
chaingang 355.28 540.24
chair 245.03 530.11
chairman 516.03
chaise 453.21
chalice 461.35 552.36 613.27
chalk 077.11 319.10 461.28 542.34
chamber 032.16 354.01 622.07
chambermaid 075.08 148.24 212.17 594.31
chambermusic 164.15 184.04
chameleon 136.27
chamois 612.25
champagne 138.31 407.31 518.21 539.32 540.05
champion 261.14
chance 206.19 254.23 288.01
chancery 442.26 582.04
chandler 542.33
change 082.33 153.14 288.01 318.36 363.22
changer 342.31
channel 324.31
chap 020.29 196.07 233.33 253.15 416.26
chapel 395.23
Chapelizod 007.28 026.17 029.01 062.04 080.36 087.29 096.08 110.08 111.06 127.29 236.20 290.02 323.04 325.14 334.36 370.29 372.13 382.11 385.25 396.31 438.30 452.11 487.32 571.11 571.18 607.14 607.15
chaperone 269.05
chaplet 528.06
chapter 275.F4 395.23
character 098.09 302.31 314.08 518.22
characteristic 334.07 357.13
charge 348.25 431.25
chariot 279.F32 359.19
charioteer 595.23
charity 222.31 324.26 489.30 594.12
charlotte 113.16
charm 075.08 092.22 162.34 519.20 619.31
charming 280.22 280.25 427.14 427.14 458.17 569.11
chase 115.20 245.35 246.36 292.09 322.02 335.10 553.23
chaser 228.14
chastity 093.19
chauffeur 166.17 235.28
cheap 077.29 161.10 172.09 357.03 600.25
check 373.32 461.24
checker 091.30 292.03
cheek 168.11 215.19 315.11 370.35 394.18 446.10 446.10 484.16 538.33
cheer 106.19 117.23 173.26 209.36 357.06 474.17 590.30 590.30 590.30
cheerful 515.36
cheery 446.23 508.23
cheese 077.11 161.10 161.11 166.31 167.02 316.36 333.35
chemical 067.08 334.20
chemise 233.30 417.31 425.03 551.06
cherish 461.35
cherry 006.17 058.15 114.24 225.02 288.F5 446.23 508.23
cherryripe 162.35 291.11
cherub 226.19 498.33
chess 423.36
chest 227.33 227.33
chestnut 125.20 183.24 453.16
chest-of-drawers 133.17
chew 265.F5 270.F2 354.35 455.35 482.09
chiaroscuro 317.33 612.18
chicken 205.18 313.22
chickenbroth 243.13
chief 198.12 236.27 239.29 240.15 274.01
child 105.02 243.32 252.05 332.14 339.04 343.11 359.04 369.28 472.22 473.09 490.06 498.33 527.35 553.24 565.20 589.02
Childermas 330.33 355.34
childish 461.28
chilly 192.24
chime 598.30
chimney 029.05 250.06 345.26 364.27 380.17 583.33
chin 329.10 329.10 503.33 531.06
china 124.08 243.15
Chinese 461.24
chip 137.11
chirp 226.19
chitinous 416.25
chloride 035.02 613.26 616.12
chlorine 359.10 468.35
chloroform 158.10
chock 524.24
chockfull 152.26 590.13
chocolate 049.14 286.F5 587.07
choice 161.19
choirboy 543.09
choke 390.09 569.01
cholera 211.01
choose 432.36 522.01 551.36
chop 067.17 233.33 467.17
chopstick 514.08
choral 145.25 225.26 601.16
chorus 006.21 208.36 234.36 236.12 343.30 349.05 391.08
chrism 326.33
chrisom 326.33
christen 138.25 201.35 562.09
christendom 053.04
Christian 022.17 053.04 080.20 086.04 141.05 142.11 177.09 245.28 312.32 326.15 326.33 331.32 344.16 396.19 455.27 491.06 518.36 531.06
Christianity 618.34
Christlike 267.L3
Christmas 006.15 011.14 130.07 141.05 142.11 197.15 236.14 346.05 412.10 416.26 455.27 518.36 534.01 562.09 619.05 624.06
chronicler 254.07
chrysanthemum 326.15
chum 464.03
church 067.13 137.10 141.12 326.04 533.23 559.29 568.27
churchmouse 416.13
churchyard 034.08 096.08 201.31 213.01 246.01 388.02 621.34
churl 303.24 426.25
churn 362.33 537.24
cicatrice 564.36
cigar 341.17 417.13
cigarette 236.02 351.12
cinder 532.03
cinnamon 006.18
cipher 283.04
circle 119.23 134.16 298.15 480.24
circuit 460.09
circulation 135.28
circumcise 170.19

circumference 298.15
circumspect 230.32 433.34
circumstance 297.07 342.12 354.14
circus 319.06 375.28 460.09
cirrhus 375.28
citadel 062.01
citizen 012.02 298.01 494.22
citron 171.08 171.11 171.11
city 053.03 098.29 143.05 205.24 332.33 347.35 435.01 532.06 564.28
civic 610.08
civil 353.09 399.04 546.35
civilise 550.23
civilised 350.35
clack 464.19
clap 023.03 044.19 284.14
claretcup 613.26
clarion 474.17
class 025.21 152.08 167.20
classic 357.16
clatter 475.23 621.15
claudication 126.14
clay 478.21
clean 038.10 086.10 138.10 353.17 421.02 510.21 548.15 625.17
cleaner 364.34
clear 138.10 381.22 459.08 488.25
clearance 266.12
cleave 505.18
cleft 229.23 583.36
clematis 059.13 360.30
cleric 459.08
clerical 338.11
clerk 485.36 510.21
clever 159.30 285.26 352.23 422.02 478.25 508.33
click 044.20
climax 222.11
clitoris 239.18 406.19
cloak 211.01 243.26 276.12 553.14 567.18
clock 111.08 213.16 328.11 371.04 510.21
cloister 265.02
close 053.12 148.23 165.04 355.19 390.06 569.14 582.07 602.24
closet 111.17 438.01 553.10
closingtime 451.08
cloth 320.17 542.34
clothe 366.15 528.22
clothes 023.11 053.12 148.23 236.01 322.12 324.30 366.33 375.29 434.23 453.15 510.28 510.29 537.15 545.30
cloud 186.23 279.F29
cloudburst 091.03 509.30
cloudcapped 607.32
clover 478.25 508.33
club 409.24 476.16
clubfoot 015.31
clue 528.14
clumsily 149.29
clumsy 344.30
cluster 026.13
Clydesdale 553.35
coach 355.32 364.05 568.04
coachman 420.06
coagulate 349.17
coal 108.25
coalblack 294.28 447.05
coalesce 029.16
coalman 278.F3 443.27
coalmine 539.13
coalscuttle 160.27
coast 447.27 482.13
coat 031.28 035.13 051.15 087.34 116.14 317.35 319.29 329.27 373.14 408.35 522.17 543.21 546.16 553.14 567.18 611.36 624.34
cobber 398.27
cobbler 265.12
cobblestone 132.01 313.24
cock 051.23 090.32 136.17 171.10 282.23 310.34 390.17 394.07 567.24
cockade 348.35
cockadoodledoo 461.27 584.22 595.30 615.08
cockahoop 128.10
cockalorum 241.02
cockatoo 461.27
cockeyed 189.10
cockhorse 121.23
cockroach 415.10
cocksure 551.01
cocoa 033.03 036.20 072.13 073.10 118.13 120.22 162.14 171.10 192.08 238.32 294.24 327.35 327.36 349.17 354.21 356.27 357.20 358.01 376.09 378.14 382.05 409.12 417.36 439.04 483.35 509.20 516.13 516.20 518.29 537.23 538.19 584.27 584.30 597.01 609.14
coconut 376.09
cocoon 483.35 519.03
cod 286.13
coefficient 284.12
coeliac 516.35
coffee 059.29 199.18
coffeecup 542.13
coffeehouse 177.20 416.36
coffer 416.04
coffin 026.26 356.03 444.14 482.10 578.10
coign 313.17
coin 016.31 313.17 538.16 579.16
coincide 551.34
coincidence 299.08
colander 102.10 347.02 408.34 578.22
cold 024.31 086.06 110.16 117.31 139.26 152.26 187.19 194.29 213.04 213.28 241.12 241.27 279.02 316.14 326.17 345.12 365.13 365.13 367.28 367.28 414.34 452.01 502.18 502.24 581.13 593.20 596.32
coldcream 526.29
colder 188.27
collaborate 342.34
collapse 005.27 580.07
collar 022.34 322.36 341.11 370.33 614.10
collation 071.08
collect 059.34
collection 162.13 550.06
college 106.35 189.35 279.F14 315.01 594.36 623.32
colon 152.16 222.36 244.17 289.17
colonel 351.32 607.29
colonial 488.31
colossal 128.32 181.03 241.08 261.12 551.35 551.35
colossus 625.22
colour 051.26 063.13 146.16 158.10 173.17 176.10 205.09 223.06 443.34
colouringmatter 359.10
colporteur 221.03
colt 246.36
column 335.28
comb 238.32 243.23 390.32 423.25 442.35 529.19 550.20
combination 200.35 351.26 361.01
come 232.16
comedian 033.03
comely 143.16 550.20
comet 177.26 350.33
comether 325.13 325.30
comfit 521.01
comfort 136.32 147.16 340.23 355.31 521.01 620.06
comical 334.20
comically 263.25
comma 374.10
command 552.24
commander 034.05
commander-in-chief 240.15
commandment 326.02 615.32
commence 130.11
commentary 162.06
commercial 069.35
commission 141.23
commit 130.11 147.06 172.31 434.34
committal 616.18
committeeman 529.08
common 029.30 130.21 228.12 283.07 539.23
commonplace 159.15
commons 261.F2
commonwealth 238.32 593.12
communicate 536.04
communion 227.30 227.30 380.10 498.30 624.28
communist 438.18
community 042.14
company 230.20
comparably 529.06
comparative 140.33 598.23
compass 382.20 410.10 543.12
compasses 295.27
compassionate 192.28
compel 434.28
compensation 616.25
compere 337.36
complanate 553.16
complementary 612.21
complete 296.23
completely 232.20 540.01
complex 607.20
complexion 407.07
compliment 271.F4 456.06
compline 553.16
compos 516.29
compose 066.19 155.21
composer 162.02
compound 036.02
comprehend 285.28 612.01

compression 115.24
compulsory 271.F3
comrade 036.20 089.07 329.04 551.15
con 044.21
conan 019.25
conceal 453.02
conceive 237.19
concept 032.03
concert 243.11
concertpitch 584.02
conclude 155.09 617.04
concord 590.17
concrete 285.F5 358.06 581.28
concubine 117.15 284.F4
concupiscent 432.10
condemn 142.22 252.34 418.30 421.02
condemnation 362.03
condition 077.35 229.29
condole 585.17
condom 142.22 252.34 255.22 613.03
conduce 310.13
conduct 310.13 537.14
conductor 420.33 553.33
conduit 537.14
cone 278.04
confectioner 339.15
confederacy 349.34
confederate 537.18
confess 156.31 459.07
confession 261.F3 353.25 387.01
confessional 333.06 520.12 619.15
confirmation 339.28
confiteor 531.02
conform 268.29
confound 415.02 542.11
confront 564.14
confuse 156.31 193.21
confusedly 365.04
confusion 035.36 252.19 353.25 417.15 485.35 542.11
congenital 525.05
conger 165.21 229.22
congratulation 234.21 535.12
congregational 167.16
conic 385.12 602.27
conjecture 608.08
conjugation 143.13
conk 181.22
conquer 116.11 170.14 305.R1 328.25 357.08
conquest 167.36
conscience 368.21
consciously 224.23
consciousness 224.17
conscription 364.19
consequence 178.03 284.23
consequent 298.24
conservative 535.17
consider 061.08
consideration 451.36
consolation 581.13
consonant 337.08 485.11
conspicuously 173.02
constable 015.35 429.19 443.05 548.16
constabulary 086.01
constantly 618.32
constellation 340.30 450.13
constituent 537.22
construct 036.09
consul 581.13
consumation 194.07
consume 336.35
contain 355.28
contemn 355.28
contemptible 352.01 497.35
content 322.29
continent 337.08
contingency 298.24
continuation 284.20
continue 067.16 359.27
continuously 294.31
contract 374.20
contradict 096.03
contraption 364.19
contrary 061.10 148.35
contrite 229.29 341.25
conundrum 085.22 352.34
convenience 024.02 551.27
convent 527.22
conversation 071.08 413.20
convert 021.29
conveyance 024.02
convince 425.13
convulse 138.34
coo 095.32 244.17
cook 162.15 170.16 221.14 245.02 279.F25 295.F1 324.29 420.09 511.08 511.08 550.15
cool 010.25 095.22 178.33
coombe 532.28
cooper 255.22
cop 243.24 417.33
copper 096.35 280.L2 416.04 433.30
Coptic 419.25
copulation 525.06 557.17
copy 221.29 464.05
copycat 267.F6
copyright 133.18 185.30
coral 363.03
corduroy 085.33 208.20
core 049.09
cork 160.27 176.30 352.09 375.34 497.28 519.24
corkscrew 341.18
corky 132.35
corn 110.17 589.36
corncrake 144.33
corner 067.13 116.11 118.36 186.29 190.25 219.10 291.01 496.34 533.24 602.16
cornucopia 137.30 451.07 457.01
corollary 294.07 298.18
coronation 230.24
coronet 250.35
corporal 346.35
corporation 251.13 368.12 568.20
corps 049.09
corpse 055.08 178.36 224.05 336.02 595.10 616.06
corpulence 294.22
corrective 300.24
correctly 042.17 162.28
correspond 457.28
correspondent 602.20
corroborate 575.13
corrugate 057.27
corrupt 300.24
corsage 468.31
corsair 323.03 343.03 444.27 626.28
corset 106.23 236.36
Corsican 333.11 465.16
cosecant 298.24
cosine 293.01 298.23 354.33 532.21
cosmopolitan 309.10
cosmos 118.21
cossack 311.29
cosy 429.22
cot 044.21 231.05
cottage 466.25
cotton 234.09 319.22
couch 476.31
cough 089.30 095.08 380.22 423.26 511.14
count 272.27 288.04 365.18 408.35 497.10
countenance 198.35 252.14 304.01
counterclockwise 119.18
counterfoil 191.18
counterparts 187.07
countess 039.30 448.10
countinghouse 135.01 267.05 575.26
country 035.14 148.35 241.35 253.29 286.16 353.26 500.36
countryman 490.28
county 186.25 446.35
couple 053.10 151.17 331.03 432.13 433.30 553.16 607.20 607.34
couplet 495.29
coupon 170.35 242.04
courage 395.28 534.34
courier 125.14 570.10
course 037.10 097.03 143.11 224.05 254.32 311.07 311.28 322.05 322.19 372.03 410.02 414.29 474.05 516.33 561.33 575.33 586.02 615.11
court 076.17 120.31 232.13 376.01 378.32 548.35 557.12 618.14
courtmartial 349.02
courtyard 455.01
cousin 053.03 071.30 207.12 238.25 298.23 354.33 393.32 413.20 436.09 577.25 608.07
covenant 321.27 527.22 552.06
cover 141.15
covertly 606.27
covetousness 318.34 620.06
cow 199.07 204.18 236.14 241.22 325.34 346.21 356.03 452.16 486.06 529.34 599.06 608.20
coward 344.07 480.27
cowboy 105.35
cowpuncher 386.30
cowslip 511.31
crab 009.31
crack 173.25 262.12 332.07 449.32
cracked 056.24
crackle 082.26 142.01
cradle 276.F5 444.13 562.16
crag 051.28
crake 144.33
cramp 392.05 392.11
crash 017.25 230.26 338.08

crater 129.34
craven 262.F3
crawl 134.02 186.19 497.15
crazy 009.08 528.07
cream 292.22 461.03 526.29
creamy 337.16
creation 350.14 585.01
creative 300.20 300.24
creator 129.34 386.25 411.15
creature 004.29 386.25 465.34 487.20 549.29
credible 536.32
credulous 568.03
creed 412.29
creep 075.21 158.08 158.08 323.05 467.10
cremate 366.17
cremation 342.19
cress 491.19
crest 023.19 312.32 596.06
crick 334.19
cricket 037.20 055.07 056.24 249.35 549.29
crime 243.09
crimson 119.17 326.33 350.28 570.34 578.04
crinkly 275.27
crinoline 008.30 460.10
criterion 150.04
crocodile 570.34
crook 178.33
croon 186.19
cropper 382.19
cross 029.09 029.09 137.22 222.24 245.13 256.31 288.03 326.06 331.15 336.02 339.32 343.08 374.33 390.18 527.15 542.14
crossbones 308.F2
crosslegged 297.28
crossquestion 487.27
crossword 178.04
crouch 008.22
crow 134.30 262.F3 347.05 427.03
crowbar 086.13
crowd 233.36 420.36
crown 043.32 610.11
crowner 567.30
crozier 104.14
crubeen 258.35
crucifixion 192.18
crudity 538.10
cruel 159.30 206.08
cruelty 285.F2 505.36 538.10
cruise 186.19
cruiser 085.01 480.25
crumb 304.29 563.24
crupper 010.13
crusader 464.14 516.31
crush 344.16 376.11
crusher 516.31
crust 042.33 624.36
crusty 144.33
crwth 041.22
cry 087.18 093.13 164.19 199.19 233.36 316.22 325.34 395.32 535.03
crybaby 300.17 423.05
crystal 378.19
crystallization 086.04
cteis 522.30 539.03
cube 284.14
cuckoo 378.14 511.08
cucumber 279.F27
cuddle 330.25 376.23
cuff 322.36 339.12 614.10
culpa 023.16 072.04 105.18 139.35 175.29 238.21 238.21 238.21 297.10 311.26 331.03 332.32 363.20 426.17 433.30 506.09 536.09 606.23 618.01
culpable 363.32 396.23 406.33
culprit 504.26 538.15
culture 213.14 303.21 523.14 569.35
culvert 178.12
cumulus 375.29 624.28
cuneiform 198.25 524.20
cunning 223.28 576.28 579.15
cunningness 590.14
cunt 075.16 084.23 131.35 139.05 185.14 189.19 198.25 201.33 203.12 221.06 288.04 295.28 297.09 305.R1 310.13 338.17 345.30 357.14 357.16 357.30 378.13 390.31 394.31 497.10 504.11 524.20 525.05 538.16 553.33 581.16 603.32 611.04 622.10
cup 008.12 038.16 236.31 383.20 428.27 448.14 462.06 519.33 542.10 542.13
cupboard 321.28
cupola 242.04
cur 214.30 258.01 601.03
curate 242.03 301.19
curd 241.25
cure 110.22
curfew 145.34 244.08 436.02 586.21
curiosity 014.02 157.26 434.30 472.03
curious 093.06 261.25 278.F2 508.11
curl 234.15 331.18
curly 080.35 143.20
currant 075.12 141.35 183.22 288.F5
current 075.12
curry 404.31 456.05
currycomb 550.20
curse 145.34 180.11 222.30 241.25 251.02 311.07 317.22 319.27 319.29 320.02 320.12 322.01 322.05 322.09 322.17 322.18 322.19 323.08 328.04 339.06 343.02 361.23 404.32 459.24 594.36 600.11
cursorily 447.07
cursory 162.11
curtsy 623.11
curvature 409.17
curve 178.36
cushion 393.32
cushy 562.31
custard 464.30 555.19
custom 322.07 406.26 532.01 534.02 560.33
customary 349.25
customer 312.28
cut 179.11 285.16 365.04 534.32
cutaway 548.16
cute 019.02
Cuticura 237.29 291.F6
cutlass 516.05
cutthroat 091.11
cycle 115.16 119.23 134.16
cyclist 145.11 245.21
cyclometer 614.27
cygnet 341.10
cynically 370.09
cynosure 234.13
cypress 550.03
cyst 596.28
czar 072.03 341.17 344.33

dachshund 548.15
dactylo 478.27
dad 273.F8 283.F2 353.11 481.20 539.12 626.10
dada 271.03 518.30
daddy 024.14 104.08 161.23 179.17 628.08
daddylonglegs 498.03
dado 291.F3
daedal 179.17
Daffeydowndilly 040.29
daffodil 350.17 475.09 530.03
daft 221.33 225.17
dagger 180.11
dail 256.28
daily 198.06 411.19 500.15 501.20 531.01 603.08 608.28
daintily 236.22
dainty 060.36 276.16
daisy 597.23
dam 210.07 338.25 525.18
damage 541.19
damn 022.10 052.05 057.08 078.33 093.34 107.36 113.05 118.22 139.18 143.27 172.36 214.23 223.21 225.18 262.09 289.F4 300.06 320.14 326.13 347.29 353.01 353.08 357.07 363.05 365.21 365.21 376.16 417.21 424.12 424.32 441.33 442.22 445.22 455.24 463.36 464.21 469.20 471.02 471.03 484.16 509.09 513.27 515.06 521.08 521.09 536.16 545.36 547.25 568.03 599.31 607.02 615.26 619.06 619.33 624.14 625.20
damnation 058.08 068.34 561.28 593.21
damp 488.19
damsel 226.16 226.16 585.07 595.06
dance 089.28 105.10 330.34 333.08 341.01 346.06 513.11 513.13
dancer 098.12 513.16
dandelion 535.01 587.26
Dane 079.35 252.19 340.09 369.12 518.23 593.02 593.11 593.11 594.12
dangerous 296.16 296.17
Danish 105.18
dapper 199.14
dapple 007.02
dare 353.10 405.05
dark 096.01 207.08 269.03 313.19 351.09 359.02 385.35 478.35 523.17 582.28
darkest 442.33
darkness 407.12 427.11 470.07 607.25 625.27

darling 232.13 242.08 252.28 300.R1 413.25 550.23 601.17 624.23
darn 177.02 201.03 448.07 513.27
dart 357.09
dash 172.36
date 347.08 377.35 550.32
daughter 019.29 068.14 127.02 135.34 199.35 215.14 245.22 314.30 326.07 333.29 358.21 372.03 376.10 379.21 396.25 396.26 396.26 396.26 411.34 413.07 415.13 444.26 472.21 498.14 514.24 520.14 526.35 543.15 558.22 584.32 595.05 616.04
dawn 091.24 130.13 350.28 455.24
day 006.23 009.05 051.01 052.17 053.05 070.03 071.23 074.06 074.06 095.06 136.27 156.07 177.20 192.19 199.04 203.20 231.07 240.09 257.31 279.F26 283.F2 285.29 310.18 316.26 338.33 346.27 379.20 398.27 413.10 453.13 453.23 485.20 493.27 519.32 531.01 562.16 597.19 608.36 608.36
dayboy 179.08
daybreak 546.23
daylight 328.23 412.06 427.17 617.15
daze 617.29
dazzle 089.28
deacon 055.30 369.11 440.01
dead 006.10 011.07 013.31 025.23 034.06 054.05 055.05 089.28 134.36 185.31 186.08 221.07 239.05 251.16 251.24 258.09 264.F1 277.13 283.F2 309.03 310.24 317.04 321.29 323.36 328.28 340.20 342.03 344.09 378.18 409.02 416.30 420.30 424.05 424.21 467.17 496.04 499.06 499.06 499.06 499.18 516.25 539.12 540.24 580.16 620.19 621.03
deadly 040.12
deaf 016.12 073.20 087.24 088.25 089.33 136.29 138.27 149.03 175.25 200.16 221.32 268.L4 288.23 354.33 467.17 476.21 491.30 496.04 512.14 517.02 535.31 571.03 619.10
deafmute 016.14
deal 229.23 366.30
dealer 325.16
dean 015.06 047.23 047.24 077.14 084.04 086.22 129.12 139.22 201.08 237.18 288.19 323.36 330.06 334.13 353.31 359.14 372.17 379.36 385.16 389.10 414.01 420.29 438.14 452.02 479.32 480.10 496.08 503.21 562.30 594.27 622.20
deanery 261.16
dear 007.05 049.21 079.24 079.28 092.21 105.18 105.34 116.11 136.20 140.08 140.08 160.08 161.14 178.28 180.05 196.15 197.17 206.17 208.29 224.10 224.10 225.32 244.29 277.L4 291.28 299.21 299.21 305.07 317.34 319.24 329.17 333.33 337.26 344.32 365.33 366.24 370.09 371.06 372.22 374.18 375.32 395.14 407.02 413.17 426.09 466.23 476.21 479.02 527.07 557.22 570.03 578.20 580.11 601.08 601.17 601.18 603.26 608.36 608.36 625.31
dearchase 553.23
dearest 527.03 528.10 583.19 617.07
dearly 488.20 489.31 600.24
dearth 392.34
death 008.22 011.32 079.17 095.30 158.15 167.30 199.01 318.13 349.26 379.20 407.12 416.09 416.10 626.31 626.31
deathless 481.22
deathwatch 517.36
debacle 011.01
debauch 169.21 319.04
debauchery 350.16
debility 607.03
debt 172.17 458.19
Decameron 561.24
decasyllabic 386.06
decease 069.15 423.27 574.05
deceased 242.02
deceiver 412.23
December 024.11 087.07 282.26
decent 006.23 262.01 405.28 578.14
deception 270.F4
decide 008.32
decidedly 468.21
deciduous 580.19
decimal 440.15 566.12
deck 601.02
declination 603.23
decline 083.24
decode 482.35
dedicate 243.25
deener 170.03
deep 095.30 196.18 241.24 277.13 287.F3 367.35 532.28
deepest 506.06
deeply 320.01
deepsea 029.24 075.13 366.14
deerchase 553.23
deface 448.11
defamation 509.28
defame 092.24
defence 084.22
defend 092.24
defendant 523.07
defiance 084.22
defile 075.05 233.33 335.06
define 051.06 389.16 510.10
definitively 613.35
degenerate 422.08
degree 279.F13
deity 143.04
delay 084.08 492.14
delete 272.08
deliberate 300.21 300.23
delicately 525.02
delicious 128.29 148.01 247.20 266.F3 351.23 370.18 392.33 421.04 486.34 528.17 616.10
deliciously 038.04
delight 027.21 135.30 136.07 183.36 195.02 232.01 272.08 345.31 450.12 484.08 504.21 540.06 615.15
delightful 118.32 291.25 497.24
delinquent 107.10
deliquesce 251.09
delirium 379.17 502.30
deliver 542.31
Delphic 140.09
delta 229.23 568.32
deltoid 531.05
deluge 136.07 331.18
demented 279.F06
demerara 334.05
demijohn 229.23 268.07
democracy 291.08
demon 142.23 225.26 261.L1 577.32 577.32
denominational 614.27
denominator 283.07
deny 043.30 061.34 162.16
depart 222.29 536.02 625.31
department 364.07
depend 310.05
dependent 602.17
deplorable 224.10
deploy 009.12
deponent 269.31 602.17
deprave 536.25
depravity 328.17
deprecate 569.18
deprive 421.36
depth 199.01
deputy 277.09
derby 062.06 180.15 325.06 448.14
derelict 513.32
derivative 505.26
Derryman 045.20
Dervish 513.16
descend 222.35 317.31 610.28
describe 338.17
description 270.F4 414.05
desert 013.27 265.28
deserve 366.11
desiccate 026.31
desirously 470.13
desperate 267.F3 354.07
desperation 257.25 257.25 257.25 257.26 463.21
despot 354.07
destiny 162.03
destruction 140.18
detain 174.29 567.33
determine 170.11
detonate 353.24
detriment 353.04
detrimental 452.03
Deuteronomy 537.26
devalue 543.02
development 394.10 578.34
device 585.16
devil 005.23 021.06 024.25 028.04 037.18 043.26 050.02 106.26 147.02 149.06 149.07 178.35 183.33 186.09 186.09 186.10 186.10 205.10 220.28 222.25 227.22 239.33 243.22 297.22 300.04 303.F1 306.F1 314.05 315.13 316.36 317.03 321.29 329.03 332.06 332.06 364.25 473.21 499.18 503.17

505.32 511.12 535.15 545.29 566.20 578.13 580.14 583.27 622.35 626.31 626.33 626.33 627.04
devilish 513.16
devilment 578.34
devine 560.35 599.13
devise 340.22
devoid 072.11
devote 413.20
devotion 072.24
devour 023.32
devout 243.35 340.22
devoutly 319.35
dew 136.36 279.F02 330.11 367.24 597.31 598.09
dewdrop 439.18 568.10
dextrous 423.06
diadem 239.33
diagnose 254.01
diagnosis 411.29 421.26
diagonal 297.24
diagram 164.36 292.05
dialect 374.12
dialectic 322.31
dialectically 614.33
diamond 134.07 365.04 365.04 377.20 391.18 453.34 476.15 528.06
diarrhoea 467.19
diary 467.19 603.17 603.17
dibble 029.22
dickens 239.25 261.31 348.09 373.34 423.06 424.19 428.05 439.24 440.01 517.27 568.02 610.03
dictate 170.03 243.08
dictator 170.22 423.18
die 106.24 130.24 143.26 185.32 237.12 258.18 276.F2 321.04 335.02 375.13 376.29 392.08 392.11 392.11 407.36 420.13 448.09 452.16 486.06 488.18 506.06 514.25 527.23
diet 143.04 358.36 531.36
different 059.34 342.35 614.05 620.16
difficult 303.F1
difficulty 366.20
dig 586.13 586.13
digamma 300.26
digest 338.12
digestible 236.28
digestion 023.20
dilate 484.08
dim 536.16 617.31
dimension 367.27
dimensional 395.01
diminutive 278.F2
din 350.09 350.09 350.09 350.09
dingle 360.33
dinkum 373.34
dinner 110.03 121.34 131.04 262.F5
dinnertime 026.28
diocese 433.05
diode 319.24
dip 062.08
dirge 198.25 570.04
dirigible 006.02
dirt 387.10 394.18 600.25
dirty 007.06 049.21 076.25 095.10 105.18 136.21 160.08 178.28 180.15 196.15 197.18 199.14 206.17 305.07 317.34 319.24 333.33 337.26 366.24 370.09 374.18 492.16 521.19 548.06 570.03 601.17 615.12
disagreeable 301.F4
disappear 427.07 448.17
disappoint 090.16
disaster 338.12
discharge 431.25
disclose 063.27 543.14
discontent 318.20
discover 291.16 540.33 577.18
discovery 294.12 326.31
disdain 153.15 153.16
disease 415.11
disembark 388.20
disembowel 515.12
disentangle 161.13
disgrace 057.23 071.19 338.13
disguise 232.33 363.09 532.27
disgust 136.07 321.06
disgusted 610.01
dish 007.09 317.12
dishevel 608.05
dislike 163.12
dismal 301.27 440.15 566.12
disobedience 343.36
disorder 540.19
dispel 305.04
dispensation 095.01
displace 292.04
display 009.12 227.22
displease 292.04
dispute 043.36
dissect 073.02
dissolute 081.12
dissolve 215.22 608.05
distant 358.03 472.06
distend 169.20 317.31
distinct 297.21
distinguish 063.26 066.29
distinguished 342.13
distoma 597.21
distraction 140.18
distress 486.20
distribute 220.20 371.12
disturb 353.06 378.20 457.12 585.34
disunite 417.04
ditch 008.22
ditto 255.33 442.27
diversion 009.35 285.F3 332.36
divert 203.11
divide 212.17
dividend 451.19
divine 212.31 252.04 389.16 536.18
divinity 373.20
divorce 243.35 255.24 315.01 348.15 365.29 370.05 388.07 616.15
divulge 255.24 285.F3
Djinn 023.22
dobbin 316.36 600.23
dock 224.07 287.F2
doctor 044.02 134.18 170.22 241.15 314.30 413.07 492.22
doctrine 326.33
document 350.28 358.30 369.24 386.20 390.29 482.20 528.33 619.19
dodecane 100.30 435.09 523.26
dodge 394.07 578.13
dog 188.18 215.04 267.F6 278.23 282.F3 511.32 597.19
dogbox 225.21
doggerel 294.23 498.16
dogmatic 411.23
dogooder 358.16 602.09
dogwatch 517.36
doldrum 051.34
dollar 189.22 278.F2
dolomite 317.34
dolphin 211.21 513.09 566.20 601.22
domestic 038.11 411.23
domination 498.34
dominican 424.03
donkey 020.25 285.14 347.10 373.04 383.23 405.06 427.11 555.13 566.31 568.23 568.26
doom 011.04 326.04 548.13 586.30 624.15
doomsday 347.08 588.34 602.20
doomster 545.30
door 014.20 020.18 021.16 021.17 021.19 067.19 198.29 200.18 224.25 257.27 279.F26 333.01 333.03 334.30 354.30 371.16 388.02 395.13 556.34
doorbell 463.17
doorknocker 572.03
doornail 329.24
doorpost 221.32
doorway 086.26
dope 319.18 326.24
dormer 327.22
dormitory 593.21
dory 398.18
dose 376.13
dot 542.14
dotage 074.16
dote 327.06
double 113.18 267.L2 267.L2 267.L2 294.01 297.22 445.31 450.22 515.29 583.27
doublebarrelled 286.F4
doublebedded 245.30
doublebreasted 320.07
doublejointed 310.31
doubloon 432.20
doubt 089.13 339.26 462.22 513.03
doubtful 478.07
dough 317.01
dove 136.13 136.30 148.07 202.08 245.18 358.05 365.23 377.22 403.16 579.15 626.33
downside 356.34
downstairs 219.03
doze 438.36
dozen 155.27 212.20 330.07 335.27 415.06
drachma 182.24
drag 624.32
dragon 017.35 358.29 479.32
drain 049.32 335.02
drake 363.07
drama 302.32
dramatise 133.26
dramaturge 496.24

draper 529.12 608.05 608.06 608.06
draught 316.26 327.06 413.25
draughts 128.18
draw 616.25
drawbridge 389.35
drawer 133.17
drawers 065.19 068.33 205.12 224.23 224.23 224.27 238.01 276.F1 379.04 396.18 457.26 465.06 491.18 511.29 546.07 566.11 610.36
drawingroom 126.20
dray 133.29
dread 473.11
dreadful 347.16 348.14 609.35
dream 017.17 049.32 056.18 069.14 110.11 115.32 143.27 148.27 198.34 198.35 199.06 199.09 277.17 293.12 295.13 302.32 320.21 327.22 342.30 351.17 370.18 378.10 381.19 399.34 406.27 462.09 488.19 517.02 527.06 527.06 571.13 598.02 601.17 601.28 614.03 623.31
drear 491.30
dreary 600.02
dreg 025.14
dress 366.33 407.28 555.19
dribble 337.24 555.19
drink 017.35 129.06 182.24 321.29 345.24 348.11 408.36 416.10
drinker 311.03
drip 337.24 549.04 571.13
drive 078.24 136.29 214.35 276.F2 395.36 539.29 583.35 622.02
driver 224.03
droll 444.35
dromedary 005.26 443.31
drone 099.16 321.28 333.22
droop 415.02
drop 023.22 034.06 074.17 089.01 089.19 204.24 344.09 484.04 491.18 568.10
drown 321.28
drug 316.30 358.35
drughouse 256.34
druid 078.24 279.F27 320.21 378.28 549.13
druidess 331.09
drum 122.07 464.21
drumhead 349.02
drunk 017.35
drunkard 049.29
dry 078.21 447.13 540.36 584.09
dual 089.04 238.31 251.33 290.23 360.10 372.18 565.03
dub 037.31
Dublin 003.08 003.23 007.06 007.12 013.04 013.14 016.35 017.12 018.07 019.12 020.16 021.06 024.01 024.25 029.22 034.01 037.03 044.11 057.32 060.35 061.02 064.03 066.18 072.34 072.34 076.25 079.29 081.31 095.10 097.09 098.28 099.34 105.18 106.26 116.13 129.20 136.01 136.02 136.21 138.23 139.13 139.24 140.27 153.18 158.04 160.27 160.29 169.23 174.26 178.35 180.15 196.08 196.15 197.05 197.18 197.20 197.20 197.26 199.14 201.19 206.18 208.33 215.14 219.08 222.25 227.22 232.05 243.22 244.24 244.34 245.14 248.07 250.36 254.17 264.15 266.06 287.05 290.16 293.12 295.31 301.27 303.07 305.07 309.13 310.07 311.16 311.32 314.05 315.24 316.36 317.34 319.25 320.07 323.35 326.25 326.34 328.03 328.03 329.03 329.14 329.19 331.19 332.06 332.06 332.10 333.33 335.28 337.26 337.26 337.29 341.17 342.25 346.15 347.35 350.15 353.19 362.02 362.36 364.25 365.18 366.24 367.22 368.33 368.34 370.09 370.19 372.16 373.19 373.20 374.18 375.06 376.11 377.22 383.23 403.16 413.25 426.18 432.20 437.06 443.16 445.31 447.23 448.11 461.02 462.19 479.18 480.28 480.28 480.30 480.30 480.30 484.21 488.26 489.21 490.17 492.16 495.04 514.06 520.25 534.29 535.15 539.24 546.17 546.17 548.06 550.34 553.27 555.14 555.14 560.12 565.22 566.20 566.20 569.20 570.03 578.14 580.22 582.21 583.25 583.27 586.15 590.29 593.24 596.12 600.11 602.19 603.27 603.29 615.12 620.03 622.35 623.24 625.27 625.36
Dubliner 049.22 193.02 339.31 594.05
ducal 182.23
duchess 171.25 171.26 171.27 209.06 229.33 391.36 461.09
duchy 498.14
duck 008.19 363.07 364.34 456.15
duckling 177.35 456.23
duel 441.28 442.27 565.03
duke 008.19 010.12 010.14 071.19 071.35 137.11 138.27 162.04 171.26 209.04 295.F1 329.29 354.19 354.19 367.18 367.20 371.36 375.04 417.30 441.07 456.31 519.26
dulcet 360.05
dull 031.24 327.35 427.17
duly 162.05
dumb 073.20 089.33 149.03 175.25 223.21 225.18 236.30 237.08 241.01 261.17 299.16 329.27 365.21 455.24 496.04 517.03 517.04 545.36 595.02 619.06
dumbbell 604.11
dumbfound 482.21
dumbshow 120.07 163.13 507.23
dumdum 238.31 353.35 354.01
dummy 372.05
dump 097.26 120.07 619.09
dumpling 028.19
dunghill 050.30
duodecimal 566.12
duodenum 437.13
dupe 157.29
duplicate 157.29
duplicator 534.05
during 243.11
dusk 158.08 158.09 158.19 158.20 594.30
dust 004.12 158.08 158.09 158.19 158.20 190.01 190.01 240.16 333.32 439.10 550.21 588.28 588.28 603.10 603.10
dusty 357.05
Dutch 021.20 070.04 105.18 105.23 140.03 364.34 371.06 485.13 553.33 622.20
Dutchman 327.23
dutifully 237.08
duty 143.04 150.06 327.01 568.25 600.25
Dvapara 595.28
dwell 064.04 199.10 264.F2
dwelling 209.33
dwindle 549.13
dye 358.36 593.03
dyke 100.31 431.12
dynamite 291.03
dynasty 567.15

each 016.08 209.27 295.33 527.29 537.34 546.16 562.21
eager 132.07 340.18 435.14
ear 020.27 103.05 117.15 154.10 214.09 225.29 231.30 278.L3 289.F6 371.25 421.23 485.21 485.27 533.33 588.27 588.28
earl 130.33 313.15 574.15
early 060.30 060.31 155.12 224.16 253.09 257.10 257.18 279.09 360.14 360.14 390.06 435.23 465.28 507.31
earn 024.05 291.06 324.03 433.31
earnest 141.23 233.20 534.08
earring 074.11 272.20 524.26
earth 018.04 036.35 069.03 090.15 104.03 158.16 178.07 207.22 208.03 231.22 240.28 313.36 326.34 494.12 496.11 590.13 615.24
earthcloset 551.25
earthquake 221.09
eartrumpet 247.32
earwig 020.23 021.01 031.11 048.16 083.06 091.11 098.28 098.32 098.32 134.16 149.13 173.09 175.25 193.13 221.28 238.31 243.17 243.17 255.05 284.25 301.08 311.11 312.16 315.26 320.26 320.27 327.27 327.32 339.14 351.25 359.26 360.32 360.32 367.33 373.24 375.19 382.25 390.04 393.13 413.23 414.36 421.12 434.11 435.19 445.36 467.28 485.21 491.30 496.12 496.15 496.15 496.35 512.25 520.06 537.19 539.04 552.21 553.26 559.25 560.15 565.14 568.26 581.06 588.34 593.03 602.21 615.16 619.12 622.32 625.02 625.17
ease 418.29 434.24

easily 231.13
east 018.35 203.15 325.22 373.03 374.31 418.27 494.14 502.06 523.05 534.15 557.02 571.11 571.18 578.30 595.01 595.01 597.11
Easter 210.35 407.08 413.08 584.09 623.08
eastern 604.26
eastward 569.28
easy 024.16 027.22 152.01 176.22 198.12 314.27 516.09 542.31
eat 012.10 142.02 224.03 300.16 318.15 376.36 378.03 385.16 392.05 397.25 405.18 433.11 480.22 597.35
eatable 181.23
ecclesiastic 447.34
echo 146.21 180.25 215.25 230.34 242.33 245.18 274.01 291.F1 291.F1 450.21 604.08
eclipse 603.02
economic 230.34 599.17
economical 131.31
economy 540.27
ecumenic 440.35
Edda 597.06
Eden 053.13 069.10 069.10 104.03 130.03 183.08 263.21 324.36 597.35
edge 506.26
edgewise 288.05
eel 165.21 229.22
e'en 237.35
effect 081.24 116.01 341.12 474.05
effervescence 452.19
effigy 018.34
effort 560.16
egad 518.12 520.10
egg 012.14 019.09 069.13 088.17 088.21 090.28 124.14 178.33 184.13 184.27 184.30 199.06 199.16 229.01 257.19 308.14 308.F2 339.03 352.05 366.26 379.19 381.06 405.34 406.16 406.16 406.36 463.28 485.10 584.09
eggnogg 026.03
egoarch 525.10
egotist 137.08
egregious 143.10
Egyptian 005.23 198.01
eight 187.20 202.02 283.09 354.29 382.13 397.20 601.14 601.15 617.27
eighteenth 567.15
eighth 138.33 539.33
Eire 227.01 324.07 331.23 344.31 353.32 358.21 361.28 365.13 500.14 501.19 515.01 547.32 601.06 604.24
either 029.09 053.04 201.34 209.22 458.23 578.34
ejaculate 129.10 243.08 338.27
ejaculation 089.10 145.25
eject 182.35
elastic 447.34
elbow 036.16 060.14 208.01 303.04 372.01 494.29 535.31 557.17
elbowroom 052.25
elder 017.19 372.34
elect 510.35 622.03
election 346.13
elector 374.17
electrical 415.01
electrically 309.24
electricity 284.L1
electrolyse 067.08
electrolysis 163.31
elegant 014.04 129.17
elegiac 156.26
element 163.02 286.L4
elephant 244.35 427.22 502.10 545.36 599.06
elevation 160.11 338.06
eleven 019.24 201.27 215.22 220.21 329.06 341.20 347.04 378.23 388.12 403.02 517.33 517.33 517.34 586.25 597.05 606.18
elevenhundred 274.L3
eleventh 032.31
elf 079.29 261.03
elfin 203.31
elicit 196.21
eligible 482.21
eliminate 131.32 394.33
elixir 133.19
ell 293.16 535.28
elm 153.10 293.14
elocution 381.18
elocutionist 072.16
elopement 394.10
eloquent 283.08
else 197.07 620.09
elude 448.27
elysium 453.32
emancipate 239.21 322.35
emancipation 310.36
emancipator 342.26
embalm 277.F1 499.01
embark 388.20
embarrass 354.17
embarrassment 375.26
embattle 227.36
embattled 140.33
embellish 356.30 357.32
ember 527.29
embezzle 352.30
embezzlement 375.26
emblem 467.11
emboss 404.29 546.10
embrace 244.29 354.17 365.35 388.05 467.05 537.06 581.18
embroil 324.17
emerge 310.24
emergency 241.06
eminence 494.27 504.20
emolument 409.25
emperor 070.25 175.11 273.16
emphasis 329.34
empire 353.29 367.25 497.29 516.15 549.16
empress 548.02
empty 295.24 517.33
empyrean 516.15
enamored 092.27 158.11 180.03
enchant 237.11
enclose 356.07 537.15
encomium 278.04
encompass 543.12
encounter 186.24 321.28
encyclopedia 334.03
end 048.17 048.17 054.05 111.15 214.01 272.05 313.20 331.12 346.08 417.23 458.08 505.12 537.12 598.16
endear 092.21 519.20
endless 226.36
endlessness 613.27
endorse 127.28
endure 234.29 368.35
enema 282.21
enemy 008.23 160.22 339.09 542.18 549.22 620.06
engagement 159.08
engager 313.29
engine 005.31 207.29 207.30 224.03 361.11
engineer 146.19 457.32
English 008.23 016.06 124.07 233.33 275.F6 351.08 468.18 485.12 485.29 532.10 539.36 584.04 609.15
Englishman 181.01 284.L1 537.01
engulf 306.06
enisle 605.20
enjoin 244.29
enjoy 060.08 185.28 456.01 465.10
enjoyable 529.36
enlist 353.34
enough 078.36 158.18 246.11 251.21 308.02 469.21 502.01 535.21 623.19 623.20
enquire 003.21 229.31
enquiry 475.19
ensign 112.08 357.14
ensue 336.13
enter 350.15 552.20
entertain 348.29
entertainment 335.26 413.10 534.08
enthuse 129.33
enthusiasm 425.15
enthusiast 260.18
enticement 239.08
entire 229.17
entirely 004.36 059.13 299.25 537.16
entirety 597.07
entitled 070.16 104.04
entity 336.32 538.07
entomology 101.17
entrance 240.29 407.05 423.06
entreat 246.06 302.24
entreaty 329.32
entrust 356.29
entry 235.28
envelop 244.15 324.29 339.09 378.35
envy 318.35 541.16 582.12 620.06
epaulette 343.24 623.17
epexegesis 296.10 511.18
ephemeral 369.33
epicene 019.11 523.34
epidemic 539.36
epidermis 497.15
epilepsy 232.30
epiphany 626.05
episcopally 513.11
epistemology 374.17
epistle 411.15 617.05

epitaph 420.11
epithalamion 040.14
epithet 226.06
epoch 236.31
eponymous 210.35
equal 297.07 505.17
equality 133.32
equanimity 599.17
equation 131.32
equiangular 286.21
equilateral 286.19 297.27
equine 254.31
equinox 134.18
equivalent 285.16
era 256.23
ere 057.30 256.01
erection 343.18 539.03 545.33
erector 126.10
erg 167.07
Erin 016.21 017.23 021.24 022.09 053.13 062.19 112.33 127.26 130.03 130.34 136.26 138.21 144.18 148.33 180.06 182.06 198.12 207.21 228.04 228.15 232.16 242.01 264.31 265.29 267.13 272.20 288.F6 305.33 312.01 313.17 315.12 316.04 320.24 321.17 328.16 328.17 338.26 338.32 358.21 362.22 362.23 363.33 364.21 371.36 379.11 389.06 391.01 391.16 392.27 394.22 398.05 398.20 405.19 412.25 421.14 426.15 426.18 427.06 446.21 465.27 469.21 491.36 492.35 493.13 493.27 510.24 510.27 521.01 524.26 525.06 525.21 530.21 537.10 538.18 538.26 589.28 600.07 604.08
ermine 357.08
errand 232.16
errant 229.11
erroneous 617.30
error 036.35 140.32 419.34 431.14
Erse 273.27 273.28 314.27 489.09 507.22
erstwhile 319.04
erupt 386.35
escape 004.36 076.19 158.17 579.05
escapement 151.19
escatology 428.22
escort 203.21
Eskimo 198.02 276.F4 572.16 572.17 585.24
especially 436.19 440.19
espouse 503.18 548.11
esquire 102.16 205.22 254.20 420.22 570.15 557.01
essay 137.25
essence 608.04
establish 290.26
establishment 523.27
estate 343.17
estimation 204.02
etcetera 152.10 152.10 160.05 235.17 303.21 379.31 379.31
etch 205.27 423.35
eternal 527.23 532.06
eternally 298.17
eternity 240.20 406.28
ethical 354.10
Ethiop 223.28
etiquette 556.30
etymologist 107.13 113.04
etymology 077.26 101.17 417.04
eucharist 304.R3
eunuch 291.01 562.33
European 088.01 191.04 205.29 419.14 598.15
eustachian 535.26
evaporate 004.24
eve 017.26
evening 222.32 285.27 538.31 613.30
evensong 350.08
event 238.07
eventide 204.14
eventime 051.32
eventual 405.36
evergreen 014.34 019.23 032.29 221.19 279.03 285.L2 329.06
everlasting 222.30 414.29 499.02 503.30
everybody 113.34 228.36 234.13 315.20 321.15 324.11 329.18 356.10 361.12 361.12 378.05 460.12 475.20 516.10 534.01 568.04 597.21 612.15
everyman 534.14
everyone 209.27 557.09 624.26
everything 299.02
everytime 130.35
everywhere 131.07
evidence 094.28 366.03 374.32
evident 186.33
evidently 166.11
evil 140.03 435.18 466.32
evince 090.06
evocation 178.18
evolution 073.32
ewer 348.25 493.19
exaggerator 619.30
examination 087.34 143.08 497.02
example 099.33 254.01 280.23 304.24 342.08 521.32 561.09
exarchon 285.09
exasperate 251.31
excellency 084.14 521.04 535.12
excess 159.25 524.01 625.02
excessively 138.09
exchange 016.08
exchequer 308.04 423.19
excise 457.16
exclaim 093.19 315.19
exclamation 342.19
exclude 189.08
excommander 240.15
excuse 016.05 086.01
execute 086.01 346.06
executive 363.09
exercise 231.27 286.08 437.12
exhaust 013.12 091.27 542.30
exhibit 602.22
exile 127.26 148.33 392.27 415.09
existence 148.18 222.28 387.12
exit 171.36 368.19 534.30
exodus 353.18
expand 298.27
expanse 385.36
expectation 245.31
expedient 317.10 317.15
expedition 455.06
expel 176.07 230.05 420.25 488.22 618.34
experimentally 296.26
expertly 240.10
expiration 058.08
explain 149.30 369.02 505.28
explanation 063.31
explication 369.02
explode 172.19 249.15
exploit 124.29
expose 344.16 503.18 548.11
exposition 419.11
expostulate 581.13
express 501.20
expression 064.31 316.34
expressly 240.10
expulsion 518.23
expurgate 219.06
exquisite 412.08
exserviceman 429.20
extend 005.28 086.22 476.07
extension 371.24
extent 524.30
extenuation 558.12
exterior 105.11 254.13
extinction 083.25 371.24
extol 258.15 258.15
extra 324.29 419.04 601.33
extract 284.15
extraordinary 295.17 505.14
extreme 227.32 432.31
eye 018.16 038.16 088.17 114.01 114.02 143.14 152.03 182.22 183.15 189.20 198.09 199.06 202.02 207.08 241.12 244.32 247.31 254.30 275.18 292.24 304.R1 310.30 311.33 311.33 314.33 314.34 317.26 317.26 319.27 331.09 349.27 353.34 357.33 419.26 425.25 425.30 426.15 426.16 434.13 451.25 463.30 481.35 482.35 504.16 505.18 509.28 552.08 585.04 598.25 598.25 604.25 607.31 620.15
eyeball 075.17 247.21 389.28 557.12 616.14
eyebrow 389.28
eyeglass 405.20
eyelash 482.05
eyelet 533.02
eyesore 107.23 394.30 484.05
eyewitness 254.10 515.30
eyrie 048.16 053.05 207.08

fable 113.15 422.22
fabler 419.13
face 004.22 012.09 056.18 077.18 077.18 083.36 085.30 124.12 160.19 177.36 177.36 266.22 266.22 285.F5 311.31 323.08 331.03 333.23 344.35 358.03 373.14 374.11 374.11 383.21 388.05 408.01 415.28 416.05 416.06 432.32 461.02 509.32 542.11 578.27 593.05
face-to-face 153.21
facsimile 358.03 484.34
fact 086.05 150.11 199.33 248.26 288.09 288.13 300.03 345.04 345.07 493.02 510.17 516.26 523.33 532.15 532.29 576.02 607.03

factotum 516.24
fade 528.13
faeces 301.04 358.35 418.11 461.02
fagend 452.34
fail 143.24 424.01
fain 251.18 623.18
faint 008.31 157.24 269.F1 278.F4 331.29 603.36 621.14
fair 018.07 117.05 171.34 178.03 323.09 366.11 420.26 528.11 541.31
fairest 206.17
fairheaded 562.24
fairly 278.F4
fairy 011.09 048.14 149.22 176.07 242.25 281.03 298.28 319.12 328.31 340.09 340.10 353.27 389.23 412.13 553.22 600.34 617.18 628.02
faith 091.36 105.30 141.06 222.30 379.21 381.09 489.30 569.35 603.24
faithful 034.06 552.24 613.28
faithfully 124.32 424.12
fake 264.19
fall 004.15 112.33 130.14 143.24 208.31 215.36 234.02 239.35 251.16 261.03 344.34 345.11 361.18 368.19 377.26 386.08 443.06 464.05 490.05 597.12 603.22
fallingsickness 530.02
false 127.04 247.22 365.36 378.12 423.28 492.07 615.33
falsehood 131.18 291.20 411.22
fambles 269.16
fame 163.02 241.18 370.28
familiar 237.35 345.02
familiarity 606.22
familiarly 414.34
family 196.15 273.L2 299.F4 314.36 340.15 441.02 582.05
famish 251.12 451.35
famous 007.12 073.09 167.24 192.24 272.28 314.36 451.35 462.17 463.33 550.29
fanatic 450.27
fanciful 426.21 446.03
fancy 004.31 061.22 112.36 226.14 302.31 340.29 346.18 458.07
fandango 187.01
fanny 171.27 171.28 230.20
fantastic 182.04 470.18
fantasy 112.36
far 292.19 298.28 375.31 452.20 471.19
farce 004.17 301.04 340.35 356.12
fare 323.09 454.28 469.21 480.21 553.34
farer 102.21 365.01
farewell 225.29 225.30 225.30 242.21 244.22 345.14 345.14 363.19 371.28 379.32 382.28 590.16 626.33
farfamed 022.36 085.25 241.18 370.28
farm 434.02 566.14
farmer 164.11 236.09 240.31 372.29 424.04 440.20 577.13
faroff 129.36
farrier 404.19
fart 005.15 085.09 116.29 127.09 127.10 248.14 252.30 258.04 316.28 369.12 369.12 371.05 415.05 450.23 553.34 581.09 596.15 596.15 599.08 610.06 613.23
farther 202.16
farthing 202.02 451.01 567.34
fashion 148.09 320.07 333.21 339.10
fashionable 396.25
fast 435.25 473.24 512.15 552.08
faster 061.20
fat 239.17 296.22 531.07
fatal 563.10
fate 300.22 300.23 463.21
father 011.23 027.03 029.07 052.16 057.04 065.32 071.20 093.20 115.21 129.04 147.20 153.31 157.16 161.27 164.11 164.12 180.35 182.18 202.02 202.16 203.11 213.32 229.01 232.28 235.05 240.22 241.20 242.10 276.14 279.F32 281.F1 286.22 288.F7 310.35 322.12 326.24 329.07 329.33 331.14 333.26 339.36 361.21 365.01 368.04 378.25 378.35 396.22 413.16 414.36 419.09 424.04 467.12 481.19 481.32 483.16 494.31 496.26 530.36 536.34 551.14 565.20 566.24 589.21 595.06 596.07 599.06 612.30 614.31 617.25
father-in-law 267.F5 325.15
fathom 312.07
fatuous 527.34
fault 354.18 357.04 581.30
favour 052.33 124.31 456.05
favourite 012.18 294.19 347.36
fay 331.02
fealty 543.21
fear 161.01 263.F2 343.35 370.31 451.17 497.16 519.15
fearless 493.27
feast 086.12 405.31 408.23 514.04 598.11 600.34 613.09
feather 005.20 565.20
featherweight 559.27
feature 004.22 173.33 493.02
February 015.35 473.03
federal 336.22
feeble 160.33 160.34 346.01
feed 172.08 172.09 516.12 597.17 619.17 626.10
feedkeeper 142.24
feel 006.08 126.17 144.13 144.14 201.19 276.06 295.33 313.32 323.15 366.25 422.32 455.33 490.05
feeling 537.29
feign 157.24
felicitation 491.30
felicity 154.34 494.22 540.26 610.08
feline 072.22 268.18
felix 023.16 072.04 105.18 139.35 175.29 263.29 297.10 311.26 331.02 332.31 363.20 426.17 433.30 506.09 606.23 618.01
fell 440.24 526.22
fellah 029.07 338.27
fellow 162.24 229.19 278.F1 355.27 357.32 436.19 444.13 506.16 506.18 569.25
fellowship 349.18
felly 447.04
felon 007.31
female 437.31 539.22 564.03 581.18 617.23
feminine 093.14 237.01 241.15 251.31 268.18 434.20
femininity 166.25 606.22
feminiser 242.13
fend 224.26
fender 223.26
Fenian 277.05 277.F7 346.27 481.13 506.17 521.33
Fenland 245.16
ferment 132.29 221.36
fern 571.10
ferocious 182.05
ferociously 423.04
ferrule 547.23
ferry 367.20
fervid 568.02
festive 074.09
festoon 256.09
fetch 014.28 494.34 506.07 594.09
feud 141.23 498.14
feudal 354.07
fever 015.35 171.27 372.09
few 316.24
fib 569.08 601.21
fickle 266.28
fiction 248.05 285.26 336.20 532.15
fiddle 131.28 198.26 603.04
fiddlefaddle 531.28
fiddler 569.24
field 099.29 136.13 142.15 142.15 193.04 246.04 247.35 273.L3 310.26 326.04 340.08 340.22 366.25 422.32 543.14 602.15
fieldday 009.05
fiend 223.26 345.33
fierce 018.02
fiercer 335.18
fife 370.28 370.28 464.20
fifteen 601.13
fifth 087.04 323.20 616.10
fifthly 288.11
fifty 025.34 114.23 208.26
fig 169.23
fight 090.13 282.11 423.17 442.27
fighter 566.10
figure 282.11 298.17 335.30 354.30 420.09 452.34
Fijian 546.18
filch 594.09
filial 613.04
filibeg 099.11
filing 246.24
fill 006.08 050.33
film 264.19
filmfun 398.25
filter 189.05 324.30 474.07 492.18 537.06
filth 128.24 160.12
filthy 229.30 360.05

final 269.29 455.14
finance 541.07
finch 486.17
find 106.25 156.16 302.17 332.04 418.15 529.02 537.15
finder 223.26
fine 005.11 071.07 093.08 301.07 330.18 343.25 347.01 622.35
finery 493.22
finest 357.01 380.10
finger 144.35 250.08 282.11 341.11 349.01 349.30 352.29 357.11 357.14 419.26 449.24 455.33 496.18 511.31 548.19 612.35 617.02 621.04
finish 004.17 007.15 017.14 040.18 130.11 228.14 230.07 322.20 325.12 380.09 452.36 621.01
finite 452.36 505.24
Finnish 285.22 287.F4 288.09
fire 128.19 185.27 209.04 222.30 225.24 244.12 322.10 322.23 347.35 350.12 368.07 370.34 394.09 436.29 438.17 483.15 553.10 538.27
firebird 024.11 595.33
fire-escape 150.32 228.29 388.03
firefly 029.07 199.36
fireplace 461.19 624.34
firm 476.12 571.10
firmament 258.23 274.23 449.02 494.03
firmly 610.05
first 049.32 113.06 135.25 138.32 141.06 157.15 162.04 167.20 202.32 203.16 227.05 228.33 238.24 262.12 282.25 285.11 285.12 286.09 286.19 288.09 291.27 298.11 303.03 309.13 311.16 326.08 328.19 334.13 338.16 340.35 342.24 343.36 350.13 356.01 356.12 356.32 366.01 378.13 380.10 408.36 435.25 444.18 481.34 506.15 506.17 546.12 566.35 576.27 607.28
firstborn 178.10 210.04
firy 319.34 553.22 628.02
fiscal 064.31
fish 007.08 013.34 050.33 051.13 051.15 073.06 085.29 098.24 137.11 198.09 199.16 264.07 318.20 320.16 325.21 371.22 407.17 451.13 525.20 525.31 546.06 572.04
fisherman 153.29 256.25
fishfry 356.17
fishmonger 029.26 144.30
fist 083.29 311.31 323.16 557.10
fisticuffs 202.20
fit 333.03 603.04
five 077.14 183.13 282.30 282.30 282.31 282.31 282.32 283.04 323.20 352.29 403.04 420.27 457.13
fivepence 142.01 266.L1 425.14
fix 200.05 516.12
fizz 421.09
flabbergast 496.15
flabby 304.R3
flag 267.14
flagrant 051.36
flame 080.24 089.10 246.05 289.13 464.06 473.19 499.13 502.20 547.15
flannel 101.18 452.09
flap 383.09
flash 182.12 222.22 263.F2 395.36 426.29 594.16
flashlamp 377.27
flask 141.08 370.33
flat 121.34 162.09 549.13
flattery 139.04
flaxy 140.16
fleece 320.10
fleet 388.18
Flemish 376.05 397.24
flesh 073.06 137.11 138.08 149.05 205.08 220.28 254.12 325.21 341.33 378.04 422.03 505.32 571.29 621.33
fleshmarket 378.08
fleshpot 192.29 347.11 550.14
flick 199.35
flippant 468.10
flirt 449.26
flirtation 352.07
float 023.35 082.20 501.31
flog 514.06
flood 072.35 209.30 388.18
floor 021.13 086.01 104.14 107.18 107.18 136.09 142.07 143.04 268.01 313.05 389.07 606.34
floorwalker 443.21
flora 086.01
floral 250.27 406.36
flossy 265.21
flotsam 292.14 312.18 354.31 513.32
flounce 494.16
flour 265.07 531.12
flourish 171.10
flout 050.34 263.F2 536.22
flow 319.12 327.10 397.01
flower 086.01 092.21 130.09 143.04 171.10 226.32 256.09 268.01 269.10 272.12 313.05 337.25 339.25 350.11 359.14 370.19 514.28 531.12 546.32 561.20 621.22
flowerpot 386.26
flowery 007.12
flurry 204.25
fluster 501.31 546.04
flute 012.08 200.35 451.08 514.06 536.22
fluter 063.27 335.31 363.15 444.08
fluvial 526.25
fluxion 299.18
fly 010.36 019.33 020.19 136.09 199.36 287.F1 347.05 418.32 427.04 468.29 519.36
focus 266.16 332.27 516.19
fodder 009.20 011.23
foe 131.22
fog 005.33 565.18
foggy 116.12 277.07
foil 191.18
fold 350.25 619.20 619.21
foliage 008.04 143.19
folio 197.18
folk 106.22 264.20 352.17 444.15 455.09
folklore 419.12
follow 091.09 334.04 335.31 343.07 353.01 379.10 389.17 466.02 602.19 623.22
follower 364.04
follow-my-leader 042.17 579.19
folly 050.33 510.15
fond 107.14 224.10 238.35 241.17 257.26 315.28 463.15 547.07
fondest 489.11 601.02
fondle 291.14
fondly 119.19 357.14
fondness 542.07
font 620.19
food 034.07 164.17 224.05
foodstuff 007.13
fool 536.16 617.19
foolhardy 434.19
foot 059.09 070.15 072.35 154.34 181.19 215.34 224.10 291.04 317.19 364.16 382.24 384.28 405.30 408.23 419.05 437.20 437.27 473.15 581.04 603.24
footing 224.20
footrest 279.08
footstep 442.15
forbid 303.16 376.35 466.22 541.36
force 162.02 292.F2 345.32 365.36 418.11 565.04
ford 224.06 342.18 570.21
fore 606.34
forebear 084.36 132.32 428.04
forecast 324.24 332.27 516.19
forecastle 382.22 411.32
forecourt 232.13
foredoom 586.30
forefather 281.F1 288.F7
forefinger 612.35
forefoot 423.28
foreground 293.14
forehand 080.16
foreign 235.27 374.24 500.35 570.05
foreigner 385.32 541.14
foreman 354.07
foremast 590.15
foremost 519.21 590.15
forenoon 079.20
forepaw 438.04
foresee 245.23
foreshorten 121.36
foresight 079.03 290.10
foreskin 621.25
forest 112.06 339.25 464.20 506.15
forestall 411.01 444.11
foretell 390.24 411.01
forewarn 421.05
forget 130.26 153.14 247.07 339.24 440.24 515.30 625.18
forgetful 350.34
forgive 060.11 128.34 153.16 287.03 434.13 564.35 587.28 587.29 615.36
forgiveness 498.27
fork 089.12 370.12 408.33
forlorn 142.35
form 129.26

former 310.33 331.25 353.14 455.04 536.14 589.21
fornication 080.06 333.30 417.27 529.07 557.17
forsake 119.05 346.31 405.35 441.06 442.10 601.35
fort 316.28
forth 156.07 200.13 289.01 313.04 516.13 597.12 608.29 608.30
forthright 596.16 612.26
fortify 514.27 548.16
fortnight 357.24 409.21
fortress 278.25 279.08
fortune 221.12 434.05
forty 020.28 176.13 194.27 243.04 243.24 283.01 285.F3 312.09 312.10 357.04 372.18 432.25 432.26 450.23 519.07 519.07 561.34 619.20 619.21 622.24
fortyfive 188.07 514.27
fortyninth 153.34
fortysecond 177.26
fortythird 156.33
fortytwo 093.08 177.26
forward 113.09 357.36
forwards 018.32 279.F21
fossil 013.32 266.16
foster 178.36 489.13
fosterfather 215.14 329.07 596.07
foul 130.14 130.15 425.11 492.07
foulest 419.35
found 482.21
founder 328.08
foundling 227.26
fountain 542.09
fountainpen 563.06
four 005.36 013.23 082.14 094.15 134.07 160.33 199.03 240.11 271.F2 282.31 282.31 283.03 283.04 285.F5 324.28 332.27 352.29 355.33 361.02 361.02 372.18 372.34 377.29 382.20 385.35 390.36 408.03 456.09 457.13 513.30 533.34 546.28 587.01 589.27 602.16 612.35
foursome 555.11
fourteen 601.13
fourth 377.14 415.05 473.10 549.21
fowl 088.19
fowler 197.08
fox 089.12 097.13 152.14 249.02 449.06 480.23 489.02 567.24
fraction 269.F3 285.26 385.12
fragrance 265.08
fragrant 051.36 206.31
frame 315.30
frank 351.23
fraternity 133.31
fratricide 167.10
freckle 204.23 602.04
free 071.09 090.02 130.34 330.26 516.09 542.31
freebooter 388.19
freemason 500.15 501.19 552.05
freeschool 358.36
freeshooter 378.26
freewheel 285.F4
freeze 112.36 265.08 327.01 346.01 602.35
french 083.30 363.19
French 233.09 311.33 486.17 495.03
frenchy 603.08
fresco 564.17
fresh 034.32 088.29 098.24 117.29 129.29 209.13 264.07 268.F6 407.17 411.15 525.20 525.24 540.23 546.05 571.32 588.08
freshener 072.35
freshest 543.09
friar 338.05 432.23 468.31
Friday 005.24 184.32 301.21 409.29 487.34 492.06
friend 107.14 224.24 273.L1 311.33 315.30 337.07 345.33 358.35 406.18 434.28 440.25 449.16 579.20 617.31
friendship 313.27 354.19 542.18 603.08
Friesian 346.01
frighten 115.23 157.10 243.06 521.23 626.16
frightful 068.03 396.27 411.35
frightfully 167.11 615.35
frightfulness 224.10
frill 451.24
fringe 233.09
frisky 513.20
frolic 537.33
frond 153.15
front 153.15 405.28 435.17 507.11
frontispiece 191.32
frostbitten 424.09
froth 353.30
frothblower 303.R2
fruit 012.19 148.29 171.18 341.16 343.36 366.06 376.13
fruitful 513.08
fry 184.32 356.17
fryingpan 438.17 538.27
fuck 034.32 059.24 150.05 177.29 231.21 231.29 262.L1 267.L3 279.F21 302.16 304.R3 320.05 379.16 381.36 416.16 419.12 432.16 439.01 451.16 466.04 466.15 466.16 466.21 468.03 469.27 480.04 480.05 480.31 480.31 480.32 480.32 481.09 512.07 532.30 581.09 599.08 609.18 617.16 617.17 626.27
fucker 316.32 507.35 509.03
fuddle 323.08
fulcrum 384.18
full 014.03 160.12 164.17 228.33 238.24 238.35 382.07 426.17 475.09 502.22 624.23 626.11
fullback 129.32
fullface 388.04
fullstop 020.13 210.26 222.23 370.13 595.32
fully 113.13 426.17
fulmen 167.34
fulminate 551.11
fulmination 283.13
fulsome 242.20
fumble 176.04
fume 208.24 243.02 548.08
fun 345.09 375.16 398.25 499.13
fund 575.28 617.31
fundamentally 610.01
funeral 013.15 018.35 111.15 120.10 130.09 137.12 277.04 304.12 332.26 336.22 346.13 365.03 369.33 414.35 458.22 617.20 617.26
funicular 319.28
funk 502.33
funning 256.12
funny 065.33 208.31 242.29 288.09 495.20 519.14 519.14 589.11
funnyman 025.32
fur 476.12
furibund 243.05
furlined 419.29
furlong 545.24
furnace 289.13 319.34
furnish 414.32
furry 375.32 375.32
further 229.01 426.19
furthermore 288.10 314.15
furze 044.02
fuse 346.01 551.03
fusilier 176.13 335.18 412.34 451.14
fuss 145.33
futhorc 329.33
futile 143.08
futtock 018.34 329.33
future 072.23 143.08 233.02 348.06 518.28 527.34 593.17 608.21
futurism 130.01
futurity 292.19

gab 093.20
gabardine 276.12
gadfly 418.32
Gael 321.23 326.08 352.31 377.05
Gaelic 054.14 063.06 174.15 260.F1 315.36 378.28
gaff 375.17
gaffer 330.01
gaga 270.31
gaiety 411.15
gain 018.23
galaxy 524.29 604.15
gale 011.05 043.27 321.12 321.23 326.08 339.13 352.31 604.24
gall 043.36
gallant 157.04 187.13
gallery 057.21
gallon 283.17
gallowglass 008.25
gallows 489.07
galore 496.13
gamble 343.03
game 028.07 332.26
gamete 259.06
gamin 256.25
gamut 259.06 492.04
gander 287.02 450.30
gang 355.28
ganger 443.21

gangrene 196.18 503.23 576.31
gangster 219.23 350.09
gap 616.22
gape 417.22 529.14
garden 034.27 069.10 075.01 140.36 151.21 176.18 191.21 192.29 224.24 224.32 226.23 252.32 253.17 253.32 272.03 281.03 324.07 347.12 350.02 354.22 532.22 552.19 553.09 622.36
gardener 108.17 133.23 336.21
gardenia 564.35
gardenparty 059.12
garland 238.11
garlic 174.15 550.10
garment 181.29
garter 008.19 144.27 211.01 247.19 266.03 349.21
gascooker 323.13
gaseous 394.35
gasmask 603.03
gasometer 559.24
gassy 175.31
gasworks 221.09 555.12
gate 069.24 071.11 214.22 258.08 318.01 531.04 551.34 551.35 616.30
gateway 260.13 372.13 558.02
gather 155.26 226.22 602.11
gathering 186.25
gauge 070.23 105.32 331.27
Gaul 377.05
gauntlet 567.31
gauze 531.19
gay 306.R2 331.32 332.18 332.18 570.28
gayatri 297.18
gaze 056.11 064.06 531.19
gazelle 362.21
gee 411.19
geezer 193.10
gem 193.09 318.05
general 026.03 105.22 116.06 176.20 192.03 243.10 265.28 292.F1 335.20 337.34 338.19 340.27 341.07 341.29 342.13 346.12 346.20 349.19 350.06 352.01 352.23 354.35 365.07 368.08 369.34 372.06 375.24 388.34 390.04 423.33 492.29 531.28 531.36 620.04
generality 523.04
generally 220.14 220.15
generous 268.25
generously 084.18
Genesis 004.24 106.13
gent 310.25 381.13 540.23
Gentile 509.19
gentleman 010.18 150.26 152.16 173.13 177.08 228.35 236.12 322.17 343.14 348.13 350.09 365.04 370.07 371.26 462.02 510.31 523.22 524.07 569.31 573.35 617.25
gentlemanly 034.18
gentry 609.03
genuflect 271.F4
geography 234.12
geologer 302.13
geometer 297.01
geometry 286.L4
Georgian 242.06
geriatry 265.F2
German 127.13 176.20 230.33 392.15 625.02
germane 020.03 235.29
gesticulate 243.19
gesture 227.27 267.09 350.10 535.03
gewgaw 548.24 605.01
ghastly 346.20
ghost 015.01 081.30 153.32 235.05 245.13 265.03 299.14 323.35 331.15 349.19 359.26 368.04 390.03 397.22 409.06 414.08 419.10 440.15 467.27 551.03 580.12 612.30 614.32
ghoststory 051.13 359.26
ghoul 377.34 518.35
giant 015.07 018.11 020.16 055.27 069.06 080.02 241.17 284.F5 310.33 391.18 503.01
gibber 504.30
gigantic 099.09
gill 283.17
gimble 567.36
ginger 055.18
gingerbread 542.34
ginpalace 597.13
girdle 349.21 548.17 618.03
girl 044.08 065.23 101.16 112.30 178.33 182.22 201.25 206.14 228.14 234.07 234.31 283.F1 302.25 314.31 331.18 341.07 346.08 351.12 354.31 361.17 375.12 379.16 434.07 445.09 448.24 448.25 469.32 469.32 491.31 508.30 508.34 567.33 571.31 587.27 601.01 601.18 618.03 626.03
girlfriend 384.24
girly 601.17
girt 287.19
girth 138.36
give 105.15 148.20 209.28 231.03 257.31 367.13 487.34 531.01
glad 354.22
gladden 358.10
glaive 006.29
glance 226.28 226.28
glass 014.34 124.07 183.36 262.F2 294.08 405.20 453.23 459.04 470.33 526.36 609.15
glasses 304.F3
glassful 512.09
glasshouse 537.01
gleam 379.23
glean 038.10 221.20
glee 146.16 183.36
glen 105.29 340.10 526.23
glide 202.12
glimpse 122.01 130.03
glitter 236.02
gloaming 232.07
globe 054.29 055.01 305.31 354.11
globetrotter 435.12
gloomy 198.29 600.36
glorious 498.36
glory 089.35 141.30 286.31 324.21 327.17 333.31 338.28 339.24 372.29 498.19 557.03 557.04
glossary 113.02 339.24
glottal 117.13
glove 204.25 205.18 369.19 434.06 468.13
glow 056.18 404.12 528.23
gluttonous 416.24
gluttony 370.36
G-man 133.10 202.20
gnash 222.27
gnat 416.15
gnosis 224.14
goad 076.10 076.11
goat 005.34 007.27 051.13 051.15 069.25 081.30 141.09 143.05 197.07 299.F3 305.05 339.04 343.13 346.25 379.19 466.34 467.01 488.22 551.03 589.12 589.13
Gobelins 308.01 501.09
goblet 031.11
goblin 600.23
God 009.26 009.27 010.36 023.06 034.10 053.27 054.20 055.19 060.11 070.01 071.18 073.06 073.06 076.31 085.17 087.03 089.36 094.29 094.31 107.16 108.12 114.25 141.30 144.02 148.20 153.35 156.22 162.36 171.30 177.06 177.08 178.31 178.33 180.07 191.23 192.35 198.13 200.16 201.28 202.05 207.23 215.34 229.03 233.13 240.13 240.35 241.26 241.28 246.13 247.16 251.02 254.19 257.34 258.01 258.28 271.29 276.11 279.F34 305.05 310.34 313.08 313.13 313.18 317.09 317.11 317.28 324.21 330.28 332.10 339.04 340.24 344.28 345.23 346.34 347.15 350.20 352.11 352.35 353.02 355.36 356.03 356.34 357.29 364.01 364.02 373.20 375.16 377.31 397.22 409.15 412.31 412.31 413.28 415.27 419.30 421.30 427.20 438.31 440.14 440.14 445.02 445.07 448.32 449.05 451.04 480.02 481.19 485.05 485.10 487.07 487.17 499.04 502.22 520.12 531.19 534.08 538.16 551.02 558.35 561.27 561.28 562.33 565.21 566.28 580.11 586.30 587.02 596.22 596.36 597.09 597.24 602.10 612.31 612.31 613.01 613.01 613.12 617.01 626.06
godchild 167.08
goddamn 024.17 052.05 118.22 277.L5 320.14 361.13 441.33 538.33
goddess 242.09
godfather 279.F32 325.18 326.24 585.14
godforsaken 346.31 405.35
godhead 233.16
godlike 551.29
godliness 378.04
godmother 011.09 146.05 149.23 242.25 353.27 449.36 617.18
godsend 117.04 327.02
godspeed 600.14
gold 028.11 084.04 129.31 131.05 140.15 176.24 327.28

340.01 390.35 479.05 578.23 602.11
golden 079.35 102.24 225.16 234.36 394.27 619.24 619.29 619.30
golflinks 567.36
gondolier 317.15
goner 497.17 588.11
gonorrhea 192.03
good 017.16 028.10 076.10 076.11 087.26 095.18 095.18 097.34 155.19 164.02 232.18 241.28 256.16 264.F1 275.10 276.12 302.25 356.18 519.16 520.35 521.31 593.09 596.36
goodbye 073.16 215.07 225.34 262.F7 382.28 453.16 521.36 535.27 595.07
goodness 227.25 237.07 242.09 345.22 460.06
goodnight 534.01
googly 584.09
goose 071.04 185.06 197.14 227.25 268.11 299.11 353.27 394.27 450.30 493.30 557.07
gooseberry 142.02 170.35 270.F2
goosegrease 548.03
gorgeous 152.27 406.07
gospel 038.23 155.19 343.08 343.32 349.16 480.33
gossamer 278.F1
gossip 623.04
goster 219.08 532.04
goulash 291.23 406.06
gout 199.22
government 273.06
governor 325.01 375.23 531.29
governor-general 243.10 338.19 342.13 531.36
gown 208.25 624.08
grab 018.13 457.28
grace 158.17 158.19 161.16 177.06 214.18 227.23 267.04 310.34 417.11 432.35 489.04 502.22 509.30 535.05 546.02 598.10 604.11
graceful 220.09
gracefulness 136.09 136.09
gracious 186.31 227.25 237.07 242.09 353.03 387.34 415.25 460.06 568.25 570.06 607.34 623.11
graciously 379.29
grain 457.09 603.35
grammar 388.31
grand 072.34 078.28 146.35 197.31 257.04 329.29 332.20 336.21 418.12 423.18 457.09 553.26 624.12
grandest 503.33
grandfather 027.03 029.07 070.28 242.10 361.21 368.04 378.25
grandmother 299.10 585.14
grandpa 198.29 268.26
grandpapa 007.08 065.12 065.19 362.08 587.32
granny 007.09 058.11
grant 078.29 221.31 372.08 466.22 513.28 581.26 605.07
grape 009.31 072.10 105.27 360.25 364.25 365.15 365.20 418.32 432.35 457.28 465.35 489.04 561.26 568.11 579.13
grapeshot 366.20
graph 317.36
grapple 456.15
grasp 561.26
grasshopper 063.01 087.23 105.28 147.16 197.27 257.05 268.12 331.16 338.18 338.35 339.36 343.23 360.36 393.12 417.01 417.02
grassplot 284.07
grasswidow 291.09
grassy 158.19
grateful 273.F6
gratefulness 136.09 136.10
grave 018.13 240.04 353.10 364.09 545.34
gravel 366.20
gravestone 146.34
graveyard 568.27
gravingdock 224.06
gravy 375.03
grease 176.17 206.32 267.04 278.F1 548.03 549.02
great 013.33 102.33 113.01 134.07 135.10 140.04 167.12 177.35 225.35 241.09 249.09 254.28 289.21 317.30 329.30 337.01 342.14 343.17 344.27 345.08 361.21 365.06 409.15 444.20 464.31 497.28 503.27 550.06 601.05 603.22 603.28 604.12
greatcloak 016.34
greatcoat 553.14 567.18
greater 324.21 512.28
greatest 387.34 425.15
greatly 037.03
greatness 061.07
greedily 532.23
greediness 318.35
Greek 011.35 113.02 145.25 155.27 214.22 234.09 242.13 343.17 416.18 563.09 620.30
green 019.23 023.01 143.25 176.24 221.20 267.13 279.03 279.F32 285.L2 292.03 329.06 338.36 339.28 345.14 397.35 432.30 469.16 503.23 516.08 596.21 603.28
greenhouse 575.26
Greenlander 378.11
greenwashed 553.20
greet 308.17 377.01
greeting 288.19
gremlin 057.14
grey 071.31 247.35 257.06 317.36 503.23 567.18 588.13
grief 241.31 353.10 565.13
grievously 234.02
griffin 418.27
grig 620.30
grim 379.23
grime 078.32 094.08
grin 330.06
grip 482.13
grisly 016.35
gristle 406.11
groan 177.17 223.32
grocer 565.22
grocery 367.02
groggy 418.19
groom 318.06
grouch 252.21 541.17
ground 223.31 477.35 481.15 500.01 624.12
grouser 268.11
grove 371.16
grovel 356.05
grow 117.07 138.36 239.32 344.11 344.11 433.19 504.32 506.13
grumble 356.05
grunt 605.07
guarantee 255.13 574.34
guard 197.07 258.30 258.30 347.14 567.04 596.22
guardian 252.32 324.07 483.26
guardsman 599.19
guess 093.11 233.12 561.07
guesswork 224.26
guest 240.03 393.35 511.02
guffaw 149.04
Gugerati 498.17
guilt 159.13
guilty 072.29 406.33
guinea 182.12
guineapig 072.15
gulfstream 319.27
gullible 396.23
gumboot 023.01
gumjube 273.17
gun 083.35 246.21 603.32
gunman 371.26
gunner 443.21
gunpowder 142.11 364.26 410.25
gush 326.05 492.24
gust 323.35 369.04
gutta-percha 224.02
gutter 320.14 320.14 382.17
guttersnipe 199.03
guttural 116.29 117.13 493.13
Gypsy 230.20 359.18
gyre 245.14

habeas 362.17 423.31
habit 171.09
habitat 057.07
habitually 004.31
hack 180.35
hackney 042.27 284.F3
Hades 229.13
haft 136.24
hagiography 234.12
hail 027.15 081.28 177.05 243.18 345.01 350.35 440.36 488.32 532.06 583.28 604.10
hailstone 416.33 502.20
hair 004.10 004.29 065.04 102.24 131.34 164.31 206.16 239.24 275.05 295.25 317.34 338.16 342.05 342.05 362.31 449.20 468.36 498.31 526.26 534.32 580.02 610.03
hairy 207.08 224.12 351.31 390.31 546.10 584.31
halcyon 351.05
half 043.23 075.18 248.21 249.34 292.27 292.27 300.20 300.22 320.02 347.14 367.33 370.31 397.16 463.26 506.03 526.02 610.11 610.12
halfbrother 066.26
halfhearted 121.07
halfmourning 566.07
halfpence 144.17

halfpenny 011.21 041.20 265.F3 321.25 351.21 437.18 550.01 586.23
halfpennyworth 578.27
halidom 155.15
hall 092.03 185.08 264.F2 301.18 450.19 551.05
halleluiah 083.34 083.34 236.17 304.31 456.03 456.04
hallo 256.11 321.14
hallow 007.33 019.25 104.02 304.F5 536.35 553.22 599.05
Hallowe'en 237.35 488.23 537.28
halt 359.23
halter 326.21
halve 136.24
ham 124.13 229.01
hamburger 496.03 560.07
hammer 140.15 310.19 439.23
hand 004.29 028.02 132.21 174.09 209.26 241.31 245.05 285.10 318.14 318.14 320.09 326.20 365.23 365.23 374.07 395.27 460.30 463.28 464.25 520.34 535.33 550.30 622.22
handkerchief 010.10 089.36 158.34 265.F3 471.23 495.09 537.15 612.25
handle 054.27 295.28 615.19 618.02
handlebar 270.24
handmade 420.08
handmaid 008.32 239.10 278.12 420.08 561.26
handsome 161.31 384.28 384.28 415.12 415.12 527.16 618.02
handy 066.29
hang 225.10 347.12
hanger 586.29
hangman 177.22
hansom 391.35
hansomcab 487.10
haphazard 016.09 615.07
happen 075.11 324.35 342.26 348.18 600.15 604.12
happily 261.05
happiness 261.F1 443.10 471.04
happy 041.23 328.19 358.09 386.08 414.22 417.17 452.16
happy-go-lucky 332.24 358.09 499.04
harbour 136.32 227.20
harbourmaster 358.18
hard 059.34 275.14 315.21 331.03 332.20 533.20
hardly 051.14 089.19 129.14 222.03 257.18 344.04 354.14 419.03 485.27 512.31 547.04 550.05 570.33
hardship 448.23
hardware 614.15
hardy 434.19
hare 423.03
harem 295.25 532.32 547.06 566.16
hark 096.01 096.01 096.01 493.25
Harlene 237.28
harm 271.17 532.32 566.16
harmless 197.29 474.03
harmonise 466.25
harmonium 377.15
harmony 456.21 462.06
harp 100.02 103.10 286.16 306.F2 454.27 488.36 624.28
harpist 508.33
harpsichord 239.16 415.18
harrow 537.28 599.05
haruspication 100.18
harvestrose 427.20
hasbeen 162.21
haste 131.15 237.20 328.09 405.01 506.26
hasten 135.11 535.06 563.16
hat 043.23 056.07 320.08 322.05 334.07 347.30 439.16 509.22 607.03
hatchet 613.30
hate 597.18
hater 566.36
haven 076.33 315.22 365.13 604.12
hawk 133.01 207.08
hawser 154.10
hawthorn 160.06 184.07
hay 097.26 097.26 097.27 097.27
haymarket 068.05
hazel 180.12 577.11
head 006.08 056.30 065.04 158.33 240.22 268.27 324.20 338.08 347.19 383.15 385.33 444.24 468.36 517.08 535.22 535.26 535.27 538.29 562.24 578.07
headache 127.31 362.20
headhunter 497.07
headquarters 344.19
health 060.08 076.09 091.28 197.18 313.36 569.02 619.12
healthy 530.09
heap 356.26
hear 015.08 015.09 039.15 039.23 044.17 044.18 048.09 117.02 117.02 145.21 160.26 201.24 204.35 213.16 223.01 227.06 280.21 313.17 326.25 331.03 331.03 332.20 363.26 370.01 371.05 371.28 378.07 409.03 409.03 410.31 464.18 464.22 485.25 485.26 485.27 485.28 491.16 538.29 572.16 584.36 593.05 593.06 595.07 603.02 627.32
hearer 160.35 164.36
hearing 021.01
hearsay 112.29 263.L4
hearse 323.08 328.15
heart 011.26 037.11 051.36 106.27 116.23 121.07 152.01 168.02 188.31 188.31 224.35 245.06 247.18 251.07 259.07 300.16 309.24 322.29 329.07 329.16 339.08 345.03 345.08 346.21 352.22 440.20 460.17 460.25 476.15 490.05 499.30 535.16 570.04 577.22
heartache 362.20
hearth 137.06 138.26 309.24 346.31 352.22
hearthrug 126.20
heartiest 616.02
heartily 547.04
heartless 458.36
heartsease 434.24
hearty 235.31
heat 053.35 111.11 239.17 317.32
heathen 264.06 289.01 424.11 426.21
heather 081.16 081.16 566.36
heaven 053.26 059.21 064.24 104.03 139.08 144.34 173.24 175.17 225.31 239.18 244.29 258.14 258.14 258.14 261.14 284.10 392.06 416.01 416.31 426.21 435.23 475.33 496.04 506.26 531.01 533.05 536.35 541.01 541.01 557.03 590.14 599.05 601.18 601.18 601.19 603.28 617.01 620.34
heavenliness 548.11
heavenly 177.21 234.10 234.13 603.07
heavensent 348.29
heavier 376.14 376.14 376.15
heavy 215.36 348.29 421.07 426.12
hebdomadary 071.16 581.27
Hebrew 228.34 497.24
hedge 571.10
hedgerow 327.10
hedgeschool 533.26
heed 151.23
heel 152.32 342.26 448.04 449.27
heelless 468.25
heeltapper 480.09
hegerite 062.03
hegoat 005.07
height 004.36 158.29 448.02 536.14
heir 280.21 483.34 627.30
heliotrope 089.19 223.11 223.28 223.28 223.28 235.05 273.24 280.24 303.F1 326.15 509.22 603.28 626.17
hell 028.09 029.21 082.32 083.08 092.03 107.36 131.24 185.08 200.34 231.29 258.02 299.F1 315.27 323.15 335.28 349.26 370.34 416.32 421.12 426.01 434.19 440.36 449.27 469.16 518.35 520.27 547.02 561.08 565.02 594.23
hellfire 409.23 436.29
hellish 518.35
hellishly 289.14
helm 594.13 613.32 613.32
helmet 530.14
helot 613.01
help 076.09 118.28 136.24 137.32 141.13 141.13 249.34 292.27 300.20 300.22 323.15 333.13 348.27 348.27 352.35 356.26 375.15 445.07 463.26 524.30 538.16 590.26
helpmate 242.25
hem 465.29 465.29
hemicycle 375.13
hemisphere 081.25 129.21 346.07 453.22
hemlock 031.24 450.31
hemp 616.14
hen 012.17 151.12 205.30 482.16 616.20
henceforward 357.36
henna 379.23
henpecked 364.36

hepatite 441.08
herald 324.28
heraldry 005.06
herb 230.07
hereabouts 602.06
hereafter 141.13 618.30
hereditary 013.20 303.26 410.02
heredity 614.02
heresiarch 188.16
heresy 240.13 376.05 463.18
hereupon 231.10
hermit 203.18
hero 068.25 117.02 136.13 146.24 271.L3 328.25 427.20
heroic 284.10
heroine 261.24
herring 007.19 187.19 268.F6 289.F6 391.16 394.34 524.26 578.07
herringbone 268.16
herself 333.13 557.05
hesitancy 016.26 016.30 026.35 097.26 119.18 146.34 187.30 296.F4 305.04 305.09 350.12 379.07 421.23 599.14 599.14 623.34
hesitate 097.25 149.16
heterodox 252.21
heterosexual 120.35
Hibernian 376.12 567.35
hiccup 004.11 140.13 321.22 616.23
hidalgo 281.F3 388.19
hide 066.17 208.11 305.24 305.25 359.33 373.07 373.07 373.07 373.07 374.21 549.31
hidinghole 581.20
hidingplace 127.11
hierarchy 409.35
high 054.26
highbrow 012.08 228.34
higher 204.02 561.01
highest 340.22
highfalutin 448.35
highho 612.35 617.02
highjinks 439.33 547.22
highkick 067.19
highland 168.02 331.11 392.34
highly 070.15 110.35 344.02 553.14
highness 337.29 623.18
highpitched 121.16
highwayman 542.36 546.36
hiker 410.08
hill 007.33 007.34 009.29 015.24 124.33 128.12 338.36 541.01 617.32 619.12
hillock 566.29
hillside 542.25
himself 003.20 032.07 086.05 114.23 130.20 143.26 157.13 168.01 170.17 171.04 184.10 187.04 193.31 199.05 222.25 240.11 288.08 308.F2 313.33 317.28 352.36 373.13 416.14 426.13 460.11 557.01
hinder 363.34
hindmost 167.25 364.25
hindquarters 410.04
Hindu 010.06 010.09 010.14 198.18 513.24
hinterland 276.F7
hip 258.09 258.09 348.27 348.27 377.33 377.33 495.13 495.14 569.25 569.25 594.16 594.16
hippodrome 245.02
hippopotamus 064.17 210.35 449.32
hire 448.21
hirsute 391.20
hiss 314.31
historic 266.R1
history 052.05 064.06 143.12 161.22 162.12 163.25 214.01 280.L1 280.L1 319.06 418.28 535.18
hit 006.15 054.01
hitch 461.01
hither 325.13 325.30 359.34 365.22
Hittite 427.29 484.20
hoar 006.27 320.22 449.28
hoard 243.34
hoarse 029.27
hoarsely 150.12
hoary 352.13 382.12
hobbledehoy 063.30
hobgoblin 600.23
hock 033.27 033.27 033.27 548.01
hogmanay 053.34
hogshead 015.31
hold 081.31 167.13 204.01 227.05 315.31 362.19 480.34 481.05 552.16 598.03 606.21 624.26
holder 054.25
hole 069.05 076.09 077.10 090.21 090.22 124.11 143.01 248.12 311.08 320.05 379.36 415.07 492.15 561.06 563.32 612.35
holiday 058.05 069.32 129.13 192.19 264.04 353.07 553.16
holiest 266.14
holiness 158.27
Hollander 126.16
hollow 553.22 596.28
holly 059.09 236.13 331.14 376.13 421.06 465.13 468.10 485.22 502.02 502.04 505.03 508.09 552.10 556.03 557.10 616.32
holocaust 596.28
holy 005.30 023.35 027.15 057.06 070.02 072.25 089.34 111.18 111.18 111.18 138.25 152.03 153.31 176.12 177.05 231.21 235.05 238.27 245.13 264.F3 271.F5 310.35 312.11 318.12 326.01 326.11 331.14 349.19 352.13 380.10 396.12 419.09 424.04 424.33 466.26 471.31 481.20 515.25 552.10 612.30 614.32
holyness 091.35 351.31
homage 623.12
home 030.09 080.18 080.18 092.30 093.15 098.08 124.33 129.23 173.29 242.33 244.09 256.11 261.05 276.F2 310.01 316.33 326.18 330.24 338.16 367.30 371.01 371.01 374.19 379.36 465.35 481.21 485.16 494.02 606.16 613.32 613.32 616.04 619.13 624.15
homebound 560.01
homegrown 611.35
homely 173.29 450.13
homerule 185.05
homestead 026.26
homonym 490.13
honest 290.22 411.29 627.30
honester 177.14
honesty 325.08
honey 029.32
honeymoon 329.19 377.15 417.14
honeymooner 340.20 395.13
honeysuckle 417.17
honorary 240.03 533.34
honour 034.12 243.33
honourable 050.23 325.27 328.13
hood 186.08 307.F1 411.24 551.08
hooded 088.03 223.29
hoodwink 078.22
hook 330.26
hoop 434.02 436.34
hop 063.36 232.30 331.16 597.23 602.33
hope 008.30 020.28 137.32 222.30 239.11 302.25 304.F4 312.20 328.29 349.11 360.24 434.02 439.34 441.06 450.35 489.30 527.23
hopper 581.19
hopscotch 620.32
horde 371.05
horizon 449.28 623.26
horn 049.15 236.30
hornet 290.22
hornpipe 315.24
horoscope 105.28 261.25
horrible 016.18 438.17 452.34 538.10 545.12
horribly 202.35
horrid 169.04 578.26 610.03
horror 184.07 455.06 545.13
horse 017.08 040.13 067.05 106.01 126.20 137.17 143.23 164.18 188.23 219.15 273.23 273.23 285.L2 317.32 322.25 323.06 323.08 328.15 334.16 342.18 347.01 348.35 373.15 373.15 373.16 376.05 379.05 379.14 388.17 476.28 480.06 567.17 570.33 594.29 602.23 607.33
horseback 535.08
horsehair 362.31
horseman 276.26 557.01
horsemanship 547.25
horsepiss 203.02 510.30
horsepower 008.36 178.27 248.21
horserider 581.19
horsesense 194.16
horseshoe 063.22 246.23 447.17 595.23
horsie 531.22
hose 178.01 313.05 453.09 545.30
hosiery 032.35 414.33
hospice 024.04 071.13 392.07 416.15 514.25
hospital 040.36 441.12 448.15
hospitality 345.29

hostage 096.05 346.32
hostelry 371.25
hostile 335.12
hostler 521.30
hot 014.30 289.05 289.14 395.29 485.03 623.08
hotel 196.01 420.25 514.18 586.18
Hottentot 333.27 540.29
hotwaterbottle 610.30
hound 031.29 232.28 322.14 339.08 603.31
hour 194.29 251.27 320.22 326.14 389.20 435.23 556.34 566.32 628.08
hourglass 101.29 408.24
house 007.05 009.22 010.27 029.01 055.13 059.21 081.12 088.01 094.04 104.16 106.33 126.15 129.16 135.01 154.09 177.20 194.29 197.03 201.04 240.29 245.36 267.05 313.05 320.11 330.35 337.11 369.03 380.07 388.17 491.18 506.05 511.34 525.22 527.23 528.07 530.14 533.18 538.16 545.30 589.21 614.03 619.25 621.35
household 242.05 606.21
householder 054.25
housekeeping 422.14
housetop 422.13
housewife 512.13
housework 397.10
houyhnhnm 101.07 465.29 490.13 623.24 623.24
howl 205.04
Howth 004.05 007.30 015.24 023.27 030.11 036.26 042.18 077.21 077.30 081.12 081.16 081.16 106.33 116.15 126.15 128.23 130.33 131.07 133.01 140.23 175.15 197.03 223.29 253.32 254.29 276.26 287.09 289.14 313.05 317.32 318.12 324.20 340.06 346.26 346.31 359.25 359.25 365.13 376.14 376.14 376.15 383.15 385.33 394.28 426.01 448.02 452.11 468.30 468.36 497.07 535.27 536.14 538.16 538.34 588.16 588.16 595.03 607.27 619.12 619.25 624.26
huckleberry 025.33 130.14 132.36 137.12 297.20 616.01 622.17
hug 004.29
huge 371.36 541.14 567.21 567.21
hugely 620.26
Huguenot 085.05 517.07 541.14
hullaballoo 239.33 322.07 339.02
hum 166.09
human 029.30 036.06 295.01 597.33
humanity 042.14
humble 029.30 214.32 390.32 568.25 588.33 620.01
humbly 356.05
humid 450.13
humiliation 593.15
humility 588.25
hummer 140.15
humour 102.27 331.33
humouristic 594.28
hump 619.12
humus 029.30
hundred 029.01 032.31 054.25 078.05 081.04 155.29 188.36 188.36 220.21 240.28 243.01 265.26 265.26 274.L3 329.09 330.33 341.20 347.19 376.02 389.25 420.26 507.22 541.29 567.03 577.14 596.02 597.05 608.24 618.36
Hungarian 287.F4
hunger 586.29
hungry 101.35 126.22 406.30
hunt 233.08 293.F2 295.09 335.10
hunter 124.33
hurdle 224.06 316.29 447.30 570.21 608.29 608.29
hurdygurdy 354.14
hurlyburly 257.18
hurrah 258.09 338.03 594.16
hurray 329.04 341.22 569.25 593.02
hurricane 227.30 233.31 245.05 589.30
hurry 029.22 445.04
husband 062.10 104.16 104.16 104.18 104.18 146.20 162.21 226.18 279.F18 317.06 319.32 320.23 364.36 393.16 459.33 494.35 511.28 533.20 540.20 556.29 561.32 578.20 617.07
hush 023.27
husky 339.31
hussy 101.04 162.20 589.33
hustler 521.30
hyacinth 181.26 563.16 603.28
hydrazine 067.10
hydrocephalic 310.06
hydrogen 067.10 327.10
hydrolic 452.01
hyena 010.04
hymn 183.15 330.07 465.29 550.33
hypnotise 261.F1
hysteria 528.11

iamb 386.05
Iberian 197.29
ibis 436.24 562.17
icedcoffee 059.29
Icelander 378.11
icicle 453.14
icon 205.27 279.F12 312.03 349.18
icy 358.01
idea 348.07
ideal 280.26 384.24
identical 016.36 295.27
identify 051.05 051.06 133.28 510.10
identity 049.36
ideology 352.19
ides 040.10 354.25 603.15
idiot 037.14
idle 395.02 547.05
idly 357.21
idol 351.25 455.03
idyll 351.25
ifrit 446.12
ignite 594.02
ignition 614.17
ignorance 121.23 540.32
ilk 321.10
ill 007.33 057.11 320.25
illegible 420.23
illgotten 434.05
illigate 014.04
illiterate 082.17 284.15 336.31
illness 568.26
illuminate 167.07 461.18
image 082.19 486.34
imaginable 004.19
imagination 251.17 299.05 565.29
imagine 337.18 337.20
imbibe 378.03
imitate 460.12 535.03
immaculacy 528.20
immaculate 601.22
immaterial 378.34
immemorial 600.26
immense 528.09
immodest 085.30
immodesty 034.18
immortal 149.07
immortality 145.26 580.13
impart 324.20
impassive 386.29
impecunious 363.28
impediment 463.11 515.33
imperative 187.31
imperial 353.29
impervious 377.13
importance 158.26
important 138.05 464.07
impose 066.19
impossible 298.18 340.05 499.19 614.10
impressible 609.06
impression 115.24
improbable 538.05 538.12 609.05
impromptu 093.14
improper 366.23
impropriety 617.35
improvement 603.03
impulsive 386.29
inaccessible 285.28
inaudible 016.23
incapable 363.32
incarnate 250.35
incense 279.F29
inceptive 541.02
incest 263.06
inch 495.30
inchoate 404.07
incidental 222.01
incidentally 254.31
incisor 563.02
incite 437.05
incline 165.03 284.L2
include 026.10 356.07
income 182.23 567.24
incometax 191.18
incomparably 533.05
incompetent 325.04
incomplete 325.04
incontinent 388.05
incorporate 228.20
increment 043.32
incriminate 366.17
incubus 013.11
incur 324.31
indecent 534.30

indeed 079.16 089.18 201.03
347.05 363.20 411.29 440.26
503.22 505.21 560.18
indelible 015.33 391.06 432.21
independent 501.19 602.17
indescribable 298.32
Indian 008.29 079.20 207.30
224.03 274.02
India-rubber 224.03
indigestible 236.28
indigestion 023.20 536.07
indignation 153.21
indigo 143.25 203.28 277.F4
284.28 339.29 432.31
individual 572.15
indulgence 187.16 531.02
inebriate 029.29 098.21 429.23
ineffable 183.14
ineffectual 118.28
inexhaustible 091.27
inexpressible 357.28
infallibility 245.12
infallible 153.26
infant 483.27 538.30 621.26
infantry 348.35
inferior 154.11
inferiority 291.F8
infernal 300.07
inferno 497.23
infest 256.09
infinity 284.11
inflamatory 348.35
influence 221.11
influenza 026.27
information 059.34 137.34
374.26
infrared 316.03 590.08
infuriate 138.28
infuse 249.02
ingenious 425.17
ingle 201.22 226.22
ingrate 318.01
inhabit 224.11 437.14 602.22
inhabitant 258.22 348.16
inherit 224.11
inhibit 224.11 602.22
inhuman 615.04
inhume 097.24
initial 451.19
initiate 535.03
injurious 234.29
ink 027.07 088.17 240.08
349.18 534.16 606.27
inn 089.18
inner 546.21
innermost 341.04
innkeeper 144.07
innocence 229.35 332.24
538.30
innocent 059.09 204.19
innuendo 425.18
innumerable 608.31 615.04
innumerous 158.11
inoculate 541.27
inquisitive 505.09
insane 129.15
inscribe 179.23 496.05
insect 029.30
insense 536.19
insensitive 465.12
inside 415.01 428.24
insidious 580.19
insincerity 415.26
insinuation 412.15
insolence 562.32
inspect 537.32
inspire 374.08
instance 173.34 337.21 435.10
instant 143.08 227.05 353.18
instanter 534.35
instead 061.13 137.22 598.04
instruct 295.22
instrument 043.32
insulate 291.05
insult 010.14 051.30 353.18
373.17
insure 197.18
integer 131.32
integument 245.10
intention 241.05 301.30
interact 284.01
intercept 232.10
intercession 449.15
interdiction 060.21
interest 055.24 388.02 538.03
interestedness 055.25
interfere 060.24
interference 504.18
interim 187.36 529.15
interject 320.23
interlock 289.11
interlope 551.01
intern 254.14
international 128.27 128.28
240.14
interpretation 338.29
interpreter 467.05
interrogate 601.33
interrogation 224.14
interrupt 368.04
interruption 332.36
intersect 284.01
interview 058.35
intimate 238.06 248.31 417.20
523.23
intoxication 447.29
introduce 607.05
introvert 425.28
intruder 082.18
inundate 589.25
inundation 194.32 372.23
invader 581.03
invalid 320.15
invaluable 404.25
invasion 626.28
invective 412.13
invent 425.28 517.34
invention 341.14 412.29 424.20
526.35
invert 034.25 284.09 374.10
investigation 150.07
invincible 232.26
inviolate 285.02
invisible 419.03 527.12 594.33
invite 054.35 523.17 623.08
invoke 368.13
involuntary 358.02
involve 080.12
ionise 323.29
ire 406.15
Ireland 006.35 040.19 062.25
069.08 073.02 129.27 139.20
169.24 171.06 261.F2 264.31
270.30 288.13 290.18 294.04
316.32 320.21 323.20 323.26
347.11 348.16 353.16 353.19
359.26 362.07 374.19 378.06
391.28 392.31 392.34 421.27
446.25 522.04 525.30 539.18
541.19 546.33 582.25 583.20
595.10 604.24 605.04 613.01
613.01
iridescence 494.04
iridescent 484.09
iris 354.25 432.04
Irish 070.04 130.19 141.21
144.10 182.15 229.07 238.32
285.27 318.34 320.13 354.25
354.25 378.09 410.33 424.03
498.01 501.19 605.05 611.05
Irishman 071.34 086.21 091.22
463.25 463.26 489.31 612.20
616.03
irk 410.08
iron 071.35 112.33 127.26
207.21 219.20 242.34 247.22
310.20 347.06 358.21 390.10
392.17 392.27 433.31 491.36
493.13 547.32 614.11 620.09
ironbound 461.23
ironical 014.30
ironore 359.03
irreconcilable 434.20
irreparable 057.18
irreverence 249.24
irrigate 601.33
irritate 009.03
isinglass 415.28 486.24
island 290.18 294.04 605.04
605.20
isle 019.17 062.12 291.09
353.04 391.16 464.29 605.17
605.20
islet 605.20
isletshore 605.28
issue 062.03 228.02
isthmus 623.10
Italian 569.29
itch 465.29
itself 611.21
ivory 019.23 027.13 327.28
ivy 029.04 059.09 147.11
186.25 236.14 291.01 408.28
421.07 465.13 468.11 502.02
502.04 508.09 523.08 556.03
557.11 616.32 619.36

jack 155.16 309.22
jackal 589.15
jackdaw 276.06
jacket 339.12
jacktar 316.36
Jacobite 542.30
jail 228.33
jam 241.34
jamboree 236.15 236.15 236.16
236.17
jamjar 316.36 537.24
January 015.35 112.26 332.25
473.03
Japanese 090.27
jar 223.08 316.36 537.24
jargon 198.18
jaunt 055.24
jauntily 223.33
jaw 305.03
jealous 009.07 068.18 161.21
232.22
jealousy 417.23

jellyroll 461.16
jeremiad 229.32 575.09
jerk 567.36
jessamine 229.23 450.11
jest 227.27 407.25 468.05 489.11
jesuit 240.28 349.19 489.14
jetsam 312.18 354.31 513.32
Jew 066.30 466.18
jewel 105.20 153.29 236.02 291.12 313.25 329.29 394.08 559.15
Jewess 331.09
jiffy 501.10
jig 523.31
jiggery 535.13
jigsaw 376.13
jingo 238.18
job 204.30
jock 033.28
jocular 587.07
join 006.18 020.16 058.14 244.29 370.22
joint 027.02 181.30 192.35 231.31 310.31 534.18
joke 033.28 063.31 126.07 162.04 208.23 270.03 337.24 375.04 376.13 417.30 449.32
jolly 112.32 113.35 236.13 248.13 254.15 272.15 278.F1 347.29 451.01 463.12 463.27 590.23
jonah 160.18
joss 338.27
jostle 092.06 568.08
journal 228.33 500.15 501.20
journey 215.09 469.18 472.34 621.02
jovial 405.20
joviality 006.19 058.14 351.15
jowl 168.11 215.19 245.30 315.11
joy 162.35
joyride 613.22
jubilant 084.02 338.17
jubilee 031.20 087.05 205.07 305.19 329.30 340.06
judge 246.02
jug 153.07 341.04
jugjug 450.17
jugular 300.31 511.35
juice 067.17 171.18 229.26 229.27 334.21 351.09
jujitsu 352.28
July 070.03 082.28 097.03 569.13
jumble 112.04
jump 231.31 232.30
June 015.35 082.28 087.05 203.20 231.02 245.12 473.10 569.13
jungle 084.16 268.03
junk 156.06 179.28
junta 316.36
jurisdiction 574.34
juror 536.33 575.36
jury 242.14 447.09 519.26 575.25 603.17 603.17
juryman 516.03
just 011.07 030.18 031.10 042.15 048.01 130.24 180.07 229.26 229.27 233.03 245.22 258.04 292.20 359.22 363.10 363.10 416.12 419.30 440.26 448.06 486.10 491.06 502.07 511.11 517.08 565.14 599.19 626.05
justice 100.15 134.34 351.09
justification 241.36
justify 488.17
jut 441.24
Jute 175.12

kaffir 614.10
kalander 040.34
kaleidoscope 143.28
kalekannon 174.22 391.33 456.07
kangaroo 165.21 244.10 244.10
keenly 421.05
keep 062.08 206.24 208.23 243.22 415.24 422.14 467.24 531.22 540.36 565.15
keeper 144.07 229.09 255.22 305.16 352.26 366.02
keepsake 438.19
ken 031.28 225.16
kepi 015.34
kerchief 051.14
kettle 073.08 151.14 267.F5 316.20 320.16 330.25 332.02 549.13 585.30 596.32
kettledrum 122.07 356.19 531.09
key 093.23 095.14 133.09 135.23 141.22 196.20 205.08 282.29 434.15 511.30 535.07 540.23 570.29 601.23
keyhole 379.36
kick 113.07 210.06 245.02 388.02 490.05 503.08 511.32 584.20 584.21 614.06
kidglove 205.18
kidney 059.20 350.23 464.36
kill 413.27
kind 059.10 099.14 289.05 608.23
kindergarten 191.21 253.31 483.25
kindly 499.16 528.22
king 026.29 052.25 058.19 058.20 108.11 187.20 267.05 285.L2 285.L2 322.33 353.31 363.05 388.02 393.07 457.07 457.08 498.11 499.13 499.14 557.06 569.23
kingdom 018.21 104.02 241.22 255.22 333.31 373.15 536.35 594.06 600.10
kingsman 087.25
kish 110.23
kismet 316.06
kiss 083.13 137.22 210.06 264.11 313.13 375.16 383.18 461.30 467.07 475.24 475.25 494.29 512.08 568.24
kitchen 494.34 531.06
kitchenmidden 503.08
kith 394.28
kitten 239.23 370.03
kitty 239.18
klyster 406.19
knack 113.07
knapsack 011.19 350.34
knave 274.F2 267.06 370.15 405.29 414.05 420.23 552.07
knead 498.20
knee 376.10 388.04 534.19 547.05
kneesknob 274.F2
knickerbockers 177.04 208.15 208.16 549.04 611.34
knickknack 288.18
knight 277.14 346.06 489.31 501.28 501.29
knob 274.F2
knobbly 064.30
knock 139.35 302.F1 476.06 515.07 556.34 557.05 606.19
knocker 572.03
knockkneed 241.24
knot 267.09
know 010.26 021.02 059.34 079.29 129.15 133.16 141.17 233.07 248.03 269.26 274.F2 315.29 322.13 323.26 341.16 344.04 353.15 379.01 379.02 392.06 413.28 512.31 550.05 561.05 597.22
knowledge 233.07 623.32
knuckle 507.11 602.33
knut 395.23
kohl 359.10
Koran 020.10 040.05 056.19 089.05 177.09 242.32 297.32 312.35 368.26 443.01 597.15
kowtow 090.01 325.34 550.28 552.11 608.20 623.12

label 246.20
labial 116.28
labour 091.14
laburnum 509.24
labyrinth 310.21 485.26
lace 548.33
lacewing 417.25
lack 162.23 378.04
lacrimose 569.02
lad 290.25
ladder 006.10 150.08 323.14 337.12 370.28 425.01 518.04 590.15
laddy 263.18
laden 585.16
lady 071.07 071.09 126.02 152.16 177.08 228.35 232.15 263.18 277.L4 328.24 330.10 332.22 343.21 350.08 415.03 465.36 510.31 523.22 568.23 573.35
ladybird 534.36
lady-in-waiting 275.12
ladylike 111.23 246.14 370.10 437.01 438.26 461.19 531.23
ladylove 530.15
ladymayoress 510.11 550.28
ladyship 229.21
laetification 372.24 551.20
lagoon 327.29
laird 510.18
lake 378.04 427.02 600.36 617.31
lamb 070.07 524.31 562.24 562.35 566.09
lament 221.27 440.35 601.05
lamentation 340.09 571.22
Lammas 296.01 421.02
lamp 019.31 318.14 338.31 377.27 411.28 427.16 583.33

lampblack 207.18
lampshade 445.04
land 116.11 137.09 168.02 319.17 320.22 370.28 382.28 395.14 447.33 614.08
landlocked 023.29
landowner 568.06
landscape 011.10 464.35 474.02 502.36 595.04
landslide 323.09
landsman 372.23
lane 444.29 534.18
lang 087.06 096.23 112.08 238.13 398.26 398.28
language 073.01 096.11 116.28 141.21 232.21 275.F6 323.05 327.20 338.20 339.01 357.18 378.23 466.32 478.09 485.13 579.33 584.04 621.22
languish 357.18 508.34
lantern 184.17 321.04 338.35 549.02 621.05
lap 578.24
lapel 397.19
large 364.07
largely 412.28
lark 021.03 381.22 624.28
larynx 489.17
lascivious 068.12
lash 060.15 227.07 322.22 482.05
lashing 029.32
lass 140.16 270.21 290.25 329.03
lassitude 270.08
lassy 324.09
last 063.24 069.10 123.04 130.03 142.03 149.23 155.28 214.01 227.09 232.06 254.13 282.26 285.12 298.10 300.11 302.F2 350.14 356.01 356.33 398.10 409.10 414.29 433.10 433.23 444.25 453.12 480.20 503.30 515.26 601.05 615.15
latch 459.26
late 021.33 022.21 224.15 242.29 329.35 346.09 601.04
later 526.36 604.08
lateral 477.19
latest 106.11 232.15 320.07 365.05 620.03
Latin 093.09 113.02 155.27 183.20 205.27 393.01 519.16
latish 174.29
latitude 050.17 441.09
latter 369.35 393.20 450.26 510.16
latterly 502.16 502.16 502.16 502.16
laud 605.14
lauds 605.14
laugh 011.33 023.25 070.12 149.07 175.23 175.23 203.30 229.04 254.13 273.22 314.20 319.31 420.13 420.34 511.13
laughter 092.02 222.34 463.11
launch 162.31
laurel 264.26 561.19
lavatory 068.07 357.22 420.11
lavender 331.27
law 027.08 049.15 067.36 139.29 153.19 200.36 220.23 267.F5 312.13 325.15 448.15 532.25 603.25
lawful 529.18
lawgiver 545.32
lawn 089.10 325.14
lay 203.08 240.04 405.34 624.01
layer 013.17 323.30 552.26
layman 038.07 062.01 488.04
lazily 427.01
lazuli 293.11
lazy 530.21
lead 072.08 096.03 332.22 561.22 594.06
leaden 412.10 620.31
leader 042.17 330.10 579.19
leaf 107.15 117.01 140.25 240.24 265.14 357.21 426.13 444.25 601.02 608.28
leafy 146.23
league 256.36 260.F1 310.17 347.14
leak 449.33 462.30 467.03
lean 251.22
leap 141.04 197.11 201.18 250.22 427.02 433.34 451.15 484.29 499.13 626.02
leaper 540.31
leapyear 127.02 143.01 159.16 327.07 430.03
learn 149.06 200.36 239.02 251.22 255.21 288.23 378.25 479.23
learner 292.23
learning 222.25
least 063.24 214.10 323.33 452.06 489.05
leather 390.07
leave 015.24 027.08 032.06 062.09 068.07 080.29 088.34 118.34 136.28 142.03 168.02 203.01 203.10 221.12 249.30 293.16 304.F4 311.33 341.07 344.10 371.17 420.23 437.14 439.34 476.27 490.25 540.35 549.33 600.07 621.33
leaven 517.33
leavings 027.10
lecherous 181.08
lecture 241.16 333.35
lee 466.06
leer 590.02 610.09
leeward 279.F30
left 027.04 119.02 138.21 183.29 226.26 256.36 282.20 301.29 334.26 397.11 417.18 490.25 498.05
lefthanded 374.07
leg 028.05 082.05 294.11 297.28 337.03 449.20
legate 497.08
legend 277.22 431.04
legible 356.21
legion 380.23 576.34
legitimate 364.29 495.25
legpull 057.17
leisure 024.16 131.15 263.23 328.09 373.19 609.11
leisurely 427.01
leman 038.07 062.01 110.28
lemon 110.28 171.12 215.20 296.03 302.R1 331.17 361.24 373.23 560.14 571.22 596.01 601.05
lemonade 236.03
lemonsoda 604.09
lemonsquash 270.L1 296.01 318.27 386.09 390.32 392.36
lend 206.26 278.L3 293.23 378.23 607.09
length 023.02 208.05 238.24
lengthy 130.08
lentil 302.02 540.21 607.09
leopard 422.13 483.14 483.21
leper 257.06
leprechaun 419.17
lesbian 116.28
lesion 436.20
less 053.05 078.28 379.24
lessen 477.07
lesson 026.34 436.20 477.07
lest 016.02 069.30
lethargy 334.01 432.32
Lethe 166.07
letter 017.28 066.25 073.29 093.24 100.02 100.02 114.17 114.18 157.08 157.17 159.05 159.06 202.02 278.20 278.21 284.15 286.22 289.19 301.02 323.14 329.35 337.12 355.33 364.05 369.32 369.35 369.36 370.06 382.13 390.01 413.16 419.17 420.35 422.35 423.11 424.20 425.01 456.27 479.27 490.27 510.16 511.22 534.21 534.34 561.11 570.18 590.15 593.13 593.13 602.18 603.03 603.17 604.08
letterbox 618.12
letterpress 356.21
lettuce 020.24 424.20 511.22 540.23
lever 076.13 230.34 563.30
lewd 337.09 340.02 507.28 580.36
lexicon 083.25
liability 240.20
liable 425.13
liar 364.32 499.19 540.23
libation 442.36
libel 603.29
liberally 465.25
liberate 300.21 300.23
libertine 211.05
liberty 133.31 233.18 577.34 604.09
libidinous 524.35
libitum 541.28
library 440.05 442.36
libretto 365.09 425.20
licit 445.10
lick 551.05
lie 044.10 099.30 291.21
lieu 051.24 069.22
lieutenant 299.16 338.19
lieutenant-colonel 607.29
lieutenant-governor 325.01
life 011.29 023.33 138.31 145.27 162.05 227.17 230.25 255.02 279.F12 299.29 309.02 316.27 326.30 340.13 341.17 345.07 361.18 368.12 372.07 416.09 418.06 425.20 427.12 427.20 441.06 447.23 506.08 513.23 580.13 595.08 617.07

lifeline 178.06
lifelong 547.33
lifesize 230.28 571.21
lifetime 088.34 230.19 361.26 394.34 444.25
Liffey 003.24 007.35 026.16 042.18 174.26 203.06 204.05 224.29 230.25 254.11 308.20 310.05 317.32 328.17 328.17 342.25 382.27 387.09 420.34 445.34 452.19 496.27 553.04 619.20 619.29 624.22 625.33 628.07
lift 037.02 118.34 415.34 593.07
light 090.12 123.34 127.27 139.11 159.32 202.28 348.25 350.28 362.22 395.33 412.06 427.17 517.20 525.03 549.17 565.17 583.14 594.11 615.24 617.15
lightly 237.07
lightning 222.22 263.F2 299.16 335.11 339.17 347.34 367.28 378.09 415.20 468.21 520.10 607.26
likelihood 312.03
liken 013.17
likeness 153.32 621.27
likewise 366.24 369.34
lily 318.04 326.03 331.27 338.21 340.22 352.22 366.25 396.25 396.25 396.26 396.26 422.32 433.13 450.29 452.19 491.22 501.30 561.19 583.09
lilywhite 584.15
limb 319.17
lime 319.13
limestone 319.10 331.04
limit 198.13
limousine 595.04
line 209.18 358.05 365.24 419.29
lingo 621.22
lingual 298.06
lining 367.28
link 567.36
linoleum 391.21
lion 054.21 148.36 155.06 155.06 193.04 244.32 277.22 350.30 371.36 449.11 541.16 545.36 590.07 599.06
lioness 359.16
lionise 323.29 465.15
lip 251.16 376.20 395.33 395.33 403.16 489.27 528.13 619.20 619.20 628.15
lipstick 093.25 460.02
liquid 234.17 280.32 394.35 465.23
liquor 316.19 434.29
lisp 023.23 302.F2 553.18 619.20
lissom 236.06
list 364.29 508.34
listen 013.17 021.02 021.02 023.29 101.06 148.26 148.26 201.04 207.24 209.24 245.09 290.02 290.08 367.13 384.19 394.20 394.20 432.21 477.07 588.26 619.20 619.22 621.17 624.06
listener 013.13 477.18
literally 321.01 408.09 444.28 534.09
literary 422.35 530.10
literate 166.04 336.31
literature 570.18
litter 183.10
little 004.28 018.34 029.08 048.04 105.10 180.06 183.13 191.20 198.05 207.26 208.05 226.29 226.29 241.04 259.04 265.14 270.21 282.F3 287.07 295.05 315.05 327.03 379.15 394.20 394.20 395.32 407.04 416.18 417.04 432.21 448.25 461.13 471.10 491.22 496.18 496.19 496.20 504.14 527.11 528.04 533.23 542.22 547.05 553.23 561.24 562.14 577.13 583.22 587.26 588.26 601.19 613.27 621.24 625.23
littlebriton 152.05
littlego 279.F12 327.07 507.09
liturgy 432.32
live 012.02 153.30 230.25 254.11 353.10 390.30 392.14 463.28 495.21 511.34 533.35 534.29 548.01 562.25 625.27
livelihood 012.33
liveliness 568.04
liver 059.19 097.30 230.34 234.30 334.15 424.11 552.26
liverish 590.02
livid 524.35
lizzard 324.04
load 583.04
loaf 023.32 243.28 375.33 385.15 451.12 587.02 623.19
loan 184.01 212.27 378.23 578.26
loathe 023.31 336.06 336.07 336.07 428.14 627.17 627.17 627.18 627.33 627.33
lobe 208.11
lobster 094.17 311.10 337.21 351.06 408.19
local 051.26 051.26 237.22 324.32
localise 087.18
lock 013.13 023.29 196.20 248.23 257.27 289.11 289.12 415.33 545.27 604.07
locker 316.19
locket 485.09
lockkneed 241.24
locksmith 148.32 197.11
locust 318.15 419.09 435.35
lodger 489.03
lodging 233.07
lodginghouse 506.21
loft 170.21
log 428.20
logical 296.26
loneliness 325.35 627.34
lonely 194.21 627.34
lonesome 026.15 206.24 450.09
long 006.26 017.03 021.05 167.27 172.28 244.25 270.F2 323.25 335.32 338.21 396.29 406.28 434.33 439.16 499.14 525.31 547.33 579.33
longer 331.06 349.35
longitude 542.06 566.35
look 013.13 052.35 058.06 058.06 071.27 079.21 079.21 123.13 125.09 127.19 223.31 226.26 245.30 262.F2 268.F6 295.33 314.17 343.14 343.27 447.14 485.09 493.07 529.20 534.31 541.16 578.17 597.24 601.04 601.07 604.07
looker 270.21
lookingglass 014.34 193.16 294.08 415.28 459.04 526.35 528.17
loop 097.08 097.08 108.27 214.04
loose 082.25 082.33 082.33 151.23 234.15
loquacious 099.02
loquacity 424.34
lord 017.08 027.08 063.27 083.07 090.03 091.19 097.31 141.16 180.07 193.01 214.19 215.08 230.05 232.23 239.10 242.36 243.10 253.32 257.31 258.13 258.13 258.25 258.26 259.03 259.04 259.07 268.28 278.12 282.04 286.31 288.25 299.06 299.06 301.22 326.19 331.09 370.31 385.18 409.15 413.05 431.27 435.10 456.10 469.21 483.34 485.25 507.17 540.34 547.08 552.25 587.15 590.05 604.10 609.03 613.15 615.36 626.06
lord-lieutenant 338.19
lordmayor 248.07 342.28 372.02 379.05 498.29 510.10 550.28 625.36
lordship 053.31 312.16 332.23
lose 006.26 080.15 245.07 263.L4 347.15 426.28 493.05 528.34 547.07 603.01 610.34 615.25 627.17 627.17 627.18 627.33 627.33
loss 312.05
lot 011.25 051.16 176.16 201.36 375.16 410.26 512.23 607.16
lottery 518.18
lotus 062.11 229.13
loud 208.12 232.22 479.33 580.36 609.10 624.20
louder 460.11
loudmouth 329.33
loudspeaker 459.28
lousy 336.06 336.07 516.09
lout 484.10
love 010.27 017.36 146.36 172.11 196.24 207.23 245.07 245.13 250.17 262.F2 263.23 270.21 293.21 293.22 324.09 340.07 354.28 375.33 385.15 408.19 418.24 440.30 454.06 460.04 466.25 468.13 494.07 495.17 518.02 531.11 532.22 539.33 541.14 551.02 601.02
loveliest 265.29 561.15 624.22
lovelight 441.16 615.24
lovely 011.23 023.31 140.23 182.27 204.14 226.26 226.26 226.27 226.27 241.13 273.19 300.F4 318.01 357.17 365.02 365.23 416.34 470.14 528.04 613.29 617.24
lovematch 143.29

lovenest 290.15
lover 093.07 327.32 388.03 395.34 513.32 540.31 540.35 546.32
lovesong 328.06
low 023.11 071.09 198.23 279.F32 327.27 359.19 531.15 549.18
lower 206.31 315.35 421.11
lowest 283.07
lowly 499.31
loyal 021.07
lozenge 405.24
Lucan 037.32 051.26 053.24 087.18 110.08 255.21 476.24 497.18
lucifer 069.12
luck 257.27 425.28
lucky 035.03 326.35 332.25 358.09 424.21 499.04
lug 506.12
lugger 026.04
lull 098.03
lullaby 450.29 462.15
luminous 282.29
lump 137.01 511.12
lunch 028.09 121.34 127.31 131.04 162.31 222.10 405.17
luncheon 015.33 069.33 191.28 248.20 322.02 372.30 373.20
lunge 396.29
lungfish 525.31
lurch 249.31
lure 310.24
lurk 381.22 510.18 606.31
luscious 062.11
lust 318.35 338.17
lusty 176.29
lute 105.27
Lutheran 021.30 110.08 141.16 195.02
luxuriously 451.32
luxury 451.31
lymph 580.25 583.33
lyre 391.28
lyric 528.23

mace 165.02
machine 495.23
mackerel 525.08
mackintosh 346.02
mad 064.17 151.06
madam 158.01 232.17 232.18 240.12 272.F1 315.21 316.11 333.34 351.31 624.08
madcap 415.07
maddest 296.20
madness 032.05 182.07
madonna 433.04 490.06
magazine 013.14 116.18 137.17 262.26 294.25 314.13 314.13 314.15 331.30 334.24 553.24 560.15 615.31
maggers 379.30
magic 203.31
magical 514.02
magistrate 106.23
magma 595.27
magnanimous 331.22 545.32
magnate 246.23
magnesium 397.27
mahamanvantara 020.17
maid 013.26 015.11 040.10 117.29 126.24 177.02 184.04 201.17 239.10 239.18 243.26 278.12 289.19 314.13 316.23 335.36 387.21 394.26 436.12 436.32 461.24 496.11 526.36 565.09 590.20 601.31
maiden 021.01 235.01 424.11
maidenhead 250.09 582.26
mail 421.02 461.25 545.27
mailbag 337.11
mailcoach 364.05
mainbrace 316.09
mainly 260.L2 313.23 406.31 527.24
mainstay 431.35
mainstream 547.31
majestic 008.18
majesty 031.10 112.28 116.24 120.17 171.25 175.23 239.22 278.F6 334.17 334.18 335.02 340.34 369.30 379.30 420.07 535.06 535.07 568.25 569.02 623.16 624.02
major 088.20
make 019.08 020.10 037.21 096.14 101.09 135.01 154.10 206.09 229.22 239.22 245.29 251.06 271.F4 296.05 314.03 326.06 350.13 362.19 374.01 395.19 418.10 420.09 433.28 518.31 519.24 525.13 525.19 542.13 593.14 602.19
maker 290.27 352.36 619.28
makeshift 205.17 603.14
malady 279.F04
male 437.31
malevolence 350.13
maliciously 414.30
mallow 208.32
malt 319.09
maltreat 322.29
maltster 338.01
mamma 332.13 373.34 501.32 571.12
mammal 451.23
mammifer 421.35
mammoth 054.25 510.04
manage 450.23
manager 108.18
manciple 338.25
mandarin 089.24 171.16 338.26
mange 145.01
mangy 228.03
manhood 054.25 329.09 484.03
manifest 261.21
manifestation 106.34
manifesto 104.04 106.34
manikin 017.02 058.10 207.14 267.F2 329.04 334.35 532.33 576.15 576.15
mankind 252.05 270.F4 297.F4
manmade 309.22
manner 247.27 365.05 444.26 464.33
mannerism 608.01
manoeuvre 344.17 432.23 480.17 570.05
manor 128.08 242.36 365.05 396.05
man-o'-war 272.10 338.24 525.32
mansion 197.24 242.06
mansionhouse 491.18 617.22
manslaughter 433.29
manufacture 310.10 466.12
manufacturer 173.17
Manx 496.08
marble 064.04 319.10
march 064.13 078.22 246.23 260.08 276.F2 364.09 365.27 377.15 412.10 614.17
March 015.36 040.10 085.27 134.12 353.02 366.30 423.03
mare 138.24 276.08 379.05 411.08 485.26 568.30 588.13
marigold 561.21 562.12
mariner 315.21 316.11 324.08 426.03
mariposa 417.28
maritime 209.05 325.30
mark 023.23 078.08 083.10 083.15 249.03 266.09 280.14 491.17 491.17 491.17 506.24 551.07
market 034.10 068.05 378.08 532.25 533.20
marketplace 368.09
marmalade 223.08 235.32 236.06 285.06 464.06 586.36
maroon 426.03
marquis 386.18
marriage 196.24 239.13 340.28 514.04 607.21
marriageable 584.32
marrow 016.03
marrowbone 550.10
marry 006.11 105.20 131.15 208.35 226.18 232.15 256.08 276.F2 375.27 492.31 501.32 563.26
Mars 494.12
marshal 132.24
marshmallow 208.32 491.15
marshy 624.24
martial 349.02 539.27
martially 063.33
Martinmas 310.25 517.34
martyr 091.23 214.23 326.02 348.11 569.08 575.01
marvellous 148.24 443.36
masculine 166.24 166.26 237.03 268.18
mash 491.15
mask 237.30 300.21 300.24 390.10 512.09 603.03
masquerade 206.14 515.25
mass 064.13 199.09 203.31 212.08 243.35 300.24 310.25 336.02 347.13 366.08 382.13 514.27 596.02 604.06 613.25 623.36
massage 531.05
masseur 432.23
master 037.08 054.21 062.03 149.08 154.03 177.30 186.35 191.35 224.20 256.21 271.04 275.F5 324.20 324.28 326.10 337.28 338.01 355.29 384.06 391.08 393.08 395.03 499.15 506.05 511.28 515.32 530.32 568.17 576.18 603.12 607.31
masterbuilder 077.03 126.10 274.11 296.07 309.13 377.26
masterkey 560.29
mastertailor 613.32
mastery 166.36

masthead 322.11
mastodontic 510.03
masturbate 209.08 515.32 585.34
match 064.32 143.29 297.16 415.13 584.10
matchbox 010.18 562.14
mate 165.25 172.07 242.25 313.18
mater 531.19
material 205.20 274.32
mathematical 286.23
matinee 219.05 397.16
matins 540.31
matrimony 010.03 423.30 451.12
matter 016.16 037.10 066.25 089.26 150.11 166.19 166.27 225.32 230.08 254.32 345.04 345.07 389.06 465.34 516.26 596.05
mattress 326.10 585.06
maturity 230.14
maudlin 057.27 153.36 206.01
Maundy 128.13 149.05
mausoleum 261.13 553.10
mavrodaphne 406.25
maximus 532.09 567.31
May 027.12 082.36 245.06 245.06 267.29 285.03 352.36 364.13 569.13
maybe 093.31 280.20 623.30
mayhap 425.27 514.29
mayor 029.02 248.07 342.28 364.26 372.02 379.05 498.29 510.11 550.28 568.16 625.36
mayoress 510.11 550.28
maypole 596.21
maze 244.21 493.07
mazurka 437.29
mead 236.21 518.31
meadow 278.18
meal 333.31 579.22
mean 214.34 311.27 313.28 333.02 511.22
meander 333.23
meanest 396.21
meaning 151.31 267.03 267.03 313.23
meaningless 247.16
means 161.19 405.30 505.24
meantime 085.36 192.06 312.25 528.05
meanwhile 243.14
measles 523.29
measure 331.22 336.05 336.05 356.20
meat 143.19 224.07 270.F2 313.34 356.18 362.03
Meathman 067.25
meat-safe 311.12
mechanic 258.17 471.14
medalist 336.21
mediaeval 423.28 538.12
medical 413.07 492.24 514.02
medicine 025.04 413.11
Mediterranean 120.29 289.20
meek 423.13
meerschaum 050.30 241.14
meet 060.29 105.08 118.20 176.24 228.19 236.21 287.F3 305.28 340.07 350.35 467.31 520.26 541.15
meeting 129.13 540.31 567.08 610.34
megaphone 229.21 258.21
melancholic 453.07
melancholy 555.23 565.20
melodious 412.07
melody 106.08 279.F04 341.04 492.34 516.32
melon 453.07 555.23
melt 151.26 477.30
melting-pot 346.15
member 242.28 277.09 390.29
memoir 387.34
memorable 294.07
memorial 008.35 009.34 027.33
memorise 180.29
memory 254.18 270.30 310.23 460.20 490.14 507.30 535.27 535.30 551.04
mend 329.35 346.09
menhir 025.11 492.17 539.03
mensuration 269.F3
mental 282.08
mention 052.26 265.05 620.21
mentis 516.29
mercenary 609.03
mercery 548.31
merchandise 210.02
merchant 061.28 105.01 197.33 317.24 340.23 435.02 536.31
merciful 104.01 353.02
mercury 247.21 251.15 261.25
Mercury 494.12
mercy 055.19 184.09 205.16 208.36 212.26 259.07 288.25 326.19 409.16 548.31 552.30 607.35
merely 224.19 245.28 365.29
meretrix 008.08 060.06 211.33
merge 496.23
meridian 406.01
mermaid 352.08 464.06
merman 312.10
merriment 062.07 074.10 375.27
merry 011.14 223.01 227.01 453.19 493.07 525.16 534.01 563.26 569.24
merrygoround 309.24 525.17 550.27
merrymaker 619.28
mesial 492.24
mess 179.11 568.12
message 004.20 298.07 324.18 460.20 506.35 510.12 536.02
messenger 026.18 108.18 235.01 352.10 405.07 497.07
metal 313.27 344.22 359.04 551.32
metamorphose 434.32 513.31
metaphysically 319.34
meteor 194.16
meteorite 518.12
methinks 239.22
method 032.04 316.31
methylated 266.09
metre 531.19
metropolis 316.15 582.34
metropolitan 080.01 543.01 565.04
mezzotint 552.24
miasma 236.22 568.01
Michaelmas 215.21 413.24 556.05 567.16
microcephalic 525.08
microcosm 151.01 468.21
microscope 275.L2 300.17
mid 209.21 328.18 519.35
midden 393.23 595.25
middle 086.19 141.33 191.29 311.07 346.27 347.01 357.05 378.29 393.23 410.17 491.12 506.02 541.35
middleage 491.08
middleclass 152.08
midland 295.19 447.33
midnight 067.03 067.03 067.03 067.04 339.05 391.33 470.07 475.21 519.35 543.12
midst 007.17 008.04 339.34 339.35 350.02 563.03
midsummer 502.29
midweek 349.25
midwife 588.36
midwinter 502.29
mighthavebeen 408.16
mightiest 269.19
mighty 009.26 088.17 093.31 296.19 301.08 310.33 314.30 416.26 417.10 445.14 482.13 623.05
migraine 004.04
mild 212.26
mildew 057.27 196.17 221.11
mile 020.19 200.19 246.19 410.34 628.03 628.03
milestone 462.25
militant 495.10
military 125.10 338.20
militia 347.09 351.23 451.13
milk 097.19 111.12 141.09 183.30 243.32 262.22 277.F5 318.15 326.23 354.32 370.19 416.11 420.33 425.10 613.11
milkcart 538.08
milkingstool 559.07
milkman 277.F1 337.06 366.17 435.28 586.16 618.03
milkwhite 111.30 596.32
milky 395.01
miller 341.05
millinery 338.20
million 117.22 129.16 239.03 265.25 285.24 382.18 613.25
millrace 541.15
millstone 322.33 375.31 504.32
mime 106.10
mince 113.13
mind 016.27 141.25 252.16 300.24 333.12 333.12 421.11 425.25 434.04 472.05 509.28 530.14
mine 146.31 314.22 315.31 469.11 538.28 565.30
mineral 556.36
minister 508.22 552.03 609.11
ministry 228.14 338.35 370.05
minor 026.04 082.05 112.34
Minotaur 272.10
minstrel 062.31 515.28 528.32 609.11
mint 146.31
minus 412.27
minute 177.27 238.34 469.01
mirabilis 539.29
miracle 326.31 327.30 365.01 425.20 617.25
miraculous 229.32
mirage 613.29

mire 417.33 569.06
mirror 295.05 310.24 471.04 471.04 613.29
mirth 392.34
miry 493.07
misbeliever 520.19
miserliness 148.36
misery 260.F2 270.22 348.09 432.22
misfire 322.10
misfortune 149.23 492.28
mishap 313.32
mislead 349.11 523.29
misogyny 175.31
misplace 418.11
misprint 020.11
miss 197.23 224.20 224.20 248.21 290.25 299.F1
misselthrush 384.03 385.02 586.26 616.32
missile 586.26
mission 106.19 620.21
missionary 228.14 348.09
missive 395.36
missus 186.36 238.15
mist 235.06 324.32 566.36
mistake 063.29 097.06 317.26 420.26 532.21 625.01
mister 004.18 050.23 058.16 107.02 126.10 144.20 271.04 291.F4 309.13 337.28 338.01 355.30 383.01 395.03 437.33 453.17 466.30 477.21 515.32 516.03 528.28 530.32 576.28 578.10 615.18
mistletoe 009.19 097.36 147.10 236.15 349.11 360.25 376.13 384.03 385.02 392.24 465.14 465.27 468.26 485.30 491.29 556.05 588.26 588.35 616.32
mistress 112.29 189.25 228.17 326.10 370.05 406.30 437.33 442.01 453.17 538.06 578.19
misty 155.24
misunderstand 363.36
misunderstanding 175.27
misuse 228.03
mix 070.32 166.14 196.24 299.13
moan 512.26
moat 118.20
mobile 448.29
mocha 199.18
mock 308.02 320.06 393.11
model 311.07 435.05 435.15
modern 289.F6 353.29 355.21 377.12 395.10 396.36
modest 085.30
modesty 034.19
moggy 258.21
mogul 277.03
mole 422.32 499.23
molecule 353.26
molest 334.03
molybdenum 056.13
moment 165.12 231.08 353.06 357.12 404.14 568.13 628.06
monarch 468.29 525.17
Monday 117.05 128.13 149.05 205.17 301.20 324.33 338.18 350.12 364.33 409.28 453.13 457.19 492.05 532.31
money 135.01 172.11 184.30 219.19 451.12 451.12 462.06
monger 029.26
mongrel 095.34 095.34
monkey 192.03 337.29 397.20 595.26 611.10
monocotyledon 056.13
monolith 105.12
monologue 182.20 254.14 424.34
Monseigneur 243.31
monster 088.16 249.03 528.28 576.18
montage 223.08
month 078.19 177.25 324.26 331.29 348.16 421.34 536.22 598.32
monthly 387.35
monument 025.16 318.31 595.22
moon 141.25 244.26 245.07 267.03 267.22 382.10 399.05 411.27 561.12
moonbeam 225.22
moonlight 147.25 202.28
moonrise 485.26
moonshine 440.31
moonstone 225.22
moor 426.08
mop 527.31
moral 583.24
more 007.15 053.05
moreover 172.11 213.09 274.16
morganatic 530.13 545.27
Mormon 534.14
morn 005.10 091.24 203.10 212.26 584.03
morning 006.07 006.14 012.14 023.31 031.29 090.08 106.08 131.28 139.11 222.18 247.18 277.07 320.20 322.15 331.06 335.18 378.36 387.31 395.16 452.02 512.26 525.03 530.27 584.25 593.09 608.19 613.30 614.08 623.27
morrow 037.02 095.18 158.16 516.10
mortal 080.22 147.17 149.08 227.31 317.33 577.04
mortar 005.27 315.06
mortification 058.08
mosaic 037.24
mosque 136.01 541.31
mosquito 211.28
moss 602.11
mote 005.27
moth 561.26
mother 017.24 020.07 055.19 060.31 089.26 107.19 116.02 116.03 116.03 116.04 116.04 131.07 132.05 132.34 135.05 139.15 146.05 157.14 158.27 166.27 177.06 187.13 206.09 207.29 212.15 213.30 220.04 223.05 224.10 224.18 225.32 238.25 240.23 294.04 295.05 296.21 297.01 298.29 325.13 330.36 330.36 336.06 340.16 341.14 354.24 360.14 377.25 378.27 388.21 388.29 397.12 408.32 411.17 411.25 412.31 415.13 423.01 426.04 433.30 443.34 469.14 469.26 496.27 535.35 542.20 558.29 566.19 568.01 608.16 615.04 617.18 623.03
mother-in-law 049.15 139.29
motherlove 250.17
mothermilk 425.09
motion 377.10
motley 338.11
motorcraft 623.19
motto 485.03
mould 142.03
moulder 364.09
moult 378.12
mound 007.31
mount 128.13 181.19 405.30
mountain 008.01 044.01 128.03 136.35 136.36 227.20 317.34 327.22 331.18 331.20 338.17 354.20 372.28 478.31 608.19
mountebank 055.04
mourn 304.F4 439.34 512.26
mourner 385.32 496.35
mournful 347.07
mournfully 158.27
mourning 335.18 428.17 428.18 566.07 566.25
mouse 416.13 626.23
moustache 087.03 182.27 288.F7 532.21
mouth 088.18 144.35 165.05 172.22 338.17 354.34 395.23 536.22 562.26 587.34 595.01
mouthful 441.15
mouthorgan 315.24
move 215.34 377.14 593.14
mow 278.18
muchness 294.17 505.20
muck 090.31
muddle 084.25
muezzin 310.25
muffinman 491.28
mufti 300.25
mugwump 268.11
mulberry 105.08 237.05 265.01
mule 468.31
mulga 321.33
mulligatawny 309.23
multiplication 026.36
multiply 283.05 446.01 586.24
mummery 378.33
mummify 333.06
mummy 176.12
mumps 523.29
mundane 333.23 350.12
munificence 302.07 549.21
munition 011.15
murder 008.24 017.24 020.07 063.21 090.34 131.07 151.31 206.09 219.20 224.18 250.17 259.05 305.12 320.13 326.02 340.16 345.07 353.20 354.14 354.25 354.25 397.12 412.31 433.30 445.31 449.21 499.07 517.11 535.35 540.29 558.29 569.08 624.26
murderer 566.19 566.24 617.18
murderous 374.12
murmur 092.13 101.33 160.25 254.18 335.18 354.18 387.34 396.34 540.15 541.31 551.04 604.11
murram 006.06
muscat 078.24 354.26
muscle 531.06

muscleman 491.28 491.28 -491.29
muscular 166.24
muse 061.04 064.06 541.32
museum 333.16
mushroom 142.10 625.19
music 198.24 340.34 565.17 570.02
musical 013.09 237.30 417.09 492.24 497.07 588.09 613.18
musichall 450.19
musket 517.09 539.35
musketeer 379.36 412.35
muskrat 615.16
Muslem 005.16 243.28 245.27 422.16 491.28 553.10
muslin 553.10
mustard 230.08 279.F23 322.11 446.22
mutant 508.27
mutate 496.07
mute 517.03
mutiny 323.11
mutter 623.03
mutton 007.06 327.22 467.16 549.04
muttonchop 067.17
mutual 230.14 434.28
mutually 164.02
Mycenaean 178.36
myopia 454.01
myopic 139.16
myriad 375.10
myrmicine 415.13
myself 161.01 168.05 444.18 447.10 469.12 487.18 538.08 612.24 623.33 627.21 627.27
mysterious 015.33
mystery 060.20 166.36 270.22
mystically 510.18
mystify 393.33
myth 243.06
mythological 373.21

nag 250.36
nail 516.12
naked 288.F4 359.10 551.12
name 029.19 075.20 141.30 155.32 204.05 236.30 270.28 363.13 420.04 420.23 476.35 482.03 505.22 536.35 599.05 601.30
namely 414.31
namesake 442.05 489.20 619.13
narcissism 526.34
narcissus 234.14
narration 205.14
nasal 577.11
nasturtium 320.04 624.26
nasty 395.02 456.17 536.36
nation 107.19 128.16 297.F1 309.12 365.27 426.20 475.21 614.17 614.17
national 057.21 128.27 240.14 428.17 440.05 498.06 610.35
native 288.16 538.11
natural 313.21 598.17
nature 524.06
naughtily 222.35
naughty 054.21 068.03 105.10 196.24 261.24 284.11 411.34 512.21 512.21
nauseous 233.36
nautical 622.10
naval 480.17
navel 583.03
navigate 320.07
navy 179.19 322.04 323.05 396.21
Neanderthal 018.22 019.25
neap 141.06 244.36
Neapolitan 172.23
nearer 506.24
nearest 460.04
nearly 151.07
nearsighted 143.09
neat 312.24
neath 200.01
neatly 469.12
nebulous 256.33
necessary 237.36
necessity 412.28 526.34 613.27
neck 039.06 039.06 258.10 258.17 310.34 334.19
necklace 548.33
needle 104.20 120.27 143.09 239.36 320.17 327.03
needless 532.24
ne'er 012.08
neigh 010.15 010.15 010.15
neighbour 005.21 023.29 091.14 209.07 270.27 414.05 460.04 487.12 536.19 552.19 552.20 579.18 585.34 598.35 598.35 598.36 615.33
neighbourhood 235.16 248.35
neither 008.26 027.27 140.04 201.34 256.05 415.31
neolithic 576.36
Neomania 244.05
neon 020.35
neophite 425.31
nephew 388.03 536.19
nest 290.15 298.08
nestle 243.23 571.17
net 236.33 390.07
nether 151.17 197.13
nethergarment 508.14
nettle 159.19
neuter 268.18
nevermore 315.35
nevernever 451.29
nevertheless 050.36 061.07 318.18 415.33 523.03 581.36 619.36
new 076.20 111.01 117.24 138.20 141.17 148.18 162.10 199.14 213.20 289.F6 331.31 335.13 348.30 395.33 448.31 493.19 497.13 527.18 620.16
newborn 291.28
newcastle 018.06
newlaid 405.34
newmade 138.08
newsboy 363.06
newsletter 382.13 390.01
newspaper 560.23 607.34
newsreel 489.35
next 445.14 614.13
nice 029.08 092.18 188.03 200.29 225.17 281.F2 295.26 295.26 312.24 320.16 361.16 361.17 370.05 516.11 532.24 556.28 604.03 615.15
nicely 242.09 469.12 552.04
nicest 326.33
niche 563.35
nick 625.33
nickle 602.33
nickname 067.26 234.22 330.13 468.13 506.01 546.04
niece 388.04
nigger 423.33 423.33 423.33 423.33
night 065.12 085.34 087.35 087.35 126.18 159.19 191.30 222.18 229.16 243.06 244.33 245.22 247.03 253.18 315.02 329.10 335.26 339.05 339.24 346.06 346.27 347.01 368.36 409.21 412.06 415.14 436.28 462.05 470.14 475.21 502.12 502.29 515.26 519.36 526.10 534.01 543.12 555.05 555.05 555.05 555.10 555.10 556.23 556.23 558.21 558.21 558.21 558.21 589.25 597.05
nightcap 334.10
nightdress 157.08
nightingale 040.25 359.32 360.02 406.24 450.17 541.30
nightmare 138.24 364.26 411.08 485.26 568.30
nightshirt 388.03
nighttime 349.06
nihilist 346.32 349.14
nil 282.32
nimbus 375.31
nine 075.04 187.20 202.02 206.04 207.16 283.09 358.28 451.21 601.14
ninehundred 420.26
ninepence 549.36 618.07
ninety 255.36
ninetynine 451.21
ninth 153.34 326.33 327.03
Nipponese 339.01
nirvana 619.29
nitric 167.21
nobility 235.13 536.12
noble 584.23
noblesse 277.11 567.26
nobody 028.10 113.36 236.08 448.20 505.17 569.25
nocturne 064.16
nod 625.33
nogg 026.03
noggin 382.09 548.32 560.18 560.19 581.12
noise 059.13 064.02 098.03 154.09 168.05 314.27 418.10 448.34 620.16
no-man's-land 022.08 265.02
nomen 318.06
nomenclature 147.21
non-Aryan 508.02
nonbeliever 520.18
nonce 004.17
nonconformist 362.05
nondescript 039.09
nonentity 336.32 538.07
noninebriate 542.10
nonpareil 283.22
nonplussed 410.10
nonsense 149.22 162.18 245.21 326.21 378.33 457.29 535.19 562.32 619.18
nook 231.35 231.35
noon 523.17

no-one 173.29 275.F5 348.26
noose 241.04
nor'-east 311.35 375.03 523.34
normal 597.33
Norman 321.14 386.28 387.21 510.20
Norse 279.F20 314.27 340.24
north 324.25 329.07 329.08 387.02 494.14 534.15 553.30 557.02 578.30 620.16
Northman 578.11
Norwegian 021.01 023.11 028.27 049.28 067.13 241.18 311.09 311.22 312.02 312.05 316.34 320.25 325.27 343.10 511.02 618.34
nose 053.13 088.06 088.18 102.03 112.31 114.02 114.02 154.19 162.21 208.28 225.05 228.28 329.11 344.29 344.35 349.28 398.30 453.17 476.36 489.17 524.21 524.34 531.11 534.21 577.11
nosebag 377.08
nosegay 612.24
nostril 450.11 624.26
note 224.14 339.24
notecase 356.23
notepaper 457.34
noteworthy 241.30
nothing 113.03 231.22 253.08 253.08 455.22
notice 164.31 224.14
notion 309.12 354.21 409.06 414.08 426.20
notonecta 416.11
notwithstanding 616.17
nought 018.04 294.06 356.12 418.26 475.21 536.18
novena 601.14 619.29
nowadays 561.06
nowhere 007.15 155.12 626.04
nude 037.21
nugget 537.19
nuggety 277.07
nuisance 147.06 275.F6 479.20 551.10 616.18
nullify 462.05
numb 476.35
number 003.08 010.28 198.11 222.32 242.05 313.25 358.30 373.02 374.34 386.21 390.29 420.25 485.30 502.11 528.34 529.24 531.04 546.25 546.26 611.19 619.19
numerous 450.19
nuncupative 432.10
nuptial 167.30 324.36
nurse 203.07 279.F20 370.05
nursery 584.16 619.18
nurture 252.22
nut 226.22 314.36
nutmeg 333.33
nutriment 416.25
nutshell 276.L2 455.29
nymph 539.19 577.11

oar 367.21
oath 346.31 571.29
oats 239.32
obedience 389.03 605.29 610.07
obedient 347.35 422.21
obeisance 347.35 358.08 476.10
obey 333.34
obiter 183.13
object 340.05 624.24
oblation 606.24
obligation 270.03
oblige 277.12 495.26
oblivious 080.25 251.04 317.32
oboe 359.36
obscene 017.15 034.10 068.33 403.16 523.34
obscenest 535.19
obscenity 236.30
obscurity 150.31 602.28
obsequious 291.08
observatory 551.25
observe 156.25
obsidian 403.16
obsolete 019.11 575.05 609.02
obtainable 397.33
obviously 161.18
ocarina 007.03 007.03
occasion 160.12 324.31
occasionally 005.25
occur 271.08 320.18 322.19
ocean 123.25 139.22 197.29 326.18 385.36 421.25
oceanic 102.05 481.13
ochone 006.35 176.27 246.05 297.11 297.11 392.15 536.12
o'clock 026.27 035.18 070.29 127.07 138.29 155.02 353.15 371.04 382.13 584.03 599.03 599.04
octagon 284.L2
October 186.14 481.28
octoroon 468.36
octroy 538.07
oddity 614.02
odious 059.10 487.36
odour 204.34 321.23 364.24 538.31
Odyssey 396.32 419.29
oesophagus 319.12
offal 374.24
offend 131.08
offer 279.F30 342.30 585.06 601.02
office 369.34 374.24 534.21
offing 311.05
offspring 030.08 162.14
ogham 027.05 338.22
ogle 076.28 082.12
ohm 301.03
oil 017.13 069.36 182.22 322.02 596.13
oilcan 461.29
oilpaint 550.30
oily 411.26
old 021.05 021.05 024.34 054.04 063.36 072.34 087.06 088.02 089.29 089.35 095.06 096.20 096.23 107.22 112.08 114.23 117.30 128.05 136.15 141.27 146.35 183.15 197.03 197.24 207.26 213.20 230.03 230.26 231.05 237.18 238.13 245.36 257.14 257.17 257.21 257.24 309.24 329.19 329.33 331.19 335.13 336.10 338.33 348.17 350.06 355.11 366.33 373.19 381.21 382.15 384.17 388.29 389.11 393.16 398.14 398.26 398.27 406.28 415.03 421.14 437.30 438.22 449.24 453.15 469.14 484.21 486.06 489.36 493.27 499.23 527.07 536.09 580.04 593.20 617.16 621.11 624.23 624.27
oldcastle 018.06
older 053.04
oldest 135.18 540.19
oldworld 019.11
oleaginous 361.27 520.33
olive 244.04 499.26 550.18 564.21
Omama 571.12
omasum 097.15
omelette 230.07
omen 318.06 370.34
omit 222.15 245.34
omniannual 127.14
omnibus 006.01 098.12 410.17 415.17 488.11 542.35
onanism 040.25 143.03 464.01
oneirist 397.02
onerous 318.04
onion 162.26 456.23 566.03
onlooker 186.24
onomatomancy 370.15
onomatopoeic 468.10
ontological 310.21
onus 151.01
onward 567.03
onwards 325.09
opal 223.28
open 067.16 313.02 315.32 319.12 342.26 349.31 364.15 395.12 395.23 499.31 528.21 562.26 572.10 609.19
openair 425.16
opening 492.30
operatic 439.25
opium 153.26
oppidan 497.15 539.36
opportunity 366.21 395.34
oppose 338.12
opposite 318.06 324.14 382.16 420.21 436.17 581.18 611.24
opposition 527.12
opulence 126.16
opulent 282.22
oracle 412.15
oracular 157.22
oral 545.12
orange 132.29 143.25 203.27 241.03 277.F4 327.32 339.28 344.26 432.30 541.34 555.19 596.01 611.06
orangoutang 541.34
oratorio 041.28
orb 494.22 593.09
orbit 598.28
orchard 133.30 613.30
orchestra 128.26
ordain 291.F4 512.30
order 229.01 285.01 287.17 344.17 378.13
orderly 125.11 373.23
ordinary 109.03
organ 513.08
organisation 086.21
orient 003.13
oriental 357.18
orifice 356.06 414.27
oriflamme 080.24 084.34
origin 161.08 504.14

original 431.35 619.02
originally 115.14
originate 004.36
orison 598.13
ornament 208.08 227.20
orotundity 055.36
ort 067.05
orthodox 152.28 252.20 312.32 358.29 425.20
oscillate 165.13
oscillation 279.04
osmosis 455.36
osprey 325.33
ostensibly 151.14
ostler 521.30
ostrich 070.01 136.15 162.32
other 016.08 053.12 067.30 085.03 091.25 113.07 150.35 153.14 164.05 180.16 181.29 222.28 245.05 245.06 275.09 275.09 280.19 280.27 285.22 295.33 300.19 322.09 379.21 397.34 411.34 450.03 513.09 593.11 598.20 598.20
otherwise 040.10 056.20 263.19
otiose 163.26 310.21
otter 275.09 275.09 450.03
Ottoman 419.25
ouch 354.20
ourselves 311.17 311.17 324.15 324.15 378.31 607.19 623.28
outback 221.22
outburst 066.19 091.03
outer 228.12
outherod 127.11
outhouse 319.23 319.30 320.11
outlander 581.03
outlast 444.25
outlaw 169.03
outlet 169.03
outrage 062.02
outrageously 285.02 541.08
outrigger 335.13
outright 534.35
outside 031.32 333.20 374.14 507.07
outstretch 033.08
outward 227.23
outworn 597.18
oval 156.15
ovalloid 157.05
oven 541.35
overall 051.12 315.16 619.36
overalls 085.30
overboard 557.15
overcoat 035.13
overcome 246.01
overdraught 340.15
overdue 604.17
overflow 397.01
overgrown 504.32
overhead 383.15
overlord 193.01 541.09
overreach 138.06
overripe 542.29
overseer 493.31
overstamp 456.28
overtake 627.04
overthrow 326.22
overtone 318.33 565.05
overture 064.14
overweight 421.07
overwhelm 356.35
owe 178.33 183.15 229.29
owl 408.24
own 138.01 202.06 204.02 209.23 223.13 408.24 421.08 457.12
owner 025.19 568.06
ox 599.01 621.14
oxide 128.11 239.12 247.21 392.27 480.10
oxidise 183.33
oxter 085.11 324.03 393.32
oxygen 067.07 284.L2
oyez 553.04 553.04 553.04 585.26 585.26 604.22 604.22 604.22
oyster 277.F7 317.12
ozone 241.19

paddle 430.09 582.24
paddysnap 312.14
paddywhack 064.07 064.25 086.17 289.17 346.22 353.17
padlock 069.25 423.25
pageant 319.12 597.05
pain 055.30 243.07 349.01 357.10 370.03 403.11 434.28 522.29 533.20
painfully 158.04
paint 434.18 550.30 581.32
pair 075.17 098.14 186.36 205.02 311.29 365.06 372.08 375.25 389.23 445.24 451.25 539.26 571.17 584.09
palace 543.10 551.01 597.13
paladin 596.25
pale 145.12
paleface 078.27
palfrey 154.15
palliasse 380.25 495.15
palm 016.30 363.18
palmbearer 115.18
palmleaf 600.36
palmoil 440.25
palpably 187.02
palpitation 276.F1
paltry 112.05 391.36
pan 296.22 438.17 463.28 538.27 547.29 596.32 610.32
pancake 162.09 575.16 619.02
pandemonium 285.15
pane 456.34
pangs 628.05
panic 606.30
panicstricken 599.28
panoply 530.16
panorama 143.03 502.36
panpipe 237.15
pant 349.10
pantaloons 509.34
panther 565.19
pantomime 032.11 180.04 285.15 455.27 509.34 531.21 587.08 615.24 626.27
pants 061.21 234.06 257.20 415.19 434.09 538.14 600.24 614.07
papa 173.26
papal 095.01 245.12 287.31 392.20
paper 020.10 023.31 141.10 157.28 170.15 210.13 237.04 279.F23 281.F2 292.07 332.05 560.23 560.29 563.08 607.34
paperboy 363.14
paperchase 475.28
paperseller 529.19
papilla 417.12
papoose 348.24
papyrus 568.34
parachute 237.02
paradigm 298.28
paradisal 610.14
Paradise 053.13 069.10 230.13 263.L4 296.07 435.18 493.05 610.34 611.19 615.25
paradox 611.19
paragogical 338.07
parallel 284.02
paralyse 612.19
paralysis 352.14
paranymph 548.02
parapet 461.35
parasite 131.09 418.01 616.26
parasol 315.19 569.20
parcel 011.23 280.15 364.07 364.07 365.02 412.22 617.25 619.05
parch 625.20
pardon 293.01 302.06 607.19
pardonable 537.36
parent 331.12 388.16 576.27
parish 265.20 280.L2 281.L4 289.03 289.05 343.30 432.12 458.04 625.20
Parisian 021.17 143.36
park 012.24 039.17 096.03 201.02 324.07 346.32 359.36 371.35 373.20 406.10 407.19 407.19 407.21 407.21 413.36 473.18 491.18 625.21
parliament 189.34 252.05 392.35
parliamentary 338.20
parlour 135.02 170.15 346.18 454.20
parlourmaid 526.36
Parnellism 243.09
Parnellite 334.14 542.21
parochially 533.28
paronomasia 502.36
paroxytone 288.11 487.02
parrot 011.09 197.21
parsimonious 545.28
parsnip 256.20
parson 039.23 365.02 432.18
part 041.10 167.31 318.13 326.33 327.03 373.33 512.28 553.34 620.34
Parthalonian 015.30
participate 337.24
particular 166.29 315.30
particularly 004.31 087.09 088.13 191.19
partner 004.29 537.25 571.28
partnership 575.28
partridge 447.29 478.34
parts 187.07
party 012.24 046.27 054.12 059.12 072.23 157.30 182.27 247.15 247.15 513.06
paschal 302.03 561.20
pass 051.02 204.01 316.27 373.33 594.17 622.33
passim 106.13 356.32
passion 198.17 230.18 356.32 396.25
passive 386.29

Passover 553.08
past 039.14 186.36 236.31 314.21 395.36 603.12
pastoral 086.21 374.17
pastrycook 486.17
Patagonian 512.18
patch 093.04 516.23
patent 419.23 492.35 519.03 546.10
path 018.32 284.04 599.04
patience 568.05
patient 053.05
patriarch 074.11 153.27 269.24 531.11 531.33 624.15
patrician 078.23
patricide 167.10
patriot 228.07 230.34
patriotic 178.17
patrol 323.31 340.19 546.36
patron 328.08
patronage 342.13
patronise 032.12 520.07
patronship 539.31
patter 507.31
pattern 068.35 253.20 537.10
pauper 140.13 175.09 422.20
pause 157.13 221.14
pawn 340.19 377.14
pawnbroker 074.15
pawnshop 209.31 516.28
pay 140.13 362.32 379.08
paynim 141.07
pea 050.05 265.F5 456.22 602.36
peace 092.22 102.16 134.35 150.07 202.30 259.04 275.F4 301.04 346.19 349.25 361.32 424.26 424.26 440.10 545.36 549.31 602.36
peaceably 014.30
peaceful 043.31 222.32
peach 225.06 603.36 604.01
peachfed 185.10
peage 006.32
peagreen 086.35
peahen 205.30
peak 057.19
peal 167.35 206.36 302.11 332.11
peanut 314.35
pearl 044.01 199.12 202.08 394.35 424.27 434.06 443.34 549.20 576.25 601.22
peartree 176.08
peasant 111.23
peasantry 344.18
peascod 313.07
pease 038.05 289.05 395.28
pebble 424.27 537.30
peccadillo 336.29
peck 364.36
peculiar 019.03 606.30
peculiarity 241.05
pecuniary 511.17
pedal 137.33 582.24
pederast 153.28 155.23 344.27 349.33 387.26 410.35
pedestal 513.36 542.17
pedestrian 565.01
pedigree 513.14
peeler 323.30 347.15 589.12 603.31
peeper 567.33
peer 063.28 332.27
peerless 092.12
Pekinese 595.32
Peloponnesian 008.20
pelota 567.35
pen 066.15 069.06 238.01 377.29 519.03 615.10
penchant 435.33
pencil 098.30 173.10 261.10 425.18 492.30 566.09
pending 575.35
penetrate 310.09
penguin 577.27
peninsula 135.18
penis 061.36 150.05 173.10 188.32 349.01 357.10 438.29 465.05 495.23 538.14 548.23 581.01 594.23 596.06
penman 093.13 517.18 558.07
penniless 581.01
penny 006.01 007.25 014.22 129.08 137.01 141.07 142.02 144.17 170.01 188.32 204.31 231.03 236.10 242.30 265.F3 266.L1 268.13 321.26 342.02 367.05 437.18 442.03 465.23 466.02 485.02 495.23 527.01 549.36 568.13 578.27 586.23 588.18 606.19 611.04 618.07 618.33
pennyfarthing 567.34
pennyless 203.06
pennyworth 288.F1 548.23
pension 230.18 373.20
pentacle 513.17
pentagon 513.17
pentameter 386.05
Pentateuch 004.25 071.18
Pentecost 152.27 160.07
people 260.L2 273.07 273.07 273.07 334.24 346.32 369.10 390.26 443.30 454.35 537.13 556.26 567.33 568.21
pepper 173.26
peppercaster 279.F23
peppermint 521.01
per 061.09 165.31 378.03
perambulator 314.11 490.03
perceive 609.30
percent 329.09 370.05 618.36
perch 153.10
peremptory 364.24
perfect 156.34 181.02 242.23 404.32 501.10
perfection 094.10
perfectly 090.19 395.20 419.32 527.26
perfidious 264.F3 343.09
perfidy 480.12
performance 219.05
perfume 236.02 624.24
perfumery 511.17
perhaps 016.03 062.25 089.33 130.35 154.03 237.35 238.19 309.08 339.34 352.21 357.09 415.17 443.23 510.09 595.20 602.24 608.24 625.03
peri 579.05
peril 424.27 434.06
perimeter 298.28
periodical 070.06 106.11
peripatetic 226.06 417.32
perish 091.23 130.05
periwig 423.03
periwinkle 388.06 515.04
permanent 328.17 596.05
permeate 162.14
permit 480.07
perpendicular 493.10
perpetrate 077.01 364.16
perruque 020.32
persecute 503.29 594.14
persevere 092.01
Persian 018.22 038.11 280.15 286.08 324.19 357.09 419.24
person 011.23 048.16 060.25 063.11 141.25 149.34 149.36 280.15 324.19 357.10 420.24 599.21 617.25
personal 083.03 174.24 183.07 230.20 485.05
personally 449.04
personifier 378.24
personify 589.24
persuade 078.17 298.23 603.17
pertinent 363.30
pertinently 055.09
peruser 060.27 156.13
pervert 238.23
pest 524.31
pet 144.17 273.20 614.16
petal 087.29
petard 497.08
peter 202.11
petition 390.32
petname 561.10
petrify 087.11 405.35
petrol 340.19
petticoat 043.20 225.33 407.36 497.32 513.14 545.29 546.16 611.36 624.34
petty 261.02
phalanx 346.35
phallus 257.28
phantom 565.19
phenomenal 244.13
phenomenon 258.22
philosopher 072.14
philosophy 119.04 417.15 435.10
Phoenician 221.32
phoenix 023.16 038.04 039.17 080.06 116.18 196.11 219.02 238.24 311.26 324.07 331.02 346.35 454.34 461.10 473.16 516.35 518.26 518.27 520.01 534.12 564.08 576.28 590.05 608.32 610.08
phooey 481.35 481.35 520.21
phosphor 415.05
phosphorescence 378.08
phosphorus 505.33
photo 233.02 593.24
phrase 358.03
phthisis 415.12 437.09
physical 437.12
piano 200.35 360.09 362.32
pianoforte 162.04
pianotuner 327.21
pick 489.36 614.15
picket 565.35
pickpocket 082.14 093.02 507.26 507.28
picnic 141.35 240.02 292.19 599.28
Pict 204.07 210.26 565.35 619.11

pictorial 106.11 584.36
picture 104.20 160.08 164.04 233.01 299.05 304.R2 415.07 438.13 531.15 587.14 598.21
picturebook 351.24
picturesque 427.33
piddle 137.33 551.10 561.36 562.02 562.03 582.24 600.08
pidgin 584.04
pie 059.20 287.16 298.01
piebald 071.29
piece 014.14 023.09 137.07 189.06 191.32 202.14 232.06 257.15 257.22 301.F1 390.05 416.24 463.27 618.33
piecemeal 582.16
pied 338.05
pier 490.22
pierce 090.30 106.05 117.15 363.06 556.35 626.25
pierceable 616.32
piety 149.26
pig 089.15 173.08 185.10 273.15 279.F17 359.26 368.11 424.20 613.27
pigeon 374.35
piggy 368.10 496.19 496.20
pigsty 176.29 538.32
pigtail 435.24 609.04
pike 231.33 371.35 379.36
pikestaff 296.29
pilgrim 248.13 384.18 483.33 600.35
pilgrimage 305.33 312.27 423.08
pillar 128.36 540.24 556.33
pillarstone 006.24
pillow 556.33 617.10
pillowfight 453.03
pilsen 492.30
pimpernel 564.28
pimple 537.30 538.13
pin 053.01 239.35
pinafore 007.25 226.25 354.26 453.03
pinch 618.06
pine 055.30
pineapple 121.11 167.15 246.29
ping 032.02
pingpong 058.24 072.33 189.23 233.28 243.07 245.25 245.26 327.24 344.22 367.05 379.07 528.18 541.24
pink 296.12
pinprick 011.10
pint 537.29
pioupiou 533.03
pious 156.20 189.01 425.36
pipe 007.34 221.29 298.05 341.17 351.14 411.11 450.10 464.20
pipedream 602.24
piper 188.20 541.29
pipette 014.08 096.14 143.31 144.17 147.29 232.25 272.F4 366.01 413.22 413.24 449.31 449.31 459.25 502.09 540.14 601.28 624.09
pipistrelle 178.27 276.20
pirate 301.19
piratical 337.23
piss 017.02 058.10 176.02 203.02 225.06 267.11 287.31 329.04 334.35 363.27 406.19 406.20 456.02 456.04 472.06 492.18 510.30 532.33 534.21 587.19 587.24 587.31 588.29 588.35 619.17
pissabed 397.25 600.08
pistol 237.03
pitch 254.01
pitcher 587.14
pith 007.14
pitiful 240.05
pituitary 037.01
pity 043.20 244.20
pixillate 011.12
pixy 316.17
place 055.31 133.30 159.15 166.01 243.23 299.14 350.19 368.09 368.20 422.29 461.20 465.34 528.05 539.20 543.17 617.20
placenta 585.23
plagiarist 182.03 525.07
plague 378.20
plaid 174.02 381.21
plain 023.36 128.03 139.23 160.06 296.29 333.27 394.34 541.22 609.15
plainly 164.17
plaint 478.16
plait 526.32
plankton 477.25
planxty 566.28 593.04
plash 246.14 463.18
plaster 184.21 543.10
plateau 236.24
platinum 164.11
plausible 138.09
play 231.06 243.23 388.07 451.18 553.34 562.03 562.03 562.15 567.35 583.25 625.21
playboy 027.09
player 224.22
playful 119.10 200.31 562.01
playhouse 435.02
plead 327.13
pleasant 062.12
pleasantly 595.07
please 089.01 113.24 113.25 113.25 113.34 113.36 150.03 154.16 166.01 191.21 199.20 262.08 264.29 265.19 278.24 286.18 297.08 310.26 313.07 328.35 337.27 347.15 349.03 349.25 350.18 350.19 356.34 358.10 358.29 371.26 372.03 372.05 379.06 379.06 379.06 381.21 396.04 412.31 412.31 419.30 420.30 432.18 445.08 488.27 488.27 488.28 495.01 502.23 537.15 543.17 546.24 568.06 571.21 590.11 607.31 617.20 623.15
pleasure 070.03 160.35 263.23 370.18 496.01 549.27 554.07 568.15 581.22 619.01
pleat 526.32
plebiscite 331.17 331.17 523.24
pledge 105.01 496.01
pleistocene 165.26
plenary 319.07
plenitude 241.07
plenty 028.03 143.05 240.16 439.15 457.01 519.25 566.28 593.04
plethora 542.02
plight 453.27
plough 600.14
plougher 318.13
ploughshare 018.31 549.27
pluck 053.24 053.24 160.20 566.28
plum 225.17 288.F5
plumcake 236.17 446.10
plump 624.14
plumpudding 418.19
plunder 525.22
plural 138.08 224.25 269.04 290.24
plus 231.13 231.14 231.14 282.30 282.30 282.30 282.30 407.30 617.03
plush 562.01
pneumatic 315.34
pneumonia 313.12
poach 297.14
pocket 029.07 058.35 236.13 242.30 507.28 617.08
poem 080.22 080.22 230.36 528.16
poet 056.22 337.24 345.17 414.29 429.18
poetry 023.10 111.23 145.24 178.17 391.36 466.11 509.35 543.07 547.17 597.16
pogrom 443.08
poignancy 343.01
point 050.02 155.23 160.32 164.11 191.36 295.30 309.04 356.14 369.23 532.09 617.35
pointblank 468.17
pointer 622.27
pointless 374.11
poise 498.33
poison 085.29 143.19 165.10 177.12 212.24 451.06
poisonous 039.14
poke 236.16
poker 606.33
polar 328.01 370.27
polarbear 602.30
pole 164.04 277.10 580.11 596.21
polecat 513.13
police 023.15 072.16 113.36 128.22 186.21 281.F2 324.20 340.28 543.01
policeforce 565.04
policeman 057.03 202.15 624.19
polish 137.29 281.F2
polite 186.21 543.01
politician 173.16
polka 341.01 513.13
poltroon 423.07
polygamous 241.05
polygon 231.30
pomposity 493.22
pond 553.21
ponder 089.25 580.01
pong 032.03
pontifex 242.35 293.F2 345.29 532.09 567.31
pontifically 155.08
pony 464.22 627.24
pool 320.03 338.15 377.35
poop 442.31
poor 005.36 013.25 024.34 031.25 054.04 096.19 107.22

135.10 141.27 163.09 224.36 245.36 290.22 291.04 295.05 314.09 328.01 339.05 350.20 474.01 498.22 533.35 612.18 617.25
poorbox 165.31
poorer 318.13
pop 072.09 135.03 396.32 425.36
Pope 084.06 084.17 091.35 095.01 146.08 220.34 269.27 310.35 416.32 440.06 441.06 442.31 480.19 531.02 560.27
popery 388.21
popgun 331.01
popish 370.34
poplin 133.20
poppinjay 621.15
poppy 009.20 351.12 379.25
popular 039.12 155.32 248.29 351.12 523.24 599.26
population 140.13 362.04 525.06
porch 209.29
porpoise 362.08
porridge 074.13 280.L2 281.L4 289.05 395.29 458.04 487.16 614.12
port 130.35
portcullis 240.15
porter 069.26 327.34 368.11 372.04 531.25 548.12 570.15 570.19 570.20 571.20 622.27
portfolio 083.31
portion 397.18
portmanteau 113.02
portrait 059.08 114.32
posh 556.36
position 245.13 390.32
poss 372.04 417.07
possession 198.17 245.13 379.05 529.18
possible 152.30 158.10 432.26
possibly 014.30 118.15 161.21 236.35 397.25 417.21 619.08
post 067.32 070.11 092.13 096.20 099.35 106.04 221.32 345.17 395.36 409.06 441.06 453.22 454.06 469.29 498.32 603.05
poster 373.23
postern 236.30
posthaste 405.01
posthorn 236.30
posthumous 408.13
postman 370.01 408.13
postmaster 462.02
postmistress 412.23
postmortem 150.07 263.11
postoffice 534.21
postprandial 417.11
postscript 124.32 370.10
posy 265.14
pot 151.15 268.13 279.F23 333.34 345.26 347.11 368.20 386.26 395.28 435.26 463.28 609.25 622.07
potash 393.11 616.12
potato 111.01 286.03 323.17 495.10 595.11 604.15
pottage 393.11 607.09
pottery 023.10
pound 013.02 082.34 169.24 210.23 211.20 321.26 599.05
pour 027.24 064.17 145.19 189.31 300.30 326.05 515.24
powder 023.33 128.12 142.11 147.32 200.06 272.L3 364.26 540.36 550.18 618.15
power 283.21 498.33
pox 144.32 263.08
poxy 083.33
practicable 269.13
practically 316.05
practice 353.01
practise 458.35
praise 141.36 310.35 333.28 338.33 485.10
prancer 484.19
praty 031.24 137.11 351.07
pray 011.18 188.08 228.03 231.06 237.19 240.11 240.14 279.F17 336.10 350.25 438.10 522.29 522.30 537.34
prayer 059.18 222.29 342.11 351.25 461.29 541.24
preach 113.17 249.35 281.L4 297.14 318.19
preacher 465.34
precarious 363.28
precede 275.F4
precious 237.08 332.23 350.16
precisely 089.04 177.33 224.21 358.05
precocious 052.14 224.36
precursor 541.11
predecease 423.27
predominant 076.02 617.23
prefect 181.25
prefer 141.22 276.L1
prefix 162.13
prehistoric 266.R1
prejudice 344.32
prelate 497.08
prelude 337.09
premise 005.28 238.15 409.34 440.13 535.11
premises 179.10
premium 590.11
preparatory 274.30 446.36
prepare 364.05 413.01 516.28
prepay 590.11
preposition 178.04
prepossession 156.08
preposterous 016.03 094.13 178.03
preposterously 153.25
Presbyterian 120.02 294.01 381.15
prescribe 436.10
presence 294.20 347.36 363.31 536.24 563.37 596.11
present 116.21 155.18 165.16 221.17 224.04 280.15 304.22 370.05 498.31
presently 295.29 595.07
preserve 548.10
press 056.28 183.29 232.06
pressure 324.32 455.17
pretend 003.11 013.18 069.22 191.22
pretension 511.17
preterite 269.08 301.03
pretty 012.24 020.32 021.17 124.27 139.23 157.30 186.36 186.36 201.07 224.28 242.17 264.28 285.F3 314.30 336.24 351.29 467.32 502.14 513.06 513.20 546.16 600.17 600.32 609.02
prevalent 160.05
prevention 505.36
preventive 585.09
previous 321.01 338.06 606.16
price 036.13 054.21 251.34 256.31 257.22 280.24 327.29 366.02 375.34 433.33 485.20 502.09 614.16
priceless 237.08 535.08
prick 011.10 224.36 284.04 538.15 554.03
pride 054.21 286.L3 318.34 434.21 561.16
priest 074.12 094.36 225.11 281.L4 289.05 343.30 432.12
primate 141.36 513.20 604.22
prime 101.35 129.26 240.36 242.11 287.10
primrose 327.16
primus 604.22
prince 137.17 280.22 289.02 346.29 387.20 447.16 484.19 537.05
princess 396.08
principal 405.32 626.27
principality 498.33
print 137.17 425.24
priory 607.02
prism 127.03
prison 127.03 498.31
prisoner 313.14
privacy 138.19 328.17
private 138.19 351.20 412.27
privateer 327.36
privatesecretary 177.19
privilege 605.07
privy 338.06
prize 054.21 155.16 155.17 264.22 398.27 419.01 498.31
probably 337.22 608.23 619.10
problem 182.21 286.20
proboer 491.32
proceed 268.19
proceeding 352.18
procession 379.05
proclamation 540.13
prodigious 414.05
produce 087.31
production 285.F2
profane 562.32
professional 141.24
professor 124.09 124.15
proffer 585.06
profile 335.30
profit 240.32 305.01 520.29
profound 378.24 535.29
profoundly 342.28
progenitor 027.03
programme 443.08
progress 234.20 284.22 384.18 465.08 609.31
prohibit 085.09
promentory 623.06
promiscuous 361.09 386.24
promise 323.11 409.34 422.08
prompt 466.22
promptly 003.20 338.15
pronominally 490.08
pronounceable 478.19
pronto 353.19

pronunciation 089.26
proof 303.14 606.27
prop 274.30
proper 162.13 279.F06 366.23
prophecy 153.02 358.15
prophesy 520.29
prophet 068.28 189.31 240.32
proportion 343.19
proposal 575.32
propose 582.02
propriety 519.04 617.35
proscenium 180.03
prose 337.16 423.16
prosecute 503.29 594.14
prosepoem 528.16
prosperity 136.32
prosperous 230.35
prostitute 117.15 117.35 235.02
285.29 350.15 616.17
prostitution 365.17
prostrate 235.02 417.11
protection 285.F2
protem 524.27
protend 476.07
protest 577.33
protestant 126.22 328.10 456.23
prototype 324.01
proud 316.02 482.31 484.19
proverb 242.12
proverbial 060.32
providence 062.07 147.17 190.22
325.02
provincial 144.10
prowl 546.36
prowler 484.19
prune 006.17 288.F5
Prussian 539.30 608.11
prussic 359.07
pry 375.34
psalm 163.03 391.28 457.30
pseudonym 332.32 420.05
psyche 094.16
psycho 115.21
psychoanalyse 522.34
psychological 396.14
psychopannychy 094.16 340.25
pub 243.22 454.35
public 185.02 604.05
publican 593.17
publication 071.16
publicly 458.36
publish 160.20
pudding 083.29 179.34 311.32
405.34 418.19 617.20
puddle 016.21 106.05 208.30
600.08
puff 529.30
puffcake 146.07
puisne 090.36
pulchritude 340.26
pull 057.17 568.14 568.14
588.23 589.35
pullman 055.19
pullover 325.12
pulp 442.31
pulverise 550.18
pump 010.09 040.12 340.19
343.29 516.28 625.10
pumpkin 236.17 353.27 627.23
pun 377.29
punch 124.11 257.23 415.19
422.05 594.35 617.14
puncture 160.08
Punic 156.03 270.30
Punjabi 498.16
punk 263.F2 612.16
punning 184.24
puny 055.12 350.22 477.22
pupil 542.18
purchase 339.14 443.30
pure 112.04 160.05 163.09
180.06 181.23 243.08 328.01
364.24 483.21 561.09
purely 048.22
purest 241.05
purgatory 266.L1 352.36
purge 379.33
purity 325.08 436.22
purlieu 236.21
purloin 419.29
purple 200.04 296.13 392.20
539.11
purpose 018.31 076.13 341.25
348.24 396.24 427.21 437.30
623.14
purse 154.10
pursuance 061.09
pursuit 181.23 441.14 609.06
push 423.34
pusher 608.11
pushpull 317.04
puss 008.07 008.07 008.07
072.35 072.35 072.35 415.03
531.22 622.11
pussy 083.33 275.L1 275.L1
pussycat 445.19
put 144.35 164.17 270.04
286.F5 295.04 330.25 364.16
365.27 370.30 373.35 437.20
548.05 603.13 615.10 622.06
putrifaction 078.21
putsch 423.34 519.03
puttee 011.20
puzzle 223.25 234.03 393.32
pygidium 414.26
pyre 244.03 553.10

quack 195.06 243.33
258.04 294.14 491.25
595.02
quadrilateral 477.19
quadruped 397.15
quai 105.02 601.23
quaintly 167.06
quake 221.09
quaker 129.13 587.01
qualify 179.15
quality 083.22
qualm 623.25
quarrelsome 254.12
quarry 097.02
quarter 011.02 077.30 119.06
300.30 344.19 384.01
403.02
quasi 359.07
quaternion 138.02
queen 102.10 128.17 238.32
245.28 269.21 285.L2 328.31
348.34 389.23 508.28 531.13
queer 016.01 067.15 128.02
215.13 294.31 303.26 313.31
343.22 343.22 395.32 413.29
442.19 492.19 581.09 587.13
query 132.32 442.19 512.33
545.06
quester 476.36
question 056.28 110.14 183.01
199.01 239.06 269.20 270.14
487.27 528.36 602.18
queue 538.16
quick 196.07 202.21 302.18
quickchanger 342.31
quicker 019.17
quicksilver 226.24
quid 413.23
quiet 040.32 314.03 571.31
quince 550.33
quincunx 206.35 278.L1
quite 053.23 086.03 154.21
290.20 299.08 358.02 374.10
quiz 126.06
quondam 157.29
quorum 368.26
quotation 183.22
quoth 049.11 260.F1 487.13
595.02
quotient 254.04

rabblement 424.36
race 541.15
rackets 366.10
racoon 256.26
radio 151.02 231.34 324.18
445.09
radish 346.03
radius 256.30 298.14
rafter 005.15 130.20
rag 105.16
rage 285.02 541.08
ragged 019.05
ragwort 478.09
rail 513.23
railway 236.23 604.12
rain 007.26 039.14 064.16
068.21 129.28 213.09 231.33
242.17 312.12 312.17 332.15
335.02 348.22 355.17 519.24
531.13 568.34 578.23 607.25
rainbow 003.14 011.12 063.12
143.24 165.22 176.18 203.27
285.15 304.09 319.05 351.05
379.17 493.30 527.30 548.28
590.10
rainladen 503.34
rainmaker 583.28
rainy 347.07
raise 032.08 265.07 279.F22
338.31 373.09 411.28 421.11
542.01 547.22 552.20 557.04
623.36
raisin 006.18 212.17 288.F5
497.31 550.32
rake 073.13 553.20
ram 328.03
ramp 440.04
rampant 374.13
rampart 324.20
ramshackle 452.21
rancid 204.30
rancour 613.25
rann 256.06 256.06 256.07
256.07 348.33 348.34 376.33
376.33 376.33 504.01 504.01
504.02 504.03 604.08
rapture 533.32
rare 207.07 540.31
rascal 323.32 324.13
rascally 156.10
rash 594.17

rat 154.13 182.32 209.10 275.L1 511.33
rather 174.29
rathole 370.20
ratification 369.06
rattattat 490.27
rattlesnake 516.06
rave 192.27 595.21
ravel 361.33
raven 049.11 136.13 203.36 238.25 243.10 276.F2 358.04 365.23 377.22 622.02
ray 051.26
raze 623.36
reacher 533.32
react 345.32
reactionary 310.19
read 018.06 018.18 052.04 201.01 201.28 283.22 566.36
reader 063.10 249.14 285.02 476.21
ready 036.19 042.11 043.25 204.10 314.03 335.15 348.35 421.06 521.31 541.13
readymade 525.13 525.19
real 049.14 064.25 064.26 064.26 093.05 339.31 467.35 482.29
reality 292.31
really 027.01 037.32 089.36 090.31 099.27 162.28 174.29 231.12 362.02 373.30 378.09 445.07 455.27 512.20 512.20 520.32 527.25 560.33 593.03 593.03 593.04 593.04
ream 098.32 381.30
reap 072.10 196.23
reappearance 162.10
rear 019.14 080.31 235.26 329.28 332.34 350.02 467.35
rearadmiral 553.13
rearise 053.13 277.14 610.04
rearouse 055.11
reason 146.05 154.31 159.25 166.20 296.04 478.10 496.14 575.34 581.32
rebellion 151.14
recalcitrant 371.23
recall 160.35
recension 410.36
recess 607.25
recipient 100.15
recite 343.31 543.06
reckon 208.35 253.29 283.23
reclaim 546.22
recluse 472.07
recognise 089.17 334.10 344.35 455.04 465.03
recollect 234.26 340.13
recommend 444.15
reconcile 371.23 434.20
reconjugation 143.13
reconstruct 036.09
recorder 210.03
recourse 423.30
recreation 491.35 585.01
recross 029.09
recruit 491.35
recruiter 364.19
rectangle 298.25
rectify 313.08
recuperate 059.05
red 007.19 020.01 023.01 052.04 083.19 176.23 176.24 219.20 225.09 244.14 256.09 262.F3 277.F4 286.14 298.14 307.F1 309.16 313.34 327.32 328.35 338.09 339.28 344.18 356.18 364.08 392.06 411.24 432.30 515.02 551.08 557.14 568.02 569.33 582.28 611.06
redbreast 537.09
redden 378.08 445.17
redeem 363.13
redemption 154.06
redundant 179.12
reed 427.11
reek 208.24
reel 083.22 292.20
reeve 397.34
referee 379.32 521.32
reflect 160.04 523.02 612.16
reflection 299.18 455.09 589.29
reform 072.25
refract 345.32 612.16
refresh 088.29
refreshment 082.10 129.29
refuge 552.06
refugee 379.32
refund 457.16
refuse 242.16
regal 099.27 131.22 622.08
regale 397.34
regard 566.26
regatta 366.10 551.24
regent 132.01
regicide 161.17
regiment 350.34
register 364.21 439.26
regular 130.05 291.28 610.10
regulate 340.13
rehearse 315.16
reign 174.23 213.09 312.12 339.27 437.35 533.10 568.34 607.25 627.11 627.13
rejoice 493.09
relation 358.03
relay 517.30
release 224.35
relentlessly 610.07
relevance 325.35
relevant 324.26
relict 340.15
religion 317.02
relinquish 381.34
rely 517.30
remain 044.10 134.17 239.34 262.F7 302.25 320.36 370.13
remainder 283.11
remark 083.15 222.03 333.13
remember 016.28 017.23 135.33 264.26 295.04 328.20 338.27 339.31 360.24 371.11 396.36 445.13 460.34 488.18 493.17 493.27 608.22 628.14
remembrance 054.02 226.32
remind 144.15 159.34
reminiscence 319.17
reminiscent 084.05
remnant 323.21 611.24
remove 579.10
rename 363.13
rend 088.26
renounce 243.21 341.19 365.01 581.05
rent 089.15 450.02
renunciation 537.03
rep 196.36
repair 057.18 421.03
reparation 507.06
repast 584.35
repeat 345.20
repel 518.20
repent 131.15 328.09
repetition 492.28
replenish 381.34
repletion 110.07
reply 129.02
repopulation 362.04
report 324.20
reporter 061.06 523.02
reproach 274.11
reproductive 298.17
republic 105.23
republican 053.28 172.23
repudiate 513.22
reputation 374.29 467.26
request 130.09 238.15
requiem 499.11
rescue 034.30 500.04
resemble 338.27 373.14 538.27 608.23
reservation 434.20
resident 524.14
resin 130.16
resolve 538.08
resourceful 194.26
respect 207.13
respectable 351.31 386.16
respond 214.08
response 408.15
responsibility 189.06
responsible 029.35
rest 003.23 102.04 187.22 224.07 348.09 392.27 393.34 436.16 545.36 547.13
restaurant 602.18
restore 434.05
resurge 596.06
resurrection 499.01 593.02
retail 003.17
retain 557.22
retina 443.02
retire 395.06
retort 093.07 150.12
retractable 477.20
retreat 521.19
retrograde 351.27
retrospection 445.29
return 018.05 143.30 304.27 472.34 614.08
reunite 395.33
reveal 220.33
revel 579.04
revelation 338.06 350.31
revenge 328.27
reverberate 492.27
revere 492.27
reverence 052.07
reverend 003.01 050.22 061.28 130.08 144.30 203.18 328.26 341.26 420.35
reverse 161.18
revile 595.21
revolution 338.06 346.08 350.31 462.34
revolutionise 545.33
revolve 177.10 270.25 518.17

revolver 060.07 352.09 538.31
revulsion 151.10
reward 471.13
Rheato-Romanic 327.11
Rheingold 578.23
rheosilver 467.35
rheumatism 241.25
rhinestone 279.02
rhododendron 135.31 445.17 588.32
rhombus 165.22 176.18
rib 261.L2
ribald 177.12 198.25 364.01
ribbon 219.20 250.04 555.10
rice 329.22 456.22
richer 318.13
richly 162.22
rickshaw 553.36
riddance 007.19
riddle 198.25 231.01 270.11 338.08 356.12 607.11
ride 100.13 121.22 197.35 307.F1 348.35 367.34 434.07 449.30 464.22 613.22
rider 315.13
ridge 324.32
ridiculous 553.15
ridinghat 622.28
ridinghood 033.01 551.08
rifle 352.18
rift 105.27
right 019.36 027.04 113.07 167.33 186.18 190.12 225.31 226.27 229.26 229.27 231.27 242.24 256.36 279.F25 282.20 284.01 301.27 303.22 328.13 334.26 358.24 365.27 373.28 396.03 417.18 437.04 487.14 490.25 519.10 563.09 595.19 603.03 606.13
righteous 497.36
righteousness 005.18 137.34
rightly 252.23 319.06
rime 178.05 619.18
ring 147.18 319.07 349.01 569.04 569.04 569.05 569.05 583.17
ringlet 208.10
ringworms 059.12
rinse 204.30 370.33 371.04 624.19
ripe 346.29 508.23 542.29
ripper 361.28 511.36 611.01 611.02
rise 025.32 199.24 204.02 210.28 363.10 363.10 363.10 375.34 485.26 610.04 626.06
riser 253.09
rival 352.18
river 017.01 086.01 245.14 300.16 586.23
riverpool 266.03
riverside 547.18
roach 449.16
road 064.03 068.31 081.09 096.03 197.26 203.13 208.26 315.23 323.35 328.03 341.17 359.20 369.11 434.07 514.05 565.22
roam 098.31 588.03
roar 198.04
roast 171.01 224.07
robber 112.35 154.08 160.19 224.03 328.01 510.20 568.02 579.14
robe 328.01
robin 211.27 537.09
robot 622.29
robust 622.29
robustly 368.17
rock 019.05 124.07 229.14 449.16
rockabye 384.03
rocky 064.03 197.26 244.24 315.23 323.35 328.03 341.17 514.05 565.22 623.24
rod 029.07
roebuck 622.29
roguish 091.34
roister 341.29
role 405.20 614.06
roll 133.20 456.25
roll-call 362.07
Rolls-Royce 005.30 205.29
Roman 070.02 084.05 123.17 214.22 239.21 242.13 243.16 344.15 347.31 440.04 485.01 489.16 518.22 519.26 611.24
romance 243.16 404.14 518.22
Romanic 327.11
Romany 472.22 600.30
Romish 072.24
roofless 420.27
rookery 231.34 231.35
room 101.09 126.20 243.11 391.31 465.08 538.12 543.13 593.14
roomy 416.03
roost 244.10 244.10 279.F31
rooster 371.28
root 183.07 231.11 284.14 448.18
rosary 072.25 264.F3 411.17 528.06
rose 096.02 227.17 286.14 337.16 391.30 405.20 414.03 423.16 427.20 541.36 577.13
roseate 231.20
rosetree 304.F4
Rosicrucian 099.28 122.25 155.28 346.13 351.06 352.33
rotate 018.05 590.07
rote 160.15
rotter 204.28 345.10
rough 384.26 623.20
round 186.29 309.24 319.24 320.22 387.36 487.16 499.34 533.23
roundabout 057.25 242.05
route 279.F31 343.07 570.31 606.31
routeless 577.30
routine 340.05
rove 563.13
rover 228.24 566.31
row 283.F1 444.30 553.31
royal 099.27 227.29 243.35 287.05 315.01 347.08 365.29 378.09 388.07 423.03 616.15 623.18
rub 136.13 210.02 440.27
rubber 224.03
rubbish 079.31 151.34 260.F1 261.L2
rubbishy 580.14
rubicund 382.02
ruby 379.24 395.33 395.33
rucksack 137.31 621.06
rude 247.16 309.16 324.06 424.17 515.02 564.23 601.24
rudiment 485.30
rue 347.15
rueful 198.35
ruffian 366.23
rugby 449.35
ruin 019.36 283.F2
ruinous 140.09
rule 067.20 279.F19 279.F31 411.30 445.32 520.32
rumba 176.18 257.04 353.25
rumble 353.24
rumen 097.15
rump 268.11
run 009.28 009.35 021.22 021.22 021.22 022.09 022.09 022.09 022.18 022.18 153.06 247.06 364.30 583.08
rune 207.07
rush 199.22 297.31 494.19 509.07 509.13
rushlight 123.34
Russian 009.18 040.07 042.11 072.04 080.15 089.07 105.22 192.02 198.18 199.22 220.15 290.F7 292.F1 335.14 335.20 335.24 337.34 339.11 340.27 340.35 341.06 341.29 344.33 346.12 346.20 347.31 349.20 350.06 352.01 352.33 354.34 365.07 368.08 372.06 375.24 388.33 423.32 471.19 492.09 494.19 509.07 509.13 610.12 620.04
rustle 625.15
rut 379.20 570.31
rye 242.31 329.22 578.32 600.30

sabbath 129.13 343.24 409.29 493.02
sabbatical 365.09
Sabonian 539.27
saccharine 230.33
sacerdotal 607.06
sacerdote 440.22
sack 206.09 493.20 621.07
sackbut 252.35 552.28
sackcloth 542.34
sackfull 626.11
sacrament 082.03
sacred 009.10 147.27 293.F2 416.07 433.28 506.26 537.33
sacrilege 365.03
sacristan 173.17
sad 130.16 130.16 224.09 488.22
saddle 342.16
safe 234.27 311.12 612.33
safest 314.20
safety 205.10 412.28
saffron 172.20 625.30
saga 275.09 551.04
sagacity 108.28
sage 289.25
sail 198.11 244.25 311.28 325.25 326.19 428.08 521.35 565.31

sailor 202.14 208.25 256.27 297.29 317.07 319.21 324.09 325.24 326.16 440.30 594.34 620.07
saint 007.10 012.22 012.22 060.16 095.16 138.26 142.06 176.28 179.09 214.31 235.19 241.16 243.34 247.20 253.12 253.12 253.12 253.12 277.F6 324.31 328.24 335.27 353.01 361.03 407.19 419.08 432.36 440.19 440.20 455.05 471.05 480.33 482.22 492.34 498.03 498.13 498.30 549.24 557.03 561.19 587.34 600.22 613.06 618.15 621.07 624.18 624.21
sake 112.08 178.35 389.36 433.14 438.19 442.05 489.20 606.32 619.13
salad 235.01
salary 413.01
sale 196.15
sallow 426.16
salmon 007.18 069.34 100.30 139.03 198.03 264.17 279.F22 362.06 387.31 416.26 451.11 531.03 538.20 557.36 615.18 625.16
saloon 032.36 323.27 337.33
salt 107.15 199.14 359.10 359.17 536.23
saltcellar 570.36
saltpetre 059.17 167.21 393.22
saltwater 247.23
salute 008.14 333.12 520.11
salvage 553.08
salvation 351.33 623.29
same 162.28 177.33 215.23 249.22 259.28 505.31 510.02 568.15 620.16
sample 323.14 338.25
sanctify 417.35
sanction 498.13 531.02
sand 058.32 124.08 294.26 440.20 601.26
sandblind 379.20
sandwich 142.01
sandy 323.02
sanitary 014.13
Sanskrit 215.26
sapphire 601.11
Saracen 370.24 516.31
sardine 368.21
Sardinian 221.32
saros 571.24 600.05 601.33
Sassenach 552.29 595.03 596.14
satanic 338.23
satellite 155.25 583.14
satin 302.12 505.08
satiric 288.18
satisfaction 161.02 445.08 446.06 452.06 512.07
satisfactory 084.15
satisfy 014.02 234.24 238.17 313.11
satrap 014.18 344.26
satsuma 241.11
saturation 319.35
Saturday 088.14 088.15 192.19 205.16 280.07 301.21 355.25 355.26 355.27 366.15 390.06 409.29 415.14 436.27 460.29 488.26 492.06 583.19 602.22
Saturn 415.09
satyr 230.28 254.23 280.07 602.22
sauce 064.24 376.14 569.27
saucepan 531.05 562.14
saucer 008.12 251.12 336.04 433.26 519.34
saucy 003.12 324.12
saunter 627.05
sausage 324.12 595.11
savage 350.35
save 107.22 180.07 240.17 301.F1 340.24 363.31 561.08 613.01 613.01
saviour 146.24 534.23 606.13
saw 231.15 489.30 505.34
sawyer 299.28 372.06
Saxon 015.35 022.35 175.12 363.35 388.31 411.30 516.31 532.11 565.35
say 006.13 007.08 012.20 018.35 032.08 059.23 065.36 068.27 068.27 068.27 085.29 125.23 164.27 164.34 168.12 177.27 193.10 213.16 215.08 240.32 251.10 281.F4 289.F1 308.10 340.24 356.33 365.36 423.20 435.26 444.16 461.29 482.18 485.04 485.13 486.26 487.13 512.01 513.09 533.20 551.07 558.34 565.08 597.02
sayer 366.25
sayso 092.32
scaffold 014.25 355.27
scald 324.17 551.04
scallywag 172.35
scalp 445.07
scan 223.33
scandal 080.34 223.33 255.36
Scandinavian 157.16 223.33 310.30
scapegoat 329.36 346.25 488.22
scapula 011.20
scarce 078.23 224.18
scarcely 227.20
scare 561.01
scarecrow 134.30
scarface 496.11
scarlatina 059.12
scarlet 060.04 352.06
scatological 134.34
scatologically 412.03
scatology 482.33
scatophily 190.34
scatter 073.34 243.18 345.18 370.06
scatterbrain 594.01
scatterer 340.01
scavenger 491.28
scene 052.36 053.02 114.23 404.09 600.21
scent 222.35 600.22
scheme 176.18
schismatic 424.36
scholar 292.23 326.29 482.17
school 127.11 151.09 198.20 220.19 223.18 255.36 265.06 265.06 308.F2 314.35 350.33 358.36 364.09 467.25 487.34 514.19 533.27
schoolgirl 101.16
schoolmaster 149.08 224.20
schoolmistress 228.17 571.07
schooner 332.02 393.33
science 279.F13 608.03
scissors 250.08 375.25 433.26 449.15 600.24
sclerosis 498.23 541.36
scold 228.36
scone 459.12 459.13
scoop 346.25
scope 302.21
scopolamine 183.01
scorch 531.10
score 332.27
scorn 330.23 410.08
scortatory 434.33
Scot 177.35 245.28 345.08 352.01 518.21 518.22 619.11
Scotch 019.16 163.08 204.06 206.34 232.14 454.33
Scotsman 391.04
Scottish 577.22
scrap 343.22 623.32
scrape 158.17
scraper 543.30
scratch 397.26
scream 331.08 348.27
screen 443.35 587.13
screw 341.18
scribble 182.13 301.10 442.33
script 124.32
scripture 293.F2
scrivener 423.15
scruff 133.03
scull 010.13
scullerymaid 239.18
scurrilous 495.03
scuttle 160.27
scythe 341.10
sea 027.07 048.01 050.34 075.13 138.23 162.07 208.31 209.08 254.29 320.02 325.16 366.14 370.31 371.08 371.09 371.09 371.20 371.32 372.27 373.11 375.35 389.26 393.35 416.30 436.13 445.26 453.24 540.23 588.15
seacrest 023.19
seal 101.25 297.03 328.33 360.30 493.31
sealevel 508.03
seaman 095.15 245.08 331.29 549.18
seamless 468.25
seamstress 324.33 326.10
search 012.10 167.12 203.04 322.17 416.14 597.22
searcher 298.15
searchlight 292.18
seaside 294.21
season 279.03
seat 057.25 061.14 061.25 198.34 209.08 354.29 382.19 452.09 461.28 541.04 545.28 550.21 590.13
seawind 201.20
seaworthy 599.21
sebum 594.13
second 005.25 138.33 153.01 177.26 288.09 315.22 340.36 342.34 356.15 360.04 602.01
secondclass 444.04
secret 009.10 082.03 248.26 416.07 491.13 537.33
secretary 166.18 177.19

sect 267.R1
section 221.03 385.12
secular 492.32
sedan 492.20
sedate 389.17
sediment 192.22
seduce 004.09
see 018.33 027.04 034.10 048.01 114.01 114.18 153.23 154.33 223.13 234.31 245.23 246.10 247.31 262.F2 295.25 335.21 336.10 339.02 360.28 370.13 403.11 505.17 509.36 513.13 538.30 540.11 549.20 558.34 595.08 626.07 626.07
seed 106.32
seek 035.09 066.17 202.02 373.07 373.07 373.07 373.07 374.21 418.06
seeker 237.31
seem 053.01 265.18 309.16 404.09 407.11 480.31 509.19 511.04 619.26
seemingly 057.18 415.24
seemly 352.18
seer 612.23
seesaw 237.07
seize 208.01 308.02 408.19 479.28
selection 111.12 252.28 504.33
selene 019.11
self 049.33
selfabuse 040.23
selfish 357.25 497.36
selfishness 238.14
selfrighteous 497.36
selfrighteousness 137.34
selftaught 147.09
sell 025.18 184.10 264.20 327.28 359.26 362.19 366.01 421.08 433.33 459.36 570.36 614.16
seller 123.23 529.19
selvedge 459.08 553.08
semaphore 522.33
semblance 317.33
semen 245.08 549.18
semicolon 152.16 222.36
semidetached 079.06
semiliterate 166.04
seminal 296.04
seminary 085.09 594.08
senap 037.33
senate 219.13 280.01 352.13 353.28 372.11 454.35
senator 372.12 475.23 475.24 475.27 475.29
send 117.04 302.F2 348.29 420.30 488.06 593.01 593.01 593.01
sender 330.01 412.23 414.02 532.03
sennet 280.01
sensation 123.12
sense 083.12 106.29 130.01 194.16 227.31 239.02 251.05 364.24 538.30
sensitive 527.27
sentiment 239.03 300.R1
sentimental 171.18 440.19 621.02
sentry 014.13 388.27
sentryman 085.36
separable 404.21
separate 451.32
sephiroth 029.13 479.08
sepoy 010.14 010.15 010.19
September 450.12
septic 536.05
Septuagesima 102.15 578.22
seraph 226.20 344.25 498.33
Serbian 126.19
serene 192.30 230.33
serenely 513.01
serfdom 395.01
sergeant 341.15 596.28
serial 263.24 545.27
seriocomically 263.24
serious 286.08 426.24 512.02 570.25
seriously 513.01 522.12
sermon 152.07 163.03 167.16 538.20 615.18
servant 200.18 598.36 605.15
serve 376.15 456.13 468.27 499.16
service 082.03 125.10 349.25 585.06 602.26
serviceman 208.36 429.20
sesame 333.01
session 618.14
set 127.17 220.31 229.26 262.17 333.34 353.31 354.28 552.03
settle 030.09 559.06
seven 048.14 090.02 187.20 199.10 202.02 203.27 225.31 283.08 330.01 354.29 469.30 495.08 552.17 590.08
seventh 284.10
seventyfifth 616.09
seventyseven 541.01
sever 260.04
several 019.02 126.19 296.04 339.15 616.09
sewer 266.30
sex 247.06 273.F7 297.22 550.33
sexappeal 441.33 508.29
shabby 005.16
shackle 354.08 452.21 541.21
shade 009.02 051.02 167.02 231.08
shadow 197.23 238.07 255.02 354.01 355.30 358.05 365.23 504.07 512.35 513.01
shaft 133.30
shag 450.01 627.26
shake 028.02 241.30 275.F5 362.20 409.22 464.25 527.17 541.18
shallot 352.06
sham 190.33
shaman 468.19
shame 029.04 092.28 124.27 141.06 177.30 231.04 424.08 502.28 509.11 565.30 580.18 580.18 619.31 622.07
shamer 192.08
shampoo 206.30
shamrock 180.06 465.08 467.10 600.31
shanty 312.30 408.33 408.34 408.34
shape 278.F2 313.18 373.13
shaper 098.30 255.02
share 528.30 549.27
sharp 233.33 539.31 558.18 617.27
sharpen 341.03
sharpener 098.30
sharpshooter 352.26 360.20
shave 225.29
shawl 381.21 497.30
sheaf 612.25
shed 350.28
sheep 143.06 172.09 240.34 313.18 340.15 343.13 373.13 453.15 535.16 551.02
sheepfold 325.31
sheepskin 387.05
sheer 061.07
sheet 228.10 614.06
sheetlightning 449.28
sheik 275.F5 614.06
shell 008.30 206.26 276.L2 321.16 455.29
shellshock 357.36
shelter 102.01
shepherd 276.12 396.17
sheriff 006.17 226.20 471.24
shewolf 049.28
shield 159.01
shillelaghlaw 511.15
shilling 008.06 036.13 159.01 169.24 234.04 280.L2 281.L4 416.04 520.14 526.33
shimmer 342.07
shin 531.18
shine 092.28 266.08 387.05 489.27 528.22 601.32 613.10
shiner 221.10
ship 010.09 077.28 106.14 229.21 317.06 319.32 320.14 372.13 387.25 453.15 471.25 516.28 532.13 539.31 608.29
shipahoy 255.31
shipshape 563.02
shipwreck 155.09
shirt 009.04 023.09 028.02 064.18 067.31 247.29 298.33 299.01 352.05 388.03 425.02 434.20 434.33
shirtsleeve 446.32
shirttail 493.01
shit 057.35 093.18 144.17 251.10 288.27 290.F7 318.21 354.01 360.26 366.30 415.35 499.09
shithouse 057.34
shiver 140.18 240.05 478.31 497.23
shoal 078.10 078.10 177.10
shock 011.18 199.22 524.24
shoe 246.23 286.21 391.09 417.34 449.28 487.34 536.13 603.04 603.04 603.04
shoehorn 556.36
shoemaker 320.17
shoeshiner 221.10 224.30
shoo 181.20
shoot 011.18 042.11 069.13 105.21 116.06 138.13 177.21 192.02 220.15 241.30 244.32 265.F5 288.27 290.F7 305.26 319.03 335.13 337.33 341.29 346.11 346.20 352.14 353.21 354.01 365.06 368.08 388.33 420.27 423.04 423.32 502.20 514.09 514.27 612.33 620.04

shooter 352.26 360.20 378.26
shooting 060.12
shop 209.31 289.07 311.24 434.30 499.21 553.10 595.32 617.27
shopkeeper 123.24 229.09 352.26
shoplifter 273.11
shoppinghour 414.33
shore 197.21 266.08 527.08 539.35 601.01 601.35
short 247.29 320.19 419.24 446.31 494.20
shortest 230.10
shortly 609.19
shortness 166.09
shorts 295.F1
shot 366.30
shoulder 029.06 035.13 073.17 157.10 161.13 161.13 207.19 252.01 320.19 330.21 404.20 446.33 446.33 511.30 621.12
shout 249.34 320.19 342.19
shove 352.28
show 112.34 112.36 265.F5 288.09 565.30 578.13
shower 601.35
shrapnel 341.03
shriek 138.34 200.01 474.21
shrine 173.19
shrink 015.31
shrivel 063.15
shun 344.22
shut 244.06 305.05 324.15 370.34
shutter 161.24 363.09 372.05 595.31 612.33
shuttlecock 051.23 390.17
shy 467.12 619.31
Siamese 235.30 329.02 344.08 354.24 408.27 411.13 425.16 425.22
Siberian 567.35 604.12
sibling 491.04
sick 170.17 397.23 416.13
sickle 339.32
sickness 062.07
side 011.36 027.08 029.27 058.27 090.13 109.01 249.02 279.F13 299.01 320.04 325.22 338.18 354.30 542.25 597.13 607.18 623.29
sidereal 378.13 604.12
sideroad 577.28
sidesaddle 342.16
sideways 236.36 474.09
siege 580.17
sift 376.35
sigh 264.11 503.28 512.30 568.09
sight 005.25 227.20 240.09 369.19 405.28 415.26 420.27 461.27 595.36 623.29
sign 222.24 227.23 336.01 374.33 420.24 580.17
signal 324.28 336.05 607.14
signet 377.28
signify 417.35 515.08
signpost 075.04
silence 044.04 052.36 147.35 602.14 602.26
silhouette 056.07
silicate 604.09
silk 021.06 133.20 133.33 315.28
silken 342.06 393.08 532.08 535.16
silkhatted 056.07
sill 200.24
silly 031.25 149.29 200.19 364.30 465.31
silt 537.07
silver 016.31 028.11 104.09 146.21 148.08 187.19 200.28 202.28 225.16 226.25 299.23 305.22 310.04 314.24 342.16 345.20 352.15 371.33 428.08 497.35 564.25
silvery 140.27
simp 360.17
simple 107.34 112.04 338.25 408.20 612.29
simply 242.16 267.F3 364.24 451.31 600.01
simultaneous 161.12
simultaneously 285.10
sin 028.34 205.17 224.22 263.27 268.F6 332.28 349.10 487.36 498.28
sinamite 494.33
sine 298.22
sinecure 014.25
sinful 140.18 344.17
sinfully 267.F3
sing 119.24 236.14 244.35 267.08 300.R1 379.17 409.02 415.14 466.36 549.03 577.29 581.10 603.10
singe 625.16
singer 254.33
single 159.13 299.22 306.06 310.04 515.12
singsing 511.13
singular 468.09
sink 175.04 275.F5
sinker 311.02
sinner 455.04 626.14
sinople 263.F4
sip 406.12 406.12
siphilis 422.07
siphonaptera 417.01
sir 016.20 031.26 072.03 073.04 079.01 100.14 154.25 173.01 181.02 182.21 238.31 279.F06 322.17 336.22 336.23 352.09 353.09 378.23 387.30 421.29 425.12 476.02 551.02 624.08
sire 073.04 089.28 174.12 245.27 523.15
sireland 446.25
sister 003.12 022.02 061.20 067.23 090.02 094.11 096.13 104.10 109.19 148.05 157.08 158.06 162.01 170.04 192.02 234.14 250.08 267.L1 280.21 314.31 335.08 375.25 413.06 431.29 433.26 436.14 448.34 452.08 458.10 465.17 468.35 469.23 489.16 493.11 500.21 500.21 511.11 526.34 528.11 528.12 528.14 528.16 528.17 538.25 551.29 561.16 564.36 578.29 587.19 598.13
sister-in-law 067.36
sisterliness 354.18
Sistine 157.08
sit 006.07 012.02 017.11 028.20 093.18 114.26 171.08 224.07 230.17 239.05 240.08 250.12 276.13 324.15 332.33 340.36 371.30 382.19 394.02 432.21 469.35 492.20 496.07 499.19 552.29 564.36 587.23 603.23
sitter 012.02
situation 319.35 385.30
six 008.36 123.08 148.08 161.22 179.34 202.02 283.08 354.28 356.15 385.24 403.02 495.27 517.25 550.33 583.30 584.03 605.30
sixfooter 384.28
sixpence 129.08 242.30 236.10 568.13
sixteen 157.08 529.02 552.23
sixth 186.14 484.07
sixty 077.13 234.13
sixtyfive 420.26
size 006.13 144.21 184.01 230.28 571.21
skeleton 397.22 422.09
skewer 344.29
skidoo 258.05
skill 237.13
skin 024.03 205.21 387.05
skintight 373.27
skipper 315.14 315.34
skirmish 021.19 022.30 347.05
skirt 023.09 044.08 227.05 298.33 364.10 434.33
skirty 197.33
skite 200.04
skull 203.13 224.20 308.F2 516.06 602.24
skyblue 240.33
skylark 383.04
skylight 358.01
skyscraper 004.36 543.30
slang 270.15
slapstick 094.02
slate 165.36
slaughter 008.17 500.17 539.28
Slav 253.04
slave 159.30 253.04
slaver 294.25
slavetrade 316.29
sledge 334.28
sledgehammer 439.23
sleep 007.28 026.24 230.19 244.35 250.17 250.17 250.18 277.13 299.10 328.23 345.11 368.20 377.26 379.30 383.20 394.15 398.14 423.06 435.26 477.23 495.15 541.30 562.16 571.30 595.31 597.12 603.13 614.13 619.26 619.33 626.02
sleepwalker 472.21
sleepy 075.08 426.18
sleeve 083.30 199.23 305.23 446.33
sleight 595.36
slice 007.18
slick 100.11
slide 006.02 100.11 188.22 323.09 505.07
slight 595.36
sling 207.18 233.09

slip 116.20 156.13 161.32 299.10 379.30 495.15 563.10
slipper 295.10 314.35 342.16 492.27
slippery 311.01 626.12
slippy 267.06
slipshod 426.36
slipstream 171.35
slither 195.03
sloppy 560.27
slosh 349.16
slot 188.32 436.24 495.23
sloth 263.23 318.35
slothfully 415.28
slouch 342.01
slough 326.36
slow 239.04 348.08 468.12 565.17 568.04
slowly 252.22 337.26 607.25
slowmotion 377.10
sluggard 415.32 416.20 516.01 579.12
sluggish 436.19
slumber 394.04 570.07 580.15
slush 346.02
slut 188.32 442.35 526.16
sly 377.10 377.10
small 083.35 318.06
smallpox 263.08
smart 262.F1 601.36
smatter 417.04
smattering 245.04
smear 170.16
smegma 294.25
smell 397.21 603.01 624.25
smile 208.26 209.33 411.25 426.15 509.26 550.29 562.28 603.01
smirk 089.09 294.20
smite 005.33
smith 357.01 595.17 595.17
smoke 089.09 143.30 241.14 294.20 298.06 320.06 343.24 347.36 417.12 607.08
smoky 583.33
smooth 340.18 621.25
smother 242.25
smuggler 327.01 548.08
smut 594.11
smutty 100.05 524.29
snack 233.33 407.04
snag 407.04 436.12
snake 019.13 206.05 233.33 516.06 560.35 597.36 615.28 616.17 618.05
snap 312.14
snatch 502.04
snatcher 026.17
sneak 019.12
sneeze 417.22
snigger 172.32 192.31
snivel 037.35
snood 468.13
snore 257.36 266.07 345.11
snort 326.21
snotty 204.29
snout 179.06
snow 205.21 287.04 302.F2 305.20 622.02
snowdrift 503.32
snowfall 552.35
snowflake 017.28 570.06
snuff 625.17
snuffbox 545.23
snuggle 345.15 436.07
soak 342.06
soandso 229.33
soap 419.22 544.35 578.23 594.12
soapy 075.08
sob 292.27 491.04 535.29
sober 230.32 343.25 353.03 353.03 353.09 353.09 536.21
sobriquet 506.17
soccer 174.25
socialism 230.09
socialist 072.23 132.19 144.05 491.06
society 186.22 229.07 413.20 435.31 459.10
sock 233.09 305.03
socket 508.01
sockeye 542.22
sod 346.21 353.16 370.23
soda 604.09
sodawater 155.01
sodden 324.32
sofa 114.26 360.10
soft 075.17 114.23 162.07 162.23 197.11 286.F5 302.F2 327.10 360.06 427.24 567.30 600.05 621.08
soften 338.10 338.14
softer 037.21
softly 018.08 333.04 628.14
softsoap 045.31
softspot 286.F5
soil 019.06 542.02
solace 470.07
solderingiron 582.22
soldier 073.17 093.35 124.30 142.09 161.13 161.13 202.14 222.09 256.27 317.07 317.22 322.03 362.10 379.08 380.28 520.18 563.31 571.13 619.30 620.07
soldierboy 336.04
sole 036.30 182.34 230.23 376.36
solely 131.11 598.19 600.01 610.09
solemn 310.35 416.05 577.08 599.12 599.12 599.12
solemnly 126.16 337.10 512.35
solfa 450.18
solicit 356.05
solicitor 087.02 270.05
solicitous 622.03
solid 394.35 567.34
solidly 163.20
soliloquise 425.15
solitaire 567.34
solitary 598.04
solution 166.27 338.08
solve 356.11 491.04
sombre 198.34 271.11
somebody 176.36 204.21 207.16 361.15 415.17 620.09
somehow 242.20
someone 007.18 141.28 163.03 241.02 298.19 345.10 346.26 362.06 387.31 477.09 546.15 594.09 594.10 603.30
someplace 489.10 568.09
somersault 132.20 380.31
something 149.03 208.24 224.11 226.26 284.08 341.11 349.27 415.18 454.26 562.34
sometime 083.09 228.34 496.29 527.28 576.31
sometimes 133.19 267.19 365.14 506.13
somewhat 245.10 448.34 524.25
somewhere 145.04 292.32 346.26 347.10 580.15
son 112.05 117.04 135.24 150.12 153.31 162.15 202.30 228.15 235.05 278.23 286.23 310.03 314.28 322.05 322.08 331.14 333.29 339.36 340.02 358.21 360.03 362.10 415.22 419.09 437.29 481.27 510.33 543.09 603.32 612.30
song 192.17 224.35 236.14 242.30 300.R1 328.06 330.08 352.17 396.31 596.08 610.22
songster 186.31
sonny 603.16
sooner 093.24 314.18
sooterkin 311.23
sooth 311.34
sop 240.22
sorceress 251.12
sore 222.27 394.30
sorra 624.14
sorrow 051.01 053.26 230.11 425.15
sorrowful 301.15 512.25 527.10
sorry 011.35 114.01 159.18 229.29 264.F1 265.F5 281.21 299.F1 319.03 336.04 360.17 361.36 392.16 471.02 607.22
sort 016.01 043.35 053.23 067.15 111.31 141.08 162.21 326.36 395.18 539.29 546.16
soubrette 531.16 590.11
soul 014.03 026.14 036.30 093.36 144.04 149.08 167.36 180.25 208.25 236.36 297.21 304.F5 317.03 321.29 326.19 329.31 359.26 367.29 415.25 488.17 499.17 524.09 534.33 542.02 568.29 569.24 580.02 593.20 612.08
soulful 512.25
sound 214.10 419.06
soup 240.22 318.20 491.06 506.22 563.24
soupcan 199.18
sour 072.10 221.34 485.03 542.11
source 023.19 209.14
souse 241.28
soutane 288.15
south 117.25 171.35 240.17 251.14 373.01 387.02 494.14 497.13 539.14 553.30 557.02 597.12 620.16
southsea 162.07
souvenir 302.F2
sovereign 059.30 243.10 313.14 455.07
Soviet 414.14
sow 041.26 130.17 154.10 196.23 356.18
sowterkins 317.22 324.12
soyabean 140.31
sozzler 415.14

space 025.23 112.14 153.17 160.10 165.05 209.12 251.14 263.F2 292.06 293.18 316.29 365.33 417.25 456.20 504.28 550.09 574.17 616.27
spacious 153.17
spade 134.08 198.19 198.19 338.23 338.23 476.15
span 140.31 515.03 572.05
Spaniard 180.11
spaniel 350.30
Spanish 199.17 233.35 548.08
spar 130.17
spare 131.14 450.14 485.19
spark 346.32
spasmodical 515.16
spate 318.12 613.17
spatial 154.35
spatialist 240.03
speak 016.06 023.04 066.15 080.20 087.36 178.07 186.11 229.07 238.36 240.28 322.01 323.36 323.36 378.27 407.09 421.27 455.28 463.06 479.33 485.12 485.13 533.06 535.15 536.02 611.10 611.11 619.20
speakable 181.23 496.31
spear 267.04
special 140.04 154.35 287.F2 358.05 417.12
specialist 149.19 240.03
speciality 172.09
specially 113.16
species 161.09 419.07 504.14 504.28 600.03
specious 150.36
spectacles 386.16 397.35
spectral 015.32
spectre 015.32 299.05
speech 023.04 086.01 181.03 299.22 303.08 307.F7 349.26 378.32 432.25 448.17
spell 097.25 299.F3 328.24 420.33 461.03 461.35 508.33 540.26
spend 414.08 416.16
spendthrift 335.34 418.07
spermatic 296.26
spew 078.20
sphere 222.12 346.07
spice 616.27
spider 131.18 287.F1 417.24
spiderweb 374.08 481.05
spike 231.33
spill 496.19
spin 214.08
spinach 241.03 611.36
spindle 354.30
spindrift 335.34
spire 023.35 266.04 473.18
spirit 234.02 318.12 343.21 363.17 431.09 439.22 570.28
spiritual 482.02
spirt 363.17
spit 262.F2 323.08 323.36 326.20 363.17 417.26 535.15 594.21
spite 111.01 263.F2 537.32
spitfire 539.11
splash 072.35 172.25 460.28 488.28 562.15
splatter 454.14
splendidly 357.02
splinter 352.09
split 084.03 124.08 365.06
splutter 454.14
spokesman 517.12
spontaneously 414.01 542.09
spoof 619.20
spook 323.36
spool 426.05
spoon 240.22
spoonful 286.F5
sport 231.06
spot 220.07 291.F7 422.13 534.24
spouse 451.21
sprawl 004.11 437.11
spray 198.05 209.17
spread 007.09 058.11
sprig 161.28
spring 023.30 030.08 162.14 349.27
springflower 059.11
spume 072.36
spur 111.22
spy 251.14 301.01
squad 516.09
square 029.06 139.36 151.15 252.01 384.10
squash 183.22 270.L1 296.02 318.27 366.10 390.36 392.36 520.27
squat 343.13 438.13
squeak 151.22 455.28
squeal 426.05
squeamish 462.17
squeeze 296.03
squint 180.25
squirrel 550.24
stable 077.23 253.34 328.11
stablecart 610.17
stack 472.02
staff 296.30
stag 590.29
stage 071.34
stagewhisper 059.05
stagger 413.16
stain 011.22 075.14 128.02 199.17 225.24 420.12 528.17
stainedglass 277.F5 609.15 609.15
stair 109.19 219.03 222.36 266.13 354.01 533.17 562.20 579.02 588.05 607.26 624.09
staircase 557.03
stake 091.23 237.34 603.14
stalemate 313.18
stalk 126.11 615.25 624.10
stall 240.09
stammerer 547.25
stamp 356.07 421.07
stand 005.14 056.14 251.04 277.L3 300.32 346.27 583.36
standpoint 309.04
star 029.13 134.07 152.01 171.27 188.31 198.29 199.07 210.14 222.33 253.18 259.07 265.L2 266.02 291.F4 315.01 338.09 345.03 390.09 395.02 415.18 427.10 440.20 460.17 490.05 519.36 531.11 537.10 560.34 624.09
starboard 077.06
stardust 439.10
stare 143.22 199.24 616.29
stargazer 143.26 471.09
starling 466.17
start 017.14 266.13 322.20 488.27 496.25 553.32
starve 070.16 456.13 466.17 468.27 550.06
state 105.36 185.31 186.22 320.15 329.31 545.32
statement 236.35 313.18
station 343.07
stationer 106.12
statistics 616.22
statue 322.33 334.18
statuette 378.12
statute 495.31
staunch 084.22
stay 139.08 251.10 262.22 349.35 350.01 431.35 538.25
stead 026.26
steadfast 552.08
steadily 349.18
steak 059.20 142.05 170.33 456.22 563.03
steal 132.11 142.04 460.17 461.13 600.32
stealer 325.16
stealth 236.26
steam 176.02 225.07 531.09
steamer 324.33 326.10
steed 553.35
steel 068.29 303.05 460.17
steeple 004.34 077.23 141.05 327.15 342.07
steeplechase 322.02
steer 267.04 599.06
stem 104.10
stench 524.30
step 064.01 105.31 232.30 299.10 442.15
stepbrother 070.26
stepdaughter 472.21
stepson 481.27
stereotype 611.25
stern 303.06 450.07 602.30
sternly 454.21
stevedore 395.09 398.18
stew 295.30 371.17 406.11 460.32
steward 498.01
stick 004.22 019.06 050.05 092.16 093.25 214.09 225.09 270.L1 332.34 345.17 460.02 514.08 534.35 612.34
stickingplaster 101.24
sticky 555.23 555.23 555.24
stickybud 553.23
stiff 334.15 366.31
stifle 301.18
stile 093.31 445.33
stilly 040.13
stink 371.01 379.17
stirabout 155.25
stirrup 310.20 462.08
stitch 252.26
stock 085.11 106.18
stocking 144.21 154.34 368.31 459.08 495.09
stomach 053.31 061.17 097.29 145.04 187.03 199.21 243.07 344.35 355.30 599.20
stone 006.24 011.22 098.04 111.03 150.12 169.18 173.17 187.19 225.24 230.36 247.04

255.31 287.19 313.24 416.33 450.09 454.27 460.17 462.25 467.15 502.20 529.02 538.32 552.30 594.22 602.11 624.27
stonedeaf 522.28
Stonehenge 005.31 069.15
stony 291.11
stool 240.08 251.22 622.13
stoop 232.18
stop 020.13 074.19 081.16 210.26 222.23 312.01 312.01 332.10 361.03 365.27 370.13 560.16 560.16 560.17 595.32
storage 614.12
store 412.25
stork 443.25
storm 335.17 335.18 335.19
story 020.23 117.11 153.26 242.23 359.26 367.15 485.31
storybook 336.17
storytelling 424.35
stout 063.33 310.29 348.04 490.20 565.11
stoutness 537.17
stowaway 370.36
straight 012.25 183.34 252.25 291.17 294.02 315.23 318.12 344.09 413.18 491.09 499.33 617.36
straightway 315.30 340.32
strain 384.18 386.10
strait 491.09
strand 547.20
stranger 336.20 531.12
strangle 339.32
stranglehold 371.02
strategy 008.32
straw 041.08 112.34
strawberry 020.25 207.10 604.17
stray 404.15
streak 474.21
stream 086.20 104.10 171.35 203.24 228.13 319.27
streamer 374.10
street 003.17 032.26 083.36 110.33 110.34 117.15 132.06 156.29 169.23 183.34 207.23 236.20 236.23 242.24 245.19 245.22 274.13 294.F1 296.F2 300.F4 310.12 318.12 346.33 351.18 364.31 372.21 393.30 413.14 420.28 424.07 481.06 491.09 512.15 537.22 539.22 542.16 543.17 549.15 553.35 602.21 626.11
streetwalker 243.22 545.28
strength 023.03 102.25 341.11 359.17
stretch 033.08 443.25 595.04
strew 152.27 245.31
strict 512.15
strictly 119.08 237.36
strike 004.22 018.16 190.02 358.10 444.17 598.30
string 376.12
stripe 265.L2 564.24 623.16
strive 340.13 569.34
stroke 377.29 598.30
strong 004.10 082.13 276.22 343.04 547.31
strongly 011.29
struggle 145.26 340.13
struggler 132.09 247.30
Struldbrug 623.23
strumpet 421.07
struth 613.12
stub 552.26
stuck 153.20
study 432.22
stuff 161.16 354.33 456.24
stuffing 456.24
stumble 033.36 183.20 223.12 423.24
stun 423.24
stupid 445.22
stupify 437.28
stuprate 437.28
stutter 096.31 537.08 584.01 596.27
stutterer 016.15 337.18
sty 176.29 225.24 538.32
style 191.01 250.05 347.13 505.22
suave 048.10 287.31
subconscious 377.28
subconsciously 394.31
subconsciousness 224.17
subjection 053.05
subjugate 508.22
subjugation 525.04
sublimate 508.22 607.21
subordinate 156.11
subpoena 066.16 096.30
subscriber 523.31
subsection 221.03
subspecies 374.08
substitute 314.26 487.11
substitution 055.35
subtitle 314.26
subtle 270.15
subtropical 090.27
suburb 454.30 596.12
suburban 139.16
succeed 105.30 156.10 462.28
such 023.24 023.24 157.30 157.30 223.12 419.04 420.24 497.13
suck 230.09 437.29 606.31 610.19 612.15
sucker 241.03 362.15 371.01 446.11 524.05
sudden 324.32
suddenly 315.29 344.09 345.10 441.24 514.09 514.27 553.31 566.28
suet 205.30 313.34
suffer 078.03 118.18 223.01 241.07 312.04 352.36 418.29 434.04 454.24 625.30
suffice 481.24
suffocate 172.20 439.35 534.28 569.18
suffragette 242.24 542.19
suffusion 184.30
sugar 100.19 137.01 141.34 286.F5 357.02 397.17 405.35 415.06 608.20
sugarcane 424.28
sugarloaf 243.28
suggestion 369.27 406.32 525.04
suggestiveness 222.32
suicidal 040.31
suit 023.11 086.02 167.19 180.25 251.27 277.01 301.F1 311.23 311.27 322.11 324.02 324.30 366.33 391.20 411.22 510.28 520.08 527.27 620.04
suitor 326.27
sulk 061.11 342.06
sulphate 086.02
sulphide 359.03
sulphur 183.01 222.25 415.06 537.30
sultan 034.06 616.11
Sumerian 504.06
summarise 602.07
summer 069.32 152.21 157.08 302.F2 327.20 331.26 371.15 415.27 433.10 453.16 502.29 517.29
summon 163.03
sun 014.11 280.04 312.06 385.10
sunbaked 139.11
sunbath 129.28 493.02 548.14
sunbeam 127.15
sunbonnet 176.36
Sunday 005.11 007.24 138.17 141.24 147.25 196.19 205.17 219.05 227.31 235.34 289.08 295.07 338.18 350.33 355.25 355.26 355.27 409.28 432.33 436.27 457.19 492.07 493.02 539.16 593.01 593.01 593.01
sunder 207.11
sundown 138.36
sundry 310.13 339.25 343.32 539.16 547.33
sunflower 350.11
sunlight 517.20 578.23 594.11
sunset 353.31
sunshine 603.02
sunup 593.23
sup 406.12 406.12
super 221.07
superannuate 441.12
supercilious 025.15
superficies 524.31
superfluous 526.25
superior 404.18
supernatural 341.30 598.17
supernaturally 524.20
superposition 299.08
supersonic 123.12
superstition 378.12
supper 121.35 131.04 326.32 453.12 626.12
supplicate 569.18
support 232.22 454.31
supporter 372.09
suppose 090.25 105.20 232.22 332.07 337.16 337.18 356.19 406.19
supposedly 366.23
sura 312.35
surd 352.09
sure 004.14 026.14 058.20 058.20 089.35 198.09 202.05 203.09 277.15 333.15 341.28 341.34 354.05 387.30 459.23 490.30 517.07 540.11 561.03 565.19 565.30
surely 089.13 110.04 277.F5 621.09
surface 050.10 089.32 124.11 354.11 429.20 496.11
surfeit 086.02
surgeon 450.15

surly 499.22
surname 441.29
surplus 204.31 279.F35 404.28
surprise 345.08 370.24 493.36 582.17 606.36
surprised 222.09
surrender 130.34 232.19
surrogate 149.29
survival 145.27
susceptible 230.28 343.18
suspender 531.05
suspicious 254.08 443.34 527.33
suttee 025.03
swab 485.24
swain 254.03 326.36 426.25
swallow 018.03 181.03 257.18 394.06 406.12 449.04
swamp 328.20 451.29
swan 326.36 372.16 372.16
swap 070.04
swarm 019.13 238.33 430.20
swarthy 199.07
swastika 514.30 566.10
sway 254.03
swear 021.24 022.11 083.07 113.17 131.22 163.25 228.04 264.12 264.13 292.23 312.02 348.14 374.26 434.13 436.12 557.12
swearword 501.13
sweat 017.24 198.06 291.06 324.03 336.28 408.01 563.28
Swede 141.12 211.03 557.28
Swedish 360.02 590.20
sweep 230.25 391.06 391.06
sweepstake 237.34 603.14
sweet 017.24 065.05 110.24 116.01 137.07 154.30 156.15 170.04 295.32 302.F2 309.12 345.31 356.18 359.19 387.19 395.20 431.33 443.19 474.12 533.22 533.22 539.36 557.28 604.07 617.36
sweeter 354.34
sweetheart 051.36 116.23 247.18 302.14 360.12 431.19 454.03
swell 199.23 325.26
swift 303.06 347.20
swig 132.34
swim 188.23 229.04 600.31
swimmingpool 377.35
swindle 426.27 598.03
swine 173.19 187.02 202.09 424.27 434.29
swineherd 254.03
swing 279.F32
swipe 547.28
Swiss 093.06 129.34 620.35
switch 349.27
switchback 009.12 620.35
swivel 157.12
sword 090.10 222.22 250.35 262.F2 352.09 353.14 354.30 379.21 464.13 539.29 549.27
sycamore 281.20 460.23 476.14
sycophant 094.16 340.25 349.10
syllable 129.08 267.20 292.27 292.27 292.27 299.F3 424.33
sylvan 019.02 388.26 495.36
symbol 612.29
symbolically 292.25
symbolise 607.10
sympathise 226.07
sympathy 092.10 159.27 409.10 522.33
symphony 341.08
symposium 066.19
synagogue 136.01 240.10 244.07 244.07
synchronise 349.10
syndic 223.04
syndrome 582.30
syne 087.06 096.23 305.29 398.28
synod 352.13
syntax 183.20 269.03
synthesis 092.10
syrup 225.16
systematically 157.22

tabernacle 244.06 405.31 438.13 507.11 584.31 613.09
table 326.01 434.31
tablespoon 038.20
tabloid 219.18
taboo 225.08
taciturn 099.02
tack 063.36 139.30 142.07
tactful 388.03
tactic 009.06 139.29
tactics 089.24 396.27 418.34 418.34 534.03 534.03
tag 105.16
tail 007.11 089.35 143.15 165.21 227.12 247.01 354.36 361.08 415.32 425.02 462.31 493.01 524.24 531.22 607.01
tailfeather 383.13
tailor 023.11 061.28 067.14 070.20 202.14 311.06 311.24 311.26 312.03 317.07 323.19 325.16 325.24 326.01 356.10 365.33 372.03 375.34 511.29 594.36 613.32
take 004.29 037.06 118.34 151.23 157.24 197.13 206.25 287.29 311.33 315.31 322.05 322.08 359.02 363.18 363.18 364.25 373.19 376.13 396.27 441.32 451.24 484.17 487.36 504.12 514.06 525.12 585.31 603.14 607.03 613.30 614.14 617.20
taker 396.27
tale 006.03 007.05 007.05 105.09 117.31 143.24 203.17 324.05 341.31 350.23 354.36 423.04 598.21
talent 606.30
talk 016.05 016.06 106.29 167.19 177.29 317.07 326.30 332.10 426.18 461.28 499.21 599.09
talker 503.17
talkie 541.18
tall 019.25 334.07 427.23
taller 082.04
tally 468.36
Talmud 030.10
tambour 510.19
tambourine 415.09
Tamil 498.17
tam-o'-shanter 227.22 229.21 315.25
tan 510.19 540.21 563.31 588.18
tank 586.29
tantalise 251.23
tantalising 149.35
tantamount 247.34
tapioca 275.08
tapper 483.19
tar 130.04
tarboy 362.08
tarbrush 491.26
tariff 365.17
tarnation 366.27
tart 051.36 079.08 407.04 535.16
Tartar 105.25 136.21 233.34 407.04 491.14
taskmaster 037.08 271.04
tassle 465.30
taste 132.34
tat 139.30 359.11
tata 065.17
tattoo 238.17
taut 336.28
tautological 468.08
tavern 265.23
tax 191.18 448.33 567.25
taxi 304.17
tea 012.16 026.07 038.16 054.12 054.12 102.20 106.01 110.11 111.20 117.18 117.30 119.23 124.13 137.08 145.05 145.05 184.30 199.18 229.26 235.28 247.18 262.17 262.L2 277.F5 330.06 330.26 331.02 332.03 355.30 367.12 371.31 376.30 406.28 421.09 435.12 453.12 490.28 553.13 586.35 599.03 601.11 601.11 603.05 603.06 621.14
teach 021.29 147.09 292.24 441.15
teacher 251.29 284.16
teacup 232.35 236.31 616.23
tealeaf 427.02 608.26 608.28
teaparty 247.15 247.15
tear 110.09 118.34 145.12 190.21 245.10 344.03 426.15 505.16 509.26 598.19
tearer 070.20
tearose 248.02
tease 247.14 342.36 563.04
teatime 191.28 548.32
teem 395.02
teetotal 181.21 260.02
teetotally 330.06
tegular 416.35
telephone 086.14 485.22
telescope 008.35 009.34 010.13 275.L2 431.14 449.34
television 338.09 338.14 345.35 349.28 489.21 597.36 610.35
tell 007.05 015.25 018.07 020.14 044.09 056.34 117.31 167.15 203.16 206.24 209.17 216.03 248.26 268.F1 275.24 316.33 324.05 347.19 347.22 378.18 390.24 425.02 512.28 519.18 520.36 555.13 563.27 566.09 571.13 572.17 572.17
telltale 007.02 510.29
telly 437.27
temper 317.03 360.09

temperature 597.32
template 272.23
temple 290.03 520.10 607.30 621.34
tempt 015.26 250.14
temptation 362.04 561.22
temptress 480.04
ten 051.33 077.14 150.35 172.01 181.31 187.20 202.02 283.02 283.09 330.33 371.04 421.18 495.27 564.19 582.35 588.18 593.10 610.18
tenant 414.06
tender 335.11 594.18
tenderly 368.17
tenement 538.10
tenor 182.23
tenpenny 466.02
tenpound 082.34
tenterhooks 133.34
tenure 539.33
term 478.11
termite 057.12
terrace 105.35 199.31 265.11 420.28 553.11
terracotta 071.22 119.02 133.30 134.18 240.19
terrible 132.18 138.17 205.29 224.12 344.13 353.24 381.24 477.21 520.02 628.05
terribly 283.28 303.F1
terrier 182.15 404.19
terrific 396.34
terrify 053.35 060.21 191.23
territorial 082.25
territory 359.03
terror 105.35 343.08 602.15 626.28
terse 165.18
tersely 150.12
testament 413.17
testify 382.02
testily 417.06
testis 116.36
testmatch 584.10
tetrain 129.28
tettigoniidae 416.35
thank 009.31 035.27 044.23 054.11 145.06 150.05 151.35 343.20 487.07 527.28 533.36 534.02 584.32 585.08 619.33
thankful 543.13 599.21
thanksgiving 061.21 618.26
theatre 059.09 214.14 587.08
theatrical 363.28
theft 335.33
themselves 357.32 368.16 373.13 547.24
theocrat 029.15 295.33
theology 374.17
theorem 156.02 292.05
theory 163.25
Theosophy 277.L5
thereby 224.08
thesis 278.L2 278.L2 278.L2 356.11 357.22 358.05 487.26 532.12 533.02 533.14 533.31 534.10 537.14 539.07 586.22
thick 017.27 416.33 506.04 541.35 608.26
thicket 087.30
thief 021.23 176.13 243.24 312.01 411.05 622.24
thimble 038.20 295.F2
thin 584.33
thine 102.01 593.04
thing 018.35 149.03 162.35 176.14 201.21 296.20 432.29 460.16 466.06 487.24 503.18 505.18 505.28 515.06 532.29
thingamejig 332.24 479.14 613.19
Thingmote 018.16 053.06 058.01 058.02
think 009.31 024.15 095.17 141.32 151.35 152.33 153.31 177.29 214.19 224.25 250.08 258.09 317.03 336.30 342.27 344.18 375.18 422.27 499.18 504.12 512.30 532.28 556.34 561.14 586.31 588.11 608.22 628.10
thinkable 173.36
thinker 151.09
third 138.33 156.34 314.29 319.20 373.15 532.09 598.30
thirst 311.16 319.34 497.23 599.06
thirsty 137.24
thirteen 378.22
thirty 283.01 284.16 320.22
thirtynine 283.10 534.12 535.29
thirtysecond 084.32
thirtythree 173.07 444.12
thirtytwo 073.15 093.12 274.12 274.L3 286.10 347.04 378.22 389.25 516.17 517.30 574.26 584.24 606.18
thong 511.31
thoroughbred 317.01 411.22
thoroughfare 085.09
thoroughly 465.10 609.26
thought 049.31 302.26 328.07 342.03 378.12 440.24 450.26 527.02
thoughtful 537.04
thousand 070.08 070.09 230.13 265.26 268.26 285.24 285.25 295.03 438.24 478.03 505.06 567.02 597.05
threaten 248.27 361.10
three 011.02 019.22 041.18 051.11 053.36 053.36 058.24 060.36 094.14 094.15 094.15 094.15 094.15 100.06 105.30 106.19 106.19 115.17 126.08 134.07 134.09 146.34 150.02 166.10 202.01 238.31 240.11 246.15 247.08 248.27 251.33 272.20 282.31 282.31 283.03 283.04 299.01 315.14 332.02 337.16 339.12 346.28 348.27 348.28 350.24 352.29 354.11 354.28 361.02 372.18 398.20 403.04 420.08 457.13 469.27 506.16 506.18 546.27 556.19 569.24 581.23 588.36 616.09 621.04
threepence 141.07 266.L1 425.14
threepenny 190.19 485.02 485.17
thrice 361.02 594.32
thrift 335.33
thrill 145.32 563.27
throat 160.24 162.33 165.05 374.06 457.33 493.24 511.12 601.23
throne 148.22 336.13 348.14 378.05 417.11 498.34
throneroom 498.07
throw 120.28 279.F11 326.22 537.01
thrush 588.08
thrust 319.34 388.06 395.36 454.03 599.06
thud 156.34
thumb 283.20 340.26 341.11 352.28 357.21 381.19 533.11 608.22 612.34
thumbstall 240.09
thunder 093.26 176.01 187.15 221.21 227.06 295.14 314.29 334.27 335.11 339.16 347.34 353.24 365.22 405.35 415.20 468.21 525.20 565.17 607.25 607.26 623.24 624.05
thunderbolt 106.15 140.17
thunderclap 284.14
thunderhead 274.08
thunderstruck 018.16
thunderweather 283.L2
thurible 132.18 138.17 205.29 628.05
Thursday 005.13 006.14 086.11 100.17 137.24 182.26 301.21 325.06 409.29 491.27 492.05 514.22 520.17 581.16
thwart 139.07
thyme 394.10
thyself 579.18
tick 141.33 180.22
ticket 428.26 604.14
tickle 013.17 212.33 293.30 331.12 363.18 405.06 511.11
ticklesome 295.30
ticklish 038.17
tictac 139.29
tiddlywink 583.35
tide 196.23 204.14 308.17 432.33 590.22
tidemark 262.F1
tidy 206.13
tie 123.20 138.23 225.33 226.24 250.04 379.05
tiger 202.34 322.21 599.06 624.31
tight 265.21 342.16 373.27 379.05 426.20 478.23
tighten 583.17
tightrope 301.01
tile 183.05
tillage 545.14
tilt 316.01
timbre 209.36
time 012.19 020.24 022.21 026.28 029.21 051.32 065.11 090.07 114.01 138.15 138.15 140.22 149.17 150.23 161.04 161.06 161.28 163.13 172.05 181.30 196.22 196.22 200.31 210.01 223.08 236.27 250.14 275.24 284.09 292.06 317.03 320.36 322.27 327.09 342.36 364.15 371.25 377.11 408.23 412.18 424.01 424.03 448.28 453.20 453.20 454.03 465.36 501.05 501.19 516.01 516.01 519.25 538.31 598.27 599.23 602.36 607.17 607.17 607.17

607.17 607.22 607.22 608.12 610.11 612.07 614.08
timeless 053.04
timepiece 416.24 590.11
timetable 579.24
timetaker 396.27
time-time 149.21
timorous 356.34
tin 068.08 262.F3
tincture 286.05
tingle 395.19 419.12
tinker 317.07 338.25 351.26 405.06 409.21
tinkle 405.06
tinpan 310.11 547.29
tintack 063.36
tintinabulate 497.35
tiny 224.31 594.21 626.09
tip 111.31 262.F2 333.18 334.04 334.11 334.16 337.03 376.05 419.26 470.32 510.30 547.30 595.18 595.18 598.04
tipple 534.30
tiptoe 150.03 207.34 562.09
tiptop 512.20
tire 261.17 394.16 584.13
tissue 183.23
tit 139.29 359.11 371.25
titbit 101.05 172.32
titivate 346.03 374.04
title 070.16 212.34 314.26
titlepage 212.34
titty 260.02 583.03
toad 389.24
toadstool 040.23
toast 184.31 199.17 298.F3
tobacco 243.21 427.13
tocher 584.32
tock 141.30
today 060.28 087.08 102.28 111.02 144.13 172.06 172.24 315.32 324.35 342.29 381.23 381.23 381.24 381.24 407.36 408.22 534.01 548.31 593.02 598.02 598.23
toe 199.26 349.01
toecap 260.04
toenail 110.14
together 015.02 155.27 332.12 334.22 334.22 453.16 517.14
toiler 372.03 385.33
toilet 221.23 344.12 525.03
token 484.17
toller 522.08
tomb 006.10 006.11 532.28
tombowler 584.07
tomboy 385.10 385.10 561.04 561.04
tombstone 253.34
tomorrow 011.14 012.14 060.29 087.08 102.28 104.12 126.18 141.35 172.24 315.33 324.33 338.12 346.12 377.25 407.36 408.19 408.22 455.12 455.13 455.13 470.14 548.31 563.37 565.21 579.23 597.33 598.10 625.14
tomtit 338.26 505.01
tomtom 231.05 338.26 608.32
ton 132.26 540.26
tong 511.31
tongue 015.12 117.15 158.14 177.05 185.11 260.F1 411.21 453.19 485.22 511.31 598.04 599.09
tonguetied 123.20
tonic 261.18 450.18
tonight 011.13 126.02
tonsil 236.35
tonsure 234.11
tooth 015.05 024.03 222.27 311.34 311.34 323.04 349.11 598.26 598.26 602.30
toothache 233.01
toothbrush 348.32
toothpick 025.16 071.03 183.30 410.24
top 048.17 211.21 533.35
tophat 347.30
topical 020.15 275.08
topmast 504.23
topper 510.04
topple 481.14 534.30
topsyturvy 275.14 470.32
torch 027.13 443.25
torment 230.13
tornado 416.34
torpedo 077.07 310.03 364.29 530.24
torrid 381.24
torso 084.27 607.33
tortoise 238.22 241.07
tosh 151.34
toss 222.26 322.21 415.12
tot 626.09
total 006.28 042.27
touch 027.13 284.17 319.11 463.16 465.29 599.20
toucher 557.10 557.11
tough 624.17
tourmaline 021.27 022.14
tow 201.27
toward 523.04
towards 078.31 120.22 237.01 584.33
towel 594.09
tower 027.13 320.22 327.28 353.34 523.32 527.22 536.08 541.06
town 130.24 311.06 316.29 331.36 342.17 355.24 382.26 415.08 481.14 540.21 540.26 577.29 593.02 593.02 593.11 599.22
towncrier 427.03
township 532.13
toxin 255.07
trace 348.27
trackless 028.29
trade 230.35
trademark 114.32 378.12 547.33
tradesman 551.13
tradition 151.20
tragedy 005.13 061.07
trail 608.23
train 074.19 077.35 444.03 484.04 571.29
trainer 370.22
traitor 019.07 378.05
tram 081.16 378.10
tramconductor 420.33
tramp 078.21 078.21 078.21 246.22 246.22 246.22
trample 016.27 483.36
tramticket 428.26
trance 199.10
transatlantic 311.21 326.09
transcript 111.09 374.03 393.31 623.36
transfix 613.09
transit 415.04
transition 100.01
transitive 594.03
translate 233.09 275.F6 281.F2 419.24
transparency 548.25
transport 056.03 452.14
trapdoor 224.25 288.02
trapeze 086.02 257.04
trapezium 165.22
trauma 115.32 601.28
travail 569.19
travel 137.16 344.34 453.13 569.19
traveller 286.F2
treacherous 088.18 148.19
treacherously 541.08
tread 161.01 337.19
treason 575.34
treasure 144.22
treat 105.26 300.12
treatise 440.02
treaty 440.02
treble 330.06 450.22 465.23 628.05
tree 060.20 105.09 176.08 304.F4 379.05 526.22 551.13 600.20
treetop 152.34
trefoil 526.22
tremble 016.27 258.23 341.09 462.26 506.13 506.14 506.14
trembler 283.13
tremens 502.30
tremulous 185.28
trench 009.19
trenchcoat 051.12
trend 200.34 327.09
trepan 248.27
trespass 302.06 363.26 594.27
trespasser 345.28 503.29 594.14
triad 389.24
triangle 165.13 286.20 297.27
triangular 297.24
tribulation 094.13
tributary 210.04
tribute 011.02 385.14 387.34
tricastle 018.06
trick 147.14 436.05 515.33 531.15
tricky 282.L2
tricoloured 339.12
tricycle 567.34
trident 547.22
trifle 174.34 430.24 469.17 478.25 485.24
triforium 224.02
trilabial 548.29
trilby 075.15 075.15 285.F1 548.29
trinity 315.02
tripartite 003.10 012.24 086.02 087.35 265.09 312.20 405.31 465.14
triple 462.20 465.23
triplex 133.30

tripod 452.10
tripos 286.24
triptote 477.28
triptych 477.28
triumph 022.28 328.34
triumphal 590.10
triumvirate 271.05
triune 422.26 422.26 590.09
troglodyte 252.34
trolley 498.06 577.14
trollop 520.25
troop 237.02
trooper 350.26 510.04
troth 511.12
trotter 435.12
troubadour 165.07 224.25 288.02 411.29 439.09 462.26
trouble 330.06 354.29 589.06
trousers 011.36 065.20 085.35 126.13 144.22 262.F2 268.26 276.F1 276.F1 280.L3 311.29 319.22 319.29 324.19 354.29 433.31 450.26 507.14 598.03
trousseau 560.35
trout 148.19 362.06
truce 478.25
truculence 360.21
true 049.33 074.09 337.27 370.04 410.05 411.29 483.36 510.20 520.25 528.12 564.21 597.20
trueblue 076.32 328.09
truelove 340.07 370.04 567.08
truly 089.36 090.29 090.31 094.28 129.02 313.10 396.34 406.21 498.06 520.32 533.06 534.08 610.14
trump 023.26 023.27 244.35
trumpet 247.33
trumpeter 553.36
trunk 244.35
trust 104.24 433.34
trusty 365.33 521.22
truth 015.25 044.09 107.16 113.12 122.09 132.05 162.33 209.17 288.03 325.08 336.19 336.19 336.19 336.20 343.08 349.16 353.09 364.01 378.06 410.36 413.29 413.30 459.23 493.24 505.19 520.12 534.08 597.24 613.12
try 129.22 160.33 196.10 196.10 225.04 238.31 328.19 362.06 438.10 538.07 552.17
try-out 357.03
tryst 388.06
tsetse 299.26 423.04
tub 105.09 117.32 423.04 423.24 598.21
tuberculosis 541.36
tuck 142.02 240.35
Tudor 504.21
Tuesday 221.06 227.31 301.20 408.19 409.28 457.19 492.05 617.21
tuffet 413.19
tulip 015.01 570.04
tumble 175.17 520.10
tumult 555.01
tundish 448.06
tune 247.29 486.06
tuningfork 450.27
tunnel 201.02 583.35
turbulence 338.17
turf 086.10 111.31 346.21 353.16 363.25 388.17 606.36 625.18
Turk 581.10
turkey 456.32 483.08 510.08 542.28 559.28 594.34
turkeycock 310.34 394.07
Turkish 248.20 281.F2 294.19 347.36 350.22 530.36
turn 116.14 140.34 213.23 236.35 319.23 346.28 353.17 353.34 356.23 357.21 363.25 382.01 382.01 408.23 408.23 557.09
turnabout 142.10
turncoat 579.34
turnpike 132.32 231.33 371.35 570.04
turpentine 206.34 478.13
turpitude 523.28
turquoise 215.21 235.08
turret 077.19
turtle 007.06 039.15 091.09 406.12
tutelage 343.16
twaddle 006.28 319.13
twain 425.30
'twas 059.34
twelve 076.02 199.03 248.21 309.14 353.15 403.02 437.13 479.14 524.30 549.10
twenty 177.27 228.24 242.18 284.16 312.21 436.01 601.14
twentyeight 469.30 601.15
twentyfour 130.27
twentyfourth 473.10
twentynine 010.29 075.04 223.09 279.F18 499.05
twentyone 601.14
twentysix 396.17
twentytwo 364.04 364.05 438.24 438.24 505.05 505.06
twice 361.02 594.31 594.32
twilight 331.28 344.12 492.09 525.03
twin 111.17 143.18 211.06 330.30 354.24 436.11
twine 396.24
twinge 279.F33
twinkle 222.34 279.F33 297.13 620.15
twinkling 256.04
twist 204.25 205.10 424.06 427.19
twitter 037.17
two 060.36 094.15 094.15 115.17 154.26 169.08 169.09 177.26 198.11 198.11 202.01 226.21 226.21 238.31 246.15 246.34 251.33 272.20 274.L3 282.30 282.31 282.32 283.03 283.04 285.13 286.10 288.23 295.30 314.28 314.28 331.08 337.16 346.27 347.04 348.22 350.24 360.29 361.02 361.22 364.05 364.05 369.25 378.23 438.05 438.24 457.13 469.27 505.05 505.06 517.30 538.21 541.29 541.29 546.26 557.09 581.23 584.24 586.25 601.11 601.11 606.18
twofold 359.32
twogun 083.35
twohandled 615.19
twopenny 041.20 232.05 268.13 442.03 465.23 611.04
twotoned 063.20
tympanum 224.19
typhoon 325.14
typical 031.22
tyre 567.34

udder 180.16 240.15 417.33
ugly 070.23 082.12
ultimatum 336.09 336.09
ultramarine 225.05
ultraviolet 316.02 425.35
Ulyssean 123.16
umbrella 007.26 022.20 024.33 106.32 227.36 284.04 338.07 361.19 373.21 492.23 530.29 569.20
umpire 516.15
unaccompanied 607.32
unappealed 452.22
unawares 371.26
unbearable 162.02
unbelieve 468.16
unbeliever 352.15
unbiassed 110.18
unborn 370.07
unbuttoned 341.02
uncaparisoned 152.05
unceasingly 445.36
uncertain 449.02
uncle 076.28 101.09 228.17 235.16 237.13 250.13 288.06 367.14 467.12 467.14 480.17
unclean 421.02
unclosed 569.14
unclothed 366.15
unconditionally 232.23 326.08
unconscious 123.22
unconsciously 300.25
uncouth 227.27 365.18
uncrowned 043.32
unction 227.32
undefiled 075.05 233.33
undergarment 181.29 245.10
underground 481.15
understamp 421.07
understand 272.21 363.36 378.22 456.28 492.17 581.17
understatement 236.35
understudy 432.22
undertake 613.30 625.09
underwear 085.03 365.11 371.35 547.08
underworld 147.28 385.04 593.23
undesirable 456.30
undies 008.32
undo 291.17 353.17
undulate 243.28
undying 527.23
uneatable 181.23
unending 276.11
uneven 475.33
unfiltered 474.07
ungallant 157.04
ungentlemanly 034.18
ungirdle 548.17
unhappy 257.02
unheard 017.15 223.01 363.26
unhindered 330.33
unholy 396.12

unhorse 137.17
unicorn 156.25 157.03 291.01 422.15
unicycle 567.34
uniform 222.13 344.10 413.31
uninterested 538.03
uninvented 517.34
union 162.26 186.25
unique 462.20
unison 060.11
unite 105.36 320.15 489.31
universe 054.23 356.12 410.17 607.11
university 551.28
unkempt 013.08 541.02
unkind 059.10 465.31
unknown 091.28 323.26 353.15
unladylike 438.26
unlatch 459.26
unleavened 517.33
unless 350.34
unlocalised 087.18
unmarried 226.18
unmentionable 052.26
unpardonable 537.36
unperishable 130.05
unpierceable 616.32
unprincipled 594.02
unprohibited 085.09
unpronounceable 479.09
unqualified 005.16
unravel 361.33
unready 204.10
unruly 332.07
unseemliness 352.18
unshackled 354.07
unskilled 237.13
unspeakable 181.22 496.31
unspeakably 238.36
unsure 540.28
unsyllabled 183.15
unthinkable 173.36
untiringly 261.17
unusable 324.29
unusual 510.28 516.32
unveil 354.22
unwashed 049.22 159.27 435.31
unwittingly 124.15
uphold 586.26
upholsterer 276.F5
upholstery 271.F3
upper 454.01
upright 239.19
uproarious 121.27
uproot 448.18
upsadaisy 597.23
upset 127.17 284.26 333.34
upside 205.28
upstairs 109.19 266.13
upstart 266.13
urination 269.F3
urine 171.28 253.27
urn 210.31 433.31
usable 324.29
use 338.20 462.01 465.09 580.05 593.09 593.11
useful 510.28
uselessly 179.26
usual 510.28
usucapion 035.29 537.23
usurp 426.06
utensil 053.18
utmost 058.14 424.08 460.16
utter 222.28 378.33
utterly 229.35 485.25

vacant 553.15
vacuum 136.34 309.21 362.25 364.33 473.06 514.12
vagina 625.34
vagrant 010.29
vain 597.25
vale 007.12 074.02 110.09 190.21 199.10 466.35 472.01 608.01
valediction 077.25
valentine 439.17
Valhalla 005.30 069.07 091.30 348.10 359.34 609.18
valid 493.03
valley 158.19 338.21 345.31 478.12 526.21 528.23
valuation 619.04
value 283.10 478.23 543.02
valve 297.27 314.20 349.12
vamp 176.34
vampire 551.02
vanish 061.18 177.17 192.24 339.11 427.07 473.20
vanity 178.03 354.05 354.05 493.18 493.18 493.18 493.18 502.25 502.25 502.25 502.26 625.07 625.07
vanquish 379.10 490.01
vapour 208.13 569.18
variation 450.19
variegated 015.03 115.26
various 373.30
vary 324.28
vast 338.14
vaticinate 152.23
vaudeville 294.18 580.01
vault 403.16 549.16
vaunt 549.16
vegetable 357.34 455.30
vegetarian 171.03
vehicle 490.03
veil 354.22 528.22 610.14
velar 424.26
velleity 625.07 625.07
vellum 478.12
velocity 154.34
velum 242.01
Vendidads 432.30
vendor 408.36
venerate 167.30
veneration 356.33
venery 355.36 581.11
Venetian 356.36
venial 227.31 463.11
venison 055.06 093.17
vent 351.30
ventriloquence 360.21
veracity 151.06
verbatim 037.15
verbiage 183.13
verbigeration 037.13 611.29
verdant 231.07
verdure 110.10
verey-light 344.23
verge 203.29
verger 412.17
verisimilitude 404.12
veritable 010.34 059.11
veritably 410.10
vermilion 352.17
vernacular 082.12 319.28
versatile 468.02
verse 173.25 270.L3 395.22 553.25 566.35
versify 044.09
versus 196.21 272.31 272.31 301.10 454.30 443.11 518.13
vertically 297.12
vesper 038.14
vespers 569.18
vessel 023.35 201.23 316.29
vestal 234.15 599.07
vestment 323.10
vestpocket 058.35
vestry 146.09 204.32
viaduct 604.14
vibrate 157.01
vicar 330.13 349.25 495.17
viceregal 033.30 131.22 622.08
viceregent 438.28 564.13
viceroy 100.05
viceversa 173.25 384.27 453.17
vicious 134.16 141.09 414.02 481.29
victorious 298.14 353.12
victory 009.13 082.12 395.36 537.10
victual 116.01 164.17 242.12 405.36
view 160.32 293.12 344.22
vigil 569.16
vignette 600.12
viking 018.13 053.26 157.17 241.18 279.F21 310.10 326.07 331.20 338.30 433.04 546.03 565.19 626.27
vile 360.18
vilest 231.20 390.12
villa 128.08
village 265.29 381.04
villager 548.18
villain 219.20 242.01 545.14
vindicate 370.32
vine 381.04
vineyard 542.12
vintage 355.29
vintner 072.10
viol 164.17
violence 285.F6 316.02 432.31
violet 207.11 253.18 261.02 277.F4 285.02 285.F6 339.29 403.15 425.35 432.31 461.17 604.14
viper 569.18
virgin 088.33 270.25 395.22 432.11
virginity 279.F15
virile 439.36 440.01 564.22
virtual 396.20
virtue 498.33 510.06 537.05
visa 183.14
visage 296.12
visibility 324.34
visible 016.24 053.04 472.03 527.12 594.33
vision 423.05
visit 493.19
visual 079.28
vital 097.30 599.07
vitamin 456.20
vitriol 101.24 603.35
vituperate 157.01
vivisection 489.03

vixen 383.24
viz 041.32
vocabulary 419.12
vocal 224.19
voce 261.F4
voice 016.23 039.15 068.26 142.19 153.36 160.26 182.23 312.05 435.10 441.26 487.11 513.12 536.22
void 378.29
volatile 020.34
volcanic 240.26
Vollapük 040.05 116.31
volley 334.26
volume 048.19 155.27 242.01
voluminous 155.20
voluntarily 364.06
vomit 492.03
vote 243.36 393.13
vouchsafe 234.27
vowel 116.28 116.28 485.11 563.14
vulcanise 481.14 545.33
vulcanology 387.12
vulgar 211.13 242.29 256.22 329.17 385.12 422.30 481.14 563.14 613.28 626.27
vulva 492.33

wadding 214.09
waddle 257.18
wade 178.15
waft 318.32
wage 098.32
wagon 141.17 253.10 553.34 582.32
wagoner 577.13
wail 078.03
waistcoat 242.34 404.25
wait 007.36 155.19 223.36 232.13 257.18 275.12 375.08 491.32
waiter 537.19 594.32
waitingroom 589.29
waitress 255.33
wake 148.35 158.23 176.16 257.18 276.22 294.F3 295.14 310.10 320.22 338.30 351.02 358.23 358.26 368.13 368.19 375.17 375.19 435.28 469.04 497.01 499.13 519.04 531.26 549.18 584.22 593.14 597.12 596.06 608.34 617.17
walk 245.12 368.09 383.10 518.33 545.29 609.31
walkabout 242.15
walker 243.22 603.15
wall 020.27 111.11 209.03 262.26 314.09 314.13 314.14 331.30 365.16 415.07 497.25 553.22 615.31
wallaby 165.20 497.13
wallflower 269.09
Walloon 376.05
wallpaper 416.21
walrus 056.07 248.21 324.09
waltz 236.20 248.12 255.24 281.F1 320.10 378.31 435.10 513.13 578.16 601.25
waltzer 443.21
wander 013.33 049.06 056.22 229.14 336.16 368.08 414.29
wanderer 245.24 355.33
wanderlust 576.21
want 138.07 138.08 164.07 223.35 245.23 278.19 278.21 359.18 361.25 446.02 487.21 499.31 516.21
wapping 533.17
war 156.03 272.10 379.11 493.19 528.32
warble 270.F2 452.01 597.29
warden 526.20
warfare 350.35 518.02
warm 356.35
warmingpan 610.32
warmth 348.25
warn 423.30
warning 107.31
warp 034.24 174.02 403.04
warrior 350.33 596.11
wart 305.10
wary 316.34
wash 004.22 049.22 064.20 282.22 290.17 318.19 340.03 432.33 435.32 525.02 553.20 595.08
washer 026.17 066.16 105.33
washerwoman 287.L1 336.12
washhouse 614.03
wassail 588.17
waste 017.28 062.11 162.17
wastefully 164.07
wasteland 335.12
wastepaperbasket 523.25
watch 076.23 187.06 275.F1 296.02 297.17 436.03 525.02
watchman 245.16
water 008.32 009.21 012.09 064.20 064.20 070.09 130.04 135.06 155.01 178.25 206.31 227.29 229.23 239.20 241.12 245.22 315.21 331.27 341.12 351.24 371.07 371.20 371.31 372.26 373.06 373.06 373.10 373.33 376.08 393.13 492.24 495.26 510.27 519.24 551.36 551.36 551.36 578.20 587.26 594.10 601.06 610.20 610.20 610.30
watercress 225.12 225.13 491.19
waterfall 383.23
wateringcan 518.18
waterlog 344.14
waterproof 155.29 290.19
watershoot 502.20
waterway 153.23
waterworks 067.09
wave 105.02 194.32 349.12 371.28 463.32 552.15
wavy 041.23
wax 149.13 333.22
waxy 010.07
way 086.26 154.16 175.20 236.36 249.20 257.19 304.06 324.31 347.32 395.01 413.35 542.36 558.02 595.09 621.33
wayfarer 365.01
wayward 351.08
weak 626.03
wealth 091.28 238.32 593.12
wean 005.23 546.31
weapon 339.10 566.22 615.19
wear 093.36 345.14 414.03 534.18 614.16
weary 053.05 433.19
weasel 540.15
weather 039.14 085.03 178.30 283.L2 324.24 347.07 396.25 445.32 594.32 603.15 604.34
weave 318.32 330.12
web 374.08
wed 140.21 260.17 309.05 391.33 416.10 452.31 588.09 620.22
wedding 116.21 228.30 314.33 376.11 377.15 377.20 409.29 461.18 619.24
weddingguest 511.02
weddingnight 446.05
wedlock 560.30
Wednesday 058.29 062.28 088.15 301.21 375.35 376.11 409.29 457.20 492.05 565.05
wee 625.24 626.03
weed 426.21 526.33
week 019.25 082.27 138.16 196.13 320.22 519.04 537.34
weekday 219.04
weep 519.36
weeper 368.29
weevil 369.12 613.21
weft 034.24
weigh 421.07 457.07
weight 338.35 407.05 559.27 583.30
weird 424.20 426.21
welcome 260.04 553.34 617.21
welkin 106.17 588.17
well 598.22
Welsh 160.27 160.28 327.22 340.03
welter 597.29
wench 578.23
wend 278.25 520.25
werewolf 225.08 244.11 444.32 467.15 565.06
west 018.36 019.32 028.31 064.01 072.02 112.26 114.20 153.27 160.28 160.28 203.15 204.25 251.15 300.29 309.13 323.10 326.12 359.23 372.17 373.05 383.20 390.25 394.15 411.31 424.30 469.04 469.24 482.11 482.12 494.14 516.04 523.05 557.02 578.30 597.11 601.21
westbriton 491.32
westend 058.35
westward 235.07 245.08 265.27
westwards 324.31
wet 201.23 223.36 406.11 502.06 521.17
wether 238.26 396.25
whack 360.08
whale 013.34 245.12 325.31 463.32 519.04 536.33
wharf 332.19 547.04
whatnot 507.14
whatsoever 253.08
whatyoumaycallit 608.25
wheel 119.30 285.F4 497.14 563.32
wheelbarrow 015.24 017.04
whenever 077.14
whereabouts 239.30 255.07 379.07 506.25 541.05
where'er 250.32

wherefore 208.35 226.06 239.26 326.22 565.06
wheresoever 576.19
whereupon 300.09 617.03
wherever 110.10
whether 089.09 224.18 239.20 326.29 488.02 618.25
whey 542.36
whiddle 620.23
whig 132.19
whilom 607.22
whimper 149.04
whine 261.04
whip 622.26
whirlpool 300.09
whisht 376.34
whisker 117.07
whiskey 006.27 070.30 091.28 139.08 157.06 319.04 326.05 470.33 497.23 497.23 499.31 499.31 499.32 510.33 516.07 587.12 600.32
whiskeybottle 071.03
whisper 121.12 138.10 148.01 158.06 257.02 291.20 410.30 414.29 460.07 516.07
whist 193.14
whistle 060.04 072.09 199.27 406.11 433.35 521.17 556.27 587.12 620.23
white 004.05 013.34 043.24 064.21 100.26 111.30 135.21 139.04 176.23 223.17 229.27 241.09 247.19 247.31 252.15 300.F4 310.26 320.08 334.16 342.22 352.15 358.23 387.25 388.16 403.14 568.02 584.15 596.21 607.03 614.14
whitehead 535.22 535.26 535.27
whiteheaded 240.22 472.05
whitehot 322.05
whiteness 241.36
whiter 026.08
whitewash 282.22
Whitsun 170.13 204.24
Whitsuntide 432.33
whiz 436.08
whoever 202.13 246.01
whole 019.01 139.01 143.15 163.01 169.12 224.34 284.19 309.22 330.28 336.19 350.06 370.32 403.15 407.25 415.07 463.16 496.11 512.28 539.24 540.17 587.16 593.03 593.12 610.02
wholesale 326.23
wholly 163.11 299.13 358.29
whomsoever 239.19
whoop 308.F2 506.22
whooping 095.08
whoopingcough 397.24 423.26 511.14
whopping 533.17
whore 020.36 150.13 185.12 349.01 364.23 416.11 547.06 610.02
whoreson 350.33 369.21
whosoever 364.23 426.03 618.25
wicked 108.23 527.05 527.16 527.17 527.25
wicker 375.19
wicket 337.03 583.34
wicketkeeper 366.02
wide 079.19 234.07 300.F4 320.08 345.30 403.15 469.11 596.21 612.29 613.21
wideawake 608.34
widespread 628.10
widow 009.21 209.05 243.36 282.F1 291.09 340.14 351.10 376.02 399.13 456.35 457.36 526.32 577.22
widower 024.09 587.10
width 168.07 549.26
wife 014.27 038.09 098.01 114.23 172.30 197.18 227.02 336.30 350.14 411.11 493.19 527.11 532.30 534.29 547.28 577.01 578.32 579.01 612.24 615.33
wifebeater 356.09
wifie 004.28
wig 423.03
wight 143.11 358.23
wigwam 553.26
wild 040.13 106.01 209.20 233.12 256.23 263.19 345.04 382.25 622.25
wildebeest 571.28
wilderness 055.28
wildgoose 197.14
wildlife 113.03
wilful 305.12 433.30
will-o'-the-wisp 404.15
willow 360.03
willy 377.14
willynilly 339.33
wily 010.07
wind 020.35 201.20 206.05 213.23 261.04 362.19 448.20 519.22 552.16 552.17 607.24
window 010.28 101.04 141.18 182.34 198.23 340.14 351.10 371.33 388.03 415.29 519.22 567.28 586.31 597.28
windowsill 274.25
windward 351.08
wine 024.13 078.20 088.21 154.15 183.33 256.07 265.23 518.21 596.07 610.22
winecup 383.19
winepress 020.09
winestain 528.17
wing 433.18
wink 595.08
winkle 388.06
winner 246.15
winsome 200.19
winter 318.20 502.29 561.20
wintery 331.05
wipe 111.32 222.26 353.17
wireless 021.22 053.04 172.25 219.16 223.34 407.21 469.29
wiry 200.33
wisdom 584.16
wise 040.10 204.22 269.11 366.24
wish 162.27 189.01 199.13 319.35 407.11 407.11 457.30 469.24 587.12
wishful 333.34
wistaria 482.11
wistful 568.12
wistfully 164.07
wit 083.15 085.10 085.14 225.12 234.02 372.34
witch 129.13 151.13 221.14 226.01 546.35
witchcraft 269.F4 468.24
witchery 225.02
wither 134.22 260.14
within 604.07
without 102.02
witness 204.22 241.36 247.22 316.04 364.01 376.11 449.28 597.19 615.33
wizen 521.17
woad 348.12
wobble 079.31 198.24 270.F2 452.01
woe 387.21 408.15 562.10
woebegone 007.17 104.12 240.06
woeful 369.12 503.21 503.22
wold 593.03
wolf 074.04 088.22 350.25 385.17 385.17 535.15 565.05 565.05
woman 012.03 013.26 022.08 055.10 098.01 101.04 101.07 101.08 122.15 149.09 167.31 170.14 277.04 279.F23 323.19 331.30 331.30 339.26 348.25 375.16 465.28 471.32 475.21 596.07 610.22 616.04
womanhood 375.09
womb 296.31 465.08
wonder 280.11 280.34 314.36 597.29
wonderful 059.13 265.15 265.15 265.16 543.11 624.23
wonderland 276.F7 528.18 618.22
wonderment 449.02
wondrous 004.35
woo 152.20
wood 126.03 221.29 225.19 250.16 251.19 287.F3 290.18 325.30 340.20 366.34 388.06 551.09
wooden 082.16 325.31 409.01 535.05
woodman 077.16
woody 348.12
wool 070.07 300.F3 337.24 481.29
woollen 376.05
woolly 225.20 578.07
woolworth 004.35 127.35 357.03 398.23 539.05 541.06
word 017.14 056.11 083.12 112.04 172.22 183.08 223.34 250.35 262.L3 262.F2 275.06 280.26 285.23 305.10 352.07 378.29 379.02 425.13 487.21 515.05
work 284.21 287.L1 310.17 465.08 491.34 497.03 544.22 555.12 609.31
workday 553.15
workman 616.25
world 006.24 011.07 019.11 059.10 073.28 080.13 147.22 147.28 150.13 152.30 163.27 167.29 175.12 220.28 225.31 248.24 255.18 258.21 272.04 277.F7 316.13 336.10 336.17 345.31 354.22 354.23 403.15 441.19 450.29 498.24 505.02

505.32 535.28 549.25 563.32 564.24 582.20 588.03 608.34 612.29 613.21
worldly 540.34
worm 019.12 084.30 163.10 225.14 318.14 465.28
worry 125.16 225.20 255.18 257.18 258.21 337.24 467.07 511.32
worse 084.27 119.02 421.18 453.11
worship 154.18 289.07 408.35 547.27 628.11
worst 017.28 158.10 245.02 365.08
worth 012.02 056.27 233.11 241.08 578.27
wouldbe 028.32
wound 361.25 499.31
wounder 483.16
wrack 130.05
wrangle 454.02 508.02
wrap 020.10 542.34 546.16
wrath 016.27 134.30 252.14 292.02 303.15 340.16 379.21
wrathfully 229.27
wreath 142.36 414.03
wreathe 589.27
wreck 123.23 155.10 275.19 387.20 463.31 518.09 557.06
wrecker 313.15
wren 363.05 363.05 604.08
wrestle 586.01
wrestler 143.21
wretched 565.10
write 041.21 066.17 167.33 283.22 301.07 387.34 422.34 424.36 606.16
writer 291.28 313.11 495.02
writing 482.32 490.29
wrong 019.36 098.10 167.32 349.27 407.04 508.02 595.19

X ray 051.25 530.08

yacht 335.29
yahoo 348.01 387.10 490.13 585.04
Yank 308.22 329.01
Yankee 258.05 464.21
yap 343.15
yard 034.09 088.19 096.08 201.31 229.01 243.01 246.01 388.02 492.25 568.27 624.16
yarn 620.36
yashmak 234.26 547.14
yawn 314.32 538.01
year 024.09 024.09 054.03 091.21 127.02 156.19 156.21 159.11 159.16 173.07 182.20 237.31 239.11 279.03 295.03 295.05 318.07 331.29 346.08 377.29 415.32 513.23 593.10 593.10 594.15 598.32
yearly 119.25
yearn 143.29
yellow 023.01 092.02 171.16 180.06 226.31 233.32 277.F4 327.32 338.15 339.28 416.34 427.18 432.30 434.06 485.29 577.26 577.26 611.06
yelp 323.16
yester 624.25 624.25
yesterday 004.21 087.08 104.12 126.18 295.01 295.01 346.22 407.36 570.09 570.12 590.19 598.11 598.20 628.11
yestereve 214.01 473.11
yesteryear 212.31 318.07 327.13
yew 009.13 553.03 590.19 601.03
Yggdrassil 504.35
yield 346.08
yodel 236.21 469.16
yoghurt 305.03 387.10 424.13
yolk 613.11
yon 015.18
yonder 007.29 057.15 365.22 617.32
yore 237.31 594.15
young 010.03 051.01 100.06 115.22 134.22 170.06 225.17 231.09 245.06 253.28 253.29 267.03 267.08 267.L3 268.F3 299.25 314.31 361.17 370.07 388.01 431.35 467.14 487.16 519.20 590.11
youngest 135.19
youngster 130.15 162.33
yourself 301.08 425.05 499.22
yourselves 337.25
youth 310.17
youthful 129.26 231.06
yoyo 123.02 305.R1 583.10
Yugoslav 137.33
Yule 082.28 236.11 236.11 245.06 582.26 620.17
Yuletide 097.03 308.17
yum 446.03
yumyum 306.F5

zany 101.28
zeal 529.24
zealot 543.19
Zend 234.15
zenith 038.03
zephyr 418.29
zero 310.08
zigzag 111.08 288.18 330.21 363.36 364.30
zircon 323.19
zither 222.33
zodiac 056.23 512.07
zone 057.07 101.28
zoo 266.07
zoological 165.21
zouave 287.31

NUMBERS

00 086.34 369.04
0009 488.29

10 284.17
100 063.02 284.17
1000 015.05 032.32 073.20
10,000 262.01 282.26 564.19
100,000 016.34 081.04 081.06 123.15 188.36 305.10 317.08 404.36
1000,000,000,000 117.21 117.21
1001 005.28 041.33 051.04 064.34 135.20 210.05 238.20 254.19 295.03 325.07 341.33 342.15 357.18 433.18 519.07 570.31 597.05 604.25 609.14 617.04 627.15 628.14
101 507.22
1014 324.20
105 386.32 386.32
109 567.03
11 054.32 083.02 084.04 126.05
1100 073.20
111 008.15 019.20 019.24 032.31 038.13 072.04 101.34 117.20 153.01 201.29 220.21 243.01 273.16 273.17 283.F1 303.32 325.05 327.08 328.07 330.33 341.20 425.32 507.22 516.18 577.14 583.10 583.13 597.05 617.03 627.14
1112 617.03
1132 019.20 054.12 070.33 073.15 077.06 082.07 084.32 095.14 119.25 120.25 256.22 274.12 274.L3 285.13 338.05 347.04 378.22 388.12 389.25 448.03 497.09 513.05 516.17 517.30 574.26 606.18 617.24
118 242.16
12 048.13 199.03
120 126.06
13 054.32 335.06 335.27 435.09 498.26
132 182.23
133 155.29 156.02
140 101.16
15 282.32
160 405.12
180 429.08
1823 138.32

200 519.35
20,000 413.23
206 084.26
21,999 412.27
22,000 364.04 364.05 412.26 412.27 438.24 438.24 505.05 505.06
222 327.08
22,200 375.09
2,280,960 265.25
234 043.14
24 543.05 558.06
25 282.32
250,000 317.08
26 264.22
28 093.12 147.07 279.F15
29 075.04 092.12 092.12 161.29 170.02 223.09 242.17 358.28 433.03 469.30 558.22 582.35 601.13 601.14 601.14 601.15

30 623.05
300 541.29
31 283.01 283.F1
32 073.10 119.25 264.22 396.17 494.33
33 155.30 173.07
333 444.12
357 386.32
360 331.15 619.27
365 128.31
366 211.17
37 173.28
39 396.18

40 102.11 312.21
400 264.20
41 283.01
432 499.16 612.26
4.32 618.13
4320 283.03
47 083.02
479,001,600 285.17 285.23
500,000 129.16
501 084.26
5050 589.02
543 240.11
55 200.05
566 497.26
5.73 508.02
58 430.09
6 032.03
60 079.10 620.04
600 349.15
606 478.09
63 264.21
7 134.15
70 029.26 079.10
700 347.19
732 123.06
74 084.04
75 616.09
753 386.32
78 248.32
80 332.27 346.24 580.06
800 285.F3
9 348.27
90 105.04
930 535.29
932 584.24
939 133.17
99 255.36
999 086.15 102.31 357.18 604.25
999,000,000 398.32

ABBREVIATIONS

A 080.09 090.28 113.18 143.13 263.F1 283.26 340.16 453.09 458.36 560.34
AB 087.32 283.26 288.05 553.03 571.07
ABC 019.08 019.09 044.12 051.34 090.28 091.22 099.10 107.34 140.14 167.08 179.13 179.16 198.20 208.20 247.35 249.18 250.34 272.12 285.01 303.29 314.10 327.34 327.34 352.35 389.03 392.11 397.25 484.23 514.26 552.07 553.02 568.32 571.07
ABCDEF 089.33
AD 077.07 347.19 365.16 484.21 513.05
AEIOU 259.09 532.03
AEO 278.10
AI 082.02
AIM 329.05
AM 481.06 603.19
AMDG 282.06 324.23 418.04
ANN 113.18 575.07
AO 090.28 090.28 287.15 414.36 503.32 553.04 601.19
A1 245.35
AP 296.24
APGQNE 072.08
ASS 609.09
AZ 104.19 263.F1 560.34
B 120.07 260.F1 283.26 392.23
BA 315.01 608.02
BAD 072.16
Bart 293.F2
BBC 039.07 343.03 489.03
BC 481.09
BCDFSMNV 178.02
BVM 568.04 618.14
C 048.01 254.29 284.17 308.02
CAC 499.10
CBA 179.13
CCB 039.08
CD 571.08
CEH 559.21
COD 270.R1
CQ 593.05
CRC 499.10
CUTT 527.27
D 123.02 198.26
DBC 149.27 433.16
DCC 386.35 389.26
DUD 574.26
DV 300.04 306.F1 316.19 451.19
E 120.19 143.14 254.30 340.16
ECH 023.04 072.14
EHC 559.22
F 120.33 280.12
FFF 284.15 464.15
FNG 018.34
G 042.05 042.05 120.21 133.10 188.27 284.F5
GBD 437.07
GG 042.05 120.21
GHIJ 089.33
GHOTI 299.F3
GLUGG 223.12
GNG 042.05
GPO 265.28 369.34 454.16
H 121.16 254.29 337.07 581.19
HCE 254.29 593.05 595.32
HCF 284.05
HIM 166.18
HOD 087.12
I 023.36 121.17 143.14 210.26 372.03 542.14
IAPO 086.20
ICNC 563.19
ICUR 201.02
IHVH 478.11
IOM 183.15
IOU 183.15 251.31
J 121.17 284.F5
JP 134.35 386.26 387.06 486.12
K 133.09
KKK 085.33 095.22 120.02 137.12 171.10 176.30 177.09 178.33 186.19 193.24 203.35 245.02 279.F25 324.29 353.14 361.16 372.14 375.03 379.01 421.04 464.15 464.19 503.08 505.34 511.08 531.25 533.24 556.29 584.21 585.30 612.11
KO 085.04 221.06 333.03 379.36
KOK 282.23
L 369.36 475.05
LBW 337.03
LCM 284.07
LDS 282.F2 325.03 418.04
LP 296.26
LSD 325.03
LSK 205.07
M 123.01 198.28 207.35 404.30 419.19
MA 112.29
MARIE 300.12
MBD 228.15
MCC 584.09
ME 198.18
Messrs 534.15
Mrs 391.36
MUD 527.15
MUG 588.02
N 113.18
NB 606.13
Nth 298.21 312.17
NVI 235.24
O 143.13 207.36 340.16 453.09 458.36
OBE 489.13
OF 363.36
OHMS 301.03 408.14
OIU 584.34
OK 063.04 085.04 089.34 221.06 282.23 299.09 302.21 305.18 305.19 306.09 317.05 322.17 332.18 332.18 333.03 338.25 340.01 360.26 360.26 368.10 368.14 379.36 542.22 601.02
OUM 584.34
OUT 461.13
P 296.05
PBI 370.15
PC 496.32
PG 072.08 419.30
PGG 089.34
PGOEO 006.32
PL 296.25 296.26
PM 113.02 455.11 517.25
PMG 603.12
PP 085.05 085.20 093.14 120.02 343.30 533.26
PPP 249.17
PQ 019.02 019.03 029.18 061.16 061.16 072.08 119.35 119.36 128.22 280.16 314.19 319.24 344.02 349.03 350.17 374.10 377.18 412.28 469.18 472.06 492.19 508.06 508.19 508.23 508.24 508.26 508.28 536.06 550.32 606.30

PS 111.18 406.20 513.06
PUR 310.11

QED 299.03
QEF 298.04
QP 412.28
QT 314.03

R 034.10 122.06 404.30 405.19 453.09
RIP 325.01
RMD 232.25
RSVP 495.32
RU 102.06

SAD 069.15
SAG 621.07
SAP 099.34
SOS 252.24 316.18 479.36 499.10 588.28
SPQR 454.35 484.22
SSOS 479.36
SUM 421.02

T 302.09 369.32 542.14
TC 308.02
TCD 112.30 315.01
TT 260.02
TU 553.03

U 023.36 340.17 477.32
UI 626.07
UOM 183.15
US 320.15

VC 529.25

W 019.11 120.28 336.12
WC 279.F22 296.01 489.03
WW 351.12 372.14 377.13 459.06 467.15 610.36 613.21 614.03

X 019.20 123.02 205.09 284.17 308.F2 355.06 625.02
XX 579.09
XYZ 167.07 281.F3 288.05 432.35

Y 019.20 285.04
YOYOY 123.02
YWCA 141.18
YWCU 141.18
YZ 283.27 578.17

Z 028.29 051.28 123.04 263.F1 285.03 560.34 578.17

23025031R00299

Made in the USA
San Bernardino, CA
31 July 2015